The Kingfisher

ILLUSTRATED
HISTORY
OF·THE
WORLD

The Kingfisher
ILLUSTRATED
HISTORY
OF·THE
WORLD

Foreword by Magnus Magnusson
Introduction by Professor Jack Zevin

40,000 B.C. to Present Day

Kingfisher Books

NEW YORK

Consultant Editor
Professor Jack Zevin

General Editor
Charlotte Evans

Project Designer and Art Editor
Stefan Morris

Project Editors
Annabel Else, Lee Simmons, Nina Hathway, Margaret Younger

Designers and Art Editors
Branka Surla, Jackie Moore, Smiljka Surla

Editorial Manager
Catherine Headlam

Design Manager
Louise Jervis

Picture Research
Elaine Willis, Su Alexander

Contributors
Hazel Martell, Theodore Rowland-Entwistle, Fiona Macdonald,
Ken Hills, Elizabeth Longley, Teresa Chris, Neil Grant, John Paton

Advisers
Ellie Bowden, John Harrop, Robert Guyver

KINGFISHER BOOKS
Grisewood & Dempsey Inc.
95 Madison Avenue
New York, New York 10016

First American edition 1993
2 4 6 8 10 9 7 5 3
Copyright © Grisewood & Dempsey Ltd. 1992

Library of Congress Cataloging-in-Publication Data
The Kingfisher illustrated history of the world: 40,000 B.C. to present
day/foreword by Magnus Magnusson: introduction by Jack Zevin: [general editor, Charlotte
Evans: contributors, Hazel Martell . . . et al.]. – 1st American ed.
p.   cm.
Includes index.
Summary: Traces the history of the world, from the ancient world
of 40,000 B.C. to the present day, covering such aspects as war,
society, religion, people, buildings, arts, science, and communication.
1. World history–Juvenile literature. [1. World history.]
I. Evans, Charlotte.   II. Kingfisher Books.
D20.K56   1993
909–dc20   92-29123   CIP   AC

ISBN 1-85697-862-1

Printed in Italy

Foreword

To me, history is the most fascinating subject there is. I am not a professional historian: I am a lover of history, in the sense that I love the "story" of our times, past, present, and future.

This ambitious enterprise is, to my mind, immensely important. It is the kind of book that I would have liked to have had when my own interest in the subject began to form. When I was a youngster, history was presented to us in schools only from our Western perspective of civilization; of man's development based on the imperatives of conquest and empire building which made our own society the fortunate and inevitable outcome.

This *Illustrated History of the World* shows how much we have learned to respect other and equally valid aspects of civilization; to respect the achievements of other peoples. History is, above all, a matter of perspective. For the past to be comprehensible, and accessible, it requires an overall framework of time. Throughout this book, chapter by chapter, and theme by theme, we are given the chronological context within which we can place properly the events that interest us most closely.

The style of the book is as up-to-date as it is informative. Once, history was presented as a portrait gallery of rulers—good, bad, and indifferent—but that approach was only a superficial illustration of events. Today we recognize the significance of new and broader perspectives as a way of illuminating our understanding, rather than simply illustrating the written word.

An overview of history—even a book as good as this one—cannot be the last word; but it can be a marvelous incentive to learn more, and to give us a reliable basis from which to launch our curiosity. Enjoy this treasure house of knowledge about the past. It is the door to the future.

Magnus Magnusson KBE

Introduction

The Kingfisher Illustrated History of the World takes you back in time through the stories of the many diverse peoples of our earth. See across the ages—from the Stone Age through the agricultural revolution and the creation of the first cities, to the rise of great empires, and finally to the nations of today, which use technology to meet their needs and seek their dreams.

Humankind's story is told for Asia, Africa, Europe, the Americas, and Oceania, and almost all major cultures and societies are pictured and discussed. There are accounts of wars and conflicts, leaders and tyrants, but there is also information on developments in science and the arts and the way of life of ordinary people. Find out what was happening in the ancient Greek City States; look into the lifestyle of the Indian peoples under the Mauryan Empire; be an amateur archaeologist and examine the evidence presented about the Vikings. Ask yourself provocative questions: when Columbus came to the New World, what did he really discover? Why were two world wars fought in the twentieth century?

The evidence of history is sometimes a detailed chronicle of events; sometimes just a few intriguing artifacts or fragments of writing for us to interpret. Often we must create theories to explain human actions—mystery and interpretation are part of history, so play detective and build your own views. Investigate connections between places and cultures. Jump to Europe during the Renaissance and then move over to the Middle East and Asia to see what events, leaders, and technological inventions were on the rise there. Choose several time periods and seek out those events, people, or developments that had an impact on the world. Judge for yourself which had the most influence.

As communication develops among the people of our world, the earth grows smaller. New products, inventions, and problems are rapidly shared across boundaries and over time. Political decisions in one capital produce an immediate reaction in capitals across the globe. How and why international organizations arose is part of history. The lives we now live are also a part of the human story. Why do we live in different places and speak different languages? Are we better off than our ancestors or worse off? Have we solved all our conflicts and learned to cooperate? Use the *History of the World* to try to answer these questions and others you may think of, and make the human story come alive as you travel through time.

Professor Jack Zevin
Queens College, City University of New York

Contents

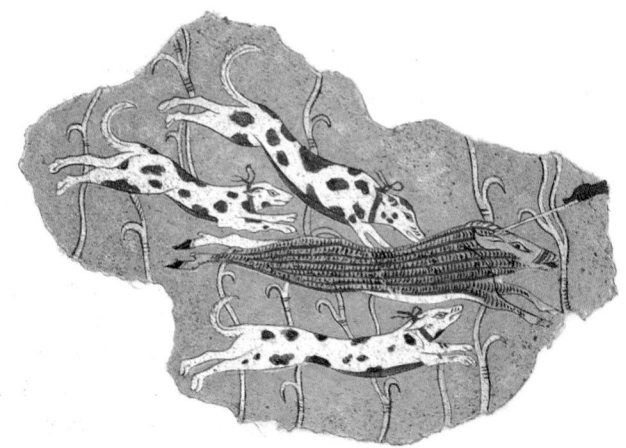

How to get the most from your History of the World

The *Kingfisher Illustrated History of the World* is full of interesting information about the people, places, and events that have shaped history. It contains many features to help you look up things easily, or simply to have fun just browsing through. Every page is illustrated to complement the informative text; there are fact and date boxes as well as boxes on important historical figures. Each section has ten special feature spreads which take an overall look at a particular theme, such as the arts, so drawing together what was happening in that area during the time period. Over these two pages you will find many of the features of the *History of the World* explained in more detail.

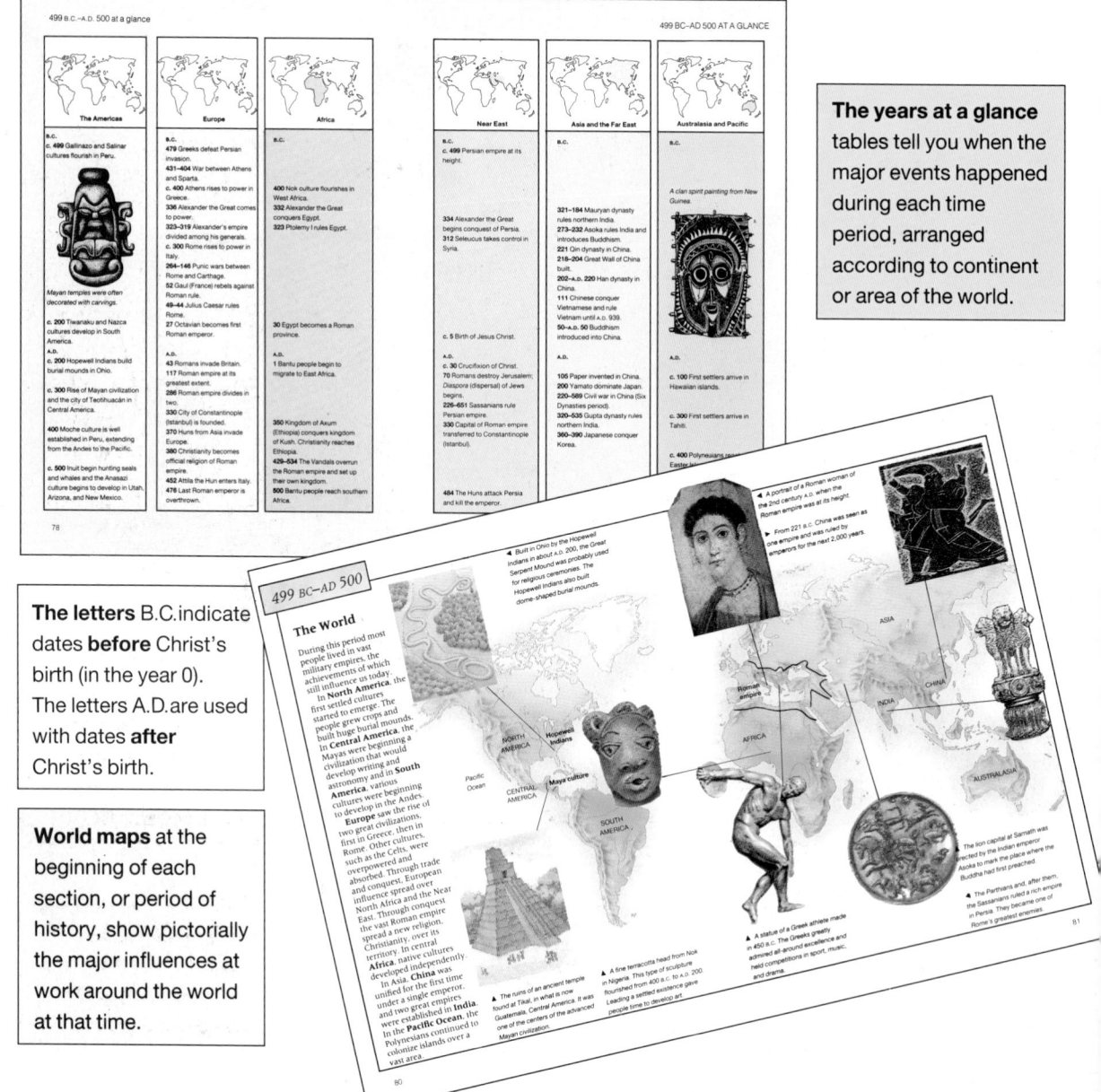

The years at a glance tables tell you when the major events happened during each time period, arranged according to continent or area of the world.

The letters B.C. indicate dates **before** Christ's birth (in the year 0). The letters A.D. are used with dates **after** Christ's birth.

World maps at the beginning of each section, or period of history, show pictorially the major influences at work around the world at that time.

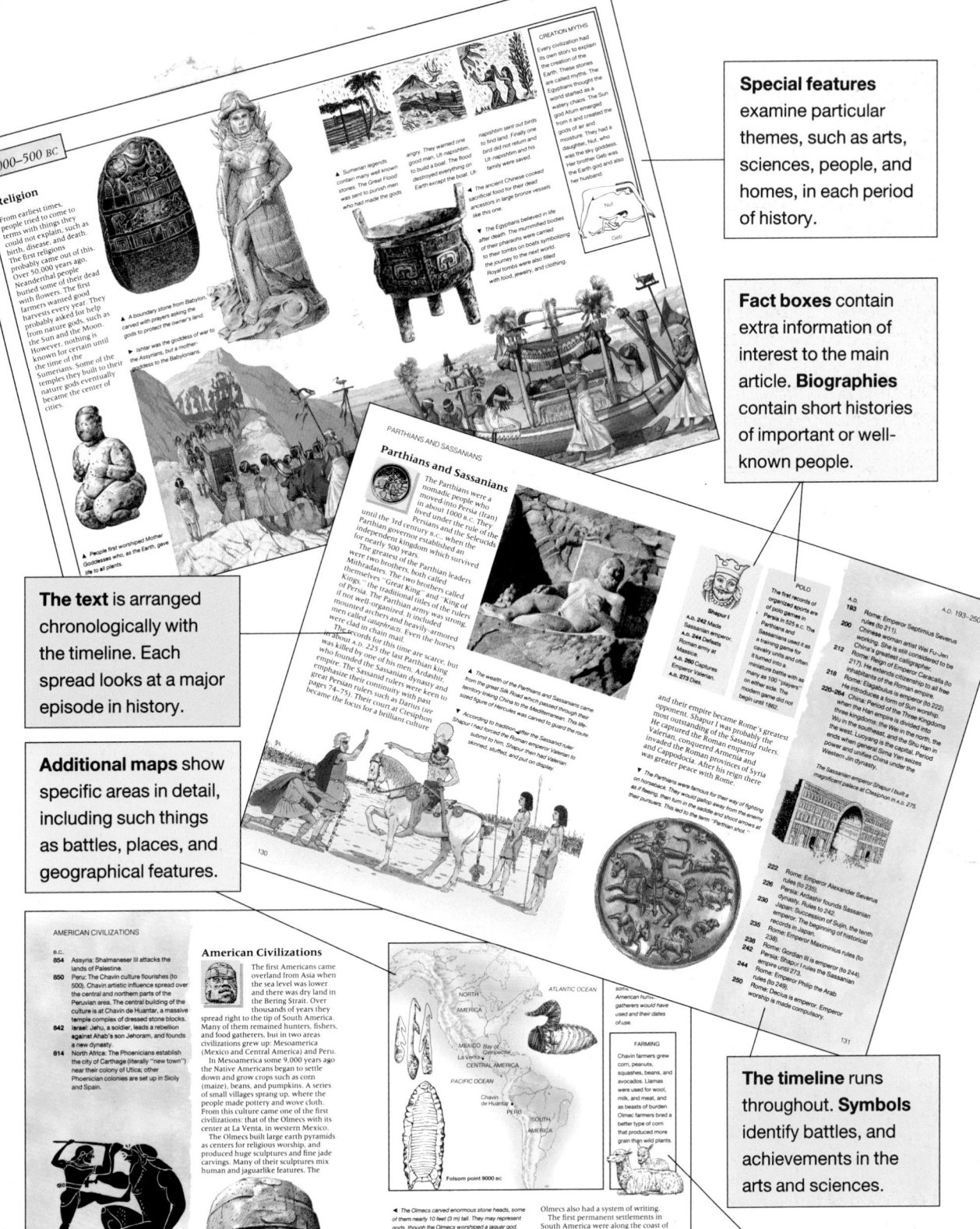

Special features examine particular themes, such as arts, sciences, people, and homes, in each period of history.

Fact boxes contain extra information of interest to the main article. **Biographies** contain short histories of important or well-known people.

The text is arranged chronologically with the timeline. Each spread looks at a major episode in history.

Additional maps show specific areas in detail, including such things as battles, places, and geographical features.

The timeline runs throughout. **Symbols** identify battles, and achievements in the arts and sciences.

Illustrated boxes contain information on particular places, people, and goods.

1000–500 BC

Religion

From earliest times, people tried to come to terms with things they could not explain, such as birth, disease, and death. The first religions probably came out of this. Over 50,000 years ago, Neanderthal people buried some of their dead with flowers. The first farmers wanted good harvests every year. They probably asked for help from nature gods, such as the Sun and the Moon. However, nothing is known for certain until the time of the Sumerians. Some of the temples they built to their nature gods eventually became the center of cities.

▲ A boundary stone from Babylon, carved with prayers asking the gods to protect the owner's land.

▲ Ishtar was the goddess of war to the Assyrians, but a mother-goddess to the Babylonians.

▲ People first worshiped Mother Goddesses who, as the Earth, gave life to all plants.

▲ Sumerian legends contain many well known stories. The Great Flood was sent to punish men who had made the gods angry. They warned one good man, Ut-napishtim, to build a boat. The flood destroyed everything on Earth except the boat. Ut-napishtim sent out birds to find land. Finally one bird did not return and Ut-napishtim and his family were saved.

▲ The ancient Chinese cooked sacrificial food for their dead ancestors in large bronze vessels like this one.

▲ The Egyptians believed in life after death. The mummified bodies of their pharaohs were carried to their tombs on boats symbolizing the journey to the next world. Royal tombs were also filled with food, jewelry, and clothing.

CREATION MYTHS

Every civilization had its own story to explain the creation of the Earth. These stories are called myths. The Egyptians thought the world started as a watery chaos. The Sun god Atum emerged from it and created the gods of air and moisture. They had a daughter, Nut, who was the sky goddess. Her brother Geb was the Earth god and also her husband.

Parthians and Sassanians

The Parthians were a nomadic people who moved into Persia (Iran) in about 1000 B.C. They lived under the rule of the Persians and the Seleucids until the 3rd century B.C. when the Parthian governor established an independent kingdom which survived for nearly 500 years.

The greatest of the Parthian leaders were two brothers, both called Mithradates. The two brothers called themselves "Great King" and "King of Kings," the traditional titles of the rulers of Persia. The Parthian army was strong, if not well organized. It included mounted archers and heavily armored men called cataphracts. Even the horses wore records in chain mail.

The records for this time are scarce, but about A.D. 225 the last Parthian king was killed by one of his men, Ardashir, who founded the Sassanian dynasty and empire. The Sassanid rulers were keen to emphasize their continuity with past great Persian rulers such as Darius (see pages 74–75). Their court at Ctesiphon became the focus for a brilliant culture

▼ The wealth of the Parthians and Sassanians came from the great Silk Road which passed through their territory linking China to the Mediterranean. This tile-sized figure of Hercules was carved to guard the route.

According to tradition, after the Sassanid ruler Shapur I had forced the Roman emperor Valerian to submit to him, Shapur then had Valerian skinned, stuffed, and put on display.

and their empire became Rome's greatest opponent. Shapur I was probably the most outstanding of the Sassanid rulers. He captured the Roman emperor Valerian, conquered Armenia and invaded the Roman provinces of Syria and Cappodocia. After his reign there was greater peace with Rome.

The Parthians were famous for their way of fighting on horseback. They would gallop away from the enemy as if fleeing, then turn in the saddle and shoot arrows at their pursuers. This led to the term "Parthian shot."

Shapur I
- A.D. 242 Made Sassanian emperor.
- A.D. 244 Defeats Roman army at Massice.
- A.D. 260 Captures Emperor Valerian.
- A.D. 273 Dies.

POLO
The first records of organized sports are of polo games in Persia in 529 B.C. The Parthians and Sassanians used it as a training game for cavalry units and often it turned into a miniature battle with as many as 100 "players" on either side. The modern game did not begin until 1862.

▼ The Sassanian emperor Shapur I built a magnificent palace at Ctesiphon in A.D. 275.

A.D. 193–250

A.D.	
193	Rome: Emperor Septimus Severus rules (to 211).
200	Chinese woman artist Wei Fu-Jen working. She is still considered to be China's greatest calligrapher.
212	Rome: Reign of Emperor Caracalla (to 217). He extends citizenship to all free inhabitants of the Roman empire.
216	Rome: Elagabalus is emperor (to 222). He introduces a form of Sun worship.
220–264	China: Period of the Three Kingdoms when the Han empire is divided into three kingdoms: the Wei in the north, the Wu in the southeast, and the Shu in the west. Luoyang is the capital. Period ends when general Sima Yen seizes power and unites China under the Western Jin dynasty.
222	Rome: Emperor Alexander Severus rules (to 235).
226	Persia: Ardashir founds Sassanian dynasty. Rules to 242.
230	Japan: Succession of Sujin, the tenth emperor. The beginning of historical records in Japan.
235	Rome: Emperor Maximinus rules (to 238).
239	Rome: Gordian III is emperor (to 244).
242	Persia: Shapur I rules the Sassanian empire until 273.
244	Rome: Emperor Philip the Arab rules (to 249).
250	Rome: Decius is emperor. Emperor worship is made compulsory.

130

131

AMERICAN CIVILIZATIONS

B.C.
- **854** Assyria: Shalmaneser III attacks the lands of Palestine.
- **850** Peru: The Chavin culture flourishes (to 500). Chavin artistic influence spread over the central and northern parts of the Peruvian area. The central building of the culture is at Chavin de Huantar, a massive temple complex of dressed stone blocks.
- **842** Israel: Jehu, a soldier, leads a rebellion against Ahab's son Jehoram, and founds a new dynasty.
- **814** North Africa: The Phoenicians establish the city of Carthage (literally "new town") near their colony of Utica; other Phoenician colonies are set up in Sicily and Spain.

▼ Episodes from Homer's Odyssey were often shown on Greek vases. Here the hero Odysseus drives a stake into the eye of the cyclops, the one-eyed giant, to kill him.

- **800** Greece: Traditional date for the composition of Homer's epic poems the Iliad and the Odyssey. Mexico: The Olmecs build the earliest American pyramid at La Venta.

American Civilizations

The first Americans came overland from Asia when the sea level was lower and there was dry land in the Bering Strait. Over thousands of years they spread right to the tip of South America. Many of them remained hunters, fishers, and food gatherers, but in two areas civilizations grew up: Mesoamerica (Mexico and Central America) and Peru. In Mesoamerica some 9,000 years ago the Native Americans began to settle down and grow crops such as corn (maize), beans, and pumpkins. A series of small villages sprang up, where the people made pottery and wove cloth. From this culture came one of the first civilizations: that of the Olmecs with its center at La Venta, in western Mexico.

The Olmecs built large earth pyramids as centers for religious worship, and produced huge sculptures and fine jade carvings. Many of their sculptures mix human and jaguarlike features. The

some American hunter-gatherers would have used and their dates of use.

FARMING
Chavin farmers grew corn, peanuts, squashes, beans, and avocados. Llamas were used for wool, milk, and meat, and as beasts of burden. Olmec farmers bred a better type of corn that produced more grain than wild plants.

▲ Folsom point 9000 bc

▼ The Olmecs carved enormous stone heads, some of them nearly 10 feet (3 m) tall. They may represent gods, though the Olmecs worshiped a jaguar god.

▼ This fine stone bowl carved in the form of an animal was the work of a Chavin sculptor.

Olmecs also had a system of writing.

The first permanent settlements in South America were along the coast of northern Peru, where there are traces of fishing and farming communities. About 2,800 years ago a more advanced culture appeared, called Chavin after Chavin de Huantar, the site where it was first found. The Chavin people made pottery, wove cloth on looms, built in stone, and made elaborate carvings. The largest building at Chavin de Huantar, the "castle," is three stories high. Inside is a maze of rooms, corridors, and stairs.

The Chavin culture extended to several other parts of Peru. From their temples and carvings, we know that they worshiped a sacred jaguar or puma.

62

63

Using this Book

The Kingfisher Illustrated History of the World is very easy to use. All the entries are arranged in chronological order. There are two main ways to find the information that you want. The first is by looking up a date that you know of in the timeline, or by looking through the Contents under the time period you want to read about. There you will find the area you are interested in. The second way, if the subject that you are looking for does not have its own essay or particular date entry, is to look in the Index at the back. This will lead you to the information you are seeking.

•

Throughout each time period in the *History of the World* there are a number of special thematic essays that provide an overview of important developments in that period. There are ten themes as follows: **Arts and Crafts**; **Buildings**; **Communication and Transportation**; **Food and Farming**; **People**; **Religion**; **Society and Government**; **Science and Technology**; **Trade and Money**; and **War and Weapons**. If you want to compare how, for example, people's lives and occupations have changed during history, you can refer to each special essay in the time periods and observe the differences.

•

The running timeline provides information about dates and developments from 40,000 B.C. to the present day. You can also use it to give a flavor of the main preoccupations of a period of years. For easy reference, subject symbols appear next to entries of major events in the arts 🎭, developments in science and technology ⚙, and main battles ✖.

In addition to the main text of each essay, there are many boxed features giving the details of important people's lives, of the various plants and commodities that have driven trade through the ages, and telling some of the "stories," associated with historical events.

•

Throughout essays in the *History of the World* you will find page references. You can look these up to discover other events that have a direct bearing on the subject you have been reading about.

•

If you want to find out the dates of a particular ruler or leader, or for example, who came before Julius Caesar, along with the Index there is a large Ready Reference section containing extensive lists of names and dates for easy access.

•

Use your *History of the World* to discover a wealth of information about the events of the past and how people lived their lives years ago.

What is History?

The word "history" comes from the ancient Greek command *histo*, "know this." In Greek "I know" also meant "I have seen," and *historeo* came to mean "learn by inquiry." The Greeks realized that to know something you must see it for yourself or make an inquiry about it. The historian Thucydides wrote that too many people believe the first story that they heard!

The ancient Greeks understood the essence of what history is. First, historical knowledge must be based on evidence (evidence literally means "that which has been seen"). Second, history is not just one story, but several. And third, that everything must be looked at in a critical way, to check for any errors. Historians try to find out not only what happened but why it happened.

The word "history" has many meanings. It is an account of past events, in sequence of time; it is the study of events, their causes and results; and it is all that is preserved or remembered about the past, especially in written form. For evidence historians use written

▲ Buildings tell us a lot about the past. The Romans erected huge public buildings and many, such as the Colosseum, Rome, still stand.

◄ Events in modern history are often well documented, such as the meeting of the "Big Three" war leaders, Churchill, Roosevelt, and Stalin, at Yalta after World War II.

accounts, artifacts such as weapons and tools, and oral, or spoken, accounts.

To remember something people write it down, or commemorate it in some way. This is because events, even important ones, quickly disappear from human memory. Our lives today seem very different from the past, but not everything changes. Roman roads are still used every day and games like chess were invented centuries ago.

The Work of Archaeologists

Archaeology is the study of people of the past by the scientific analysis of the things these people left behind. Archaeologists study objects (artifacts), features (buildings), and ecofacts (seeds or animal bones). Archaeology can tell us about societies that existed before written records were made, as well as adding to our knowledge of literate societies.

Archaeologists are like detectives. They treat the things they find as clues to the lives of the people who used them. Like historians, archaeologists can sometimes discover the reasons for great changes in the societies

they are studying. Kathleen Kenyon, digging at the site of ancient Jericho in 1952, found out that its famous walls were destroyed in biblical times, not by resounding trumpets, but by fire!

Archaeology can often present historians with evidence that makes them reexamine their views of early societies. In 1939 at Sutton Hoo in England, the remains of an Anglo-Saxon treasure ship were discovered. The artifacts found there show a far from primitive society of the so called "Dark Ages."

Since the 1950s, archaeologists have been concerned with finding general theories that

▲ *Undersea archaeologists carefully plot the position of artifacts aboard a shipwreck. The silt on the seabed often preserves objects in a remarkable condition.*

▼ *It is very important that the exact position, size, and condition of finds is recorded. Great care is taken in excavating to prevent damage.*

▶ *A grid is used to locate and record finds. All earth removed from a site is collected in buckets and later sifted in case any small find has been missed.*

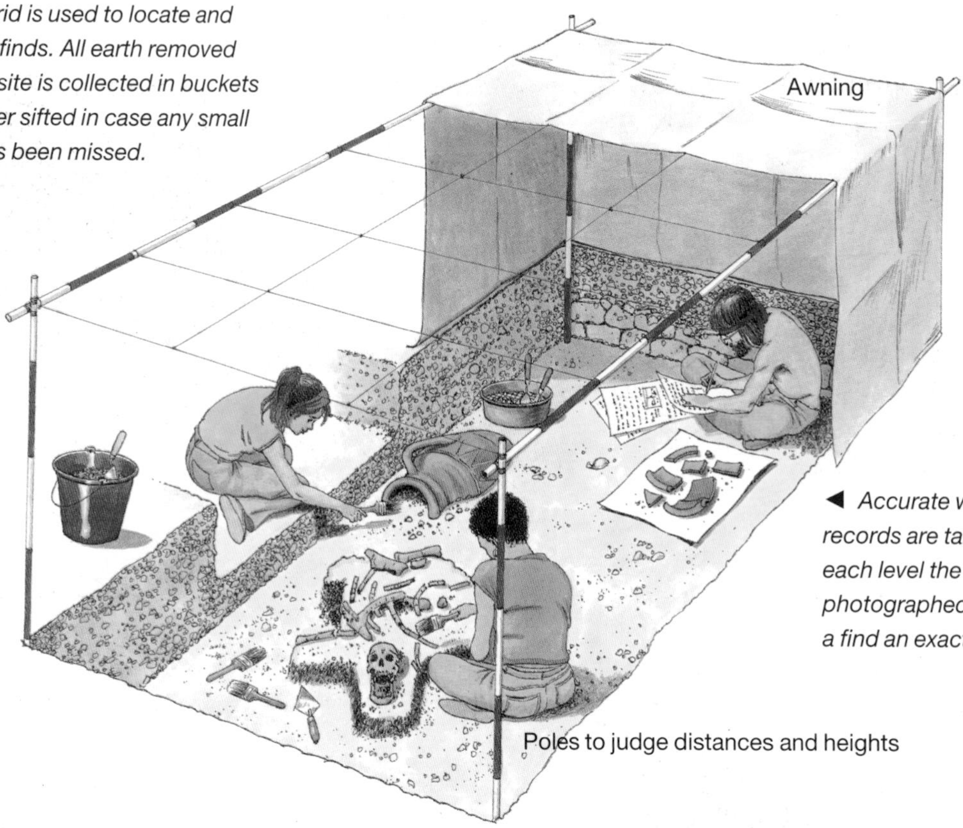

Awning

◀ *Accurate written records are taken. At each level the site is also photographed. This gives a find an exact position.*

Poles to judge distances and heights

WHEN IT HAPPENED

1748 Town of Pompeii is discovered, Italy.

1799 The Rosetta Stone is discovered, Egypt.

1870 Heinrich Schliemann begins excavating site of Troy in what is now Turkey.

1879 Prehistoric cave paintings are found in Spain.

1900 Sir Arthur Evans begins excavating Knossos, Crete.

1922 Howard Carter discovers Tutankhamun's tomb, Egypt.

1925 Flint points found at Folsom, New Mexico.

1939 Sutton Hoo treasure ship is found, England.

1952 Kathleen Kenyon excavates Jericho, Jordan.

1970 "Tollund Man" is discovered, Denmark.

1974 Tomb of Shi Huangdi is found in China.

1991 A diver discovers cave paintings in France; 6,000-year-old body found in the Alps.

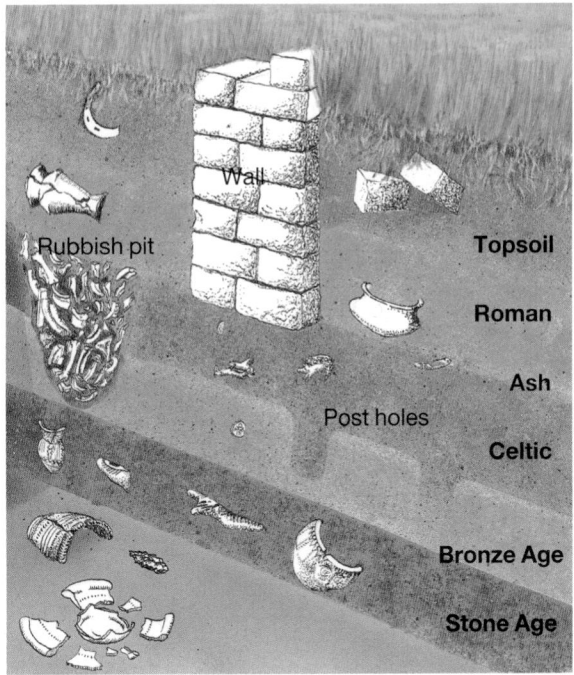

explain the changes that occur in human societies. They now try to find out why farming developed in Mexico around 7000 B.C. or why the first cities grew up in the Near East. Archaeologists also study specific problems not just sites. In the 1960s Richard MacNeish studied cave sites in Mexico to document making bread from corn. Computers are used to process the statistics and have made this sort of study much faster and more efficient.

▲ *A site's history is revealed in layers. The post holes show that a Celtic stockade on this site was replaced by a stone wall during Roman times. An ash layer indicates that the site burned down.*

Schliemann

Heinrich Schliemann (1822–1890) excavated Troy, the city of Homer's *Iliad*. The site in Turkey had nine cities built, one on top of the other. Homer's Troy was probably the sixth city.

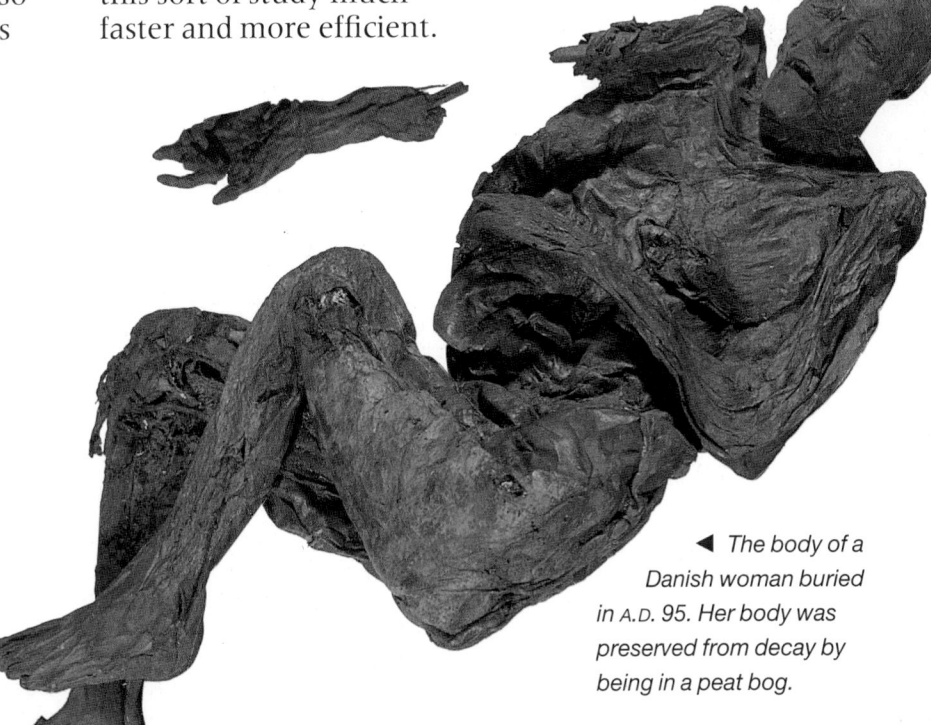

◄ *The body of a Danish woman buried in A.D. 95. Her body was preserved from decay by being in a peat bog.*

Buildings often reveal clues about how people lived in the past. Stonehenge in England is linked with the phases of the Sun and Moon and archaeologists believe it is an ancient calculator or computer, used to find the best times for planting and harvesting, two important times of year.

Artifacts, such as coins, pottery, tools, weapons, and ships are sometimes found in great abundance. Their study can add to our knowledge of social and military history. Ecofacts (often found near artifacts), such as animal bones, skins, and plant seeds, help identify the jobs people did and what they had to eat.

Pictures can provide valuable information. We

▶ *For the centuries before photography paintings are the only enduring record of what people looked like. This wall painting from the Roman town of Herculaneum in Italy shows a mother watching her daughter's music lesson.*

▼ *Aerial photography can sometimes help archaeologists where books, maps, and documents may not provide clues. Crop-marks seen from the air show the outlines of Roman forts or Celtic settlements. This picture shows a Roman street plan.*

► *Wooden objects can be dated using dendrochronology, or tree ring dating. Tree growth is affected by the weather and this can be seen in its rings. Over a period of years a pattern develops in the rings. Known patterns can be traced in wooden objects up to 8,000 years old to date them.*

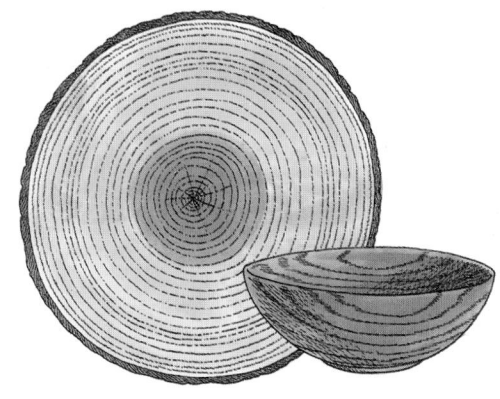

Carter

In 1922 Howard Carter (1874–1939), working with the Earl of Carnarvon, found the fabulously rich tomb of Tutankhamun, who ruled Egypt in 1333 B.C. The discovery of the tomb was one of the most sensational moments in the history of archaeology.

◄ *Radiocarbon dating is used to date specimens up to 60,000 years old. All living things constantly absorb carbon-12 and carbon-14. Carbon-14 is unstable and, after death, decays, so decreasing the ratio of carbon-14 to carbon-12. Using a particle accelerator, scientists measure the amount of carbon-14 to carbon-12. The lower the ratio, the older the object is.*

can tell a lot about what people looked like and what they did before photography was invented from cave paintings, frescoes, portraits, and pictures in stained glass. Pictures can also tell the story of a society. The Bayeux Tapestry (which is really an embroidery) tells the story, in pictures and words, of the Norman invasion of England in 1066. It also tells a less well-known story – that of Harold Godwinsson' being shipwrecked off the coast of France and his encounter with Duke William, his future rival.

▼ *We know a lot about the lives of ancient people because of their belief in life after death. The tombs of rich Egyptians were filled with things that would make the afterlife more comfortable. They made models of their servants; the ones below show a servant making beer and the crew of a ship.*

The Work of Historians

Before the age of writing, history was passed on by word of mouth (the oral tradition) from generation to generation. The Vikings told *sagas*, or stories, many of which have now been confirmed as fact. Long before Columbus, Leif Ericsson sailed to North America and named it Vinland. Many ancient stories were written down a long time after they happened. Homer's *Iliad*, the story of the siege of Troy around 1250 B.C., was probably written down centuries after it happened. No one can be sure how true the story is, but the site of Troy has been found.

The oral tradition forms the history of many African and Aborigine people and can be found in many poems and songs. These tell of migrations, power struggles, and battles as dramatic as any that happened in the Europe of ancient times.

Some events recorded in the Bible are now thought to have really happened. For example the area known as Mesopotamia lay between two rivers and was prone to flooding. This was probably the origin of the story of Noah's Ark.

The first real historian was Herodotus. He used the Greek word *historia* to mean "investigation." Although Herodotus was writing at a time when everyone believed their lives were controlled by the gods, he also looked for rational explanations and was the first person to look at the causes and effects of events.

Sometimes history is written by those who play a major part in it. Julius Caesar (100–44 B.C.) wrote about the wars in Gaul (France) and, according to his own account, was merciful to the defeated Gauls. He granted them Roman

◄ *The Rosetta Stone, found by Napoleon's invading army in Egypt, was the key to deciphering Egyptian hieroglyphic writing.*

Parkman

Francis Parkman (1823–1893) wrote *The Oregon Trail* about his life with Sioux Indians. His multi-volume work *France and England in North America* includes the role played by Native Americans in the struggle for power in North America.

Ranke

Leopold von Ranke (1795–1886) wrote histories of 16th and 17th century France and England and of Germany and Prussia. He also wrote a history of the world up to time of Otto I the Holy Roman emperor, who died in A.D. 973.

Herodotus

Called "the father of history," Herodotus c.485–425 B.C. set out to write a true and systematic record, based on evidence. He wrote about the Greek and Persian wars and the Pyramids of Egypt.

citizenship as a way of establishing order. Caesar may have written his history to show his actions were not done just for personal glory.

Diaries are a valuable source for historians. John White accompanied the 1584 expedition to establish the first English colony in America. He brought back to England his writings and drawings about the daily life of Native Americans. His records are firsthand accounts of events which would otherwise have been lost, because the rest of the colony perished.

Not all historians witness the events they write about. Most depend on accounts and documents produced at the time. Those who write history must always be aware of bias or prejudice in themselves and in

other writers. Bias means being influenced by a particular point of view and prejudice literally means "judging before" – before all of the facts have been looked at. Historians must also avoid the mistake of writing about the past as if all events

▼ *The Dead Sea scrolls are the oldest known biblical manuscripts and may have been written at the time of Christ.*

▲ *A 19th century print showing the American Declaration of Independence in 1776. It set out the idea that all people have rights.*

were leading with a fixed purpose to the present. The events in eastern Europe and the former Soviet Union between 1989 and 1991 show that change can be sudden, and that trends, thought to be fixed, can be reversed.

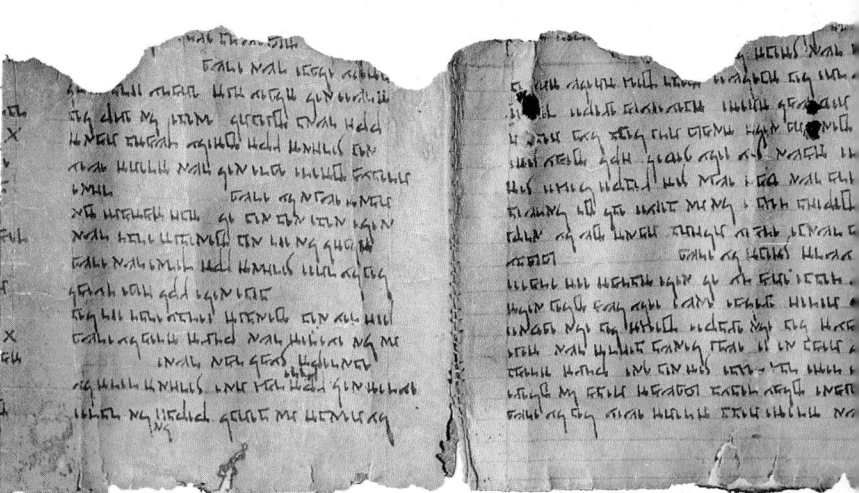

Local History

Oral history is a good source of local history. Listening to older people's recollections, looking at their photographs, and sharing their memories reveal a lot about life in the past. They may have objects or mementos that they kept from their early lives or that have been passed on to them by their parents or

were often recorded in the front of a family Bible. When women married in the past, they usually changed their names; this meant every generation of married women would introduce a new family name. It is unusual for one family to be based in just one place for any length of time and many people who study family

diaries, letters, census returns, old photographs, records of large properties (in towns and the country), school registers, and business accounts from firms that have long since closed down. Church records give details of births, marriages, and deaths. In England, families that have had a connection with one place stretching back

▲ Letters, diaries, menus, and bills can give us a vivid picture about everyday life in the past.

▶ This old family photograph taken in 1909 shows three generations of the same family.

grandparents.

Family history is a branch of local history. Photographs of family members may reach as far back as great-grandparents or even great-great-grandparents. Important family events

history try to find out the reasons why members of their families moved to other places. Was it a job, a sweetheart, or some other reason, such as war or religious and even racial persecution?

Local record offices store

a very long time (over 1,000 years) may find a reference to their family in the *Domesday Book*, compiled in 1086 by order of William the Conqueror. No survey of the British Isles was conducted again until 1801.

The Ancient World

When this period of history begins the world was still in the grip of the last Ice Age. Vast ice caps and huge glaciers covered northern Europe, Asia, and North America. Farther south, however, in what is now Africa, the Sahara was green and fertile. While people in the north shivered in caves, hippopotamuses splashed around in the warm waters of the Sahara.

The earliest humans learned how to use fire to keep themselves warm, cook food, and scare away wild animals. From being hunters and gatherers of wild fruit, berries, and seeds, they slowly found out how to grow crops and keep animals. Eventually they settled down to build houses, villages, and the first cities.

The first civilizations began on the banks of river systems where the land was extremely fertile: the Euphrates and Tigris in what is now Iraq; the Nile in Egypt; and the Huang He or Yellow River in China. For a time another ancient people flourished on the banks of the Indus River in present-day Pakistan, and a little later advanced civilizations grew up in the Americas.

Many of the greatest inventions, such as the wheel and writing, occurred during this period, but with events that happened before the invention of writing, archaeologists can only give approximate dates. Later in the period, historians often disagree about the exact dates of events. Nevertheless, it is fascinating to compare what happened in different places at about the same time.

For example, while Pharaoh Cheops (Khufu) was urging his workers to finish the Great Pyramid in Egypt, ancient Britons were building Stonehenge in England; farmers in Peru were growing cotton at the same time as the people of the kingdom of Kush in Africa were learning to work metal; and only a few years after the first Olympic games were held in Greece, Chinese astronomers first observed an eclipse of the Sun.

▼ *A village on the Nile River, Egypt in about 3000 B.C. The early Egyptians used papyrus reeds, not only for their huts but also to build boats.*

NOTE: Most dates in the period before Christ (B.C.) are approximate.

The Americas

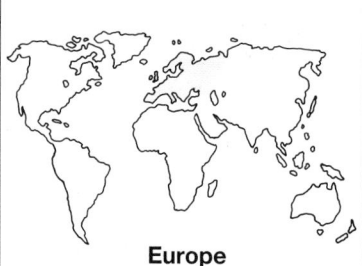

Europe

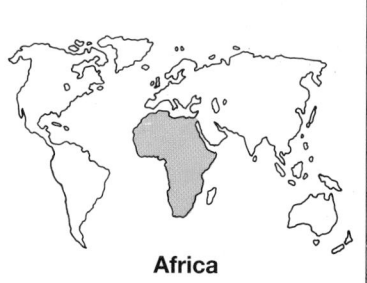

Africa

The Americas	Europe	Africa
35,000 First Americans cross from Asia.	**40,000** Cro-Magnons enter Europe from the Near East.	
25,000 People live in caves in Brazil.	**30,000** Neanderthals disappear.	**30,000** Neanderthals die out.
	25,000 Cave art flourishes in Spain and France.	**15,000** Last rainy period in northern Africa.
		6000 Early rock paintings.
5000 Corn (maize) cultivated in Mexico.	**5000** Land bridge between England and France disappears.	**5000** Civilizations develop in Fayoum and Nubia.
3500 Potatoes grown in South America.		
3372 First date in Mayan calendar.		**2920** Menes rules a united Upper and Lower Egypt.
3000 Agriculture develops in Mexico; coastal towns built in Peru.	**3000** Windmill Hill culture in England.	**3000** Lake Chad drying up, Sahara becoming a desert.
		2630 Step Pyramid in Egypt.
	2700 Building of Stonehenge, England begins.	
	2500 Skara Brae in Scotland destroyed.	**2551** Great Pyramid begun.
2000 Cotton grown in Peru.	**2000** Minoan Crete dominates the Mediterranean.	
	1900 Mycenaean culture in Greece develops.	**2000** Bantu begin migrating from central Africa.
	1450 Thera (Santorini) volcano erupts, Greece.	**1640** Hyksos usurp Egyptian throne; people from Palestine settle in Egypt.
1500 Stone temples built in Mexico.	**1400** Knossos, Crete, destroyed.	**1550** New Kingdom in Egypt.
1200 Olmec civilization develops in Mexico.	**1100** Dorians invade Greece.	
	900 Etruscans flourish in Italy.	*c.* **1270** Israelites leave Egypt.
	814 Foundation of Carthage.	**1179** Sea People attack Egypt.
850 Chavín culture appears in Peru.	**700** Homer's the *Iliad*.	**1140** First Phoenician colony in Africa at Utica.
	776 First Olympic games.	**1070** End of Egypt's New Kingdom.
	753 Foundation of Rome.	**750** Kush conquers Egypt.
	621 First written laws in Athens.	
	539 Greeks defeat the Carthaginians.	
	510 Last king of Rome deposed, republic formed.	

Near East

Asia and the Far East

Australasia and Pacific

Near East

10,000 Beginnings of agriculture.
6000 Çatal Hüyük in Anatolia flourishing.

3760 Bronze in use.
3200 Sumerians invent writing.

3000 Wheeled vehicles in use.

2300 Semites invade Mesopotamia.
c. 2100 Abraham leaves Ur.
1950 End of the empire of Ur.
1595 Hittites conquer Babylon.

1300 Medes and Persians move into Iran.
1116 Assyrians conquer Babylon.
922 Israel splits into Israel and Judah.
612 End of Assyrian empire.

550 Cyrus the Great founds the Persian empire.
525 Persia conquers Egypt.

Asia and the Far East

18,000 Earliest human sculpture.

4000 Yang Shao period in China.
3500 Copper in use in Thailand.

2697 "Yellow Emperor" in China.
2690 Indus Valley civilization.

2200 Jomon culture in Japan.
2150 Aryans begin invasion of Indus Valley.

1500 End of Indus Valley civilization. Shang dynasty in China.

1200 Aryans in India.
1122 Zhou dynasty in China.
1000 *Rig Veda* compiled in India.
800 Development of India's caste system.
722 Period of loose confederations in China.
563 Birth of the Buddha.
551 Birth of Confucius.

Australasia and Pacific

30,000 First people reach Australia.

4000 Colonization of the Pacific islands begins.

Canoes were used for transport.

2000 First settlers arrive in New Guinea.

1300 First settlers arrive in Fiji, Tonga, and Samoa.

The Ice Age

Changes in the Earth's orbit around the Sun may cause ice ages. When they occur, the climate at the North and South Poles becomes extremely cold. Ice caps form, and spread south and north from the Poles. Life becomes impossible under the ice, and difficult near it. The climate of the whole world changes.

The Ice Age was at its height around 16,000 B.C. This was the most recent of a series of ice ages that have occurred over the last 2.3 billion years. It is the one that most affected humans.

During the Ice Age, the Arctic ice cap spread south to cover northern Europe and Asia, the whole of Canada, and the Great Lakes area of the United States. With so much water locked up in ice, the sea level fell by about 300 feet (90 m).

As a result, there was dry land between northern Asia and Alaska, between Australia and New Guinea, and many Indonesian islands. The British Isles and Europe were linked by land that covered the southern part of the North Sea. The Thames was a tributary of the Rhine.

▲ During the Ice Age people were limited in the areas where they could live, but they managed to exist in caves on the edges of the ice. In the caves they left wall paintings as a record of the animals they knew. In this re-created scene ibex are being pursued by huntsmen armed with spear-throwers.

▶ The Leakey family – Louis, Mary, and their son Richard – spent many years looking for fossils of early humans in Africa. Here Mary Leakey is examining footprints of a human-type creature that are about 2.5 million years old. It was warm in Africa while ice covered most of Europe.

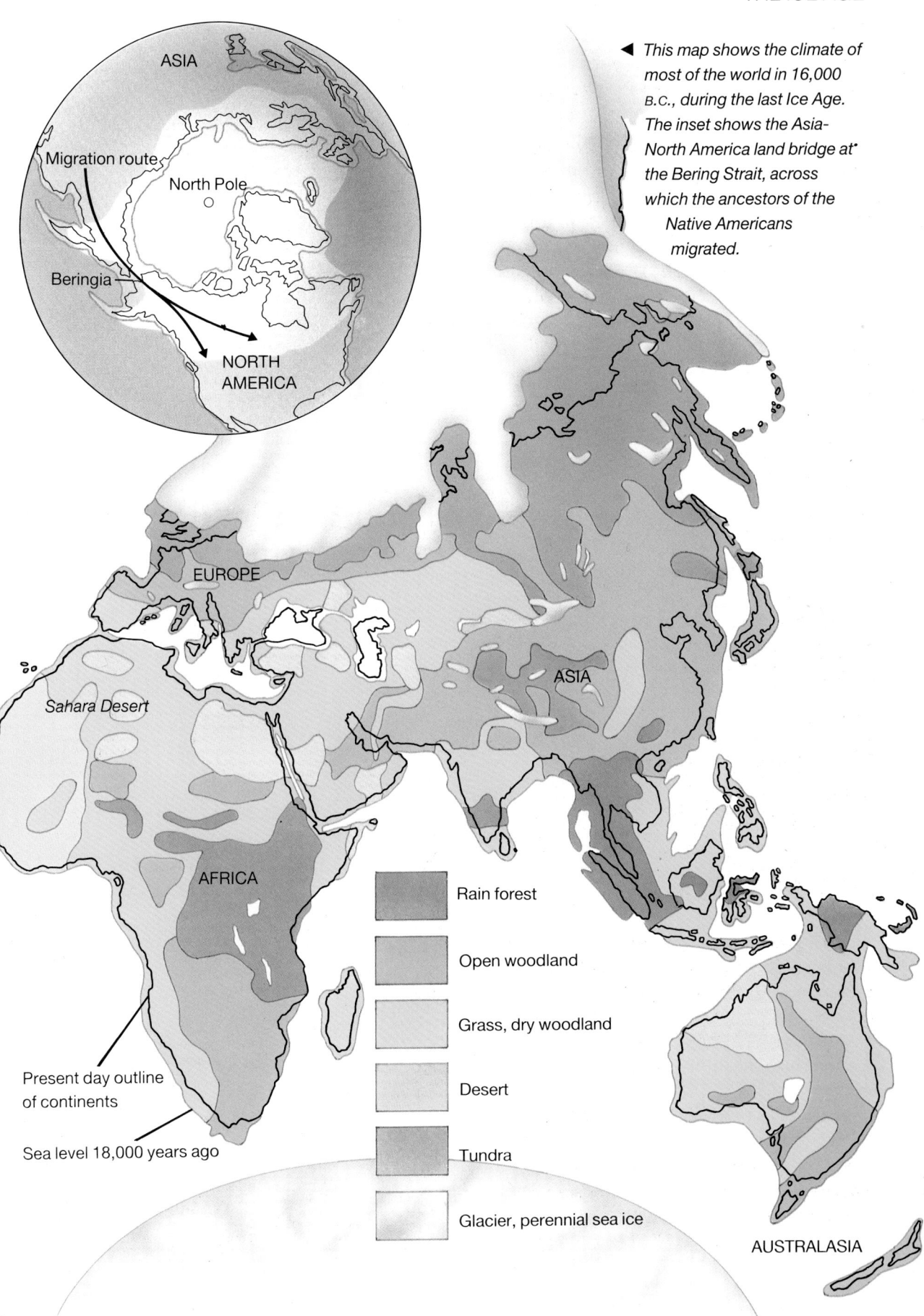

◄ This map shows the climate of
most of the world in 16,000
B.C., during the last Ice Age.
The inset shows the Asia-
North America land bridge at
the Bering Strait, across
which the ancestors of the
Native Americans
migrated.

ASIA

Migration route

North Pole

Beringia

NORTH
AMERICA

EUROPE

ASIA

Sahara Desert

AFRICA

Rain forest

Open woodland

Grass, dry woodland

Desert

Tundra

Glacier, perennial sea ice

Present day outline
of continents

Sea level 18,000 years ago

AUSTRALASIA

The First People

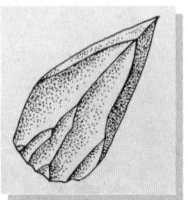

The earliest hominids, or humanlike creatures, are called Australopithicines. Many of their bones have been found in Africa. They walked upright and made simple tools from pebbles. They were probably not true humans because their brains seem to be very small.

The earliest species of true humans, belonging to the genus *Homo* (human), first appeared about two million years ago. Called *Homo habilis* (handy human), they lived alongside the last of the Australopithicines.

The most advanced of these early humans is known as *Homo erectus* (upright human) and their remains have been found in Africa and Asia. By learning to use fire, this species was able

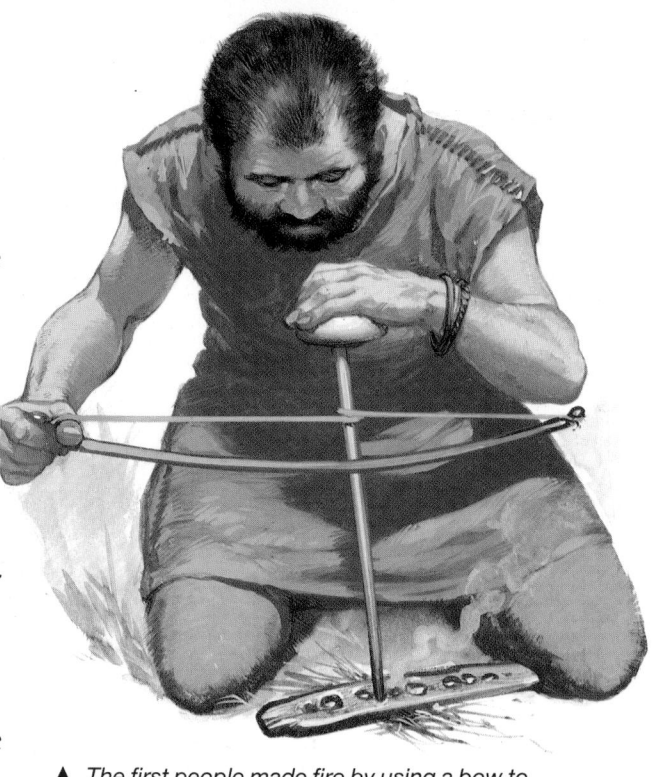

▲ *The first people made fire by using a bow to spin a stick against another piece of wood.*

TOOLS AND HOMES

Knife

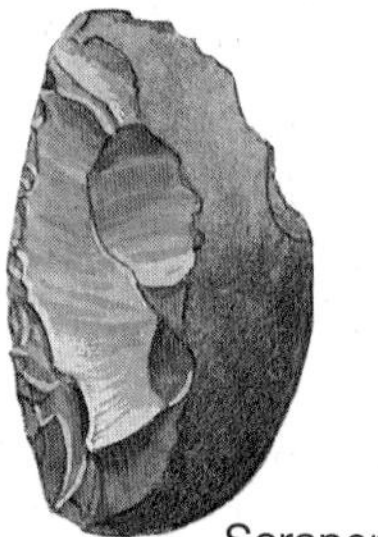

Scraper

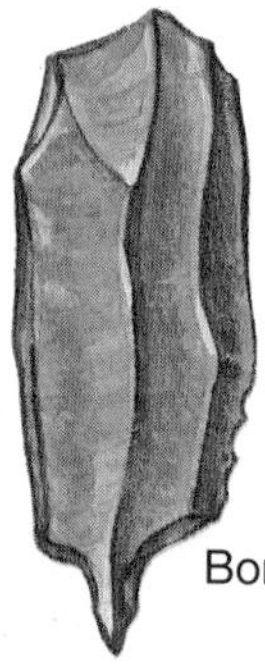

Borer

Arrowhead

Bone needle

The first people used flint for making tools such as scrapers, knives, arrowheads, and borers. These were often set into wooden handles. They also made needles from bone. They built shelters and when timber was scarce, they used large mammoth bones to make a framework for their dwellings. The hut shown here was discovered at Mezhirchichi in the Ukraine. The builders usually hollowed out the floors of the huts below ground level, as protection from the bitter Arctic winds. They probably covered the framework with skins or sod to make the huts weatherproof.

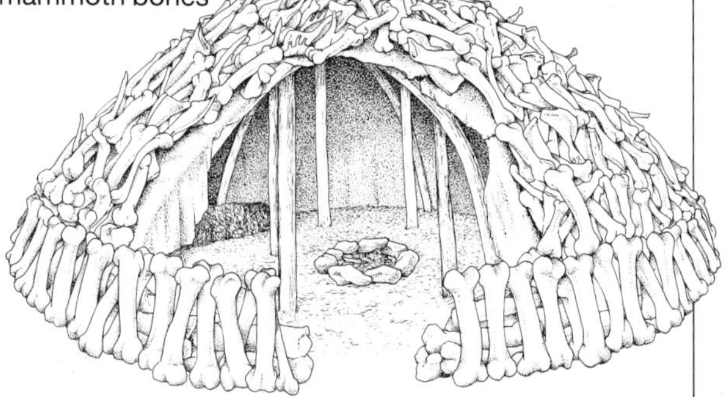

Shelter made of mammoth bones

PIGMENTS

The first people used many natural pigments (paints) to decorate their bodies and their homes. In Europe, Cro-Magnons painted the animals they hunted using black, yellow, red, and white pigments. More than a hundred decorated caves have been found in Europe and many rock paintings exist in Africa and Australia.

EARTH MOTHER

One of the earliest statues known is called the Venus of Willendorf, named after the place in Austria where it was found. It was probably carved between 25,000 and 15,000 years ago. Archaeologists think it represented a goddess, probably the Earth Mother.

to move into icy Europe, cook and keep warm, and drive away wild animals. Next followed *Homo sapiens* (wise human), which flourished from about 200,000 years ago. One type, called the Neanderthals, were particularly adapted to living in a cold climate and were able to survive in northern Europe. They developed many types of stone tools.

The humans who live today are probably descended from the Cro-Magnons who seem to have entered Europe from the Near East and replaced or mixed with the Neanderthals. The first people lived by gathering fruits, berries, and roots, and hunting wild animals.

▲ Early artists painted animals, like this bison, deep inside caves.

▼ An encampment of hunters in eastern Europe about 25,000 years ago. Hunting in groups, they could kill very large animals such as the mammoth. The hide was used for clothing and shelter and the meat and bones were cooked in large pit fires.

Arts and Crafts

The mammoth hunters who lived in Europe over 25,000 years ago made little clay models of women and of animals. No one knows whether these were just works of art or whether they were religious. Later hunters painted pictures of animals deep inside caves. Once people started leading more settled lives, they had more time to make pottery and other items. In China the people of Yang Shao painted pots with geometrical patterns on them. As bronze replaced stone for weapons and tools, metalworkers became important craftsmen. They made objects which were not only practical, but beautiful. As towns and cities grew, temples and important buildings were decorated with carvings and paintings.

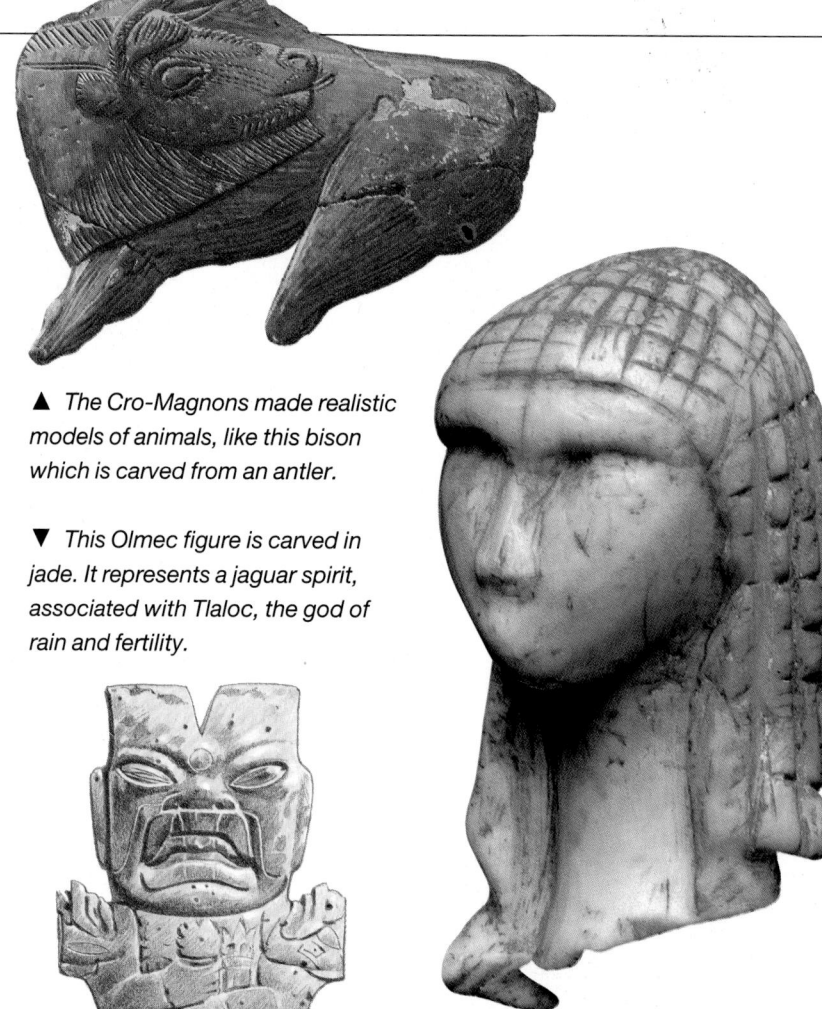

▲ The Cro-Magnons made realistic models of animals, like this bison which is carved from an antler.

▼ This Olmec figure is carved in jade. It represents a jaguar spirit, associated with Tlaloc, the god of rain and fertility.

▲ This delicately-carved ivory head found in France may be the world's earliest known portrait. It was carved over 24,000 years ago.

▲ This fish from the Egyptian New Kingdom is a bottle for cosmetics. It was made from strips of colored glass wrapped around a core. The ripples were made by drawing a point across the glass before it hardened.

WHEN IT HAPPENED

c. 27,000 B.C. Mammoth hunters in Europe make clay figures of women and animals.

c. 25,000 B.C. Hunters paint animals on the walls of the caves at Lascaux in France.

c. 6000 B.C. People at Çatal Hüyük, Turkey, have necklaces made from shells.

c. 3500 B.C. At Yang Shao, China, pottery painted with geometric patterns is made.

1323 B.C. Tutankhamun is buried in Egypt.

c. 1200 B.C. The Olmecs, Mexico, carve huge human heads out of basalt.

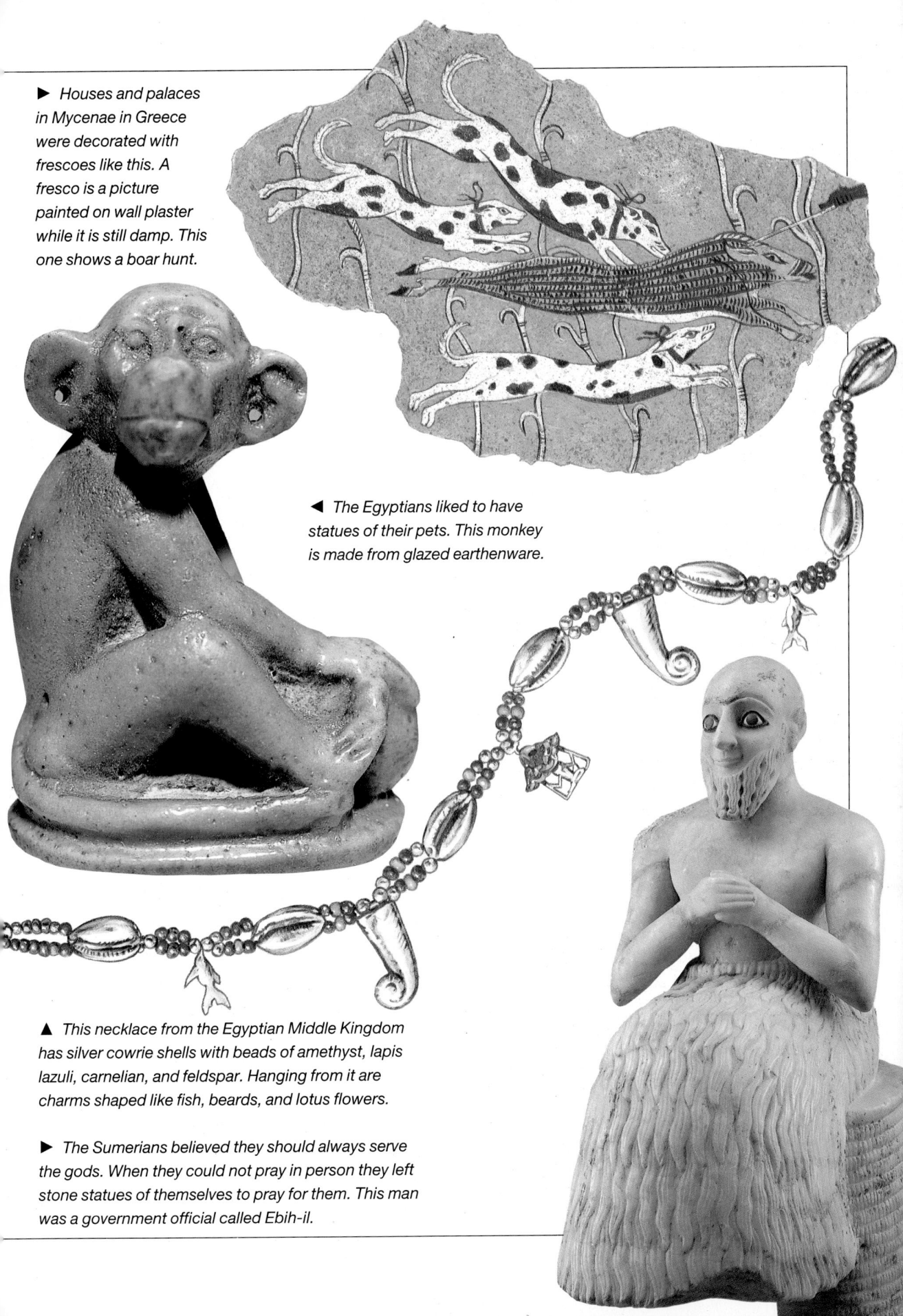

► Houses and palaces in Mycenae in Greece were decorated with frescoes like this. A fresco is a picture painted on wall plaster while it is still damp. This one shows a boar hunt.

◄ The Egyptians liked to have statues of their pets. This monkey is made from glazed earthenware.

▲ This necklace from the Egyptian Middle Kingdom has silver cowrie shells with beads of amethyst, lapis lazuli, carnelian, and feldspar. Hanging from it are charms shaped like fish, beards, and lotus flowers.

► The Sumerians believed they should always serve the gods. When they could not pray in person they left stone statues of themselves to pray for them. This man was a government official called Ebih-il.

NOTE: Most dates in the period before Christ (B.C.) are approximate.

B.C.

40,000 Last Ice Age: Cro-Magnon people, the first modern humans, begin to enter Europe from the Near East.

35,000 Around this time humans cross the Bering Strait land bridge to America from northeastern Asia.

30,000 First humans reach Australia from southern Asia, partly by land bridges, partly by boat. Neanderthal people seem to disappear in Africa and Europe after existing for about 70,000 years. Hunters roam southern Europe.

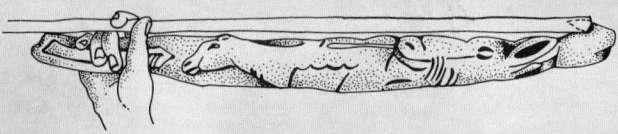

A spear-thrower lengthened the hunter's throwing arm and meant that he could throw his spear farther. This was probably the first machine ever invented.

25,000–20,000 Cave art flourishes in southern Europe, especially at Lascaux, France and Altamira, Spain. Figurines of Great Mother-Goddess, made of stone and ivory in Europe, found in Nile mud in Egypt. People in southeast Asia use rafts. Early cave settlement, with wall decoration, flourishes in northeastern Brazil.

18,000 Earliest known human sculpture made in Asia.

15,000–10,000 Africa cooler than today – last rainy period in northern Africa.

10,000 End of the last Ice Age. Hunting weapons develop. Disappearance of large mammals in North America. Humans reach the tip of South America.

10,000–9000 Beginnings of agriculture in the Near East and eastern Asia. Ceremonial burials of bodies coated in red ocher in Czechoslovakia and Iraq, associated with goddess worship.

The First Farmers

People's lives changed with the development of agriculture. Slowly people discovered that certain plants could be grown or cultivated to provide crops, and certain animals could be protected or domesticated (tamed) to provide meat, milk, hides, or wool. Gradually many people began to rely on the steady supply of food from their crops and animals and instead of moving from place to place to gather their food, they started to settle in fertile areas of land.

Farming and civilizations grew up in several parts of the world, including China, Africa, and Central America. Some of the earliest farmers settled nearly 10,000 years ago in what is often called the "Fertile Crescent." This was an area of land which was watered by the Tigris, Euphrates, and Nile rivers. Here people grew wild wheat and wild barley, and

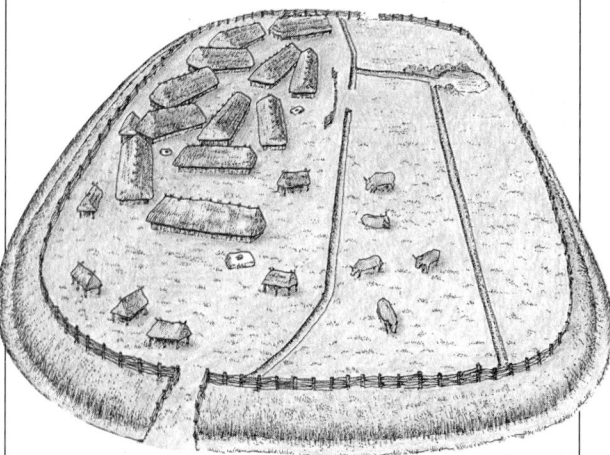

EARLY VILLAGE LIFE

An aerial view of a European farming village about 4500 B.C. The large enclosure contains shelter for cattle and pigs. Peas, beans, and lentils grew in vegetable patches in front of the houses. Villages of up to 50 dwellings are known to have existed. In time, the crops and grazing animals exhausted the soil and the people had to move to new sites.

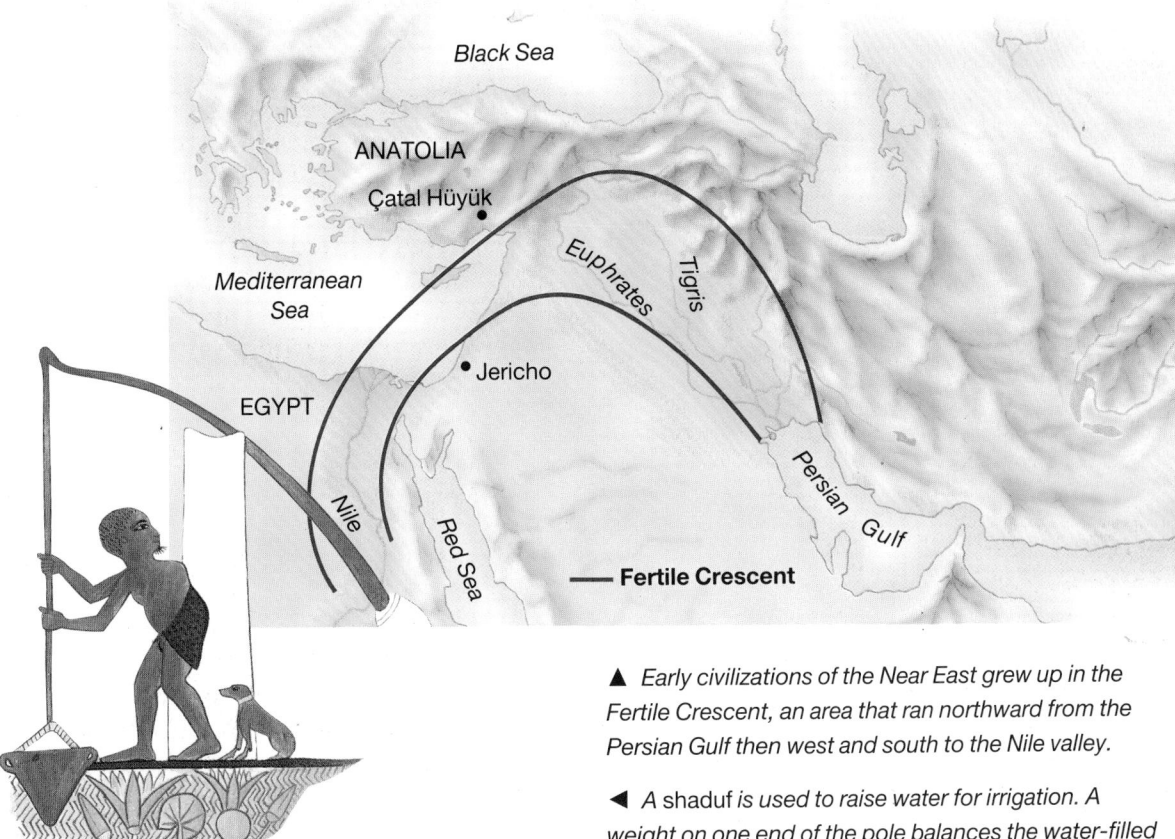

▲ Early civilizations of the Near East grew up in the Fertile Crescent, an area that ran northward from the Persian Gulf then west and south to the Nile valley.

◀ A shaduf is used to raise water for irrigation. A weight on one end of the pole balances the water-filled leather bucket on the other end.

kept goats, sheep, pigs, and cattle.

The first animal to be domesticated was the dog, and it is likely that dogs adopted humans just as much as humans began to keep dogs. This probably began as far back as 10,000 B.C. Dogs were used to herd other wild animals, who in turn were domesticated. Soon breeding began to change the animals.

One of the most important inventions for agriculture was irrigation, a system of supplying cultivated land with water. Farmers in the Fertile Crescent and America dug out channels to carry water from the river to their crops. Using reservoirs and sluice gates, land lying far from the river could be made fertile.

After many generations these farming settlements grew and established the first cities and civilizations.

CROPS

The early farmers harvested wild wheat and barley. They then sowed some seeds to raise new crops. Farming grew rapidly when wild wheat crossed naturally with a kind of grass. It produced a new form of wheat with plump seeds. People were able to cultivate this wheat and use it to make a new kind of food: bread. Farmers used simple tools such as hoes and crude plows. They reaped the crops with sickles made of flint.

Wheat

Barley

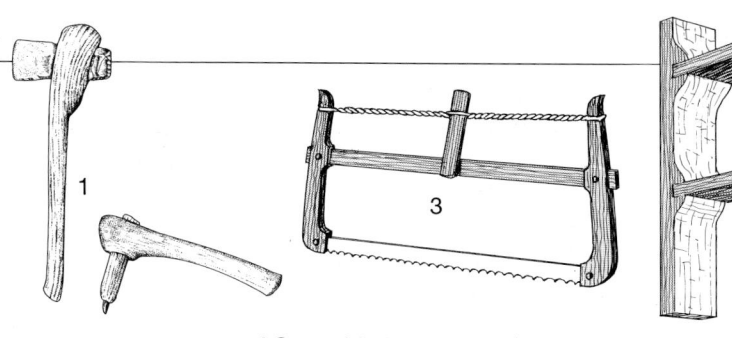

Buildings

The earliest humans lived in caves or any other natural shelter they could find. The first buildings they made were like tents of animal skins supported on wooden poles. In places where wood was scarce, they used mammoth bones for supports. Eventually they started making more comfortable homes for themselves. Many of these were made of mud and wood and so they have long since rotted away. Luckily archaeologists have been able to find enough evidence to show us what some of these houses looked like and how they were built. However, not all buildings were made for people to live in. Some were made for religious purposes and others were made as tombs for the dead. Often these were built from stone and so they have survived to the present day. They include the pyramids and temples in Egypt, and Stonehenge in England.

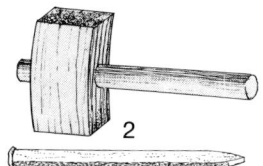

1 Stone-bladed ax and pick
2 Wooden mallet and bronze chisel
3 Bronze-bladed saw
4 Plumb line

▲ *The first builders used stone tools in constructing their houses. Later builders had metal tools which were more efficient.*

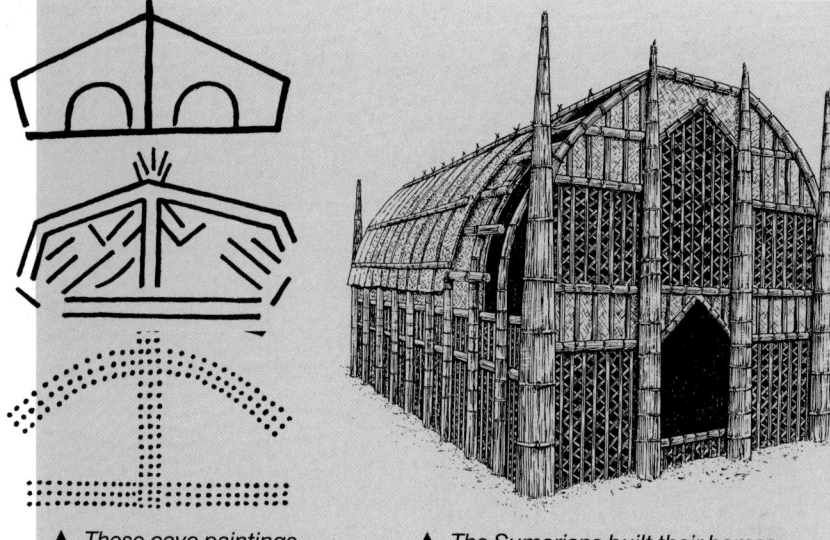

▲ *These cave paintings may show plans for huts.*

▲ *The Sumerians built their homes out of marsh reeds.*

▼ *Pyramids were usually built on the edge of the desert with a causeway connecting them to the Nile River. The funeral procession landed by boat and then went along the causeway to the mortuary temple where the funeral was performed. The body was then buried in the pyramid. The pyramid was seen as a ramp to the sky.*

Causeway

Mortuary temple

Pyramid

WHEN IT HAPPENED

c. **9000 B.C.** Walls of Jericho are built.
c. **5000 B.C.** The Chinese build circular huts of wood and mud by the Yellow River.
c. **2700 B.C.** The building of Stonehenge begins.
c. **2630 B.C.** Pyramids built at Giza, Egypt.
c. **2000 B.C.** Minoans build Knossos in Crete. Mohenjo-daro is built in Pakistan.
c. **1250 B.C.** Egyptians add to the Karnak temple.

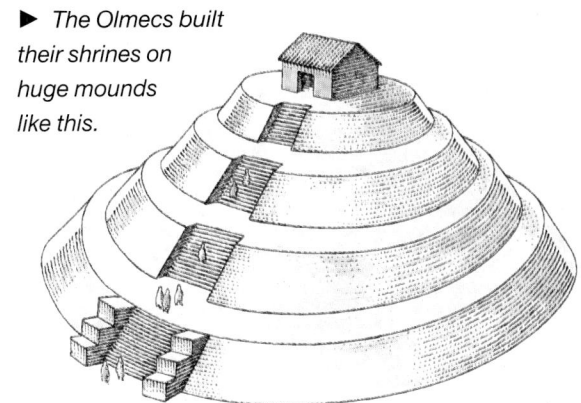

▶ *The Olmecs built their shrines on huge mounds like this.*

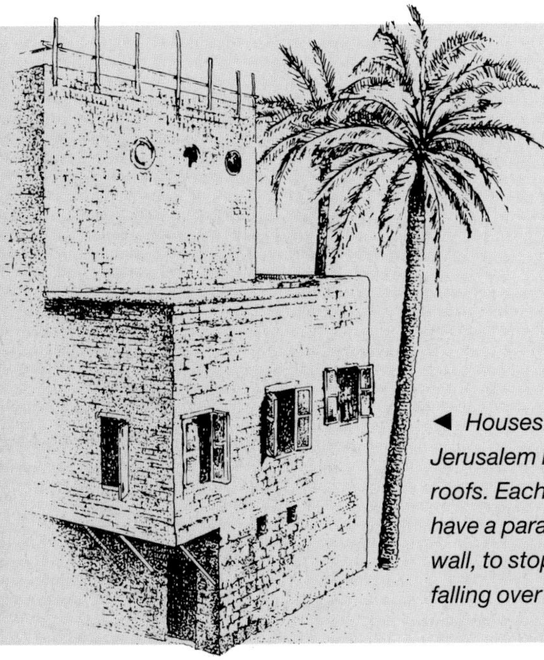

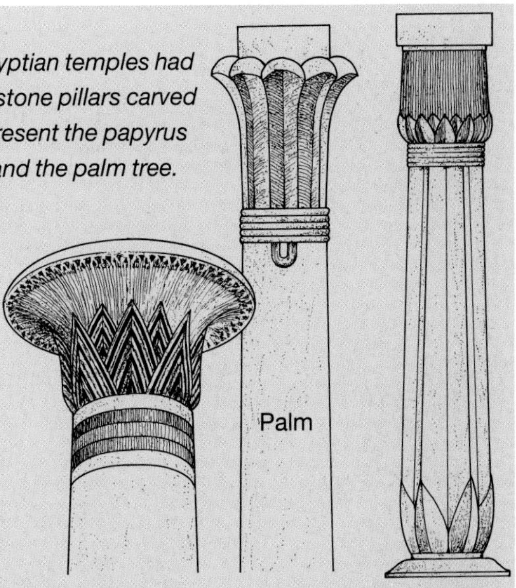

▼ *Egyptian temples had many stone pillars carved to represent the papyrus plant and the palm tree.*

Palm

Open papyrus

Bundle papyrus

◀ *Houses in Jerusalem had flat roofs. Each one had to have a parapet, or low wall, to stop visitors falling over the edge.*

▼ *In Europe the first farmers made their house walls of panels of woven twigs, plastered with clay to keep out the wind and rain.*

The First Cities

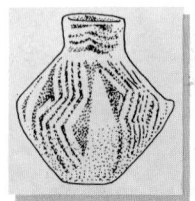

One of the oldest cities known is Jericho, which lay on the west bank of the Jordan River. The battle of Jericho, which is described in the Bible as when the walls came tumbling down, was fought about 3,500 years ago. But the ruins of some of the city's walls are 11,000 years old. They were massive structures of stone, and some may have been as high as 23 feet (7 m).

The walls of ancient Jericho were rebuilt at least 16 times. They were probably destroyed not by a series of battles, but by earthquakes. Inside the city walls, the houses and other buildings were built from mud bricks and had flat timber roofs.

Çatal Hüyük is another ancient city. Its ruins are in Anatolia, Turkey. It may well have been as ancient as Jericho, but

THE EARLY USE OF POTTERY

Pottery developed at about the same time as agriculture because pots were needed to store grain and to hold water. This pot was discovered near Çatal Hüyük and it is nearly 8,000 years old. It was decorated to resemble braided reeds. At first people made pots out of clay dried in the sun, like their mud bricks. They soon found that baking the clay in a fire made it much harder and longer lasting. Pottery of advanced craftsmanship and decoration was made both in the Near East and in the Yang Shao settlements of China.

▶ *The builders of Çatal Hüyük built their houses with a framework of posts and beams, then constructed the walls with mud bricks before filling in any holes with daub (mud and straw).*

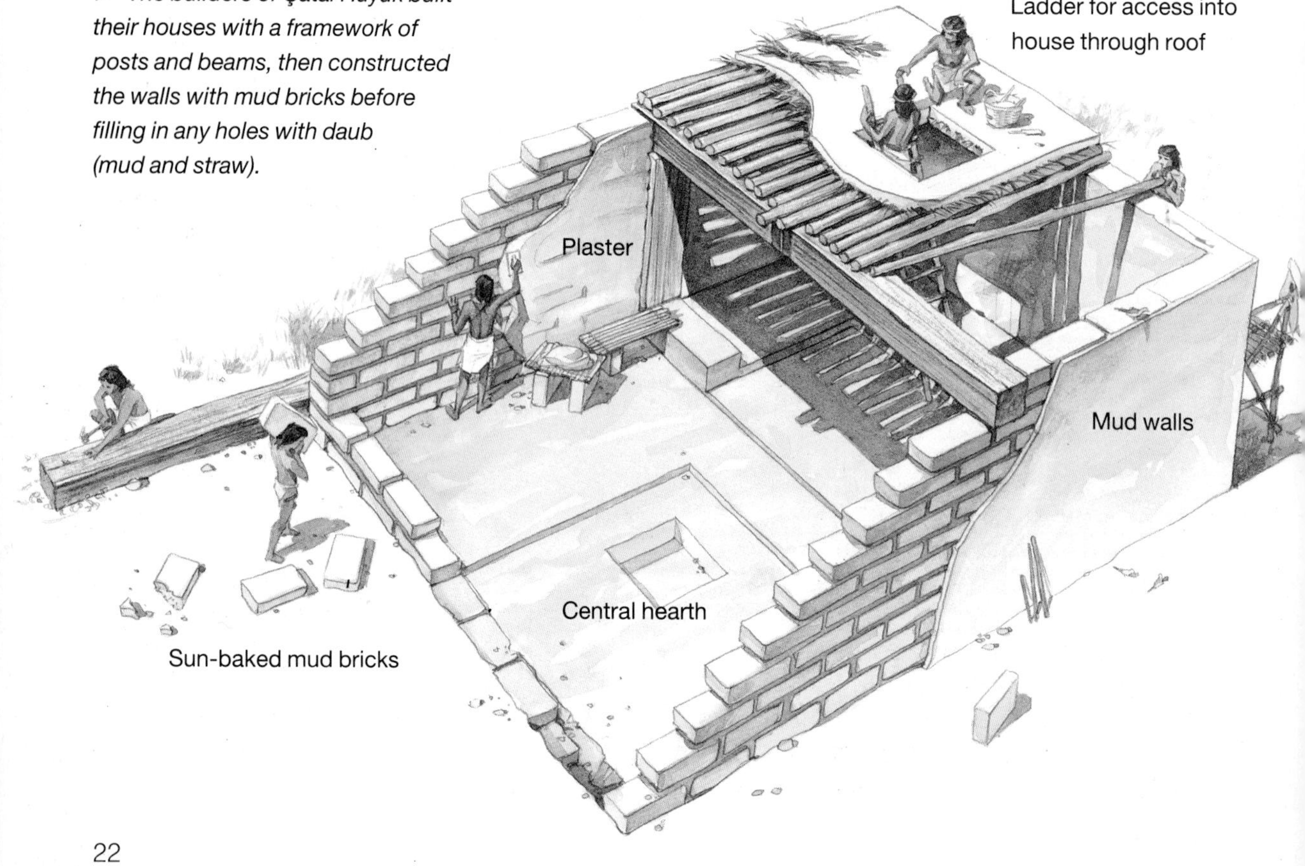

Ladder for access into house through roof

Plaster

Mud walls

Central hearth

Sun-baked mud bricks

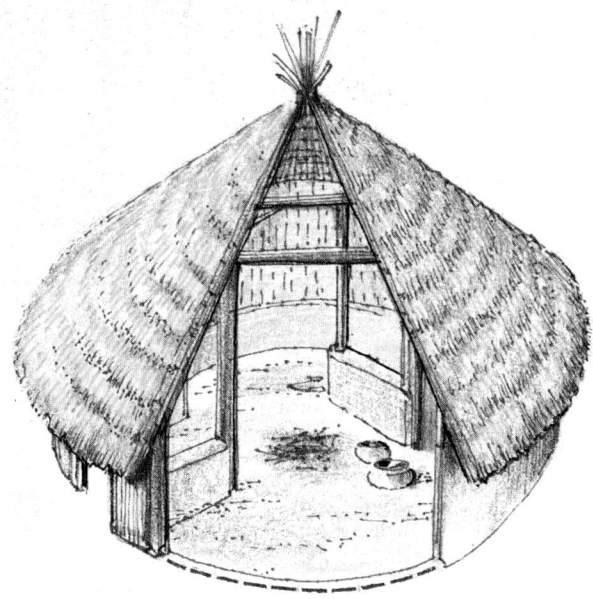

▲ *A model of a Chinese house from about 2000 B.C. The roof was held up by wooden posts. Remains of posts have been found where the Yang Shao lived.*

▼ *The houses in Çatal Hüyük were so tightly packed that there were no streets. People had to walk along the rooftops, then use ladders to enter their homes. This also meant it was difficult for enemies to get in.*

the earliest ruins we know of date from about 6250 B.C. By then about 6,000 people lived in Çatal Hüyük in mud-brick houses. They covered the walls inside their houses with fine plaster, on which they painted decorations in a red pigment. Some of their furniture was made, like the walls, from mud bricks.

While cities were growing up in western Asia, other settlements were rising in the east, in what is now China. The Yang Shao people, who lived in a fertile river valley between the Huang He and its tributary the Wei He, built a number of small, self-contained villages.

B.C.

9000 Near East: Sheep, goats, cattle, and pigs are domesticated; development of Middle Stone Age culture. Earliest walled settlement built at Jericho. Americas: Humans at Folsom in North America.

8400 Americas: First known dog was kept in the Idaho Valley.

8000 Europe: Spread of agriculture to Europe. Near East, and Eastern Asia: Copper is in use. Anatolia: Early settled villages in eastern part of the region. North America: Humans hunt bison. Japan: Pottery is being made.

7600 About this time, the Irish Sea and then the Strait of Dover begin to open up as the sea level rises, gradually separating Ireland from Great Britain, and Great Britain from Europe.

The first bricks were made of mud and left to harden in the Sun.

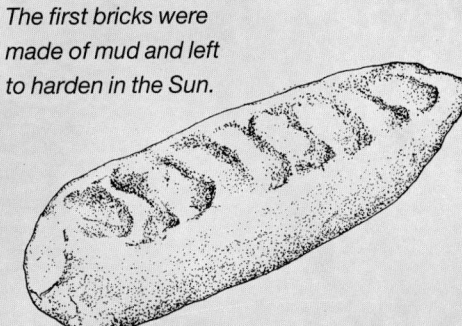

7000 Near East: The city of Jericho continues to flourish despite repeated destruction. First shrines to the Mother Goddess erected there. Pottery develops. The use of brick for building begins in the Near East.

6000 Near East and Europe: The Neolithic (New Stone Age) period begins. Anatolia (modern Turkey): The settlement at Çatal Hüyük is already flourishing and contains 6,000 people. Shrines to the Mother Goddess are set up there.

6000–5000 Near East: The earliest known use of looms for weaving at this time. Crete: The earliest settlements are established. There is trading in obsidian and flint.

North Africa: Early rock paintings are made in the Sahara region.

B.C.

5000 Africa: New Stone Age people work polished stone. Development of civilizations begins at Fayoum and Nubia in the Nile River valley. Agriculture begins to spread southward. China: Yang Shao people establish village farm communities along the banks of the Huang He. Mesopotamia: Sumerians establish their first agricultural settlements in the river valleys of the Tigris and Euphrates. Europe: As the ice cap continues to melt, the rising sea level severs the last land bridge between Great Britain and mainland Europe. Mexico: People begin cultivating corn 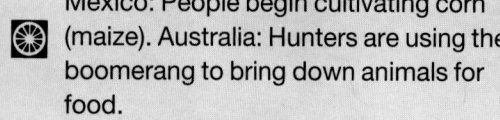 (maize). Australia: Hunters are using the boomerang to bring down animals for food.

4500 Sumer and Egypt: Real metalwork begins, heating and pouring metal into molds.

4000 China: Yang Shao farmers cultivate rice.

A drawing of an alabaster vase found in the temple at Uruk. It shows the fruits of the harvest being given to a priestess.

4000–3500 Sumer: First towns are founded including Ur and Uruk (Eridu). The potter's wheel is first used. Disastrous floods hit the region, probably giving rise to the biblical story of Noah's Ark. Colored pottery from Russia reaches China. Egypt: White painted pottery is produced. Crete: Ships sail in the Mediterranean Sea.

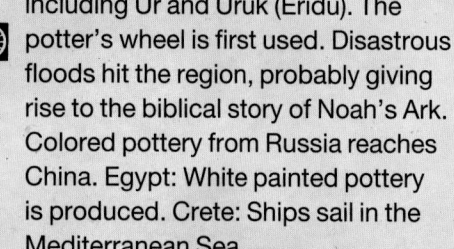

Mesopotamia and Sumer

The first people to settle in Mesopotamia were the Sumerians who arrived there more than 7,000 years ago. Their civilization consisted of a number of city-states or cities that were also independent nations.

Each city-state had fine public buildings, a water supply, and drainage. It had a royal palace for its ruler and a *ziggurat* or tower, on top of which was a temple dedicated to the god that the city worshiped. Around the public buildings were the houses of the people. Beyond them lay the fields of the farmers. Farther out were the marshlands for which southern Mesopotamia was noted.

The Sumerians devised the first known writing system. From about 3200 B.C. they wrote on clay tablets. Thousands of these tablets have survived, containing accounts and letters revealing that as

▼ *Mesopotamia lay between the Tigris and Euphrates rivers. Its name came from the Greek for "between the rivers." Some of its more powerful city-states, shown on the map, conquered their neighbors.*

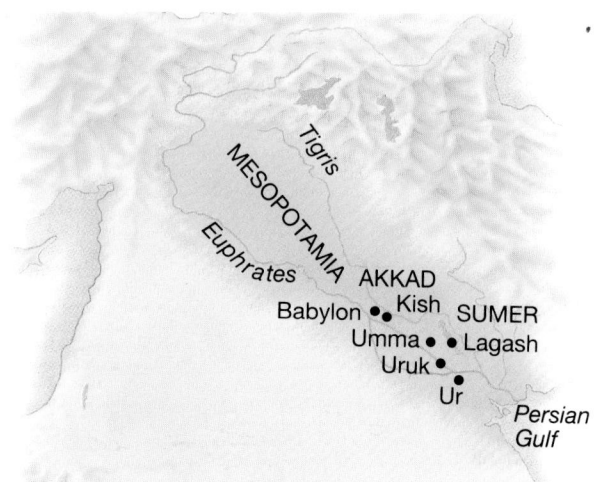

24

Sargon of Akkad

Sargon of Akkad founded a Sumerian empire in 2360 B.C. From his city-state of Akkad he conquered other Sumerian cities. His empire reached as far north as Syria.

▲ *A reconstruction of the ziggurat at Ur. On the top was the temple, where the king (who was also the high priest) performed religious rites and sacrifices. The ziggurat was built of sun-baked clay bricks.*

well as textbooks and history, the public services were highly developed. Royal graves have also been found containing treasures that show the Sumerians' wealth and the skill of their craftsmen.

Many Sumerian traditions have been passed on to us today. Their ancient poem *The Epic of Gilgamesh* describes a flood that is very similar to the biblical story of Noah's Ark (*see* pages 44–45).

The rulers of one city-state called Ur extended their lands to form an empire which included Babylon. The Babylonian language was spoken throughout Ur.

THE WHEEL

No one knows when the wheel was invented. The first wheel was probably the potter's wheel, used to make perfectly round vessels. Carts like this were certainly in use in Sumer more than 5,000 years ago. An important weapon of war developed from the cart: the chariot. Warriors from the north in chariots later overwhelmed Sumer. The wheel was also used as a pulley to lift heavy loads.

▼ *The Sumerians of Mesopotamia built and lived in reed houses on the southern marshlands. This picture of present-day Marsh Arabs on the banks of the Tigris in southern Iraq shows that people still do the same.*

Ancient Egypt

The civilization of the whole of ancient Egypt depended on the Nile River, which flooded every year, depositing rich silt (soil) along its banks. With this, the Egyptians were able to cultivate a long, narrow strip of land on either side of the river. Here the workers grew wheat and barley to make bread and beer, and flax for linen with which they made most of their clothes. They reared cattle mainly as beasts of burden.

For most of their history, the ancient Egyptians were united under one ruler. At the top was the *pharaoh* (king). He was worshiped as a god. The Egyptians believed in an afterlife, so they developed the custom of embalming (preserving) the bodies of the dead. They also built elaborate tombs for them and decorated them with paintings and inscriptions in Egyptian picture-writing, or hieroglyphic ("sacred writing") script.

In between the pharaohs and workers were officials who ran the government, priests who served in temples, and merchants who traded.

UPPER AND LOWER EGYPT

When the small communities along the Nile River became two larger states in the 4th millennium B.C., Lower Egypt occupied the Nile delta and Upper Egypt ran south from the delta for about 500 miles (800 km). In about 2920 B.C., Menes, king of Upper Egypt, became ruler of both states.

The pharaohs of Egypt are generally grouped in dynasties (families). The most important periods are the Old Kingdom (2575–2134 B.C.), from the 3rd to the 6th dynasties; the Middle Kingdom (2040–1532 B.C.), the 11th and 12th dynasties; and the New Kingdom (1550–1070 B.C.), the 18th to 20th dynasties. The Pyramids and the Sphinx at Giza were built during the Old Kingdom.

▶ *A group of funeral urns, known as canopic jars, were used to contain the vital organs taken from a body before it was embalmed. The lids show the heads of four minor Egyptian gods called the Sons of Horus, represented as a jackal, a baboon, a hawk, and a man. They were often made from stone, wood, or pottery.*

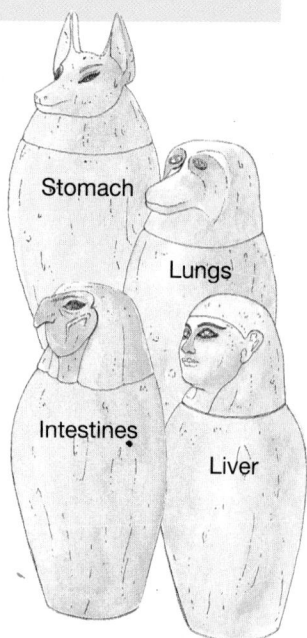

Stomach

Lungs

Intestines

Liver

◀ *Plowing the fields with a pair of oxen, as shown in a tomb painting from about 1300 B.C. The annual flooding of the Nile River kept the land very fertile.*

▶ *The white crown stood for Upper Egypt and the red crown, Lower Egypt. After the two lands were united the pharaohs wore a double crown.*

Mediterranean Sea

Rosetta
Alexandria
Tanis

LOWER EGYPT

Cairo
Giza
Memphis
Saqqara

El-Amarna

Nile

Red Sea

Karnak
Valley of the Kings • • Luxor (Thebes)

UPPER
EGYPT

Abu Simbel •

NUBIA

▲ Important places in Egypt throughout its early history.

B.C.

3800 Sumer: Earliest known map, inscribed on a clay tablet, it shows the Euphrates River.

3760 Earliest date in the Hebrew calendar, for long the traditional date of the Creation. Egypt and Sumer: Early use of bronze is recorded.

3500 Near East: Flax is being grown for making linen; irrigation canals are dug in Mesopotamia. Egypt: Two kingdoms of Upper Egypt and Lower Egypt flourish side by side. The earliest known numerals and a hieroglyphic script are invented. Development of the mastaba, a burial pit covered by a brick platform. South-East Asia: Copper tools come into use in what is now Thailand. South America: farmers grow potatoes.

3372 North America: First date in the Mayan calendar.

A mastaba was a platform built over a burial pit and was the forerunner of the pyramid. Mastabas were also the tombs of noblemen.

The first pyramid was built at Saqqara and is called a step pyramid because of its shape.

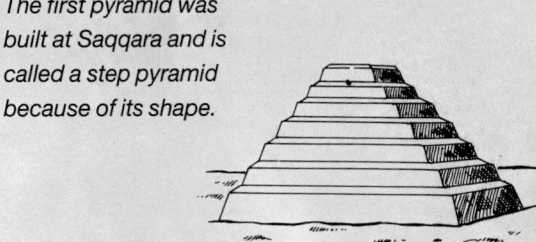

The true pyramids of Giza were the largest of all and the most carefully built.

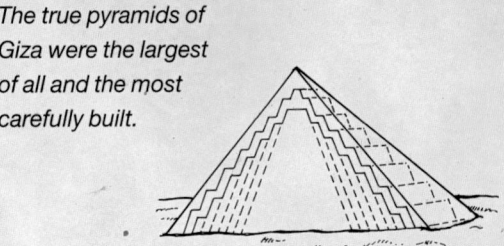

27

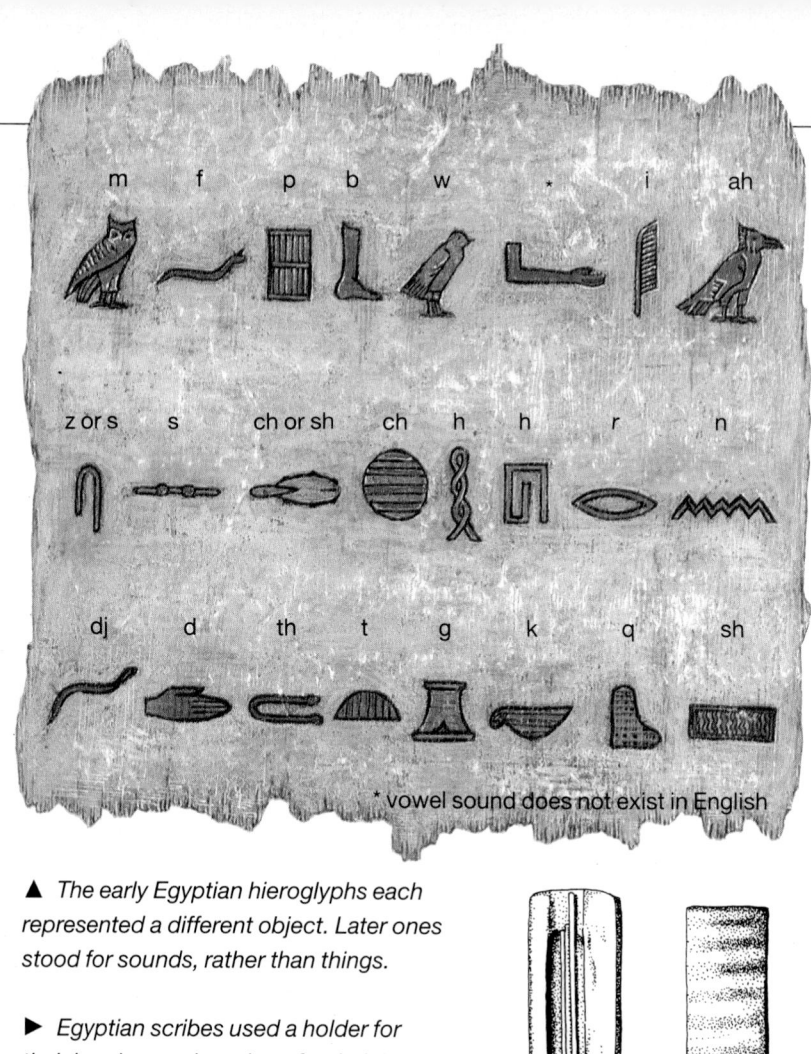

m f p b w * i ah

z or s s ch or sh ch h. h r n

dj d th t g k q sh

* vowel sound does not exist in English

Communications

Once people started trading with each other, they had to find ways of keeping a record of the goods they bought and sold. One way of doing this was by writing the information down. The earliest writing to be discovered so far dates from around 3200 B.C. and comes from Mesopotamia. Here the Sumerians drew tiny pictures on clay tablets. These were probably records and accounts of traders. Over the next 200 years these pictures were replaced by wedge-shaped patterns made with a chopped off reed. Each pattern represented a sound or a syllable. This sort of writing is called cuneiform. The Egyptians knew about it, but they invented a writing system that used pictures, or glyphs. They wrote on sheets of papyrus, made from the papyrus reed. These were lighter and more convenient than clay tablets. In China the earliest surviving examples of writing are from the Shang dynasty. Over 2,000 different characters have been found on oracle bones from this time, suggesting that writing was already well developed.

▲ The early Egyptian hieroglyphs each represented a different object. Later ones stood for sounds, rather than things.

▶ Egyptian scribes used a holder for their brushes and a palette for their ink.

▼ Scribes were important people in Egypt. Their training took up to twelve years. They became civil servants, teachers, or librarians.

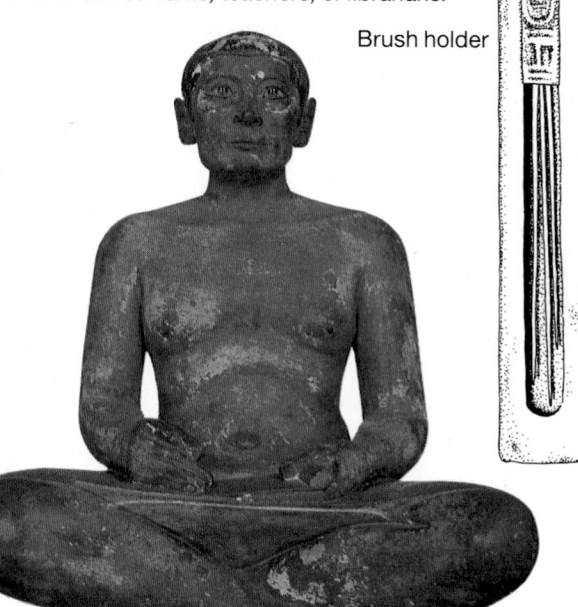

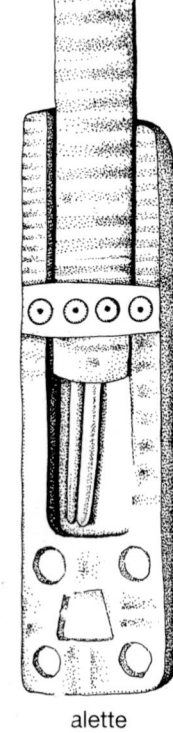

Brush holder

alette

► Mycenaean writing, found on baked clay tablets at the palace of Knossos in Crete. This script is called Linear B. The tablets tell us what was in the palace storeroom, such as weapons and chariot wheels. This writing probably developed into the modern Greek alphabet.

► This map shows where four of the earliest known forms of writing developed. They were all based on pictures that were later simplified.

Cuneiform

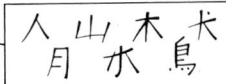

Chinese characters

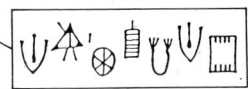

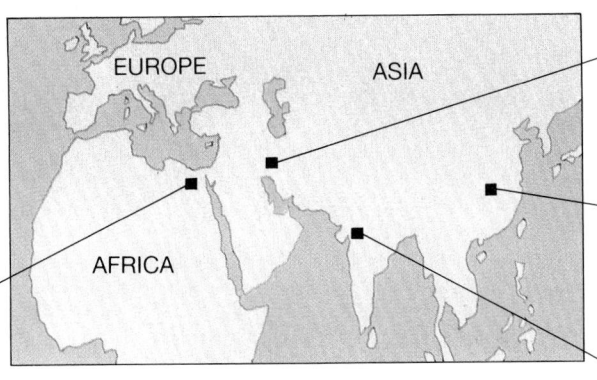

Egyptian hieroglyphs

EUROPE

ASIA

AFRICA

Indus Valley glyphs

► There was more than one Chinese language, but everyone who could read could understand Chinese writing. This was because each symbol stood for an object, not a sound.

WHEN IT HAPPENED

c. 3200 B.C. First writing appears in Mesopotamia.

c. 3200 B.C. Sumerians develop cuneiform writing.

c. 2600 B.C. Papyrus used in Egypt. Before this, the Egyptians wrote on stone.

c. 2000 B.C. Basis for the modern alphabet appears in the eastern Mediterranean countries.

c. 1500 B.C. Chinese writing appears on oracle bones, but Chinese have probably been using writing since c. 2800 B.C.

c. 1400 B.C. Mycenaeans use the script called Linear B for their palace records.

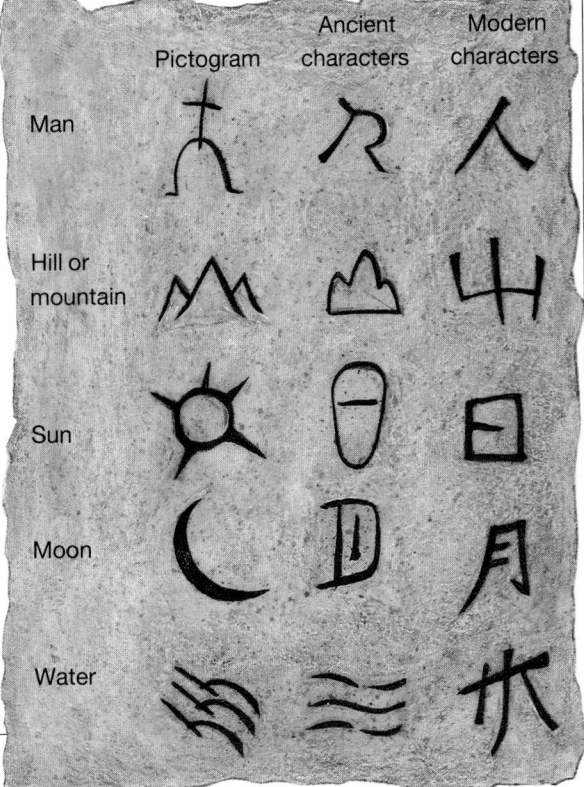

	Pictogram	Ancient characters	Modern characters
Man			
Hill or mountain			
Sun			
Moon			
Water			

Megalithic Europe

All around the coast of western Europe are ancient Stone Age monuments built of megaliths, which means "huge stones." The most impressive of these monuments is Stonehenge, in southern England. It was built in three stages from 2750 B.C. onward, forming a circle of huge, dressed (shaped), upright stones linked by lintels (beams). Scientists think that it was used as a temple and a place to study the stars.

Even older than Stonehenge is the Avebury stone circle, a few miles to the north. It is a much larger ring of stones which have not been shaped.

Stone circles are found elsewhere in the British Isles. One example is the Ring of Brodgar in the Orkney Islands, off northeastern Scotland, which is about the same age as Stonehenge. The stones there are all tall, thin, and pointed.

At Carnac in Brittany, northwestern

▲ Skara Brae, in the Orkney Islands, was a Stone Age village that was buried by sand at the height of a fierce storm 4,500 years ago. The people fled, leaving pottery, bone pins, stone tools, and even a necklace behind.

▼ Stonehenge on Salisbury Plain, England, is one of the most elaborate megalithic monuments in Europe. Its layout was arranged to mark the midsummer sunrise and the midwinter moonrise. To erect the largest stones the people must have used ramps, ropes, and levers. The huge blocks of stone were dragged many miles using only wooden rollers.

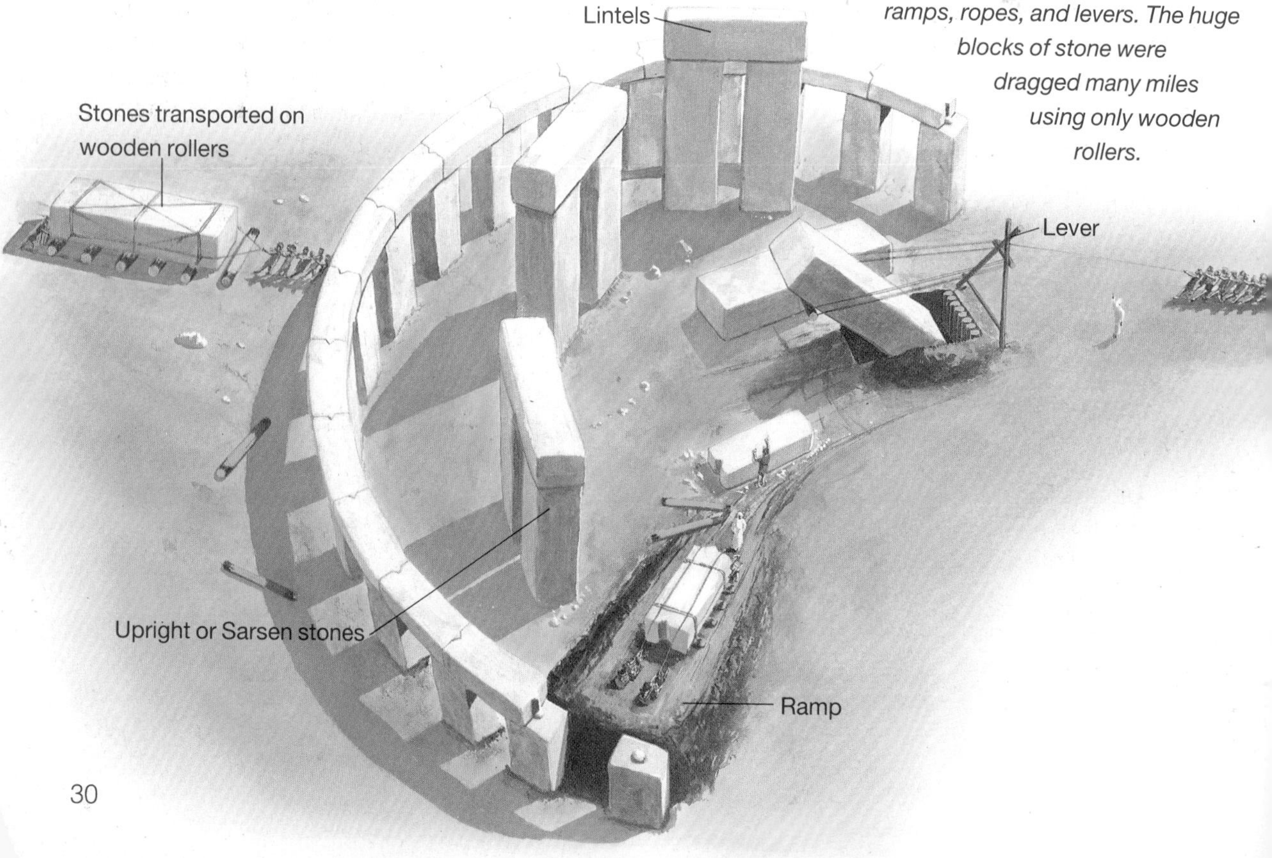

Lintels

Stones transported on wooden rollers

Lever

Upright or Sarsen stones

Ramp

France, there is a series of avenues of standing stones, stretching for several miles and erected in the New Stone Age. Brittany also has many single standing stones, called menhirs.

Many barrows or stone-built graves covered with soil and sod are found in France and England. In some cases the soil has been removed, leaving standing stones with flat slabs resting across them.

Another remarkable collection of megalithic monuments is in Malta and its sister island of Gozo. Some of the oldest have walls made of huge stones 20 feet (6 m) or more long and 11 feet (3.5 m) tall. Several of the temples, such as those at Hagar Qim and Tarxien, contain dressed stones carved with simple designs. The most remarkable Maltese monument is the Hypogeum, an underground temple carved on three levels deep into the rock. ·

RELIGIOUS BELIEFS

We can only guess at the religious beliefs of Stone Age people. Undoubtedly stone monuments, like this one at Carnac in Brittany, France, had a great significance, possibly as meeting places for worship and sacrifice.

Stonehenge, and some other circles, were positioned either to help with observations of the heavens, or as vast outdoor calendars. They suggest some form of Sun worship was practiced.

Some of the stone temples contain altars. The Hypogeum on Malta has an "oracle hole," which magnified the voice of a priest or soothsayer.

B.C.

3200 Sumerians devise first known system of writing, using 2,000 pictographic signs inscribed with a stylus on clay tablets. The script appears in an inscription on the temple of the Mother Goddess at Uruk, under her title Queen of Heaven.

Sumerian farmers grow barley, and make wine and beer. First harps and flutes are made. Scotland: First houses are built at the village of Skara Brae, in Orkney.

3000 Ukraine: Wild horses are domesticated. England: Settlers at Windmill Hill, Wiltshire make pottery; Avebury stone circle in Wiltshire is begun, and also nearby Silbury Hill. Phoenicia: Settlers occupy the eastern Mediterranean coast. Iran: The Elamite civilization flourishes. Africa: Lake Chad begins to dry up and the Sahara begins to form as a desert. Egypt: Pharaoh Menes unites the kingdoms of Upper and Lower Egypt, founding the first dynasty. Mexico: Development of agriculture in the Tehuacan Valley. People make their first pottery. Peru: Villages and towns are built on the coast. Anatolia: Troy flourishes as a city-state. Bronze Age begins. Crete: Stone villages are built. Trade flourishes with Egypt, the Levant, and Anatolia.

Mesopotamia: The first iron objects are made; Sumerians first use wheels on vehicles. Europe: Weaving loom introduced from the Near East.

A tomb in Portugal, built using giant stones (megaliths). Tombs like this have been found all over western Europe dating from 4,000 B.C..

The Indus Valley

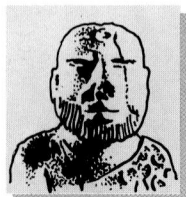

The early peoples of the Indian subcontinent lived around the Ganges and Indus rivers. The first civilization sprang up in the Indus Valley, now in Pakistan. The two largest cities in the valley were Mohenjo-daro (which lay about 200 miles (320 km) northeast of Karachi), and Harappa (which was some 120 miles (200 km) southwest of Lahore). At the center of both Mohenjo-daro and Harappa lay an artificial mound, which served as a citadel (stronghold). On this mound stood a large well-aired granary. Beyond the citadel were stores and the workers' houses.

Each house was built around a courtyard, and had several rooms, a toilet, and a well. All the buildings were built of bricks, baked in wood-fired ovens. The citadel at Mohenjo-daro even had a bathhouse, with private baths around the outside of a much larger public one.

Among other crops, the farmers of the

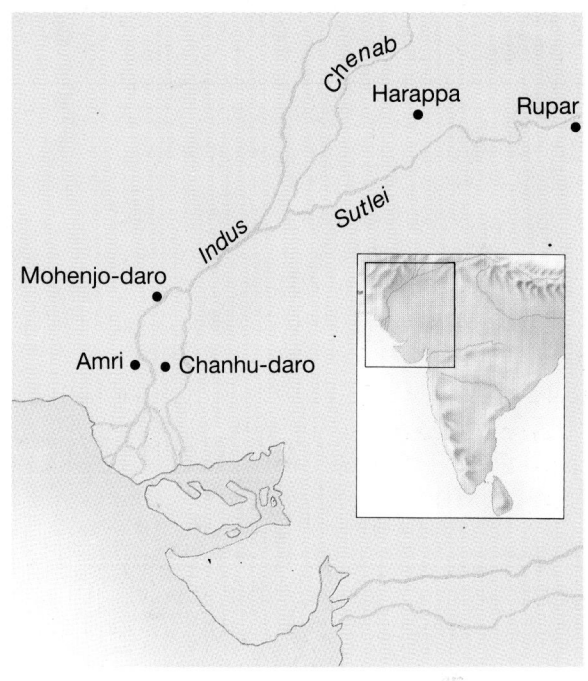

▲ The main places of the Indus Valley civilization. It flourished at a time when the climate of the region was much wetter than it is today.

▼ An artist's impression of Mohenjo-daro as it may have looked at the height of its prosperity. This city was built on a grid pattern like modern U.S. cities.

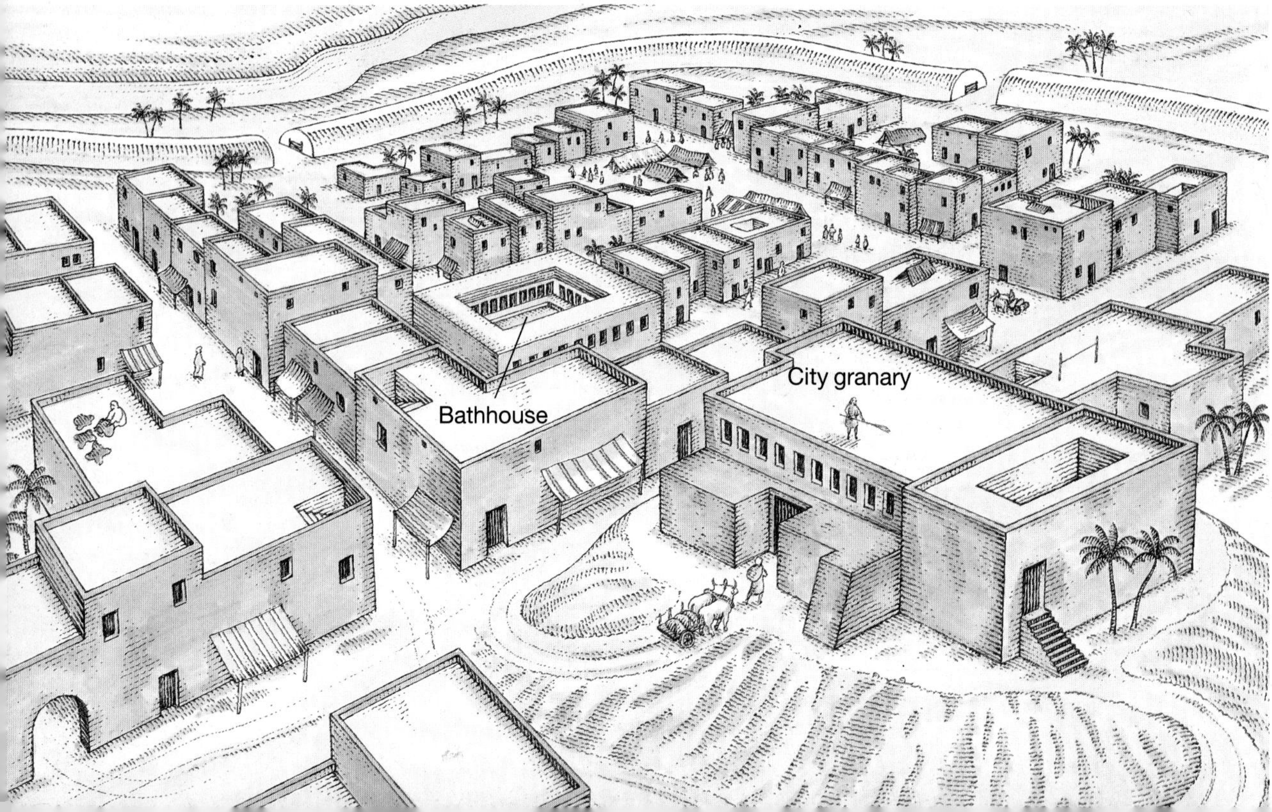

Bathhouse

City granary

Indus Valley grew barley, wheat, melons, and dates. Elephants, water buffalo, and rhinoceroses roamed the region. The area had many skilled potters, who used the wheel for throwing pots. People also used stone tools, and made knives, weapons, bowls, and figures in bronze.

The Indus Valley civilization came to an end about 3,500 years ago. No one knows exactly why this civilization ended but possible causes include flooding, as the Indus River changed its course, and attacks by Aryan invaders from the northwest which eventually drove the Indus Valley people away.

▼ *Brick-lined shafts like this have been found in the courtyards of houses in Mohenjo-daro. They may have been wells or used to store jars of grain or oil.*

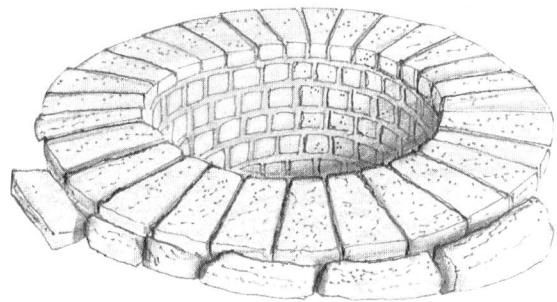

Weaving was an important activity for both women and men. This Egyptian loom dates from 1,900 B.C. and was used to weave linen.

SEALS AND WRITING

More than 1,200 seals like this have been found in Mohenjo-daro. They were used by merchants to stamp bales of goods. No one has yet worked out what the writing on them means.

TRADE AND TRADERS

The people of the Indus Valley carried on a busy trade across the Arabian Sea and up the Persian Gulf to Dilmun (now Bahrain). Polished stone weights found at Bahrain are identical to those that have been identified in Mohenjo-daro and Harappa. Soapstone stamping seals used in the Indus Valley have also been found in Bahrain and the ruins of Ur (now in Iraq).

B.C.

2500 Egypt: The first mummies are embalmed. Europe: Metalworking spreads through the continent. Norway: The first picture of skiing is made – a rock carving in southern Norway. Scotland: Village of Skara Brae, in Orkney, is destroyed by a sandstorm.

2360 Sumer: Sargon the Great of Akkad begins the conquest of Sumer, and founds the Akkadian empire, the largest to date (lasts until 2180).

This Bronze Age rock engraving from Scandinavia shows a sledge with some animals, probably oxen or deer. It was made by chipping away the surface rock.

2300 The chief priestess of Sumer, Enheduanna, daughter of Sargon I, 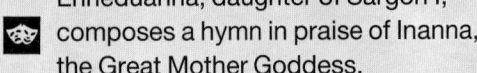 composes a hymn in praise of Inanna, the Great Mother Goddess.

2300 Mesopotamia: Semites from Arabia migrate to Mesopotamia and begin to set up the Babylonian and Assyrian kingdoms.

2250 China: According to tradition, this is the period of the Hsia dynasty; Yu is the emperor.

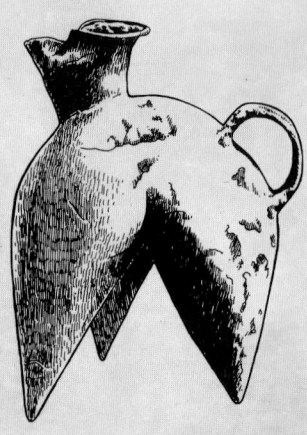

This three-legged earthenware pot was made in China in the 2nd century B.C. on a potter's wheel.

The Great Migrations

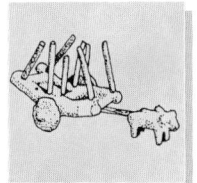

All through history people have been on the move. As populations expand some people travel to places where there is more room for them. They also tend to move as the climate becomes colder or dryer.

By 500,000 years ago humans had spread to all parts of Africa, southern Europe, and southern Asia. During the last Ice Age when the sea level was lower, even isolated parts of the world, such as Australia, were occupied.

But the biggest movement, and growth of the number of people, came when the last Ice Age ended and the sea rose. People began moving north, both in North America and Europe to occupy the now ice-free land.

A great change took place to the east of the Atlantic Ocean around 4,000 years ago. A group of peoples known as Indo-Europeans or Aryans moved from their homeland in southern Russia. Some Indo-Europeans traveled south into

VEHICLES

The Indo-Europeans from southern Russia lived on the Steppes (the wide plains). They were wanderers who traveled with their families and possessions in wagons covered with felt. These wagons also served as living quarters. The wagon wheels were made of solid oak boards pegged together, though later spokes were used. The wagons were drawn by pairs of oxen. From such wagons the war chariot evolved.

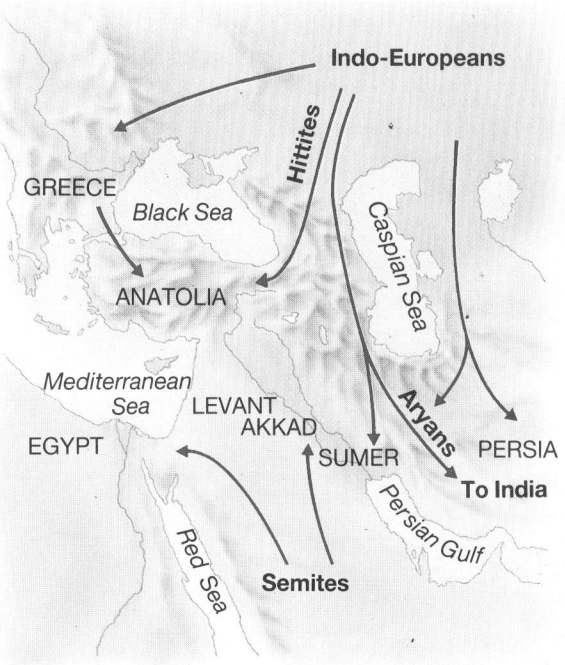

▲ *Nomads made camp from time to time so that their animals could graze the rich grass. When it was all eaten, the nomads traveled on. They moved to low ground in winter and higher ground in summer.*

▼ *This map shows the main movements of people in Europe and the Near East after the end of the Ice Age. The arrows indicate the direction in which the Indo-European and Semitic peoples moved.*

what is now Iran (the name is adapted from the word "Aryan"), and from there into India. Others moved into Anatolia and the Fertile Crescent. A farther group of Indo-Europeans occupied the Balkan peninsula and Greece, and the Celts later spread into western Europe.

The Indo-Europeans came into conflict with Semitic people (a group of people who all speak a Semitic language, such as Arabic, Hebrew, Akkadian, or Phoenician) who had migrated into the Fertile Crescent earlier and settled in Sumer. These Semitic people also moved about, particularly the Hebrews.

In the East, China too was affected by migrations. After 2000 B.C., people from central Asia invaded the area several times. However, China remained fairly isolated from the rest of the world.

Indo-Europeans

Hittites

GREECE

Black Sea

Caspian Sea

ANATOLIA

Mediterranean Sea

LEVANT

AKKAD

Aryans

EGYPT

SUMER

PERSIA

To India

Persian Gulf

Red Sea

Semites

People

The first people worked a few hours a day, hunting, trapping, and gathering food. They wore animal skins to keep warm and spent their free time making works of art and jewelry to decorate their bodies. Once people settled down in farming communities, all their time was taken up with agriculture to feed a growing population.

However, as cities grew up and flourished, rich men and women dressed to be fashionable. They looked at themselves in mirrors made of glassy rock called obsidian. Egyptians used cosmetics and wore perfumed wax cones on their heads; as the wax melted it released the perfume. Rich people entertained themselves by playing board games similar to chess and checkers, and listened to music. The Chinese had a musical instrument rather like a huge xylophone, made from jade or bronze.

In contrast, poor people were too busy working to care about fashion and entertainment. For both rich and poor, however, life was short. Many children died as babies and adults often died from accidents or diseases before they were thirty.

► *Egyptian children had many games and toys. Games, with balls made of leather or wood were very popular. There were also toys with moving parts, like this wooden lion and wheeled horse.*

▲ *Egyptian women wore a pleated robe over a straight shift of fine linen. Rich noblewomen used cosmetics and perfume. All social classes wore sandals.*

▲ *Minoan women wore long, flounced skirts with a tight-fitting bodice which had short sleeves. A shaped metal belt pinched in the waist. The cloth was very colorful.*

Game board

Dice

Counters

▲ A gaming board, counters, and dice dating from between 3000 and 2000 B.C. Sadly the rules of the game have not survived.

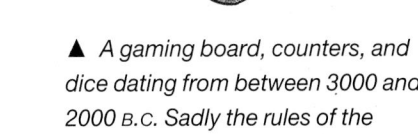

▲ An Egyptian cosmetic spoon and comb. The comb was worn in the hair for decoration.

▼ The Chinese particularly valued jade and carved a lot of jewelry from it, like this open ring.

▲ Sumerian princesses wore elaborate headdresses, earrings, and necklaces, made of gold and silver, decorated with lapis lazuli and carnelians.

▲ Etruscan women wore a long, straight garment with sleeves. It was sometimes gathered at the waist with a sash. They liked to trim their clothes with colored braid.

Ancient Crete

The very first European civilization began on the island of Crete about 4,500 years ago. It is called the Minoan civilization after the legendary king Minos. Stories say that he built a labyrinth (maze) in which he kept a monster known as the Minotaur. It had the head of a bull and the body of a man. The Minoan civilization was at its height from 2200 to 1450 B.C. The Minoans owed their prosperity to their abilities as seafarers and traders.

The Minoans built several large cities, connected by paved roads. At the heart of each city was a palace, with a water supply, good drainage, windows, and stone seats. The capital, Knossos, had the grandest palace. It had splendid apartments for the king and queen, rooms for religious ceremonies, workshops, and a school. The internal walls were plastered and decorated with magnificent painted pictures. Minoan craftsmen were renowned for their skills as potters and builders. They also made

ATLANTIS

The Aegean island of Thera (Santorini) suddenly blew up about 3500 years ago. It was one of the most violent volcanic eruptions in history and it caused a huge tidal wave. This wave swept across the Aegean Sea and the Mediterranean Sea, causing great damage wherever it struck land.

The disappearance of most of Thera gave rise to the legend of the lost land of Atlantis. The Greek philosopher Plato said Atlantis had sunk into the sea because its people were so wicked.

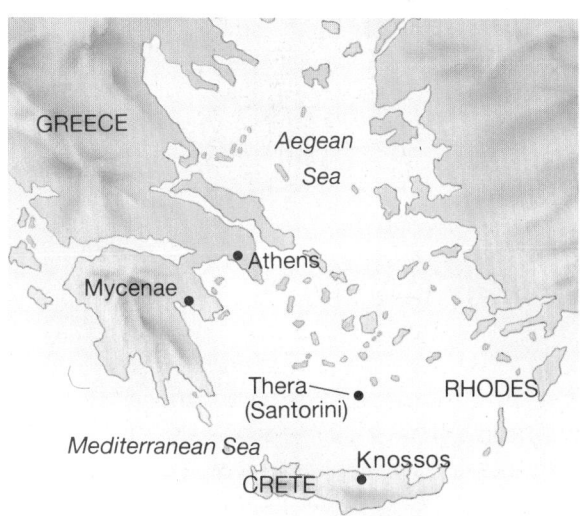

▼ Decorating one of the state rooms at the royal palace at Knossos. The wall painting shows the dangerous sport of bull leaping, which may have given rise to the legend of the Minotaur.

▲ This map shows where the Minoan civilization was located. The Minoans greatly influenced other Aegean civilizations, especially the Mycenaeans who developed later on the Greek mainland.

▼ *A view of the royal palace at Knossos as it looked in Minoan times. It was built of stone and wood and the royal apartments lay around a central courtyard, with public rooms upstairs.*

beautiful jewelry from silver and gold.

The advanced Minoan civilization came to a sudden and mysterious end in about 1450 B.C. Its collapse followed the eruption of a huge volcano on the island of Thera (Santorini) which overwhelmed much of Crete. Knossos was invaded by the Mycenaeans who greatly admired the Minoans and took back their ideas to the European mainland.

SHIPBUILDING

Minoan craftsmen were skilled at shipbuilding. In ships like the one shown below, Cretan traders traveled to other islands in the Aegean Sea and to eastern Mediterranean countries, including Egypt. Minoan artifacts, such as their beautiful pottery and metalwork have been found in many lands. These finds show that trade for the Cretans was very profitable. It contributed to their great wealth.

B.C.

2200 Crete: Greek speakers arrive on the island; they use a Minoan script known as Linear A (which is still undeciphered) and Linear B, an early form of Greek writing (deciphered in 1952). Japan: The Jomon culture flourishes.

2150 Indus Valley: First invasion by Aryans from the north.

c. 2100 Mesopotamia: The Hebrew patriarch Abraham migrates north and west from Ur. Indus Valley: Aryans continue their invasion.

2040 Egypt: Start of the Middle Kingdom. Lasts to the end of the 14th dynasty (1532).

2030 Mesopotamia: The decline of Sumer is now under way.

The double-ax, labrys, was a symbol of Crete's Mother Goddess and was painted on the walls throughout the palace at Knossos.

2000 Indo-Europeans (early Greeks) invade and settle mainland Greece. Minoan Crete dominates the Aegean Sea region; Minoans start building the palace at Knossos. Anatolia: Hittites, an Indo-European tribe, move in; they monopolize the secret of working iron.

Egypt: Locks and latches come into use. Europe: The Bronze Age begins. England: Construction of the second stage of Stonehenge begins. Scotland: Work begins on erecting the Ring of Brodgar, a stone circle in Orkney. Peru: Cotton is cultivated. New Guinea: First settlers arrive.

1950 Assyria: Building begins of a great temple and palace at Mari. Egypt: Armies of Pharaoh Sesostris I invade Canaan (modern Palestine). Mesopotamia: Decline of the empire of Ur.

1920 Anatolia: Assyrian merchants establish a colony at Cappadocia (to 1850).

B.C.

1900–1600 Greece: Development of the Mycenaean culture.

1800 Micronesia: First settlers arrive.

1830 Babylon: Founding of the first dynasty. Its armies conquer the city-states of northern and southern Mesopotamia.

1792 Babylon: Accession of Hammurabi the Great, who produces a code of laws (reign lasts to 1750).

1783–1550 Egypt: Dynasties 13 to 17.

1760 China: Shang dynasty is founded.

1750–1500 Anatolia (Turkey): Old Kingdom of the Hittites.

1730 Egypt: The Hyksos, a Semitic tribe, begin the conquest of the country, founding the 15th dynasty; about this time the Israelites settle in Egypt, possibly under Hyksos protection.

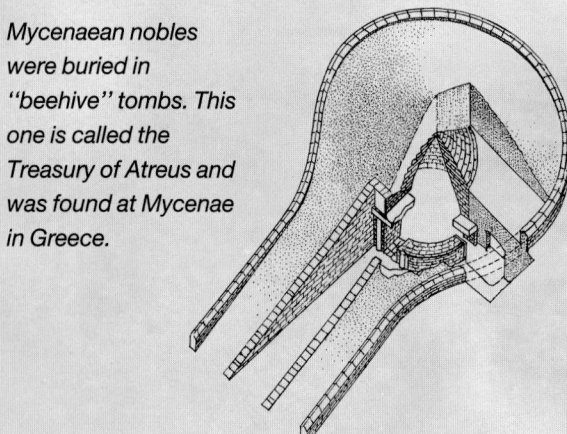

Mycenaean nobles were buried in "beehive" tombs. This one is called the Treasury of Atreus and was found at Mycenae in Greece.

1700 Syria: Invasion by the Hittites. England: Third phase of building Stonehenge begins.

1650–1450 Greece: Growth of Mycenaean power, centered on Mycenae and Pylos.

1600 Mycenaeans trade by sea throughout the Mediterranean. Syria: The Hittites capture Aleppo on Mediterranean coast.

1550 Egypt: Beginning of the New Kingdom (till 1070); the Hyksos are driven out; Temple of Amun at Karnak is begun.

1504–1450 Egypt: Period of expansion under Thutmosis I, who soon controls Palestine, Syria, and south along the Nile into Kush (Nubia). Mexico: Stone temples built.

The Mycenaeans

Mycenae was a city in Peloponnesus, the southern peninsula of Greece. It was the center of the first Greek civilization, which grew up at about the same time as that of the Minoans in Crete. The city has given its name to the whole of the late Bronze Age in Greece.

The Mycenaean civilization originally began as a series of little hillside villages, occupied by people speaking an ancient form of Greek. In time, many villages grew into great fortified towns, with palaces and luxurious goods that rivaled those made by the highly-skilled craftsmen of King Minos.

Before they built fortresses the Mycenaeans began to bury their important people in elaborate graves, known as "beehive tombs" from their shape. These tombs were built of large

---

AGAMEMNON AND THE TROJAN WAR

Homer's epic poem the *Iliad* tells the story of the Greek siege of Troy, a city lying on the coast of Anatolia. Paris, son of the king of Troy, eloped with Helen, the wife of Menelaus who was king of Sparta. Menelaus's brother Agamemnon, King of Mycenae, raised an army to attack Troy and get Helen back. Much of the story is legend, but Troy existed, and Agamemnon was almost certainly a real king of Mycenae. This gold mask was found in a grave at Mycenae by a German archaeologist, Heinrich Schliemann. He thought it was the mask of Agamemnon, but today scholars think it was that of a man who lived 300 years earlier.

stone blocks, shaped to form a great dome. One tomb at Mycenae, known as the Treasury of Atreus, has a doorway nearly 20 feet (6 m) high, opening into a chamber more than 42 feet (13 m) high and 46 feet (14 m) wide. It was once lined with bronze plates.

The richness of these tombs shows that a great deal of money and effort was spent on royalty and the aristocracy. To judge by the treasures found in many of the tombs, wealthy Mycenaeans were very fond of gold, imported from Egypt. Craftsmen made golden cups, masks, flowers, jewelry, and inlaid swords and armor with gold. It is no wonder that the poet Homer described Mycenae as ''rich in gold.''

LION GATE

The ruins of the Lion Gate which was the main entrance into Mycenae and was built around 1300 B.C. It was almost the only way through the city walls, which were built of great stone boulders. The lions, now without their heads, stand above a massive stone lintel (beam). Walls flanked the way to the Lion Gate, so that defenders could attack an enemy on both sides. The walls were built at a time when Mycenae was threatened with attacks from the north, but they did not save Mycenae from destruction.

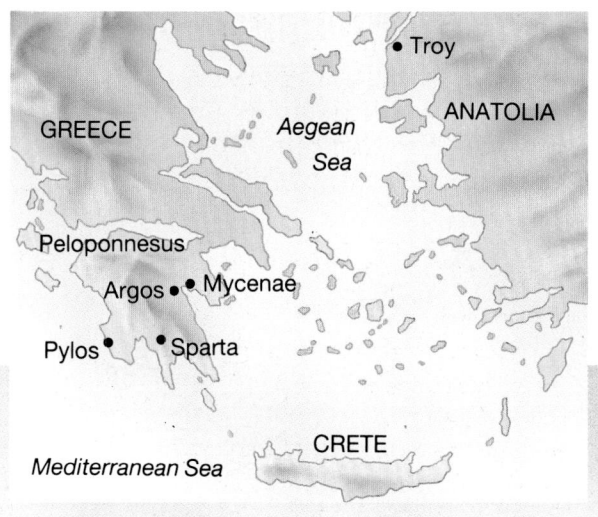

◀ The map shows the world as the Mycenaeans knew it, with the Aegean Sea bounded by Greece to the west and Anatolia to the east.

▼ A reconstruction of the city of Mycenae as it probably looked at the height of its power. The royal palace on the hilltop was built on several levels.

B.C.

1500 Crete: Minoans are facing growing competition from Mycenae. Indus Valley civilization: Aryan invaders destroy Mohenjo-daro. Anatolia: The Hittite royal succession becomes hereditary; Hittites control all Anatolia.

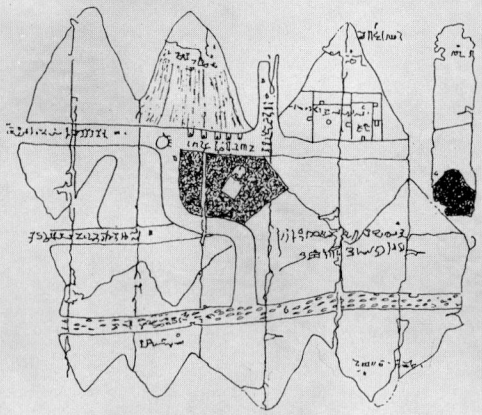

This piece of a sketch map comes from the only surviving ancient Egyptian map and is thought to show the quarries and goldmines of the Wadi Hammamat in the Eastern Desert.

1500 China: The first historical period begins under the Shang dynasty; Anyang becomes the capital. Bronze is worked in the Anyang region.

1500–1000 India: Early civilization spreads along the Ganges River valley.

1479 Egypt: Pharaoh Thutmosis II is succeeded by the young child Thutmosis III but his aunt, Hatshepsut, effectively rules for the first 22 years of his reign.

c. 1473 Battle of Megiddo – Thutmosis III of Egypt conquers Palestine.

1470 Explosion of the volcano Thera in the Aegean Sea causes widespread damage, particularly in Crete.

1450 Collapse of Minoan power begins, probably as a consequence of volcanic or earthquake damage.

1430–1200 New Kingdom of the Hittites.

1391–1353 Egypt: The reign of Amenhotep III, the country's "Golden Age;" he makes his capital at Thebes into a magnificent city and builds the Temple of Luxor and erects the Colossi of Memnon.

Shang Dynasty

Early civilizations in China grew up on the banks of the three largest rivers: the Huang He (Yellow River), the Chang Jiang (Yangtze), and the Xi Jiang (West River). Like the people of Mesopotamia and Egypt, Chinese farmers relied on the rivers for water to grow their crops and for transport. But they faced two dangers: devastating floods and raids by people from the north. The invaders were the Xiung-Nu (Huns or Mongols).

The first years of China's history are a mixture of fact and legend. According to tradition the first dynasty (ruling family) was the Hsia, who came to power more than 4,000 years ago. The first Hsia emperor was named Yu and he is credited with taming the rivers by building dikes (banks) to keep the floods at bay and building channels to supply

---

SILK

Tradition says that silk was discovered in about 2690 B.C. by the Empress Hsi-Ling Shi, the wife of the legendary "Yellow Emperor," Huang Ti. The empress found that the silkworms ate the leaves of mulberry trees so she had groves of mulberries planted to feed the insects.

Because the empress cultivated silkworms, the ladies of her court did so too. Silk was so valuable that for centuries it was used as a form of money. It remained a closely kept secret by the Chinese for about 3,000 years.

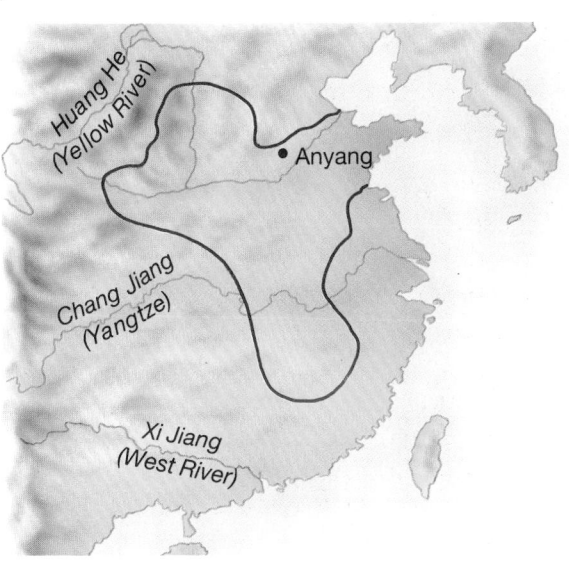

▲ *The map shows the area ruled by the Shang. According to tradition the Hsia ruled before the Shang but no historical evidence has yet been found to support this belief.*

▶ *The early Chinese were a warlike people. Shang warriors fought in cumbersome body armor, largely made of bamboo and wood, heavily padded with cloth.*

BRONZE

Shang metalworkers made this bronze cauldron. It was used in religious ceremonies of ancestor worship. Many of the bronze vessels made by the Shang were cast in molds. The craft workers decorated them with wavy lines and sometimes with symbolic human faces.

ORACLE BONE

Large numbers of animal bones like this have been excavated near the city of Anyang. They are engraved with the earliest examples of Chinese writing. Many of these bones were used for telling fortunes and are called oracle bones. The bones used were mostly shoulder blades.

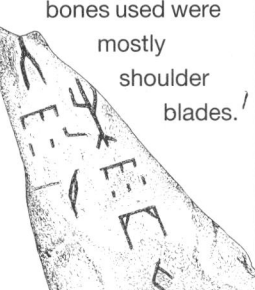

the land with regular supplies of water.

The first dynasty we know about for certain was called the Shang, and their first emperor was named·T'ang. The Shang dynasty ruled in China for more than 400 years. The people grew millet, wheat, some rice, and also mulberries. They kept cattle, pigs, sheep, dogs, and chickens, and hunted deer and wild boar. The Shang also used horses to draw plows and chariots.

Religion

From earliest times, people tried to come to terms with things they could not explain, such as birth, disease, and death. The first religions probably came out of this. Over 50,000 years ago, Neanderthal people buried some of their dead with flowers. The first farmers wanted good harvests every year. They probably asked for help from nature gods, such as the Sun and the Moon. However, nothing is known for certain until the time of the Sumerians. Some of the temples they built to their nature gods eventually became the center of cities.

▲ *A boundary stone from Babylon, carved with prayers asking the gods to protect the owner's land.*

▶ *Ishtar was the goddess of war to the Assyrians, but a mother-goddess to the Babylonians.*

▲ *People first worshiped Mother Goddesses who, as the Earth, gave life to all plants.*

▲ *Sumerian legends contain many well known stories. The Great Flood was sent to punish men who had made the gods* angry. *They warned one good man, Ut-napishtim, to build a boat. The flood destroyed everything on Earth except the boat. Ut-* napishtim sent out birds to find land. Finally one bird did not return and Ut-napishtim and his family were saved.

◀ *The ancient Chinese cooked sacrificial food for their dead ancestors in large bronze vessels like this one.*

▼ *The Egyptians believed in life after death. The mummified bodies of their pharaohs were carried to their tombs on boats symbolizing the journey to the next world. Royal tombs were also filled with food, jewelry, and clothing.*

CREATION MYTHS

Every civilization had its own story to explain the creation of the Earth. These stories are called myths. The Egyptians thought the world started as a watery chaos. The Sun god Atum emerged from it and created the gods of air and moisture. They had a daughter, Nut, who was the sky goddess. Her brother Geb was the Earth god and also her husband.

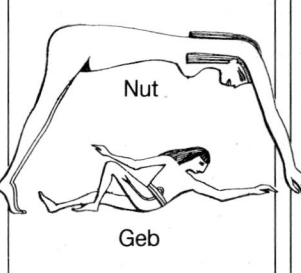

Nut

Geb

B.C.

1400 Crete: Knossos, the Minoan capital, is destroyed by fire. Mycenaeans occupy the island. Egypt: Temples at Luxor are under construction. India and western Asia: Iron Age under way.

1390–1350  Anatolia: The Hittites, led by Suppiluliumas, their greatest king, reconquer Anatolia, subdue northern Syria and make the Mitanni tribes into Hittite subjects.

1366 Assyria: Assuruballit I becomes king and begins Assyria's rise to power in Mesopotamia.

1353 Egypt: Accession of Amenhotep III's son Amenhotep IV, who begins the worship of the god Aten; he takes the name Akhenaten and abolishes the other gods.

1333 Egypt: The boy-king Tutankhamun succeeds Akhenaten; his advisers restore the worship of the traditional Egyptian gods; Tutankhamun lives only a few years, but his tomb survives almost intact until A.D. 1922.

A wall carving showing Egyptian troops attacking the Hittite fortress of Dapur.

1308 Assyria: Accession of Adadnirari I, who embarks on a career of conquest.

1307 Egypt: Pharaoh Rameses I founds the vigorous 19th dynasty.

The Hittites

The Hittites appear suddenly in the pages of history. They arrived in Anatolia, probably from farther east, but we do not know whether they made one invasion or migrated gradually. They were made up of several tribes and spoke as many as six languages.

For many years the Hittites controlled the supply of iron, and this, together with their use of chariots, gave this war-like people a great advantage. They conquered northern Syria, Mesopotamia, and Babylon before being overwhelmed by the Assyrians in about 1200 B.C.

▲ *Rock carvings left by the Hittites tell us that they were a very warlike race. Here a king hunts lions.*

▼ *The map shows the extent of the Hittite empire at its height under Suppiluliumas in about 1350 B.C.*

Babylon

The end of the Sumerian domination of Mesopotamia was followed by a series of invasions. About 3,800 years ago the Babylonians shook off their rulers, and their king Sumuabum founded a dynasty that lasted for 300 years.

They began to dominate southern Mesopotamia under their sixth ruler, Hammurabi the Great. He was a highly efficient ruler. The armies of Babylonia were well-disciplined, and they conquered in turn the city-states of Isin, Elam, and Larsa, and the strong kingdom of Mari which lay on the Euphrates.

The mathematicians of Babylonia devised a system of counting based on the number 60, from which we get the number of minutes in an hour and the degrees (60 x 6) in a circle.

▼ Gilgamesh was the legendary hero of a poem called The Epic of Gilgamesh. Here Gilgamesh sleeps and loses the plant of eternal life to a snake.

Hammurabi

Hammurabi is famous for the laws he introduced. They were designed to protect the weak from the strong, and they covered all daily activities including rates of pay and rules of trade. People who broke the law faced severe punishments.

▼ This map shows the extent of the Babylonian empire under Hammurabi and his successors.

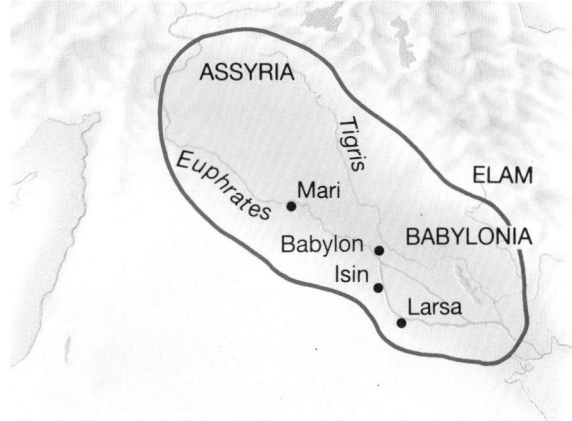

The Assyrians

While Babylonia ruled in southern Mesopotamia, the fierce and warlike Assyrians dominated the north. Their kingdom lay in the valley of the Tigris River. Its capital Assur was named after the Assyrians' chief god.

King Adadnirari I, the country's first powerful ruler, enlarged the Assyrian empire and took the boastful title "King of Everything." He and his successors were cruel dictators, ruling their empire as a whole and not allowing individual states independence. As the empire grew, rebellions were common.

Assyria's first period of power lasted for nearly 300 years. It reached its height under King Tiglathpileser I, who led brutal campaigns of conquest every year. From about 1100 B.C., Assyria and Babylonia were overrun by Aramaic tribes from northern Syria. But a hundred years or so later, Assurdan II and his successors reconquered the Assyrian empire. It reached its greatest size under Tiglathpileser III.

The last great ruler of Assyria was King

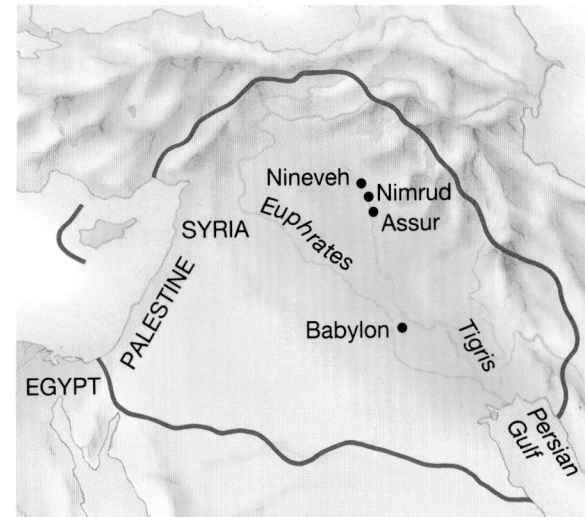

▲ The Assyrian empire at its greatest extent in 650 B.C. It extended from Syria in the north to the Persian Gulf, and included Palestine and most of Egypt. After Egypt and Babylon broke away, the empire collapsed.

▼ Under the supervision of their king, Assyrian workers toil to bring materials for building a new palace. Oarsmen in skin boats tow a raft along the Tigris.

Assurbanipal. He had a great love of the arts and during his reign he collected a huge library at his palace in Nineveh, which was then the capital of Assyria. When he died the Assyrian empire collapsed, and by 609 B.C. it had ended.

The Assyrians were great builders, erecting magnificent cities with temples and palaces. Assyrian men wore long coatlike garments, and were bearded. Women wore a sleeved tunic and draped a shawl over their shoulders. It was not unknown for men to sell their wives and children into slavery to pay off debts.

▲ *A battle scene carved on limestone shows warriors on a camel fighting off an attack by Assyrian foot soldiers carrying spears, bows, and arrows.*

LANGUAGE

The Assyrians spoke Aramaic, a language related to Hebrew and Arabic. It was the language spoken by Jesus. For a long time Assyrians wrote on clay tablets, using the cuneiform script which the Babylonians developed from earlier Sumerian. When parchment came into use they wrote on that in ink. Thousands of tablets have survived, but few parchments.

Assurbanipal

Assurbanipal ruled Assyria from 668 to 627 B.C. He was a ruthless soldier but also a great patron of the arts. He built a splendid palace at Nineveh and filled the gardens with plants from all over the world.

B.C.

1305 Egypt: Rameses I's son Seti I sets out to reconquer lands in Palestine and Syria.

1300 Iran: Medes and Persians invade. Egypt: Construction of the great rock temples of Abu Simbel begins; oppression of the Israelite colony in Egypt. Phoenicia: Sidon flourishes as a great port. Greece: The Arcadians begin settling central Peloponnesus. England: The last phase of Stonehenge is completed. Melanesia: First settlers arrive.

1290 Egypt: Accession of Rameses II, the Great; Commandment carved on the base of a giant statue of the pharaoh refers to "the Royal Mother, the Mistress of the World."

The Assyrian winged lion from Assurbanipal's palace was thought to ward off evil.

1298 Assyria: Adadnirari I reaches the Euphrates and takes the title "King of Everything."

1285 Battle of Kadesh between Egypt and the Hittites: both sides claim victory.

1283 Peace between Egypt and the Hittites.

1275 Assyria: Shalmaneser I becomes ruler, and extends Assyria's conquests.

c. **1270** The Exodus: the Israelites under Moses leave Egypt; they move into Canaan (Palestine) and adopt the worship of the one god, Yahweh.

c. **1250** Anatolia: City of Troy besieged by Greek army.

1232–1116 Assyria: Period of decline followed by new growth of power.

1232 Israelites in Canaan (Palestine): an Egyptian army under Rameses II's son Merneptah defeats them in battle.

B.C.

1200–800 India: Aryan invaders worship nature gods; they raise cattle and cultivate crops.

1200 Israel (Canaan): Period of the Judges begins; the prophetess Deborah flourishes. Anatolia: Invasion by the Sea People, a confederation of Philistines, Greeks, Sardinians, and Sicilians; the Hittite empire collapses. Sahara: Horses and chariots are in use on trade routes.

The Phoenicians sent wood from Cedar of Lebanon trees to build Solomon's temple.

1194 Egypt: Rameses III becomes pharaoh and founds the 20th dynasty with its capital at Tanis.

1179 Egypt is invaded by the Confederation of Sea Peoples, which is defeated by Rameses III.

1170 The Levant (eastern Mediterranean coast): growing power of newly independent Phoenician cities, especially Tyre.

1150–1100 Greece: Collapse of Mycenaean power.

1140 The Phoenicians create their first North African colony at Utica, which is now in Tunisia.

1125 Babylonia: the armies of Nebuchadnezzar I hold off renewed attacks by the Assyrians.

The Origin of the Jews

The Hebrews who settled in Palestine about 4,000 years ago were a tribe that came from southern Mesopotamia. Their name literally meant "the people from the other side" of the Euphrates River. Their story is told in the Bible.

According to the Old Testament, the first Hebrew was Abraham, a shepherd who lived in Ur. Abraham traveled with his family, first to Syria and then to Canaan (the old name for Palestine), where he settled. His grandson, Jacob, had 12 sons after whom the 12 Hebrew tribes were named. When famine struck Canaan, Jacob led his people to safety in Egypt. Jacob was also called Israel, and the Hebrews became known as Israelites. Later, they became slaves of the Egyptians until Moses, a religious leader, took them back to Canaan. There they fought the Philistines to establish the land of Israel.

After around 1020 B.C. the Israelites prospered under three kings, Saul, David,

▼ *The two Hebrew kingdoms of Israel and Judah.*

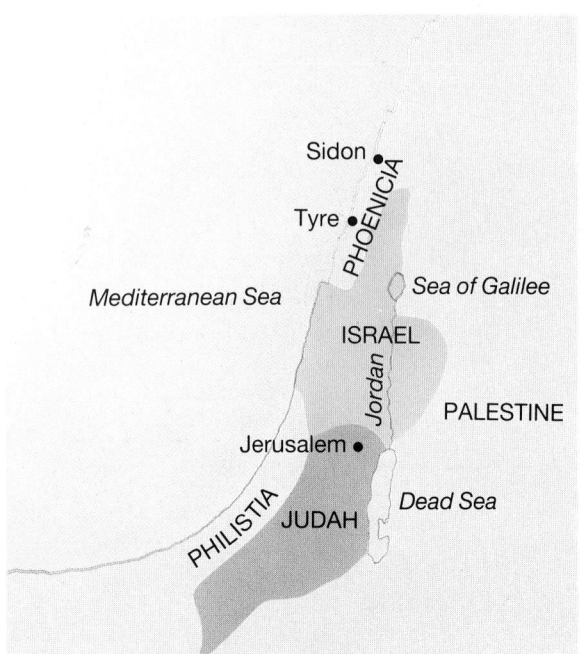

Solomon

Solomon was one of the wisest kings in history. Despite leading a life of luxury, he always carried out his royal duties. His rule brought order and peace and Jerusalem was one of the richest cities of the time.

and Solomon. David united the tribes of Israel into one nation and made the city of Jerusalem his capital. After Solomon died, the kingdom split into two: Israel and Judah. The Assyrians captured Israel in 722 B.C. and Judah in 683 B.C. From then on, the people were called Jews.

▲ This copy of an Egyptian wall painting shows a group of Hebrews asking permission to enter Egypt.

▼ Solomon built the first temple in Jerusalem to house the Israelites' holy treasure, the Ark of the Covenant, that contained the Ten Commandments. It became the focus of the cult following the one god, Yahweh.

Science and Technology

The early history of the world is often divided into periods that are named after the technology which was in use at the time. The three main divisions are Stone Age, Bronze Age, and Iron Age. These divisions cover different periods of time in different parts of the world. For example, in ancient China the Bronze Age started around 2700 B.C. and lasted for over 2,000 years, while in Africa the Iron Age started around 800 B.C. and followed straight on from the Stone Age. Apart from metal-making, probably the most important early invention was the wheel.

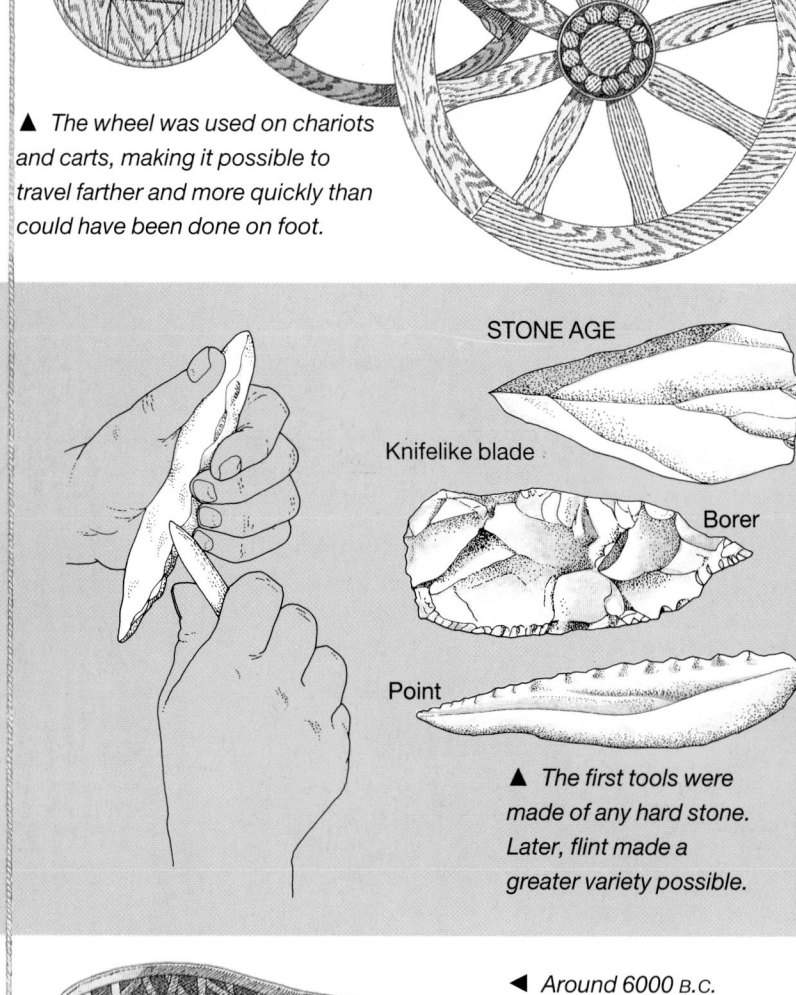

▲ The wheel was used on chariots and carts, *making it possible to travel farther and more quickly than could have been done on foot.*

STONE AGE

Knifelike blade

Borer

Point

▲ *The first tools were made of any hard stone. Later, flint made a greater variety possible.*

▼ *Using wheels in pulleys made it easier to lift heavy loads.*

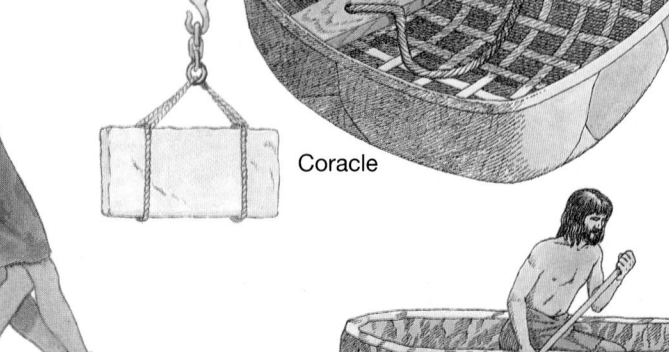

◀ *Around 6000 B.C. coracles made of animal skins fixed to a wooden frame were used as boats in Wales. Below Dugout canoes made from hollowed logs were used around 8000 B.C.*

Coracle

Dugout canoe

◀ The first farmers used plows made from wood. The plowshare was often made from a deer antler or animal bone. It made a furrow in the soil but did not turn it over like modern plows do. The earliest plows were pulled by people, but later ones were pulled by oxen, as in this scene from Egypt.

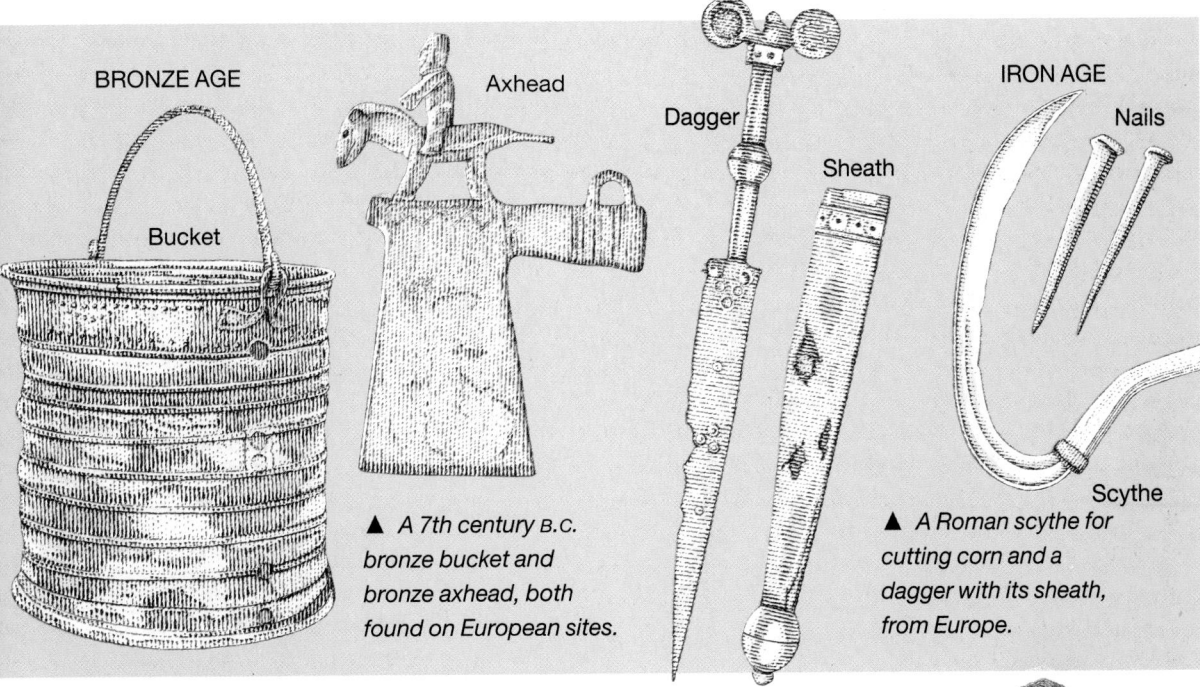

BRONZE AGE

Axhead

Bucket

▲ A 7th century B.C. bronze bucket and bronze axhead, both found on European sites.

Dagger

Sheath

IRON AGE

Nails

Scythe

▲ A Roman scythe for cutting corn and a dagger with its sheath, from Europe.

WHEN IT HAPPENED

c. **9000 B.C.** Arrowheads first made in Americas.

c. **8000 B.C.** First farming in Mesopotamia.

c. **3000 B.C.** The wheel is used on chariots in Mesopotamia.

c. **2700 B.C.** Chinese start making bronze and weaving silk.

c. **2500 B.C.** Bricks start to be used for building in the Indus Valley.

c. **1500 B.C.** Iron is smelted (heating ore to extract metal) by the Hittites, in the Near East.

▶ Early potters' wheels were made from wood. The turntable was fixed to a spindle which was turned by a foot wheel.

Egypt, the New Kingdom

A succession of feeble rulers in Egypt left the country open to an attack. It came from the Hyksos, a tribe of herdsmen from Canaan. They invaded Egypt and became its "shepherd kings," founding the 13th to the 17th dynasties. They ruled for more than a hundred years, until a group of rebellious Egyptian princes drove them out and set up the 18th dynasty.

The 18th dynasty marked the beginning of Egypt's "golden age," which is known as the New Kingdom. One of its early pharaohs, Thutmosis III, conquered Palestine, Syria, and all the lands west of the Euphrates. During the rule of Amenhotep III, the New Kingdom, which had its capital at Thebes, became rich and prosperous.

The strangest ruler was Amenhotep IV. He made Aten, the Sun in the sky, the chief god of Egypt. He changed his name to Akhenaten and even moved his capital to a new city devoted to Aten and its worship. His queen was Nefertiti, who was not of royal birth and may not have

Hatshepsut

Queen Hatshepsut was an early ruler of the New Kingdom. Widow of a weak king, Thutmosis II, she ruled as queen in her own right, and was depicted with the false beard of a pharaoh.

▼ *Models found in the tomb of Tutankhamun provide a vivid picture of the life of Egyptian people during the age of the New Kingdom.*

◀ *This temple at Abu Simbel was carved out of rock on the banks of the Nile. Four figures of Rameses II guard the entrance. It was moved in 1964 to avoid flooding when the Aswan High Dam was built.*

been Egyptian. When Akhenaten died the people returned to their old gods.

Ordinary farmers and workers lived simply but the nobility had a far more luxurious lifestyle. In law men and women were equal and women could own property and do as they wished with it. Women could choose to follow one of four professions: as priestesses, midwives, dancers, and mourners. The children of the aristocracy were well educated, especially the boys. Apart from the nobles, scribes and priests held the most important positions in Egyptian society of the time.

◀ *The dead bodies of pharaohs and nobles were embalmed so that they would "live" forever, a process called mummification. The body was put inside a coffin like this one, with a portrait painted on the outside.*

TUTANKHAMUN'S TOMB

Pharaohs were buried with many possessions in elaborate tombs such as the pyramids. But from very early on these were plundered by robbers. Thinking that it would be safer, pharaohs were then buried in the cliffs of the Valley of the Kings. Even so, only one of these has survived to the present day, that of the boy-king Tutankhamun. He succeeded Akhenaten but died when he was only 18. He was buried surrounded by treasure and beautiful furniture. This gold mask covered his face.

B.C.
1122 China: Emperor Wu Wang founds the Zhou dynasty and establishes a feudal system.
1116 Assyria: Tiglathpileser I rules; he fights off invaders from the north, conquers Babylon and controls Asian trade.

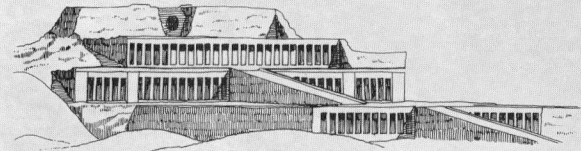

Queen Hatshepsut had this mortuary temple built for herself at Deir el Bahri.

1100–1050 Greece is invaded by Dorian and Ionian tribes from the north, bringing with them the use of iron swords and destroying the Mycenaean citadels.
1100–900 Babylonia: Aramaic tribes invade.
🎭 China: The first Chinese-language dictionary is compiled.
1093–935 Assyria and Babylonia are both overrun by Aramaeans.
1087 Egypt: The high priests of Amun become the effective rulers under a succession of weak pharaohs.
1070 Egypt: The New Kingdom ends with the death of Rameses XI; Smendes, a rich merchant, becomes pharaoh and founds the 21st dynasty; for a time Egypt splits into two kingdoms. Israel is conquered by the Philistines, who settle in Palestine. Greece: The Dorians and Ionians invade Peloponnesus.

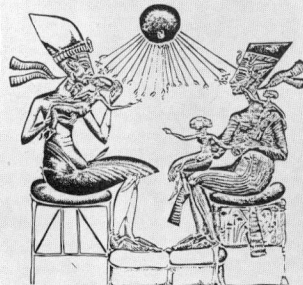

Akhenaten with his wife Nefertiti and their children. Akhenaten worshiped Aten, "the sun disk."

1045 Greece: Death of Codron, the legendary last king of Athens, possibly killed in battle with the Dorians.

55

The Phoenicians

The Phoenicians were merchants, pirates, and the greatest seafarers of the ancient world. They lived along the coastal strip at the eastern end of the Mediterranean Sea, often known as the Levant, and now part of Syria, Lebanon, and Israel. Their language was related to Babylonian and Hebrew.

They were originally called Canaanites, because they lived in the land of Canaan. From about 1200 B.C. they were called Phoenicians from the Greek word *phoinos*, or red, because they produced a wonderful reddish-purple dye.

The Phoenicians' main port was Tyre, which according to tradition they founded 4,750 years ago. The city had close links with Israel. Hiram, king of Tyre, supplied Solomon with cedar wood and craftsmen to build the Temple in Jerusalem, and Ahab, king of Israel married Jezebel, Princess of Tyre.

▲ *This is how a Phoenician warship probably looked. It was a galley with a ram for attacking other ships. It could use wind power with its square sail, and its oars made it highly maneuverable.*

▼ *The bold sailors of Phoenicia founded many colonies along the coasts of the Mediterranean. They traded throughout that sea, and even ventured into the Atlantic to Britain and down the African coast.*

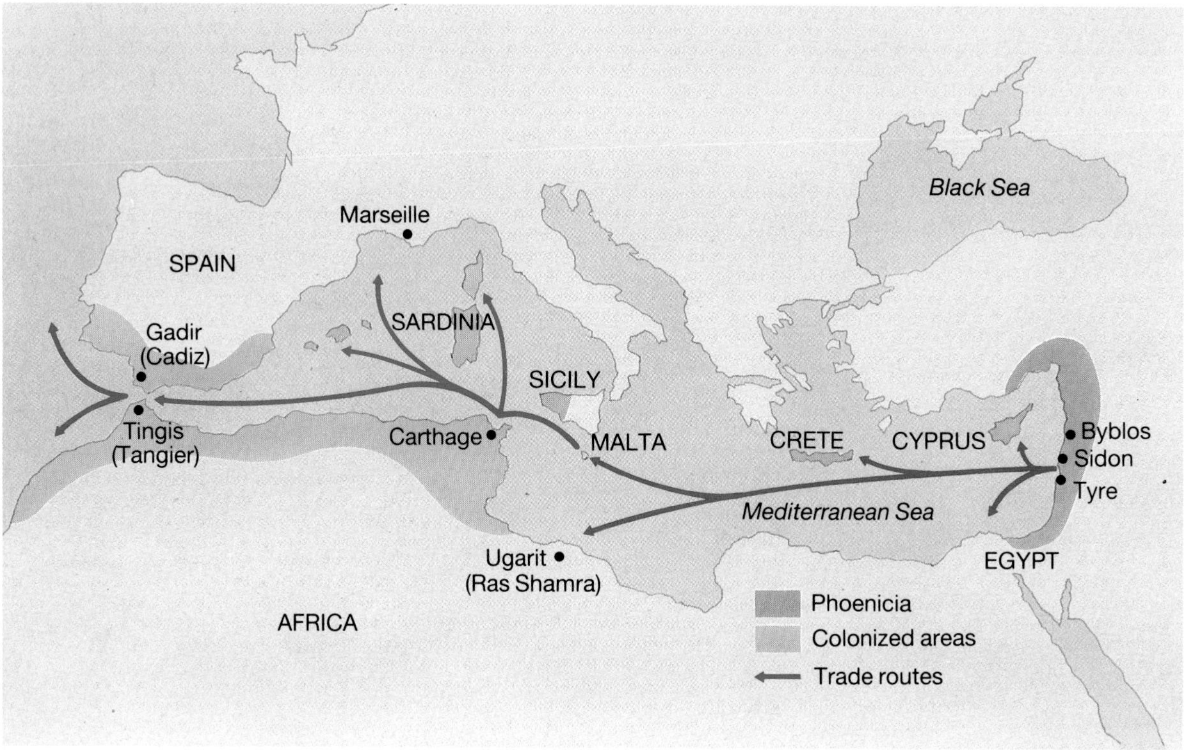

Black Sea
Marseille
SPAIN
SARDINIA
Gadir (Cadiz)
SICILY
Tingis (Tangier)
Carthage
MALTA
CRETE
CYPRUS
Byblos
Sidon
Tyre
Mediterranean Sea
Ugarit (Ras Shamra)
EGYPT
AFRICA

Phoenicia
Colonized areas
Trade routes

ALPHABET

The Phoenicians were among the first people to use an alphabet. Theirs had 30 letters, all consonants. Their alphabet is the basis of the one we use today. The word Bible comes from the name Byblos, the name of a Phoenician port. The Greeks took it as their word for book.

CARTHAGE

Carthage was founded by Dido, the daughter of a king of Tyre. When she landed in North Africa, she asked the local ruler for land. He said she could have as much land as an ox-hide would cover. Dido had the hide cut into very thin strips so that she was able to mark off a large area of land.

The Phoenicians were skilled craft workers, making glassware, weapons, jewelry, and cloth. They traded these goods all along the Mediterranean coasts and imported goods from such faraway places as Britain.

Their trading helped to spread scientific knowledge and technology. They set up many colonies, the most important being Carthage (now in Tunisia). Other colonies were Marseilles (France), Cadiz (Spain), and Malta, Sicily, and Cyprus.

GLASSWARE AND PURPLE DYE

The Phoenicians were the first people to make, on a large scale, transparent glass, like this perfume bottle. They invented the process of glass-blowing. They made the dye for which Tyre was famous (Tyrian purple, a rich dark violet shade) from a gland in the murex, a sea snail. Cloth dyed in this rich color was expensive, and it was worn by Greeks and Romans as a sign of rank. But the process of making it was smelly. Other peoples did not like to visit Tyre because of the tremendous garliclike stench.

B.C.

1020 Israel: Samuel, last of the Judges, anoints Saul as the first king of the Israelites; Saul leads a successful revolt against the Philistines.

1000–774 Phoenicia: Great period of Tyre.

1000–950 China: The Western Zhou dynasty establishes its capital at Hao in the Wei Valley.

1000 Israel: Saul is killed at the battle of Gilboa; he is succeeded by David, first as king of Judah, later as king of Israel.

India: The *Rig Veda*, a Hindu religious text containing sacred hymns, is compiled about this time; iron tools are made in the Ganges Valley. Phoenicia: The people of Tyre employ a full alphabet. Greeks establish colonies in the Aegean islands.

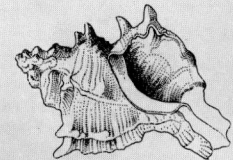

A murex sea snail, from whose glands a purple dye was made.

1000–600 Italy: The Villanova culture flourishes at this time.

994 Israel: David captures Jerusalem and makes it his capital. Central Europe: Teutonic tribes move westward to the River Rhine.

961 Israel: Death of David who is succeeded by his son Solomon; development of trade, laws, and taxes.

The Phoenicians were famous for ivory carvings, like this head of a young girl.

B.C.

953 Israel: Dedication of the Temple at Jerusalem, built by Solomon with help and materials from Hiram of Tyre.

935 Revival of Assyria begins with the accession of Assurdan II: by 860 he and his successors Adadnirari, Tukultinurta and Assurnasirapli II have re-established Assyria's ancient boundaries.

922 Israel: Death of Solomon, who is succeeded by his son, Rehoboam; a rebellion against Rehoboam's rule is led by his brother Jeroboam; Solomon's kingdom is split into Judah in the south, under Rehoboam, and Israel in the north under Jeroboam.

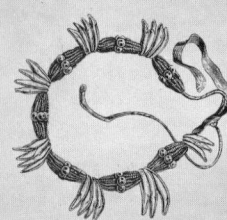

An African necklace made from beads and animal teeth.

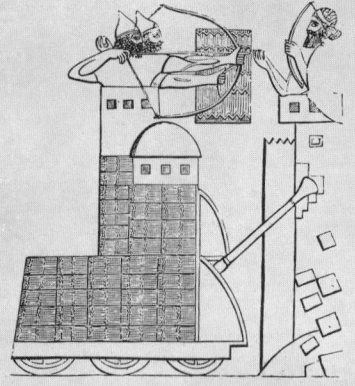

The warring Assyrians were able to knock holes in stone walls with this battering ram with movable tower.

900–625 Assyria and Babylon are constantly at war at this time.

900–700 Italy: The Etruscans flourish in upper Italy, a race with a unique language and religion.

c. **900** Africa: Kingdom of Kush becomes independent of Egypt. Nok culture of Nigeria begins.

884 Assyria: Centralized government is adopted under Assurnasirapli II.

859 Accession of Assurnasirapli II's son Shalmaneser III (reigns to 825); an ambitious ruler, he launches annual campaigns against neighboring states.

Africa

Although the earliest human remains have been found in Africa, not much is known of the continent's history before 1500 B.C. outside Egypt.

Today the Sahara forms a great desert barrier between northern and southern Africa, but in about 6000 B.C. that barrier did not exist. Rock and cave drawings and paintings show that the climate then was much wetter. One painting shows hunters in a canoe trying to spear a hippopotamus. The Sahara began to dry up after 3500 B.C., but trade routes across it remained open, providing a link between northern and southern Africa.

Egyptian culture spread to Nubia, farther south along the Nile in what is now northern Sudan. The kingdom of Kush developed in Nubia from 2000 B.C. onward. Kush was valuable to Egypt as a trading center. Egypt conquered Kush in 1500 B.C., but was in turn conquered by

▼ *The map shows the area of Nubia and the kingdom of Kush and where rock paintings have been found in the Sahara Desert.*

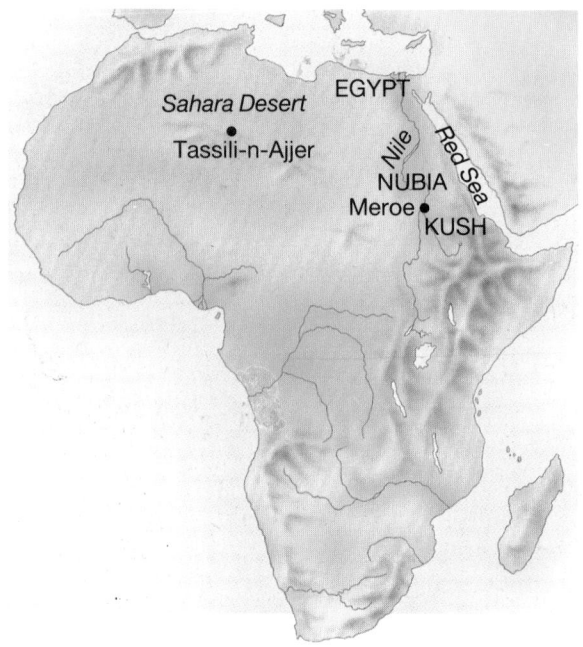

FARMING

On the fringes of the encroaching desert early farmers grew crops such as millet, sorghum, and yams. Millet was especially important because it can withstand a drier climate than sorghum. Yams are nutritious tubers. In the Sahara region pastoral peoples herded goats and sheep. Later they kept several kinds of cattle. They roamed from one oasis to another in search of water for their animals.

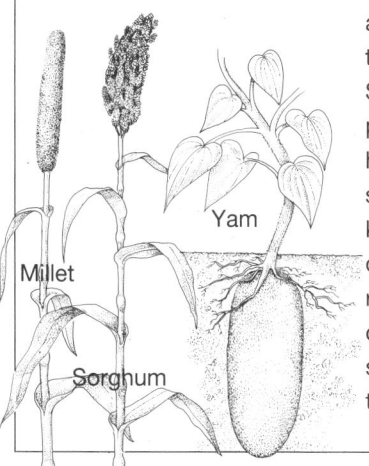

Millet

Sorghum

Yam

the Kushites in 750 B.C., who founded the 25th dynasty of pharaohs.

Kush never had a Bronze Age, but went straight from stone to iron. The capital was moved from Napata to Meroe because Meroe was surrounded by iron ore deposits. It became an important center of ironworking. From Kush the art of ironworking spread westward.

▲ This wall painting from an Egyptian tomb shows a group of Nubians, bearing gifts including fruit, jewelry, furs, and monkeys, for the pharaoh. Such paintings show that the Nubians were black Africans.

▼ Rock paintings and relief carvings are found all over Africa. This cattle herding scene was painted on a rock in the Tassili-n-Ajjer area in the Sahara. The artist has even recorded the coloring of individual cows.

Trade

Once people settled down and started farming, they began to make things like pots and baskets. Sometimes they made more than they needed in their own town or village. When this happened, they could exchange these goods for something of equal value from another community. This might be food or raw materials which they did not have in their own village. Sometimes the goods which were traded were very distinctive. By studying them and the places where they were found, archaeologists have worked out ancient trade routes. Goods traded included gold, wine, silk, pottery, grain, woolen cloth, and furs. For centuries all these goods were bartered, but slowly tokens came into use. These might be made of clay or shells or beads, or even small ingots of metal such as copper, bronze, or iron. Other people paid with cattle or horses. The Chinese probably originally traded with tools such as spades and hoes as their early tokens were shaped like them. The first coins to have a fixed value were used in Anatolia, Turkey, in the Near East around 700 B.C.

◀ The first coins were made in Anatolia, Turkey, from electrum, a mixture of gold and silver. The face stamp guaranteed its weight.

◀ Early Chinese money was shaped like a spade.

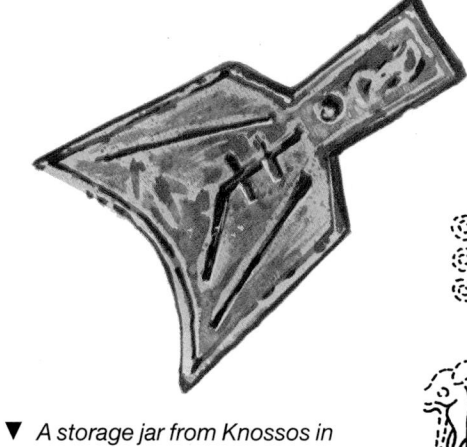

▼ Sumerian traders had their own cylinder seal for signing contracts.

▼ A storage jar from Knossos in Crete. These jars were used for transporting grain, oil, and wine.

▼ As trade grew, people needed to keep records of the goods they bought and sold. The Sumerians wrote theirs on clay tablets like this one.

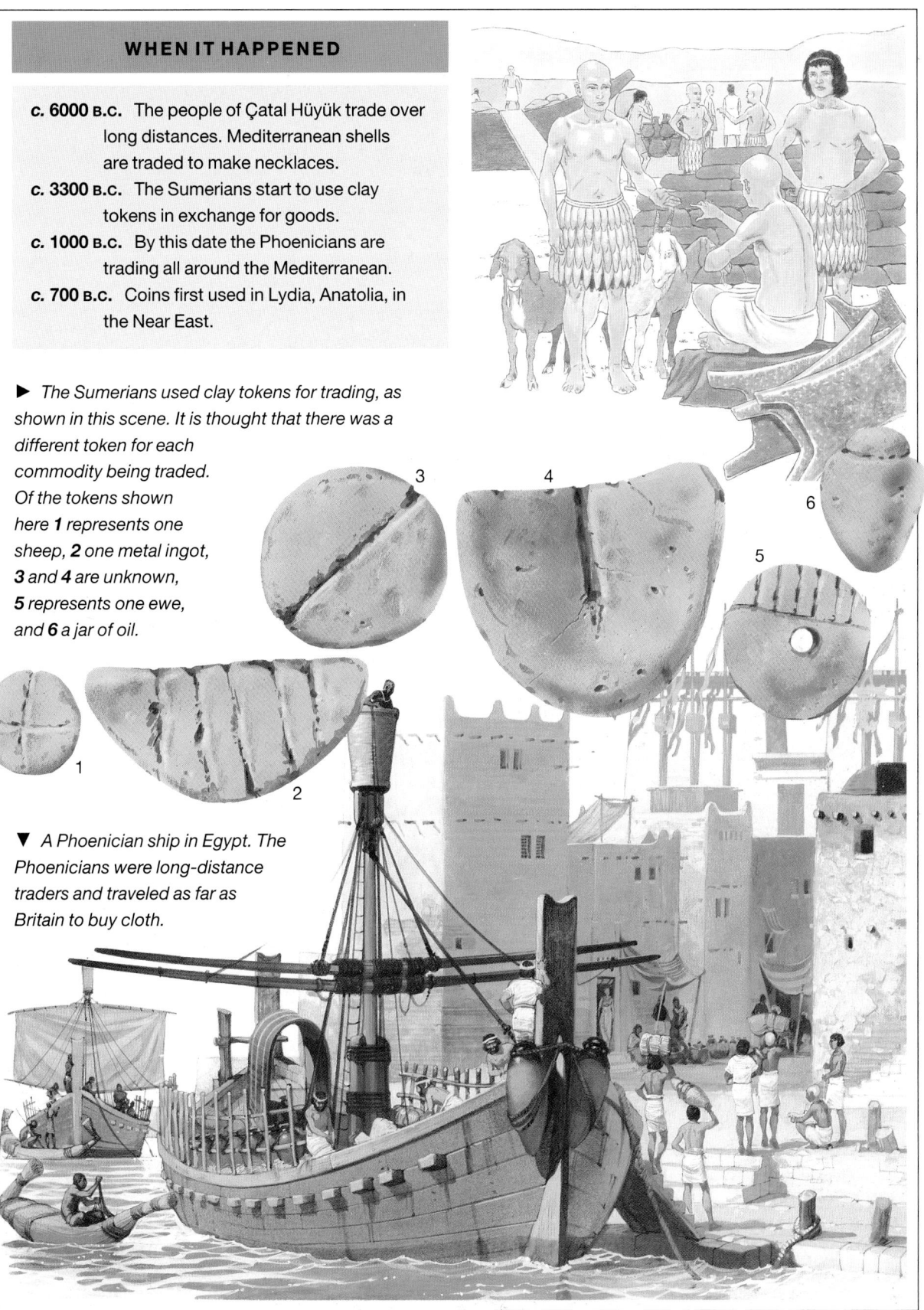

WHEN IT HAPPENED

c. **6000 B.C.** The people of Çatal Hüyük trade over
long distances. Mediterranean shells
are traded to make necklaces.

c. **3300 B.C.** The Sumerians start to use clay
tokens in exchange for goods.

c. **1000 B.C.** By this date the Phoenicians are
trading all around the Mediterranean.

c. **700 B.C.** Coins first used in Lydia, Anatolia, in
the Near East.

▶ *The Sumerians used clay tokens for trading, as*
shown in this scene. It is thought that there was a
different token for each
commodity being traded.
Of the tokens shown
here **1** *represents one*
sheep, **2** *one metal ingot,*
3 *and* **4** *are unknown,*
5 *represents one ewe,*
and **6** *a jar of oil.*

▼ *A Phoenician ship in Egypt. The*
Phoenicians were long-distance
traders and traveled as far as
Britain to buy cloth.

B.C.

854 Assyria: Shalmaneser III attacks the lands of Palestine.

850 Peru: The Chavín culture flourishes (to 500). Chavin artistic influence spread over the central and northern parts of the Peruvian area. The central building of the culture is at Chavín de Huantar, a massive temple complex of dressed stone blocks.

842 Israel: Jehu, a soldier, leads a rebellion against Ahab's son Jehoram, and founds a new dynasty.

814 North Africa: The Phoenicians establish the city of Carthage (literally "new town") near their colony of Utica; other Phoenician colonies are set up in Sicily and Spain.

Episodes from Homer's Odyssey *were often shown on Greek vases. Here the hero Odysseus drives a stake into the eye of the cyclops, the one-eyed giant, to kill him.*

800 Greece: Traditional date for the composition of Homer's epic poems the *Iliad* and the *Odyssey* (Historians now date them at 700). Mexico: The Olmecs build the earliest American pyramid at La Venta.

American Civilizations

The first Americans came overland from Asia when the sea level was lower and there was dry land in the Bering Strait. Over thousands of years they spread right to the tip of South America. Many of them remained hunters, fishers, and food gatherers, but in two areas civilizations grew up: Mesoamerica (Mexico and Central America) and Peru.

In Mesoamerica some 9,000 years ago the Native Americans began to settle down and grow crops such as corn (maize), beans, and pumpkins. A series of small villages sprang up, where the people made pottery and wove cloth. From this culture came one of the first civilizations: that of the Olmecs with its center at La Venta, in western Mexico.

The Olmecs built large earth pyramids as centers for religious worship, and produced huge sculptures and fine jade carvings. Many of their sculptures mix human and jaguarlike features. The

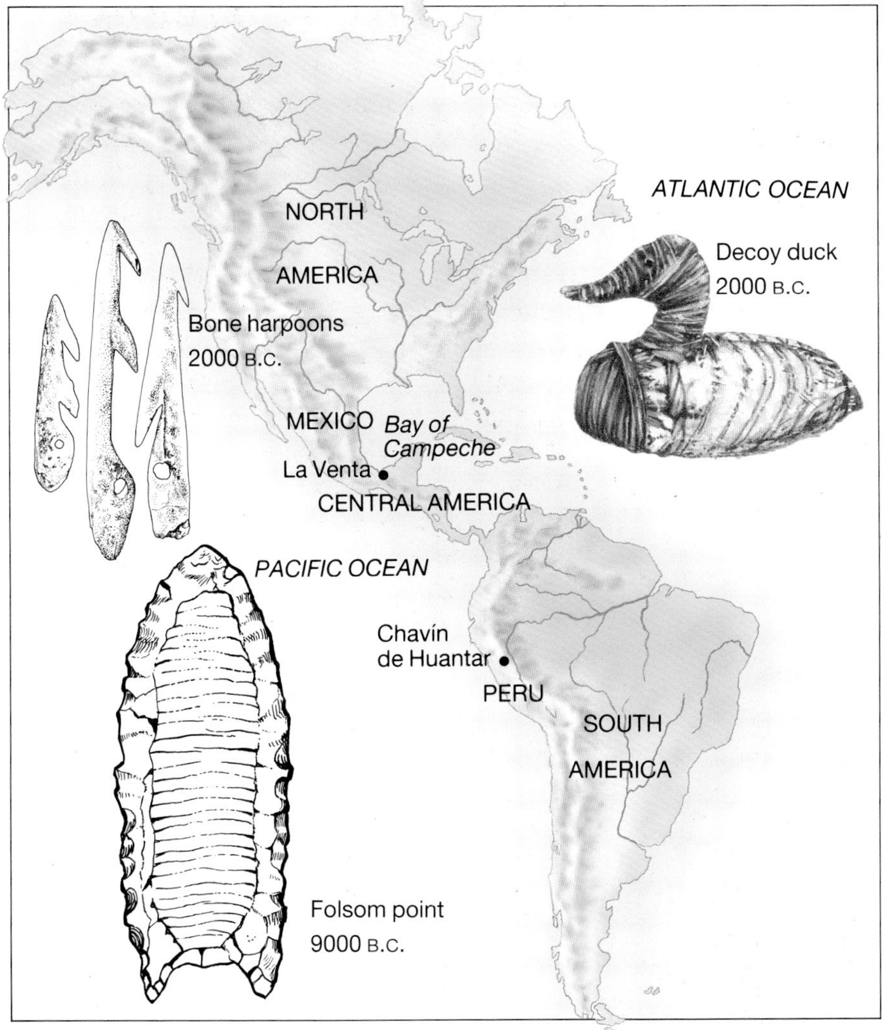

◀ *The map shows the location of the earliest American civilizations, the Olmec and the Chavín. Also shown are some of the tools early American hunters and gatherers would have used and their dates of use.*

ATLANTIC OCEAN

NORTH

AMERICA

Bone harpoons
2000 B.C.

Decoy duck
2000 B.C.

MEXICO *Bay of Campeche*

La Venta

CENTRAL AMERICA

PACIFIC OCEAN

Chavín
de Huantar

PERU

SOUTH

AMERICA

Folsom point
9000 B.C.

FARMING

Chavín farmers grew corn, peanuts, squashes, beans, and avocados. Llamas were used for wool, milk, and meat, and as beasts of burden. Olmec farmers bred a better type of corn that produced more grain than wild plants.

◀ *The Olmecs carved enormous stone heads, some of them nearly 10 feet (3 m) tall. They may represent gods, though the Olmecs worshiped a jaguar god.*

▼ *This fine stone bowl carved in the form of an animal was the work of a Chavín sculptor.*

Olmecs also had a system of writing.

The first permanent settlements in South America were along the coast of northern Peru, where there are traces of fishing and farming communities. About 2,800 years ago a more advanced culture appeared, called Chavín after Chavín de Huantar, the site where it was first found. The Chavín people made pottery, wove cloth on looms, built in stone, and made elaborate carvings. The largest building at Chavín de Huantar, the ''castle,'' is three stories high. Inside is a maze of rooms, corridors, and stairs.

The Chavín culture extended to several other parts of Peru. From their temples and carvings, we know that they worshiped a sacred jaguar or puma.

B.C.

800–550 India: Aryans expand their territory; gradual development of the caste system.

783–748 Israel: Reign of Jeroboam II: a period of prosperity.

776 Greece: First definitely dated holding of the Olympic games.

770–256 China: Eastern Zhou dynasty.

755 China: Solar eclipse sets the first verified date in Chinese history.

753 Italy: Traditional date of the foundation of Rome by Romulus and Remus; Romulus establishes the first Roman calendar: 10 months with a 60-day break in winter.

c. 750 Africa: An army of the kingdom of Kush defeats the Egyptians at Memphis.

745–727 Assyria: Reign of Tiglathpileser III: huge Assyrian expansion leads to Israel, Damascus, and Babylon paying him tribute.

Leather strips wrapped around the fists were worn by boxers at the first Olympic games.

743 Greece: Sparta begins the First Messenian War to conquer Messenia; it ends in 716.

732 Assyrian armies overthrow the city-state of Damascus.

727 Assyria: Shalmaneser V becomes king (to 722). Two years later he overruns Phoenicia, but is resisted by the Israelites under Hoshea, their 19th and last king.

722–481 China: Period of loose confederations under the Eastern Zhou dynasty.

722 Sargon II of Assyria captures Samaria and brings an end to the kingdom of Israel; 27,000 Israelites reported captive. Egypt: Kushan (Nubian) kings rule over Egypt – the 25th dynasty.

Aryan India

About 3,500 years ago a band of pastoralists crossed the mountains of the Hindu Kush into the lands which are now Pakistan and India. They were the Aryans, fleeing from their original homelands in southern Russia. A natural disaster, possibly drought or disease, made them move. They went to Anatolia, to Persia, and finally to India.

The Aryans, whom we also call Indo-Europeans, lived in tribal villages, probably in wooden houses, unlike the brick cities of the Indus Valley people. They counted their wealth in cattle and sheep and were much more primitive than the earlier peoples of the Indian subcontinent. But they were tougher; they were warriors and gamblers, beef eaters and wine drinkers. They loved music, dancing, and chariot racing.

Gradually the Aryans settled down and adopted many of the ways of the native Indians, the Dravidians. The Aryans

---

Buddha

Siddhartha Gautama was a prince who lived about 2,500 years ago. One day he saw the suffering of ordinary people and abandoned his family to search for a better way of life. He spent his time thinking and preaching. Under a fig tree he achieved enlightenment and became known as the Englightened One or Buddha. He taught a kinder religion that respected all living creatures. His teachings were popular and before long he had many followers. Buddhism is now one of the world's principal faiths.

CASTE

The Aryans introduced the caste system into India. Society was divided into four classes, or castes. The highest was the Brahman. They were educated priests and scholars and governed the country. The next was the Kshatriya who were soldiers. Third were the Vaisyas who were farmers and merchants. The native Indians of Dravidian origin, whose skin was darker and who were considered inferior, ranked below these three castes and had to serve the upper castes. It was almost impossible to change your caste or marry outside it.

Low-caste street trader in the early 1800s.

High-caste Brahman in the early 1800s.

SANSKRIT

Sanskrit was the language of the Aryans. The Aryans came from Europe so Sanskrit is related to European languages such as English, German, and Latin. It became the language of the Indian upper classes. The first teachings of the Hindu faith, the Vedas, were told in Sanskrit. Most are sacred hymns, but some explain religious rituals. Others are teachings told as a series of questions and answers.

became crop-growers as well as herders. Among the crops was rice, unknown to the Aryans but already grown in the Indus Valley. The use of the plow and the development of irrigation systems enabled the Indo-Europeans to grow more crops, and support larger towns. By 500 B.C. there were 16 major kingdoms in northern India.

The Aryans had no form of writing. Instead, like the ancient Greeks, they passed on their history and religious beliefs by word of mouth. These traditions, called *Vedas* – Books of Knowledge – were not written down until much later. The oldest is the *Rig-Veda*, a collection of more than 1,000 hymns, composed in their language, Sanskrit. The Vedas are the basis of Hinduism, one of the world's oldest religions. Because the Aryans had no written history, most of what we know about their daily lives is from the Vedas. From this we know that an Aryan wife could have many husbands.

▼ *After the Indo-European people, the Aryans, invaded the Indian subcontinent, they dominated the north. Many of the native people, the Dravidians and the Munda, moved into the south and part of east India.*

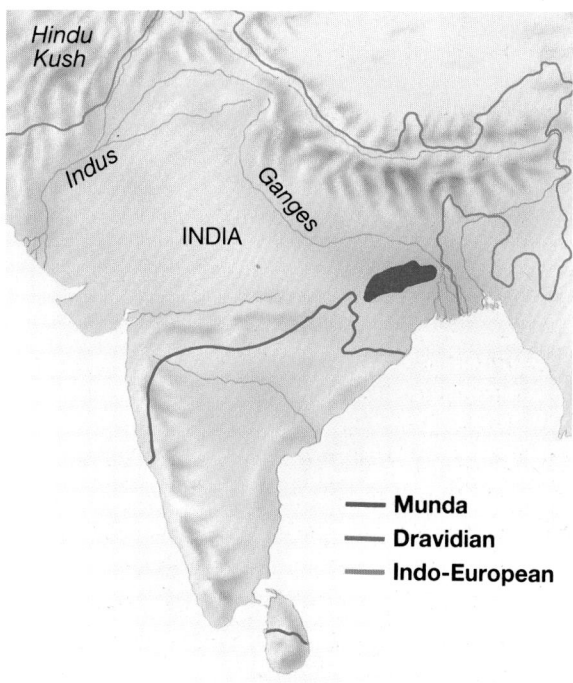

Hindu Kush

Indus

Ganges

INDIA

— **Munda**
— **Dravidian**
— **Indo-European**

The Founding of Rome

According to tradition the city of Rome was founded in 753 B.C. It was founded by the Etruscans, who chose a strong position on the top of seven hills. At that time, several different peoples lived in Italy. To the south of Rome were the Latini, or Latins.

Legends say that early Rome was ruled by Etruscan kings, of whom Romulus was the first. The citizens were a mixture of Etruscans and Latins, who in time became simply Romans. They were influenced by traders from Greece and

▼ The Etruscans have left very little writing, but their pictures are vivid. This painting from a tomb shows lyre and flute players entertaining guests at a banquet. The Etruscans were fond of music, games, and gambling.

ROMULUS AND REMUS

According to legend Rome was founded by two brothers, Romulus and Remus. They were the twin grandsons of King Numitor. The king's wicked brother Amulius put the babies in a basket to float down the Tiber River to their deaths. The basket came to land, and the babies were suckled by a she-wolf who had heard the babies' cries. They were raised by a shepherd until one day they were reunited with their grandfather. They founded Rome, but quarreled and Remus was killed leaving Romulus to become the first king.

SEWERS

Rome had a unique drainage system. It began as a ditch but was later covered by a brick vault. It ran through the whole city and was called the *Cloaca Maxima*. Part of it still exists.

GREEK INFLUENCE

The Etruscans were greatly influenced by the Greeks. They adopted their alphabet, wore togas like the Greeks did, and believed in Greek gods. Even the idea of gladiators and games was originally Greek.

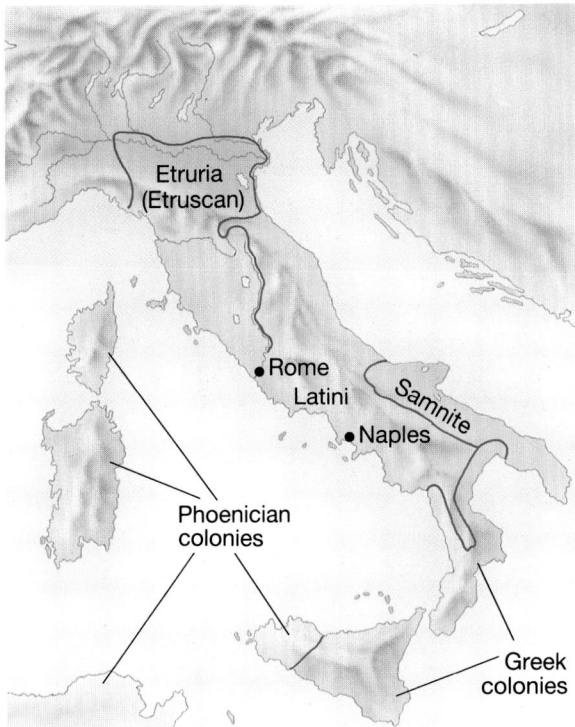

▲ *Italy at the time of the foundation of Rome. The Etruscans came from Etruria. The Greek colonies were along the coast of southern Italy, while the Phoenicians set up colonies in Sicily, Sardinia, and Corsica.*

B.C.

716 Rome: Numa Pompilius becomes the second king of Rome (to 673); he adds January and February to the earlier ten-month Roman calendar.

701 Assyria: Sennacherib establishes his capital at Nineveh.

700 North America: Early Native Americans of the Adena culture begin to build large mounds in what is now southern Ohio as burial places and as platforms for temples.

700–500 Greece: Formation of the great city-states, such as Athens and Sparta, and the rise of the *hoplites* (foot soldiers).

691–638 Judah: Reign of Manasseh: he encourages the Jews to worship the Assyrian gods.

689 The Babylonians revolt against their Assyrian rulers, who destroy the city and flood the site.

683 Judah surrenders to Assyria; Manasseh becomes a prisoner in Babylon. Greece: City-state of Athens ends the rule of hereditary kings; replaces them with nine *archons* (ministers) chosen each year from among the nobles.

681 Assyria: Sennacherib is assassinated by his elder sons.

680 Assyria: Sennacherib's youngest son, Esarhaddon, succeeds him as king (to 669). Greece: The city-state of Argos becomes powerful under its king, Pheidon.

Carthage, who brought new ideas of culture and government.

The kings of Rome wore togas (cloak-like garments) with purple borders. In processions they were preceded by attendants who carried symbolic bundles of rods with axes tied to them, called *fasces*. They were a symbol of power and represented the king's right to beat and execute people if they had done wrong. Over two thousand years later they became a symbol of the Fascist party.

Kings did not have complete power. An assembly had a say in who was king and what he could do, especially in war. The kings had armies to defend Rome. Foot soldiers were equipped like the Greeks, with thrusting spears, shields, and short swords. Those soldiers who could afford it had body armor with helmets and leg guards.

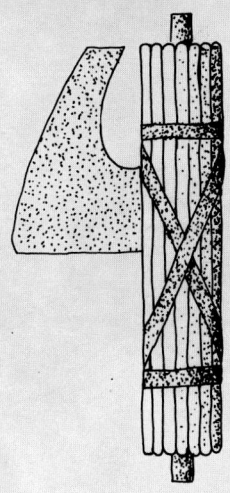

The fasces *was a symbol of power in Rome. The wooden rods symbolized punishment and the ax, life and death.*

War and Weapons

The first people probably fought over food. Their earliest weapons were just rocks and sticks, but later they had spears and arrows tipped with sharpened stones. Once people learned how to make bronze, weapons became more sophisticated. People then fought over riches and territory, but their armies were still just small groups of warriors. The Assyrians were one of the first people to organize a large army. They used cavalry (soldiers on horses) and infantry (foot soldiers), as well as men in chariots. They also had weapons which could demolish the walls built to protect towns. The Greeks also had well-organized armies, made up largely of armored infantrymen, called *hoplites*.

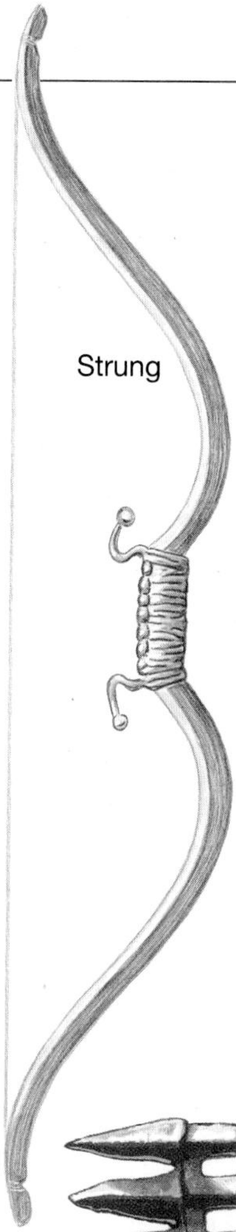

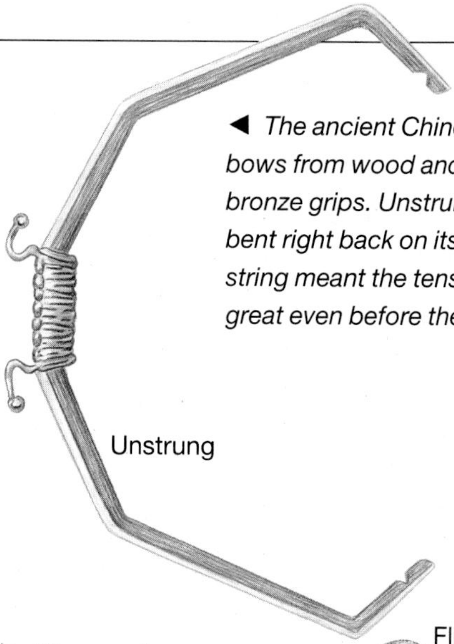

◀ *The ancient Chinese made bows from wood and bone, with bronze grips. Unstrung, the bow bent right back on itself. Adding a string meant the tension was very great even before the archer drew.*

Strung

Unstrung

Greek *kopi*

Flint knife

▶ *Three early weapons.* Below *a bronze axhead from Iran.* Right *an Egyptian flint knife with an ivory handle.* Far right *a Greek* kopi, *or curved sword.*

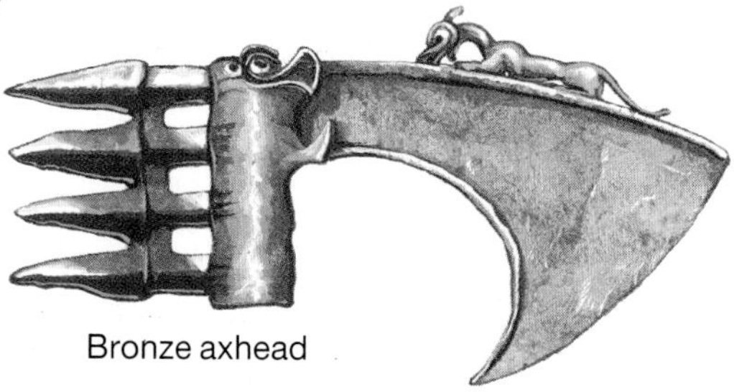

Bronze axhead

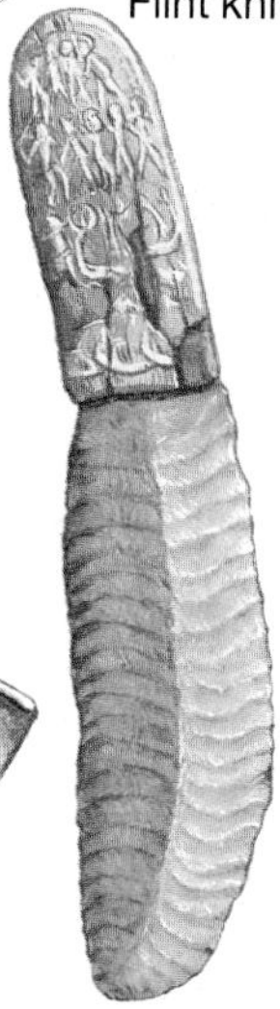

▼ *The Egyptians used fast, two-wheeled chariots in battle. Each chariot had a driver and an archer or a spearman to fight the enemy.*

▼ *The Egyptians fought with bows and arrows and a sickle-shaped sword, called a* khepesh. *They protected themselves with a shield.*

▼ *A Greek cavalryman in battle. His horse is unprotected as it was probably too small to carry his weight, plus that of horse armor.*

WHEN IT HAPPENED

c. 1500 B.C. The city of Jericho is attacked by the Israelites and destroyed.

c. 1250 B.C. The Greeks capture the city of Troy by a trick. A group of Greeks, hidden inside a large wooden horse, get inside the city, pretending the horse is a gift. Unseen, the soldiers leave the horse, open the city gates, and let their army in to defeat the Trojans.

c. 1122 B.C. In China the armies of Wu Wang defeat the armies of the Shang dynasty, bringing the Zhou to power.

689 B.C. Babylon destroyed by the Assyrians.

671 B.C. The Assyrians invade Egypt.

▶ *The Assyrians were experts at siege warfare. Their battering rams could knock holes in town walls, while scaling ladders and towers helped men climb over them. Large shields protected their soldiers.*

B.C.

680–669 Anatolia: Reign of King Gyges of Lydia, who issues the first datable coins.

669–627 Assyria: Reign of Assurbanipal, the last great king of the country.

664 Egypt: Egypt's governor, Psammetichus, rebels against Assyria and becomes pharaoh, founding the 26th dynasty.

663 Assyria: Army led by Assurbanipal sacks Thebes in Egypt.

660 Byzantium (modern Istanbul) is founded by the Greeks.

652 Babylonia: Shamash-shumuskin, governor for his half-brother, King Assurbanipal, rebels; he kills himself after four years of civil war.

The Persians were among the first people to use bows and arrows in warfare.

650–500 Greece: Period of rule by *tyrants* (self-made dictators) in the city-states.

650 Scythian and Cimmarian raiders sweep over Syria and Palestine. Greece: City-state of Sparta conquers rebellious subjects in the Second Messenian War (to 630).

626 Babylonia: The Chaldean general Nabopolassar seizes the throne and declares Babylonia independent from Assyria.

621 Greece: Athenian minister Dracon provides the city-state with its first written laws, which are severe.

612 Assyria: Medes, Babylonians, and Scythians destroy the capital, Nineveh.

609 End of the Assyrian empire.

608 Pharaoh Necho of Egypt defeats and kills Josiah, king of Judah, at the battle of Megiddo.

605 Babylonia: Reign of Nebuchadnezzar II, the Great (to 561); he defeats Necho and the Egyptians at Carcemish in Syria; Judah comes under Babylonian rule.

Babylon Revived

Tribespeople from the west, called Chaldeans, began migrating into Assyria and Babylonia in about 1100 B.C. Several Chaldeans served as kings under their Assyrian overlords. In 626 B.C., Nabopolassar declared Babylonia independent and threw off the Assyrian yoke.

Nebuchadnezzar II was one of the most famous kings of Babylonia. He came to power in about 605 B.C. and his story is told in the Bible, in the book of Daniel. Among other conquests, he captured Jerusalem and forced thousands of its people to live in Babylonia as prisoners.

Nebuchadnezzar also conducted another campaign against Egypt, but devoted most of his time to making the magnificent city of Babylon still more beautiful. He had huge walls built around the city, and named the main gate after the goddess Ishtar. Nebuchadnezzar also built himself a fine

▼ *This map shows the extent of the second Babylonian empire at its height .*

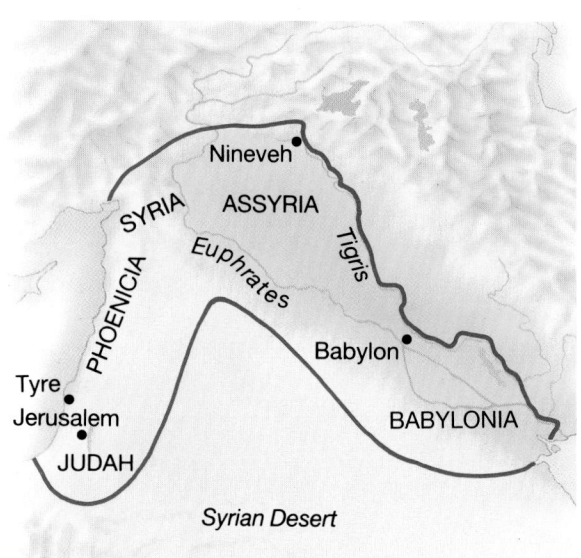

THE HANGING GARDENS

Nebuchadnezzar married a Persian princess, Amytis, who missed the hills of her native land when she moved to the flat plain of Babylon. To please her, Nebuchadnezzar built an artificial "mountain" in the city. It was made of lofty brick terraces, spread with a thick layer of soil on which flowers and trees were planted. They were irrigated with water carried up from the Euphrates by slaves. Known as the Hanging Gardens of Babylon, the ancient Greeks described them as one of the Seven Wonders of the World.

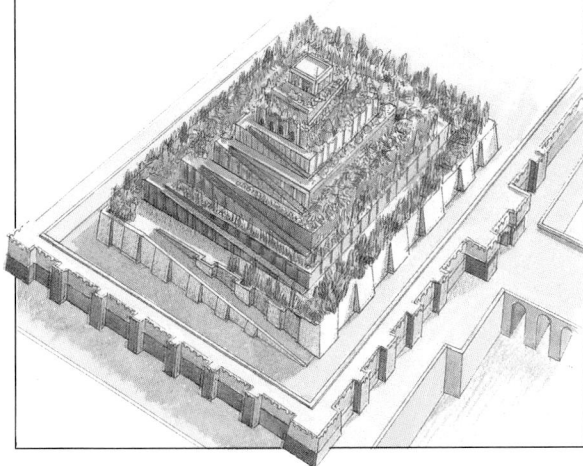

palace and improved other cities in his empire.

The king encouraged the worship of the old Babylonian city god Marduk throughout his empire, which included Syria. In his later years he is believed to have gone mad.

The Babylonian empire survived for only six years after Nebuchadnezzar died. His son, Awil-Marduk ("Evil-Merodach" in the Bible) reigned for three years, before being assassinated. Two other kings, one an infant, reigned for just three more years.

Then a Syrian prince, Nabu-Na'id, seized power, and tried to persuade the people to worship his own god, Sin, rather than Marduk. He made Belsharusur (Belshazzar) co-ruler. In 539 B.C. Naub-Na'id was deposed and his son killed by the invading Persians under their king, Cyrus II, the Great.

▼ The annual New Year festival passing through the Ishtar Gate, the northern entrance to Babylon. The gate was covered with blue glazed tiles, decorated with yellow and white figures of bulls and dragons.

Nebuchadnezzar

Nebuchadnezzar II reigned for 43 years and his reign was marked by many military campaigns. Twice he subdued revolts in Judah, and when Phoenicia rebelled he besieged its chief port, Tyre, for 13 years.

Greek Dark Age

When the Mycenaean civilization came to an end in 1100 B.C., Greece entered what is called its Dark Age. There is no written history of this period which lasted over 500 years.

The country had been invaded by the Dorians who did not have the culture or the skills of the Mycenaeans; they also spoke a different kind of Greek. However, the invaders did keep alive memories of the Mycenaean age through the tradition of telling long narrative poems. The two greatest of these poems, the *Iliad* and the *Odyssey* by Homer, tell the story of the siege of Troy and the wandering of one of its heroes, Odysseus. Grave goods found in tombs in Mycenae match Homer's descriptions.

Greek warfare developed during the Dark Age. Heavily armed foot soldiers, called *hoplites*, fought in a close formation known as a *phalanx*. In this way they could fight off attacks by fast-moving soldiers on horseback.

▼ *When two hoplite phalanxes charged each other it was essential to keep the shield wall unbroken. The end man was most vulnerable because there was no one there to protect him.*

WHO WAS HOMER?

According to tradition, Homer was a blind bard who composed the *Iliad* and the *Odyssey* around 800 B.C. His fine poetry gives vivid descriptions of people and events. Some scholars think that "Homer" was several poets who wrote over a long period. More likely he gathered together all the old legends of Mycenae and retold them. Homer would have sung or recited his poems to an audience. The stories may have been written down toward the end of his life.

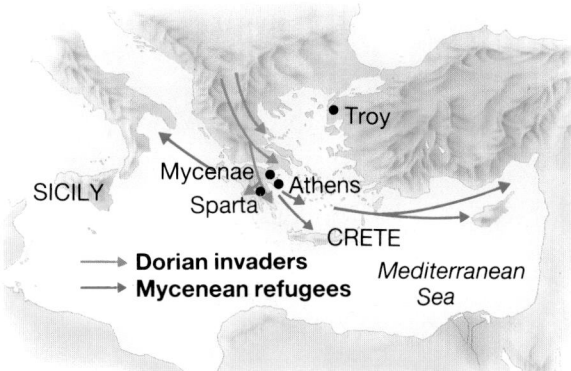

▲ *When invaders overran Greece, many of the original inhabitants left to settle elsewhere. The invaders spread out from mainland Greece to settle the islands.*

Zhou Dynasty

The Zhou dynasty ruled China for more than 800 years. The Zhou were a group of wandering herders who had settled in the fertile Wei Valley to the west. They ousted the last king of the Shang dynasty, who was cruel and a drunkard. They introduced the working of iron, which they used for weapons and for farm tools such as plows. The new metal made farming easier and gave the Zhou soldiers an advantage in war.

The Zhou domain was not a single kingdom, but a collection of large estates, whose owners owed loyalty to the king. Society was divided into the rich nobles, the common people, and slaves. A merchant class also developed.

▲ This picture of an archer mounted on horseback was stamped on a clay tile, made in Zhou times. The bow is similar to those used later in the west.

Confucius

K'ung Fu-tzu (Great Master Kung), or Confucius, was born in the Zhou period. He taught virtue and responsibility and that everyone had a place in society. His teaching has greatly influenced Chinese thought.

B.C.

600–480 Growth and expansion of Carthage.

600 Persia (Iran): Windmills are used to grind corn. India: Early cities are set up in the Ganges river valley.

594 Greece: Statesman Solon is made the sole *archon* of Athens; he introduces milder laws to replace those of Dracon, creates a court of citizens and reforms the election of magistrates.

586 Judah: Nebuchadnezzar II of Babylon sacks Jerusalem and takes the people of Judah into captivity in Babylon (the Babylonian Captivity).

580 Babylonia: Nebuchadnezzar II begins building the Hanging Gardens of Babylon, one of the Seven Wonders of the World.

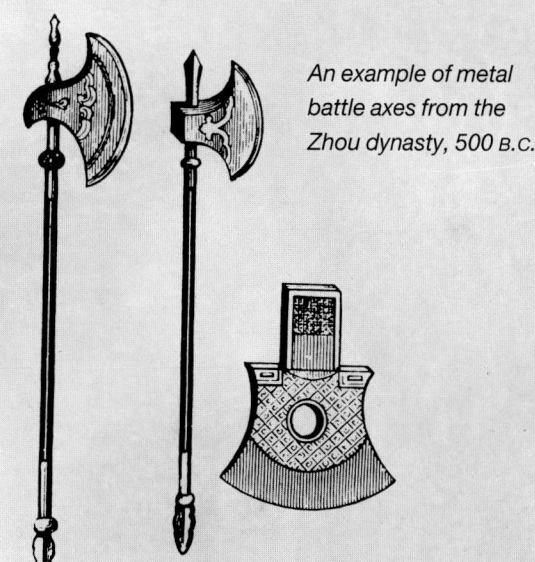

An example of metal battle axes from the Zhou dynasty, 500 B.C.

563 India: Birth of Prince Siddhartha Gautama, who later becomes the Buddha (the Enlightened One).

559 Persia: Cyrus II, the Great, becomes king (reigns to 529).

551 China: Birth of the philosopher K'ung Fu-tzu (Great Master Kung, or Confucius).

550 Persia: Cyrus the Great conquers Media and makes it part of the Persian empire.

546 Anatolia: Cyrus the Great of Persia defeats Croesus, last king of Lydia, at the battle of Sardis; the Persians overrun Anatolia.

B.C.

539 Greeks defeat the Carthaginians in battle. Persia: Cyrus the Great conquers Babylonia.

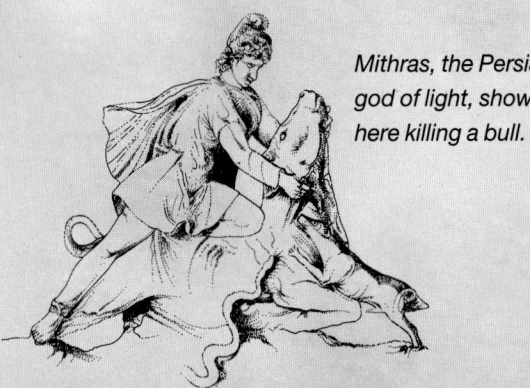

Mithras, the Persian god of light, shown here killing a bull.

538 End of the Babylonian Captivity: An edict of Cyrus the Great allows some Jewish exiles to return to Judah.

534 Rome: Tarquinius Superbus (Tarquin the Proud), becomes its last king.

530 Persia: Death of Cyrus the Great in battle against Tamyris, Scythian warrior queen and ruler of Massagetae tribe; he leaves an empire that includes Anatolia, Babylonia, Syria, and Palestine; succeeded by his son Cambyses (to 521).

525 Egypt is conquered by Cambyses of Persia; the country remains under Persian kings until 404.

521 Persia: Reign of Darius I (to 486); Persian empire is divided into 20 *satrapies* (provinces).

520 Judah: Work is resumed on the Temple in Jerusalem (completed 515).

510 Rome: Rebellion overthrows King Tarquinius Superbus.

509 Rome: Traditional date for the foundation of the Republic.

508 Greece: Statesman Cleisthenes introduces democracy in Athens. Treaty between Rome and Carthage gives Latium to Rome and Africa to Carthage.

507 Greece: City-state of Sparta attempts to restore the aristocracy in Athens.

500 Italy: The Etruscan empire is at its most powerful. India: Start of rice cultivation, writing, and coins.

The Persian Empire

The land we call Iran (from the word "Aryan") used to be known as Persia. Its people were divided into two groups, the Medes and the Persians. They migrated into Persia from the east about 3,000 years ago. At first the Medes were more powerful. Nearly 2,600 years ago Cyrus, the ruler of the Persian province of Anshan, rebelled against the Medes and seized power.

Cyrus made Persia the center of a mighty empire, the Persian empire. He became known as Cyrus the Great. His capital was Ecbatana, now buried under the modern city of Hamadan.

Cyrus commanded an army of cavalry and remarkably skilled archers. By the time he died Cyrus ruled over an empire that extended from the Mediterranean Sea to Afghanistan, and from the Arabian Sea north to the Caspian and Aral seas. He was killed in 530 B.C. defending his northern territories against

Darius I

Darius I was a good general, and extended the empire east to the Indus River. He reorganized the empire into 20 provinces called *satrapies*. Good roads allowed the royal messengers to speed to all parts of the land with orders from the king. Darius levied taxes in every part of his empire. He built a new capital city at Persepolis, in southern Iran. He introduced the domestic chicken from India to western Asia, and from Lydia in Anatolia he introduced gold and silver money to Persia. Darius's official title was Shahanshah (king of kings). The title was still in use by the Shah of Iran until the country became a republic in 1979.

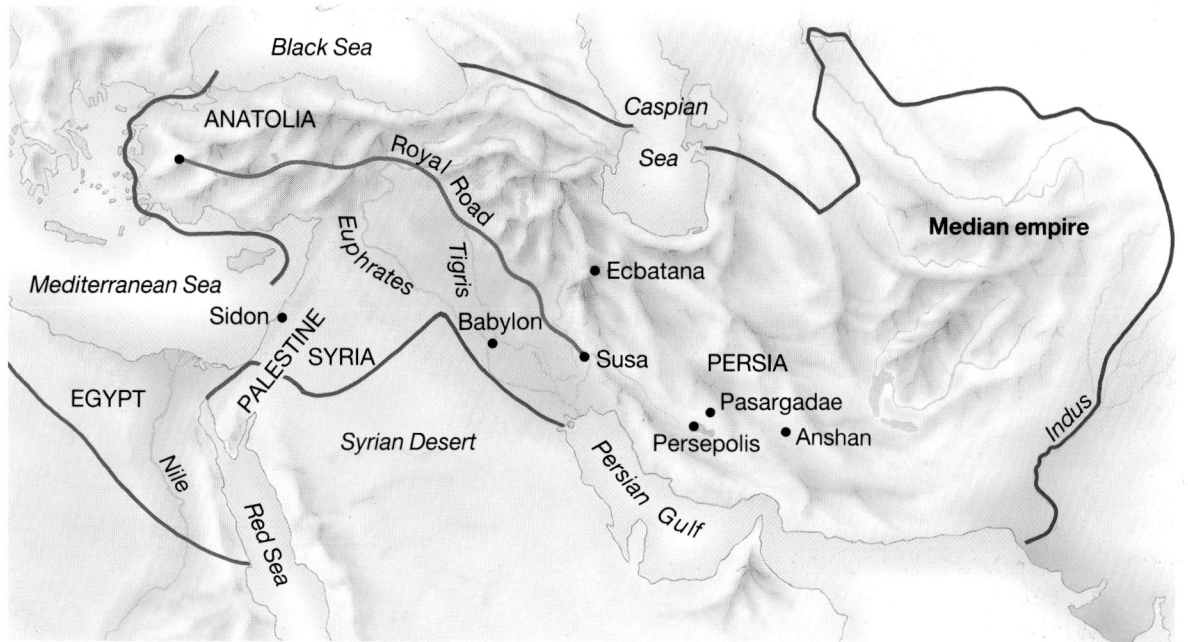

▲ *An impression from a cylinder seal shows Darius I hunting a lion from a chariot with bow and arrow. The winged figure is an image of the god Azura Mazda.*

▼ *The steps of the palace at Persepolis show people from all over the empire bringing gifts for the king.*

▲ *The Persian empire at its greatest extent under Darius I. Susa was its administrative center and Persepolis its center of state. The Royal Road was built to speed up communications.*

nomadic tribes from central Asia.

The Persian King Darius I extended and strengthened the empire. He appointed *satraps*, or governors, to each province who paid him gifts of cereals and produce. He built many roads to link his huge empire and encouraged trade by introducing a standard currency.

In religion the Persians followed the teachings of a Persian prophet named Zarathustra (in Greek, Zoroaster), who worshiped the one god Azura Mazda.

Oceania

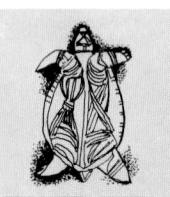

The first people migrated to Australia from southern Asia. They had to sail across the sea to New Guinea, but the low sea levels left land bridges between New Guinea, Australia, and Tasmania. They took with them the dingo, or wild dog. The ancestors of the Aborigines (native Australians) were fishers, hunters, and gatherers. They used boomerangs for hunting from very early times and gathered the seeds and fruit of the natural vegetation. The Aborigines never developed farming, but they knew how to use fire to cook their food. As the sea level rose they moved farther inland.

The first people to colonize Melanesia and Micronesia sailed from what is now Indonesia about 4,000 years ago. Their skilled craft workers built large canoes that could survive long voyages. In the canoes the explorers carried not only supplies for the voyage, but also animals and some of their favorite food plants.

They navigated across the vast distances of the oceans by studying the stars and the sea currents.

▲ The Aborigines of Australia made paintings, using simple earth colors of red, yellow, brown, black, and white. Cave and rock paintings are found in many parts of Australia, some of them at sacred sites.

▼ In addition to Australia the map shows the areas of Micronesia (Little Islands) and Melanesia (Dark Islands from the color of the people) and the approximate date they were settled.

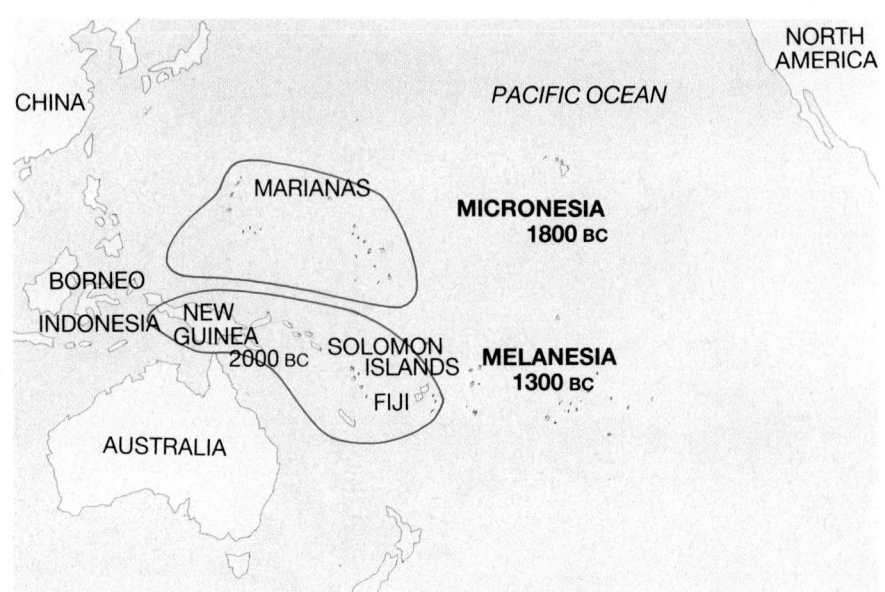

THE DREAMTIME

The Dreamtime is a religious belief that is thousands of years old. It is a creation myth that tells of the Beings that long ago shaped the world and everything in it. The Beings died, but their spirits lived on, some in the sky, others in the ground, in hills, rocks, or waterholes. Some Beings are depicted in rock paintings.

The Classical World

The great age of ancient Greece and Rome is called the classical world. These two civilizations were responsible for shaping much of the world we live in today.

Although the Greeks were continually at war with the Persians during their golden age, the discoveries they made form the basis of our knowledge of biology, mathematics, physics, literature, philosophy, and politics. By his conquests Alexander the Great spread Hellenistic (Greek) knowledge and culture over much of the ancient world. Later, the Romans, who greatly admired the Greeks, spread their culture farther afield to northern Europe and Africa.

By about the 1st century B.C. the ancient world was dominated by four great empires. The Roman empire was the most powerful; it stretched from Europe to North Africa. In the Far East, the Han dynasty controlled almost all of what is now China, and the Middle East was ruled by the Sassanians. In India, the Gupta family held power.

Inside the empires, life was mainly secure and peaceful. They had strong governments and were wealthy. Traders linked the empires and helped to spread religious ideas and knowledge. But the empires were constantly under attack from outside by tribes of nomads called barbarians. The cost of maintaining armies to protect against these attacks was high, and by about A.D. 450 the empires had collapsed.

At about the same time, one of the largest cities in the world, Teotihuacán, was at its height in Central America. Neighboring it, the Mayan people also built great cities and connected them by roads. The Mayas dominated Central America until the 15th century.

▼ *The streets of Roman towns were very busy from dawn onward. In the areas where people lived were also stores, offices, and workshops.*

The Americas

Europe

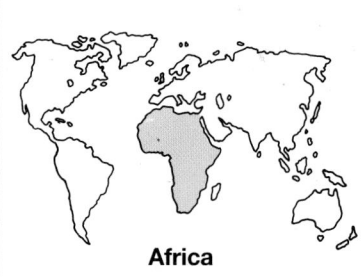

Africa

The Americas

B.C.

c. **499** Gallinazo and Salinar cultures flourish in Peru.

Mayan temples were often decorated with carvings.

c. **200** Tiwanaku and Nazca cultures develop in South America.

A.D.

c. **200** Hopewell Indians build burial mounds in Ohio.

c. **300** Rise of Mayan civilization and the city of Teotihuacán in Central America.

400 Moche culture is well established in Peru, extending from the Andes to the Pacific.

c. **500** Inuit begin hunting seals and whales and the Anasazi culture begins to develop in Utah, Arizona, and New Mexico.

Europe

B.C.

479 Greeks defeat Persian invasion.

431–404 War between Athens and Sparta.

c. **400** Athens rises to power in Greece.

336 Alexander the Great comes to power.

323–319 Alexander's empire divided among his generals.

c. **300** Rome rises to power in Italy.

264–146 Punic wars between Rome and Carthage.

52 Gaul (France) rebels against Roman rule.

49–44 Julius Caesar rules Rome.

27 Octavian becomes first Roman emperor.

A.D.

43 Romans invade Britain.

117 Roman empire at its greatest extent.

286 Roman empire divides in two.

330 City of Constantinople (Istanbul) is founded.

370 Huns from Asia invade Europe.

380 Christianity becomes official religion of Roman empire.

452 Attila the Hun enters Italy.

476 Last Roman emperor is overthrown.

Africa

B.C.

400 Nok culture flourishes in West Africa.

332 Alexander the Great conquers Egypt.

323 Ptolemy I rules Egypt.

30 Egypt becomes a Roman province.

A.D.

1 Bantu people begin to migrate to East Africa.

350 Kingdom of Axum (Ethiopia) conquers kingdom of Kush. Christianity reaches Ethiopia.

429–534 The Vandals overrun the Roman empire and set up their own kingdom.

500 Bantu people reach southern Africa.

Near East

Asia and the Far East

Australasia and Pacific

B.C.

c. **499** Persian empire at its height.

334 Alexander the Great begins conquest of Persia.
312 Seleucus takes control in Syria.

c. **5** Birth of Jesus Christ.

A.D.

c. **30** Crucifixion of Christ.
70 Romans destroy Jerusalem; *Diaspora* (dispersal) of Jews begins.
226–651 Sassanians rule Persian empire.
330 Capital of Roman empire transferred to Constantinople (Istanbul).

484 The Huns attack Persia and kill the emperor.

B.C.

321–184 Mauryan dynasty rules northern India.
273–232 Asoka rules India and introduces Buddhism.
221 Qin dynasty in China.
218–204 Great Wall of China built.
202–A.D. 220 Han dynasty in China.
111 Chinese conquer Vietnamese and rule Vietnam until A.D. 939.
50–A.D. 50 Buddhism introduced into China.

A.D.

105 Paper invented in China.
200 Yamato dominate Japan.
220–589 Civil war in China (Six Dynasties period).
320–535 Gupta dynasty rules northern India.
360–390 Japanese conquer Korea.

B.C.

A clan spirit painting from New Guinea.

A.D.

c. **100** First settlers arrive in Hawaiian islands.

c. **300** First settlers arrive in Tahiti.

c. **400** Polynesians reach Easter Island.

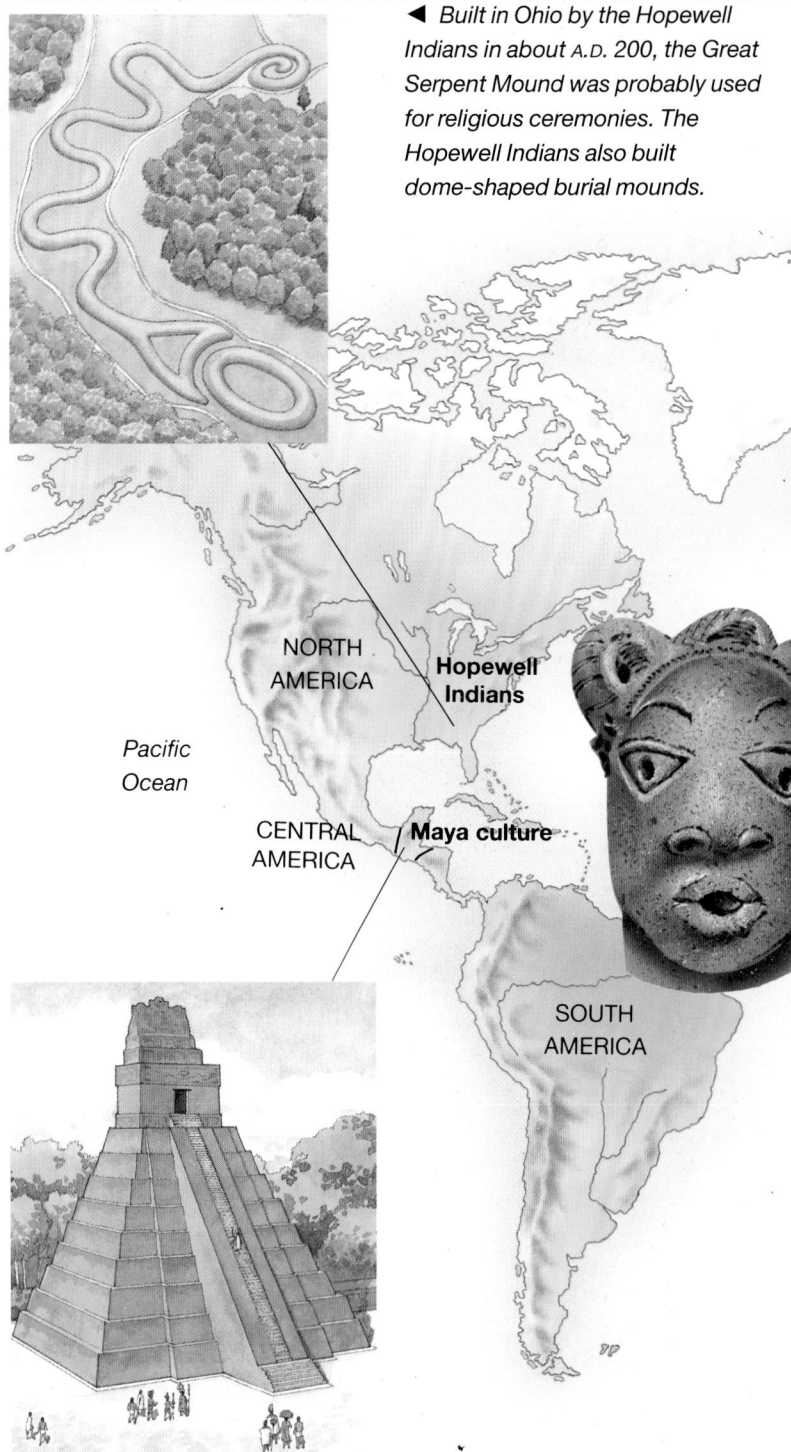

The World

During this period most people lived in vast military empires, the achievements of which still influence us today.

In **North America**, the first settled cultures started to emerge. The people grew crops and built huge burial mounds. In **Central America**, the Mayas were beginning a civilization that would develop writing and astronomy and in **South America**, various cultures were beginning to develop in the Andes.

Europe saw the rise of two great civilizations, first in Greece, then in Rome. Other cultures, such as the Celts, were overpowered and absorbed. Through trade and conquest, European influence spread over North Africa and the Near East. Through conquest the vast Roman empire spread a new religion, Christianity, over its territory. In central **Africa**, native cultures developed independently.

In Asia, **China** was unified for the first time under a single emperor, and two great empires were established in **India**. In the **Pacific Ocean**, the Polynesians continued to colonize islands over a vast area.

◄ Built in Ohio by the Hopewell Indians in about A.D. 200, the Great Serpent Mound was probably used for religious ceremonies. The Hopewell Indians also built dome-shaped burial mounds.

NORTH AMERICA

Hopewell Indians

Pacific Ocean

CENTRAL AMERICA

Maya culture

SOUTH AMERICA

▲ The ruins of an ancient temple found at Tikal, in what is now Guatemala, Central America. It was one of the centers of the advanced Mayan civilization.

▲ A fine terracotta head from Nok in Nigeria. This type of sculpture flourished from 400 B.C. to A.D. 200. Leading a settled existence gave people time to develop art.

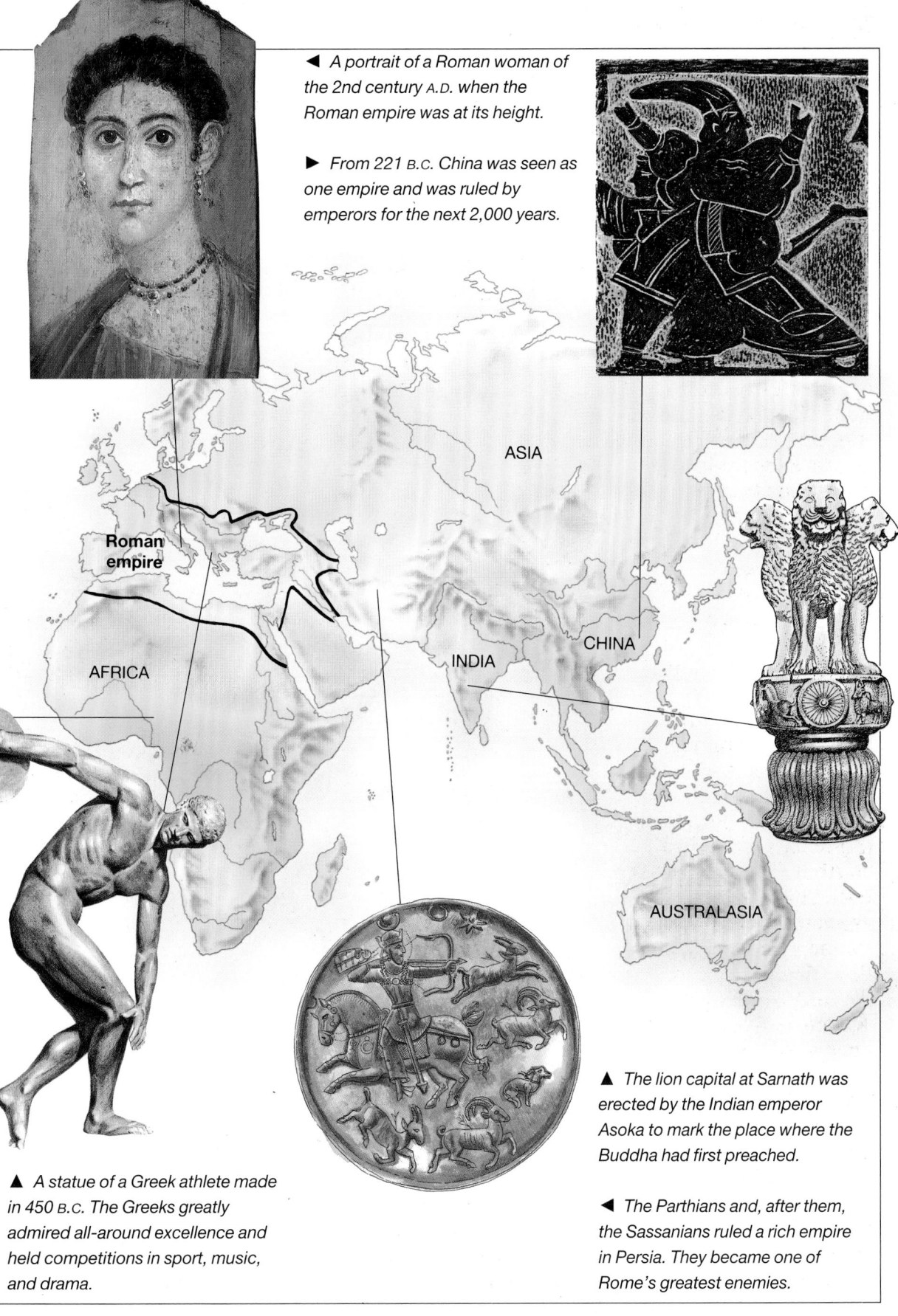

◀ A portrait of a Roman woman of the 2nd century A.D. when the Roman empire was at its height.

▶ From 221 B.C. China was seen as one empire and was ruled by emperors for the next 2,000 years.

ASIA

Roman empire

AFRICA

INDIA

CHINA

AUSTRALASIA

▲ The lion capital at Sarnath was erected by the Indian emperor Asoka to mark the place where the Buddha had first preached.

◀ The Parthians and, after them, the Sassanians ruled a rich empire in Persia. They became one of Rome's greatest enemies.

▲ A statue of a Greek athlete made in 450 B.C. The Greeks greatly admired all-around excellence and held competitions in sport, music, and drama.

B.C.

c. 499  Italy: Etruscan empire at its height. Africa: First use of iron. Nok culture becomes established in what is now northern Nigeria.

497 Greece: Death of Pythagoras, philosopher and scientist.

496 Italy: Romans defeat the Latins in battle at Lake Regillus.

494 Rome: Plebeians (common people) revolt against the patricians (aristocracy) and gain political rights.

493 Italy: Roman-Latin alliance forms the Latin League, which fights the Etruscans.

490 At the battle of Marathon on the east coast of Greece, the Athenians beat the Persians and bring to an end the First Persian War.

Persian soldiers were very well armed and protected when going into battle. They wore leather tunics strengthened with scales and carried bows and arrows, spears and daggers.

486 Persia: Reign of Xerxes I (to 465).

480 Carthage develops a naval fleet and takes control of the western part of the Mediterranean and the island of Sicily. Greeks defeat the Persians in the sea battle of Salamis.

479 Persian army defeated by the Greeks at Plataea.

477 Greece: Golden age of Athens (to 405).

469 Greece: Birth of Socrates, Athenian philosopher (dies 399).

465 Persia: Reign of Artaxerxes I (to 424).

450 Italy: Etruscan empire declines (to 400).

447 Greece: Construction of Parthenon at Athens begins. War between Athens and Persia ends with Athens victorious.

Greece

Ancient Greece was made up of independent city-states called *poleis*. Communication was not easy in the mountainous countryside, so each *polis* developed its own government and laws.

The city-states grew up on the plains, and the mountains around them provided a natural defense. For added protection, the citizens also built high, strong walls around their cities. Inside each city wall, a fort called an *acropolis* was erected in a high place. At the heart of each city was a large open space known as an *agora* which was used for meetings and as a marketplace.

The two most important Greek city-states were Athens and Sparta. Athens is probably best known for being the birthplace of *democracy* (government by the people) under Pericles in the early 5th century B.C. Athena was the goddess of Athens. She was portrayed both as a

GREEK BATTLES

A Greek archer.

490 B.C. Battle of Marathon. Persians lose.

480 B.C. Battle at the pass of Thermopylae. Leonidas and 300 Spartans die to cover Greek withdrawal. Persians victorious.

480 B.C. Naval battle at Salamis. Persian fleet forced to retreat.

479 B.C. Defeat of Persian army at Plataea.

431–404 B.C. Peloponnesian War between Sparta and Athens. Sparta won under Lysander.

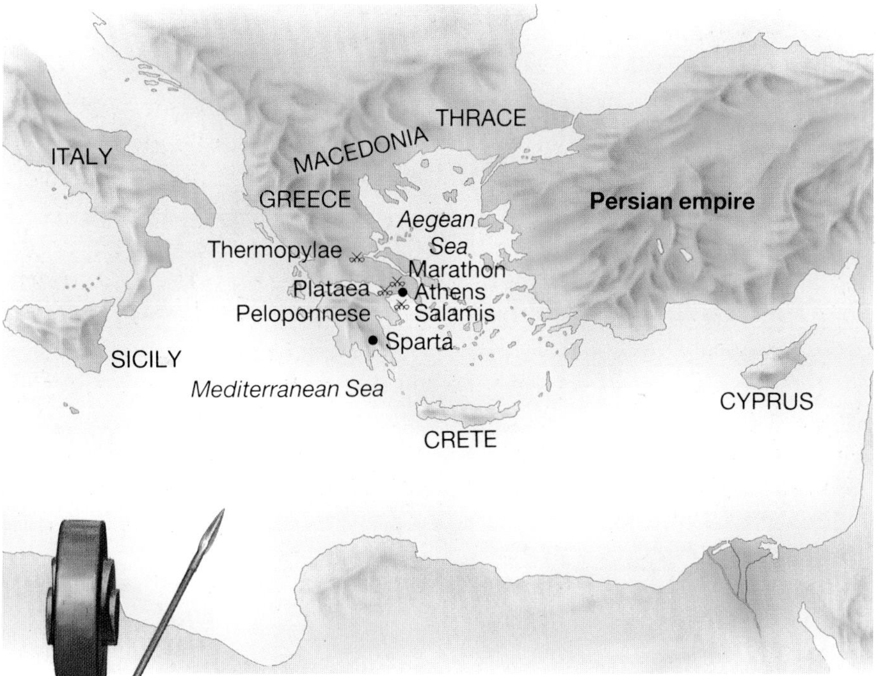

ELECTIONS

Democracy began to develop in Athens during the 5th and 4th centuries B.C. All male citizens had a say in government but non-citizens such as women and slaves, could not vote. Citizens voted in trials, using metal disks (*below*), to indicate guilty or not guilty.

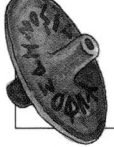

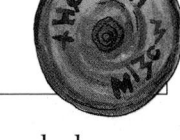

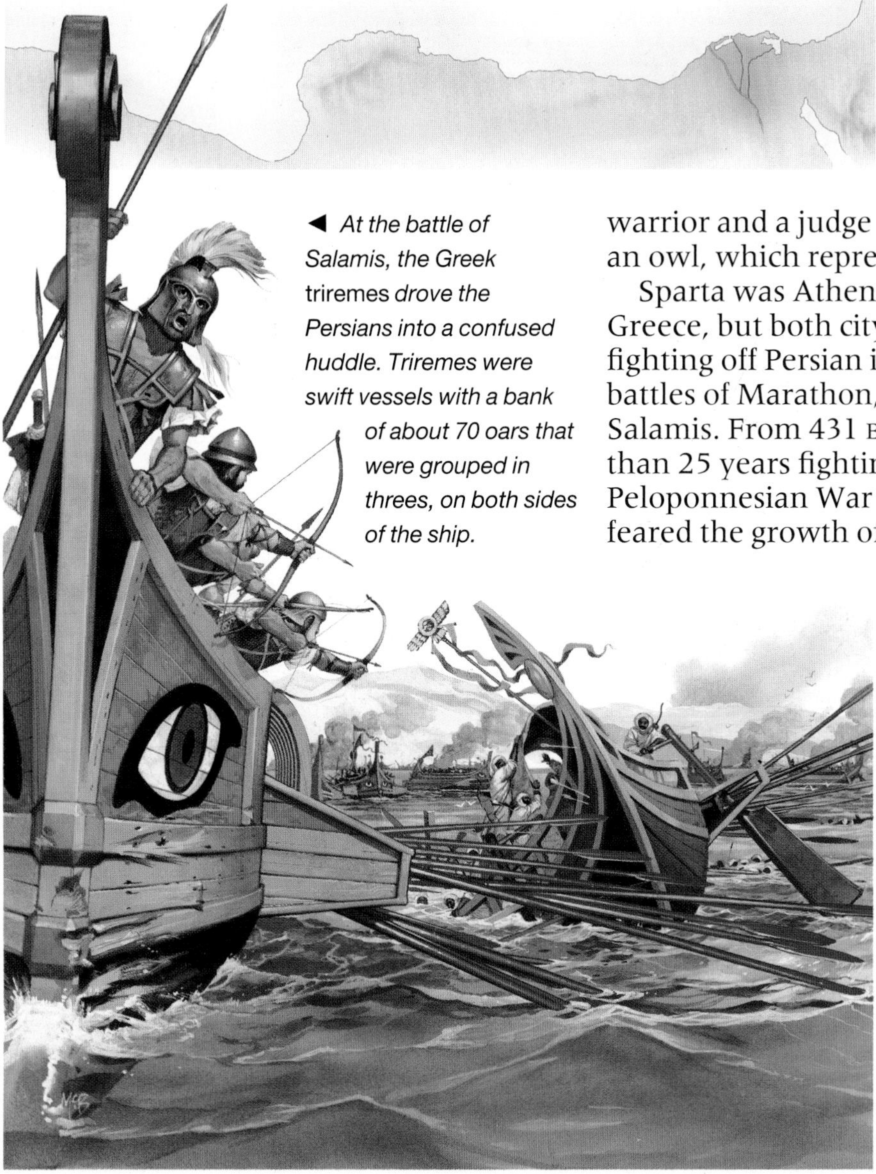

◀ *At the battle of Salamis, the Greek* triremes *drove the Persians into a confused huddle. Triremes were swift vessels with a bank of about 70 oars that were grouped in threes, on both sides of the ship.*

warrior and a judge and her symbol was an owl, which represented wisdom.

Sparta was Athens' main rival in Greece, but both city-states united in fighting off Persian invasions at the battles of Marathon, Thermopylae, and Salamis. From 431 B.C., they spent more than 25 years fighting each other in the Peloponnesian War because Sparta feared the growth of Athens' power.

OWL COIN

A silver four drachma "owl" piece was the best-known coin in the ancient Greek world. Issued in Athens, it symbolized the owl-eyed goddess, Athena.

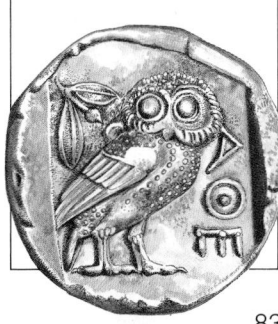

Greek City-states

As the leading city-state in ancient Greece with control over the seas, Athens was at its greatest during the 5th century B.C. It forced the other city-states to pay money to it as tribute and became even richer by trading with them as well. At this time its statesmen, soldiers, writers, architects, artists, mathematicians, and philosophers achieved so much that the period is known as the Golden Age of Greece.

Nearby, the city-state of Sparta had a superior army, but life for the Spartans was much harsher than existence in civilized, cultured Athens. The Spartan citizens had always relied on a vast population of land slaves called *helots* to provide their food. When these same slaves rebelled in 464 B.C. and continued to do so for the next 20 years, the Spartans were so frightened that they put all their energies into creating and training an army to control them.

▲ A bronze statue of a Spartan girl athlete. While Athenian girls were taught to be houswives, Spartans were trained in sports to be fit mothers of warriors.

▼ Originally a fort, the Acropolis at Athens was completely transformed in the 5th century B.C. into a complex of spectacular shrines and temples.

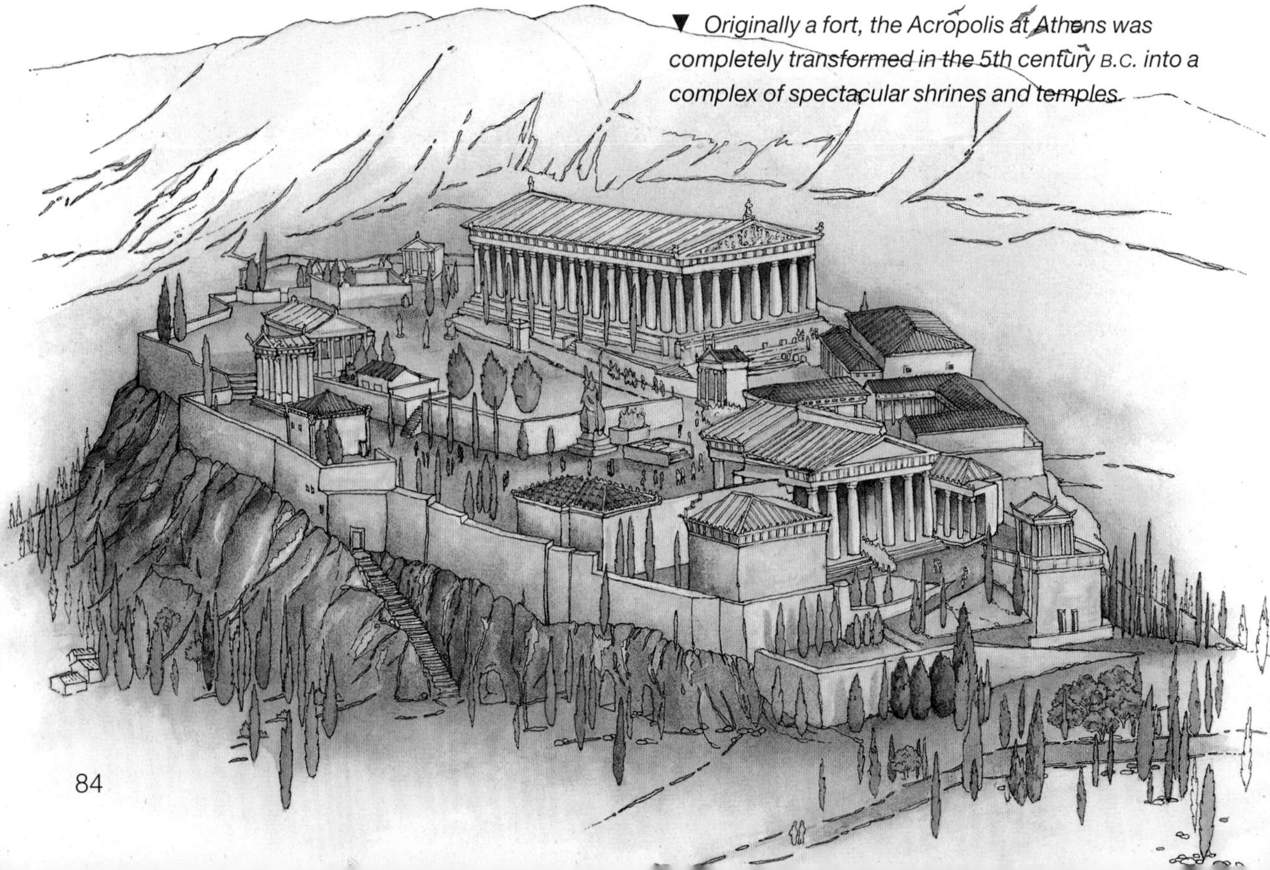

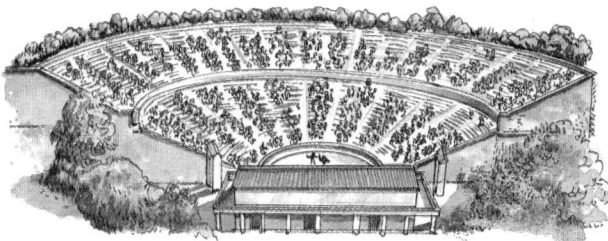

▲ *In about 320 B.C., the architect Polykleitos constructed a theater at Epidaurus which could seat more than 13,000 people. Every spectator had an equal view, and the smallest sound could be heard all over the theater. Greek plays are still performed there today.*

Spartan life was tough from birth onward. Babies who were weak or ill were left to die on the mountainside. All boys were taken from their families at the age of seven, and given a strenuous training in military skills and sport until they were 20. Then they had to join the army. Even when Spartan soldiers, or hoplites as they were known, married, they still had to eat and sleep in the army barracks. But they were renowned for their strength and courage.

GREEK WORDS

Many words in modern English have their origins in ancient Greek, but the meanings have changed. *Aristocrat* originally meant "he who fulfills the best," but now it describes a member of the upper classes. A *tyrant* was once "a master, lord, or king" and now is someone who governs harshly. An *idiot* was a "person not holding public office," but now it means someone who is stupid.

POTTERY

Athens led the way in the development of painted pottery. There were two painting techniques, known as "red figured" and "black figured." Many fine examples of this pottery still exist today.

B.C.

446 Greece: Athens and Sparta, two city-states, sign 30-year peace treaty.

c. 440 Celtic tribes begin invasions of Roman and Greek territory. Celtic La Tène culture develops in central and northern Europe. Rome: Plebeians win the right to marry patricians.

c. 431 Second Peloponnesian War between Athens and Sparta begins (to 421).

c. 430 Greece: Hippocrates founds science of medicine.

429 Greece: Birth of Athenian philosopher, Plato (dies c. 347).

424 Egypt rebels against Persia's oppressive rule. Persia: Artaxerxes I assassinated; succeeded by Darius II (to 404).

A young man from Athens beginning his compulsory two-year military training period.

421 Greece: Athens and Sparta agree a 50-year truce: it lasts for six years.

413 Athens attempts to invade Sicily, but its forces are destroyed.

411 Greece: Revolution in Athens.

404 Greece: Lysander of Sparta captures Athens and sets up government of Thirty Tyrants. Persia: Artaxerxes II becomes king (to 358).

403 Greece: Pausanias restores democracy to Athens.

400 Greek army defeated by army of Artaxerxes II of Persia. Africa: The use of iron spreads south of the Sahara. The Nok culture flourishes in what is now northern Nigeria.

c. 399 China: Period of crisis as rival groups fight each other.

Arts and Crafts

Some of the wealth of empires was used to finance the creation of works of art.

In Greece, the finest art was produced in the classical period, which reached its height about 400 B.C. Through the campaigns of Alexander the Great, Greek ideas about art spread as far as India. Roman artists often copied the work of the Greeks, but Roman quality was not as good.

Throughout the Roman empire, the houses of the rich were often decorated with bright paintings on the walls, and marble mosaics on the floors.

Art in China developed its own styles, away from the rest of the world. These styles influenced arts and crafts in Korea and Japan.

▲ This silver bowl was found in Denmark. The decorations on it show the influence of peoples from central and southern Europe.

◄ A painted drinking cup made in Athens in the 5th century B.C. Goods like these were traded all around the Mediterranean.

► A copper raven made by the North American Hopewell Indians around 100 B.C. Although they knew about metal, these Native Americans used stone tools.

▼ A sculpture from the tomb of a Roman blacksmith. The smith is working at his anvil, and his assistant is heating up the forge with bellows.

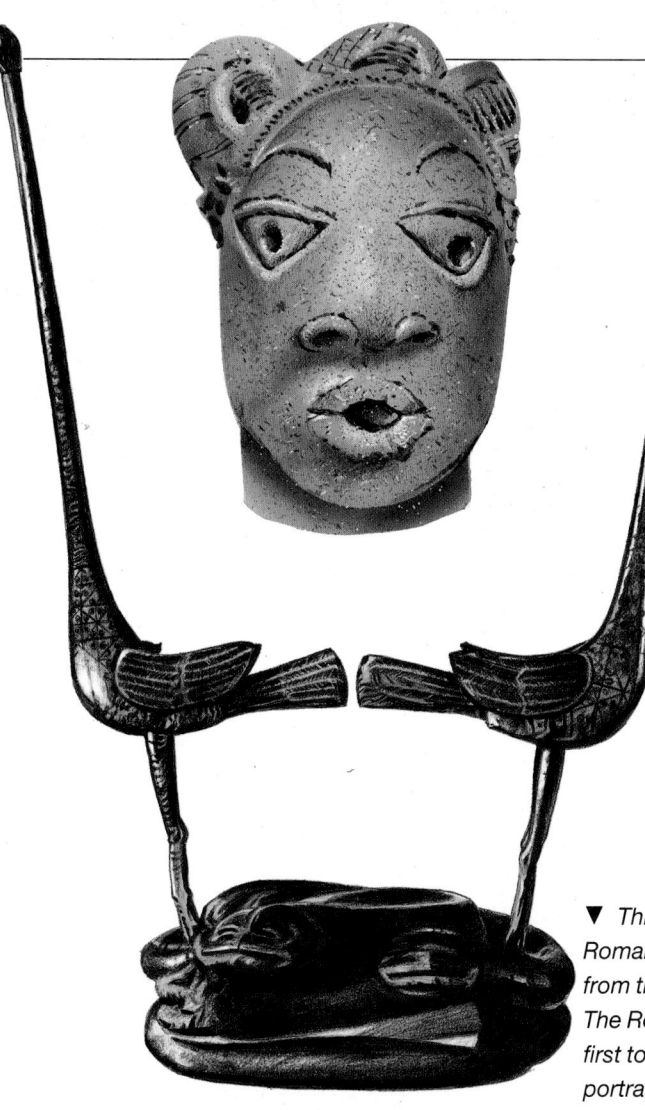

◀ *This pottery head was made by the Nok people of Nigeria between 400 B.C. and A.D. 200. It is typical of African art at this time.*

◀ *These Chinese cranes, made between the 5th and 3rd centuries B.C. are decorated with lacquer.*

▼ *This wax portrait of a Roman woman dates from the 2nd century A.D. The Romans were the first to paint realistic portraits of people.*

▲ *A Roman mosaic from the 4th century B.C. showing a goddess on a leopard. Mosaics were made from pieces of stone such as marble.*

WHEN IT HAPPENED

480 B.C. The start of the classical period in Greek art and architecture.

323 B.C. Greek sculptors portray people and, for the first time, emotions rather than gods.

310 B.C. In North America, the Hopewell Indians are skilled workers in wood and stone.

200 B.C. In Peru, the large-scale geometric and animal motifs, known as the Nazca Lines, are scratched out in the desert.

c. **150 B.C.** The Chinese make lacquerware objects, paintings on silk, and pottery figures of people and animals.

1st century A.D. The Romans make realistic portraits and sculptures.

The Greek Legacy

Like most people, the Greeks asked questions about the world they lived in. But they used reason and argument to understand why things happened. While earlier peoples wrote lists of kings and events, the Greeks wrote full accounts of their lives. The first historian, Herodotus, was Greek; he wrote studies of people and their customs. Thucydides wrote the first detailed account of a war and its causes.

The Greeks developed the idea of thinking about the meaning of life, which they called *philosophy*. Two of the world's greatest philosophers, Socrates and his pupil Plato, came from Athens. Most of the rules of geometry and arithmetic were invented by Greek mathematicians such as Euclid and Pythagoras. The Greeks were also the first to believe that citizens should have a say in making the laws of the state.

The Greeks held competitions in sports, music, and drama (producing many great tragic plays and comedies in the 5th century B.C.) in honor of their gods. The most famous were the Olympic games held every four years at the sanctuary of Zeus at Olympia. At the end of four days, oxen were sacrificed to Zeus and everyone joined in a great feast.

▲ Greek physicians made medicines from herbs and plants and kept records of them. The Greeks were the first to separate medicine from religion. They believed that disease was to do with the body, rather than a punishment sent by the gods. Hippocrates led the way by using his powers of observation and reasoning to identify many different illnesses.

Doric

Ionic

Corinthian

◄ The three types of columns that the Greeks developed for their public buildings are known as classical orders. Each type of column was more elaborate than the last and had its own proportions, molding, and decoration. From left to right they are Doric, Ionic, and Corinthian.

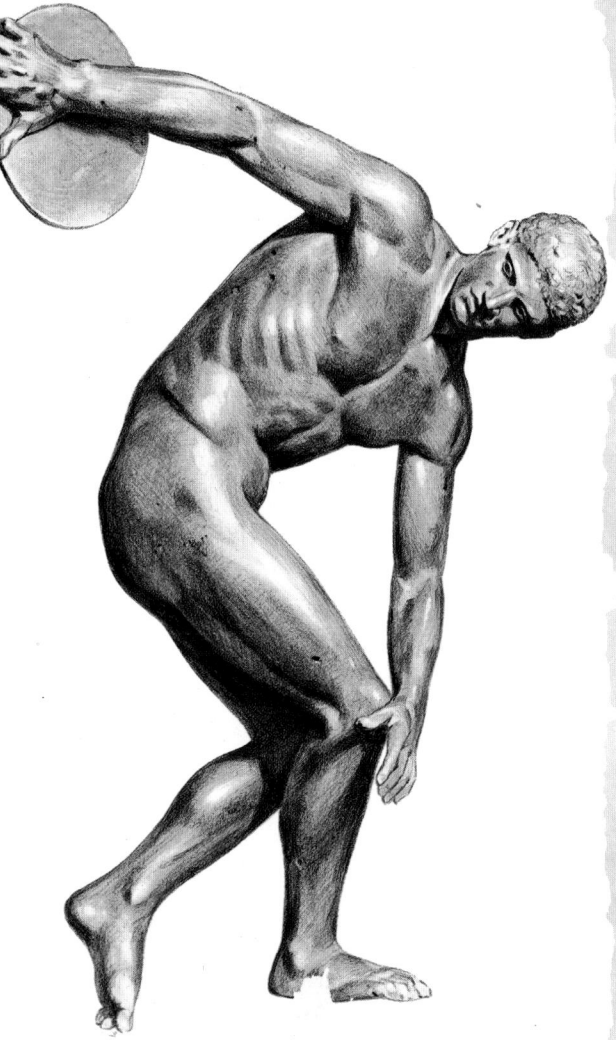

▲ *Throwing the discus was one of the five events in the pentathlon (penta is Greek for "five") in the games. The other four competitions were long jump, javelin, wrestling, and sprint. The Greeks admired all-around excellence, so the pentathlon was an important event.*

▼ *Greek schoolboys were taught to read and write. They also learned music and poetry. Girls stayed at home and probably grew up unable to read and write.*

B.C.

396 Italy: Romans defeat Etruscans following ten-year siege of Etruscan city of Veii, when Roman soldiers tunnel their way into the city.

394 Greece: Battle of Coronae in which Sparta defeats armies of Athens, Thebes, and Argos.

393 Persian fleet defeats Spartan fleet and ends Sparta's attempt to invade Asia.

390 Gauls (Celts) sack Rome.

387 Anatolia: Artaxerxes II of Persia captures Greek cities.

386 Sparta and Persia sign peace treaty, recognizing Persian rights to cities in Asia and Cyprus, and Athenian rights to three islands. All other Greek states to be independent.

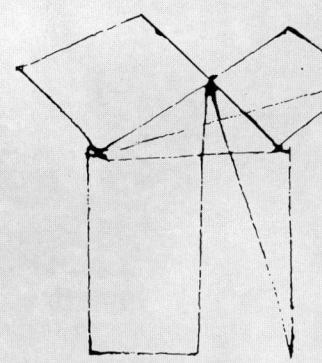

Pythagoras, a Greek mathematician, is best known for the theorem about right-angled triangles which was named after him.

384 Greece: Birth of Aristotle, philosopher (dies 322).

380 Egypt: 30th dynasty rules (to 343). It is last Egyptian dynasty to rule the country.

371 Greece: Theban general Epaminondas destroys Spartan army at Leuctra.

367 One hundred years of war between Carthage and Sicily begin.

c. 360 Greece: Thebes becomes most powerful city-state. China: Crossbow becomes most important weapon in warfare.

359 Macedonia: Philip II rules (to 336).

358 Persia: Artaxerxes III becomes king (to 338).

347 Greece: After ten years the Sacred War for possession of the oracle at Delphi ends with crushing defeat of Greeks, by Philip of Macedon.

B.C.

343 Egypt: Artaxerxes III of Persia recaptures Egypt and founds the 31st dynasty, which lasts to 332. Rome: First Samnite War between Rome and the Samnites and Latins (to 341).

c. 340 Macedonia conquers Thrace.

A head from a shrine at Taxila, India. It is thought that Greek and Roman sculptors traveled to India and taught their ideas to Buddhist artists.

339 Greece: Fourth Sacred War, between Macedonia and Athens (to 338).

338 Philip of Macedon defeats Athenian and Theban forces at battle of Chaeronea. He unites all Greece under his rule. Rome: tribes and cities of Latin League revolt against Rome. Romans are victorious at Trifanum, and the League is dissolved. Persia: Artaxerxes III is assassinated; succeeded by Darius III (336–320).

336 Greece: Philip of Macedon is murdered. He is succeeded by his son, Alexander III, known as "the Great."

334 Alexander the Great begins campaign against Persia and defeats Darius III in Anatolia.

333 Alexander the Great defeats Darius III again at battle of Issus. He takes the city of Tyre after siege. End of Phoenician empire.

332 Alexander invades and conquers Egypt. Work begins on construction of his new city, Alexandria.

331 Alexander renews Persian campaign and defeats Darius III at Arbela.

330 Darius III is assassinated, leaving Alexander in control of Persia.

Alexander the Great

After the end of the Peloponnesian War, the age of Spartan domination did not last long. In 359 B.C., a 23-year-old youth called Philip became king of Macedon in northern Greece and immediately set about building up the strongest fighting force the world had yet seen. By his death in 336 B.C. he controlled Greece.

Philip's son Alexander was only 20 years old when he became king. His father's wars had left the royal treasury empty, but Alexander realized that if he conquered the wealthy Persian empire his financial problems would be solved. His first campaign against the Persians in 334 B.C. gave him control of Asia Minor, and he soon added Egypt to his empire. In 333 B.C. Alexander defeated the Persian king Darius at Issus and by 331 B.C., all Persia had been conquered.

Alexander's last expedition was to India, where he won the battle of Hydaspes. Such terrible losses were

Alexander

336 B.C. Inherits throne of Macedon.
334 B.C. Invades and conquers Asia Minor.
331 B.C. Wins Persian empire.
325 B.C. Conquers eastern Iran and northwest India.
323 B.C. Dies in Babylon.

CATAPULTS

Both Philip and Alexander used this powerful catapult in battles. Power was supplied by springs made from twisted guts or hair. These were wound up and then let go, hurling rocks with great strength.

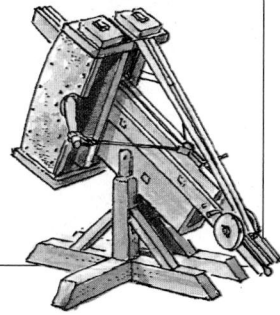

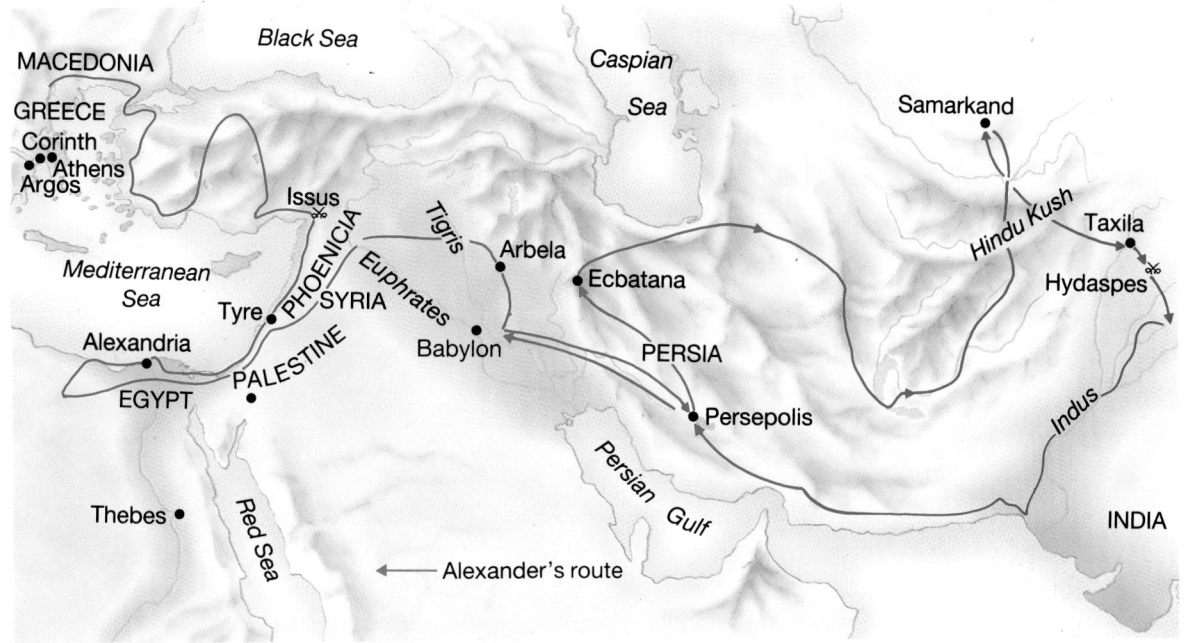

▲ Alexander's route to northwest India. His short but successful career spread the Greek language and culture over much of the known world.

▼ Alexander the Great was one of the most brilliant generals the world has ever seen. He always fought at the head of his troops and this mosaic found in Pompeii, southern Italy, shows him leading the charge.

suffered there that his soldiers refused to go any farther. Alexander was forced to retreat to Babylon, which he had made his capital. Two years later, at the age of 32, he died of a fever (some say, perhaps from poison). His generals were left to squabble over the vast empire that stretched from Egypt to India.

PETRA

Petra, now in Jordan, was part of the huge territory won by Alexander the Great. It was the capital of the Nabataeans (an Arab tribe) from the 4th century B.C. to the 2nd century A.D. A prosperous city because it was on the trade route from southern Arabia to the Mediterranean Sea, the people created some of their houses and buildings by cutting deeply into the red stone cliffs. After Alexander's conquest, many of the buildings were designed and decorated in imitation of the Greek style.

Buildings

The growth of empires and cities led to the construction of many public buildings. The most magnificent were the ones for religious use. They were often built of ordinary stone, because of its strength and permanence. Sheets of decorative marble were then added to make the building look more impressive.

The Greeks were skilled architects by the beginning of this period. The study of mathematics helped them to design well-proportioned buildings which suited their surroundings. By 300 B.C., the Greeks had also developed town planning. They worked out whole cities in detail and arranged the streets in a grid pattern.

The Romans adopted some ideas from Greek architecture, but also found new techniques. One of them was the discovery of concrete in about 200 B.C. At first they used it in foundations, but soon it become an important building material, used in huge domed roofs.

By A.D. 200, Roman cities had apartment blocks of four and five stories, called *insulae*.

▲ The Pont du Gard, a Roman aqueduct built to supply water to the town of Nemausus (now Nîmes), one of the richest towns of Roman Gaul. Towns and cities required constant supplies of water for drinking, cooking, and washing, as well as for industries such as leather tanning. This demand for water inspired some impressive feats of Roman engineering.

▼ A pottery model of a watchtower made around A.D. 100 in Han China. Towers like these were used to guard noblemen's estates from unwanted visitors.

TOOL BOX

Greek, Roman, and Chinese builders used virtually the same tools that are used today. These included saws, chisels, and planes. Iron tools were used for working stone. Bronze, which is softer, was used mainly for wood-working tools.

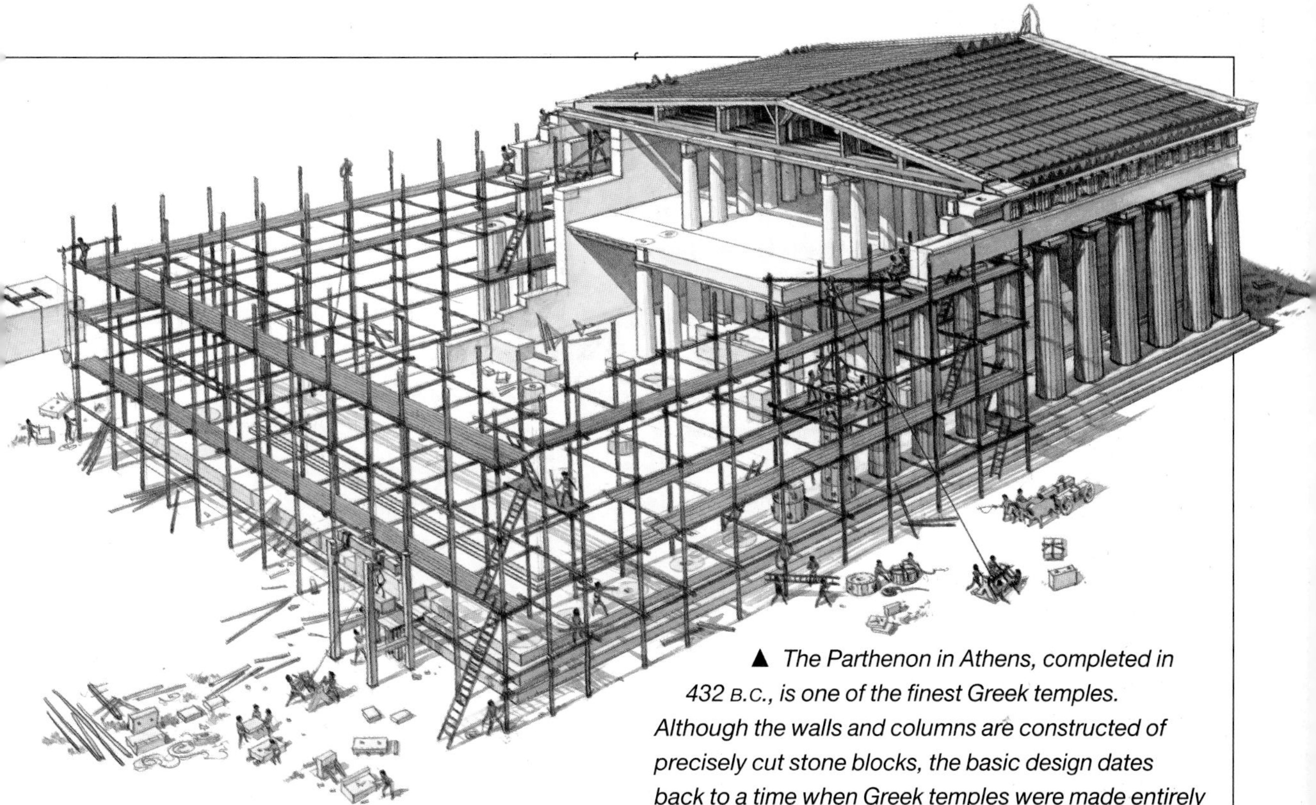

▲ *The Parthenon in Athens, completed in 432 B.C., is one of the finest Greek temples. Although the walls and columns are constructed of precisely cut stone blocks, the basic design dates back to a time when Greek temples were made entirely of wood. The fluted stone columns would originally have been tree trunks. Carved marble statues and panels added to its magnificence.*

◄ *A reconstruction of a stone, stepped Mayan pyramid at Tikal, Guatemala. At the top of the steps stands a Mayan temple. Around 300 B.C., (possibly even earlier), the Mayas began building huge temple complexes. The one at El Mirador covers more than 6 square miles (16 sq. km).*

WHEN IT HAPPENED

447–432 B.C. The Parthenon in Athens is built.

214 B.C. Work starts on building the Great Wall, China, to keep out the nomads from the north.

A.D. 50 In Mexico, the city of Teotihuacán is laid out in a rectangular grid and the Pyramid of the Sun is built. This is the largest building in the Americas until the arrival of the Europeans.

A.D. 80 The Colosseum, Rome, opens to the public. It holds up to 80,000 people.

A.D. 122–136 Hadrian's Wall in England is built.

A.D. 130 The Pantheon in Rome is built.

B.C.

327 Alexander begins invasion of India.

326 Second Samnite War (to 304). Roman troops are defeated and humiliated. During the war Appius Claudius builds the Appian Way from Rome to Capua, near Naples, to help move Roman troops more easily to the war area.

323 Alexander dies at Babylon, aged 33. His body is buried at Alexandria, Egypt. Alexander the Great's generals argue over division of his empire (to 319). Ptolemy rules in Egypt (to 285). Hellenistic period begins (to 31).

321 India: Chandragupta founds Mauryan dynasty (to 184).

320 Judah: Ptolemy captures Jerusalem. Libya: Egypt takes Libya as a province.

312 Syria: Seleucus, one of Alexander's generals, begins to take control.

310 Italy: The Etruscans join the Samnites in attacking Rome, but are defeated at Lake Vadimo.

307 Greece: Two of Alexander's generals rule the country, both taking the title of king as Antigonus I and Demetrius I. Other governors follow their example.

306 A trade treaty is agreed between Rome and Carthage.

305 Egypt: Ptolemy I takes the title of king. Babylon: Seleucus I becomes king, founding Seleucid dynasty.

These beautiful earrings are an example of the wealth of the Greek world after the many victories of Alexander the Great.

304 Italy: Rome makes peace with the Samnites and other enemies and gains land in area around Naples. India: Seleucus gives up his claim on India to Chandragupta in exchange for 500 elephants.

Alexander's Successors

After the death of Alexander the Great his empire was broken up into a number of kingdoms, each ruled by one of his generals. The richest of these kingdoms was Egypt, where a Macedonian named Ptolemy had seized control. He founded the last dynasty of kings of Egypt. His descendants ruled Egypt until 30 B.C., when the last of the line, Cleopatra VII, committed suicide when Romans defeated her navy at Actium.

The family of Seleucus, another Macedonian general, ruled land that stretched from the Mediterranean to Afghanistan. It soon split into smaller states, such as Pergamum and Bactria. Macedon itself was ruled by the Antigonids. Macedonia, Egypt, and Persia were often at war with each other. Having lost their unity, the old Greek city-states slowly declined.

Although the Greek empire broke up, Greek became the official language throughout the Near East and was also widely used by many people every day. New cities, different from the old city-states, were founded. They were much

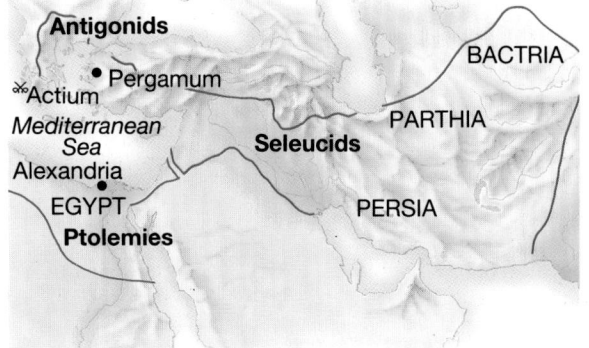

▲ *When Alexander died, his generals fought bitterly among themselves for control of his empire. Eventually it was divided up into large kingdoms.*

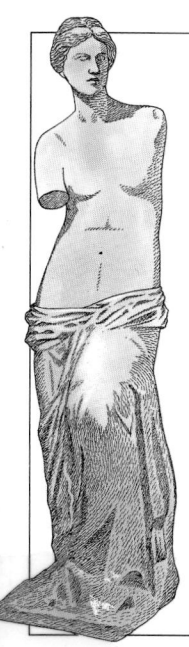

VENUS DE MILO

Alexander's many conquests spread the Greek culture over a vast area. This meant the Greeks were now living alongside many different races. It brought a new realism to the art of the period. Artists chose to represent the many facets of humanity rather than the idealized forms of classical Greece. Even statues of goddesses were given human faces. This figure of Aphrodite, the Greek goddess of love and beauty, is now known as the Venus de Milo (Venus is the Roman name for Aphrodite). It was sculpted in 130 B.C. by Alexandros of Antioch.

larger and part of a network of other towns governed by local rulers. These rulers were regarded as demigods and in Egypt the Ptolemies even called themselves pharaohs. Highly organized public services ran these new states. The cities also had theaters, gymnasiums, and places for games and festivals.

▲ *Many of the new cities in Alexander's empire were named Alexandria after him. The most famous city was Alexandria in Egypt. Its imposing lighthouse, Pharos, was one of the Seven Wonders of the ancient world.*

▼ *Cleopatra, the last ruler of Egypt, was well-known for her beauty and intelligence. Two famous Romans, Julius Caesar and Mark Antony, fell in love with her.*

Cleopatra

69 B.C. Born.
51 B.C. Becomes queen of Egypt.
c. 46 B.C. Caesarion, son of Cleopatra and Julius Caesar, is born.
31 B.C. Her forces, led by Mark Antony, are defeated at Actium.
30 B.C. Commits suicide.

The Mauryan Empire

 The first great empire in India was founded in 321 B.C. by the emperor Chandragupta. Called the Mauryan empire, it extended from Bengal to the Hindu Kush on the borders of Afghanistan and united the lands of northern India.

Chandragupta's grandson, Asoka, became the most famous Mauryan ruler. He conquered many neighboring kingdoms and enlarged his empire. His empire contained peoples of more than 60 different creeds (beliefs) and languages. Because each group was different it was difficult for Asoka to govern his empire successfully.

Asoka was originally a Hindu but he converted to Buddhism after seeing a particularly horrific battle. He immediately stopped going to war and

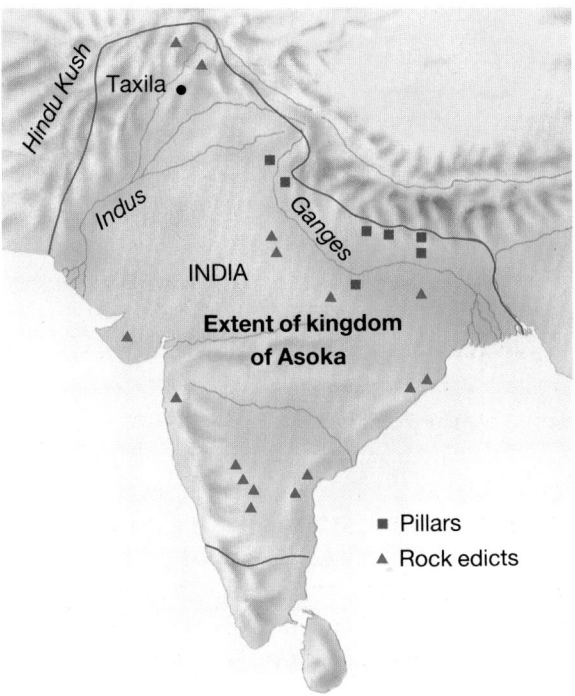

Extent of kingdom of Asoka

■ Pillars
▲ Rock edicts

Asoka

273 B.C. Becomes Mauryan emperor.
262 B.C. Converts to Buddhism.
c. **260 B.C.** Starts making rock inscriptions.
232 B.C. Dies.

◀ *Asoka said, "All men are my children." One of the many things he did to help his people was to plant banyan trees along the roads to provide shade for travelers.*

LION COLUMN

Although the Mauryan empire broke up soon after his death, Asoka was one of India's greatest leaders. Modern India adopted his lion capital at Sarnath as one of its national emblems. The column on which it stood marked the place where the Buddha preached.

◀ *The Mauryan empire ruled over nearly the entire subcontinent of India. The emperor, Asoka, left many inscriptions recording edicts and messages to his subjects on pillars and rocks throughout the empire.*

devoted himself to improving his empire.

As well as administration, the government was also responsible for promoting a set of beliefs known as *Dhamma* or "Universal Law." It preached religious tolerance, nonviolence, and respect for the dignity of people.

On a practical level Asoka tried to improve the conditions of his people. He built reservoirs and dug wells and set up rest houses at regular intervals along the roads of the empire. However, Asoka also employed a large secret police to help him run his diverse empire.

Although Asoka tried to unite the country, under his rule religious differences, in fact, became more distinctive. After his death the Mauryan empire soon began to break up.

HINDUISM

Asoka became a Buddhist, but Hinduism also thrived during his rule. This religion which worships many gods was developed gradually over thousands of years. There are many sacred writings including two great epic poems: the *Mahabharata* and the *Ramayana* which tell of the gods' deeds and their battles against evil. To the *Mahabharata*, was added the Song of the Lord or *Bhagavad Gita* which is the most important book of Hinduism. There are three gods that are more important than the rest called Vishnu, Brahma, and Shiva. Vishnu restores order; Brahma is the creator; and Shiva, the destroyer (*right*), rules over life and death.

B.C.

301 Central America: Mayan civilization begins to spread south. Greece: 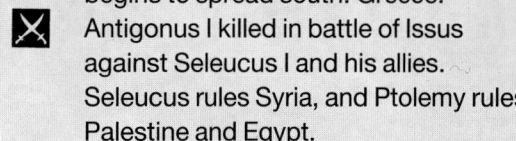 Antigonus I killed in battle of Issus against Seleucus I and his allies. Seleucus rules Syria, and Ptolemy rules Palestine and Egypt.

300 Treaty between Rome and Carthage.

298 Gauls join Samnites and Latins against Rome in the Third Samnite War (to 290). It ends in Roman victory.

287 Rome: Full equality between patricians and plebeians is agreed. Greece: Birth of Archimedes, mathematician (dies 212).

The Great Stupa at Sanchi in India was built in about 150 B.C. After the Buddha died in 480 B.C., stupas (mounds) were built throughout India, and later all over Asia. They contain relics of the Buddha or of Buddhist saints and vary greatly in size.

285 Egypt: Reign of Ptolemy II Philadelphus (to 246).

276 Greece: Antigonus II Gonatus rules (to 239).

c. 276 Greece: Birth of Euclid, mathematician (dies 194).

273 India: King Asoka rules Mauryan empire (to 232), uniting central and northern India. He becomes a Buddhist.

264 First Punic War between Rome and Carthage (to 241) begins a century of struggle for control of the Mediterranean.

254 Rome takes Panormus in Sicily from Carthage.

250 Judea is part of Ptolemaic empire based in Egypt (to 198). Hebrew scriptures are translated into Greek. Apollonius a Greek mathematician begins work in astronomy (to 220).

246 Egypt: Ptolemy III rules (to 221).

B.C.

241 Peace between Rome and Carthage. Sicily becomes first Roman province.

238 Carthaginians begin conquest of Spain.

237 Rome: Birth of Scipio Africanus, the general who leads Rome in the Second Punic War (dies 183).

The chain pump was invented by the Chinese in the 2nd century A.D. to irrigate the land near the Yellow River.

225 Romans defeat Celts at Telamon in Italy.

223 Antiochus III, the Great, succeeds his father and restores power of Seleucid empire (to 187).

221 China: Qin dynasty unites the country for the first time in one empire (to 207). Greece: Philip V rules Macedonia (to 179). Egypt: Ptolemy IV Philopater rules (to 203).

218 Second Punic War (to 202). Hannibal crosses the Alps with elephants.

217 Hannibal defeats Roman army at Lake Trasimene in Italy.

216 Hannibal wins another great victory, at Cannae, inflicting one of the worst defeats the Romans suffer.

215 Hannibal is defeated by the Roman, Marcellus, at Nola in southern Italy.

214 Rome: Marcellus begins conquest of Sicily, completed in 210. China: Construction of the Great Wall begins.

212 China: To maintain his position of power the emperor, Shi Huangdi, has all historical documents burned and books are banned. After this time a silk-based material is used for writing on, and Chinese script is standardized.

211 First Macedonian War, in which the Macedonians and the Carthaginians fight Rome (to 205).

The Qin Dynasty

In the 3rd century B.C., a powerful, warlike dynasty arose in the northwest of what is now China. Called the Qin (Ch'in) dynasty, it conquered neighboring lands and by 221 B.C. had established an empire, from which China takes its name. The first emperor, Shi Huangdi, reorganized the government, bringing everything under his control. He standardized all weights and measures, the width of wagon wheels, and introduced a single type of money.

In order to protect his empire from barbarians, Shi Huangdi, began the construction of the impressive Great Wall, much of which still exists today. He also built roads and canals, and improved the food supply by making canals to take water to the crops.

▲ *The Great Wall was originally built to keep out nomadic peoples in the north. It stretched 1,400 miles (2,250km), but if the curves are added in, it was nearer 4,000 miles (6,000km).*

▶ *Ironworking began around the 7th century B.C. in China. The people on the right are using large piston bellows to bring the furnace to a high temperature so that the ore melted before being cast in molds.*

▼ *Constructed between 214 and 204 B.C., the Great Wall was 23 feet (7 m) high. Its core consisted of earth or rubble covered by stone, bricks, and mortar. The top was paved with stone or bricks. The northern side had a parapet (low wall). Any builder who left a crack large enough to insert a nail was hanged on the spot.*

◄ *When Shi Huangdi died in 210 B.C., an elaborate tomb was built to house his body and the possessions he would need in the afterlife. It was guarded by an army of soldiers made out of terracotta.*

Shi Huangdi was an excellent warrior who used cavalry rather than chariots, but some of his actions made him extremely unpopular with many people. To cement the union of his empire, he had all writings from earlier centuries which were not about the Qin destroyed. He also tried to destroy all the writings of Confucius. This is called the "Burning of the Books" and it happened in 212 B.C. Shi Huangdi also put more than 400 scholars to death and forced large numbers of peasants to work on building the Great Wall.

He died in 210 B.C. and four years later the Qin dynasty was overthrown. China was once more broken up into a number of small states, but after the Qin dynasty the idea of a united empire had become fixed in the minds of the people.

Communications

Travel at this time was slow and uncomfortable. Those who could afford to rode on horseback, while the rest of the people had to walk. Pack animals, such as donkeys and mules, were the most common method of transporting goods by land. Even the most important news could travel only as fast as legs could run.

The Romans built a network of well-made roads connecting the chief cities of their empire. Wherever possible, Roman roads followed a straight line, using sturdy arched bridges to cross river valleys. The roads were designed for the rapid movement of Roman soldiers, but they were also used by merchants and traders to transport their goods.

▲ *The Romans were superb engineers. Their skills were developed by the army who needed surveyors and engineers to construct their forts and roads.*

◀ *The Romans used horses in chariot races. Chariots were fast and could transport individuals quickly, but were no use for moving goods, which went by ox-cart.*

WHEN IT HAPPENED
490 B.C. Phidippides runs 240 miles from Athens to Sparta in two days to request help in the battle of Marathon.
460 B.C. In Persia, stone tablets are replaced with parchment for official documents.
312 B.C. Construction starts on the Appian Way, the first Roman road.
c. A.D. 350 The Chinese start to use foot stirrups, made from wood reinforced with metal.

► In Greece and Rome, rich men and women traveled around town on couches, or litters, carried by servants or slaves. These litters had curtains for privacy, and sometimes also had a roof for protection against the weather.

◄ Oxen and cart from a Roman carving. At this time horses were rarely used as draft animals because the only harness available tended to strangle them with heavy loads. Oxen were used instead. They were strong, but very slow.

► A pottery horse and rider made in Han China about 80 B.C. Like horsemen throughout the world at this time, the rider has no stirrups. This meant that the horseman was constantly concerned with trying to stay in the saddle. Stirrups, which gave the rider a much surer seat, were probably first used in India in the late 2nd century B.C. and had come to China by the 4th century A.D. They made it easier to fight on horseback.

◄ The wheelbarrow was invented in China during the 3rd century A.D. It allowed people to carry much heavier loads than they had been able to in the past. As well as goods, the Chinese wheelbarrow was used to carry people on both long and short journeys. It remained unknown in Europe for almost another thousand years.

Africa

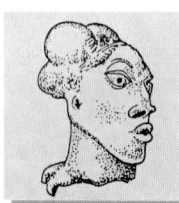

The large continent of Africa saw the rise of some of the earliest peoples, including the great civilization of Egypt. The practice of farming spread from Egypt into West Africa where village communities of farmers sprang up. Around 400 B.C., these people started to make iron tools. The first of these West African Iron Age settlements is known as the Nok culture. It existed in what is now northern Nigeria and is believed to have been the earliest center of ironworking south of the Sahara.

Africans traded gold, ivory, gums, spices, and slaves with the wider world. The powerful town of Axum (now in northern Ethiopia but then the capital of a trading kingdom) traded first with Egypt and later Byzantium. It was along this trade route that Christianity (*see* pages 128–129) eventually found its way to Africa in the 4th century A.D. Around A.D. 320, King Ezana of Axum was converted to Christianity by a missionary and about this time the huge obelisks for which the town became famous were built. In the 6th century A.D., Axum controlled western Arabia for a short time, but by A.D. 1000 the kingdom of Axum had collapsed.

▲ *This terracotta head from Nok is a fine example of the sculpture that flourished from 400 B.C. to A.D. 200.*

▼ *To smelt iron, the iron ore was put into an earthen furnace. Bellows were then used to raise its temperature so that the ore was turned into metal.*

METALLURGY

The early African peoples were skilled metalworkers who made iron weapons and tools for farming. They also made small iron figures that were used in rituals to mark birth, marriage, and death. Their skills spread all over Africa.

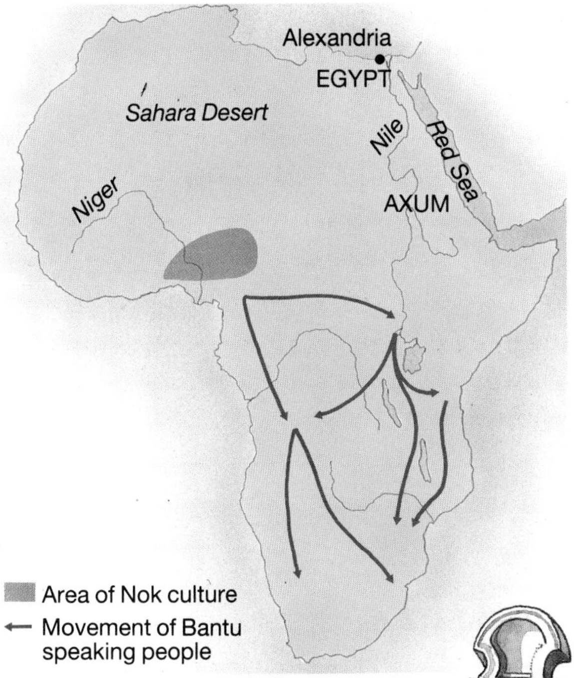

Alexandria

EGYPT

Sahara Desert

Nile

Red Sea

Niger

AXUM

■ Area of Nok culture
← Movement of Bantu speaking people

▲ *The first inhabitants of the area lying to the south of the land lived in by the people of Nok were joined by a new group from West Africa whose languages all derived from Bantu.*

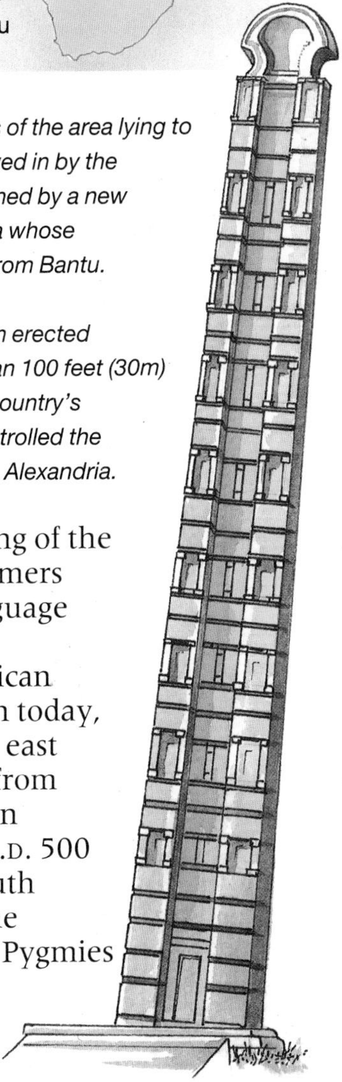

▶ *The people of Axum erected giant obelisks more than 100 feet (30m) high as a sign of their country's importance. Axum controlled the Red Sea trade through Alexandria.*

At the beginning of the Christian era, farmers who spoke a language called Bantu, the root of many African languages spoken today, moved gradually east and south away from their West African homelands. By A.D. 500 they reached South Africa, leaving the rain forest to the Pygmies and the Kalahari Desert to the Bushmen.

B.C.

206 Rome: Scipio defeats the Carthaginians in Spain.

205 Egypt: Reign of Ptolemy V Epiphanes (to 181).

203–201 Africa: Hannibal is recalled to Carthage to repel a Roman invasion by Scipio. Scipio defeats Hannibal at Zama and ends Second Punic War. Carthage surrenders Spain and Mediterranean lands and Carthaginian fleet is destroyed.

202 China: Reign of the Han dynasty (to A.D. 9), founded by Lui Pang.

200 Second Macedonian War between Greeks and Philip V of Macedon (to 196). With the help of the Romans, the Greeks are victorious, and Philip is forced to surrender Greece.

198 Judea part of Seleucid empire under Antiochus III and IV (to 166).

196 Hannibal's political reforms in Carthage make him unpopular. His enemies force him to flee into exile.

192 Syrian War (to 189). Antiochus III defeated in war with Rome.

190 Greece: Birth of Hipparchus, astronomer (dies 120).

Hinduism is represented by the symbol om, meaning the name of god. The word om is repeated many times by a Hindu during meditation.

c. **185** India: Last Mauryan king overthrown.

184 India: Reign of the Sunga dynasty (to 172), founded in the Ganges Valley, by Pushayanitra.

183 Hannibal commits suicide to avoid being captured by the Romans.

180 Egypt: Ptolemy VI Philometor rules (to 145).

180 Africa: early Meroitic writing appears.

179 Perseus, son of Philip V of Macedonia, continues war with Rome (to 167).

175 Antiochus IV Epiphanes is king of Seleucid empire (to 163).

B.C.

171 Third Macedonian War (to 167).
Macedonians under Perseus attack
Rome once again.

A plebeian (left) and patrician (right).

170 Egypt: Antiochus IV invades the country
and captures Ptolemy VI. The Egyptians
proclaim his brother, Ptolemy VIII
Euergetes, king. Antiochus withdraws,
and the two brothers reign jointly.

168 In the battle of Pydna the Romans defeat
⊠ the Macedonians and capture their
leader, Perseus.

167 Judah: Antiochus begins persecution of
the Jews. The Jewish Temple in
Jerusalem is dedicated to the worship of
the Greek god, Zeus. Judah: Jews, under
the leadership of Judas Maccabeus,
rebel against the persecution of
Antiochus IV (to 164, when Jewish
worship is restored).

160 Judah: Judas Maccabeus is killed in
battle against Syrians. His brother,
Jonathan, leads the Jews (to 143).

155 China: Early writings are compiled,
including important Taoist manuscripts.

149 Third Punic War (to 146) leads to
destruction of Carthage by Romans
under Scipio the Younger.

149 Fourth Macedonian War (to 148).
Macedon is conquered and becomes a
Roman province.

145 Egypt: Ptolemy VII rules under the
regency of his mother, Cleopatra II.
Ptolemy VIII seizes the throne (to 116).

The Rise of Rome

In about 510 B.C., the
Etruscans were driven out
of the city-state of Rome
and it became a *republic* (a
state which is run by
officials chosen by the
people rather than by an all-powerful
king). At this time, Rome had to deal not
only with the threat presented by the
warring tribes all around it but also with
its own internal problems.

Class warfare existed between the
ruling class of the *patricians* who had
inherited their land and the *plebeians* or
masses. The latter were peasants,
workers, and traders who were not
allowed to hold office. Only 300 years
later did they win a say in government.

At first the typical Roman citizen was a
peasant with a small farm. These farmers
benefited from a superb climate and rich
land. Around 200 B.C. big estates owned
by townsmen grew up. These large farms

THE SENATE

Rome was ruled by the Senate which consisted of
a group of elders who elected two consuls each
year to lead them. The role of the elders, or
senators, was to advise the consuls, but the
consuls were powerful in their own right and had a
lot of authority. The letters SC found on many
Roman coins stood for *Senatus consulto* which
means "by command of the Senate."

GEESE SAVE ROME

One of Rome's enemies, the Gauls, advanced as far as Rome itself in 390 B.C. Most of the Roman people fled, but a few took refuge on Capitol Hill. The Gauls attacked at dead of night while the Romans were asleep. Fortunately, the Romans were awakened in the nick of time by geese sacred to the goddess Juno, who cackled and flapped their wings.

MOSAICS

Mosaics are made of tiny pieces of stone. This dog was found in the entrance of a house in Pompeii. The words *cave canem* mean "beware of the dog." It was meant to discourage visitors.

▲ Rome benefited greatly from its central position in Italy. One of its earliest roads, the Appian Way, was built in 312 B.C. so that soldiers might travel south.

▼ Wealthy Roman families often had grand villas in the country. Some were run as large farms. Sheep and cows were kept, and vineyards were also profitable.

relied on slave labor to grow highly profitable crops of grain or olives.

The rise of Rome was due largely to its fertile soil and its position in the middle of Italy. It also possessed the most professional army in the world. By 266 B.C. Rome was Italy's leading power.

The Punic Wars

The North African city of Carthage was founded in about 850 B.C. as a colony of Phoenicia (now Lebanon). Carthage fought three major wars against Rome from 264 B.C. to 146 B.C. to decide who should rule the Mediterranean world. The Roman word for Phoenician was Punic, so the wars became known as the Punic wars.

The First Punic War started over a town in Sicily and grew into a conflict lasting for 23 years. Unlike the seafaring Carthaginians, Rome had no navy but it quickly built up a fleet, craftily copying a storm-wrecked Carthaginian ship. Rome eventually won control of the waters around Sicily, Corsica, and Sardinia.

The Carthaginians were determined to get revenge. Their outstanding general,

▲ Scipio was Rome's answer to Hannibal and he learned much from the Carthaginians' tactics. Scipio took an army to Africa and attacked Carthage itself.

▼ Hannibal transported his army of 50,000 men across the Alps with horses and elephants in only 15 days. Of the 38 elephants that started the difficult journey, only 12 survived.

Hannibal

218 B.C. Defeats Romans at Trebia.
217 B.C. Romans defeated at Lake Trasimene.
216 B.C. Romans defeated at Cannae.
202 B.C. Scipio defeats Hannibal at Zama.
183 B.C. Hannibal commits suicide.

▲ *Hannibal was a great general but a modest man. Many people believed his route across the Alps (*shown below*) to attack Italy was impossible.*

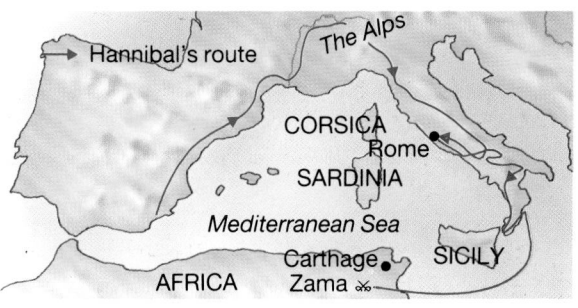

B.C.

143 Judea: Simon Maccabeus, Judas's second brother, leads the Jews (to 134).

141 Judea: Jews liberate Jerusalem. Judea proclaimed an independent kingdom.

140 China: Emperor Wu Ti expands the empire (to 87).

135 First Servile War – revolt of Roman slaves in Sicily crushed (to 132).

134 Judea: John Hyrcanus, son of Simon Maccabeus, rules (to 104).

124 China: philosophical teachings of Confucius become official.

116 Egypt: Ptolemy VIII dies; Ptolemaic empire is split up; years of strife follow.

111 China: Eastern and southern areas are subjugated (to 110). Africa: War breaks out between Rome and Jugurtha, King of Numidia.

110 India: Munda kings reign in the Deccan, central region (to A.D. 225).

108 Wu Ti, emperor of China, conquers Korea.

106 Gaius Marius elected Roman consul and sent to Africa.

105 Africa: Marius and Sulla defeat the Numidian Jugurtha. He is taken to Rome and executed.

104 Judea: Aristobulus I is king (to 103).

103 Judea: Alexander Janneus rules (to 76). Second Servile War (to 99) – a revolt by slaves in Rome.

100 China: A general history and standard religious texts are compiled, along with a list of Chinese literature.

Hannibal, cleverly decided to avoid a battle at sea and led his men across the Alps toward Rome, starting the Second Punic War in 218 B.C. Hannibal won three important victories.

Although weakened, Rome's spirit was still strong. A new army led by a brilliant general called Scipio set off for Africa to attack Carthage itself. This forced Hannibal to return home, and Scipio finally defeated the Carthaginians. In the Third Punic War, which lasted from 149 to 146 B.C., Carthage was completely destroyed by the Roman army and Africa was declared a Roman republic.

A Roman warship was called a quinquereme *from the word* quinque *which means five, because the oarsmen were ranked in fives.*

Food and Farming

Large empires need a well-organized system of agriculture. A city such as Rome, for example, with almost one million inhabitants in the 2nd century A.D., required an immense amount of food each day. In China most people worked the land.

Farming was a risky business, however. If the harvest failed, the farmer had no money. Many farms got into debt and were taken over by rich landowners. They created great estates worked by thousands of slaves.

In Europe, grains for bread, porridge, and beer, plus olive oil, dairy products, fish, and some meat, were the basis for everyday eating. In north China, wheat and millet were the most important crops while in the south rice was the main crop as it still is today.

▲ In a Roman kitchen, pans were placed on a metal stand above an open fire. The pans were made of metals that often gave the food a strange flavor.

◄ A scene from a 3rd century A.D. tomb, showing a Roman farmworker milking a goat. The screen was probably put up to protect him from the weather.

◄ Rich Roman families employed many house slaves to prepare and serve their food. They used many herbs and spices to disguise the flavor of food which was often bad.

▼ This scene, taken from a Han tomb carving, shows Chinese peasant-farmers hoeing their fields. The fields were often in terraces, on the hillside. Only rich farmers used oxen and plows.

WHEN IT HAPPENED

500 B.C. The start of wet rice culture in Japan. The increasing use of metals for tools leads to more land being cultivated in Europe.

250 B.C. In China, the River Min is brought under control, making much more land available for farming.

30 B.C. Egypt comes under Roman rule and Egyptian farmers produce much of the grain needed to feed people throughout the Roman empire.

15 B.C. Good quality tableware is made in Roman Gaul (France) and sent to Britain.

A.D. 500 In southwest North America, the Anazasi people irrigate the desert and grow corn and squash. The flooding of farmland in northern Europe leads to many Germanic peoples moving west to settle in England and parts of France.

► A 1st century A.D. farmer goes to market, where he would sell his farm produce and spend the money he received on things he could not grow or make himself.

▼ This is an idealized view of Greek agriculture. The shepherd guards his sheep, while other people press olives for oil to sell to the merchant.

B.C.

91 War between Rome and Italian cities.

90 Judea: Revolt of Pharisees occurs.

89 Rome: Roman army under Sulla regains control of Italy; all Italians are granted Roman citizenship.

88 Anatolia: First Mithradatic War (to 84). Rome fights Mithradates IV of Pontus.

Slaves in the mines worked in bad conditions and were often not well treated.

88 Civil war is waged in Rome (to 82). Sulla is victorious.

87 Anatolia: Sulla defeats Mithradates and takes Athens. China: Death of Wu Ti leads to a period of disorder.

83 Anatolia: Second Mithradatic War (to 81). Romans successfully invade Pontus.

82 Sulla becomes dictator of Rome. He launches a vicious attack on all his opponents and many are killed.

78 Rome: Sulla dies. Revolt of Lepidus is defeated by Pompey the Great, who rules with Crassus.

c. 78 India: Most of northern India is under the rule of Kanishka I of Kushan dynasty (to c. A.D. 100).

76 Judea: Salome Alexandra rules (to 67).

74 Anatolia: Third Mithradatic War (to 64). Mithradates takes Bithynia, which Rome claims.

73 Anatolia: Lucullus and the Roman army defeat Mithradates and occupy Pontus. Rome: Spartacus leads slave revolt in Third Servile War (to 71); it is crushed by Pompey and Crassus.

Judea and Palestine

Since their exile in Babylon in 597 B.C., the Jews had grown more and more apart from their Near-Eastern neighbors. They worshiped one god, Yahweh, built synagogues to pray in, and observed strict religious laws. On returning from exile in 538 B.C., they stressed their Jewish law and beliefs which set them even farther apart from the non-Jews, or Gentiles, who now lived in Palestine.

Palestine was under Greek rule (first Ptolemaic and then Seleucid) and many Jews fought hard to stop Greek influence destroying their traditions. At one point the Seleucid ruler tried to make Judaism illegal but a revolt, led by Judas Maccabeus prevented this.

▼ *Herod the Great rebuilt the Temple at Jerusalem in 37 B.C. The Western Wall is all that is left of the second Temple after it was destroyed by the Romans.*

▲ A great Jewish revolt against the Romans broke out in A.D. 66. After seven years of fighting the last Jewish forces, rather than surrender, committed mass suicide at the stronghold of Masada.

▶ This map shows the main areas, towns, and cities in Palestine at the time of the Roman occupation.

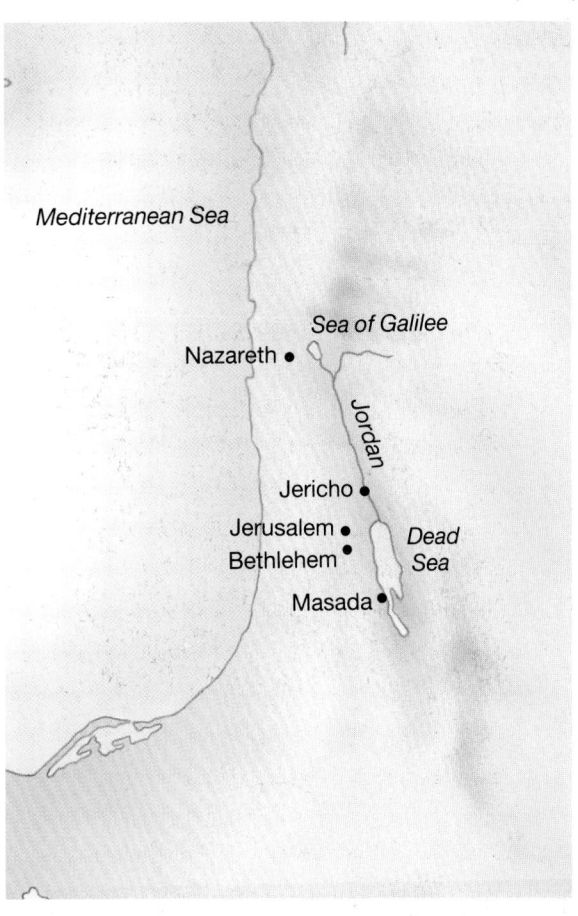

After Seleucid rule, Judea was independent for nearly 80 years before being conquered by Rome. The Roman Senate then appointed Herod the Great as king of Judea in 37 B.C.

Under Roman rule the Jewish people were free to travel and trade throughout the Roman empire, and many left Judea to settle elsewhere. Far fewer lived in Judea than in the rest of the empire, but they still regarded Judea as their homeland. Jewish people settled as far away as western India and some Roman cities, such as Alexandria and Rome itself, had huge Jewish communities.

When Pontius Pilate was made Judea's governor in A.D. 26 it was a bad time for the Jewish people. The Jews of Syria and Palestine disliked each other and also hated their Greek and Syrian neighbors. Most of all they loathed the Roman occupiers and their tax collectors.

MENORAH

Many events in Jewish history are celebrated in religious festivals, such as Passover and Hanukkah. A golden menorah, which is a seven-branched candlestick, like the one below, stood in the first Temple at Jerusalem and is still used today. Originally shaped by Moses, its branches symbolize the seven days of creation.

B.C.

70 Rome: Birth of Virgil, poet (dies 19 B.C.). His most famous work is the *Aeneid*, the story of Aeneas after the fall of Troy.

67 Judea: Hyrcanus II rules. Civil war breaks out between his forces and those of his brother Aristobulus II.

65 Pompey and the Roman army invade Syria and conquer Palestine. Rome: Birth of Horace (dies 8 B.C.), poet and satirist. He wrote *Ars Poetica* and *Odes*.

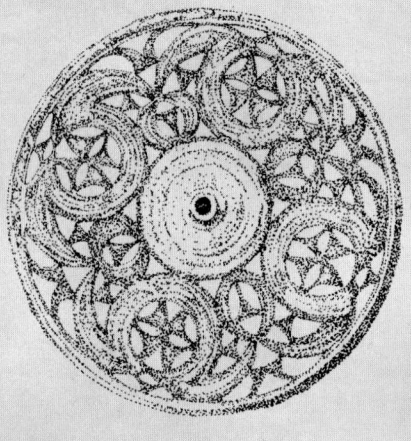

The circular compass decoration on this horse bronze is typical of the Celtic culture of La Tène. It was made in about 400 B.C.

63 Judea: Pompey captures Jerusalem, annexes Syria and Judea. Aristobulus II, King of Judea, dies; Mithradates IV of Syria commits suicide; and Hyrcanus II becomes high priest of Judea.

61 Rome: Julius Caesar wins his first major victories, in Spain.

60 Triumvirate (joint rule by three people) of Caesar, Pompey, and Crassus in Rome.

58 Caesar is appointed governor of Gaul, part of present day France. (The Gauls are a branch of the Celts.)

55 Caesar conquers northern Gaul and attempts unsuccessfully to invade Britain.

54 Second invasion of Britain by Caesar. Cassivellaunus, a powerful British leader, agrees to pay tribute to Rome.

53 Crassus is killed at battle of Carrhae against the Parthians.

The Celts

At first the Celts were a loose grouping of tribes who lived in central Europe from around 600 B.C. Gradually, they moved into southern and western Europe and established farms wherever they settled. They also built large, well-protected hill forts. The Celts traded with Rome, Greece, and other Mediterranean countries, but they were not much influenced by contact with these civilizations. Known as fierce warriors, they used iron to make weapons and tools.

They also had gifted artists: poets, musicians, and makers of beautiful decorative metalwork. Celtic artwork was quite different from that of other European cultures. Their jewelry, weapons, and drinking vessels were often decorated with abstract designs and geometrical shapes. The Celts had no written language, but the Romans left reports of their customs.

In what is now France, the Celts were called Gauls. One chieftain called Vercingetorix rebelled successfully against the Romans, but he was eventually defeated by Julius Caesar and

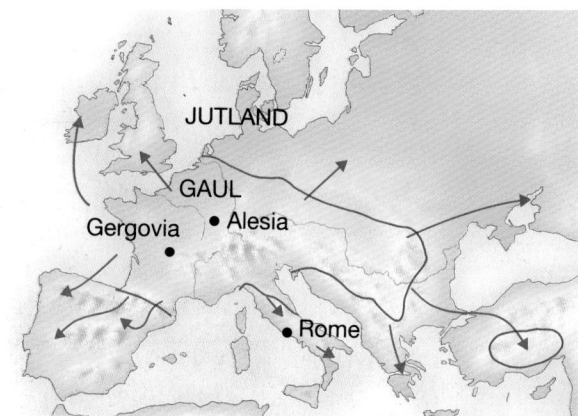

▲ *The major areas of Celtic settlement around 200 B.C. are marked by a blue line, while the arrows indicate the main direction of their expansion.*

his army. The Gauls came to accept Roman rule and later they supported the Romans against barbarian attacks (*see* pages 140–143). Most Celtic civilization in England slowly died out after the Romans invaded Britain in A.D. 43, but in what is now northern England, Wales, Ireland, and Scotland, the Celts resisted Roman rule, and their culture survived.

▼ *This bull's head appears on a huge bronze cauldron, which was found in Jutland, Denmark. Animal figures and geometric designs were a popular feature on pieces of elegant Celtic metalwork.*

Vercingetorix

In 52 B.C. Vercingetorix organized a successful rebellion against the Romans at Gergovia (now called Clermont-Ferrand), but later he surrendered.

▼ *A Celtic chief and members of his tribe feast in their timbered hall while listening to a heroic poem accompanied by music. Laws, stories, and religious rituals were handed down by word of mouth.*

The Roman Army

The key to Rome's continuing greatness as a power was its army. Originally made up of wealthy citizens, the army became a full-time professional force. Volunteers came from the poor who were willing to serve for pay. They also received the rights of citizenship in return for their service.

The army was reorganized into *legions* of 6,000 men, divided into ten cohorts. Each cohort was made up of 100 *legionaries* (foot soldiers) under a *centurion* (officer). A legion also contained cavalry and people who specialized in building roads and bridges.

Rome itself became richer. Money

▼ *Permanent camps were built for Roman army units. Sometimes known as forts or fortresses, they were like miniature cities with special areas for the commanders, ordinary soldiers, stables for horses, and so on.*

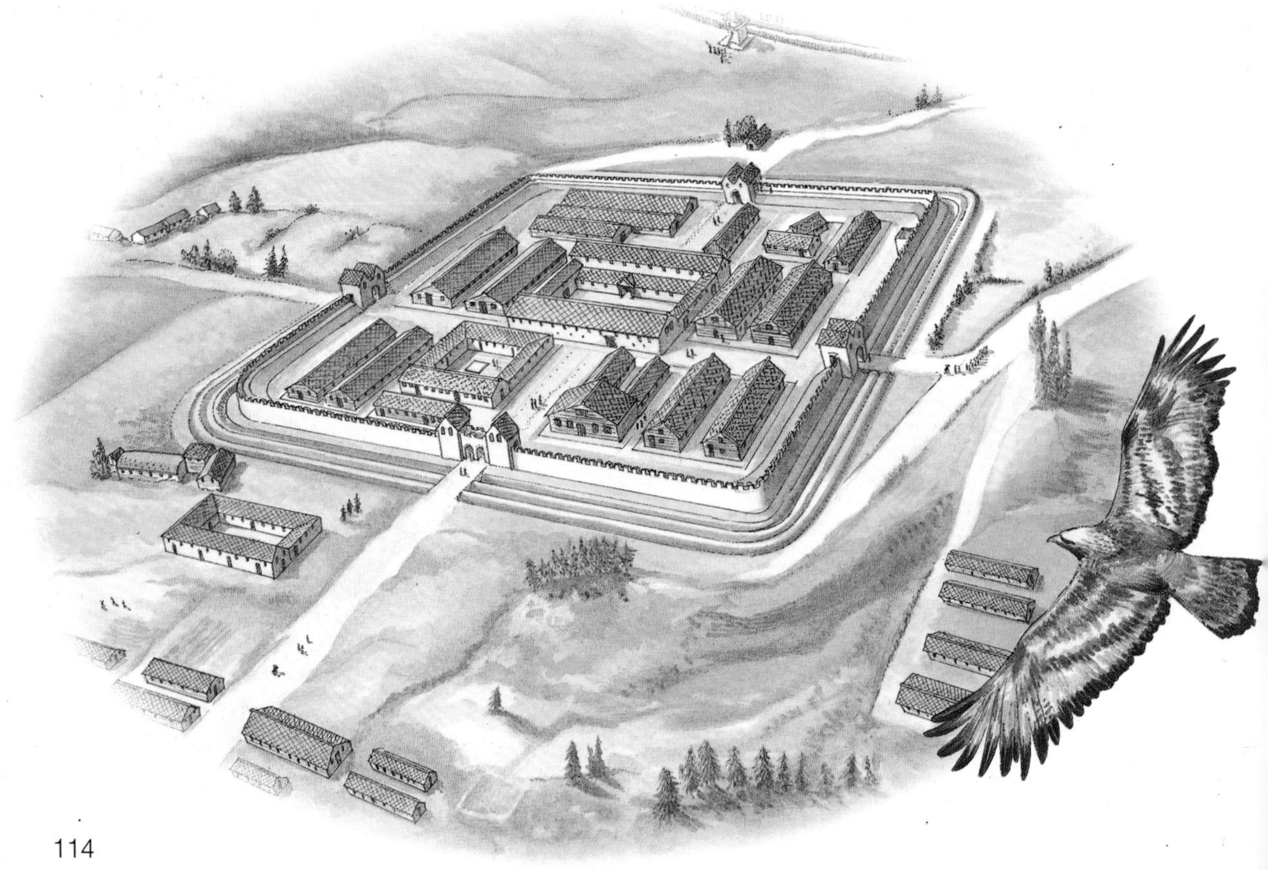

◀ *The ordinary Roman soldier wore a thick woolen tunic under his armor, and carried a sword, a dagger, and a rectangular shield. On his back he had to carry a pack weighing about 60 pounds (27kg).*

came from looting conquered cities and the selling of prisoners as slaves. New provinces were forced to pay taxes.

More contact with the east brought an increase in the influence of Greek art and learning. The Roman passion for baths, for example, came from Greece.

Successful wars produced generals who were hungry for power. Rome became a dangerous place full of political intrigue and corruption. A Roman aristocrat called Julius Caesar, used his military power to take advantage of the situation, crushed his enemies, and was made dictator (sole ruler) for life.

The Senate feared that his ambitions would not stop there. Some of them plotted to kill him and on the Ides (15th) of March 44 B.C., Caesar was murdered by two men called Brutus and Cassius.

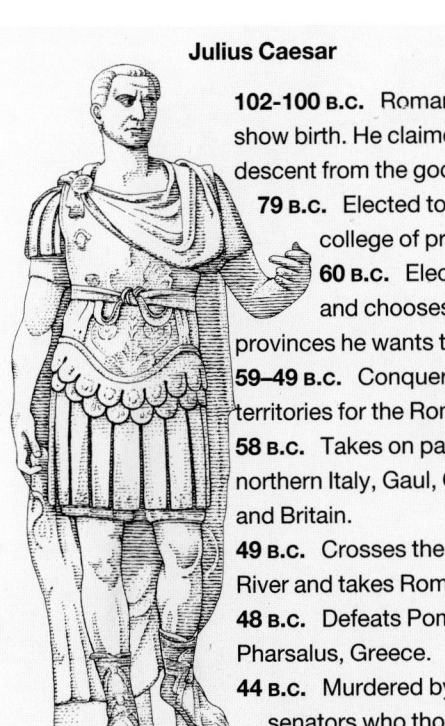

Julius Caesar

102-100 B.C. Roman records show birth. He claimed descent from the gods.

79 B.C. Elected to the college of priests.

60 B.C. Elected consul and chooses the provinces he wants to govern.

59–49 B.C. Conquers vast new territories for the Roman state.

58 B.C. Takes on parts of northern Italy, Gaul, Germany, and Britain.

49 B.C. Crosses the Rubicon River and takes Rome.

48 B.C. Defeats Pompey at Pharsalus, Greece.

44 B.C. Murdered by Roman senators who thought he wanted to be king.

B.C.

52 Pompey appointed sole consul in Rome. Gauls rebel under their leader Vercingetorix, but are crushed by the Romans.

51 Caesar completes conquest of Gaul. Egypt: Cleopatra VII and her brother, Ptolemy XIII, become joint rulers of Egypt.

The standard of the Roman emperors was called the labarum. *It had embroidered pictures of the emperors on it and at the top of the flagstaff was the Christian Chi-Rho symbol.*

50 Rome: Rivalry between Caesar and Pompey comes to a head.

***c.* 50 B.C.–*c.* A.D. 50** Buddhism spreads along the Silk Road to China from India.

49 Senate orders Caesar to give up control of Gaul. He crosses the Rubicon into Italy to start civil war. Pompey flees to Greece.

48 Caesar defeats Pompey at Pharsalus in Greece. Pompey flees to Egypt.

47 Pompey is assassinated, possibly by order of Cleopatra. Caesar conquers Cleopatra's enemies. Judea: Antipater becomes procurator of Judea; his son Herod becomes governor of Galilee.

45 Rome: Caesar defeats Pompey's son, Sextus, in Africa and crushes a mutiny in the Tenth Legion. He becomes virtual dictator of Rome. Caesar introduces Julian calendar and adopts his nephew, Octavian, as his heir.

44 Caesar is assassinated by a group of Romans led by Brutus and Cassius.

43 Rome: Second Triumvirate is formed by Octavian, Mark Antony, and Marcus Lepidus. Birth of Ovid, the poet who wrote *Metamorphoses* (dies *c.* A.D. 17). Cicero, the orator, is put to death for denouncing Mark Antony.

People

In some ways, life in large Roman towns and cities was similar to that of today. People lived in multistory buildings, there were stores and eating houses, and children went to school. Even fashions in cosmetics and hairstyles changed, and the city of Rome had a serious traffic problem, 2,000 years ago!

In China, towns were centers for trade and government. Many people could read and write. Clothes were the same for men and women, but rich people wore silks and fur while the poor made do with garments made of hemp (rough cloth).

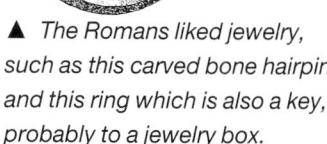

▲ The Romans liked jewelry, such as this carved bone hairpin and this ring which is also a key, probably to a jewelry box.

◄ This Japanese painted scroll from the 4th century A.D. shows court ladies getting dressed. The boxes are for cosmetics.

▼ Greek children played with wooden dolls. Other toys included pottery and wooden animals, and five-stones, or jacks. Children often also kept pets.

▲ Greek and Roman actors wore masks to identify the characters. This is the mask of the hero in a Greek play.

▲ This pot, made in Roman Britain around A.D. 200, shows the end of a fight between two gladiators. The figure on the right makes a sign asking for mercy.

◀ Street clothes of a wealthy Roman couple. The man wears a toga, or cloak, over a long shirt. The woman has a high-waisted dress. They both wear leather sandals.

▼ Some public baths in Rome. A visit to the baths for exercise, washing, and gossip, was a daily event for rich Romans. There were both cold and heated pools.

WHEN IT HAPPENED

5th century B.C. Comic and tragic drama becomes popular in Greece. Comedies include song and dance and slapstick humor. Aeschylus is famous for tragedy and Aristophanes for comedy.

240 B.C. The first Greek comedy is written in Latin for a Roman audience.

206 B.C. Pottery tomb models show that the Chinese imperial court enjoyed watching jugglers and acrobats. They also enjoyed music and dancing.

2nd century B.C. People in the Roman empire go to open-air theaters. They watch tragedies and comedies, and also see gladiators fighting each other.

A.D. 80 The newly-built Colosseum in Rome is flooded for mock naval battles.

B.C.

42 Rome: Triumvirate defeats Brutus and Cassius at the battle of Philippi.

37 Judea: Reign of Herod the Great (to 4 B.C.). Rome: Triumvirate is renewed for five years. Mark Antony, already married to Octavia (the sister of Octavian), also marries Queen Cleopatra of Egypt.

36 Octavian's fleet defeats that of Pompey's son, Sextus.

The groma was an instrument used by surveyors to mark out lines and right angles.

32 Octavian declares war on Antony and Cleopatra.

31 Battle of Actium, at which Octavian defeats Antony and Cleopatra.

30 Antony and Cleopatra commit suicide. Octavian declares Egypt a Roman province.

27 Rome: Octavian given supreme power by the Roman Senate, thus effectively ending the Roman Republic. He takes the title Augustus and becomes the first emperor of Rome (to A.D. 14).

15 Roman empire extended to the upper Danube.

12 Revolt in Pannonia (part of present-day Slovenia) quelled by Augustus' stepson, Nero.

5 Judea: Probable year of birth of Jesus of Nazareth, at Bethlehem.

4 Judea: Herod the Great dies; his kingdom is split between his three sons.

The Roman Empire

After the assassination of Julius Caesar, a power struggle erupted that affected the whole Roman world. The Republic still existed, but the idea of one-man rule had taken root in people's minds. Octavian, Caesar's nephew and heir, cleverly sought the support of the Senate for all he did, and was made Consul year after year. His power grew, but he always insisted that he was *princeps* (first citizen), not a king. Octavian was so successful that he was renamed Augustus which means "imposing one," and after he died in A.D. 14, he was declared a god.

Rome was now an empire ruled by emperors but they relied for their support on the army rather than the Senate. Although Augustus brought peace, none of the four emperors who followed him died a natural death.

The old Roman families no longer had the same power. Strength of character and ability, rather than a noble family background became all-important. The

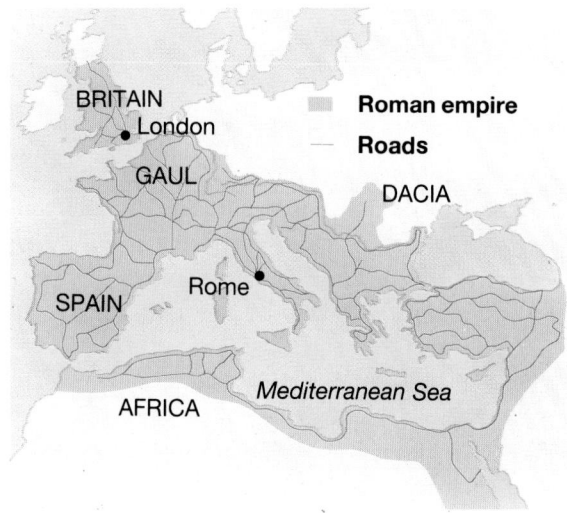

▲ *The huge Roman empire was crossed by a network of roads which linked Rome to the farthest regions. Towns or fortresses were built where roads joined.*

THE INVASION OF BRITAIN

Boudicca (Boadicea) was the ruler of the Iceni, a Celtic tribe in East Anglia, when the Romans governing Britain demanded that the Iceni kingdom join the Roman empire and ordered Boudicca to be whipped. Led by their queen, the Iceni attacked the Roman forces. They sacked the towns of Camulodunum (Colchester), Verulamium (St. Albans), and Londinium (London), killing 70,000 Romans and their allies. But a strong Roman army, led by the Roman governor of Britain, quickly crushed the rebellion and Boudicca poisoned herself.

FAMOUS EMPERORS

Augustus 27 B.C.– A.D. 14 Caesar's great nephew and the first Roman emperor.
Tiberius A.D. 14–37 Careful ruler but not popular. Feared assassination and eventually went mad.
Nero A.D. 54–68 Vain and cruel, he had his mother and first wife murdered, and executed scores of opponents.

Emperor Vespasian's grandfather had been only a centurion. A hundred years of fine government followed under the next five emperors, but three of these emperors were not even Roman.

The empire continued to grow until it was pushed to its final bounds by the Emperor Trajan who ruled from A.D. 98 to 117. He conquered Dacia (modern Romania) and extended Rome's Asian empire farther than ever before. The prestige of the emperor's position increased and the Roman people came to regard their emperors as gods.

▼ *Roman roads were usually straight and well constructed. They were built to enable troops to move quickly. Milestones were placed every 1,000 (mille) paces (passum). On them was carved the distance in* mille passum *from Rome.*

The Han Dynasty

From 202 B.C. to A.D. 220, China was ruled by emperors of the Han dynasty. They did not have as much control over their lands as the Romans did because the Han ways of governing were not so developed. But they were hungry for lands. Wu Ti, the "Martial Emperor" who reigned from 141 to 87 B.C., successfully added a large part of central Asia, southern Manchuria, and much of the southeastern coast of China to his empire. He also conquered the Thai peoples of the Mekong Valley.

Despite its large size, China remained remarkably free of influence from other cultures, mainly because it was self-sufficient. Rice, which had been introduced much earlier from either Southeast Asia or India, was one of the last major new imports before modern times.

The Han emperors tried to replace all the writings that had been destroyed earlier by the Qin (*see* pages 98–99). The ideas of the philosopher Confucius were also rediscovered and people who wanted to work as public officials had to

SILK ROAD

Silk was China's most famous export (*see* pages 42–43). Most of the trade in this material was by land and from about 100 B.C., the Silk Road was the main route to the western world. Stretching 2.500 miles (4,000 km), it linked the enormous Han and Roman empires together when both were at the height of their prosperity.

Caravans of camels led by traders took the silk through deserts and over mountains to Antioch, Syria. Here the silk was traded for western luxuries and then taken across to the Mediterranean to Greece and Rome where it was highly prized. When silk first appeared in Rome, it was so valuable it was worth its weight in gold.

▼ *City streets in Han China were crowded. The muddy roads were full of carts, chariots, and traders. Craftsmen, letter writers, storytellers, and astrologers also plied their trade noisily in the open air.*

▲ *Metalworking was important in China and iron was first used in about 650 B.C. This bronze model of a rich man in his chariot was found in the tomb of a Han official. It was probably made in the 2nd century A.D.*

take an examination on his writings.

Han China at its peak was a place of great creativity. The Chinese thought of their country as the center of the world and the finest example of true civilization. Legend has it that the empire's cities were the most beautiful in the world. Many of the exquisite objects that the Chinese produced were made of wood, paint, and silk. Unfortunately, many were destroyed during the troubles at the end of the dynasty, but a few beautiful items did survive hidden away in the tombs of the rich and noble.

▼ *The route of the Silk Road, which China used to export silk to other countries, remained much the same for hundreds of years.*

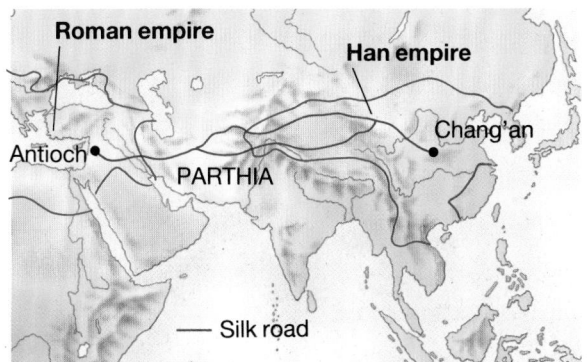

A.D.	
5	Rome acknowledges Cymbeline King of Britain. China: Wang Mang establishes the short Hsin dynasty (to 23).
14	Rome: Augustus dies and is succeeded by Tiberius Caesar.
23	Rome: Birth of Pliny, writer (dies 79).
25	China: Reign of later Han dynasty (to 220).
26	Judea: Pontius Pilate is procurator (to 36).
27	Jesus is baptized by John the Baptist.
30	Crucifixion of Jesus.
31	Martyrdom of St. Stephen.
32	Saul is converted to Christianity and becomes Paul.
37	Rome: Tiberius dies and is succeeded by Caligula (to A.D. 41). Judea: Herod Agrippa becomes king of northern Palestine.

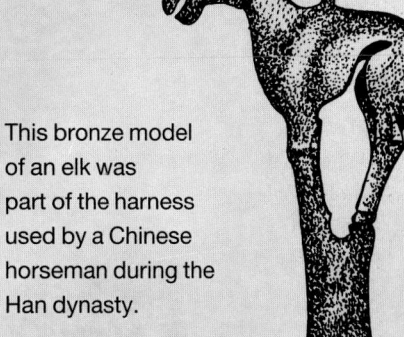

This bronze model of an elk was part of the harness used by a Chinese horseman during the Han dynasty.

41	Rome: Assassination of Caligula. Claudius becomes emperor (to A.D. 54).
42	Mauretania (modern Morocco) becomes a province of Rome.
43	Britain: Romans invade under Aulus Plautius. China: Ma Yuan conquers Tonkin and Annam.
45	Paul begins his missionary journeys in the eastern Mediterranean to spread Christianity. China: Birth of Pan Chao, (sister of General Ban Chao), historian, poet, astronomer, mathematician, and educator (dies 115).
54	Rome: Claudius is assassinated; succeeded by Nero (to 68).

A.D.

58 China: Emperor Ming Ti introduces Buddhism.

61 Britain: Boudicca (Boadicea) of the Iceni leads a revolt against the Romans. It fails and Boudicca dies.

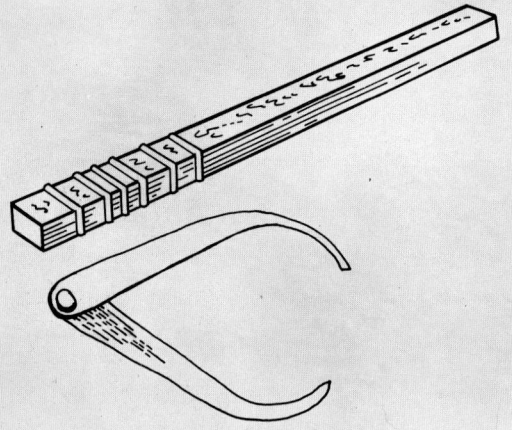

A cubit rule and curved callipers were used by Han scientists to accurately measure the width and thickness of objects.

64 Rome: Fire destroys the city of Rome. The Christians are blamed for it and they are subsequently persecuted. St. Peter is executed.

65 St. Mark's Gospel is written.

66 Jewish revolt against the Romans (to 70).

67 Martyrdom of St. Paul.

68 Rebellion in Rome. Nero commits suicide.

69 Rome: "Year of the Four Emperors:" Galba, Otho, Vitellius, and Vespasian. Vespasian defeats Vitellius to become emperor of Rome (to 79). Founds Flavian dynasty of emperors.

70 Titus (Vespasian's son) destroys Jerusalem and suppresses Jewish revolt. First Diaspora (expulsion of Jews) takes place. St. Matthew's Gospel is written.

73 Jewish stronghold at Masada falls to the Romans.

74 China: General Ban Chao brings states of Turkestan to submission and opens silk trade to the Roman empire (to 94).

75 St. Luke's Gospel is written.

77 Britain: Agricola governs Britain (to 84).

78 India: Second Kushan dynasty (to 96).

Chinese inventors were far ahead of the rest of the world and the Chinese invention which is most taken for granted today is paper. First invented around A.D. 100, paper was much cheaper to produce and easier to make than parchment (made from animal skin) or papyrus, but several centuries passed before the skill reached the West.

However, all this activity did not help the dynasty survive. The population had grown so much that rebellions among the peasants became frequent. They started because many of the peasants were landless and consequently unable to find the money necessary to pay government taxes and buy food.

At the same time, barbarians started to attack the borders of the empire. Warlords who controlled the soldiers on which the Han dynasty relied, seized power and took over the army. The last Han emperor gave up his throne in A.D. 220 and the empire fell apart.

▼ *The earliest seismographs to measure earthquakes were made in China around A.D. 100. They were pots ringed with dragons' heads. A small ball was balanced behind the teeth of each dragon. When an earthquake occurred, one ball was shaken out and caught by the frog below, showing the direction of the earthquake.*

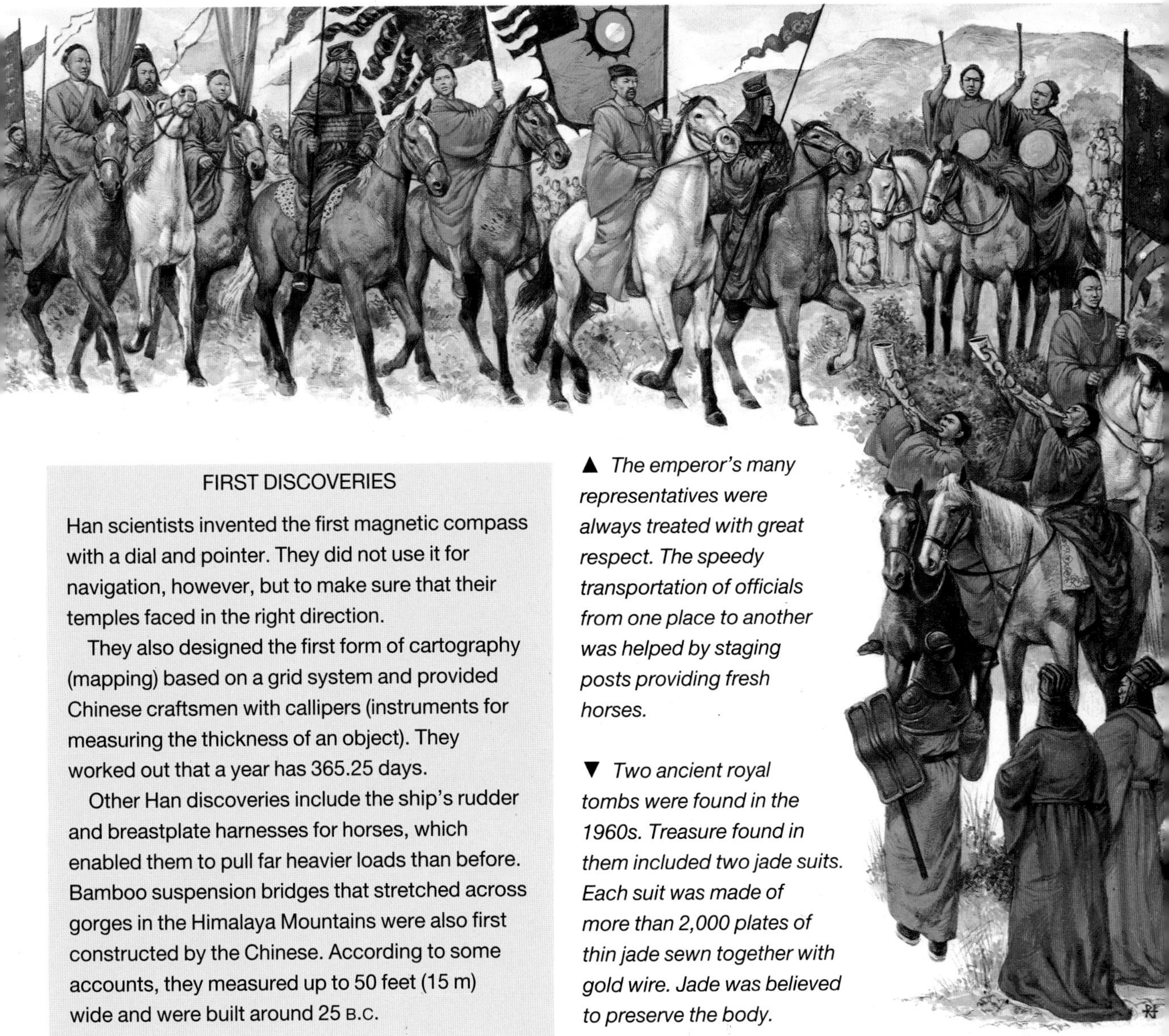

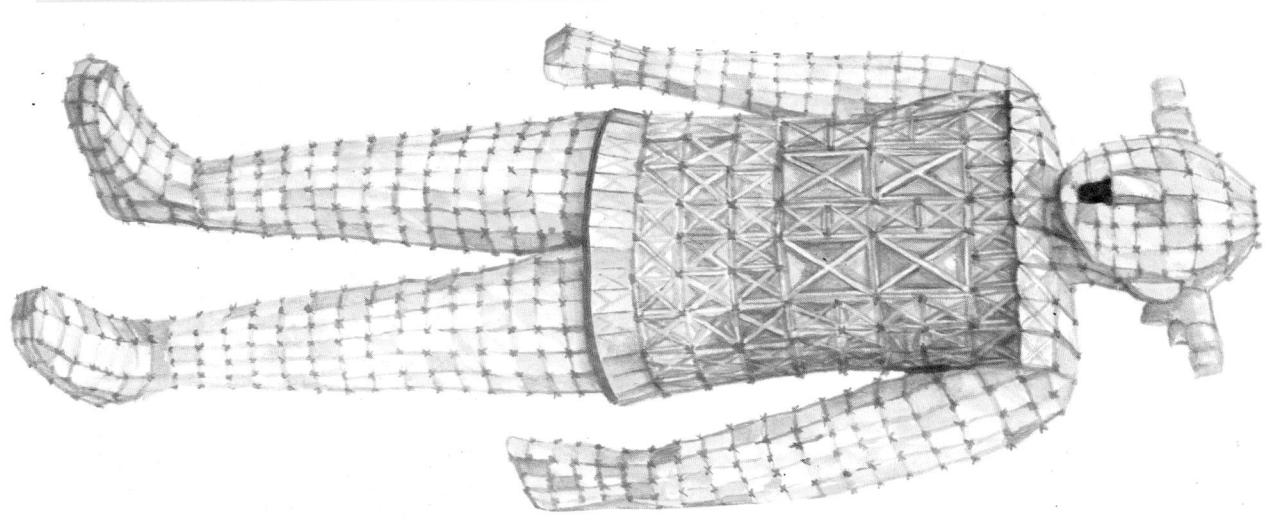

FIRST DISCOVERIES

Han scientists invented the first magnetic compass with a dial and pointer. They did not use it for navigation, however, but to make sure that their temples faced in the right direction.

They also designed the first form of cartography (mapping) based on a grid system and provided Chinese craftsmen with callipers (instruments for measuring the thickness of an object). They worked out that a year has 365.25 days.

Other Han discoveries include the ship's rudder and breastplate harnesses for horses, which enabled them to pull far heavier loads than before. Bamboo suspension bridges that stretched across gorges in the Himalaya Mountains were also first constructed by the Chinese. According to some accounts, they measured up to 50 feet (15 m) wide and were built around 25 B.C.

▲ *The emperor's many representatives were always treated with great respect. The speedy transportation of officials from one place to another was helped by staging posts providing fresh horses.*

▼ *Two ancient royal tombs were found in the 1960s. Treasure found in them included two jade suits. Each suit was made of more than 2,000 plates of thin jade sewn together with gold wire. Jade was believed to preserve the body.*

◄ Sculpted head of a Greek goddess. Some of the finest creations by Greek artists were the statues of gods and goddesses which were displayed inside temples.

Religion

This period saw the birth of several of the world's major religions. The ancient Greeks worshiped many gods and goddesses, presided over by a father figure, Zeus. The Romans adopted the Greek gods, but gave them different names, such as Jupiter for Zeus. Many Roman emperors were thought of as gods after their deaths.

From around the 1st century A.D., Christianity slowly spread across the Roman empire. In the 4th century A.D., the emperor Constantine the Great made it the official religion of the empire.

In India, Buddhism became firmly established, and gradually spread northward along trade routes. In China, Confucianism became the state religion during the 2nd century B.C.

▼ Many Romans had a shrine to their gods inside their houses. This one is from a house in Herculaneum.

▲ This Celtic god-figure with stag antlers was chiseled and hammered onto the side of a bronze cauldron around A.D. 100.

▼ A Roman wedding with the newly married couple joining hands. Ceremony and ritual were an important part of Roman life.

▲ *An early Christian painting from the catacombs under Rome. Until Christianity became an official religion, Christians were often persecuted. The catacombs, or underground burial rooms, were used for secret meetings from the 3rd century A.D.*

▶ *This carved "footprint of Buddha" is from India—such footprints were used to decorate places supposedly visited by the Buddha. Other early monuments include dome-shaped stone "stupas" and representations of the Buddha. Increasingly, Buddha was regarded as a god, which had not been his intention.*

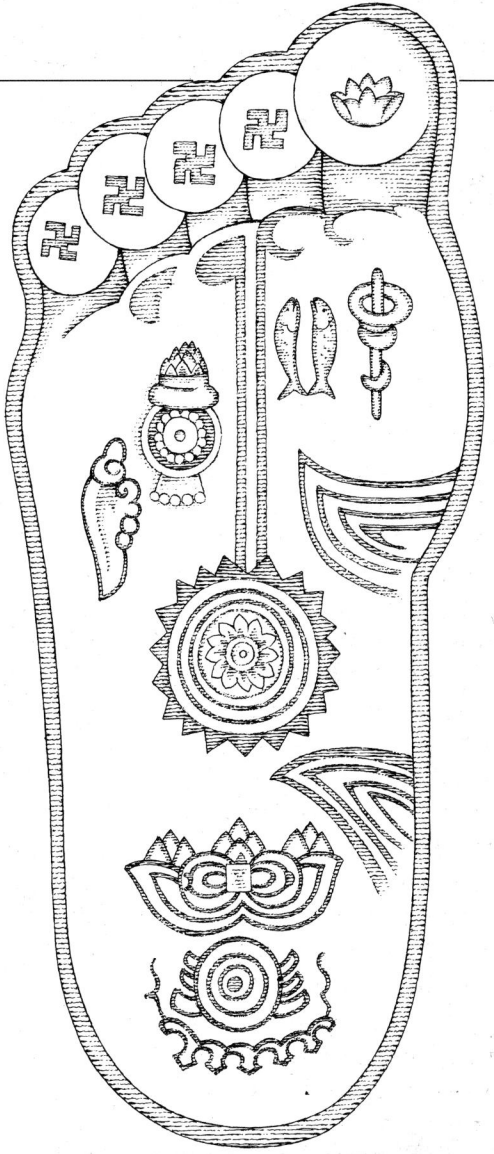

◀ *Chinese philosophy held that everything was divided into yin and yang (left). A mythical bird, (below) was associated with the south.*

Yang

Yin

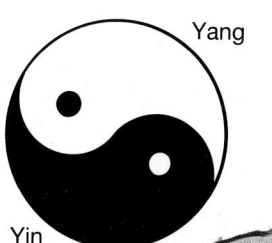

WHEN IT HAPPENED

480 B.C. The Celts bury their dead with chariots and weapons.

280 B.C. A giant bronze statue of the Greek sun god Helios is built in Rhodes harbor.

250 B.C. Buddhism reaches Sri Lanka. The first Buddhist monuments appear in India.

5 B.C. The most likely birthdate of Jesus.

A.D. 58 Buddhism reaches China from India.

A.D. 313 Christianity is tolerated in the Roman empire.

A.D. 380 Christianity is made the official religion of the Roman empire.

A.D. 400 Buddhist cave-temples are built along the Silk Road.

A.D.

79   Rome: Mount Vesuvius erupts, leaving the towns of Pompeii and Herculaneum buried in a shroud of volcanic ash and mud. About 2,000 people are killed.

81   Rome: Titus dies and is succeeded by Domitian (to 96).

82   China: The empire is ruled by a succession of women (to 132).

90   Greece: Birth of Ptolemy, astronomer and mapmaker (dies 168).

95   St. John's Gospel and the Book of Revelation are written.

96   Rome: Domitian is assassinated and Nerva becomes emperor (to 98) – first of the Antonine emperors.

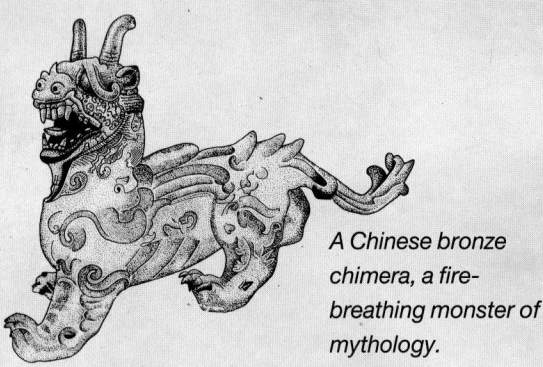

A Chinese bronze chimera, a fire-breathing monster of mythology.

97   China: General Ban Chao leads army through central Asia as far as the Caspian Sea. This is the farthest the Chinese army has ever advanced toward Europe.

98   Rome: Trajan becomes emperor (to 117). This is the last period of Roman expansion.

c. **100**   Settlement of Hawaiian Islands.

101–107   The Roman empire is at its greatest extent.

105   China: Dowager Empress Teng rules (to 121). Imperial workshops announce the invention of paper-making.

109   Central India: Gotamiputa Sri Satakani rules in Deccan (to 132).

115   Jews revolt in Egypt and North Africa; Trajan suppresses rebellion.

116   Tigris River becomes eastern frontier of Roman empire.

117   Rome: Emperor Hadrian rules (to 138).

The Influence of Rome

The Roman empire reached its peak under the Emperor Trajan around A.D. 117. During this time people from places as far apart as Gaul (now part of France) and Africa were increasingly influenced by the Roman way of life. Rich people learned Latin and Greek, wore Roman clothes and saw Roman heritage as something to be proud of. Being Roman no longer depended on living in the city of Rome. Anyone who belonged to the empire considered themselves a Roman.

Running such a huge empire was a difficult task, but the Romans managed to govern many peoples with great success. They put an end to small wars, allowing the people of the empire to farm and trade in peace. This peace is called the *Pax Romana* (Roman Peace).

POMPEII

On August 24 at 1 P.M. in A.D. 79 a cloud appeared over the Roman town of Pompeii. This was all the warning the residents had before the nearby volcano, Mount Vesuvius, erupted and rained down ash, pumice, and lava pebbles. It buried the town, and 2,000 people died of suffocation from the volcanic fumes. Pompeii was forgotten until it was rediscovered in the 18th century. Pompeii has revealed a great deal about Roman life because it was completely preserved by the volcanic ash that covered it.

Preserved bread, seeds and nuts

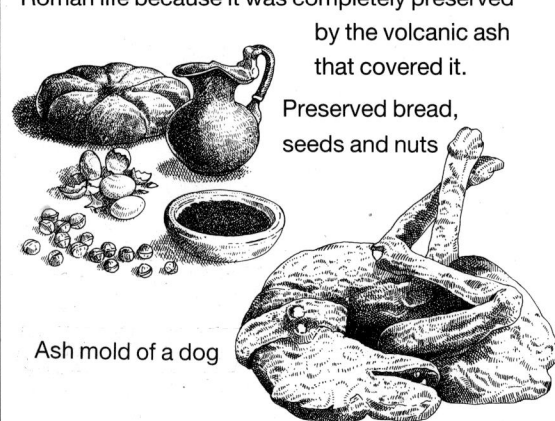

Ash mold of a dog

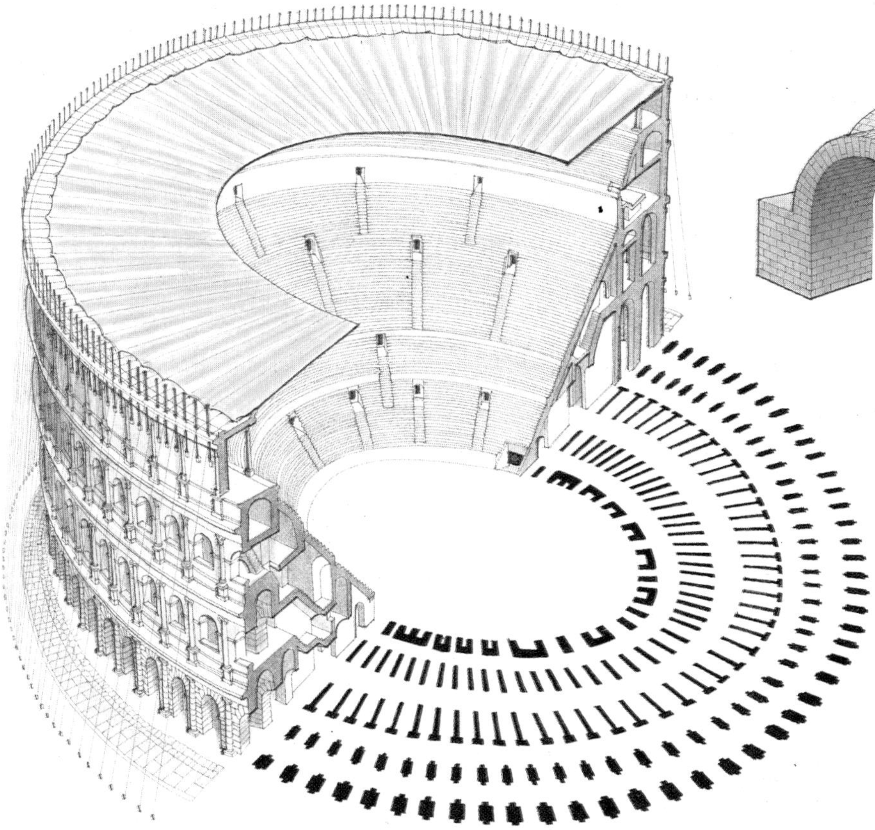

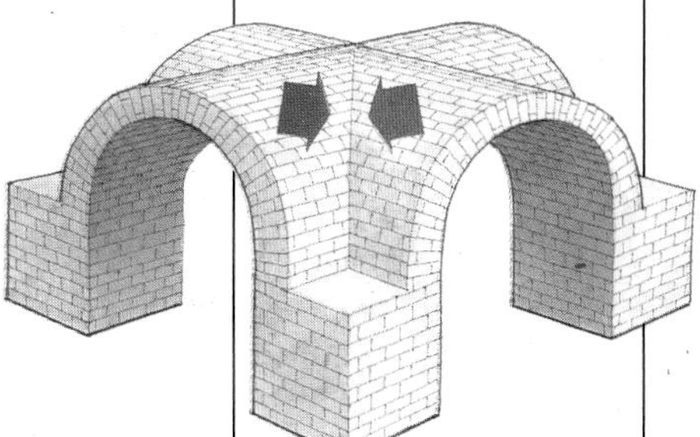

VAULTS

The Colosseum is a honeycomb of vaulted passageways. A vault is simply an extended arch. The Romans found that one vault could cross another at right angles and still stand up. They could cover a large, square area supported only by corner columns.

▲ Going to the theater was a popular entertainment but the Romans also enjoyed more gruesome sights. Arenas, such as the Colosseum (above), were built for the games, where gladiators fought to the death.

▼ The Romans entertained lavishly. Slaves prepared and served the meals while diners lay on a couch, called a triclinium that surrounded three sides of a central table that held the food.

Wherever they went, the Romans took their skills in building and town planning with them. They prided themselves on being hardy but they also had strong ideas about what was necessary to make daily life comfortable. Wherever they went they built baths, drains, and dug freshwater supplies. Roman homes were centrally heated, and plumbing for baths and toilets was considered essential. Their houses were beautifully decorated with murals of gardens and people.

The Spread of Christianity

For a long time the Jews had believed that a Messiah (savior) would be born to lead them. At the time that Jesus of Nazareth was born, Judea was under Roman rule. Jesus' followers believed him to be the promised Messiah and the son of God, but other Jews accused him of blasphemy and he was tried before the Roman governor, Pontius Pilate. Jesus was crucified, but his followers reported having seen and talked to him after his death. This resurrection formed the basis of a new religion that arose from the old traditions of Judaism: Christianity (the word comes from the Greek for "anointed one").

▼ Emperor Constantine became a Christian after seeing a cross of light in the sky. He put a Christian symbol on the shields and standards of his army and defeated his rival for the empire just outside Rome.

▲ To escape religious persecution, the Christians hid in the catacombs deep below the streets of Rome. They were used for worship and burial and were safe because Roman law held burial places to be sacred.

Jesus of Nazareth

Jesus was born in Bethlehem in about 5 B.C. in the Roman province of Judea. He grew up in Nazareth, where he probably worked as a carpenter. In about A.D. 27 at the age of 32 he began teaching and healing.

It is said that he performed many miracles. He spoke about the coming of the kingdom of God and what a person had to do to be worthy of entering it. He criticized the religious authorities and spoke of himself as God's equal, which was blasphemous for a Jew. The Roman authorities, worried about general unrest in Judea, mistrusted large crowds speaking of a new kingdom and had him arrested and put to death. Jesus was about 33 when he was crucified. Three days later news spread that he had risen and those who believed in him would share in his victory over death.

The teachings of Jesus were spread through the travels of his followers, especially Paul. They taught that Christianity was open to everyone and the new religion quickly spread. By now the Christians were completely separate from the Jews and did not join in their rebellion against Roman rule in A.D. 66. By the 3rd century A.D., Christianity had spread to most parts of the empire. But in A.D. 250 the Roman authorities began persecuting Christians, and many died a painful death in the arena.

Religious persecution stopped when the Roman emperor Constantine made Christianity legal in A.D. 313. Some 80 years later, it became the official religion of the empire. Constantine started the belief that emperors were responsible for uniting the religious and the non-religious aspects of rule. His actions greatly affected Europe and, eventually, most of the rest of the world.

A.D.

122 Britain: Hadrian starts the building of a wall (Hadrian's Wall) to defend Roman Britain from outsiders (to 126).

130 Hadrian visits Egypt. He founds a new capital at Antinopolis.

c. 130 Greece: Birth of Galen, physician (dies c. 200).

132–135 Israel: Jewish revolt attempts to establish an independent state. It fails, Jerusalem is destroyed and in the final Jewish Diaspora in 135, the Jews are dispersed around the Mediterranean.

138 Rome: Hadrian dies and is succeeded by Antoninus Pius (to 161).

144 China: Empress Liang rules on behalf of three boy emperors (to 150).

150 Korea becomes independent from China.

161 Rome: Death of Antoninus Pius; Marcus Aurelius succeeds him (to 180).

166 China: Emperor Huang Ti receives gifts from the Roman emperor Marcus Aurelius.

This Christian symbol shows the Roman victory laurel wreath combined with the Chi-Rho, the first two letters of Christ in Greek.

180 Rome: Death of Marcus Aurelius, who is succeeded by Emperor Commodus (to 192). Africa: first African Christians are martyred.

189 China: To put an end to the influence of eunuchs at the imperial court the army massacres them. Hsien Ti becomes last emperor of the Han dynasty (to 220).

Parthians and Sassanians

The Parthians were a nomadic people who moved into Persia (Iran) in about 1000 B.C. They lived under the rule of the Persians and the Seleucids until the 3rd century B.C., when the Parthian governor established an independent kingdom which survived for nearly 500 years.

The greatest of the Parthian leaders were two brothers, both called Mithradates. The two brothers called themselves "Great King" and "King of Kings," the traditional titles of the rulers of Persia. The Parthian army was strong, if not well-organized. It included mounted archers and heavily-armored men called *cataphracts*. Even the horses were clad in chain mail.

The records for this time are scarce, but in about A.D. 225 the last Parthian king was killed by one of his men, Ardashir, who founded the Sassanian dynasty and empire. The Sassanid rulers were keen to emphasize their continuity with past great Persian rulers such as Darius (*see* pages 74–75). Their court at Ctesiphon became the focus for a brilliant culture

▲ *The wealth of the Parthians and Sassanians came from the great Silk Road which passed through their territory linking China to the Mediterranean. This life-sized figure of Hercules was carved to guard the route.*

▼ *According to tradition, after the Sassanid ruler Shapur I had forced the Roman emperor Valerian to submit to him, Shapur then had Valerian skinned, stuffed, and put on display.*

Shapur I

A.D. 242 Made Sassanian emperor.
A.D. 244 Defeats Roman army at Massice.
A.D. 260 Captures Emperor Valerian.
A.D. 273 Dies.

POLO

The first records of organized sports are of polo games in Persia in 525 B.C. The Parthians and Sassanians used it as a training game for cavalry units and often it turned into a miniature battle with as many as 100 "players" on either side. The modern game did not begin until 1862.

A.D.
193 Rome: Emperor Septimius Severus rules (to 211).
200 Chinese woman artist Wei Fu-Jen working. She is still considered to be China's greatest calligrapher.
212 Rome: Reign of Emperor Caracalla (to 217). He extends citizenship to all free inhabitants of the Roman empire.
218 Rome: Elagabulus is emperor (to 222). He introduces a form of Sun worship.
220–264 China: Period of the Three Kingdoms when the Han empire is divided into three kingdoms: the Wei in the north, the Wu in the southeast, and the Shu Han in the west. Luoyang is the capital. Period ends when general Sima Yen seizes power and unifies China under the Western Jin dynasty.

The Sassanian emperor Shapur I built a magnificent palace at Ctesiphon in A.D. 275.

and their empire became Rome's greatest opponent. Shapur I was probably the most outstanding of the Sassanid rulers. He captured the Roman emperor Valerian, conquered Armenia and invaded the Roman provinces of Syria and Cappodocia. After his reign there was greater peace with Rome.

▼ *The Parthians were famous for their way of fighting on horseback. They would gallop away from the enemy as if fleeing, then turn in the saddle and shoot arrows at their pursuers. This led to the term "Parthian shot."*

222 Rome: Emperor Alexander Severus rules (to 235).
226 Persia: Ardashir founds Sassanian dynasty. Rules to 242.
230 Japan: Succession of Sujin, the tenth emperor. The beginning of historical records in Japan.
235 Rome: Emperor Maximinius rules (to 238).
238 Rome: Gordian III is emperor (to 244).
242 Persia: Shapur I rules the Sassanian empire until 273.
244 Rome: Emperor Philip the Arab rules (to 249).
250 Rome: Decius is emperor. Emperor worship is made compulsory.

Science and Technology

The wealth and security found at the heart of the great empires of this period meant great advances could be made in science and technology. Sometimes these advances were made as solutions to practical problems. Others were made by people with the leisure to do nothing but think.

The Greek thinker Aristotle (384–322 B.C.) is thought of as the founder of western science. He pioneered a rational approach to the world based on observation, and he influenced many Roman thinkers.

Cultures outside Europe placed somewhat less emphasis on this "scientific" approach. Nevertheless, they made many practical discoveries, and their astronomy matched that of Greece and Rome.

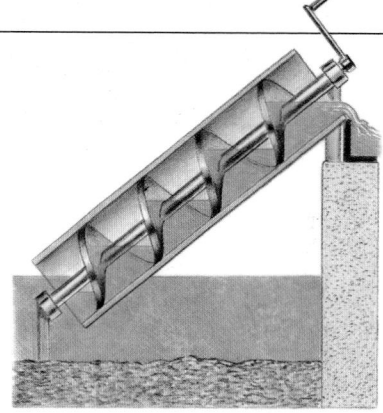

◀ The Archimedes screw is a device for lifting water from one level to another. It takes its name from the Greek inventor Archimedes (287–212 B.C.) who lived in Syracuse on Sicily.

▼ Paper-making was developed in Han China where paper documents soon became fairly common.

▲ The abacus was in widespread use throughout China from the beginning of the period. It was like an early calculator which let people do difficult sums.

◀ A Greek doctor examining a young patient. The Greeks adopted a scientific approach to medicine and made extensive studies of human anatomy. These studies also helped them to produce lifelike figures in their statues.

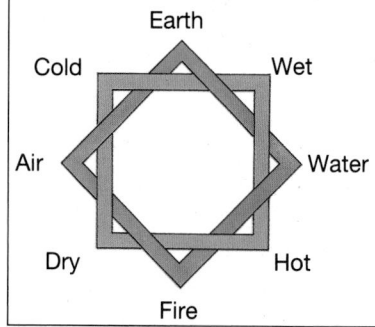

THE FOUR ELEMENTS

Aristotle developed a theory that everything was made up of a combination of four basic elements: Earth, Water, Fire, and Air. These in turn gave rise to four basic properties: Dry, Wet, Hot, and Cold.

Earth

Cold — Wet

Air — Water

Dry — Hot

Fire

WHEN IT HAPPENED

c. 450 B.C. In Africa, people of the Nok culture smelt iron in furnaces at Taruga.

c. 287 B.C. Greek mathematician and inventor, Archimedes, born in Sicily (dies 212).

200 B.C. The Romans first use concrete.

10 B.C. The Romans start using cranes.

A.D. 78 Chang Heng, the inventor of the first seismograph, is born in China.

c. A.D. 100 Paper-making is invented in China. It uses silk scraps and is very expensive.

A.D. 127 In Egypt, Ptolemy publishes his first book on astronomy. He also writes on music, mathematics and geography.

c. A.D. 270 The magnetic compass is used in China.

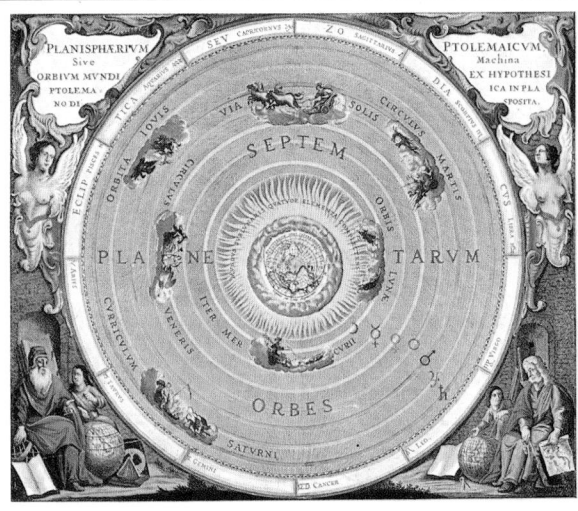

▲ *Ptolemy believed that the center of the universe was the Earth, with the Sun and planets orbiting around it.*

▼ *A Chinese acupuncture chart. The Chinese used the tips of needles to stimulate nerves within to treat illnesses. This method of treatment is still practiced today.*

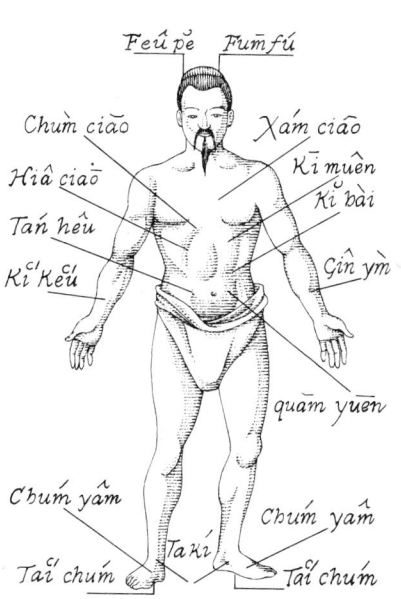

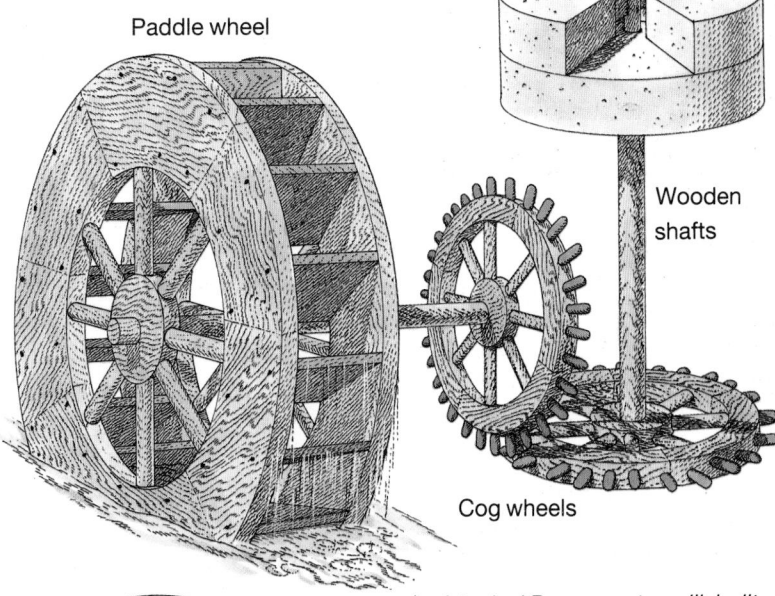

Paddle wheel

Wooden shafts

Cog wheels

▲ *A typical Roman water mill, built about A.D. 100. The water wheel's rotation is transferred through wooden shafts and cogwheels to the millstones that grind wheat. Large mills had six or more water wheels arranged in a line along a riverbank. Water wheels were also used in China, where they were important in raising water from rivers into irrigation channels to water the fields.*

▶ *A coin-operated machine for selling holy water at a Greek temple. A falling coin triggered the mechanism to release a measure of water into a container which had been brought by the buyer.*

The Americas

The early people of North America lived in the deserts, on the plains, and in woodlands. The desert people lived in caves and hunted wild animals for food. They made moccasins from animal skins and wove baskets. The people of the plains and woodlands lived in shallow pits covered with animal skins. They grew corn and tobacco.

The Hopewell Indians were one of the most interesting early Native American

▲ An eagle's claw, cut from a sheet of mica (a mineral) by the Hopewell Indians around A.D. 200.

◀ The peoples of the Americas and the sites of their major settlements.

Arctic hunters

Sub Arctic hunters

NORTH AMERICA

Pacific Ocean

Hunters and gatherers

Hopewell Indians

Atlantic Ocean

MEXICO

Teotihuacán

Mayan empires

CENTRAL AMERICA

Chavin culture

Farming tribes

SOUTH AMERICA

▲ A sculpture from Teotihuacán. It was one of the biggest cities in the world by A.D. 450. Some 250,000 people lived there.

RELIGION

Very little is known about the religious beliefs of the early Native Americans, except that some of them buried their dead in huge mounds. A holy man called a shaman chanted spells to cure sick people.

Much more is known about the religion of the people of Teotihuacán in Mexico. They prayed to a rain god, called Tlaloc and Sun and Moon gods. Their chief god was a feathered serpent called Quetzalcóatl.

tribes. They lived in and around the Ohio valley from about 1000 B.C. to A.D. 1300. In about 200 B.C., this group became the most important tribe in the region. They were very successful at trading with other tribes.

In the 4th century A.D., when the Mayan civilization (*see* pages 150–151) was at its peak, a city-state in the highlands of Mexico called Teotihuacán became very powerful. It was a city of pyramids and palaces, the earliest true city in Central America. Its people grew corn, beans, and pumpkins, and made tools from obsidian, a hard volcanic rock brought all the way from Wyoming. Craftsmen made elegant pots, fine sculptures in stone, and wall paintings. They were not warlike and it is not known why their culture declined in the 6th century A.D.

▼ *The Great Serpent Mound in Ohio was built by Hopewell Indians and is 1,600 feet (500m) long. This is one of several surviving animal-shaped mounds. This group also built cone-shaped burial mounds.*

A.D.
251 Rome: Gallus is emperor (to 253).
253 Rome: Emperor Valerian rules (to 259).
260 Shapur I captures Valerian in battle; Valerian dies in captivity. Gallienus becomes emperor (to 268). Period of Thirty Tyrants (a group who tried to control the empire) begins in Rome.
268 Greece: Goths sack Athens, Corinth, and Sparta. Rome: Emperor Claudius II rules (to 270).

Pumpkins were one of the many crops grown by the Mayas.

270 Rome: Aurelianus is emperor (to 275).
275 Rome: Emperor Tacitus rules until killed by his troops in 276.
276 Rome: Emperor Probus succeeds and rules until killed by soldiers objecting to doing peaceful work in 282.
282 Rome: Carus becomes emperor (to 283). He is killed in battle by his own troops.
284 Rome: Reign of Emperor Diocletian (to 305).
286 Diocletian divides the Roman empire into two and rules the eastern empire; Maximian rules the western empire.
287 Britain: Carausius, commander of the Romano-British fleet, revolts and rules Britain independently (to 293). He is murdered by his former ally Allectus.
296 Persia at war with Rome (to 297). At the peace, Rome gives Mesopotamia to Persia. The Tigris River now becomes the boundary between the two empires.
300 Central America: Classic period of Mayan art begins in the Yucatán (Mexico), Guatemala, and Honduras. Teotihuacán flourishes in Mexico as a religious, commercial, and manufacturing center. Its main street is over 100 feet (30 m) wide and is many miles long.

A.D.

303 Eastern Roman empire: Diocletian orders persecution of the Christians. They are banned from the army and public service. Churches and Christian books are destroyed. Many Christians are killed.

305 Diocletian and Maximian abdicate; a power struggle follows.

306 Eastern Roman empire: Constantine I, the Great, becomes emperor (to 337).

308 Western Roman empire: Maxentius, son of Maximian, is emperor (to 312).

309 Persia: Shapur II rules (to 379).

312 In the battle of Milvian Bridge, Constantine defeats Maxentius. Constantine converts to Christianity.

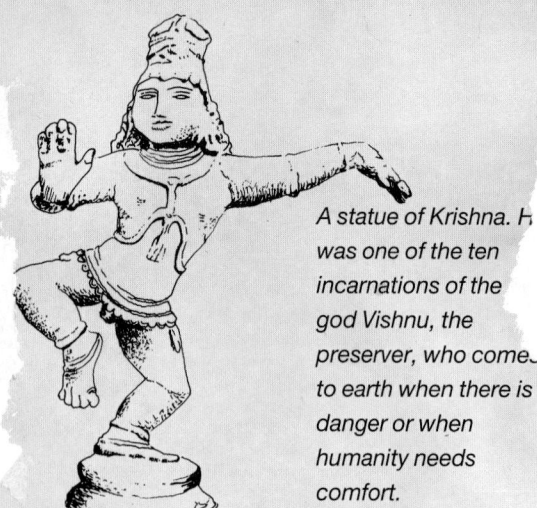

A statue of Krishna. H̶ was one of the ten incarnations of the god Vishnu, the preserver, who come̶ to earth when there is danger or when humanity needs comfort.

313 At Milan, Constantine proclaims the Edict of Toleration which allows Christianity in the empire. Construction of the first Christian basilica begins in Rome.

317 China is again divided (to 589).

320 India: Chandragupta founds the Gupta dynasty. He rules to 335. The dynasty survives to 535.

324 Constantine reunites the Roman empire.

325 The Nicene Creed, which summarizes Christian beliefs, is adopted at the first Council of the Christian Church.

330 Constantine founds Constantinople, on the site of the Greek city of Byzantium, as the capital of his empire. (The city is now called Istanbul.)

The Gupta Dynasty

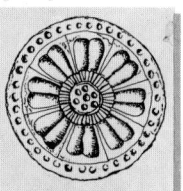

The Gupta dynasty became emperors of India in A.D. 320 and remained in power for the next 200 years. They came from a family of wealthy landowners who controlled Magadha, a kingdom in the Ganges Valley.

During the Gupta period, new Hindu villages were set up on land that had not been cultivated before. Hindu priests played an important role in these new villages. They were knowledgeable about farming and the villagers believed that the priests used magic to protect them against evil. Buddhism became increasingly popular and statues of the Buddha were set up everywhere. Both Hinduism and Buddhism preached a life of quietness and thought.

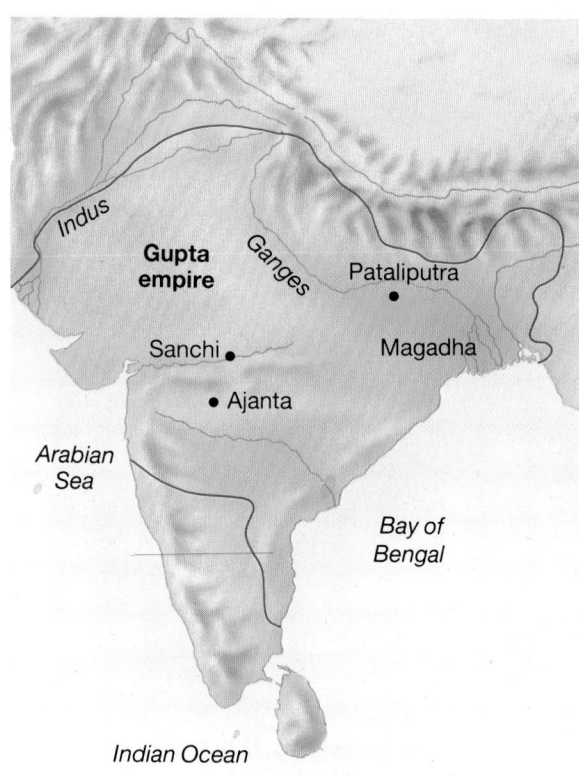

▲ *The Guptas came to rule nearly all of India.*

▲ Wall paintings from the Gupta dynasty show vivid scenes of Indian life. This picture, taken from the caves at Ajanta, shows dancers and musicians entertaining the royal household. Actors, acrobats, magicians, and wrestlers would also have taken part.

◄ Hindus and Buddhists believe that life is an endless recurrence of cycles. As a symbol of this, Buddhist temples have sculptures of the wheel of life.

The arts flourished during the Gupta dynasty. Music and dance developed into their classical Indian forms, and elaborate Hindu and Buddhist sculptures became the model for later Indian art. Kalidasa, the nation's most celebrated poet and dramatist, wrote about love, adventure, and the beauty of nature.

But at this time *suttee*, the burning of a widow on the funeral pyre of her husband, and child marriages became customs. Very young children were engaged to each other and, often, young girls were married to much older men.

SUTTEE

Suttee was a Hindu custom once practiced in India. The wife of a man who died was put to death. She was usually burned with her husband's body or a piece of his clothing.

The custom came from ancient writings which said that a good wife should follow her husband faithfully throughout her life, and even after death.

DECIMAL SYSTEM

The decimal system of counting in tens is also called the Hindu-Arabic system. Hindu mathematicians originally developed it around 100 B.C.

Arab mathematicians learned it from them after their people managed to conquer parts of India in the 8th century A.D. From them the knowledge spread to the rest of the world.

137

Society and Government

Created by conquest, the ancient empires needed strong government to keep the peace. The empires of India, China, and Rome were each ruled by one person, the emperor who drew power from either the army, or a class of nobles, or both.

The Greek city-states practiced democracy, which allowed citizens to vote. However, it proved impractical in times of war, and the experiment was ended by the conquests of Alexander the Great. Rome was also a democracy for several hundred years, but from 27 B.C. it was ruled by a succession of emperors.

Society was divided into a number of classes, which each had different rights. The rich were at the top. At the bottom were the slaves, who were the "invisible" portion of ancient society. Even in democratic Athens, about one-third of the population were slaves. Some slaves were treated as household servants, others were worked to death in mines. A few slaves were talented artists or accountants whose services were highly prized by the rich.

▲ *The attempted assassination of the Chinese emperor Shi Huangdi in 218 B.C. An emperor often had many enemies and his life was constantly in danger, so he was usually surrounded by armed guards.*

◄ *The Indian emperor Asoka erected many stone pillars to remind people of his power.*

▶ *A female slave helps a drunken Greek citizen.*

WHEN IT HAPPENED

507 B.C.	Democracy is established in Athens, allowing the citizens to vote on what will happen in their city.
279 B.C.	Asoka founds first Indian empire.
221 B.C.	Shi Huangdi becomes the first emperor of China.
212 B.C.	Shi Huangdi destroys as many books about the past as possible by burning them, to stop people thinking about "the good old days."
27 B.C.	Augustus becomes the first Roman emperor.
A.D. 50	Rome is the largest city in the world with a population of one million.
A.D. 132	A rebellion of the Jews against the Romans fails. This leads to the Diaspora, or dispersal, of Jews from Judea.
A.D. 320	The Gupta empire is founded in India.
A.D. 476	The last Roman emperor is deposed.

▼ Voting in Athens took place in the open air. At this time, Greek democracy was supposed to be government of the people, by the people, for the people. Not everyone in Athens could vote, however. Democracy did not apply to women, slaves, or foreigners. Politicians took it in turns to address the assembled citizens. Armed city-slaves, wearing caps, kept order and prevented mobs from forming.

▲ Some of the people who made up the society of the Roman Empire around A.D. 100: **1** politician, senator, or consul, and a slave; **2** wealthy citizens and people of high public standing; **3** legionary; **4** centurion; ordinary people including **5** a traveler (with hat and staff), a lawyer with scroll; **6** mother (matron) and daughter, **7** and a wine seller; **8** masked actor performing, **9** gladiator; **10** slaves working the land.

▲ Greek citizens usually voted in favor of a politician. When one became unpopular, however, the citizens could vote to ostracize (send into exile) him. They voted by scratching the politician's name onto pieces of broken pottery, called ostraka, like those shown above.

A.D.

335 India: Emperor Samudragupta extends the Gupta empire to the north-west (to 375). Although the empire expands it is still confined to northern India only and is not as large as the earlier Mauryan empire. This is the classic period of Hindu India.

337 Constantine is baptized on his deathbed. The empire is divided among his three sons, Constantius, Constantine II, and Constans I. Shapur II of Persia wages war with eastern Roman strongholds (to 350), but fails in his efforts to capture them.

339 Persia: Christians are persecuted.

350 Persians capture Armenia from Rome. Africa: Kingdom of Axum conquers Kush; Christianity reaches Ethiopia.

351 Constantius becomes sole ruler of the Roman empire.

357 Julian, half brother of Constantine the Great, defeats the Alemanni and recovers the Rhineland from the Franks.

359 Shapur II again goes to war with Rome. His army is repulsed by Julian in 363.

361 Rome: Julian becomes emperor (to 363). He reverts to paganism and tries to re-introduce it into the empire to replace Christianity. Korea: Emperor Jingo of Japan invades.

The Arch of Constantine was built in A.D. 312 to commemorate Constantine's victory over Maxentius his rival for the empire.

The Decline of Rome

The decline of the Roman empire started in the 3rd century A.D. Central government weakened as emperor after emperor was assassinated or was removed by the army. Attacks by the barbarians on the frontiers increased, and the taxpayers could not keep up with the demands from the army for money to provide the necessary defense.

When Diocletian became emperor in A.D. 284, he decided that the empire was too large for one man to rule alone and divided it into two, the east and the west. He appointed a co-emperor called Maximian to rule the western half. The army was reorganized and enlarged until it contained about half-a-million men. Provinces were subdivided to make them

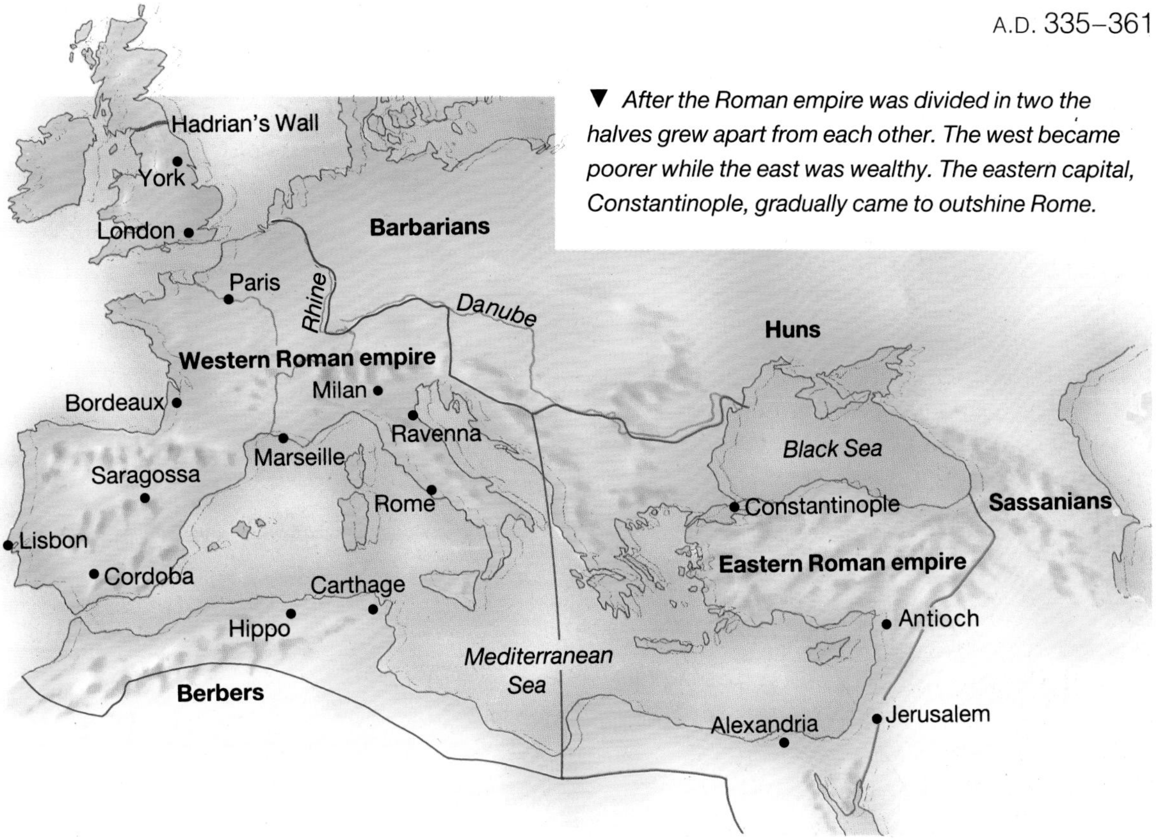

▼ *After the Roman empire was divided in two the halves grew apart from each other. The west became poorer while the east was wealthy. The eastern capital, Constantinople, gradually came to outshine Rome.*

Hadrian's Wall
York
London
Paris
Rhine
Danube
Barbarians
Huns
Western Roman empire
Milan
Bordeaux
Ravenna
Marseille
Black Sea
Saragossa
Rome
Constantinople
Sassanians
Lisbon
Eastern Roman empire
Cordoba
Carthage
Antioch
Hippo
Mediterranean
Sea
Berbers
Alexandria
Jerusalem

◄ *The Emperor Diocletian suggested a* tetrarch *(rule of four) to administer the two halves of the empire – two emperors were helped by two lieutenants.*

more manageable and regular annual taxation imposed. These were good, but expensive, plans.

The idea of the "Roman spirit" was promoted throughout the empire by placing emphasis on the divine authority of the emperor. People who did not agree that the emperor was a god, such as the Christians, were persecuted.

The emperor Constantine the Great reversed many of Diocletian's policies. After he was converted to the new Christian religion, he built churches and encouraged people to convert by giving them rewards and jobs. In A.D. 330, Constantine decided to make Byzantium on the Black Sea his capital, calling it Constantinople. This increased the division between the two parts of the empire. Constantinople in the east became as grand as Rome, while the west grew weaker and poorer.

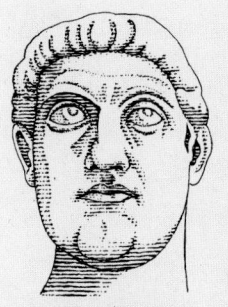

Constantine

A.D. **272** Born at Naissus, Moesia.
A.D. **306** Declared emperor by his troops.
A.D. **312** Converted to Christianity after seeing a flaming cross in the sky before a battle at Milvian Bridge, near Rome.
A.D. **330** Makes Byzantium capital of the Roman empire.
A.D. **337** Dies.

HADRIAN'S WALL

As attacks on the empire increased, the Romans became very concerned with the defense of their frontiers. Around A.D. 122, they built a wall in northern Britain to defend themselves against the barbarian Scots and Picts.

Known as Hadrian's Wall after its creator, Emperor Hadrian, it was 73 miles (117km) long and was mainly built of stone. Some 16 forts, and ditches 30 feet (10m) wide on both sides, made it the Romans' most elaborate frontier.

The western half of the Roman empire finally collapsed after Rome had been sacked for a second time in A.D. 455, and the last emperor was killed by a barbarian in A.D. 476. This part of the empire was replaced by a number of Germanic kingdoms.

The Roman empire in the east lasted longer. Ruled from Constantinople, it controlled lands stretching from Greece in the west to Egypt in the south, and to the borders of Arabia in the east.

Barbarian tribes did not attack this eastern part as much as the western empire, and one emperor, called Justinian, managed to reconquer territory that the barbarians had invaded in Africa, Italy, and southern Spain. He tried as best he could to reestablish the old Roman empire, but the lands were soon lost again. However, Roman ways were often adopted by barbarian invaders; some even became Christian. Only in Britain did the barbarians almost completely wipe out all Roman remains.

Constantinople continued to be ruled by emperors until 1453, when it was finally taken over by the Ottoman Turks.

▲ From the end of the 3rd century A.D., defensive walls were constructed around many Roman cities. Constantinople was fortified in the 5th century A.D.

▼ Emperor Justinian continued the fight against the barbarians. This gold coin was minted in A.D. 535 to celebrate his general Belisarius's defeat of the Vandals.

◄ A development of Roman-style houses in Wroxeter, near Shrewsbury, England, during the 5th century A.D. shows that Roman influence did not disappear entirely in England after the empire fell. The houses were built of wood and formed part of a city center.

The Barbarians

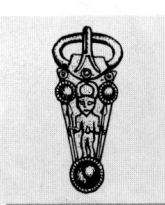

The term "barbarians" was used by the Romans to describe the peoples living outside their empire whom they thought of as uncivilized. These barbarians generally lived in small farming communities. Many of them were wild and ferocious warriors, but some were skilled craftsmen and poets, though they could only write crudely.

There were many different barbarian tribes. The Huns were nomadic Mongols who arrived in Europe around A.D. 370. The Goths were Germanic peoples, possibly from Scandinavia. In the 3rd century A.D., the Goths split into two distinct groups, the Ostrogoths (east Goths) and Visigoths (valiant or west Goths). The Vandals and Franks were also Germanic tribes. There was no real unity among them and the tribes often fought each other.

From about A.D. 167, groups of barbarians began attacking the Roman empire, especially the western part.

▼ The map shows the original homelands of the barbarian tribes, and the direction in which they traveled to invade the Roman empire.

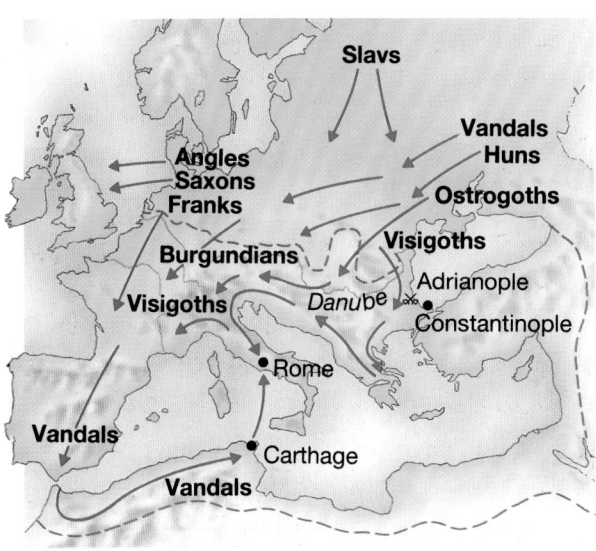

A.D.	
363	Rome: Emperor Jovianus rules (to 364). He surrenders Mesopotamia to Persia.
364	Rome: Emperor Valentinian rules (to 375). Valens rules in the east.
369	Britain: Roman general Theodosius drives the Picts and the Scots out of Roman Britain.
370	Egypt: Birth of Hypatia, noted Greek mathematician and philosopher. She died in 415 when Cyril, patriarch of Alexandria, incited a mob to torture and kill her. Huns from Asia invade Europe.
371	Shapur II at war with Rome for the third time (to 376). At this stage Persian power is at its height.
372	Korea: Buddhism is introduced into the country.
375	Western Roman empire: Emperor Gratian rules (to 383). India: Chandragupta II rules the Gupta empire.

The barbarians used the horns of cattle to make vessels from which to drink.

378	Defeat and death of Emperor Valens at Adrianople (western Turkey) at the hands of the Goths.
379	Eastern Roman empire: Theodosius the Great is emperor (to 395). Constantinople is now the center of imperial power. Persia: the death of Shapur II is followed by a series of weak Persian rulers.
380	Theodosius recognizes Christianity as the official religion of the empire.
383	Western Roman empire: Magnus Maximus is emperor (to 388). His legions begin to leave Britain to conquer Gaul and Spain, but he is executed by Theodosius.
394	Theodosius briefly reunites Roman empire. He forbids the Olympic games.
395	Greece: Stilicho, Vandal leader of the Roman army, drives out Visigoths (to 397).

A.D.

395 Honorius rules the western Roman empire (to 423) while his brother, Arcadius, rules the eastern Roman empire (to 408).

396 Africa: St. Augustine becomes bishop of Hippo. He is known as one of the Fathers of the Church and has a great influence on Christian theology. His most famous works are *Confessions* and *De Civitate Dei* (The City of God).

A brooch like this would have been used to fasten a barbarian man's cloak. It was made about A.D. 400 and was fashionable in Denmark and, later, England.

399 First known woman surgeon, the Roman Fabiola, dies. In her lifetime, she established a hospital in which she worked both as a nurse and a doctor. Eastern Roman empire: Byzantine empress Pulcheria rules (to 453).

400 South America: Incas established on parts of South American Pacific coast.

5th century Ireland: Brigid founds first women's community. Japan: First Buddhist missionaries arrive.

401 Pope Innocent I claims leadership over the Roman Church (to 417).

406 Vandals overrun Gaul.

407 Britain: Last Roman troops leave. First Mongol empire founded by Avars (to 553).

408 Eastern Roman empire: Theodosius II rules (to 450).

409 Spain: Vandals take part of Spain and establish their capital at Toledo. They convert to Christianity. Persia: Christians allowed to worship freely (to 416).

The period from A.D. 250–550 is known as the Age of Migrations because the barbarians were constantly on the move. The Huns reached the fringes of the western Roman empire around A.D. 370. They soon took over the lands of the Ostrogoths, and thousands of neighboring Visigoths fled in fear of them. When the Visigoths reached the edge of the Roman empire marked by the Danube River, they begged to be allowed to cross to safety. The eastern emperor Valens allowed them to settle on his land because he thought the Visigoths would be useful army recruits.

But the Visigoths and Ostrogoths joined forces and defeated the eastern empire's army. Eventually, the Visigoths were allowed to live around the Danube under their own rulers, if they helped defend the Romans against the Huns. The Romans were becoming increasingly

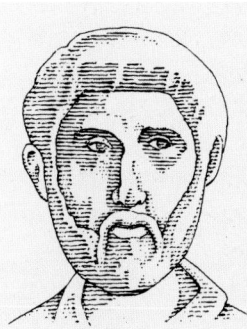

Stilicho

c. A.D. 383 Marries Serena, the niece of a Roman emperor.

c. A.D. 393 In charge of western Roman army.

A.D. 403 Drives Alaric out of Italy for a while.

A.D. 406 Wins great victory over the Goths.

A.D. 408 Beheaded after trying to make his son, Eucharius, eastern emperor.

Attila the Hun

A.D. 434 Becomes king of the Huns jointly with brother Bleda.

A.D. 445 Kills brother.

A.D. 447 Marches on Constantinople, and is paid to leave.

A.D. 451 Invades Gaul but is defeated.

A.D. 452 Invades Italy. Successful at first but has to withdraw.

A.D. 453 Dies.

dependent on barbarian help in defending the empire. Stilicho, who was half-Roman and half-Vandal, was one of the west's best generals, and became commander-in-chief of their army.

Other barbarian tribes began to invade the western empire in Gaul and Spain. The Visigoths broke their promise and invaded northern Italy in A.D. 401 led by King Alaric. In A.D. 410, Alaric sacked Rome, which had been unconquered for 800 years, striking a blow to the heart of the empire and shocking the Romanized world. At the same time, Saxons, Angles, and Jutes invaded Britain. By A.D. 417, the Visigoths had invaded Gaul. The Vandals took over Spain and then North Africa. In A.D. 455, the Vandals sacked Rome while, the Visigoths, Franks, and other tribes took over Gaul. After Attila the Hun attacked northern Italy the western empire finally collapsed.

▶ *The barbarians loved jewelry and were skillful metalworkers. This brooch of gilded bronze and garnets in the shape of an eagle was made by an Ostrogoth in Spain during the late 5th century A.D.*

▼ *A scene based on a Roman tomb carving, dating from about A.D. 200, shows Roman soldiers fighting fiercely against Germanic barbarian invaders.*

A.D.

410 Goths under leader Alaric sack Rome for three days. Rome formally renounces Britain.

420 Varaharan V of Persia declares war on Rome (to 440) when Persian Christians cross border seeking Rome's protection.

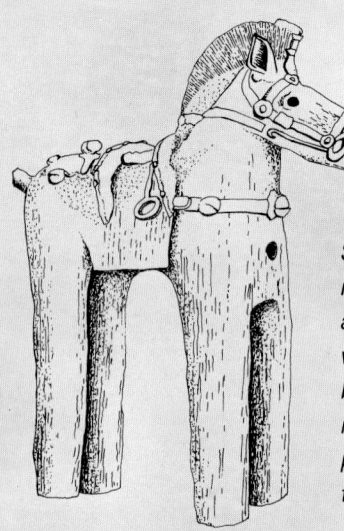

Small clay figures, representing animals and everyday objects were placed in the burial grounds of important Japanese people. Horses, like this one, stood guard.

425 Western Roman empire: Emperor Valentinian III rules (to 455). Eastern Roman empire: University of Constantinople founded. Britain: Raids are carried out by Angles and Saxons.

c. **425** The Huns settle in Pannonia (part of Hungary).

429 Vandal kingdom is established in northern Africa (to 534).

430 Africa: Death of St. Augustine.

432 Ireland: St. Patrick begins mission.

434 Attila rules the Huns (to 453).

439 North Africa: Gaiseric of the Vandals captures Carthage.

440 Leo the Great becomes pope (to 461). Persia: Yezdigird II rules (to 457). He forcibly converts Armenia to Zoroastrianism (a religion founded by the Persian prophet Zoroaster).

449 Britain: Hengest and Horsa conquer Kent.

450 Eastern Roman empire: Emperor Marcian rules (to 457).

Japan

Japan is one of the oldest nations in the world. Evidence has been found of people living there from around 30,000 B.C. From about 300 B.C. people grew crops of rice and barley. Around 250 B.C., the Yayoi tribe became the most influential in Japan. The Yayoi started using bronze and iron. These metals were probably brought from south Korea.

Around A.D. 167, an elderly priestess called Himiko became ruler of the Japanese. About 30 small independent Japanese states became unified around this time and, as their ruler, Himiko sent ambassadors to seek the friendship and support of the Chinese. As the Chinese civilization was already well established, throughout the next three centuries Chinese culture was very influential.

AINU

The Ainu were an ancient people who lived in Japan a long time before those who started the dominant race traveled over from the Asian mainland. Also known as the Ezo, they did not look at all like the Japanese. Early writings describe them as short, hairy people with light complexions. There are still a few people of Ainu descent living in northern Japan to this very day.

The Ainu had no written language of their own. However, it is believed that their religion was extremely similar to the Japanese Shinto religion and that they worshiped spirits. On the right are two Ainu elders.

Much of what is known about Japan at this time comes from Chinese reports.

From about A.D. 200, a tribe called the Yamato became the dominant people in Japan. What is called the Yamato period lasted until A.D. 646, by which time much of Japan was ruled by Yamato emperors. They gained control of most of central Japan and parts of southern Korea during the 3rd and 4th centuries A.D. Right up to the present day, Japan's emperors have always come from the Yamato family who claimed descent from the Sun goddess.

In the 5th century A.D., Yamato power increased dramatically. The Yamato attacked parts of Korea successfully and became rich from the tribute (money) that Korean kings were forced to send them. By the end of the 5th century, however, Korean horse-mounted warriors were reclaiming lands taken by the Yamato and even starting to invade parts of Japan itself.

▲ The four main Japanese islands, showing the southern Yamato Plain of Honshu where the Yamato emperors had their center of government.

◀ Shinto or "the way of the gods" was Japan's main religion. Its priests believed sacred energy or kami existed in gods, nature, and the emperor.

CREATION MYTH

Legend has it that Japan was created by a divine brother and sister who gave birth to the islands of Japan, and also to the Sun goddess, Amaterasu (above). Religious texts trace the line of Japanese emperors back to Amaterasu.

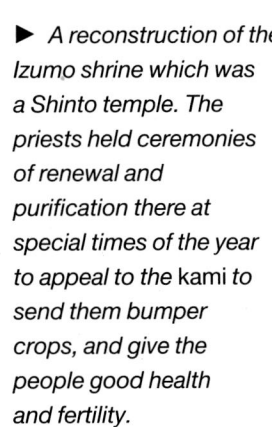

▶ A reconstruction of the Izumo shrine which was a Shinto temple. The priests held ceremonies of renewal and purification there at special times of the year to appeal to the kami to send them bumper crops, and give the people good health and fertility.

147

Trade

Despite the hazards of long-distance travel, trade was an essential part of ancient life. Stores in Athens and Rome sold a wide range of goods, not only from Greece and Italy, but from all over the known world.

By 500 B.C., Greek cities had already established trading colonies as far away as southern Italy and the northern coast of the Black Sea. The colonies sent grain and timber in return for luxury goods such as pottery and jewelry.

The trading network of the Roman empire covered the whole of Europe and extended to both China and India. The Romans prized robes of brightly colored silk from China, and Roman coins have been found in southern India.

◀ A Greek vase, once owned by a man called Leandros. The Greeks colonized the Libyan coast, and ruled Egypt.

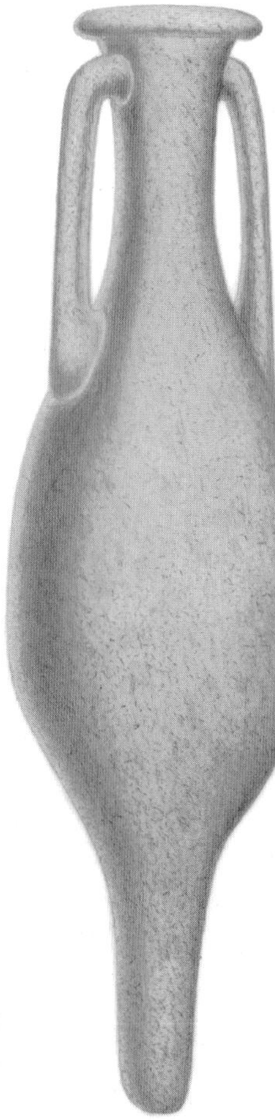

▶ Roman amphora were used to transport wine, olive oil, and other agricultural goods.

▼ A Roman butcher's shop. The butcher sold local meat and imported hams.

WHEN IT HAPPENED

500 B.C. In Africa, Darius I builds a canal to connect the Nile River to the Red Sea. In northwest India, Taxila and Charsadda are important trading centers.

310 B.C. The Hopewell Indians of North America develop a trading network.

50 B.C. Chinese silk reaches the Roman empire.

A.D. 1 Roman pottery is exported to northern Europe and southern India. Knowledge of monsoon winds leads to traders using the Indian Ocean and Red Sea.

A.D. 300 In Africa, the kingdom of Axum (Ethiopia) flourishes on trade.

▲ *A glass cup, made within the Roman empire during the 3rd century B.C., was traded to Denmark.*

▼ *Many large cargo ships could not sail into Roman harbors, so small boats were used to ferry goods to and from them.*

◄ *The Chinese emperor Kuang-wu ruled in the 1st century A.D. Within the Chinese empire, trade was very strictly controlled. The government made sure that the same weights, measures, and coins were used by everyone.*

► *Chinese money, at first shaped like knives, gradually became round and Emperor Shi Huangdi introduced a single currency. The hole meant that several coins could be strung together.*

149

The Mayas

The Mayan Indians lived in what is now southern Mexico and Guatemala, in Central America. They created a magnificent civilization in the middle of forests and jungles that was at its peak at about the same time as the Roman empire was crumbling. Many Mayas still live in parts of Central America.

The Mayas are known to have existed as long ago as 2000 B.C. Over the centuries they became successful farmers and created hundreds of great cities out of stone, each with its own character and artistic style. Every city-state was independent with no overall ruler or government. Only nobles, priests, rulers, officials, and their servants inhabited the cities. Most of the Mayas were farmers who lived in forest huts and only came to the cities to attend markets or religious festivals. The Mayas built a network of roads to encourage trade.

They were also very advanced in science, mathematics, and the visual arts. Many marvelous wall paintings in

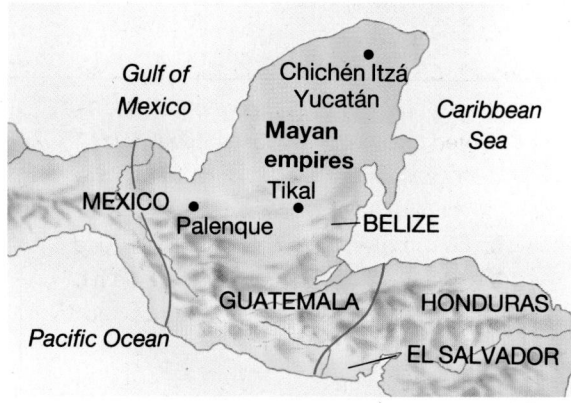

▲ The region where the Mayan civilization developed now consists of parts of Mexico, Guatemala, Belize, and Honduras.

▶ The figures found in Mayan ruins often show richly dressed people such as this priest wearing an ornate headdress.

▼ The Mayas played a ball game that had religious importance for them. In vast courts they bounced a solid ball backward and forward using hips, thighs, and elbows, aiming for a hoop in the side wall.

ASTRONOMY

In specially-built observatories, Mayan priests noted the way in which the position of the Sun, Moon, stars, and planets changed. From this they developed a calendar, and worked out the times of eclipses of the Sun and Moon.

RELIGION

The Mayas prayed to rain, earth, wind, plant, and animal gods. They built magnificent temples and shrines in honor of these gods and placed them high above the ground on pyramid platforms. Only priests and a favored few could enter the temples. At religious ceremonies they sometimes sacrificed humans.

tombs and temples, remarkable stone carvings, and decorated clay pots have been found in and around the ruins of their cities. The Mayas made pots by coiling long strips of clay into pots, then turning them around with their feet.

The system of arithmetic they invented counted in twenties and used only three symbols: a bar for 5, a dot for each unit up to 4, and a shell for 0.

▼ *The Mayas wrote in hieroglyphs (picture writing). This type of writing was found on huge stone monuments and in books they made from bark paper.*

A.D.

452 Attila the Hun invades Gaul and Italy. He is repulsed by Franks, Alemanni, and Romans at the battle of Chalons. Italy: Venice founded by refugees from the Huns. Pope Leo I negotiates with Attila the Hun for the withdrawal of the Huns from Italy.

453 Attila the Hun dies and the Huns become weaker.

455 Gaiseric of the Vandals sacks Rome.

457 Eastern Roman empire: Leo is emperor (to 474).

465 India: White Huns dominate northern part of the country.

A shell carving of a priest or official who served at Palenque, one of the main ceremonial centers of the Mayan civilization.

471 Theodoric the Great rules as king of the Ostrogoths (to 526).

475 Roman empire: Romulus Augustus becomes last emperor of the western Roman empire. He is deposed by the Goths under of Odoacer in 476. This is the end of the western empire. The eastern Roman empire continues under Zeno and Anastarius, and survives for the next thousand years.

477 North Africa: Huneric is Vandal king (to 484). India: Bliddhagupta becomes last emperor of the Gupta dynasty (to 496).

481 Clovis is king of the Franks (to 511).

483 Armenia: Volagases of Persia grants Christians in Armenia the right to practice their faith (to 485).

A.D.

484 Split between the Christian churches of Rome and Constantinople. Pope refuses to recognize Emperor Zeno's authority to change Christian doctrine and excommunicates him.

484 North Africa: Reign of Vandal king Gunthamund (to 496).

486 France: Clovis, King of the Franks, defeats Syagrius, leader of the Gallo-Romans, at Soissons and conquers much of northern Gaul.

488 After surviving attacks from barbarians and rebels Zeno pays Theodoric, King of the Ostrogoths, to expel Odoacer from Italy. Theodoric the Great of the Ostrogoths begins the conquest of Italy.

The Polynesians worshiped the god Tangaroa Upao Vahu who they believed created the world.

493 Theodoric of the Ostrogoths becomes king of all Italy.

496 Clovis and the Franks defeat the Alamanni in battle at Tolbiac near the River Rhine. The Alamanni are driven back beyond the Rhine into present-day Germany. North Africa: Trasamund, Guntamund's brother, becomes king of the Vandals (to 523).

497 Emperor Anastasius recognizes Theodoric as his representative in Italy.

498 Clovis, King of the Franks, is converted to Christianity.

c. 500 Angles and Saxons start settling in England.

500 Christian emperors forcibly suppress worship of the Great Mother Goddess and close down the last of her temples.

The Polynesians

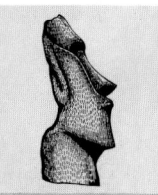

The Polynesians are now the most widely-spread people in the world. Their ancestors first lived in eastern Asia. From about 1500 B.C. many of them set sail, probably in open canoes, to find new lands to live in. They took with them animals (pigs and chickens), and fruit and vegetables (coconuts, taros, yams, breadfruit, and bananas). In time they settled in many of the smaller islands of the Pacific Ocean: in Tonga from about 1200 B.C., Samoa from 300 B.C., the Hawaiian islands from A.D. 100, and Tahiti from A.D. 300. On each island they bred their animals and used the fruit and vegetables to plant new crops. These animals and crops are found throughout the islands today.

Over a period of 1,200 years, the people developed the way of life that is now called Polynesian. They were remarkable sailors, again and again venturing into

▼ *An illustration of the type of outrigger canoe which the early Polynesians probably used in their voyages of exploration in the vast Pacific Ocean.*

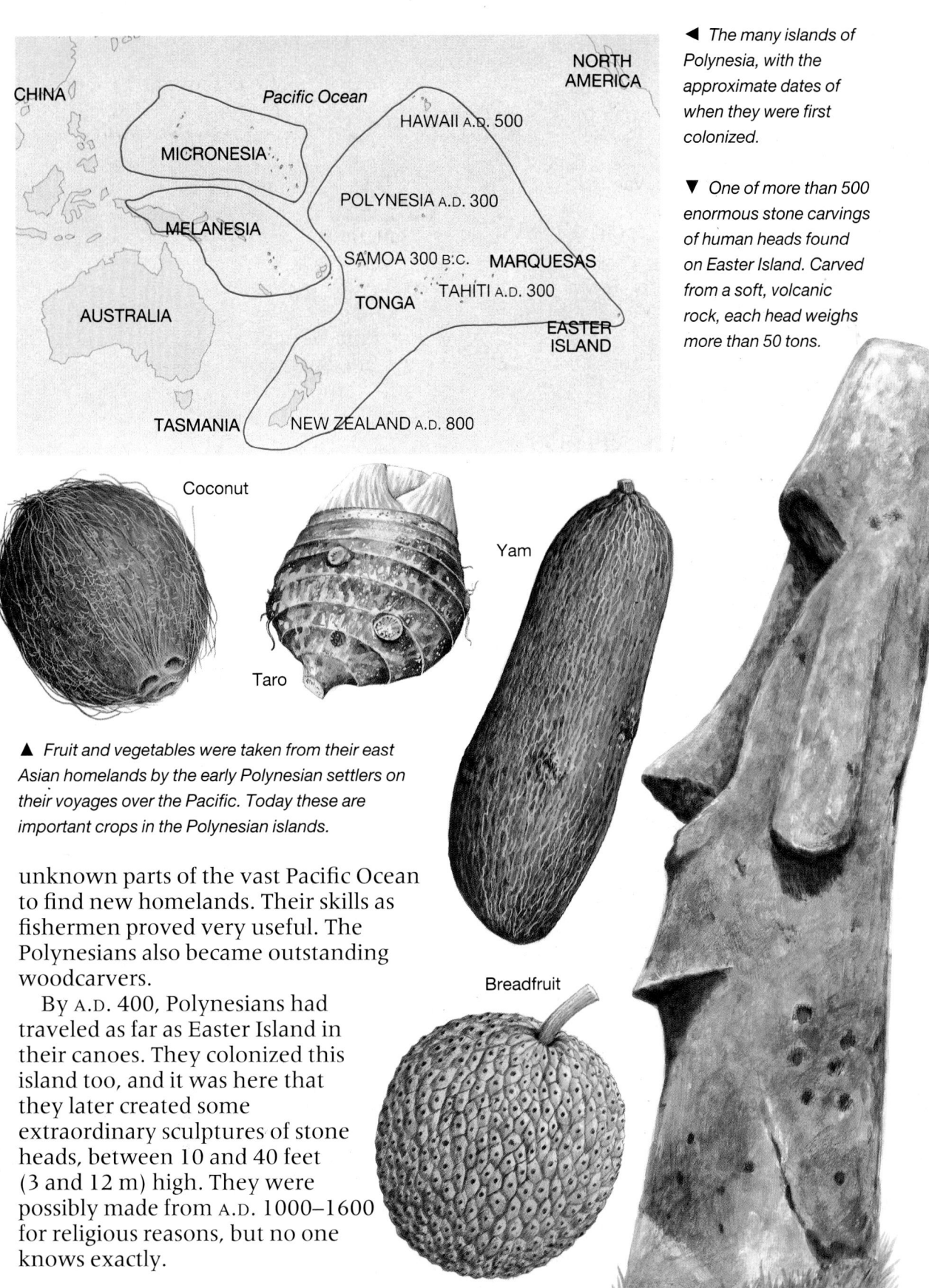

The many islands of Polynesia, with the approximate dates of when they were first colonized.

One of more than 500 enormous stone carvings of human heads found on Easter Island. Carved from a soft, volcanic rock, each head weighs more than 50 tons.

Coconut

Taro

Yam

Fruit and vegetables were taken from their east Asian homelands by the early Polynesian settlers on their voyages over the Pacific. Today these are important crops in the Polynesian islands.

Breadfruit

unknown parts of the vast Pacific Ocean to find new homelands. Their skills as fishermen proved very useful. The Polynesians also became outstanding woodcarvers.

By A.D. 400, Polynesians had traveled as far as Easter Island in their canoes. They colonized this island too, and it was here that they later created some extraordinary sculptures of stone heads, between 10 and 40 feet (3 and 12 m) high. They were possibly made from A.D. 1000–1600 for religious reasons, but no one knows exactly.

War and Weapons

The great empires of this period were created by conquest. Once they were established, their borders had to be defended against the enemies beyond. Warfare was a fact of life, and there were few years when the armies of an empire were not at war.

Although cavalry and even elephants were used, land warfare was largely conducted hand-to-hand between infantrymen. During the Greek empire, the pike (long spear) was the main weapon, but by Roman times it had been replaced by the short sword. For 300 years the Roman army was the most efficient fighting force in the world, and was rarely beaten in battle.

Land warfare had two main forms. In open warfare the two sides faced each other across clear ground. In siege warfare an enemy town was surrounded until the walls were breached.

When a naval battle was fought, ships first tried to ram each other, and then pulled alongside. The actual fighting was carried out by the soldiers who were aboard each vessel.

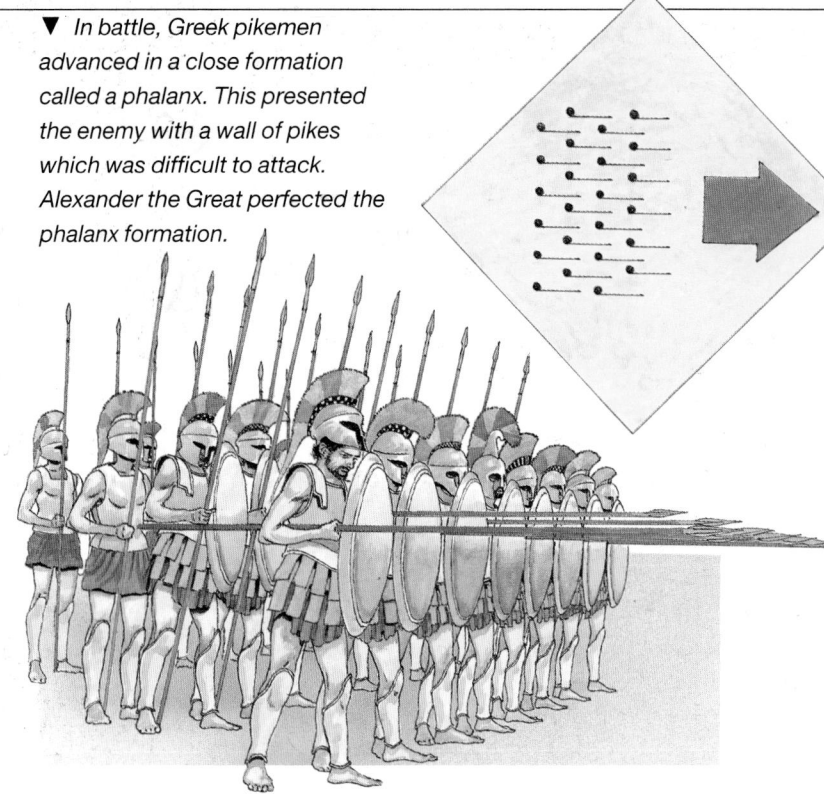

▼ In battle, Greek pikemen advanced in a close formation called a phalanx. This presented the enemy with a wall of pikes which was difficult to attack. Alexander the Great perfected the phalanx formation.

▶ This Celtic bronze shield was made around A.D. 100. It was probably for show, rather than for use in battle.

▼ The short iron sword was one of the main weapons of a Roman army. It was used at close quarters for stabbing and slashing.

WHEN IT HAPPENED

490 B.C. The battle of Marathon in which the Athenians defeat the Persians.
390 B.C. The Celts from northern Italy sack Rome.
380 B.C. Rome's defenses are improved by building the Serivan Wall.
350 B.C. The crossbow is invented in China.
334–329 B.C. Alexander the Great invades Asia Minor, conquers Egypt and Persia, and reaches India.
31 B.C. Octavian, later called Augustus, defeats Antony and Cleopatra at battle of Actium.
A.D. 43 The Romans invade Britain.
A.D. 61 Boudicca, Queen of the Iceni, leads the rebellion against the Romans in Britain.
A.D. 100 The Roman army reaches its greatest size with 300,000 regular troops.
A.D. 410 Rome is sacked by the Visigoths.
A.D. 455 Rome is sacked again by Vandals.

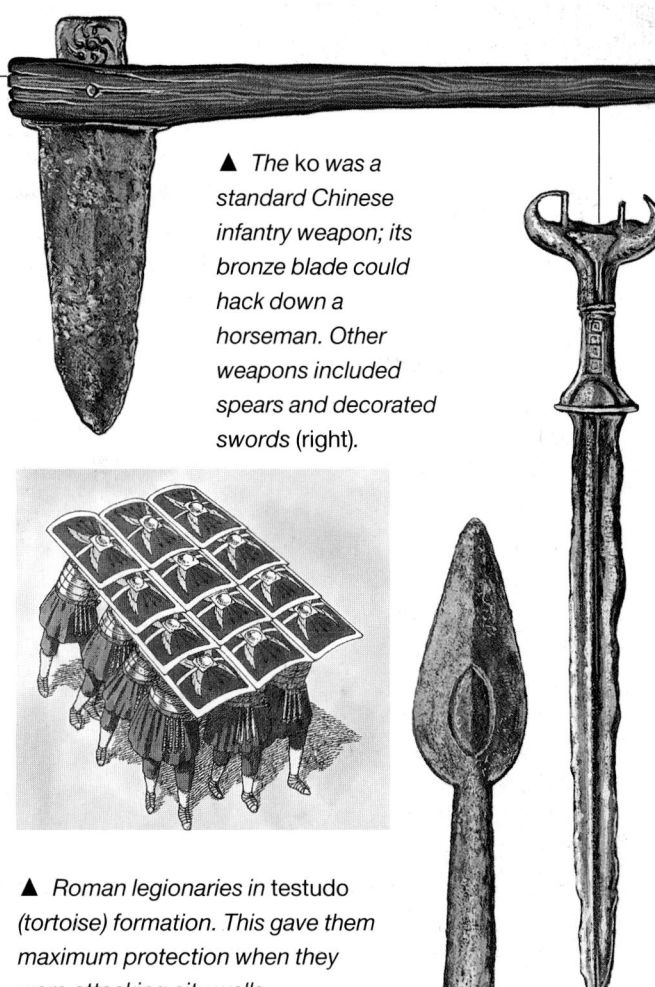

▲ *The* ko *was a standard Chinese infantry weapon; its bronze blade could hack down a horseman. Other weapons included spears and decorated swords* (right).

▲ *Roman legionaries in* testudo *(tortoise) formation. This gave them maximum protection when they were attacking city walls.*

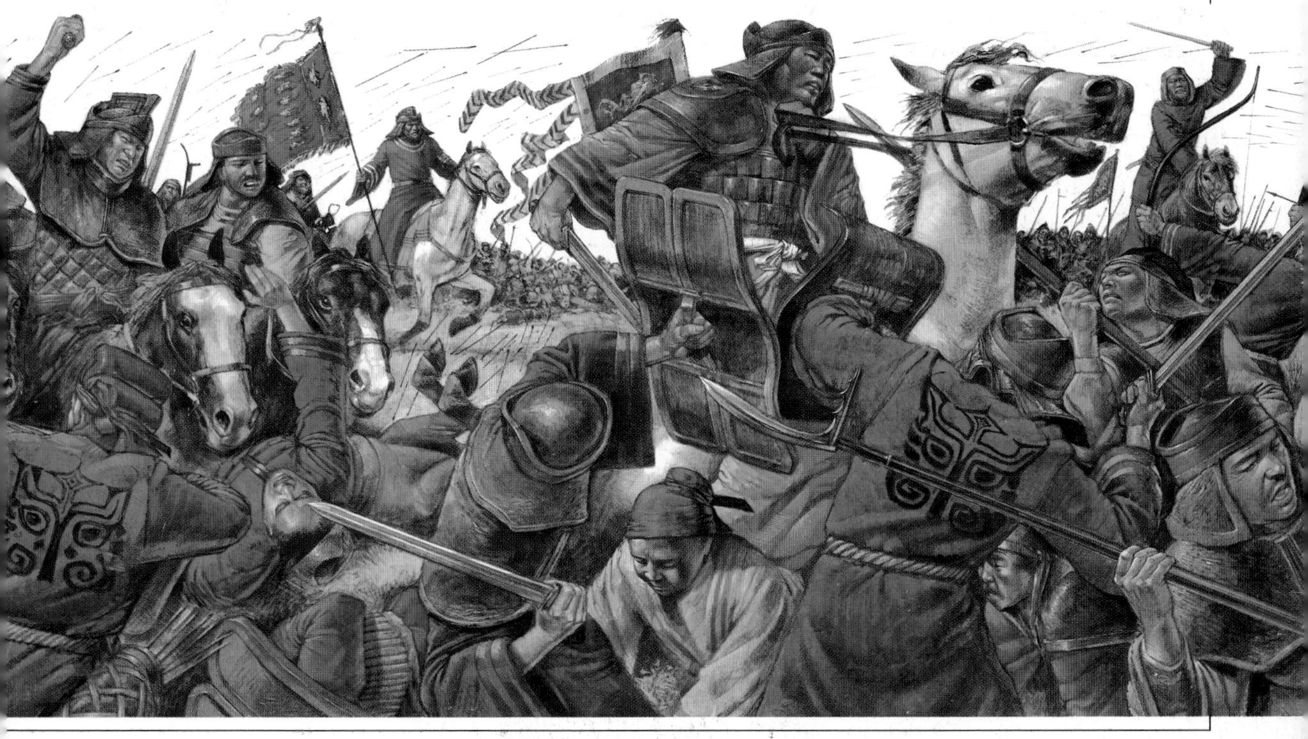

▼ *Chinese soldiers of the Han period in battle. Lacking stirrups, the horsemen on both sides were easily knocked to the ground during close-quarter fighting. Many got off their horses and fought on foot.*

Onset of the Middle Ages

After the barbarians had overrun the western half of the Roman empire, the period from A.D. 400–700 is sometimes known as the Dark Ages because there are very few written records from this time.

Europe was mostly at war during the 5th century A.D. as the barbarians sought to establish their own kingdoms, but they often kept Roman law and customs.

The Visigoth kings in southwest Gaul actively encouraged Roman ways of living. Near the end of the 5th century A.D., however, they came into conflict with the Franks led by their king, Clovis, who came from what is now northern France and Belgium.

The Franks overran the Visigoths' kingdom of Gaul, but were prevented from advancing farther to threaten Italy by Theodoric the Great and the Ostrogoths who had established a kingdom there.

As a result of all this fighting, civilization and trade developed much more slowly than before. But learning and culture was kept alive mainly by members of the Christian Church.

▲ *Monks were almost the only people who could read and write. They did all the writing for other people and they also copied books and illustrated them beautifully.*

ST. PATRICK AND IRELAND

St. Patrick was born in Britain. When he was 14 he was captured by pirates and taken to Ireland. After six years as a slave, he escaped and went to Gaul where he trained to be a Christian priest. He then returned to Britain.

After he was made a bishop, he returned to Ireland in A.D. 435 with a mission to convert its people to Christianity. Though he faced much opposition he succeeded, traveling all over the country and setting up an organized system of priests and bishops. He died in A.D. 461 at the age of 76. After his death, the priests continued his work, and by the middle of the next century most of Ireland was Christian.

MONASTERIES

The early Middle Ages saw the beginning of the Christian monasteries. These were communities of Christians who wished to concentrate on worshiping their god. They were called monks and they kept such skills as writing, painting, and sculpture alive in these troubled times.

The Early Middle Ages

The years 501–1100 were called the Dark Ages because historians thought that civilization ended when the Roman empire fell. Many people now call these years the early Middle Ages because they mark the start of the period separating ancient and modern history.

Although life after the Romans was different, the peoples who overran the western Roman empire were not all "barbarians." Many were farmers, skilled metalworkers and shipbuilders. The eastern Roman empire became the Byzantine empire. Under the Emperor Justinian, it even reconquered some land in North Africa, southern Spain, and Italy. Much of this was later lost to the Arabs, who set up an Islamic empire.

The Chinese and the Arabs led the way in science and technology, medicine, and astronomy. The Arabs adopted both the decimal system and the numbers 0 to 9 from India, and they learned how to make paper from the Chinese. This knowledge eventually passed to Europe.

Religion was spread through trade. Buddhism spread from China to Japan and other parts of Southeast Asia and many of the Vikings became Christians through trading with Christian countries. Islam was spread in a different way. As their empire grew, the Muslims converted the people they conquered. Muslim armies reached as far as France before being pushed back by new, stronger kingdoms who followed the teachings of the Christian Church.

▼ *A Viking village on the shores of a Norwegian fjord in about 800. Even the Vikings, thought to be a violent people, probably spent more of their time fishing and trading than fighting.*

The Americas

Europe

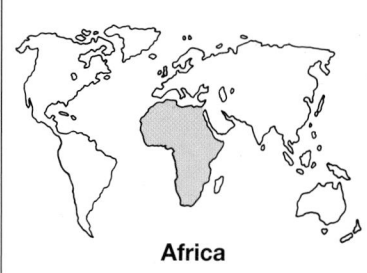

Africa

The Americas

c. **550** Huari, Moche, and Nazca kingdoms flourish in Peru.
c. **600** In Central America Teotihuacán reaches the height of its power. In South America the cities of Tiahuanaco and Huari grow in size and importance.
c. **700** In North America the Temple Mound culture flourishes and the Anasazi people start to build pueblos.
c. **750** Both Teotihuacán and the Mayan states start to decline.
c. **800** The bow and arrow is first used in the Mississippi Valley.
c. **950** The Toltecs rise to power in Central America.

c. **985** The Vikings start to settle in Greenland

c. **1000** Chimú empire develops around Chan Chan in Northern Peru.

1003 The Viking Leif Ericsson travels to Newfoundland.

1100 The Anasazi culture reaches its greatest extent.

Europe

527 Justinian becomes Byzantine emperor and tries to revive the old Roman empire.

711 The Muslims invade Spain.
732 Charles Martel leads the Franks to victory over the Muslims at Poitiers, France.
771 Charlemagne comes to power in France. Under his rule, the feudal system starts to develop.
843 Charlemagne's empire is split into three parts.
911 The king of France gives Normandy to the Vikings.

955 Otto I of Germany defeats the Magyars at the battle of Lechfeld.
962 Otto I is crowned Holy Roman emperor.

1028 Canute conquers Norway. He is already king of Denmark and England.
1066 The Normans invade and conquer England.
1096 The First Crusade begins.

Africa

535 Justinian conquers North Africa and makes it part of the Byzantine empire.
569 In Sudan, the Nubian kingdom of Makuria is converted to Christianity.

639 The Arabs invade Egypt.
c. **690** In West Africa the state of Gao is founded near the Niger River.
c. **700** The whole of North Africa is now part of the Islamic empire. Arab traders start to cross the Sahara and trade with the peoples to the south of the desert. The kingdom of Ghana starts to grow rich on trade.
c. **900** The Toutswe state (modern Botswana) is established on the edge of the Kalahari desert.
971 The world's first university is founded at Cairo in Egypt.
980 Arab merchants start to settle on the East African coast.
1000 The kingdom of Ghana is at its greatest.

1073 Ambassadors are sent to China from the East African port of Kilwa.

Near East

527 Emperor Justinian, sets out to conquer the Near East.
579 The Sassanian empire of Persia reaches its greatest extent.
622 The Hegira, when Muhammad flees to Medina. Start of the Muslim calendar.
632 Death of Muhammad; the Islamic empire starts to expand.
643 The Arabs conquer Persia and overthrow the Sassanian empire.

756 The Islamic empire starts to break up into separate countries.
762 Baghdad is founded by the Islamic leader al-Mansur.

An Islamic design from an 11th century Spanish ivory casket.

1096–99 The First Crusade reaches the Near East. Crusaders capture Jerusalem and set up a number of Christian states in the area.

Asia and the Far East

535 In India, the Gupta empire collapses.
581 The Sui dynasty is founded in China and reunites the country.
594 Buddhism becomes the official religion of Japan.
618 The Tang dynasty comes to power in China.
624 Buddhism becomes the official religion of China.
c. **775** The kingdom of the Srijaya in Sumatra conquers the whole of the Malaysian peninsula.

802 In Cambodia the Khmer dynasty establishes the kingdom of Angkor.
c. **811** The magnificent temple of Borobudur is built in Java by the island's Buddhist rulers.
868 The *Diamond Sutra* (the world's oldest surviving printed book) is printed in China.
960 The Song dynasty comes to power in China.

A Tang dynasty pottery bull

Australasia and Pacific

650 By this date all the Polynesian islands, except New Zealand, are colonized.

750 Polynesian peoples start to settle on the North Island of New Zealand.

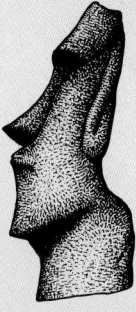

A giant head from Easter Island.

1000 The people of Easter Island start to carve huge stone statues.

The World

After the fall of the Roman empire new countries and peoples emerged in **Europe**. The lives of the people who lived in these countries were governed by the Christian Church and a rigid social system, later called feudalism.

Between Europe and the Far East there was a huge area containing many different people who all shared the same religion, **Islam**. Farther north, **Slav** countries such as Russia and Bulgaria were also forming.

China was still culturally and scientifically far in advance of the rest of the world. Its influence spread over **Asia** to Japan where there was a great flowering of the arts.

In **North America** the first towns were being built and in **Central America** the Toltec civilization developed in Mexico. In **South America** huge independent empires, such as the Huari empire, were forming.

Contact between the civilizations of the world was very limited. Only a few countries traded with each other. But Islam was spread over the whole of **North Africa** through conquest and trade.

▶ The Vikings were great seafarers and traveled enormous distances in their flat-bottomed boats. They were the first Europeans to reach North America, landing there in about 1003. Later on they tried to establish settlements there.

NORTH AMERICA

Anasazi

MEXICO

Toltecs

SOUTH AMERICA

Huari empire

▲ The Toltecs were a warlike people who flourished in Central America from 900 to 1100. Their temples were guarded by huge stone statues of warriors.

▲ The Anasazi people built pueblos (blocks of apartment-like houses). They performed elaborate ceremonies, asking for rain to water their desert surroundings.

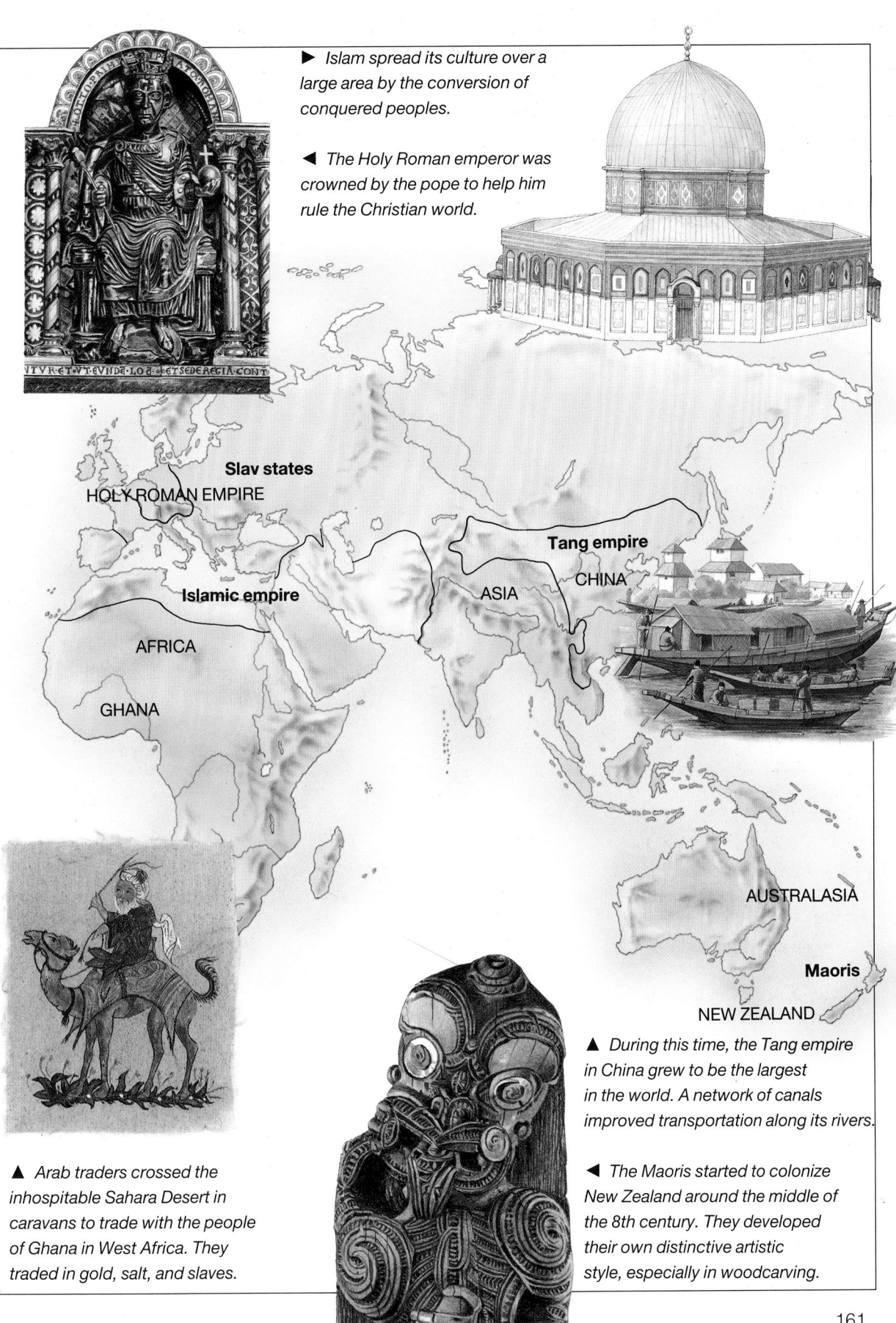

▶ Islam spread its culture over a large area by the conversion of conquered peoples.

◀ The Holy Roman emperor was crowned by the pope to help him rule the Christian world.

Slav states

HOLY ROMAN EMPIRE

Islamic empire

AFRICA

GHANA

ASIA

Tang empire

CHINA

AUSTRALASIA

Maoris

NEW ZEALAND

▲ During this time, the Tang empire in China grew to be the largest in the world. A network of canals improved transportation along its rivers.

◀ The Maoris started to colonize New Zealand around the middle of the 8th century. They developed their own distinctive artistic style, especially in woodcarving.

▲ Arab traders crossed the inhospitable Sahara Desert in caravans to trade with the people of Ghana in West Africa. They traded in gold, salt, and slaves.

161

c.501 Near East: Fighting starts between the Byzantine empire and Persia. Although they do not fight all the time, peace is not finally made until 642. Riders start to use stirrups; at first they are used for greater comfort when riding, later they are used in battle because they allow people to control their horses while fighting with swords, lances, or bows and arrows.

503 Britain: The Britons under their legendary war leader Arthur defeat the Saxon invaders from Germany at the battle of Mount Badon.

505 Fighting between the Byzantine empire and Persia ends briefly.

Christian relics were greatly prized in the Byzantine empire. Elaborate caskets, decorated with enameled pictures of Christ and the apostles, were made to hold them.

507 France: Clovis, King of the Salian Franks from 481, leads his army to victory over the Visigoths near Poitiers. He is the grandson of Merovich and founder of the Merovingian dynasty. Clovis makes Paris the capital of his kingdom and introduces the Salic Law. This is concerned with both criminal and civil law. It remains important in later times since it forbids women to inherit land.

511 Clovis dies and his empire is divided among his four sons.

523 North Africa: Hilderic becomes king of the Vandals (to 530).

524 War flares up again between Byzantine empire and Persia. It lasts until 531.

525 Byzantine empire: Theodora, previously an actress, marries Prince Justinian, heir to the empire. During his rule, she pushes through laws which give women rights of property, inheritance, and divorce.

The Byzantine Empire

Constantinople was the capital of the eastern half of the old Roman empire. It had been built on the Greek port of Byzantium and when the western Roman empire finally collapsed in 476, Constantinople became the capital of what is called the Byzantine empire.

At first, this empire controlled only a small amount of land around the Aegean Sea. Its emperors always hoped to defeat the barbarians so that they could reunite the former Roman empire. The peoples who attacked the empire also thought of its inhabitants as Romans.

During the Emperor Justinian's reign (527–565), under his general Belisarius, North Africa, Italy, and southern Spain were reconquered and the empire was expanded to include all the eastern coast of the Mediterranean. But much of this land was lost soon after Justinian's death, by the end of the 6th century.

Constantinople, now called Istanbul, stood at the entrance to the Black Sea. It was on the land route between Europe and Asia and so it became an important trading center. The empire produced

▼ *The empire reached its greatest extent under Justinian, but it was often threatened by its neighbors.*

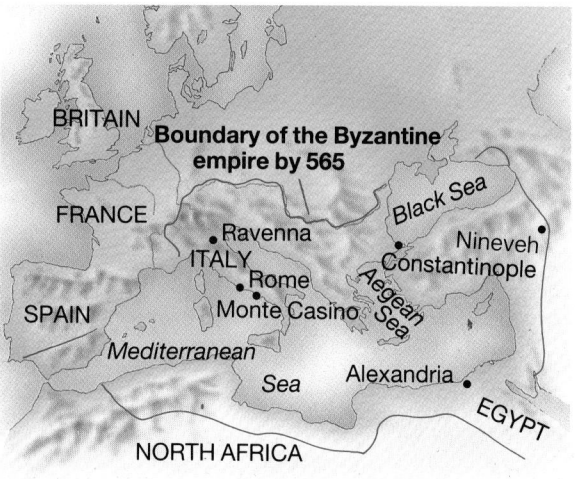

▲ *St. Sophia, or the Church of Holy Wisdom, was built in Constantinople for Justinian between 532 and 537. It took over 10,000 people to construct it.*

gold, grain, olives, silk, and wine, and these were traded for goods such as spices, precious stones, furs, and ivory, from the Far East and from Africa.

The Byzantine empire was a center of learning, where the knowledge of the Ancient Greeks was combined with the newer teachings of the Christian Church. It also had its own form of Christianity in the Orthodox Church. For centuries the greatest church in Christendom was St. Sophia in Constantinople. The emperor was thought to be God's viceroy, or representative, on Earth and this idea later passed to the tsars of Russia.

JUSTINIAN AND THEODORA

Justinian *(below)* ruled the Byzantine empire with his wife, Empress Theodora. They believed their empire was the guardian of civilization and true religion. They also believed that laws should be something made by rulers, rather than something which was handed down as a custom. Under Justinian the old Roman law was reorganized and his ideas later spread back to western Europe. Justinian's wife, Theodora helped him govern the empire. She had been an actress before her marriage and was considered very beautiful. Justinian relied on her for advice and support, and she changed laws to improve the lives of women and the poor.

▼ *The Byzantine empire was often attacked from both the land and the sea. Its navy had a secret weapon called "Greek fire." It was a mixture of quick-lime, petroleum, and sulfur which burst into flames once the quicklime touched the water. Greek fire was very successful at keeping the enemy at bay and some people have called it the first modern weapon.*

Arts and Crafts

During this time much art was used for religious purposes. Byzantine churches were decorated with mosaics and with holy pictures called icons. In monasteries monks spent long hours copying out books by hand. To make the pages more attractive, they illuminated, or decorated, the capital letters. Muslims concentrated on calligraphy, or beautiful handwriting, and used words from the Koran to decorate buildings. The Germanic peoples were skilled metalworkers who made gold and silver jewelry. So did the Byzantines. The Chinese made pottery and porcelain, while others carved out patterns in wood and stone.

▲ This Byzantine mosaic is inside the church of San Vitale in Ravenna, Italy. Ravenna was briefly the capital of the Byzantine empire. It shows Theodora, wife of the Emperor Justinian presenting a gift for the church to two bishops.

▼ Maori woodcarvings, such as this totem pole, were cut out with stone axes. The patterns were then carved with stone points.

▲ In the Song dynasty many of these pale green bowls, called celadons, were made for export from China. They were said to crack or change color if poison was put into them.

◄ Under Islamic law, artists were not allowed to paint or draw pictures of human beings or animals. Instead they practiced calligraphy, and decorated their texts with geometric designs or with flowing patterns of flowers and leaves. They often used gold leaf for the borders.

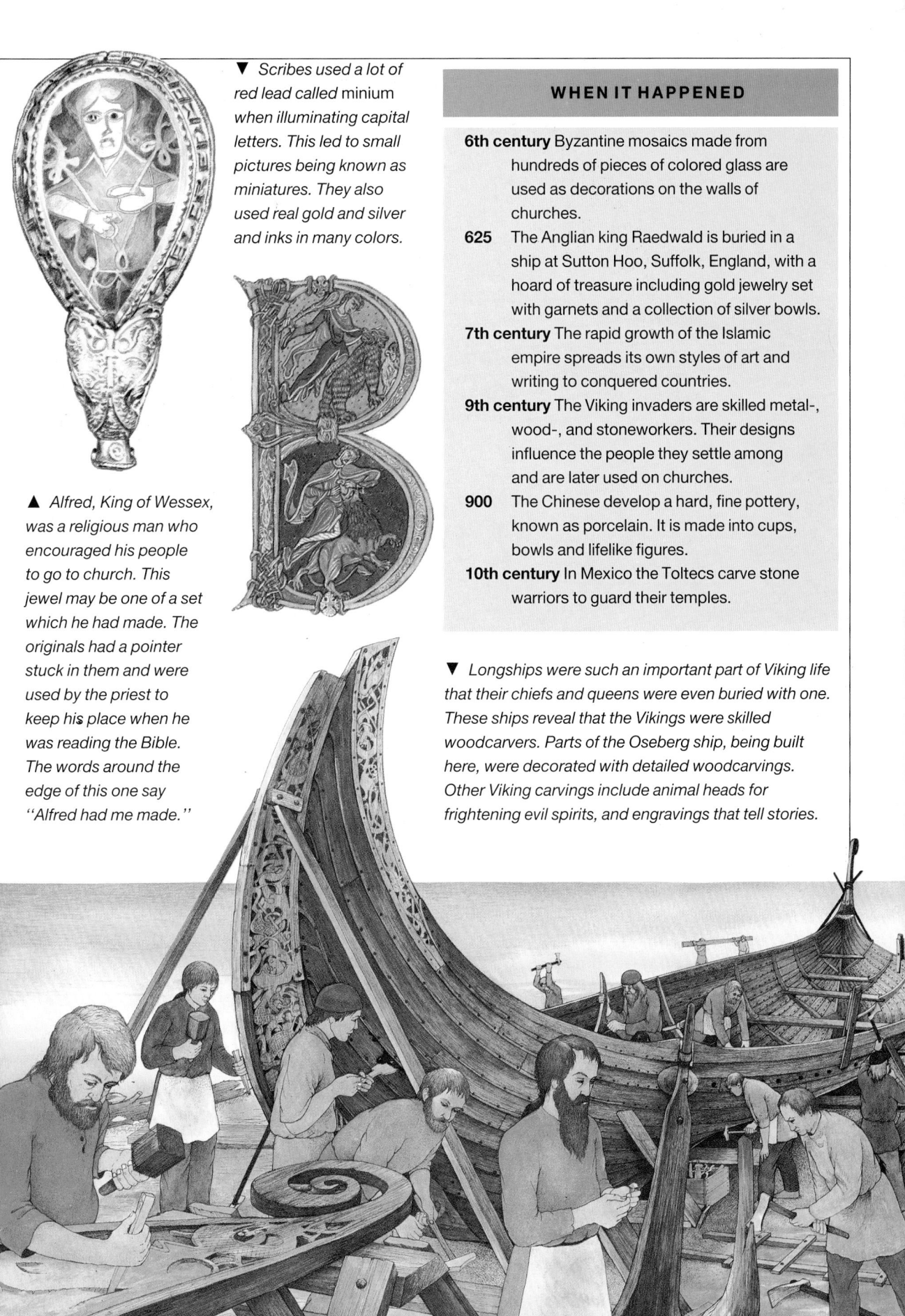

▼ *Scribes used a lot of red lead called* minium *when illuminating capital letters. This led to small pictures being known as miniatures. They also used real gold and silver and inks in many colors.*

▲ *Alfred, King of Wessex, was a religious man who encouraged his people to go to church. This jewel may be one of a set which he had made. The originals had a pointer stuck in them and were used by the priest to keep his place when he was reading the Bible. The words around the edge of this one say "Alfred had me made."*

WHEN IT HAPPENED

6th century Byzantine mosaics made from hundreds of pieces of colored glass are used as decorations on the walls of churches.

625 The Anglian king Raedwald is buried in a ship at Sutton Hoo, Suffolk, England, with a hoard of treasure including gold jewelry set with garnets and a collection of silver bowls.

7th century The rapid growth of the Islamic empire spreads its own styles of art and writing to conquered countries.

9th century The Viking invaders are skilled metal-, wood-, and stoneworkers. Their designs influence the people they settle among and are later used on churches.

900 The Chinese develop a hard, fine pottery, known as porcelain. It is made into cups, bowls and lifelike figures.

10th century In Mexico the Toltecs carve stone warriors to guard their temples.

▼ *Longships were such an important part of Viking life that their chiefs and queens were even buried with one. These ships reveal that the Vikings were skilled woodcarvers. Parts of the Oseberg ship, being built here, were decorated with detailed woodcarvings. Other Viking carvings include animal heads for frightening evil spirits, and engravings that tell stories.*

Monasticism

From the earliest years of Christianity, some deeply religious people had chosen to live apart from everyone else, so that they could spend their time in prayer. They were known as hermits, and usually lived in remote places such as islands or deserts. In the 4th century, an Egyptian hermit, St. Anthony of Thebes, brought several hermits together to form a community. This idea spread to other Christian countries and more communities of religious men, called monks, and women, called nuns, were established.

Some of these communities were

▲ St. Benedict thought that the only way to escape evil in the world was to live a secluded and religious life.

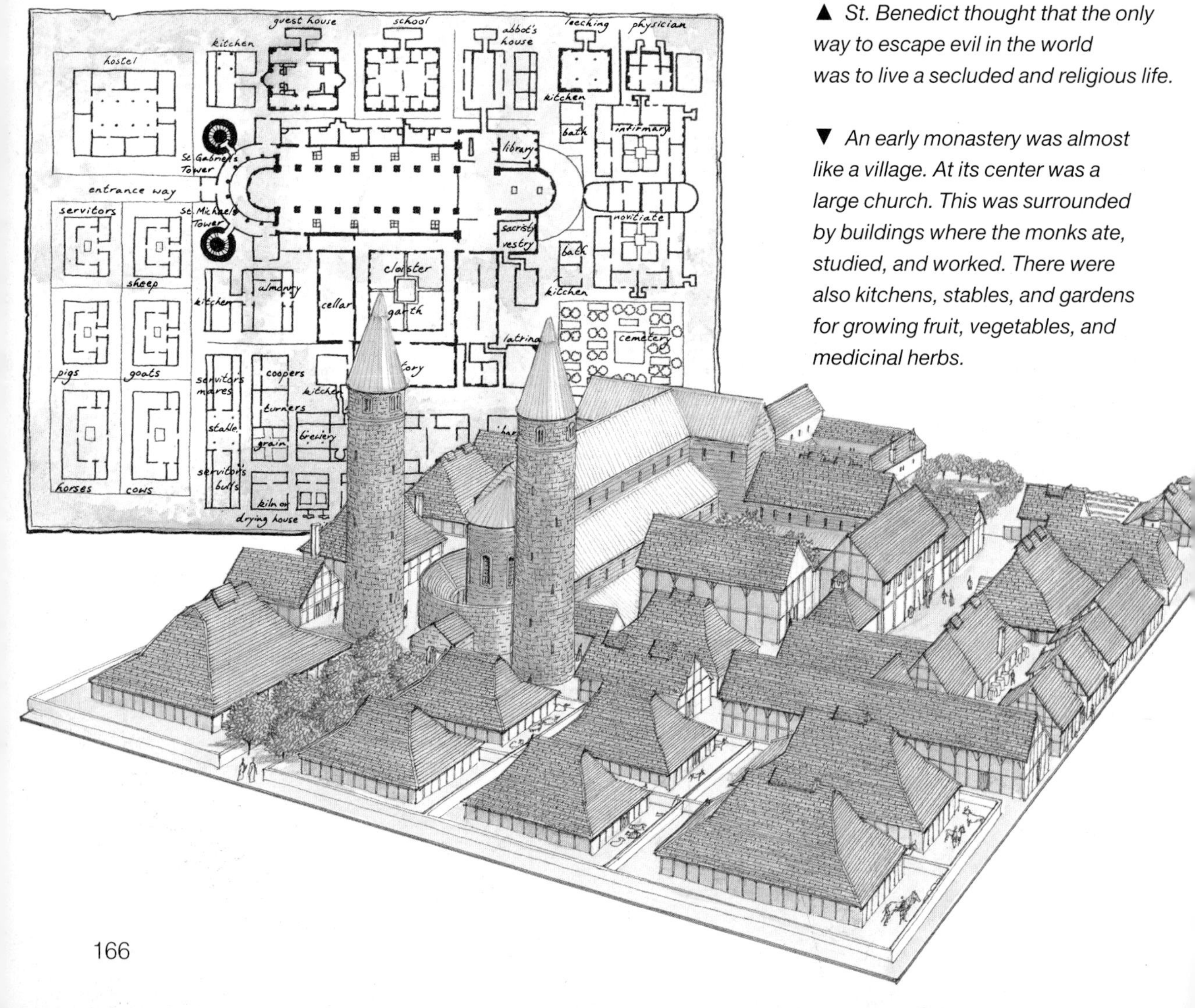

▼ An early monastery was almost like a village. At its center was a large church. This was surrounded by buildings where the monks ate, studied, and worked. There were also kitchens, stables, and gardens for growing fruit, vegetables, and medicinal herbs.

linked to each other by following the same "rule." This was a guide to how the community should live and was drawn up by a monastic leader. The most famous was the rule of St. Benedict who founded the monastery of Monte Cassino in Italy in about 529. He said that a monk's life should be one of manual labor, as well as prayer and worship. Monks and nuns who followed his rule belonged to an order, or group, known as Benedictines. They built communities all over Europe where they prayed and worked together as well as preaching to the local people.

By the 10th century other orders had developed their own versions of the rule of St. Benedict. One of these was the Cluniacs, who had their center at Cluny in France. They spent most of their time in prayer and hired servants to do the daily chores. Another Order, the Cistercians, disagreed with this idea and divided their community into "choir monks," who spent their time in prayer and administration, and "lay brothers" who did the heavy work.

▲ Both nuns and monks were supposed to lead good, simple lives. As well as studying and praying, they had to grow food and look after the sick.

527 Justinian becomes ruler of the Byzantine empire (to 565).

529 Italy: The monastery of Monte Cassino, near Naples, is founded by St. Benedict of Nursia. The monks who follow his rule are known as Benedictines. Although they lead a life of prayer and manual labor, the monks also provide almost all medical care and, by copying manuscripts, preserve much classical learning that would otherwise be lost.

A page from the Book of Durrow, *made by Irish monks. Monks produced beautifully decorated books completely by hand. Scribes copied the text and artists decorated the borders and capital letters. One book may have been a lifetime's work.*

529 Byzantine empire: Justinian starts to codify the laws that are based on the old Roman ones. They fill three volumes and it takes him until the end of his reign to complete them. (They go on to influence the law of nearly all European countries.) Justinian's empire also has its own form of Christianity, which exists today as the Eastern Orthodox Church.

530 North Africa: Gelimer becomes king of the Vandals (to 534).

533 The so-called "Eternal Peace" treaty is signed between the Byzantine empire and Persia. It lasts for seven years.

534 North Africa: Belisarius, the Byzantine general, conquers the Vandals and adds their territory to the Byzantine empire. France: The Franks conquer Burgundy.

535 Byzantine forces start the reconquest of Italy from the Ostrogoths (completed 554). India: The Gupta empire finally collapses.

540 War breaks out again between Persia and the Byzantine empire (to 562).

542 Byzantine empire: An epidemic of plague starts. It lasts until 546.

550 Wales: St. David brings Christianity. He becomes the first abbot of Menevia, now known as St. David's. He dies in about 601 and later becomes the patron saint of Wales.

552 Buddhism is introduced into Japan.

553 Egypt becomes part of the Byzantine empire and Justinian reforms its administration.

554 Byzantine armies conquer southeastern Spain and add it to the empire.

561 France: Civil war breaks out among the Merovingians.

562 Japanese power ends in Korea.

563 St. Columba, a monk from Ireland, founds a monastery on the island of Iona off the west coast of Scotland and begins to convert the Picts to Christianity.

In early manuscripts initial letters were highly decorated and often took up most of the page.

565 Justinian dies and his nephew, Justin II, rules the Byzantine empire (to 578).

568 Italy: A Germanic people known as Lombards conquer the north under the leadership of their king, Alboin. In 572 he establishes the kingdom of Lombardy, with Pavia as its capital.

570 Muhammad, the Prophet of Islam, is born in Mecca.

572 The Persians take control of Arabia (to 628). A new war starts between the Byzantine empire and Persia (to 591).

WAY OF LIFE

Religious communities tried to be self-supporting. Most monks never left the monastery. They grew the crops and vegetables they needed and kept animals for milk, eggs, and wool. They wove cloth for their clothes and blankets. Many monasteries had a forge where tools could be made and mended. Monks worked as potters, masons, carpenters, and glaziers, constructing and repairing the monastery buildings.

Life in a monastery or convent was simple but not too harsh. Time was divided between praying, sleeping, and working. Every day each monk or nun was given a loaf of bread, a measure of wine, and two cooked meals. They had a roof over their heads and a bed to sleep in, as well as clothes to wear. They were also looked after if they were old or ill. This was far more than many people got in the world outside and so there was never any shortage of new members to live in monasteries or convents.

Although monks and nuns lived apart from the rest of the world in order to devote themselves to God, monasteries soon began to play an important role in everyday life. For centuries monks were almost the only people who could read or write and the only way to get an education was by taking holy orders. Not everyone who did this stayed in the monastery, however. Some became priests and went out to work in the parishes, while others became secretaries to kings and other rulers. Many monks and nuns looked after the sick and the dying, caring for them in an infirmary. They used herbs from the gardens to make medicines and prayed for people's souls when everything else failed.

NUNS

At a time when women had to obey their fathers if they were single and their husbands if they were married, becoming a nun was almost the only way they could exercise any control over their own lives. They could work and study and some had power as abbesses in charge of convents.

RULE

The Rule is the name for the guidelines along which convents and monasteries were organized. The Benedictine Rule is the best known, but in Britain it had a rival in the Rule of St. Columba. He was an Irish monk who founded a monastery on Iona, off the west coast of Scotland.

▲ *Many monasteries had schools and large libraries where trained monks copied out books by hand. Some of the more learned monks wrote new books as well.*

Almost all monasteries provided accommodation for travelers, and especially for pilgrims who were making long journeys to holy places. Most monasteries also had a library of classical and biblical texts. These were often copied out by hand in the *scriptorium* and were the basis for much of the learning of the time. Some monks wrote histories. One of the most famous was St. Bede who wrote the *Ecclesiastical History of the English People* in 731.

▼ *Monks spent months or even years illuminating (decorating) a manuscript with beautiful pictures. The Celtic monks of Britain and Ireland drew very individual illuminations. This page is from the* Book of Kells, *a copy of the Gospels begun by monks on the island of Iona in Scotland and completed in Ireland. It shows St. John the Evangelist surrounded by designs which are typically Celtic in origin.*

MONKS IN OTHER RELIGIONS

Christianity was not the only religion to have monks and monasteries at this time. Both the Jainist and Buddhist religions had monks who lived in monasteries. Their lives, however, were different from those of the Christian monks. Buddhist monks spent much of their time in prayer, but they did not have to be monks for all of their lives. They could leave the monastery whenever they wanted. The Jains believed that becoming a monk was the only way to escape a cycle of rebirth after death.

Sui and Tang Dynasties

The Sui dynasty was founded in 581 when Yang Chien seized the throne of north China. By sending an army across the Yangtze River and reconquering the south of the country, he was able to reunite China for the first time since the end of the Han dynasty in 220. Before he came to power, taxes were high and people were conscripted into the armies for long periods of time. Yang Chien cut both the amount of taxation and the period of conscription. He governed firmly from his capital, Chang'an, and during his rule Buddhism began to spread from India. He also encouraged agriculture by setting up irrigation schemes so that more rice and grain crops could be grown. This helped to make the country wealthy again.

The second Sui emperor was Yang Di. Under his rule, the Grand Canal was rebuilt on a large scale. He also had palaces and pleasure parks built for himself and raised money for them by ordering people to pay ten years' tax in advance. The peasants rebelled and in 618 Yang Di was killed.

Li Yuan, an official from the Sui

▲ This pottery camel from the Tang dynasty is loaded with bales of silk, China's most important export. Chang'an at the end of the Silk Road grew to become the largest city in the world at this time.

▼ The Grand Canal linked the main rivers of China and made it possible to travel from the south to the north of the country without using the dangerous sea route. Because they were easier to use than roads, the waterways were the most important trading routes in China and goods of all sorts were carried along them.

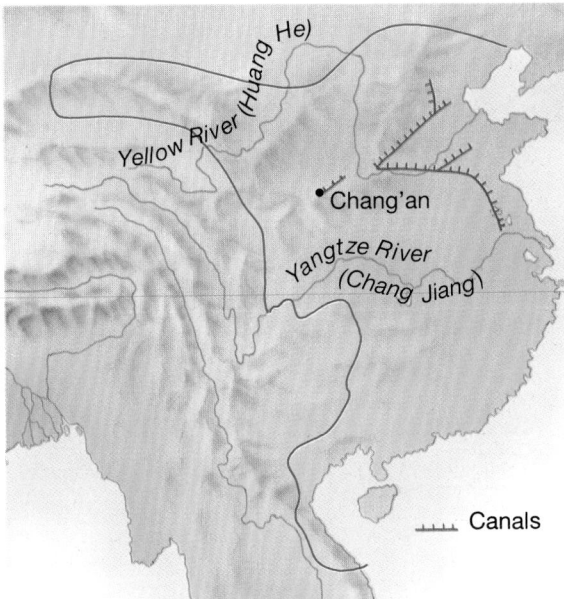

▲ *From its original boundaries (shown above) the Tang empire grew to be the largest empire in the world. An efficient canal system helped transportation.*

dynasty, then founded the Tang dynasty. This lasted until 907 and was a time of Chinese excellence in the arts, science, and technology. The silk trade flourished with merchants from many countries transporting cloth by land and by sea. The making of fine porcelain and gunpowder for fireworks were invented and printing was developed.

GUNPOWDER

One of the most important inventions of the Tang dynasty was gunpowder. It was made accidentally by a scientist who was trying to make a potion to give everlasting life. At first, it was made into fireworks, which were used to frighten an enemy. Later it was used in weapons.

PRINTING

By the 10th century, the Chinese were printing books using wooden blocks. These made it possible to print pictures and text, as both could be carved into the wood. It took a long time to carve each page, but it was worthwhile because many copies could then be printed.

581 China: Yang Chien, formerly chief minister of the Chou, founds the Sui dynasty and starts to reunite the country for the first time since the fall of the Han dynasty in 220.

584 England: The Anglo-Saxon kingdom of Mercia, roughly spanning the modern Midlands, is founded.

585 China: Reconstruction work starts on the Great Wall. Many thousands of people are conscripted to do the work and many of them die in the harsh conditions.

587 Spain: The Visigoths become Christians.

589 Persia: The Arabs, Khazars, and Turks invade, but are defeated. China: The country is finally united under the Sui.

A pottery figure of a lady from Tang China. Tombs were filled with models of servants, animals, and businessmen such as merchants and traders. The figures were meant to serve the dead person in the afterlife.

590 Gregory I, also known as Gregory the Great, becomes pope (to 604). Famous for his charitable works, after his death he is made into a saint.

593 China: The first printing press is invented. Japan: Suiko becomes empress of Japan (to 628). Buddhism takes root and becomes the official religion in 594.

594 Muhammad enters the service of Khadija, a rich widow, whom he later marries. They have six children.

596 Pope Gregory I sends Augustine to convert the Anglo-Saxons to Christianity. Legend says that this happened after Gregory saw some people who had been taken to Rome to be sold as slaves. He asked who they were and was told they were Angles. He then said "They are not Angles, but angels."

501–1100

Buildings

Building styles varied throughout the world. In hot countries, buildings were made to shelter people from the Sun. Cold countries had buildings to protect people from wind and rain. Where trees were plentiful, houses were made entirely of wood. This was especially true in northern Europe. Even the first castles were made of wood, but they were later built in stone. In warmer climates sun-baked bricks, or adobe, were used.

Early villages developed around a spring or well. Sometimes they were surrounded by a ditch with a wooden fence on top for protection.

Many Roman towns in northern Europe were abandoned. In their place, towns developed around castles and manor houses. The houses had a solid timber frame, but their walls were made of wattle and daub (woven twigs covered with mud or plaster). In southern Europe, however, many Roman towns survived and people continued to live in their houses.

▶ A sanctuary knocker on an abbey door was so-called, because criminals could find temporary refuge there.

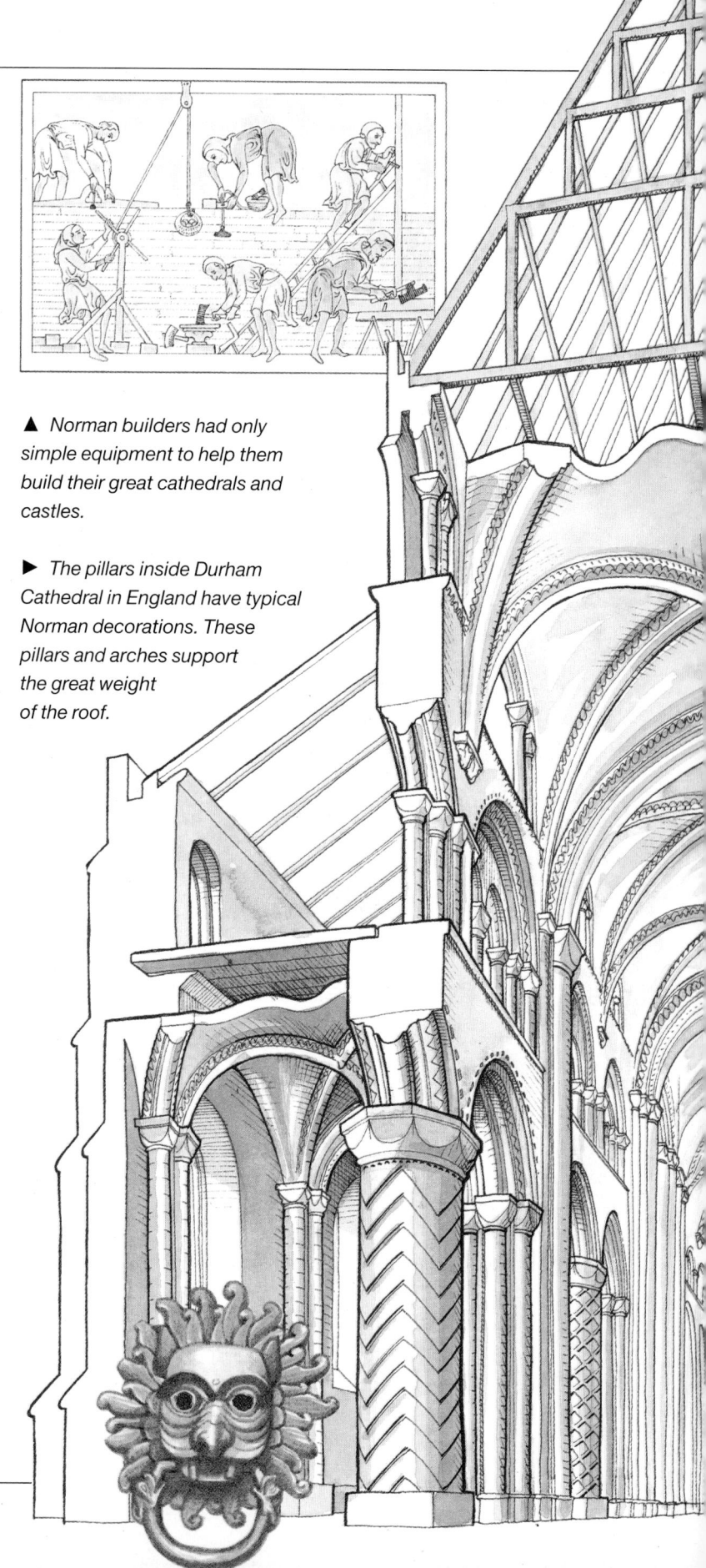

▲ Norman builders had only simple equipment to help them build their great cathedrals and castles.

▶ The pillars inside Durham Cathedral in England have typical Norman decorations. These pillars and arches support the great weight of the roof.

700   In America the Anasazi people start to build pueblos, or communal villages.

7th century The first mosques are built.

1067   The Normans start to build the Tower of London to impress the defeated English.

1093   Durham Cathedral is begun.

▲ *Motte-and-bailey castles* (above) *were common all over western Europe. The outer wall was replaced with stone* (below) *to stop attackers setting fire to them.*

◄ *Most Muslims lived in hot climates and so built their mosques to be as light and airy as possible. There are over a thousand pillars in the Great Mosque at Cordoba in Spain.*

▼ *Most Anglo-Saxon settlers built their houses and barns from wood and thatched the roofs with straw or reeds. Often, houses did not last as the wood rotted. Also, fire was always a danger.*

597 St. Augustine lands in England with 30 missionaries. They go to Kent where the ruler, Ethelbert I, has a Christian wife. Augustine converts Ethelbert and his people to Christianity.

7th century Ireland: Laws are passed against using women in battle. This reverses a Celtic tradition of female fighters which goes back at least 3,000 years.

604 Japan: First written constitution.

605 China: Yang Di, the second Sui emperor, orders the complete rebuilding of the Grand Canal. Both men and women do the work which takes five years.

606 India: Harsha becomes emperor in the north (to 647).

610 Muhammad has a vision in which the Archangel Gabriel commands him to proclaim the one true god, Allah.

618 China: The second Sui emperor is assassinated and Li Yuan founds the Tang dynasty (until 907).

The symbol of Islam is a crescent Moon and a star. Today this symbol often appears on the flags of countries which have a majority of Muslim people.

622 Muhammad flees from persecution in Mecca to Yathrib, later called Medina. This is known as the Hegira and marks the start of the Islamic calendar.

624 Muhammad marries Aisha. China: Buddhism becomes the official religion although others are allowed.

625 Muhammad begins dictating the Koran, the holy book of Islam. The Persians attack Constantinople, but fail to take it.

626 Egypt: The Byzantine emperor Heraclius I expels the Persians.

The Foundation of Islam

The prophet Muhammad, who founded the religion called Islam, was born in Mecca in 570. At this time the Arab peoples worshiped many different gods. Muhammad, however, was influenced by the Judeo-Christian belief in just one god. When he was about 40 years old, he had a vision in which the Archangel Gabriel told him to preach about one god, who was called Allah. The word Islam means "submission to the will of Allah." When Muhammad started preaching in Mecca, the people felt that the new religion threatened their old gods. In 622 Muhammad and his followers had to flee to the nearby town of Medina.

In Medina, Muhammad and his followers organized the first Muslim state and built the first mosque. Muhammad taught that people could be saved through regular prayer and by avoiding the pollution of their bodies with

MUHAMMAD

Muhammad was brought up by his uncle who was the chief of a small tribe. He spent his early years looking after sheep and camels. Then he went to work for a wealthy widow called Khadija, whom he later married. He started preaching in Mecca when he was about 40 years old, but his life was threatened, so he fled to Medina in 622. His journey is known as the Hegira. This date marks the start of the Muslim calendar. There are many pictures of Muhammad, but Islamic traditions forbid artists to show his face. Because of this, he is often shown with a veil, as in this picture.

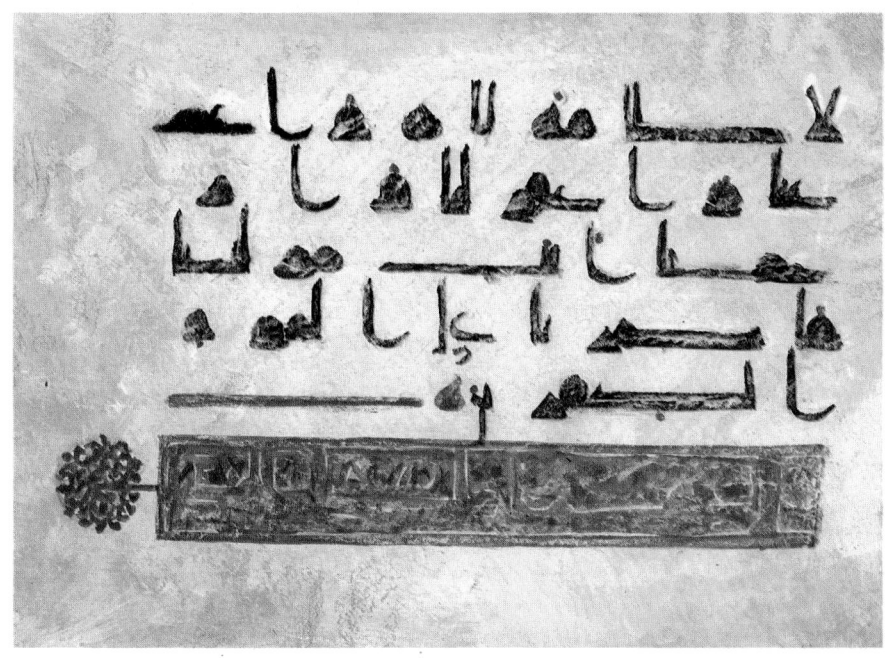

THE SPIDER

When Muhammad was fleeing from Mecca to Medina, he went into a cave to hide from his pursuers. While he was in there, a spider spun a complete web across the entrance. His pursuers saw the web and decided Muhammad could not be in the cave because otherwise it would be broken. They passed on and Muhammad was saved.

▲ *This page from the Koran was written in the 9th century. It was important to Muslims to make the words of Allah look as beautiful as possible.*

certain foods and drinks. These teachings, together with Muhammad's prophecies, were written down in the Koran, the holy book of Islam. Muhammad insisted that the words were those of Allah, speaking through him.

During his stay in Medina, Muhammad's following grew quickly. Most of the Arabian people were very poor. They were attracted to Islam because they felt its teachings offered them the chance of a fairer society.

In 630 Muhammad recaptured Mecca. He became its ruler, and banned the worship of idols. He also kept non-believers out of the city and, to this day, only Muslims are allowed into it. Under Muhammad's rule, the Islamic empire gained control of most of the Arabian peninsula. After his death in 632 the Islamic religion began to spread beyond Arabia to Europe and India.

▶ *The Dome of the Rock in Jerusalem is the third most important Muslim shrine, after Mecca and Medina. It was built over the rock from which Muhammad is said to have ascended to heaven. Completed in 691 and decorated with complex geometric patterns, it is one of the earliest Muslim buildings still in existence.*

The Islamic Empire

After Muhammad's death, Muslim armies began to spread the Islamic religion. In 633 they moved north toward the Byzantine and Sassanian empires. Although the Byzantine empire was rich and powerful, it had just fought a costly war against the Sassanians. Early in 634, the Muslim leader, Abu Bakr, called for a *jihad*, or holy war. He sent an army to Syria and defeated the Byzantine forces at Ajnadain. By the end of 635 the Arabs had conquered most of Syria and Palestine and in 636 they defeated the Byzantine army again near the Yarmuk River. Continuing the successful military expeditions, the Muslims advanced east into Mesopotamia and west into Anatolia. By 643 they had gained control of Persia.

The Muslims pushed east into Afghanistan and reached India early in the 8th century. Another army headed west to capture Egypt from the Byzantines by 642. By 700 most of the north coast of Africa was under Muslim

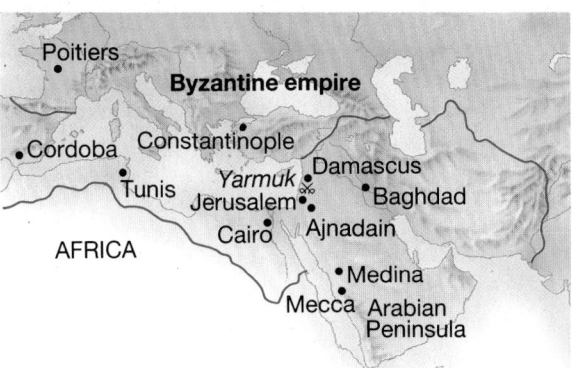

▲ *The Islamic empire spread rapidly. Its capital moved from Medina to Damascus and later to Baghdad.*

control. Berbers and Arabs from Morocco invaded Spain in 711. They did not reach the rest of Europe because they were defeated by the Franks at Poitiers in 732.

Most of the conquered peoples became Muslims and Arabic became the most important language in all parts of the Islamic empire except Persia. This helped ideas and knowledge to spread quickly and easily from one place to another.

▼ *The Arabs were fierce and fearless warriors. At the battle of Yarmuk, an Islamic army of 25,000 men defeated 50,000 Byzantine troops.*

▲ *As well as their religion, the Arabs brought their style of architecture to the lands they conquered. Mosques were built all over the Islamic world.*

627 Near East: The Byzantine emperor Heraclius defeats the Persians at Nineveh. China: T'ai Tsung the Great becomes emperor (to 649) and there is a period of military conquest. Arts and letters also flourish at this time.

629 Dagobert I reunites the Frankish kingdom.

630 Muhammad captures Mecca, and sets out the principles of Islam.

632 Muhammad dies and is succeeded as leader of Islam by his father-in-law, Abu Bakr. He is the first caliph and leads the Muslims until his death in 634.

633 England: The Mercians under Penda defeat the Northumbrians.

634 Omar I becomes caliph of Mecca (to 644). He continues the holy war first called by Abu Bakr.

By using an astrolabe Arab sailors could plot their position at sea.

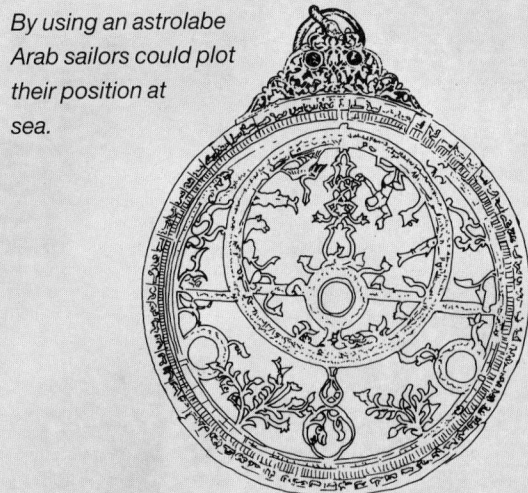

635 The Muslims begin the conquest of Syria, which takes three years, and of Persia, which takes eight years.

638 Islamic empire: The Muslims capture Jerusalem.

639 The Muslims start on their conquest of Egypt (completed in 642).

642 England: The Mercians under Penda again defeat the Northumbrians.

643 Islamic empire: The Arabs finally defeat the Persians at Nehawand.

644 Mecca: Following the assassination of Omar, Othman becomes caliph of Islam (to 656).

▲ *Islamic scientists built on the discoveries of Hellenistic and ancient Greece, Persia, and India. Through them this knowledge spread to Europe.*

645 Egypt: Byzantine forces recapture Alexandria, whose people have risen against the Arabs. Japan: The Taikwa edict of reform nationalizes land in Japan and reorganizes the government. The Japanese still tend to imitate the Chinese way of life.

646 Islamic empire: The Arabs recapture Alexandria.

649 The Arabs conquer Cyprus.

c.650 The Babylonian Talmud, a record of Jewish religious law, is finalized.

655 England: Oswy, King of Northumbria, defeats and kills Penda of Mercia. Islamic empire: The Arabs have their first naval victory when they defeat the Byzantine fleet at the battle of the Masts off the Egyptian coast near Alexandria.

656 Following the assassination of Othman by supporters of Muhammad's brother-in-law Ali, Ali becomes caliph of Islam (to 661).

661 Islamic empire: Mu'awiya founds the Umayyad dynasty (to 750). Mu'awiya rules as caliph until 680.

664 England: At the Synod of Whitby, King Oswy of Northumbria abandons the Celtic Christian Church and accepts Rome's form of Christianity with the pope as its leader. The Celtic Church, which has kept Christianity alive in the west and north of Britain since the Romans left, starts to decline.

668 Korea: The kingdom of Silla reunites the country and marks the start of the Silla period which lasts until 935.

669 The Greek monk Theodore of Tarsus is sent to England as archbishop of Canterbury to reorganize the Church in England and make it like the Church in the rest of western Europe.

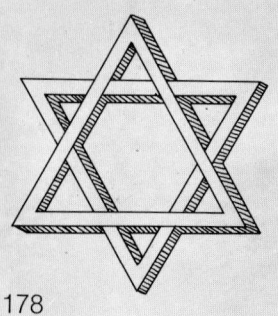

The Star of David, or the Shield of David, is a very ancient symbol. It first appeared as a symbol of Judaism around 960 B.C..

Persecution of the Jews

After the destruction of Jerusalem in A.D. 70, most Jews moved into exile. In what is called the Diaspora, or dispersion, they gradually spread out all over Europe and northern Africa. Large numbers of them went to Spain, where they were called Sephardim, and Germany, where they were known as Ashkenasim. They formed small, usually separate communities in various cities and kept to their own traditions in religion and learning.

Many were skilled craftsmen, but others earned their living by trade or by moneylending. Lending with interest was forbidden to Christians so Jews often filled an important but difficult service for European societies. Moneylending made some of the Jews unpopular, but at first they were usually allowed to live in peace.

By the 11th century, however, Europe had become very religious. Anyone who was not a Christian was also not part of European society. This made people turn against the Jews. They were forced to

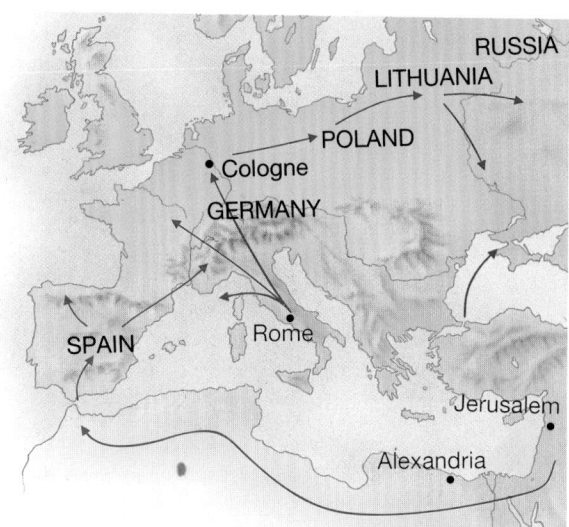

▲ *The arrows show the approximate movement of Jewish people during the Diaspora and, later on, in the early stages of persecution in the 12th century.*

▲ *Jewish boys went to schools where they were taught by the rabbis. They kept their traditions alive by learning to read, write, and speak Hebrew.*

▼ *In the persecution, many Jews were burned to death, like these in Cologne. Sometimes whole communities were wiped out in this way.*

GHETTOS

Once the persecution began, all the Jews in a city were forced to live in small areas of cities which became known as ghettos. They were usually in a poor part where nobody else wanted to live. Although the Jews were forced to stay there, the ghettos did not protect them.

YIDDISH

The Jews' own language was Hebrew. It has an alphabet of 22 letters and is written from right to left. The Ashkenasic Jews in eastern and central Europe developed a trading language called Yiddish. It was a mixture of German and Hebrew, but written in Hebrew letters.

live in separate areas known as ghettos.

The situation grew worse when many Christians began to blame the Jews for the death of Jesus, forgetting that Jesus himself was a Jew. As a result, Jews were persecuted, killed, or expelled from their homes. Many fled east to Poland and Lithuania. In the 12th century, even the Moors in Spain turned against them and in 1290 England became the first country to expel all Jews.

ARAB TOLERATION

Because of the persecution the Jews faced from Christian rulers many of them welcomed Arab conquests which brought greater toleration. In the Near East, Spain, and North Africa, especially Cairo, Jewish communities prospered. Under Islamic rule, Jews (and other recognized non-Muslim religions) enjoyed security and protection from their enemies, freedom of worship, and took a large part in deciding their own affairs. But they had to pay heavier taxes than Muslims and could not bear arms.

Communications

In western Europe the Roman empire left behind a good system of roads, but over the years they were neglected and the stones used by farmers and builders, until only dirt tracks were left. This made it easier to travel on foot or on horseback than in a wheeled vehicle. In wet weather the tracks became impassable. Then, many people stayed at home or traveled by boat.

At this time, not all countries had suitable horses. For example, those in China were generally small, while in America there were no horses at all until the arrival of Europeans. In Africa camels were more suitable for journeys across the desert, but horses were used in the grasslands.

Writing flourished in the Byzantine, Islamic, and Chinese empires. In northern Europe, however, it mainly survived in monasteries. Even kings such as William the Conqueror could not read or write. In court and on their travels they always dictated their letters and records of events to a scribe. Most communication was by word of mouth and so news traveled slowly.

◄ Bede was a monk at Jarrow in England. He is sometimes called the "Father of English History." This is because he wrote a book called the Ecclesiastical History of the English People. He was the first historian to date events from the birth of Jesus.

▼ Before printing came to Europe, all books had to be copied out by hand, which could take months or years to do. There was no paper and so animal skin, called parchment, was used. Mistakes and blots had to be scraped off with a sharp knife.

أرسلنا عليكم الريح

◀ Most writing was done with a quill, usually a goose feather. It was sharpened to a point and dipped in ink. It was resharpened with a little knife, later known as a penknife. The Chinese wrote with brushes made of horse hair.

▲ In many places it was easier to travel by water than overland. During this period the Grand Canal was rebuilt in China. It connected the main rivers and meant that people going north or south could avoid the dangerous coast. Many people made their homes on boats and lived on the canal.

▲ The earliest known printed book is the Diamond Sutra *which was printed in China in 868. The text and pictures were engraved on wooden blocks, which were then spread with ink and printed.*

WHEN IT HAPPENED

593 The Chinese start using woodblocks for printing. They have used paper for about 500 years.

618 The Sui emperor Yang Di is assassinated in China. He employed over 2,000,000 people to rebuild the Grand Canal.

731 Bede completes his *Ecclesiastical History of the English People*. It is written in Latin, but translated into English in the reign of King Alfred (871–899).

863 St. Cyril is sent to Moravia to convert the Slavs to Christianity. He introduces the Cyrillic alphabet for the Slav languages.

▲ *In China both horses and camels were used for transportation. The native horses were very small, but in the 2nd century* B.C. *large horses were introduced from Central Asia. Known as celestial horses, they became status symbols for officials and the rich. This ornament from the Tang dynasty shows one of them.*

673 The Arabs start an unsuccessful, five-year siege of Constantinople.

674 Islamic empire: The Arab conquest reaches the Indus River in what is now Pakistan.

675 The Bulgars settle south of the River Danube and found their first empire.

680 Islamic empire: Civil war breaks out among the Arabs.

685 Abdalmalik becomes caliph of Islam (to 705). In this time, he sets up a new system of administration in the Arab empire.

687 Pepin the Younger reunites the Frankish kingdom after his victory at the battle of Tertry.

A Central American funerary urn showing Cocijo, the rain god, who has a forked tongue. Funerary urns were at first carved by hand, but later on they were mass-produced using molds.

697 North Africa: The Arabs destroy Carthage, the former Vandal capital.

700 England: The Psalms are translated into Anglo-Saxon and the Lindisfarne Gospels are started. Germany: Thuringia becomes part of the Frankish kingdom. Islamic empire: The Arabs capture Tunis and Christianity in North Africa disappears almost completely.

8th century North America: The first true towns appear. Africa: Bantu Africans cross the River Limpopo taking iron working to southern Africa.

702 The Ethiopians attack Arab ships in the Red Sea. In return, the Arabs occupy Ethiopian ports. Arabic is declared the official language of Egypt.

707 North Africa: The Arabs capture Tangier.

709 North Africa: The Arabs capture Ceuta.

710 Spain: Roderic, the last Visigothic king, comes to the throne.

North America

The first true North American towns appeared in the middle Mississippi Valley around the beginning of the 8th century. Remains of them have been found as far apart as Cahokia in Illinois, Aztalan in Wisconsin, and Macon in Georgia. Now called the Temple Mound culture, each town had a central plaza with up to 20 rectangular mounds of earth arranged around it. On top of these were temples and houses for the dead. The plaza was separated from the rest of the town by a wooden fence, or palisade. Around the plaza up to 10,000 people lived in long houses with mud walls and thatched roofs. The villages were fortified and the people were farmers, growing corn, sunflowers, beans, and pumpkins. After about 800 they stopped using spear-throwers and darts for hunting and used bows and arrows instead.

In the southwest people known as the Anasazi started building houses above

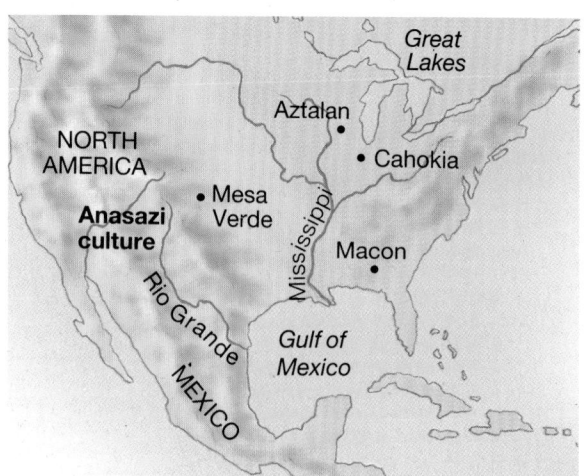

▲ *The Temple Mound culture gradually spread over much of the east of North America from the Great Lakes to the Gulf of Mexico. Many settlements were connected to each other by rivers. The pueblo builders lived in the southwest.*

◀ *Religious ceremonies played an important part in pueblo life. These masked men are performing a ceremony to try and make rain fall on the desert so that their crops will grow.*

ground around 700. They used stone and adobe to build pueblos, which were rather like apartment houses. By 1100 some of these were three or four stories high and housed up to 250 people. They lived by farming. Water was valuable because there was very little rainfall. They built irrigation channels to water their crops. The villages gradually grew in size as farming improved and the Anasazi started to build *kivas* or sunken ceremonial chambers.

▼ *The Cliff Palace at Mesa Verde, Colorado, was built by the Anasazi. It housed about 250 people. The cliff sheltered it in bad weather.*

711 Spain: The Moors (Arabs and Berbers from Morocco) invade. They defeat Roderic and end the Visigothic rule.

712 Birth of Rabi-ah al-Adawiyyah, the famous female Sufi (Muslim) mystic and religious teacher (dies 801). Islamic empire: The empire expands to include Sind, which is now in Pakistan.

716 The Arabs start a second siege of Constantinople (it fails in 717). Bulgaria: The Bulgar state is recognized by the Byzantine empire.

This silver plaque is one of the few things to have survived from the once wealthy Slav kingdom of Moravia, after it was invaded by the Magyars in 899. Coins and jewelry have also been found.

718 Spain: Pelayo, a Visigoth prince, founds the kingdom of Asturias in the Spanish mountains. The Moors hold most of the rest of Spain and Portugal and advance northward. The Christians defeat them in Spain at the battle of Covadonga.

725 Egypt: Coptic Christians rebel against Muslim rule.

726 England: King Ine of Wessex levies the first "Peter's Pence." This is a tax to support a religious college in Rome. Byzantine empire: Emperor Leo III begins the Iconoclast movement. This is a violent protest against sacred images and is opposed by Pope Gregory II.

730 Pope Gregory II excommunicates Leo III.

731 Bede completes his history of the Church in England.

732 France: Charles Martel, ruler of the Franks, defeats the Moors at Poitiers.

733 Byzantine empire: Emperor Leo III removes the Byzantine provinces in southern Italy from papal jurisdiction.

735 England: Death of Bede.

737 France: Charles Martel defeats the Moors again in a battle at Narbonne.

Bulgars and Russians

The people known as Slavs settled in eastern Europe and western Russia in the 8th century, after many generations of wandering across Europe. The first Slav state was in the south and was ruled by people known as Bulgars. Their state was recognized by the Byzantine empire in 716, but the two countries did not live at peace with each other. After the Bulgars had sacked Constantinople and killed the Byzantine emperor, the empire sent men to try and convert the Bulgars to Christianity. The most important were St. Cyril and St. Methodius. Eventually a Bulgarian king agreed to be baptized, but the quarrels did not end until the Bulgars were beaten by the Byzantines in 1014.

Other Slav communities developed in the east along many of the Russian rivers. These were ruled by Viking traders from Sweden who were known as the Rus. From this came the name Russia. The first leader of the Rus was

▲ *Vladimir, Grand Prince of Kiev, chose the Eastern Orthodox Church when he became a Christian.*

Rurik. He founded Novgorod and then Kiev and all Russian nobility afterward claimed to be descended from him.

In 988 the Russian prince Vladimir was converted to Christianity and married a Byzantine princess. He then forced Christianity on the rest of the Russian nobility. By the 11th century the Russian capital Kiev was a center of splendor and influence to rival Constantinople. Its greatest ruler was Yaroslav the Wise, who set up diplomatic relations with other courts. In this period many churches were built, the first Russian laws were written, and so were the first works of Russian literature.

◀ *Most of the Slav states followed the Eastern Orthodox religion. Churches and homes were decorated with religious paintings, called icons.*

▼ *When the Bulgars killed the Byzantine emperor Nicephorus in 811, they made his skull into a goblet for Krum, who was their king or khan. The Byzantine emperors called Bulgarian kings tsars or caesars.*

CYRILLIC

In the 9th century St. Cyril and his brother St. Methodius invented the Cyrillic alphabet which they mostly based on the letters of the Greek alphabet. Later, Christian missionaries sent to convert the Slavic people from Constantinople and Rome spread the alphabet throughout eastern Europe and Russia.

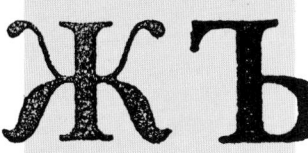

739 Egypt: The Christian Copts rebel for a second time against their Muslim rulers.

740 India: The Gurjaru-Prathi-Nara dynasty is founded in the north (to 1036).

741 Pepin the Short succeeds his father, Charles Martel, as "mayor of the palace." In reality this means that he rules the Franks, but he is not yet their king.

746 The Greeks retake Cyprus from Arabs.

This gold image of Charlemagne, inset with many semi-precious stones and made in Germany, is a reliquary. It was made in about 1350 to hold parts of his skull.

750 Islamic empire: The Umayyads are overthrown and the Abbasid dynasty is founded. The capital is Baghdad.

751 Pepin the Short is crowned king of the Franks. He founds the Carolingian dynasty to replace that of the Merovingians. Italy: The Lombards, led by Aistulf, capture Ravenna from the Byzantine empire. Asia: The Arabs defeat the Chinese at Samarkand.

756 Spain: Abd al-Rahman ibn Mu'awiya establishes an independent Umayyad dynasty at Cordoba. Italy: Pepin the Short's army protects Pope Stephen III from the Lombards. The Papal States are founded.

757 England: Offa becomes king of Mercia (to 796). During his reign he builds a large earthwork, known as Offa's Dyke, from the Dee River to the Severn River, to keep the Welsh out of his kingdom.

767 Egypt: Another Coptic revolt starts. It lasts until 772.

771 Pepin's son, Charles, becomes king of the Franks (to 814). He is also known as Charlemagne or Charles the Great.

772 Charlemagne conquers Saxony in Germany and converts the people to Christianity.

Charlemagne

After the Franks invaded part of the Roman empire they settled in what is now central France. Their leader, Clovis, founded the Merovingian dynasty. When he died, the kingdom was divided among his sons, but this weakened it so much that power fell into the hands of Charles Martel, who had led the Franks against the Muslims at Poitiers. In 751 Charles's son Pepin overthrew the Merovingians and began the Carolingian dynasty. After his death in 768 his sons, Carloman and Charlemagne, inherited his kingdom. Three years later Carloman died and Charlemagne took full control.

Charlemagne soon conquered the rest of France and then extended his kingdom into what is now Germany, Italy, and the Netherlands. In central Europe he forced the Saxons and the Avars to accept Christianity. He supported the pope and extended the power of the church in his own kingdom. In return, the pope recognized

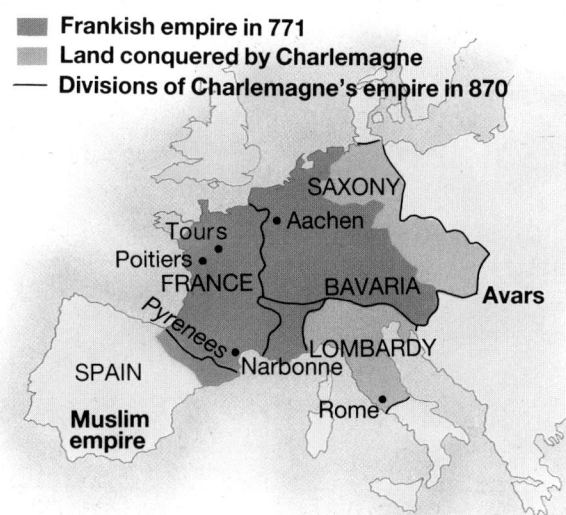

■ Frankish empire in 771
■ Land conquered by Charlemagne
— Divisions of Charlemagne's empire in 870

▲ *After Charlemagne's empire was split, the boundaries of present-day France, Italy, and Germany became recognizable.*

EDUCATION

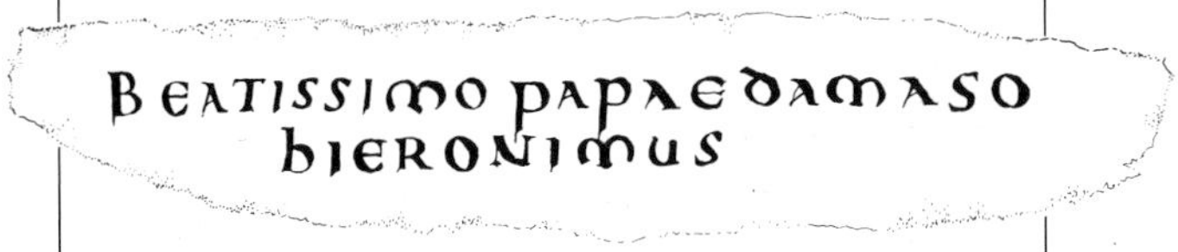

BEATISSIMO PAPAE DAMASO
HIERONIMUS

Scholars at Charlemagne's court in Aachen developed a new style of script for use in books. It was known as miniscule and was formed with clear, rounded letters. At this time all books were written in Latin. Charlemagne himself learned to speak and read Latin, but he did not manage to write it.

▼ *When Pope Leo III crowned Charlemagne as Holy Roman emperor in Rome on Christmas Day 800 he laid the foundations for the Holy Roman Empire which included Germany, France, and part of Italy.*

Charlemagne's power in 800 by creating him Holy Roman emperor. Charlemagne also encouraged scholars by founding schools in cathedrals and monasteries. The palace school in his capital city of Aachen was the most important center of learning in western Christendom.

After Charlemagne's death in 814, his empire was troubled by Viking raids and civil war. In 843 it was divided among his three grandsons. They and their descendants ruled Germany until 911 and France until 987.

▲ *Charlemagne was a great military leader and his kingdom became the most powerful in Europe. He also tried to improve conditions in his lands, where most of the people were poor farmers.*

Food and Farming

The use of iron tools made it possible to create much more farmland in this period. In Britain, both the Anglo-Saxons and the Vikings began to farm more and more land. When the Normans invaded, the feudal system (*see* pages 226–227) was introduced. In Europe horses and pigs were the most important animals but by 1100, sheep had become more important, because of their wool.

In China new irrigation schemes created more land for rice growing. In North America Native Americans grew corn, and in Central America crops such as squash, beans, and tomatoes were grown.

▲ Under Norman rule, woods were cleared to provide additional land for farming. People known as bordars *were encouraged to set up smallholdings in clearings on the edge of woods.*

▼ *The development of plows with iron plowshares and wheels, pulled by a team of oxen made it easier and quicker to plow through heavy soil. This meant more wheat could be sown.*

▲ *Grain crops were cut with a scythe* (above) *or a sickle* (right) *which had metal blades. The grain was then threshed with a wooden flail* (left) *to separate it from the chaff (the outer husks). When tossed up into the air, the lighter chaff blew away.*

◄ Honey was the only source of sweetening in Europe at this time, so many people kept bees. Hives were often made of basketwork, and were known as skeps.

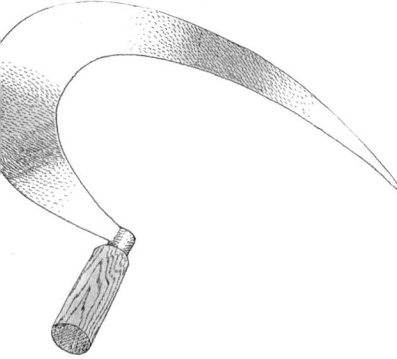
◄ Many people kept a pig, because it could forage for its own food in the woods and on common land. In winter most of the animals were killed because there was not enough food for them.

WHEN IT HAPPENED

c. 501 Many farmers go to England after their villages in northern Europe are flooded.

610 In China, a network of canals allows rice to be traded widely.

Late 8th century A shortage of good farmland is one reason why the Vikings start to leave their homelands.

1066 William the Conqueror brings the feudal system to England.

1100 Sheep become important as the European wool trade expands.

▼ The Norman system of farming, where large fields were divided up into long strips to be farmed by villeins or peasants, can still be seen in England today.

▼ In Europe, harvest was a busy time. The grain was needed for bread and beer. If there was not enough, people starved in winter.

773	Charlemagne adds the kingdom of Lombardy to his Frankish empire.
778	Spain: The Moors and the Basques defeat the Franks at the battle of Roncesvalles, in the Pyrenees.
779	England: Offa, King of Mercia, becomes king of all England.
780	Constantine VI becomes the new Byzantine emperor. He is only a child and is influenced by his mother, Irene.
782	Charlemagne summons the monk and scholar Alcuin of York to head the palace school at Aachen. This event marks the revival of learning in mainland Europe.
786	Harun al-Rashid becomes caliph of Baghdad. His rule lasts until 809.

An elaborately decorated Islamic tile from Persia (present-day Iran). It was made in the 12th century and may have been used as a tombstone.

787	Papacy: The Council of Nicaea orders the restoration and use of images in churches.
788	Bavaria becomes part of Charlemagne's empire.
789	England: The first Vikings arrive. They land on the south coast and kill the messenger who is sent to meet them.
791	The Byzantine emperor Constantine VI imprisons his mother because of her cruelty, and assumes power.
793	Viking raiders attack the monastery of Lindisfarne off the coast of Northumbria. They kill some of the monks and take others away to sell as slaves. They also steal the monastery treasures. This is their first serious raid in England. The *Anglo-Saxon Chronicle* records that the people of Northumbria had been "sorely frightened" by "immense whirlwinds, flashes of lightning, and fiery dragons . . . flying in the air" just before the raid.

The Abbasid Dynasty

In 750 the Abbasid family took power from the Umayyad family and started a new dynasty of caliphs which ruled the Islamic empire until 1258. The Abbasids were descended from Muhammad's uncle, al-Abbas. Under the rule of their first caliph, al-Mansur, the Abbasids moved the capital of the empire from Damascus to the newly-founded city of Baghdad. Their most famous ruler was Harun al-Rashid who was the fifth Abbasid caliph and succeeded his brother, al-Hadi, in 786. At first he ruled with the aid of the wealthy Barmecide family, but in 803 they fell from favor and he imprisoned them all. After that date, he ruled alone.

In 791 Harun al-Rashid became involved in a war against the Byzantine empire. This war lasted until 806, when he finally defeated the Byzantines. At the same time he had to fight against rebellion in his own empire when Tunisia

HARUN AL-RASHID

When Harun al-Rashid became caliph in 786, he ended a decade of uncertainty and rivalry in the Islamic empire. The military had backed his older brother, al-Hadi, but the officials wanted Harun to become caliph. When al-Hadi died suddenly, it was rumored that Harun had plotted to murder him, but this was never proven. Harun soon won the support of the military and brought political unity to his empire. He is even thought to have sent ambassadors to the court of Charlemagne. After Harun's death, however, rival caliphates appeared in Spain and North Africa, but the world of Islam was still bound together by its rich culture.

ISLAMIC ART

At a time when Christian countries were often divided by disagreements between popes and emperors, Islam and its culture flourished. Muslim artists concentrated on intricate designs and beautiful handwriting. They decorated books, tiles, and pottery, such as this Persian bowl.

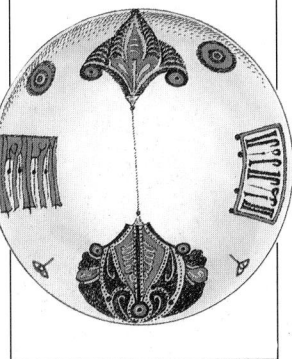

began a struggle for independence, but he managed to defeat this, too.

In spite of these wars, Harun al-Rashid found time to encourage learning and the arts. His court was also a center for the Islamic culture which unified the empire. It was his court in Baghdad that was the setting for many of the stories told in *The Thousand and One Nights* which are still enjoyed today. Legend says that the stories were written by a woman called Sheherezade. She married a king who had been so unhappy with all his other wives that he had killed each one on the first morning after their wedding. Sheherezade prevented this by telling the king a different story every night.

▶ *Arab traders carried cargo and passengers across the Indian Ocean in ships called* dhows. *They also helped to spread Islamic culture and ideas.*

▲ *The stories for* The Thousand and One Nights *came from many different countries, including India, Syria, and Egypt. The stories feature Ali Baba, Sinbad the Sailor, and Aladdin.*

796 England: The death of Offa ends Mercian supremacy.

797 The Byzantine empress Irene has her son Constantine blinded and then rules by herself (deposed 802).

800 onward Europe: Feudalism (*see* pages 224–225) is established by the Franks mainly for military purposes. Horses start to be bred as big as possible for war. The lateen (or triangular) sail comes into use in the Mediterranean. It makes it possible for boats to beat into the wind. Africa: The trans-Sahara trade grows between west and north Africa. Cities such as Gao develop. Ghana is known as the "Land of Gold" because of its growing wealth. India: The north is divided into many little states.

A beautiful gold Viking ring. Viking chiefs often gave rings or swords as a reward.

800 Pope Leo III crowns Charlemagne Holy Roman emperor of the west, recognizing his protection and expansion of Christian Europe. Germany: The Vikings invade.

802 England: Egbert becomes king of Wessex (to 839).

803 Islamic empire: Harun al-Rashid suddenly ends the power of the Barmecide family in Baghdad.

813 Mamun the Great becomes caliph of Baghdad (to 834). His 20-year-reign is a great period for art and also a time of liberal religious attitudes.

814 Louis the Pious, son of Charlemagne, inherits the Frankish empire (rules to 840). During his reign the political importance of his empire declines.

The Kingdom of Ghana

The ancient kingdom of Ghana was much farther north than the present country of that name. It was probably founded in the 4th century and was first ruled by the Maga dynasty. The Maga were a Berber family, but most of the people of Ghana were from the Soninke tribes. In 770 the Soninke ousted the Maga dynasty and began to build up an empire. This grew under the rule of Kaya Maghan Sisse who was king around 790. Its capital was Koumbi Saleh which was populated by Africans and by Berbers, who by this time had become Muslims.

The empire grew rich on trade and commerce and in the 9th century Arab traders described it as "the land of gold." The gold came from Asante and Senegal to the south and west. To the north was the Sahara Desert and many of the routes across it from the Near East and the Mediterranean ended in Ghana.

ETHIOPIA

Ethiopia became a Christian country in 350, but after Egypt became Muslim in 642, it was cut off from the main centers of Christianity for 800 years. In the Middle Ages a legend grew up about a king called Prester John who was said to rule over a Christian empire in the heart of Africa. Many Europeans thought that Ethiopia was this country and later medieval explorers and emissaries of the pope were sent to try to find him.

Ghana reached the peak of its powers in the 10th century when it controlled both the gold and the salt trade. Other goods which passed through Ghana included woolen cloth and luxury items from Europe, and leather goods and slaves from countries to the south. In 990 Ghana took over the Berber kingdom of Andaghost and at its greatest extent was 500 miles (800 km) across. In 1070, however, Ghana fell to the Berber family of Almoravids and much later, in 1240, it became part of the Mali empire.

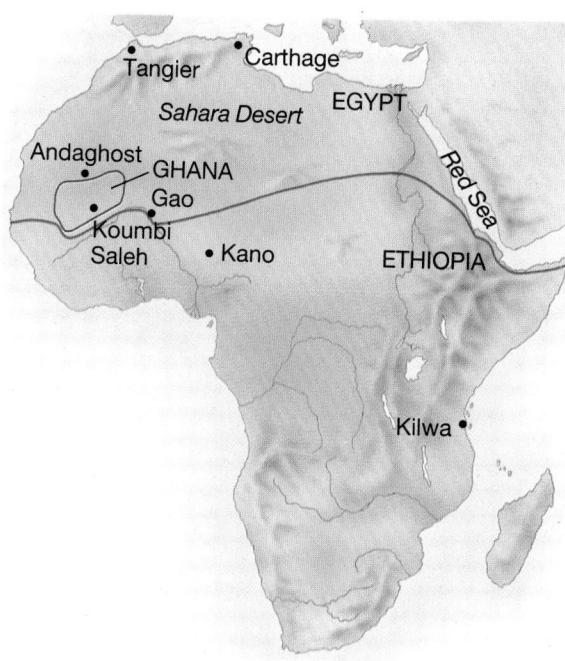

▲ Some important places in Africa during this period. By 1100 most of North Africa was Muslim, as indicated by the blue line on the map.

▼ Arab traders transported goods across the Sahara Desert on camels. They went in large groups called caravans and could travel 200 miles (320 km) in a week.

SALT

Salt was an essential commodity, found in vast quantities in the desert. A huge trade network was set up to bring it to Ghana by camel. From here it was then taken to countries farther south on horseback.

SLAVES

People captured in southern Africa were brought to Ghana to be sold as slaves. Arab traders took them across the Sahara to be sold again as servants to rich people in the Mediterranean and Near East.

Scotland

The early inhabitants of Scotland formed a number of tribes, each with its own leader. Very little is known about them until the 7th century when some of the tribes united to make two kingdoms north of a line joining the Clyde to the Forth. These kingdoms were Pictavia, which was the land of the people known as Picts, and Dalriada, which was a Christian kingdom made up of people called Scots who had come originally from Ireland. In the south, the Britons colonized the west, which they called Strathclyde, and the Angles settled in the east, which they called Bernicia. Vikings settled in the far north and west.

In 843 Kenneth MacAlpin, King of the Scots, also claimed the throne of Pictavia because his grandmother had been a Pictish princess. This united all the land north of the Clyde and Forth and it became known as Scotland. By 1018 Kenneth's successors, Kenneth II and Malcolm II, had united most of present-

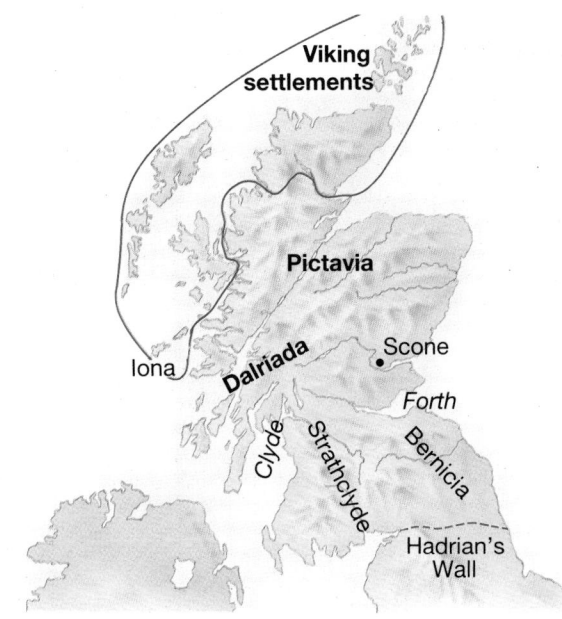

▲ While the king of Scotland ruled the mainland, many of the islands were occupied by Viking people. In time these people too became part of Scotland.

▼ In the 9th century many Vikings moved to the Orkney and Shetland islands to the north of Scotland. They lived by farming and trading with Viking neighbors. Ruled by the king of Norway, the islands became the center of the Norwegian empire based on the North Sea.

day Scotland. Malcolm's son, Duncan, was killed by a chief called Macbeth in a battle at Bothnagowan in 1040. Macbeth then ruled Scotland until he was killed by Duncan's son, Malcolm III, in 1057. Malcolm III was called Cranmore meaning "big head." He married a Saxon, Margaret, who was later canonized as a saint. In 1072 he became a vassal of the English king, William the Conqueror. This did not stop Malcolm raiding England, where he was killed in 1093.

BODY PAINT

The Romans gave the name Pict to all the people who lived north of a line from the Clyde to the Forth Rivers. The name means "painted people" and the Romans used it because the Picts tattooed their bodies with patterns in different colored vegetable dyes.

Macbeth

Macbeth became king in 1040 after killing Duncan in revenge for the murder of his brother-in-law. Macbeth ruled for 17 years and was a strong and good king.

▶ *The Scots moved to western Scotland from Ireland and forced the Picts to move farther east. They were fierce warriors who dressed like the man in this picture and they were the first people in Scotland to accept Christianity. In the 8th century the Picts claimed all Scotland from their court at Scone, but in the 9th century the king of the Scots was powerful enough to claim the Pictish throne and unite northern Scotland.*

817 Louis the Pious divides the Frankish empire among his sons Lothair, Pepin and Louis the German. Later, in 829, a share is also given to his fourth son, Charles the Bald.

828 England: Egbert of Wessex is recognized as overlord of the other English kings.

835 The start of 15 years of Viking attacks on England.

839 England: Ethelwulf, son of Egbert, becomes king of Wessex (to 858).

840 Lothair I is emperor of the Franks (to 855), but his brothers are allied against him. Central Europe: Under Mojmir, a confederation of Slav tribes is formed in Bohemia, Moravia, Slovakia, Hungary, and Transylvania.

The monastery on the island of Iona, off western Scotland.

841 Ireland: The Vikings start to build bases, called *long-phorts*, where they stay over winter. The earliest is Dublin, which soon attracts merchants and craftsmen. The others are Limerick, Cork, Wexford, and Waterford. China: Wu Tsung persecutes all religions except Buddhism (to 846).

843 The Treaty of Verdun leads to the division of the Frankish, or Holy Roman, Empire. Louis the German rules east of the Rhine River, Charles the Bald rules France, and Lothair rules Italy, Provence, Burgundy, and Lorraine. Scotland: Kenneth MacAlpin, King of the Scots, defeats the Picts and unites the country.

850 England: The Vikings stay over winter for the first time. Vikings from Sweden go to Russia. Africa: The Bantu build Great Zimbabwe.

People

Most people dressed for comfort, not fashion. In northern Europe the women wove woolen and linen cloth and made it into simple garments for their families. Men began to wear trousers made from either cloth or leather, with a tunic or doublet over the top. Women wore long dresses with belts and shawls. Both men and women wore cloaks in cold weather. People who lived in hot climates wore long, flowing clothes and cotton began to be used. In southern Europe, Roman fashions still influenced the way people dressed.

Clothing in the Byzantine empire was very decorative. Crowns decorated with pearls and precious stones were later a model for the crowns of northern rulers. In China rich people wore thin silk robes with long sleeves in hot weather and thick silk ones when it was cold.

▲ During the 11th century people started to wear clothes made from sheep's wool. First, the wool was combed and spun. Then it was dyed with vegetable dyes and woven. This meant that checks, stripes, and other patterns such as tartans could be woven into the fabric.

▼ Many people had leather shoes or boots. Only the poorest had to go barefoot.

▲ Ironing boards were used during this period. The stone was known as a smoothing stone.

◄ Viking jewelry was often practical. Two large brooches held together a woman's tunic while a chain held keys, scissors, and a comb.

529 St. Benedict founds the order of Benedictine monks. Monasteries become an important part of medieval life.

c. 750 The feudal system appears in Europe. It changes the lives of many people and leads to stricter government of countries.

9th century Vikings who visit Constantinople start to wear Arab-style clothing.

11th century In Song dynasty China, people believe small feet are a sign of great beauty. Girls' feet are bound so they will not grow.

▲ *Chinese men and women were entertained separately. They sat on the floor or on little stools. These Tang court ladies are listening to a music concert.*

▶ *In cold climates, life centered around the hearth, placed in the middle of the room. It gave out heat and light and was also used for cooking meals. The family would sit around the fire when carrying out their daily tasks.*

851	The crossbow is used in France.
855	Louis II, son of Lothair, becomes emperor of the Franks until 875. Lothair's lands are again divided.
858	England: Ethelbald, eldest son of Ethelwulf is king of Wessex (to 860). Japan: Fujiwara Yoshifusa is regent.
860	England: Ethelbert, second son of Ethelwulf is king of Wessex (to 865). Iceland: Norwegian Vikings arrive.

Japanese horses wore many ornaments, especially bells, on their harnesses. This horse bell would probably have been worn on the horse's hindquarters.

862	Russia: Swedish Vikings, led by Rurik, seize power in the north and found a trading post at Novgorod. From there they attack Constantinople.
865	England: Ethelred I, third son of Ethelwulf, rules Wessex (to 871).
867	England: Viking invaders conquer Northumbria, East Anglia, and Mercia. Photius, head of the Eastern Orthodox Church, quarrels with the pope. In 879 they excommunicate each other.
869	Malta is part of the Islamic empire.
871	England: The Danes attack Wessex. Ethelred defeats them at Ashdown. Later Ethelred dies and his brother Alfred becomes king of Wessex (to 899).
874	The Vikings settle in Iceland.
875	Charles the Bald becomes emperor of the Franks (to 877). Anarchy (disorder) follows his death.
878	England: Alfred defeats the Danes at Edington. By the Treaty of Wedmore, England is divided into Wessex in the south and the Danelaw in the north. The Vikings can live in the Danelaw on condition that they become Christians.

Fujiwara Japan

From the beginning of the 4th century, Japan was ruled by an emperor. If an emperor died while his oldest son was still very young, a regent was chosen to help the child rule. The regent was usually from the emperor's family. In the 9th century the Fujiwara family became very important at the Japanese court when Fujiwara Yoshifusa's daughter married the emperor. When the emperor died in 858, their son became emperor in his place. Fujiwara Yoshifusa then became the first regent from outside the imperial family. This was the start of what is called the Fujiwara period in Japan.

More Fujiwara daughters were married to emperors and the power of the Fujiwara family grew. Soon it became customary for every emperor to have a Fujiwara regent. While the regent controlled the running of the country, the emperor spent his time on religious matters. For three centuries the Fujiwara

▼ *Court life was very formal, with rules for everything. This man is reading a letter. Even the color of the paper and the way it was folded were very important.*

family dominated the imperial court.

During the Fujiwara period art and literature flourished in Japan. Many people wrote poetry and some of the ladies at the court wrote books that are still read in Japan today. Families who were in favor with the Fujiwaras prospered until late in the 11th century. Then other families began to grow more powerful. These families fought among themselves and the Fujiwaras could not control them any longer. In the 12th century there were many rebellions until finally war broke out and the Fujiwara period ended.

▼ *This clay figure is of a god who protected holy buildings from demons. Most Japanese people practiced the Shinto religion. This was influenced by Buddhism which was used for funerals and other ceremonies. The clothing worn by this figure is typical of a Japanese warrior from the 8th century.*

THE TALE OF GENJI

Japanese courtiers spent a lot of time entertaining each other. A novel called *The Tale of Genji* tells us a great deal about the sort of life they led. It was written by Lady Murasaki who was a lady-in-waiting to an 11th century empress. She wrote the story to be read out in installments. At this time, many women were novelists, diarists, or poets.

GARDENS

Buddhist gardens in Japan were very distinctive. They were usually set out to the south of the house and were rectangular or oval. Each had a narrow pond or lake with an island in the middle. Usually a man-made hill and waterfall stood on the northern shore of the lake.

EARTHQUAKES

During the Fujiwara period the capital city, Kyoto, suffered many fires and earthquakes. Many people thought these were caused by the spirits of officials who had been banished by the Fujiwaras. To calm the spirits, shrines were built and offerings made to them.

Magyars and Bohemians

The Magyars were a race of people who came from the steppes (open plains) of Russia, between the Volga River and the Ural Mountains. Under their leader, Prince Arpad, they entered what we now call Hungary in the late 9th century. This was a fertile area where wheat and grape vines had been grown since Roman times. This area also had rich veins of gold and silver.

Although the Magyars only numbered around 25,000 they soon defeated the local inhabitants. They raided their neighbors for slaves and treasures and also harassed the kingdom of Germany. After the German king, Otto I, defeated them at the battle of Lechfeld in 955, however, they decided to make peace. In the year 1000, Pope Sylvester crowned Stephen as the first king of Hungary. He unified the country and introduced

▲ The Slav states of Bohemia, Moravia, and Poland looked to western Europe for their culture while the rest were strongly influenced by Byzantine culture.

▼ The Magyars' arrival in Hungary is shown in a manuscript called the Kepes Kronika. It shows the army accompanied by groups of women and children, and cattle. Set in a flower-strewn landscape, the picture gives a peaceful impression, at odds with the Magyars' reputation as fierce warriors and raiders.

▲ *According to Hungarian tradition, this crown was given to King Stephen by Pope Sylvester at his coronation on Christmas Day 1000, as a reward for converting his people to Christianity.*

880 Italy: The Byzantine emperor Basil drives the Arabs out of the mainland.

881 Charlemagne's empire (except Burgundy) is reunited when the emperor of Germany, Charles III, becomes king of the Franks.

886 England: Alfred recaptures London from the Danes.

889 Hungary: The Magyars led by Arpad invade the Hungarian plain.

890 Nailed horseshoes are used for the first time. They protect horses' feet and so longer journeys can be made. The shoes are cheap enough for peasants to afford them for their farm horses.

891 A history of England known as the *Anglo-Saxon Chronicle* starts under Alfred's instructions.

893 France: Charles the Simple becomes king. He reigns until 929.

899 England: Alfred the Great dies and Edward the Elder is king of Wessex (to 924). Moravia: Magyars from the east invade.

Wenceslas

Wenceslas became prince of Bohemia in 921. He tried to make his people Christian. His brother opposed him and killed him in 929. Wenceslas was later made a saint.

HORSEMANSHIP

The Magyars were expert horsemen. They came from the flat Russian steppe where the nature of the countryside made riding easy. Their skills on horseback helped them to go raiding in central France and Italy. They also fought on horseback and could usually outride their enemies.

The Magyars rode strong horses, which could cover many miles. This helped the Magyars to carry out their devastating raids.

Christianity to it. His reign was a time of peace and prosperity and, after his death, he was made into a saint.

North of Hungary were the Slav states of Moravia and Bohemia. In the 9th century Bohemia was part of the Moravian empire, but in 1029 Bohemia became stronger and made Moravia part of its kingdom. Christianity, introduced in the 9th century, was not completely accepted until the country came under the influence of the Holy Roman Empire.

900 Central America: The Mayas emigrate into Yucatán. North America: The Vikings arrive in Greenland. Spain: Alfonso III of Castile begins to reconquer the country from the Moors. Europe: Castles become seats of the nobility. In eastern Europe, the Bulgars accept the Eastern Orthodox Church. Africa: The Hausa kingdom of Daura is founded in northern Nigeria. Zimbabwe in southern Africa becomes a major power. Islamic empire: The tales of *The Thousand and One Nights* are started.

Anglo-Saxon Britain

After the Romans left Britain in the 5th century, Germanic peoples began invading the country. The Jutes settled mainly in Hampshire, Kent, and the Isle of Wight, while the Angles and Saxons had by 600 settled most of the rest of England. The invasions pushed many of the Romano-British people into Wales and Ireland.

England was divided into seven kingdoms: Essex, Wessex, and Sussex, which were ruled by the Saxons; East Anglia, Mercia, and Northumbria, which were ruled by Angles; and Kent, which was ruled by the Jutes.

These kingdoms often fought battles to decide which one of them had authority over all the others and claim the title *Bretwalda* (Lord of Britain) for their king. In the 7th century the Northumbrian kings Edwin, Oswald, and Oswy claimed supremacy, while in the 8th century the Mercian kings Ethelbald and Offa claimed to be in control.

In 789, however, the first Vikings appeared in England and by the 850s they had started to settle. When Alfred became king of Wessex in 871, the Vikings were threatening to overrun his kingdom and he fought nine battles against them in one year. He finally

▲ The Angles, Jutes, and Saxons were skilled metal-workers who used iron for tools and weapons. They also used bronze, gold, and silver to decorate items such as this helmet from around 625.

▼ Most of the invaders were farmers looking for new land. Their society was divided into three classes – noblemen, churls (yeomen or freemen), and slaves. In this picture, farm workers are harvesting wheat.

▲ *The seven kingdoms of England. From 878 Northumbria, East Anglia, and much of Mercia came under Viking control and formed the Danelaw.*

defeated them in 878, and made them sign the Treaty of Wedmore. This allowed the Vikings to live in the north and east of the country, which became known as the Danelaw. Alfred ruled the rest. The Danelaw was gradually won back from the Vikings, and the last Viking king of York died in 954. From that date, England was one kingdom.

CHRISTIANITY

Christianity first came to Britain in Roman times, but the Angles, Saxons, and Jutes worshiped many gods. In 597 Pope Gregory sent Augustine to convert the Anglo-Saxons to Christianity. Several monasteries were set up and crosses were erected where monks preached or said Mass. The Ruthwell cross *(left)* was carved in the 8th century and is decorated with scenes from the Gospels and poetry.

901	England: Edward the Elder takes the title "King of the Angles and Saxons."
906	Germany: The Magyars, from the area around the Volga River, begin invading.
907	Russia: Commercial treaties are made between Kiev and Constantinople. Silks, spices, and silver from the east are traded for slaves and furs from the north. China: The fall of the Tang dynasty leads to civil wars which last until 960. At the same time, the Mongols begin their capture of Inner Mongolia and northern China (completed 1126).
909	Islamic empire: The Fatimids start to conquer north Africa by seizing power in Tunisia. They claim descent from Muhammad's daughter, Fatima, and found the Fatimid dynasty (to 1171).

This lion, symbol of St. Mark, is taken from the manuscript used by the Anglo-Saxon monk St. Willibrod on his travels as a missionary.

910	France: Cluny Abbey is founded. It becomes the center of the Cluniac order which later builds monasteries in other parts of western Europe.
911	France: The King of France grants Normandy to the Viking Rollo and his followers, on condition that they help to keep the other Vikings out of the country.
912	Rollo is baptized with the name Robert.
913	England: Edward the Elder recaptures Essex from the Danes.
916	Africa: The Arab scholar, al-Masudi, travels from the Gulf down the African coast as far as Mozambique.

Religion

At the beginning of this period, only some parts of Europe were Christian. The Vikings, together with the Angles, Saxons, and Jutes, had many different gods. The main Viking ones were Odin, Thor, and Frey. Some early Vikings also worshiped Tyr. The Angles, Saxons, and Jutes had the same gods, but called Odin, Woden, and Tyr was called Tiw. From the names of these four gods, we get Tuesday, Wednesday, Thursday, and Friday. By 1100, however, the whole of Europe had accepted Christianity, though the old gods were often remembered in place names. Beyond Europe, Buddhism had begun to spread north and east from India. It became the official religion of Japan in 594 and China in 624.

In Arabia, Muhammad, the founder of Islam, was born in Mecca in 570. He started preaching about Allah, the one true god, after a dream in which the Archangel Gabriel spoke to him. After Muhammad's death in 632, his followers carried his teachings to other countries and built up an Islamic empire which stretched from Spain to northern India.

▲ A Viking cremation was described by the Arab ambassador Ibn Fadlan. On the ship with the dead chief was food and belongings for the next life and a slave girl who was sacrificed. The pyre was lit by his nearest relative, who was naked.

▲ Muslims believe that the Archangel Gabriel was Allah's messenger. In this painting from Baghdad, Gabriel is dressed as a Muslim.

▶ Before they became Christians, the Angles buried their kings in ships with their possessions, such as this gold clasp from the famous burial at Sutton Hoo, in England. They believed that the treasures would go with the king to the afterlife.

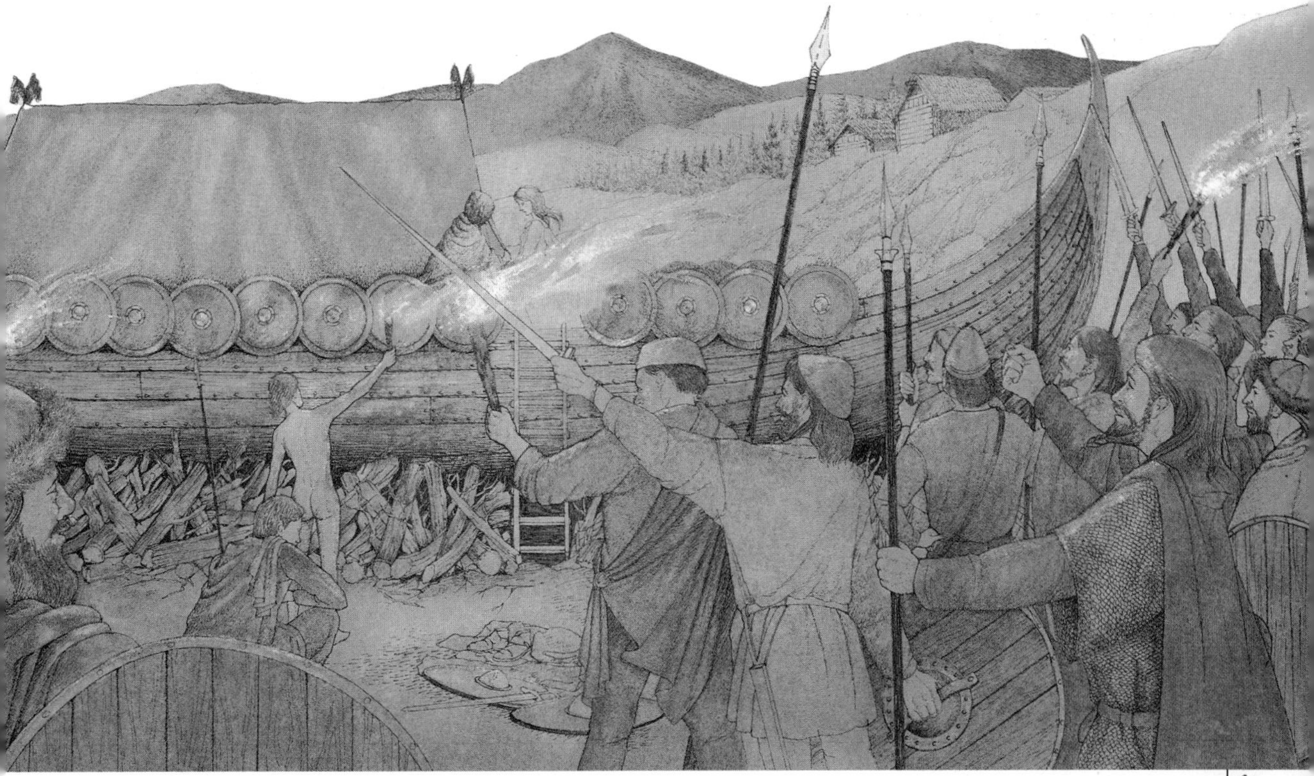

► *During the Sui dynasty, Buddhism became the official religion of China. Over 100,000 statues of Buddha were made, some carved out of solid rock. Many of them showed Buddha with a laughing face. Almost 4,000 temples were built in this period. There were also many temples in caves along the Silk Road.*

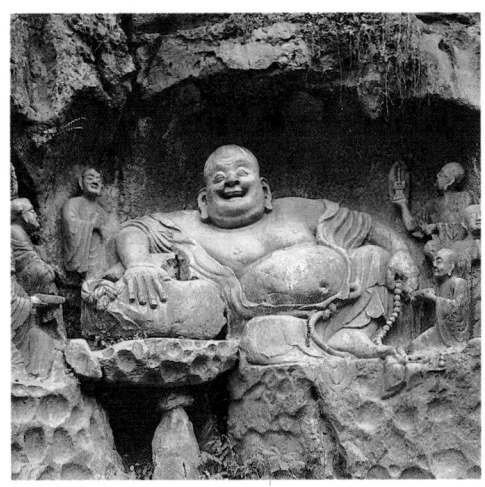

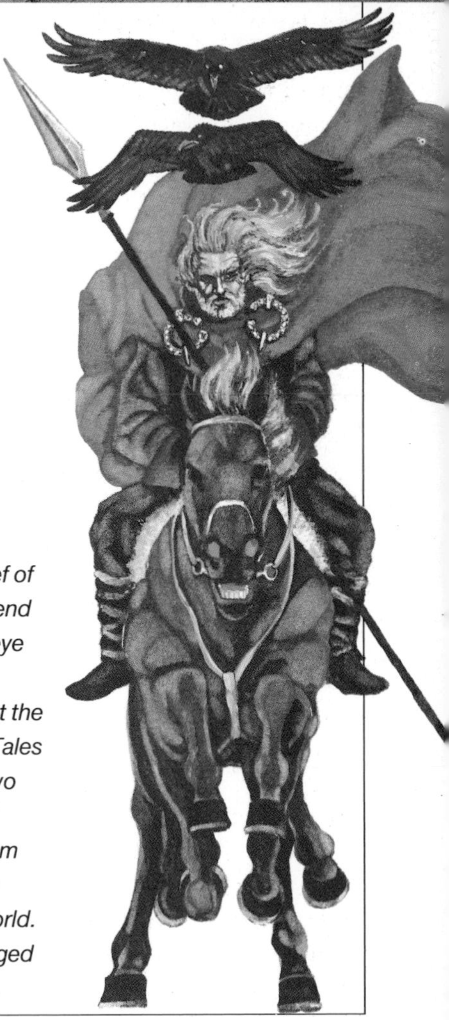

► *Odin was the chief of the Viking gods. Legend says that he lost his eye to gain knowledge in payment for a drink at the Well of Knowledge. Tales also say he owned two ravens, Thought and Memory. He sent them out daily to report on happenings in the world. He rode an eight-legged horse called Sleipnir.*

WHEN IT HAPPENED

532	Justinian starts to build the church of St. Sophia in Constantinople.
622	Muhammad's flight to Medina marks the start of the Islamic calendar.
632	Muhammad dies.
664	King of Northumbria accepts the Roman Catholic Church, abandoning Celtic one.
1000	The Vikings in Iceland become Christian.
1096	The First Crusade to the Holy Land starts.

The Holy Roman Empire

Although the idea of a Holy Roman Empire was founded by Charlemagne in 800, the land he ruled was usually called the Carolingian empire. Its area covered present-day France, Austria, Germany, and Switzerland, but after his death the empire gradually broke up and France became separated.

Otto I, who became king of Germany in 936, wanted to revive the old Roman empire. In 962 he had the pope crown him Emperor Augustus, founding a line of emperors that lasted until 1806. Otto was a powerful ruler who brought stability by subduing his vassals (the

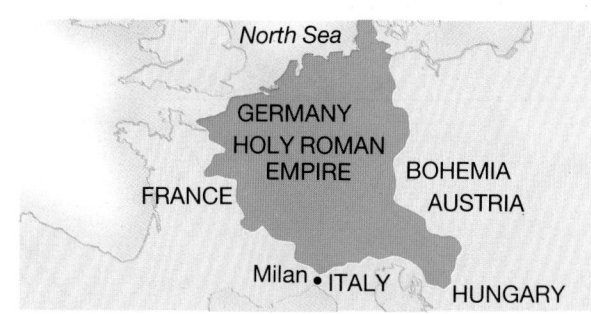

▲ By 1100 the Holy Roman Empire stretched from the North Sea and the Baltic, nearly to the Mediterranean. At this time it was ruled from Germany.

▼ The Holy Roman emperor had the right to be crowned by the pope in Rome. However, many emperors and popes disagreed with each other over questions of authority. This led to problems, especially if one side wanted to interfere in the other's affairs.

▲ *Otto I, also known as Otto the Great, came to the throne of Germany in 936. He gave a lot of land to the bishops to try to limit the power of the nobles.*

nobility who owed him allegiance) and defeating the Magyars. He conquered Bohemia, Austria, and north Italy. His empire became the Holy Roman Empire.

The empire was made up of many separate duchies, counties, and bishoprics (districts ruled by a bishop). Although they all owed allegiance to the emperor, they were independent of each other. After Otto died there were clashes as one or another struggled for power. The emperor was chosen by members of the nobility called electors, but they usually "chose" the king of Germany.

The popes who helped to create the Holy Roman Empire thought that its emperors would help them to rule over Christendom. Instead, the powerful Holy Roman emperors were often in dispute with the popes and were sometimes even at war with them.

918 England: Aethelflaed, daughter of King Alfred dies. During his reign this "Lady of the Mercians" helped to unite England by rebuilding the fortifications of Chester and building new fortified towns, including Warwick and Stafford. She fought in Wales and led her own troops to capture Derby from the Vikings. She also received the peaceful submission of Leicester and York.

A Peruvian pottery figure of a god made between 600 and 1000. Its body is decorated with corn. Most Peruvians were farmers and worshiped many different land gods.

919 Germany: Henry I, or Henry the Fowler, becomes king (till 936).

920 Africa: The golden age of the kingdom of Ghana begins. It lasts until 1050.

922 North Africa: The Fatimids seize power in Morocco.

924 England: Athelstan, son of Edward the Elder, becomes king of Wessex. He annexes Northumbria, and forces the kings of Wales, Strathclyde, and Scotland to submit to him.

929 Bohemia: Wenceslas, attempting to convert his people to Christianity by asking German missionaries to come to Bohemia, is murdered by his younger brother, Boleslav, a pagan.

930 Spain: Cordoba becomes the seat of Arab learning.

935 Korea: Rebel leader Wanggon overpowers the Silla and founds the state of Koryo from which the name Korea is derived. The Koryo period lasts until 1392.

936 Germany: Otto I, King of Germany, revives the Holy Roman Empire. In 962 he has himself crowned Emperor Augustus. He reigns until 973.

The Americas

Apart from the Vikings' brief visits around 1003, the peoples of the Americas remained isolated from the rest of the world. By 900 the city-state of Teotihuacán (*see* pages 134–135) had been destroyed and Mexico was overrun by barbarian tribes from the north. In 968 one of these tribes, the Toltecs, established their capital at Tula. It became the center of a military state and a trading network which reached as far as Panama and Colombia. They invaded the Mayas (*see* pages 150–151) and built new administrative centers, such as Chichén Itzá, in Yucatán. The Toltecs' kings were also their religious leaders and one of them was called Topiltzin Quetzalcoatl. Legend says that he was driven from Tula by a rival religious group and sailed east vowing to return one day. The Toltec empire came to an end in the 12th century when it was overrun and the city of Tula was destroyed.

The great civilizations in South America at this time were based in the Andes Mountains and along the northern coast of Peru. One was based on Tiahuanaco, a large city and ceremonial

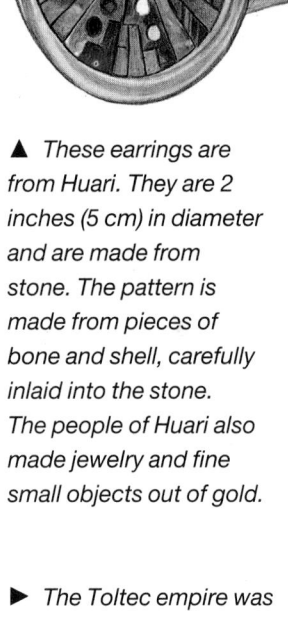

▲ These earrings are from Huari. They are 2 inches (5 cm) in diameter and are made from stone. The pattern is made from pieces of bone and shell, carefully inlaid into the stone. The people of Huari also made jewelry and fine small objects out of gold.

▶ The Toltec empire was arranged along military lines. The temples in their capital of Tula were guarded by stone statues of warriors like this one. The Toltecs believed in a god called Quetzalcóatl, the "plumed serpent," who was the legendary founder of Tula.

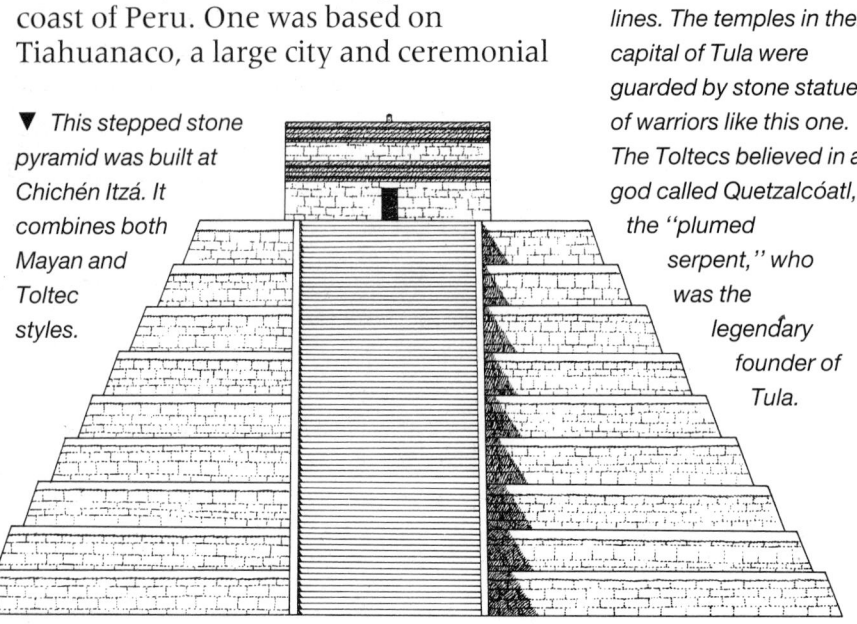

▼ This stepped stone pyramid was built at Chichén Itzá. It combines both Mayan and Toltec styles.

site near Lake Titicaca in what is now Bolivia. Up to 100,000 people lived there when the city was at its greatest between 600 and 1000. The people of Tiahuanaco made distinctive pottery and jewelry.

The other great South American civilization was based on the city of Huari. Unlike Tiahuanaco, Huari was the center of a powerful military empire, covering more than half of modern Peru. Both cities had many stone temples decorated with intricate carvings and may have followed the same religion. The two cities prospered for over two centuries until about 1000 when they were suddenly abandoned.

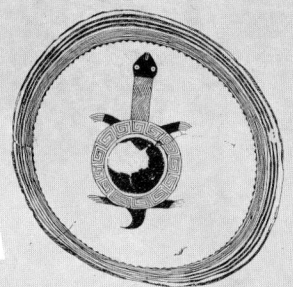

A 12th century pottery bowl from New Mexico. The hole in the center was made on purpose to "kill" the dish so that it could then be buried with the dead.

▲ *The civilizations of Central and South America had no contact with other parts of the world. Contact between them was limited by the large areas of thick jungle which covered the narrow width of Central America. They built great stone pyramids, studied mathematics and astronomy, and used a calendar.*

937 Britain: At the battle of Brunanburh, Athelstan defeats an alliance of Scots, Celts, Danes, and Vikings, and takes the title of "King of all Britain."

939 England: Athelstan dies and his brother, Edmund, becomes king of England. In Japan the first of a series of civil wars starts.

942 Scotland: Malcolm I is king (to 953).

943 England: Dunstan becomes abbot of Glastonbury. He rebuilds its monastery and starts a revival of monasticism in England.

945 Britain: The Scots annex Cumberland and Westmorland from the English.

946 England: Edmund is assassinated and his younger brother Edred becomes king (to 955). He appoints Dunstan as his chief minister.

950 Otto I, King of Germany, conquers Bohemia. Europe: The invention of the padded horse-collar means horses can pull heavier loads and wagons. Central America: Yucatán is invaded by the Toltecs, who take control of Chichén Itzá.

951 Otto I campaigns in Italy.

954 England: Eric Bloodax, the last Viking king to rule in York, is killed at the battle of Stainmore.

955 England: Edwy, son of Edmund, becomes king until 959. Germany: Otto I defeats the Magyars at Lechfeld and stops their westward expansion.

956 Edwy sends Dunstan into exile.

957 Mercia and Northumbria rebel against Edwy.

959 Edgar the Peaceful, younger brother of Edwy, becomes king of England (to 975). He recalls Dunstan from exile and makes him archbishop of Canterbury.

Popes and Emperors

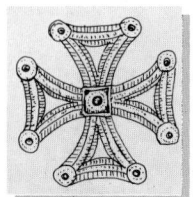

At this time, the most important ruler in western Europe was the pope. As head of the Roman Catholic Church, he was in charge of a wealthy organization. The Church owned vast areas of land and had estates in many different countries. In addition to this, the Roman Catholic Church had become the only church in Western Europe. All the people had to obey the pope and so he could influence the way the leaders of countries behaved. Eventually this power led to conflict between the popes and the rulers of the Holy Roman Empire. Strong popes thought they had the right to choose the emperor and strong emperors thought they had the right to choose the pope.

Emperor

Pope

Nobility

High clergy

▲ *In disputes the pope was supported by most of the bishops and the abbots and, through them, monks and priests.*

Soldiers

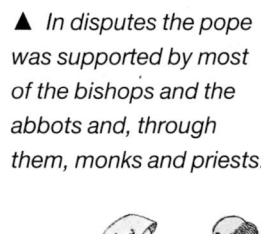

Monks

▲ *The noblemen usually supported the emperor against the pope, but sometimes they rebelled against him. The knights supported the baron, or nobleman, who gave them their land.*

Farmers

▶ *The disputes had little effect on the daily lives of peasants, the majority of the population. They were more worried about producing enough food to keep themselves alive and keeping a roof over their heads.*

Laborers

▲ *When the Holy Roman emperor Henry IV went to see the pope at Canossa, Gregory kept him waiting outside for three days in a snowstorm before forgiving him and removing the ban of excommunication.*

The Holy Roman emperors tried to control the Church's affairs in their lands. They wanted the right to choose bishops but the Church disagreed. In the 1070s this led to a big dispute between Emperor Henry IV and Pope Gregory VII over who should become the next archbishop of Milan. This was an important post in the Church. It was also important to the Holy Roman Empire as Milan controlled the mountain passes between Germany and Italy. In 1075 Gregory said Henry had no right to choose any of the bishops. In revenge, Henry said that Gregory was no longer pope. Since not many people supported Henry in this, Gregory excommunicated him. This meant Henry was no longer a member of the Church and would go to Hell after he died. It also meant his subjects did not have to obey him. In 1077 Henry went to the pope and asked to be forgiven. The quarrel over choosing bishops was finally settled in 1122. There were many more disputes over land and power, and neither side ever really won.

960 Poland: Mieszko I becomes the first ruler (to 992). China: The Song dynasty is founded (to 1279).

961 The German king Otto I makes another expedition to Italy to protect the pope.

962 Pope John XII crowns Otto emperor in Rome, reviving the Holy Roman Empire.

966 Holy Roman Empire: Otto I makes a third expedition to Italy. His son, Otto II, is crowned as future emperor.

971 Scotland: Kenneth II becomes king to 995.

973 Otto II is Holy Roman emperor to 983.

975 England: Edward the Martyr, son of Edgar, becomes king until 978.

976 China: T'ai Tsung starts to reunite the country. It takes until 997 to complete.

978 England: Edward the Martyr is murdered at Corfe Castle. He is succeeded as king by his younger brother, Ethelred II, also known as the Redeless. China: The writing of an encyclopedia in 1,000 volumes begins.

980 England: The Danes raid again, attacking Chester and Southampton. East Africa: The Arabs begin settling along the coast.

An astronomical clock built during the Song dynasty in China. It was powered by a controlled flow of water over a wheel. The hours were marked by the striking of an internal gong.

983 Venice and Genoa start trading with Asia.

985 North America: The Viking, Eric the Red, sets out from Iceland with 25 ships of people who want to settle in the land he has called Greenland to make it attractive to them. Denmark: Sweyn Forkbeard is king (to 1014).

Science and Technology

Many advances in science and technology were made by the Chinese and the Arabs. The Chinese knew how to make medicines from herbs, and understood how vaccination worked. They also made a magnetic compass and invented gunpowder for fireworks and as a signaling device. The Chinese progressed from using wooden blocks for printing to using movable type.

The Arabs were skilled at astronomy and mathematics, and used the decimal system of numbers which had been invented in India. They drew the most accurate maps available at that time. They knew how lenses worked and, like the Chinese, they made herbal medicines to treat people. Cairo in Egypt, and Baghdad in Mesopotamia (Iraq) were great centers of learning.

In Europe, the Germanic peoples were skilled metalworkers. The village blacksmith was a central figure of their society because he made and mended all the iron tools.

◄ *The Arabs were great astronomers. They invented the astrolabe, a device which measures the angle of a star in relation to the horizon, so they could navigate by measuring the altitude of stars and planets. At Baghdad there was an observatory and a "House of Learning" where scholars translated ancient Greek works into Arabic. Arab astronomers, like the ancient Greeks, drew star constellations as human figures. The one shown here is called Cepheus.*

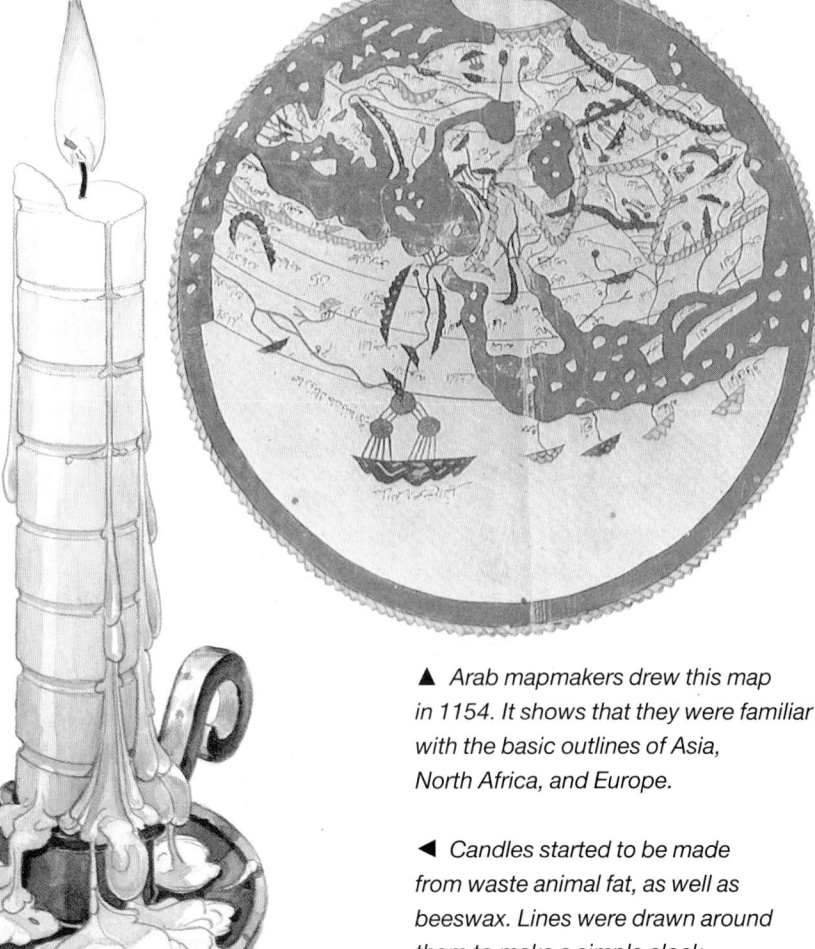

▲ *Arab mapmakers drew this map in 1154. It shows that they were familiar with the basic outlines of Asia, North Africa, and Europe.*

◄ *Candles started to be made from waste animal fat, as well as beeswax. Lines were drawn around them to make a simple clock.*

▶ *The Chinese mostly used fireworks in religious rituals. A scientist discovered gunpowder by accident when the potion he was mixing exploded, setting his beard on fire.*

◀ *This Chinese compass is made of magnetic stone. The figure on top always points south.*

▼ *Charcoal, which was used in metal smelting, was made from wood. Branches were piled up, then covered with earth, leaving an opening at the top. A fire was lit at the bottom and the wood dried out slowly, leaving charcoal behind.*

987 France: Hugh Capet is elected king (to 996) and founds the Capetian dynasty.

988 Russia: Vladimir of Kiev introduces the Christian Eastern Orthodox Church into his lands.

991 England: At the battle of Maldon, Byrhtnoth of Essex is defeated by Danish invaders. Later Ethelred II buys off the Danes with 10,000 pounds of silver.

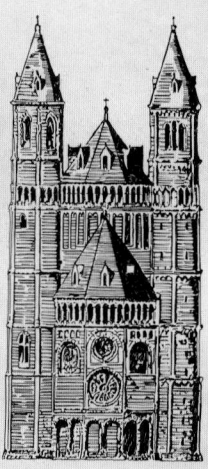

In about the 11th century Europe began a period of prosperity. This growth in wealth was marked by the construction of many impressive buildings, such as this huge Romanesque cathedral at Worms in Germany.

992 Ethelred makes a truce with Duke Richard I of Normandy. Boleslaw the Brave, son of Mieszko, becomes king of Poland. He rules until 1025.

993 Sweden: Olaf Skutkonung is the first Christian king. He rules until 1024.

994 England: The Danes under Sweyn Forkbeard and the Norwegians under Olaf Tryggvason sail up the river Thames and besiege London, until Ethelred buys them off.

995 Olaf Tryggvason returns to Norway, deposes Haakon the Great, and makes himself king. Japan: A literary and artistic golden age starts under the rule of Fujiwara Michinaga. It lasts until 1028.

996 France: Richard II becomes duke of Normandy until 1027. Hugh Capet's son, Robert, also known as Robert the Pious, becomes king of France (to 1031).

998 Asia: Mahmud, the Turkish ruler of Ghazni (to 1030), founds an empire in northern India and eastern Afghanistan.

The Capetians

In France the Carolingian dynasty was followed by that of the Capetians in 987. Capet was a nickname which had been given to the dynasty's founder because of the short cape he wore when he was lay (not a clergyman) abbot of St. Martin de Tours. As Hugh, Duke of Francia, he was the most powerful vassal of Louis V, the last Carolingian king of France. Duke Charles of Lorraine claimed a right to the throne by descent from Carolingian monarchs, but Hugh schemed to have himself elected as king by seeking the support of wealthy, land-owning bishops.

Although Hugh Capet was king, his position was not very strong. From his capital in Paris, he ruled directly over a large part of northern France. In the rest of the country, however, some of his vassals were almost as powerful as he was. These included the dukes of Normandy, Burgundy, and Aquitaine. Luckily for Hugh, no single one of them was strong enough to overthrow him

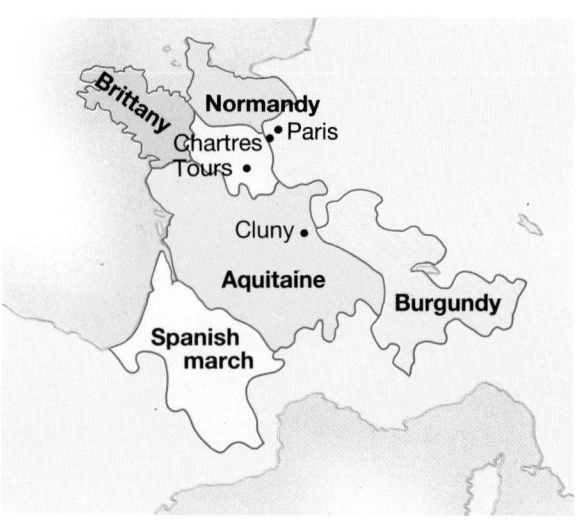

▲ *When Hugh Capet came to power, France was divided into large duchies. The most important of them were Normandy, Burgundy, and Aquitaine.*

and they were all too jealous of each other to make an alliance against him.

Hugh Capet made sure the succession passed to his son by having him crowned as king of France while he was still alive. In this he was copying the Holy Roman emperors who had their sons crowned king of the Romans. This meant that no one could contest the throne. The practice continued for the next two centuries, helping to make France into a stable country. Later Capetian kings enlarged royal territory, increased the powers of the king, and gave the country a strong central government.

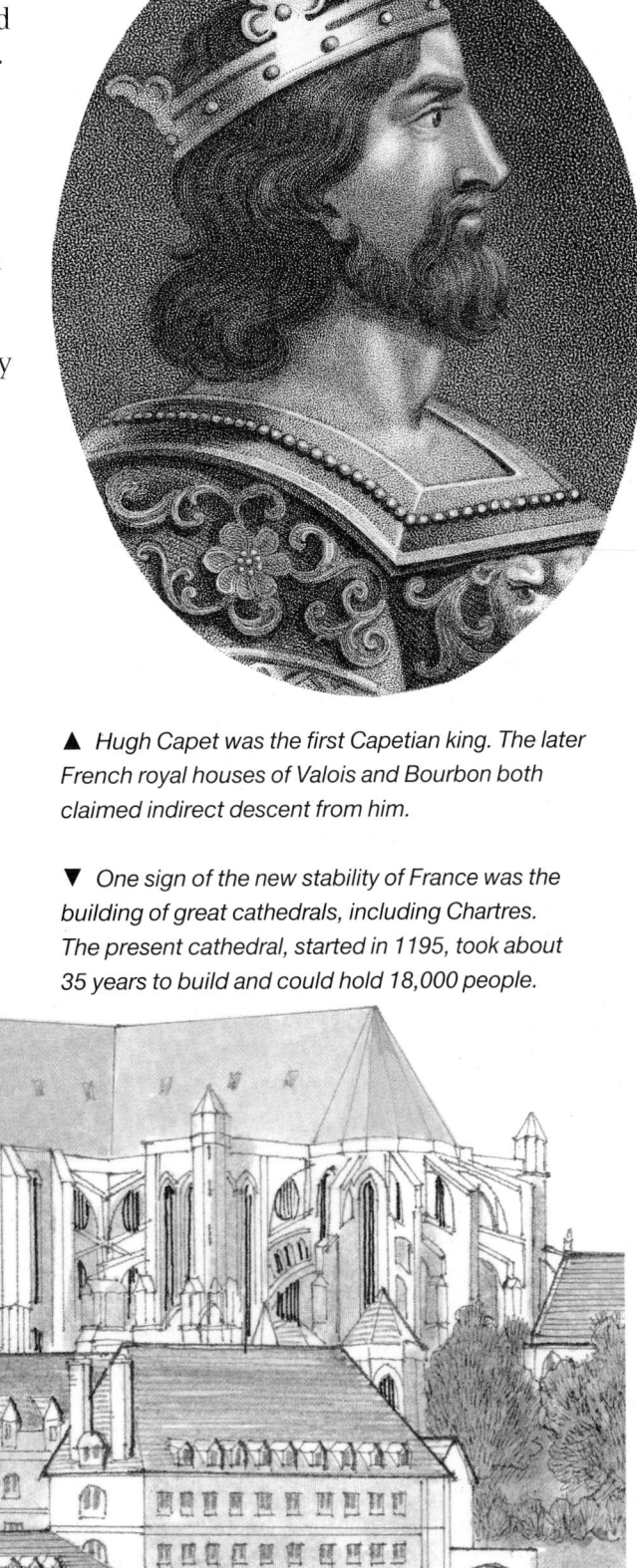

▲ Hugh Capet was the first Capetian king. The later French royal houses of Valois and Bourbon both claimed indirect descent from him.

▼ One sign of the new stability of France was the building of great cathedrals, including Chartres. The present cathedral, started in 1195, took about 35 years to build and could hold 18,000 people.

The Vikings

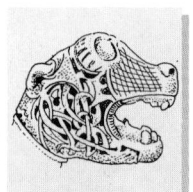

In the late 8th century, the Vikings began to venture from their homelands of Norway, Denmark, and Sweden in search of treasure and better farmland. They made excellent wooden ships, lightweight and flat-bottomed, which could sail up rivers as well as on rough seas. They could also land on beaches and so could go to places where there were no harbors. At first their targets were monasteries, but later they attacked coastal towns. They sailed along the Rhine, Seine, and Loire rivers to attack inland cities such as Paris and Cologne. Local rulers bought them off with large amounts of silver or gold.

Not all Vikings were raiders, however. Many were farmers looking for new land

▲ The Vikings were skilled metalworkers. This is a die, used for stamping an identifying pattern onto a metal sheet. It shows two legendary warriors about to attack a ferocious beast. The Vikings also made gold and silver jewelry, and swords and axes from iron.

▼ Viking warriors sailed in longships which often had a dragon's head at the front. Although the Vikings usually fought in small groups they were fearless fighters both at sea and on land. Viking ships had a keel, a long narrow piece of wood attached to the underside. This made their ships faster and easier to steer.

as there was not enough for everyone in their homelands. In Britain they settled mainly in northern and eastern England, northern Scotland, the Isle of Man, and Ireland. In France they settled in Normandy which was given to their leader, Rollo, by the king of France in 911. Others settled in Iceland and some went on from there to Greenland and the east coast of North America. The Vikings often married local people. They adopted local languages, but added words of their own to them (our days of the week are named after the gods Tyr, Odin or Woden, Thor, and Frigg). They wrote in runes, sticklike letters, which were carved on stone, wood, or metal.

▲ *A Viking man and woman in everyday clothes. These were practical, rather than fashionable. Their silver jewelry was sometimes cut up and used as money.*

999 Africa: Bagauda becomes the first king of Kano (now in Nigeria). Europe: As the year 1000 approaches, people fear the Last Judgement and the end of the world will come. The Poles conquer Silesia.

The seven warriors depicted on the Lindisfarne stone, shown here, are thought to represent the Vikings who raided the monastery in 793.

1000 Hungary: Stephen I, later to be known as St. Stephen, becomes the first king. He rules until 1038. North America: The Viking Bjarni Herjolfsson sights the coast of North America when he is blown off course in a storm. Denmark: At the battle of Svolder, Sweyn Forkbeard kills Olaf of Norway and annexes Norway. England: Ethelred II ravages Cumberland. China: The invention of gunpowder is perfected. Africa: The kingdom of Ghana reaches the height of its power. It controls Atlantic ports, as well as trade routes across the Sahara.

1002 England: King Ethelred marries Emma, sister of Duke Richard of Normandy. In the Massacre of St. Brice's day, Ethelred orders all Danes in southern England to be killed.

1003 England: Sweyn Forkbeard, King of Denmark, lands to avenge the massacre. North America: Leif Ericsson, son of Eric the Red, journeys down the coast, possibly as far as Maryland.

1007 England: Ethelred buys two years of peace from the Danes for 36,000 pounds of silver.

1012 The Danes sack Canterbury, before being bought off for 48,000 pounds of silver.

1013 Sweyn lands in England again and is made king. Ethelred flees to Normandy.

1014 Sweyn Forkbeard dies suddenly and the English recall Ethelred II from Normandy to be their king. Ireland: The king, Brian Boru, defeats the Vikings at the battle of Clontarf. He allows them to stay in Ireland, however, because they bring wealth to the country through their trading ports.

1015 England: Sweyn Forkbeard's son, Canute, now king of Denmark, invades and war between the Saxons and the Danes starts.

1016 England: Ethelred II dies. His son, Edmund Ironside, becomes king, but then agrees to share the country with Canute. Edmund rules Wessex, while Canute rules the north. When Edmund is assassinated, Canute becomes king of England. Olaf II becomes king of Norway.

1017 Canute divides England into four earldoms: Wessex, Mercia, Northumbria, and East Anglia.

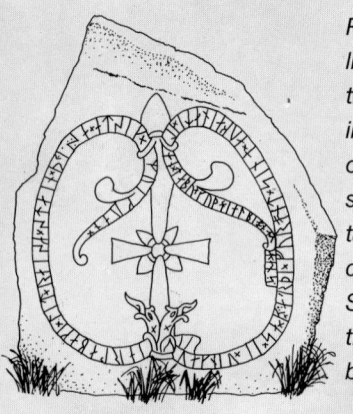

Runes, straight stick-like letters, were used by the Vikings to write inscriptions in wood or on stone. Many stones still stand and have taught historians a great deal. This one in Sweden commemorates the building of the road by which it stands.

1018 India: Mahmud of Ghazni pillages the sacred city of Muttra.

1019 To strengthen his claim to the English throne Canute marries Emma of Normandy, widow of Ethelred II.

1021 Islamic empire: Caliph al-Hakim declares himself divine and founds the Druse sect.

1024 Holy Roman Empire: Conrad II, becomes king of Germany and Holy Roman emperor until 1039.

1027 France: Robert the Devil is duke of Normandy. He rules until 1035.

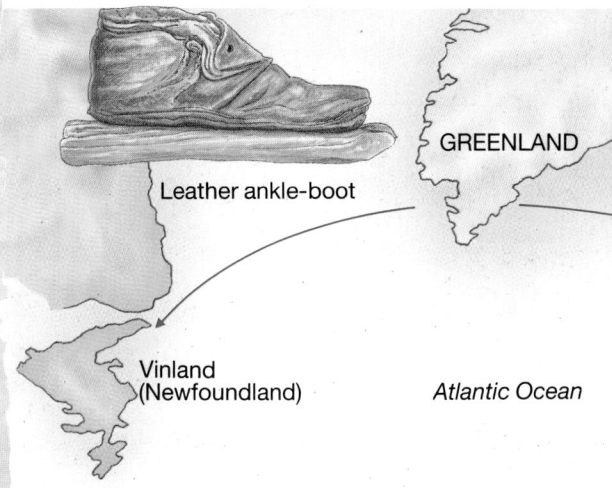

Leather ankle-boot

GREENLAND

Vinland (Newfoundland)

Atlantic Ocean

The Vikings sailed across the Atlantic Ocean at a time when most people did not dare to sail out of sight of land. From Iceland they colonized Greenland around 985. At the same time Bjarni Herjolfsson saw the coast of North America when he was blown off course by a storm. He did not land there, but told people in Greenland of what he had seen. Leif Ericsson went in search of this new land, which he called Vinland, the Land of Grapes (the grapes were probably gooseberries or cranberries, used to make wine). The Vikings settled there briefly around 1003. Traces of settlement have been found in Newfoundland, Canada, and Maine in New England.

Swedish Vikings sailed east across the Baltic and into Russia (*see* pages 184–185). They were traders rather than settlers and set up trading posts at Novgorod and Kiev. From there they sailed down rivers to the Black Sea and Constantinople where they traded for goods from as far away as China. Some sailed into the Mediterranean and visited Jerusalem and Greece. Others sailed into the Mediterranean from the west and fought with the Arabs and the southern Europeans. Descendants of the Norman Vikings in France later colonized southern Italy and the island of Sicily.

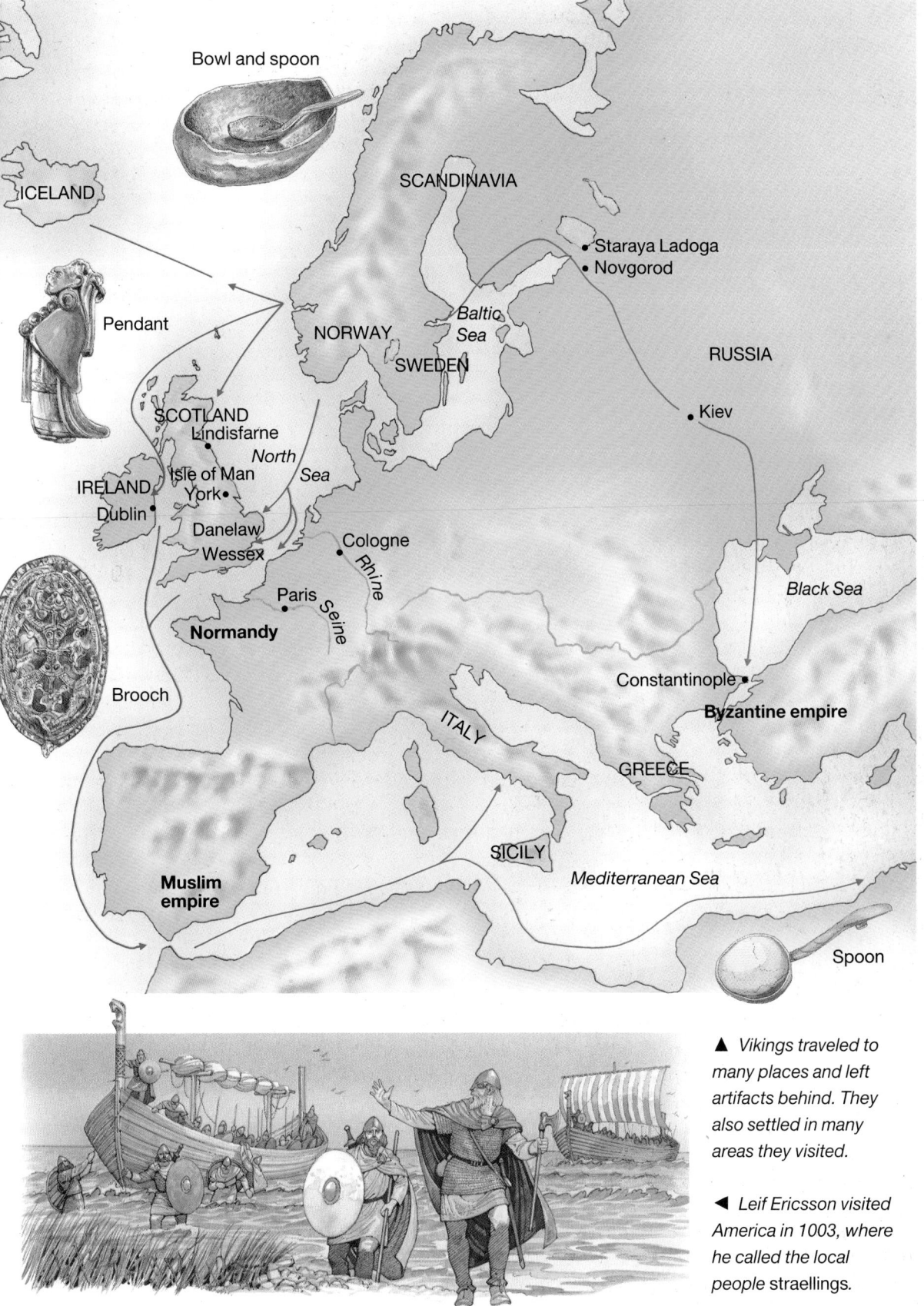

Bowl and spoon

ICELAND

Pendant

SCANDINAVIA

Staraya Ladoga
Novgorod

Baltic
Sea

NORWAY

SWEDEN

RUSSIA

Kiev

SCOTLAND
Lindisfarne

North

IRELAND   Isle of Man   Sea
Dublin   York

Danelaw
Wessex

Cologne

Rhine

Paris

Seine

Normandy

Black Sea

Constantinople

Byzantine empire

Brooch

ITALY

GREECE

SICILY

Muslim
empire

Mediterranean Sea

Spoon

▲ Vikings traveled to
many places and left
artifacts behind. They
also settled in many
areas they visited.

◄ Leif Ericsson visited
America in 1003, where
he called the local
people straellings.

219

Society and Government

In China all power was concentrated in the hands of the emperor. He could conscript people into his army or force them to work for him. Japan also had an emperor, but he spent a lot of his time studying religious matters while a regent ran his country for him.

In the Islamic empire, people were governed by Islamic Law. This included laws on food and drink, prayer, and pilgrimages.

The Byzantine empire under Justinian based its laws on those of the old Roman empire. Farther north and west, however, society was governed differently. The emergence of strong kings like Charlemagne led to the development of the feudal system. In contrast, the Vikings had no kings at all until the late 9th century. Instead, they were governed by *things*, which met to solve disputes and make new laws. Every freeman could vote. Those who refused to accept the law of the thing became outlaws. Many Viking laws were similar to Saxon laws. One law said a criminal had to pay compensation to his victim.

▲ Muslims traveled widely (part of their faith decreed that they had to make at least one pilgrimage to the Ka'aba in Mecca). Their travels helped to spread ideas, as well as trading goods. Not all societies approved of merchants, however. In China and Japan the poorest soldier was considered to be more important than a trader.

▲ Under the Vikings and Saxons, people were often tried by a jury of 12 men. Later, trial by fire or hot water became more common. The accused person had to walk barefoot across hot coals or (right) put his hand into boiling water. He was innocent if the burns healed.

◄ *A wall painting from the tomb of the Chinese princess Yung T'ai. Yung T'ai was forced to commit suicide at 17 for criticizing her grandmother, Empress Yu. In Chinese society, ancestors and parents were highly respected and children had to obey their parents, even when they became adults.*

▼ *In England, the Normans adopted many of the old laws. The lord of the manor dealt with small offenses. The shire court was used for more serious crimes, or those involving property. This one, held in 1072, met to decide whether some lands belonged to the Bishop of Bayeux or to Canterbury Cathedral.*

WHEN IT HAPPENED

622 Islam attracts many poor people in Arabia because its teachings offer a fairer society.

858 Regents start to rule Japan for the emperor.

1086 By this date most land in England belongs to the Normans. The feudal system gives the nobility all the power.

1028 Norway: The Danes under Canute conquer the country. His son, Sweyn, becomes king of Norway. Byzantine empire: Zoë starts to rule the country in her own right. Arabia: Asma, the ruling queen of the Yemen, is succeeded by her daughter-in-law, Arwa, bypassing the sultan, al-Mukarram, with his consent.

1030 Norway: Olaf tries to regain the throne, but is killed at the battle of Stiklestad.

1031 France: Henry I rules until 1060.

1034 Scotland: Duncan is king (to 1040).

1035 Canute dies and his possessions are divided. His illegitimate son, Harold Harefoot, rules England as Harold I until 1040. Harthacanute becomes king of Denmark. France: William, the illegitimate son of Robert the Devil, becomes duke of Normandy.

1039 Holy Roman Empire: Henry III, also called Henry the Black, becomes emperor (to 1056).

The top border of the Bayeaux Tapestry is embroidered with many fantastic animal figures from mythology.

1040 England: Harthacanute becomes king. Scotland: Macbeth kills Duncan in battle and becomes king (to 1057).

1042 England: Harthacanute dies and is followed by Edward the Confessor, son of Ethelred II. Real power is in the hands of Earl Godwin of Wessex and his sons. Denmark: Magnus the Good, son of Olaf II, becomes king to 1047.

1046 Harald Hardrada becomes king of Norway.

1047 Canute's nephew, Sweyn II, becomes king of Denmark until 1076.

1051 England: Godwin is banished for opposing the king. He returns in 1052 with a fleet to win back his power.

1052 England: Edward the Confessor founds Westminster Abbey, near London.

England

In 978 Ethelred II became king of England. He ruled until 1016, but it was not a peaceful time. Armies of Danes and Norwegians kept attacking and Ethelred had to bribe them to go away. This made him unpopular with the people, who had to provide the money. In 1013, Sweyn Forkbeard, King of Denmark, landed in England and was proclaimed king. Ethelred fled to France.

Ethelred returned the next year when Sweyn died, but in 1015 Sweyn's son, Canute, came to England and in 1016 he became its king. He ruled until his death in 1035, when he was succeeded by his son, Harthacanute. When he died in 1042, Edward the Confessor, son of Ethelred II, was chosen as king of England. He had been brought up in Normandy and was very religious. He relied heavily on Godwin, Earl of

▼ *A panel from the Bayeux Tapestry showing the deathbed of Edward the Confessor when he is said to have named Harold as his successor even though he had already promised William the throne of England.*

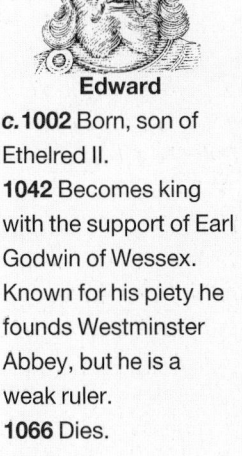

Canute

c. **994** Born.
1016 Invades England and becomes king.
1018 Becomes king of Denmark.
1019 Marries Emma, Ethelred's widow.
1028 Invades Norway, makes his son king.
1035 Dies.

Edward

c. **1002** Born, son of Ethelred II.
1042 Becomes king with the support of Earl Godwin of Wessex. Known for his piety he founds Westminster Abbey, but he is a weak ruler.
1066 Dies.

▲ *Canute's kingdom included Denmark, England, and Norway, along with Danish lands in southern Sweden.*

▼ *The battle of Hastings took place just 19 days after Harold had defeated Harald Hardrada at Stamford Bridge. Harold had marched south and raised a fresh army, but he was killed and his troops were defeated.*

Wessex, and Godwin's son, Harold, to govern the country for him.

When Edward died without an heir in 1066, Harold Godwinsson was chosen to replace him. Harald Hardrada, King of Norway, also claimed the throne and attacked England, but Harold defeated him near York. Three days later a Norman army invaded England and Harold was defeated in the battle of Hastings by William, Duke of Normandy.

The Feudal System

Feudalism was a system under which people held land in exchange for services, rather than for rent. It developed in the 8th century under the Franks and gradually spread across western Europe. William the Conqueror brought it to England when he became William I. He believed that all the land in the country belonged to him. To help him raise money and have an army

▶ *Early medieval society was strictly divided and everyone knew his or her place. At the top was the king who granted land to barons and to the church. The barons built castles for defense 1 and lived in large manor houses 2. In return for military service they granted land to knights 3. By the side of the manor house were farm buildings 4 and the house of the bailiff 5 who managed the estate. The farm work was done by villeins and brodars who, to protect their lord's privacy, lived some distance from the manor house in the village 6.*

when he needed one, he allowed his barons to hold some of this land. In exchange for these estates, they paid him taxes and provided him with knights to help him fight his enemies.

In turn, the barons allowed their knights to hold some of their land. In exchange for these manors, each knight had to give the baron 40 days' military service each year. For this he had to be armed and on horseback and also have a certain number of soldiers with him.

Each knight allowed people known as *villeins* to hold land from him. They were the largest group in society at this time. They usually lived in villages near the manor house and farmed around 30 acres (12 ha) of land each. They had to work two or three days a week for the lord of the manor. They also had to give him some of their crops or an equal amount in money. There were also *brodars* who had about 5 acres (2 ha) of land. A village was largely self-supporting and people rarely traveled beyond its boundaries.

1053 England: Earl Godwin dies. His son Harold succeeds him as earl of Wessex.

1054 The final break comes between the Byzantine empire and the Roman Church; the Eastern Orthodox Church becomes completely independent. West Africa: Abdallah ben Yassim begins the Muslim conquest.

1055 England: Harold Godwinsson's brother, Tostig, becomes earl of Northumbria.

Hunting was a popular sport for both noblemen and noblewomen.

1056 Holy Roman Empire: Henry IV is emperor (to 1106). His mother is regent.

1057 Scotland: Duncan's son, Malcolm, defeats and kills Macbeth. Macbeth's stepson, Lulach, becomes king for a year.

1058 Scotland: Malcolm (Canmore) becomes king after killing Lulach in battle (until 1093). Poland: Boleslaw the Bold becomes king and conquers Upper Slovakia.

1060 France: Philip I is king (to 1108).

1061 Scotland: Malcolm invades Northumbria. North Africa: The Muslim Almoravid dynasty is founded and later conquers Spain.

1062 North Africa: Yusuf ben Tashfin founds Marrakesh, in Morocco.

1063 England: Harold and his brother Tostig subdue Wales. Africa: The kingdom of Ghana under Tunka Manin has an army of 200,000.

1064 France: Harold Godwinsson is shipwrecked in Normandy and is possibly tricked into swearing an oath to support William of Normandy's claim to England.

The Normans

William the Conqueror was crowned William I of England on Christmas Day 1066. In Normandy, however, he was still only a duke and a vassal of the king of France. At first many people in the north and east of England protested against his rule. He put down these rebellions brutally, taking the land and giving it to his followers. To keep the peace, he introduced the feudal system (*see* pages 224–225). He gave much land to the church and replaced most of the English bishops with French ones. He also encouraged traders and craftsmen from France to settle in England.

In William's reign, the landscape of England and Wales started to change. He

▶ William I was followed by two of his sons. William II ruled from 1087 to 1100 and Henry I from 1100 to 1135. They established firm Norman rule, but it collapsed under the next king, Stephen.

▼ The Normans enjoyed hunting and created many areas known as forests. These did not all have trees. Instead, they were places where animals were kept to be hunted by rich people. It was forbidden for anyone to enter a royal forest with bow and arrows or dogs, without a special warrant.

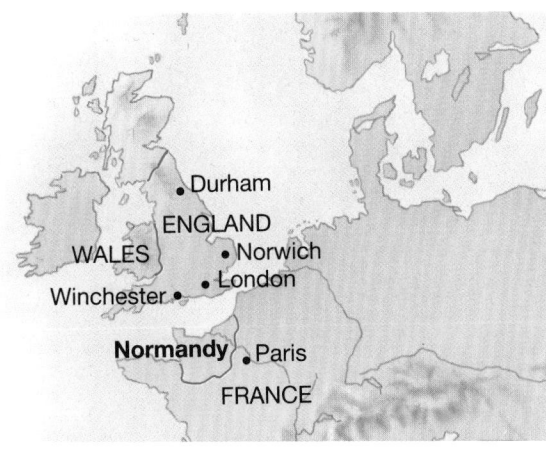

▲ *The connection between England and Normandy gave the English monarch control of land in France.*

▼ *In 1085 William ordered a survey of England to find out who owned the land, who lived there, how much it was worth, and what taxes he could expect. The survey was written up in the* Domesday Book, *shown here.*

and many of his followers built large castles, and towns grew up around them. The old churches were replaced by bigger ones and the great cathedrals such as Winchester and Durham were begun. Monks and nuns from France set up large monasteries and convents in the countryside and attracted new followers from the local populations. French became the language of the nobility.

Although Norman rule was harsh, it brought advantages: castles provided refuges for local people when attacked; the civil service (the work of running the country) was started; and the first survey of English land was carried out.

1066 England: Edward the Confessor dies on 5 January. Although he was married, he has no children. Harold Godwinsson claims the throne and is crowned as King Harold II of England on 6 January. Harold's brother, Tostig, joins forces with Harald Hardrada of Norway to invade England in September. Harold's army defeats and kills them both at the battle of Stamford Bridge. While Harold and his army are in the north, William of Normandy lands on the south coast of England. Harold marches south and meets William's army at the battle of Hastings just 19 days after the battle of Stamford Bridge. Harold is killed and his army defeated. William declares himself king of England and is crowned in Westminster Abbey on Christmas Day.

Manuscripts telling stories about courtly love and romance between lords and ladies were very popular in Norman England.

1067 England: Work starts on building the Tower of London. Italy: Monte Cassino monastery is rebuilt.

1068 England: The Norman conquest continues until 1069. William subdues the north of England by laying it waste. This is known as the "Harrying of the North." China: Shen Tsung is emperor (to 1085). His minister Wang Anshi carries out some radical reforms.

1069 Egypt: A famine there lasts until 1072.

1070 England: Hereward the Wake begins a Saxon revolt in the Fens, East Anglia.

Trade

After the collapse of the Roman empire, trade became more difficult in Europe. Roman roads fell into disrepair and traders were at the mercy of robbers. Most goods went by sea if possible.

From the East, merchants traveled with camels along the Silk Road and across the Sahara Desert. Important commodities included salt and spices. The greatest traders were the Vikings and the Arabs. They traded with each other in Baghdad and Constantinople, where furs, walrus ivory, and slaves were exchanged for silk, spices, and silver.

▲ This Viking coin was made in the 9th century. Coins were valued for the silver or gold they contained.

◄ A Tang model of an Armenian trader. The Chinese preferred to let foreigners handle their trade.

▼ The Vikings used sturdy ships called knarrs to transport their goods down the rivers of Russia to the markets of Constantinople.

▶ This statue of Buddha was found at Helgo in Sweden. It was buried in about the 8th century, and shows that even before the Viking age, Swedish traders had found their way East.

▲ As populations expanded, more people went to live in the towns. Some became weavers, but they did not own their own sheep. They bought wool from merchants who traveled around from farm to farm, buying up any wool the farmers did not need. Soon nearly all wool was sent to the towns.

WHEN IT HAPPENED

c. 501 In South America the powerful Tiahuanaco empire controls the trade of drugs used in religious ceremonies.

800 The kingdom of Ghana starts to trade in gold and salt and grows rich.

841 The Vikings build a settlement at Dublin in Ireland. It attracts both merchants and craftsmen.

850 Vikings from Sweden start to visit Russia. Soon after this date, they set up trading posts and make their way down the rivers in Russia to Constantinople.

1071 The East African ports of Kilwa and Gedi send ambassadors to China in order to set up trading links.

▲ Arab traders who crossed the deserts of Asia and North Africa carried their goods on camels. They could travel 200 miles (320 km) in a week. If a well or oasis was dry, however, they might all die.

The Seljuk Empire

Nomadic Turks from the steppes of central Asia founded their first kingdom in Afghanistan in the late 10th century. As it expanded, it attracted more tribes of Turks into the area. In the late 900s, a tribal chief called Seljuk and his followers settled around the oasis of Merv, near Bokhara in Uzbekistan. There they were ruled by the Ghaznavid Turks from Afghanistan. In 1037, however, the Seljuks occupied Merv and in 1040 they defeated the Ghaznavids. After that, the Seljuks started to build up their own empire.

Under the leadership of Toghril Beg (990-1063), the Seljuks swept through present-day Iran and Iraq to conquer Baghdad in 1055. Toghril Beg was expelled for a short time by an uprising, but came back to power. When he died his nephew, Alp Arslan, took power.

Alp Arslan continued to expand the

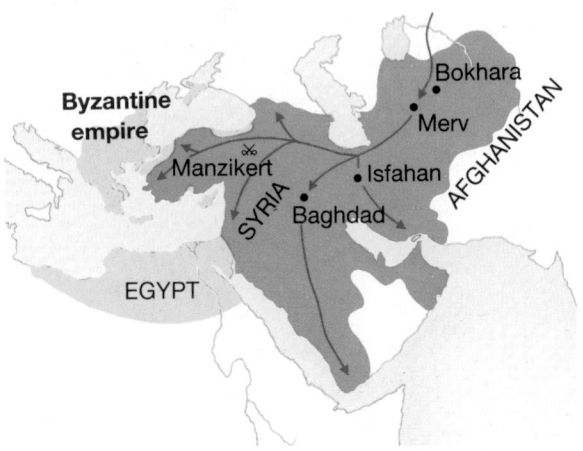

▲ The Seljuks made great conquests between 1037 and 1092. After the death of Malik Shah the empire started to split into separate countries.

▼ Like most people from the steppes of Central Asia, the Seljuks were great horsemen. They used stirrups and could fire arrows from horseback very accurately. This picture shows them beating the Byzantines at Manzikert. This victory gave the Seljuks control of Anatolia, which was later part of the Ottoman empire.

THE LION HERO

The Seljuk leader Alp Arslan (whose name literally means the Lion Hero) was sultan from 1063 to 1072. He was a skillful and brave commander who devoted his energies to extending the Seljuk empire. His victory at Manzikert opened up Anatolia to the Muslims. He was killed in a struggle with a prisoner while fighting in Persia. His son later conquered Syria and Palestine.

▲ *The Seljuks became Muslim around 970. This minaret at the Jami Mosque in Simnan, built around the time of the conquest of present day Iran, has typical Seljuk patterns in its elaborate brickwork.*

Seljuk empire. In 1064 he captured the capital of Armenia and raided Constantinople. In 1071 the Byzantine emperor decided to fight back. While Alp Arslan was in Syria, the Byzantine army marched into Armenia from the west. Alp Arslan heard of this and marched in from the south. The armies fought at Manzikert. The Seljuks won because they pretended to be defeated and ran away. When the Byzantines went after them, they turned around and defeated the Byzantine army heavily. The Seljuks captured the Byzantine emperor and held him for ransom. This victory laid the foundation for what later became the Ottoman empire (*see* pages 304–305).

The Seljuk empire reached its greatest power under the rule of Alp Arslan's son, Malik Shah (1072-1092). He was a patron of science and the arts and built fine mosques in his capital, Isfahan.

1071 Anatolia: At the battle of Manzikert, the Seljuk leader Alp Arslan defeats the Byzantine empire's army and conquers most of Anatolia.

1072 Mediterranean: Normans invade Sicily. By 1091 they have conquered the whole island. England: William I invades Scotland; in East Anglia Hereward the Wake submits. Spain: Alfonso VI is king of Castile.

1073 Gregory VII becomes pope until 1085.

1075 A dispute starts between the pope and the Holy Roman emperor over who should appoint bishops. Near East: The Seljuk leader Malik Shah conquers Syria and Palestine.

1076 Holy Roman Empire: At the Synod of Worms, the bishops depose Pope Gregory. Pope Gregory then excommunicates Emperor Henry IV.

This bronze deer was made as a fountain in Muslim Spain. The water was drawn up through the legs and body and came out of the mouth.

1077 Holy Roman Empire: The dispute between the emperor and the pope leads to civil war starting in the empire. Henry, frightened of losing his throne, does penance to Pope Gregory at Canossa. Africa: In Ghana the Almoravid dynasty takes control.

1080 Denmark: Canute IV rules (to 1086). Holy Roman Empire: Henry IV is again excommunicated and declared deposed by Pope Gregory. The civil war ends.

1081 Alexius I Comnenus becomes the Byzantine emperor (to 1118).

1083 The Holy Roman emperor Henry IV attacks Rome.

1084 Robert Guiscard, Duke of Apulia, forces Henry IV to retreat to Germany.

1085 Spain: Alfonso VI captures Toledo from the Moors.

1086 The Danish threat to England ends when Canute IV of Denmark is assassinated. England: The *Domesday Book* is completed and the feudal system established.

1087 England: William I dies, leaving Normandy to his oldest son, Robert, and England to his second son, William Rufus. To his third son, Henry, he leaves some money.

1088 Urban II becomes pope (to 1099).

1090 Persia: The Assassin sect is founded by Hasan ibn al-Sabbah, the first "Old Man of the Mountain."

1093 Scotland: Donald Bane becomes king, after the death of his brother, Malcolm III, in battle against the English.

During the Song dynasty, Chinese emperors had factories built to make porcelain especially for their palaces.

1096 The First Crusade begins, after Pope Urban II appeals for volunteers to free the Christian holy places in Palestine from the Muslims or Saracens.

1097 Scotland: Malcolm's second son, Edgar, becomes king of Scotland after William II of England helps him to defeat Donald Bane.

1098 France: The first Cistercian monastery is founded at Citeaux. The Crusaders defeat the Muslims at Antioch.

1099 Palestine: The Crusaders capture Jerusalem and elect Godfrey of Bouillon as its king.

1100 England: Henry, youngest son of William I, becomes king after the assassination of William II. Italy: Bologna University is founded. Palestine: Some parts are ruled by Crusaders; Baldwin of Bouillon is count of Edessa, Raymond of Toulouse is count of Tripoli, and Bohemund of Otranto is prince of Antioch.

The Song Dynasty

After the fall of the Tang dynasty in 907, five emperors in 53 years tried to reunite China and start new dynasties. None of them succeeded until the first Song emperor who came to the throne in 960. He finally reunited the country between 978 and 979, but the Chinese empire was smaller than it had been in the past. In the northwest was Tibet and in the northeast was Lao, to whom the Song paid a tribute in silk. The first Song emperor worked hard to bring peace to his country. Agriculture expanded and the population grew rapidly. By the end of the Song period there were probably around 100 million people living in China.

In 1068 the prime minister, Wang Anshi, tried to reform the government of China. He made the tax system simpler and cut the huge army down to a reasonably sized fighting force. Although these cuts saved money, they also made it easier for other peoples to invade China, especially from the north.

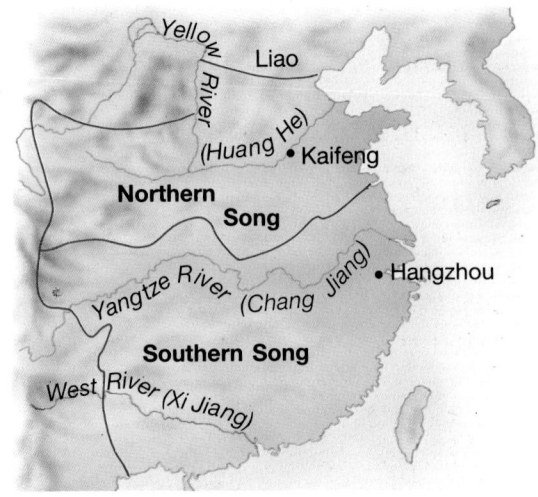

▲ *The Song dynasty was split into two parts. The first is the Northern Song, with its capital at Kaifeng. Later the Southern Song ruled only the south of the empire.*

◄ *This picture is painted with ink on silk. At this time the Chinese often painted natural objects such as animals, flowers, or landscapes, but they did not always make them look realistic.*

The Song emperors managed to keep defeating the invaders until 1126. In that year the emperor and his family were captured and the Song lost control of the north. Only one son escaped because he was away from home. He moved to Hangzhou and made it the capital of a new empire, known as the Southern Song. This lasted until 1279 when it was overrun by the Mongols (*see* pages 270–273) under Kublai Khan.

In spite of the threat of invasions, the arts flourished in the Song dynasty. Pictures were painted on silk and paper. Fine porcelain was produced and exported to places such as India and the east coast of Africa. Many poems were written and professional storytellers wandered around the countryside, performing in exchange for money.

► *This wine vessel in a lotus-shaped warmer is one of the many beautiful, fine porcelain objects that were produced during the Song dynasty.*

LILY FEET

The Chinese thought women should have tiny feet, called lily feet. The feet were tightly bound from birth to stop them growing normally. As a result, most rich women could hardly walk.

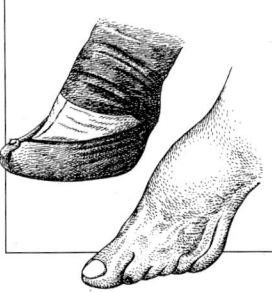

INVENTIONS

Chinese technology was more advanced than that of the west. Under the Song they made firearms and bombs. They built ships, used a compass, and made clocks. In medicine, they understood how vaccination worked. They made the best silk in the world and their pottery was so fine that today we call porcelain "china."

War and Weapons

Weapons became more effective with the introduction of iron. Swords and knives were made from it, as were the heads of battleaxes and spears. In turn, this meant that soldiers needed better protection. At first they used wooden shields covered in leather. Later chain mail was worn. It was expensive to make, so many wore a thick leather breastplate instead.

Early battles in this period were fought on foot. Later, when stirrups were introduced into Europe, horses became more important in war.

In Europe, armies were still quite small, while in China and Arabia they numbered thousands.

▼ *Stirrups, introduced into Europe in the 8th century, gave horsemen a more secure seat in battle.*

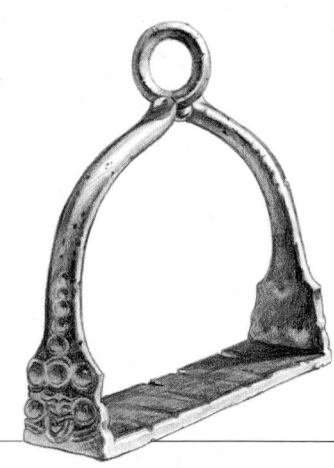

▲ *At the battle of Hastings the English fought on foot with axes and spears. Although they were protected behind a wall of shields, they could not match the Normans, who fought on horseback.*

WHEN IT HAPPENED

553	The Franks are defeated and massacred at the battle of Casilinum, near Capua, in Italy.
636	The Arabs defeat the Byzantines at Yarmuk.
732	Charles Martel defeats the Moors at Poitiers.
793	The Vikings raid the monastery of Lindisfarne off the north coast of England.
1066	King Harold of England defeats King Harald of Norway at the battle of Stamford Bridge. Then Harold is defeated by William, Duke of Normandy at the battle of Hastings.
1071	The Seljuk Turks defeat the Byzantines at Manzikert and conquer most of Anatolia.

◄ *Viking soldiers often carried a spear in battle. It was made of ash wood and had an iron head. These were thrown at the enemy and gathered up after the battle.*

► *Viking raiders went in search of treasure and slaves, often traveling in small numbers. Their raids were usually successful because they came to the towns and villages without warning.*

▲ Chain mail consisted of looped metal rings. These protected a soldier's body and a metal helmet protected his head and face.

▲ A 6th century Frankish warrior carried a number of weapons into battle. These included a battle-ax and an angon, a barbed spear used for throwing or stabbing.

▲ Swords were highly valued by the Vikings. They often decorated them with gold and silver.

New Zealand

People from the Polynesian Islands in the Pacific probably first reached New Zealand by canoe around 750. They settled mainly on the North Island which was much bigger and cooler than their homelands. It had plants, birds, and other animals that were unlike those the Polynesians were used to. At first the Maori culture was based on hunting. One favorite food was a flightless bird called the moa. When this had been hunted to extinction, the Maoris turned to farming to provide food. They lived in wooden houses in large, fortified villages and their main crops were sweet potatoes and fern rhizomes. They were fierce warriors and could use either male or female lines of descent to claim rights to land. Their religion was based on taboos which meant that certain objects, persons, and places were sacred and forbidden to certain members of the group.

▼ *As well as being farmers and warriors, the Maoris were also skilled woodcarvers and decorated their houses with complicated designs. They had no metal tools and so used stone for axes to cut wood.*

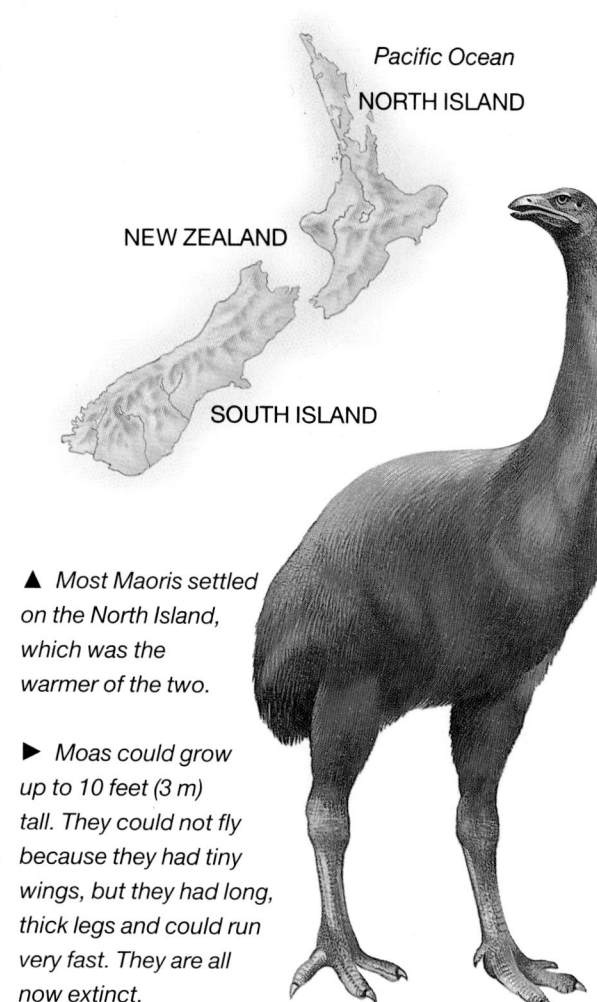

Pacific Ocean

NORTH ISLAND

NEW ZEALAND

SOUTH ISLAND

▲ *Most Maoris settled on the North Island, which was the warmer of the two.*

▶ *Moas could grow up to 10 feet (3 m) tall. They could not fly because they had tiny wings, but they had long, thick legs and could run very fast. They are all now extinct.*

The Middle Ages

Travel could be dangerous and difficult in the Middle Ages; nevertheless people journeyed as far afield as China and what were then other unknown places to those living in Europe. Trade was the reason for much of this travel. Silk was carried from China along the Silk Road through Central Asia to the markets of the West. In Africa, caravans trudged across the Sahara, while in the Mediterranean Sea, Venetian ships sailed to and fro with their goods. Meanwhile, the merchants of northern Europe grouped themselves together into a trading alliance, the Hanseatic League.

At this time most of Europe was a mass of small kingdoms, principalities, duchies, and city-states, that made alliances with each other and then broke apart again. But nationalism, or the sense of belonging to a particular country, was growing, especially in England, France, and Scotland.

Empires rose and fell. The Mongol empire, the biggest the world has ever known, came into being and fell apart all within a hundred years. In West Africa, the Mali empire grew powerful, while in eastern Europe the Ottoman empire took the place of the Byzantine empire. Across the Atlantic Ocean, the Incas and the Aztecs were starting to build empires of their own in the Americas.

Many wars were undertaken in the name of religion. Early in the period, Christian knights of Europe set out on crusades to free the Holy Land from the "infidels," as Christians called the Muslims who controlled Palestine. Later Ottoman Turks captured Constantinople from the people who were "infidels" to them: the Christians of the Byzantine empire. Meanwhile, the Christian Church was itself divided. At one time there were no fewer than three popes.

By far the most important invention of the Middle Ages came at its close: printing. Suddenly learning came within the reach of everyone who could read.

▼ *Caernarvon Castle in north Wales was built by Edward I of England during his wars with Wales. It was one of the last great castles to be built in Britain.*

The Americas

Europe

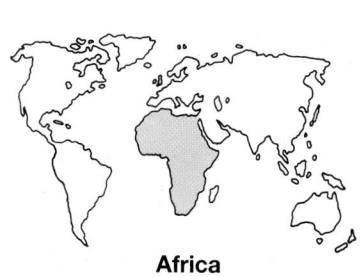

Africa

The Americas	Europe	Africa

1109–1113 War between England and France.
1135 Henry I, King of England, dies.
1143 Portugal becomes independent.

1145–1150 Almohades of North Africa conquer Spain.

1151 End of the Toltec empire.

1152 Eleanor of Aquitaine marries Henry of Anjou.
1170 Thomas à Becket is murdered.

1168 Aztec migration begins.
1191 Second era of Mayan civilization begins.

1190 Henry VI becomes Holy Roman emperor.

1190 Lalibela becomes emperor of Ethiopia.

1200 Hunac Ceel revolts.

1204 France captures Normandy.
1215 Magna Carta agreed.
1223 Mongols invade Russia.
1240 Mongols capture Moscow.

1220 Manco Capac founds the Inca people.

1240 New empire of Mali founded.

1270 Philip III becomes king of France in succession to Louis IX.
1305 Papacy removed to Avignon.

1270 Yekunà Amlak becomes emperor of Ethiopia. Louis IX of France dies in Tunis.

1325 The Aztec city of Tenochtitlàn is founded in Mexico.

1326 Queen Isabella leads rebellion against her husband, Edward II, in England.
1337–1453 Hundred Years' War between France and England.
1347–1350 Black Death sweeps Europe.
1378–1417 Great Schism.

1307 Mansa Musa becomes ruler of Mali. The empire of Benin is established in Nigeria.
1324 Mansa Musa visits Mecca.

1438 Inca empire established in Peru.

1460 Wars of the Roses start in England.

1440 Oba Ewuare becomes ruler of Benin.

Near East or Middle East

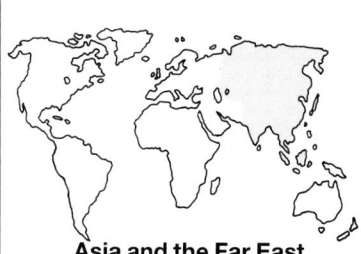

Asia and the Far East

Australasia and Pacific

1113 Knights of St. John founded, Jerusalem.

1143 Manuel Comnenus becomes Byzantine ruler.
1147 Second Crusade begins.
1171 Saladin overthrows Egyptian caliph; becomes sultan (1174).
1190 Crusader Emperor Frederick Barbarossa drowned.

1204 Crusaders sack Constantinople.

1261 Michael VIII becomes Byzantine emperor.

1291 End of the Crusades.
1299 Ottoman empire founded in Turkey.
1326 Orkhan I becomes ruler of the Ottoman Turks.

1369 Ottoman Turks attack Bulgaria.

1453 Fall of Constantinople.

1113 Work starts on Angkor Wat.

1190 Temujin begins Mongol conquests.
1192 Minamoto Yoritomo becomes shogun of Japan.
1206 Temujin becomes Genghis Khan.
1218 Mongols conquer Persia.
1219 Hojo clan become shoguns in Japan.
1260 Kublai Khan conquers China.
1271 Marco Polo sets off for China from Venice.

1290 Turkish leader Firuz founds Khalji dynasty in India.
1293 Vijaya founds the Majaphiat Empire in Java, the last Indianized Kingdom in Indonesia.
1325 Nō plays are first performed in Japan.

1336 Revolution in Japan.
1368 Ming dynasty begins in China.
1411 Ahmad Shah rules in west India.

A sea slug. Indonesian traders collected them from Australia's north coast.

c. **1200** Tahitians migrate to Hawaii and win control over earlier settlers.

c. **1300** Marco Polo refers to a mythical southern continent.
14th century A second wave of Maoris migrate to New Zealand from the Marquesas, Polynesia.

15th century Indonesian traders regularly visit the northern coast of Australia.

The World

During this period trade increased people's knowledge of many parts of the world, but it also helped to spread the Black Death, a disease carried by fleas that lived on ships' rats. In **Europe** the Black Death killed a quarter of the population.

Information about **Africa** was spread by Arab traders who sailed down the east coast of the continent. They brought stories of vast inland empires, rich with gold, and centered on large stone cities. In West Africa, the kingdom of Mali flourished.

In the **Far East**, the Khmer empire of Cambodia was at its height. In **Japan**, military rulers called shoguns, supported by samurai warriors were virtual dictators.

The **Mongols** conquered much of Asia and Europe to form the largest empire of all time. Their success was based on brilliant military tactics and superb horsemanship.

In the **Americas**, the Aztecs built their capital city of Tenochtitlán in the center of a lake in Mexico, while in South America, the Inca empire was expanding by conquering neighboring tribes.

◀ The Aztecs worshiped many gods, including Quetzalcóatl, the feathered serpent. He was associated with civilization and learning. By the 1400s the Aztecs dominated Central America.

NORTH AMERICA

▼ Pachacuti ruled the Incas from 1438. He expanded the Inca empire, leading his troops into battle.

Aztec empire

CENTRAL AMERICA

ATLANTIC OCEAN

PACIFIC OCEAN

SOUTH AMERICA

Inca empire

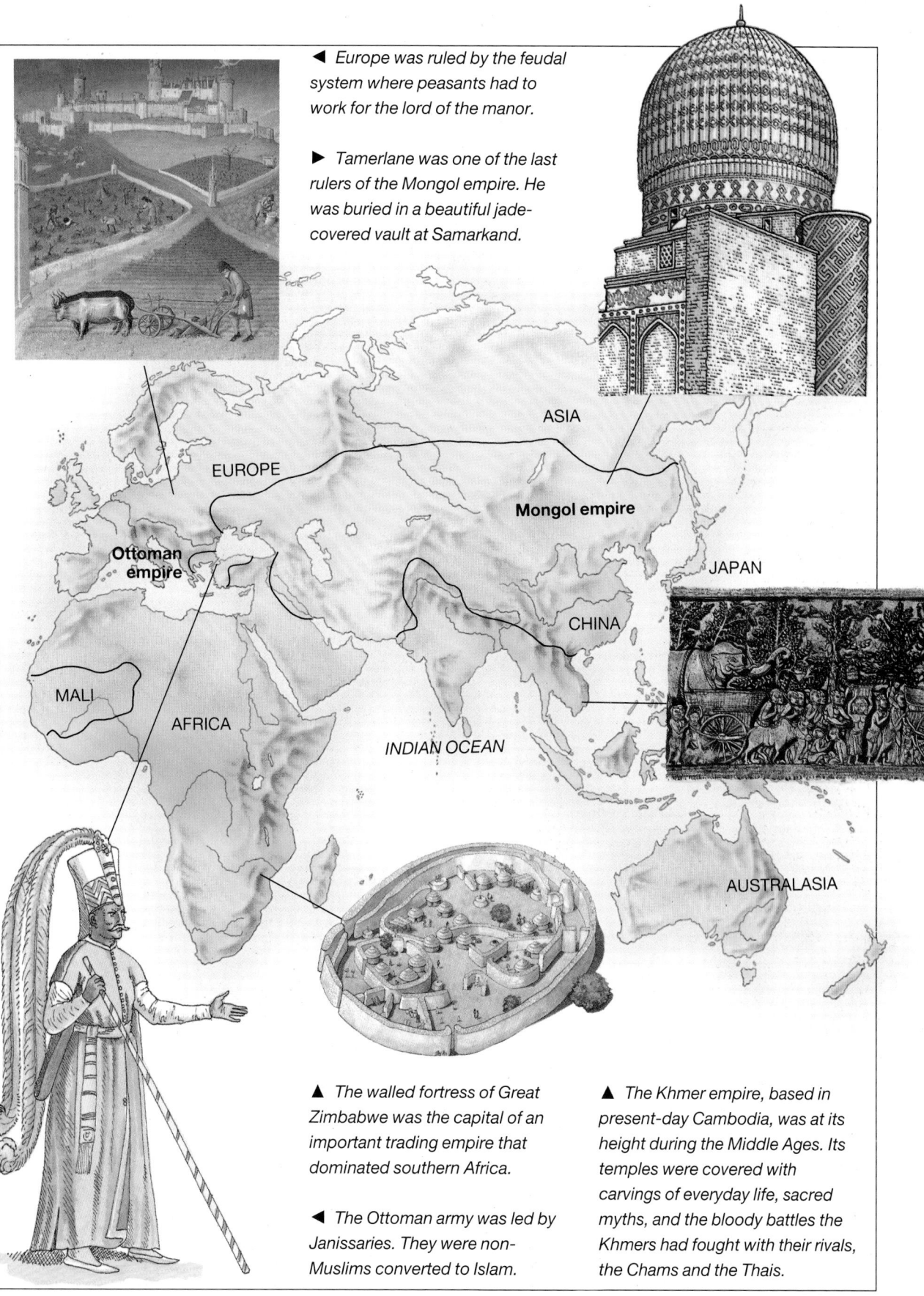

◀ *Europe was ruled by the feudal system where peasants had to work for the lord of the manor.*

▶ *Tamerlane was one of the last rulers of the Mongol empire. He was buried in a beautiful jade-covered vault at Samarkand.*

ASIA

EUROPE

Mongol empire

Ottoman empire

JAPAN

CHINA

MALI

AFRICA

INDIAN OCEAN

AUSTRALASIA

▲ *The walled fortress of Great Zimbabwe was the capital of an important trading empire that dominated southern Africa.*

◀ *The Ottoman army was led by Janissaries. They were non-Muslims converted to Islam.*

▲ *The Khmer empire, based in present-day Cambodia, was at its height during the Middle Ages. Its temples were covered with carvings of everyday life, sacred myths, and the bloody battles the Khmers had fought with their rivals, the Chams and the Thais.*

1104 Palestine: Crusaders capture the Muslim city of Acre.

1106 Germany: Henry V becomes Holy Roman emperor (to 1125). England: Henry I defeats his brother Robert, Duke of Normandy, at battle of Tinchebrai: Robert remains captive for life.

1107 Scotland: Alexander I is king (to 1124).

1108 France: Louis VI is king (to 1137).

1109 War breaks out between England and France (until 1113).

1111 Holy Roman emperor Henry V forces Pope Paschal II to acknowledge his power.

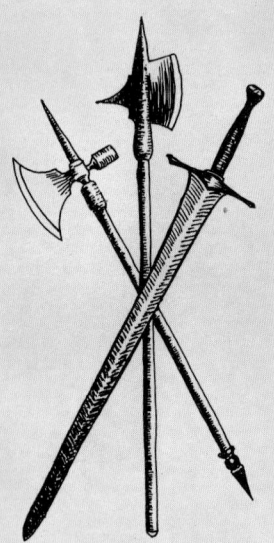

Weapons like these axes and sword were commonly used in battle by knights during the Crusades.

1113 Palestine: Knights of St. John founded. Cambodia: Work starts on Angkor Wat.

1114 England: Matilda (Maud), daughter of King Henry I, marries Holy Roman emperor Henry V.

1115 France: St. Bernard founds the Abbey of Clairvaux, and becomes its first abbot. Hungary: Stephen II is king (to 1131). China: The Jin dynasty is founded by Akuta.

1118 Byzantine empire: John II Comnenus becomes emperor (to 1143); he revives Byzantine power.

1119 Palestine: Hugues de Payens founds the Order of Knights Templar.

c. 1120 China: Playing cards are invented.

The Crusades

To Christians everywhere, Palestine, where Jesus Christ lived and died, was the Holy Land. Pilgrims traveled there from all over Europe from the 2nd century onward. Even after the Muslim Arabs conquered Palestine, pilgrims were free to come and go as they wished. But when the Seljuk Turks, who were also Muslims, invaded the land from central Asia, they persecuted the Christians.

Pope Urban II called on Christian leaders to free the Holy Land from the infidels, as Christians called the Muslims. Because the knights who went to Palestine wore a cross, the expeditions are known as the Crusades, from the Spanish word *cruzada* which means "marked with the Cross."

The first Crusaders were a disorganized band, led by two well-meaning men named Peter the Hermit and Walter the Penniless. They never reached Palestine. Later a well-disciplined army recaptured Jerusalem and set up four Christian kingdoms in Palestine. At first the Saracens, as the Crusaders called the Seljuk Turks, left the kingdoms alone.

▼ *Armies from France and Italy journeyed across Europe to the Holy Land. They traveled by way of Constantinople, capital of the Byzantine empire.*

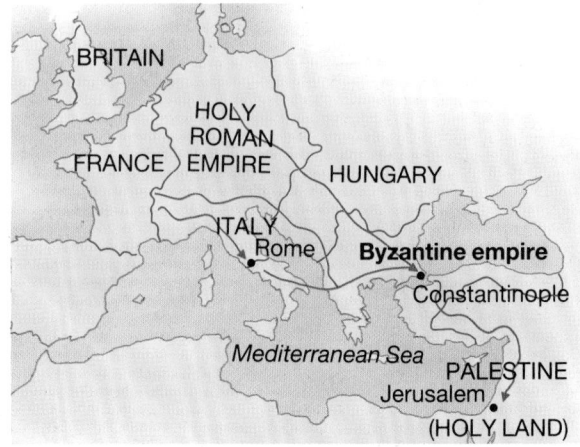

▲ *A 14th century picture of Crusaders boarding ship and loading supplies at a French Mediterranean port.*

But eight more Crusades followed, and by the end of the 13th century the Christians had been thrown out.

Many of the Crusaders were more interested in personal gain than religion, and they quarreled among themselves. By the 14th Century, Europe had lost interest in the Crusades. Although there were several more attempts to organize Crusades, they all failed.

▼ *Richard I of England led an army to Jerusalem, but was unable to recapture it from the Saracens.*

CHILDREN'S CRUSADE

In 1212, several thousand boys and girls decided to march and save the Holy Land. Some were sold into slavery on the way, others were turned back. From this may have come the legend of the Pied Piper of Hamelin, who lured a band of children away.

▼ *The crossed legs of this effigy on the tomb of a Norman knight show he had been on a crusade.*

Knighthood

Warfare was the most important occupation for a young man of good family at the time of the Crusades. But knighthood was not just about fighting. A knight was expected to be just and honorable as well as brave, to help the weak and protect the poor. These qualities formed the ideal known as chivalry, though many knights did not live up to these high standards.

Boys began their training at about the age of seven, as pages in the household of a knight or nobleman. At the age of 14 or 15 a page was promoted to squire, the personal attendant of a knight. A squire served at table, helped his master to put on his armor, and accompanied him into battle. He spent many hours practicing riding and the use of the sword and lance. After a few years he too was made a knight, especially if he had fought well in battle.

▶ *Two orders of knights active during the Crusades were the Knights Templar (left) and the Knights of St. John (right), also known as Hospitallers because they set up a hospital for pilgrims in Jerusalem. Their long robes, or surcoats, kept the hot sun off their armor.*

◀ *Two knights jousting (fighting) in a tournament. They used blunt swords and lances, but even so, knights were often killed or maimed. Tournaments showed the skills and bravery of knighthood. They became very organized in the 15th century with rules on issuing a challenge, fighting, and scoring points. Mock sieges and assaults on castles were also staged.*

▲ *The troubadour tradition of poetry and music first started in the 11th century in southern France. These minstrels sang songs of love, chivalry, and religion.*

Knights continued to practice their skills, often in mock battles called tournaments. During these, most knights carried a token from a lady, such as a scarf or glove, to show they were fighting on her behalf. Two kings, Richard I of England and Louis IX of France, were famous for their support of the romantic ideals of chivalry.

▼ *A squire kneels to help his master arm for battle. Plate armor of steel was introduced in the 14th century. Before that knights wore chain mail.*

1122 The Concordat of Worms, a conference of German princes, ends the dispute between the pope and the Holy Roman emperor over appointing bishops.

1123 Persia: Death of poet Omar Khayyam.

1124 Scotland: David I, younger brother of Alexander I, becomes king (to 1153).

1125 Holy Roman Empire: Lothair of Saxony is elected emperor (to 1137).

1126 Spain: Alfonso VII, King of Castile (to 1157). China: The Song dynasty loses control of north China.

1129 France: Matilda, widow of Henry V, marries Geoffrey of Anjou.

c. 1135 England: Geoffrey of Monmouth writes *History of the Kings of Britain* which includes stories about King Arthur.

The highest duty of a chivalrous knight was to protect vulnerable people.

1135 England: Stephen of Blois seizes the crown on the death of his uncle, Henry I; a rival claim by Matilda causes civil war.

1137 France: Louis VII becomes king (to 1180).

1138 Scotland: David I is defeated at the battle of the Standard while fighting on behalf of Matilda. France: Louis VII marries Eleanor of Aquitaine. Holy Roman Empire: Conrad III becomes emperor (to 1152).

1139 England: Matilda arrives from France.

Arts and Crafts

In Europe, the arts of stained glass and tapestry flourished. They were used to show illustrated versions of Bible stories, so that people who could not read might learn from them instead.

Later artists began to paint pictures as though they were "windows on the world." The colors they used were brighter and they painted on wood, walls, and canvas.

Many plays were on religious subjects. These included Mystery Plays which were based on the Bible. Poems were about popular heroes such as Charlemagne and King Arthur. Poets began to write in the national languages instead of Latin.

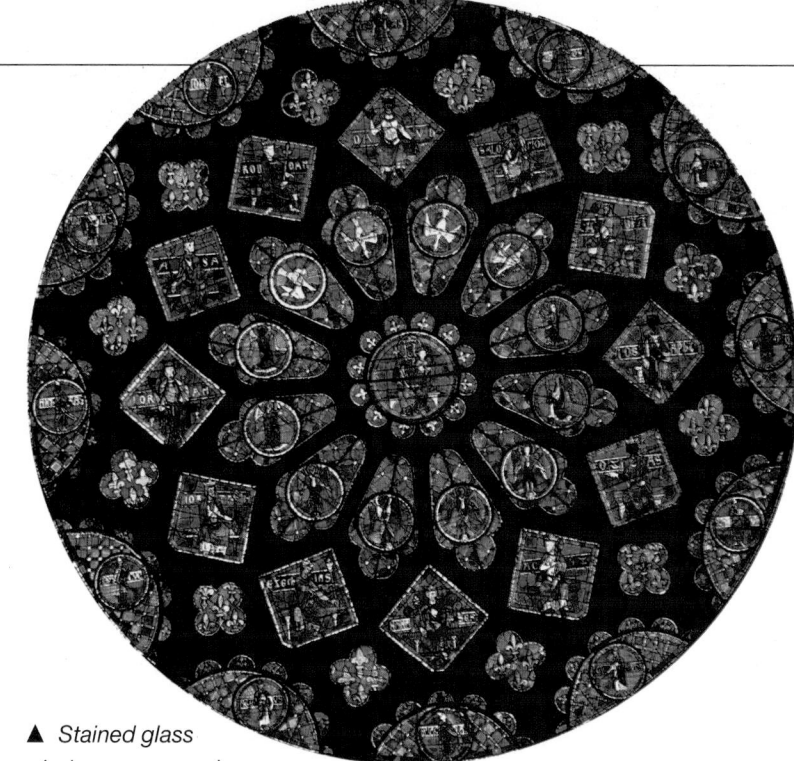

▲ *Stained glass windows were made from pieces of colored glass, joined together with strips of lead. This is the Rose of France window at Chartres Cathedral.*

▼ *There were no theaters in Europe in the Middle Ages. Plays were performed in the street, with a cart for the stage.*

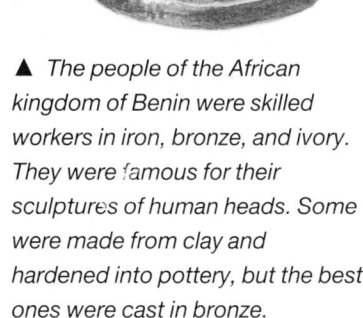

▲ *The people of the African kingdom of Benin were skilled workers in iron, bronze, and ivory. They were famous for their sculptures of human heads. Some were made from clay and hardened into pottery, but the best ones were cast in bronze.*

▲ Wooden furniture and wall panels were often carved or painted with scenes from stories. This scene is from The Pardoner's Tale by Chaucer. It shows Death teaching a lesson to three men.

▶ These two Aztec women are making cloth. One is spinning raw cotton into yarn for the other to weave on a belt-loom. It is given this name because one end is attached to the woman's belt.

◀ During the Ming dynasty (1368–1644) the Chinese started to make blue-and-white pottery in imperial factories. Later, much of it was exported to Europe.

▼ Jan van Eyck painted The Arnolfini Wedding in 1434. By then portraits were more realistic and rich people commissioned them for their homes.

WHEN IT HAPPENED

1307 Dante Alighieri in Florence, Italy, writes *The Divine Comedy*.

1348 Giovanni Boccaccio starts to write *The Decameron*, a book of stories told by people fleeing from the plague.

1360 William Langland, the English poet, writes *The Vision of Piers Plowman*.

1368 The Persian poet Há fiz, publishes the love poem *The Diwan*.

1388 The English poet, Geoffrey Chaucer, writes *The Canterbury Tales*.

1415 Following Roman models, Donatello sculpts unusually realistic statues of St. Mark and St. George in Italy.

1140 Venice: The power of the doge (Venetian ruler) is transferred to a Great Council.

1141 England: Matilda captures Stephen at the battle of Lincoln. Her reign is disastrous, and Stephen is restored.

1143 Alfonso Henriques, Count of Portugal, makes Portugal independent of Spain and becomes king (to 1185). Byzantine empire: Manuel Comnenus rules (to 1180).

1145 Spain: Almohades, North African Berber dynasty, begin the conquest of Moorish Spain (to 1150).

1147 England: Matilda leaves for France. Palestine: The Second Crusade begins (ends 1149). Crusaders fail to capture Damascus.

***c.* 1150** First paper made in Europe.

1150 France: Founding of Paris University. Cambodia: Temple at Angkor Wat completed by Suryavaraman II.

1151 France: Geoffrey of Anjou dies. Mexico: Toltec empire comes to an end.

The seal of Paris University, first used in 1215. In 1258, Robert de Sorbon founded a religious college at Paris University, now called the Sorbonne.

1152 France: Marriage of Louis VII and Eleanor of Aquitaine is annulled. Eleanor marries Henry of Anjou, adding Aquitaine to the regions of Anjou and Normandy that Henry already rules. Holy Roman Empire: Frederick I Barbarossa becomes emperor (to 1190).

1153 England: Henry of Anjou, son of Matilda, invades England and forces Stephen to make him heir to the throne. Scotland: Malcolm IV, "The Maiden," grandson of David I, rules (to 1165).

1154 England: Henry of Anjou becomes King Henry II (to 1189); he also rules more than half of France. Papacy: Nicholas Breakspear becomes Adrian IV (to 1159), the only English pope.

Henry of Anjou

The way to the throne was not an easy one for Henry II of England. His mother, Matilda, was the daughter of Henry I, who wanted her to be the next ruler of England. But the throne was seized by her nephew Stephen and civil war broke out. Matilda was the widow of the Holy Roman emperor, Henry V. She next married Count Geoffrey of Anjou, in France. Their son, Henry, forced Stephen to make him his heir.

By the time Henry II became king of England at the age of 21, he had inherited Anjou, Maine, Touraine, and Normandy in France from his parents. He gained Aquitaine when he married its beautiful duchess, Eleanor.

Henry chose capable people for his ministers, among them Thomas à Becket, a priest who became chancellor. As the king's chief minister, Becket led a life of pomp and power. But when Henry made

▼ *Henry II ruled over a greater area of France than the French king Louis VII, though Louis looked after Henry's French lands.*

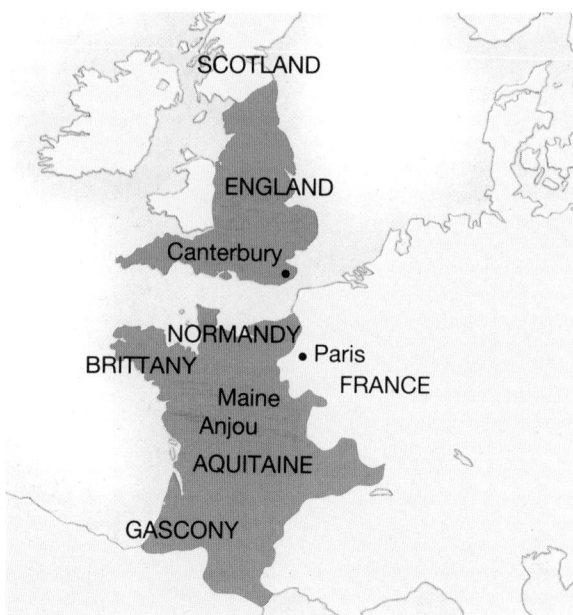

Eleanor

Eleanor of Aquitaine (c. 1122–1204) married Louis VII of France in 1138. The marriage was annulled and in 1152 she married Henry of Anjou becoming queen of England in 1154.

PLANTAGENET

Henry II's father, Geoffrey of Anjou, wore a sprig of broom (called *planta genista* in Latin) in his cap. Because of this people called him Plantagenet and the name passed to his descendants.

him archbishop of Canterbury, Becket changed his ways. He led a frugal life and began to assert the rights of the Church. After years of quarrels, Henry exclaimed crossly, "Who will rid me of this turbulent priest?" Four knights took him at his word and killed Becket. Henry did penance for this crime, but it made little difference to him. He forced the king of the Scots to do homage to him, invaded Ireland, and subdued the Welsh.

▲ *Eleanor of Aquitaine's tomb in the abbey church at Frontrevault, in western France, lies next to one of her sons, Richard I. Her husband Henry II lies nearby.*

▼ *The Archbishop of Canterbury, Thomas à Becket, was brutally murdered by four of King Henry II's knights on the altar steps of Canterbury Cathedral.*

Thomas à Becket

Becket (1118–1170) became archbishop of Canterbury in 1162. He opposed the king and fled to France. On his return in 1170 he was murdered. He was made a saint in 1173.

Ireland

Ireland in the early 12th century was made up of more than 100 small kingdoms that often fought each other. Even so, the Irish were united because they all spoke the same language, Irish-Gaelic, and belonged to the Celtic Christian Church. Most of them were Celts, but some descendants of the Vikings lived in the east.

The five largest kingdoms were Ulster, Leinster, Munster, Connaught, and Meath. One of their kings usually held the title of *Ard Ri* (high king). The last really strong high king was Turlough O'Connor, King of Connaught. After he died, his son Rory made himself high king. But the King of Leinster, Dermot MacMurrough, also wanted the title.

Dermot asked for help from the Normans who ruled England. Eventually Richard de Clare, Earl of Pembroke, known as "Strongbow," agreed to back him in return for marrying Dermot's daughter, Aoife, and inheriting Leinster. As King of Leinster, Strongbow, and other Normans, seized Irish lands for themselves. This alarmed the king of England, Henry II, who proclaimed himself overlord of Ireland.

► *Ireland was divided into five main provinces. The smaller kingdoms all recognized as overlord the king of one of the provinces. The number of provinces changed from time to time.*

Ulster
Connaught
The Pale
Clontarf
Dublin
Meath
Kilkenny
Leinster
Munster

HIGH KINGS OF IRELAND

The first high king of Ireland was Cormac mac Airt of Tara in the 3rd century. The greatest of them was Brian Boru, King of Munster, who died after defeating Viking invaders at the battle of Clontarf in 1014. For the next 100 years the kingdoms fought bitterly among themselves until Turlough O'Connor, King of Connaught, became the most powerful king in Ireland. He built fortresses and weakened his rivals by dividing their kingdoms.

▼ *On the Rock of Cashel stand the ruins of St. Patrick's Cathedral. Given to the Church in 1101, the cross (far left) is where the kings of Munster were crowned.*

BREHON LAWS

Each Irish kingdom had its own judge, called a brehon. Over hundreds of years, the brehons built up a system of laws called the Brehon Laws. These laws covered property, trade, and contracts. They allowed a woman to manage her own property, but never that which belonged to her husband.

Strongbow

Richard de Clare, known as Strongbow, (c. 1130–1176) became earl of Pembroke in 1148. In 1170 he invaded Ireland and afterward was made king of Leinster in 1171.

Like the Vikings before them, many Normans adopted the customs of the Irish. In 1366, Edward III's son, Lionel, who was in charge of Ireland, ordered the Normans to stop speaking Irish and forbade them to marry Irish women. But the Irish gradually reclaimed their lands and by the late 15th century English rule was confined to a small area around Dublin called "the Pale."

▼ *The marriage of the tough Norman warrior Strongbow to Aoife, daughter of the King of Leinster, paved the way for the Normans to take over Irish lands.*

1155 England: Henry II makes Thomas à Becket Chancellor. Pope Adrian IV grants Henry II the right to rule Ireland.

1156 Japan: Civil wars start between rival clans (to 1185).

1158 Spain: Alfonso VIII becomes king of Castile (to 1214).

1159 England: Henry II demands scutage (payment in cash) instead of military service. Papacy: Alexander III becomes pope (to 1181).

1161 China: Explosives are used at the battle of Ts'ai-shih.

1162 England: Becket appointed archbishop of Canterbury; at once he quarrels with Henry II over the Church's rights.

1164 England: Becket flees to France.

1168 Mexico: Aztecs begin to migrate.

The knight from the Canterbury Tales, *written in 1388 by Geoffrey Chaucer.*

1169 Egypt: Saladin (Salah al-Din), becomes vizier (to 1193) and sultan from 1174.

1170 England: Becket is apparently reconciled with King Henry II and returns to Canterbury, but is murdered soon afterward. Oxford University is founded. Ireland: Normans from England invade under the command of Strongbow.

1171 England: Henry II breaks the power of Strongbow and annexes Ireland.

1173 England: Henry's sons, Henry, Richard, and Geoffrey, rebel, supported by their mother, Eleanor of Aquitaine. Thomas à Becket is declared a saint.

1174 Palestine: Saladin conquers Syria.

Buildings

Most people in Europe built their houses with wood because it was cheap and plentiful. Unfortunately, it caught fire easily. This was a big danger in towns where houses were close together and a fire could spread quickly. In time, wood rotted, so important buildings were built with stone. Special stone was sometimes brought long distances to build cathedrals and churches.

Cathedrals were built in a new style called Gothic which replaced the Romanesque style. This change meant that instead of rounded arches and sturdy pillars, churches had pointed arches and slender pillars. They also had larger windows.

Castles were also built with stone, and towns without a castle to protect them were usually surrounded by a high stone wall.

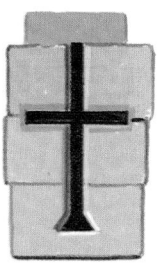
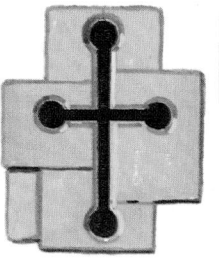

▲ *Most castle walls had slots called loopholes. They were narrow on the outside and wide on the inside. This let the defenders shoot arrows out, but attackers could not shoot arrows in. Some sloped at the bottom so that the archer could fire downward.*

▼ *A baron's castle was his home. It was also the place from which he looked after his estates and defended the surrounding countryside. Many castles were built on hills or beside rivers to make it more difficult for any enemies to get close.*

Carpenter

Mixing mortar

Blacksmith

◄ *Hundreds of workmen were needed to build a cathedral, an abbey, or a castle. Carpenters cut the wood to the right length and shape. They also made the scaffolding for the builders to climb on. Other men burned lime and mixed it with sand and water. This made the mortar which was used to stick the stones together. Meanwhile the blacksmith made nails, and made and mended tools.*

▶ *Gothic style churches were taller and lighter than earlier ones. They took many years to build. Note the pointed arches.*

▲ *Two important workers were the* stonecutter (above) *and the* mason (below). *The cutter shaped stones and numbered them so that the mason knew where they went.*

WHEN IT HAPPENED

1163 Work starts on the Gothic cathedral of Notre Dame in Paris, France.

1200 Early English Gothic style starts.

1300 Decorated phase of English Gothic architecture starts.

1370 Perpendicular phase of English Gothic architecture starts (ends about 1540).

1420 Filippo Brunelleschi starts work on Florence Cathedral, Italy.

▶ *Stone carvers left their own special marks to identify their work. Some of them also carved the faces of the people they knew on the gargoyles and other decorations around the churches they built.*

1177 Palestine: Baldwin IV of Jerusalem defeats Saladin at Montgisard.

1179 Palestine: Saladin besieges Tyre. Truce agreed between Baldwin IV and Saladin. Mongolia: Temujin becomes leader.

1181 Cambodia: Jayarvarman VII is made king (to 1220).

1183 Byzantine empire: Reformer Andronicus I becomes emperor.

1185 Portugal: Sancho I is king (to 1211). Byzantine empire: Andronicus I is executed, a period of corruption follows. Isaac II becomes emperor (to 1195). Japan: Kamakura period (to 1333).

1187 Palestine: Saladin captures Jerusalem.

Saladin, Sultan of Egypt and Syria and great Muslim warrior, taken from a Persian portrait.

1189 England: Richard I becomes king of England (to 1199). Palestine: Third Crusade starts (to 1192). North America: The Vikings visit for the last time.

1190 Holy Roman Empire: Frederick Barbarossa is drowned on his way to Palestine. Henry VI becomes Holy Roman emperor (to 1197). Ethiopia: Lalibela is made emperor (to 1225). Mongolia: Temujin begins conquests.

1191 Palestine: Richard I of England conquers Cyprus and captures Acre in Third Crusade. North America: Second era of Mayan civilization begins.

1192 Palestine: Richard I of England captures Jaffa, makes peace with Saladin but on the way home he is captured by his enemy, Duke Leopold of Austria. Japan: Minamoto Yoritomo becomes shogun.

Shoguns and Samurai

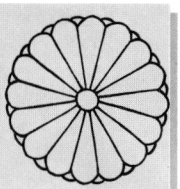

The Fujiwara family had held power in Japan from the 9th century (*see* pages 198–199). The influence of the Fujiwara broke down when they ran out of daughters, the traditional brides of the emperor. For a time retired emperors ruled. Then the Taira clan took over briefly until a rival clan, the Minamoto, whom the Taira had defeated, rallied under Minamoto Yoritomo and seized power. Yoritomo assumed the title of *sei-i dai-shogun* which means "barbarian conquering great general." His appointment in 1192 was without limit to his authority and from then on shoguns ruled Japan as hereditary military dictators until 1868. Minamoto set up his military government in Kamakura, after which his shogunate is named. When Minamoto died in 1199 the Hojo family, a branch of the Taira

▼ *The ruthless general Minamoto Yoritomo lived from 1147 to 1199. A brilliant organizer, he let others take command in battles and had his rivals murdered.*

clan, took control of Japan.

The shoguns were members of a warrior class, called *samurai*. Samurai were prepared to fight to the death for their *daimyos* (overlords), to whom they swore undying loyalty. Like the medieval knights in Europe, samurai believed in the values of truth and honor.

In battle a samurai fought hand to hand, on foot, or on horseback. Before combat he shouted his name and those of his ancestors, and boasted of his own heroic deeds. If he was dishonored he was expected to commit suicide. The samurai also lost their status in 1868.

▲ A samurai took a long time to arm himself for battle. He always took a bath first so that he would be clean and sweet-smelling if he were killed.

▼ A samurai's chief weapons were a bow of boxwood or bamboo and a single-edged sword. Samurai were trained from childhood and followed a strict code called Bushido (warrior's way). Battles were almost ceremonial, with a series of individual duels accompanied by chants, flag signals, drums, and gongs.

ARMS AND ARMOR

A samurai wore elaborate armor, made of enameled iron plates sewn onto fabric. He carried a sword and a dagger and often a fan reinforced with iron plates, which was used as a shield. His mask was designed to make him look fierce.

European Trade

The early Middle Ages were a period of great prosperity for Europe. The population was growing, which meant more land needed to be cultivated to grow food. Eventually this led to an agricultural surplus which could be traded. Towns grew up as trade centers and markets. Some, such as the French town of Troyes, were the site of regular trade fairs. Others, such as Paris or London, stood on important road and river links. Many were seaports because it was often easiest to travel by water.

Italy was one of the main trade centers. The Crusades weakened Islam's control of the Mediterranean Sea and through Venice, Genoa, and other ports came spices, silks, and other riches of the East. Goods from Asia traveled either overland along the Silk Road (*see* page 120), or by ship from India to the Red Sea and overland to the Mediterranean. They were exchanged for cloth, furs, hides, iron, linen, timber, and slaves.

Most of Europe's money was silver, but the Asian countries traded in gold. This

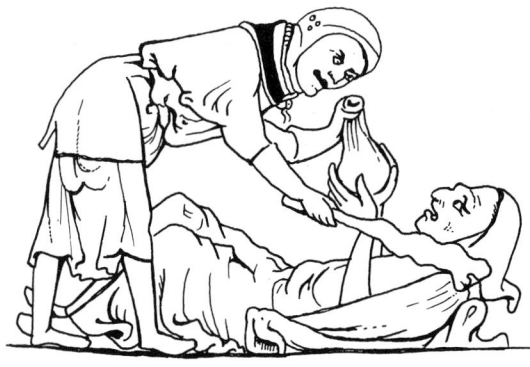

▲ The perils of medieval travel are shown by this drawing of a highwayman robbing a traveler of his money. Highwaymen often lay in wait at roadsides.

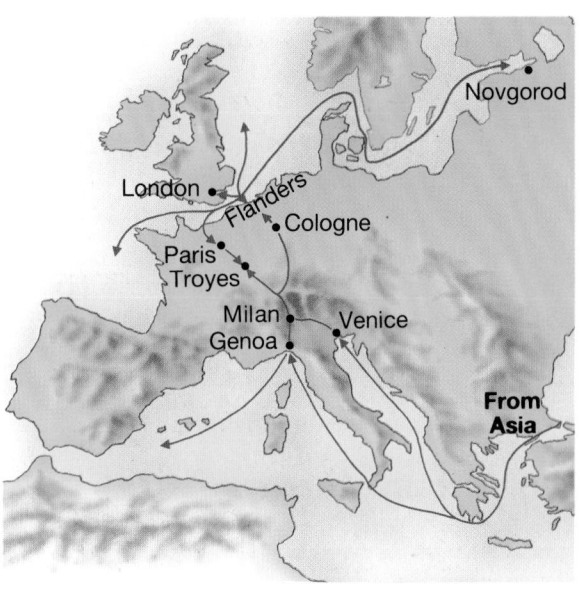

▲ Trade routes in the 12th century. Italian merchants attended fairs such as Troyes to buy Flemish cloth and sell Asian goods.

▼ Market day in a medieval town. Markets were usually held once a week. Livestock, food, metal, leather, and woodwork were all sold.

caused problems, so Italian merchants invented banking, with bills of exchange which could be used instead of cash.

In northern Europe trade was centered on the Rhineland in Germany, with the city of Cologne at the height of its prosperity. The Low Countries (now Belgium and the Netherlands) imported raw materials such as copper and wool and sold manufactured (finished) goods. During this time England began to sell most of its surplus wool to Flanders (now part of Belgium) where it was made into richly colored cloth.

THE GUILDS

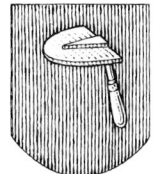
Masons

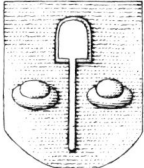
Pastrymakers

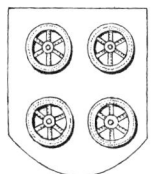
Wheelmakers

Glassmakers

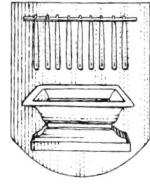
Candlemakers

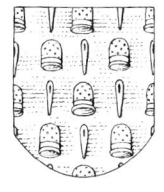
Needle and thimblemakers

Guilds had existed on a family basis since Anglo-Saxon times but were eventually formed for all merchants and craftsmen. They regulated trade and set standards. Apprentices could serve for up to 12 years before becoming a master. To qualify, an apprentice submitted a piece of work, called a masterpiece. Shown are some emblems of guilds.

Barbers

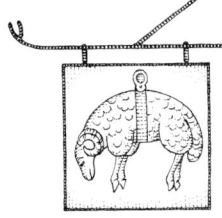
Wool merchant

1193 Austria: Leopold hands Richard I of England over to Holy Roman Emperor Henry VI, who demands a ransom. Palestine: Saladin dies and Al-Aziz Imad al-Din succeeds him (to 1198). India: Muslims capture Bihar and Bengal under Muhammad of Ghur (Mu'izz-ud-din).

1194 Holy Roman Empire: Henry VI conquers Sicily. Richard I is ransomed and returns to England. According to legend the place where Richard I is imprisoned was found by his troubadour, Blondel, who had accompanied him on the Crusades.

1195 Spain: Pedro II becomes king of Aragon (to 1213). Byzantine empire: Alexius III is made emperor (to 1203).

A money balance was used by both bankers and merchants to weigh solid silver coins to find out their value.

1197 Holy Roman Empire: Henry VI dies and civil war breaks out. Bohemia: Ottakar I becomes king (to 1230).

1198 Holy Roman Empire: Otto IV becomes emperor (to 1212). Papacy: Innocent III is made pope (to 1216).

1199 England: Henry II's youngest son, John, becomes king (to 1216).

c. 1200 Europe: Compass first used. Trade undergoes great expansion owing to the growing number of towns that require goods of all types. Polynesia: People from the island of Tahiti arrive in Hawaii and win control over the earlier settlers.

1200 North America: Hunac Ceel revolts against the Mayas of Chichén Itzá and sets up a new capital at Mayapan.

1202 Palestine: The Fourth Crusade begins.
Italy: Leonardo Fibonacci, a Florentine mathematician, publishes work on the Arabic numbering system which leads to use of modern numerals in Europe.

1203 England: John orders his nephew Arthur, Duke of Brittany, the true heir to the throne, to be murdered.

1204 France: Philip II captures Normandy and Touraine from England. Fourth Crusade: Crusaders, unable to pay Venice for transportation, agree to loot Constantinople on Venice's behalf.

By the 14th century skilled, Chinese iron workers knew how to forge metal objects such as this huge ship's anchor.

1206 Mongolia: Temujin is proclaimed Genghis Khan, "Emperor of All Men."

1207 England: Pope Innocent III appoints Stephen Langton archbishop of Canterbury but King John does not allow him to take office.

1208 Ghengis Khan conquers Turkestan.

1209 England: Innocent III excommunicates John for attacks on Church property.

1210 Holy Roman Empire: Innocent III excommunicates Emperor Otto IV. Italy: Francis of Assisi founds the Franciscan Order. Mongolia: Genghis Khan begins the invasion of China.

1211 Portugal: Alfonso II is king (to 1223).

1212 Holy Roman Empire: Frederick II is made emperor (to 1250). Children's Crusade: thousands of children from France and Germany set off for Palestine.

The Rise of Venice

When the Roman empire fell in the 5th century, a group of Roman citizens from the northern end of the Adriatic Sea fled to the safety of lagoons farther down the coast. They settled on some muddy islands and so began one of the greatest Italian cities: Venice.

The people built on stilts. There was no land to farm, so the early Venetians turned to the sea to fish. Their small boats then ventured farther afield to trade. The Venetians constructed more permanent homes, on piles driven into the mud, and channeled the sea so that it flowed in canals between the islands.

By 1100 Venice was a wealthy place. Protected by the sea, it did not have to spend time and money building elaborate fortifications. Its rich traders lived in sumptuous palaces and expanded their influence in the Near East by taking an active part in the Crusades. After fighting off its great trading rival Genoa, Venetian ships handled most of the trade between northern Europe and the Far East. Venice reached the height of its power during the 15th century with an empire which included many Greek islands, Cyprus, the Dalmatian coast (now in

▲ *The Lion of St. Mark has been Venice's emblem for centuries. The lion is often shown straddling the land and sea symbolizing Venice's dominance of both.*

▶ *Venice in the Middle Ages was well placed both for safety and for trade. It was Europe's greatest port for hundreds of years, and the main trading link between west and east.*

▼ *Four bronze horses, dating from the 4th century B.C., were seized by the Venetians at the sack of Constantinople in 1204 during the Fourth Crusade. The Crusades enabled Venice to grow even richer.*

GOODS TRADED

Twice a year a fleet of ships sailed from Venice to the Levant in the eastern Mediterranean, guarded by war galleys. It carried amber, metals including gold and silver ware, linen, timber, and woolen cloth. The fleet returned with cotton, silk, and porcelain from China, spices from Zanzibar and the East Indies, gems and ivory from Burma (Myanmar) and India, and dyewood from which dyes and pigments were extracted. Venice itself was famous for its lace and glassware and for a long time the only mirrors made were made in Venice.

Croatia), and part of northeastern Italy.

Like other places in medieval Italy, Venice was a city-state, largely independent. Its rulers were called *doges*, from the Latin word *dux* which means a leader. Doges were elected for life and came from among the most powerful and wealthy families in Venice. They had almost absolute power over government, the army, and church. But after 1140 they lost most of their powers, which were transferred to a Great Council.

Communications

The biggest revolution in communications in Europe came in the middle of the 15th century when Johannes Gutenberg began to print books with movable metal type. Although there had been some wood block printing in Europe before this time, it took a long time to cut each block and it could only be used for one page in one book. With movable type, many copies of one page could be printed, then the type could be rearranged and used for another page. This was far quicker than copying out books by hand, and so more books became available for those who could read.

For most people, however, the only form of communication was by word of mouth. Traders often spread news as they went on their travels, and villagers brought it back from market. This meant that news was months out of date, and often wrong.

The reason why news traveled slowly was that people themselves traveled slowly. On land the top speed was still that of the fastest horse, while at sea ships depended on the wind to provide them with power.

▲ Early medieval books were completely handmade. Scribes wrote them on sheets of parchment which were bound together with covers made of wooden boards. This made books both rare and expensive. In libraries, books (left) were often chained to the desks.

▲ Once people started printing with movable type, books could be produced more quickly and more efficiently. Although this made books cheaper, only the rich could afford them or knew how to read.

◀ Travelers in Asia and the Middle East often had to cross vast areas of desert with no towns or villages to stay in or buy food. To solve the problem, caravansaries were built along the main routes. They provided food and rooms for the travelers, and fodder, water, and shelter for their horses and camels. The caravanserais also gave travelers the chance to meet up and pass on information about the road ahead.

▼ Mediterranean sailors, copying Arab boats, started to use a triangular or lateen sail, which could be swung into the wind.

WHEN IT HAPPENED

1271 Marco Polo sets out from Venice to visit China. He later writes about his travels.

1397 The oldest surviving books printed with movable type are produced in Korea.

1434 Portuguese sailors round Cape Bojador off the coast of West Africa.

1440 Gutenberg starts using movable type in Germany.

▼ In Europe posting stations were built along main roads. They served refreshments to travelers, who could also change their horses or have them reshod.

Charter and Parliament

King John of England, the youngest son of Henry II, was given to violent bursts of temper. Not surprisingly, he soon annoyed his barons in English-ruled Anjou and Poitiers, and he lost those lands. In England, he taxed his barons heavily and ignored their rights until they rebelled. The barons demanded that John should confirm their ancient rights. They met him in a meadow called Runnymede, beside the river Thames. There they forced the king to put his seal to the Magna Carta, which means "great charter."

No sooner had John agreed to the Charter than he went back on his word. But he died the following year, leaving the throne to his nine-year-old son, who

▼ A 19th century artist's impression of King John signing the Magna Carta. In fact he did not actually sign it, and possibly could not even write.

▲ The Great Seal of King John affixed to the bottom of the Magna Carta. John's seal showed his agreement and so turned the Charter into the law of the land.

▼ *Simon de Montfort as pictured in a window at Chartres Cathedral in France. Born and brought up in France, he inherited the earldom of Leicester through his grandmother.*

1213 England: Pope Innocent III declares John deposed. John hurriedly makes peace with him. John surrenders the kingdom to the pope and becomes his vassal. Spain: James I, the Conqueror, becomes king of Aragon (to 1276).

1215 England: The barons force John to agree to a statement of their rights in the Magna Carta. France: St. Dominic founds the Dominican Order of friars at Toulouse.

1216 England: Henry III, aged nine, becomes king (to 1272). Papacy: Honorius III is made pope (to 1227).

1217 Fifth Crusade (to 1222); the venture fails to capture Egypt. Severe famine in central and eastern Europe.

1218 Genghis Khan conquers Persia.

1219 Mongols conquer Bokhara. Japan: Hojo clan rules (to 1333), after they overthrow the Minamoto family.

1220 According to tradition, Manco Capac founds the Inca civilization in Peru.

1223 France: Louis VIII becomes king (to 1226). Russia: Mongols invade.

became Henry III. The barons had the Charter reissued, and in 1225 it became the law of England. The Charter stated that the king could continue to rule, but must keep to the laws of the land and could be compelled to do so.

Henry III was incompetent and spent large sums of money. Again the barons got together, led by Simon de Montfort. They forced Henry to agree to rule with the help of a council of barons if they paid off his debts. Like his father, Henry III went back on the deal, but de Montfort defeated him in battle at Lewes and ruled the country in Henry's name. In 1265, de Montfort called a Parliament (governing body) at which he asked for two knights from every shire and two burgesses from every town to attend. This was the first time commoners had attended; up to then parliaments had consisted only of barons and bishops.

Images of monkeys were often used to mock people who took things too seriously. Rabbits, geese and foxes were also used to make fun.

1226 France: Louis IX, aged 12, becomes king of France (to 1270). His mother, Blanche of Castile, becomes regent and dominates European politics for the next quarter of a century.

1227 England: Henry III, now aged 20, begins to rule. Papacy: Gregory IX becomes pope (to 1241). Mongolia: Genghis Khan dies.

1228 Sixth Crusade (to 1229): Led by Holy Roman Emperor Frederick II, Crusaders recapture Jerusalem.

1229 Mongolia: Ogodai, son of Genghis, is elected khan (to 1241).

1232 The earliest known rockets are used in a war between Mongols and Chinese.

1233 Rome: Pope Gregory IX establishes the Inquisition.

1234 China: Mongols annex the Chin empire of north China.

1235 Mali: Sundiata Keita is king (to 1255).

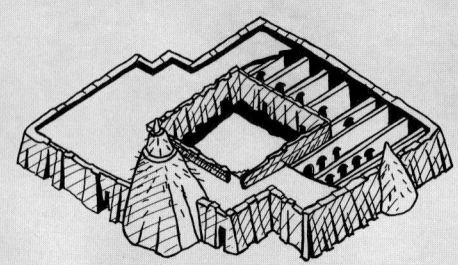

The great mosque at Timbuktu was designed by As-Saheli, an Egyptian.

1236 Russia: Alexander Nevski is made prince of Novgorod (to 1263).

1238 Spain: First European paper mills appear at Sativa.

1240 Russia: Alexander Nevski of Novgorod defeats the Swedes at the battle of Neva. Mongols capture Moscow and destroy Kiev. West Africa: Old empire of Ghana is incorporated in the new kingdom of Mali.

1241 Mongols invade Hungary and cross the River Danube into Austria; they are forced to withdraw from Europe following the death of their leader Ogodai Khan.

1242 Russia: Batu, grandson of Genghis Khan, establishes Mongol khanate of Kipchak, known as the Golden Horde, on the lower Volga River.

1243 Papacy: Innocent IV becomes pope (to 1254). Palestine: Egyptians capture Jerusalem from the Christians.

1245 Holy Roman Empire: Pope Innocent IV calls the Synod of Lyon, which declares Emperor Frederick II deposed.

Mali and Ethiopia

In 1240 Sundiata Keita, ruler of the small West African kingdom of Kangaba, brought to an end the empire of Ghana and established a new empire, Mali. Under his rule the empire soon became rich and powerful, reaching its peak under Sundiata's grandson Mansa Musa in the early 14th century.

The empire covered a large part of what is now Gambia, Senegal, Guinea, and Mali. Its merchants traded gold, kola nuts, and slaves for cloth, copper, dates, figs, metal goods, and salt. All these traveled by caravans of camels across the Sahara from northern Africa.

Timbuktu, on the Niger River and now in modern Mali, became the capital and chief trading center. When Mansa Musa converted the empire to Islam, Timbuktu became a center of Muslim scholarship

▼ *Mansa Musa as shown in the Catalan Atlas of 1375. He made a famous pilgrimage to Mecca, accompanied by 500 slaves and many camels carrying gold.*

CHURCHES

Ethiopia was the only Christian country in Africa. During the 13th century, the emperors of Ethiopia had 11 Christian churches carved out of solid rock. One of the most remarkable was the Church of St. George at Lalibela, in the mountains north of Addis Ababa. To build the church, workers had to cut a hole 36 feet (11 m) deep in the rock, leaving a cross-shaped block standing in the middle. They then hollowed out the middle of this block to form the interior of the church.

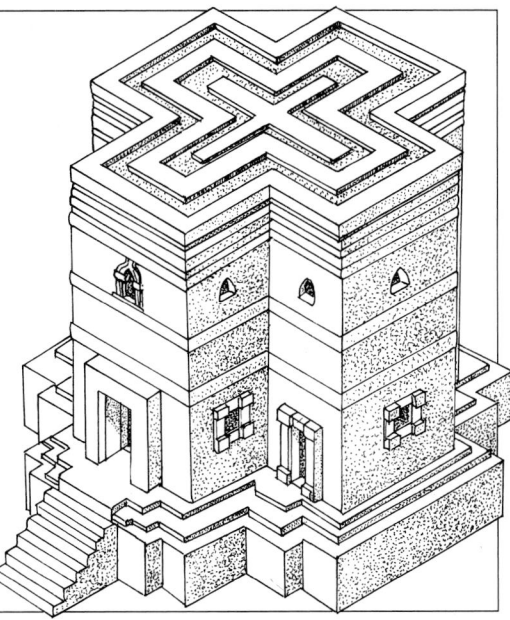

FALASHA JEWS

Ethiopia had about 20,000 people, called Falashas, who follow the Jewish faith. Because they have no ancient Jewish traditions, it is thought they were converted at the beginning of the Christian era. The Falashas, like the former emperors of Ethiopia, claim descent from Solomon and the Queen of Sheba.

as did another trading city, Djenne, now in Guinea. Mali was later swallowed up by another empire, Songhay, which had been a province of Mali.

On the other side of Africa, the Christian empire of Ethiopia was cut off from the Christians of Europe by the spread of Islam in northern Africa. After Lalibela became emperor in 1190, he moved the capital from Axum (see pages 102–103) to a town called Roha, later renamed Lalibela in his honor.

In 1270 Yekuno Amlak seized the throne. His family claimed descent from Solomon and the Queen of Sheba. The very last emperor of Ethiopia, Haile Selassie (who ruled from 1930 to 1974) was a descendant of Yekuno.

▼ A mosque has stood at Djenne since the days of the Mali empire. The present Great Mosque, finished in 1907, was built of mud brick in traditional style.

The Friars

Giovanni Bernadone, son of a cloth merchant from Assisi in central Italy, dreamed of becoming a chivalrous knight. He was known as *Il Francesco*, the little Frenchman, from which came the name Francis. One day he realized that his true vocation (calling) was to follow the teachings of Jesus, give up all his possessions and preach the word of God. So he founded the first order of friars, later called the Franciscans or Friars Minor (Little Brothers). He is now known as St. Francis of Assisi.

Friars supplied a real need in the medieval world. Nuns and monks in their cloisters had withdrawn from the world in order to worship God. But in the expanding towns, teachers and

▼ *Robes worn by friars showed to which order they belonged. On the far left is a nun. To her right are a Franciscan friar, a Dominican friar, a Carmelite friar, and an Augustinian or Austin friar.*

UNIVERSITIES

The University of Bologna in Italy, founded in 1100, is believed to be the oldest university in Europe. Universities were set up to educate priests and monks to a higher level than that found in monastery schools. Many friars taught at them. The Dominicans were a clever and industrious order, but always followed a set doctrine. The Franciscans were more independent thinkers and interested in science. One Franciscan, Alexander of Hales, became a professor at the University of Paris, founded in 1150.

St. Francis

Francis (1182–1226) was born in Assisi, Italy to a wealthy family. He gave up this life in 1205 and devoted himself to the poor and sick. In 1210 he founded the Order of Franciscans. After his death he was made a saint in 1228.

RULES FOR FRIARS

St. Francis of Assisi drew up a number of rules for his friars to follow. They were to adopt a life of poverty, owning nothing themselves except the simplest clothes. Friars were to practice strict self-denial, abstaining from all worldly pleasures (Francis himself ate only the plainest food). Above all, each friar was expected to preach the Gospels (in the Bible) to as many people as possible.

1245 Papacy: Pope Innocent IV sends Friar John of Pian del Carpine to explore Mongolia (returns 1249).

1247 Italy: Bitter war between Holy Roman Emperor Frederick II and papal allies (to 1250). Japan: Mongols invade.

1248 The Seventh Crusade begins, led by Louis IX of France (to 1270).

1250 Holy Roman Empire: Conrad IV becomes emperor (to 1254). Seventh Crusade: Saracens capture Louis IX in Egypt, but he is ransomed.

1252 Italy: Golden florins minted at Florence.

1253 France: Louis IX sends Friar William of Rubruquis to Mongolia (returns 1255).

1254 Holy Roman Empire: The Great Interregnum starts. It is a bitter struggle for the imperial crown (to 1273).

1256 Wales: Prince Llewellyn sweeps the English from his country. Papacy: Alexander IV founds the Augustinian Order from several groups of hermits.

preachers could help in the community. The friars lived and worked among the people. They addressed each other as "brother," and the name friar came from the Latin word for brother, *frater*.

Francis intended that his friars should work for their living, and only beg if they were unable to work. In time friars became so busy teaching that they had no time to earn a living. So begging became their means of survival and they were known as *mendicants* or beggars.

A second order of friars was founded in southern France six years later by Dominic, a Castilian canon from Spain. Its members were called Dominicans. Other important orders were the Carmelites, founded at Mount Carmel in Palestine, and the Augustinians, or Austin Friars, who followed the teachings of St. Augustine of Hippo.

Some friars were known by the color of their robes. The Franciscans were Gray Friars (though they later wore brown), the Dominicans were Black Friars, and the Carmelites, White Friars.

This illustration, taken from a medieval manuscript, symbolizes St. Francis of Assisi's love of nature as he stands surrounded by birds, a lion, and an oak tree.

1258 England: Barons compel Henry III to accept a series of reforms called the Provisions of Oxford.

1260 China: Mongol chief Kublai is elected khan by his army at Shan-tu. Germany: The Hanseatic League is formed.

1261 England: The pope allows Henry III to break his promise to keep the Provisions of Oxford. Papacy: Urban IV becomes pope (to 1264). Byzantine empire: Michael VIII restores Byzantine authority.

Food and Farming

In Europe the peasants lived mainly on a diet of bread, cheese, and beer. Occasionally they killed one of their pigs and ate its meat. They might also kill an old sheep if it was no longer producing lambs or very good wool. Its meat would be tough, however, and so it would be stewed for a long time to try and make it more tender. Herbs from the garden, together with vegetables and beans, were sometimes added.

In contrast, rich people ate meat or fish. Some meat and fish came from their farms and special fish ponds. Some was hunted, such as swans and herons, as well as deer, rabbits, and hares.

Everyone had the problem of getting enough food to last through winter. If the harvest was poor, then the old and the weak could easily starve. Even strong people could die because hunger left them more likely to catch diseases. A great plague swept through Europe in 1347 after a series of bad harvests. Although it was devastating at the time, it led to improved sanitary conditions.

▲ Aztec farmers grew vegetables on reed platforms called chinampas. *These were built in a lake and were covered with fertile mud. The Aztecs also caught birds and fish to eat.*

▼ *About 90 percent of the people in England lived and worked in the countryside. In spring, they plowed the land and sowed seeds by hand. As they worked children scared the birds away. Later all the weeds had to be pulled out by hand.*

► The heavy plow made it possible to use the clay soils of central Europe, as well as parts of England. It was pulled by a horse or a team of oxen. Few farmers were rich enough to own their own plow. Often, the plow and the draft animals would be shared by many villagers.

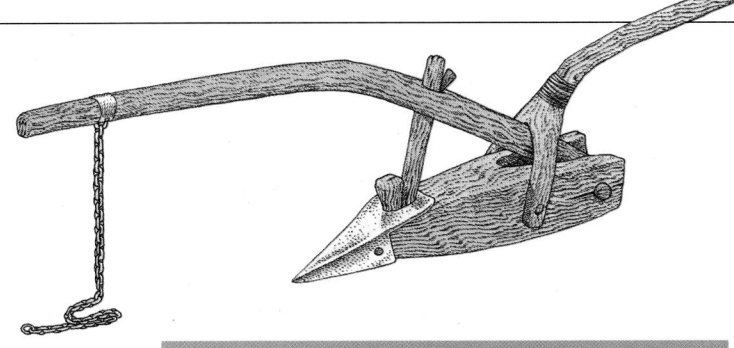

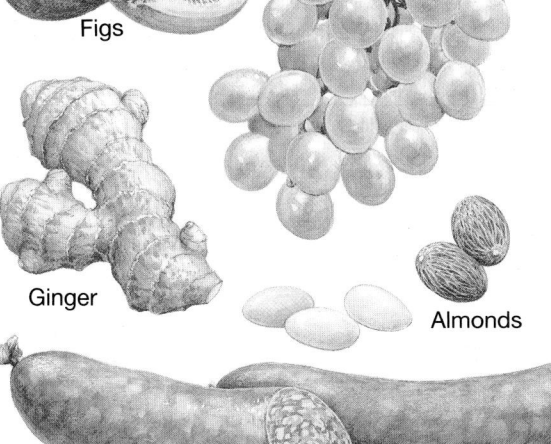

Grapes

Figs

Ginger

Almonds

Spices for preserving meats

WHEN IT HAPPENED

1100 Men returning from the First Crusade bring back spices from the Middle East. They also bring back the knowledge of how to use them for cooking.

1347 The Black Death arrives in Europe and lasts until 1353. Those who survive ask for higher wages and better living conditions.

c. **1400** Many landowners turn arable land to sheep pasture as the demand for wool increases.

c. **1450** By this date, farmers are practicing seed selection to try and improve their crops.

◄ When the Crusaders came home from the Near East, they brought with them many different sorts of food. These included oranges and lemons, figs, raisins, and dates. They also brought sugared almonds at a time when sugar was unknown in most of Europe. Like the Vikings, they also brought back spices which came to the Near East from India and the islands of the Moluccas. These included ginger, cinnamon, and pepper. They were used to hide the taste of meat which was going bad or which had been salted to preserve it over the winter. This led to the development of the spice trade. After the fall of the Ottoman empire, Europeans started looking for routes to India and the Moluccas, so they could trade directly with the spice growers.

1264 England: Simon de Montfort and other English barons defeat Henry III at the battle of Lewes, and take him prisoner. Mongolia: Kublai Khan reunites the Mongol empire. He transfers China's capital to Yen-ching and builds Khanbaliq (modern Beijing) on the sight of the former Chin capital.

1265 England: Simon de Montfort asks leading citizens from the main towns to take part in Parliament. Henry III's son Edward defeats and kills Simon de Montfort at battle of Evesham. Papacy: Clement IV becomes pope (to 1268).

Mongols moved easily from place to place by transporting their yurts (tents) on wagons.

1266 English philosopher and scientist Roger Bacon invents the magnifying glass.

1268 Papacy: following the death of Clement IV, the Holy See remains vacant until 1271. Palestine: Muslims from Egypt capture Antioch which had been held by the Christians.

1270 France: Louis IX dies on the Seventh Crusade. He is succeeded by Philip III, the Bold (to 1285). Ethiopia: Yekuno Amlak becomes emperor (to 1285).

1271 Venice: Merchant Marco Polo, his father and his uncle set off to visit the court of Kublai Khan in north China along the Silk Road (return 1295). Papacy: Gregory X becomes pope (to 1276).

1272 England: Edward I is king (to 1307).

1273 Holy Roman Empire: Rudolf I is made emperor (to 1291).

1274 Japan: Kublai Khan's Mongols invade but fail to gain a foothold.

The Mongol Empire

In 1180 a 13-year-old boy suddenly became the leader of his tribe when his father was poisoned. The boy was named Temujin, and his tribe were a warlike nomadic people who lived in Mongolia, the Yakka Mongols. Two-thirds of the tribe promptly deserted him, but very soon Temujin reunited them. He went on to conquer other Mongol tribes. In 1206, a meeting of the *khans* (chiefs of tribes) hailed Temujin as Genghis Khan, "Emperor of All Men." He promised that future generations of Mongols would lead lives of luxury.

Genghis Khan began a career of conquest by training a ruthless, well-disciplined army. His hordes terrified their opponents, killing people who did not surrender and often butchering those who did. In a series of brilliant campaigns, Genghis Khan conquered northern China and Korea, then swung westward to overrun northern India, Afghanistan, Persia, and parts of Russia.

After Genghis died, his son Ogodai conquered Armenia and Tibet, then

▼ *Mongol horsemen were trained to shoot with bow and arrows while riding at full gallop. In this way they hunted game, and in battle their sharp arrows could pierce an enemy's armor.*

▲ *Mongol sports were designed to train their warriors for war and make them fit. From boyhood on they practiced archery and wrestling.*

turned toward Europe, ravaging Hungary and Poland. His nephew, Kublai Khan, completed the conquest of China and made himself emperor of China. He was the first ruler of the Yuan dynasty which held power until 1368.

A Venetian merchant called Marco Polo (*see* pages 282–283) spent 17 years at the court of Kublai Khan. His account of life there showed that the Mongols in China now lived the life of luxury promised them earlier by Genghis.

HOW THE MONGOLS LIVED

The Mongols were wandering herdsmen, roaming over the bleak plains of Mongolia with their cattle and sheep, and riding small, sturdy ponies. They lived in *yurts*, tents made of hides or cloth stretched over a collapsible wooden frame. A hole at the top let out the smoke from the fire. The tents were transported on ox-drawn carts.

It was a male-dominated world: the warriors sat nearest the fire and ate the best food, while the women sat farther away and ate what was left. Children had to make do with scraps, or whatever small animals they could catch for themselves.

▼ *In battle Mongol warriors wore helmets of iron or hard leather. Their armor was made of iron plates linked together by strong leather thongs.*

Genghis Khan

1167 Born Temujin.
1206 Becomes Genghis Khan.
1210–14 Conquers northern China.
1218–25 Overruns Persia, Turkestan, and Afghanistan.
1227 Dies after a fall.

Tamerlane
1336 Born in Samarkand.
1370 Becomes ruler of Turkestan.
1383 Conquers Persia.
1391 Occupies Moscow.
1398 Invades India.
1401 Defeats Syria.
1405 Dies in Kazakhstan.

▼ *A charge by the mounted archers and sword-wielding cavalry of the Mongol armies struck fear into any force that opposed them. News of Mongol victories spread throughout Europe and travelers told horrifying tales of their ferocity. The Mongols were said to eat their captives. The Mongol invasion cut off Russia, Asia, and the Far East from Europe.*

▲ *The ancient Persian game of polo, played there since the 6th century B.C., was adopted by the Mongols because it helped to give their warriors the excellent skills in horsemanship necessary for fighting battles.*

After the death of Kublai Khan in 1294, the mighty Mongol empire that he had tried to rule from Khanbaliq (now Beijing) broke up. But other Mongol khans carved out smaller empires for themselves in central and western Asia, such as Kipchak, which included a large area of Russia. Russians called it the Golden Horde because of the magnificent tent in which its khan lived.

Cruel though the Mongols were, none was as barbarous as the great Mongol chief, Tamerlane (Timur-i-Lenk) sometimes called Timur the Lame

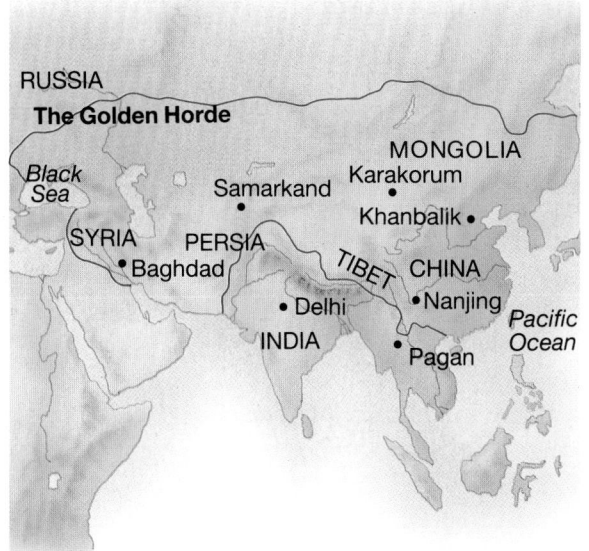

▲ *At its greatest extent in the 13th century during the reign of Kublai Khan, the Mongol empire extended from the Pacific Ocean to the Black Sea.*

because of his battle wounds. He ruled from Samarkand in Turkestan but overran Persia (Iran), Mesopotamia (Iraq), Armenia, Georgia, Azerbaijan, and the Golden Horde. For a year he occupied Moscow. He died marching on China. Despite his cruel reputation he was a great patron of the arts and brought many craftsmen to beautify his capital city of Samarkand.

TAMERLANE'S TOMB

When Tamerlane died he was buried in a beautiful jade-covered tomb just outside the city of Samarkand in central Asia. Called Gur Amir, the tomb was finally opened by archaeologists in 1941, and is thought to be one of the finest examples of Islamic art from this period.

1275 China: Marco Polo enters the service of Kublai Khan and travels widely in the Mongol empire during the next 17 years.

1276 Papacy: Innocent V is the first Dominican to become pope. He dies five months after election and is succeeded by Adrian V who dies five weeks after being elected. The successor Pope John XXI dies after eight months in office.

1277 England: Roger Bacon is exiled for heresy (to 1292). Papacy: Nicholas III becomes pope (to 1280).

1278 Holy Roman Empire: Rudolf I defeats and kills Ottakar of Bohemia at battle of the Marchfeld.

A pottery figure of an actor made at the time of the Yuan dynasty, when China was ruled by the Mongols.

1279 Holy Roman Empire: Rudolf I surrenders claims to Sicily and the Papal States. China: Kublai Khan completes the Mongol conquest of the whole of China and founds the Yuan (Mongol) dynasty (to 1368).

1281 Papacy: Martin IV becomes pope (to 1285). Japan: The second Mongol invasion ends in disaster.

1283 Wales: Edward I of England defeats and kills Llewellyn, Prince of Wales, and also executes Llewellyn's brother David. The English conquest of Wales is complete and Edward I orders the building of Caernarvon castle.

1285 France: Philip IV becomes king (to 1314). Papacy: Honorius IV is made pope (to 1287).

1286 Scotland: Margaret, the Maid of Norway, becomes queen, succeeding her grandfather Alexander III (to 1290).

1287 Burma (Myanmar): Mongols pillage Pagan, the capital.

1288 Papacy: Nicholas IV becomes pope (to 1292).

John Balliol reigned in Scotland from 1292 to 1296. Unwillingly, he paid homage to Edward I, King of England and in 1295 he tried to ally himself with France. This led England to invade Scotland. Balliol gave up his throne and retired to his estates in France where he died in 1314.

1289 China: Friar John of Montecorvino becomes the first Christian archbishop of Beijing.

1290 Scotland: Margaret dies; many men claim the Scottish throne. India: Turkish leader Firuz founds the Khalji dynasty (to 1320) in Delhi. England: The Jewish population is expelled.

1291 Scotland: Scots acknowledge Edward I of England as their sovereign; he arbitrates in the succession dispute. Palestine: Saracens (Muslims) capture Acre, the last Christian stronghold in Palestine. Although the Crusades continue, their great age is at an end.

1292 Holy Roman Empire: Adolf, Count of Nassau, emperor (to 1298).

1293 China: First Christian missionaries arrive. Southeast Asia: A Mongol expedition to attack Java ends in failure.

1294 Papacy: Celestine V (the hermit Peter of Morrone) becomes pope but he resigns after five months. Boniface VIII, lawyer, diplomat, and believer in the magic arts, becomes pope (to 1303). China: Death of Kublai Khan.

Robert the Bruce

A little girl of three became Queen of Scotland in 1286 when her grandfather, Alexander III, died. She was Margaret, known as the Maid of Norway because her mother was the wife of the King of Norway. She died at sea four years later, on her way to Scotland. There was no obvious heir, and 13 men claimed the throne.

Some of the claimants asked Edward I of England to decide who should rule Scotland. There were two leading contestants, John Balliol and Robert Bruce. Edward chose Balliol, but in 1296 Balliol defied Edward. Edward at once invaded Scotland and ruled himself.

Many Scots resented this treatment. In 1297 a Scottish knight, William Wallace, led a rebellion. It was crushed and

▼ *Robert I was born in 1274. He was enthroned at Scone, near Perth, as were all Scottish kings. Robert died in 1329 and was succeeded by his son, David II.*

THE SPIDER'S LESSON

Legend says that Robert the Bruce, in despair after a defeat, was sheltering in a cave when he saw a spider trying again and again to climb a thread. Eventually it succeeded and Bruce decided never to give up the fight.

SCOTTISH CLAIMANTS TO THE THRONE

The question of the Scottish succession (who has the right to rule) was a complicated one and it was made worse by the number of claimants to the throne after Margaret, the Maid of Norway, died.

Alexander III was the direct descendant in the male line of the first ruler of a united Scotland, Duncan I (1034–1040). John Balliol and Robert Bruce were both very distant cousins of Alexander, being descended through the female line from David, Earl of Huntingdon, the younger brother of Alexander III's grandfather, King William "the Lion."

Robert I's son David II had no children, so the throne descended through Robert's daughter Marjorie, who married Walter Fitzalan, High Steward of Scotland. His position gave the family its name, the house of Stuart. Robert II became the first Stuart king of Scotland.

Wallace was beheaded, but a new champion appeared: Robert Bruce's grandson, who was also named Robert and is known as Robert the Bruce.

Bruce was ruthless. He and his followers killed his only rival, John Comyn, Balliol's nephew. Bruce began a fresh rebellion. He suffered several defeats, but was saved when Edward I died on his way to subdue Scotland again. Edward's son, Edward II, did not have his father's iron will and Bruce defeated him in 1314 at the battle of Bannockburn. In 1328, Scotland finally became independent from England and Bruce was crowned King Robert I.

► *The Great Seal of John Balliol, King of Scotland, showing him on horseback.*

▼ *At the battle of Bannockburn, a Scottish army of about 7,000 defeated an English force three times the size.*

▼ *Leprosy was common at this time. There was no cure, so everyone was frightened of it. Lepers often begged in the streets and rang a bell to warn of their approach.*

People

Life was harsh for poor people in Europe. Many died as babies, but if they survived to the age of 12, they were thought to be adults. They might live to be 60, if they were lucky. People did not know where diseases came from and many died of plagues, smallpox, and influenza. A small cut could be fatal because no one knew how to keep wounds clean.

The poor spent most of their time working or begging for food. The rich were entertained by singers, dancers, and musicians at home. Acrobats and bear-trainers performed in the streets.

▶ *Japanese women always used white makeup on their faces, but this made their teeth look yellow. To hide this, the women painted their teeth black.*

▼ *An illustration of a Chinese Song dynasty tomb painting. It shows a wealthy couple at their table, waited on by four servants. At this time China was the wealthiest and best run state in the world.*

▼ *A Japanese court lady in her underclothes. Over them she wore several silk kimonos.*

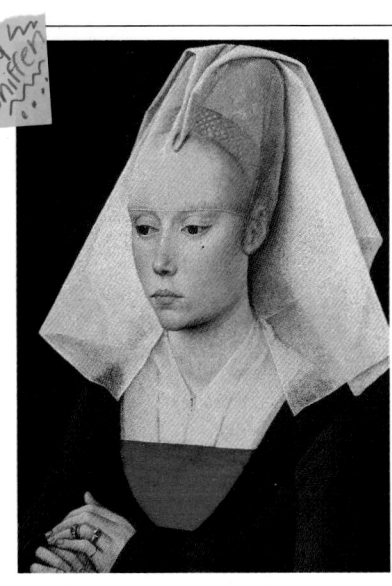

▲ European women wore very little makeup. Instead, they plucked their eyebrows and pinned their hair back tightly. It was also fashionable to pluck the forehead.

▼ The clothes people wore showed where they belonged in society. Peasants (left and below) were not allowed to wear scarlet and certain shades of blue or green. Workmen used a certain kind of cloth, friars used another kind, and servants made their clothes from cloth with a striped band. Only the rich (right) could afford to be fashionable. Both men and women wore two tunics: a close-fitting one underneath, with a heavier, flowing coat over the top, usually in different colors. Women in northern Europe wore a wimple, a headdress that framed the face.

▲ People played games that we still have today. These included chess, bowls, cards, and hide-and-seek. They also played soccer.

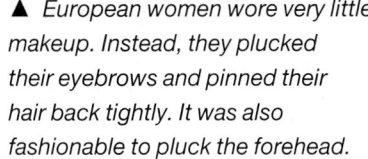

WHEN IT HAPPENED

1100 Crusaders returning from the Near East bring back the Muslim idea of regular washing.

1381 English peasants, led by Wat Tyler, march on London to demand better working conditions.

15th century Illuminated manuscripts, such as the Duke of Berry's *The Very Rich Hours*, depicting everyday life, are made.

Aztecs and Incas

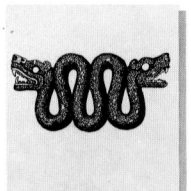

Two great civilizations were founded within a hundred years or so of each other: the Inca empire in Peru and the Aztec empire in Mexico. According to tradition, Manco Capac and his sister, Mama Ocllo, were the first rulers of the Incas around 1200. They called themselves "the Children of the Sun" and, if they existed at all, they were probably the leaders of a wandering tribe. Little is known about the emperors who followed except Pachacuti, who succeeded in 1438 and was a brilliant general. He conquered neighboring tribes and founded the Inca empire.

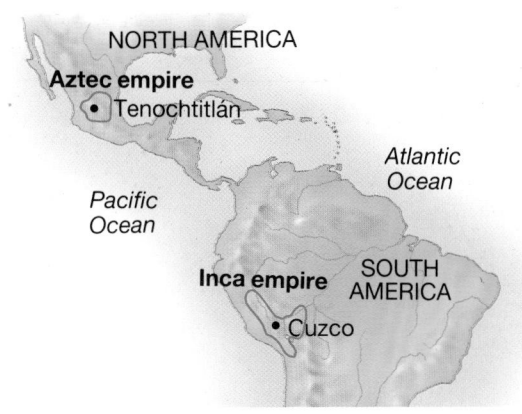

▲ The location of the Aztec and Inca empires.

▼ The Inca ruler Pachacuti leads his army into battle. Inca soldiers used slings, bolas, which were stones linked by lengths of string, wooden spears and swords, and star-shaped clubs.

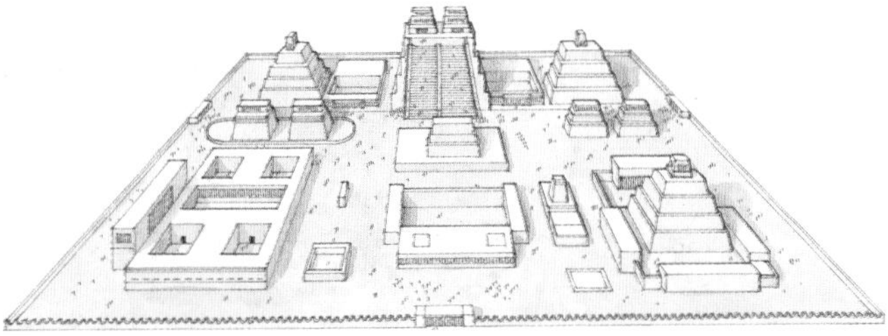

▲ The center of the Aztec city of Tenochtitlán showing the Temple of Huitzilopochtli (back), priests' quarters (left front), and the Temple of the Sun (right front).

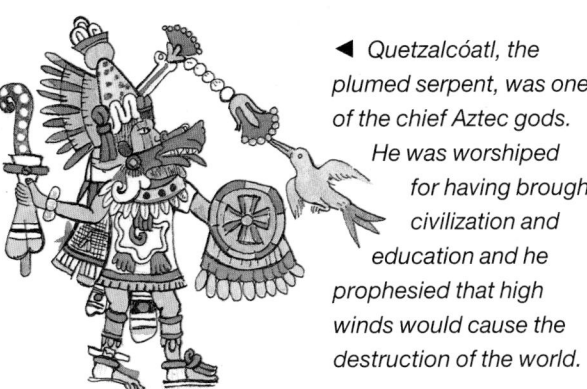

◀ *Quetzalcóatl, the plumed serpent, was one of the chief Aztec gods. He was worshiped for having brought civilization and education and he prophesied that high winds would cause the destruction of the world.*

The Incas probably looked very like their descendants, the Quechua Indians, who live in the highlands of Peru today. Short and stocky, with straight black hair, they are well adapted to life in the thin air of the mountains.

Legends say the Aztecs came from northern Mexico. In 1168, on the instructions of their god Huitzilopochtli, they began to migrate. They eventually settled in the valley of Mexico. In 1325, the Aztecs started to build a city, Tenochtitlán, on an island in Lake Texcoco which is now the site of Mexico City. In the 15th century they went on to conquer the other cities of the valley, and founded the Aztec empire.

AMERICAN FOOD

The Incas mainly lived on potatoes and bred ducks and guinea pigs for eating. Aztecs hunted for fish and birds and bred turkeys. The Aztecs made a chocolate drink from cocoa beans (the tree, pod and beans of cocoa are shown here). Both peoples grew corn, chilies, tomatoes, peanuts, avocados and beans. The Incas made beer from corn.

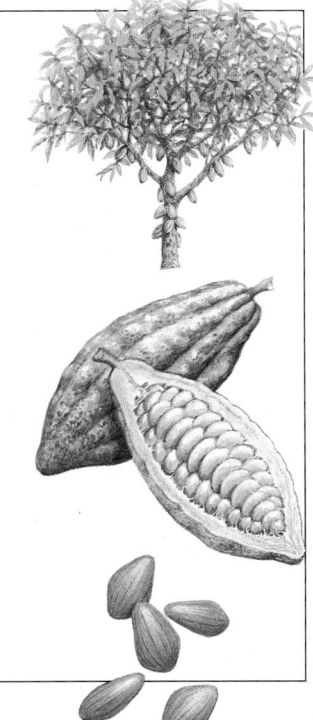

1295 England: Knights and burgesses from English shires and towns are summoned to the Model Parliament of Edward I. China: Temur Oljaitu (Ch'eng Tsung), grandson of Kublai Khan, becomes emperor of China (to 1307). He is the last effective ruler of the Yuan dynasty.

1296 France: Conflict between Philip IV and Pope Boniface VIII over papal powers in France (to 1303).

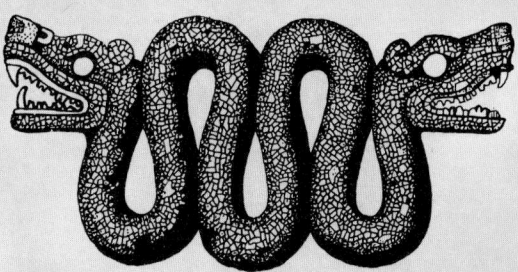

The Aztec god Huitzilopochtli was depicted as a snake. This image is made of wood covered with turquoise. It was probably worn on the back of the head as part of a headdress.

1297 Southeast Asia: The Burmese become vassals of the Chinese Mongols. Scotland: Rebellion against the English led by William Wallace. He defeats an English army at the battle of Stirling.

1298 Scotland: Edward I of England defeats Wallace at the battle of Falkirk and reconquers Scotland. Holy Roman Empire: German barons depose Adolf and elect Albert I (to 1308).

c. **1299** Turkey: Osman I founds the Ottoman empire.

1300 Italy: Bologna University appoints Dorotea Bocchi as professor of medicine, and Maria di Novella as professor and head of mathematics. Peru: Incas begin period of expansion.

14th century Polynesia: A second wave of Maoris arrive in New Zealand from the Marquesas.

1301 Wales: Edward I of England invests his baby son, Edward, as prince of Wales. Byzantine empire: Osman, founder of the Ottoman Turks, defeats the Byzantines.

Benin and Zimbabwe

The modern country of Benin, formerly called Dahomey, took its name from one of the most powerful empires of West Africa. Called Benin, this empire was situated in eastern Nigeria. Its capital, Benin City, was founded in about A.D. 900. At its most prosperous in the 15th century, the city had walls 25 miles (40 km) long and wide streets, lined with large wooden houses. The palace of the *oba* (king) was richly decorated with bronze plaques.

The city stood on a major trade route, and its merchants dealt in cloth, ivory, metals (especially bronze), palm oil, and pepper. It was the custom for warring black African states to make their prisoners slaves, so when the Portuguese reached Benin in the 15th century (*see* pages 306–307), they took advantage of this and bought slaves. The slave trade became one of Benin's greatest sources of money. Benin reached its height during the reign of Oba Ewuare the Great, who ruled from 1440 to 1481.

Benin is renowned for its art, especially

▲ This Benin bronze shows an oba seated on his throne, with two subjects kneeling beside him. Benin craftsmen cast bronzes by the "lost wax" process. A mold is made by covering a wax model with clay, then the wax is melted away and molten bronze poured in.

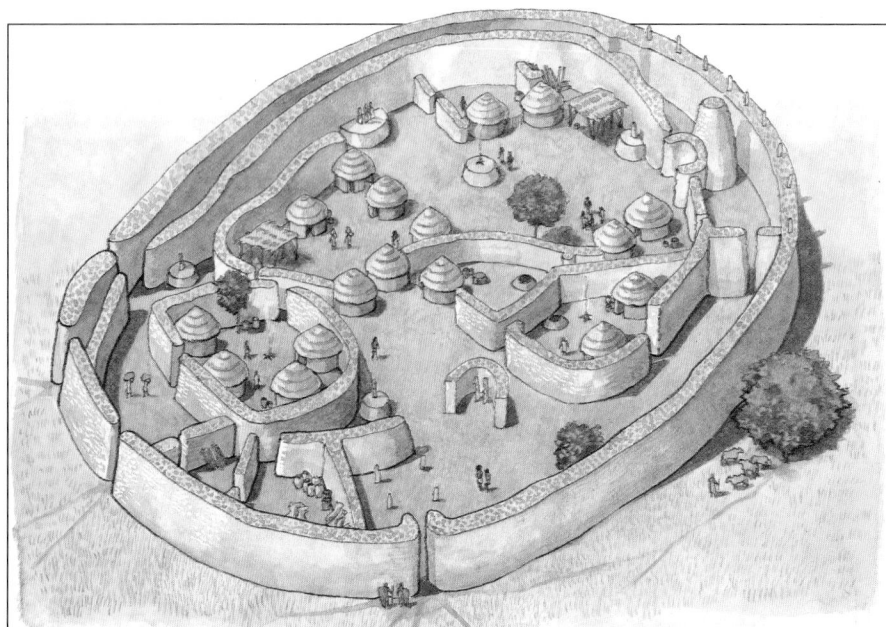

GREAT ZIMBABWE

One of the greatest African mysteries is the walled city of Great Zimbabwe, after which modern Zimbabwe is named. The massive stone ruins were built of granite blocks from the 11th to the 14th centuries, but nobody knows why or by whom. Great Zimbabwe appears to have been a center for religion and the gold trade.

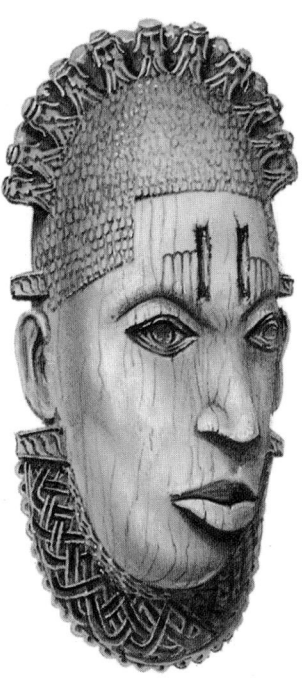

◀ *This lifelike ivory mask shows an oba of Benin. The oba hung it around his waist on ceremonial occasions. This particular sculpture must have been made after Portuguese explorers began visiting the area in the 15th century, because the headdress depicts a row of Portuguese sailors. According to a traditional Benin belief, wearing representations of strangers in this way enabled the oba to "take over" the newcomers.*

the bronze and ivory sculptures of the heads of its rulers and their wives. But there was a darker side to the empire: although the people were friendly to strangers, there existed a tradition of human sacrifice which later earned Benin City the name "City of Blood."

▼ *Some African civilizations during the Middle Ages.*

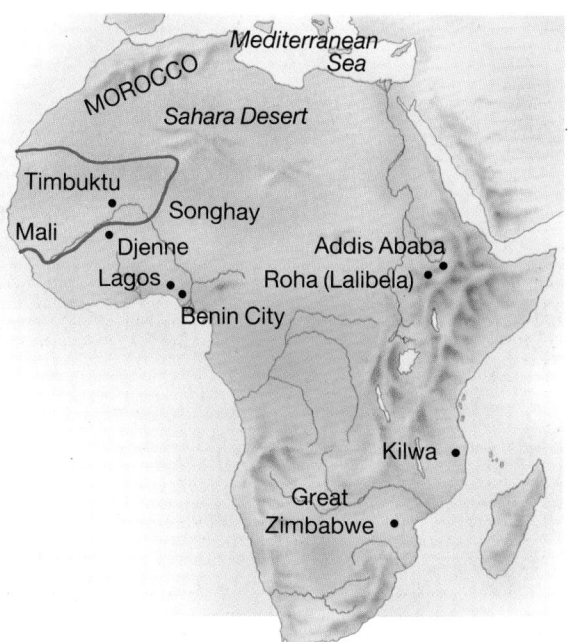

1302 Flanders: The Flemish defeat the best French soldiers at the battle of Courtrai and save their country from French occupation. Papacy: A decree called *Unam Sanctam* declares papal authority to be supreme.

1303 Papacy: Guillaume de Nogaret, emissary of Philip IV of France, captures Pope Boniface VIII at Anagni, Italy, and ill-treats him. The pope is rescued by the citizens of Anagni, but dies soon after. Benedict XI becomes pope (to 1304).

1305 Scotland: The English capture and execute William Wallace. Papacy: Clement V (Bertrand de Got, Archbishop of Bordeaux) is made pope (to 1314).

1306 Scotland: Robert Bruce leads a rebellion against English rule. He is crowned Robert I (to 1329) at Scone.

A 14th century bronze head of an oni, or king, of Ife, a kingdom in what is now Nigeria. He is wearing the headdress of a sea god. This sculpture has been called one of the finest surviving sculptures of medieval African art.

1307 Africa: Mansa Musa is made king of Mali (to 1337). Around the same time Benin emerges as an empire in West Africa. England: Edward I dies marching north to crush Robert of Scotland: his son Edward II becomes king (to 1327).

1308 Holy Roman Empire: Henry VII becomes emperor (to 1313).

1309 Pope Clement V transfers the papal see (capital) from Rome to Avignon, France; it remains there until 1377.

1312 Order of Knights Templars is abolished for malpractices, including dishonesty in business and heresy. A French ship discovers the uninhabited Canary Islands.

Medieval Explorers

Many bold men made long, and often dangerous, journeys in the Middle Ages. The first good account of central Asia was written by a Franciscan friar, John of Pian del Carpine, who was sent on a mission in 1245 to the Great Khan of Mongolia by Pope Innocent IV. Another "official" traveler was the Chinese admiral, Zheng He. Between 1405 and 1433, he led seven naval expeditions to extend China's political sway over maritime Asia. He returned with many luxuries such as spices.

Trade was the reason for many of these journeys. The greatest European traveler was Marco Polo, a young Venetian

▼ The incredible journeys of medieval travelers covered thousands of miles. Many suffered hardships such as frostbite, but others enjoyed luxury.

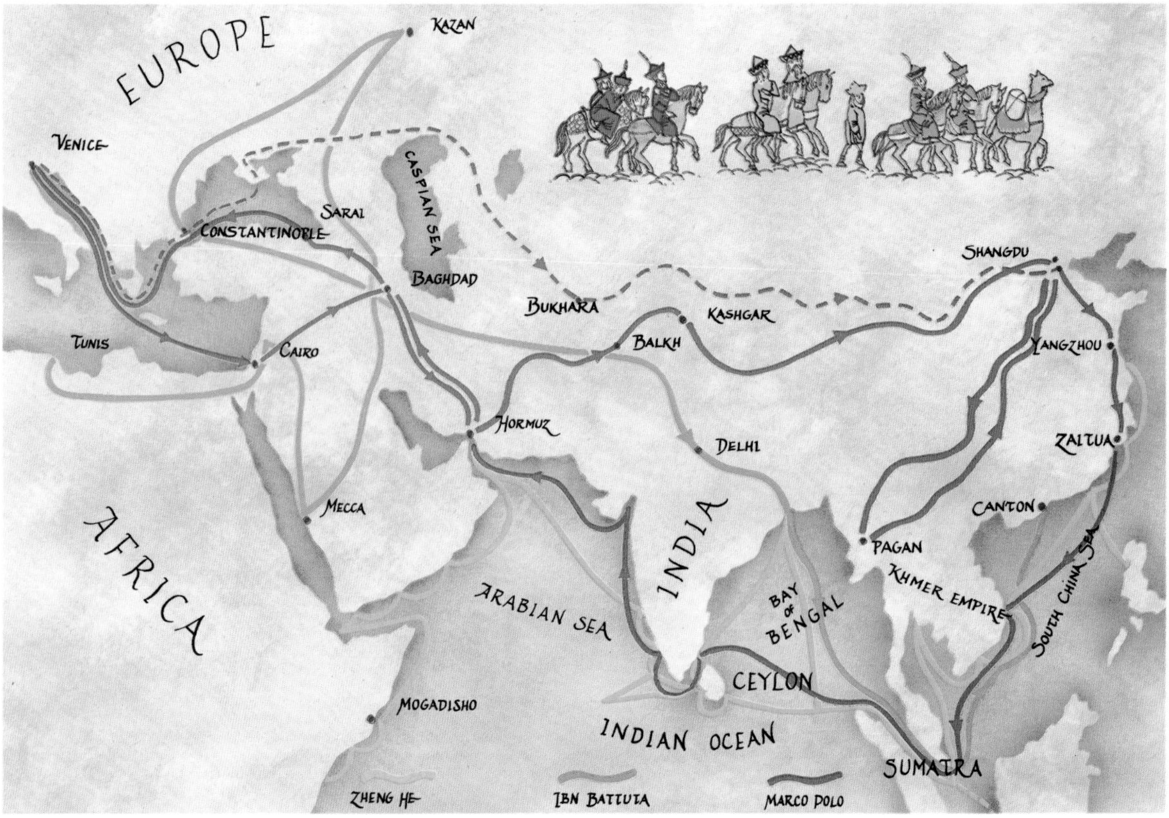

▲ The first giraffe seen in China was brought back from Africa by Admiral Zheng He. It had its portrait painted by order of the emperor.

Marco Polo

Marco Polo (1254–1324), his father, and uncle took three years to reach China in 1275. In 1284, Marco became China's envoy to India. His return to Venice in 1295, sparked great interest in the East.

Ibn Battuta

Ibn Battuta (1304–1368) left Tangier on a pilgrimage to Mecca in 1325. He went on to visit East Africa, India via Russia, and China before returning home in 1349. Finally he toured West Africa.

merchant. He traveled to the court of Kublai Khan in China and worked there for many years. Returning in 1295 laden with jewels, he later composed a vivid account of his travels. But the greatest travelers at this time were the Arabs. Ibn Battuta, a Moroccan lawyer, visited Russia, India, and Africa and left a detailed description of his travels.

▼ Huge ships like this one were specially built for Zheng He's expeditions; 62 sailed on his first voyage.

1314 Scotland: Edward II of England invades but Robert I defeats him at the battle of Bannockburn. France: Louis X, the Quarrelsome, becomes king (to 1316). Holy Roman Empire: Louis IV becomes emperor (to 1347): civil war follows with his rival, Frederick of Austria.

1316 France: Philip V, the Tall, is made king (to 1322). Papacy: John XXII becomes pope (to 1334): the papacy sends eight Dominican friars to Ethiopia in search of Prester John, a legendary Christian leader.

1317 France: Women are excluded from succeeding to the French throne, through the Salic Law.

1320 India: Tughluk dynasty in Delhi (to 1413), is founded by the Turk Ghidyas-ud-din Tughluk. He encourages agriculture, reforms taxes, and creates a postal system.

A mask of the demon Hannya. It was used in the Japanese Nō theater. Developed in the 14th century, Nō plays are still performed in Japan. All the actors are men and very little scenery is used.

1322 France: Charles IV, the Fair becomes king (to 1328).

1323 Flanders: Peasants' revolt begins. It is eventually suppressed by the French army in 1328.

1324 Mansa Musa, King of Mali, travels to Mecca. The magnificence of his court astonishes all who see him.

1325 Japan: Development of Nō plays. Mexico: Traditional date when Tenochtitlán (now Mexico City) is founded by the Aztecs. Arabia: Ibn Battuta begins his travels to Mecca, India and Africa.

Religion

Fighting between Christians and Muslims broke out in the Near East because they both shared the same holy places. People of all religions had been allowed to visit peacefully until the Seljuk Turks refused to let Christians visit Jerusalem. The Christians tried to recapture the city in a series of Crusades. In Europe, many Christians went on pilgrimages. If they could not go, they paid people called palmers to go in their place.

Meanwhile, the Arabs continued to spread the Islamic faith across Africa Africa until Ethiopia was the only Christian country left in northern Africa. Muslims, too, went on pilgrimages, but their destination was Mecca.

In Asia, Buddhism, spread by missionaries, was split into many branches as it combined with local beliefs.

▼ *This Buddhist wisdom text was written on a palm leaf in 1112. It is written in Sanskrit, an ancient Indian language used by Buddhists and Hindus all over India. Buddhism and Hinduism were the main religions in India at this time.*

▲ *During the twelfth century, Zen, a branch of Buddhism, spread to Japan from China. Its strict code appealed to Japanese warriors, the samurai. Buddhist temple buildings, such as this gateway, were also built in the Chinese style.*

► *The remains of the mosque at Kilwa, East Africa, founded by Arab traders. Trade spread the Muslim faith throughout Africa.*

▼ *Reliquaries contained holy relics and the bones of saints. People made long journeys to see them.*

WHEN IT HAPPENED

1204 The Crusaders seize Constantinople.
1209 St. Francis of Assisi starts the Franciscan order of friars.
1345 The Aztecs arrive in Central Mexico. Their religion includes human sacrifice.
1453 Constantinople falls to the Ottoman Turks who convert the great Christian church of St. Sophia into a mosque.

▼ *Early medieval churches had no furniture. People stood during services, but there were special ledges for old people to lean on.*

1326 England: Queen Isabella, Edward II's wife, and her lover Roger Mortimer sail from France with an army to lead a rebellion against Edward. Turkey: Orkhan I becomes the first real ruler and organizer of the Ottoman Turks (to 1359). The Ottomans capture the city of Bursa, Anatolia.

1327 England: Parliament declares Edward II deposed, and his son becomes Edward III. Edward II is murdered nine months later. Holy Roman Empire: Emperor Louis IV invades Italy and declares Pope John XXII deposed.

In medieval Europe peddlers traveled from door to door to display their wares. Here a woman inspects the goods, hung up outside her home. Peddlers also acted as a means of spreading news and stories.

1328 England acknowledges Scotland's independence. France: Philip VI becomes king (to 1350), the first French ruler of the house of Valois.

1332 Scotland: Edward Balliol, son of John Balliol, attempts to seize the Scottish throne but he is defeated.

1333 Scotland: Edward III invades Scotland on Edward Balliol's behalf and defeats the Scots. Japan: Emperor Daigo II overthrows the Hojo family of shoguns and rules himself (to 1336).

1334 Papacy: Benedict XII becomes pope (to 1342).

1336 Japan: Daigo II is exiled. Ashikaga family rule Japan as shoguns (to 1568); civil war starts (to 1392). India: The Hindu Kingdom of Vijayamagar is founded in southern India.

1337 Edward III of England declares himself king of France starting the Hundred Years' War (to 1453).

The Hundred Years' War

The Hundred Years' War between England and France was not one long war, but a series of short ones. It began in 1337 and ended in 1453, so the conflict actually lasted for 116 years. English kings tried to dominate France, while the French strove to throw the English out of their country.

In 1328, Charles IV of France died without a direct heir. French barons gave the throne to his cousin, Philip VI, but Charles's nephew, Edward III of England, challenged him. When Philip declared that Edward's French lands were confiscated, war broke out.

The English defeated a French fleet in the English Channel at Sluys, then invaded France and won a major land battle at Crécy. Edward captured Calais. But both sides ran out of money and had to agree a truce, which lasted from 1347 until 1355.

In 1355, a fresh English invasion took place, led by Edward's heir, Edward, whose nickname was "the Black Prince." The Black Prince won a resounding victory at Poitiers, capturing Philip's successor, John II. The Treaty of Brétigny in 1360 gave England large parts of France. But a new campaign followed the peace treaty and England lost most of her French possessions.

For a while, both the French and English thrones were occupied by children, Charles VI of France and Richard II of England. Richard's uncle, John of Gaunt (Ghent), Duke of Lancaster, ruled for him. In 1396 Richard II married Charles VI's daughter, Isabelle, and a 20-year truce was agreed.

▶ *At the battle of Crécy in 1346 an English army of 10,000 men defeated a French force of 20,000. The English archers easily outshot the French crossbows. Over 1,500 French died, but only 40 English.*

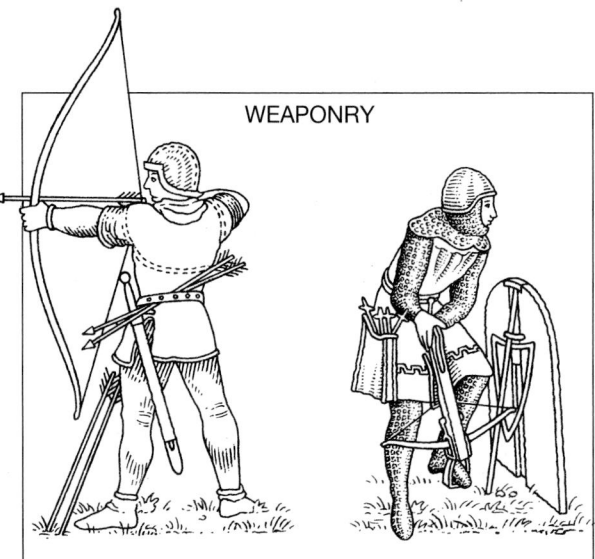

WEAPONRY

The longbow *(left)*, made of yew, was developed in England during the 13th century. English archers could fire six carefully aimed arrows a minute, each a "cloth-yard" (1 meter) long. They were accurate at a range of up to 1,000 feet (320 m).

French archers and other European soldiers used the crossbow *(right)*. Its bolts (missiles) did not carry as far as the longbow's arrows. It was easier to fire than a longbow, but much slower.

John of Gaunt

John of Gaunt (1340–1399), born at Ghent, was one of the sons of Edward III. In 1372, he claimed the throne of Castile through his wife. As regent (1377–1386) for Richard II he was the most powerful man in England.

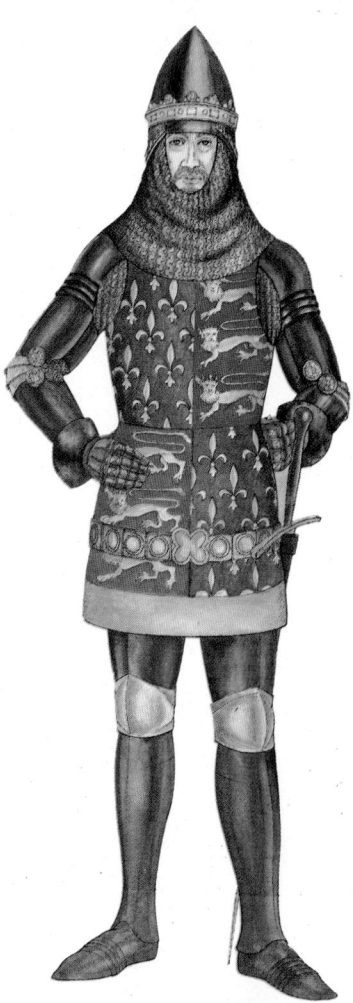

► *Edward, Prince of Wales, got his nickname the Black Prince from the color of his armor.*

1338 Holy Roman Empire: Electors of the empire declare it to be independent from the papacy. The Treaty of Coblenz forms an alliance between England and the empire.

1339 Moscow: Construction begins on the Kremlin.

1340 Hundred Years' War: A naval victory at Sluys gives England the command of the English Channel.

Gold florins from Florence had a lily on one side and St. John the Baptist on the other.

1341 Mali: Sulaiman becomes king (to 1360).

1342 Papacy: Clement VI is made pope (to 1352).

1344 Germany: By now, almost all larger German towns along the Baltic and North seas belong to the Hanseatic League.

1345 Ottoman Turks first cross the Bosporus into Europe.

1346 Hundred Years' War: Edward III of England invades France and defeats a large army under Philip VI at the battle of Crécy. Scotland: David II of Scotland is defeated and captured by the English. Serbia: Stephen Dushan, King of the Serbs, is crowned "Emperor of the Serbs and Greeks."

1347 Hundred Years' War: The English capture Calais. Holy Roman Empire: Charles IV becomes emperor (to 1378). Italy: Patriot Cola da Rienzi assumes power in Rome, taking the title of "tribune," but he is soon driven from office. The Black Death reaches Genoa from Central Asia.

The Hanseatic League

Trade routes in the late Middle Ages were often threatened by pirates at sea and robbers on land. In 1241, two north German towns, Hamburg and Lübeck, agreed to protect each other's merchants by setting up a *hansa* or trading association. Two groups of traders formed the Hanseatic League in 1260. North German merchants based in Lübeck had a virtual monopoly (sole rights) of trade around the Baltic Sea, while merchants based in Cologne and other Rhine cities traded with England and the Low Countries (now Belgium and the Netherlands).

The Hanseatic League brought food and raw materials from eastern Europe in exchange for manufactured goods from the west. From Russia and lands to the south and east of the Baltic, Hanse ships carried charcoal, flax, grain, hemp (rope), honey, pitch, and timber. Hanse merchants secured a monopoly of Norwegian cod and whale oil, and Swedish iron mines and herrings. They also traded overland to Venice and Constantinople (now Istanbul).

NOVGOROD

The fortified city of Novgorod, in western Russia, was the farthest into Russia that Hanse merchants reached. Novgorod traded in amber, furs, and wax.

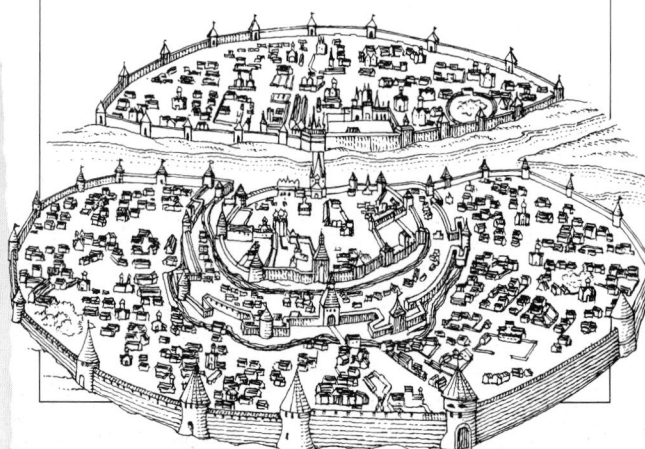

The Hanseatic League
had depots, called
kontore, in some
countries. In Bergen,
Bruges, London, and
Novgorod, the kontore
obeyed the laws of the
League rather than
those of the countries
they were in. Traders
in London were called
"Merchants of the
Steelyard" from the old
German word *stalhof*
(a yard used for
displaying samples).

The Hanse towns safeguarded their
ships with lighthouses and they fought
off pirates at sea. The League also took
political action to safeguard its
monopolies. Member towns were
forbidden to fight each other and
highway robbery was put at an end. If
other countries or towns would not
cooperate, it forced them to do so by
applying financial pressure. The League
also had its own army and navy.

▲ When it was at its peak, the main trading routes of
the Hanseatic League covered Europe. The League
began to collapse in the early 17th century.

▼ It was in small, sturdy ships like these that the goods
of the Hanseatic merchants were carried. Western
cloth, linen, silverware, and wool were exchanged for
eastern spices, silk, and raw materials.

The Black Death

The Black Death is sometimes said to have been the worst disaster in history. It killed about 25 million people in Europe alone (about a quarter of the total population), and nobody knows how many millions more in Asia.

The Black Death was a form of bubonic plague. It got its name from spots of blood that formed under the skin and turned black. The first symptoms were the swelling of glands in the groin and armpit. Victims usually died within a few hours. The plague was first carried by rat fleas which could also live on humans. Bubonic plague is not carried by human contact, but the Black Death later changed to pneumonic plague, which spreads from person to person.

The disease seems to have been carried from central Asia to the Crimea by a Tartar (Mongol) raiding party, and from there to the Mediterranean by ship, arriving at Genoa, in Italy, in 1347. It

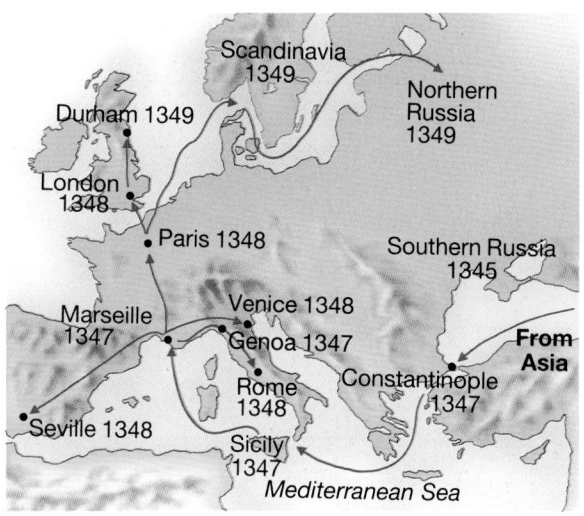

▲ The Black Death came from Asia to Europe in 1347 and reached its peak in 1349. Only a few areas were unaffected because people managed to isolate themselves and stop the disease from spreading.

▼ A typical European town street in the Middle Ages had filthy open sewers, rats and refuse everywhere. Human waste was hurled from the windows with the cry "Gardez-loo!" to warn passersby. It was no wonder the plague spread, but many people thought it was the judgment of God on a wicked world.

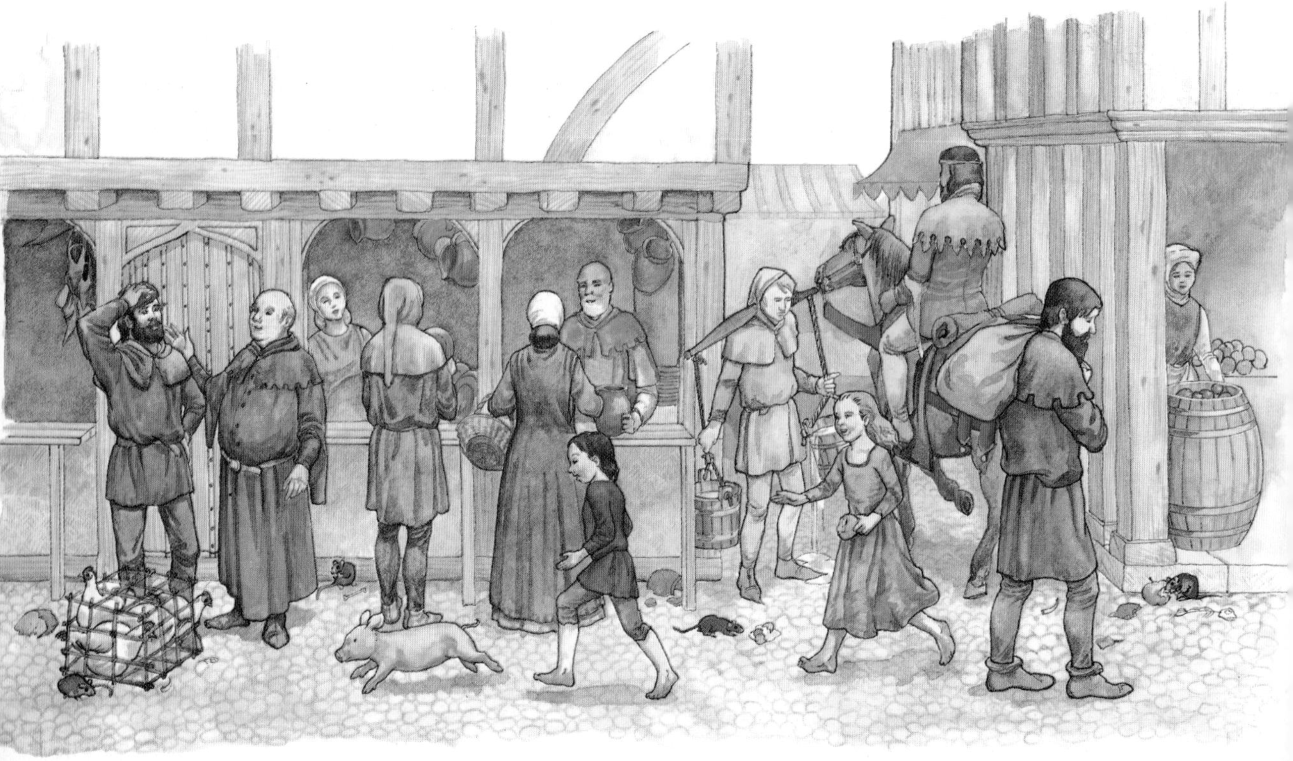

▲ *The feelings of fear and helplessness were reflected in the art and literature of the time. Pictures showed the Black Death as a skeleton riding on horseback.*

spread west and north, reaching Paris and London in 1348, and Scandinavia and northern Russia in 1349. It devastated regions: houses stood empty and towns were abandoned. Fields became littered with unburied corpses.

The effects of the Black Death were widespread. Before it, Europe had had a surplus of labor and wages were low. Afterward there was a severe shortage of workers. As a result wages soared and attempts to hold wages down led to revolts (*see* pages 298–299). The already weak feudal system collapsed.

▼ *People burned the clothes of the dead to try to stop the infection spreading. The plague killed rich and poor alike and sometimes whole towns were wiped out.*

1348 England: Edward III establishes the Order of the Garter. The Black Death ravages Europe, reaching Paris and London. In England it kills about one-third of the population.

1348–1353 Italy: The poet Boccaccio writes the *Decameron*, which is about ten young people who leave Florence to escape the plague and tell each other tales for ten days.

1349 The Black Death reaches northern Russia.

1350 France: John II becomes king (to 1364). Hayam Wuruk's reign (to 1389) is the most glorious period in Javanese history.

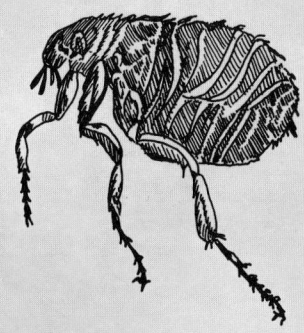

The Black Death, which wiped out over one-third of the population of Europe, was spread by fleas that lived on rats. The rats made their nests in houses and so infected humans.

1352 Mali: Ibn Battuta spends time here after exploring the Sahara. China: The Black Death arrives.

1354 Italy: Rienzi returns to power in Rome and is killed by his opponents.

1356 Hundred Years' War: Edward the Black Prince, son of Edward III, defeats the French at the battle of Poitiers, and captures the French king, John II.

1358 France: A revolt by the peasants is suppressed by the Regent Charles, son of John II.

1360 Hundred Years' War: Treaty of Brétigny ends the first stage of the war; Edward III of England gives up his claim to the throne of France. France: The first francs are coined.

1363 Burgundy: Philip the Bold, son of John II, is duke of Burgundy. Asia: Mongol leader Tamerlane begins his conquest.

1364 France: Charles V, the Wise, becomes king (to 1380), on the death of his father, John II, in captivity in London.

Science and Technology

Both the Chinese and the Arabs were still ahead of the rest of the world in science and technology. Crusaders returning to Europe from Palestine carried Arabic knowledge of astronomy and mathematics. Ideas from classical Greek medicine were also introduced.

Knowledge of how to make paper also spread to Europe from Arabia toward the end of this period. Along with the development of printing, this made books more plentiful, although most people could not read.

More knowledge from ancient Greece came to Europe after the fall of the Byzantine empire, when many scholars fled from Constantinople to Italy. It was this knowledge which led to the new interest in learning that swept through Europe in the 15th and 16th centuries.

▲ *Muslim scholars studying in the library at Hulwan, near Baghdad. Islam preserved many important scientific manuscripts from ancient Greece which would otherwise have been lost.*

◄ *This servant is washing dishes in a castle kitchen. Diseases were common because no one understood the connection between dirt and disease.*

▶ *The padded horse collar was originally invented in China. It was introduced into Europe in the 11th century and became widely used by the 12th century. It enabled horses to pull heavy weights, such as plows and carts, without the risk of choking themselves as they had sometimes done in the past.*

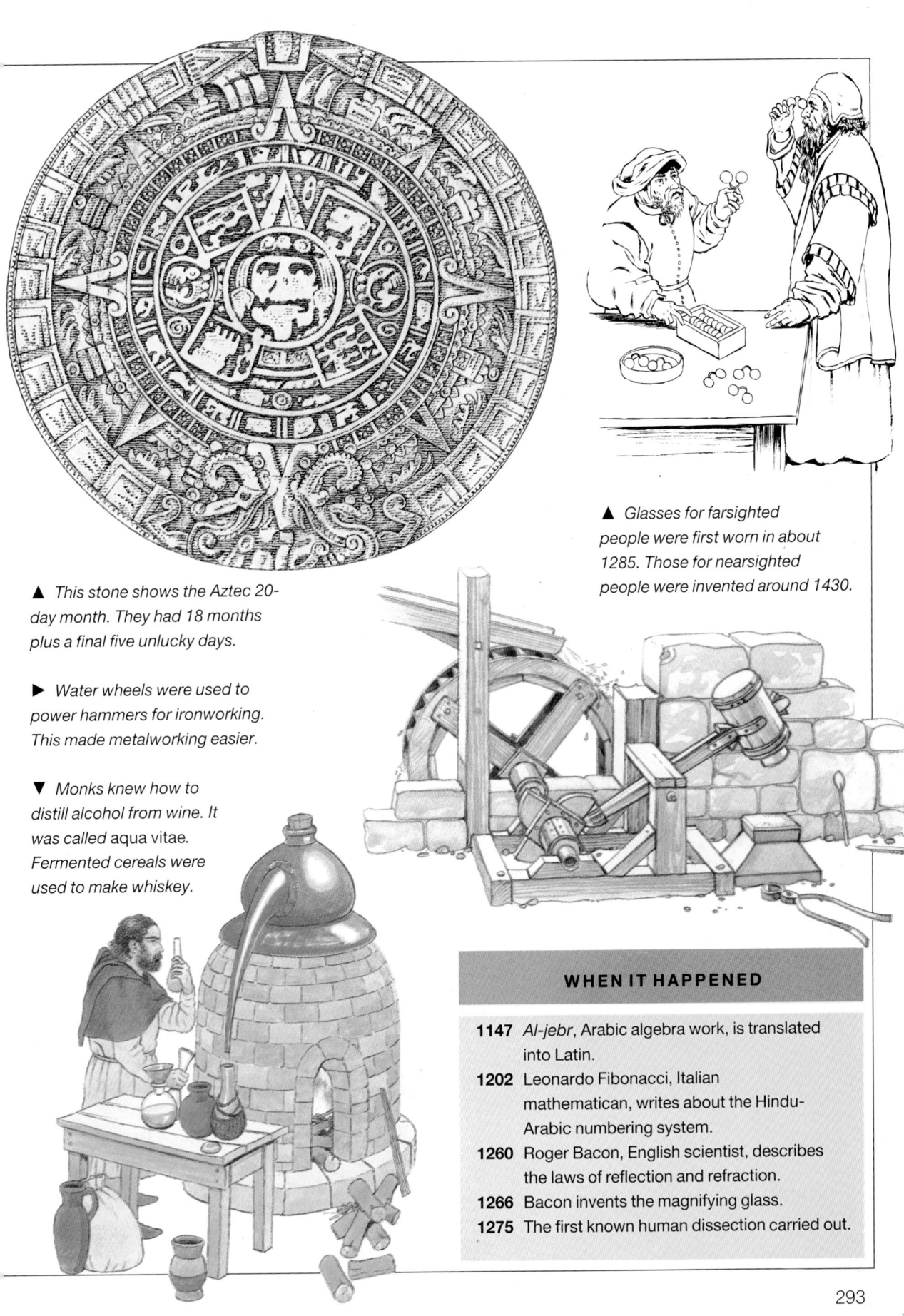

▲ This stone shows the Aztec 20-day month. They had 18 months plus a final five unlucky days.

▲ Glasses for farsighted people were first worn in about 1285. Those for nearsighted people were invented around 1430.

▶ Water wheels were used to power hammers for ironworking. This made metalworking easier.

▼ Monks knew how to distill alcohol from wine. It was called *aqua vitae*. Fermented cereals were used to make whiskey.

WHEN IT HAPPENED

1147 *Al-jebr*, Arabic algebra work, is translated into Latin.

1202 Leonardo Fibonacci, Italian mathematican, writes about the Hindu-Arabic numbering system.

1260 Roger Bacon, English scientist, describes the laws of reflection and refraction.

1266 Bacon invents the magnifying glass.

1275 The first known human dissection carried out.

The Ming Dynasty

After the death of Kublai Khan in 1294, the Yuan (Mongol) dynasty of China had a succession of relatively feeble emperors. The last Yuan emperor, Sun Ti, was a bad ruler. The Chinese people were tired of being ruled harshly by foreigners. They found a Chinese ruler in Chu Yuen-Chang, who had been a monk and a beggar. He was a bandit chief, so he had a ready-made army. He also proved to be an excellent general.

After a 13-year campaign he captured Beijing, drove the Mongols back to Mongolia, and became emperor. He founded a new dynasty called the Ming, which means "brightness," and took the name Hung Wu, which means "very warlike." He moved the capital to the fortified city of Nanjing.

Hung Wu ruled China for 30 years as a dictator, but he restored order and prosperity to his land. Any minister who opposed him was executed. The many

THE CIVIL SERVICE

The emperor Hung Wu set up colleges for the sons of public officials; other boys were allowed in if they showed promise. The ambition of every scholar was to obtain one of the 100,000 civil service posts or a post in the 80,000-strong military service. Candidates had to pass examinations in literature and philosophy.

Civil servants had little real power, which lay in the hands of the emperor and the court favorites. However, Ming officials adorned many fine jade carvings of the period.

THE FORBIDDEN CITY

The Ming emperors were great builders. Their masterpiece was Beijing. The two main cities, the Outer and the Inner, were linked by the Tiananmen (Gate of Heavenly Peace). Inside the Inner City was the Imperial City, and inside that, the Forbidden City. It was "forbidden" because it was built for one man, the emperor, and only his household was allowed into it.

CRAFTS

The Ming period is famous for its blue-and-white porcelain. Some of the porcelain made during Yung Lo's reign is of eggshell thinness. The center of porcelain manufacture was at Jingdezhen, south of Nanjing, where there is a good supply of clay. Ming craft workers also made enamelware, carpets, carvings, and exquisite embroideries.

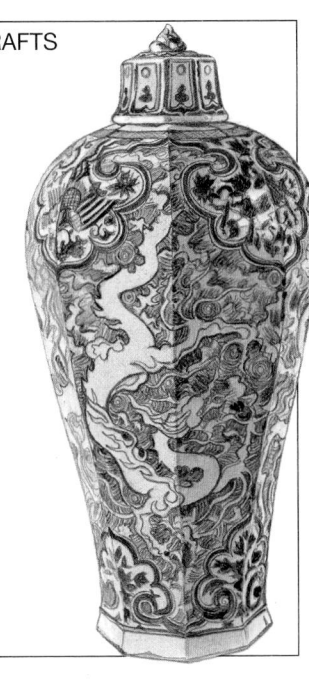

soldiers who had fought in the long civil wars were made farmers, especially on land along the frontier where the Mongols might counterattack. Hung Wu left the throne to a young grandson, Hui Ti, but Hui Ti was soon overthrown by his uncle, who became the third Ming emperor with the title of Yung Lo. Yung Lo moved the capital back to Beijing, where he built an imperial city.

▼ A later plan of Beijing, first built in 1410.

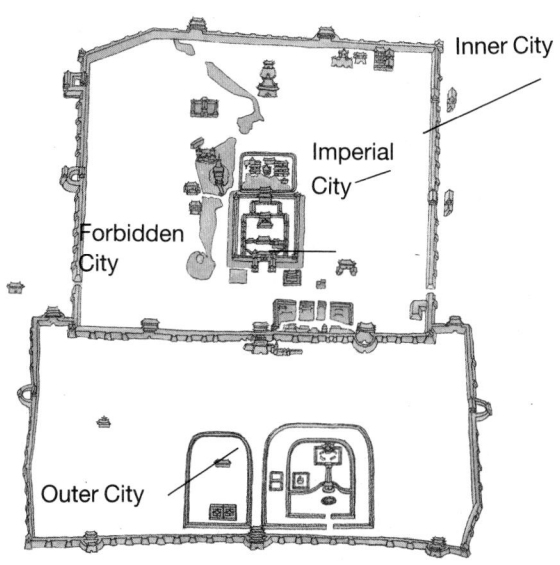

Inner City

Imperial City

Forbidden City

Outer City

1365 Turks make Adrianople their capital.
1367 Confederation of Cologne: 77 Hanse towns prepare for a struggle with Denmark.
1368 China: Rebellion led by Chu Yuen-Chang overthrows the Yuan dynasty and founds the Ming dynasty (to 1644).
1369 Hundred Years' War: Second stage of conflict between England and France begins. China: Korea submits to the Ming dynasty. Central Asia: Tamerlane becomes king of Samarkand.

Kublai Khan founded the observatory at Beijing in the 13th century to observe important planetary events. China had a special government astronomy department.

1369 Ottoman Turks begin conquest of Bulgaria (completed 1372).
1370 Hundred Years' War: Edward the Black Prince of England sacks Limoges. Holy Roman Empire: Peace of Stralsund establishes the power of the Hanseatic League over the Danish. Papacy: Gregory XI becomes pope (to 1378). Turkestan: Tamerlane becomes ruler.
1371 Scotland: Robert II becomes king (to 1390), the first Stuart monarch. Balkans: Ottoman Turks defeat Serbs, and conquer Macedonia. Spain: John of Gaunt, Duke of Lancaster, younger son of Edward III of England, marries Constance, daughter and heiress of the King of Castile and Leon. John lays claim to the throne of Castile.

1372 Hundred Years' War: French troops recapture Poitou and Brittany; naval battle of La Rochelle gives the French control of the English Channel again.

1373 Hundred Years' War: John of Gaunt leads a new English invasion of France.

1374 John of Gaunt returns to England and takes charge of the government.

1375 Hundred Years' War: Truce of Bruges halts hostilities between England and France. Papacy: Catherine of Siena negotiates the return of the papacy from Avignon to Rome.

A pardoner was an agent of the Church who was licensed to sell indulgences. These documents forgave people the sins they had committed and eased their consciences. They were sold to raise money for the Church.

1376 England: The Good Parliament, called by Edward the Black Prince, introduces many reforms. Later in the same year the Black Prince dies. John Wycliffe, an Oxford University teacher, calls for Church reforms.

1377 England: Acts of the Good Parliament are reversed. Edward III dies. Richard II, son of the Black Prince, is made king (to 1399). Papacy: Pope Gregory XI returns the papal see to Rome.

1378 The Great Schism (to 1417): rival popes are elected: Urban VI, pope at Rome (to 1389), Clement VII, antipope at Avignon (to 1394). Holy Roman Empire: Wenceslas IV becomes emperor (to 1400).

The Great Schism

In the late 14th century, the Christian Church underwent a split, known as the Great Schism. For a short time there were three popes at one time.

In the Middle Ages, the Roman Catholic Church was the only Christian Church in western Europe. The pope was head of a state in Italy as well as a spiritual leader. But at this time Italy was torn by feuds and wars, so in 1309 Pope Clement V, a Frenchman, moved the papal headquarters to Avignon, in southern France. For many years his successors were Frenchmen, and the papacy remained in Avignon until 1377, when Gregory XI decided that it would be better to go back to Rome.

The next year Gregory XI died and, under pressure from a group in Rome, the cardinals elected an Italian pope, Urban VI. But Urban so upset the cardinals that 13 of them rebelled and elected a Swiss cardinal, Robert of Geneva instead. The two popes each had their own College of Cardinals and claimed to be head of the Church. Some

CHURCH REFORM

The first great English leader of Church reform, John Wycliffe (c. 1320–1384), was a professor of theology at Oxford University. He denounced the corruption and wealth of the Church and its involvement in politics, and began to question some of its basic beliefs. He was supported by the king.

▲ *The French Palace of the Popes stands on a hill in the middle of Avignon, a city in southeastern France. The palace is also a fortress. It was begun in 1314 and not finished until 1370.*

kings supported one, some the other.

In 1409 a council of churchmen meeting at Pisa, in Italy, declared both the current popes deposed and elected another. There were now three popes. This was too much and, in 1417, another council elected Martin V as the only rightful pope. The Great Schism was finally over. The popes elected in Rome were regarded as the rightful ones. The others were called antipopes.

▲ *In the Middle Ages, St. Peter's, the church of the popes in Rome, looked like this. Constructed in about 325, it was based on a Roman basilica (meeting hall). St. Peter's had slender walls and a light wooden roof. It was demolished in 1506.*

▼ *Europe during the Great Schism. The rulers of Aragon, Castile, France, Navarre, Portugal (to 1381), Savoy, and Scotland supported Avignon; England, Flanders, the Holy Roman Empire, Hungary, Italy, Poland, and Portugal (from 1381) supported Rome.*

LIFESTYLE OF POPES

The popes and the College of Cardinals who elected them, enjoyed a luxurious lifestyle. The Church's leaders lived in palaces and had many servants to wait on them. The popes headed a large administration. Many of them were as much concerned with power and prestige as with spiritual matters.

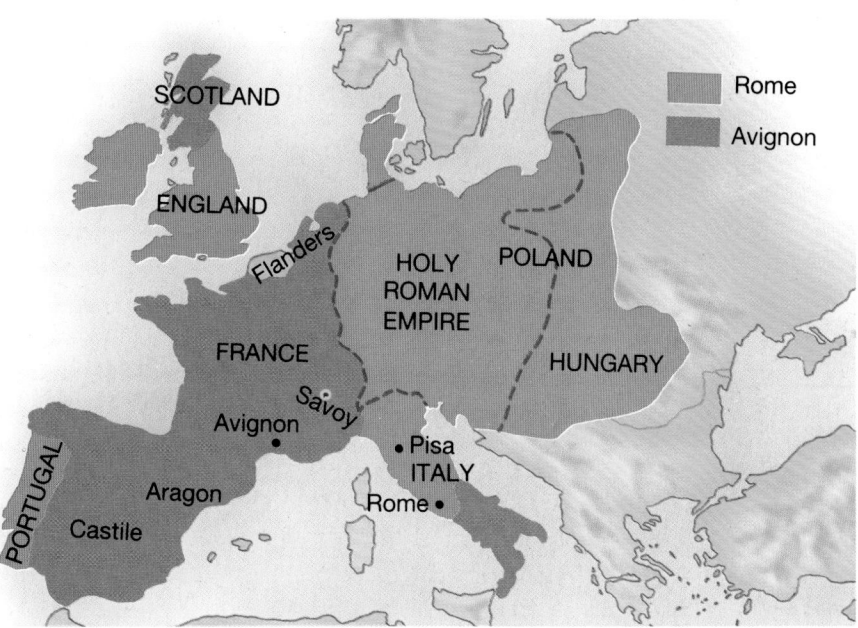

The Peasants' Revolts

After the Black Death killed over a third of the people in Europe, there was a great shortage of labor. Many peasants, laborers, and smallholders secured higher wages. But there were more wars, and the cost of maintaining armies soared. As a result, people had to pay more taxes.

Most peasants lived in great poverty. They ate mainly porridge, bread, and vegetables, with a little meat or fish occasionally. They became dissatisfied with these harsh conditions and three rebellions happened in the 14th century.

The first revolt was in Flanders (now in Belgium). It began in 1323 and lasted until 1328. The peasants and farmers refused to pay their taxes. The landlords resisted them, and civil war erupted. A French army finally crushed it.

In northern France, the second revolt was a protest against hordes of mercenary soldiers ravaging the

1 **Norfolk**
2 **Huntingdon**
3 **Cambridge**
4 **Suffolk**
5 **Hertford**
6 **Essex**
7 **Middlesex**
8 **Surrey**
9 **Kent**

▲ *The counties shown are the main areas involved in the English Peasants' Revolt of 1381. The towns marked were also areas of discontent.*

▼ *As the Lord Mayor of London killed Wat Tyler on the left, the young Richard II faced the angry mob of peasants and shouted, "I will be your leader."*

JOHN BALL

A priest and a leading agitator of his day, John Ball was in jail in Maidstone, Kent when the Peasants' Revolt began. The rebels broke open the prison and freed him, planning to make him archbishop of Canterbury. At Blackheath he preached to the rebels, "When Adam dalf (dug) and Eve span, wo was thanne the gentilman?" After the revolt, Ball was tried and hanged.

▲ *A typical scene taken from the Duke of Berry's book,* The Very Rich Hours. *It shows peasants still bound by society into working for the lord of the manor.*

countryside in 1358. Known as the *Jacquerie* because the term of contempt for a peasant was Jacques Bonhomme or "Goodman Jack," the rebellion was savagely put down. Some 20,000 French peasants were killed.

The third revolt was in England. In 1381 people had to pay a new tax, called Poll Tax, of one shilling. That was a week's wages for a skilled laborer and peasants protested in Essex, Kent, and six other counties. Led by Wat Tyler and the priest John Ball, 60,000 Kentish and Essex men marched on London, demanding to see King Richard II.

The 14-year-old Richard met the rebels on Blackheath (now in southeast London), and agreed to an end to serfdom and better labor conditions. Tyler was killed by the Lord Mayor of London, William Walworth, but Richard prevented an ugly scene by promising to be the rebels' champion. They went away satisfied, but parliament did not honor any of Richard's promises.

1380 France: Charles VI becomes king (to 1422). England: John Wycliffe and others translate the Bible into English. Rome: Death of the Christian mystic Catherine of Siena.

1381 England: Peasants march on London burning and killing in the Peasants' Revolt. Richard II promises reforms.

1382 England: John Wycliffe is expelled from Oxford University because he opposes Church doctrines. Portugal: John I is king (to 1433), founder of the Avis dynasty.

1383 Tamerlane conquers Persia.

1386 Switzerland: The Swiss defeat and kill Leopold III of Austria. Spain: John of Gaunt leads an expedition to Castile (fails 1388).

1388 Mongolia: Chinese forces drive the Mongols out of their capital, Karakorum.

A plow of the 12th century was pulled by oxen to increase the amount of work that could be done. The design remained almost unchanged until the 16th century.

1389 England: Richard II, aged 22, assumes power. Scotland: A truce halts fighting between England and the French and Scots. Great Schism: Boniface IX becomes pope at Rome (to 1404).

1390 Scotland: Robert III, king (to 1406). Ottoman empire: Turks complete conquest of Anatolia.

1391 First siege of Constantinople by Turks (to 1398): Constantinople pays Turks tribute (money). Russia: Tamerlane defeats Toqtamish, khan of the Golden Horde.

1392 France: Charles VI goes mad. Korea: Yi Song-gye seizes power and founds the Yi dynasty (to 1910).

Society and Government

There were many different types of government at this time. In China, the emperor had complete power over a vast area of land. In contrast, towns in Italy such as Venice made their own rules separately.

In theory, England was ruled by a king and his council, but in reality the king had all the power. In Europe, the feudal society still kept people firmly in their places for most of this period, but a class of wealthy merchants was gradually developing.

Throughout the world, religious leaders also had a lot of power. The Aztecs and Incas were ruled by priests, as well as by emperors. The Arabs were ruled by Islamic Law and in Europe the pope and his envoys were more powerful than many kings and emperors. The balance of power between religious leaders and kings and emperors frequently led to conflict.

▶ *In the Islamic empire, the Koran gave women important rights over property. For example, when she married, the bridegroom had to give his wife a dowry. This became her own property, even if she was later divorced.*

▲ *Edward I of England in Parliament in 1274. The Church taught that kings were appointed by God and that it was everyone's duty to obey them. But a weak king could find himself overthrown.*

▶ *The Incas celebrated two festivals of the Sun. One was in June, the other in December. The emperor led the ceremonies in the great square at Cuzco. Officials from all over the empire attended.*

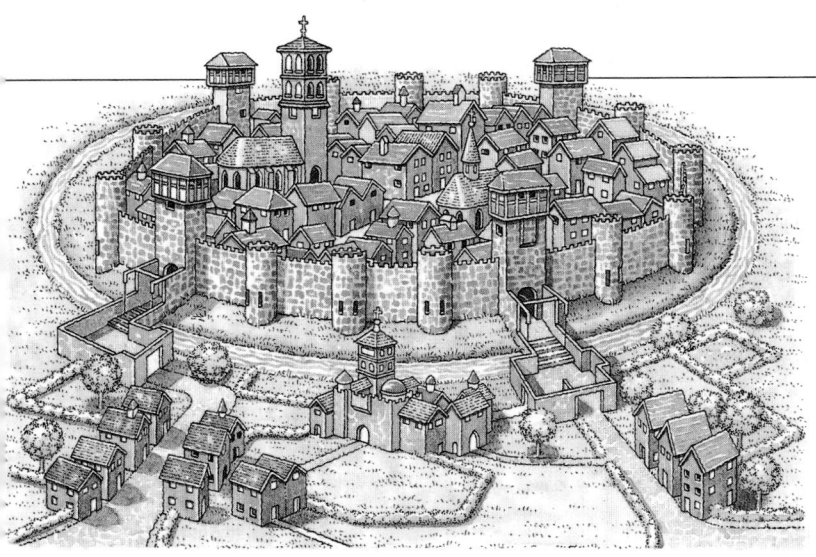

WHEN IT HAPPENED

1192 Minamoto Yoritomo becomes shogun of Japan and takes over real power.

1215 In England, the Magna Carta gives rights to the barons.

14th century Peasants revolt in much of Europe demanding better pay and conditions.

▲ *Most medieval towns were built in the same pattern. This example is Feurs, in the south of France. The walls protected the town from attack and also helped to control trade – tolls could be collected from strangers carrying goods.*

▲ *Rich men carried their money in purses on their belts to prevent robbery. Rich and poor people could usually be told apart by their clothes.*

1393 Tamerlane takes Baghdad and subdues Mesopotamia (present-day Iraq).

1394 Ireland: Richard II of England leads expedition to conquer Ireland. The Great Schism: Benedict XIII antipope at Avignon (to 1423).

1396 England: Richard II marries seven-year-old Princess Isabelle of France. Anatolia: Abortive crusade by about 20,000 European knights against Turks is defeated at Nicopolis. Ottoman empire: Turks conquer Bulgaria.

A Turkish door knocker in the shape of two winged dragons. Dragons had an astrological significance and were thought to protect the buildings on which they hung.

1397 Scandinavia: Union of Kalmar unites Norway, Denmark, and Sweden under Eric of Denmark. Ottoman empire: Turks invade Greece.

1398 India: Tamerlane ravages kingdom of Delhi and massacres 100,000 prisoners.

1399 England: John of Gaunt dies and his eldest son, Henry of Bolingbroke, is banished by Richard II. Bolingbroke invades England, deposes Richard and becomes Henry IV (to 1413).

1400 England: Richard II is murdered at Pontefract Castle. Wales: Owen Glendower proclaims himself prince of Wales and begins rebellion. France: Jean Froissart finishes his *Chronicles* of the chivalric world.

15th century By this date, Indonesian traders regularly visit Australia's north coast to collect sea slugs and sandalwood. These goods are traded as far away as China.

1402 Ottoman empire: Tamerlane overruns most of it, which saves the Byzantine empire.

1403 England: Henry IV defeats and kills Harry "Hotspur" Percy at the battle of Shrewsbury after the Percy family rebel.

The Fall of Constantinople

In eastern Europe and the Near East two empires vied for power in the late Middle Ages. One was the remains of the Christian Byzantine empire (*see* pages 162–163). The other was the Muslim Ottoman empire, founded in about 1299 by the Turk Osman I.

The Ottoman Turks built up their empire quickly. From 1326 they proceeded to conquer large parts of the Byzantine empire. They controlled most of Greece, Bosnia, Albania, and Bulgaria by 1450, and tried to conquer Hungary. All that was left of the Byzantine empire was Constantinople, which was founded on a village once called Byzantium.

In 1453 the Turks, under their leader Muhammad II, made a final assault on the city. The last Byzantine emperor, Constantine XI, had about 10,000 men under arms whereas Muhammad had between 100,000 and 150,000 soldiers. Muhammad could not send his warships

◄ *A janissary, an elite soldier of the Ottoman army. The name came from the Turkish word for "new forces," because the first janissaries were prisoners of war.*

into the Golden Horn, a channel of sea which runs through Constantinople, because it was guarded by a huge iron chain. So he dragged 70 small ships overland to launch an attack. Protected by strong walls, the Byzantine forces held out for 54 days before Muhammad's best troops, the *janissaries*, overran the city. This was the end of the Byzantine empire.

▲ *After Constantinople fell the Turks converted the Christian church of St. Sophia into a mosque.*

▲ *Turkish decorative arts were very distinctive. This panel dates from the Seljuk period.*

▼ *Teams of oxen and thousands of soldiers dragged the 70 small galleys (oared warships) of Muhammad II's fleet along a wooden track over a neck of land into the unprotected part of the Golden Horn.*

1403 Tamerlane withdraws from Anatolia. China: Yung Lo is emperor (to 1424). A 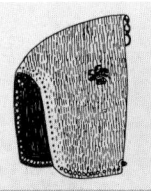 Chinese encyclopedia in 22,937 volumes is compiled (only three copies made).

1404 The Great Schism: Innocent VII, pope at Rome (to 1406). Persia: Shah Rukh (fourth son of Tamerlane) rules (to 1447).

1405 Mongolia: Tamerlane dies on his way to campaign in China; his empire disintegrates. Ottoman empire: Civil war starts (to 1413). China: Zheng He embarks on his first expedition.

1406 The Great Schism: Gregory XII is pope at Rome (to 1415). Scotland: James I, aged

The standard of the French heroine and war leader, Joan of Arc.

12, is king (to 1437); the English seize him on his way to France and hold him captive (to 1423). Wales: Henry, Prince of Wales, defeats Glendower.

1409 The Council of Pisa is called to resolve the Great Schism; it deposes the rival popes and elects Alexander V (to 1410).

1410 John XXIII (Baldassare Cossa), is antipope at Pisa (to 1415). Holy Roman Empire: Sigismund is emperor (to 1437). Peru: The Inca empire is expanded under the leadership of Viracocha Inca.

1411 India: Ahmad Shah, ruler (to 1422), builds the beautiful city Ahmadabad as his capital in western India.

1413 England: Henry V is king (to 1422). Ottoman empire: Muhammad I consolidates Ottoman power (to 1421).

1414 Italy: The Medici family of Florence become bankers to the papacy.

1415 Hundred Years' War: Henry V of England defeats French at Agincourt. North Africa: Prince Henry the Navigator of Portugal captures Ceuta.

End of Hundred Years' War

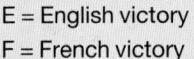

After a long truce the Hundred Years' War started up again in 1415. Henry V, England's adventurous king, revived his country's old claim to the throne of France. England still held Calais and parts of Bordeaux.

Henry captured the town of Harfleur in Normandy, and also heavily defeated the French at Agincourt losing only about 1,600 men to France's 10,000. He next occupied much of northern France and forced the French king, Charles VI, to disinherit his own son and make Henry heir to the French throne. He also married Charles's daughter, Catherine of Valois. However, Henry died only 15 months later, leaving his infant son Henry VI. Charles VI died soon after.

In support of the claim Henry's uncle, John, Duke of Bedford, besieged Orleans. French forces led by a 17-year-old peasant girl, Joan of Arc, successfully defended the town. Joan saw visions and heard voices telling her to free France. Joan escorted the new uncrowned

MAIN BATTLE DATES

1340 Sluys (E)*
1346 Crécy (E)
1347 Calais (E)
1356 Poitiers (E)
1370 Pontvallain (F)
1372 La Rochelle (F)*
1415 Agincourt (E)
1428 Orleans (F)
1429 Patay (F)
1448 Le Mans (F)
1450 Formigny (F)
1451 Bordeaux (F)

E = English victory
F = French victory
* = Naval battle

Joan of Arc

At 17, Joan of Arc (1412–1431) led the French against the English. At her trial she was accused of being a witch and found guilty. The verdict was later changed. In 1920 she was made a saint.

▲ A stained-glass window shows Joan of Arc, France's heroine.

French king, Charles VII, to Reims to be crowned. But shortly afterward she was defeated at Paris and captured by the Burgundians. They sold her to the English who burned her as a witch.

Sporadic fighting carried on for some years. The French recaptured their lands, effectively ending the war and leaving only Calais to the English.

▲ Joan of Arc kneeling before the King of France. She said she was guided by the voices of saints Michael, Catherine, and Margaret. She is shown in the armor she wore from the start of her campaign to her death.

▼ At the battle of Agincourt, Henry V commanded only about 900 men-at-arms and 3,000 archers. The French had at least three times as many heavily armed troops, but they were badly led and poorly organized.

Henry the Navigator

Prince Henry the Navigator was not a navigator (a sailor who plotted a ship's direction) and never attempted to explore, but he was called the Navigator because through his encouragement Portuguese sailors began to explore the coast of Africa.

Henry was the third son of King John I of Portugal. At the age of 21, he led a Portuguese army to capture the Moorish city of Ceuta in North Africa. There he found treasures that had been brought across the desert from the Senegal River in West Africa. He wondered if this river could be reached by sea.

The date of his first expediton is not known, but between 1424 and 1434, Henry sent 14 expeditions along the west coast of Africa. None of them would sail beyond the dangerous seas off Cape Bojador, on the coast of the western Sahara. But the 15th expedition did.

Encouraged by this, Henry built a school of navigation at Sagres on the southern coast of Portugal. From his home there he sent more expeditions to

▲ *The Portuguese developed what was then the perfect ship for exploration, the caravel. It was small, with a crew of only 30 men. Its triangular or lateen sails enabled it to sail very close to the wind.*

◄ *At Sagres, Henry established a school which brought together the best navigators and geographers of Europe. They helped to plan and equip his expeditions, and to train the crews. His captains and pilots were taught navigation, astronomy, and cartography (map making). New designs were produced for the expeditions' ships. Henry also had an observatory built to aid ships to navigate by the stars.*

Prince Henry

Henry (1394–1460) captured Ceuta in 1415. He was made governor of the Algarve in 1419 and lived at Sagres. In 1443 he was given a monopoly of African exploration.

THE PHOENICIANS

The Portuguese were not the first sailors to try to sail around the coast of Africa. The Phoenicians (*see* pages 56–57), under contract to the ruler of Egypt, sailed around Africa in about 600 B.C. Their ships were driven by oarsmen and it must have taken over two years for them to complete the voyage. On their return, however, the Egyptian ruler did not make use of their discoveries.

1416 Wales: Owen Glendower dies.

1417 The Great Schism ends when the Council of Constance elects Martin V as the only rightful pope.

c. 1418 Portugal: Prince Henry the Navigator organizes the first of many expeditions to West Africa. The Portuguese discover the islands of Madeira.

1420 Hundred Years' War: Henry V of England is acknowledged as heir to the French throne.

1421 Ottoman empire: Sultan Murad II becomes emperor (to 1451). China: the capital is moved to Beijing.

1422 Hundred Years' War: Henry V of England and Charles VI of France die. They are succeeded by Henry VI, a baby, as King of England (to 1461) and Charles VII as King of France (to 1461).

explore the west coast of Africa. Gradually his sailors overcame their fear of falling off the edge of what they believed was a flat Earth. By the time Prince Henry died in 1460, Portuguese explorers had reached the coast of what is now Sierra Leone. Henry's work inspired later Portuguese explorers (*see* pages 338–339) to sail around the Cape of Good Hope and find a sea route to India and the Far East.

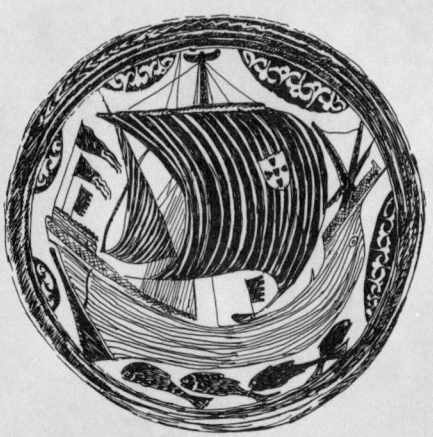

This early 15th century bowl from Valencia, Spain, shows a Portuguese sailing ship.

ANCIENT BELIEFS

Sailing in the Middle Ages was an unknown and frightening experience. Apart from believing the Earth was flat many sailors were terrified of what they might meet in unknown waters. They told each other colorful stories of the fabulous monsters they believed lurked in the deep Atlantic Ocean. Many could easily crush a ship.

1424 Hundred Years' War: John, Duke of Bedford, defeats the French at Cravant. Portuguese sailors start the attempt to sail around Cape Bojador, West Africa.

1428 English begin the siege of Orleans. Joan of Arc sees visions and hears voices telling her to free France.

1429 Joan of Arc is appointed military commander and wins the siege of Orleans. Charles VII is eventually crowned king of France at Reims.

1430 Burgundians capture Joan of Arc and hand her over to the English.

Trade

The Middle Ages saw a great revival in trade within Europe. Towns and markets sprang up and many large cities held trade fairs. Merchants established contacts with the Near East again and so luxury goods such as silks and spices came into Europe once more.

Within Europe the most important trade was in wool. At first England supplied the fleeces for the cloth makers of the Low Countries to spin and weave. Later the situation changed and most of the cloth was then made in England. Banking started at this time, as did the slave trade. Merchants grew rich through buying and selling, but they also risked losing their money when they sent goods overseas. Ships might be wrecked or attacked by pirates and the cargo lost.

▲ *Merchants sold local produce in the market towns of Europe. At the larger fairs merchants sold silk, brocade, and porcelain from China, spices from Southeast Asia, gold from Africa, and jewels from India.*

▼ *Although going by sea was the easiest and safest way of moving goods, shipwrecks did happen. To avoid losing all their money in a shipwreck, merchants had shares in several ships. Each ship was shared among several merchants.*

▲ *The seal of Danzig. Danzig, on the Baltic, was one of the leading towns in the Hanseatic League which dominated the trade of northern Europe.*

► *The first modern European bank was set up by merchants in Venice in 1171. Its purpose was to lend money to the government. Soon merchants realized that banks were useful places to deposit their money and to invest it safely. The success of the bank in Venice led to the formation of banks in all the major cities of Europe. People began to realize that banks helped to develop trade and commerce, as well as making a profit for their owners. Venice went on to establish a series of trading ports around the Mediterranean and by 1400 it had become the richest commercial city in Europe.*

WHEN IT HAPPENED

1241 Hanseatic League begins when two ports agree to protect each other's merchants.

c. **1290** Guilds are established in Europe.

1400 By this date there are over 150 ports in the Hanseatic League.

▲ *The use of paper money began in China in the 7th century A.D. Marco Polo wrote about it in the 13th century. This note from the 14th century is made of bark paper.*

◄ *A slave market in the Yemen in 1237. The Koran did not ban slavery, but forbade people from making other Muslims into slaves. Slaves were mostly bought from central Asia and Africa.*

309

1431 Joan of Arc burned as a witch at Rouen. Henry VI of England is crowned king of France in Paris. Cambodia: Khmer city of Angkor is abandoned; the Thais and Chams, supported by the Mongols, rebel against their Khmer overlords and overrun most of the empire.

1432–1434 Portuguese explorers discover the islands of the Azores.

1433 West Africa: Tuaregs from the Sahara sack Timbuktu.

1434 Portuguese sailors successfully round Cape Bojador, West Africa, and go on to explore the west coast of Africa.

1436 Hundred Years' War: English troops withdraw from Paris.

Heavenly dancers carved on a temple at Angkor in about 1200.

1438 France: Pragmatic Sanction of Bourges declares the French Church independent of the papacy. Holy Roman Empire: Albert II is made emperor (to 1439). Peru: Pachacuti becomes Sapa Inca and expands the Inca empire farther.

1439 Papacy: Felix V becomes last of the antipopes (to 1449).

1440 Holy Roman Empire: Frederick III, emperor (to 1493); in Mainz goldsmith Johannes Gutenberg begins printing with movable type. Benin: Ewuare the Great takes the title of oba (king) (to 1481); he institutes many reforms and his powerful army conquers the Yoruba. Mexico: Montezuma becomes ruler of the Aztecs and begins the conquest of tribes outside the valley of Mexico.

The Khmer Empire

The Khmer empire (now Cambodia) was created in 802 when the Khmer people were united by King Jayavarman I. The Khmers wrote books on paper, palm leaves, and vellum. Fire, rot, and termites have long since destroyed them, but we can learn a lot about the Khmers in ancient Chinese histories, and from the carvings in the ruins of Angkor Thom, which means "great city," and Angkor Wat, the city's "great temple."

Angkor Thom, originally called Yasodharapura, was begun just before 900. Angkor Wat was built between 1113 and 1150. The Khmer empire reached its height during the reign of Jayavarman VII (1181-1220).

The Khmer were builders, fishermen, farmers, and warriors. Many lived in houses perched on stilts around the lake of Tonle Sap, as today's Cambodians still do. Their main food was rice and they developed an irrigation system which produced three crops a year.

The kings were Hindus, but most of the people were Buddhists. They held religious feasts to celebrate the start of

▼ *The Khmer empire was at its greatest extent during the reign of King Jayavarman VII (1181–1220).*

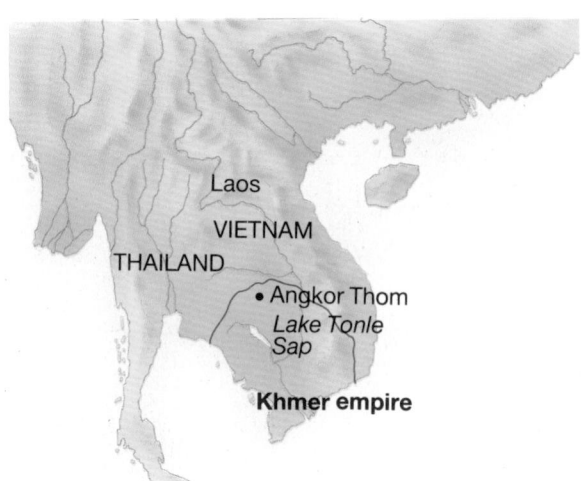

plowing and harvest. They traded with China, bartering spices and rhinoceros horn for porcelain and lacquerware.

Sculptures show that the royal women of the court wore skirts, but left the upper part of the body bare. They were encouraged to study law, astrology, and languages. Most men only wore a loose covering around their loins.

The Khmer armies, which may have included hundreds of war elephants, fought many battles and conquered most of the surrounding lands. But in the 15th century, invading armies from Thailand forced the Khmer to abandon Angkor.

▲ *Many of the temple carvings at Angkor Wat show the daily lives of the Khmer people as well as telling the stories of their sacred myths and bloody battles.*

▼ *A reconstruction of Angkor Wat. The huge, elaborate temple complex is surrounded by walls and a moat that was 600 feet (180 m) wide and 2½ miles (4 km) long. The temple was made up of three main enclosures (representing the outer world) surrounding an inner holy shrine. After the temple and the city were abandoned in the 15th century, they were swallowed up by the jungle and not rediscovered until the 1860s.*

1451 Hundred Years' War: French take Bordeaux and Bayeux from the English. Scotland: Glasgow University is founded. Ottoman empire: Muhammad II becomes sultan of Turkey (to 1481).

1452 Hundred Years' War: English recapture Bordeaux from the French. Italy: Leonardo da Vinci, artist, architect, and engineer is born (dies 1519).

1453 England, driven out of France, retains only Calais. The Hundred Years' War ends. Byzantine empire: Constantinople falls to the Ottoman Turks after a siege of 54 days; it marks the end of the Byzantine empire. England: Henry VI declared insane; Richard of York is declared Protector and rules in his place.

Johannes Gutenberg who introduced printing to Europe and made it possible to produce the books we know today.

1455 Henry VI recovers. Richard of York is replaced by the Duke of Somerset, a Lancastrian. The Wars of the Roses start. Yorkists defeat Lancastrians at the first battle of St. Albans.

1456 Germany: Johannes Gutenberg publishes the Bible in Latin, the first to be printed with movable type.

1458 Pius II becomes pope (to 1464).

1459 Ottoman empire: Turks conquer Serbia.

1460 England: Richard of York is defeated and killed at battle of Wakefield; Earl of Warwick captures London for the Yorkists; Yorkists capture Henry VI at battle of Northampton. Scotland: James II killed in battle against the English, is succeeded by eight-year-old son James III (to 1488). Mexico: the end of the great age of Mayan civilization. West Africa: The Portuguese explore the coast as far as Sierra Leone.

Printing in Europe

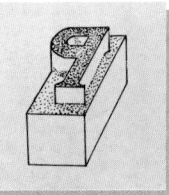

One of the most exciting developments in the Middle Ages was the European development of printing. Before then books had to be slowly and laboriously copied by hand, and only a few rich people could afford to own them. Suddenly, knowledge was within the reach of anyone who could read.

Printing was developed around 1440 by Johannes Gutenberg, a goldsmith from Mainz in Germany. His invention consisted of three parts: a mold for casting the letters in an alloy of lead, a "sticky" ink, and a winepress that had been adapted to make a printing press. Paper had been brought to Europe from Morocco in the 12th century.

This new method had an advantage over woodblock printing, already used for printing playing cards. Block printing needed a new block for every job, but Gutenberg's metal letters or type could be used over and over again.

▼ *The spread of printing in Europe during the first fifty years of its existence. England's first printer was William Caxton, a retired businessman.*

Gutenberg was the first of many printers who began producing books in the 15th century. They tried to match the beautiful handwritten manuscripts that had been made by the monasteries, mostly in Gothic or black-letter script. So in the first printed books Gothic type was used. Roman type, which is used in this book, was invented by Italian printers.

By 1500 there were 1,700 printing presses in Europe. They had already produced around 40,000 books which were made up of nearly 20 million volumes. The invention of printing made possible the sudden spread of learning which was later called the Renaissance (*see* pages 330–333).

▲ *The early books were made to look as much like the familiar handwritten manuscripts as possible. Color was added by hand after the initial printing.*

EASTERN ORIGINS

Chinese and Korean printers experimented with movable type before Gutenberg, using wood, pottery, and bronze. None of their attempts was satisfactory because they faced one enormous difficulty: Chinese writing uses a minimum of 5,000 different characters, and the full range is ten times as many. Even allowing for capital and small letters, numerals, punctuation marks, and so on, Gutenberg needed only 300 different letters to print his first book in 1456, an edition of the Bible.

▼ *Block printing (top) required a carver to cut the letters in reverse in one solid piece of wood, which could be used for only one job. Gutenberg's metal type (bottom) could be broken up and reused.*

► *Early printing was carried out by rubbing a sheet of paper onto an inked woodblock. Gutenberg adapted a wine press to apply pressure quickly and evenly over the whole sheet of paper. This kind of press remained in use for the next 350 years. The ink was spread on a metal plate and then dabbed on the type with a leather-covered tool. Later on, a roller was used to apply the ink more evenly.*

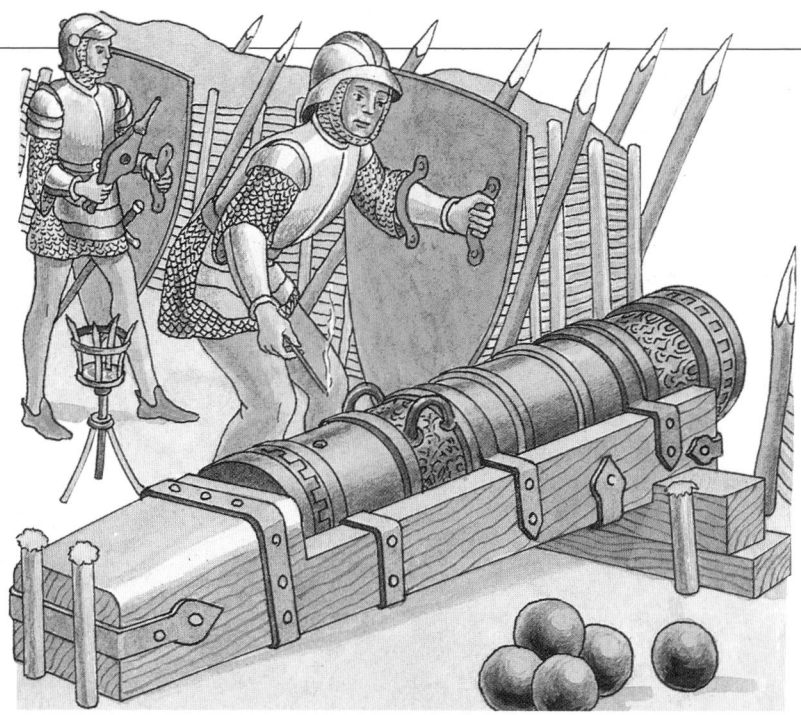

War and Weapons

As the struggle for power continued, there were wars in many parts of the world. In Europe, the most important soldiers were the knights. In Japan they were the samurai. Both had very strict codes of chivalry and relied on warhorses to carry them into battle.

European knights wore heavy chain mail and metal helmets. Gradually, this was replaced by armor made from flat metal plates, which made the knight extremely heavy. An elaborate suit of armor could weigh over 100 pounds (45 kg). They also began to use longer swords which were sharpened to get through plate armor.

In the 12th century, much fighting took place around castles, rather than on battlefields. Despite the development of heavily fortified castles, the technique of seige warfare differed little from that used in ancient times. By the middle of the 14th century the use of gunpowder had spread to Europe from China. Once cannons were able to knock down castle walls, the castle could no longer protect its inhabitants.

▲ A cannon from the 14th century. It is made of strips of iron, held together with hoops. The arrival of gunpowder from China in the 13th century completely changed warfare and weapons. The first guns appeared in the 14th century and were very like simple cannons mounted on long, wooden shafts. By the middle of the 15th century the matchlock had been invented, but it was unsafe to load.

▼ A Japanese samurai warrior on horseback was a frightening sight. Samurai armor was made of enameled metal links or very thick strips of leather, which made it flexible. They fought with bows and arrows and with long curved swords. A samurai's sword was his most treasured possession. It had a razor-sharp edge for cutting but a soft iron core, enabling it to withstand many blows.

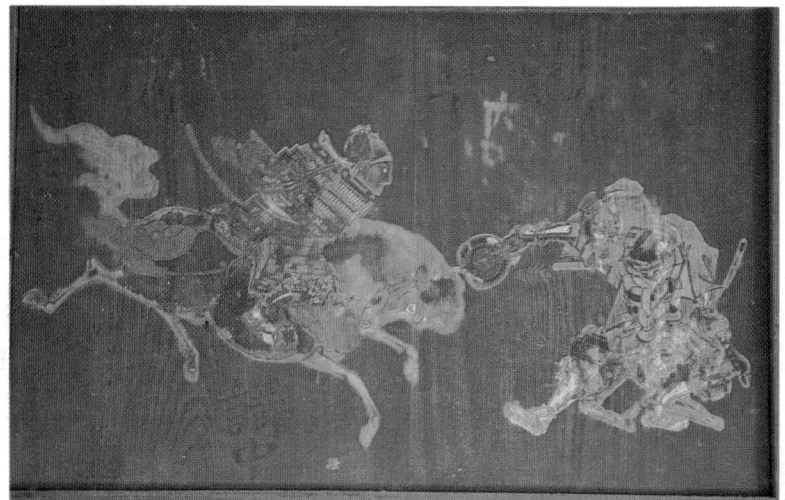

WHEN IT HAPPENED

13th century   The English develop the longbow.
1291   Christian Crusaders are finally expelled from the Holy Land (Palestine).
1304   Arabs start using the first guns.
1337–1453   The Hundred Years' War is fought between France and England.
1453   Constantinople falls to the Ottoman Turks after a 54-day siege.

▶ *The art of heraldry grew out of the need for knights to recognize each other on the battlefield, so that they did not kill people on their own side. To make this easier, they painted their shields with simple patterns. Soon all the men in the same army used the same pattern.*

▼ *During a seige, catapults hurled stones, and giant, soldier-laden seige towers were wheeled up to the walls. Archers kept up a hail of arrows to keep defenders back.*

The Wars of the Roses

The Wars of the Roses is the name given to the struggle between two branches of the Plantagenet family (*see* pages 248–249) for the English throne. Called the House of York and the House of Lancaster, both were descended from Edward III.

Trouble began in 1453 when King Henry VI, of the House of Lancaster, went mad. His distant cousin, Richard, Duke of York, became Lord Protector (regent) and ruled for him. When Henry suddenly recovered, war broke out between Richard of York and his supporters and the Lancastrian advisers to Henry VI. Although Richard was killed, the Yorkists triumphed and in 1461 Richard's son became Edward IV. Henry VI was later murdered.

When Edward died 12 years later, his young son Edward V succeeded him, under the care of his uncle, Richard, Duke of Gloucester. After a few weeks Richard seized the throne, saying that Edward V was illegitimate. Edward and his younger brother were possibly murdered. The remaining Lancastrian heir, Henry Tudor, defeated and killed Richard, becoming King Henry VII. He married Edward IV's daughter, Elizabeth of York, and ended the Wars of the Roses.

THE ROSES

The Wars of the Roses get their name from the emblems of the two principal families involved: the red rose of Lancaster and the white rose of York. When Henry VII became king and married Elizabeth of York he combined the two to form the Tudor Rose which is shown here.

Richard III

1452 Born. Brother of Edward IV.
1471 Murder of Henry VI. Richard possibly present.
1483 Becomes Lord Protector for his nephew, Edward V; takes the throne.
1485 Dies at the battle of Bosworth Field.

Henry VII

1457 Born; his mother a great granddaughter of John of Gaunt.
1471 Flees to Brittany.
1485 Defeats Richard III, becomes king.
1486 Marries Elizabeth of York, Edward IV's daughter.
1509 Dies at Richmond.

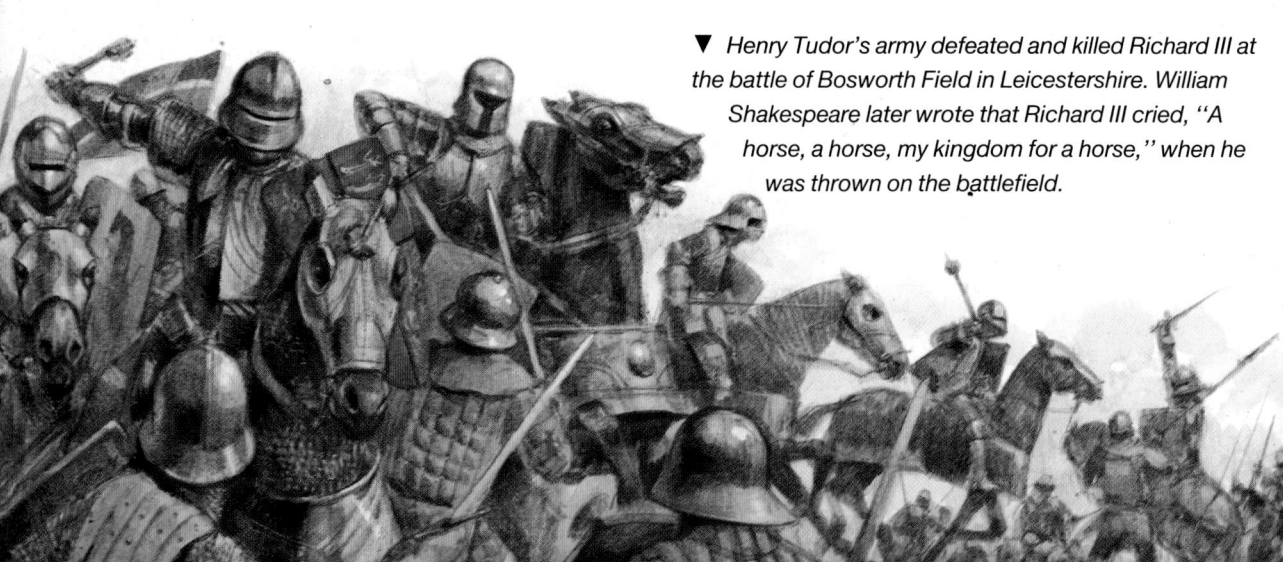

▼ Henry Tudor's army defeated and killed Richard III at the battle of Bosworth Field in Leicestershire. William Shakespeare later wrote that Richard III cried, "A horse, a horse, my kingdom for a horse," when he was thrown on the battlefield.

The Renaissance

The period from 1461 to 1600 marks the start of modern history. Europeans started to emerge from the narrow confines of the Middle Ages to travel beyond their own continent. The movement now called the Renaissance was given support by Greek scholars, fleeing from the fall of Constantinople who brought with them the knowledge of ancient Greece and Rome. Education, art, science, and architecture were all affected as people began to question what they were told.

Largely unknown to most Europeans at the start of this period, other civilizations were flourishing elsewhere in the world. In India the Mogul empire was founded. It expanded under the rule of wise emperors who, although Muslim themselves, treated their Muslim, Hindu, and Sikh subjects equally.

In the Far East, China was fairly peaceful and prosperous under the rule of the Ming, but Japan was being torn apart by civil wars as its feudal lords struggled with each other for control.

From 1460, European explorers set out to find new routes to the Far East. The Portuguese sailed south along the coast of Africa and on to reach the Moluccas, China, and Japan. Trading posts were established but settlers were rarely allowed farther than the coast. In contrast, the Spanish set out to conquer the lands they explored. When Columbus arrived in the West Indies in 1492, he claimed them for Spain, although the Arawak and Carib Indians already lived there. By 1535 the Spaniards had turned the people of South and Central America into slaves; the original inhabitants were nearly wiped out by disease and ill-use.

▼ *The Renaissance was a time of great prosperity in Italy, but some Christians condemned the luxury and vanity of the rich. One such was Savonarola, who ruled Florence from 1494 to 1498. He had great bonfires built on which people burned their precious possessions.*

The Americas

Europe

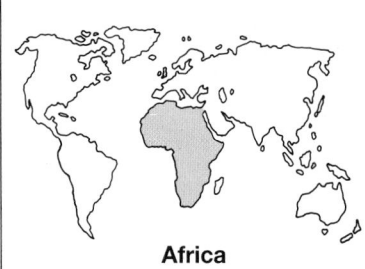

Africa

1466 The Incas under Topa overrun the Chimu empire.
1492 Christopher Columbus reaches the Caribbean islands.
1494 The Treaty of Tordesillas divides the known world between Spain and Portugal.
1497 The Italian navigator John Cabot reaches North America.
1498 Huayna Capac extends the Inca empire into Colombia.

1462 Ivan III becomes ruler of Muscovy and much of Russia is freed from Tartar control.
1485 The end of the Wars of the Roses in England.

1464 The kingdom of Songhay becomes independent of the Mali empire in West Africa.
1482 The Portuguese start to settle the Gold Coast (Ghana).
1488 Bartholomeu Dias sails around Cape of Good Hope.

1503 Montezuma becomes ruler of the Aztecs.
1513 Juan Ponce de León, former governor of Puerto Rico, claims Florida for Spain.
1521 Hernán Cortés conquers the Aztec empire.
1525 Civil war in Inca empire.
1533 Francisco Pizarro conquers the Incas.
1535 Large silver mines are discovered in Peru and Mexico. The local people are forced to work in them, but the silver is sent to Spain.
1535–1536 Jacques Cartier sails to Canada and explores the St. Lawrence River.
c. **1570** The Portuguese set up the first sugar plantations in Brazil.
1585 Sir Walter Raleigh tries to set up an English colony in Virginia but fails.

1517 Martin Luther, a German priest, starts the Reformation.
1519 Charles I of Spain becomes Charles V of the Holy Roman Empire.
1529 The Ottoman Turks beseige Vienna.
1534 Henry VIII becomes head of the Church in England.
1543 Nicolas Copernicus states that the Earth moves around the Sun.
1545 The first meeting of the Council of Trent starts the Counter-Reformation.
1562–1598 Wars of Religion in France.
1568 A revolt against Spain starts in the Netherlands.
1571 The battle of Lepanto ends Ottoman ambitions in the Mediterranean.
1588 Defeat of the Spanish Armada in the English Channel.
1600 Foundation of the English East India Company.

1502 The first African slaves are taken to work in the Americas.
1505 The Portuguese set up trading posts along the east coast of Africa.

1571 In the Sudan the Kanem Bornu empire flourishes.
1574 The Portuguese colonize Angola in southern Africa.
1578 The Moroccans destroy Portuguese power in north-western Africa.
1591 The Moroccans overrun the Songhay empire.
1600 In West Africa the Oyo empire starts to flourish.

Middle East

1463–1479 War between Ottoman empire and Venetians.

1491 Ottomans and Mamelukes reach a peace agreement after six years of war.
1501 The Safavid dynasty is founded in Persia (Iran).
1520 Suleiman I becomes sultan of the Ottoman empire.
1526 Ottomans defeat Hungary at the battle of Mohacs.

1534 Suleiman conquers Baghdad in the Safavid empire.

1566 The golden age of the Ottoman empire enters a period of decline.

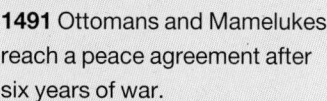

A Turkish velvet, saddle-cover.

Asia and the Far East

1471 The Vietnamese conquer their neighbors, the Champa.

1498 Vasco da Gama reaches India.
1512 Portuguese traders reach the Moluccas.
1519 Guru Nanak founds the Sikh religion in India.
1526 Babur conquers Delhi and founds the Mogul empire.

1542 Portuguese explorers arrive in Japan.
1549 Jesuit missionaries arrive in Japan and start converting the people to Christianity.
1550 The Mongols under Altan Khan invade northern China.

1571 Spain conquers the Philippines.
1581 Russian settlement of Siberia starts.
1592–1593 The Japanese invade Korea, but are defeated by the Chinese.
1595 The Dutch begin to colonize the East Indies.

Australasia and Pacific

1520 Ferdinand Magellan sails around Cape Horn and into an ocean which he names the Pacific. He then sails northeast until he reaches the Philippines, where he is killed.

An Aboriginal bark drawing of a lightning spirit

The World

In 1461 European seafarers, traders, and colonists were on the brink of setting out to explore and exploit the rest of the world. For the first time continents were brought into direct contact with each other.

In **Central** and **South America**, the Aztec and Inca empires were at their height, but with the arrival of Europeans the Aztec capital Tenochtitlán was destroyed and the Incas were forced to retreat to the highlands of Peru. The invaders turned their attention north, but it was not to be for several decades that **North America** would feel the real effects of their arrival.

African civilizations too came under European influence, but it was confined to the coast. The heart of **Africa** remained undisturbed.

China was still ruled by the Ming. Although the arts flourished, society had begun to stagnate under their rule.

In **Europe** itself, many new ideas led some people to question their religion. By 1600, half the population of Europe had left the Catholic Church and joined a new one: the Protestants.

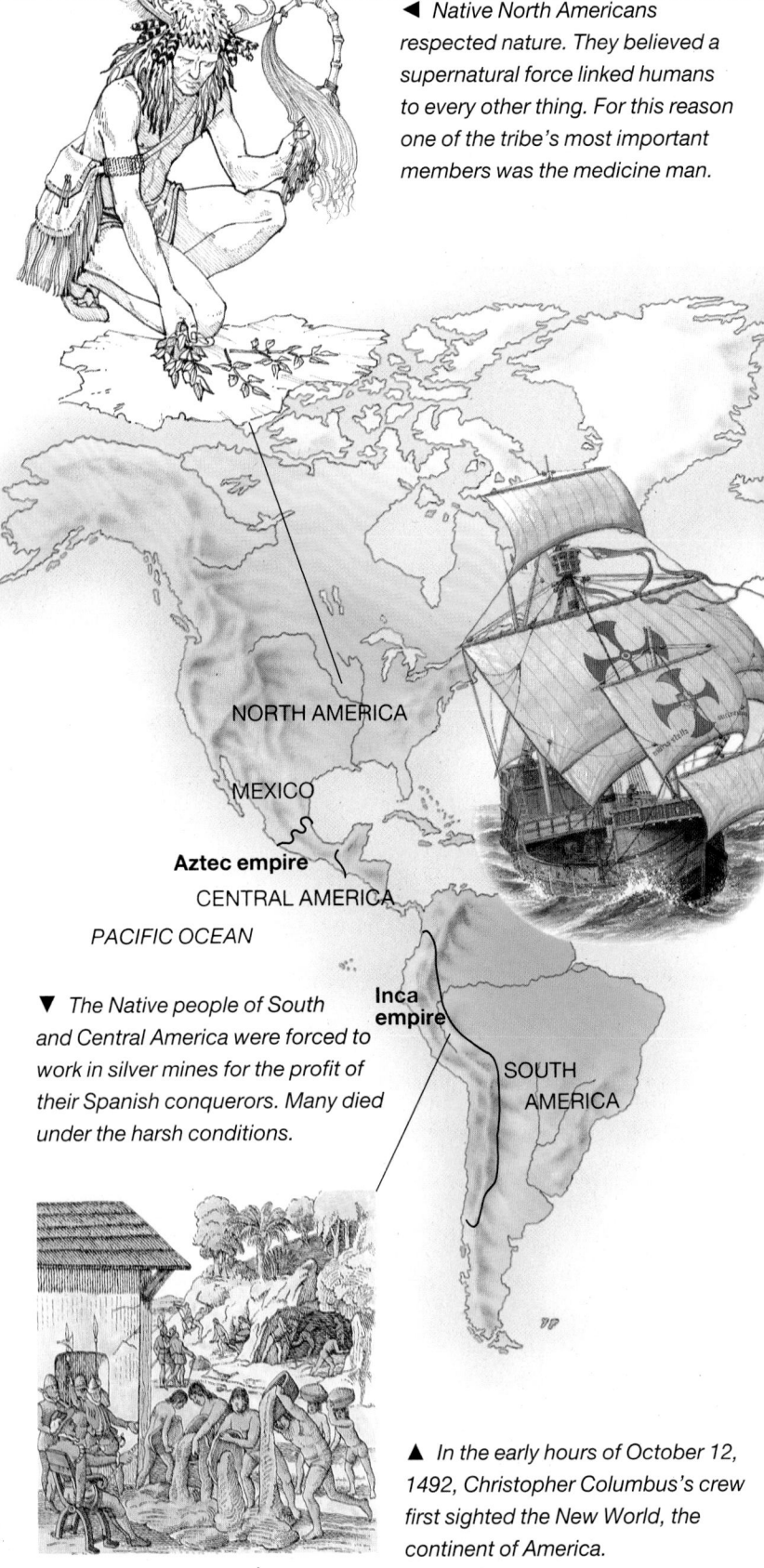

◄ *Native North Americans respected nature. They believed a supernatural force linked humans to every other thing. For this reason one of the tribe's most important members was the medicine man.*

NORTH AMERICA

MEXICO

Aztec empire

CENTRAL AMERICA

PACIFIC OCEAN

▼ *The Native people of South and Central America were forced to work in silver mines for the profit of their Spanish conquerors. Many died under the harsh conditions.*

Inca empire

SOUTH AMERICA

▲ *In the early hours of October 12, 1492, Christopher Columbus's crew first sighted the New World, the continent of America.*

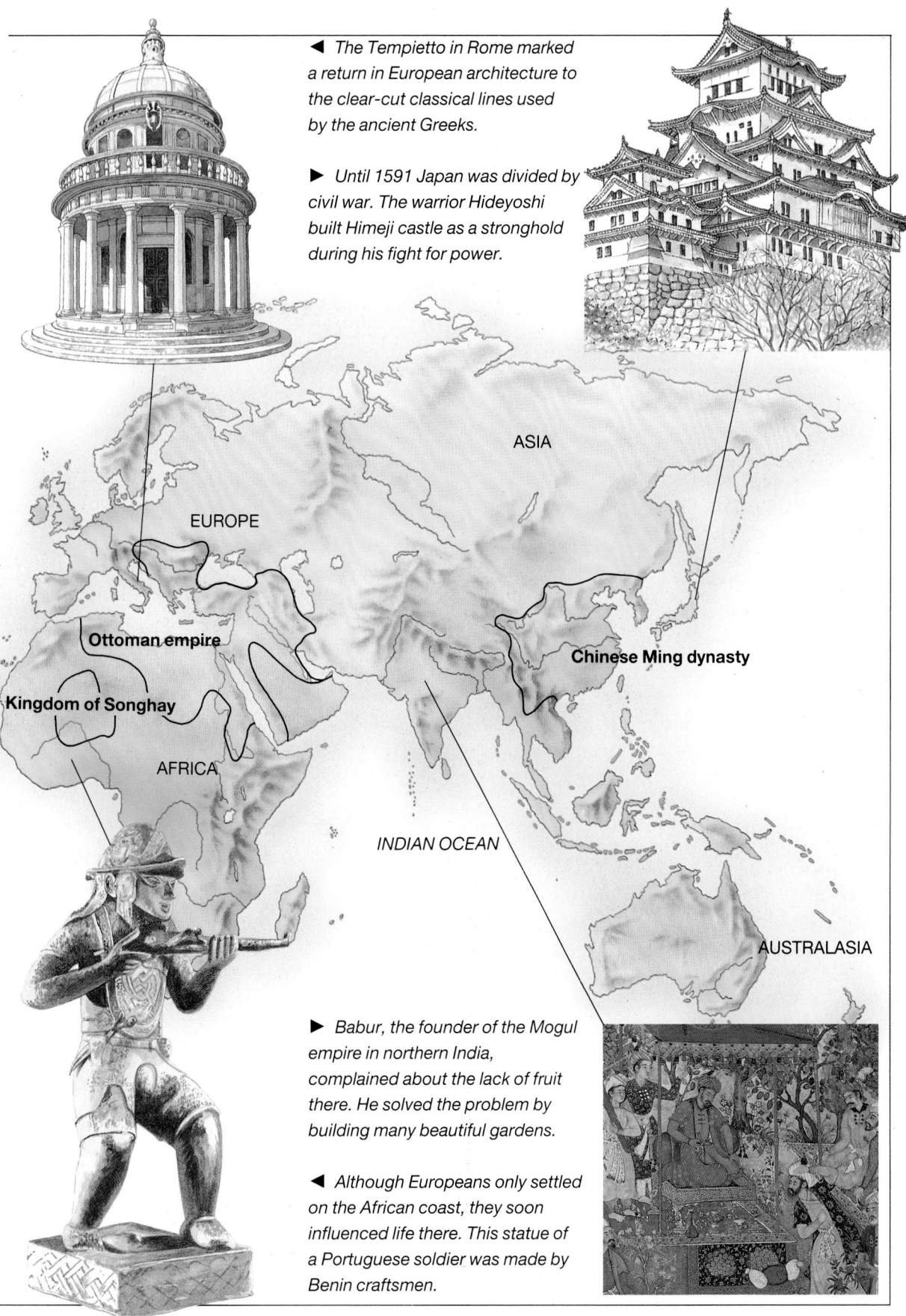

◄ *The Tempietto in Rome marked a return in European architecture to the clear-cut classical lines used by the ancient Greeks.*

► *Until 1591 Japan was divided by civil war. The warrior Hideyoshi built Himeji castle as a stronghold during his fight for power.*

ASIA

EUROPE

Ottoman empire

Chinese Ming dynasty

Kingdom of Songhay

AFRICA

INDIAN OCEAN

AUSTRALASIA

► *Babur, the founder of the Mogul empire in northern India, complained about the lack of fruit there. He solved the problem by building many beautiful gardens.*

◄ *Although Europeans only settled on the African coast, they soon influenced life there. This statue of a Portuguese soldier was made by Benin craftsmen.*

1461 England: The Wars of the Roses between the Houses of Lancaster and York continue. With the help of the Earl of Warwick, also known as the Kingmaker, Richard of York's son, Edward, defeats the Lancastrians at the battle of Towton in March and becomes King Edward IV of England (to 1470). France: Louis XI is king (to 1483). Ottoman empire: The Ottoman Turks conquer Trebizond (now called Trabzon), Turkey, the capital of the Comnenian empire since 1204.

c. 1461 Central America: The Aztec empire is at its height.

1462 Russia: Ivan III, also known as Ivan the Great, becomes duke of Muscovy (to 1505). His capital is Moscow. Spain: the kingdom of Castile captures Gibraltar from the Arabs.

The hideously grinning skull face of the Aztec god of death is shown in this terracotta statue. The Aztecs also used human skulls to make masks. They encrusted them with turquoise and seashells and lined them with red leather.

1463 War starts between the Ottoman Turks and the Venetians (to 1479). South America: Pachacuti, the Sapa Inca, wages war, successfully, against the Lupaca and Colla tribes. Quechua, the Inca language, is established in his empire. Pachacuti gives control of the Inca army to his son, Topa.

1464 Papal States: Paul II becomes pope (to 1471). England: Edward IV marries Elizabeth Woodville. West Africa: Sonni Ali becomes ruler of Songhay and makes it independent of the empire of Mali. Sonni Ali also begins to enlarge Songhay's boundaries.

The Aztec Empire

By the end of the 15th century, the Aztecs controlled a large empire in Central America. Its capital Tenochtitlán is estimated to have had a population of 150,000 people. In order to feed them all, food was grown on artificial islands, or chinampas, constructed in the lake in the middle of which the city stood (*see* page 268).

Peoples who had been conquered by the Aztecs brought food as tribute. They provided corn, beans, and cocoa, cotton cloth, as well as gold, silver, and jade for the Aztec craft workers.

Traders bought turquoise from the Pueblo Indians to the north of the Aztec empire, while from the south came brightly colored feathers. The feathers were used to make elaborately decorated capes, fans, shields, and headdresses.

Aztec society was organized along military lines. All boys had to serve in the army from the ages of 17 to 22. Some stayed on longer than this, because even a peasant could rise to be an army

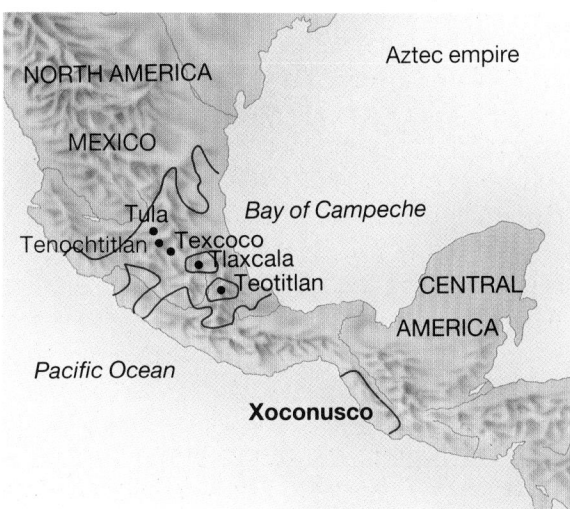

▲ *From their capital of Tenochtitlán, the Aztecs dominated most of the lands between the Gulf of Mexico and the Pacific Ocean.*

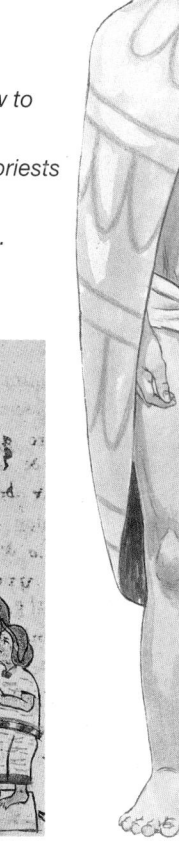

▶ Priests were a very special class of people in Aztec society. They were responsible for making the human sacrifices to keep the gods happy. Since they did not know how to use metal for making tools, the priests used stone-bladed knives on their victims.

▲ This headdress from the 16th century is made mainly of quetzal feathers. Parrot feathers in brown, crimson, white, and blue were also used.

▶ Both men and women – usually captives from other peoples – were sacrificed to the gods. The priests killed a victim by cutting out the living heart so that it jumped out of the body.

commander if he tried hard enough.

One of the main tasks of the Aztec army was to take as many prisoners as possible in a war and bring them back to Tenochtitlán. Here they were used in religious sacrifices, especially to Huizilopochtli, the god of war.

The idea of sacrifice in the name of religion was a very important part of Aztec culture. In Tenochtitlán, there were several thousand priests and several different gods. These included gods of the Sun, war, wind, and rain.

All of them were said to need large quantities of human blood. These human sacrifices were carried out at the top of huge, pyramid-shaped temples in an enormous square that stood in the middle of the city.

AGRICULTURE

The Aztecs grew many different sorts of fruit on their chinampas. These included avocados, tomatoes, and limes. None of these were known in Europe until they were taken there by explorers in the 16th century. The Aztecs did not have horses or wheeled vehicles, so all carrying was done by people.

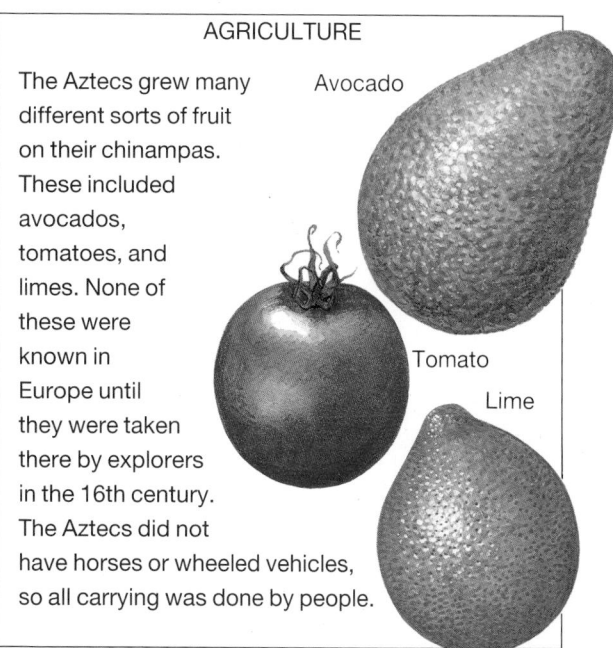

Avocado

Tomato

Lime

Arts and Crafts

In Europe, the Renaissance (*see* pages 330–333) influenced painting, sculpture, and architecture, as well as education. Artists such as Titian, Holbein, Raphael, Dürer, Leonardo da Vinci, Brueghel, Botticelli, and Michelangelo all worked at this time. In Britain there was a flowering in literature and drama.

In the Americas, the Aztecs and Incas made ornaments in gold and silver, although they did not know how to make metal tools. Art flourished in the Ottoman, Safavid, and Mogul empires and the Chinese continued to make fine porcelain.

▼ *As late as the 16th century the Incas made detailed pots from coils of clay because they had not invented the potter's wheel.*

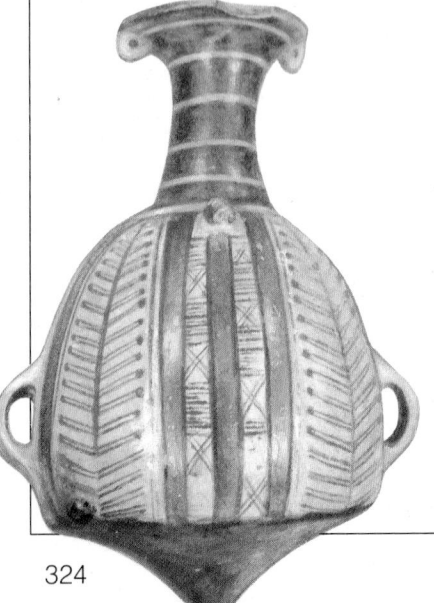

▲ *Renaissance artists started to get proportions and perspective correct. Later on, artists painted pictures full of excitement and tension, such as Tintoretto's* St. George's Fight with the Dragon.

◄ *Glazed earthenware tiles decorated the royal palace at Isfahan, Persia.*

WHEN IT HAPPENED

1482 Leonardo da Vinci paints the fresco *The Last Supper* in Milan, Italy.

1508 Michelangelo Buonarroti starts work on the Sistine Chapel while the painter Raphael works on other parts of the Vatican, Rome.

1512 Albrecht Dürer, the German painter and engraver, becomes court painter to the Holy Roman emperor Maximillian I.

1536 German-born Hans Holbein becomes court painter to Henry VIII of England.

1577 The painter El Greco moves to Spain to seek the patronage of Philip II.

1586 Kabuki theater starts in Japan.

1600 William Shakespeare writes *Hamlet*.

▲ *Theater-going was very popular in Elizabethan England. This is Shakespeare's Globe Theater which was built in London in 1599.*

▼ *People who could write or play music were admired during the Renaissance. Organs and harpsicords were popular instruments.*

▶ *During the Renaissance, more realistic statues were made. When Michelangelo carved this statue of Moses in about 1513, he included veins and muscles in the arms and legs.*

1465 England: Henry VI is captured and imprisoned in the Tower of London by Edward IV. Henry's wife and son escape to Scotland and later go to France. France: The dukes of Alençon, Berri, Burgundy, Bourbon, and Lorraine conspire against Louis XI, who had been attempting to limit their power. Italy: The first printing press is set up.

1466 Poland: Following the Peace of Thorn, Poland gains much of Prussia from the Teutonic Knights. England: The Earl of Warwick starts to quarrel with Edward IV. Later in the year, Warwick forms an alliance with Louis XI of France against Edward. South America: The Chimu empire is overrun by the Incas under the leadership of Topa.

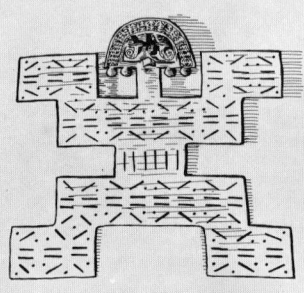

A golden pectoral ornament (worn on the chest) made by the people of South America.

1467 Charles the Bold becomes the duke of Burgundy at the age of 34. His duchy is split into two parts and includes Artois, Flanders, and Brabant (which are now in Belgium), and land within the boundaries of France. His ambition is to take control of the land between the two parts of his dukedom and make himself a king. This leads to almost continual war with Louis XI of France, who is his overlord. Japan: A period of civil war begins between the feudal lords, as each fights for control of the emperor and the country. It lasts for more than 100 years.

1468 Margaret of York, sister of Edward IV, marries Charles the Bold, Duke of Burgundy. West Africa: Sonni Ali captures Timbuktu.

The Inca Empire

The ruler of the Inca empire was known as the *Sapa Inca*. He claimed to be descended from the Sun god, who gave him the right to rule. He was also worshiped as a god himself.

Under the Sapa Inca, many officials were responsible for the everyday running of the country. They looked after the affairs of the cities and made sure the farms were working efficiently. These officials were also responsible for the factories and workshops that produced pottery, textiles, and decorative metal objects. Writing was unknown to them, so they kept all their records on *quipus*. These were thick cords of different colors that had knots tied in them to convey information.

When Pachacuti became Sapa Inca (*see* pages 278–279), he began to expand his empire from the capital city Cuzco. In

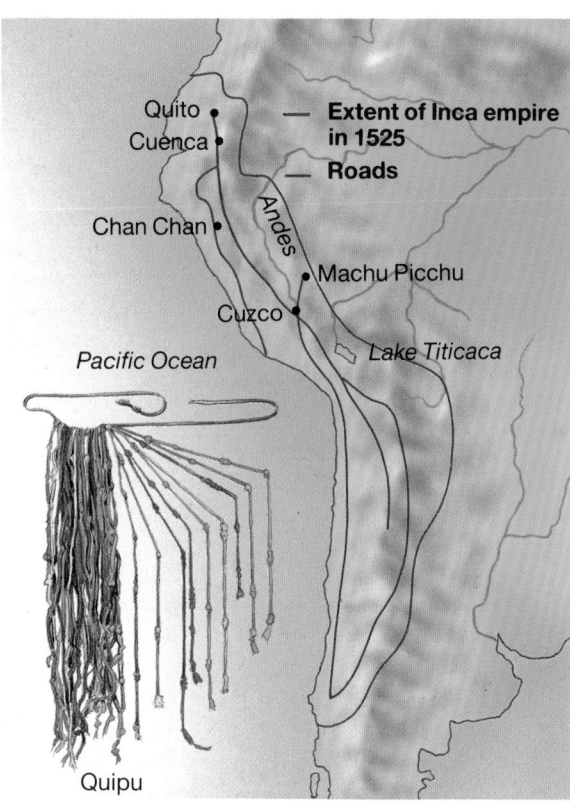

Quito
Cuenca
Chan Chan
Andes
Machu Picchu
Cuzco
Lake Titicaca
Pacific Ocean

Extent of Inca empire in 1525
Roads

Quipu

1450 he conquered the Titicaca basin, and in 1463 he went to war against the Lupaca and Colla tribes. In the same year he handed control of the army over to his son, Topa. Under Topa's command, the Inca army completely defeated the neighboring Chimu empire in 1466.

Topa continued to expand the empire after he became tenth Sapa Inca in 1471. During the next 15 years he conquered land as far south as the Maule River, and he later took control of lands to the north and west. Topa also began a period of extensive road-building. Topa's son, Huayna Capac, succeeded as Sapa Inca in 1493. He also expanded the empire and built a second capital at Quito. When Huayna Capac died in 1525, the empire was divided between his sons. Huascar ruled the south and Atahualpa, the north. This division soon led to civil war.

▲ The ruins of the Inca city of Machu Picchu still stand high in the Andes. Its temples, palaces, and houses were built of granite blocks, cleverly fitted together without the use of mortar.

◄ By 1525, the Inca empire was at its height. Stretching from the Andes to the coast, it measured 2,500 miles (4,000 km) miles from north to south. It had many different landscapes and climates. There were deserts near the coast and high mountains in the east.

▶ Two main roads ran north and south in the Inca empire. They were connected to every town and village by smaller roads. Goods were carried by llama. Quipus were delivered by relay runners.

Ferdinand and Isabella

In the 15th century, Spain was divided into four different kingdoms. The two biggest were Castile and Aragon. The first step toward uniting Spain was made in 1469 when Ferdinand, heir to the King of Aragon, married Isabella, the half-sister of the King of Castile. When the king of Castile died in 1474, Isabella and Ferdinand succeeded him as joint rulers of his kingdom. Five years later, Ferdinand inherited Aragon and made Isabella joint ruler of Aragon as well.

With the two kingdoms united, Spain grew more powerful. Both Ferdinand and Isabella were devout Catholics and the Inquisition was established under their rule. It was a religious court which punished people who did not accept the Catholic Church's teachings. It operated with great severity; people were tried in secret and tortured until they confessed. Those who did confess could be fined, while those who refused were either imprisoned or burned to death.

At this time, there were many Jews

Ferdinand

1452 Born.
1469 Marries Princess Isabella of Castile.
1478 Establishes the Inquisition.
1479 Succeeds to throne of Aragon.
1481 Rules Aragon and Castile.
1492–1512 Conquers Granada, Naples, and Navarre.
1516 Dies.

Isabella

1451 Born.
1469 Marries.
1474–1479 Campaigns for the throne of Castile.
1481 Rules Aragon and Castile jointly with Ferdinand.
1492 Finances the expedition of explorer Christopher Columbus to go to the Indies.
1504 Dies.

▼ *The army of Ferdinand and Isabella defeated the Moors in 1492. Granada became part of the kingdom of Spain and the Muslim Moors were expelled. Many of them went to live in North Africa.*

▼ *After uniting Castile and Aragon, Ferdinand and Isabella added Granada to their lands in 1492. Then Ferdinand conquered south Navarre in 1512.*

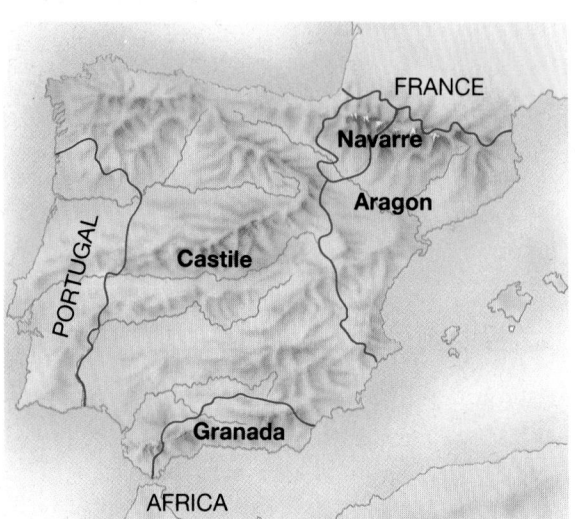

living in Spain and the Inquisition was used against them. In 1492 as many as 200,000 of them were expelled from Spain. In the same year, the Moorish state of Granada was recaptured with many Muslims being expelled or converted, and Isabella sponsored Columbus's voyage, which ended in the Americas (*see* pages 340–341).

Ferdinand and Isabella had five children. One was Catherine of Aragon who married Henry VIII of England. But they had no son and so descent passed through their daughter Joanna the Mad.

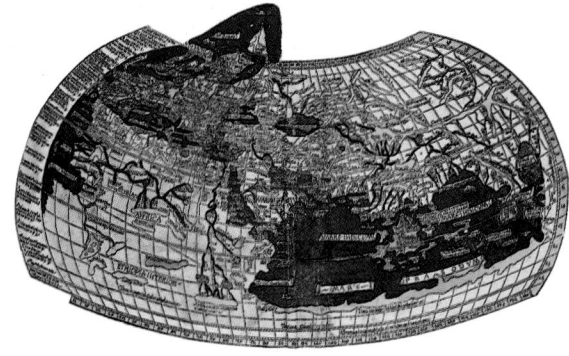

▲ *Maps at this time were based on those of Ptolemy, a 2nd century Greek mapmaker. Made in 1486, this map shows the limit of European knowledge; only half the globe is shown and Africa is joined to Southeast Asia.*

1469 Spain: The marriage of Ferdinand of Aragon and Isabella of Castile leads to the unification of Spain. Italy: Lorenzo de Medici becomes joint ruler (with his brother Guiliano) of Florence at the age of 20. England: Encouraged by Louis XI and Margaret, wife of Henry VI, the Earl of Warwick and the Duke of Clarence plan a rebellion against Edward IV.

Columbus's banner bore a green cross and the symbols of Ferdinand and Isabella.

1470 England: Having changed his allegiance and joined the Lancastrians, Warwick returns to England. Edward IV flees abroad and Henry VI is restored to the throne. Ottoman empire: The Ottoman Turks seize the Greek island of Negropont (Euboea) from the Venetians.

1471 South America: Topa becomes the tenth Sapa Inca and starts on a program of road-building to connect all parts of his vast empire with the capital, Cuzco. England: Edward IV returns to England. At the battle of Barnet he defeats and kills Warwick. He then marches west to Tewkesbury where Henry VI's wife and their son Edward, Prince of Wales, had just arrived from France. Edward IV defeats their army and captures the queen. The Prince of Wales is killed in the battle. Henry VI dies, probably murdered, in the Tower of London. Edward IV is once more King of England (to 1483). Papal States: Sixtus IV becomes pope (to 1484). Central Europe: Vladislav of Poland is elected king of Bohemia following the death of Podiebrad. North Africa: The Portuguese, led by Alfonso V, take Tangier from the Muslims. Asia: The Annamese of Vietnam begin to move southward and conquer the Champa.

The Renaissance

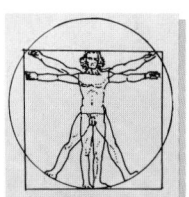

In medieval Europe, the Church was the main sponsor of the arts and the main center of education. This meant that all learning, art, and sculpture had a strong religious theme. People had to accept what they were told and not ask questions. Then, in the late 14th century, Italian scholars began to take an interest in the writings of the ancient Greeks and Romans. This grew when, in 1397, Manuel Chrysoloras, a scholar from Constantinople, became the first professor of Greek at the University of Florence in northern Italy.

His scholars found that works which were written before the birth of Jesus dealt with questions not answered by the Church. From this came the belief called *humanism* which says that people, not God, controlled their own lives. After

▼ A street scene in Florence, one of the great centers of Renaissance learning and art. Florence grew rich on trade and commerce. Its people wore fine clothes and its streets thronged with skilled craftsmen.

▲ During the Renaissance, architecture returned to the elegant, classical lines of ancient Greece as shown in this monument called the Tempietto, built in Rome to mark the probable spot of St. Peter's crucifixion.

THE AGE OF LEARNING

In the Renaissance, the ideal person was the "Universal Man or Woman." This was someone who was educated to be skillful in a wide range of subjects. These included science, travel, music, and literature, as well as philosophy and the arts.

The best example of a "Universal Man" was Leonardo da Vinci. He excelled at painting, drawing, architecture, and sculpture. Leonardo was also a competent engineer, musician, and inventor. He trained in Florence under Verrocchio and later worked in Milan, Rome, and Cloux in France. Some of his notebooks still survive. They show he was also interested in anatomy, botany, and geology.

the Byzantine empire fell in 1453, still more scholars came to Italy, bringing many old manuscripts with them.

This revived interest in learning led to the period later being called the Renaissance, which means rebirth. But the Renaissance soon meant much more than simply studying the work of ancient scholars. It affected art and science, architecture and sculpture. Paintings became more realistic and no longer concentrated only on religious topics. Statues, too, were made to look like real people and some were cast in bronze for the first time since the Roman era. Rich families, such as the Medicis and the Borgias became patrons of the arts. The development of printing helped to spread the new ideas throughout Europe.

1472 Russia: Ivan III of Muscovy marries Zoë Palaeologus, the niece of the last Byzantine emperor. He adopts the Byzantine emblem of a double-headed eagle as his own. Ottoman empire: The Venetians destroy the Ottoman port of Smyrna, now known as Izmir, Turkey. At the battle of Otluk-beli, the Turks, led by Muhammad II, defeat the Persian ruler, Uzan Hasan, who is the chief ally of the Venetians. West Africa: The Portuguese reach Fernando Po, an island off present-day Cameroon.

1473 Papal States: The Sistine Chapel is built by Giovanni de Dolci. It is the main chapel of the Vatican and is named after Pope Sixtus IV, for whom it was built.

Frescoes (wall paintings) were popular in Italy. The word is from the Italian for "fresh" because the artist painted onto wet plaster.

1474 Europe: Louis XI goes to war against Charles the Bold, Duke of Burgundy, who forms an alliance with Edward IV of England. Charles also goes to war against the Swiss Confederation. Italy: A triple alliance of the city-states of Florence, Venice, and Milan is formed. Spain: Isabella succeeds to the throne of Castile. Her husband Ferdinand is made joint ruler, as Ferdinand V of Castile. Germany: A nautical almanac for 1474–1506 by the German astronomer Regiomontanus describes the method of finding longitude by using lunar distances.

1475 France: Edward IV of England invades. Later the Peace of Picquigny is signed between the two countries. By this agreement, Louis XI pays money to Edward IV to persuade him to stay in England and not pursue his claim to the throne of France. Ottoman empire: The Ottoman Turks conquer the Crimea. Italy: Birth of Michelangelo (dies 1564).

1476 England: William Caxton sets up his printing press at Westminster. He is the first printer in England and produces a varied list of books. They include Chaucer's *Canterbury Tales* (in 1478) and *The Myrrour of the World*, which is an encyclopedia and the first illustrated book to be printed in England. Switzerland: Charles the Bold occupies Granson on Lake Neuchâtel and hangs the Swiss garrison. Bern and its allies then force Charles and his army out of Granson and later out of Morat.

This elaborate salt cellar was made c. 1540 by the Italian sculptor Benvenuto Cellini for King Francis I of Spain. It is made of gold, enamel, and ebony. Cellini was influenced by Michelangelo and besides being a sculptor was also a goldsmith, musician, and soldier.

1477 France: In January Charles the Bold is defeated and killed at Nancy in Lorraine by the armies of the Swiss Confederation. Low Countries: In Flanders, Maximilian, son of the Holy Roman emperor Frederick III, marries Charles the Bold's daughter, Mary.

▲ *Renaissance artists began to show perspective in their paintings. Here Masolino's* King Herod's Banquet *shows objects becoming smaller with distance.*

By the 16th century, the Renaissance was at its height. As well as being interested in the distant past, people looked closely at the world about them. Instead of just accepting the teachings of the Church, they began to make detailed scientific observations for themselves.

Some studied plants and animals. Others investigated geology and astronomy. Sometimes their findings brought them into conflict with the Church. When Nicolas Copernicus (1473–1543) realized that the Earth moved around the Sun, he dared not publish his views until he was on his deathbed. He feared punishment from the Church which said that the Earth was the center of the universe.

This new spirit of inquiry and interest in humanity eventually led some people to question the authority of the Church and ask for change. It also led to advances in science and art, and even led some people to set sail for unexplored lands.

▶ *The rich enjoyed life at this time. Many had country villas which they visited with friends. Hunting, telling stories, and writing poems were popular pastimes.*

▶ *Botticelli painted* La Primavera, *or* Spring, *for the Medici family between 1477 and 1478. The Greek goddess Venus, in the center, represents love, beauty, and learning.*

▼ *Leonardo's notebooks show he was interested in flight. He designed machines called ornithopters, which he thought would carry people through the air if they flapped their wings as birds do.*

Buildings

In Europe the nobility started building themselves comfortable palaces and stately homes, instead of the heavily fortified castles of the Middle Ages. More glass was available and so windows became larger. In England some houses such as Hampton Court were built of handmade bricks, but many were still made largely of wood. This could be a fire hazard in towns where narrow streets allowed flames to spread quickly. Inside the houses, furniture was made from wood and often highly carved. Walls were often paneled with wood and ceilings were decorated with plaster. Formal gardens were first laid out at this time. Especially popular were herb gardens which provided flavorings for foods and cures for simple ailments.

▲ By the 16th century, many English town houses were built up to five stories high. In the houses of the rich, windows were made up of many small panes of glass and the wood was often elaborately carved. This house has been made to look like the stern (rear end) of a galleon.

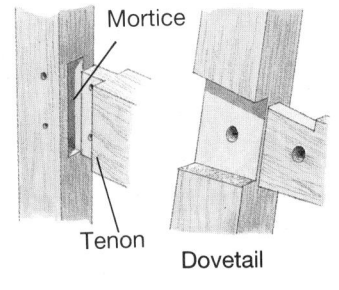

TIMBER JOINTS

The strength of a timber-framed building was in the joints between the timbers. If these were made correctly, the building would hold together even if it was pushed over (as long as the timbers themselves did not break). The most-used joints were mortice and tenon, and dovetail.

Mortice

Tenon

Dovetail

▼ In France the castles of the Middle Ages were replaced by chateaux or manor houses. Influenced by the Renaissance, they were decorated with classical Roman designs. This staircase at Fontainebleau is a typical example.

WHEN IT HAPPENED

1515 Henry VIII's Chancellor, Thomas Wolsey, starts building Hampton Court.

1547 Michelangelo becomes chief architect for St. Peter's in Rome and designs its dome.

1569 Akbar founds a new Mogul capital at Fatehpur Sikri. Its buildings are a mixture of Muslim and Hindu architecture.

1584 Philip II's palace of El Escorial is completed near Madrid.

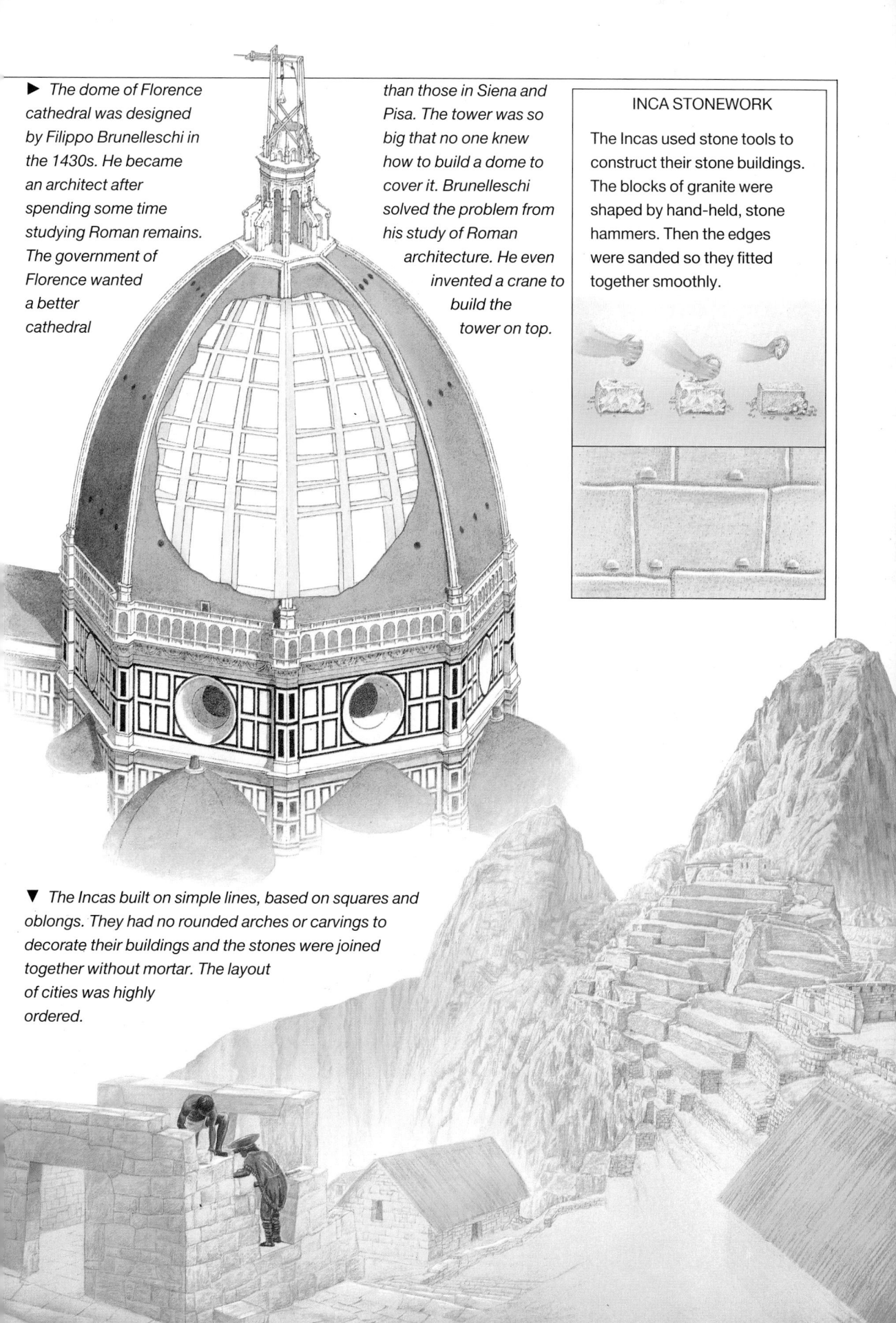

► The dome of Florence cathedral was designed by Filippo Brunelleschi in the 1430s. He became an architect after spending some time studying Roman remains. The government of Florence wanted a better cathedral than those in Siena and Pisa. The tower was so big that no one knew how to build a dome to cover it. Brunelleschi solved the problem from his study of Roman architecture. He even invented a crane to build the tower on top.

INCA STONEWORK

The Incas used stone tools to construct their stone buildings. The blocks of granite were shaped by hand-held, stone hammers. Then the edges were sanded so they fitted together smoothly.

▼ The Incas built on simple lines, based on squares and oblongs. They had no rounded arches or carvings to decorate their buildings and the stones were joined together without mortar. The layout of cities was highly ordered.

1478 England: Edward IV of England has his brother, the Duke of Clarence, executed. Spain: Ferdinand and Isabella establish the Spanish Inquisition with the consent of Pope Sixtus IV. At this time it is mainly used to punish so-called "converted" Jews who live in Spain and still practice their old faith in secret. They are burned at the stake or condemned to prison. Italy: Lorenzo de Medici becomes sole ruler of Florence (to 1492) after his brother Giuliano de Medici is assassinated. Russia: Ivan III conquers Novgorod and makes it part of the duchy of Moscow. Eastern Europe: Hungary gains Moravia and Silesia. Ottoman empire: The Ottoman Turks conquer Albania.

1479 Spain: Ferdinand, also known as the Catholic King, succeeds to the throne of Aragon as Ferdinand II. His wife Isabella becomes joint ruler with him. Spain is united by this formal union of Aragon and Castile. Eastern Europe: In the Treaty of Constantinople, Venice agrees to pay tribute to the Ottoman empire for trading rights in the Black Sea.

A coin bearing the head of Cosimo de Medici, Lorenzo de Medici's grandfather.

1480 Russia: Ivan III ends Muscovy's allegiance to the Tartars (the Golden Horde) who have controlled Russia for over 250 years. Mediterranean: Ottoman Turks besiege the island of Rhodes, held by the Knights of St. John.

1481 Ottoman empire: Muhammad II, the great Ottoman ruler, dies at the age of 51. He is also known as Muhammad the Conqueror, after his defeat of the Byzantine empire in 1453.

Italy

At this time Italy was divided into small states. Many of them were large cities, such as Florence, Venice, and Rome. Others were ducal courts such as Mantua, Urbino, and Ferrara. Most of these states were ruled by families who had grown rich on trade and commerce in the late Middle Ages.

The most powerful family of the day was the Medicis of Florence who had made a great fortune in the 14th century through banking and moneylending. The best-known is Lorenzo, who became joint ruler of Florence with his brother in 1469. He was a clever statesman and also a patron of writers, artists, and scientists. He was keen to promote his family and saw his second son become pope. Under his influence, Florence became one of the most beautiful and prosperous cities in Italy, as well as a center of the

Lorenzo de Medici

Lorenzo (1449–1492) became joint ruler of Florence at the age of 20. When his brother died, he took the title *Magnifico Signore* and was known as Lorenzo the Magnificent. He made Florence the leading state in Italy. He was a great patron of literature and art.

Lucretia Borgia

Lucretia (1480–1519), Pope Alexander VI's daughter, was married four times to further her father's ambition. Two were annulled (cancelled) and her brother killed one husband. Despite this, her court at Ferrara was a center for artists, poets, and scholars.

Renaissance. Lorenzo had a large art collection of his own and, through his writings, helped to make the form of Italian spoken in Florence into the language of the whole country.

Another famous family was the Borgias. In 1455, Alfonso Borgia became Pope Calistus III. His nephew, Rodrigo, was later made Pope Alexander VI. He had many illegitimate childen and wanted them all to be rich and powerful; but, on his death, the family's power collapsed. In contrast to the Borgias, Federigo, Duke of Urbino, spent much of his money on building churches, schools, and hospitals. Like Lorenzo de Medici, he was interested in the arts and had a famous library built in his palace. Federigo was popular with his subjects and did not need a bodyguard, unlike other Italian rulers of the time.

▲ During the Middle Ages much of Italy was controlled by the Holy Roman Empire. A power struggle between emperors and popes left them both weakened. Italian cities formed their own independent states. In the 16th century Italy came under attack from Spain.

▼ The Villa Poggio was Lorenzo de Medici's country home. Wealthy men built country villas with carefully laid out gardens. Elegant houses like this gradually replaced the fortified buildings of earlier times. At the same time, many Italians were extremely poor.

POGGIO

European Exploration

In the second half of the 15th century, European sailors and navigators began to plan voyages which would take them beyond the limits of the world they knew. This was partly a result of the new interest in the world encouraged by the Renaissance (*see* pages 330–331), but the main reason was to set up new trading links with the spice-producing countries of Asia.

Until the Byzantine empire fell in 1453, spices were brought overland to Constantinople and then taken across the Mediterranean to the countries of Europe. This made them expensive.

In spite of this, spices were an essential part of everyday life. There was no refrigeration so the only way to preserve meat was by salting it. Adding spices helped to hide the salty taste, and they also concealed the taste of meat which had gone bad despite being salted.

After 1453, direct land links between Europe and Asia were cut completely. If

Dias

In 1486, Bartholomeu Dias (1450–1500) was given the command of three ships to explore the coast of Africa. Strong gales blew him around the Cape of Good Hope, but he turned back as his crew were unwilling to go any farther. He drowned near the Cape in 1500.

Da Gama

After rounding the Cape of Good Hope in 1497, Vasco da Gama (1469–1525) sailed up the east coast of Africa and with the help of an Indian sailor crossed the ocean to Calicut in India. He sailed home with a cargo of spices. He returned to India in 1502 and again in 1522.

▼ *Vasco da Gama's small ships were a development of the caravel and its triangular, lateen sail. They had both square and lateen rigged sails which made them a great deal more maneuverable on the open sea.*

NAVIGATIONAL INSTRUMENTS

Navigation at sea was very primitive at this time. The only instruments that were available were the compass, the astrolabe, and the backstaff.

The compass was the most important navigational aid because it showed in which direction the ship was sailing. This was still a relatively new invention in Europe, but the Chinese had used it since the 12th century. Both the astrolabe and the backstaff used the Sun or a star to calculate a ship's latitude (how far north or south of the equator the ship was). But they were difficult to use if the sky was overcast. It was also difficult to work out how fast a ship was going and its longitude (how far east or west the ship was).

Astrolabe

Backstaff

Compass

spices were to reach Europe, then a sea route to the East had to be found. When the Portuguese began exploring the west coast of Africa in the 1460s (*see* pages 306–307), they set up forts and traded in gold, ivory, and silver.

Gradually they sailed farther south and Bartholomeu Dias reached the Cape of Good Hope at the tip of Africa in 1488. Ten years later, he helped Vasco da Gama to plan a voyage which took him around the Cape and across the Indian Ocean to Calicut. Da Gama was followed by Pedro Cabral who returned from India with a cargo of pepper. This encouraged other navigators to try and sail farther east. In 1517, the Portuguese reached China, and nearly 30 years later they arrived in Japan. The Portuguese were not only driven by trade but also by a determination to spread Christianity.

1482 West Africa: The Portuguese navigator Diego Cao starts an exploration of the Congo River (to 1484). Portuguese traders establish settlements on the Gold Coast, now known as Ghana, where they trade for gold and ivory.

1483 England: Edward IV of England dies. His 12-year-old son becomes Edward V. Edward IV's youngest brother, Richard Duke of Gloucester, is made Protector of Edward V during his childhood. However, Richard takes the throne as Richard III. Edward V and his younger brother Richard are imprisoned in the Tower of London, where they die, possibly murdered. France: Louis XI dies and Charles VIII succeeds to the throne (to 1498). Italy: Raphael, Italian painter and architect, is born (dies 1520).

1484 England: Caxton prints *Morte D'Arthur*, the poetic collection of legends about King Arthur compiled by Sir Thomas Malory. Papal States: Innocent VIII is elected pope (to 1492).

1485 England: Henry Tudor, Earl of Richmond and a descendant of Edward III, lands in England from France. He defeats and kills Richard III at the battle of Bosworth Field. Henry Tudor is then crowned as Henry VII (to 1509), the first of the Tudor monarchs. Eastern Europe: Hungary becomes the most powerful state by capturing Vienna and acquiring lower Austria. South America: The Incas under Topa conquer all of what is now Chile as far as the Maule River. They also conquer the south coast of Peru and the northwest of Argentina.

A woodcut of a blacksmith from a book published by Caxton in 1483.

1486 England: Henry VII of England marries Elizabeth of York, daughter of Edward IV, and so unites the houses of York and Lancaster. Germany: Maximilian becomes king (to 1493). Mexico: The Great Temple of Tenochtitlán is inaugurated.

1487 West Africa: The Portuguese reach Timbuktu by traveling overland from the coast.

1488 South Africa: The Portuguese navigator, Bartolomeu Dias, rounds the Cape of Good Hope, Africa's southernmost point. Scotland: After defeating and killing his father at Sauchieburn, James IV becomes king (to 1513).

1490 Italy: Aldus Manutius sets up the Aldine Press in Venice to make more classical works available. West Africa: The Portuguese sail up the Congo River for about 200 miles (320 km) and convert the king of the Congo to Christianity.

1492 Americas: Christopher Columbus crosses the Atlantic and arrives in the Caribbean islands, which he calls the West Indies. Spain: Ferdinand conquers Granada and ends Muslim influence in his country. The Moors and the Jews are expelled from Spain. Jews are also expelled from Sardinia. Papal States: Rodrigo Borgia is elected as Pope Alexander VI (to 1503).

⚙ Germany: First modern globe is made by Martin Behaim of Nuremberg.

The world map of Henricus Martellus, published in 1490, showed advances on previous maps. It showed sea separating Africa and Asia, and mapped approximately three-fourths of the globe.

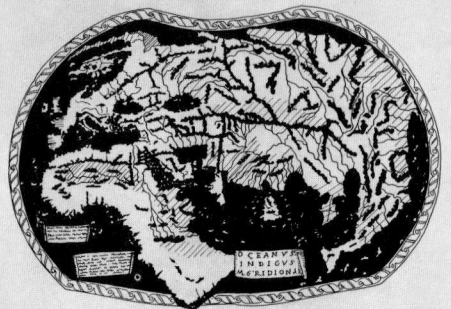

While the Portuguese sailed east, the Spanish sailed west. In 1492, Queen Isabella sponsored Christopher Columbus, a navigator from Genoa in Italy, to find a route to India. Existing maps showed the world to be much smaller than it really is. When Columbus reached a group of islands across the Atlantic, he was sure he had reached his goal and called them the West Indies. In fact, they were the Caribbean Islands off the coast of North America. Columbus made three more voyages there, but he never realized his mistake.

Another Italian, Amerigo Vespucci, reached the northeast coast of South America in 1499. On a second voyage in 1501 he explored as far as the Rio de la Plata, Uruguay, and realized he had found a new continent. A map in 1507 named the continent America after him.

Other Europeans tried to find a northern route to India. One was John Cabot, a Venetian who was sponsored in 1497 by Henry VIII of England, to

Magellan

Ferdinand Magellan (c. 1480–1521) led the first expedition to sail around the world in 1519. The voyage took three years but he only survived as far as the Philippines. He gave the Pacific Ocean its name. The Magellan Straits in South America, are also named after him.

Columbus

Christopher Columbus (1451–1506) first went to sea as a pirate. In 1476, he settled in Portugal after being shipwrecked. When the Portuguese king would not sponsor his voyage to reach India by sailing west, he asked the Spanish monarchs. They took six years to say yes.

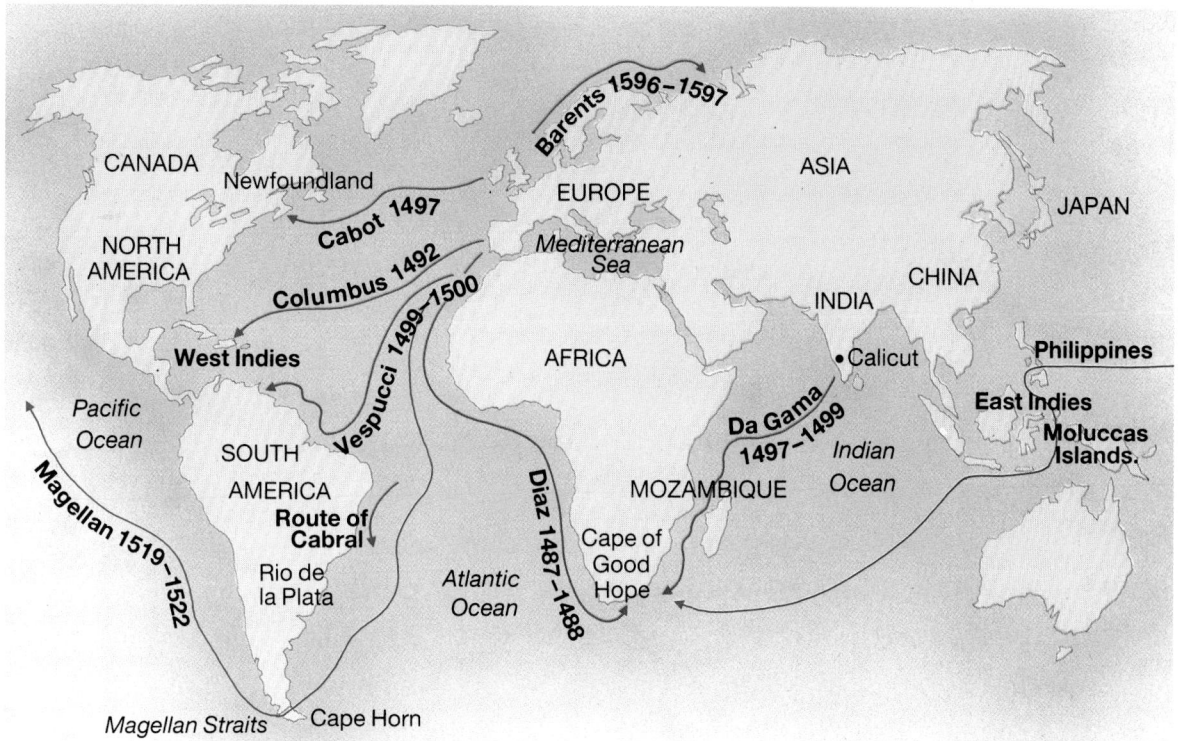

explore the northern ocean. Another explorer called Jacques Cartier sailed up Canada's St. Lawrence River in 1535 and claimed land near it for France.

In August 1519, Ferdinand Magellan left Spain to find a western route to the Spice Islands (Moluccas). He crossed into the Pacific, but was killed in the Philippines. Juan Sebastian del Cano then took over, arriving back in Spain in September 1522 with just one ship.

▲ Navigators from Spain, Portugal, England, and France tried many different routes to reach the spice-producing islands of the Moluccas. This widened European knowledge of the world, led to increased trade, and the setting up of new empires.

▼ Columbus set sail on his voyage in a ship similar to this one. He took three ships; the flagship Santa Maria, was only 120 feet (36 m) long but it was twice the size of the other two, the Pinta and the Niña. The crew had no accommodation and their food was cooked on deck.

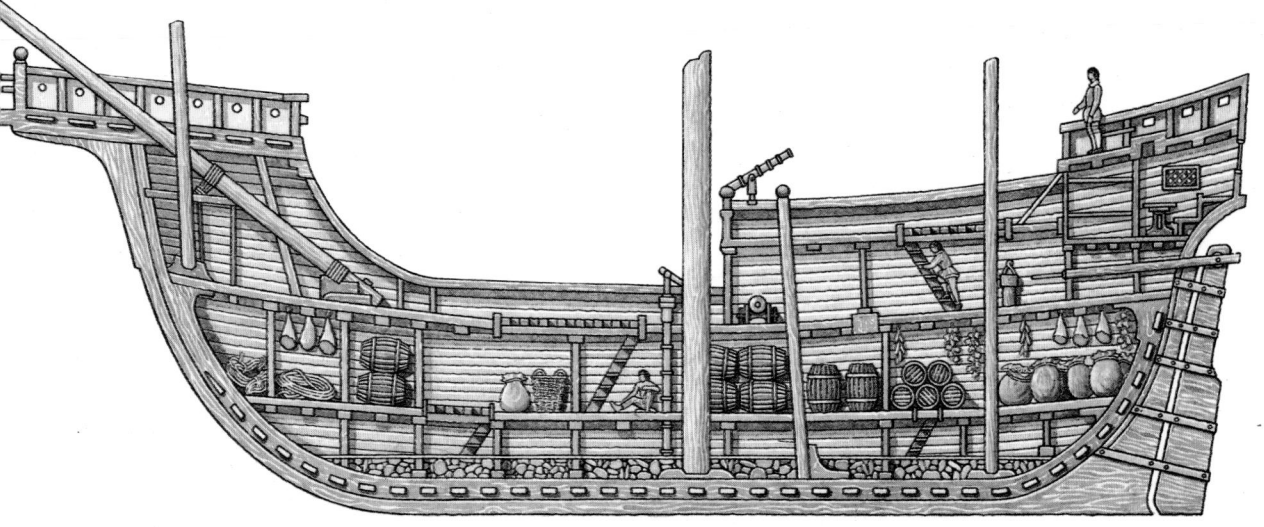

Communications

As the knowledge of printing spread through Europe, many more books were published. More people learned to read. New ideas in science and the arts reached various countries at the same time and so people everywhere knew the same things. However, nothing could travel faster than the speed of a horse. Most news was passed on by word of mouth and there was no postal service as we know it today. Most roads were so badly maintained that it was often faster to travel by sea or river. When the Spanish arrived in America, they found the people knew nothing about horses or wheeled vehicles. It took weeks for messages to go to and from Europe, which made government very difficult.

▶ Christopher Columbus crossed the Atlantic with three small sailing ships in 1492. The journey took 30 days to complete. His ships bore the cross of Christianity.

▲ The Aztecs used little pictures, or glyphs, for written words. The ones here represent a mountain, the emperor Montezuma, a tree, Tenochtitlán, teeth, and a stone.

Mountain Montezuma

Tree

Tenochtitlan

Teeth Stone

▲ In 1588, a chain of beacons was set up on hilltops in England. Each one could see the next in either direction. Their fires were lit to warn of the Spanish Armada.

1476 William Caxton sets up the first printing press in England.

1500 Wynken de Worde sets up a printing press in Fleet Street, London. The street is a center for printing for almost 500 years.

c. **1530** By now the Incas are using a code of knots tied in strings of different thicknesses.

1539 The Spaniards set up the first printing press in the Americas. It is in Mexico City.

▲ *In the Inca empire, relay runners carried official messages and packages. The first set off and ran about a mile (1.5 km) to a shelter. From there a second runner took the message for another mile. Each runner blew on a shell to announce his approach.*

▲ *The publisher Aldus Manutius set up the Aldine Press in Venice in about 1490. There he produced some of the first printed copies of ancient Greek and Roman classical works. These pages are from* The Dream of Poliphilus *which he published in 1499.*

▶ *During the 15th century, books were very expensive, but Lorenzo de Medici was able to collect together a great private library in Florence. In 1571, it was refounded as a public library in a building designed by Michelangelo.*

1493 Americas: Pope Alexander VI divides newly discovered lands between Spain and Portugal using an imaginary line of demarcation. Spain can claim land to the west of it and Portugal can claim land to the east. West Africa: The Songhay empire reaches its greatest extent under Askia Muhammad who takes over much of the Mandingo empire. Holy Roman Empire: Maximilian I becomes Holy Roman emperor (to 1519). South America: Huayna Capac becomes the 11th Sapa Inca. He founds a second capital at Quito in the north of his empire.

1494 Italy: Charles VIII of France invades Italy. Inspired by Girolamo Savonarola, the people of Florence depose the Medici family. Iberian Peninsula: By the Treaty of Tordesillas, Spain and Portugal move the pope's line of demarcation farther west. This will eventually give Portugal territory in eastern Brazil.

1495 Italy: Charles VIII enters Naples. The Holy League, made up of Milan, Venice, Maximilian I, Pope Alexander VI, and Ferdinand of Spain, forces Charles to withdraw.

1496 England: Henry VII of England joins the Holy League. Western Europe: A commercial treaty is drawn up between England and the Netherlands.

1497 North America: Italian-born John Cabot crosses the Atlantic and arrives in Newfoundland. He is probably the first European to go there since the Vikings, five centuries before. Africa: Vasco da Gama sails around Africa.

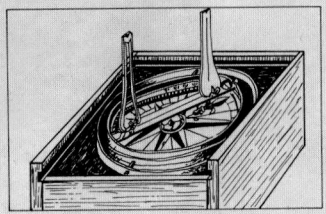

Magnetic compasses such as this were used in the 1500s by explorers to plan their routes across unknown waters.

The Songhay Empire

When Europeans first went to Africa in the 1460s, the continent was made up of many different states and kingdoms. They had their own trade networks and practiced advanced forms of farming. In some areas gold and copper were mined and in others cloth making and metal-casting were important activities.

One of the most important kingdoms was Songhay in West Africa. Tradition says that it was founded in the 7th century by a Berber Christian called al-Yaman. It later became part of the Mali empire and was a Muslim state from the 11th century onward (*see* pages 264–265). In 1464 Sonni Ali made Songhay independent again and expanded its territory, taking over what had been the Mali empire and adding to it. Writers in the city of Timbuktu described him as cruel and immoral.

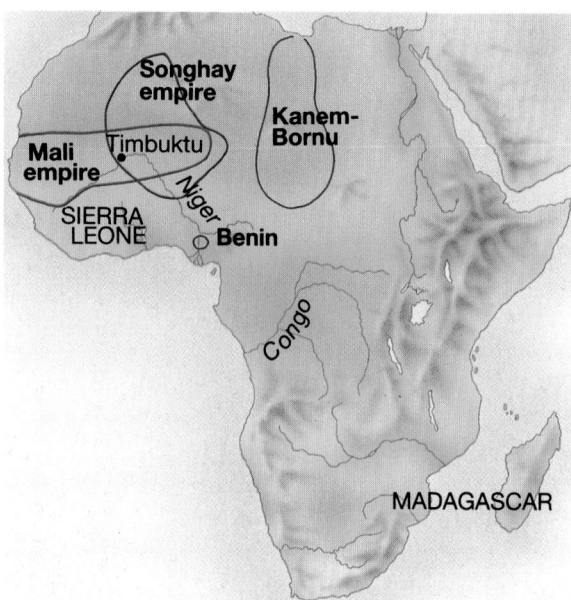

▲ *Early European explorers who settled on the coasts of Africa knew nothing about its rich interior. Songhay traded its gold and slaves for luxury goods and salt.*

◀ *Although Europeans only settled on the coast, they soon influenced Africa. This cast-iron model of a Portuguese soldier was made in Benin.*

They also said that he persecuted men of religion, while pretending to be a Muslim. When Sonni Ali died by drowning, he was succeeded by his son, Bakari. However, Bakari was weak and the al-Yaman line died out with him.

In 1493, Askia Muhammad I founded a new dynasty in Songhay and made it the most important empire in West Africa. Its wealth was built on the trading cities of Gao and Timbuktu. Here gold from the south was exchanged for salt from the north. Leo Africanus, a Spanish Muslim, visited Timbuktu in the early 16th century and wrote that the king had "many plates and scepters of gold." He also noted that "manuscripts and books . . . are sold for more money than any other merchandise." Askia was followed by weak rulers, and in 1591 the Songhay empire fell to the Moroccans.

▼ *Timbuktu, first controlled by the Mali empire was taken over by the Songhay. It had a university, a mosque, and more than 100 schools. Gold, ivory, cloth, salt, copper, and slaves were all sold in its markets.*

KANEM-BORNU

Kanem-Bornu was an African empire which grew up around Lake Chad. Kanem became a center of Muslim civilization in the 11th century and was situated on the eastern trade routes through Africa. When its king was expelled in 1389 he founded a new dynasty in Bornu. In the 16th century Bornu conquered Kanem. It reached its peak under Idris Aloma who came to power in 1571 and ruled till 1603.

1498 Columbus finds his way to Trinidad and the coast of South America. Huayna Capac extends his Inca empire north of Quito into what is now Colombia. The Andes highway is completed. France: Louis XII, king (to 1515). Italy: In Florence, Savonarola is burned at the stake by his political rivals. Vasco da Gama reaches India.

1498 Modern-style toothbrushes are being used in China. Columbus leaves on his third voyage.

1499 South America: Amerigo Vespucci explores the northeast coast of South America.

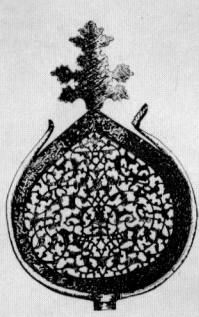

A standard from Safavid Persia. It was probably used in a religious ceremony and would have been carried in the annual procession to honor those who were killed in battle in 1080.

1500 Blown off course on his way to India, Pedro Cabral lands on the coast of Brazil and claims the country for Portugal. Italy: Louis XII conquers Milan; in the Treaty of Granada, he and Ferdinand of Spain agree to divide Naples between them.

1501 Amerigo Vespucci explores the coast of Brazil. Italy: France and Spain occupy Naples. Russia and Poland are at war (until 1503). Shah Ismail founds the Safavid dynasty in Persia (now Iran).

1502 The first Africans arrive as slaves in the Americas. Columbus lands in Nicaragua. Mexico: Montezuma II becomes chief of the Aztecs. War breaks out between France and Spain.

1503 Italy: France is defeated by Spain at the battles of Cerignola and Garigliano. Papal States: Julius II is elected pope (to 1513); he demolishes the old St. Peter's and plans a new church in the Renaissance style of architecture. Italy: Leonardo da Vinci paints the *Mona Lisa*.

Safavid Persia

The Safavid dynasty came to power in Persia (now Iran) at the start of the 16th century. It was founded by Ismail I who captured the city of Tabriz in 1501 and had himself crowned *shah* or ruler. The name Safavid came from one of Ismail's ancestors called Safi od-Din who lived in the 13th century.

By 1508, Ismail controlled the whole of Persia and most of Mesopotamia (now Iraq). In contrast to the rest of the Muslim world, which followed the Sunni branch of Islam, he established Shiism as the state religion in his country. The Sunnis believed that the *caliph* or leader of Islam should be chosen by the people, the Shiites believed that only the descendants of Muhammad's family should be caliphs. These differences, together with disputes over lands, led to a long series of religious wars between the Safavids and the Ottoman empire (*see* pages 358–359). They started in 1514 when the Ottoman sultan, Selim I, invaded western Persia.

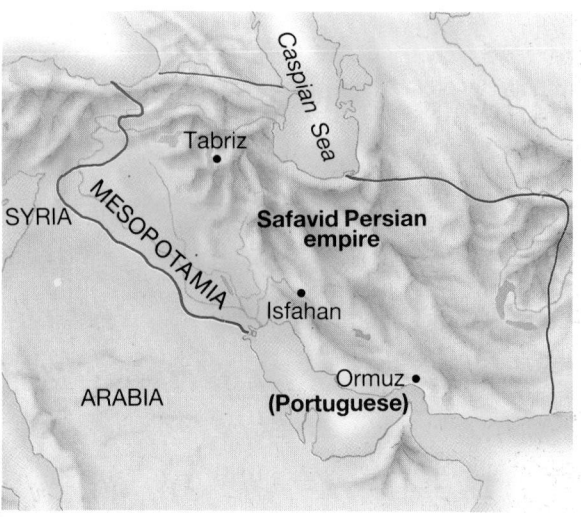

▲ *The heart of the Safavid empire was Persia. Isfahan became the capital during the long reign of Abbas I. In 1497, the Portuguese occupied the island of Ormuz.*

◄ *Many fine carpets were made during the Safavid dynasty. They were handmade from wool which was dyed in different colors. The carpets were covered in patterns similar to ones used on pottery and tiles. This carpet was made in 1539.*

Abbas I

1557 Born.
1587 Becomes fifth Safavid shah.
1590 Ends war with the Ottoman Turks.
1598 Drives Uzbek Turks from north-eastern Persia.
1602 Goes to war with Ottoman empire.
1604 Defeats Ottomans at Tabriz.
1628 Dies.

The Safavid dynasty reached its peak under Shah Abbas I, known as the Great. A good military leader, he moved his capital to Isfahan and made it into a beautiful city, building a magnificent palace and mosque. Covered *bazaars* or shops surrounded the main square, trees and streams flanked the market square, and a central avenue had gardens growing on both sides of it. However, Abbas is said to have had his children blinded because he feared them as rivals.

▼ *Part of the mosque at Isfahan built by Abbas the Great in honor of his father-in-law. It is decorated with patterns based on geometric designs and plant shapes. Some of the patterns are carved into the stone, but most of them are painted onto ceramic tiles.*

Food and Farming

When Europeans arrived in the Americas they found many foods they had never seen before, such as potatoes, tomatoes, new varieties of beans, pineapples, and bananas. They brought some back to Europe and found that many would grow there too.

Europe still had famines when the harvest failed. It was still not possible to feed all the animals over the winter and so many were killed in the autumn. The population, however, was increasing so more marshland was reclaimed for farming, especially in England and the Netherlands.

◀ Windmills first appeared in northeast Europe in the 12th century. At first they were used for grinding wheat into flour. By the 15th century, however, they were being used to pump water from marshy land to make it suitable for farming and building. Many were used in the Netherlands.

▼ Babur, the first Mogul emperor of India, was very fond of gardens. He complained about the lack of grapes and good fruit in India. He put this right by building beautiful gardens. Babur introduced grapes and melons from the Near East to India.

▲ An early drawing of a pineapple. It was one of the fruits Columbus discovered in the West Indies.

◀ Some of the Native Americans in Virginia lived by growing corn and hunting. So that the corn did not all ripen at once, they planted three crops of it each year.

▲ By now the feudal system had almost disappeared from Europe. Everyone still worked together at harvest, however, as this 16th century Dutch painting shows.

▶ To grow crops, the Incas had to cut terraces in the steep slopes of the Andes. They then harvested the crop with a wooden digging-stick, called a taclla. On the high ground, llamas and alpacas grazed. Both men and women worked in the fields.

WHEN IT HAPPENED

1492 At the time of Columbus's arrival, Caribbean Arawaks grow yams, cotton, and tobacco.

1512 The Portuguese start trading in cloves, and nutmeg from the Moluccas.

1534 To stop landlords evicting tenants, Henry VIII bans flocks of more than 2,000 sheep.

1570s After a slave revolt on Sâo Tomé, off the coast of West Africa, the Portuguese set up sugar plantations in Brazil.

1504 Central Asia: Babur captures Kabul in Afghanistan. It will later be the base from which he sets out to capture northern India and founds the Mogul dynasty. Germany: The watch is invented by Peter Henlein of Nuremberg. It has only a single hand.

1505 Italy: By the Treaty of Blois, France keeps Milan but cedes Naples to Spain. This gives Spain control of southern Italy. East Africa: The Portuguese establish trading posts on the Malabar coast and found Mozambique. Russia: Basil III, son of Ivan III, becomes ruler of Moscow.

1506 Spain: Columbus dies in poverty, still convinced that the lands he has visited are part of Asia.

1507 Germany: Martin Waldseemuller produces a world map. It is the first to show South America as separate from Asia and uses the name America, after Amerigo Vespucci.

The great seal of Henry VIII.

1508 Europe: In the League of Cambrai, the Holy Roman emperor Maximilian I, Louis of France, and Ferdinand of Spain ally against Venice. Papal States:  Michelangelo starts painting the Sistine Chapel in the Vatican. The artist Raphael (Raphaello Sanzio) also begins work on decorating the Vatican for the pope. Searching for a northwest passage, Sebastian Cabot reaches Hudson Bay.

1509 England: Henry VII dies and is succeeded by his 17-year-old son, Henry VIII (to 1547).

The Early Tudors

When Henry Tudor became Henry VII of England in 1485 (*see* page 316), he started a dynasty that ruled until 1603. Henry strengthened his position by banning private armies. He also executed and took estates from any lord who opposed him. Henry's policies of harsh taxation and careful spending also increased the wealth of the Crown. In 1492, Henry even persuaded the French king to pay him money each year for not going to war against France.

When Henry VIII came to the throne in 1509, England was an important power in Europe. Henry married Catherine of Aragon, the daughter of Ferdinand and Isabella of Spain. He went to war successfully against France in 1513, and in the same year defeated the Scots at Flodden and killed their king.

Henry VIII

1491 Born.
1509 Becomes king.
1521 Supports the pope against Martin Luther; is made "Defender of the Faith."
1534 Severs English Church from papal authority and becomes head of the Church of England.
1536 Closes many monasteries.
1547 Dies.

HENRY'S WIVES

Henry married six times. He divorced two of his wives and had two more executed. After divorcing Catherine of Aragon, he married Anne Boleyn. She gave birth to Elizabeth, but was beheaded in 1536. Only his third wife, Jane Seymour, provided him with a son, Edward. Jane died in 1537. Henry divorced Anne of Cleves after six months of marriage, and beheaded Catherine Howard, but Catherine Parr survived him.

THE MARY ROSE

Henry VIII was always at war with the French, so he strengthened the English navy. His pride and joy was a ship called the *Mary Rose*. After it had been refitted in 1536, Henry and his court went to watch it sail on the English Channel. Some 700 sailors, soldiers, and archers stood on deck. This affected the ship's balance so that, when a gust of wind blew, it capsized and quickly sank.

Although Catherine of Aragon had five or six children, they all died except Princess Mary. As Henry wanted a son to make the Tudor dynasty secure, he decided to divorce Catherine and marry again. To do this he needed the pope's permission. The pope refused to agree so, with the help of Thomas Cromwell his chief minister and Thomas Cranmer then Archbishop of Canterbury, he broke from the Roman Catholic Church and made himself supreme head of the Church in England. This new Church granted him a divorce and he married Anne Boleyn in 1533. Three years later Henry began to close the monasteries and nunneries in England and Wales. He sold most of their land to help pay for wars against France.

▼ *Sir Thomas More, shown here with his family, was Lord Chancellor from 1529 to 1532. He resigned when Henry broke away from the Catholic Church and he was executed for treason in 1535.*

The Portuguese Empire

When the Portuguese explorers reached the East Indies in the early 16th century, they found that these islands were rich in the spices that Europe wanted. To control this valuable trade, the Portuguese conquered the Moluccas Islands and seized the main ports in the Indian Ocean. As Portuguese traders had to sail around the Cape of Good Hope to return to Lisbon, forts were set up at various places along the coast of Africa to protect them. From Africa, the Portuguese took gold and also slaves to work on the sugar plantations.

At first, they had plantations on the African island of Sâo Tomé. When the slaves there revolted in the 1570s, the Portuguese set up sugar plantations in Brazil. A large part of this country was in their empire and the African slaves were taken to work there instead.

▶ *This ivory carving from West Africa shows Portuguese soldiers standing in a miniature crow's nest on a ship. It dates from the 16th century.*

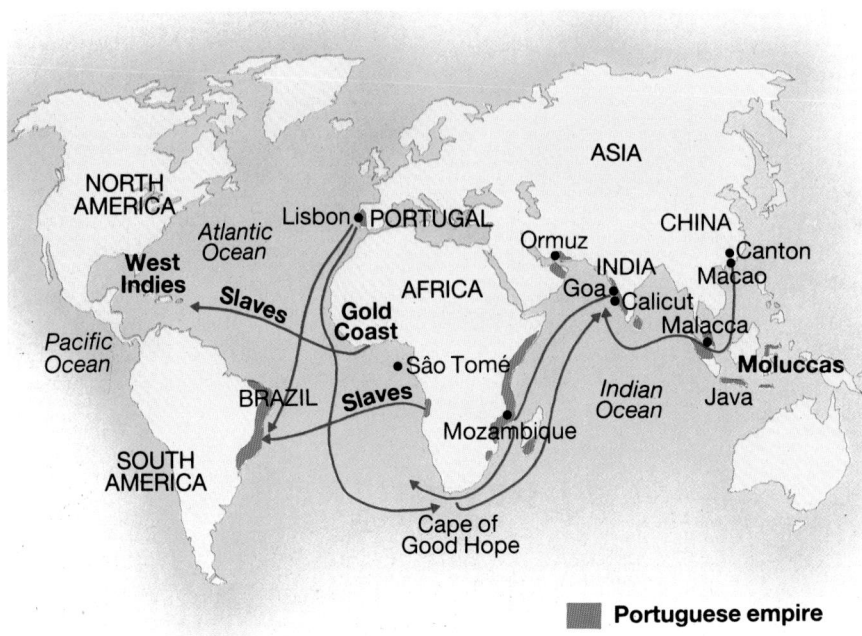

◀ *The Portuguese empire at its greatest extent in about 1600. As well as trading, the Portuguese tried to spread Christianity. Missionaries had little influence in the East where there was no colonization beyond the trading posts, but they were much more successful in Brazil. The Portuguese monopoly on spices ended after 1600 when England and the Netherlands set up East India Companies to trade in spices for themselves.*

Portuguese empire

▲ *An ivory carving made in 1540 shows a Portuguese nobleman and his wife at the dinner table. Many Portuguese grew rich on trade. In Brazil and India they lived in splendor, surrounded by many servants.*

At its height in the 16th century, the Portuguese empire also included the islands of Cape Verde, Madeira and the Azores, and narrow strips of land on the east and west coasts of Africa. The Portuguese occupied long stretches of Angola and Mozambique, the bases of Ormuz, Goa, Calicut, and Colombo in the Indian Ocean, and trading posts in the Far East, such as Macao in China, the Celebes, Java, and Malacca.

▲ *Before the Portuguese arrived in the Moluccas its rulers enjoyed the profit from the lucrative spice trade. But under Portuguese rule local people were forced to harvest cloves and nutmeg for them. Other spices from the East included pepper, cinnamon, and ginger.*

1510 Italy: Pope Julius II and Venice form a Holy League to drive Louis XII of France from Italy. Europe: Sunflowers are introduced to Europe from America.

1511 Europe: Ferdinand of Spain and Henry VIII of England join the Holy League against France. Caribbean: The first African slaves reach the New World.

1512 Italy: The Swiss join the Holy League and drive the French from Milan. Eastern Europe: Russia is at war with Poland (to 1522). Ottoman empire: Selim I becomes sultan (to 1520).

1513 Vasco Nuñez de Balboa reaches the Pacific. Scotland: James IV of Scotland is killed at the battle of Flodden Field. His son becomes James V (to 1542). Italy: At the battle of Novara the French are defeated and driven out of Italy. Papal States: Giovanni de Medici is elected Pope Leo X (to 1521).

1514 France: Mary, sister of Henry VIII, marries Louis XII of France. Near East: War breaks out between the Ottoman and Safavid empires.

This collar was designed to stop African slaves from lying down or escaping.

1515 England: Thomas Wolsey is made Lord Chancellor of England and a cardinal. France: Louis XII dies and Francis I becomes king of France (to 1547). Italy: At the battle of Marignano, the French defeat the Swiss and regain Milan.

1516 Europe: In the Treaty of Noyon France gives up its claim to Naples. Spain: Ferdinand of Spain dies. His grandson becomes Charles I (to 1556). Ottoman empire: War breaks out with Egypt; Selim I defeats the Egyptians at the battle of Marjdabik. Europe: Coffee is introduced.

The Reformation

By the early 16th century, the new ideas of the Renaissance led some people to challenge the teachings of the Roman Catholic Church. At the same time, the way its leaders ran the Church was strongly criticized. It seemed that many monks and nuns no longer led lives of poverty, and some popes and bishops thought more about money and power than religion. People felt the Church should be reformed.

The movement which started this was called the Reformation. It began in Germany in 1517 when a priest called Martin Luther nailed a list of 95 statements to the church door at Wittenberg. It gave details of all he thought was wrong with the Church. Most of all, Luther hated the Church's sale of Indulgences. These certificates forgave people their sins, and could be bought from the Church for money.

Luther

Martin Luther (c. 1483–1546) believed that man was saved by faith alone, not by good works or by the sale of Indulgences. He wanted faith to be based on scriptures in the Bible and not on religious ceremonies. He also believed Bible reading was important and that services should be in the local language, not Latin.

Calvin

John Calvin (1509–1564), born in France, was originally named Jean Chauvin. He studied law and theology, before becoming involved in the Reformation. He believed in predestination (that God had already ordained the future) and that only people chosen by God, the Elect, would be saved.

▶ The Protestant faith had become the main religion of Sweden and Finland by 1529. In 1536, it was adopted in Denmark and Norway. The seven northern provinces of the Netherlands followed the teachings of Calvin, but they were ruled by the Catholic king of Spain, who tried to suppress the new religion. Most of Scotland became Protestant, as did England and Wales, but Ireland and southern Europe stayed Catholic. Divisions between the two religions in France later led to civil war.

■ Roman Catholic
■ Protestant
■ Roman Catholic and Protestant

NORWAY
FINLAND
SCOTLAND
SWEDEN
IRELAND
DENMARK
WALES ENGLAND
NETHERLANDS
• Wittenberg
• Paris
SWITZERLAND
• Zurich
FRANCE
PORTUGAL
SPAIN
• Rome
Ottoman empire (Muslim)

▲ *The sale of Indulgences, shown in this illustration based on a Protestant woodcut of the time, was used to raise money for the Roman Catholic Church.*

1517 Germany: The Reformation begins when Martin Luther protests about corruption in the Church. He is especially concerned about the sale of Indulgences to raise money for a new St. Peter's church in Rome. Ottoman empire: The Mameluke empire collapses when the Ottoman Turks capture Cairo.

1518 Italy: Forks are first used at a banquet in Venice. Germany: The first fire engine is constructed by Anthony Blatner.

1519 Switzerland: Ulrich Zwingli leads the Reformation in Switzerland. Holy Roman Empire: Charles I of Spain becomes Holy Roman Emperor Charles V (to 1556), after his grandfather, Maximilian I, dies. Spain: Ferdinand Magellan sets out to circumnavigate the world. Mexico: Hernando Cortes lands at Vera Cruz and marches on Tenochtitlán.

1520 France: At the Field of the Cloth of Gold, Francis I of France meets Henry VIII of England but fails to gain the latter's support against Charles V, the Holy Roman Emperor. Instead, Henry makes a secret treaty with Charles. Ottoman empire: Suleiman I, also known as the Magnificent and the Lawgiver, becomes sultan (to 1566). Europe: Chocolate is introduced.

Luther hoped his list would lead to debate in the Church, but instead he was accused of heresy (going against Church beliefs). He refused to take back his words and he was excommunicated (excluded) from the Catholic Church in 1521. By this time, Luther had gained support in northern Germany and in Switzerland. He set up his own church and his followers were called Lutherans. After 1529, they were renamed Protestants when they protested against attempts to limit their teachings.

Ulrich Zwingli led the Reformation in Switzerland. His views were more extreme than Luther's. In 1524 he banned Catholic mass in Zurich. This led to a civil war in which Zwingli was killed. Zwingli was followed by John Calvin. He completed the Reformation in Switzerland and influenced John Knox who took the Reformation to Scotland.

A woodcut illustration for The Art of Dying Well, *published in Germany in about 1470 and used by the Church as a sermon in pictures.*

355

People

By 1500, the population of Europe had grown again to the size it had been before the Black Death in the 14th century. Most people still lived in the country, but there was no longer enough land for everybody. Many people moved into towns. Some found jobs, but others became beggars. By 1600 some Europeans lived in colonies overseas.

While the ideas of the Renaissance affected the lives of the rich, many poorer people were more concerned with just staying alive. It was a time when plagues still killed thousands and lack of food meant diseases such as influenza had high death rates. In spite of this, people still enjoyed street entertainments and going to see plays.

Whistle

Rosary

Comb

Pocket sundial

▲ *This selection of items from the ship* Mary Rose *shows what a sailor was likely to take to sea in 1536. They include a pouch, a whistle, a comb, and a rosary.*

▼ *European children played many different games. These included leapfrog, tag, follow-the-leader, and rolling bowls or hoops.*

▶ *The Native North Americans of the Eastern Woodlands wore moccasins made from a single piece of leather. On the Great Plains, they made wooden pipes for smoking tobacco and decorated them with colorful woven cloth.*

◀ Many children died young, and so people often had large families in the hope that some would survive to be adults. This church memorial records the 24 children born to a woman in Cornwall.

◀ This couple are wearing clothes which were fashionable at court in Europe around 1570. The men usually wore plainer colors than the women, but their doublets were often encrusted with jewels. Most rich women wore luxury fabrics such as velvet, brocade, silk, and lace.

▼ In most countries, sons were thought to be more important than daughters. Some dynasties died out because there was no son to continue the line. The birth of a son to a popular ruler was often the cause for a celebration, as shown in this Indian picture of the birth of the Mogul emperor Akbar's first son in 1569.

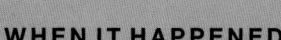

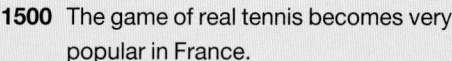

WHEN IT HAPPENED

1500 The game of real tennis becomes very popular in France.

1535 Angela Merici founds a teaching order of nuns called the Ursulines. Joining a convent is still one of the very few options apart from marriage open to women at this time.

1540 In Germany there is a fashion for men to wear jackets with huge padded shoulders and brightly colored doublets.

1590 In France women start to wear a whalebone farthingale under their dresses. It is shaped like a wheel and makes the skirt stand out as much as 2 feet (60 cm) from the hips.

1521 Hernán Cortés captures Tenochtitlán, the Aztec capital. Germany: The Diet of Worms, condemns Martin Luther as a heretic and excommunicates him (cuts him off from the Roman Catholic Church). England: Henry VIII is made "Defender of the Faith" by Pope Leo X for opposing Luther. The Ottoman Turks capture Belgrade. Ferdinand Magellan dies in the Philippines.

1522 Italy: Emperor Charles V drives the French out of Milan. Spain: One ship from Magellan's expedition completes the first circumnavigation of the world. The Ottoman Turks take the island of Rhodes from the Knights of St. John.

A sipahi, or cavalryman, of the Ottoman empire. In return for providing military service in times of war they received a land grant from the state. They remained important until the 18th century.

1523 Papal States: Clement VII is elected as pope. Sweden: Gustavus Vasa of Sweden leads the revolt against the Danish rulers of his country and is elected King Gustavus I of Sweden.

1524 Italy: France invades and recaptures Milan. England: The first turkey from South America is eaten at court.

1525 South America: Huayna Capac dies and civil war breaks out in the Inca empire, between Huascar, the 12th Sapa Inca, who rules in the south, and his brother, Atahualpa, who rules in the north. Italy: At the battle of Pavia, Francis I of France is captured by the Spaniards. He is released a year later in return for giving up his claim to Milan, Genoa, and Naples. He fails to keep this promise and instead forms an alliance with Pope Clement VII, Milan, Venice, and Florence against Charles V.

The Ottoman Empire

When Constantinople fell in 1453 (*see* pages 302–303), the Ottoman empire started its golden age. The former Christian capital of the Byzantine empire was renamed Istanbul and it became the center of an empire that eventually covered more than a million square miles (2.5 million sq.km). At its peak, the Ottoman empire stretched from Algeria to Arabia and from Hungary to Egypt. Most of these conquests were made during the rule of Suleiman I who became sultan in 1520.

To his own people he was known as *Qanuni*, the Lawgiver, because he reformed administration and the legal system. However, Europeans called him Suleiman the Magnificent because of the splendor of his court and his military victories in Europe. These included a series of campaigns in which he captured Belgrade in Yugoslavia, the island of

▲ *Suleiman's greatest victory was at the battle of Mohacs in 1526 when he crushed the Hungarian army. This picture is taken from a painting commemorating the battle in which the king of Bohemia was also killed.*

Rhodes, and the whole of Hungary. In 1529 his armies even reached Vienna, the capital of the Holy Roman Empire, but they failed to conquer it. The Turkish fleet, under the pirate Barbarossa (Khayr ad-Din Pasha), attacked and ravaged the coast of the Mediterranean.

Suleiman also waged three campaigns to the east against the Safavid empire of Persia (*see* pages 346–347). In these he gained control of Mesopotamia (Iraq), but the eastern border of the empire was never secure. Wars between the two empires lasted throughout the 16th century and helped to stop the Ottoman Turks advancing farther into Europe.

When Suleiman died, his son Selim II became sultan. He led a life of leisure while his ministers and generals ran the empire. By 1600, the Ottoman empire was in decline.

▲ *The women of the Ottoman empire led a secluded life. When they went outside the house, they had to be fully veiled and accompanied by a servant. They could only meet men from their own families.*

▼ *By 1566, the Ottoman empire stretched into three continents. Suleiman had built up a strong navy and won control of the Mediterranean. He also dominated the Red Sea and Persian Gulf.*

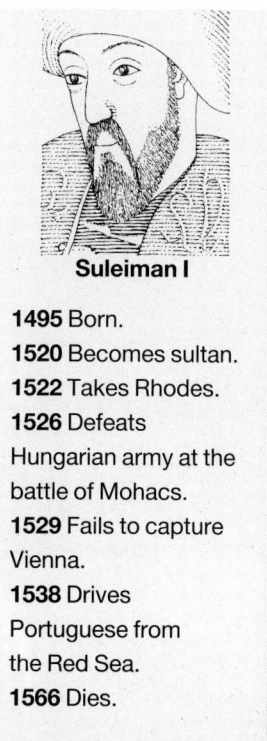

Suleiman I

1495 Born.
1520 Becomes sultan.
1522 Takes Rhodes.
1526 Defeats Hungarian army at the battle of Mohacs.
1529 Fails to capture Vienna.
1538 Drives Portuguese from the Red Sea.
1566 Dies.

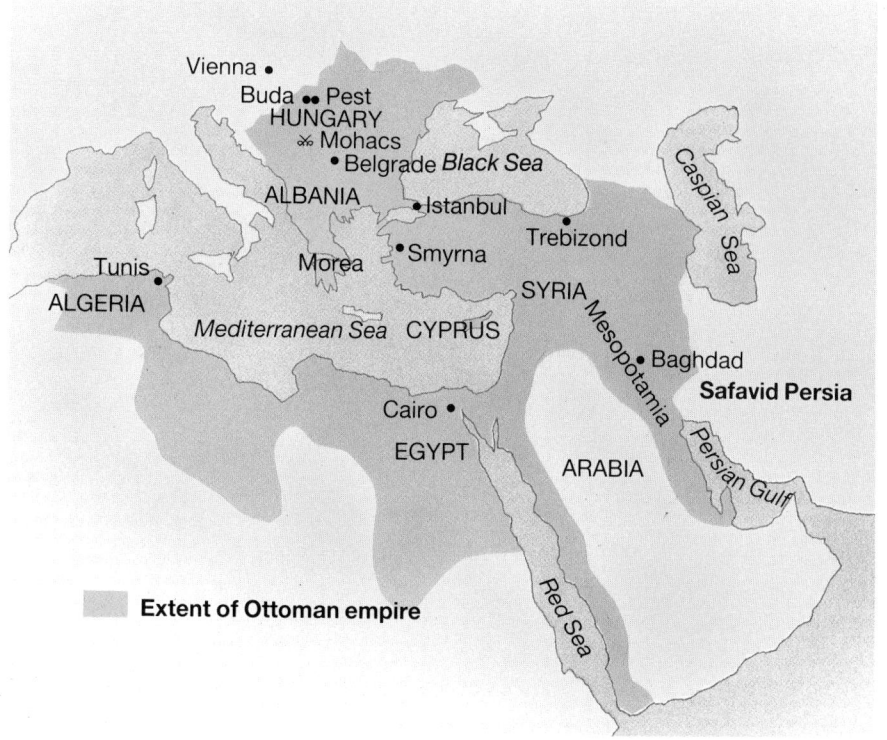

Extent of Ottoman empire

The Mogul Empire

Babur founded the Mogul empire when he invaded northern India from Afghanistan in 1526. He was a descendant of Tamerlane (*see* pages 272–273), who in turn claimed descent from Genghis Khan. The name Mogul is a variation of the word Mongol.

Babur and his followers were Muslims. When they invaded India, the Ottoman empire supplied them with guns and soldiers. Babur's troops also rode swift horses which easily outmaneuvered the Indians' slower elephants. This helped them to defeat a much larger Indian army at a battle in which the sultan of Delhi was killed. After this victory, Babur made Delhi his capital.

When Babur died in 1530, his son Humayun became the next ruler. He could not hold the throne, however, and in 1540 he was chased out of India and into Persia. He returned in 1555 to win

▲ *The founders of the Mogul dynasty were* (from left to right): *Babur, Timur, and Humayun. Here they are shown with their chief attendants.*

▼ *Babur only ruled over north India. Akbar expanded the empire to include lands to the east and south.*

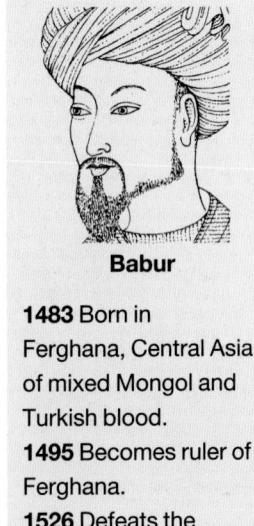

Babur

1483 Born in Ferghana, Central Asia of mixed Mongol and Turkish blood.
1495 Becomes ruler of Ferghana.
1526 Defeats the sultan of Dehli at the battle of Panipat, and becomes first Mogul emperor of India.
1530 Dies at Agra.

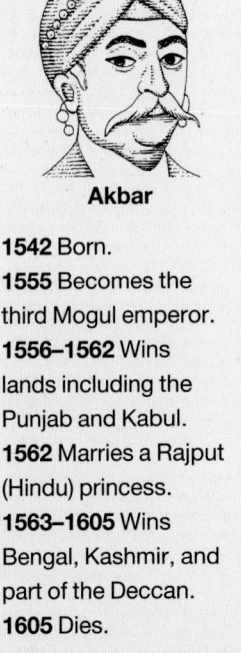

Akbar

1542 Born.
1555 Becomes the third Mogul emperor.
1556–1562 Wins lands including the Punjab and Kabul.
1562 Marries a Rajput (Hindu) princess.
1563–1605 Wins Bengal, Kashmir, and part of the Deccan.
1605 Dies.

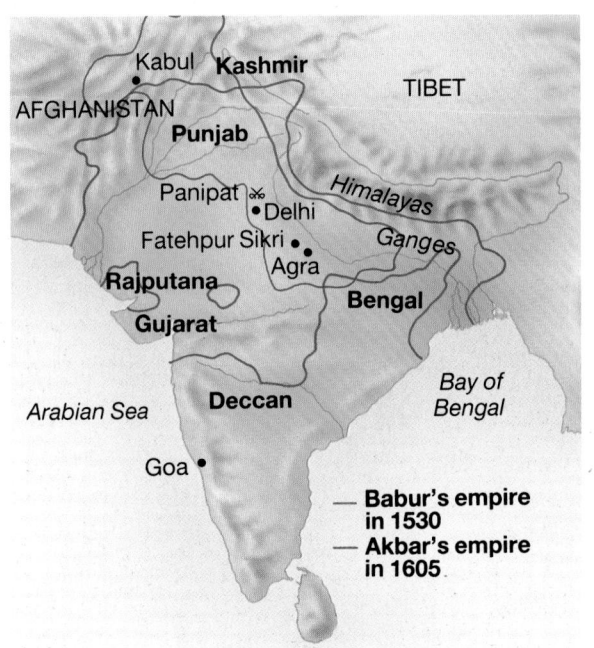

Kabul **Kashmir** TIBET
AFGHANISTAN **Punjab**
Panipat ⚔ Delhi *Himalayas*
Fatehpur Sikri Agra *Ganges*
Rajputana **Bengal**
Gujarat
Arabian Sea Bay of Bengal
Deccan
Goa

— **Babur's empire in 1530**
— **Akbar's empire in 1605**

the empire back, but before he could do so, he was killed in an accident. His 14-year-old son, Akbar, became emperor and ruled until his death in 1605.

Under Akbar, the Mogul empire expanded and flourished. He was a great military leader who defeated the neighboring Rajputs and conquered Gujarat and Bengal. This was the richest province in the north of India. It produced rice and silk which provided Akbar with his main source of income.

Akbar was also a very wise ruler. Although he was a Muslim, many of his subjects were Hindu. To keep the peace he married a Hindu princess. He allowed his subjects freedom of worship and let them be tried according to their own religious laws. Akbar built schools for the children and also constructed a new capital city at Fatehpur Sikri. It combined Muslim and Hindu styles of architecture.

▼ *Although some people rebelled against Akbar, they were soon defeated. This picture shows the rebel Bahadur Khan submitting to him.*

1526 Central Europe: At the battle of Mohacs, the Ottoman Turks defeat and kill Louis II of Bohemia and Hungary. A dispute over the Hungarian succession starts between Ferdinand and the Ottoman empire (to 1528). India: Babur defeats the last sultan of Delhi at Panipat and founds the Mogul empire. Mexico: Dominican monks arrive in Mexico.

1527 Papal States: Spanish and German troops sack Rome and capture the pope.

1528 Hungary: Ferdinand of Austria succeeds to the Hungarian throne. Switzerland: The first manual of surgery is written by Paracelsus, a physician.

An illustration from Babur's magnificent account of Hindustan, in northern India.

1529 England: Henry VIII dismisses Lord Chancellor Thomas Wolsey for failing to obtain the pope's consent to his divorce from Catherine of Aragon. Sir Thomas More is appointed Lord Chancellor. Henry VIII summons the "Reformation Parliament" and sets about cutting ties with Rome. Europe: In the Peace of Cambrai between France and Spain, France renounces claims to Italy. The Treaty of Barcelona is signed by Pope Clement VII and Charles V. Austria: The Turks unsuccessfully besiege Vienna.

1530 Malta: Knights of St. John are given the island by Charles V. England: Thomas Wolsey dies on his way to be tried for treason. Switzerland: Civil war breaks out between the Catholic and Protestant cantons. The Protestants are defeated.

The Conquistadores

Soon after the navigators had found their way to the Americas, Spanish adventurers, known as *conquistadores* (conquerors), started to make their way to what they called the New World. After conquering many Caribbean islands, they started exploring the mainland of Central and South America in the hope of finding treasure.

In 1519, a group of about 500 Spanish soldiers, led by Hernán Cortés, attacked the Aztecs in their capital city of Tenochtitlán. The Aztec emperor, Montezuma, had been awaiting the return of the god-king Quetzalcóatl and may have thought that Cortés was he. Montezuma. allowed himself to be captured and Cortés ruled in his place. When Cortés went back to the coast, however, the Aztecs rebelled and defeated the Spaniards that were left behind. With the help of an interpreter, Cortés then won the support of neighboring tribes who had been

NORTH AMERICA

MEXICO

Tenochtitlán

Aztec empire

— **Route of Cortés 1519–1522**

— **Route of Pizarro 1532–34**

Line of Demarcation 1494

Quito

Amazon

PERU

Machu Picchu

Lima

Cuzco

Inca empire

SOUTH AMERICA

▲ *Both Cortés and Pizarro lived in the West Indies before exploring the mainland of Central and South America. Cortés found the Aztec empire easily, but Pizarro had problems finding the Incas. He set out in 1530, but it took him three expeditions to find them.*

▶ *When Cortés and his men arrived in Tenochtitlán, they had with them horses and guns, both of which the Aztecs had never seen before. They also took a local interpreter called Dona Martina. She told them that the emperor Montezuma thought they were all gods because of their clothes. Because he believed this, Montezuma showered them with gifts. Cortés made him a prisoner and ruled the Aztecs in his place.*

conquered by the Aztecs. In 1521 he returned to Tenochtitlán with a large native army and destroyed the city.

Another conquistador, Francisco Pizarro, landed in Peru in 1532 intending to conquer the Inca empire. A civil war was in progress there, between Huascar and Atahualpa who were the sons of Huayna Capac (*see* pages 326–327). Atahualpa killed Huascar, but Pizarro then had Atahualpa executed. The Incas soon surrendered and by 1533 their empire was in Spanish hands.

▲ *Atahualpa, the Inca ruler, tried to buy his freedom by filling a room with gold treasures and offering them to Pizarro, but Pizarro had him executed.*

Cortés

Hernán Cortés (1485–1547) was born into a noble Spanish family and lived in the West Indies as a young man. After conquering the Aztecs he returned to Spain and died there in poverty.

Pizarro

Francisco Pizarro (c. 1475–1541) arrived in Panama in 1513. Hearing about the Incas, he marched on them in 1532. He founded Lima before being murdered by a rival in 1541.

1532 South America: Huascar is defeated and Francisco Pizarro begins his conquest of the Inca empire for Spain; he takes Atahualpa captive. England: Sir Thomas More resigns over the question of Henry VIII's divorce; Thomas Cranmer becomes archbishop of Canterbury. Germany: The Peace of Nuremberg allows some Protestants to practice their religion freely. France: Calvin starts the Protestant movement. Rabelais publishes his first book, *Pantagruel*.

1533 South America: Francisco Pizarro captures the Inca captial, Cuzco, and conquers Peru. Atahualpa is executed for crimes against Spain. England: Henry VIII marries Anne Boleyn and is excommunicated by the pope. Eastern Europe: Peace is made between the Ottoman empire and Ferdinand of Austria. Russia: Ivan IV, also known as Ivan the Terrible, becomes ruler of Russia (to 1584), at the age of three.

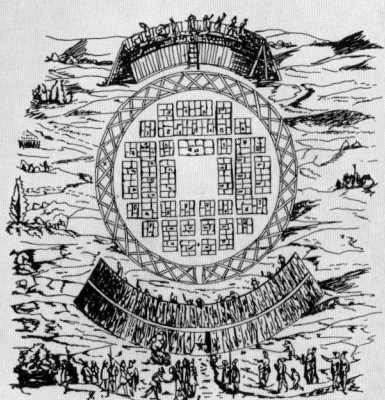

A map of Hochelaga, now Montreal, a Huron Indian town that was discovered by Jacques Cartier on his second voyage to America.

1534 England: By the Act of Supremacy, Henry VIII is declared supreme head of the Church in England. Spain: Ignatius Loyola founds the Society of Jesus, also known as Jesuits. Papal States: Paul III is elected as pope. Ottoman empire: The Ottoman Turks capture Tunis, Baghdad, and Mesopotamia (Iraq).

Religion

This period saw splits in both the Islamic and the Christian worlds. The Islamic world was divided between the Sunnis, who thought that the leader of Islam should be chosen by the people, and the Shiites who thought that he should be descended from Muhammad.

Following the Reformation, the Christian world divided into Roman Catholics whose leader was the pope, and Protestants who were divided into many different groups. Catholic missionaries converted the Aztecs and Incas, but had less success in Japan and none at all in China. In India, Akbar's fair and wise government kept the peace between Muslims and Hindus.

◀ Many Native North Americans had no contact with Europeans at this time, so they followed their own religions without any interference. Their beliefs were closely tied to nature and magic. The most important religious person was the medicine man. He used plants and herbs to prepare cures and took part in religious and magic ceremonies.

▶ In Central and South America, the Spanish conquistadores were soon followed by Roman Catholic missionaries. They were determined to win souls for God and convert the people there to Christianity. They did not hesitate to use force if other methods failed. They destroyed Aztec and Inca temples and made the Native Americans build Christian churches in their place. Indians who refused to abandon their old gods were usually burned to death.

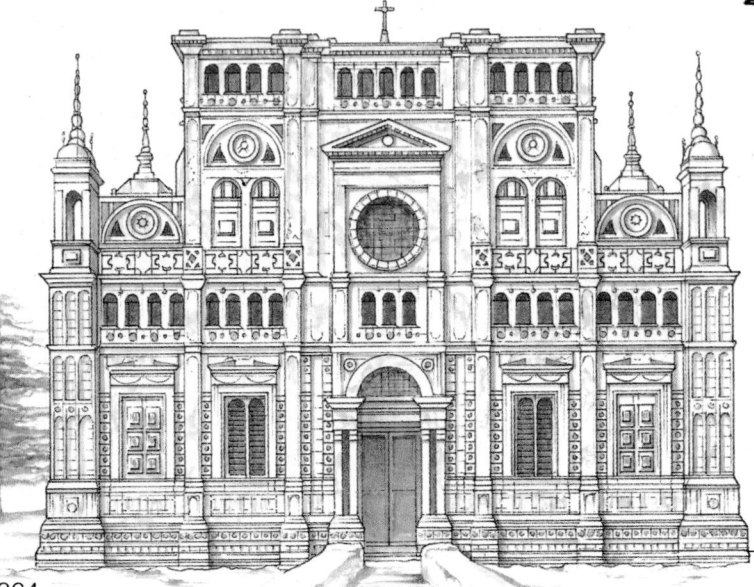

◀ During this period many new churches were built in Europe and old ones were extended or replaced. Those belonging to the Roman Catholic faith were usually very ornate, like this one at Pavia in Italy. It was started in 1491, and the outside was decorated using different colored marbles. Roman Catholic churches had rich carvings, paintings, and stained-glass windows. In contrast, the new Protestant churches were very plain and simple in style.

▶ *Aztec priests used stone-bladed knives like this one to cut out the hearts of their victims. Thousands of people were sacrificed to the god of war Huitzilopochtli.*

◀ *This cartoon is thought to be an anti-Lutheran picture. It is supposed to show that the devil dictated Luther's sermons to him.*

▼ *People found guilty of heresy (holding beliefs contrary to that of the established Church) could be burned at the stake in punishment.*

WHEN IT HAPPENED

1517 The Reformation starts in Europe.
1519 In India, Guru Nanak founds Sikhism.
1534 Ignatius Loyola founds the Society of Jesus, or Jesuits.
1536 Dissolution of the Monasteries in England.
1545 Meeting of the first Council of Trent to try and reform the Roman Catholic Church.
1549 St. Francis Xavier arrives in Japan to convert the people to Christianity.
1560 The first Puritans preach in England.
1562 The French Wars of Religion start.

◀ *In the 16th century, Buddhism flourished in China and Japan, with many temples and thousands of monks. Around their temples in Japan, the Zen Buddhists laid out gardens of contemplation, like this one at Ryoan-ji in Kyoto, then the capital of Japan. It has no plants. Instead it has an oblong of raked white sand, with 15 rocks of different sizes set in it.*

1535 The French explorer Jacques Cartier navigates the St. Lawrence River and claims Canada for France. Silver mining in Peru and Mexico greatly benefits Spain (the crown is entitled to one-fifth of any silver mined). The Spanish explore Chile. England: Sir Thomas More is executed for refusing to take the oath agreeing to the Act of Supremacy.

1536 England: Anne Boleyn is executed and Henry VIII marries Jane Seymour. The Dissolution of the Monasteries starts (completed 1540). The money from selling monastic lands is used to help pay for wars with France. The Pilgrimage of Grace, a Catholic uprising in the north, is suppressed. The German artist Hans Holbein becomes court painter to Henry VIII. Switzerland: Calvin leads the Protestants in Geneva. Italy: France invades Savoy and Piedmont and makes an alliance with the Ottoman Turks. South America: Pedro de Mendoza founds the city of Buenos Aires.

1537 England: Jane Seymour dies after the birth of a son, the future Edward VI.

1539 Holy Roman Empire: The Truce of Frankfurt is made between Charles V and the Protestant princes of the empire.

This bronze gun was found in the wreck of the Mary Rose, *which sank in 1544.*

1540 England: Henry VIII marries Anne of Cleves following negotiations by Thomas Cromwell. Henry soon divorces her and marries Catherine Howard. Thomas Cromwell is executed for treason. Low Countries: Gerhardus Mercator finishes his first map of the world. Italy: Philip, son of Charles V, is made duke of Milan. Papal States: Pope Paul III approves Ignatius Loyola's Society of Jesus.

The Spanish Empire

After the conquest of the Aztecs and the Incas, the king of Spain added their territories to his empire. He divided the lands into two viceroyalties, each ruled by a viceroy. The Aztec empire became the Viceroyalty of New Spain in 1535. Later in the 16th century it also included parts of California, Arizona, and New Mexico. The land of the Incas became the Viceroyalty of Peru.

Many people from Spain went to live in the new Spanish empire. The colonies were ruled by the Council of the Indies based in Spain. Many of the laws made for the colonies show that the Spanish government tried to make sure that the

NEW FOODS FOR EUROPE

The Spanish explorers brought many new foods back to Europe. These included pineapples, tomatoes, capsicums, and sunflowers which were grown for their seeds. They found the potato in the high mountains of Peru and took some samples back to Europe where at first they were grown for their flowers, rather than for food. The Aztecs used cocoa beans as money and also ground them to make a chocolate drink. In 1528, Cortés took some beans to Spain and cocoa gradually became a popular drink in Europe. The Spanish and the Portuguese introduced sugar cane to the West Indies and Brazil. Native American slaves first worked on the plantations then African slaves were brought over.

▲ *The Spanish exploited the gold and silver of the New World. The harsh conditions and new diseases brought by the Spanish meant the population of Mexico fell from 25 million in 1519 to just over 1 million in 1600.*

▼ *Spain tried to stop other countries trading with its empire, but did not succeed. By 1600, France, England, and the Netherlands were challenging its might.*

Native Americans were not ill-treated. But it was impossible to prevent the ruling Spaniards from treating them very cruelly. The Native Americans were forced to mine silver and to work as slaves. Thousands died because they had no resistance to European diseases such as measles and smallpox.

The conquistadores and colonists were followed by Spanish missionaries. They destroyed the existing temples and idols and set up Roman Catholic churches in their place. They tried to force all the Indians to become Christians.

The Spanish empire continued to expand during the reign of Philip II (1556–1598). Most of the islands of the Philippines were conquered in 1571. Then King Sebastian of Portugal was killed in battle against the Moroccans in north Africa in 1578. As Philip was Sebastian's nearest relative, he was able to add the Portuguese empire to his own.

By 1600, the Spanish empire was the biggest in the world, but it had begun to lose its power. Philip's desire to stamp out heresy had led him into wars which used up most of the gold and silver that had been taken from the New World.

Spanish Netherlands
SPAIN
Kingdom of Portugal
Franche-Comté
Duchy of Milan
Kingdom of Naples
Kingdom of Sicily
Kingdom of Sardinia
Tangier
Viceroyalty of New Spain
Viceroyalty of Peru
Atlantic Ocean
Indian Ocean
Pacific Ocean
Philippines

■ Spanish empire

EL DORADO

The conquistadores were spurred on in their explorations by the legend of *El Dorado*, which means "the Golden Man," whose kingdom was said to be full of gold. This promised land was never found and silver gradually became more important. It eventually made up 90 percent of the precious metals sent back to Spain.

1541   North America: Hernando de Soto discovers the Mississippi River. Hungary: Ferdinand of Habsburg is defeated at Pest by the Turks. Hungary becomes a Turkish province.

1542   England: Catherine Howard is executed. Scotland: At the battle of Solway Moss, James V of Scotland is killed. His one-week-old daughter, Mary, becomes queen of Scotland (to 1567). Japan: First Portuguese sailors arrive.

1543   England: Henry VIII marries Catherine Parr and forms an alliance with Charles V. Europe: Vesalius publishes his work on human anatomy. Poland: On his deathbed, the astronomer and priest Nicolas Copernicus states that the Earth moves around the Sun. North America: Oil is found in Texas by the Spaniard Luis de Moscoso.

A silver pomander made in about 1580. It carried perfume to keep away disease.

1544   France: Henry VIII and Charles V invade France. Western Europe: Spain and France sign The Treaty of Crepy.

1545   Europe: Pope Paul III opens the Council of Trent which, under Jesuit guidance, is to reform the Roman Catholic Church.

1547   England: Henry VIII dies and his 10-year-old son becomes King Edward VI of England (to 1553); the Duke of Somerset acts as Lord Protector. France: Francis I dies and his son Henry II succeeds to the throne (to 1559). Germany: Charles V defeats the Protestant Schmalkaldic League at the battle of Muhlberg. Russia: Ivan IV is crowned tsar, or emperor, of Russia. France: French becomes the official language, rather than Latin.

The Counter-Reformation

In 1522, Pope Adrian VI admitted there were many problems in the Roman Catholic Church, but he died before he could start putting them right. Nothing more was done until 1534, when Paul III became pope. He started to reform the Church in a movement known as the Counter-Reformation. He began by encouraging the preaching and missionary work of an Italian order of friars, called the Capuchins. Six years later he approved the founding of the Society of Jesus, or Jesuits, which had been founded by Ignatius Loyola to spread Catholicism.

With the encouragement of the Holy Roman Emperor, Pope Paul III called a meeting known as the Council of Trent in 1545 to decide what else needed to be done to reform the Roman Catholic Church. One of the suggestions was better education for clergymen and Church colleges, called seminaries, were set up. The Council of Trent also decided that monks, nuns, and priests should obey their vows of poverty.

▲ *The religious conflict in this period led to an inceased concern with witchcraft. Both Catholics and Protestants began witch hunts which often led to harmless women being burned or drowned.*

Loyola

Ignatius Loyola (1491–1556) was born in Spain. He turned to religion after being wounded in battle. In 1534, he founded the Society of Jesus. This aimed to spread the Catholic faith largely through teaching and set up missions as far away as India, China, and South America.

Erasmus

Desiderius Erasmus (c. 1467–1536), born in the Netherlands, was a traveler and scholar. He published an edition of the Greek New Testament. He was a Catholic, but his views clashed with those of the Church. In 1559, his books were placed on the Index of forbidden books.

▲ *The Council of Trent met three times between 1545 and 1563. It reformed the Roman Catholic Church and tried to stop the spread of Protestantism.*

In 1554, Charles V's son, Philip, the future king Phillip II of Spain, married Mary I of England, daughter of Henry VIII and Catherine of Aragon. Mary had made England Catholic again when she came to the throne in 1553. The marriage was a failure and when Mary died, England became Protestant again. Later Philip tried to restore Catholicism in England and the Netherlands by force. He failed and in the process also helped to ruin Spain's economy.

▼ *The Spanish Inquisition questioned people accused of heresy. This included reading books that were forbidden by the Catholic church, and having Protestant beliefs. Heretics were burned at the stake.*

The Habsburgs

The Habsburg family dominated European politics for over 600 years from the 13th century onward. It took its name from the family castle in Switzerland which was called Habichtsburg or "Hawk's Castle." By the 13th century, Austria and Styria formed part of their lands and, from 1438 onward, the Holy Roman emperor was nearly always a member of the Habsburg family. In the late 15th century, Maximilian I made sure that their power would continue by arranging very advantageous marriages for his family. His son, Philip of Burgundy, was married to Joanna the Mad, a daughter of Ferdinand and Isabella of Spain. Their son, who became Charles V, was to be the most powerful Habsburg of all.

When Philip died in 1506, Charles inherited Burgundy and the Netherlands. In 1516, Ferdinand of Spain left him Spain and Naples, and in

▼ After Charles died, Austrian Habsburgs ruled the Holy Roman Empire and Spanish Habsburgs ruled Spain, the Netherlands, and part of Italy.

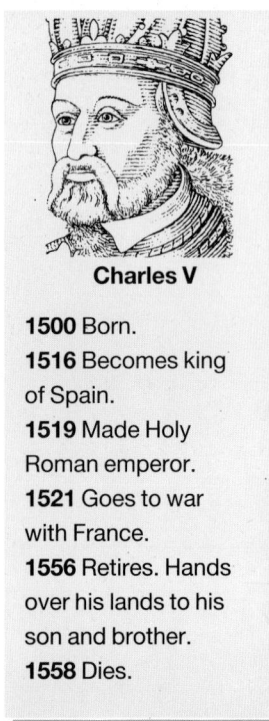

Charles V

1500 Born.
1516 Becomes king of Spain.
1519 Made Holy Roman emperor.
1521 Goes to war with France.
1556 Retires. Hands over his lands to his son and brother.
1558 Dies.

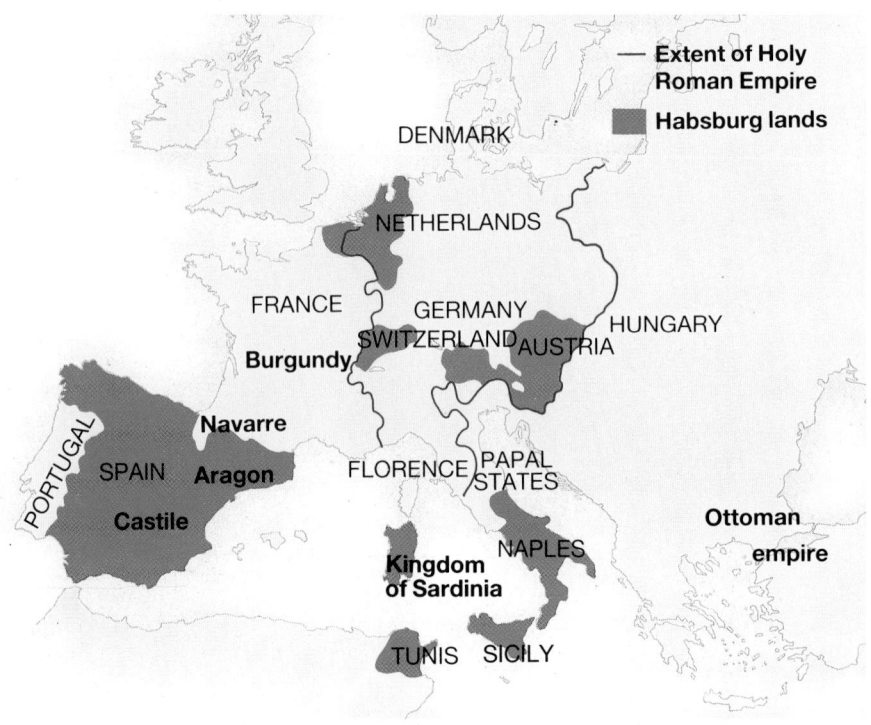

— Extent of Holy Roman Empire

■ Habsburg lands

DENMARK

NETHERLANDS

FRANCE GERMANY HUNGARY
SWITZERLAND AUSTRIA
Burgundy

PORTUGAL Navarre
SPAIN Aragon FLORENCE PAPAL STATES
Castile

Ottoman empire

Kingdom of Sardinia NAPLES

TUNIS SICILY

◄ *Rudolf IV founded Habsburg power. He was elected king of Germany and became Holy Roman emperor although he was never crowned. The Holy Roman Empire remained in Habsburg hands until 1806.*

1519 he inherited the Holy Roman Empire from Maximilian. This led to rivalry with Francis I of France, who also wanted to be Holy Roman emperor, and their countries were at war for most of Charles's reign.

A devout Catholic, Charles also had to deal with problems in the Holy Roman Empire caused by people in Germany who had become Protestants after the Reformation (*see* pages 354–355). In 1546, Charles took up arms against some of them who had formed the League of Schmalkalden. He defeated them in 1547, but four years later he was forced to agree to their demands.

By 1556, Charles was exhausted by all these wars. He retired to a monastery, having divided his lands between his son Philip (who ruled Spain and the Netherlands) and his brother, Ferdinand (who ruled Germany and Austria).

THE HOLY ROMAN EMPIRE

First used in the 13th century, the double-headed eagle was the emblem of the Holy Roman Empire. The eagle was a symbol of power, but in the 16th century the power of the emperors began to decline. Some of the German states grew more powerful and wanted to become independent of the Holy Roman Empire. This was especially true

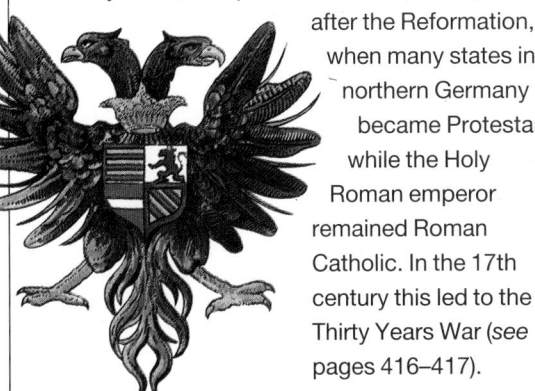

after the Reformation, when many states in northern Germany became Protestant, while the Holy Roman emperor remained Roman Catholic. In the 17th century this led to the Thirty Years War (*see* pages 416–417).

1549 England: A uniform Protestant service is introduced in the Church of England, using Edward VI's first *Book of Common Prayer*. Japan: The Christian missionary St. Francis Xavier arrives.

1550 Papal States: Julius III becomes pope (to 1555). Florida: The Spanish bring the first beef cattle to North America.

Violins as we know them today appeared in about the middle of the 16th century.

1551 War starts between the Ottoman Turks and Hungary (to 1562).

1552 War breaks out between Spain and France (to 1556). France seizes Toul, Metz, and Verdun. England: Second *Book of Common Prayer*.

1553 England: On death of Edward VI, Lady Jane Grey is proclaimed queen of England by the Duke of Northumberland. Her reign lasts nine days. Mary I, daughter of Henry VIII and Catherine of Aragon, then becomes queen (to 1558). She is a devout Roman Catholic.

1554 England: Lady Jane Grey is executed. Mary I marries Philip, heir to throne of Spain, on condition that he will not be allowed to rule England in the event of her death. North Africa: The Ottoman Turks start to conquer the coast.

1555 England: With Mary on the throne England returns to Roman Catholicism. Protestants are persecuted and about 300, including Thomas Cranmer, are burned at the stake. Papal States: Paul IV is elected pope. Germany: At the Peace of Augsburg, Protestant princes are granted freedom of worship and the right to introduce the Reformation into their own territories. Russia: Building starts on St. Basil's Cathedral in Moscow. India: Akbar, grandson of Babur, becomes Mogul emperor (to 1605).

Science and Technology

The revival of learning in 15th century Europe led people to start observing the world about them and do experiments, rather than just accept what they were told. Sometimes this led to clashes with the Church, when new ideas were contrary to the Church's teachings. Even though scientists were threatened with stern punishments, many brilliant ideas and inventions were produced such as the first successful watch, invented in 1504, and the microscope, invented in 1590. People also studied the human body and in 1543 Andreas Vesalius published some of the first accurate descriptions of human anatomy. His teachings, however, were unpopular.

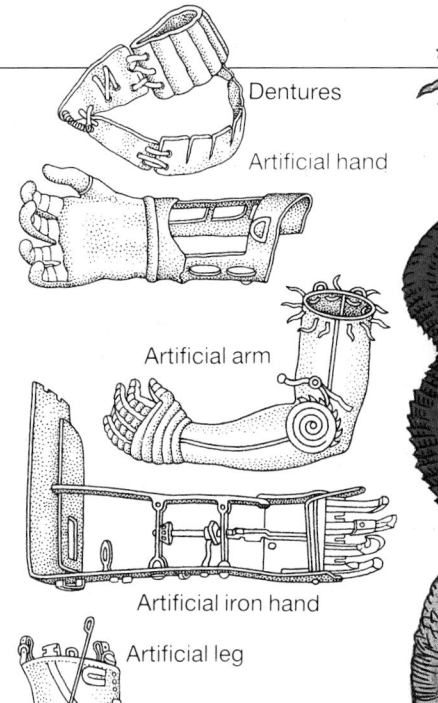

Dentures

Artificial hand

Artificial arm

Artificial iron hand

Artificial leg

▲ *Wars in Europe, led to growing interest in surgery. Amboise Paré, a great French surgeon, designed useful aids for crippled soldiers. His artificial hand had fingers which moved by springs and cogwheels.*

▲ *This drawing is meant to show the "essence of mercury," an element that many scientists thought was present in all matter.*

▼ *During the Renaissance people began to study mathematics seriously. This helped them with their scientific experiments.*

▼ *Leonardo da Vinci drew many sketches of flying machines. In this one a man flaps the four wings with a system of pulleys and treadles.*

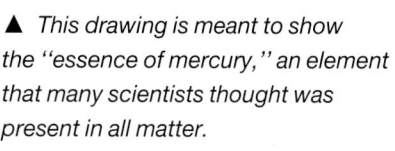

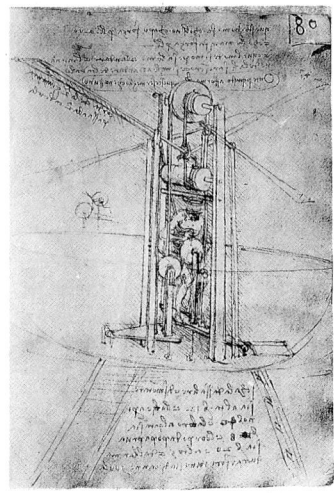

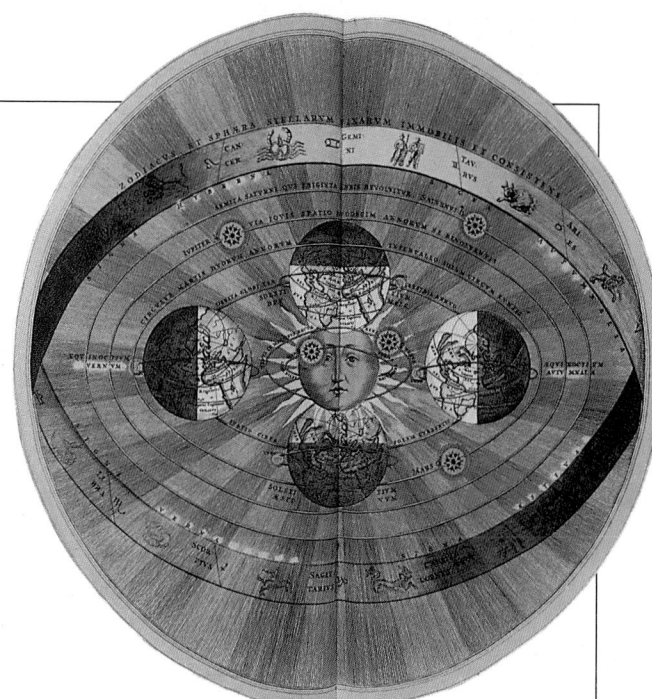

▶ *In the 16th century scientists had many strange theories to explain reproduction. This drawing shows a lamb growing like a plant. They also believed that more minerals would grow underground to replace those removed by mining.*

▲ *This is the Solar System as described by Nicolas Copernicus in 1543. He said that the Earth and planets moved around the Sun and that the Earth turned on its own axis every day. Many people thought that this was not only against the teachings of the Church, but against common sense. They thought that if the Earth turned it would make a great wind.*

◀ *Tycho Brahe (1546–1601) was a Danish astronomer who came to the attention of King Frederick II of Denmark after observing a star called a nova. The king had two observatories built for him on the island of Hveen. In the observatory shown here he had a library, laboratory, living apartments, and rooms for his instruments. From his observations he believed that the planets moved around the Sun, but that the Sun then moved around the Earth. The telescope had not been invented then, but Brahe established the positions of 777 stars by naked-eye observations.*

Elizabethan England

During the reign of Queen Elizabeth I, England became a prosperous trading nation. From the start of the 16th century, sailors from Devon and Cornwall sailed across the Atlantic to fish for cod in the seas off Newfoundland. Then English sailors started trading with Spanish America. In 1562, the seaman John Hawkins bought slaves in Sierra Leone, Africa, and took them to Hispaniola in the West Indies where he traded them for hides and sugar. He sold these goods in England for such a profit that Queen Elizabeth herself invested money in his next voyage.

Other sailors turned to piracy, attacking Spanish treasure ships taking silver back from America. This, and the fact that Elizabeth had sent a military force to the Netherlands to help Dutch

Drake

Francis Drake (c. 1543 –1596) was born in Devon. He became a sea captain and later an admiral. His first voyages were to Guinea and the West Indies. In 1580 he became the first Englishman to sail around the world in his ship the *Golden Hind*. He helped defeat the Spanish Armada.

Elizabeth I

1533 Born. Only child of Henry VIII and Anne Boleyn.
1558 Becomes queen of England and Ireland on her sister Mary's death.
1559–1563 Sets up a moderate Protestant Church in England.
1588 English fleet defeats the Spanish Armada.
1603 Dies.

▶ *When this portrait was painted after England's victory over the Spanish Armada, Elizabeth was 56 years old. Well-educated and a skillful politician, she was made to look younger as a symbol of her power. She never married and was succeeded by James VI.*

◀ *Philip II sent his Invincible Armada to attack England in August 1588. The Spanish had more ships, but the English sailors knew the seas better. The English ships were more maneuverable than the heavy Spanish galleons and defeated the Armada off Gravelines in France.*

SHAKESPEARE

One of the most famous Elizabethans was the playwright and poet William Shakespeare. He was born in the market town of Stratford-upon-Avon in 1564, the son of a rich tradesman. He married Anne Hathaway in 1582 and they had three children. After becoming an actor in London, he wrote his first four plays between 1589 and 1592. These were *Richard III* and the three parts of *Henry VI*. Between 1593 and 1600 he wrote comedies, including *A Midsummer Night's Dream* and *The Taming of the Shrew*. By 1599 he held shares in the Globe Theater at Southwark in London. He then started to write tragedies, including *Hamlet* and *Macbeth*. Shakespeare lived until 1616 and wrote 37 plays in all.

rebels in their fight against Spanish rule (*see* pages 386–387), angered Philip II of Spain so much that in 1588 he sent a fleet of fighting ships called the Armada to attack England. It was unsuccessful but the war with Spain continued until after Elizabeth's death in 1603.

England prospered in spite of war with Spain. Elizabeth was a hard-working and

1556 Holy Roman Empire: Charles V abdicates. Spain and its colonies, the Netherlands, Naples, Milan, and Franche-Comté are to go to his son Philip. The Holy Roman Empire and the Habsburg lands go to Charles's brother, Ferdinand. An alliance is made between Pope Paul IV and Henry II of France.
⚔ India: By his victory at the battle of Panipat, Babur's grandson, Akbar, establishes his rule as Mogul emperor.

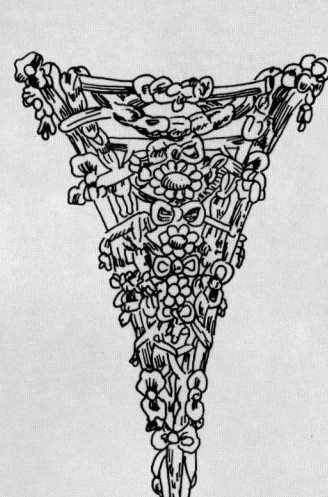

Elizabethan women wore elaborate clothes such as this jeweled stomacher, worn over the chest and stomach.

1557 At the battle of St. Quentin, Spain and ⚔ England defeat France. The Livonian War, a dispute over the succession to territories in the Balkans, between Poland, Russia, Sweden, and Denmark, starts (to 1582). Russia invades Poland. China: Portuguese traders are allowed to settle in Macao.

1558 France: England loses Calais, its last possession in France. England: Mary dies and is succeeded by Elizabeth I (to 1603). Catholic legislation in England is repealed. Mary, Queen of Scots, marries Francis, Dauphin (heir to the throne) of France. Holy Roman Empire: Ferdinand I becomes emperor (to 1564). Papal States: Pius IV becomes pope (to 1565).

1559 The Treaty of Cateau-Cambresis ends war between Spain and France; France gives up all its conquests except Toul, Metz, and Verdun. Spain controls most of Italy. The king of France, Henry II, dies of a head wound received in a tournament celebrating the peace. His son, Francis II becomes king (to 1560) at the age of 16.

1560 Scotland: The Church of Scotland is founded. The Treaty of Edinburgh is agreed between England, Scotland, and France. England: The first Puritans appear. Many of them are Protestants who went abroad to escape persecution in the reign of Mary I. They want to purify the Church of England of anything left over from Roman Catholicism. France: Francis II dies and is succeeded by his 10-year-old brother, Charles IX (to 1574). Catherine de Medici, widow of Henry II, rules France as regent. The Huguenots, (French Protestants) try to overthrow the Guise family who are strong supporters of the Catholic cause. Jean Nicot imports tobacco seeds and leaves into France (nicotine is named after him). Moscow: Construction of St. Basil's cathedral is completed.

A contemporary illustration of the beheading of Mary, Queen of Scots, in 1587. Elizabeth I had kept her under guard for 18 years before signing her death warrant.

1561 Scotland: Mary, Queen of Scots, and widow of Francis II, returns to Scotland. Spain: Madrid becomes the capital. England: The English sea captain, John Hawkins, starts England's involvement in the slave trade when he takes 300 African slaves from a Portuguese ship bound for Brazil. India: Portuguese monks in Goa introduce printing to India.

▲ *Elizabeth I traveled a great deal around England so that people could see her. She took her courtiers with her and stayed at large country houses. After hunting, she often enjoyed an elaborate meal in the open air.*

intelligent monarch. She established a rule with the aid of her chief adviser, William Cecil, that made her popular with her people. Art, music, and literature flourished as the country enjoyed a time of stability.

Elizabeth hoped to satisfy most of her subjects by reestablishing the Church of England along mostly Protestant lines. She passed two laws called the Religious Settlement of 1559. Although Catholics and Protestants alike criticized her settlement for being too moderate, there was no open warfare and Protestantism was slowly reestablished.

Under Elizabeth's rule the textile and iron industries expanded and towns grew in size. Poor Laws were passed recognizing that some people might be genuinely unable to find employment and were in need of support from the parish. The Poor Laws were also designed to try to prevent starvation in years when the harvest failed.

Mary, Queen of Scots

Mary became queen of Scotland in 1542 when she was just one week old. Her father, James V, was the nephew of Henry VIII and this eventually led Mary to claim the English throne. Mary's mother, Mary of Guise, took her daughter to France in 1547 and brought her up at the French court. In 1558, Mary married the *Dauphin* (heir to the French throne), soon to be Francis II. He died two years later and in 1561 Mary returned to Scotland.

By this time Scotland was a Protestant country, but Mary was a Catholic. She married Lord Darnley, her Catholic cousin, and they had a son, later James VI. When Mary tired of Darnley, she became friendly with her private secretary, David Rizzio. He was murdered in 1566 and later Darnley died when his house was blown up. The Earl of Bothwell was thought to be involved. When Mary married him, the Scottish lords rebelled and forced her to abdicate. In 1568, she fled to England where she was kept until her execution in 1587.

Mary

1542 Born.
1558 Marries the Dauphin Francis.
1560 Is widowed.
1561 Returns to Scotland.
1565 Marries Lord Henry Stuart Darnley.
1567 Marries the Earl of Bothwell. Loses battle of Carberry to Scottish lords and flees to England.
1587 Is executed.

Knox

John Knox was a Scot who became attracted to Protestantism in 1543. He fled to Geneva in 1553 and met John Calvin. In 1558, he wrote *The First Blast of the Trumpet Against the Monstrous Regiment of Women*, protesting against Mary of Guise who ruled Scotland for her daughter.

▼ *After nearly twenty years of imprisonment, Mary was executed at Fotheringay Castle in 1587 on a charge of treason. She was said to have plotted against Elizabeth I of England many times.*

French Wars of Religion

The spread of the Protestant faith led to problems in some parts of Europe. In France, the majority of the people stayed Roman Catholic, but the number of Protestants was growing. They were called Huguenots and at first they were tolerated.

King Henry II of France died in 1559 from an injury he received while celebrating the Peace of Cateau-Cambresis between France and Spain. His oldest son, Francis, succeeded him, but he died the following year.

Ten-year-old Charles then became king of France. He was under the complete control of his mother, Catherine de Medici. She supported the Catholics and objected when Charles came under the influence of the Huguenot leader, Admiral Gaspard de Coligny, in 1572.

▲ Henry IV of France signed the Edict of Nantes in 1598. This brought the French Wars of Religion to an end because it gave the Huguenots freedom to worship as they wanted.

▼ The St. Bartholomew's Day Massacre started in Paris on August 24, 1572. As many as 20,000 Huguenots may have been killed throughout France in the course of that day and the next.

Catherine de Medici

Catherine de Medici (1519–1589) was born in Italy, the daughter of Lorenzo de Medici, Duke of Urbino. She married Henry II of France in 1533. She acted as regent for their second son, Charles IX, but her influence waned in Henry III's reign.

Henry of Navarre

1553 Born.
1572 Becomes king of Navarre and marries Margaret of Valois. Is held prisoner at court.
1589 Becomes Henry IV of France, the first Bourbon king.
1593 Converts to Catholicism.
1600 Marries Marie de Medici.
1610 Dies.

When an attempt to have Coligny assassinated failed, Catherine plotted a massacre of the leading Huguenots who were in Paris for the marriage of her daughter, Margaret, to the Huguenot Henry of Navarre. The killings began at dawn on St. Bartholomew's Day and were repeated all over France. Coligny was killed, but Henry was spared.

In 1574, Henry III, another son of Catherine de Medici, became king of France. He was also influenced by his mother, and the civil war continued. In 1585, he banned the Protestant religion, and the War of the Three Henrys started.

It involved Henry III of France, the Huguenot Henry of Navarre, and the Catholic Henry of Guise. The war only ended in 1589 after Henry III had Henry of Guise murdered for trying to seize the throne. Henry III was then assassinated by a fanatical monk, and Henry of Navarre, his rightful heir, became King Henry IV of France.

1562 France: The Wars of Religion start in France, after the murder of over 60 Huguenots by the Guise family during a Protestant church service. Ireland: The Earl of Tyrone leads two unsuccessful rebellions against Queen Elizabeth I. The Ottoman Turks sign a eight-year truce with the Holy Roman Empire.

1563 England: The Thirty-Nine Articles combining Protestant beliefs with Roman Catholic organization and stating the ruling monarch is the head of the church, are adopted. English soldiers catch the plague while in France and bring it back to England; it kills over 20,000 people in London alone. Russia: Ivan the Terrible, conquers part of Livonia.

1564 Western Europe: The Peace of Troyes ends the war between England and France. Holy Roman Empire: Ferdinand I dies and is succeeded by his son, Maximilian II (to 1576). Europe: Michelangelo and John Calvin die. William Shakespeare and Galileo Galilei are born (Shakespeare dies 1616, Galileo 1642).

1565 Russia: A "reign of terror" begins as Ivan the Terrible sets out to destroy the power of the nobles. America: Pedro Menendez de Aviles founds the first European colony in North America at St. Augustine in Florida. Scotland: Mary, Queen of Scots, marries her cousin, Lord Darnley. Malta: The Ottoman Turks besiege Malta, but are defeated by the Knights of St. John. Switzerland: First known use of pencils. England: Sir John Hawkins introduces sweet potatoes, and possibly tobacco as well.

During the reign of Henry IV, the French began breeding silkworms. This grew to become a national industry of France.

Society and Government

This period saw changes in both society and government in Europe. In many places the decline of the feudal system meant people were able to leave the land and look for work in towns if they wanted. More powerful kings emerged, especially in England, France, and Spain. They ruled over the whole of their countries and controlled the rich noblemen more successfully than their predecessors had.

Other parts of the world were governed differently. In the Inca empire, the old, the frail, and the young were looked after by the state in a way that would not be equalled in Europe for over 400 years, but healthy young people were still sacrificed to the gods. In China, and later in Mogul India, the emperor's word was law, but both countries had a vast number of civil servants to make sure everyone obeyed. By 1600, the Ottoman empire controlled parts of northern Africa, southwestern Asia, and southeastern Europe, as well as the area we call Turkey. The sultans made all important decisions for the empire.

▲ *In North America, Great Plains Indians led a nomadic life hunting the buffalo. Different tribes had different customs, but storytelling was an important part of all their cultures. Tribal customs and lore were passed from one generation to the next by word of mouth. A tribal council settled quarrels.*

▼ *Members of the Aztec royal family were carried around on litters. No one was allowed to look at the emperor and if they did they were risking death. Tribes conquered by the Aztecs had to send them tributes, while the army went to war to capture more people to sacrifice to the gods in Tenochtitlán.*

1498 Girolamo Savonarola is burned for heresy by his political rivals in Florence.

1513 Machiavelli writes *The Prince*. He says that all actions are fair to secure a stable state.

1520 Suleiman I becomes Ottoman emperor and reforms the laws and administration.

1555 In Russia, Ivan IV reforms the legal code and local administration.

1572 Each parish in England is allowed to levy a tax from its parishoners to help the poor.

▶ *Leonardo Loredano was doge of the Venetian Republic from 1501 to 1521. Although he was head of state, the real power was in the hands of the Great Council, whose members came from the leading families of Venice.*

▲ Utopia, *by the English lawyer and scholar, Sir Thomas More, was published in 1516. It was about a mythical island with an ideal social system; everyone shared equally in government, education, and wars.*

▶ *To be pope was to be one of the most powerful men in the world. He not only ruled his own country, but, before the Reformation, was responsible for the spiritual welfare of nearly everyone in Europe (and later on of people all over the world). During the 15th and early 16th centuries, some popes worked hard to advance the fortunes of their own families. Pope Sixtus IV, shown here with four of his nephews, helped one of them to become Pope Julius II.*

Russia

Until the middle of the 15th century, much of southern Russia was under the control of the Mongol rulers of the Golden Horde (*see* pages 272–273), who were also known as Tartars. In 1462, however, a new ruler came to the throne of Muscovy, a small region of Russia that included Moscow. Ivan III, also known as "the Great," succeeded in making his lands independent of the khanate of the Golden Horde. In 1472, he married the niece of the last Byzantine emperor and appointed himself as protector of the Eastern Orthodox Church.

By 1480, he had brought Novgorod and other cities under his control and called himself the ruler of all Russia. He made Moscow his capital and rebuilt its *kremlin* (citadel) which had been damaged by fire. When Ivan III died, he was succeeded by his son Vasili. Vasili ruled until 1533, then he was succeeded by Ivan IV, his three-year-old son.

Ivan III

1440 Born.
1462 Succeeds to the throne of Moscow.
1471–1478 Invades Novgorod three times before finally conquering it.
1480 Becomes ruler of all Russia.
1497 Introduces a new legal code.
1505 Dies an alcoholic.

Ivan IV

1530 Born.
1547 Is crowned tsar and grand prince of all Russia.
1547–1549 Pushes through legal and administrative reforms.
1565 Starts a "reign of terror" to break the power of the nobility.
1581 Kills his heir, Ivan.
1584 Dies.

▼ *The Kremlin was the center of Moscow. It was like a fort and many palaces, churches, and cathedrals were built within the protection of its walls.*

▲ *St. Basil's Cathedral in Moscow was constructed between 1555 and 1560 to celebrate Ivan IV's victories in Kazan and Astrakhan.*

Ivan IV also became known as Ivan the Terrible. He was the Grand Prince of Muscovy from 1533 to 1584 and was crowned as the first *tsar* (emperor) of Russia in 1547. His harsh upbringing left him with a violent and unpredictable character, but his nickname meant "Awe-inspiring" rather than "Terrible."

He changed the legal system as well as reforming trading links with England and other European countries. Ivan also expanded his lands by capturing Kazan and Astrakhan from the Tartars. At home he reduced the power of the *boyars* – the Russian nobility – by inventing a kind of secret police.

In 1581, he killed his eldest son in a fit of rage and so was succeeded by his second son, Fyodor. Boris Godunov acted as regent until Fyodor died in 1598. Then he became tsar.

1566 Papal States: Cardinal Michaele Ghislieri is elected as Pope Pius V (to 1572). Netherlands: Religious riots break out between Catholics and the followers of John Calvin. Scotland: Mary, Queen of Scots gives birth to a son, the future James VI of Scotland and James I of England. Ottoman empire: Suleiman the Magnificent dies and is succeeded by his son, Selim II (to 1574).

1567 In Brazil, the Portuguese found Rio de Janeiro. Netherlands: The Duke of Alba is sent from Spain to quell the riots. Scotland: Lord Darnley, husband of Mary, Queen of Scots, is murdered, probably by the Earl of Bothwell who marries Mary in a Protestant ceremony. Later, Mary is forced to abdicate. Her son succeeds to the throne as James VI.

1568 An 80-year-long war of independence starts between the Netherlands and Spain. Mary, Queen of Scots escapes to England, but is held by Elizabeth I. Selim II of the Ottoman empire and Maximilian II of the Holy Roman Empire make a peace agreement which results in the Sultan's receiving large annual payments from the emperor.

1569 Poland: The Union of Lublin merges Poland and Lithuania under Sigismund II of Poland. India: The Mogul emperor Akbar conquers Rajputana.

Grand Prince Ivan III married the niece of the last Byzantine emperor. He took the double-headed eagle of the Byzantine empire as his emblem.

1570 France: The Peace of St. Germain-en-Laye ends the Third War of Religion, giving the Huguenots conditional freedom of worship. Ottoman empire: The Ottoman Turks attack Cyprus and declare war on Venice for refusing to hand over control of Cyprus. Russia: Ivan IV razes Novgorod.

1571 At the battle of Lepanto in the Mediterranean, a combined Papal and Venetian fleet under Don John of Austria defeats the Ottoman Turks under Ali Pasha. The Ottoman fleet loses all but 40 of its 230 galleys, while the Christian fleet loses just 12 ships.

1572 Papal States: Pope Pius V dies and is succeeded by Pope Gregory XIII (to 1585). France: Over 20,000 Huguenots are killed in the St. Bartholomew's Day Massacre. England: Ben Jonson, dramatist, and John Donne, poet, are born (Jonson dies 1637, Donne 1631). Caribbean: Francis Drake attacks Spanish harbors and loots Spanish ships.

Iznik pottery of the Ottoman empire was influenced by Persian craftsmen. The pieces were often decorated with sailing vessels.

1573 Ottoman empire: Venice abandons Cyprus and makes peace with the Ottoman Turks. North Africa: Don John captures Tunis from the Ottoman Turks. India: The Mogul emperor Akbar conquers Gujurat. China: The Ming emperor Wan Li comes to power (to 1620). Italy: Michelangelo Caravaggio is born (dies 1610).

1574 France: Charles IX dies and his brother, Henry III, succeeds him (to 1589). North Africa: The Ottoman empire regains Tunis from Spain. Southern Africa: The Portuguese begin to settle in Angola.

1575 Spain faces bankruptcy and cannot afford to pay its troops in the Netherlands. Plague sweeps through Italy and Sicily.

Mediterranean Struggle

The Ottoman empire tried to gain control of the Mediterranean as its navy grew powerful during the reign of Suleiman the Magnificent (*see* pages 358–359). In 1522, it conquered the island of Rhodes where the Christian order of the Knights of St. John (also called the Knights Hospitaller), had lived since 1282. This left the Knights without a home until the Holy Roman Emperor Charles V gave them the island of Malta in 1530. The Knights remained at war with the Muslim Turks over religion.

In May 1565, Suleiman decided to attack the Knights of St. John and besieged Malta with a large fleet of ships. There were four times as many Turks as Knights, but the Knights had a strong leader in Jean Parisot de la Valette. Fighting continued until September,

▼ *The leader of the Knights of St. John, Jean Parisot de la Valette, founded a heavily fortified city to defend the island of Malta. It was called Valetta in his honor.*

▶ *At Lepanto, Don John of Austria commanded 204 galleys and 6 galleasses (huge oar-driven ships) against 230 Turkish galleys. The Turks lost all but 40 ships, and their hopes of controlling the Mediterranean.*

▶ In the 16th century, the Ottoman empire and the Holy Roman Empire clashed on land and sea. The Ottoman Turks controlled the south and east of the Mediterranean, while the Holy Roman Empire, with Spain, controlled the west and Italy. Suleiman was followed by weaker rulers and the power of the Turks declined.

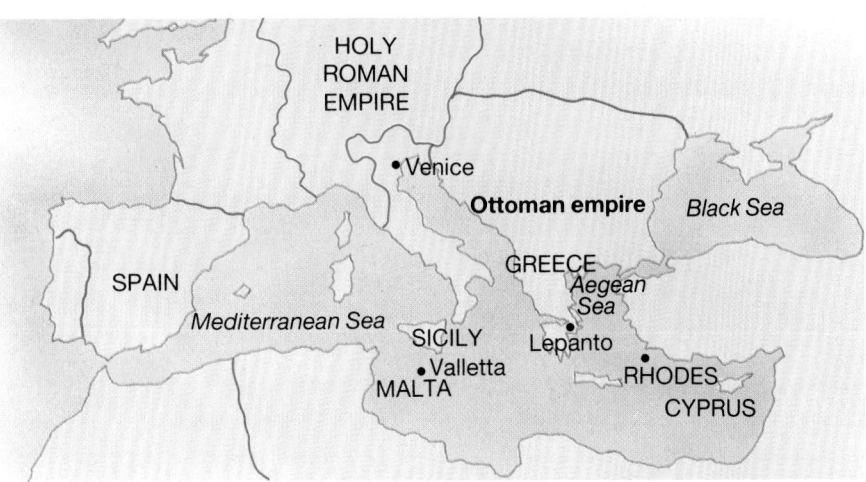

when reinforcements arrived from Sicily, and the Turks withdrew.

Selim II then tried to expand the Ottoman empire by invading Cyprus in 1570. At that time Cyprus belonged to the Venetians. They immediately appealed to Pope Pius V for help and he assembled a fleet from the navies of Venice, Spain, and the Papal States under the command of Don John of Austria. This fleet met the Turkish galleys at the battle of Lepanto off Greece in October 1571, and defeated them in three hours.

THE MALTESE CROSS

The Knights of St. John wore a cross on their uniforms to show that they were Christians. To distinguish them from the other orders of Knights, their cross had four triangular arms. It was later called the Maltese Cross.

1576 Rudolf II becomes Holy Roman emperor (to 1612) on the death of his father, Maximilian II. In the Pacification of Ghent, all the provinces of the Netherlands unite to drive out the Spaniards. Protestantism is forbidden in France. India: Akbar, the Mogul emperor, conquers Bengal.

1577 Europe: An alliance is made between England and the Netherlands against Spain. England: Francis Drake sets out to sail around the world. Low Countries: The Flemish painter, Peter Paul Rubens is born (dies 1640).

A sketch of an Indian setting a parrot trap, first drawn by one of Francis Drake's companions during his voyage around the world.

1578 The Duke of Parma subdues the southern provinces of the Netherlands. North Africa: Sebastian of Portugal invades Morocco. His troops are defeated and he is killed at the battle of Alcazar. Sebastian has no children and is succeeded by Cardinal Henry. The Cardinal asks the pope's permission to marry so he can start a new dynasty.

1579 Netherlands: The Northern provinces form the Union of Utrecht to fight against Spain. India: The Portuguese set up trading colonies in Bengal.

1580 Portugal: Cardinal Henry dies. Philip II of Spain, Sebastian's uncle, invades and declares himself king. Francis Drake returns to England after sailing around the world. The Moguls invade Afghanistan.

1581 The United Provinces of the Netherlands, declare themselves independent of Spain and elect William of Orange as their ruler. Russia: Ivan the Terrible kills his eldest son in a fit of rage. Poland invades Russia.

Dutch Independence

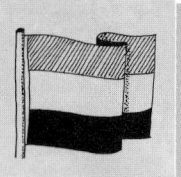

The Netherlands were made up of 17 provinces in what is now Belgium, Luxembourg, and the Netherlands. From 1482 to 1506 they were ruled by Philip of Burgundy, son of the Holy Roman Emperor. Philip's son, Charles, inherited them and made them a Spanish possession when he became king of Spain in 1516.

The fight for independence started after Charles's son became King Philip II of Spain. He strongly resisted the Protestant threat to Catholicism and tried to take complete power over the Low Countries. In 1567, Philip made the Duke of Alba governor of the Netherlands with orders to use terror to crush any opposition. The Duke of Alba started by executing two leaders of the opposition and this led to the Dutch Revolts led by

▼ *The Netherlands were called the Low Countries, because they were low-lying lands, close to the sea. They became rich through trade in the 16th century.*

William of Orange

1533 Born.
1544 Becomes Prince of Orange.
1559 Governs Holland, Zeeland, and Utrecht.
1567–1572 Leads the Dutch Revolts.
1573 Joins the Calvinist church.
1580 Philip II declares him an outlaw.
1584 A Catholic fanatic assassinates William.

▲ *Amsterdam's wealth grew after 1576. The city was built largely on land reclaimed from the sea. It consisted of more than 100 islands linked by canals.*

▶ *A caricature (exaggerated drawing) of the Duke of Alba trying to stamp out heresy in the Netherlands by trampling on the bodies of executed Protestants.*

William of Orange. As Alba became more ruthless, so the opposition spread. There were public executions. Towns were pillaged and their populations massacred. In 1576, Spanish troops sacked Antwerp, ending its prosperity. Many merchants and bankers moved to Amsterdam.

Spain brought the southern provinces back under its control, but in 1581 seven northern provinces declared themselves independent. These provinces were where most of the Protestants lived. Under William of Orange, they called themselves the Republic of the United Netherlands, but Spain did not recognize their independence until 1648.

Trade

In the 16th century the most important trading centers in Europe were Antwerp and Amsterdam. Wool from England and grain, fish, and timber from the Baltic reached the growing population of Europe through these cities. New markets were opening up for goods produced on a large scale such as woolen cloth, iron goods, and firearms.

Spain's exploitation of its South American empire meant a flood of silver into Europe. This encouraged business but it also brought inflation. The first African slaves were taken to the Americas in 1502. The need for cheap labor led to more and more Africans being taken there to work.

▲ *Quentin Massys painted this picture,* The Moneychanger and his Wife, *in 1500. For a small sum, gold was exchanged for silver coins or one currency for another.*

▶ *Europe suffered rapid inflation. Prices rose by up to 400 percent in ninety years.*

◀ *China attracted many visitors, but not all of them were as welcome as these going to Beijing. European traders were regarded as little better than pirates. The Chinese were prepared to sell silk and porcelain, but they did not want European goods in exchange.*

WHEN IT HAPPENED

1460s The Portuguese set up forts in Africa to trade in gold, silver, and ivory.

1498 Vasco da Gama becomes the first European to reach India by sea.

1502 The first African slaves are taken to South America by Spanish settlers. They are used as a source of cheap labor on plantations.

1576 Antwerp is sacked by Spanish troops.

1600 In England the East India Company is set up to trade with India.

▲ *As trade increased in Europe, towns and cities grew larger. In London, shops, houses, and inns were even built on London Bridge. The weight of them caused many maintenance problems.*

◄ *Ship navigation was very basic at this time. Some captains relied on the Sun and stars. Others used a compass and charts when possible. They told the time on board with a sandglass in which the sand took half an hour to run through. They could also use a board like this to tell the time by the stars at night.*

▼ *Russia was cut off from Europe for nearly 250 years. In the late 15th century Russian merchants like these, by order of the tsar, began establishing links in fur trading.*

▶ *A Portuguese map, drawn in 1558. Maps showing sea routes were jealously guarded to stop other countries stealing them and taking the trade.*

North America

When the Europeans first arrived in America in the 16th century, there were hundreds of different tribes of native people living there. Each tribe had its own customs, language, and way of life, according to where it lived. For example, on the Great Plains where wild animals were plentiful, the North American Indians lived by hunting and trapping. The animals they caught provided them with meat and also with skins to make into clothing and shelters. Tribes who lived on the coast or by lakes where trees were plentiful, made wooden canoes and went fishing.

In the southwest, people living in villages called *pueblos* grew crops of corn, squash, and beans by building dams to irrigate the dry land. They also set up trading links with the Aztecs and other native peoples.

Native North Americans on the east coast also lived by farming. They grew corn and tobacco in plots around their villages. The people hunted and trapped animals and gathered fruit, nuts, and

▲ The Miami tribe made clothing from hides and furs. First the skins were cleaned and stretched, then cut and sewn into garments and moccasins. In many tribes women were responsible for raising crops while men hunted. Women, however, did play an important part in tribal affairs; some became chiefs while others took part in tribal councils, held to settle quarrels.

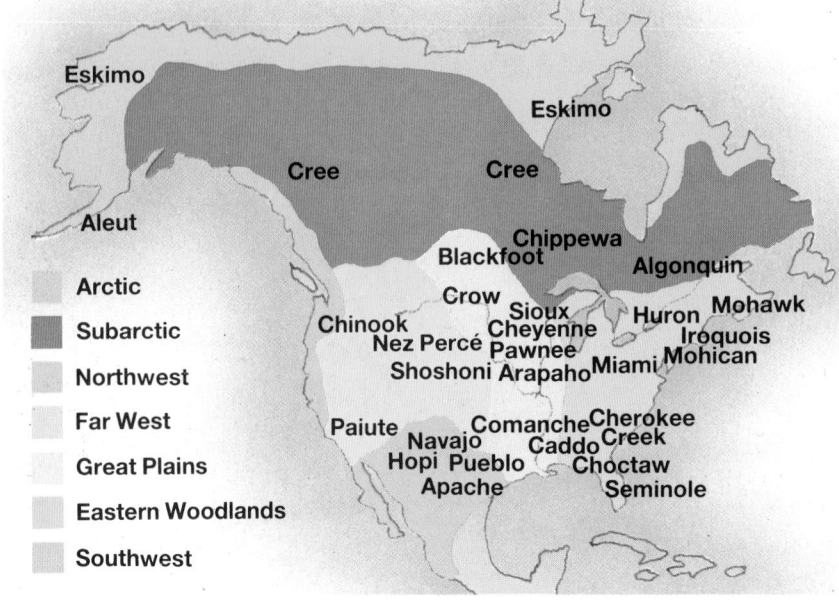

Eskimo
Eskimo
Cree
Cree
Aleut
Chippewa
Blackfoot
Algonquin
Crow
Chinook
Sioux
Cheyenne
Huron
Mohawk
Nez Percé
Pawnee
Iroquois
Shoshoni
Arapaho
Miami
Mohican
Paiute
Comanche
Cherokee
Navajo
Caddo
Creek
Hopi
Pueblo
Choctaw
Apache
Seminole

Arctic
Subarctic
Northwest
Far West
Great Plains
Eastern Woodlands
Southwest

◄ The map shows where the main tribes of Native North Americans lived in 1500, before Europeans arrived and started driving them off their own lands. At that time there were between one- and six-million Native North Americans. They did not believe that they "owned" the land but thought that it was held in common for the entire tribe. The colored areas shown indicate regions in which tribes shared a similar way of life.

▲ *Hunters on the Great Plains sometimes camouflaged (disguised) themselves in animal skins when they went in search of prey.*

▲ *The Chippewa lived in wigwams. The frame was made from bent branches and covered with an outer layer of animal skin or birch bark.*

berries from the surrounding forests.

Like the Aztecs and the Incas, none of these tribes had horses or wheeled transportation before the Europeans arrived. Their knowledge of metal was also very limited and most of their tools were made from either wood or stone. Their main weapon was the bow and arrow. It was used for hunting and also in occasional wars between tribes.

The arrival of the Europeans in the late 16th and early 17th centuries soon had a disastrous effect on the native peoples. Many died from diseases, such as smallpox and measles, which had been unknown in America up to then. Others were killed in disputes and the rest were gradually driven off their lands.

1582 Europe: The Gregorian calendar is introduced into Roman Catholic countries. Peace is declared for Russia, Poland, and Sweden. Mogul empire: Akbar abolishes slavery.

1583 North America: The English explorer Humphrey Gilbert takes possession of Newfoundland on behalf of Queen Elizabeth and founds the first English settlement in the Americas.

1584 North America: Sir Walter Raleigh names Virginia after Queen Elizabeth I. Netherlands: William of Orange is murdered. England sends aid to the Netherlands. Russia: Ivan the Terrible dies and is succeeded by his second son, Fyodor (to 1598).

1585 Papal States: Sixtus V is elected as pope (to 1590). France: the "War of the Three Henrys" starts. Japan: Hideyoshi comes to power in Japan. Low Countries: The Dutch use the first time bombs at the seige of Antwerp. North America: A group of English colonists led by Sir Richard Grenville reaches Roanoke Island.

1586 England: Mary, Queen of Scots, is involved in a plot against Elizabeth I. Persia: Abbas I becomes shah (to 1628). India: Akbar conquers Kashmir.

1587 England: Mary, Queen of Scots, is executed. England is at war with Spain. Sir Francis Drake destroys the Spanish fleet at Cadiz. Savoy and the Catholic cantons form an alliance with Spain.

The tribes of the Iroquois wore masks during important tribal ceremonies. They represented spirits of mythological creatures.

1588 The Spanish Armada is defeated by the English fleet under Lord Howard of Effingham, Sir Francis Drake, and Sir John Hawkins, but the war between Spain and England continues (to 1603). France: Henry of Guise is murdered.

Japan and China

In 1467, civil war broke out among the great feudal lords of Japan. The emperor had lost most of his power and even the shogun had very little influence over the running of the country. For over 100 years private armies of samurai fought against each other in the struggle to control Japan.

During these civil wars, Europeans started visiting Japan. The first to arrive were Portuguese sailors in 1542. Seven years later a Spanish missionary, St. Francis Xavier, arrived to try and convert the Japanese to Christianity. Other traders and missionaries followed and were made welcome at first.

As well as introducing a new religion to Japan, the Europeans also brought firearms. Some samurai looked down on these, saying they were the weapons of cowards, but others quickly saw their advantages in battle.

One samurai called Oda Nobunaga equipped his men with muskets (guns) and captured Kyoto in 1568. His own efforts to reunite Japan ended when he was killed, but his work was continued

▲ *When he was shogun, Hideyoshi managed to break the power of the feudal lords and the Buddhist monks, but his plans for an empire failed.*

by Hideyoshi. He became shogun in 1585 and planned to built a great Japanese empire which would include China. Hideyoshi invaded Korea twice, in 1592 and 1597, but failed to conquer it. The second campaign was abandoned when Hideyoshi died. Hideyoshi had appointed Tokugawa Ieyasu his son's guardian and on his death a power struggle broke out. Civil war followed until Ieyasu defeated his rivals at the battle of Sekigahara in 1600, becoming shogun in 1603.

▼ *At the battle of Nagashino in 1575, Nobunaga armed his 3,000 men with muskets. They were able to defeat a much larger force of mounted samurai, armed with a mixture of swords and bows and arrows.*

By 1500, the Ming dynasty in China was weakening. The emperor forbade Chinese ships to sail beyond coastal waters, but allowed foreign ships to visit China. From 1517, Portuguese and other Europeans traders visited the coast. In 1557, the Portuguese were allowed to settle in Macao and some Jesuit priests were allowed into Beijing. The expense of defeating Hideyoshi's invasion of Korea in 1592 helped to destabilize China. A time of famine also led to unrest and in the 17th century the Manchus invaded from the north.

◀ *Missionaries from Europe had converted 150,000 Japanese to Christianity by the year 1580. This lessened the power of the Buddhists, whom the Japanese ruler Hideyoshi distrusted. But later he regarded Christianity as a dangerous threat to Japanese beliefs. In 1587, Christianity was banned and Christians were persecuted and put to death.*

TEA CEREMONY

The Japanese tea ceremony is called *cha-no-yu*. It was originally brought to Japan by Buddhist monks from China, but the ceremony spread beyond the monasteries in the 15th century. Japanese society was very formal, so strict rules developed over the way the tea was prepared, served, and drunk. The ceremony had to take place in a simple but elegant room. A tea master was in charge.

1590 Near East: Peace is declared between the Ottoman and Safavid empires. England: Around this time Shakespeare begins writing plays. Netherlands: The first microscope is made by Hans and Zacharias Janssen. India: Akbar, the Mogul emperor, conquers Sindh. Virginia: John White, governor of Roanoke Island, returns to America to find settlement mysteriously abandoned.

A Chinese mine-layer barge.

1591 West Africa: The Songhay empire is destroyed by Spanish and Portuguese mercenaries in the service of Morocco.

1592 Papal States: Clement VIII becomes pope (to 1605). Japan: Hideyoshi invades Korea with plans to conquer China, but is forced to withdraw the following year.

1593 War starts between Austria and the Ottoman empire.

1595 The Treaty of Teusina between Sweden and Russia, gives Estonia to Sweden.

1597 Ireland: Under Hugh O'Neill, Earl of Tyrone, the Irish rebel again.

1598 The Edict of Nantes ends civil wars in France by giving Huguenots equal political rights with Roman Catholics. Spain: Philip II dies and his son becomes Philip III (to 1621). Russia: On the death of Fyodor, Boris Godunov becomes tsar (to 1605). Persia: Abbas I drives out the Uzbek Turks.

1599 Ireland: Irish rebels defeat the Earl of Essex and his English army.

1600 England: The East India Company is founded. Ireland: The king of Spain sends an army to support the Earl of Tyrone's rebellion.

War and Weapons

In Europe the increasing use of gunpowder meant that castles were no longer an adequate defense against the enemy. This led to more open battles, instead of the long sieges there had been in the Middle Ages. Both cannons and handguns were used, adding artillery to the two divisions of infantry and cavalry. Although the flintlock was developed, firearms were not very reliable and often injured the person firing them rather than the enemy.

Most soldiers lived in poor conditions. They were often underfed and underpaid. They were also poorly disciplined and more likely to die from disease than enemy fire.

▲ *The warrior ruler of Japan, Hideyoshi, built Himeji castle in 1577. It was his stronghold in the civil wars which tore Japan apart for almost 100 years.*

◀ *Aztec warriors decorated their ceremonial shields with bright feathers. This one was a gift sent to Spain in the early 1500s.*

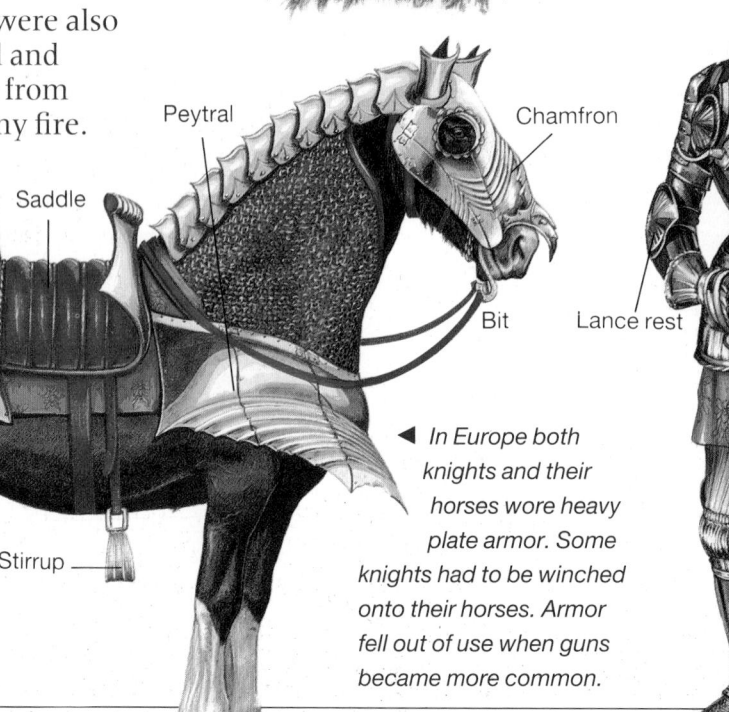

Visor

Breast plat

Chamfron

Peytral

Crupper

Saddle

Bit

Lance rest

Stirrup

Leg harne

◀ *In Europe both knights and their horses wore heavy plate armor. Some knights had to be winched onto their horses. Armor fell out of use when guns became more common.*

1526 The battle of Panipat in India. Babur founds the Mogul empire.

1525 At the battle of Flodden Field, Scotland is heavily defeated by England. The Scottish king James IV is killed in the battle.

1571 The sea battle of Lepanto takes place in the Mediterranean. Although the fleet of the Holy League is outnumbered they defeat the Ottoman navy in three hours.

1578 The king of Portugal is killed in battle against the Moroccans.

▼ *In 1520, Henry VIII of England and Francis I of France met in Flanders at the "Field of the Cloth of Gold" to make an alliance between their countries. Instead the event turned into a contest between the two kings with each trying to outdo the other in the splendor of his arrival.*

▶ *Most European armies were made up of professional soldiers who assembled groups of mercenaries for hire to the highest bidder. Many mercenaries found work in Southeast Asia, along the trade routes. This Mogul miniature shows Portuguese mercenaries fighting the Indians.*

The Calendar Change

The calendar which is used in most parts of the world today is known as the Gregorian calendar. This is because it was worked out by the astronomers of Pope Gregory XIII in the 16th century. Before then Europeans used the Julian calendar, established by Julius Caesar in 46 B.C.

In this calendar a period of three years, each of 365 days, was followed by a leap year with 366 days. This meant that the average length of a year was 365.25 days. However, the amount of time which the Earth actually takes to orbit the Sun is 365.2422 days. This made a year in the Julian calendar 11 minutes and 14 seconds longer than the actual year, and so an extra day appeared about every 128 years.

By the 1580s the Julian calendar was 10 days ahead of the seasons. To correct this, Pope Gregory made October 5, 1582 into October 15. To prevent the error happening again, he decided that every year which could be divided by four would be a leap year with 366 days. But only century years divisible by 400 (such as 1600) would be leap years.

Roman Catholic countries adopted the new calendar at once, but many Protestant kingdoms did not change until 1700. Britain altered its calendar in 1752, by which time there was a difference of 11 days. Russia kept the Julian calendar until 1918.

The use of different calendars in the 16th century can be very confusing. For example, the date when the Spanish Armada was seen off the coast of England can differ by ten days, depending on whether a Spaniard or an English person recorded it. Also, in England, the New Year started on March 25, and not January 1, until the Gregorian calendar came into use.

▲ All through the centuries, scholars tried to find ways of measuring the passage of time. On this 13th-century French manuscript they are comparing the lunar (Moon) year with the solar (Sun) year.

ROMAN CALENDAR

As well as calculating the Julian calendar, the Romans divided the year into 12 months. To this day the names for them are based on the Roman ones. January was named after Janus, the two-headed god of beginnings who could look both ways at once. February was named after *februa*, a Roman feast which took place at that time. March was named after Mars, the god of war, and April comes from the Latin *aperire* (to open) as it is the month when the earth opens up to produce new plants. May is named after the goddess Maia and June after the goddess Juno. July takes its name from Julius Caesar and August from Augustus Caesar. September, October, November, and December were originally the seventh, eighth, ninth, and tenth months.

Trade and Empire

In Europe, the 17th century was a period of contrasts. It was a violent century, filled with wars and revolutions. Its most terrible conflict, the Thirty Years' War, involved most of the European nations and devastated the German states, where most of the fighting took place.

At the same time, the discoveries of its scientists and the achievements of its artists made it a golden age. Louis XIV of France built the world's grandest palace at Versailles. It was decorated by leading craftsmen, and filled with the finest works of art. The findings of scientists such as Newton, Kepler, and Harvey were not only important in themselves, they also established valid methods of scientific enquiry. This period also saw the beginnings of religious toleration in the Protestant countries of Europe and in the North American colonies.

In India, Europeans were making their presence felt. The high tide of Spanish and Portuguese expansion had passed and now French, Dutch, and English merchants negotiated trade treaties with local rulers. For a time, the whole East Indies became the private empire of the Dutch East India Company. European trading posts were also dotted along the Chinese coast. Only Japan held out against European penetration and deliberately closed its doors to foreigners.

However, Europe's greatest impact was felt in America. While South and Central America remained locked in the grip of Spanish and Portuguese colonists, a wave of settlers flooded into North America from Europe. Before the century was out these newcomers had begun to take over the continent. The Native American peoples had no answer to their guns or their sheer numbers.

▼ *The first Thanksgiving feast in 1621 was held to celebrate the first successful harvest by the Pilgrims.*

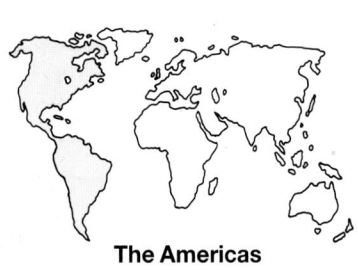

The Americas

Europe

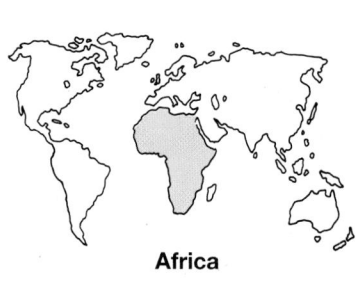

Africa

The Americas	Europe	Africa

1607 English found Virginia.
1608 Champlain establishes Quebec.

1619 First elected assembly meets in Virginia.
1620 Pilgrims land near Cape Cod.

1626 Dutch found New Amsterdam and buy Manhattan Island.
1629 Foundation of colony of Massachusetts.
1633 Colony of Connecticut founded.
1642 French establish Montreal.
1654 Portuguese drive Dutch from Brazil.
1655 English seize Jamaica from Spain.
1663 New France formed in Canada.
1664 English seize New Amsterdam.
1670 Hudson's Bay Company founded.

1682 French claim Mississippi Valley. William Penn founds Quaker colony in Pennsylvania.

1603 James VI of Scotland becomes James I of England.
1608 Protestant Union formed.
1610 Catholic League formed. Henry IV of France murdered; Louis XIII succeeds him.
1612 Gustavus Adolphus becomes king of Sweden.
1618 Defenestration of Prague begins the Thirty Years' War.
1624 Richelieu becomes chief minister of France.
1625 Charles I becomes king of England.
1628 Huguenots defeated at the siege of La Rochelle.
1642–1649 English Civil War.
1643 Louis XIV becomes king of France.
1648 Thirty Years' War ends.
1649 Charles I is executed.
1652 Anglo-Dutch Wars.
1660 Charles II is restored to the English throne.
1685 Louis XIV revokes the Edict of Nantes.
1686 League of Augsburg is formed.
1688 Glorious Revolution. William of Orange becomes king of England. War of the League of Augsburg.
1700–1721 Great Northern War.
1701–1713 War of Spanish Succession.
1707 Union of England and Scotland.

1618 English and Dutch found West African companies.

1637 Dutch drive Portuguese merchants from Gold Coast (now Ghana).
1645 Capuchin monks explore the Congo River.
1652 Dutch East India Company founds Cape Town as a supply base for Dutch ships trading with the East Indies.
1670 Alafin Ajagbo founds the Oyo empire in Nigeria.
1680 Akaba, fighter for his nation's independence, becomes king of Dahomey.
1686 France annexes Madagascar.
1687 First Huguenots settle at Cape of Good Hope.
1689 Osei Tutu founds the Asante nation.

Middle East

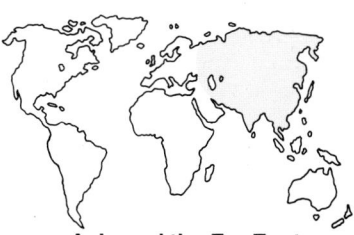

Asia and the Far East

Australasia and Pacific

1602 Holy war starts between Persia and the Ottoman empire.
1603 Ahmad I becomes ruler of the Ottoman empire.
1604 Persians defeat the Ottoman Turks at Tabriz.

1638 Ottoman Turks recover Baghdad from the Persians.
1640 Ibrahim is made ruler of the Ottoman empire.
1648 Ibrahim is deposed and murdered; his son succeeds him as Mehmet IV.
1656 Venetian fleet routs the navy of the Ottoman empire in a battle off the Dardenelles.

1683 Ottoman Turks fail to capture Vienna.
1687 Suleiman II becomes the ruler of the Ottoman empire.
1688 An earthquake destroys Smyrna in Asia Minor.
1691 Ahmet II is made ruler of the Ottoman empire.

1603 Tokugawa Ieyasu becomes shogun of Japan.
1604 The Russian settlement of Siberia begins.
1605 Jahangir succeeds his father Akbar as Mogul emperor of India.
1611 The Dutch are the only Europeans permitted to trade with Japan.
1615 The Dutch seize the Moluccas from the Portuguese.
1616 The Manchu army invades China.
1619 Dutch East India company sets up headquarters at Batavia on the island of Java.
1622 Christian missionaries are driven from Japan.
1623 Dutch massacre English merchants at Amboina in the Moluccas.
1627 Shah Jahan succeeds as emperor of India.
1637 Russian explorers make the first crossing of Siberia.
1638 Japanese put down the Shimbara uprising and slaughter Christians.
1644 Manchus found Qing dynasty in China.
1659 Aurangzeb becomes emperor of India.
1669 Aurangzeb persecutes Indian Hindus.
1690 English set up a trading post at Calcutta.

1606 Dutch sea captain Willem Jansz sights Cape York peninsula; it is the first time a European catches sight of Australia. Spaniard Luis Vaez de Torres sails through the Torres Strait and proves New Guinea is an island.
1616 Dutch captain Hartog makes first European landing on the west coast of Australia.

1622 Dutch expeditions continue to make several landings on Australia's southeast coast.

1642 Dutchman Abel Tasman is the first European to land on the islands of Tasmania and Tonga. He is also the first to sight New Zealand.

1699 William Dampier leads an English expedition along Australia's northwest coast and names the island New Britain.

The World

The 17th century was the age of the absolute ruler. In **Europe**, **India**, **China**, and **Japan**, power was increasingly concentrated in the hands of the kings, emperors, and shoguns who ruled the land. The great exception was in England where an elected, rebellious Parliament overthrew and executed the king, Charles I. Although his son, Charles II, was later invited to return, he was only granted limited powers as a monarch.

At this time, Europe spread its influence worldwide, while countries such as India and China enriched Europe with their products, art and ideas. Many thousands of Europeans went overseas to **North America** to seek a better life or to found a society where they could worship as they wished, free from the interference of a hostile government.

The 17th century also saw another kind of movement of people. The terrible trade in slaves tore millions of **Africans** from their homes and transported them across the Atlantic Ocean to toil until they died far away in an alien land.

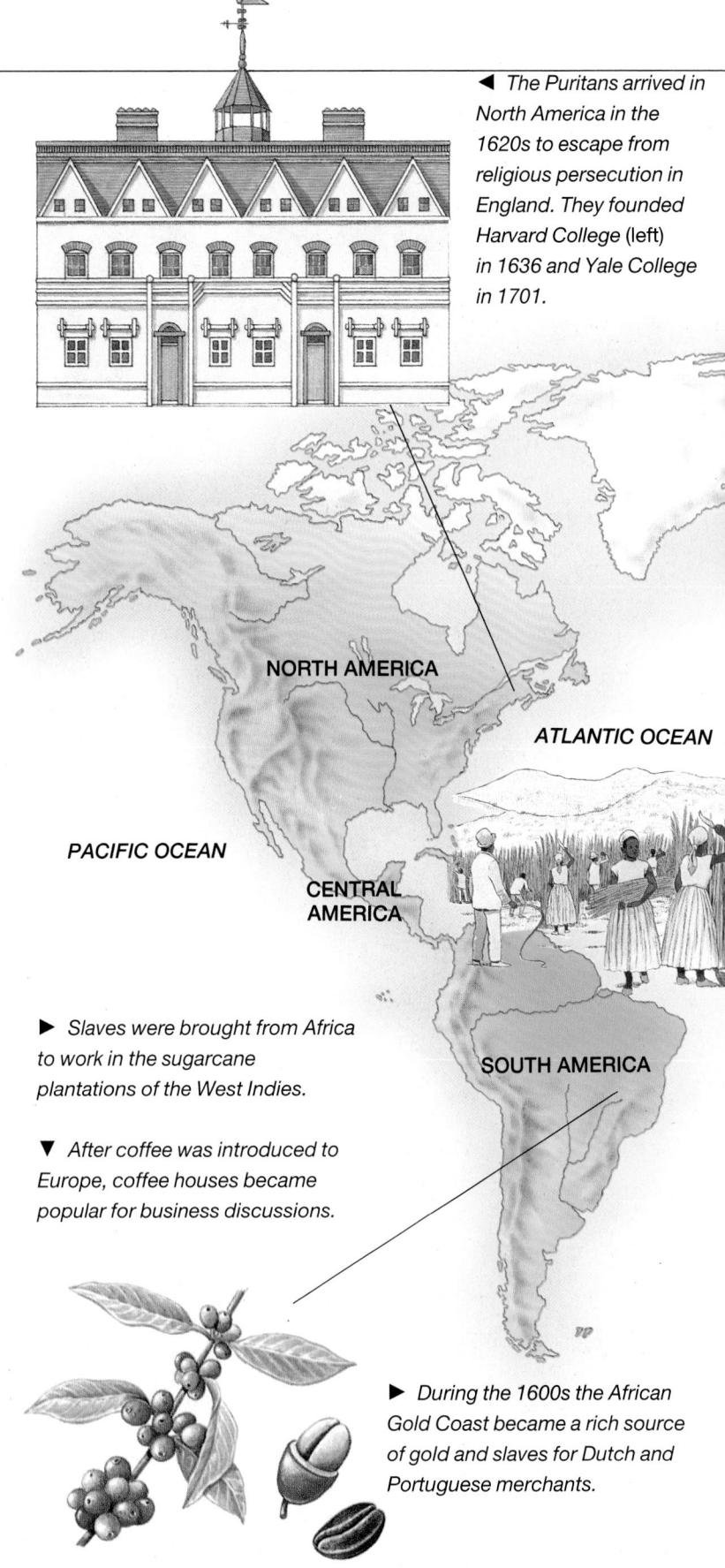

◀ The Puritans arrived in North America in the 1620s to escape from religious persecution in England. They founded Harvard College (left) in 1636 and Yale College in 1701.

NORTH AMERICA

ATLANTIC OCEAN

PACIFIC OCEAN

CENTRAL AMERICA

SOUTH AMERICA

▶ Slaves were brought from Africa to work in the sugarcane plantations of the West Indies.

▼ After coffee was introduced to Europe, coffee houses became popular for business discussions.

▶ During the 1600s the African Gold Coast became a rich source of gold and slaves for Dutch and Portuguese merchants.

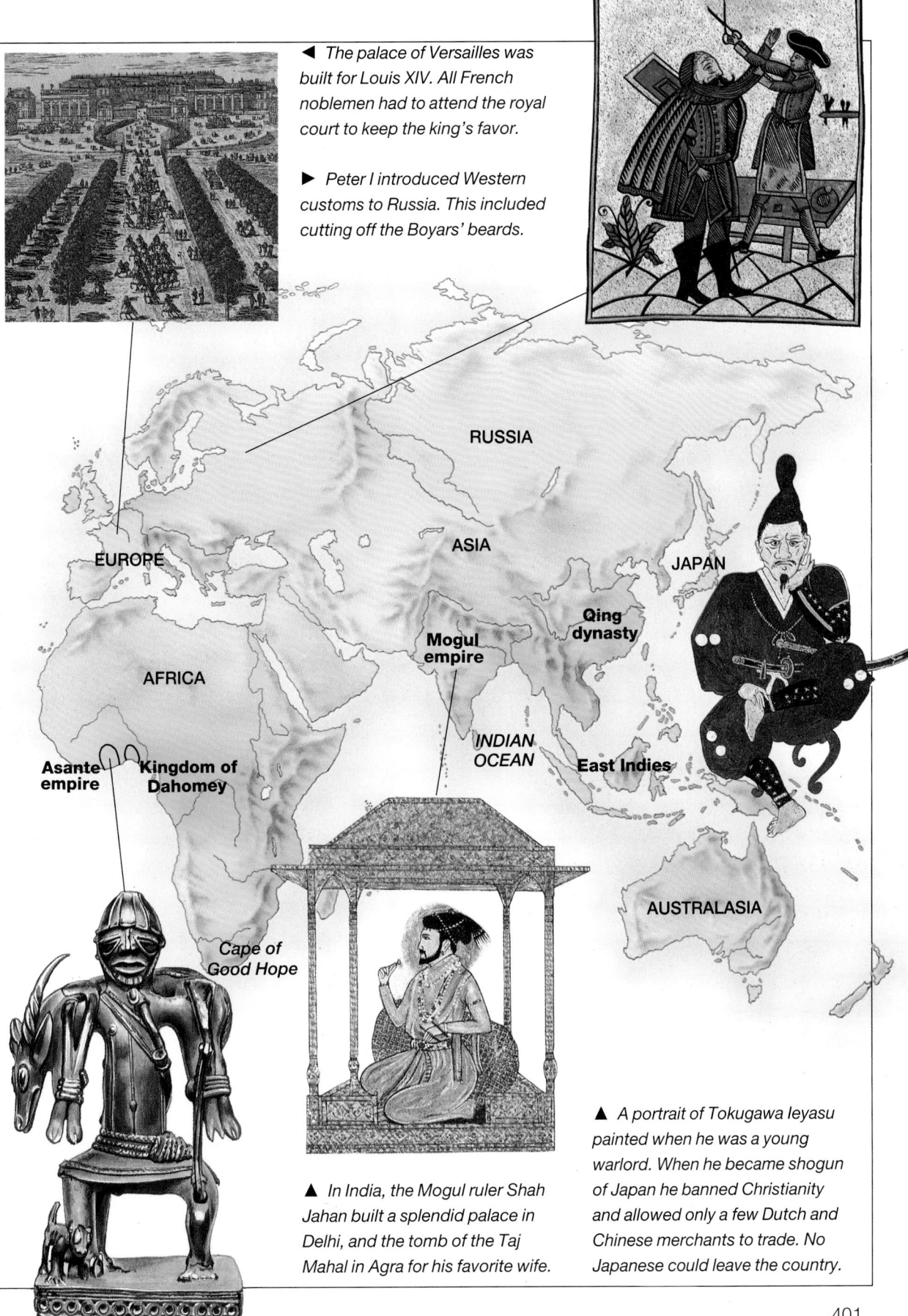

◀ The palace of Versailles was built for Louis XIV. All French noblemen had to attend the royal court to keep the king's favor.

▶ Peter I introduced Western customs to Russia. This included cutting off the Boyars' beards.

RUSSIA

ASIA

EUROPE

JAPAN

Qing dynasty

Mogul empire

AFRICA

INDIAN OCEAN

East Indies

Asante empire

Kingdom of Dahomey

Cape of Good Hope

AUSTRALASIA

▲ In India, the Mogul ruler Shah Jahan built a splendid palace in Delhi, and the tomb of the Taj Mahal in Agra for his favorite wife.

▲ A portrait of Tokugawa Ieyasu painted when he was a young warlord. When he became shogun of Japan he banned Christianity and allowed only a few Dutch and Chinese merchants to trade. No Japanese could leave the country.

401

1601 England: The Earl of Essex, attempts to organize a rebellion against the chief minister Robert Cecil. He fails and is executed.

1602 The Italian kingdom of Savoy attacks Geneva in Switzerland. Netherlands: The Dutch East India Company is formed. Persia: Shah Abbas I starts a holy war against Ottoman Turkey (to 1618). Hungary: The Counter Reformation gathers force with the persecution of Protestants in Bohemia and Hungary.

Ikebana, *the Japanese art of flower arranging, was mostly a pastime followed by men during the 17th century.*

1603 Japan: Tokugawa Ieyasu is made shogun of Japan. Ottoman empire: Ahmet I becomes ruler (to 1617). Scotland: On the death of Elizabeth I of England, James VI of Scotland becomes James I of England (to 1625). He is the first Stuart king of England. He is a firm believer in the Divine Right of Kings. Canada: The Frenchman Samuel de Champlain explores the St. Lawrence River.

1604 Russia: The Time of Troubles starts (to 1613), during which there are several rivals for the throne. The settlement of Siberia begins and the city of Tomsk is founded. France: French East India Company is founded. England: James I bans Jesuits from England. England and Spain make peace. Persia: Persians defeat Ottoman Turks at Tabriz.

Japan in Isolation

In 1603, Tokugawa Ieyasu, the head of a leading Japanese family, became shogun of Japan. He set up his government at Edo (later renamed Tokyo) and began to change what was then a small fishing village into an enormous fortress-city. From Edo he ran most of the country's affairs. Ieyasu abdicated in 1605, but he continued to control the government until he died in 1616.

During this time, contact between Japan and the outside world had grown. European merchants came to trade and Catholic priests from Spain and Portugal set up missions, converting many thousands of Japanese to Christianity.

The teachings of the new faith alarmed the Tokugawa rulers. They feared their authority might be undermined by this outside influence. When Japanese Christians were found to have joined in a revolt against oppression in 1637,

◀ *Tokugawa Ieyasu when he was a young warlord. When he became shogun, Ieyasu was the real ruler of Japan. The emperor in Kyoto had little real power.*

▲ *The Japanese tortured Christian priests by testing their faith.*

▼ *Nagasaki, where the Dutch were allowed to trade, was as far as possible from the heart of Japan.*

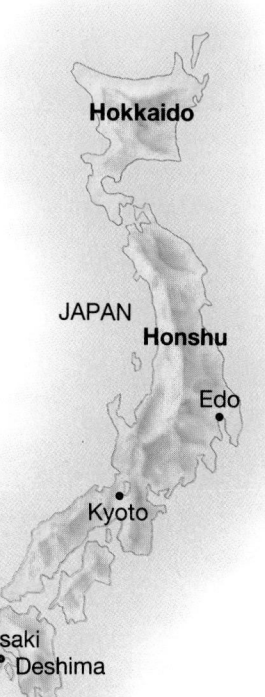

▲ *The Dutch had never tried to convert the Japanese and so were not regarded as a threat. They were allowed to send one trading ship a year to Japan and were given a tiny island, Deshima, in Nagasaki Bay to use as a trading base. Even so they were closely watched and forbidden to cross the bridge to the mainland.*

Ieyasu's grandson Iemitsu issued decrees banning the Christian religion.

The persecution of Christians continued under his successors. All priests were ordered to leave or be killed and their churches were torn down. Japanese Christians who refused to give up their religion were executed. To make sure that foreign ideas did not enter the country, Japan was sealed off from the outside world. No one was allowed to enter or leave and the penalty for doing so was death. Tokugawa rule gave Japan almost 250 years of relative peace.

The Arts

A new style of art and sculpture called Baroque, developed in western Europe during the first half of the 17th century. Painters, sculptors, and architects aimed to produce spectacular grand effects and also to represent reality. It was the age of great portrait painters such as Rubens, Rembrandt, and Van Dyke from the Netherlands, and Velázquez from Spain. Ruisdael and Hobbema from the Netherlands, Salavator Rosa from Italy, and Claude Lorraine of France were the leading landscape painters of the day.

Many new forms of music also began to appear during this period. European composers wrote the first concertos, sonatas, operas, and oratorios (a type of opera that was sung without any acting or scenery).

▲ The Night Watch *was painted by the Dutch artist Rembrandt in 1642. Other military paintings of the time portray soldiers in rigid formal poses, but Rembrandt shows them in action, assembling for duty.*

◀ *A bronze mask from the West African kingdom of Benin. Heads and masks representing gods and spirits were centerpieces in the annual ceremonies of sacrifice, chanting, and dancing.*

◀ *Lacquered objects from India, China, and Japan were highly fashionable in the 17th century, but very expensive. Craftsmen in the West produced imitations using a process called "japanning."*

▶ *Molière (1622–1673) wrote plays and ballets to entertain the court of Louis XIV of France. Best known are his comedies which laugh at human failings such as stinginess and snobbishness.*

▶ *Kabuki drama was developed in Japan in the 17th century. It combined dialogue, songs, dances, and music. Men took all the parts in the plays. Kabuki was performed on huge stages and many plays are still performed in Japan today.*

WHEN IT HAPPENED

1605 The Spanish author, Miguel de Cervantes, publishes the first part of *Don Quixote*.

1634 Flemish painter Peter Paul Rubens paints the *Adoration of the Magi*.

1658 English poet John Milton begins his epic poem *Paradise Lost*.

1677 Aphra Behn, the first known English woman dramatist, writes *The Rover*.

1678 The Puritan preacher John Bunyan publishes *Pilgrim's Progress*.

1689 The English composer Henry Purcell produces his opera *Dido and Aeneas*.

▲ David slaying Goliath *by Giovanni Bernini (1598–1680) who was the leading Italian sculptor and architect of his day. He designed and decorated churches, chapels, monuments, and tombs for eight successive popes.*

▶ *A cloisonné flask made in China in the 17th century. Cloisonné is a method of decorating metal surfaces. The design is first outlined with thin wires and the spaces between are then filled with different colored enamel.*

The Stuarts

Queen Elizabeth, the last Tudor monarch of England, died in 1603. James VI of Scotland succeeded her as James I of England. James was descended from Elizabeth's aunt, Margaret Tudor, who had married the Scottish king, James IV, in 1503. His family, the Stuarts, had ruled Scotland for more than 200 years.

Although England and Scotland now had the same king, they remained separate countries. James dreamed of uniting them as ''Great Britain'' but strong, steadfast English opposition frustrated his plans.

At first James was successful in foreign affairs. In 1604, he ended the war with Spain. Britain was at peace for the next 20 years, but in 1624 James was drawn into war on the side of his Protestant son-in-law, the German prince Frederick, Elector Palatine.

At home, James got deeply into debt. The costs of running the country were growing and James himself was a lavish spender. He was also convinced that

▲ James had his failures but his reign also saw some great triumphs. He ordered a new translation of the Bible, the Authorized Version. In the early years of his reign, William Shakespeare wrote his finest plays.

▼ In November 1605, a Catholic plot to blow up King James as he opened Parliament was discovered. The conspirators, including Guy Fawkes, were caught, tortured, and horribly put to death.

since he was God's choice as king, Parliament should obey him and grant whatever he asked for. He fell out with Parliament when his demand for more money was refused.

James was also unpopular with many of his English subjects merely because he was Scottish. They also disliked the fact that his Danish wife, Anne, became a Roman Catholic. James' son Charles succeeded him as king in 1625.

Boris Godunov wearing the traditional robes of the Russian tsars. During his reign he waged war against Poland and Sweden. His last years were marked by civil war.

▲ *Many English towns were largely rebuilt in late Tudor and early Stuart times. It was a sign of the growing prosperity of the age. But the opportunity to replan the towns completely was not taken. Instead the new houses were built following the lines of the old, narrow, winding streets. Wood was still the main building material. This meant that few towns escaped serious fires at some time during the period.*

1605 Paul V becomes pope (to 1621). England: Following the discovery of the Gunpowder Plot to blow up Parliament, Guy Fawkes and other conspirators are arrested, tried, and executed. Shakespeare writes *King Lear*. Russia: Tsar Boris Godunov dies. His successor Fyodor II is deposed and murdered. India: Jahangir becomes Mogul emperor (to 1627).

1606 England: Laws are passed against Roman Catholics. Ben Jonson writes the play *Volpone*. Russia: Basil Shuisky is made tsar (to 1610) but there are several attempts by pretenders to gain the Russian throne. Cossack and peasant uprisings start (to 1608). Turkey: Treaty of Zsitva-Torok signed with Austrians. Austrians abandon Transylvania. The Dutch sea captain Willem Jansz is the first European to sight Australia.

1607 England: Parliament rejects proposals for union between England and Scotland. North America: English colony of Virginia is founded at Jamestown (named after King James I of England) by John Smith. Henry Hudson begins a voyage of discovery to what is now eastern Greenland and the Hudson River.

1608 Canada: French explorer Samuel de Champlain founds the settlement of Quebec on the St. Lawrence River.
 Netherlands: Hans Lippershey invents the telescope. The first checks are used for money transactions.

1609 The Twelve Years' Truce ends fighting between the Netherlands and Spain. Bavaria: The Catholic League, led by King Maximilian, is formed in opposition to the Protestant Union. Germany: Johannes Kepler publishes his first two laws of planetary motion. Germany: The first weekly newspaper is published in Augsburg. North America: Henry Hudson sails up the river near Manhattan Island (the Hudson) and finds that it does not lead to the Orient.

The arms of the Hudson's Bay Company set up in 1670 to establish a fur trade in Canada.

1610 England: Ben Jonson becomes the unofficial Poet Laureate. Italy: The first observations of the stars using a telescope are made by Galileo. Germany: Frederick V becomes Elector Palatine (to 1623). France: Henry IV is assassinated and is succeeded by Louis XIII (to 1643). Canada: Henry Hudson discovers Hudson Bay. Netherlands: Tea is first shipped to Europe by the Dutch East India Company. Russia: Tsar Basil Shuisky is deposed and the throne is offered to Vladislav, son of the King of Poland.

Colonies in America

For a century after Columbus arrived in 1492, the peoples of Europe regarded North America merely as an obstacle that prevented ships from sailing westward to trade with the countries of the East. Not until the early 17th century did Europeans begin to realize that the new lands might be valuable in themselves.

The first successful English colony in North America was established at Jamestown, Virginia, in 1607. Disease, hunger, and battles with the Native Americans almost wiped out the settlement, but it survived under the leadership of Captain John Smith. In 1612, John Rolfe introduced tobacco-growing to the settlers. The crop earned them money and they prospered. As the demand for tobacco increased, so the tobacco growers needed more land and took it from the local people. This struggle for land led to bitter wars between the colonists and the Native

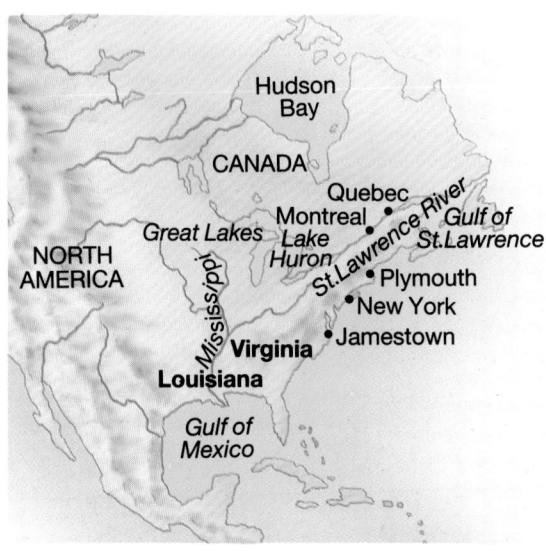

▲ *The place names of modern northeast America show that most of the successful early European settlers came from either England or France.*

North Americans around them.

In 1620, a ship called the *Mayflower* sailed from Plymouth in England bound for North America. Its 102 passengers were Puritans. English laws did not allow them to follow their religion freely, so they decided to risk the perilous journey to find a new land where they could worship in peace. They landed near Cape Cod and founded a small settlement there which they named Plymouth.

Plymouth was the first successful settlement in New England and it became the origin of the United States.

▲ *The Pilgrims, the settlers from the* Mayflower, *landed in America in November. Establishing settlements meant land had to be cleared for building, even in the bitter cold. The first settlers knew nothing about living in this new wilderness. Food ran short and many died from disease and exposure. Nearly half of them died that winter and only 54 were still alive by the following spring.*

TOBACCO

By the early 17th century, tobacco smoking had become popular in Europe. It was easy to grow and did not require many workers. This, and the fact that the climate of Virginia suited it, made tobacco the ideal crop for the colonists to grow for export.

THANKSGIVING DAY

In November 1621 the Pilgrims gave thanks for the first successful harvest in their new home. The local Wampanoag Indians joined in. Their advice on farming and fishing had helped save the colony. This first Thanksgiving Day is now commemorated every year all over North America.

FUR TRADING

During the 17th century there was a huge demand for wild animal furs and skins throughout Europe. Beaver skins fetched particularly high prices because beaver-skin hats were then in fashion. Native Americans were skilled hunters and trappers. They readily exchanged animal pelts for European goods such as guns, beads, or whiskey.

French explorers had visited North America many years before the English began to settle in New England and Virginia. In 1535, a French sea captain, Jacques Cartier had sailed into the Gulf of St. Lawrence and claimed the land around it for France. The Huron Indian word for village, "kanata," which the French pronounced "Canada," eventually became the name for the land north of the St. Lawrence River.

Later Cartier explored the St. Lawrence River as far as where Quebec now stands and onward to the site of present-day Montreal city. He attempted to found a colony at Montreal but failed.

The first successful French settlement in Canada was made in 1608 by Samuel de Champlain at Quebec. Champlain devoted his life to creating a French empire in Canada. He called it "New

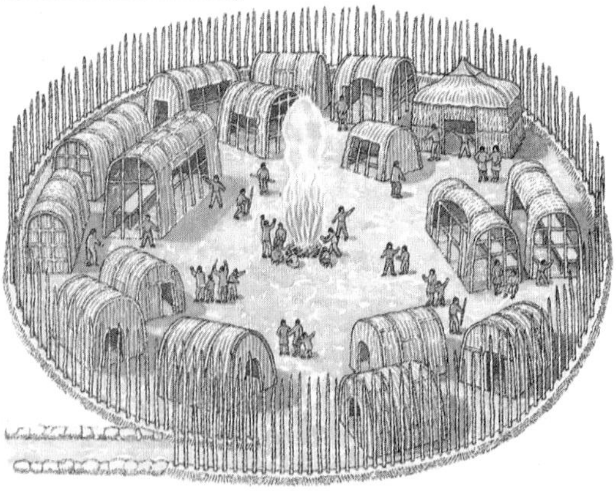

◄ *Many parts of North America were already well populated before the Europeans arrived there. Customs and ways of life differed greatly from place to place. Both the French and English took detailed accounts of the Native North Americans they encountered.*

◄ *Father Jacques Marquette was chosen to explore the interior of North America because he spoke several Indian languages.*

Champlain

Samuel de Champlain (1567–1635) made 11 journeys of exploration into Canada, traveling beyond the St. Lawrence River to the Great Lakes as far as Lake Huron. He became governor of the French colony of Quebec and made it a base for exploring the Canadian interior. He later died there.

La Salle

Frenchman René Robert Cavelier, Sieur de La Salle (1643–1687), arrived in Canada in 1666 and made a fortune as a fur trader and farmer in Montreal. Native North Americans taught him how to survive in the wilderness; these skills helped him to explore the length of the Mississippi River.

1611 England: The Authorized Version or King James Bible is published. Ireland: The Plantation of Ulster begins as English and Scottish colonists settle there. Sweden: Gustavus Adolphus becomes king (to 1632). Japan: Dutch merchants are permitted to trade with Japanese. Italy: Marco de Dominis publishes the first scientific explanation of a rainbow.

1612 Holy Roman Empire: Matthias, King of Bohemia is elected emperor (to 1619). North America: Dutch merchants begin fur-trading on Manhattan Island. Settlers plant tobacco in Virginia. Germany: The decimal point is used for the first time in mathematics. Netherlands: The Amsterdam Stock Exchange opens.

1613 Russia: Michael Romanov becomes tsar (to 1645) and founds the Romanov dynasty (to 1917). India: Mogul emperor Jahangir allows English merchants to settle at Seurat. The Ottoman Turks invade Hungary.

1614 France: An advisory body called the Estates-General is summoned to curb the powers of the nobility. They do not meet again until 1789, the outbreak of the French Revolution. England: James I dissolves the "Addled Parliament," which has failed to pass any legislation. North America: Virginian colonist John Rolfe marries Pocahontas, a Native North American princess.

France" and Quebec became its capital. French lands in North America grew hugely in the later half of the 17th century. In 1673, Father Jacques Marquette and Louis Jolliet explored the northern reaches of the Mississippi River. Later the explorer La Salle sailed down the Mississippi to the Gulf of Mexico and claimed the entire Mississippi Valley for France. He called the territory "Louisiana" in honor of the then French king, Louis XIV.

Unlike the English, who arrived in North America intending to settle permanently, the French came for wild animal furs and to convert native Americans to Christianity. Later explorers, thinking they were in uncharted territory, would often find French-Canadian fur trappers already trading there. However, French colonization lagged behind the English.

James I was portrayed on the seal of the Virginia Company, the first English trading company in North America.

Buildings

Buildings and works of art produced in the same area at the same time usually have many features in common. Like the art of the 17th century, the architecture which developed in western Europe is called Baroque. Louis XIV's palace at Versailles in France, the churches of Bernini and Borromini in Italy, and St. Paul's Cathedral in London, all had spectacular effects.

Cities such as London and Paris were largely rebuilt. The new buildings consisted mainly of brick or stone and were more permanent and comfortable than their wooden predecessors. Fireplaces and chimneys replaced the often dangerous braziers or open hearths that had been used before.

▶ A row of houses built in Amsterdam mid-17th century. They are constructed of brick and decorated with finely carved stonework. Since good building land was scarce in Amsterdam, the city authorities declared that building plots should be long, narrow strips not more than 30 feet (10m) wide. These measurements did not allow for any space to be left around each house, so even the most expensive dwellings were joined together in rows.

◀ Muhammad Aga built this mosque in Istanbul for Sultan Ahmet I of Turkey. It was finished in 1616. Under the vast dome, the interior is covered with patterned tiles from which it gets its name, the Blue Mosque.

▼ The William and Mary College in Williamsburg, Virginia was founded at the end of the 17th century. Williamsburg was specially built as the state capital of Virginia.

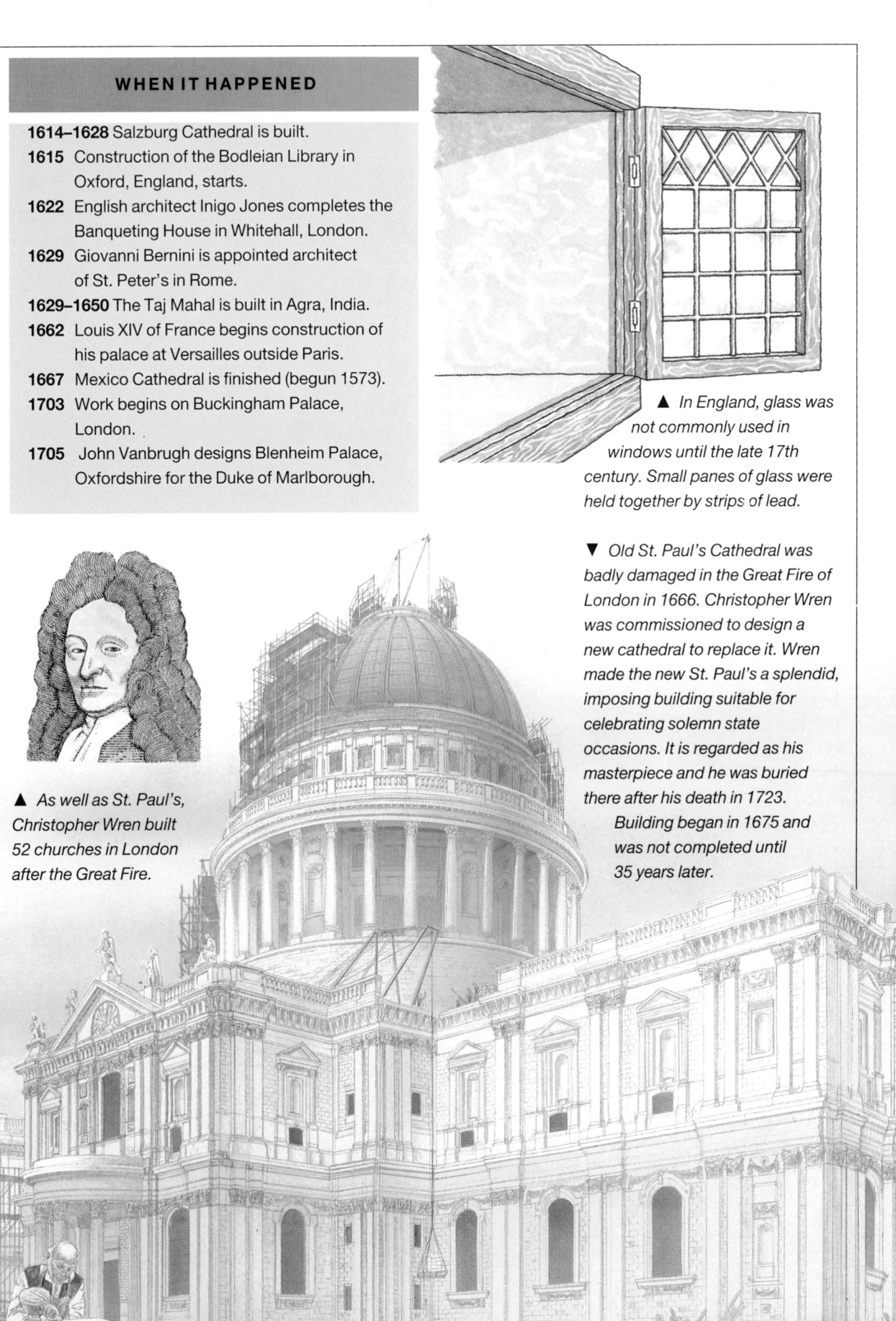

▲ In England, glass was not commonly used in windows until the late 17th century. Small panes of glass were held together by strips of lead.

▼ Old St. Paul's Cathedral was badly damaged in the Great Fire of London in 1666. Christopher Wren was commissioned to design a new cathedral to replace it. Wren made the new St. Paul's a splendid, imposing building suitable for celebrating solemn state occasions. It is regarded as his masterpiece and he was buried there after his death in 1723.

Building began in 1675 and was not completed until 35 years later.

▲ As well as St. Paul's, Christopher Wren built 52 churches in London after the Great Fire.

1615 The peoples north of China combine to form powerful military organizations, known as Manchus. East Indies: The Dutch seize the Moluccas (Spice Islands) from the Portuguese.

1616 Dutch navigator Willem Schouten rounds Cape Horn, at the tip of South America. The Manchu army invades China. England: British East India Company starts to trade with Persia (Iran). Turkey: The Blue Mosque in Istanbul is completed.

1617 England: Sir Walter Raleigh leads an expedition to find the mythical land of El Dorado in South America. The Peace of Stolbovo ends war between Russia and Sweden. Sweden gains Karelia.

Sir Walter Raleigh was an English explorer who sent an expedition to America in 1584 and set up an English colony in Virginia. He introduced tobacco and potatoes into Britain from America.

1618 Bohemia: After Bohemian nationalists throw Catholic officials out of a window in Prague Castle, the Thirty Years' War begins (to 1648). England: Sir Walter Raleigh returns from his expedition and is executed for treason. The English West African Company is founded. Netherlands: Dutch West African Company begins trading.

1619 North America: The first elected assembly meets at Jamestown, Virginia. African slaves arrive to work on the first tobacco plantations. Protestant Bohemians depose Emperor Ferdinand II and elect Frederick V, Elector Palatine, as Holy Roman emperor. East Indies: Dutch East India Company makes Batavia (now Djakarta) its headquarters.

Gustavus Adolphus

Gustavus Adolphus was born in 1594. He became king of Sweden in 1611, when only 17 years old, but he was to be Sweden's greatest king.

Gustavus was the marvel of Europe. He was a devout Protestant and in an age when most princes learned little more than dancing and royal manners, he spoke German, Latin, Dutch, French, and Italian and could understand several other languages.

Sweden's frontline army was only 40,000 strong but Gustavus made it the best in Europe and soon showed his skill as a general. By 1629, he had defeated in succession the hostile armies of Denmark, Russia, and Poland, and made Sweden the leading military power of northern Europe.

But across the Baltic Sea, his fellow Protestant princes in Germany were facing defeat in the Thirty Years' War (*see* pages 416–417) by the armies of the Catholic emperor Ferdinand II of Austria.

If Germany became Catholic, Sweden would be isolated. Gustavus saw the danger clearly and declared war on Ferdinand. In July 1630, he landed an army on the German coast and advanced inland. At Breitenfeld near Leipzig, in September 1631, the Swedish force utterly defeated the emperor's army. The following spring, Gustavus moved south. He occupied Munich and advanced against Ferdinand's capital at Vienna.

The two armies clashed at Lützen. After a day-long battle the emperor's forces retreated in disorder. Gustavus himself did not survive. He died leading his men in a charge against the enemy.

▲ As well as creating a strong army, Gustavus also built a powerful and efficient fleet and made Sweden the strongest naval power in the Baltic Sea. Through military conquest, Sweden gained most of Finland from Russia. Tragically, his flagship the Vasa, *shown here, capsized and sank on its maiden voyage in 1628.*

▼ *Gustavus, called the Lion of the North, was a brave and inspiring leader. He always fought at the head of his men. After he died his heart was taken back to Stockholm.*

The Thirty Years' War

In 1618, the Protestant nobles of Bohemia rose in revolt against their ruler, the Catholic Ferdinand II of Austria, the Holy Roman emperor. In his place they appointed Frederick, Elector Palatine, the foremost Protestant prince of Germany.

In order to recover his throne, Ferdinand immediately declared war on his rebellious subjects. In 1619, the German rulers who elected the Holy Roman emperor met at Prague. They deposed Ferdinand and made Frederick emperor in his place. The outcome was a series of wars which eventually involved most of Europe for the next thirty years.

The first war ended in complete victory for Ferdinand. The Protestant army was defeated near Prague. Frederick fled and

▲ In 1618, the Protestant nobles of Bohemia met at Prague castle to protest against Ferdinand's order that Protestant churches should be pulled down. Three officials sent to the meeting by the emperor were seized and thrown out of the window. This violent action is known as the "Defenestration of Prague."

Spanish
Austrian
Prussian
Swedish
— **Holy Roman Empire**

SWEDEN

North Sea

Baltic Sea

DENMARK

ENGLAND

Magdeburg

NETHERLANDS

Breitenfeld

POLAND

Lützen

BOHEMIA

FRANCE

Prague

Vienna

Munich

AUSTRIA

Bavaria

ITALY

Ottoman empire

PORTUGAL

SPAIN

•Rome

Mediterranean Sea

◄ The Treaty of Westphalia ended the Thirty Years' War in 1648. It drew up a map of Europe which lasted for more than 100 years. The war ruined Germany. The treaty split it into more than 300 states. France became the dominant power in Europe.

► The matchlock musket the Austrians used was slow to fire and had to be supported on a forked rest because it was so heavy. Gustavus Adolphus introduced an improved version. He halved the weight and adopted cartridges, which doubled the rate of fire to a shot a minute.

a Catholic prince, Maximilian of Bavaria, was appointed in his place.

The struggle then moved northward. Led by Count Wallenstein, the emperor's army defeated the Danes and overran northern Germany. It seemed that nothing could stop Ferdinand from forcing the whole of Germany to become Catholic until, in 1630, Gustavus Adolphus of Sweden entered the war on the Protestant side. He soundly defeated the Catholic forces in battles at Breitenfeld and Lützen.

But in 1635 the war swung in Austria's favor when the Protestant princes of Germany gave up the struggle. France entered the conflict and, after a dozen years of war, forced the new emperor Ferdinand III to ask for peace.

1620 North America: The Pilgrims reach Cape Cod, Massachusetts in the *Mayflower* and found Plymouth colony. Bohemia: The Holy Roman emperor Frederick V is defeated by Maximilian of Bavaria in the battle of the White Mountain near Prague. Poland: War begins with Sweden. Italy: Giovanni Bernini begins his finest sculptures, including *Apollo and Daphne*.

1621 Netherlands: Dutch West India Company is founded. Canada: An English attempt to colonize Newfoundland and Nova Scotia fails. Spain: Philip IV becomes king (to 1665). Netherlands: 12-year truce with Spain ends; war is resumed. Gregory XV becomes pope (to 1623).

The gunpowder for muskets was carrried separately from the shot. Some powder bottles were decorated, such as this highly carved wooden powder bottle showing a hunting scene.

1622 Spain: After the Spaniards occupy the Valtelline Pass, war with France follows. Thirty Years' War: German Protestant forces are defeated in the battles of Wimpfen and Rochst. Japan: Christian missionaries are savagely persecuted (to 1624).

1623 East Indies: Dutch massacre English merchants at Amboina. England: Duke of Buckingham and Charles, Prince of Wales, unsuccessfully attempt to negotiate a marriage treaty with Spain. Papal states: Urban VIII becomes pope (to 1644). North America: Dutch begin trading on the Hudson River. Colonists at New Plymouth establish the system of trial by 12-man jury.

417

1624 France: Cardinal Richelieu is made first minister (to 1642). France and England become allies. Prototype submarine tried out on the Thames River by Dutch scientist Cornelius Drebbel. North America: Virginia becomes a crown colony. First English settlers arrive in West Indies.

The state flag of France (1640–1790) was the forerunner of the Tricolor we know today.

1625 England: Charles I is crowned king (to 1649). He marries Henrietta Maria, sister of Louis XIII of France and also dissolves Parliament for refusing to vote him money. First passenger coaches for hire appear in London, called "hackney" carriages. Thirty Years' War: Denmark enters the war on the side of the Protestants. West Indies: Barbados is settled by the English. North America: Dutch found New Amsterdam (now New York) as a trading post.

1626 Germany: Catholic armies under Count Wallenstein defeat Protestants at Dessau, Germany. Italy: Physician Santorio Santorio measures the temperature of the human body for the first time with a thermometer.

1627 France: Government forces led by Richelieu besiege the Huguenot port of La Rochelle. An English attempt to relieve La Rochelle fails. Germany: Kepler compiles tables giving the positions of 1,005 stars. Thirty Years' War: Count Wallenstein's victories continue with the occupation of Silesia. India: Shah Jahan becomes emperor (to 1658).

France and Richelieu

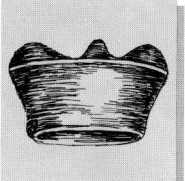

In 1610, Henry IV of France was assassinated by a fanatical monk. He was succeeded by Louis XIII, his nine-year-old son. When he took power as king, Louis appointed as his chief minister the man who was to make France the leading nation in Europe. His name was Cardinal Richelieu.

Richelieu's one ambition was to make France great. To achieve it he destroyed all rivals to his power at home and followed an aggressive policy abroad. In 1628, he dealt with the troublesome French Protestants, the Huguenots, by capturing their stronghold of La Rochelle. After this they had no power to cause him any further trouble.

Next, Richelieu destroyed the power of the noble families of France. Any suspicious activity was reported to him by his spies. All who plotted against him risked imprisonment or death.

Louis XIII

1601 Born.
1610 Becomes king.
1615 Marries Anne of Austria.
1617 Overthrows his mother's regency.
1624 Appoints Richelieu as chief minister.
1643 Dies.

Marie de Medici

Louis XIII was a child when he became king and too young to govern. His mother, Marie de Medici (c. 1573–1642), ruled France as Regent. She clung to power after Louis had grown up, but was imprisoned.

◀ *Richelieu personally oversaw the defeat of his Protestant enemies the Huguenots, who had for a long time resisted the king's power. For over a year they were besieged in the Atlantic port of La Rochelle. Richelieu supervised the construction of a breakwater (a wall) across the mouth of the harbor. This meant that British ships could not bring in supplies of food and goods. The starving Huguenots were forced to surrender in 1628. Richelieu went on to destroy the last Huguenot refuge at Montauban. The political and military privileges of the Huguenots were over.*

Abroad, Austria and Spain were the main threats to France. Members of the Habsburg family ruled both countries and, if they were to combine, France would face an overwhelming attack on two fronts at the same time. Richelieu's aim was therefore to weaken and divide the Habsburg powers.

By 1631, in the course of the Thirty Years' War, Habsburg Austria had overrun most of Germany and threatened to dominate Europe. To weaken Austria, Richelieu paid the Swedes, the Dutch, and the Danes to support their armies in war against their common enemies, the Habsburgs.

In 1635, France declared war on Spain. The fighting went on until 1648 and outlasted Richelieu. He died in 1642, but as he would have wished, by the end of the war the French armies had become the finest in Europe.

Richelieu

Armande Jean du Plessis, Duke of Richelieu (1585–1642) was made a cardinal in 1622 and ruled France as the king's chief minister from 1624 until 1642. He was hated for his harsh rule and heavy taxes.

INTENDANTS

Intendants were royal officials who made tours of inspection around the country on behalf of the king. In the 1630s, Richelieu gave them wider powers as a means of uncovering and crushing opposition to his rule. They acted as his spies.

The Intendants supervised taxation, the local police, and the courts of law. They had the authority to try and sentence people on the spot.

Communications

Communication of all kinds improved during the 17th century. Travel overland became more reliable, speedier, and more comfortable. By the late 1600s horse-drawn coaches ran between major towns. A traveler could cover up to 40 miles (65 km) a day by coach.

Heavy goods were transported by ship around the coasts and inland by rivers or canals. Letters were carried over short distances by couriers on foot and by relays of post-horses on longer journeys. Postal services across western Europe became more reliable. Regular and punctual correspondence by scholars and businessmen began to be possible, which was an immense benefit to both learning and trade.

▲ *Sedan chairs were available for hire in England to carry people through muddy city streets.*

◄ *By the late 17th century, coffee houses, first introduced by the Turks, were to be found in most of the cities of Europe and in North America. Politicians, businessmen, and people of wealth and influence met there to do business and read the newspapers. They also discussed literature, theater, and affairs of the day.*

◀ *An elderly merchant ship called the Mayflower was converted to carry settlers to North America in 1620. The 102 passengers and the crew made the 65-day voyage across the Atlantic in a ship only three yards longer than a modern tennis court. The living space for each person was the size of a single bed.*

▶ *Town and city authorities were responsible for keeping people informed. A roll on the drum brought the citizens out to hear the town crier read the latest news.*

◀ *Newspapers began in the 17th century. Among the first to appear was the Antwerp Gazette which was just a single sheet.*

The Decline of Spain

When Philip III became king of Spain in 1598, his country was bankrupt. The Spanish army was outdated and the government corrupt and incompetent. Yet Spain's empire was still the largest in the world, consisting of most of South and Central America and settlements throughout Asia and Africa.

Philip had no interest in government and Spain was run by his ministers. The first of these, the Duke of Lerma, used his position to make himself immensely rich. His greatest mistake was to expel the Moriscos, descendants of the Moors who had once ruled Spain, on the grounds that they were plotting against the government. The Moriscos were extremely hard-working and Spain could ill afford to lose them. More powerful than the king or his ministers, however, was the Roman Catholic Church. Through the Inquisition (*see* page 328–329) it supervised and controlled

CERVANTES

Much Spanish writing of this period reflects the pursuit of unobtainable ideals. The most famous author in Spain at the time was Miguel de Cervantes (1547–1616). His novel *Don Quixote*, which was published in two parts in 1605 and 1615, tells the story of a foolish landowner who sees himself as a brave knight and has a series of amusing adventures with his "squire," the peasant Sancho Panza.

THE HABSBURGS

The Spanish Habsburg kings may have died out because marriages were always arranged within their own family. Six of Charles II's great-grandparents were Habsburgs. Charles II was the last Spanish Hapsburg king.

▲ *Velázquez was the official court painter to Philip IV. His many portraits of the royal family included this painting of the seven-year-old Prince Balthasar Carlos.*

every aspect of Spanish life.

In 1621, Philip was succeeded by his son Philip IV. His reign was disastrous. Supporting the Catholic cause in the Thirty Years' War and wars with France all proved very costly. By now the flow of treasures from America had dwindled. At home a revolt in Catalonia plunged Spain further into debt. In December 1640, a mass rising in Portugal ended the union with Spain. Philip IV was followed in 1665 by his four-year-old son, Charles II. Charles was the last Habsburg king of Spain. Failing to produce an heir, he was succeeded by Philip of Anjou, the grandson of Louis XIV of France.

◄ *Wealth from the New World was not only spent on wars. Philip II built his palace at El Escorial at the end of the 16th century. Its library, shown here, housed his collection of Greek, Latin, and Arabic manuscripts.*

1628 France: Huguenots surrender at La Rochelle. Their political power is destroyed. Bohemia: A new constitution confirms hereditary rule of the Habsburg family. Thirty Years' War: Catholic forces under Counts Tilly and Wallenstein subdue most of Protestant Germany. England: Charles I accepts the Petition of Right, which states Parliament's rights and grievances, forbids taxation without Parliament's agreement and arrest without cause. In return Charles receives a grant of money to help with wars against France and Spain. Oliver Cromwell is elected for the first time as Member of Parliament. Physician William Harvey demonstrates how blood circulates around the human body.

1629 England: Charles I dissolves Parliament and rules without it until 1640. Peace is agreed with France. Thirty Years' War: The Treaty of Lübeck is made between Ferdinand II, the Holy Roman Emperor, and Christian IV of Denmark. Ferdinand issues the Edict of Restitution which entitles Catholic churches to reclaim lands lost to Protestants. North America: Colony of Massachusetts is founded. Italy: Bernini is appointed architect to St. Peter's, Rome. India: Shah Jahan orders the building of the Taj Mahal in memory of his wife Mumtaz Mahal.

An intricately engraved knife bearing the coat of arms of its owner. Knives were still commonly used in 17th century warfare.

1630 England: Peace treaty signed with France and Spain. Thirty Years' War: Gustavus Adolphus of Sweden enters the war against Ferdinand II. North America: Large numbers of English colonists settle in Massachusetts; by 1642 there are about 16,000. South America: Dutch colonists invade Brazil.

1631 Thirty Years' War: The German city of Magdeburg is sacked by Catholic forces under Count Tilly. But at the battle of Breitenfeld near Leipzig, Swedish and Saxon forces defeat Tilly. North America: Dutch found a settlement on the Delaware River. West Indies: English start to colonize the Leeward Islands. England: William Oughtred, a mathematician, suggests the symbol x should be used for multiplication.

1632 Thirty Years' War: The Swedish army wins battle of Lützen in Germany but King Gustavus Adolphus is killed in the action. England: Flemish artist Anthony van Dyck is appointed painter to the court of Charles I. North America: A royal charter is issued for Maryland, named in honor of Henrietta Maria, the wife of Charles I.

1633 Italy: The Inquisition forces Galileo to deny the theory that the Earth goes around the Sun. India: The English establish their first trading post in Bengal. England: A mass trial of witches takes place in Lancashire. Scotland: Charles I of England is crowned king of Scotland in Edinburgh.

1634 Thirty Years' War: The Swedes are defeated at the battle of Nordlingen. Germany: The first Passion play (about the life of Christ from the Last Supper to his death on the Cross) is performed to mark the end of the plague.

Ships previously used for trading purposes were also put to use during times of trouble and converted into warships. This one was part of the Dutch East India Company's fleet.

East India Companies

In 1600, the English East India Company was formed in London. Its purpose was to unite the English merchants doing business in Southeast Asia. There was cutthroat competition for trade in this area which had first been controlled by the Spaniards and the Portuguese. In the 17th century the contest for trade with the East was among the Dutch, English, and French.

▲ *During the 17th century many European travelers visited India. Through them knowledge of the history and culture of India began to reach Europe.*

The Netherlands followed England and set up the Dutch East India Company at Batavia on the island of Java in 1602. The French formed their own East India company later, in 1664. These organizations became immensely powerful. Trading was only one of their activities. They armed their ships to fight at sea and maintained private armies. The East India companies set up military as well as trading bases and made treaties with local rulers around them. They waged war on the nations around them and on each other. In many ways the East India Companies behaved as

▶ By the beginning of the 17th century, France, the Netherlands, and England had joined Spain and Portugal in the race to build empires overseas. The map shows their colonies in 1650. European nations were prepared to fight to keep the trade with their colonies to themselves. The wars between England and the Netherlands in the mid-17th century were the first to be fought for trade rather than territory.

independent states in their own right.

The English lost the contest to control the spice trade of the East Indies to the Dutch. India then became the center of their activities. The Mogul rulers of India had little interest in foreign trade and gave trading rights to foreign merchants. By 1700, England had sole trading rights with a number of key ports, notably Calcutta, Madras, and Bombay.

▲ In India, the English East India Company employed local women to make cotton cloth especially for export.

◀ The English colony of Madras was a major port for shipping cotton goods overseas. It was also the center of a region noted for making cloth. The weavers of Madras specialized in cloth printed with brightly colored designs and scenes from Indian life.

The Dutch Empire

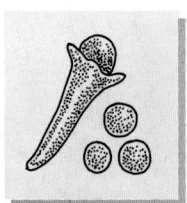

By the early 17th century the Dutch had taken the spice islands of the Moluccas from the Portuguese (*see* pages 352–353) and founded an empire in the East Indies. In 1602, they formed the Dutch East India Company to unite all the Netherlands merchants engaged in the spice trade.

In 1619, the company established its headquarters at Batavia (Djakarta) on the island of Java. The company maintained an army and a powerful fleet. With their aid it drove the English and the Portuguese out of the East Indies and seized Ceylon (now Sri Lanka), Malacca, and several ports in India. The company even set up a trading post in Japan, the only Europeans allowed to do so. In 1652, the Dutch occupied the Cape of Good Hope on the southern tip of

Stuyvesant

Peter Stuyvesant was the harsh governor of the New Netherland colony from 1647 to 1664. He was hated both by the Native Americans and the colonists themselves. In 1664, the colonists surrendered gladly to a small English fleet without fighting.

▶ A servant holds a vast sunshade over a Dutch merchant and his wife. In the background is the bay of Batavia (Djarkata) in the East Indies. The 1600s were a golden age for the Netherlands. Their merchant fleet tripled in 50 years and Dutch ships supplied half the world's shipping. They enjoyed the highest standard of living in the world. Dutch artists produced many fine works of art during this period.

▼ Spices were prized for the strong flavors they gave to food. Many grew in the East Indies.

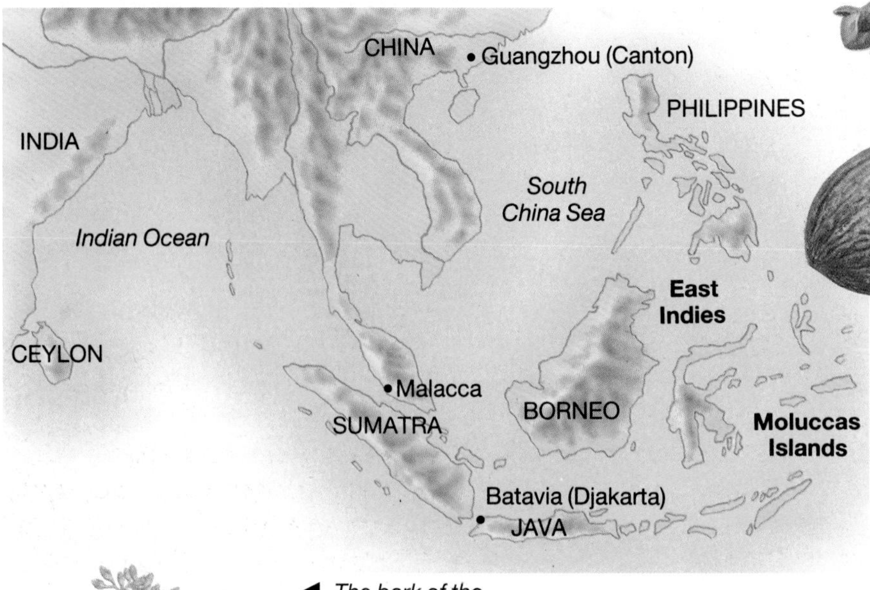

▲ Cloves (above) were used to flavor meat and nutmeg (left) puddings.

Map labels: CHINA • Guangzhou (Canton), PHILIPPINES, INDIA, South China Sea, Indian Ocean, East Indies, CEYLON, •Malacca, SUMATRA, BORNEO, Moluccas Islands, Batavia (Djakarta) • JAVA

◀ The bark of the cinnamon plant was used in candies and jams.

▶ Mace, from the outer covering of the nutmeg, was used in pickles.

▲ Pepper, grown in India and the East Indies, was used to season food and flavor soups.

Africa. From there Dutch ships were able to take the shortest route to the East Indies, straight across the Indian Ocean.

The huge merchant fleet of the Netherlands was also busy elsewhere. In 1621, the Dutch West India Company was founded across the Atlantic and by 1623, 800 Dutch ships were engaged in the Caribbean, trading in sugar, tobacco, animal hides, and slaves. The company established a colony in Guiana, captured Curaçao and other islands off the Venezuelan coast and, for a while, controlled northeastern Brazil.

In North America, the company founded the colony of New Netherland along the Hudson River in 1624.

NEW AMSTERDAM

In 1625, the Dutch colonists of New Netherland built a trading post on Manhattan Island in the Hudson River and called it Fort Amsterdam. Later it became New Amsterdam. When the English captured it in 1664 they renamed it New York.

1635 Bohemia: Ferdinand II makes peace with Saxony and the Treaty of Prague is signed. It is accepted by most Protestant princes. France: War breaks out with Spain (to 1648). Richelieu sets up the French Academy to maintain the standards of the French language. West Indies: The English occupy the Virgin Islands and the French establish a settlement in Martinique. China: The Dutch occupy Formosa (now Taiwan).

1636 Manchuria: The Manchus found the Qing dynasty and establish their capital at Mukden. The Dutch settle Ceylon (now Sri Lanka). France: Tea appears for the first time in Paris. North America: John Harvard founds the first American university at Cambridge, Massachusetts.

The cultivation of tulips became a boom industry in the Netherlands in the 1700s.

1637 Russian explorers make the first crossing of Siberia and reach the Pacific Ocean. Bohemia: Ferdinand III becomes Holy Roman emperor (to 1657). Africa: The Dutch expel last Portuguese merchants from the Gold Coast (now Ghana). China: English merchants establish base at Canton (Guangzhou). France: Pierre Corneille's play *Le Cid*, the earliest classical tragedy in French, is first performed.

Food and Farming

In 17th century Europe, all but the rich depended on the food produced in their own neighborhood. The rich ate too much. The poor ate too little and they often starved if harvests were bad.

Although farming methods changed slowly, more food was being produced in Europe. The extra food came from additional land. Old pastureland was fenced off and forests were cut down. Marshes were drained and the Dutch reclaimed thousands of acres from the sea which became farmland.

At first the colonists in North America just tried to produce enough food to stay alive. But land was plentiful and as time went by, they grew crops and raised livestock for export.

▲ In 1652, the Dutch East India Company founded a colony at the Cape of Good Hope in South Africa. Here their ships could take on supplies and fresh food on the long voyage to the East Indies. The land was very fertile and grapes for making wine were introduced from Europe.

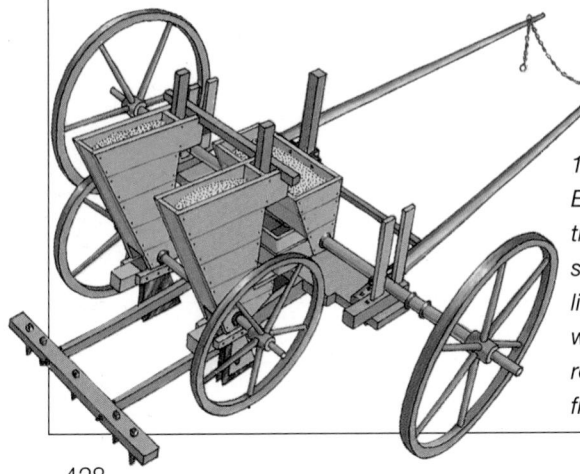

◄ Scattering seed by hand is a wasteful process. In 1701, Jethro Tull, an English farmer, invented the seed drill. It sowed seed evenly in straight lines that allowed weeding between each row. The drill was the first farm machine.

▲ New England's first colonists were not farmers. They might have starved in their new home but a Native North American called Squanto befriended them. He taught them how to grow corn and how to grind it. He also showed them where to catch the best fish. Farming and fishing soon became the colonists' most important ways of making a living.

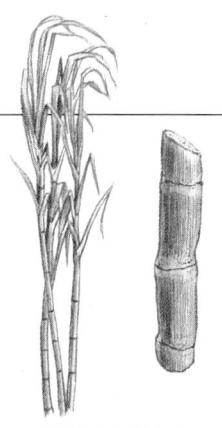

◄ Sugar was first brought to the Americas by Columbus on his second voyage. By 1700, sugar production in America was the largest industry in the world. Slaves from Africa supplied the workforce.

▲ Jan Vermeer (1632–1675) like other 17th century Dutch artists, painted scenes from life. His pictures show both imported and homegrown food of the time.

▲ Hungry sailors landing on the island of Mauritius off East Africa found the dodo easy to catch and good to eat. It was about the size of a turkey and had little wings, so it could not fly. Pigs and monkeys introduced to the island destroyed the dodo's eggs. An English sailor killed the last dodo in about 1680.

COFFEE AND TEA

Legend has it that coffee was first found in Ethiopia, Africa. It reached Italy in the early 17th century and quickly became a popular drink in coffee houses throughout Europe.

The Dutch East India Company brought tea to Europe from China and Japan. Tea was first drunk in a coffee house in 1657.

Early in the 18th century the company introduced coffee to their colonies in South America and the Caribbean.

Coffee

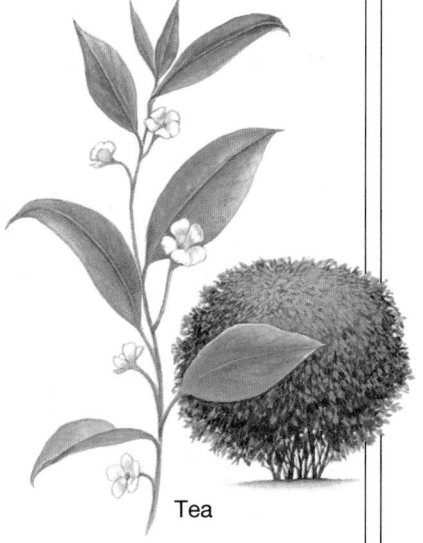

Tea

1638 Mesopotamia (Iraq): Ottoman Turks conquer Baghdad. England: Act of Parliament abolishes the use of torture to extract confessions. Japan: The Shimabara uprising near Nagasaki is put down. For several months 40,000 Christians have held out against the shogun's army. The Christians are slaughtered. The few surviving Christians in Japan practice their religion in secret.

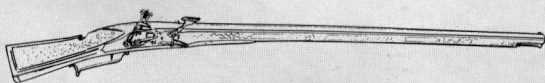

A 17th-century musket used by infantry soldiers, with a view of its internal mechanism.

1639 Scotland: First Bishops' War with England over religion ends with Pacification of Dunse. India: The English settle in Madras.

1640 Portugal: Independence is won from Spain. England: Charles I summons the Short Parliament (April to May), and dissolves it for refusing to grant him money. His lack of funds forces him to call the Long Parliament in November (to 1653). Scotland: In the Second Bishops' War, the Scots invade England and defeat the English army. Charles I agrees to pay Scotland £860 per day until a settlement is reached. Germany: Frederick William, the Great Elector, becomes ruler of Brandenburg (to 1688).

1641 Ireland: The Catholic Irish revolt and massacre Protestants in Ulster. Thirty Years' War: Emperor's army victorious at Wolfenbüttel, north Germany. North America: French set up trading posts in Michigan.

1642 England: First Civil War starts (to 1646) between the Royalists (Cavaliers) and Puritans (Roundheads). Canada: French found Montreal. Australasia: Dutch navigator Abel Tasman discovers Van Diemen's Land (now Tasmania) and New Zealand. Netherlands: Rembrandt van Rijn paints the *The Night Watch*.

The English Civil War

The English Civil War was fought between supporters of King Charles I and supporters of Parliament. Like his father, Charles believed in "divine right," claiming his right to rule came directly from God. This belief put Charles at odds with Parliament.

Charles became king in 1625 and immediately quarrels began over taxes, his right to imprison people who opposed him, and over religion. In 1629, Charles dissolved Parliament. For the next 11 years he tried to rule alone.

In 1640, Charles recalled Parliament to ask for money to put down a rebellion in Scotland. Civil war broke out after he tried to arrest his five leading opponents. Fighting broke out all over the country between Royalists (supporters of the king) and supporters of Parliament.

The king's forces at first held the advantage. However, in the long run

Charles I

1600 Born.
1625 Comes to throne; marries Henrietta Maria of Spain.
1642 Start of civil war.
1646 Surrenders to the Scots.
1647 Escapes to Isle of Wight.
1649 Tried and executed.

Cromwell

Oliver Cromwell (1599–1658) was first elected to the English Parliament in 1628. In the civil war he recruited and trained Parliament's New Model Army. He was a strict Puritan and felt that God had chosen him to perform his will.

COMMONWEALTH AND PROTECTORATE

After Charles' execution England became a Commonwealth. Parliament governed but it quarreled with the army, and its members fell out among themselves. In 1653 Oliver Cromwell emerged as a strong leader and ruled the country as Lord Protector. This period is known as the Protectorate. Cromwell clashed with Parliament and was forced to govern through army generals. In 1658, Cromwell died and was succeeded by his son Richard. However, he was not an effective ruler and the army soon removed him. The English people wanted a king again and in 1660 Charles I's son took the throne as Charles II.

▼ The first major battle of the civil war took place at Edgehill in 1642; the last at Worcester in 1651.

SCOTLAND   Dunbar

Marston Moor
Preston
ENGLAND
Nottingham
Naseby
Worcester   Edgehill
Oxford
London

Isle of Wight

■ Parliament's Headquarters
● Royalist Headquarters

Parliament proved superior, for it had the money to maintain a professional army. This New Model Army led by Sir Thomas Fairfax decisively defeated Charles's forces at Naseby in 1645.

Charles was imprisoned on the Isle of Wight where he plotted to begin the war again with Scottish help. A second civil war broke out but was swiftly crushed. In 1649, Charles was tried by Parliament and executed for treason.

THE KING'S TRIAL

Charles was unpopular because he married a Roman Catholic princess. He also revived ancient taxes to pay for wars his people did not want, and he tried to limit the powers of Parliament. However, at his trial and execution he behaved with dignity. This won him support and sympathy, and helped his son Charles return later as king.

China and the Manchus

The Ming dynasty of emperors had ruled China since 1368. But heavy taxation had made their rule unpopular and rebellions broke out all over the country. The last Ming emperor hanged himself as peasant rebels overran his capital Beijing. In the confusion that followed, the Manchu chieftain Dorgon led an army south from his homeland of Manchuria. He occupied Beijing and set up the Qing dynasty which was to rule China from 1644 until 1911.

Resistance to the Manchus persisted in the southern provinces and 40 years went by before all China submitted to their rule. The Manchus lived apart from the Chinese in separate areas. Marriage between Chinese and Manchus was forbidden. Chinese men were compelled to wear their long hair in pigtails to show they were inferior to the Manchus. However, Chinese as well as Manchus were employed as civil servants to run the empire. As time passed, the Manchus adopted Chinese customs.

China prospered under the Qing. The

▼ The Chinese silk industry employed many thousands of workers, especially women, to weave silk on looms. Silk cloth was produced both for home use and for export to Europe. The weavers of the port of Su-Chou were particularly famous for their silk.

▼ Under the Manchus, porcelain (or "china" as it became known) grew to be a very large export to the West. Europeans paid for it in gold and silver since the Chinese had little use for goods made in Europe. Here porcelain is being carefully packed for export.

TIBET

Tibet (Xizang) was ruled by a Buddhist leader called the Dalai Lama. The third Dalai Lama rebuilt the Potala monastery in Lhasa, the capital, as his residence in 1645. The Dalai Lamas came under the influence of the Mongols, who were the enemies of China. In 1720, the Qing army invaded Tibet and made it part of the Chinese empire.

empire grew and trade increased, particularly with Europe, where Chinese goods and styles became fashionable. Chinese silk and porcelain were the finest in the world and their cotton goods were cheap and of high quality. Huge quantities of Chinese tea were sold abroad when tea-drinking became all the rage in Europe during the 18th century.

The empire became so rich and powerful that its rulers were able to treat the rest of the world with contempt. Under emperor Kangxi (1662–1722) foreign merchants were forced to kneel whenever his commands were read out.

▲ The Manchus came from lands lying to the north of the Great Wall to conquer China.

1643 England: Parliament signs the Solemn League and Covenant, which allies it with the Scots. The Scots provide military aid in return for £30,000. France: Louis XIV, aged five, becomes king (to 1715). France defeats Spain in battle of Rocroi. Sweden: Goes to war with Denmark over Baltic supremacy (to 1645). Italy: Evangelista Torricelli invents the barometer.

1644 China: Manchus establish Qing dynasty (to 1912). England: Oliver Cromwell defeats Prince Rupert at the battle of Marston Moor. Quaker leader William Penn born (to 1718).

A gold flower-shaped ornament made during the Qing dynasty in China. It was probably worn as a brooch.

1645 Mediterranean: Venice and Turkey go to war over Crete (to 1669). Cromwell's New Model Army defeats Royalists at battle of Naseby. Africa: Capuchin monks explore the Congo River. The Dutch establish a settlement on the island of Mauritius.

1646 England: First stage of the civil war ends with the surrender of the Royalist headquarters at Oxford. Charles I gives himself up to the Scots. Thirty Years' War: Swedish army captures Prague and invades Bavaria with help from the French. West Indies: English occupy the Bahamas. Germany: Athanius Kircher makes the first magic lantern.

People

For nine years, between 1660 and 1669, Samuel Pepys recorded each day's events in minute detail in his diary. Only once did he note that his wife took a bath. Like most other wealthy English women, Elizabeth Pepys rarely bathed but instead wore rich and elaborate clothes and used perfumes and spices in abundance to make herself smell sweet.

The discoveries in science and technology made by Isaac Newton and others did little to alter ancient superstitions. Late in the 17th century in England and New England witches were being tried by law and condemned to death. Thousands of parents still brought their children to court for the monarch of the time to touch to cure them of skin diseases.

▲ How rich people dressed in 1640. The clothes of men and women were trimmed with large quantities of lace and adorned with rosettes, ribbons, jeweled brooches, and buttons.

▶ A French officer's campaign wig of 1670. Wigs were made in all shapes and sizes, often of horse or goat hair. Women's hairstyles, like that of this Spanish lady from the 1650s, often favored tightly curled ringlets tied with golden wire.

◀ Furniture during the 17th century became as ornamental as the people who used it. For the first time chairs were upholstered, using rich fabrics for greater luxury. They were also highly carved. This English chair was made in 1680.

◄ Commedia dell'arte *was a form of comedy that was popular in Italy. It was the ancestor of pantomime. The same characters appeared in each play and the actors made up their lines as they went along.*

◄ *Sumo wrestling, the national sport of Japan, dates from 1624. Wrestlers are selected when young and train for many years.*

▼ *The real ruler of India in the reign of Emperor Jahangir (1605–1627) was his wife Nur Jahan. When she knew her husband was dying, Nur Jahan murdered their eldest son in order to stay in power. Her favorite pastime was lion hunting.*

WHEN IT HAPPENED

1614 Native North American princess Pocahontas marries English settler John Rolfe.

1618-1648 Thirty Years' War reduces population of Germany from 17 million to 8 million.

c.1660 Women begin to take acting parts on the English stage.

1667 "Mad Madge," Duchess of Newcastle, becomes the first woman member of the Royal Society, London.

1669 Madame de Sévigné begins her letters to her daughter, detailing life in Paris and at the French court.

KEEPING CLEAN

Even the rich rarely washed their whole bodies regularly in 17th-century England. The face and hands were washed in soap and water each morning. The rest of the body was occasionally rubbed down with a cloth dipped in rose water.

The Sun King

When Louis XIII of France died in 1643 his son Louis XIV was five years old. Because he was so young, his mother, Anne of Austria, ruled as regent on his behalf for eight years until 1651.

For years the French people had been burdened by heavy taxes and in 1648 the citizens of Paris rose in revolt. The troubles spread to include the nobility and Louis was forced to flee the city.

The revolt, called the Fronde, eventually collapsed in 1652 and Louis reentered Paris in triumph. But he was determined that when he was old enough to rule he would make sure that nothing like it ever happened again.

In 1661, when he was 22, Louis personally took over the government of France. One of his ministers at the time wrote, "he sees everything, hears everything, makes every decision, gives every order." France became an absolute state where power was concentrated in Louis' hands. Louis once said *L'état c'est moi* "I am the state."

In 1665, Louis appointed Jean Colbert as his Controller-General of Finance. Colbert made France the most efficiently run country in Europe. He reorganized French taxes and reformed the legal system. New industries were set up on his orders. He had new roads, canals, and bridges built to improve communications within France and he greatly enlarged the French navy and merchant fleet.

ROYAL PATRONAGE

In 1440, a dye-works factory was established on the River Seine in Paris by Jean Gobelin. In 1662, Louis XIV bought the Gobelins factory. He made it a center where artists and craftsmen were employed to produce works which glorified him as monarch. The factory was renowned for its beautiful wall hangings. This detail taken from one of 14 tapestries glorifying the Sun King, shows artists with an enormous silver urn.

▼ *Louis ruled France from Versailles. He saw his ministers there, approved new laws, and received foreign princes and ambassadors. Spectacular entertainments were put on, stressing the king's magnificence and glorifying his position.*

Louis and the royal family made their home in his superb new palace of Versailles, waited on by 15,000 guards, courtiers, and attendants. The heads of the noble families of France were made to live there too so that Louis could keep an eye on them. The whole life of France revolved around the king like the planets around the Sun. For this reason he was given the name the "Sun King."

Louis XIV

1638 Born.
1643 Becomes king.
1660 Marries Maria Theresa of Spain.
1661 Takes control of government.
1715 Dies; succeeded by Louis XV.

▲ *Louis did not like Paris. None of its palaces was grand enough for him and after the revolt of 1648 he never trusted the Parisians. So he built himself the most magnificent palace in Europe at Versailles, a short distance from Paris. It took 36,000 workers 47 years to complete. The palace was surrounded by splendid formal gardens while inside the finest artists were hired to decorate the huge building with carvings, sculptures, paintings, and beautiful tapestries.*

1647 England: Scots sell Charles I to Parliament for £400,000; he is kidnapped by the army but escapes and makes a secret treaty with dissident Scottish nobles. France: The bayonet is invented at Bayonne.

1648 Thirty Years' War: Treaty of Westphalia ends the war. Dutch and Swiss republics become independent. France: Riots in Paris mark the outbreak of a revolt known as the Fronde (to 1652). The Scots try to invade England, but they are defeated by Cromwell at the battle of Preston. George Fox founds the Society of Friends (called the Quakers after 1650).

1649 Charles I is tried and executed. England becomes a Commonwealth (until 1660). Cromwell invades Ireland and puts down the Catholic rebellion there with great severity. English replaces Latin as language of all legal documents. Russia: Serfdom is established by law. North America: Maryland Assembly passes an act allowing any form of Christian worship in the colony.

1650 Scotland: Charles Stuart lands and is proclaimed Charles II. North America: Dutch and English settlers make an agreement over the frontiers of their colonies. England: First coffee house opens in Oxford.

1651 England: Charles II invades with a Scots army. He is defeated at the battle of Worcester by Cromwell and escapes to France.

Louis XIV's personal emblem was the golden, shining Sun. It can be found throughout his palace at Versailles.

1652 First Anglo-Dutch War starts (to 1654). London's first coffee house opens. South Africa: Dutch found Capetown. France: Lawful government is restored and Louis XIV returns to Paris. Spain: Barcelona surrenders to Philip IV, ending the Catalan revolt.

1653 England: Cromwell becomes Lord Protector of England. France: Mailboxes and postage stamps are first used in Paris.

1654 Brazil: Portuguese drive out the last of the Dutch colonists. England: Treaty of Westminster ends First Anglo-Dutch War. Russia is at war with Poland (to 1660). France: Louis XIV is crowned. Germany: Otto von Guericke gives the first demonstration of an air pump.

1655 England: Cromwell divides the country into 11 military districts, each governed by a Major General. West Indies: English seize Jamaica from Spain. Poland: War starts with Sweden after the invasion of Charles X of Sweden (to 1660).

This vase from Versailles celebrates French victories during the reign of Louis XIV.

1656 Mediterranean: Venetian fleet routs the Ottoman Turks off the Dardanelles. Switzerland: First Villmergen War starts between Protestant and Catholic cantons. Poland: Charles X of Sweden is victorious at the battle of Warsaw.

THE PEASANTRY

The nobility and the clergy of France paid no taxes. The burden of taxation fell on the peasants in the countryside and the workers in the towns. They, of all the people in France, could least afford to pay. An observer at the time described the peasants as "sullen animals, male and female, filthy, blackened and scorched by the Sun, living in hovels on black bread, water, and grapes." About three-fourths of the French population lived by farming. It was reckoned that it took 20 acres (8 ha) of land to support a family and very few of the peasants owned as much as this. If there were two bad harvests in a row or a plague among the cattle, hundreds of thousands starved. This widespread misery led to numerous protests and revolts. The government crushed all such uprisings with merciless severity.

By the time that Louis took up the reins of government in 1661, two great cardinals, Richelieu (*see* pages 418–419) and Jules Mazarin, had turned France into the most powerful nation in Europe. At the same time, many of France's neighbors had been weakened both by revolts within their own countries and expensive wars with other lands. In Louis' mind, the natural boundaries of France were the Alps, the Pyrenees, and the River Rhine. His intention was to push the frontiers of France out to these limits as well as win glory for himself.

As a result, Louis plunged France into 30 years of foreign wars trying to achieve his ambition. During his reign, the French army was enlarged to consist of between 300,000 and 400,000 men. It became the biggest, most formidable fighting force in Europe. The navy was also increased from 20 to 270 warships.

On the home front, a religious conflict developed during the later years of Louis's rule. Ever since the Edict of Nantes in 1598, French Roman Catholics and Protestant Huguenots had enjoyed equal rights. However, as Louis grew older he became more and more attached to the Catholic religion. He was determined to banish Protestantism and turn France into a solely Catholic nation.

In 1685, Louis overturned the Edict of Nantes. Faced with imprisonment or death if they did not give up their religion, some 300,000 Huguenots fled abroad. Since many of France's most skilled and hardworking craftsmen were Huguenots, the country could ill afford to lose their valuable services.

After ruling for more than 70 years, Louis died in 1715. He was succeeded by his great-grandson who became Louis XV at the age of five. He left the little boy a land that was under rigid control, nearly bankrupt from years of war, and a people who deeply resented the heavy taxes they were asked to pay.

THE WARS OF LOUIS XIV

1667–1668 War with Spain. France gains part of Flanders.
1672–1678 The Dutch War. Invasion of the Netherlands is halted when the Dutch, led by William of Orange, flood their land with the sea.
1689–1697 War of the League of Augsburg against English-led powers. France, defeated at sea, loses important fortresses to the Dutch.
1702–1713 War of the Spanish Succession. The English and German army is victorious in Flanders. Ended by the Peace of Utrecht.

▶ Jean Colbert was Louis's Controller-General of Finance. His policies provided the wealth which made France the leading nation in Europe.

▼ By the end of his reign in 1715, Louis XIV had succeeded in establishing secure frontiers for France.

THE HUGUENOTS

Many thousands of Huguenots left France when the legal protection they had been given ended in 1685. They fled to the Protestant countries of Europe and some eventually settled as far away as North America and the Cape of Good Hope in southern Africa. The best silk-weavers and the finest silversmiths in France were Huguenots. Their new homes benefited from the skills they took with them. In England, Huguenots played an important role in the growth of the textile industry.

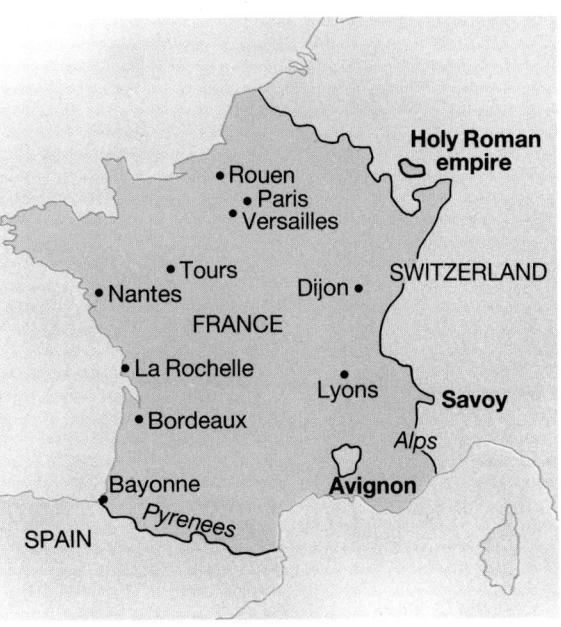

1657 Netherlands: War starts with Portugal (to 1661). Mathematician Christiaan Huygens invents the first pendulum clock. England: Parliament offers Cromwell the throne but he rejects it. France: First stockings and fountain pens are made in Paris.

1658 England: Lord Protector Cromwell dies. His son Richard succeeds him (to 1659), but he is not a good ruler. Poet and political writer John Milton starts to write his epic poem *Paradise Lost* (finished in 1663). France: Combined English and French armies defeat Spaniards at the battle of the Dunes. England gains Dunkirk. Holy Roman Empire: Leopold I is elected emperor (to 1705), succeeding his father Ferdinand III. Sweden: Financier Johann Palmstruck devises the first bank note.

1659 England: The army forces Richard Cromwell to resign and flee the country. Months of confusion follow. France: Peace of the Pyrenees ends war between France and Spain. The frontier between the two countries is agreed. Germany: Elector Frederick William drives the Swedish out of Prussia. India: Aurangzeb, the last of the great Mogul rulers, becomes emperor (to 1707).

Many beautiful textiles were made in India. They were highly sought after in Europe. This embroidered detail is from a Gujarati bedspread. It shows angels playing among birds and trees. It was made in about 1600.

Decline of Mogul India

Akbar, the founder of the Mogul empire in India, (*see* pages 360–361) died in 1605. His son Jahangir succeeded him. Jahangir's name means "holder of the world" but he experienced great difficulty in holding on to his empire. Jahangir was not interested in the ruling of his lands. He preferred the company of painters and poets, so he lavished his energies and much of his money on constructing splendid buildings and elaborate gardens. Meanwhile, his beautiful and ambitious wife Nur Jahan became virtual ruler of the country.

▲ *Emperor Aurangzeb is presented with the head of one of his three brothers. He killed them all because they were his rivals for the throne.*

Shah Jahan succeeded his father Jahangir as emperor in 1627. He enlarged the Mogul empire and by 1636 he had conquered the Deccan in central India. His end was tragic. In 1657, he fell sick and became so ill that he was incapable of ruling the country. His sons quarreled over who should succeed him. The third son, Aurangzeb, was the victor. He killed his three brothers, imprisoned his father, and seized the throne. Shah Jahan died in captivity and was buried next to his wife in the Taj Mahal.

Aurangzeb was the last great Mogul emperor. Under his rule the empire reached its greatest extent. Aurangzeb conquered most of the rest of India but was unable to overcome the warlike Maratha people on the west coast. He was a fanatical Muslim. Most of his subjects were Hindus and he persecuted them without mercy. Opposition to him grew. The Marathas overran the Deccan and revolts broke out all over the country. After Aurangzeb died in 1707, the Mogul empire began to break up. All real power was lost in 1803 when the British captured the capital city of Delhi.

▲ Shah Jahan rebuilt Delhi as the capital of his empire. He spent his last years imprisoned by his treacherous son Aurangzeb.

▼ The Taj Mahal near Agra was built of white marble inlaid with intricate patterns of semi-precious stones. It took 11 years to complete it.

▶ Empress Mumtaz Mahal was Shah Jahan's favorite wife. He built the Taj Mahal for her, after she died in childbirth. She was then buried there.

The Restoration

When Cromwell died in 1658, the Commonwealth he had ruled as Protector collapsed (*see* pages 430–431). A new Parliament was elected, which invited Charles II back from exile.

On May 29, 1660, Charles traveled from France to Dover. Happy crowds along the route cheered him all the way to London. After years of wandering abroad in poverty, Charles was determined to keep his throne at all costs. Real power now lay with the aristocracy and the country squires who had seats in Parliament. They were out for revenge over their Puritan enemies and passed acts to bar Puritans from all government jobs, and to put them in prison if they held religious services.

In 1665, thousands of Londoners died in an outbreak of the plague. It was the first of three calamities. The following year the heart of London was destroyed in the Great Fire. In 1667, the Dutch navy sailed up the Thames and burned part of the English fleet.

Charles II

1630 Born.
1642 Present at the battle of Edgehill in the English Civil War.
1646 Flees to France.
1660 Restored to English throne.
1662 Marries Catherine of Braganza; they have no children.
1685 Dies; succeeded by his brother, James, Duke of York.

THE GREAT PLAGUE

The Great Plague (1664–1665) was a disasterous outbreak of bubonic plague in London and southeast England that killed almost one-fifth of London's population. Large red crosses were painted on the doors of infected households to warn others of the danger.

▼ *The Great Fire of London in 1666 destroyed many of the close-packed slums in which the plague had flourished. Plans to rebuild London included a new St. Paul's Cathedral by Sir Christopher Wren.*

▲ *The filthy streets of London meant many people traveled by river. Boatmen offered a frequent service.*

In 1670, Charles signed a treaty with Louis XIV of France in which he agreed to join France in a war against the Dutch. Secretly, and in return for an annual payment, Charles also promised to restore the Catholic religion in England. But his plans miscarried.

First, Parliament refused to grant toleration to Catholics and passed the Test Act in 1678 which banned them from holding official positions. Then it withdrew England from the war against the Netherlands (*see* pages 448–449) and made arrangements for Charles's niece, Mary, to marry the Dutch Protestant leader William of Orange.

1660 England: Parliament invites the exiled Charles II to return as king (to 1685). Women replace boys in female roles on the stage in England (and Germany). Samuel Pepys begins keeping a daily diary (to 1669).

1661 India: Drought and famine strikes some parts owing to lack of rain since 1659. France: Louis XIV takes absolute power as king. China: Formosa is captured from the Dutch by supporters of the defeated Ming. Russia: In the Treaty of Kardis, Russia and Sweden agree to restore all conquests to each other. North America: Pastor John Eliot founds the first church for Native Americans in Massachusetts.

A contemporary woodcut showing Londoners fleeing from the Great Plague to seek refuge in the countryside.

1662 England: Charles II marries Portuguese princess Catherine of Braganza and receives Bombay, Tangier, and £300,000 as a dowry. He sells Dunkirk to France for £400,000. In London, the Royal Society receives its charter. France: Louis XIV begins to build the palace at Versailles. First eight-seater, horse-drawn buses are used in Paris. China: Kangxi becomes second Qing emperor (to 1722).

1663 Balkans: War is declared between the Ottoman empire and Holy Roman Empire. The Ottoman Turks invade Transylvania and Hungary. Canada: French colonies join together as Province of New France with their capital at Quebec. England: Travelers have to pay turnpike tolls (road charges).

Religion

In the 17th century people believed that the events of everyday life were acts of God. God caused floods and droughts and sent rain, hail, and snow. Bad harvests were regarded as a punishment and good harvests a reward.

Families prayed daily and went to church on Sunday. People believed in the Devil and witchcraft. In colonial America, a number of so-called witches were tried and some were executed.

Most countries passed religious laws. People who refused to obey them were severely punished. Those who could went abroad and settled in places where they could worship freely.

▲ Protestant England distrusted Catholics. Several were executed in 1680 on suspicion of murder.

▼ The Golden Temple in India is the holiest shrine for followers of the Sikh religion.

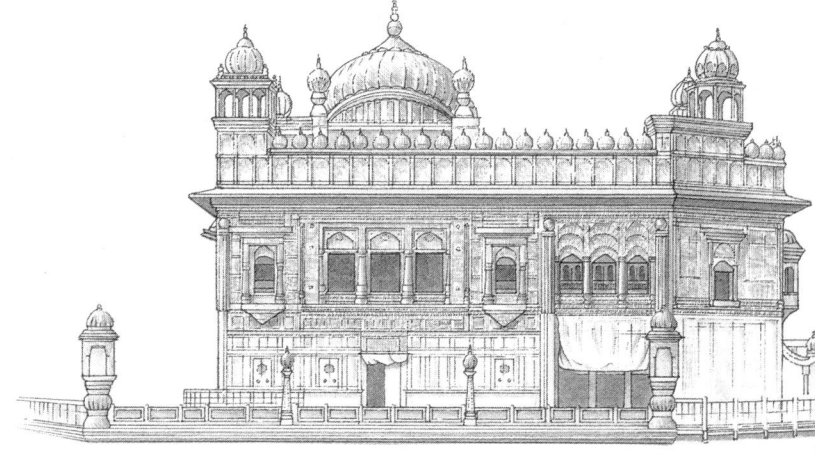

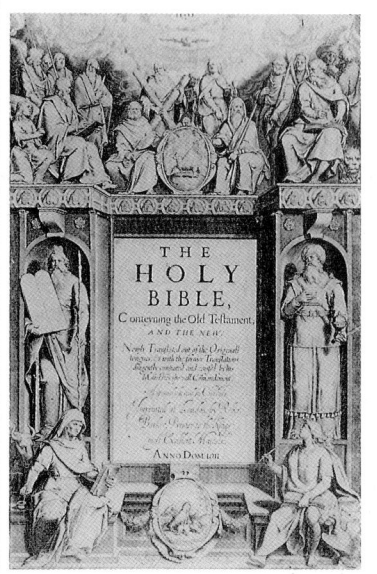

▶ Colonists in New England, trudging to church through the snow. They wear the simple Puritan dress of black cloth and white linen collars. Native North Americans were not always friendly so the settlers carry guns for protection as well as bibles.

◀ In 1604, a conference of religious leaders at Hampton Court Palace agreed that England needed a new translation of the Bible. Fifty eminent scholars took several years to complete it. The result, published in 1611, was the Authorized or King James Version.

► Portuguese priests were the first Christian teachers to arrive in Japan. The Japanese were Buddhists but they let the priests preach Christianity and build churches. By the beginning of the 17th century, about 300,000 Japanese had been converted. But the priests' success alarmed Japan's rulers. They ordered the priests to leave and invented ingenious tortures to persuade Japanese Christians to give up their faith. In April 1638, the last 30,000 Christians were trapped in the castle of Hara near Nagasaki. They held out for three months. All were killed in the final massacre.

WHEN IT HAPPENED

1611 The Authorized Version of the Bible appears in England.

1641 George Fox, the founder of the Quakers, starts to preach in England.

1645 The Dalai Lama, religious ruler of Tibet, founds a monastery in Lhasa, Tibet.

1661 The Bible is translated into Algonquin, a Native North American language.

▼ A 17th-century Muslim artist of Mogul India painted this tender picture of the baby Jesus in the arms of his mother, the Virgin Mary.

445

1664 North America: English seize New Amsterdam from the Dutch and rename it New York. France: The French East India Company is established.

1665 England: The worst attack of plague since the Black Death in the 15th century, the Great Plague (July–October) kills more than 60,000 people in London alone. Scientist Isaac Newton invents calculus and begins to formulate laws of gravitation. The Second Anglo-Dutch War begins (to 1667). Italy: Sculptor and architect Giovanni Bernini completes high altar of St. Peter's, Rome. Spain: Charles II becomes king (to 1700). He is the last of the Spanish Habsburg kings.

1666 England: The Great Fire of London destroys thousands of homes. The fire, beginning in a baker's shop, rages for four days, destroying 87 churches and more than 13,000 homes. It is stopped by blowing up buildings in its path. Samuel Pepys includes an eyewitness account of the blaze in his diary. The first Cheddar cheese is made. Isaac Newton measures the Moon's orbit. Italy: Antonio Stradivari starts to make violins. West Indies: English privateers capture the island of Tobago. France: Jean Thevenot invents the level for measuring.

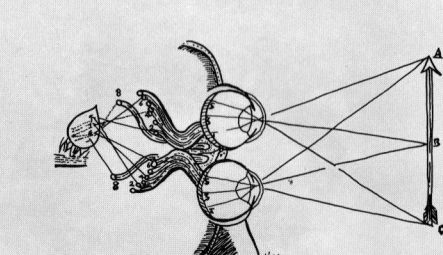

A diagram showing French philosopher Descartes' theory concerning the co-ordination of the senses. He thought that a visual stimulus traveling from the eye to a gland beneath the brain stopped attention being given to the sense of smell.

The Age of Reason

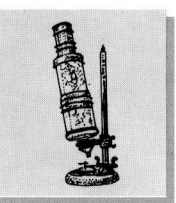

By the middle of the 17th century the ideas of the Renaissance (*see* pages 330–333) had spread through most of Europe. People began to question and doubt the truth of some of these ideas. It was no longer believed that everything that was true had already been written in the Bible or discovered by philosophers in ancient Greece. Many began to believe in the power of people to think things out for themselves. At the same time, new discoveries were made about the world and human beings which led to a revolution in scientific methods and ways of thinking. This revolution became known as the Age of Reason, and later in the 18th century the Enlightenment (*see* pages 504–505).

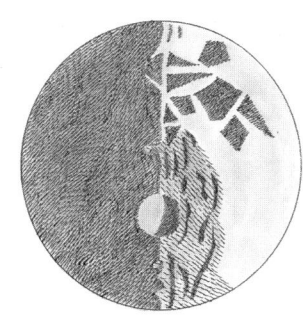 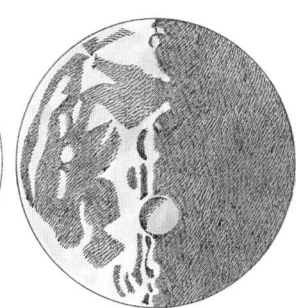

▲ *Galileo watched the Moon change as it circled around the Earth. He drew its surface as he saw it through his telescope. He guessed, wrongly, that the dark areas he saw were seas, but because of this, some areas of the Moon are named as seas.*

▶ *Galileo also built his own telescopes. He was the first to use the telescope in astronomy.*

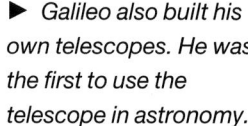

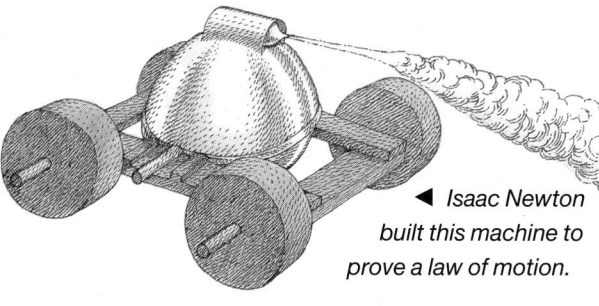

◀ *Isaac Newton built this machine to prove a law of motion.*

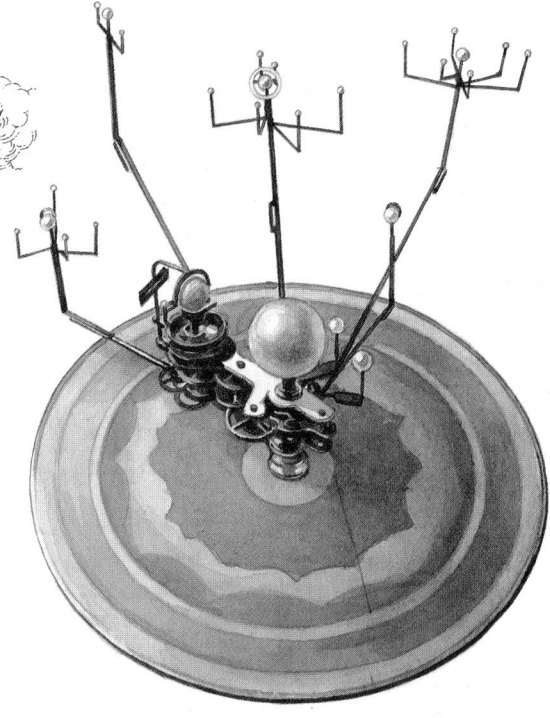

▶ *The first orrery was made in 1700 to demonstrate the movements of the planets around the Sun and moons around the planets. A handle turns the planets.*

At the center of this thirst for knowledge was an intense curiosity about the place of the Earth in the universe. In 1633, when an Italian professor named Galileo claimed that the Earth and the planets circled around the Sun, he was sentenced to imprisonment for life for his beliefs. He had challenged the authority of the Roman Catholic Church which taught that the Earth was the center of the universe and that the Sun and the stars moved around it.

But nothing could stop the progress of the new ideas. The work of René Descartes, Isaac Newton, Francis Bacon, Galileo himself, and many others, formed the foundations on which today's knowledge of the world is built.

▼ *Until the 17th century the Church forbade people to cut up human corpses for study. But a growing interest in how the human body worked led to more dissections as this painting by Rembrant shows.*

NEW IDEAS

The Frenchman René Descartes made the first clear statement of the ideas of the Age of Reason. He argued that only ideas that could be proved to be true by evidence or by reasoning, were true. All other ideas were not to be trusted.

Among other important discoveries, the English scientist Isaac Newton explained the world and the Universe in simple statements and mathematical equations. The English doctor William Harvey discovered that the blood circulates around the body.

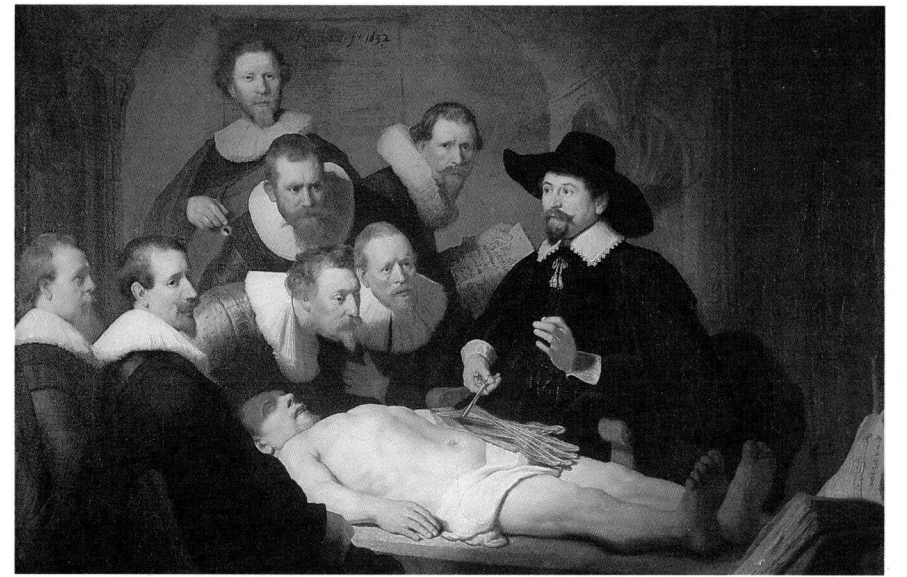

The Anglo-Dutch Wars

 England and the United Provinces of the Netherlands went to war with each other three times during the 17th century. The English and the Dutch were rivals in the slave trade between Africa and America. They also quarreled over fishing rights in the North Sea, over trading in spices with India and the islands of Southeast Asia, and over colonies in the Americas. Since the wars were fought between the navies of the two countries, they became a battle for command of the seas.

In 1651, the English Parliament passed a law requiring that all goods entering England should be carried in English ships. This was a deliberate attempt to limit Dutch trading and led to a war which lasted for three years. War was again declared in 1665. There was fighting off the coast of West Africa, where the English first captured, but then lost, the Dutch slave ports. In North America an English expedition occupied New Amsterdam, which was renamed New York. But in 1667 the Dutch, under Cornelius van Tromp sailed up the Thames and burned part of the English fleet at anchor in Chatham docks. Peace was signed soon afterwards at Breda.

In 1672 England, together with France, was again at war with the Netherlands. This was unpopular with the English people and peace was signed in 1674. The quarrels between the two countries ended when the Dutch prince, William of Orange, became king of England in 1688.

▼ *The Four Days' War raged at the mouth of the Thames in 1667. The Dutch destroyed 25 English ships but both sides withdrew after the battle was finished.*

1667 England: Poet and political writer John Milton publishes *Paradise Lost*, an epic poem about sin coming into the world. Peace of Breda ends the war between England, France, and the Netherlands. Charles II of England and Louis XIV of France sign a secret treaty against Spain. A truce ends the 13-year war between Russia and Poland. Russia gains Kiev, Smolensk, and the eastern Ukraine.

1668 Netherlands: England, Sweden, and the Netherlands form an alliance against France. Portugal: Spain recognizes Portugal's independence. The Treaty of Aix-la-Chapelle ends the War of Devolution between France and Spain. France keeps most of her conquests in Flanders. England: Isaac Newton invents the reflecting telescope.

1669 Mediterranean: Venice surrenders Crete to Ottoman Turks. India: Emperor Aurangzeb bans the Hindu religion and starts to persecute Hindus. North America: Robert Cavalier explores the Midwest – probably the first European in the region.

1670 England: Charles II of England and Louis XIV of France sign the secret Treaty of Dover in which Charles agrees to restore Roman Catholicism to England in return for an annual pension. Canada: The Hudson's Bay Company of England is formed. Russia: Peasants and Cossacks start a series of uprisings (to 1671).

An illustration taken from an anti-Dutch poster which describes the Dutch as "lusty, fat, two-legged cheeseworms."

1671 Ottoman empire: Turks declare war on Poland. West Indies: Sir Henry Morgan, a former pirate, is made Deputy Governor of Jamaica. France: Dramatist Molière (Jean Baptiste Poquelin) writes *Le Bourgeois Gentilhomme*, one of his most famous plays.

1672 Netherlands: French declare war (to 1674) and invade. William of Orange is appointed Captain General of the United Provinces of the Netherlands. Nicholas and Jan van der Heijden invent the first effective hose pipes for firefighting. England: Third Anglo-Dutch War starts (to 1674).

1673 England: The Test Act excludes Roman Catholics and Non-Conformists from filling public offices. Austria: Holy Roman emperor Leopold I declares war on France. North America: French explorers Jacques Marquette and Louis Joliet sail down the Mississippi to Arkansas.

1674 England: Public opposition to the war with the Netherlands forces peace to be made. But the war continues between Holland and France. France: French surgeon Morel invents the tourniquet to reduce the amount of blood lost during amputation of limbs.

1675 North America: New England colonists fight a war against Native North Americans, the Wampanoags, who are led by their chief Metacomet, known as King Philip, (to 1676). England: Greenwich Observatory is founded.

The pirate Blackbeard carried six pistols into battle and wore burning matches in his hair. His favorite drink was rum and gunpowder.

Plantations and Pirates

Within a hundred years of Columbus's first landing in 1492, most of the original peoples of the Caribbean islands were dead. The Europeans killed many of them and gave others diseases that proved deadly because the native people had no immunity to them. By the early 17th century the Caribbean was a battleground. Spanish, French, English, and Dutch all fought for the islands they called the West Indies. Some islands changed hands more than once in a fierce contest for trade and for land to establish European colonies.

In Europe, tea and coffee were

▲ *Slaves harvesting sugar cane on a plantation on one of the islands in the Caribbean. The high price of sugar in Europe made some owners immensely rich. They built themselves superb houses to live in and were waited on by many servants.*

becoming fashionable drinks and this gave rise to a huge new demand for sugar to sweeten them. Sugar grew well in the climate of the West Indies, but sugar cultivation needed many workers. Local workers were not to be found, because the original islanders had died out. So, the colonists imported slave labor from West Africa.

◄ The Caribs were a fierce and warlike people who lived in the islands of the eastern Caribbean. The most ferocious Caribs were found on the island of Dominica. Some explorers believed they were cannibals. Europeans on nearby islands lived in great fear of their attacks. Not until many Caribs had been killed by the English in 1683, did the settlers feel at all secure.

At this time Europeans saw nothing wrong in using Africans as slaves. Africans in West Africa were almost defenseless against bands of determined slave raiders armed with guns. They were simply rounded up, crammed by the hundred into ships, and taken away. Nearly a third of them died on the three-month voyage to the West Indies. On arrival, the slaves were sold to plantation owners. One in three died within three years of landing from disease or over work, or after brutal ill-treatment. But the number of slaves still grew. By the end of the 17th century, about 90 percent of the West Indian people had originally come from West Africa.

▼ Pirates of all nationalities roamed the Caribbean attacking merchant ships. Some like Henry Morgan, turned respectable on the proceeds of their piracy. He became the Deputy Governor of Jamaica.

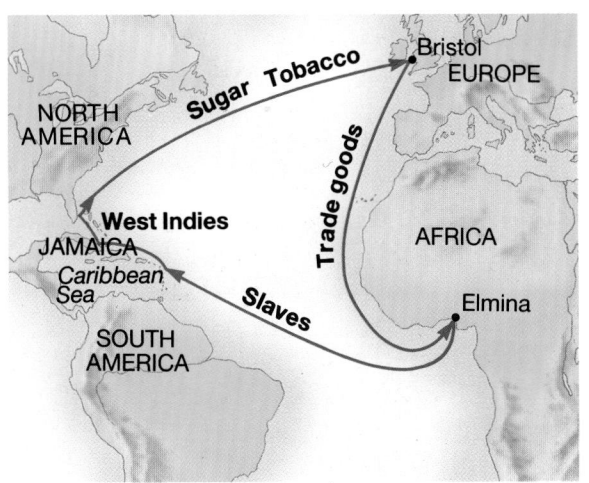

◄ The slave trade followed a route shaped like a triangle. A typical voyage might set out from Bristol carrying cloth and other finished goods for sale in West Africa. Once the goods had been sold in Africa, the ship would load up with slaves and take them to the West Indies. The final leg of the voyage would bring a cargo of sugar back to Europe.

Science and Technology

In the 17th century scientists began to understand how nature worked and how to harness it for use. They made scientific discoveries which led to advances in technology. By using this new technology they were able to make further discoveries. For example, for the first time heat could be accurately measured with the newly-invented thermometer.

Advances in mathematics kept pace with those in science. The invention of calculus, logarithms, and the slide-rule enabled scientists to make calculations to support their theories.

▼ *Galileo realized in 1581 that a swinging pendulum keeps accurate time but it was not till 1657 that Christiaan Huygens designed the first successful pendulum clock.*

NEWTON'S THEORIES

Sir Isaac Newton showed that sunlight is made up of a mixture of colors *(right)*. He demonstrated that a beam of white light shone through a glass prism splits up into the colors of the rainbow.

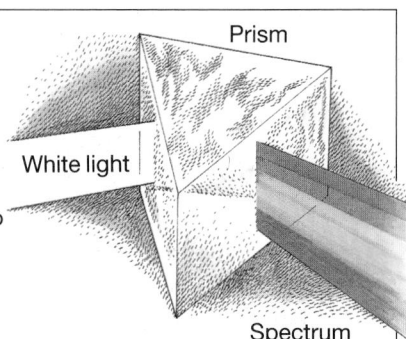

White light

Prism

Spectrum

Newton drew this diagram *(left)* to show how objects move if launched at great heights at different speeds.

Stars seen through early telescopes had fuzzy colored edges. By using a curved mirror to reflect the light, Newton produced a telescope *(right)* that was able to correct this fault.

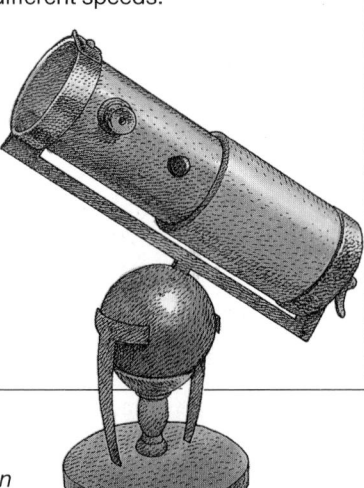

▼ *Otto von Guericke demonstrated air pressure by pumping out the air between two half spheres. Horses could not part them.*

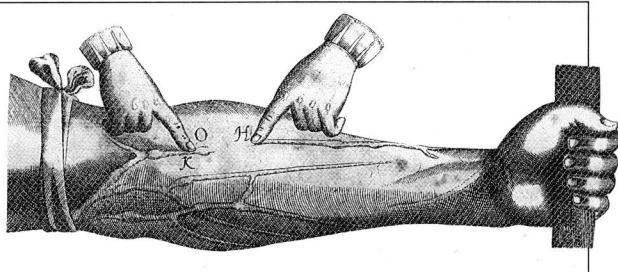

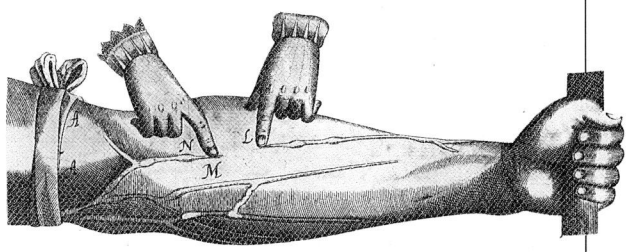

WHEN IT HAPPENED

1608 Hans Lippershey, a Dutch optician, invents the first telescope.

1609 The British inventor Cornelius Drebbel makes the first thermostat.

1631 The multiplication sign x is first used.

1644 Evangelista Torricelli, an Italian scientist, invents the barometer.

1650 Otto von Guericke invents the air pump.

1654 The first accurate thermometer is used.

1660 A barometer is used to forecast weather. The Royal Society is founded in London.

1666 The Royal Academy is started in Paris. Isaac Newton devises calculus.

1668 Newton invents the reflecting telescope.

1680 Clocks now have a minute hand.

1684 Newton publishes his theory of gravitation.

1705 The English astronomer Edmond Halley predicts the return of a comet in 1758.

▲ *In 1628 an English doctor, William Harvey, described how the blood circulates in the human body. He showed that blood moves around the body in only one direction, along arteries and veins.*

▼ *New ideas in science and philosophy were discussed by leading figures of society at salons run by women such as Ninon de Lenclos (below left). The new interest in science influenced the way people thought about the world. The English philosopher John Locke (below right) studied medicine and science before carrying out a systematic enquiry into the nature and scope of human understanding.*

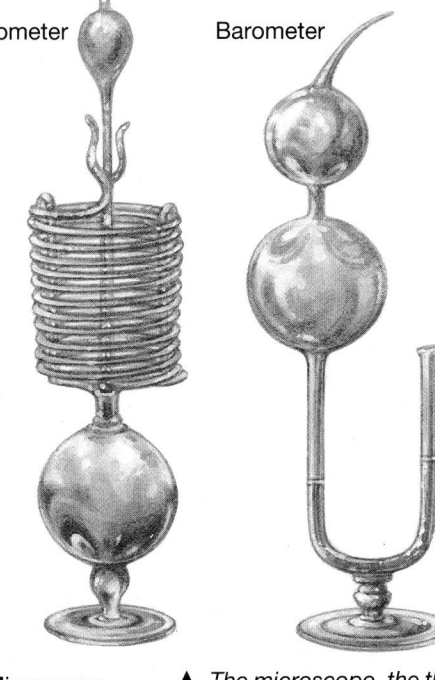

Thermometer   Barometer

Microscope

▲ *The microscope, the thermometer, and the barometer all made their first appearance in the 17th century. Scientists invented them as tools to help them carry out experiments more accurately. With the aid of instruments such as these, they produced a revolution in human knowledge.*

Oceania

During the 17th century, Dutch seamen explored the southern Pacific and Indian Oceans. By the 1620s, they had found parts of the northern and western coast of Australia. They named the new land "New Holland" but its shape and size remained unknown.

In 1642, the Dutchman Abel Tasman discovered the island that now bears his name, Tasmania. He had sailed from Mauritius and traveled so far south that he did not sight Australia. Farther to the east, Tasman reached another unknown coast: the south island of New Zealand. After a fight with its Maori inhabitants he set off for Batavia in the Dutch East Indies, discovering Tonga and Fiji on the way. The next year, he sailed along the northern coast of Australia.

Tasman and other Dutch explorers proved that Australia was an island. But the Dutch did not settle there. So the Pacific remained largely unknown as it was too distant and too poor to attract trading interest from the Europeans.

▲ Tasman's drawing of Fijian craft shows that the Pacific islanders were superb boat-builders. They used their larger vessels to make long voyages of thousands of miles across the Pacific. Paddled at full speed they could overtake European ships.

▼ Tasman did not sight all the shore of Australia, but he proved it was an island by sailing right around the area where it was known to be. Knowledge of Australia remained vague until James Cook's voyages more than a hundred years later.

Tasman

Originally the navigator Abel Tasman (c. 1603 –1659) called the island of Tasmania Van Diemen's Land, after the governor of the Dutch East Indies, Anthony van Diemen who sponsored the expedition. The British then renamed it Tasmania in 1853. The Dutch authorities changed Staten Land (Tasman's original name for these islands), to New Zealand which means "new sea-land."

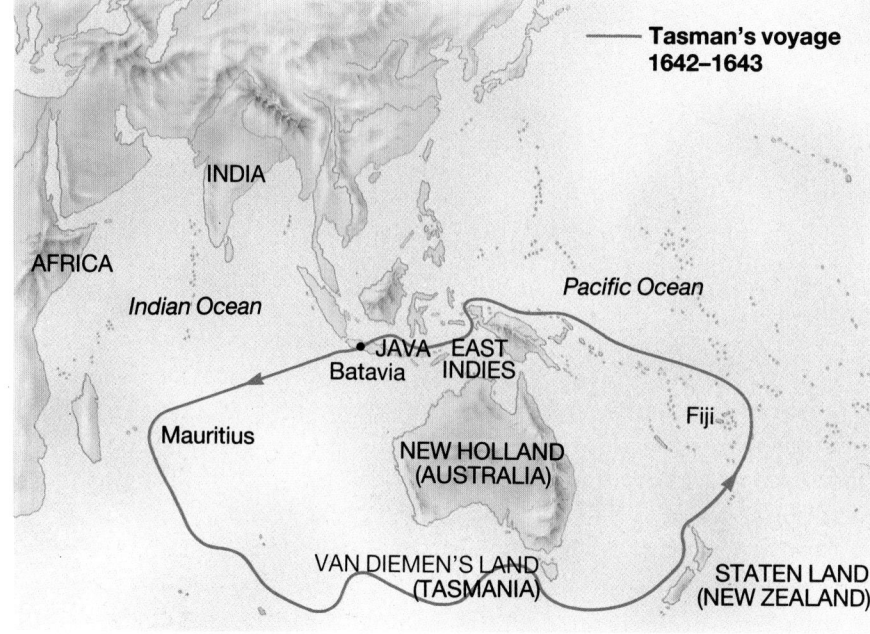

Tasman's voyage 1642–1643

INDIA

AFRICA

Indian Ocean

Pacific Ocean

• JAVA EAST
Batavia INDIES

Mauritius

Fiji

NEW HOLLAND
(AUSTRALIA)

VAN DIEMEN'S LAND
(TASMANIA)

STATEN LAND
(NEW ZEALAND)

Decline of Ottoman Power

In the reign of Suleiman the Magnificent (1520 to 1566), the Ottoman empire reached its height (*see* pages 358–359). It stretched from Egypt through Syria and Turkey to the Balkans. During the 17th century the empire began to show signs of decay. The Turkish civil service had become corrupt and inefficient. At the top, the authority of the sultans was weakened by a series of bloody contests for power among the ruling families.

In 1683, a Turkish army, besieging Vienna in Austria, was destroyed by a force under the command of King John of Poland. After this defeat the Ottoman empire went into a spectacular decline. Hungary was lost to Austria and Russia seized territories along the Black Sea. Austria now challenged Ottoman Turkey as the major power in the Balkans.

▲ The siege of Vienna in 1683 marked the farthest point of the Ottoman Turks' advance into Europe. The defenders of Vienna held out for two months, just long enough for a slow-moving army of Germans and Poles to arrive. The Turks were utterly defeated in a 15-hour battle on September 12, 1683.

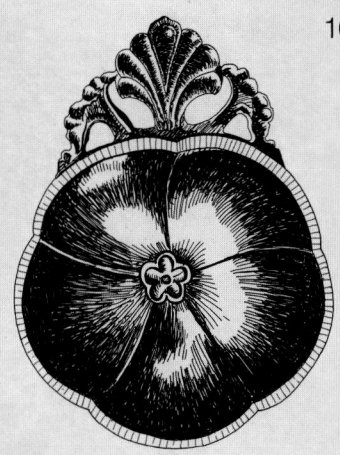

The idea of carving cups in natural forms such as flowers came to Turkey from China.

1676 Poland: War with Ottoman empire ends. The Turks gain Polish Ukraine. India: Sikh uprising starts against Mogul rulers (to 1678). Russia: Fyodor III becomes tsar (to 1682). Denmark: Astronomer Ole Romer calculates the speed of light. North America: The first coffee house is licensed in Boston, Massachusett.

1677 England: William of Orange marries Mary, daughter of James, Duke of York, heir to the English throne. Aphra Behn, first known English woman dramatist, writes *The Rover*. Russia: At war with the Ottoman empire (until 1681).

1678 England: Titus Oates pretends there is a Catholic plot to murder Charles II and several innocent Catholics are executed as a result. Roman Catholics are excluded from both Houses of Parliament. Netherlands: Treaty of Nijmegen ends Franco-Dutch War. Dutch import the first chrysanthemums to be seen in Europe from Japan.

1679 England: Act of Habeas Corpus forbids imprisonment without trial. Charles II blocks a parliamentary bill to exclude his Catholic brother James, Duke of York, from succeeding to the throne. He also rejects petitions (to 1680) calling for a new Parliament: petitioners become known as Whigs, their royalist opponents known as Tories. North America: French fur-traders are the first Europeans to see Niagara Falls. France: Scientist Denis Papin invents the pressure cooker.

1680 France: *Comédie Française* formed in Paris. On the island of Mauritius in the Indian Ocean English sailors kill the last surviving dodo. England: Merchant William Dockwra establishes the Penny Post (letters carried for one penny) in London. First musical entertainments performed at Sadlers Wells, London.

1681 England: Christopher Wren elected president of the Royal Society. Russia: Treaty of Radzin signed with Ottoman Turks; Russia gains most of Turkish Ukraine. The Academy of Sciences is founded in Moscow.

Peter the Great, seen here portrayed as a cat, became a very unpopular ruler when he broke with tradition and shaved off his beard.

1682 North America: French explorer La Salle claims entire Mississippi Valley for France. Ottoman empire is at war with Austria (until 1699). Russia: Peter I and Ivan V become joint tsars (to 1689). France: Louis XIV excludes Protestants from his court and from the civil service. Thousands of Huguenots are forced to become Roman Catholics.

1683 Austria: Ottoman Turks besiege Vienna but are driven off by a German and Polish army. China: Manchus conquer the island of Formosa. England: Newton gives the first mathematical explanation of the rise and fall of tides. Henry Purcell is appointed composer to Charles II's court. A plot to murder Charles II is discovered. North America: First German colonists settle in Pennsylvania.

Peter the Great

Peter I, known as Peter the Great, became joint tsar of Russia with his half-brother Ivan in 1682. Ivan was feeble-minded, and in 1689 Peter took complete control. At the beginning of his reign Russia was a backward state compared with the countries of western Europe. Peter's ambition was to make Russia a great European power.

He realized that Russia would remain in isolation until it secured an outlet to the west through either the Baltic or Black seas. Accordingly Peter captured, but later lost, Azov on the Black Sea. In 1700, he went to war successfully against Sweden. In the peace treaty he gained

▶ *Peter had enormous energy and was constantly at work making laws, drilling troops, planning towns, building ships, and even extracting teeth. He was careful with money and gave most of his income to the state. He died after diving into the Neva River in winter to rescue drowning sailors.*

▲ *The boyars had been the hereditary ruling class in Russia since the 10th century. When Peter returned from Europe, he abolished their powers. He cut off their beards as a sign that he had done so.*

▼ *Peter abandoned Moscow and founded a new Russian capital, St. Petersburg, on land taken from Sweden. He hired European architects to build the city.*

▶ *Peter the Great encouraged fine craftsmanship. He gave this jeweled cup to his little son Alexis in 1694. But he could also be cruel. Much later he imprisoned Alexis who died after torture.*

Estonia and Livonia which gave him the foothold he needed on the Baltic coast.

In 1697, Peter began an 18-month tour of western Europe traveling dressed as an ordinary citizen. He visited factories, hospitals, almshouses (houses for the poor), and museums. He worked as a carpenter in dockyards to learn the art of shipbuilding. He hired hundreds of craftsmen and technicians to teach their skills to the Russian people.

On his return Peter created a new civil service organized on European lines and made his courtiers adopt western dress and manners. He built factories, canals, and roads, and founded new industries. Both the army and navy were reformed.

Peter's work was only half-complete when he died in 1725, but he began a process that was to make Russia one of the superpowers of the modern world.

1684 Austria: Emperor Leopold, with Poland and Venice, forms Holy League of Linz against the Ottoman Turks. Germany: Peace is made between the Holy Roman Empire and France.

A Delft plate from the Netherlands bearing the portraits of William III and Mary II. It was made to celebrate their succession as joint monarchs of England, Scotland, and Ireland.

1685 France: Louis XIV revokes the Edict of Nantes. More than 50,000 Huguenots flee abroad. James II becomes king of England and Scotland (to 1688). Monmouth Rebellion is put down after the battle of Sedgemoor.

1686 Germany: Led by Emperor Leopold the League of Augsburg is formed against France. Russia declares war on Turkey. England: James II ignores the Test Act and appoints Roman Catholics to public positions. North America: New England colonies are united in a federation.

1687 England: James II issues the Declaration of Indulgence giving freedom of worship to all religions. Isaac Newton publishes his *Principles of Natural Philosophy* establishing the basis of modern mathematics. Greece: Venetians bombard Athens and badly damage the Parthenon. Hungary: At the battle of Mohács the Ottoman Turks are routed. The victory assures Habsburg succession to the Hungarian throne.

1688 Seven lords invite William of Orange to save England from Roman Catholicism. James II flees to France. Austria captures Belgrade from the Ottoman Turks.

The Glorious Revolution

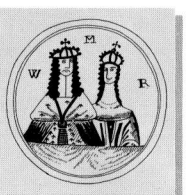

After Charles II of England died in 1685, his brother succeeded him as James II. James was a Roman Catholic and he immediately appointed Catholics to important positions throughout the country. When James's second wife gave birth to a son, a line of Catholic kings seemed assured.

The English were Protestant and had no wish to be ruled by Catholics. To keep England Protestant, a number of leading men invited James's nephew, the Protestant prince William of Orange, to England. William's wife Mary was the daughter of James and she, like her husband, was a Protestant.

William landed in England with an army in November 1688. James's fighting force quickly melted away and by Christmas he had fled abroad to France. The following year, Parliament passed the Bill of Rights which formally offered the English throne to William and Mary. It also stated that future rulers should

▲ *This medallion was made to commemorate the marriage of William and Mary in 1677. Since they both had a claim to the English throne they occupied it as joint sovereigns, William III and Mary II.*

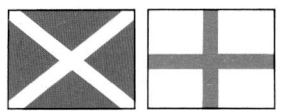

▶ *James I drew the first Union flag in 1606. It combined the blue and white cross of Scotland's St. Andrew with the red and white cross of England's St. George. It came into use after the Act of Union in 1707. The red and white cross of Ireland's St. Patrick was added in 1800, creating the present-day flag.*

▼ *William of Orange landed at Torbay on England's southwest coast with a small army of Dutch soldiers. He was warmly greeted as the deliverer of England from Catholicism. The welcome grew as William marched toward London and James II's own army refused to fight for him.*

not be, or marry, Roman Catholics. So William and Mary became rulers of England in a transfer of power that was accomplished with no bloodshed. It was later called the Glorious Revolution.

But William and Mary's position was not secure yet. Backed by Louis XIV of France, James tried to win back his throne. In 1689, he landed in Ireland and besieged the Protestant stronghold of Londonderry. He failed to take it, and in July 1690 his army was utterly defeated by William at the battle of the Boyne.

GLENCOE MASSACRE

When the chief of the Scottish clan called Macdonald of Glencoe arrived six days late to swear an oath of loyalty to King William, he was, in a sense, guilty of treason. The Campbells, long-standing enemies of the Macdonalds, swore to destroy them. At dawn on the February 13, 1692 a band of Campbells sheltering with the Macdonalds turned on their hosts and murdered them.

Society and Government

The history of 17th century Europe is marked by a series of strong sovereigns. Some, like Louis XIV of France or Peter the Great of Russia, had absolute authority within their kingdoms.

In England, however, the elected Parliament demanded more power as its role in government grew. After Charles I was tried and executed for treason the powers of the monarchy were restricted and by the early 1700s Parliament had gained nearly total control over the monarchy.

The government and laws of European colonies overseas mirrored those of their home countries. In the English colonies of North America, elected assemblies and not the monarch, made the laws.

▲ The first elected representatives of the colony of Virginia, together with its governor and council, met in 1619 at Jamestown to formulate the laws.

▼ Punishment was usually inflicted in public in order to bring disgrace upon the offenders. The ducking stool was used to punish minor misdeeds such as swearing, drunkenness, brawling, and stealing.

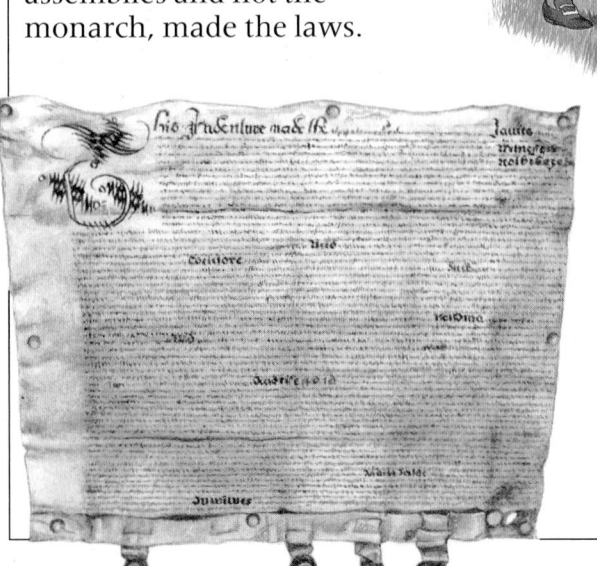

◀ The letters patent issued in 1621 by King James I gave the Mayflower Pilgrims the right to own the land where they had settled in Plymouth Colony, New England. A letters patent is a public document in which a king or queen confers certain rights on the holder.

1628 Charles I of England is forced to accept Parliament's Petition of Right.

1649 New laws in Russia make serfdom legal.

1679 Act of Habeas Corpus is passed in England, forbidding imprisonment without trial.

1682 The legal system of Pennsylvania is established.

1695 Press censorship is abolished in England.

▲ The Mogul emperor Aurangzeb (1659–1707) gained the throne by violence, murdering his brothers and imprisoning his father. He ruled India as a merciless tyrant. His brutal army put down many rebellions and kept the country subdued. He alienated the many different communities of his empire, particularly the Hindus who were persecuted for their religion. Many people were taxed to starvation to pay for his excesses.

▶ Also known as the Society of Friends, the Quakers are a religious group founded in England in the mid-17th century. They have always believed that men and women are equal so women were encouraged to preach. Here a woman talks to people assembled at a Quaker meeting.

▶ Louis XIV of France was one of the most powerful kings of the period. He ruled his glittering court in splendor. But he was very conscious of acting the role of supreme monarch. Even getting up in the morning and going to bed at night were attended by elaborate ceremonies. Each nobleman had a role at these rituals and strict etiquette governed who should hand Louis his shirt or his shoes.

African States

In the 17th century, Africa south of the Sahara was a patchwork of different peoples, kingdoms, and empires. Each had its own customs and forms of government, spoke its own language, and worshiped its own gods. The people were expert farmers and workers in cloth and metals. They mined for gold and by this time had developed many other crafts and skills.

A number of states occupied the forest zone along the West African coast. In 1625, the new kingdom of Dahomey was set up by King Akaba. Dahomey was

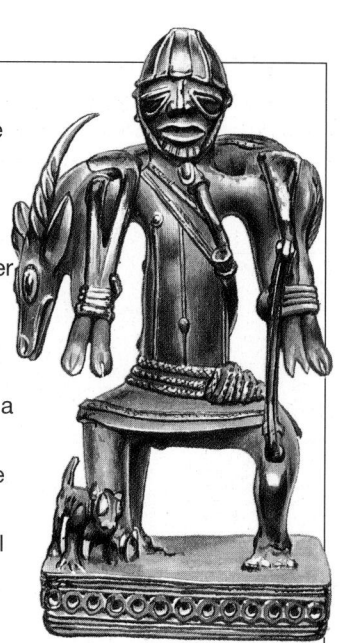

THE GOLD COAST

Europeans named the land north of the Portuguese fort of Elmina, the Gold Coast. This region later became part of the Asante empire. The symbol of power for the Asante rulers was a stool made of solid gold. The Asante were very skilled goldsmiths. This small golden figure was used to weigh gold.

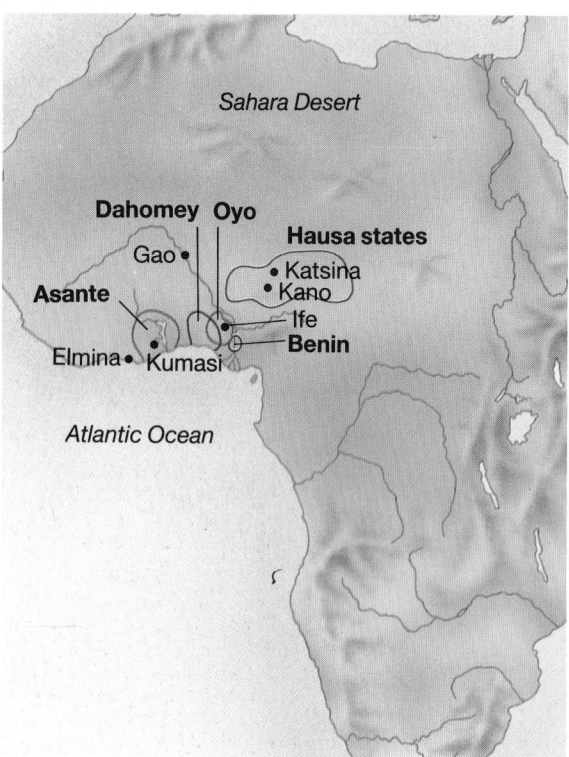

overrun a hundred years later by the Yorubas of the kingdom of Oyo (now part of Nigeria). In 1689, Osei Tutu founded the powerful Asante empire and built its capital at Kumasi. It grew wealthy from trade, particularly cola nuts and gold, and by selling slaves.

All these states were by no means isolated from the outside world. Arab merchants crossed the Sahara to trade with centers such as Ife in Oyo, and Benin. Europeans built small forts along the coast and traded cloth and firearms for slaves and gold. The Portuguese, Dutch, English, and French all set up trading posts on the African coast.

▼ An oba (ruler) of Benin in a procession of his people. Once the richest state in West Africa, by the 18th century the kingdom of Benin's power was on the wane. It too was overwhelmed by the growing strength of the Yoruba people and the kingdom of Oyo.

▲ The Muslim religion was brought to West Africa across the Sahara by the Arabs. The kings of Gao became Muslims as early as 987 A.D. The Hausa states of Katsina and Kano also adopted the faith of Islam, but the coastal kingdoms kept their own religions. Much of northeast Africa was under Ottoman control. They also plied a lucrative slave trade for the Muslim world.

▼ *Captured enemies in a slave war were marched off to the slave markets on the coast. There slaves were examined and branded to show that they were strong enough to survive the voyage to America.*

Africa provided the slaves needed to work the rapidly growing plantations in the Americas. Millions were shipped across the Atlantic. Many died either during slave wars between different African states to capture slaves or on the terrible voyage across the Atlantic. To lose such an enormous number of its people was a catastrophe for Africa.

1689 Germany: The war between France and the League of Augsburg is now joined by England and the Netherlands (to 1697). France invades the Palatinate. England: Parliament passes the Bill of Rights which establishes a constitutional monarchy in Britain and bars Roman Catholics from succeeding to the throne. William III and Mary II become joint monarchs of England and Scotland (to 1694). The Toleration Act grants freedom of worship to dissenters in England. Russia: Peter the Great becomes tsar (to 1725). West Africa: Osei Tutu founds the Asante empire.

1690 Ireland: At the battle of the Boyne the former James II's Irish and French force is greatly outnumbered by a Protestant army led by William III of England. James is defeated and returns to exile in France. The victory confirms William III's control of Ireland. England: French defeat an Anglo-Dutch fleet at the battle of Beachy Head. Balkans: Ottoman Turks recapture Belgrade from the Austrians. India: English establish a trading settlement at Calcutta.

An Asante helmet decorated with gold animal horns and charms. Europeans, unable to buy slaves with gold from the Asante because they had all they needed, bought them with guns instead and increased Asante power.

Ireland

The Irish never took kindly to English rule. Henry II of England conquered them in 1171, and for the next 400 years English monarchs struggled to maintain their authority there. Relations between the English and the Irish became more and more strained as time passed.

Part of the problem lay in the different religions of the two countries. Since the 16th century the Irish had been Catholic while the English were Protestant. Irish priests taught that the English were heretics with no rightful authority over Ireland and maintained that it was lawful to rebel against them. The English were well aware of this hostility and took strong measures to keep the Irish in subjection. The Irish reacted with frequent revolts.

From an English point of view, the solution to the growing Irish hostility seemed to be to replace the Catholics with loyal Protestants. This policy was applied in the province of Ulster. By the middle of the 17th century, Protestant settlers from England

▲ Kilkenny was the center of the Irish revolt of 1641–1649. In 1641 the Catholics massacred the Antrim Protestants. Cromwell butchered the garrisons of Drogheda and Wexford in 1649.

▼ After James II's defeat at the battle of the Boyne in 1690 he lost all hope of regaining the throne of England from William.

PLANTATION

The Plantation of Ulster was the policy adopted to replace the Roman Catholic Irish living there with Protestant settlers from England, Wales, and Scotland. Plantation started under the Tudors and was not just confined to Ulster. By 1665, Irish Catholics owned only one-fifth of the land in Ireland.

and Scotland outnumbered the original Catholic inhabitants of the province.

The Irish were already in revolt in 1642 when civil war began in England (*see* pages 430–431). Oliver Cromwell was therefore not able to tackle the problem of Ireland until 1649. When he arrived with a large army, the Irish uprising was crushed with a brutality that has never been forgiven.

Irish hopes were briefly raised when the Catholic James II became king of England, but he was forced to give up the crown and flee abroad. In 1689, he landed in Ireland with a French army to try to win back his throne. After failing to capture the Protestant town of Derry, James was defeated by William III of England. After this the Protestant English conquest of Ireland seemed complete.

The emblem of the Bank of England gave it its name "the Old Lady of Threadneedle Street."

1691 Balkans: Austrians win a decisive victory over the Ottoman Turks at Szalankemen and strengthen their grip on Transylvania. Rome: Innocent XII becomes pope (to 1700). England: Naturalist John Ray writes a book suggesting that fossils are the remains of animals from the distant past. Ireland: Treaty of Limerick formally ends the conflict between William III and James II.

1692 England: An Anglo-Dutch naval force destroys a French fleet at the battle of La Hogue and ends the planned French invasion of England. North America: Witchcraft trials take place at Salem, Massachusetts. West Indies: An earthquake destroys the city of Port Royal in Jamaica.

1693 Netherlands: French defeat William III of England at Neerwinden. England: The National Debt is established. North America: The colony of Carolina is divided into North and South. Jamaica: Kingston is founded to replace Port Royal as the capital city. New Mexico: Governor Ponce de Leon completes the reconquest of New Mexico for Spain.

1694 England: Queen Mary II dies. William survives as sole ruler of England and Scotland (to 1702). France: French Academy publishes the first French dictionary.

1695 England: The government ends the censorship (restrictions on what can be reported) of the press.

▲ *James Butler, Duke of Ormonde, governed Ireland under Charles I of England. Cromwell drove him out in 1649 but he returned as Governor under Charles II.*

1696 Peter the Great takes Black Sea port of Azov from the Ottoman empire. He also sends 50 young Russians to study shipbuilding and defense in England, the Netherlands and Venice. England: The currency is reorganized under Isaac Newton and philosopher John Locke.

1697 France: Nine years of war between France and the allies of the League of Augsburg ends. France returns lands conquered from Spain. Charles Perrault publishes the first collection of European fairy stories. China: The Manchus conquer western Mongolia.

An early example of a baling machine, an agricultural machine that was used to make bales of hay.

1698 Russia: Palace guards rebel against Peter the Great. The rebels are executed. Spain: Charles II names the Elector of Bavaria as his heir. Germany: The future King George I of England becomes the Elector of Hanover. Vietnam: The Cambodians evacuate Saigon.

1699 Austria: The war ends between Turkey and Austria and her allies Poland and Venice. Oceania: English navigator William Dampier explores the northwest coast of Australia and the Pacific islands.

1700 Russia: The Great Northern War starts with Sweden over supremacy in the Baltic (to 1721). Spain: In his final will Charles II of Spain names Philip of Anjou, grandson of Louis XIV of France, as his heir. Philip succeeds as Philip V (to 1746). Rome: Clement XI becomes pope (to 1721). Germany: Academy of Science founded in Berlin.

The Great Northern War

The Great Northern War was fought between Sweden and other northern European powers led by Peter the Great of Russia. It cost Sweden most of its empire and Russia became the leading power in the Baltic.

In 1700, Sweden was attacked by Denmark, Poland, and Russia. Sweden's King Charles XII was only 18-years-old and the leaders of the other powers hoped to take advantage of his inexperience. But Charles proved to be a born leader. By the end of the year, he had inflicted a crushing defeat on the Russian army at the battle of Narva in Estonia, and forced both Poland and Denmark out of the war.

Eight years later Charles invaded

▲ *The extent of the Swedish empire at the beginning of the 17th century. At this time Sweden was the greatest military power in northern Europe. It was well placed to invade Russia, as it did in 1708.*

Russia. The Russians retreated, destroying everything as they went. This caused the Swedes to run short of food and, throughout the bitter winter of 1708–1709, the hungry Swedes struggled for survival against repeated Russian attacks. By spring Charles's army had been reduced to half its size. At the battle of Poltava in June 1709, the Swedes were beaten by the Russians. Charles was forced to flee to Turkey.

He returned to Sweden in 1714, beating off a planned Danish invasion two years later. He invaded the Danish province of Norway and was killed there in 1718. Without Charles to lead them, and exhausted by 20 years of fighting, the Swedes agreed peace terms in 1721.

◀ A 17th-century Swedish soldier's kit including a scythe and knapsack. At the battle of Narva, 8,000 Swedish soldiers defeated 40,000 Russians.

▼ The battle of Poltava, near Kiev, in 1709 marked the end of Charles XII's advance into Russia. His army was beaten by a much larger, well-equipped Russian force.

Trade

World trade grew steadily throughout the 17th century. The increase was partly due to the development of long-distance trading between America and Southeast Asia on the one hand, and trade between America and Europe on the other.

In North America, once the colonists had mastered growing the crops that were necessary for their survival, they began to export a variety of raw materials to England. The pine forests of northern New England provided timber, turpentine, pitch, and resin for shipbuilding, and offshore the seas teemed with fish. The middle and southern colonies exported flax, wheat, oats, rice, corn, and tobacco.

Raccoon

Beaver

THE FUR TRADE

The French and English were rivals in the North American fur trade but they operated in different ways. The English waited in their trading posts for the American trappers to bring in their loads of furs. French traders went out with the Native North Americans to hunt beaver, raccoon, bear, fox, and mink on journeys far into the interior. Here two famous French traders, Medard Chouart and Pierre Radisson, meet Native North Americans near Lake Superior.

◄ Amsterdam was the center of European trading in the 17th century. A bank was founded there in 1609 for depositing and lending money. Customers were not allowed to overdraw their accounts, but it did extend credit to institutions such as the city of Amsterdam and the Dutch East India Company. Three years later a Stock Exchange (left) was set up to buy and sell commodities such as furs, corn, and timber. The Bank of England was founded in 1694 to lend money to William III to pay for the country's war against France.

1602 Dutch East India Company founded.

1609 Bank of Amsterdam is set up.

1612 Stock Exchange founded in Amsterdam.

1641 Wampum (shell beads) becomes the coinage in Massachusetts.

1651 English Navigation Acts insist that all imports are carried by English ships or by ships from the country of origin.

1652 First Anglo-Dutch War starts over trade.

1661 First banknotes are issued in Stockholm in Sweden.

1670 Hudson's Bay Company is set up in London.

1694 Bank of England is founded.

1696 London weavers riot in protest against cheap cloth imports from India.

▲ *Tobacco was the main export of the colony of Virginia. Shops advertised tobacco with signs that often showed Native North Americans smoking pipes.*

▲ *This 1699 note is the oldest surviving English banknote. Although Europe had known about paper money from China since the 13th century, it was not until the 1600s that it came into use. Banks issued individually written notes which could be exchanged for gold or silver coins. In North America some of the first paper money was made out of playing cards. When the French colonies ran out of cash the colonial government issued playing cards, signed by the governor, instead of money.*

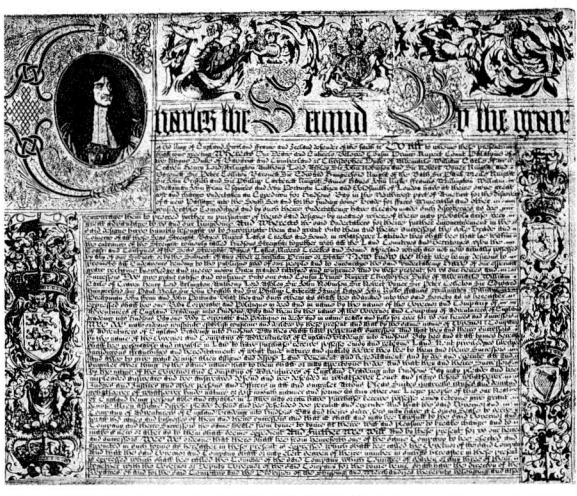

▲ *By the 17th century coins had been in use in India for centuries. The Mogul rulers continued the practice. This coin was issued in 1611.*

◄ *A charter granted by Charles II of England in 1670 to the Hudson's Bay Company in Canada. It gave the company the right to trade and to govern its territory.*

The Spanish Succession

When Charles II of Spain died in 1700 he had no children to succeed him. The question of who was to become king of Spain and the Spanish empire led to the War of the Spanish Succession.

The Bourbons of France and Habsburgs of Austria both claimed the Spanish throne. Since neither side wanted to go to war to win it, before Charles II died they signed an agreement dividing his empire between them. But Charles made a will leaving his lands to Louis XIV of France's grandson, Philip of Anjou.

Louis decided to ignore his agreement with the Habsburgs and accept the will on behalf of his grandson. The prospect of an alliance between the power of France and the huge Spanish empire was not acceptable to other European nations. They were ready to fight to prevent it and by the end of 1701 western Europe was at war.

In September 1701, England, the

ENGLAND SPANISH NETHERLANDS
• Utrecht
Oudenaarde ⚔ ⚔ Ramillies
Malplaquet
⚔ Blenheim
Vienna •
FRANCE GERMANY AUSTRIA
Savoy
ITALY
PORTUGAL
SPAIN
Naples
SARDINIA
• Gibraltar
SICILY •

■ To Spain   ■ To France
■ To England ■ To Savoy
■ To Austria

▲ At the Peace of Utrecht in 1713, France retained her frontiers. Austria took the Spanish Netherlands and Naples. England gained Gibraltar and Newfoundland. Philip V remained king of Spain.

▼ Only a third of Marlborough's army at the battle of Blenheim was English. The majority of his troops were Germans in British pay. Without the help of the Austrian army led by Prince Eugène, it is unlikely that Marlborough would have won.

Marlborough

John Churchill, Duke of Marlborough (1650–1722), was made commander-in-chief of the allied forces in 1702. He won four great battles at Blenheim (1704), Ramillies (1706), Oudenarde (1708), and Malplaquet(1709). As a result of these victories, the French had to seek peace.

Prince Eugene

Prince Eugène of Savoy (1663–1736) joined the Austrian army to fight the Turks at the siege of Vienna in 1683. He was a gifted soldier, and by 1701 had risen to be commander-in-chief of the Austrian forces. He fought together with Marlborough at the battles of Blenheim and Oudenarde.

1701 England: To prevent the Roman Catholic Stuarts regaining the throne, after the death of Princess Anne's (queen in 1702) last surviving child, the Act of Settlement establishes that the line of succession to the throne lies in the Protestant House of Hanover. English agricultural reformer Jethro Tull invents the horse-drawn seed drill. France: The former King James II of England dies in exile. Louis XIV recognizes his son as James III of England (the Old Pretender). The War of Spanish Succession starts (to 1713). It is fought between France and a Grand Alliance of England, the Netherlands, the Holy Roman Empire, and several of the German states. Michigan: Antoine de La Mothe Cadillac establishes a French fort at Detroit.

1702 Britain: Princess Anne, daughter of James II becomes queen of England and Scotland (to 1714). She is the last Stuart sovereign. The Duke of Marlborough is appointed captain-general of English forces in the War of Spanish Succession against France. Poland: Charles XII takes Warsaw and Cracow.

Netherlands, most of the German states, and Austria formed a grand alliance against France. The first phase of the war ended in disaster for the French. In 1704, a French army was overwhelmed by a combined English, German, and Austrian force commanded by a brilliant general, the Duke of Marlborough. The battle took place at Blenheim on the Danube River. The fighting then moved to the Spanish Netherlands on the northeast frontier of France where Marlborough won three more great victories.

By the end of 1706 an Austrian army under Prince Eugène had driven the French from Italy. The allies invaded Spain but the French pushed them out, allowing Louis's grandson Philip V to remain on the Spanish throne. The long war had exhausted both sides and in 1713 peace was signed at Utrecht.

Pendants of this kind, displaying the insignia of the Spanish Inquisition on the reverse (a cross, feather, and sword), had to be worn at public and religious functions by order of King Philip III of Spain in 1603. This pendant was made in the late 17th century.

War and Weapons

During this period great changes took place in the way wars were fought. The invention of a quick firing flintlock musket, armed with a bayonet (dagger) fixed to the top was a powerful weapon in battle. It quickly caused an alarming rise in the number of casualties.

Many commanders of armies therefore tried to avoid fighting pitched battles in the open. Instead they attempted to outmaneuver the enemy and then retired behind strong defenses. Only well-trained troops could cope with the new tactics.

Governments found it cheaper to maintain properly-paid regular armies than to rely on men who joined up for a few months and then went home to gather the harvest. Many professional standing armies appeared.

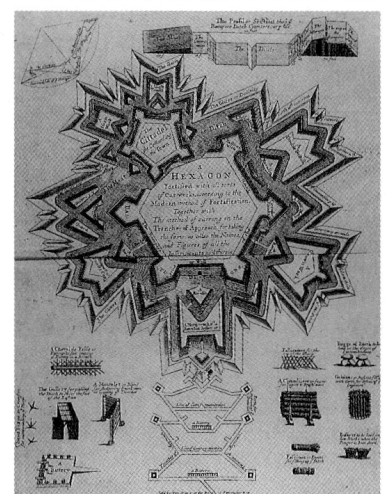

◄ Sieges of fortified places became major features of 17th-century wars. At the outset, the attackers held the advantage. Their improved siege guns easily knocked down the medieval walls which served as the defense of most cities at this time. As a result, much effort was put into designing fortifications strong enough to withstand the latest weapons and tactics. The French engineer Sébastien de Vauban built or reconstructed 160 fortresses on the frontiers of France.

◄ Gustavus Adolphus of Sweden equipped his army with 3-pounder guns that could be easily carried by the soldiers. Their canister shot tore holes in enemy armies.

▲ Parliamentary Roundheads fought Royalist Cavaliers in England's civil wars. Officers on both sides wore armor but Roundheads had simpler uniforms.

◀ Indian
soldiers of the
17th century
fought dressed
in coats of thick,
quilted cloth. The
cloth was tough
enough to deflect
the edge of a
sword while still
allowing the wearer
ease of movement.

WHEN IT HAPPENED

1618–1648 The Thirty Years' War.

1642–1651 The English Civil War.

1652 The Anglo-Dutch Wars begin.

1655–1660 The First Northern War. Sweden
fights Russia, Poland, and Denmark.

1675–1674 War between France and Holland.

1683 The Ottoman Turks are defeated at Vienna,
Austria by a combined European force.

1689–1697 The War of the League of Augsburg.

1700–1721 The Great Northern War.

1701–1714 The War of the Spanish Succession.

▼ Firearms such as these kept monarchs safely on
their thrones. Only kings could afford to equip their
armies with them. As a result, many kings grew too
powerful for rebel subjects to overthrow.

Double-barreled wheel-lock pistol

Flemish matchlock

▶ The 17th-century
battlefield as shown by
the battle of Naseby in
1645 when the Royalist
army of King Charles I of
England was soundly
beaten by Parliament's
Roundheads. The
Roundheads are in the
foreground. Both sides
have drawn up their army
in the same way. Each
army is made up of
infantry (alternate
companies of musketeers
and pikemen) in the
center and cavalry on the
outer wings.

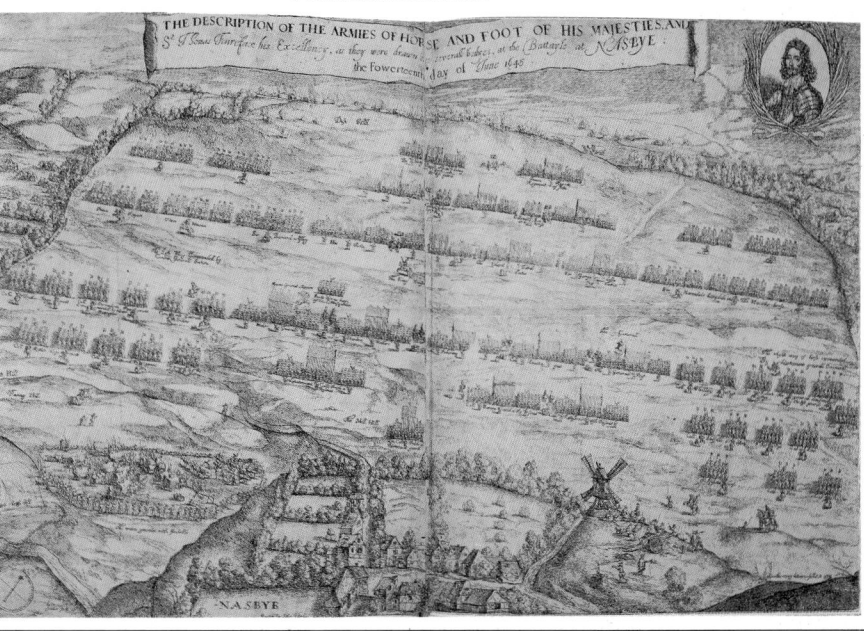

1703 Hungary: Revolt against Austria begins (to 1711). Russia: Peter the Great founds St. Petersburg on the Baltic coast to replace Moscow as Russia's capital city. North America: Delaware in New England breaks away from Pennsylvania and becomes a separate colony.

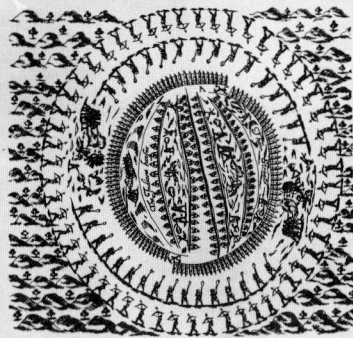

A plan of an attack on a Pequot Indian village by colonists after one of them was murdered.

1704 War of Spanish Succession: An English fleet captures Gibraltar. Allied English and Austrian armies under Marlborough and Prince Eugène defeat the French at the battle of Blenheim in Bavaria. England: Isaac Newton publishes *Optics* defending his theories on the nature of light. Germany: Earliest subscription library opens in Berlin. Boston: A regular weekly newspaper, the *Boston News-Letter*, begins publication.

1705 Austria: Joseph I becomes Holy Roman emperor (to 1711). England: Astronomer Edmond Halley predicts the return in 1758 of the comet which last appeared in 1682. Russia: Peter the Great's campaign to modernize his country meets with armed resistance.

1706 War of Spanish Succession: Marlborough defeats the French at the battle of Ramillies in the Netherlands. Prince Eugène also beats the French at the battle of Turin in Italy.

1707 England: Act of Union unites England and Scotland under the name of Great Britain. India: Aurangzeb's death leads to the break up of the Mogul empire.

Colonial America

The French were the first Europeans to settle in North America (*see* pages 410–411), but many more English people crossed the Atlantic to settle there. The majority were Puritans. After 1620, the anti-Puritan laws in England became more severe, which encouraged people to leave. In 1630, a group of about a thousand settlers landed in Massachusetts Bay and founded the city of Boston. Within 20 years of the first Puritans arriving in America there were 20,000 English people living in Massachusetts. Some of these colonists moved to Rhode Island and Connecticut. In 1681, the English king gave Pennsylvania to a group of Quakers led by William Penn. Penn helped poor people to settle in this new colony and many English, Scottish, Irish, and German settlers quickly moved there. These northern colonies were called New England and grew rapidly.

THE SUPPLY BOAT

Ships from the mother country brought the basic necessities of life to new colonies. Their cargo included spinning wheels and looms; lengths of cloth and canvas; copper pots and frying pans; lanterns, lamps, and candlesticks; plates, mugs, knives, and spoons; spades, scythes, axes, saws, hammers, and nails; muskets, powder, and shot.

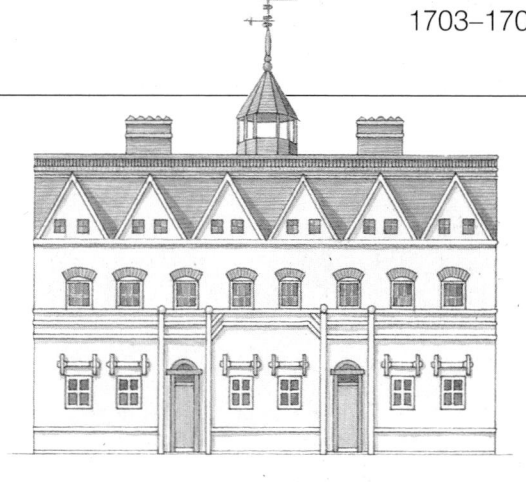

HARVARD COLLEGE

The Puritans of New England had a high regard for education. By law all parents had to ensure that their children learned to read. In 1636 the Massachusetts government founded a college in Cambridge. They called it Harvard College in memory of John Harvard, who left it his library of books and a large sum of money in his will.

▲ A small family farm of about 20 acres (8 ha) in Maryland. The houses and farm buildings are neat, strong, and well cared for. They look very like those being built in England at the time. The family kept cattle, pigs, and chickens, and grew tobacco, cotton, wheat, and vegetables.

▼ In 1692, several young girls in the town of Salem, Massachusetts, claimed that they had been bewitched by a West Indian slave. Most people of the time believed in witchcraft and the Puritans of Salem took fright; 15 women and 4 men were tried and hanged as a result.

In the far southwest, Spanish pioneers under Juan de Oñate had pushed north out of Mexico and claimed a vast new territory for Spain. Onate gave it the name New Mexico and established its capital at Santa Fe in 1609. With Florida also in their hands, the Spaniards might have won the whole of North America. But Spain lost its control over the seas. French settlers started to arrive but they were eclipsed by English colonists who made the journey in large numbers.

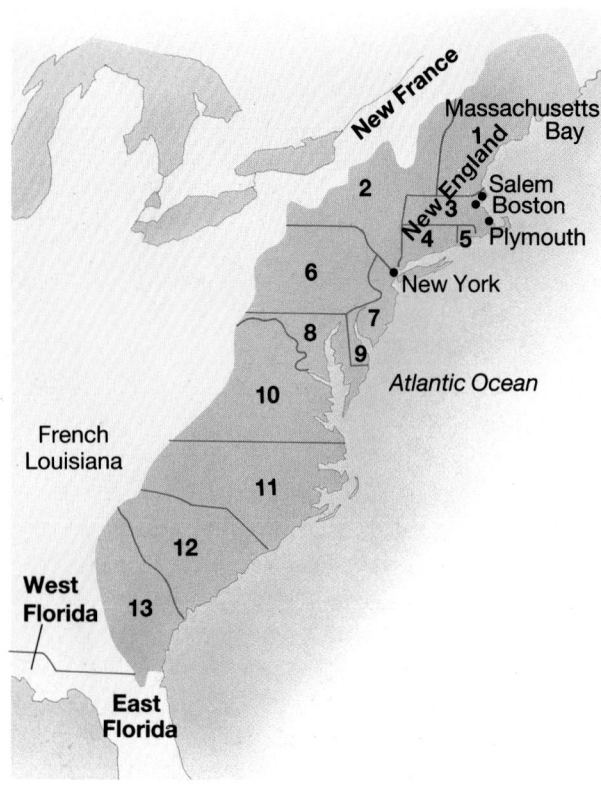

New France

New England

Massachusetts Bay

1

2

Salem
Boston

3

4   5   Plymouth

6

New York

7

8

9

Atlantic Ocean

10

French Louisiana

11

12

West Florida   13

East Florida

THE 13 ENGLISH COLONIES

1 New Hampshire 1680

2 New York 1664

3 Massachusetts 1629

4 Connecticut 1633

5 Rhode Island 1635

6 Pennsylvania 1681

7 New Jersey 1664

8 Maryland 1632

9 Delaware 1702

10 Virginia 1607

11 N. Carolina 1670

12 S. Carolina 1670

13 Georgia 1732

Penn

The wealthy Quaker William Penn (1644 –1718) founded Pennsylvania in 1682. Penn called it a "holy experiment" where people could worship as they wished. He also founded the city of Philadelphia, "the city of brotherly love."

COLONIAL ART

The colonization of North America is well documented in arts and crafts, such as this Delft tile commemorating the sailing of the *Mayflower*. Many settlers took the arts and crafts of their home countries with them. For example, in 17th-century England it was the custom for wealthy people to have their portraits painted. English settlers followed this custom and as a result portraits of several leading colonists have survived.

▲ *The 13 original English colonies stretched from New France in the north to the Spanish territory of Florida in the south. They later became the first 13 states of what came to be called the United States of America.*

Unlike the Spaniards in South America, the English and French found no gold or silver so they mostly had to make a living by farming, fishing, and the fur trade. Neither were there many Native North Americans in the areas where they settled, so they had to provide the labor themselves. The only exception was Virginia which exported large quantities of tobacco with the help of slaves brought over from Africa.

The first European settlers built simple log cabins to withstand the cold winters; but as they cleared more land, they built bigger and more comfortable houses. By 1700 there were 12 English colonies on or near the Atlantic coast. Some 250,000 people from England had settled in North America by this time compared with only 20,000 from France.

Revolution and Independence

The 18th century is often called "the century of revolutions." In the years 1708 to 1835, there were revolutions against governments in many parts of the world; some were successful, others were not. There were also revolutions in farming and industry, in science, technology, and medicine, in transportation, and in the arts, especially literature.

Political revolutions happened because people felt dissatisfied with the way their country was run. In North America, North Africa, and Greece, they rebelled against rule by a foreign power. They wanted to govern themselves. In France the citizens executed their weak king and tried to introduce a democracy.

However, not all rebellions were successful. In Britain the Jacobites – supporters of the exiled Stuart king, James II – who wanted to replace the existing king with their claimant to the throne, were easily defeated. In India the local peoples who fought against growing colonial power also faced defeat.

In Europe landowners and engineers pioneered new inventions that revolutionized farming and industry. Bigger and better crops were produced.

Steam-powered machines turned out enormous quantities of clothes and tools, in place of traditional handmade goods. Steam was also used to drive ships and the first-ever railroad trains.

Important discoveries were made in all branches of learning. Philosophers developed a new respect for human intelligence. Poets celebrated freedom and imagination. For the first time, scientists understood how electricity worked and started to classify animals and plants into separate species. Advances were made in chemistry and, in medicine, vaccinating against smallpox saved thousands of lives.

▼ *The first passenger train in England opened in 1825 and ran between Stockton and Darlington. It reached speeds of up to 15 mph (24 km/h).*

The Americas

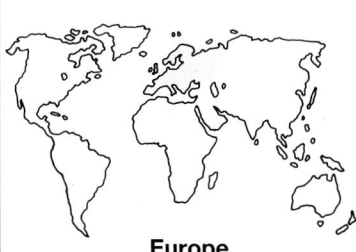

Europe

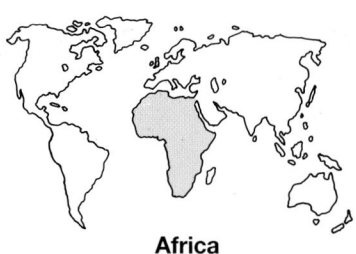

Africa

1720 Population of British colonies is 474,000. Boston is largest city at 12,000.
1728 Bering begins to explore Alaska.
1732 Benjamin Franklin publishes *Poor Richard's Almanac*, an immediate success.
1753 The Liberty Bell is hung in Pennsylvania State House and cracks with first stroke of the clapper.
1759 British capture Quebec from the French.
1763 Britain wins control of Canada.
1775–1783 The Revolutionary War.
1776 Declaration of Independence.
1789 George Washington becomes the first president of the United States.
1803 Louisiana purchase.
1808–1828 Independence movements in South America.

1819 U.S. buys Florida from Spain.

1709 Battle of Poltava, Russia defeats Sweden.
1713 Treaty of Utrecht ends War of Spanish Succession.
1715 Jacobite rebellion in Scotland and England.

1740 Frederick the Great comes to power in Prussia.
1740–1748 War of Austrian Succession.
1745 Jacobite rebellion in Scotland and England.
1756–1763 Seven Years' War.
1762 Catherine the Great comes to power in Russia.
1783 Russia takes over the Crimea.
1789 French Revolution.
1791–1794 Russia wins control of the northern Black Sea coast from the Ottoman empire.
1792 French Republic founded.
1793 Louis XVI of France is executed.
1799 Napoleon comes to power.
1807 Slave trading abolished in British empire.
1812 Napoleon invades Russia.
1815 Battle of Waterloo. French monarchy reestablished.

1710 Algeria becomes self-governing.
1714 Tripolitania becomes independent from Ottoman empire.

1730 Kingdom of Borno (central Sudan) becomes powerful.

1776–1786 Fulani set up Muslim states in West Africa.
1779–1781 and **1793** Wars between Xhosa peoples and Boer (Dutch) settlers in South Africa.
1798 Napoleon invades Egypt.
1800s Kingdom of Buganda grows powerful in East Africa.
1804 Fulani nation conquers Hausa peoples in West Africa.
1806 Britain takes control of Dutch Cape Colony.
1811 Mehemet Ali comes to power in Egypt.
1818–1828 Zulu kingdom ruled by the Shaka.
1822 State of Liberia founded.
1829 Greece becomes independent from Ottoman empire.
1830 France invades Algeria.

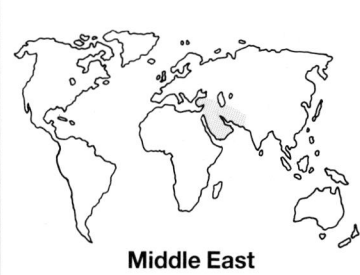

Middle East

Far East

Australasia and Pacific

1700–1800 Long period of civil war in Easter Island region.

1727 The Persians and Ottomans form an alliance against Russia.

1736 Nadir Shah seizes control in Persia and overthrows the Safavid dynasty.

1747 Durrani dynasty founded in Afghanistan.

1793 Sultan Selim III reforms the Ottoman empire.

The lion and Sun became the national symbol of Persia (now Iran) in 1834.

1736 Emperor Qianlong comes to power in China.
1739 Nadir Shah, ruler of Persia, attacks Delhi.

1757–1824 Burma united under Konbaung dynasty.
1757 Battle of Plassey. Britain controls much of India.
1761 Capture of Pondicherry. Britain defeats French power in India.
1769 The French East India Company is dissolved.

1795–1804 White Lotus rebellion against the Chinese government.
1799 Tipu Sultan, ruler of Mysore, killed by the British.
1803–1818 Marathas fight against growing British power in India.

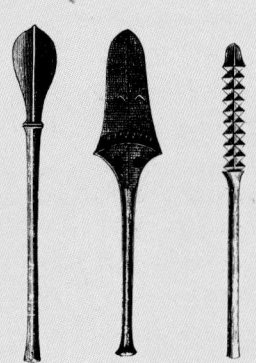

South Sea islanders' war clubs.

1768–1779 Captain James Cook explores the South Pacific until his death.
1788 Britain establishes New South Wales as a penal colony.
1789 Mutiny by British seamen on the *Bounty* leads to Pitcairn Island's being settled.
1793 First free settlers arrive in Australia.

1824 A penal colony is established in Brisbane.
1829 Britain claims western Australia as part of its empire.

The World

In **North America**, the United States won its independence from British rule, but this brought problems for Native North Americans. Many people emigrated from Europe and took more and more land. In **South** and **Central America**, the colonies there too fought for freedom from Spain and Portugal and won.

In **Europe**, Prussia and Russia rose to become major European powers, while the French Revolution of 1789 marked the end of the old-style monarchy in France. In Britain new inventions led to revolutions in farming, transportation and industry that quickly spread to the rest of the world.

In **Africa**, the Fulani, Zulu, and Buganda peoples established new kingdoms. African states in the north threw off Ottoman control.

The Mogul empire in **India** collapsed and Britain and France fought for control of its land. **China** conquered Tibet, but faced problems at home. **Japan** banned contact with the West. In the Pacific the arrival of Europeans threatened the traditional way of life.

NORTH
AMERICA

CANADA

PACIFIC
OCEAN

UNITED STATES
OF AMERICA

ATLANTIC
OCEAN

CENTRAL
AMERICA

Caribbean

▲ The first of many battles during the Revolutionary War took place at Bunker Hill, near Boston.

▼ Pierre Dominique Toussaint L'Ouverture led the slave revolt against the French colonists in Haiti.

SOUTH
AMERICA

▶ British colonials in India enjoyed a life of wealth and luxury. They employed many Indian servants to attend to their every need.

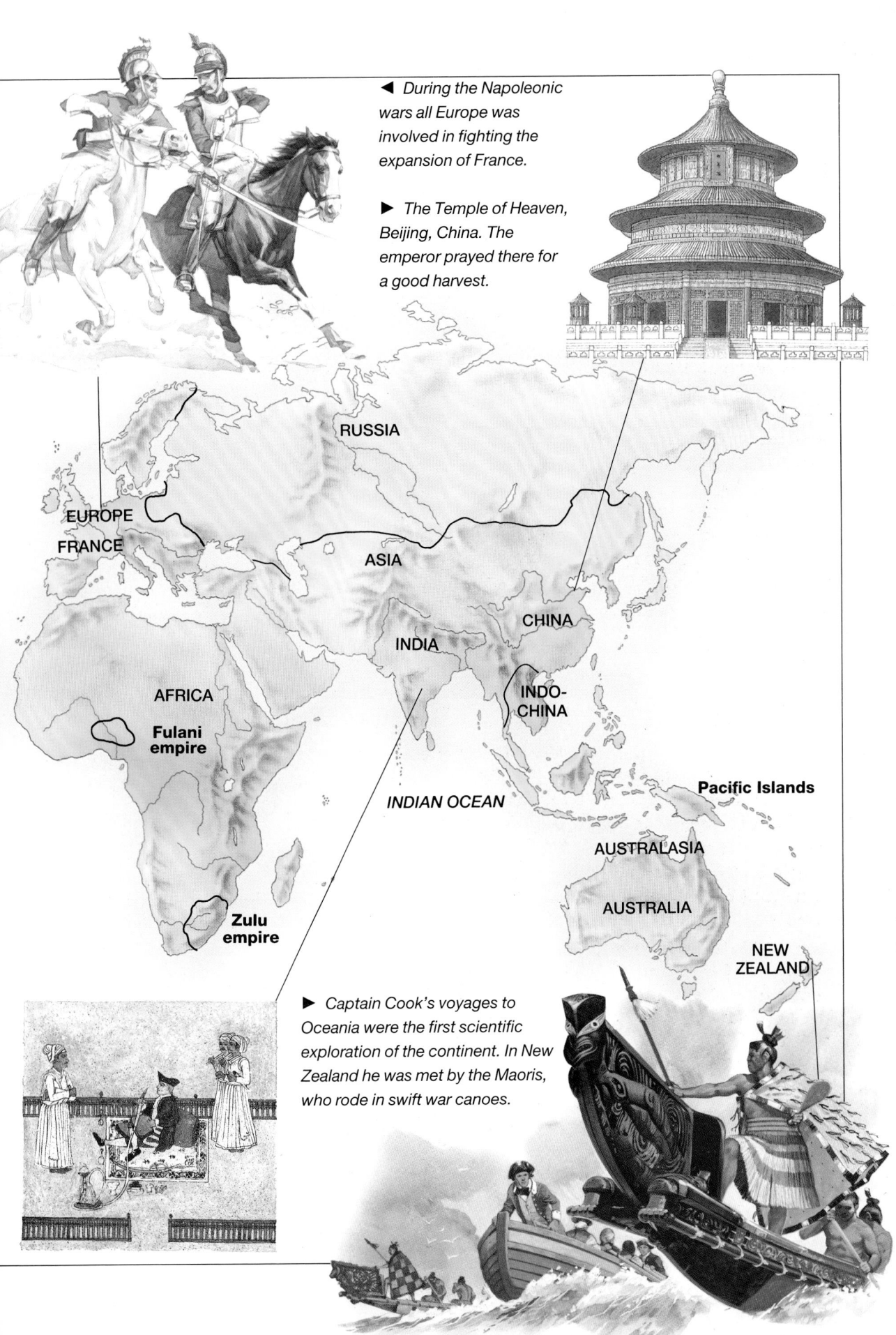

◄ During the Napoleonic wars all Europe was involved in fighting the expansion of France.

► The Temple of Heaven, Beijing, China. The emperor prayed there for a good harvest.

RUSSIA

EUROPE

FRANCE

ASIA

CHINA

INDIA

INDO-CHINA

AFRICA

Fulani empire

INDIAN OCEAN

Pacific Islands

AUSTRALASIA

AUSTRALIA

Zulu empire

NEW ZEALAND

► Captain Cook's voyages to Oceania were the first scientific exploration of the continent. In New Zealand he was met by the Maoris, who rode in swift war canoes.

1708 War of Spanish Succession: British and Austrian troops defeat the French at the battle of Oudenarde. The Grand Alliance of Austria, Netherlands, and England fight against France, which is allied with German and Italian states. Russia: King Charles XII of Sweden invades Ukraine. Peter the Great, Tsar of Russia, introduces government reforms.

1709 Britain: Abraham Darby produces a coke furnace to smelt iron ore. Russia: Peter the Great defeats the Swedish army.

1710 Russia: As a result of Peter's policy of expansion, Russia is at war with Turkey.

1711 Charles VI of Austria becomes Holy Roman emperor (to 1740). Carolina: Indians attack colonists on Roanoke and Chowan rivers, starting Tuscarora War.

The Schonbrunn imperial summer palace in Vienna was built between 1696 and 1730.

1712 Britain: Thomas Newcomen builds the first steam-driven engine to use pistons.

1713 The Peace of Utrecht ends the War of Spanish Succession. King Philip V of Spain gives up his claim to the French throne and loses Spain's lands in Europe. France's domination in Europe is checked. Holy Roman Empire: Emperor Charles VI issues "Pragmatic Sanction" to ensure that his children inherit his lands undivided. By 1720, it is clear that his daughter Maria Theresa will be his heir. Prussia: Frederick William I becomes king (to 1740). He sets up a new army of 80,000 men, making Prussia a leading European power. Vietnam: In a continuing war against Christianity, French missionaries are driven out of Tongking.

Austria and Prussia

In 1711, Charles VI, the Archduke of Austria, became Holy Roman emperor. This made him the most powerful man in Europe, and added the lands of the Holy Roman Empire, which stretched from Silesia in the north to Hungary in the south, to his territory in Austria. As he had no sons he wanted his daughter, Maria Theresa, to rule after him and he spent his last years trying to get the other powers to agree to this.

After Charles died in 1740, three men claimed that they, not Maria Theresa, should be crowned. The rivals to the throne were Charles of Bavaria, King Philip V of Spain, and Augustus of Saxony. The situation became more complicated as other European states joined in. The War of the Austrian Succession broke out in 1740 when the Prussians invaded the Austrian province of Silesia. Prussia was supported by France, Bavaria, Saxony, Sardinia, and

▼ *Frederick the Great was king of Prussia from 1740 to 1786. He was stern, brave, and ambitious. Under his leadership, Prussia became a strong nation. But many men died as a result of his wars.*

Maria Theresa

1717 Born in Vienna.
1740 Inherits Austria,
Hungary, Silesia,
Bohemia, Italy, and the
Netherlands on the
death of her father.
1765 Co-ruler of Holy
Roman Empire with
her son, Joseph.
1780 Dies.

Spain. However, Britain, Hungary, and
the Netherlands backed Maria Theresa.

In 1742, Charles of Bavaria became
Holy Roman emperor and Prussia was
given Silesia. But Charles of Bavaria died
in 1745 and Maria Theresa's husband,
Francis of Lorraine, became Holy Roman
emperor in his place. The war ended in
1748, and under the terms of the treaty
of Aix-la-Chapelle Maria Theresa kept
Austria, Bohemia, and Hungary.

Prussia's rise to the status of major
European power began during the reign
of Frederick William I. He became king
in 1713, and built up the Prussian army.
His successor, Frederick the Great, used
the army to challenge the great powers
of Austria, France, and Russia and by the
end of his reign in 1786 he had doubled
the size of Prussian territory.

▶ *Prussia was originally just one of many small
states in northern Germany. It grew rapidly in size
between the 16th and 18th centuries, as Prussian rulers
conquered many new lands. During his reign Frederick
the Great added Silesia and part of Poland.*

▲ *During the War of Austrian Succession, French and
British foot soldiers fought at the battle of Fontenoy in
1745. Britain and France supported opposing sides in
the wars to decide who should govern the Holy Roman
Empire. The French won the battle and captured the
Austrian Netherlands (now Belgium).*

Austrian
Papal States
Prussian
Spanish Bourbons
Venetian
Great Britain
— Boundary of Holy Roman Empire

The Arts

The 18th century saw tremendous achievements in arts of all kinds. In China, jade carving showed great skill. In Japan, woodblock printing grew more advanced and haiku poetry became popular.

In Europe, the composers Handel, Beethoven, and Schubert wrote brilliant works. Constable, Ingres, and Goya were the famous artists of the day. Novelists, essayists, and journalists introduced new forms. Neoclassical poets aimed for elegance, while the later Romantic poets chose bold, emotional styles. In the theater, ballet developed and operas attracted keen, discriminating audiences who demanded realistic plots and characters.

▲ For many years, Europeans tried to copy the techniques used by Chinese porcelain makers. This figure was made in the Meissen factory near Dresden in 1765.

▲ The Wave, a print by the Japanese master Hokusai (died 1848). It is part of a famous series which all include Mount Fuji. Woodblock printing had a revival in Japan during the 17th century and became very popular. Hokusai developed it into an art form.

▼ The magnificent King's Theater in Turin, Italy. It opened in 1740 and staged operas. During the 18th century, operas were written which put more emphasis on the story and characters, instead of just the music. Mozart was one of the most famous composers of this time; among his operas are The Marriage of Figaro and Cosí fan Tutte.

◄ The famous ballet dancer, Marie-Anne de Cupis de Camargo (1710–1770). As ballet dancers became more skillful they started to perform in public, rather than just for monarchs and the court. Camargo was famous for her technical skill, although others were thought to be more graceful or better at telling a story through dance.

► This 18th-century Chinese jade pot is very finely carved. It was made to hold brushes used in calligraphy (writing), an important Chinese art form, sometimes described as "dancing on paper."

▼ A clavichord made in the 1720s, which produces a clear, light, delicate sound. Johann Sebastian Bach (1685–1750) wrote many pieces especially for the clavichord. During his lifetime his music was unknown outside Germany.

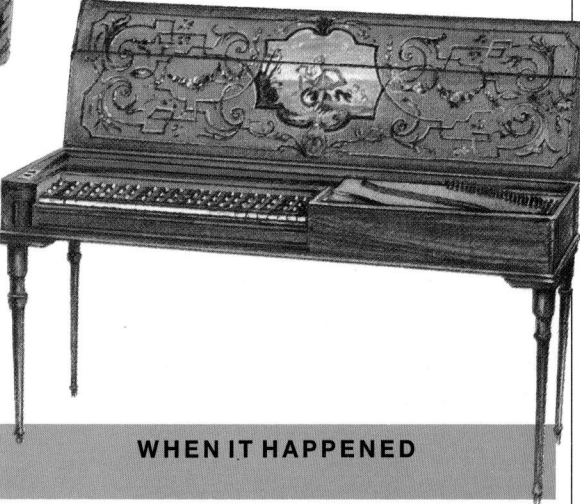

▼ Chintz (expertly-printed cotton fabric) was made in India for export to Europe. Designs like these were popular for clothes and furnishings. The word chintz is now applied to cotton fabric that has a glazed finish.

WHEN IT HAPPENED

1709 The first piano is made by the Italian Bartolomeo Cristofori.

1742 First playhouse opens in New York.

1755 Samuel Johnson publishes his mammoth *Dictionary of the English Language*.

1775 German poet Johann Wolfgang von Goethe begins his greatest work *Faust*, published in two parts in 1808 and 1832.

1798 The poems of English poets William Wordsworth and Samuel Taylor Coleridge start a new fashion for Romantic poetry.

► The musical genius, Wolfgang Amadeus Mozart (1756–1791), performing in public with his father and sister. Mozart was only seven, but he was already famous. He had played for the Austrian empress when he was six years old.

◄ The African American poet Phillis Wheatley was sold into slavery as a child, and shipped to America in 1761. Her poetry was admired by many other writers, as well as by the first president of the United States, George Washington.

The Jacobites

In Britain, Queen Anne died in 1714. As she had no surviving children, the Act of Settlement passed in 1701 said that the throne should go to the Protestant heirs of James I. Her cousin George of Hanover (a German state) became the new king. He was the great-grandson of James I and a Protestant, but he was a foreigner. Some people felt that the Scot, James Stuart, had a better claim. He was also a great-grandson of James I and the son of James II, but he was a Catholic. Also many Scots were unhappy because their nation had been joined with England to form a "United Kingdom" in 1707 (*see* page 459).

The Jacobites, who supported James Stuart, invaded England in 1715 and were defeated in November at Preston, Lancashire. James Stuart arrived in Scotland from France in December, but support for him was weakening, so early in 1716 James fled back to France.

In 1745, James's son, Charles Edward led another uprising. After a series of

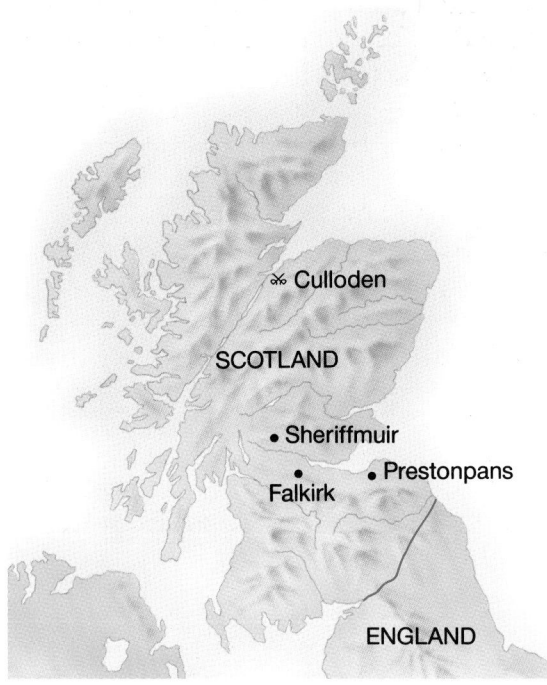

▼ In 1715, at the battle of Sheriffmuir, 12,000 Jacobite troops led by the Earl of Mar fought against 4,000 English troops led by the Duke of Argyll. Both sides claimed it as a victory.

▲ During the "Fifteen" Jacobite rebellion, battles were fought at Sheriffmuir and Preston, and during the "Forty-Five" rebellion at Prestonpans (1745), Falkirk, and Culloden (1746).

successful battles in Scotland "Bonnie Prince Charlie," as he was called by his followers, marched into England. He reached Derby but English supporters did not join him as he had hoped and he retreated to Scotland. Early in 1746 the Jacobites were defeated at the battle of Culloden. With most of his followers dead, Bonnie Prince Charlie fled north. After a few months he managed to escape disguised as Flora Macdonald's maid. He then returned to France.

The English reprisals were severe. A lot of the Highland chiefs were executed. The clansmen were disarmed and, until 1782, they were forbidden to wear their clan tartans or play the bagpipes.

▲ At the battle of Culloden the Jacobites were defeated by English troops led by the Duke of Cumberland. He earned the title of "Butcher" because all the wounded Jacobites were killed and any who escaped were punished when they were caught.

1714 Britain: Queen Anne dies. Prince George of Hanover is named as the new king, George I (to 1727). Finland: Russians conquer Finland after winning victory at the battle of Storkyro. Germany: Scientist Gabriel Daniel Fahrenheit invents thermometer filled with mercury, plus a new scale of degrees for measuring temperature. Ottoman empire: North African state of Tripolitania wins independence from the Ottoman empire.

Flora Macdonald (1722–1790) helped Charles Stuart (1720–1788) to evade capture by the English by disguising him as her maid.

1715 Jacobite rising, the "Fifteen," in Scotland and England (to 1716), led by James Stuart, who claims the throne of Great Britain as James III. Thomas Foster leads the English rebels in the north and the Earl of Mar commands the Scots. Forster is compelled to surrender at Preston in Lancashire and Mar fights an inconclusive battle at Sheriffmuir in Scotland, all but ending the rebellion. James escapes to France. France: Louis XIV, the Sun King, dies after ruling for 54 years. He is succeeded by his five-year-old great-grandson Louis XV (to 1774). Philip, Duke of Orléans is regent.

1716 Britain: Swedish engineer, Martin Triewald, installs the first hot-water-based central heating system in an English greenhouse. The Agricultural Revolution begins about this time. Louisiana: The first slaves are brought to French territory in North America.

This figure represents a farmworker. He is holding and wearing many agricultural tools, including a scythe and a plow.

1717 Britain: Lady Mary Wortley Montague introduces Turkish practice of smallpox vaccination into Britain. Because she is a woman the medical profession ignore her work. Tibet: Mongol peoples invade.

1718 The Quadruple Alliance formed among European nations: Austria, Britain, France, and Netherlands unite to fight against Spain (to 1719). Britain: The first machine gun is patented by James Puckle of London. Austria: After many years of experiment, porcelain is manufactured for the first time outside China. North America: The Collegiate School of America is expanded and reformed as Yale University.

1719 Britain: Novelist Daniel Defoe publishes his novel *Robinson Crusoe* based on adventures of Alexander Selkirk. Scotland: Jacobite rising in the West Highlands, supported by Spain, fails.

The Agricultural Revolution

Until the late 17th century, European farming methods had not changed for centuries. But by the 1700s, landowners, botanists, and livestock breeders were all busily discussing better ways of running farms and growing crops. For the first time, there was scientific investigation into animals and plants and how they grew.

This new interest in farming and sudden enthusiasm for change led to the Agricultural Revolution, a period when new crops were grown, better animals were bred and new farming methods were introduced. In Europe, advances in medicine and a better diet led to a population increase. Also more people were now living in towns which meant there was a bigger demand for food. As farm profits rose, landowners began to study and experiment even more.

There were other major changes in the countryside during the 18th century. In many parts of Britain, land was still

▼ *In some villages, poor people were forced to leave their homes, so space could be cleared for the new enclosed fields.*

▼ *The old open fields were enclosed either by bank fences planted with trees (right), or wall fences (left), which were built of large blocks of stone.*

farmed in large open fields. Villagers rented scattered strips in these fields, where they worked alongside their neighbors. This system provided enough food to keep people alive, but it did not produce enough to give a surplus which could be sold for profit.

Landlords decided that their fields could be more efficiently farmed if they were enclosed. The open fields were divided up into smaller plots, separated by newly-planted hedges, to provide small, easily worked units. The Acts of Enclosure passed by Parliament between 1759 and 1801 also meant that common grazing land was enclosed. In total, over 7 million acres of land were enclosed during the Agricultural Revolution.

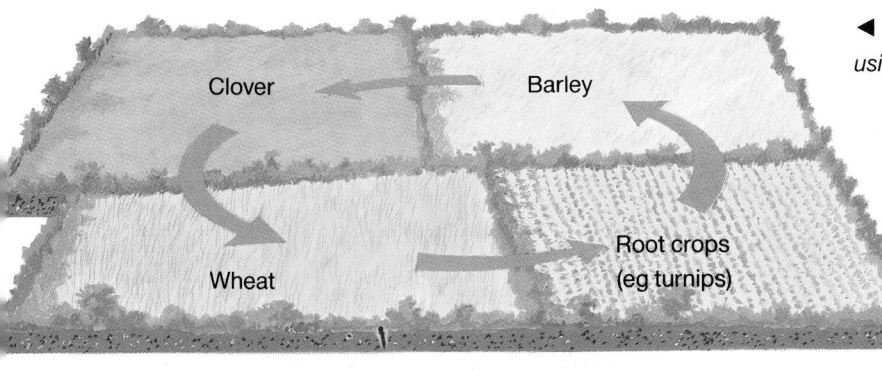

Clover

Barley

Wheat

Root crops
(eg turnips)

◀ *By the 1700s, farmers were using new methods to increase soil fertility. Instead of leaving one field fallow (with no crop) each year, they planted wheat, turnips, barley, and clover in turn. The clover put goodness back into the soil, improving it for the other three crops.*

▶ *Wealthy landowners, such as Thomas Coke, Earl of Leicester, encouraged experimental breeding of sheep and cattle, to produce new, improved, more profitable strains. Every year Coke held a grand assembly at Holkham Hall, his country house. Guests came from all over Europe to discuss new farming ideas.*

The Industrial Revolution

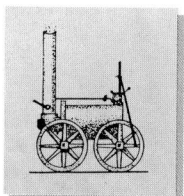

In the early 1700s, most people worked at home, making goods in the slow, traditional way, usually by hand. Men were carpenters, blacksmiths, and weavers. Others were farm laborers, who worked on the land to grow crops to feed their families. Women worked in the home, looked after the animals, cleaned sheep fleece, and spun wool into yarn for clothes.

By the middle of the 19th century, all this had changed. Many British people now lived in towns, and worked in enormous factories, or in stores, offices, railroads, and other businesses designed to serve the inhabitants of these industrial (manufacturing) centers.

British inventors continued to develop revolutionary new machines, which performed the traditional tasks of spinning and weaving much faster. Machines also made iron and steel. These metals were in turn used to make more machines, weapons, and tools.

Factories housing the new machines made Britain "the workshop of the world." Four main factors helped bring

▲ *Early 19th-century workers in a flax mill. Fibers from flax (a plant rather like a nettle) were spun into thread. This was woven to make linen cloth. Workers were mostly women and girls. They earned lower wages than men, and so were cheaper to employ. The mill looks clean, but its machines were dangerous and noisy.*

▼ *The first multi-reel spinning machine, the Spinning Jenny, was made by James Hargreaves in 1764. At first, it was powered by hand, but steam-driven versions were soon built and used successfully.*

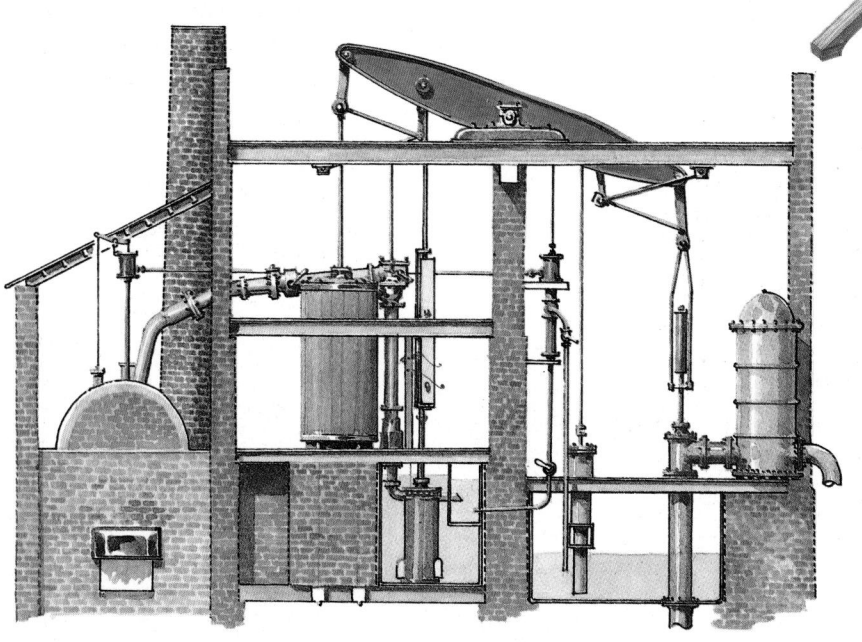

◄ *The first steam engine built by Thomas Newcomen in 1712 was used to pump water out of mines. In 1765, James Watt, a Scotsman, improved Newcomen's design, and patented his own steam engine in 1775. It was soon used in factories throughout Britain.*

▲ *The Ironworks at Coalbrookdale in England produced more iron than anywhere else in Europe.*

1720 Europe: Year of financial crisis in England and France following failure of two high-risk investment companies, the South Sea Company in England and the Mississippi Company in France. Around this time gin-drinking becomes very popular in Britain. Far East: China takes control of Tibet. Japan: The government removes the ban on the study of all European books, but Christianity is still outlawed. North America: Spanish troops invade Texas. The population of the British colonies is 475,000. Boston with 12,000 people is the largest city.

1721 Germany: Composer Johann Sebastian Bach completes the *Brandenburg Concertos*. China: Rebellion in Chinese island of Taiwan (Formosa). Britain: Sir Robert Walpole becomes first lord of the treasury. He came to be known as the prime (first) minister. First regular postal service is established between England and the colonies in North America.

1722 France: Scientist René de Reaumur publishes the first technical book describing the production of iron and steel. Pacific: Dutch navigator Jacob Roggeveen is the first European to visit Samoa and Easter Island.

1723 Germany: Engineer Jacob Leupold starts to publish his massive nine-volume work on the theory of mechanical engineering (to 1739). Leupold suggests designs for many new machines.

about this change: coal mining, a canal system, capital (money), and cheap labor. Coal was used to smelt iron and steel, and to make steam to power the new machines. Barges carried bulky raw materials and finished goods along the canals. Profits from Britain's colonies meant there were merchants with money to invest in industry. Poor farmworkers flocked to the towns to find work.

The Industrial Revolution did not reach America until after the Revolutionary War in 1783.

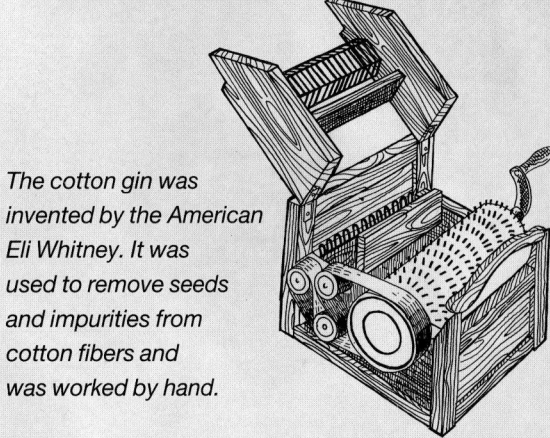

The cotton gin was invented by the American Eli Whitney. It was used to remove seeds and impurities from cotton fibers and was worked by hand.

Buildings

A number of styles were used for buildings designed during the 18th century. In many parts of the world, such as Africa, Russia, and the Far East, traditional designs using local materials remained popular. In Europe, too, houses built for ordinary people did not change.

Among fashionable Europeans and Americans, some architects stopped using the swirling curves of the Baroque. Instead they were influenced by the earlier, simpler designs of classical Greece and Rome. Others started to design for a big city environment (in America) or use new industrial techniques (in Britain). Architects designed new types of building using new materials.

▶ After 1776 politicans, architects, and philosophers in the United States all discussed how to build the ideal city. Cities were built to a pattern. Buildings were put up at a regular distance from each other, and groups of buildings formed a block. The blocks were separated by streets, usually of the same width. Earlier cities had irregular arrangements of buildings, but with the grid system cities could be extended in any direction.

▲ Traditional Russian peasant housing was made of rough-cut logs. Homes like these could be built cheaply using wood from nearby forests. They were decorated with local designs.

▼ The first cast-iron bridge, was built at Coalbrookdale, England, in 1779. The builders used the same methods of construction they used for wooden buildings as they did not know how cast-iron behaved.

▼ *The Royal Crescent, Bath, England is a group of 30 row houses built during the late 18th century to plans by John Wood the Younger. He was strongly influenced by classical Greek designs.*

◄ *The Temple of Heaven, Beijing, China. It was rebuilt in 1751, following traditional Chinese designs. The wooden prayer hall inside is over 100 feet (30 m) wide and is supported by a marble platform. Color was used to create an effect in Qing-dynasty buildings. The roof is covered with blue ceramic tiles.*

WHEN IT HAPPENED

1720 Rococco style begins in France.

1741 Italian architect Bartolomeo Rastrelli designs Winter Palace at St. Petersburg.

1751 Lancelot "Capability" Brown sets up as a landscape gardener to English nobility.

1762 Summerhouse, "Petit Trianon," built for French king's mistress Madame Dubarry.

1792 Building of original Palladian style (using classical Greek and Roman designs) White House, in Washington D.C. starts.

▲ *During the 18th century, houses were built with large windows which let in light and fresh air. But in 1784, a window tax was introduced in England. In order to save money many people, especially the rich, blocked up some of their windows* (on the left in the picture).

► *A Zulu settlement consisted of several houses which were guarded by a strong outer stockade. The houses were built around a central kraal or cattle-pen. They were made of wooden poles covered with matting and straw thatch. There was one for each wife of the man who built the kraal, plus some for storing grain.*

1724 India: The great Mogul empire begins to collapse. The state of Hyderabad breaks away from Mogul control. There are upheavals on the Indian border and in the Middle East. The Russians and Turks agree to divide conquered Persian (Iranian) lands between them. Afghanistan: The ruler Mahmud becomes insane. Russia: Peter the Great sets up an Academy of Sciences in St. Petersburg. Many leading mathematicians go to study there. Germany: Johann Sebastian Bach's *St. John Passion* is performed in Leipzig on Good Friday.

1725 Alliances between rival groupings of European powers: Treaty of Vienna between Austria and Spain; Treaty of Hanover between Britain, France, Prussia, Sweden, Denmark, and the Netherlands. Italy: Composer Antonio Vivaldi writes *The Four Seasons* concertos.

1726 Ottoman empire: Persian armies defeat Turkey. Ireland: Novelist Jonathan Swift writes *Gulliver's Travels*.

1727 A border agreement between Russia and China is signed. Brazil: First coffee trees planted. Coffee soon becomes a major crop as coffee drinking in fashionable coffee houses and private homes grows more popular throughout Europe. Britain: The religious Society of Friends (Quakers) demands the abolition of slavery. George II becomes king (to 1760). War breaks out between England and France against Spain (to 1729).

Ivory carving is a very ancient Indian art form. This 18th century ivory comb, made in Mysore, shows Lakshmi, the goddess of good fortune and prosperity.

India in Chaos

In 1707, the Mogul emperor Aurangzeb died. During his long reign he had spent many years trying to maintain power (*see* pages 440–441).

After his death and throughout the 18th century, India was at war as separate groups tried to gain control. Local rulers, trusted by Mogul emperors to protect distant states, instead built up their own private kingdoms in Oudh, Hyderabad, and Bengal. In western India and the Punjab, rebellions were organized by the Hindu Maratha states and Sikh princes. In 1739, the Persian emperor attacked the Mogul capital, Delhi, and killed 30,000 of its inhabitants.

The fragile Mogul empire was also threatened by ambitious Europeans. The British and French East India Companies (*see* pages 424–425) had acquired vast possessions in India, centered on their

▼ *The ruler of Persia (now Iran) Nadir Shah was a brilliant general. In 1739 he led his troops in a successful attack on Delhi, the Mogul capital.*

Dupleix

As governor-general of the French East India Company, Joseph-François, Marquis de Dupleix (1697–1763), built up a Sepoy army and challenged British interests in southern India. The appointment of Robert Clive as commander of British troops finally defeated French plans.

▲ As Mogul power declined, the Hindu kingdom of the Marathas grew. The Maratha leader, Mahadji Scindia (1727–1794) ruled large parts of northern India.

▲ Robert Clive meets Mir Jafar in 1757. Mir Jafar was employed by the Moguls to fight against the British. But he thought he could do better by changing sides. He received large gifts of money from Clive and in return he allowed trade advantages for the British East India Company goods. Mir Jafar's support eventually helped the British to win power in India.

▼ War in Europe between France and Britain spread overseas. Several major battles involving French, British, and Indian troops took place from 1756 to 1763.

profitable trading posts. They made alliances with discontented Indian leaders, using a mixture of diplomacy, bribes, and bullying. The British and French also fought one another, training many Indian troops to help them. At the battle of Plassey in 1757, 3,200 British soldiers, led by East India Company official Robert Clive, won a victory over 50,000 French and Indian troops.

After the battle, Britain gradually took over control of the rich province of Bengal. The end of real Mogul power in India came when the British captured the Mogul capital Delhi in 1803.

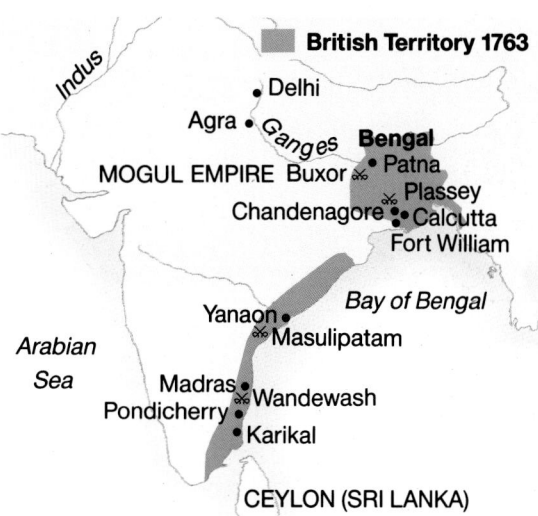

The Seven Years' War

For much of the 18th century Austria, Prussia, Russia, and France all wanted to take control of Europe, but none of them was strong enough to do so on their own. As a result, there was an uneasy balance of power. States made alliances with one another and went to war, in the hope of weakening their enemies. But wars were expensive in time, money, weapons, and lives, and also drained the warring states' resources.

The fighting that followed the death of Emperor Charles VI in 1740 (*see* pages 482–483) ended in 1748. But peace did not last long. The grievances that had led to war were still not settled. Austria wanted to recapture Silesia from Prussia, and England and France still saw each other as enemies because of conflicts in their Indian and Canadian colonies (*see* pages 494–495 and 498–499).

Fighting started again in 1756, and lasted for seven years. The European states divided themselves into two power blocks: Austria, France, Russia, and Sweden against Britain, Hanover (a German state), and Prussia.

At first, it seemed as if the Austrians and French would win. But Prussian

Pitt the Elder

William Pitt the Elder (1708–1778), was British prime minister from 1757 to 1761. Under his leadership, Britain won many victories in the Seven Years' War, but he upset fellow ministers.

▲ Art was used in the service of politics. This medal was designed by the French artist François Boucher. It was made in honor of the alliance made at the palace of Versailles in 1756 between France (right) and Austria (left).

◀ The Seven Years' War was a battle between the European powers for control at sea and in their colonies. It was also a battle for power between Austria and Prussia over control of Silesia. The British navy defeated the French at the battle of Quiberon Bay, and the Prussians fought battles against the French and the Russians.

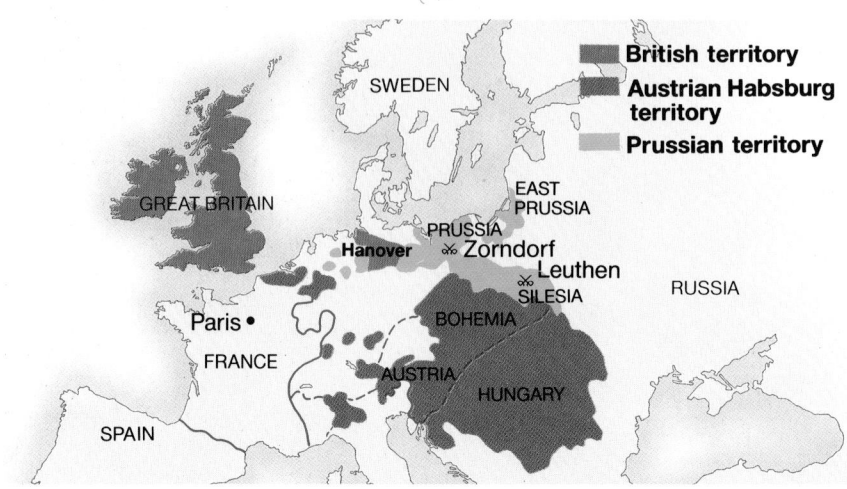

SWEDEN

British territory
Austrian Habsburg territory
Prussian territory

GREAT BRITAIN

EAST PRUSSIA

PRUSSIA
Hanover ⚔ Zorndorf
⚔ Leuthen
SILESIA

RUSSIA

Paris •

BOHEMIA

FRANCE

AUSTRIA

HUNGARY

SPAIN

▲ *The battle of Zorndorf was one of the battles of the Seven Years' War. It was fought in 1758 between the Russians and Prussians. The Russians, who were allies of Austria, attacked troops led by Frederick the Great of Prussia. The battle was fierce and neither side won.*

victories at the battles of Rossbach and Leuthen in 1757, and the British success at Plassey in India and Quebec in Canada restored the balance of power.

The war ended when a new tsar, Peter II, came to power in Russia. He wanted peace and a treaty ending the fighting was signed in Paris in 1763. As a result, Britain gained land in Canada and India from France, and the Prussians were allowed to keep Silesia.

THE BREAKUP OF POLAND

Countries fought over by opposing sides suffered badly in war. Poland was the scene of many battles during the Seven Years' War (and in the years that followed), because its neighbors, Austria, Russia, and Prussia, all wanted its land for themselves. Since Poland was divided into several small states, this made it easy to attack.

In 1772, 1793, and again in 1795, Polish territory was divided among the three strong neighboring nations. The Poles protested in 1794 but were defeated by Russian and Prussian troops. After 1795, Poland ceased to exist as an independent country. However, the Polish people kept their own language, and strong sense of national pride, and waited for a chance to win back their freedom.

1728 The Danish navigator Vitus Bering explores Bering Strait in cold northern seas between Siberia (Russia) and Alaska (North America).

1729 China: Emperor Yung Cheng bans opium smoking.

1730 India: Maratha state controls large parts of India as Mogul empire weakens. Britain: "Norfolk Four-Course" system of crop-rotation is introduced by Viscount "Turnip" Townshend. John Wesley preaches a new form of Christian worship – Methodism. North Africa: Kingdom of Borno (in central Sudan) becomes more powerful. China: Qing emperor Yung Cheng begins to abolish slavery.

1731 Farther alliances formed in Europe as competing nations jostle for power: new treaty made at Vienna between Britain, Holland, Spain, and the Holy Roman Empire. Russia, Prussia, and the Empire also agree to fight together against Poland. Britain: Factory workers banned from emigrating to America because the British government does not want American colonies to develop industrial power. Scotland: First book on dieting published by Dr. John Arbuthnot.

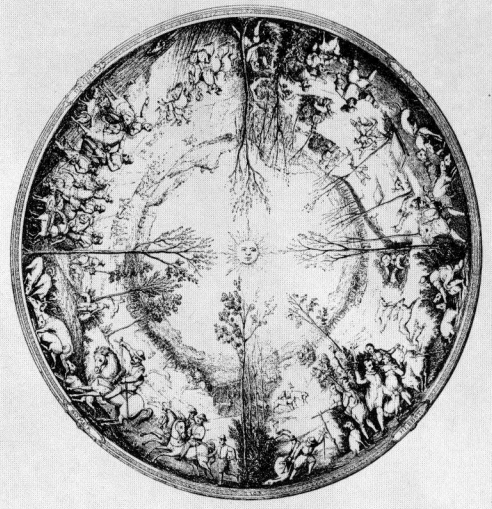

Scenes from the four seasons decorate this 18th-century German shield. Small round shields like this were called bucklers.

1732 Japan: Famine begins (to 1733). North America: James Oglethorpe obtains a royal charter (license) to set up a new colony (the 13th) in Georgia. Conflicts between Britain and other European powers spread to North American lands. Britain: Molasses Acts forbid American trade with French colonies in the Caribbean.

1733 North America: First settlers arrive in new colony of Georgia. New York City and Philadelphia are struck by first major influenza epidemic in the colonies. Britain: Inventor John Kay patents the flying shuttle, a mechanized loom for weaving cloth. Prussia: Military service becomes compulsory for all young men.

1734 Ottoman empire: War between Turkey and Persia.

1735 Swedish doctor and botanist Carolus Linnaeus publishes his book *The System of Nature*. In it he sets out the method of classifying species that is still used today. North America: European settlers begin to expand their lands westward. A French colony is established at Vincennes in Indiana. Rivalry between different groups of settlers (and their Native American allies) grows.

Struggle in North America

French and British colonists had been fighting in North America for many years. First came King William's War (1689–1697), then Queen Anne's War (1702–1713) and finally King George's War (1744–1748). Sometimes fighting was sparked off by local disputes, but mostly these wars mirrored quarrels between rival European powers. Both sides had a long-term aim: they wanted to control the American and Canadian lands.

In 1754, fighting broke out again in what was called the French and Indian War. (After 1756, this became part of the wider European conflict known as the Seven Years' War.) French colonists moved onto land in the Ohio Valley, which the British claimed as theirs. The French built a chain of forts along the border, and refused to leave. The fighting soon spread to Canadian territory.

The French won important battles in 1755 (Fort Duquesne) and 1756 (Fort

In 1812 American troops tried to invade Upper Canada during the war against Britain. This medal celebrates the Canadian victory.

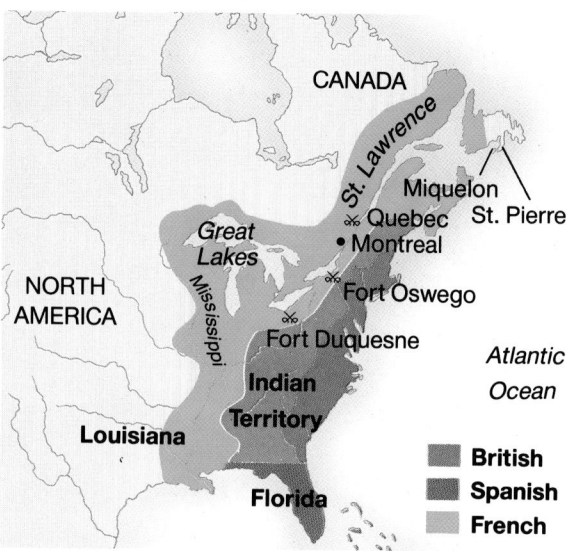

▲ *European possessions in America and Canada at the beginning of the Seven Years' War in 1756. By the end, Britain had won most of France's lands.*

Joseph Brant

Born a Mohawk (1742–1807) called Thayendanega, he fought on the British side in the French and Indian War when he was 13 years old. He became friends with an English official and so received an English name and education. Later he went to London and was received at court.

▲ *British troops landing from their warships at the siege of Quebec in 1759. They climbed up the steep slopes overlooking the French city, and fought against French soldiers gathered in the fields just outside the city. The British and French generals, James Wolfe and the Marquis de Montcalm, both died during the battle.*

Oswego). The British were also successful, capturing Acadia in 1755, Quebec in 1759, and Montreal in 1760. Peace terms agreed in 1763 gave Britain many former French colonies.

The Europeans were helped by Native North American troops who fought in all the wars, hoping in return to receive support in their own disputes with colonists who were stealing their land.

In 1791, the British Constitutional Act split the territory held by Quebec into the colonies of Upper and Lower Canada. Upper Canada was English speaking and Lower Canada French speaking.

◀ *In 1755, the British captured the French territory of Acadia (Nova Scotia), forcing all the inhabitants to leave. By 1763, Acadia had become officially British.*

Communications

People, goods, and news began to travel faster in the 18th century as new forms of transportation and communication were introduced. The demands of war and trade brought about these changes.

Army commanders needed to move their troops to trouble spots, quickly and easily. When fighting overseas, they also needed to keep in touch with their governments at home.

The increase in trade meant that raw materials needed by the factories had to be transported as cheaply as possible. Then the finished goods had to be moved to the new centers of population in the big cities, where they would sell more quickly.

► *Post-riders, like the one shown in this woodcut of 1734, carried the mail from town to town. In America letters could take weeks or months to reach their destinations as the distances between settlements were vast.*

◄ *In France the Montgolfier brothers pioneered flights by hot-air balloon. The first successful journey was made in 1783 when a balloon traveled 6 miles (9 km) over Paris.*

▼ *In winter, Tsarina Catherine the Great often traveled through the snowy Russian countryside and along frozen rivers in a traditional sleigh pulled by horses.*

▲ *In 1804, the first steam train to be built in England ran along a private railway track in a coal mine. The new invention spread quickly and soon railroads were being built to carry people as well as goods. Second-class passengers had to travel in coaches open to the air.*

WHEN IT HAPPENED

1710 Three-color printing process invented.
1783 First paddle-steamer boat sails in France.
1785 First crossing of English Channel by hot-air balloon.
1804 The electric telegraph is first successfully demonstrated in Barcelona, Spain.
1808 First typewriter is made.
1811 Friedrich Koenig invents first steam-powered printing press.
1825 First passenger train runs between Stockton and Darlington, England. In the USA the Erie Canal opens, joining the Great Lakes' ports and New York City.
1829 Braille alphabet is first used in Paris.

▲ *Although some roads had been improved by 1750 it took about 10 days to make the journey from London to Scotland by stage coach (so called because it stopped at stages on the way). During that time, passengers were at risk from attack by highwaymen, who might rob them of their money and possessions at gunpoint.*

◀ *Canals were being built throughout Europe so horse-drawn barges could carry bulk goods cheaply and easily. People traveled by stage coach which was faster but more expensive.*

▶ *After 1794, coded messages could be sent by the Chappe telegraph using semaphore. Movable metal arms on top of towers sent coded messages rapidly across the countryside.*

1736 China: Qianlong becomes emperor (to 1795). He faces problems of governing China with a vast, inefficient bureaucracy and rejects suggestions for reform. Persia: Nadir Shah becomes ruler (to 1747). French expedition led by Swedish scientist Anders Celsius explores Lapland, north of the Arctic Circle.

1737 India: Earthquake in Calcutta kills about 300,000 people. North America: In Connecticut, John Higley mints the first copper coins in the colonies, inscribed with the words, "I am good copper."

1738 Persia: Nadir Shah invades northern India. Poland: End of war of Polish Succession. France gains new eastern territory of Lorraine, formerly part of the Holy Roman Empire. Introduces hated "corvee" system of forced labor to build national roads. Germany: First cuckoo clocks are made.

1739 Ottoman empire: Turks advance toward Belgrade in Serbia, part of the Holy Roman Empire. Emperor Charles VI agrees peace treaty. India: Nadir Shah's troops attack Delhi, capital of Mogul India, loot its buildings and massacre thousands of inhabitants. Nadir Shah takes the beautiful Peacock Throne of Shah Jahan back to Persia. Britain and Spain are at war because of rivalry at sea, especially in the Caribbean.

This Chinese map from c. 1800 shows China at the center of the world. China deliberately isolated itself from all other countries.

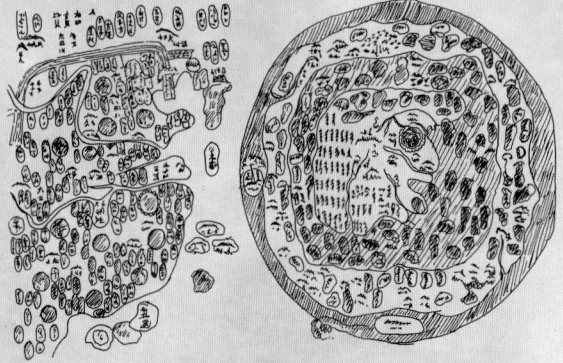

Trade with China

Throughout the 18th century Chinese silk and porcelain remained highly prized in Europe. Both were very expensive because they were in very short supply. Merchants from Portugal, Britain, Italy, and the Netherlands eagerly looked for the chance to expand their trade with China. But the powerful Chinese emperors, who controlled all contact between their people and foreigners, were simply not interested. Soon European merchants looked for other ways to trade. They established links with Chinese drug dealers (*see* page 568), and sold them vast quantities of opium (5,000 barrels per year by the 1820s), from countries such as Burma. In return they received precious Chinese goods for Europe.

The Chinese emperors were not keen to develop trade because they had more urgent problems to deal with at home. Years of peace and prosperity had led to

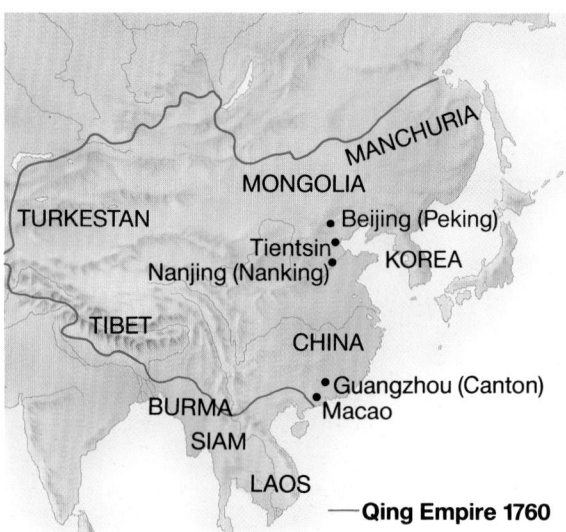

— **Qing Empire 1760**

▲ *Emperor Qianlong (1736–1795) expanded the Chinese empire. His armies conquered Mongolia, Turkestan, and Tibet. At this time, China described itself as the "middle kingdom, surrounded by barbarians."*

▼ *A scene in Canton harbor where a few British ships were allowed to trade with China each winter. Some Portuguese traders had a base at Macao and the Russians had signed a trade agreement with China in the 17th century. Otherwise all other merchants were banned.*

an increase in population (400 million by 1800). But the amount of food being grown was not enough to feed everyone. This caused food shortages. Protests and uprisings resulted, including the White Lotus peasant rebellion which lasted from 1795 to 1804 and weakened the control of the Qing dynasty.

Even China's control of the world supply of tea was almost over. During the 1830s, Englishman Robert Fortune stole several tea plants while traveling in China. He took them to India and set up rival plantations there.

▼ *In 1793, the British diplomat Lord Macartney visited China to encourage trade. But illegal deals proved more profitable. British traders supplied the Chinese with the drug opium, which they smoked like tobacco.*

▶ *Emperor Qianlong received European visitors with coldness. He was not interested in making contact with the Western world.*

1740 Frederick II, the Great, becomes king of Prussia (to 1786). The War of Austrian Succession (to 1748) starts after Frederick the Great of Prussia invades Silesia. Frederick also introduces freedom of the press and freedom of worship in Prussia, and founds the Berlin Academy of Sciences. Britain: Smallpox epidemic sweeps the country. North America: University of Pennsylvania is founded.

1741 Britain: Scottish philosopher David Hume publishes *Essays, Political and Moral*, a very influential book about politics and philosophy. Sweden: Carolus Linnaeus sets up a scientific Botanical Garden at Uppsala.

1742 Ireland: German (later British) composer George Frideric Handel conducts the first performance of his oratorio, *The Messiah*, in Dublin. Sweden: Anders Celsius invents new temperature scale, now named after him. Britain: First cotton factories set up in Birmingham and Northampton.

Voltaire (1694–1778) was one of France's most famous authors. He wrote plays and philosophical works and the novel Candide.

1743 North America: Benjamin Franklin helps set up the first scientific and philosophical society in the Americas – the American Philosophical Society in Philadelphia. Thomas Jefferson conducts some of the earliest scientific excavations of archaeological remains. He studies Native American burials, and also fossils.

The Enlightenment

Scholars, writers, and artists living at the time of the Age of Reason (*see* pages 446–447) or the Enlightenment felt they had all awakened after hundreds of years of darkness. They believed that the truth about how the world around them functioned could be worked out by reason, instead of accepting the ideas and superstitions of the past. It was also a time when people began to find things out by scientific experiment and observation. A major scientific achievement during this period was the start of modern chemistry and advances were also made in biology. Both these developments were to help scientists in the future.

The Enlightenment produced many remarkable works of scholarship and literature; the most famous being the French *Encyclopédie*, which was planned by the philosopher Denis Diderot. Articles in each book were written by

▼ *An imaginary portrait by the British artist and poet William Blake. It shows Isaac Newton working out how the universe is held together by the law of gravitation.*

▼ *A lecture being given in the salon of Madame Geoffrin in Paris in 1725. Wealthy, well-educated men and women often met in the drawing rooms of noble ladies to discuss the latest books, music, and plays. Some rich noblewomen also acted as generous patrons of learning and the arts. Madame Geoffrin is seated on the right in the blue dress. She was famous for her gatherings of philosophers.*

▶ *An illustration taken from a cartoon drawn about 1791. It shows Thomas Paine as the champion of liberty. Paine supported the ideas behind both the French and American Revolutions. In his book,* The Rights of Man, *he said he saw "a dawn of reason rising on the world."*

▼ *Diderot's* Encyclopédie *was published between 1751 and 1772. The 28 volumes included 17 books of text and 11 books of pictures. Each volume was censored by his publisher if they did not agree with his enlightened views.*

subject experts, who tried to explain the scientific discoveries that were being made at the time. Other important Enlightenment figures included the French thinker Voltaire, the Scottish economist Adam Smith, the French political thinker Jean Jacques Rousseau, and the Scottish philosopher David Hume. Their style was to ridicule or question the established way of doing something. In France, the ideas of Voltaire and Rousseau on government and citizens' rights began to influence political events. Enlightenment ideas also spread to America, where they influenced the British-born, revolutionary writer, Thomas Paine.

The Asante people of West Africa became more wealthy and powerful during the 18th century. These brass figures are shown pounding grain before cooking it.

Africa

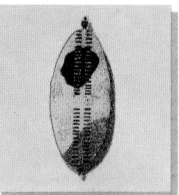

During the 18th century, the continent of Africa was relatively peaceful. In the north, the Ottoman empire, which controlled Egypt, continued to decline. The Asante people (*see* pages 462–463) on the west coast continued to grow rich by selling slaves. In the southeast, the Portuguese were slowly building up a colony in Mozambique. The lands of the east coast (now Kenya) were ruled from Oman, a kingdom to the north on the Arabian Sea. At the Cape of Good Hope, Dutch settlers began to explore the territory inland.

By about 1820, there had been many developments in the African kingdoms. The military leader Mehemet Ali had established a new empire in Egypt for the Ottoman Turks by overthrowing the Mamelukes who had ruled there since

1744 North America: War between Britain and France, known as King George's War (to 1748). Germany: Tune of British National Anthem, *God Save the Queen*, is published. France: First national geographic survey is undertaken. It results in the production of the first map drawn on modern scientific principles.

1745 The "Forty-Five" Jacobite rising. Charles Edward Stuart, son of James Stuart arrives from France to lead Scottish troops. He invades England and reaches Derby, but retreats. Holy Roman Empire: Francis II, husband of Maria Theresa of Austria, becomes emperor (to 1765).

1746 Scotland: The Jacobites are defeated at the battle of Culloden. Charles Edward Stuart escapes with the help of Flora Macdonald, and flees to France. New Jersey: Princeton University is founded.

1747 Germany: Chemist Andreas Marggra discovers sugar in beets. This marks the beginning of the European sugar beet industry. Afghanistan: The country is reunited under Ahmad Shah who founds the Durrani dynasty at Kandahar.

1748 Treaty of Aix-la-Chapelle ends the War of the Austrian Succession. Maria Theresa abandons Silesia to Prussia. Italy: First excavations of ruins at Pompeii.

1749 North America: Benjamin Franklin conducts experiments to investigate lightning and electricity in Pennsylvania.

1750 West Africa: Asante kingdom at its most powerful. Its wealth is based on trading in gold and slaves with Europe. North America: The population of the colonies passes the one million mark.

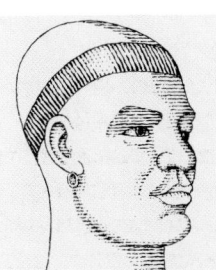

Shaka Zulu

Shaka (1787–1828) took over as the leader of the Zulus in 1816. He taught them to use different weapons, and improved their battle skills with a new fighting formation. He also used women in his army. Shaka was murdered by his half-brother.

◀ *Zulu warriors were armed with spears known as assegai. They were designed for stabbing, having short handles and long, sharp blades. Warriors wore feathered headdresses, and carried ox-hide shields painted with easily-recognizable designs, so that they could find their fellow warriors in battle.*

▶ *The city of Kano in northern Nigeria became rich through trade. In 1809, it was captured by the Muslim leader Uthman dan Fodio who was building up a new empire in the region. He converted the people to the Islamic religion.*

▲ *After Mehemet Ali had conquered the Mamelukes in 1811 and taken control of Egypt, he invited all the surviving Mameluke commanders to a banquet in Cairo. There he killed them. Although Mehemet Ali ruled Egypt for the Ottoman empire, he was allowed to do what he wished. He made Egypt the leading power in the eastern Mediterranean.*

the middle of the 13th century. The Muslim leader of the Fulani people, Uthman dan Fodio, created a powerful kingdom in what is now northern Nigeria. Other Muslim rulers in Senegal expanded their lands. The Dutch fought with the Xhosa people at the Cape.

But the greatest changes happened in southern Africa. Led by a fierce warrior called Shaka, the Zulu people rapidly took control of a large area of land. They fought constantly with their neighbors. The bloodshed was so great that the years from 1818 to 1828 became known as *mfecane,* or the time of troubles.

◀ Farmers planting rice seedlings in a flooded paddy in China. During the 18th century the population of China increased dramatically, and traditional methods of farming, which in the past had produced excellent crops, were unable to produce the amount of rice needed. Soil erosion also added to the farmers' problems. There were many food shortages and famines in parts of Asia in the late 18th century.

Food and Farming

The 18th century was a time of problems and opportunities for people concerned with food and farming. Problems arose because the population, especially in towns and cities, was rising rapidly. It seemed as if demand would overtake the food supply. The economist, Thomas Malthus, first recognized this in 1798 in his *Essay on the Principle of Population*.

Opportunities came after experiments with crops and livestock breeding programs led to better yields and bigger animals. There were also attempts to improve food storage and processing, although these were threatened by unscrupulous merchants, eager to sell low quality goods at high prices.

▶ Oranges from Spain were introduced to America by Christian missionaries during the 18th century. They grew well in the warm climate of Florida and California.

▼ Sheep were first taken to Australia by European settlers in 1797. They were so successful that vast flocks were raised and, by 1803, the wool was being exported.

▲ This illustration based on early 19th-century cartoons protested about shopkeepers who mixed all kinds of substances, often poisonous, with pure foods, to make them go further. Sand was mixed with brown sugar, plaster with flour, and milk was watered down.

▲ An early canning factory. Canning and bottling food were new techniques during the early 1800s. The first canning factory opened in England in 1811. The methods used were not always reliable, but further demands for preserved food came from armies and European explorers.

▶ The fantail windmill was invented by Edmund Lee in 1745. The small fantail was attached to the main sail and kept it turned toward the wind. This meant it was more efficient and could therefore grind more grain. As the main sail turned, the millstone ground wheat into flour.

1751 India: British troops led by Robert Clive defeat French in siege of Arcot. This is a major turning point in struggle between French and British in India.

1753 North America: French troops from Canada invade the Ohio Valley, a British colony. Benjamin Franklin and William Hunter are chosen to run the postal service in America.

1754 Russia: Start of a great period of Russian culture under Tsarina Elizabeth, Tsar Peter III, and Tsarina Catherine the Great. Building work starts on the Winter Palace in St. Petersburg. North America: Start of French and Indian War (to 1763).

1755 Russia: University of Moscow founded. Burma: Alaungpaya founds the Konbaung dynasty which is constantly at war with Siam (now Thailand). His successors expand Burma so that it reaches the boundary of India.

1756 India: Local ruler, Nawab Siraj-ud Daulah imprisons 120 British people in the "Black Hole of Calcutta;" many die. Seven Years' War begins (to 1763). North America: A stagecoach service is opened between New York and Philadelphia. Journey takes three days.

1757 India: British defeat the French army at the battle of Plassey.

1759 North America: British defeat the French at the battle of Quebec.

1760 Britain: George III becomes king (to 1820).

1761 India: British capture French fort at Pondicherry. French lose all power in India.

1762 Russia: Catherine the Great becomes tsarina (to 1796).

Foreigners, envious of Catherine the Great's success, said she was working with the devil.

Catherine the Great

Russia's most famous tsarina was not Russian at all. Catherine II, usually known as Catherine the Great, was born into a poor but noble Prussian family. Like many women at the time, she recognized that marriage was the only career open to her. So Catherine married the heir to the Russian throne in 1745. Her husband, Peter III, became tsar in 1762. He was a weak man and Catherine despised him.

Six months after the coronation, he was killed in a brawl. The rightful new tsar was Catherine's son Paul, but she declared herself empress and ruled in his place. Catherine carried her private ruthlessness into public life. She

▲ *Catherine the Great (1729–1796) ruled for 34 years. Other European leaders respected Catherine for her achievements in foreign policy, but feared her power.*

► Catherine supported the ideas of the Enlightenment. She read the works of French writers who contributed to the 28-volume *Encyclopédie* (encyclopedia). They included Voltaire (second from left) and Diderot (seated on his left).

▼ From the 16th to the 18th centuries, the Russian empire more than doubled in size. It gained ports on the Baltic and Black Sea coasts through expansion.

—— **Extent of Russian territory 1762**

SWEDEN
Baltic Sea
POLAND
• Archangel
• St. Petersburg
• Moscow
RUSSIA
Siberia
EUROPE *Black Sea*
Ottoman empire
ASIA
Caspian Sea
MONGOLIA

▼ Life at the Russian court was rich and elegant, and Catherine encouraged the introduction of Western ideas. Many schools were opened but they were mainly for the nobility. In contrast, the peasants lived in poverty. They were very badly treated by their landlords and by their ruler. When Catherine traveled through Russia in 1787 to see how her subjects lived, the streets of the towns were lined with healthy, well-dressed actors. The real peasants were kept hidden from view.

won new lands for Russia through wars with the Ottoman empire in 1774 and 1792 and Sweden in 1790. She also seized most of Poland when it was partitioned (divided up).

But Catherine was also terribly cruel. Courtiers were flogged and peasants who dared to complain about their miserable conditions were punished. She brutally crushed a peasant revolt in 1773. Its leader, Pugachev, was a man who claimed to be her dead husband.

Many poor people faced starvation, yet Catherine continued to collect heavy taxes to pay for her wars and extravagant lifestyle. Although she planned to improve the education system, and to reform old Russian laws, these changes never took place.

Exploration of Oceania

During the 17th century, Dutch explorers had sighted parts of the coast of Australia and New Zealand (*see* page 454), but the first scientific exploration of these southern lands was undertaken by Captain James Cook. He made three voyages to the Pacific region between 1768 and 1779.

Cook's first voyage (1768–1771) took him right around New Zealand. Then he landed at Botany Bay on the east coast of Australia and claimed the land for Britain. On his second voyage (1772–1775) he sailed toward Antarctica and explored many of the Pacific islands. On his last voyage (which started in 1776) he visited New Zealand and then went on to explore the Pacific coast of South America, but had to turn back because of ice. Then he sailed south to Hawaii, where he was killed in a quarrel with the islanders.

BOTANY BAY

Cook took well-trained artists with him on his expeditions as he was determined that the findings should be scientifically recorded. Among the many beautiful plants they found growing on the shores of Botany Bay, was this Australian red honeysuckle.

◀ The Maori people were skilled sailors and craftworkers who decorated their war canoes with elaborate carvings. When Cook arrived, about 100,000 Maoris lived in New Zealand. Many were killed in wars with the settlers.

▶ On Cook's first voyage he sailed from the tip of South America to New Zealand and proved there was no large continent in between, as many people thought.

◄ *Back home in Europe, the general public was fascinated to hear details of the "new" countries and islands visited by explorers. This 19th-century illustration aimed to show the many different peoples met by Captain James Cook and the French traveler La Perouse on their journeys through the Pacific region. But although it looks very attractive, it is full of mistakes.*

The "new" land explored by Cook had been inhabited for hundreds of years. The Maoris lived in New Zealand, and the Aborigines lived in Australia. Both peoples lived according to ancient traditions. Understandably, they were wary of Cook and his men – the first Europeans they had ever seen.

Before long, more Europeans arrived. The first settlers in Australia were convicts who had been transported there from Britain in punishment for their crimes. Free settlers started to arrive there in 1793. In New Zealand, whalers, hunters, and traders were soon followed by missionaries. The settlers introduced diseases which often killed the local peoples who had no resistance to them.

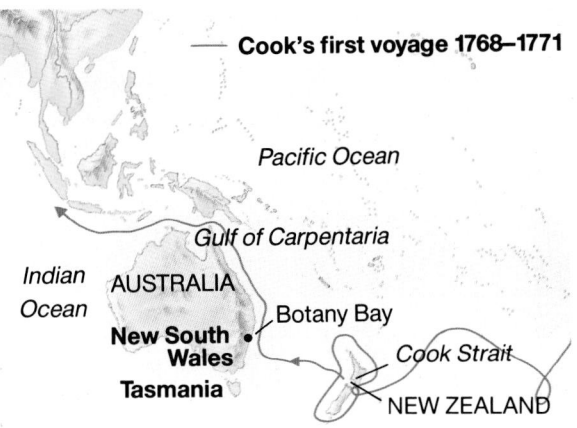

— Cook's first voyage 1768–1771

Pacific Ocean

Gulf of Carpentaria

Indian Ocean AUSTRALIA

New South Wales

Tasmania

Botany Bay

Cook Strait

NEW ZEALAND

1763 Seven Years' War: Peace of Paris between Britain, France, and Spain ends war. North America: Chief Pontiac leads Native American rebellion against British settlers in America.

1764 Britain: Spinning Jenny invented by James Hargreaves. Britain imposes new taxes on American colonies. Russia: Catherine the Great seizes Church lands.

1765 North America: Delegates from nine American colonies meet in New York to protest about the Stamp Act, a British tax. City merchants in Boston organize a boycott of luxury imports from Britain. Potatoes introduced from North America become the most popular European food. Austria: Composer Wolfgang Amadeus Mozart writes his first symphony at the age of nine.

1766 North America: The Mason-Dixon line is marked out. It separates Pennsylvania and Maryland, and it soon becomes the boundary between slave and non-slave owning colonies. Benjamin Franklin invents bifocal glasses.

One of the crew of Captain Cook's ship the Endeavour *barters with a Maori in New Zealand for a crayfish.*

1767 Britain: Neville Maskelyne starts to publish the *Nautical Almanac*, an important navigational aid.

1768 Britain: First edition of *Encyclopaedia Britannica* is published. Navigator Captain James Cook begins his exploration of the Pacific. He improves his sailors' diet, with orange juice, cabbage, malt, fresh eggs, and milk. He also makes important astronomical observations of the southern skies.

Japan and Southeast Asia

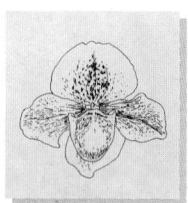

Since 1603 Japan had been dominated by the Tokugawa shoguns (*see* pages 402–403). Under their rule the country prospered. The population tripled in size, and four times as much rice was grown. Towns flourished, and skilled craftworkers made beautiful goods, especially clothes and fabrics woven from colored silks. Many Japanese people received a good education. In spite of these achievements, Japan had problems. Heavy taxes led to riots. Cruel laws meant that many minor crimes were punished by death.

A small number of Dutch traders (*see* pages 426–427) were still the only foreigners allowed into Japan. They were treated scornfully, but made so much money that they put up with the insults.

In Southeast Asia there was no such ban. European spice traders had visited there since medieval times and had

▲ *Japanese civilization was refined and elegant. These porcelain figures were made around 1700 and show no signs of foreign influence.*

▼ *In 1824, the British commander, Sir Archibald Campbell, led 11,000 soldiers on a river journey of 400 miles (640 km) to capture the city of Rangoon in Burma. The raid was planned in revenge for the Burmese king's attack on British lands in India.*

▲ The "floating world" district of a Japanese town was a special area with pleasant streets where people could go to enjoy music, plays, poetry, and paintings.

◄ Sir Thomas Stamford Raffles, founded the British colony of Singapore in 1819. He worked hard to increase British power in Southeast Asia.

established trading posts. During the 18th century these trade links began to turn into political battles. In 1786, the British took control of Penang in Malaysia. They also established Singapore as a free port in 1819, with special privileges for their own traders. This led to a conflict with Dutch merchants, who felt that the British were trespassing on their territory.

European nations also became involved in wars between the Southeast Asian states. They used these local conflicts to settle European-based disputes among themselves. The British, French, and Dutch all fought in Siam (now Thailand). From 1824 to 1826, the Anglo-Burmese War flared up after Burma supported Britain's enemies close to the rich Indian lands of Bengal.

1769 Britain: Richard Arkwright invents a water-powered spinning machine. France: Engineer Joseph Cugnot builds a steam-powered vehicle that can carry four people. Pacific: James Cook circumnavigates New Zealand.

1770 North America: British troops fire on a crowd and kill five civilians during the "Boston Massacre." France: Inventor Alexis Duchateau makes lifelike false teeth from porcelain. The first public restaurant is opened in Paris.

1772 Poland: First partition of the country between the European powers.

1773 Britain: Richard Arkwright builds his first spinning mill (factory). North America: Protests against British tax on tea result in the Boston Tea Party. The British pass the "Intolerable Acts," closing the port of Boston and suspending the charter of Massachusetts.

1774 North America: Continental Congress meets at Philadelphia and bans the import of British goods.

1775 India: War starts between British and Marathas (to 1782). North America: The Revolutionary War starts (to 1783). Second Continental Congress meets and makes George Washington commander-in-chief of the Continental (American) army.

1776 North America: American Declaration of Independence. West Africa: The Fulani set up the states Futa Toro, Futa Jallon, and Masina.

1777 North America: Revolutionary War continues. Some Native Americans support the British; others join the Colonists.

Sword guards protected the hand during close fighting. This decorative Japanese sword guard dates from the 18th century.

People

In the 18th century there was a wide gap between the rich and poor. In Europe life for the privileged few, which now included a growing middle class, could be very pleasant. Good manners, "civilized" behavior, elegant clothes, amusing entertainments, and charming music were all highly prized.

Life for the poor, especially in the cities, could be very difficult. However, better hygiene helped to reduce the death rate. Few people received a good education, and even fewer could vote to elect their country's government. The divisions between rich and poor meant that social tensions in some countries led to revolution.

▲ Japanese clothes had no pockets so things were carried around on a cord attached to the belt by a small, beautifully carved netsuke or toggle.

▼ Spa towns became fashionable in Europe. Drinking the local water was believed to benefit health.

▼ A sans-culotte *of the French Revolution. Instead of the usual tight breeches they wore trousers held up by suspenders, and a short jacket. They ruled the streets of Paris armed with swords and pikes.*

◄ An 18th-century Chinese painting, showing nobles practicing archery. The Chinese ruling dynasty came from Manchuria, where there was a long tradition of archery among their horsemen.

▼ Public baths became popular in cities in 18th-century Japan, as the population grew and houses became more cramped. Few houses had bathrooms.

► As farming became more profitable in England, landowners found themselves with money to spend. Some used this new wealth to improve their estates. Mr. and Mrs. Andrews in this portrait by Gainsborough (1717–1788), chose to be painted proudly surrounded by their own private property. They also put up walls and planted hedges which was unusual at that time.

WHEN IT HAPPENED

1719 A smallpox plague kills 14,000 people in Paris.

1749 Portuguese Gaicobbo Pereire invents sign language for deaf people.

1750 The population of Europe is now about 140 million.

1766 Benjamin Franklin invents bifocal glasses.

1800 A change in fashion leads men and women now to favor short hair. Greek-style dresses become popular.

1813 The waltz becomes a popular dance.

► An English cricket match in 1740. Although an early form of cricket had been played in the country for centuries, it was not thought of as a sport until fashionable London clubs took it up in the 1700s.

American Independence

At the end of the Seven Years' War in 1763 (*see* pages 496–497), both the British government in London and the colonists in America felt satisfied. They had defeated Britain's traditional enemy, the French, and had gained territory from them in Canada and also land as far west as the Mississippi. Now that the threat from the French had gone, the colonists did not need to rely on Britain for their defense. This did not suit the British government. It wanted to govern the old French territories and collect higher taxes to pay for soldiers to defend these newly-won lands. In 1763, British troops were sent to North America. In 1764, the Sugar Act put a tax on imported molasses and the Stamp Act the following year also added tax on documents.

The British lands in America were divided into 13 colonies (*see* page 476). The local colonial assemblies argued that it was unfair for Britain to tax the American colonies, since they had no say at all in how the British

▼ *British troops attack American defenders at the battle of Bunker Hill on June 17, 1775. Fighting actually took place nearby, on Breed's Hill. The British captured both sites, but lost more than a thousand soldiers.*

▲ *The Americans fired the first shot in the Revolutionary War (1776–1783). America's success influenced the French Revolution.*

George Washington

1732 Born in Virginia.
1754–1763 Wins respect as a soldier.
1775 Made a commander in the Revolutionary War.
1789 Becomes first president of the U.S.A.
1799 Dies.

▲ *American colonists objected to paying taxes to Britain on imports. In what became known as the Boston Tea Party, colonists disguised as Native North Americans raided British ships in Boston harbor on December 16, 1773. They threw the cargoes of tea overboard.*

1778 North America: France joins war against Britain and sends troops and ships.

1779 Britain: First cast-iron bridge is completed by Abraham Darby at Coalbrookdale. Captain Cook is killed in a quarrel in Hawaii.

1780 South America: Peruvians, led by Inca Tupac Amaro, rebel against Spanish colonial rulers. Britain: Riots break out in London against the Catholics (the Gordon Riots). North America: American Academy of Arts and Sciences founded.

1781 North America: The British surrender at the battle of Yorktown, virtually ending the Revolutionary War. Thailand: Rama I founds new dynasty; its capital is Bangkok. This challenges British power in Southeast Asia.

1783 Russia conquers the Crimea and gains access to the Black Sea and the Mediterranean. Japan: Growing population results in famine. France: Montgolfier brothers conduct the first flight of their hot air balloon. Frenchman Louis Lenormand makes the first successful parachute jump. North America: Revolutionary War ends and Britain recognizes American independence at the Peace of Paris.

1784 India: Britain makes peace with Tipu Sahib, Sultan of Mysore, a fighter for Indian independence.

1785 Russia founds a whaling base in Aleutian Islands, close to Japan. This marks the beginning of European commercial colonization in the North Pacific.

1786 Britain takes over the spice trade center of Penang, Malaysia.

government was run. They said "taxation without representation is tyranny." The colonies reacted to the British taxes by banning all British imports. In 1776, colonial leaders signed the Declaration of Independence (*see* pages 520–521), claiming the right to rule themselves.

The Revolutionary War began in 1775. At first the British were successful, despite the problems of fighting nearly 3,000 miles (5,000 km) from home. But the Americans had an advantage because they were fighting on home territory. Six years later the British army surrendered at Yorktown, Virginia in 1781, after being defeated by George Washington's troops. Britain officially recognized American independence in 1783.

The Liberty medal was struck (made) to mark the victory of the American states over the British in 1781.

1787 United States: Assembly of newly independent American former colonies meets at New York. It imposes duties on imported foreign goods, to protect the United States' own products and industries and to raise revenue for a new government. A convention, called to revise the Articles of Confederation, meets in Philadelphia and drafts an entirely new constitution. The federal system of government is agreed for the new United States. Russia: Catherine the Great encourages publication of an *Imperial Russian Dictionary*. It contains 285 words in 200 languages. Switzerland: French climbers reach the summit of Mont Blanc, the highest mountain in Europe. France: The *Parlement* of Paris demands that the king summon the Estates-General. King Louis XVI delays, resulting in political crisis. West Africa: Britain sets up a colony in Sierra Leone.

Patchwork was one of the handicrafts that flourished during the American colonial period. Quilts were given as wedding gifts.

1788 United States: New constitution comes into force. New York declared Federal Capital of the United States. Australia: First convicts transported to new British colony of New South Wales. France: Political crisis worsens after *Parlement* of Paris draws up lists of complaints against the king and his ministers, and there are riots for bread. Britain: *The Times* newspaper first published in London.

American Constitution

In 1776, rebel colonists guided by Thomas Jefferson, drew up the American Declaration of Independence. It said: "We hold these truths to be self-evident, that all men are created equal, that they are endowed (given) by their Creator with certain inalienable (fixed) rights, that among these are Life, Liberty and the pursuit of Happiness."

In 1783, after signing the peace treaty with the British, the people of the new United States of America had to decide on the best way to run their country. They decided to have a president, elected every four years. He would rule with the help of a Congress (divided into a House of Representatives and a Senate, both made up of representatives from the states), and a Supreme Court. The draft Constitution (set of rules) for the new government contained three important statements about the American nation.

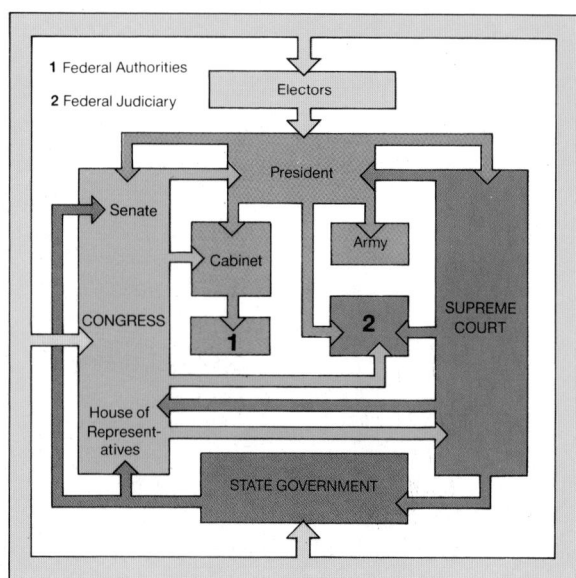

▲ *The American Constitution was designed to make sure that policymakers, government officials, and supreme court judges, all had a fair share of power.*

Thomas Jefferson

1743 Born in Virginia.
1776 Writes first draft of the Declaration of Independence.
1789 Becomes first U.S. secretary of state.
1801 Made president.
1805 Reelected.
1826 Dies.

▶ *The American Constitution was drawn up in 1787, and adopted in 1789. It began with the words, "We the People of the United States..." and stated that the United States of America was to be a democracy, where all citizens had a right to take part in government.*

▲ *The draft Constitution was discussed at a series of meetings held in Philadelphia during 1787. Thirty-nine delegates attended. They came from 12 of the 13 states that made up the new nation. George Washington was in the chair. Once the draft was agreed, copies were sent to each state to be agreed by its leaders.*

First, it was to be a union. The colonists who had fought against the British would now stay together to govern their new country. Second, each of the states would hold their own assembly, and run their own state government as they liked. Third, neither the president, the Congress, nor the Supreme Court would ever be allowed to control the central government on their own. A carefully designed system of checks and balances made sure that the power was shared among these three parts of government.

The French Revolution

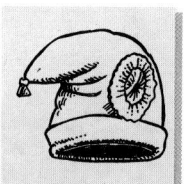

On July 14, 1789, a furious mob attacked the Bastille prison in the center of Paris. The riot marked the beginning of a bloody revolution in which the rebels demanded, "Liberty, Equality, Fraternity."

In the 18th century, France was in crisis. Food was scarce, prices were high, and the government was facing bankruptcy. To get more money, Louis could either borrow it or raise taxes, but first he would have to recall an ancient assembly, the Estates-General, which had not met for 175 years. Discontent among the middle class led to the Estates-General turning itself into a new National Assembly which demanded reform. Louis sent troops to try and dismiss the

Robespierre

Originally trained as a lawyer, Maximilien Robespierre (1758–1794) became the leader of a revolutionary group called the Jacobins in 1793. He was head of the Committee of Public Safety and helped protect France from invasion. In 1794, he was accused of treason and executed.

Marie Antoinette

1755 Born, the daughter of Maria Theresa of Austria.
1774 Her husband, Louis XVI, becomes king of France. She is a popular queen at first, but is soon hated for her extravagance.
1792 Is arrested by revolutionary troops. She shows courage and dignity in prison.
1793 Executed.

◄ Around 18,000 people were executed in France during the 1793 Reign of Terror. Anyone who was considered an enemy of the revolution was beheaded on the guillotine. A similar device had been in use since the Middle Ages. The guillotine was designed as a "kind" way of killing.

► Ordinary people were badly treated before the French Revolution. This cartoon shows them overloaded with work to support the extravagant tastes of the nobility and clergy, who paid no taxes.

▲ *In 1789, a group of women marched to the palace at Versailles. They seized the royal family, and brought them back to Paris as captives.*

Assembly, but when the Paris citizens heard this, they rebelled. In the countryside, the peasants also rioted.

The Assembly introduced a new government in 1791, with laws based on freedom and equality. The royal family tried to escape, but were arrested and imprisoned, as were thousands of nobles. In 1793, Louis XVI and his wife, Marie Antoinette, were tried and executed. By this time the revolutionary government was at war with most European states, who were frightened that revolution might spread to their countries. To defend France, a Committee of Public Safety seized power. They executed anyone who opposed them in a Reign of Terror, but they saved France from invasion.

1789 France: The French Revolution begins. Revolutionaries make the Declaration of the Rights of Man. Austrian Netherlands (Belgium): Declares its independence from Austria. Pacific Ocean: Mutiny breaks out on the British ship *HMS Bounty*. The mutineers are set adrift and settle on Pitcairn Island, South Pacific. U.S.: George Washington becomes the first president (to 1797).

1790 Britain: First steam-powered iron rolling mill built. Russia: Alexander Raditcheff calls for freedom for poor and badly treated Russian serfs (landless peasants). Belgium: Austrians invade and end its brief independence. North America: British naval officer, George Vancouver, explores the Pacific Ocean coast. The first census taken in the United States shows the population to be 3,929,625.

Members of the lower classes celebrate the end of the Reign of Terror in July 1794. The tree is decorated with rosettes in the national colors. The Reign of Terror had lasted from September 1793. During this period about 18,000 people were sentenced to death. They included supporters of the king and anyone who disagreed with the government. The Reign of Terror ended with the execution of the Jacobin leader, Robespierre.

◀ Hindu "thugs" killed travelers in India as an offering to Kali, the goddess of death.

Religion

In Europe and America, calls for religious change were prompted by two powerful emotions: dissent (disagreement with established ways of worship) and enthusiasm (extreme religious feeling). Some dissenters, like John Wesley, called for reform. Others, like the Shakers, set up new, independent churches.

In the Muslim world, a movement known as Wahhabism spread from Arabia to nearby lands. Its followers wanted to return to a stricter observance of Muslim laws.

In Africa and India, traditional religious beliefs continued. But problems came when European colonial powers challenged the existing order for political reasons. The Europeans saw religious ecstasy as a threat to their rule.

▶ There was strong anti-Catholic feeling in England in 1780. During the Gordon Riots people and property were attacked. Newgate prison was also set alight. Catholics were only granted civil rights in England in 1829.

▶ A Shaker meeting. Shakers (from the way they trembled with religious feeling) believed in purity, peace, love, and justice. They believed "Mother Ann" was the reincarnation of Christ.

1715 Christian missionaries banned in China.

1731 Protestants expelled from Salzburg (now in Austria) settle in America.

1738 The Methodist John Wesley begins preaching at open-air meetings in England.

1744 Arabian ruling family encourages Wahhabi movement.

1766 Catherine the Great allows religious freedom in Russia.

1772 Ann Lee founds the Shakers in Manchester, England. In 1776, she and eight followers emigrate to America.

1781 German philosopher Moses Mendelssohn calls for better treatment of Jewish people.

1826 New scholarly edition of the writings of Chinese philosopher Confucius published.

◄ *The Church of Jesus Christ of Latter-day Saints (or Mormon Church) was founded by Joseph Smith in 1830, after he received a message from God. He translated this into* The Book of Mormon. *Mormons believe that Christ's Church did not survive in its original form and was restored by the prophet Joseph Smith.*

▲ *Crowds of people gather to celebrate the Yam Festival held by the Asante people of West Africa in 1817. Yams were an important food crop and so the harvest was celebrated every year.*

▲ *The English priest John Wesley who founded Methodism. Methodists take their beliefs directly from the Bible and see Christian tradition as secondary.*

The bird-catcher, Papageno, from the opera The Magic Flute. *It was the last of 22 operas written by Wolfgang Amadeus Mozart (1756–1791). He also composed symphonies, church music, and orchestral works.*

1791 Canada: Constitutions Act divides Canada into British- and French-speaking territories. U.S.: Bill of Rights introduces 10 important Amendments (changes) to the Constitution. France: Louis XVI tries to escape from France but is recaptured. Inspired by the French Revolution, the British writer Thomas Paine publishes his book *The Rights of Man.* Caribbean: Slave rebellion in French colony of Haiti (Santo Domingo). Britain: William Wilberforce speaks in Parliament, campaigning for the abolition of the slave trade.

1791–1794 Russia wins control of the northern Black Sea coast from the Ottoman empire. Odessa is founded in 1794 and becomes the principle port for Russian exports to the Mediterranean.

1792 U.S.: First chemical society founded in Philadelphia. Original silver dollar is minted. Britain: Gas first used to light an office. France: French Republic established. France declares war on Austria and Prussia. Denmark becomes the first nation in the world to abolish the slave trade. China invades Nepal, and Chinese troops fight along Tibetan border. Britain: Mary Wollstonecraft publishes her book *Vindication of the Rights of Women.*

Slaves in Revolt

The revolution in France spread quickly to the French colonies. In 1791, the National Assembly in Paris decided to give the vote to all slaves in Santo Domingo (now Haiti), a French island in the Caribbean. But plantation owners living on the island refused to obey the Assembly's new laws. When they heard this, about 100,000 of the slaves immediately rebelled.

Slave owners were killed, houses were destroyed, and plantations of sugar cane and coffee were set on fire. The French sent a fleet of warships carrying troops to the island. Thousands of slaves joined in the fighting, which developed into a long civil war led by Toussaint L'Ouverture.

▲ *Pierre Dominique Toussaint-Breda (1743–1803) was usually known as Toussaint L'Ouverture after he had opened a gap in the ranks of the enemy during a battle. He led the slave rebellion in Santo Domingo.*

526

▼ Although Toussaint's actions had impressed many Europeans, in 1802 the French sent a force to reassert their control over the Caribbean. His army of freed slaves was defeated and Toussaint was arrested and taken back to France.

The son of Santo Domingo slaves, he was a slave himself until he was almost 50 years old. L'Ouverture declared himself ruler of the island in 1801, but he was captured and taken to France the following year, where he died in prison.

Most slaves in the Caribbean had been brought over from West Africa (*see* pages 450–451). They were made to work on the vast estates carved out of the colonial lands. European settlers farmed crops there that they could sell at a high price in Europe.

Sugar was especially profitable, but coffee and cotton were also grown. All these crops needed a large number of workers to harvest them, so the slaves had to work long hours in the blazing tropical Sun. Conditions in the sugar refineries (factories) were primitive and dangerous. But most owners did not care if their slaves were injured or killed.

▲ Slaves worked in sugar refineries (above) and plantations in many parts of the Caribbean. Slave owners cruelly calculated that it was more profitable to work their slaves to death, which took about six years on average, than to feed and care for them properly. Many slaves tried to run away to freedom.

The British in India

By 1750 the British East India Company (*see* pages 494–495) controlled the very profitable trade among Britain, India, and many lands in the Far East. Its British and Indian officials were skillful businessmen, who had built up a great stock of knowledge about Indian affairs. They became friends with the Indian princes, and struck bargains with friends and enemies of the Mogul rulers.

Many British people in India lived rather like princes themselves. Even if they were working for the East India Company, they ran their own businesses as well and many became extremely rich. Some of these *nabobs*, as they were called, built fine houses in Calcutta, designed by British architects, and furnished them with expensive luxuries shipped from England. In Calcutta, they held meetings, tea parties, and dances as if they were back home. Gradually, wives and families came out to India to

▶ By 1805, the British controlled the rich cloth-making districts of Bengal in northeastern India, as well as the prosperous coastal lands in the south.

▼ Calcutta was founded by the British East India Company because seagoing ships could travel up the Hooghly River and load and unload cargoes there.

▲ This working model, called "Tipu's Tiger," shows a tiger devouring a European. It was made for Tipu Sahib of Mysore. Between 1767 and 1799 he tried to resist British control of his lands with French support.

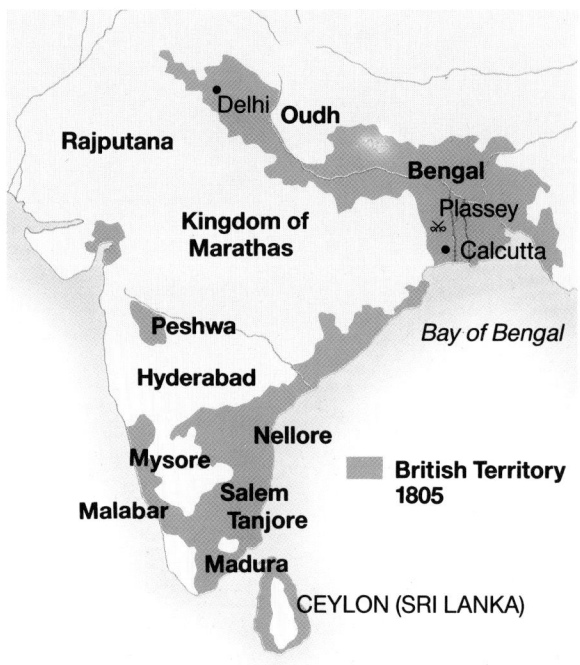

Rajputana • Delhi Oudh
Kingdom of Marathas Bengal
Plassey • Calcutta
Peshwa Bay of Bengal
Hyderabad
Nellore
Mysore
Malabar Salem
Tanjore
Madura
CEYLON (SRI LANKA)

British Territory 1805

share this English way of life.

However, other British people were attracted to Indian art and architecture, and preferred to wear Indian clothes, at least at home. They learned Indian languages and studied Indian writings.

A few Britons did not travel to India to make money. They came as missionaries, wanting to spread the Christian faith among ordinary Indian people. They made some converts and did a great deal to help many poor, sick, and starving Indian people. Some of them also ran missionary schools.

▲ *Merchants and officials who worked for the British East India Company enjoyed a wealthy, luxurious lifestyle, and employed many servants.*

1793 U.S.: A new law forces escaped slaves to return to their owners. Inventor Eli Whitney invents a machine called a "gin" (short for "engine") to process cotton fibers. France: King Louis XVI and Queen Marie Antoinette are executed. The Reign of Terror begins (to 1794). Ottoman empire: Selim II reforms the empire. These measures are unpopular and eventually cost him his throne and his life. India: State taxation and the legal system are reorganized along British lines. British East India Company troops are used to fight for Britain. Australia: The first free settlers arrive.

Tipu Sahib of Mysore is said to have owned the ivory chess set to which these two pieces belong. One side consists of Indian princes and men, and the other is the British army.

1794 Netherlands: France invades. France abolishes slavery in its colonies. France: First system of sending optical telegraph messages (semaphore) is established. U.S.: First steam engine built in the U.S. by John Hewett at Beleville waterworks. The U.S. navy is founded.

Napoleon

Napoleon Bonaparte was born on the Mediterranean island of Corsica, which had recently been acquired by the French. He was the son of an Italian nobleman who had been outlawed for reckless behavior. As a young man, Napoleon joined the French army. His boldness and quick-thinking led to rapid promotion. By the age of 26, he was a general. He led his troops in a number of successful campaigns, capturing northern Italy in 1797. After that the Directory (government committee) feared he was becoming too powerful and popular and

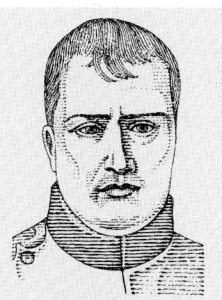

Napoleon

1769 Born in Corsica.
1793 Supports French Revolution.
1799 Seizes power. Wins wars in Europe.
1804 Made emperor.
1812 Leads disastrous invasion of Russia.
1813 Defeated at Leipzig.
1815 Final exile.
1821 Dies.

▲ *In 1796, Napoleon married Josephine de Beauharnais. When she was unable to have children he divorced her.*

▼ *In 1799, with help from dissatisfied politicians, Napoleon took control of government. His aim was to restore law and order in France, and to create prosperity once more.*

▼ *Napoleon's campaigns in Egypt led to French scholars' studying and drawing the pyramids and Sphinx at Giza. Artists also took an interest in Egypt's past and copied ancient designs. This plate is part of a dinner service made in 1798 for Napoleon.*

offered to put him in charge of invading Britain. But Napoleon suggested an invasion of Egypt, to disrupt the British trade route to India. He won success at first, but his plan failed after Nelson destroyed the French fleet in 1798.

In 1799, Napoleon suddenly returned to France from Egypt and seized control of the country. Surrounded by bodyguards, he marched into the government buildings, and dismissed the Council of 500 (a section of the Directory). He appointed three new officials, called consuls, to run the country. Napoleon was first consul.

For the next 15 years, Napoleon ruled France. The other two consuls had little real power. In 1804, he crowned himself emperor. As well as heading the government, he continued to lead the army. Napoleon introduced many lasting reforms, including new laws, a better educational system, a reorganized government, and a new national bank.

1795 France: Napoleon is made army commander in Italy. Prussia and Spain make peace with France, but Britain, Austria, Russia, Portugal, Naples, and the Ottoman empire unite to fight against France. François Appert invents a method of sealing and sterilizing glass jars. Britain: Takes over Ceylon (now Sri Lanka), and also invades the Dutch colony at the Cape of Good Hope in southern Africa. First horse-drawn railway built. West Africa: Scottish explorer, Mungo Park, travels along the Gambia and Niger rivers.

1796 France is controlled by the "Directory" government. Napoleon marries Josephine de Beauharnais. Britain: English doctor, Edward Jenner, pioneers vaccination against smallpox. (The discovery of inoculation is credited to him.) U.S.: George Washington refuses to become president for a third term. Japan: American ships trade with Japan (to 1809), on behalf of the Dutch. This marks the beginning of the end of Japan's policy of isolation from the rest of the world. China: The White Lotus Rebellion begins (to 1804). The rebellion successfully opposes Manchu troops in north China. This setback weakens the authority of the Qing dynasty.

This standard was carried by one of the regiments in Napoleon's army.

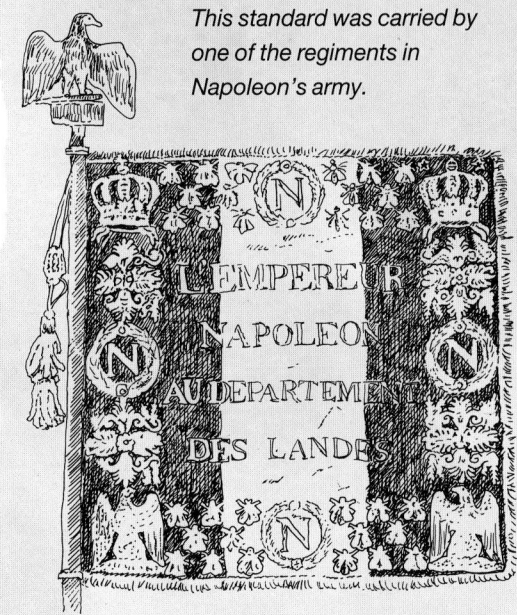

1797 Napoleon advances toward Austria. He is appointed head of a force planning to invade Italy. Britain: Pound notes, the first paper currency, are issued. Australia: Sheep farming is introduced.

1798 Napoleon captures Rome, Italy, and invades Egypt. French troops press north into Germany. Ireland: Rebellion by Irish nationalists at Vinegar Hill against the British government.

In this cartoon, drawn in 1803, Napoleon is depicted straddling the world, while the comparatively tiny John Bull (representing Britain) tries to fight him off.

1799 France: Napoleon becomes first consul. Egypt: Rosetta Stone discovered. It provides vital clues toward the understanding of Egyptian hieroglyphic writing. India: Tipu Sahib, ruler of Mysore, is killed fighting the British who now control southern India.

1800 U.S.: Washington D.C. becomes federal capital. The U.S. population is 5.3 million. France: Plot to assassinate Napoleon fails in Paris. Italy: Scientist Alessandro Volta makes the first battery. Britain: Combination Acts forbid British workers' uniting to form trade unions.

1801 U.S.: Thomas Jefferson is inaugurated president.

1800s East Africa: The kingdom of Buganda grows powerful. The people hunt elephants for their ivory to export to Europe where it is used to make piano keys and billiard balls.

The Napoleonic Wars

Napoleon was a brilliant general. He was able to move his troops quickly to where they were needed, and he developed new battle tactics. He also had vast numbers of troops to fight his wars. Robespierre's Committee of Public Safety had introduced a conscript system for the Revolutionary army. This meant that all adult men were forced to serve. The army numbered almost 750,000 soldiers in 1799 and another two million men joined up between 1803 and 1815.

Napoleon used this massive force to try and conquer Europe. At first, he was astonishingly successful. He defeated Austria and Russia at the battle of Austerlitz in 1805. The Austrian lands were shared out among little kingdoms that were allied to France and ruled by Napoleon's own relations. Prussia was

◀ *Napoleon wanted to create a society based on skill rather than on noble birth. To encourage achievement, he founded the Legion of Honor in 1802 "for outstanding service to the state." Members of the Legion received a medal and a pension for the rest of their lives.*

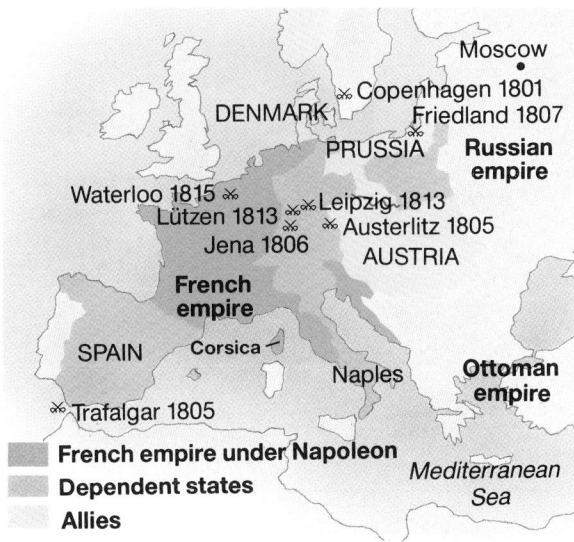

French empire under Napoleon
Dependent states
Allies

◀ *Napoleon's early success in the battles of the Napoleonic wars meant that by 1812 most of Europe was either ruled directly by Napoleon or by members of his family. Other countries were also allied with France.*

▼ *Napoleon's greatest victory was the battle of Austerlitz (now Slavkov u Brna in Czechoslovakia). Two enormous armies, made up of 73,000 Frenchmen and a combined force of 87,000 Austrians and Russians, came face to face in 1805. Napoleon first lured the enemy troops into a valley, then bombarded them with cannon. The death toll was appalling, and the Austrians and Russians retreated in complete confusion.*

Nelson

Horatio Nelson (1758–1805) was Britain's greatest admiral. His most famous victories were the battle of the Nile (1798), the battle of Copenhagen (1801), and the battle of Trafalgar (1805), where he was killed.

defeated at Jena in 1806, and Russia faced a second defeat at Friedland in 1807. After that, peace was made.

Britain won an important sea battle against the French at Trafalgar in 1805. The British admiral, Horatio Nelson, died from his wounds, but his victory saved Britain from a French invasion. In 1808, Napoleon invaded Spain when Spanish and Portuguese troops rebelled against French rule. This began the Peninsular War in which Britain supported Spain and Portugal. Many French soldiers' dying and the loss of Spain and Portugal made Napoleon unpopular.

Science and Technology

There were many developments in science and technology during this period. Discoveries were of two kinds: theoretical and practical. Throughout the 18th century, mathematicians, philosophers, and scientists published their investigations into "how the world worked," while engineers and inventors developed new and successful machines. The latest theories inspired greater invention, and more technology encouraged theoretical scientists to make further discoveries in medicine, mechanics, physics, and chemistry. The new machines brought revolutionary changes—to the workplace, to transportation and communications, and eventually to the home.

▲ The American inventor Benjamin Franklin (1706–1790) made many experiments with electricity. In 1752, he proved that lightning is electrical energy when he flew a kite during a storm and sparks came from a key tied to its tail.

▼ In 1801, the French inventor Joseph-Marie Jacquard designed the first automatic loom. It used punch cards that enabled it to weave patterned fabrics.

▲ The English scientist Michael Faraday (1791–1867) invented the first dynamo in 1831. It produced a steady electric current.

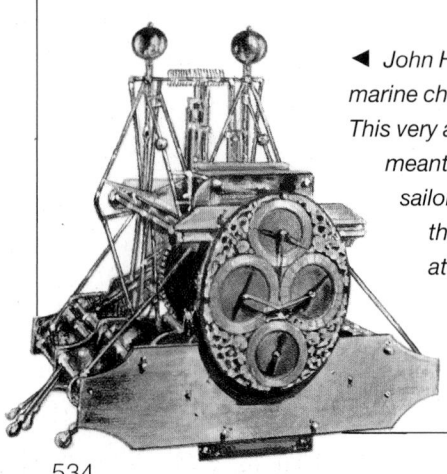

◀ John Harrison invented the marine chronometer in 1735. This very accurate clock meant that for the first time sailors could measure their precise position at sea. Harrison won a prize for his invention from the British government.

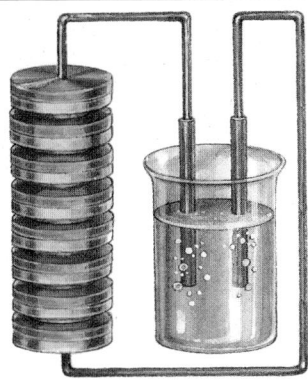

▲ In 1799, Alessandro Volta (1745–1827) designed the first electric battery, the Voltaic pile. This discovery helped later scientists.

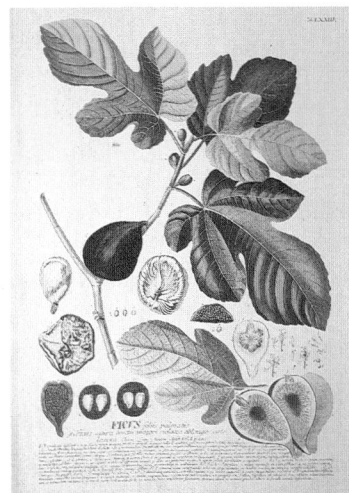

▲ The metric system using liters (for liquid), grams (for mass), and meters (for length) was introduced in France in 1795.

◄ Accurate drawings of animals, fish, and plants were published at this time. For the first time Swedish botanist Carolus Linnaeus started to name and classify living things.

▼ A table of chemical elements, drawn by the British scientist John Dalton (1766–1844), around 1803. Elements are "pure" substances – all their atoms are the same. Dalton was the first to give elements letters of the alphabet.

WHEN IT HAPPENED

1736 First successful operation for appendicitis performed in France.

1762 Carron ironworks in Scotland invent a new process for making strong, flexible iron.

1764 James Watt invents the steam condenser; the first step toward steam engine.

1774 Austrian doctor Friedrich Mesmer uses hypnotism for medical purposes.

1801 French astronomer Joseph Lalande publishes catalog of 47,390 known stars.

1823 Scottish chemist Charles Mackintosh invents waterproof cloth.

▲ Lady Mary Wortley Montagu pioneered vaccination against smallpox, which killed thousands every year.

ELEMENTS

⊙ Hydrogen	1	Strontian	46
Azote	5	Barytes	68
Carbon	54	Iron	50
Oxygen	7	Zinc	56
Phosphorus	9	Copper	56
Sulphur	13	Lead	90
Magnesia	20	Silver	190
Lime	24	Gold	190
Soda	28	Platina	190
Potash	42	Mercury	167

1801 Britain: Act of Union unites Great Britain (England, Wales, and Scotland) with Ireland to form the United Kingdom. Union flag first used in Britain. West Africa: Islamic kingdom of Sokoto founded. U.S.: Thomas Jefferson is elected president (to 1809). Engineer Robert Fulton builds his first submarine, the *Nautilus*.

1802 France: Napoleon is made first consul for life. South Africa: Cape Colony is restored to the Dutch.

1803 U.S.: Louisiana Purchase from France almost doubles the size of U.S. territory. Southwest Africa: Portuguese explorers travel through Mozambique. Austria: Ludwig van Beethoven composes Symphony No. 3, "Eroica."

1803–1818 India: The Marathas fight against the growing power of Britain in their country.

1804 France: Napoleon crowns himself emperor. West Africa: Fulani jihad proclaimed by Uthman dan Fodio. He rapidly conquers all the Hausa city-states and creates a huge empire. His son becomes sultan of Sokoto.

1805 Napoleon defeats a combined Austrian and Russian force at the battle of Austerlitz. British fleet defeats the French and Spanish at the battle of Trafalgar. Britain and the U.S. quarrel over trade with the Caribbean. Lewis and Clark reach the Pacific after an 18-month journey.

1806 Holy Roman Empire: Imperial crown is surrendered to Napoleon. Britain now employs 90,000 factory workers. South Africa: Britain takes control of Cape Colony again.

1807 Britain: Slave trade abolished in British empire. Napoleon invades Portugal.

1808 France: Napoleon invades Spain.

1809 Ecuador wins independence from Spain.

1810 Argentina breaks away from Spanish control. France: The first canned food is produced. U.S.: Population is 7.2 million.

Revolt in Latin America

Ever since Portugal and Spain had divided the rich New World between them in 1494, they had both ruled vast colonies in Central and South America. Although there had been many disagreements between colonists and governments, the colonies had not managed to break free.

In 1807, Napoleon marched into Portugal and, in 1808, he invaded Spain. For the next five years, Spain became a battleground, as British, Spanish, and Portuguese troops fought against French soldiers. This period of confusion gave the colonies the chance they had been waiting for. They began their fight for independence in 1808 by refusing to accept Napoleon's brother Joseph as the new king of Spain.

Argentina declared itself free from Spanish rule in 1810, followed by Paraguay in 1811. Peru became independent from Spain in 1821, as did Mexico, and Brazil broke free from

▼ *José de San Martín* (left) *liberator of Argentina and Chile. He led his army across the Andes mountains, a great military achievement, and secured the independence of Chile at the battle of Maipú.*

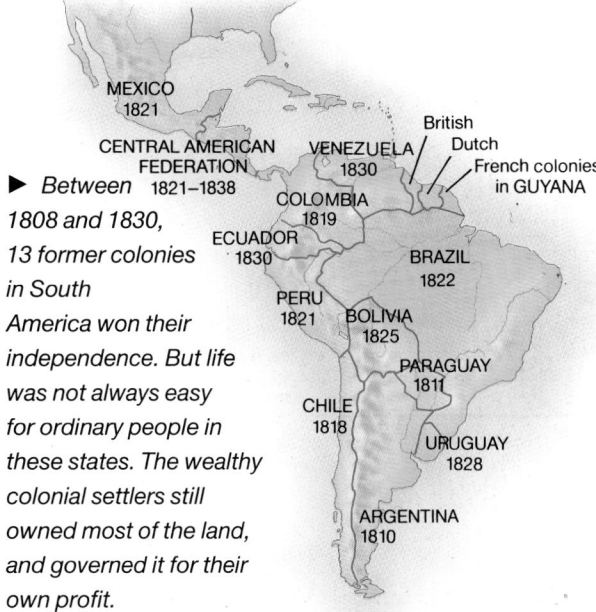

▲ *Simón Bolívar's revolutionary troops won an important victory against the Spanish colonial government at Ayacucho, Peru, in 1824.*

► *Between 1808 and 1830, 13 former colonies in South America won their independence. But life was not always easy for ordinary people in these states. The wealthy colonial settlers still owned most of the land, and governed it for their own profit.*

Simón Bolívar

1783 Born in Venezuela.
1813 Becomes dictator of Venezuela.
1819 Made president of Colombia.
1824 Becomes emperor of Peru.
1825 Bolivia is declared independent.
1830 Dies.

José de San Martín

1778 Born in Argentina.
1812 Joins rebels.
1818 Leads troops over the Andes; helps Chile to achieve independence.
1821–1822 Becomes protector of Peru.
1824 Sails for Europe.
1850 Dies.

Portugal in 1822. The Brazilians invited Dom Pedro, son of the Portuguese king, to be their first emperor. Venezuela finally gained its independence in 1830.

The South American independence movement owed a great deal to its two energetic leaders, Simón Bolívar and José de San Martín. In 1819, inspired by the French Revolution, Bolívar and other Venezuelan aristocrats defeated Spanish troops in New Granada (now Colombia) and Peru. In 1824, Bolívar met up with

San Martín who had marched across the Andes to liberate Chile. In 1826, Bolívar proclaimed the Republic of Gran Colombia (which included Venezuela, Colombia, Ecuador, and Panama), but the republic soon broke up. In 1825, Upper Peru took the name of Bolivia in his honor. Both Bolívar and San Martín had faced great hardship, and fought in very difficult conditions. But, in spite of independence, conditions in the former colonies did not really improve.

The War of 1812

In the early 19th century, the United States of America was growing. The government hoped to free all North American states from colonial rule, peacefully if possible, but otherwise through war. They almost succeeded. Only Canada in the north and Mexico in the south remained separate. The border with Canada was the site of many battles, as American settlers moved westward and northward into land still under British colonial rule.

Settlers and Canadians both fought against Native North Americans, whom they accused of helping the other side. Americans also claimed that British traders were selling arms to the North American Indians, to help them keep newcomers out of their lands. The War of 1812 (which, in fact, lasted until 1815) was fought to settle quarrels between Britain and the United States of America, particularly the question of the Canadian border. For the North American Indians it offered the chance to fight

Andrew Jackson

1767 Born S. Carolina.
1797 Becomes a senator in Tennessee.
1812 Made a major general.
1815 Wins battle against British at New Orleans.
1828 Elected president of the U.S.
1832 Elected president again, as head of the new Democratic Party.
1845 Dies.

Tecumseh

Born in the Ohio Valley, Shawnee chief Tecumseh (c. 1768 –1813) tried to agree a peaceful settlement of Native North American lands with the Americans. After Tecumseh, and other tribes, lost to the Americans at the battle of Tippecanoe in 1811, he fought for Britain in the War of 1812.

▼ The battle of Lake Erie was fought between British troops and the small American navy in September 1813. The Americans won and captured six British ships. Their commander, Oliver Perry, bravely rowed through the battle to seek safety aboard another American vessel after his own ship had been sunk.

▲ *Baltimore was an important city on the U.S. coast. In 1814, British troops bombarded it ceaselessly with cannon for more than 24 hours, but the brave citizens would not surrender.*

against Americans who were stealing their land. The great Shawnee leader, Tecumseh, became an officer in the British army. He died in battle in 1813.

At first the British had success on land, but the American navy defeated them both at sea and on the Great Lakes. American troops, including those of a future president, Andrew Jackson, also fought well. After two years, both sides were ready to sign a peace treaty restoring all conquered territories. But the news took so long to reach the battlefield that neither side knew the war was over. Jackson's victory at New Orleans in January 1815 took place after the peace treaty was signed in December 1814.

1811 Britain: Luddite riots against the introduction of new manufacturing machinery. George III is declared insane and his son George rules as regent in his place. British traveler and administrator Raffles takes over Batavia and Java for the British government (to 1816). Germany: The Krupp metalworks opens.

1812 France: Napoleon invades Russia with an enormous army, and marches to Moscow. Britain: War with U.S. (to 1814) over fights between shipping (especially in the Caribbean) and over U.S. plans to expand its territory in North America. Germany: The Grimm brothers (Jacob Ludwig Carl and Wilhelm Carl) publish the first volumes of their fairy tales *Kinder und Haus-Märchen (Grimm's Fairy Tales)*.

1813 U.S.: U.S. forces capture Toronto and Fort St. George from the British. British warship *HMS Shannon* captures the U.S. Navy ship *Chesapeake*. British troops burn the city of Buffalo. First use of words "Uncle Sam" in New York State's *Troy Post*. Venezuela: Simón Bolívar becomes ruler. Mexico declares its independence from Spain. Prussia, Russia, Britain, Austria, and Sweden join together against France. France is defeated at the battle of Leipzig. Britain: Author Jane Austen publishes her novel *Pride and Prejudice*.

This cartoon portrays the U.S. navy as wasps "stinging" John Bull (Britain) with defeats at sea during the war of 1812.

Society and Government

Throughout the world, governments struggled to keep control in the hands of the ruling classes in the face of increasing riots and levels of crime.

The ordinary people, had very different problems. With low wages and high prices their main concern was how to keep from starving. They also wanted more control over their lives. In America and France the result was revolution. This alarmed governments in other countries.

The situation was different in countries divided by war, or occupied by a foreign power. Then, when political opposition looked like rebellion, protesters were put to death.

▲ When the French invaded Spain in 1808 the Spanish rebelled. Many civilians were killed, as this painting by Francisco Goya shows.

► People became poor through illness and low wages. In 1795, it was found that some English workers were not being paid enough to keep alive. The Speenhamland system was introduced requiring districts to supplement low wages. But it was not regulated and often ignored. After 1834, poverty was a crime and the unemployed were sent to workhouses.

▲ A message in pictures from the British Governor Davey of Tasmania to the island's original inhabitants dated 1816. It shows that the Governor intended to treat Tasmanians and settlers equally. Sadly, this did not happen. The Tasmanians were killed either by the settlers themselves or by the diseases they brought with them.

▲ Russian serfs working as charcoal burners in the bleak forests of Finland. Serfdom was established in law, the serfs belonging to their owners. They could be sent anywhere, to work long hours far from home.

► Slum conditions in England drawn by the English artist William Hogarth. It shows "Gin Lane," where poor people drank to forget their misery.

▼ A Bow Street Runner, a member of the first London police force set up in 1740. They were so effective in their job that criminals feared them.

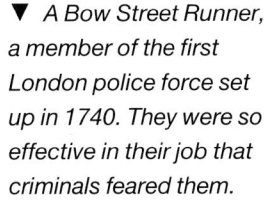

▲ After the French Revolution, even the calendar was reformed. In 1793, the government introduced new names for the months. February (top) became Ventose; November (below) became Frimaire. The calendar did not last and was abolished in 1805.

▲ Convicts in Sydney, Australia, in 1830. These men belong to a work gang, transported from England as a punishment. The first convicts were transported in 1788, but the practice was abolished in 1868.

The Fall of Napoleon

In 1808, Napoleon looked unbeatable, but he was not content. After he removed the Spanish king from his throne, many nations in Europe were outraged. The British sent troops under Arthur Wellesley (later the Duke of Wellington) to fight the Peninsular War. At first he was unsuccessful, but after the victories of Salamanca (1812) and Vitoria (1813) the French were pushed out of Spain. In 1813, Napoleon was also crushingly defeated at the battle of Leipzig by a combined European force.

At home, the Continental System (a trade blockade against Britain and its colonies) was gradually losing Napoleon support. Finally the disasterous invasion of Russia in 1812 left more than 500,000 of his soldiers dead of cold and hunger or killed at the hands of the Russians.

In 1814, Napoleon was sent into exile, but he escaped to rule for a "Hundred Days" before being defeated at the battle of Waterloo in 1815. He spent the rest of his life in exile on the island of St. Helena in the South Atlantic. He died in 1821.

Von Blücher

The Prussian field marshal, Gebhard von Blücher (1742–1819), played a major part in Napoleon's downfall. He commanded all the armies of Austria, Russia, Prussia, Britain, and Sweden at the battle of Leipzig in 1813, and if he had not arrived with his army to fight at Waterloo in 1815, Napoleon might have won.

THE CONGRESS OF VIENNA

After Napoleon's defeat at Waterloo in 1815 the major European powers met at Vienna. They were represented by Castlereagh (Britain), Frederick William III (Prussia), Metternich (Austria), and Alexander I (Russia). Talleyrand represented Louis XVIII who had been restored to the throne of France. They discussed the future of Europe and tried to re-establish stability by strengthening the power of hereditary rulers. But progress and national identity were suppressed.

▼ The battle of Waterloo was fought in Belgium on June 18, 1815. The British forces were commanded by the Duke of Wellington who described the battle as "the nearest run thing you ever saw in your life." On June 22 Napoleon signed his second and final abdication.

End of Slavery

Throughout the 18th century Britain, France, and Spain grew rich from taxes on goods produced in their colonial lands. Much of this wealth was created not by honest hard work, but by slave labor. People from West African nations continued to be sold by slave dealers, or local rulers, who saw it as a means of punishing criminals or getting rid of enemies they had captured in battle as well as making a profit.

Nobody knows how many slaves were sold in all, but historians have estimated that 15 million men, women, and children were shipped from Africa to the Americas during the period 1450 to 1870. Many Europeans disliked the slave trade, but believed it was the only way of providing the labor needed on the plantations. Fortunately, some people decided to protest.

▼ *Slaves working on a treadmill in a Caribbean sugar plantation in the 18th century. They were whipped if they did not work hard.*

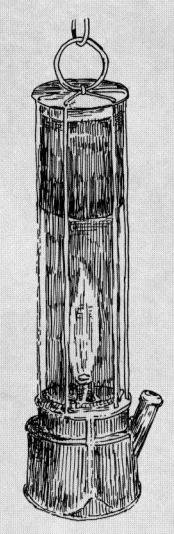

In 1815, Humphry Davy (1778–1829) devised a safety lamp for use in mines. It was important because it warned the miners of the presence of firedamp, an explosive gas made up of a mixture of methane and air. The lamp was responsible for saving many lives.

1814 France: Napoleon abdicates (gives up power) and is banished to the island of Elba in the Mediterranean. Louis XVIII becomes king of France (to 1824). Britain: Engineer George Stephenson builds first steam locomotive. U.S.: The British burn Washington. Francis Scott Key writes "The Star-Spangled Banner." The Treaty of Ghent ends the War of 1812.

1815 France: Napoleon escapes from exile and returns to France. He is defeated by British and Prussians at the battle of Waterloo, then banished to the island of St. Helena, in the South Atlantic. Britain: Chemist Humphry Davy invents miners' safety lamp. Corn Laws are passed to control grain prices.

This British medal commemorated the battle of Waterloo of 1815. It was presented to soldiers who had fought in the war.

TO BE SOLD on board the Ship *Bance-Iſland*, on tueſday the 6th of *May* next, at *Aſhley-Ferry*; a choice cargo of about 250 fine healthy

NEGROES,

juſt arrived from the Windward & Rice Coaſt. —The utmoſt care has already been taken, and ſhall be continued, to keep them free from the leaſt danger of being infected with the SMALL-POX, no boat having been on board, and all other communication with people from *Charles-Town* prevented.

Auſtin, Laurens, & Appleby.

N. B. Full one Half of the above Negroes have had the SMALL-POX in their own Country.

◀ *Advertisements like this were common in 18th-century newspapers. Black people were offered for sale just as if they were prize animals. This advertisement claims that the people are of "fine, healthy stock."*

Wilberforce

William Wilberforce (1759–1833) was first horrified by the slave trade when he became a British Member of Parliament for Hull, then a busy slaving port. In 1784, he began to campaign against the slave trade and finally succeeded in getting it banned throughout the British Empire in 1807. For the rest of his life he continued to work for the freedom of all slaves.

▼ *Some slaves escaped from plantations and set up their own villages in remote mountain areas. They were always well-armed to fight against anyone who tried to recapture them. In 1739, a group of escaped Jamaican slaves, known as the Maroons, rebelled against the British.*

During the 18th century, many people in Europe and North America began to condemn slavery, saying it was against God's law. Jean-Jacques Rousseau, a French philosopher, published *The Social Contract* in 1764, calling for greater freedom for people all over the world. "Man is born free," he wrote, "but everywhere he is in chains." His writings inspired revolutions in France and North America. Slavery had no place in these nations formed to protect human rights.

Rousseau's ideas also inspired people to fight for freedom on behalf of others who were unable to help themselves. Politicians, Church leaders, and ordinary people began to think how they might help slaves. But often moral arguments did not have as much force as the profits slavery generated.

The slave revolt led by Toussaint L'Ouverture in Santo Domingo (*see* pages 526–527) meant that in 1803 slavery was made legal again in all French colonies. In 1831, a slave

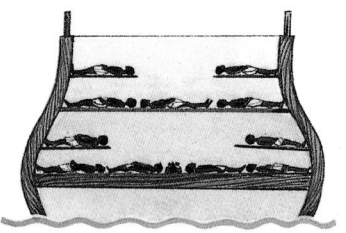

◀ *Conditions on board slave ships were cramped and unhealthy. But shipowners did not want too many of their valuable captives to die on the Atlantic voyage. So they worked out plans to make the "best" possible use of shipboard space.*

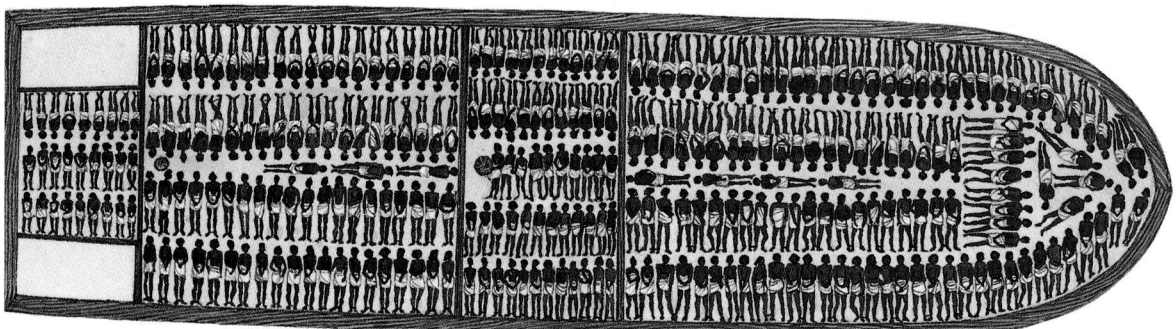

▲ *Slaves chained together waiting to be sold to European merchants at a trading post in Africa. To stop them escaping, they are guarded by men with guns.*

rising in Virginia led by Nat Turner also provoked a savage reaction. Harsh laws were passed to control slaves in the southern states of the U.S. Many southerners began to defend slavery.

In Britain, William Wilberforce led the anti-slavery campaign. He worked for more than 20 years to persuade Parliament to make new laws. Eventually, he was successful and in 1807 slavery was abolished. The problem now was to persuade or force (by attacking slavers' ships) other countries to follow Britain's good example.

▲ *The leader of the Virginia slave revolt of 1831, Nat Turner, was eventually captured and hanged. He had killed his master and encouraged 60 slaves to revolt.*

1816 France: Louis XVIII rules again as king. Europe adjusts to political and military life without Napoleon. Germany: Prince Metternich presides over new confederation of German states held at Frankfurt. Britain: British Museum, London buys "Elgin Marbles," carvings removed from the Parthenon in Athens, Greece by the Earl of Elgin. Southeast Asia: The island of Java is restored to Dutch control.

A painting from 1820 showing Pampa Indians standing outside a shop trading in hunting equipment, riding tackle, and hunting trophies.

In 1801, the Earl of Elgin took some marble sculptures from the Parthenon at Athens. Since 1816, they have been kept at the British Museum. The Greeks now want them back.

1817 Britain: Talks begin on rights to board ships suspected of carrying slaves. India: Hindu College, Calcutta, is set up to provide European-style education. Serbia: Serbs win partial independence from the Ottoman empire. U.S.: Work begins on the Erie Canal to link the Atlantic to the Great Lakes.

Unrest in Britain

The years of peace which followed Britain's victory over France at the battle of Waterloo in 1815 were a time of discontent. There was unemployment and high food prices. The government feared the ideas of the growing trade unions (workers who bargained for better working conditions) spreading in Britain, and during wars with France passed tough laws to suppress them.

Life in the new industrial towns was grim, with poor housing, accidents and disease. But events abroad had shown British people they had a right to make their voice heard. They demanded improvements in pay and working conditions and a say in government.

Many people campaigned for "one man, one vote." In 1832, the Great Reform Bill made elections to Parliament much fairer, but still only men who owned property were allowed to vote.

▶ This illustration, taken from a cartoon drawn in the early 19th century, shows a Luddite protestor disguised in female clothes. Some saw the Luddites as revolutionaries, others as against change, and others sympathized with their loss of a job.

▼ At the "massacre" of Peterloo, Manchester, in 1819, soldiers charged into a crowd of unarmed men and women. They had gathered to listen to Henry Hunt, a famous campaigner for political change. Eleven people were killed and more than 400 injured.

Richard Trevithick demonstrated his "Catch-me-who-can" steam locomotive in 1808.

1818 Southern Africa: Zulu leader, Shaka, establishes new warrior state, which he rules to 1828. Many neighboring African peoples flee the Zulu lands to avoid being attacked or killed. North America: Border between Canada and U.S. agreed upon after fighting and negotiations. Britain: Mary Shelley writes gothic novel *Frankenstein*. India: Marathas, after considerable loss of territory, are forced to accept British protection over their lands.

1819 Britain: First tarmacadam roads are laid. Laws passed to limit young peoples' working day in factories to 12 hours. The British establish Singapore as a free-trade port. Denmark: Scientist Hans Christian Oersted makes the first electromagnet. U.S.: Purchases state of Florida (a former colony) from Spain. Alabama, a slave-owning state, also joins the U.S. Economic depression in the U.S., following the war of 1812.

▲ *A cartoon of Lord John Russell, who tried to change the way in which people were elected to Parliament, taking great strides toward a fairer system in 1832.*

However, not all the protesters wanted change. Between 1811 and 1816 groups of craftsmen known as Luddites (after a mentally disabled boy who broke two knitting frames), smashed new machinery in factories in Lancashire and Yorkshire. They feared they would lose their jobs because the machines worked faster and were cheaper than paying people's wages. Six years later, a group of workers, known as "Blanketeers," because they wrapped themselves in the woolen cloth they wove, marched from Manchester to ask George, the Prince Regent, for his help.

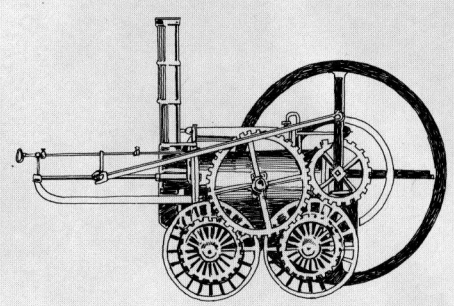

Trevithick's steam locomotive was driven by a powerful steam engine.

Trade

By 1750, raw materials were being shipped from distant lands to industrial centers in Europe and America. Merchants and factory owners did well and made high profits. Their governments designed policies to protect this trade.

However, the policies were not always good for the countries that supplied the raw materials. Their economies were distorted, as they employed more and more people to produce goods to be sold abroad. They received very little profit in return.

In Europe, the growth in trade led to the development of financial institutions, some of which were not always secure. Stock exchanges and insurance offices opened. Bank checks were produced and, at the end of the 18th century, so was printed paper money.

▲ *Whaling off New Zealand in the early 1800s. Whale oil was very valuable because it was used in lamps.*

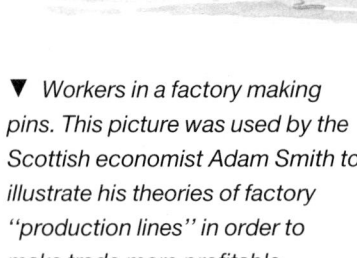

▼ *Workers in a factory making pins. This picture was used by the Scottish economist Adam Smith to illustrate his theories of factory "production lines" in order to make trade more profitable.*

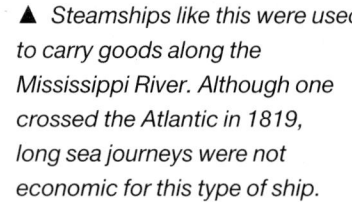

▲ *Steamships like this were used to carry goods along the Mississippi River. Although one crossed the Atlantic in 1819, long sea journeys were not economic for this type of ship.*

▲ Old Spanish dollars were known as "pieces of eight." Dollars were often cut into eight bits. Two bits, or a quarter, was the most popular division. The term is still used today.

▶ Smugglers thrived during the 18th century. Goods like wine, tobacco, and whiskey were imported illegally to avoid paying customs or to get around trade bans between countries at war.

WHEN IT HAPPENED

1719 Austrian Oriental Company founded to trade with the Far East.

1720 The Governor of New York encourages trade with Native North Americans.

1786 U.S. adopts coins based on Spanish dollar.

1797 England starts to export iron.

1802 The West India Docks, London are built.

1810 The French government starts to control the sale of tobacco.

1813 The British East India Company's monopoly of trade with India is abolished; international trade grows.

▲ European merchants making bids at a tea auction in Hong Kong, around 1800. Tea from China was in great demand in Europe. It was very expensive because tea only came from China, but in the 1830s rival plantations were set up in India by the British.

▶ The busy docks at Bristol, England, about 1760. Tobacco from North America was traded there until 1775, when the Revolutionary War stopped its export.

Regency Britain

King George III of Britain came to the throne in 1760, a confident young man who was just 22 years old. However, when he died 60 years later, he was miserable, frail, and almost certainly mad. Today doctors think George III had a disease which affects the skin and kidneys and, if not treated, the brain as well. After 1788, the king suffered from periods of confusion, which made him unable to rule. In 1811, he was replaced by his son, also called George, who ruled the country until his father's death.

Prince George was known as the Prince Regent, and the years from 1811 to 1820 are called the Regency period. The prince loved luxury, and spent a great deal of money on clothes, books, houses, paintings, and fine furniture. He also ate, drank, and gambled lavishly. Other young men were quick to follow his extravagant example.

At this time, art, music, literature, and architecture flourished in Britain, attracting the best designers and craftsmen from Europe. Regency art was elegant and graceful. Like the Egyptian style fashionable in Paris during the reign of Napoleon, Regency art was influenced by the designs of ancient history. It was also proud and confident, having been inspired by Britain's success in the war with France.

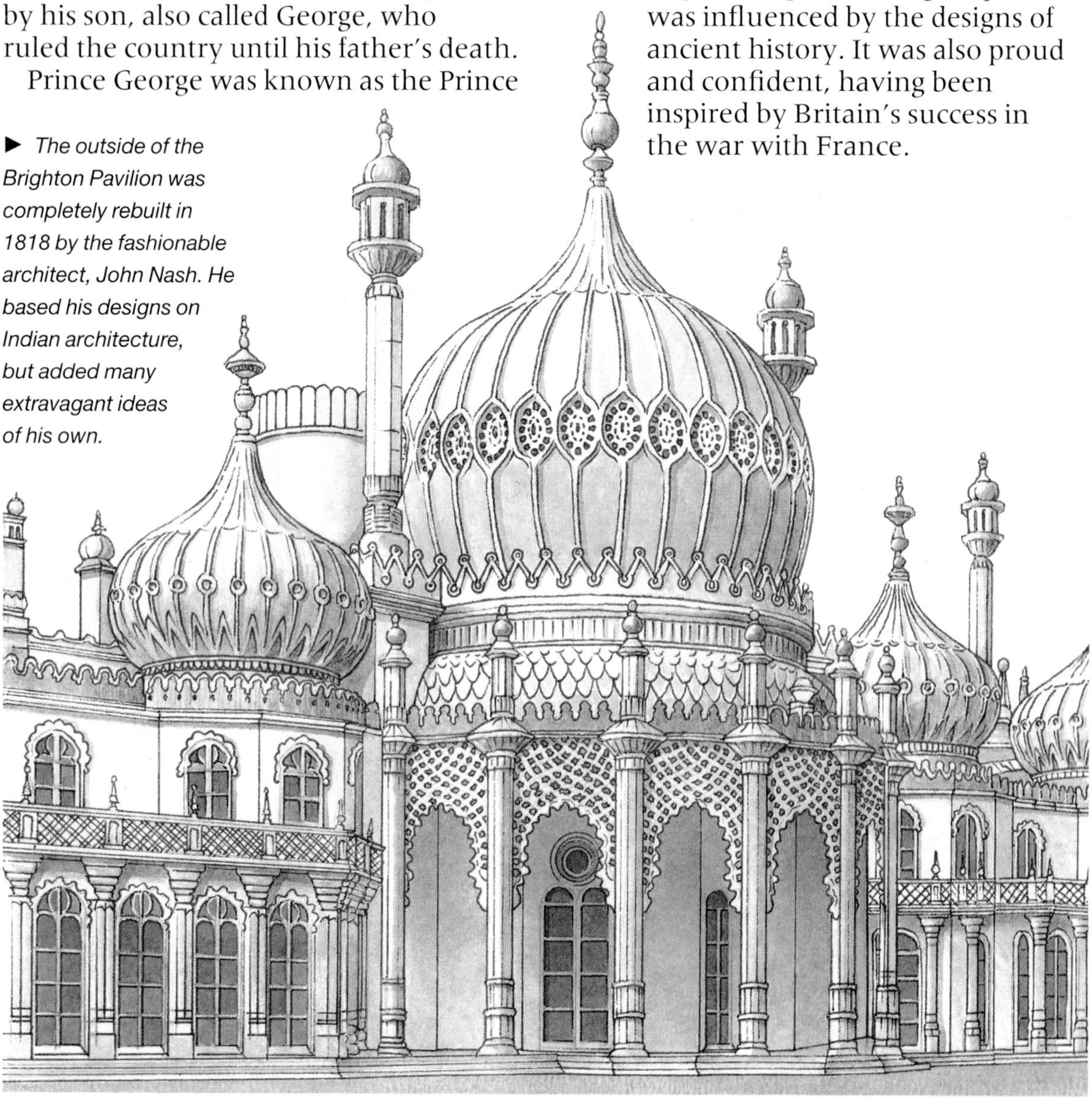

▶ *The outside of the Brighton Pavilion was completely rebuilt in 1818 by the fashionable architect, John Nash. He based his designs on Indian architecture, but added many extravagant ideas of his own.*

▲ *Vauxhall Gardens in London were a popular place for rich people to spend their leisure time. There were flowers, walks, restaurants, and theaters.*

Jane Austen

The daughter of an English clergyman, Jane Austen (1775 –1817) wrote six great novels commenting on the society and manners of her time. Her most famous novel *Pride and Prejudice*, a witty love story, is still a popular book.

▼ *A cartoon of the Duke of Wellington, who became commander-in-chief of the army in 1827.*

1820 U.S.: First American missionaries reach Hawaii. Missouri Compromise admits two new states to the Union: Missouri, as a slave state and Maine, a free state. This keeps the balance of power in the Senate. However, slavery is banned from all states north of Missouri. The population of the United States is 9,638,453, with New York the largest city at 124,000. Britain: There is disillusion with the pleasure-seeking attitude of the Prince Regent, but he succeeds to the throne as George IV (to 1830), following the death of his father George III.

1821 Greece: War of Independence against Ottoman empire begins (to 1829). South Atlantic: Napoleon dies on the island of St. Helena. South America: Venezuela, Peru, Guatemala, Panama, and Santo Domingo win independence from Spain. U.S.: Davy Crockett is elected state legislator in Tennessee.

1822 Greek War of Independence: Turks massacre Greek rebels at Chios. Ireland: Demands for independence. West Africa: Liberia is founded as a colony where escaped slaves may live.

1823 U.S.: Monroe Doctrine warns against further colonization by Europeans. Britain: Charles Babbage begins building first forerunner of the computer.

1824 Germany: Composer Ludwig van Beethoven completes his Symphony No. 9, the "Choral."

1825 Britain: Stockton-Darlington railroad line opens. It is the first railroad to carry passengers. Russia: An attempted revolt by "Decembrists" fails.

1826 First Pan-American congress held in Panama. North and South American states meet to discuss joint concerns.

1827 Russia, France, and Britain ask Ottoman Turks and Greece to make peace. The Turks refuse, and invade Athens. Russia, France, and Britain unite against Turks, and defeat the Turkish and Egyptian fleet at the battle of Navarino. France: Inventor Joseph Niépce produces first photographs on metal.

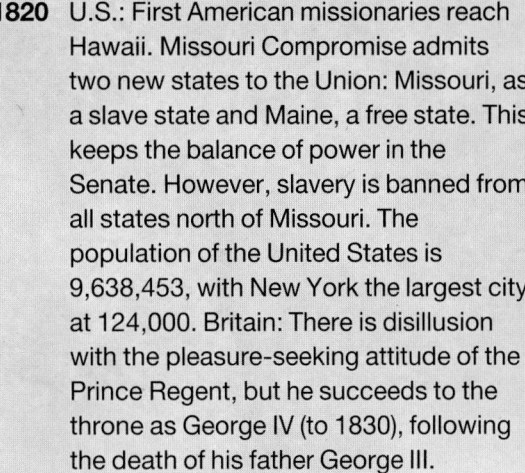

Greek Independence

For educated people in 18th-century Europe and the United States, Greece was still the home of democracy. Ancient Greek writings were studied in schools and Greek architectural styles were used in important buildings, such as the Bank of England in London and the Capitol in Washington.

But Greece itself was no longer democratic. Since the 16th century, it had been part of the Muslim Ottoman empire (*see* pages 358–359). In 1821, the Greek people rebelled against their Ottoman rulers. Thousands of people were killed. Europeans were shocked. Some, like the English poet Lord Byron, hurried to help. Austria and Russia also supported the Greeks, not because they admired the freedom fighters, but because they hoped to weaken the Ottoman Turks. In 1827, at the sea battle of Navarino, the Turks were defeated by a combined fleet of British, Russian, and French ships. Greece finally became independent from Turkey in 1829.

▲ The struggle for Greek independence lasted from 1821 to 1829. The Greeks only won freedom from the Ottoman Turks with the help of European powers. In 1833, Otto I of Bavaria, was crowned king of Greece.

▼ Greek priests (in black) fought alongside rebels after the head of the Greek Church had been murdered by the Turks, although he had nothing to do with the Greek rebellion.

Lord Byron

Like many wealthy young men of his time, George Gordon, Lord Byron (1788–1824), went on a grand tour of Europe. On his return in 1812, he wrote *Childe Harold*, a romantic poem which made him famous. He was also known for his scandalous lifestyle. He joined the Greek fight for independence in 1821, but died of a fever three years later.

The July Revolution

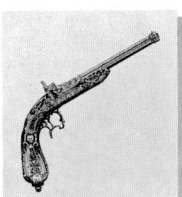

After the fall of Napoleon (*see* page 542), France was once again ruled by kings. Louis XVIII came to the throne in 1814. He was guided by a Chamber of Deputies and a written constitution, known as the Charter. Louis was succeeded in 1824 by his brother, Charles X. Charles behaved as if the 1789 Revolution had not happened. He helped the nobles, altered the Charter and dismissed the Chamber of Deputies.

This angered the French people. Fighting broke out in 1830 after Charles tried to ban all newspapers, so that no one would know what was going on. Charles fled to England and Louis Philippe, son of the Duke of Orléans, was invited to be king. Although he was a member of the royal family, he believed in the aims of the 1789 Revolution and agreed to rule as a "citizen king."

▲ *During the July Revolution of 1830, the citizens of Paris fought for several days against the king's troops. Many streets were blocked by barricades, which the soldiers were unwilling to take down since many of them were in favor of the uprising.*

1829 Greece becomes independent. Britain: First London horse-drawn omnibuses provide cheap public transportation. U.S.: patent issued for the first typewriting machine.

1830 France: July Revolution in Paris. Louis Philippe, son of the Duke of Orléans, is accepted as "the citizen king." France invades Algeria, North Africa. U.S.: Belva Lockwood becomes first American Supreme Court lawyer. Australia: Charles Stuart follows the Murray River from the north to its mouth in the south (near present-day Adelaide). Charles Freemantle lands on the southwest coast of Australia and claims the entire area for Britain.

1831 Poland: An attempt to win independence from Russia fails. Middle East: Syria is conquered by Egypt. France: Workers riot in Lyons. U.S.: The first railroad is built in South Carolina. Joseph Henry invents the telegraph and first electromagnetic motor.

1832 Britain: The First Reform Act increases the vote to middle-class men.

1833 U.S.: The first popular, cheap, daily paper, the *New York Sun*, is founded.

The first British policemen were called "peelers" after their founder Sir Robert Peel.

1834 South Africa: Fighting starts between Africans and European settlers. U.S.: Cyrus McCormick patents mechanical reaping machine.

1835 Halley's comet reappears.

War and Weapons

For many years between 1708 and 1835, the nations of Europe were at war, often against each other. There were wars in other parts of the world, including America.

European battles were fought on a massive scale; deaths and casualties were tremendous. Armies moved farther and more quickly than ever before. But even Napoleon, the most successful war leader of the age and a brilliant tactician, faced defeat when he tried to march on Moscow in winter and was forced to retreat.

New inventions were seen on the battlefield. The Prussians (Germans) introduced horse artillery (large guns drawn by horses). Colt and Derringer made new, rapid-fire pistols, and shrapnel (exploding shells) was first used by British troops in 1803. Warfare and tactics were also studied in a new, scientific way.

▼ The British "thin red line." Soldiers grouped like this could cover a wide area, and still shoot to kill the enemy.

▲ A French cuirassier (armored guard) fighting a British cavalryman at the battle of Waterloo in 1815. Cavalry still fought with swords.

► The Prussian general Karl von Clausewitz won fame for his skill as a military thinker. He was the first to try and allow for the part played by chance in winning battles.

◄ The Colt revolver was first made in 1835. Its revolving chamber (the container where bullets are held) meant that it could fire six shots before it needed to be reloaded. This was a major advance and the Colt soon became widely used.

▼ The one-man Turtle submarine was launched in America in 1755. The propeller had to be turned by hand.

▶ The inside of a Turkish arsenal, where weapons were stored. From left to right, you can see drums, swords, lances, pikes, cannon, cannonballs and barrels of gunpowder, mortars, bombs, muskets, pistols, and armor (helmets and breastplates). This illustration first appeared in the 18th century.

WHEN IT HAPPENED

1751 The *Ecole Superior de Guerre* (Academy of War) is established in Paris, France.

1774 British inventor John Wilkinson invents new system of precison-boring cannon.

1777 American inventor David Bushnell invents the torpedo.

1800 American inventor Eli Whitney makes guns (muskets) with quick-change spare parts.

1805 Rockets used as weapons by British army.

1811 Krupp ironworks are founded in Germany to make guns.

1815 First steam-powered warship built in the U.S.

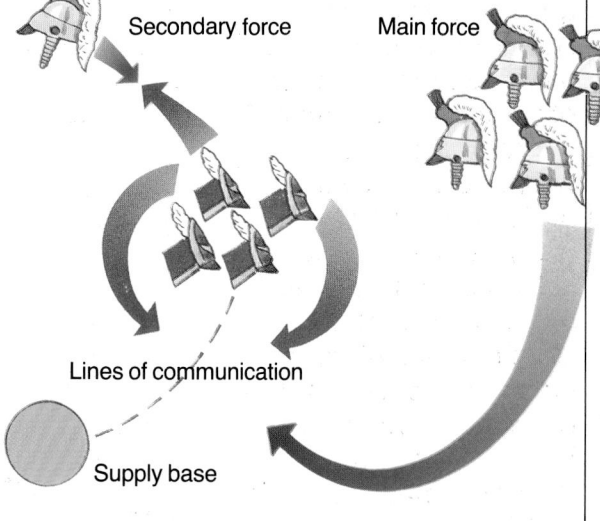

Secondary force

Main force

Lines of communication

Supply base

◀ The press-gang was loathed and feared in 18th-century Britain. It was made up of a group of sailors, licensed by the government to capture men and force them to serve in the British navy. Conditions in the navy were so bad that few men volunteered to join. The navy continued to rely on press-gangs until the 1830s, when pay and conditions improved.

▲ To move huge armies successfully battles were carefully planned. Strategy was very important in winning or losing a battle. One of Napoleon's favorite tactics in battle was to divide his forces, so only part of his force attacked the enemy while the main force circled around and attacked the enemy's supply base and communications line.

The Trail of Tears

Settlers flocked to the United States after independence was declared in 1776. They came from all over Europe, hoping to make a new life in what they called "the land of the free." The American population was around four million in 1803, but by 1861 it had increased to 31 million. The first arrivals settled in the northeastern states, but as their numbers grew, they moved farther south and west.

These lands were already occupied by Native North Americans. The government forced them to leave their homes. Many died on the long march westward, called the "Trail of Tears."

To make matters worse, the U.S. government had bought an enormous area of prairie land between the Mississippi River and the Rocky Mountains from France in 1803. Called the Louisiana Purchase, it doubled the size of the United States. These prairies were also home to many North American Indians. But the government sold the land to farmers, gold miners, railroad engineers, and ranchers.

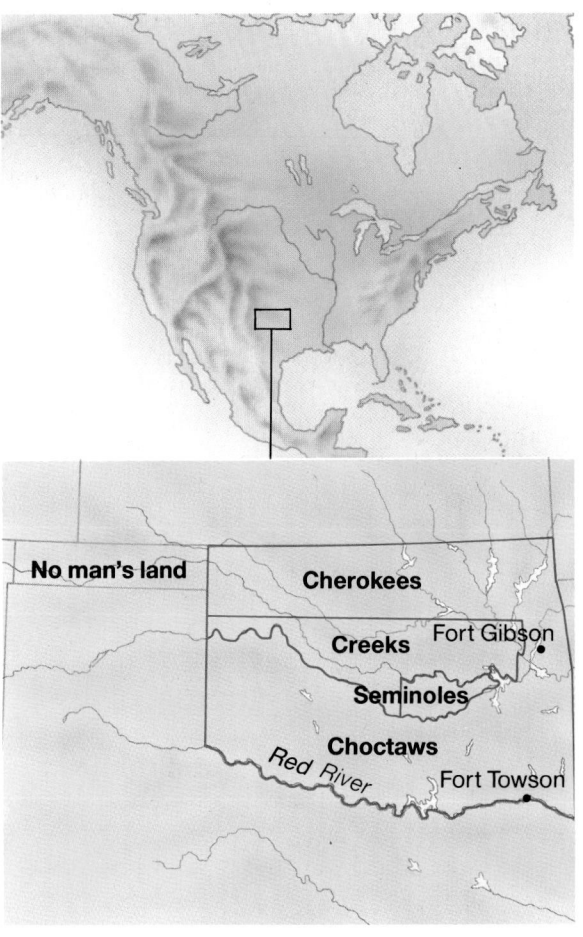

▲ Many Native North Americans were forced to leave their lands, and travel to distant "empty" regions, to make room for the new settlers from Europe.

◀ Cherokee Indians on their long journey westward in the 1830s. The U.S. government offered the Cherokees $5.7 million to move, but 90 percent of them refused. They were therefore driven from their traditional homelands in Georgia and North Carolina by government soldiers, and forcibly settled on newly created reservations in the harsh prairie lands of what is now Oklahoma.

Unification and Colonization

As the industrial revolution spread across Europe, the European nations began to carve out colonial empires to supply the raw materials needed for their factories. In the East, India became a prized colony in a massive British empire that influenced events in a large part of the world.

China and Japan both tried to keep foreigners out of their countries, but eventually they too were forced to open up to trade with Europe and the United States of America.

The United States gained territory in the west, and Texas joined the Union after winning its independence from Mexico. Economic differences and disagreements about slavery led to arguments between the states of the North and South and ultimately to the Civil War. Canada's two provinces were united and lands in the west were also added to its territory. The country later became a dominion within the British empire, as did Australia, New Zealand, and South Africa.

Disputes over territory caused wars between the newly independent nations of South America. In Europe, the collapse of the Ottoman empire led to wars between the countries that wanted control of its territories. In 1848, revolutions broke out in a number of European countries due to the desire for more democratic government and the rise of nationalism. This also affected Germany and Italy, where the small independent states were unified and both countries became major European powers.

▼ *The coming of the railroad opened up North America, but also led to the first national strike. When railroad workers had their wages cut, their protests stopped the trains. The strike spread along the railroad, from coast to coast, uniting the workers in their fight for a decent wage.*

The Americas

1836 Texas gains its independence from Mexico.
1839 Women in the United States are given legal control over their property.
1840 Upper and Lower Canada unite.
1841 Edgar Allan Poe's *The Murders in the Rue Morgue* makes detective stories popular and James Fenimore Cooper writes *The Deerslayer*.
1842 Border dispute between U.S. and Canada is settled.
1846–1848 Mexican-American War.
1861 Eleven Southern states form a Confederacy.
1861–1865 U.S. Civil War.
1863 Slavery is abolished in United States.
1864–1870 Paraguayan War.
1867 Dominion of Canada is formed.
1879–1884 War of the Pacific between Chile, Bolivia, and Peru.
1889 Brazil is declared a republic.
1890 Oklahoma Territory is created from Indian lands.
1898 Spanish-American War. Cuba gains independence. Philippines, Guam, and Puerto Rico become part of U.S.
1903 Panama becomes independent.
1910–1940 Mexican Revolution.

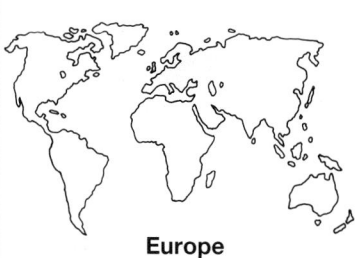

Europe

1837 Start of Queen Victoria's reign.
1844 Alexandre Dumas writes *The Three Musketeers* and *The Count of Monte Cristo*.
1845 Famine in Ireland.
1848 Revolutions in Europe. Karl Marx and Friedrich Engels publish the *Communist Manifesto*.
1853–1856 The Crimean War.
1856 Louis Pasteur discovers that bacteria cause disease.
1861 Kingdom of Italy is founded. Romania is formed.
1866 Austro-Prussian War.
1867 North German Confederation is created. Austro-Hungarian empire (Dual Monachy) is founded.
1870–1871 Franco-Prussian War.
1874 The Impressionists hold their first exhibition in Paris.
1877–1878 Russo-Turkish War.
1882 Triple Alliance is formed.
1886 First Irish Home Rule Bill.
1894 Nicholas II becomes tsar of Russia.
1896 Olympic Games revived.
1903 Entente Cordiale formed.
1905 Revolution in Russia.
1907 Triple Entente is formed.
1908 Bulgaria declares independence.
1910 Republic of Portugal is formed.

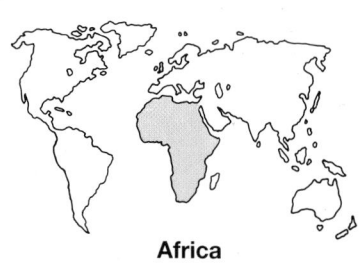

Africa

1836 Boers settle in Natal.
1838 Start of wars between the Zulus and Boers.
1840 Matabeleland is founded.
1847 Liberia is founded.
1854 Umar ibn Said Tal founds the Tukolor empire in West Africa.
1873 British-Asante War.
1877–1879 War between the Zulus and the British.
1880–1881 First Boer War between the Boers and the British.
1881 The Mahdi of Sudan leads Muslims in a holy war.
1884 Europe divides Africa up at the Berlin Conference.
1893 Matabele War against the British.
1895 Rhodesia created.
1896 Ethiopia's independence recognized by Italy.
1899–1902 Second Boer War.
1906 Algeciras conference confirms French rights to Morocco.
1910 South Africa is founded.
1911–1912 Italian-Turkish War.

Middle East

1839 Mehemet Ali of Egypt defeats the Ottoman Turks.
1839–1842 First Anglo-Afghan War.

1856–1857 Persia at war with Britain after invading Afghanistan.

1878–1880 Second Afghan War.
1879 Britain controls Afghan affairs.
1880 Abd-er-Rahman Khan comes to power in Afghanistan.

1906 Liberal revolution in Persia.

Asia and the Far East

1839–1842 First Opium War.
1841 Sarawak granted to Sir James Brooke.
1849 Death of Katsushika Hokusai, the great Japanese painter.
1850–1864 Taiping rebellion.
1852 Second British-Burmese War.
1856–1860 Second Opium War.
1857–1858 Indian Mutiny.
1858 India placed under government of British crown.
1868 Start of Meiji Period in Japan.
1869 Suez Canal opens.
1873–1903 Acheh War in Dutch East Indies.
1877 Satsuma revolt in Japan.
1884–1885 Chinese-French War.
1885 Third British-Burmese War.
1887 Union of Indochina.
1894–1895 Chinese-Japanese War.
1898 New Territories, including Hong Kong, are leased to Britain by China for 99 years.
1900 Boxer Rebellion in China.
1904–1905 Russian-Japanese War.
1908 Young Turk Revolution.
1911 End of Qing dynasty.

Australasia and Pacific

1836 City of Adelaide is founded.
1840 Treaty of Waitangi. City of Auckland is founded.
1842 French occupy Tahiti.
1845–1872 Anglo-Maori wars.
1851 Gold rush at Bathurst, Australia.
1852 New Zealand is granted a constitution.
1855 Van Diemen's Land is renamed Tasmania.

1874 Britain annexes Fiji.

1884 Britain annexes south-east New Guinea.

1901 Commonwealth of Australia is established.

1907 Dominion of New Zealand is founded.

The World

In **North America**, settlers traveled west to colonize the vast lands taken over by the United States and Canada. Railroads were built that spanned the continent. However, the opening up of new territories in the United States and **Australia** caused hardship for the people whose traditional way of life was being threatened.

In **Africa**, religious wars strengthened the influence of Islam in the kingdoms of the north. European explorers and missionaries started to visit lands in the center. Led by a desire to exploit the resources of Africa, the European powers quickly established colonies throughout the continent. The power of the great trading nations of Europe grew.

In **Asia**, Europeans took control of India, Burma and most of Southeast Asia, and began to trade with China and Japan.

Europe's expansion into other continents did not stop internal conflicts, and many wars were fought between countries or empires wanting more power and territory. During this period unrest within countries often led to conflict.

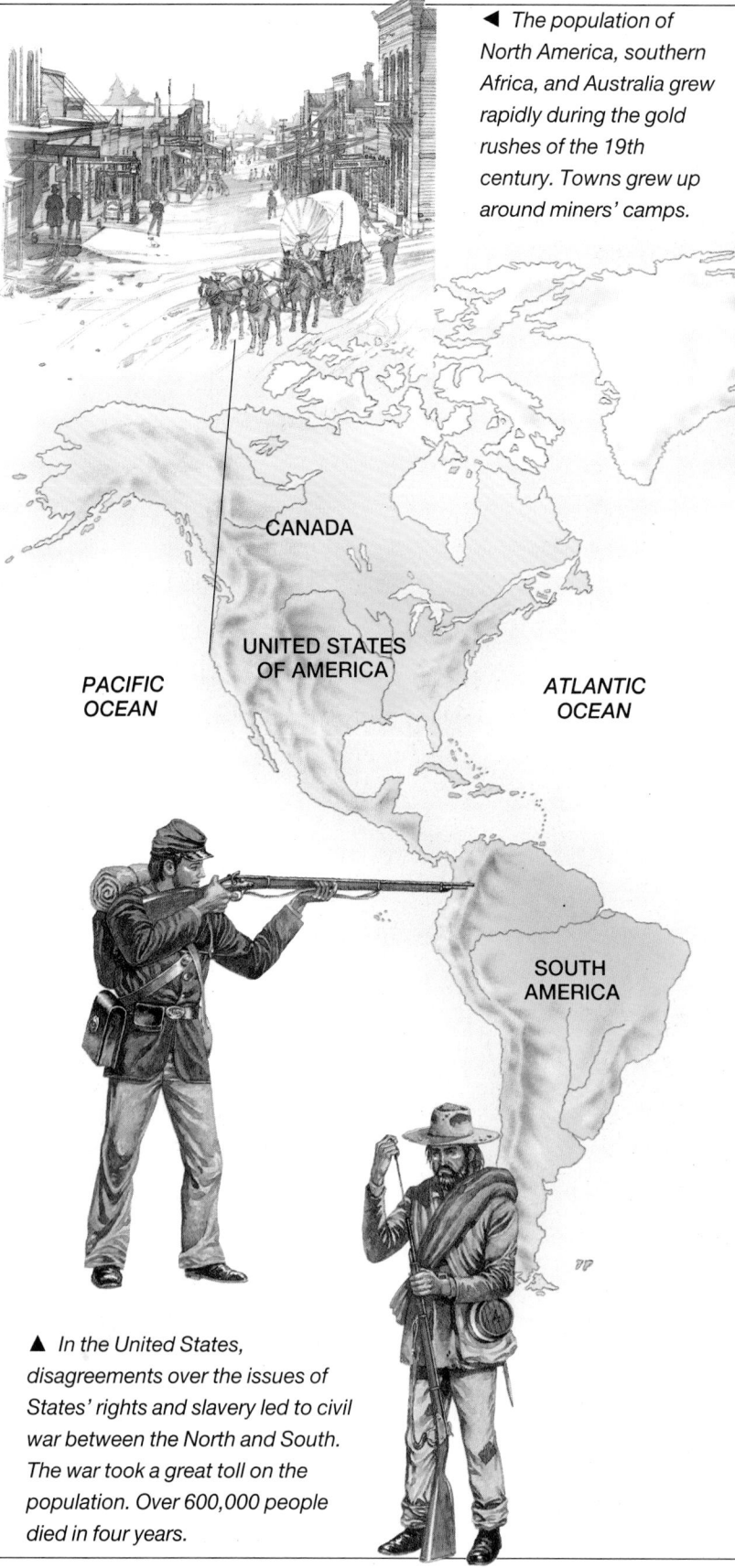

◄ The population of North America, southern Africa, and Australia grew rapidly during the gold rushes of the 19th century. Towns grew up around miners' camps.

CANADA

UNITED STATES OF AMERICA

PACIFIC OCEAN

ATLANTIC OCEAN

SOUTH AMERICA

▲ In the United States, disagreements over the issues of States' rights and slavery led to civil war between the North and South. The war took a great toll on the population. Over 600,000 people died in four years.

◄ In 1848, people all over Europe took to the streets to rebel against unjust laws. Many European rulers realized that change had to come.

► During the Boxer Rebellion, Chinese rebels murdered Europeans in protest against colonial occupation in some areas.

RUSSIA

EUROPE

Crimean Peninsula

Ottoman empire

Suez Canal

ASIA

CHINA

JAPAN

INDIA

Tukolor empire

AFRICA

INDIAN OCEAN

SOUTHEAST ASIA

Cape Colony

AUSTRALIA

NEW ZEALAND

▲ The opening of the Suez Canal. This waterway shortened the journey between Europe and the Middle East and Asia.

▲ During the colonization of New Zealand, European settlers often clashed with Maoris, who fought to defend their lands and people.

◄ During the 19th century African trading networks were set up across the continent to sell guns, ivory, and slaves.

Texas and Mexico

Mexico gained its independence from Spain in 1821 (*see* pages 536–537). At that time its borders stretched much farther north and covered many areas now in the southern United States of America. Many United States citizens settled in Texas, which belonged to Mexico, and in 1835 Texas declared its independence.

The Texans appointed Sam Houston as their military commander. He captured the town of San Antonio. His opponent, the Mexican general Santa Anna, then led a large Mexican army into Texas to

A contemporary cartoon of the ancient Aztec symbol for Mexico: a proud eagle perched on a cactus. Mexico's vast territories shrank considerably after the U.S. gradually annexed the northern areas in the mid 1800s.

1836 Britain: Chartist movement begins; demands include the vote for all men. U.S.: Texans win independence from Mexico after the battle of San Jacinto. Swedish-born engineer John Ericsson patents a screw propeller for ships. Australia: City of Adelaide founded. South Africa: Boers on Great Trek settle in Natal. Writer Nikolai Gogol's comedy *The Inspector General* is first performed in Russia.

1837 Britain: Victoria becomes queen of Great Britain and Ireland (to 1901). Sir Isaac Pitman publishes his shorthand system. Novelist Charles Dickens publishes his first work in novel form, *The Pickwick Papers* (it first appeared in monthly installments). Charles Wheatstone and William Cooke patent the electric telegraph. Canada: French reformists led by Louis Papineau rebel against British rule in Lower Canada (Quebec); the revolt spreads to Upper Canada. U.S.: Samuel Morse invents Morse code for telegraph.

THE ALAMO

Davy Crockett was one of the defenders of the Alamo, a mission in San Antonio which was sometimes used as a fort. It became a symbol of Texan resistance during the war against Mexico. About 180 Texans defended the Alamo for 11 days in 1836 against the Mexican army led by General Santa Anna. Only two women and two children survived. Other heroes killed at the Alamo include Jim Bowie (who invented the Bowie hunting knife) and William Travis. They had to use their guns as clubs because they ran out of ammunition during the siege.

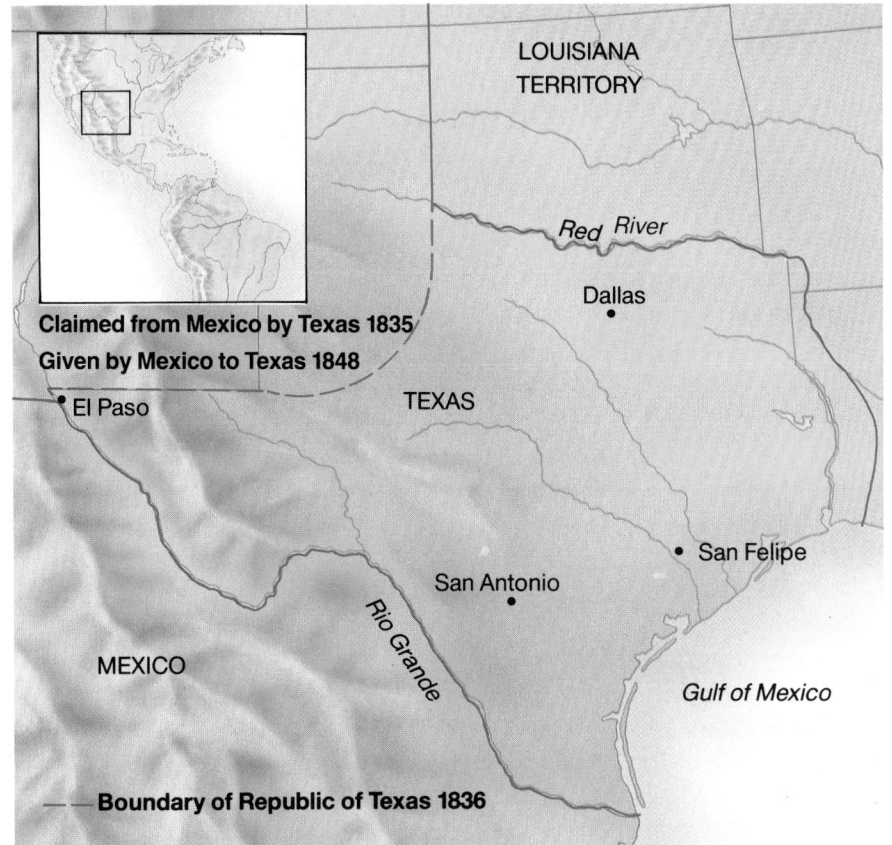

Claimed from Mexico by Texas 1835
Given by Mexico to Texas 1848

LOUISIANA TERRITORY

Red River

Dallas

• El Paso

TEXAS

• San Felipe

San Antonio

Rio Grande

MEXICO

Gulf of Mexico

— — Boundary of Republic of Texas 1836

Sam Houston

1793 Born.
1836 Defeats Mexican General Santa Anna at battle of San Jacinto.
1836–1838 and **1841–1844** Elected president of the independent republic of Texas.
1859 Elected governor of state of Texas.
1863 Dies.

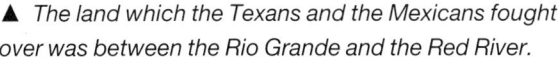
▲ *The land which the Texans and the Mexicans fought over was between the Rio Grande and the Red River.*

▶ *General Santa Anna was captured at the battle of San Jacinto, and taken to meet Sam Houston. Houston had been shot in the ankle during the battle.*

crush the rebellion. He laid siege to the Alamo, a mission in the center of San Antonio. After laying siege to the Alamo, he won San Antonio back, but was defeated by Houston's forces at the battle of San Jacinto in 1836. Texas became an independent republic. It was known as the "Lone Star" republic. After a few years of independence, the people of Texas voted to join the United States. Texas became the 28th state in 1845.

Clashes between the Texans and Mexicans continued as Texas tried to increase its territory. The U.S. president sent troops to the Rio Grande, invading land still claimed by Mexico. The Mexicans resisted, and the Mexican-American War broke out. U.S. troops captured the capital, Mexico City, in 1847, and the Mexicans surrendered.

The treaty of Guadalupe-Hidalgo, which ended the war, was signed in 1848. It gave the United States huge new territories, including the modern states of California, Nevada, Utah, Arizona, and some of New Mexico, as well as Texas.

South Africa

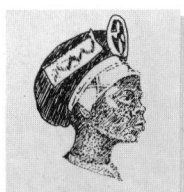

In 1836, the Cape Colony at the southern tip of Africa was ruled by the British. The Dutch settlers, known as Boers (farmers), disliked British rule. The Boers left Cape Colony, and set out on the Great Trek. They traveled northward to the areas now known as Natal and the Orange Free State. They defeated the African people who already lived in these areas.

The British took over the new Boer republic of Natal in 1843, but gave independence to the Transvaal and the Orange Free State. Fighting continued between the Boers and the Zulus, led by Cetewayo. A three-cornered struggle developed, with the British against the Zulus, and both against the Boers. In the Zulu War of 1879, the Zulus defeated the British in a battle at Isandhlwana, but lost to them at the battle of Rorke's Drift. The British won the war.

In 1880, the British tried to take over the Transvaal, and the First Boer War broke out. The Boers defeated the British, and the Transvaal remained

▲ Zulu soldiers were armed with spears and knobkerries (round-headed clubs) and carried shields. Their warfare tactics were often successful, and they inflicted heavy losses on both the Boers and the British army, even without guns. They were organized into impis (regiments) and fought with great stamina before being defeated by the British.

◄ During the Second Boer War the British troops lost to the Boers in the battle fought at Spion Kop. The Boers won a number of early battles before being defeated by the British.

► The Great Trek is an important event in Boer history. They left Cape Colony with all their belongings loaded into wagons and traveled northward, into the areas where the African peoples lived.

Rhodes

Cecil Rhodes (1853–1902) became prime minister of Cape Colony from 1890–1895. He wanted to create a British empire in Africa that would stretch from the Cape Colony to Cairo, in Egypt.

Cetewayo

Cetewayo (1826–1884) was king of the Zulus from 1873 to 1879. He led his people in the Zulu War. After their victory at Isandhlwana, the Zulus were defeated, and Cetewayo was captured.

independent. But the British still hoped to unite South Africa as one country. The prime minister of Cape Colony, Cecil Rhodes, planned the Jameson Raid to overthrow the Boer government of the Transvaal. The raid failed, but in 1899 the Second Boer War broke out. Although the Boers won some of the early battles such as Spion Kop, they were defeated by the British in 1902. The Transvaal and the Orange Free State became founding provinces of the Union of South Africa in 1910.

1838 South Africa: Massacre of 500 Boers by Zulus led by Dingaan; Boers get revenge at the battle of Blood River in which they defeat the Zulus. Britain: Anti-Corn Law League founded. France: Louis Daguerre produces an early type of photograph called a daguerreotype. Atlantic steamship service begins.

Cecil Rhodes holding the successful telegraph link between Cairo in Egypt, Britain's northernmost African colony, and the Cape Colony in South Africa, Britain's southernmost colony.

1839 China: first Opium War between Britain and China starts (to 1842). Middle East: British occupy Aden. Afghanistan: First Anglo-Afghan War starts (to 1842). Syria: Mehemet Ali, the ruler of Egypt, defeats the Ottoman Turks. West Africa: France annexes Gabon. Europe: Belgium's permanent neutrality is guaranteed by European powers in Treaty of London. Britain: Photographic pioneer William Fox Talbot claims to have invented calotype photography before Daguerre. Scottish engineer James Nasmyth perfects his steam hammer. U.S.: Charles Goodyear invents vulcanized rubber. U.S. women are given legal control over their property. France: Novelist Stendhal publishes *The Charterhouse of Parma*.

1840 New Zealand: In the Treaty of Waitangi, the islands become a British colony. City of Auckland is founded. Africa: Boers declare Republic of Natal independent. Matabeleland is founded. Canada: Act of Union unites Upper and Lower Canada. Britain: First postage stamps.

The Arts

For all the arts the period between 1836 and 1914 was a time of change and experiment. Painting and music especially showed more variety than before with an increased emphasis on nature. In European literature, far more novels were written for the growing number of readers.

Wagner invented a new form of grand opera, and the Russian ballet changed ideas about dance. Drama became more realistic with Ibsen, Chekhov, and Shaw, and by 1914 an entirely new form of performing art had appeared: the movies.

▲ This wooden carving of Queen Victoria was made in West Africa. The face is traditional, but the crown detail was carefully copied.

▶ Chinese painters often worked in ink, with a pen-like brush. In the late 19th century a broader brush style was used.

▼ Peasant with a hoe was painted by Georges Seurat in 1882. His early paintings were in the Impressionist style, an art movement that developed in the late 19th century.

▲ The stained glass lamps of Louis Tiffany belonged to the decorative style Art Nouveau, which became popular about 1890.

◄ *This scene is from* David Copperfield *by Charles Dickens, which was written between 1849 and 1850. Dickens was a popular English author, and his aim was to entertain and enlighten his readers by telling stories full of social problems. His novels were often illustrated and first appeared as serials.*

▼ Factory at Horta de Ebro *was painted by Pablo Picasso in 1909. It shows the beginning of a new art movement called Cubism. Artists depicted their subjects in basic shapes, and were often influenced by African sculpture.*

▼ *This bronze sculpture,* The Thinker, *by Auguste Rodin went on show to the French public in 1904. His figures were expressive, conveying the power of human emotion.*

WHEN IT HAPPENED

1856 French novelist Gustave Flaubert publishes *Madame Bovary*.

1869 The Russian novel *War and Peace* by Leo Tolstoy is published.

1874 First Impressionist exhibition in Paris.

1876 First performance of Richard Wagner's series of "Ring" operas.

1905 First public motion picture theater opens in Pittsburgh.

1907 Cubism movement starts in Paris, France.

1909 Diaghilev's Russian ballet company opens in Paris.

1913 Armory show introduces new styles of modern art such as Cubism to the U.S.

The Opium Wars

The Chinese had almost no contact with the rest of the world for many years. The Chinese government only allowed trading to take place at one port, Guangzhou (Canton). To get around this problem, foreign merchants began to smuggle the drug opium into the country so that the Chinese were forced into trading with them (*see* pages 502–503). The Chinese government tried to stop this, and in 1839 Chinese officials went to the British warehouses in Guangzhou where they seized and burned 20,000 chests of opium. In response, the British sent warships which threatened the

► In the "unequal treaties" the Chinese were forced to give in to European demands. The Chinese were afraid that foreign trade meant that the country would come under foreign influence. The Treaty of Nanking (Nanjing) was signed by the British and the Chinese in 1842. It opened up five ports and gave Hong Kong Island to the British. The treaties increased Western influence, and allowed foreigners to settle in China.

▲ Hong Kong Island became a British colony in 1842. It soon grew into a center of trade. In 1860 the Kowloon Peninsula was added, and in 1898 the British gained the New Territories on a 99-year lease.

◄ The Taiping Rebellion broke out in 1851 and lasted until 1864. The government overcame the rebellion with help from foreign powers who wanted Qing rule to continue.

Chinese and besieged the port. This was the first of two Opium wars fought by the British and the Chinese. When the first war was over, the British forced the Chinese to sign the Treaty of Nanking (Nanjing), which opened Chinese ports to British trade. The Chinese also gave the island of Hong Kong to the British.

The Second Opium War (1856–1860) was also won by the British, and it ended with another treaty which forced the Chinese to open even more ports to trade with European merchants. Other countries, such as France and the United States, signed more of these "unequal treaties," gaining their citizens special rights in China. Eager merchants and missionaries rushed in.

At the same time, the huge Chinese empire was gradually breaking down. The ruling Qing dynasty was faced with rebellions started by starving peasants. The Taiping Rebellion was started by people who wanted the land to be divided equally among the ordinary people. The foreign powers helped to crush the rebellion because they wanted the Qing dynasty to continue so that the treaties would be honored.

1841 Egypt: Sultan of Turkey confirms Mehemet Ali as hereditary ruler of Egypt. Black Sea region: European powers agree to close the Dardanelle Straits to non-Turkish warships. Brunei: Sultan grants Sarawak to Sir James Brooke. Belgium: Adolphe Sax invents the saxophone. US.: Edgar Allan Poe's *The Murders in the Rue Morgue* is possibly the first detective story. Samuel Morse patents the telegraph.

1842 North America: Webster-Ashburton Treaty settles border dispute between United States and Canada. Afghanistan: British leave Kabul. China: Treaty of Nanking (Nanjing) ends First Opium War; China cedes Hong Kong Island to Britain and opens its ports. Pacific: French occupy Tahiti. U.S.: First use of general anesthetic. Britain: Women and girls banned from working in mines.

1843 South Africa: Britain annexes Natal. India: British take Sind province.

1844 Britain: Co-operative movement founded in Rochdale. Artist J. M. W. Turner paints *Rain, Steam, and Speed*. France: Writer Alexandre Dumas publishes his novel *The Three Musketeers*.

1845 India: Britain at war with Sikhs (to 1849). Ireland: Famine (to 1851) after outbreak of potato blight. U.S.: Florida and Texas admitted to the Union. New Zealand: Outbreak of Anglo-Maori Wars (to 1872). Britain: Astronomer John C. Adams works out the position of planet Neptune.

The wife of an opium smoker publicly destroying her husband's pipe. The sale or smoking of opium had been banned in China by order of the emperor from the early 18th century onward.

1848, Year of Revolution

In 1848, rebellions and protests broke out in many parts of Europe. They showed that the people were not satisfied with their rulers.

The reasons for many of the rebellions were similar to those that caused the French Revolution (*see* pages 522–523). One of the main reasons was the idea that the people were more important than "the state," and that they should have a say in their government. In response to these rebellions, the rulers tried to restore the old systems of government, but the events of 1848 showed that change had to come.

The reasons for the revolutions of 1848 were not the same everywhere. One powerful cause was the desire of people who spoke the same language to form their own independent nations (nationalism). Nationalism was especially

• **Centers of Revolution in 1848**

London • GERMANY • Berlin • Warsaw
Paris • Frankfurt • Prague **Russian empire**
FRANCE Vienna •
Milan • **Austrian** • Budapest
Venice • **empire**
Catalonia ITALY **Wallachia**
SPAIN • Rome
Ottoman empire

▼ *In Britain, the last and biggest Chartist demonstration took place in 1848. The* People's Charter *demanded political reforms, including votes for all men. A large crowd gathered in London, and the meeting ended without violence.*

◀ *Most European countries experienced rebellions in 1848. Revolution had been simmering since 1815, and rebellions had broken out in the 1830s in several countries. The map shows where the most serious outbreaks were. After the revolutions were over, many countries remained unchanged, but governments realized that reforms were necessary.*

▲ *Revolutionaries, demanding "Bread or Death," stormed government buildings in Paris. They overthrew the monarchy and declared a republic, with Louis Napoleon, nephew of Napoleon Bonaparte, as "prince-president."*

strong in Germany and Italy, which were divided into many small states, and in parts of the Austrian empire. In other countries, people were demanding the right to vote (one of the reforms that the Chartist movement in Britain wanted). Other rebellions were led by people who wanted cheaper food, or for changes in land laws which would give the land to the ordinary working people.

Recent changes made rebellion easier. More people could read, and newspapers told them what was happening in other countries. Few police forces existed, so troops had to be used against rioters.

Most of the revolts of 1848 failed in their immediate demands. But over the next few years nationalist feeling grew stronger, and many governments began to see that democratic reforms would soon be necessary.

1846 Britain: Corn Laws are repealed. North America: Outbreak of Mexican-American War (to 1848). Oregon Treaty settles western border of United States and Canada. Britain: Edward Lear publishes his illustrated *Book of Nonsense.* U.S.: Elias Howe patents the first practical sewing machine. Smithsonian Institute founded in Washington D.C.

1847 U.S.: Mormons found Salt Lake City in Utah. The post office issues the first government-sponsored postage stamps. Africa: Liberia becomes an independent republic. Famine breaks out in the Netherlands and Belgium. Britain: Novelist Charlotte Brönte publishes *Jane Eyre* and her sister Emily publishes *Wuthering Heights.*

1848 "Year of Revolution" in Europe. France: Second Republic founded with Louis Napoleon as president. Italian states: Revolts widespread, but crushed by end of year. Austria: Prince Metternich resigns as chancellor, Emperor Ferdinand abdicates in favor of Franz Josef. Uprisings in Berlin, Vienna, Prague, Budapest, Catalonia, Wallachia, Poland, and Britain. National assembly meets at Frankfurt. Netherlands: A new constitution is introduced. Belgium: *Communist Manifesto* is published. U.S.: California gold rush begins. First women's rights convention held in New York State. William Thompson, Lord Kelvin, establishes absolute zero at −459.67°F (-273.15° C).

Over three million people signed the Chartist's petition in 1842. It was delivered to Parliament but then rejected by the Commons.

1849 Austria defeats Sardinia and crushes revolution in Hungary with Russian help. Germany: Frankfurt assembly collapses, ending attempt to form a constitutional German monarchy. India: British defeat Sikhs in battle of Gujerat; Punjab annexed. Rome: French troops occupy city to protect pope. New Zealand: Racial tension continues as Maoris refuse to sell their land to Europeans. U.S.: Amelia Jenks Bloomer introduces short baggy pants for women, known as "bloomers." William Hunt invents the safety pin. France: Joseph Monier produces reinforced concrete.

Whalers were among the first settlers in New Zealand and the surrounding Pacific islands.

1850 Germany: Old national assembly (diet) restored at Frankfurt. China: Taiping Rebellion against the Qing dynasty (to 1864). U.S.: California joins the Union. Novelist Nathaniel Hawthorne publishes *The Scarlet Letter*. Britain: Poet William Wordsworth publishes *The Prelude* (written 1805). France: Artist Gustav Courbet paints in realist style.

1851 France: Louis Napoleon ends Second Republic. Nigeria: British occupy Lagos, ending the slave trade. Australia: Gold rush begins. Britain: Great Exhibition is held in the Crystal Palace at Hyde Park, London. Poet Alfred Tennyson publishes *In Memoriam*. U.S.: Novelist Herman Melville finishes *Moby Dick*. Isaac Singer begins producing domestic sewing machines. Italy: Composer Giuseppe Verdi writes the opera *Rigoletto*.

New Zealand

By the 1830s, the growing number of European settlers in New Zealand's North Island (*see* pages 512–513) was beginning to cause problems. The settlers had no proper laws or government, and disputes broke out over land rights. The settlers needed large areas of land for sheep pasture. The local people, the Maoris, welcomed trade but they did not want the Europeans to settle. Maori numbers had been reduced by the diseases which the Europeans accidentally introduced.

By the 1830s, the settlers and the Maoris wanted the British to provide strong laws. In 1840, some of the Maori chiefs signed the Treaty of Waitangi with the British. The treaty said that if the Maoris gave control of New Zealand to Britain and accepted Queen Victoria as their sovereign, the British would protect all Maori rights.

The Europeans continued to take Maori land. Many of them thought they had bought it legally. But because there were two versions of the treaty, the Maoris thought that they had only

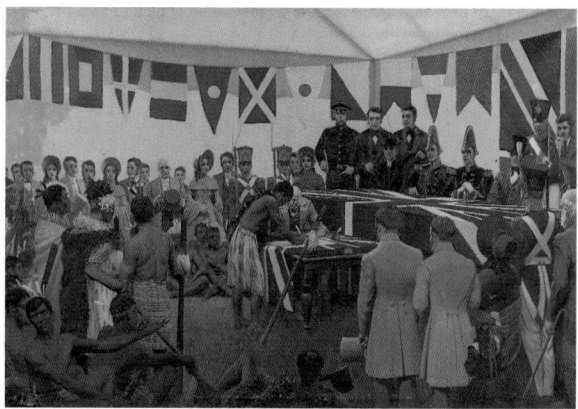

▲ *Maori chiefs signed the Treaty of Waitangi in 1840, giving New Zealand to Britain. The Maoris thought it was a promise that their lands and fisheries would be protected, but the colonial authorities did not do so.*

▲ *The colonists founded the settlement of Wellington, which became the capital in 1865. The bay had been colonized by the Maoris nearly 1,000 years earlier.*

agreed to give the British "governorship." In 1860, war broke out between the Maoris and the colonists. Although they fought bravely, the Maoris were forced to retreat to the mountains.

In 1907, New Zealand became a dominion within the British empire. New Zealand began to prosper and the numbers of Maoris began to grow again.

▼ *Until the Europeans came, the Maoris had no outside enemies. However, the different tribal groups were often at war with each other.*

THE MAORIS

Traditional Maori skills included tattooing and woodcarving. They grew crops as well as fishing and hunting. Maori folklore says that the North Island of New Zealand was created by the Maori hero, Maui. They believed that all land should be held in trust for the next generation, so selling land went against their tradition. Conflicts broke out when Maoris refused to sell land to Europeans.

Buildings

The main feature of architecture in 19th-century Europe and North America was a willingness to use all the great styles of the past, from ancient Greece to the 18th century. Sometimes, quite different styles were used in the same building.

Later in the century, a new kind of architecture developed. It was based on the use of steel to form the framework or "skeleton" of a building. As the walls did not have to support their own weight, buildings could be much larger.

In the early 20th century the style changed again. Buildings were usually large, plain, often white, and based on the form of a cube, with rows of large windows.

▲ Isambard Kingdom Brunel designed Clifton Bridge in England. It was completed in 1864, and is an early suspension bridge. The road is suspended on cables.

▼ New water mains were built under Paris streets. When cast-iron pipes became available it was also easier to build better drains.

▲ The ten-story Home Insurance Building in Chicago is often called the first skyscraper. After a fire destroyed much of the original city in 1871, the price of building land increased, and putting up taller buildings meant that less land had to be bought.

▼ The Statue of Liberty, in New York harbor, was a gift from France to the United States in 1884. The statue is 120 feet (36 m) high and weighs 204 tons. Steps and an elevator go up inside the steel skeleton to the torch.

1851 Paxton's glass-and-metal Crystal Palace is built in London for the Great Exhibition.

1871 The Mont Cenis Tunnel opens. It is the first major rail tunnel built through the Alps.

1890 The Forth Railway Bridge, near Edinburgh, is completed. It enables the railroad system to be extended from England into Scotland.

1904 Frank Lloyd Wright builds his first office building in Buffalo, New York.

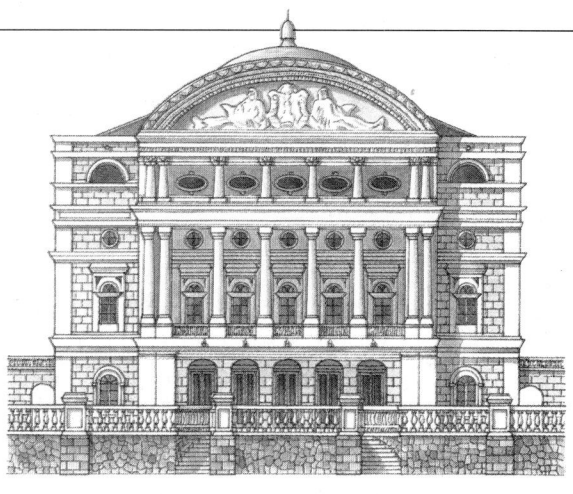

▼ The main station in Bombay was opened in 1866 and was built in a mixture of the European Gothic and Renaissance styles, but the domes are Indian in style.

▲ Opera became popular in the 19th century and elegant opera houses were built. This is the famous opera house at Manaus, in the Brazilian jungle. The town was very rich for a short time thanks to profits from the rubber industry.

▼ The most famous building in Paris was built for the Paris exhibition of 1889. It was named the Eiffel Tower after its designer, Gustave Eiffel. It is 984 feet (300m) high, and took two years to build. It is made from iron and is held together by 2.5 million rivets.

◀ The houses built for workers' families in the huge new industrial cities were small and crowded. They had no services such as running water. Some of these brick row houses have lasted well.

A defenseless Turkey seen caught up in the merciless grip of Russia; Russia was seen as the main aggressor in the buildup to the Crimean War.

1852 France: Second empire created under Louis Napoleon (Napoleon III). Burma: Second British-Burmese War; Pegu annexed. South Africa: Britain agrees to Transvaal becoming a Boer republic in Sands River Convention. New Zealand is granted a constitution. Balkans: Turkish forces withdrawn from Montenegro under Russian pressure. France: Engineer Henri Giffard builds a steam engine to power an airship. Britain: The Victoria and Albert Museum opens in London. U.S.: Author Harriet Beecher Stowe publishes *Uncle Tom's Cabin*, an antislavery novel.

1853 Black Sea region: Crimean War begins (to 1856); Russians occupy Moldavia and Wallachia and destroy Turkish fleet at Sinope. South Africa: Cape Colony becomes a British crown colony. Britain: Chloroform given to Queen Victoria in childbirth popularizes anesthetics; vaccination against smallpox made compulsory. Italy: Composer Giuseppe Verdi's operas *Il Trovatore* and *La Traviata* are first performed. France: Charles Gabriel Pravaz invents the hypodermic syringe.

The Crimean War

One of the few wars involving European nations in this period took place in the Crimea, which was then part of Russia. The war was fought by Russia against an alliance made up of Turkey, Britain, France, Piedmont Sardinia, and Austria.

The dispute was sparked off by a struggle for territory which was part of the collapsing Ottoman empire. The British were afraid that the Russians would take over the territory and gain control of the Black Sea. This would threaten British power in the eastern Mediterranean. Russia also had quarrels with France, mostly to do with religious and commercial rivalry. The Turks were anxious to get rid of the strong Russian

Florence Nightingale

Florence Nightingale, a British woman who had trained as a nurse, persuaded the war minister to send her to the Crimean War with 30 nurses. "The Lady with the Lamp" and her dedicated team carried out a revolution in the terrible conditions of the military hospital at Scutari on the Black Sea. Deaths dropped from about 50 per cent to about two per cent. Back in England, the work carried out by the nurses laid the foundations for the modern nursing profession.

▲ *Most of the fighting took place in the Crimean Peninsula, a part of Russia that projects southward into the Black Sea.*

▼ *At the battle of Balaklava, British cavalry attacked the Russian guns. They captured the guns, but one-third of them died. A misunderstanding about orders was responsible for the high death toll.*

influence in their Balkan territories of Moldavia and Wallachia.

War began in 1853 when Russia occupied Turkish territory on the Black Sea and destroyed the Turkish fleet. Turkey declared war on Russia and was backed by Britain and France. The armies fought bloody battles at the Alma River, Sevastopol, Balaklava, and Inkerman. Although they were badly supplied and managed, the allies won. The Russians were held back because a lack of railroads prevented supplies and reinforcements from getting through. The Crimean War was the first one in which the public were kept informed about the war by photographs and reports sent back by telegraph.

The war ended with the Treaty of Paris in 1856. Although thousands of soldiers had died in battles, very little changed because of the war.

Japan

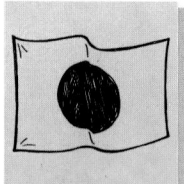

For more than 200 years Japan had been closed to foreigners, under the rule of the Tokugawa family (*see* pages 516–517). In the early 19th century, Japan began to feel the strength of Western influence. In 1853, four United States' warships sailed to Japan, under the command of the U.S. commodore Matthew Perry. The Japanese were impressed by Perry's steamships, and by other machinery he showed them. They signed the Treaty of Kanagawa in 1854 in which they agreed to open two ports to American trade. Soon, similar "unequal" treaties had been signed with Great Britain, the Netherlands, and Russia.

The Tokugawa were criticized for allowing these "unequal treaties" to be signed and for many other problems they could not solve. People were tired of isolation. They were overthrown in 1868, and the emperor was restored to his old position. Japan began to modernize.

The Japanese wanted to keep some of their traditions, but they were also keen

▲ In 1853 Commodore Matthew Perry sailed to Japan with four warships. He signed the Treaty of Kanagawa with the Japanese. This opened up some Japanese ports to trade with the United States.

▼ Many Japanese took up European fashions. They learned to play European music and dressed in European clothes. But foreigners gradually learned to respect Japanese culture and success.

▲ *The black ships of Perry's fleet were the first steam ships the Japanese had ever seen. They realized that they would be unable to beat them.*

to learn from the industrial nations of the West. They changed their government and their schools. They imported machines and introduced new industries, such as the cotton industry. By 1914, Japan was an industrial power, the first in Asia.

The Japanese began to expand their country. They tried to take over Korea, and this led to a war with China in 1894. Japan also fought Russia over this issue in 1904–1905, and finally annexed Korea in 1910. This helped make Japan the most powerful nation in its region.

1854 Black Sea region: British and French enter Crimean War; battles of the Alma, Balaklava, and Inkerman; Anglo-French forces besiege Sevastopol. Japan: United States' commodore Perry compels Japan to open ports for trade in the Treaty of Kanagawa. U.S.: In the Gadsden Purchase, America buys land from Mexico. Republican Party formed. Elisha Graves Otis demonstrates his "safety" elevator. France occupies Senegal. India: India's first cotton mill is established in Bombay.

1855 Crimean War: Florence Nightingale reforms British military hospitals; Sevastopol falls to French and British. Russia: Alexander II succeeds Nicholas I as tsar (to 1881). U.S.: Historian J. L. Motley publishes his *Rise of the Dutch Republic.* Poet Henry Wadsworth Longfellow publishes *Hiawatha.* Advances in plastics lead to the development of celluloid and rayon thread. Germany: Bunsen burner invented. Australasia: Van Diemen's Land is renamed Tasmania.

1856 Treaty of Paris ends Crimean War. Afghanistan: Persian invasion leads to war with Britain (to 1857). China: Second Opium War (to 1860). India: British take Oudh. France: Novelist Gustave Flaubert publishes *Madame Bovary.* Britain: Chemist William Perkin makes first artificial dye. Henry Bessemer invents process for turning iron into steel.

A model railway, presented to the Japanese to show the technological advances of the West.

Queen Victoria

When William IV died in 1837, the English crown passed to his niece, Victoria, who was just 18 years old. Her first prime minister, Lord Melbourne, advised her on politics and government. Later prime ministers advised her throughout her long reign. Victoria's husband, Prince Albert, also helped her in her royal duties.

India came under the control of the British government in 1858, and Victoria was made empress of India in 1876. Canada, Australia, and many parts of Africa were part of the massive British empire. The colonies provided Britain with raw materials for its factories, and the colonies became markets for British manufactured goods.

Britain changed a great deal during Victoria's reign. Social reformers campaigned to make working conditions

▲ *Queen Victoria married her cousin, Prince Albert of Saxe-Coburg-Gotha in 1840. They had nine children. The boy in this painting is their eldest son, who became King Edward VII when Victoria died in 1901.*

▼ *Victoria and Albert's children married into many European royal families. Queen Elizabeth II and Prince Philip are both descendants of Victoria.*

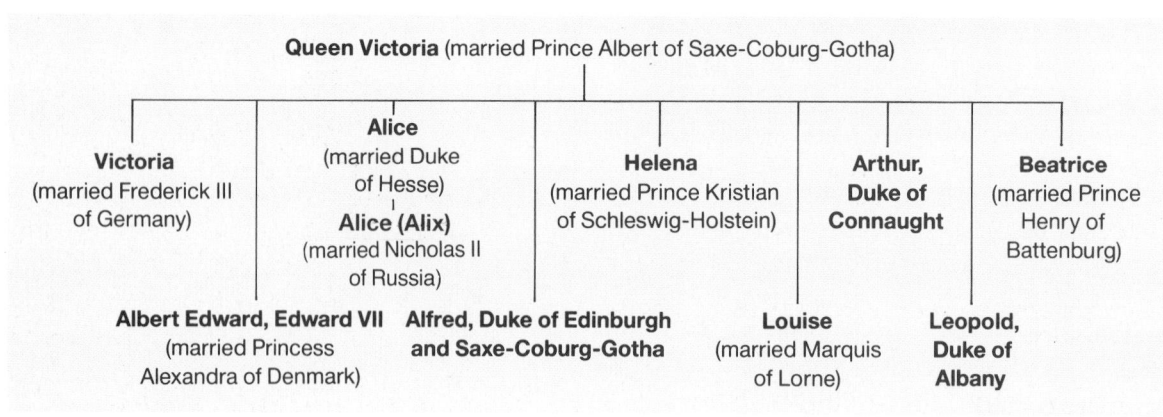

Queen Victoria (married Prince Albert of Saxe-Coburg-Gotha)

Victoria
(married Frederick III of Germany)

Alice
(married Duke of Hesse)

Alice (Alix)
(married Nicholas II of Russia)

Helena
(married Prince Kristian of Schleswig-Holstein)

Arthur, Duke of Connaught

Beatrice
(married Prince Henry of Battenburg)

Albert Edward, Edward VII
(married Princess Alexandra of Denmark)

Alfred, Duke of Edinburgh and Saxe-Coburg-Gotha

Louise
(married Marquis of Lorne)

Leopold, Duke of Albany

better for many people, and all children had to go to school. Many more people won the right to vote. Science, especially engineering, and literature also flourished. But for most ordinary people in Victorian Britain conditions were bad and their lives were hard and short.

When Prince Albert died in 1861, Victoria went into mourning and retired from public life. The monarchy became unpopular. The huge public celebrations of the queen's Golden and Diamond Jubilees made the queen (and the monarchy in general) much more popular with the people.

During Victoria's reign, the role of the monarch changed so that the monarch became more of a symbol, and had less to do with politics. When Victoria died in 1901, her reign had lasted for 63 years, the longest in British history.

▼ *In 1897 Victoria celebrated her Diamond Jubilee. It was a grand imperial event. The guests of honor included Indian princes, African chiefs, Pacific islanders, and Chinese people from Hong Kong. The queen was driven 6 miles (9 km) through the streets of London. "The cheering was quite deafening," she wrote in her diary. "I was much moved and gratified."*

Prince Albert

Prince Albert was born in Germany in 1819 and married Victoria in 1840. He introduced many reforms in education and housing, and took a keen interest in industry and the arts. He organized the Great Exhibition, held in the Crystal Palace, in 1851.

1857 Indian Mutiny against British rule (to 1858); rebels take Delhi and Cawnpore and besiege Lucknow. Anglo-Persian War ends. Britain: Scottish explorer David Livingstone publishes account of his journey across Africa. Novelist Anthony Trollope publishes *Barchester Towers*. France: Louis Pasteur discovers fermentation is caused by bacteria.

Queen Victoria was crowned Empress of India at the suggestion of Benjamin Disraeli.

1858 India: Mutiny is crushed; government is placed under the British crown; Victoria crowned Empress of India. China: Treaty of Tientsin (Tianjin) temporarily ends Opium wars; more Chinese ports are opened. Balkans: Turkish attack on Montenegro repulsed. Ireland: Irish (Fenian) Republican Brotherhood set up in Dublin and U.S. to work for independent Irish republic. East Africa: British explorer John Speke names Lake Victoria. Trans-Atlantic telegraph cable laid.

1859 Italy: France and Piedmont Sardinia declare war on Austria; Austrians defeated at Magenta and Solferino; Milan captured. China: Renewed conflict with Britain. U.S.: Antislavery campaigner, John Brown is hanged for seizing arms at Harper's Ferry, Virginia. First American oil wells drilled in Pennsylvania. Susan B. Anthony speaks increasingly on women's rights. Britain: Naturalist Charles Darwin publishes *On the Origin of Species*, explaining his theory of evolution.

The American Civil War

The United States around 1850 was a divided country. The biggest division was between North and South. The North had nearly all the trade, industry, and cities while the South was a land of farms, especially cotton plantations, which relied on slave labor. Slavery was banned in the North.

This division caused quarrels when the laws were drawn up for the new states and territories to the west. Antislavery campaigners in the North believed that slavery should be banned. The Kansas-Nebraska Act (1854) gave the new states the right to choose.

Abraham Lincoln was elected president in 1860. He belonged to the Republican Party, which opposed slavery, although he was not an abolitionist himself. Many Southern states refused to live under such a government, and they announced that they were seceding (leaving) from the Union. The government declared that they had no right to do this.

The North (Union) was made up of 23 states. They had more men, more money, and more industry than the South. The North also controlled the navy and started a naval blockade which stopped the South receiving help or supplies from abroad.

Grant

Ulysses S. Grant (1822–1885) at the age of 17 went to West Point, from which he graduated in 1843. He was appointed as commander of the Union forces in 1863. He was not a brilliant general, but tough and determined. He won by wearing the enemy down. In 1868, he was elected president.

Lee

Robert E. Lee (1807–1870) led the forces of the South. He was probably the best of all the generals. Although he had been in the U.S. army when the Civil War broke out, he resigned and became a military adviser on the Confederate side. He later took command of troops in battle.

▼ The Confederates won the first big battle of the war, at Bull Run, Virginia, in 1861. About 2,000 Confederate soldiers died in the battle. The Union lost about 3,000 men. Some of the Confederate soldiers wanted to attack Washington, the Union capital, but they decided against it. The Union now had to face the fact that the war was going to be long and hard.

▲ *Union soldiers wore the blue uniform of the U.S. army. The Confederates usually wore gray.*

The 11 states of the South (Confederacy) were much weaker, but they had good generals and great spirit.

Civil war broke out in 1861, when the forces of the South opened fire on Fort Sumter. The South won the first battles in 1861, but a turning point came in 1863, when the North won the biggest battle of the war, Gettysburg.

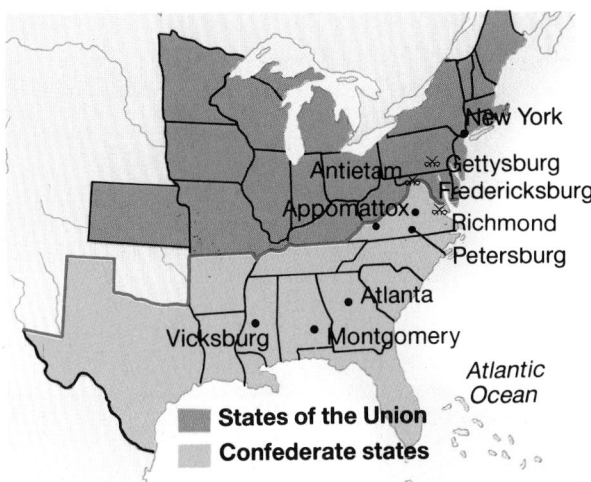

States of the Union

Confederate states

▲ *The major battles of the Civil War were fought in the east and southeast of the United States.*

1860 Italy: Piedmont Sardinia gains much of north Italy while ceding Nice and Savoy to France; Garibaldi's "Redshirts" capture Sicily and Naples; Piedmont Sardinia invades the Papal States. China: Beijing (Peking) is occupied by British and French; end of the Opium wars. New Zealand: Gold rush begins. Britain: Novelist George Eliot (Mary Ann Evans) publishes *The Mill on the Floss*. France: Engineer Etienne Lenoir constructs the first internal combustion engine.

1861 Kingdom of Italy founded under Victor Emmanuel of Piedmont Sardinia (Victor Emmanuel II). U.S.: Abraham Lincoln, an antislavery campaigner, becomes president; 11 Southern states form the Confederacy; civil war begins between the Union and the Confederacy (to 1865). Mexico: French and British forces arrive to enforce payment of debt. Russia: Serfdom ends. Balkans: Moldavia and Wallachia unite to form Romania; Serbia backs revolt against Turks in Herzegovina. Europe: Monaco gains independence from France.

A New York ferry being used as a gunboat by the Union states during the Civil War.

1862 American Civil War: Battles of Antietam and Fredericksburg. Lincoln introduces "greenbacks," first American paper money. Germany: Bismarck appointed chief minister of Prussia. Italy: Garibaldi fails to capture Rome. Far East: Cochin-China (southern Vietnam) becomes a French colony. France: Novelist Victor Hugo publishes *Les Misérables*.

1863 U.S.: Slavery is ended. Lincoln signs Emancipation Proclamation, freeing all slaves in Confederate states. The Union is victorious at Gettysburg; Lincoln gives Gettysburg Address. Poland: Uprising against Russian rule. Asia: Cambodia becomes a French protectorate. France: Artist Edouard Manet paints *Déjeuner sur l'Herbe* (Picnic on the Grass).

1864 Germany: Prussian and Austrian forces occupy Schleswig-Holstein and defeat Danish army. Poland: Revolt crushed. Russia: Social reforms introduced. French occupy Mexico (to 1867) and the Austrian Archduke Maximilian becomes emperor. U.S.: Union general Sherman marches through Georgia and burns Atlanta. South America: Paraguayan War (to 1870), Paraguay fights Brazil, Uruguay and Argentina. Britain: "First International" association of socialist workers founded. Switzerland: International Red Cross founded. Mediterranean: Greeks occupy the island of Corfu.

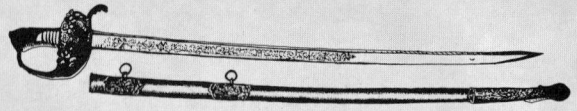

General Lee's presentation sword. It was not handed over to Grant during the surrender ceremony, as was customary. Instead, it remained by his side.

1865 U.S.: Confederates surrender, ending the Civil War; President Lincoln is assassinated. The Bureau of Freed Slaves is set up. Italy: Florence becomes capital (to 1870). Russia conquers Caucasus and Turkistan. Jamaica: Disputes between plantation owners and workers results in the Morant Bay Rebellion; it is crushed by British troops. Britain: Lewis Carroll (Charles Dodgson) publishes *Alice in Wonderland*. Germany: Wilhelm Busch writes children's tales *Max und Moritz*. Austria: Gregor Mendel explains heredity.

Harriet Tubman

Harriet Tubman (1821–1913) was an escaped slave. During the Civil War she made 19 trips through Southern territory and helped 300 people to escape to the North. She also spied for the North. General Grant said she was worth several regiments.

Abraham Lincoln

1809 Born.
1834 Begins to study to become a lawyer.
1842 Marries Mary Todd.
1861–1865 President of the United States throughout the Civil War.
1865 Shot dead in a Washington theater by John Wilkes Booth.

In 1864, in spite of Lee's skillful tactics, Grant captured Richmond, the capital of the South. General Sherman marched through Georgia and the other Southern states, destroying towns and farms.

Short of men, money, weapons, and food, Lee surrendered in April 1865, ending the Civil War. More than 600,000 soldiers had died in the conflict. Five days later the victorious president Lincoln was assassinated in Washington.

The American Civil War settled two great questions. Firstly, it confirmed that the United States of America was a single nation, and that no state had the right to break away, and secondly, it brought slavery in the South to an end.

After the war, arguments raged over how the South should be "reconstructed." This included the opening of schools and the building of railroads. Lincoln's successor, Andrew Johnson, a Democrat, wanted better conditions for Black Americans. The Republicans wanted a harsher policy, and it was they who won the argument in the end.

The people of the South resisted most aspects of Reconstruction. Many ex-slaves who had fought on the Union side came back expecting more freedom in the South. The Ku Klux Klan began a campaign of murder and terrorism in 1866 which aimed to stop Black Americans gaining civil rights.

In 1876, the Republican Rutherford B. Hayes made an agreement with the Democrats in order to gain election as president. Northern troops withdrew from the South, and the U.S. government stopped supporting equal rights for Blacks. Reconstruction ended, and the Democrats took over the South.

▼ General Lee surrendered to Grant in the courthouse at Appomattox, Virginia on April 9, 1865. His men were outnumbered, exhausted, and starving, and many of the Southern states were in ruins.

▲ The American Civil War was one of the first conflicts to be recorded in photographs. Mathew Brady, a photographer, accompanied the Union army and took 3,500 photographs of the soldiers and the conditions.

1866 German Confederation: Bismarck dissolves confederation, leading to Austro-Prussian War (Seven Weeks' War); Austria defeated, Italy gains Venice. U.S.: The racist group Klu Klux Klan is founded. Russia: Novelist Fyodor Dostoyevsky publishes *Crime and Punishment*.

1867 North German Confederation created. Dual kingdom of Austria-Hungary

The Canadian Pacific Railway stretched from the Atlantic to the Pacific.

founded. U.S.: United States buys Alaska from Russia. Mexico: French forces withdraw; rebels execute Emperor Maximilian. Dominion of Canada founded. Britain: Reform Act increases the number of male voters. German communist Karl Marx publishes first part of *Das Kapital* (Capital). South Africa: Diamonds discovered in Orange Free State. Britain: Surgeon Joseph Lister applies carbolic antiseptic during surgery to reduce risk of infection. Marquess of Queensberry draws up rules for boxing.

1868 Cuba: Uprising against Spanish rule. Spain: Revolt forces abdication of Queen Isabella II. Japan: Meiji Period ends Tokugawa shogunate and returns power to the emperor; Edo renamed Tokyo. Ethiopia: British forces release diplomats held hostage. Russia: Samarkand and Bokhara annexed. Britain: First Trade Union Congress is held. Germany: Johannes Brahms composes *A German Requiem*. U.S.: Civil rights granted to Black Americans by 14th Amendment to the Constitution.

Canada

Opposition to British rule in Canada grew during the 1830s. Rebellions broke out in both Upper and Lower Canada in 1837, led by William Lyon Mackenzie and Louis Papineau. The rebels wanted self government, and although they had some support, the most influential people in the colonies did not agree with them. The rebels were soon defeated by British troops.

The British government sent Lord Durham to Canada to investigate the causes of the rebellions. His report said that Upper and Lower Canada should be united, and should have control over their own affairs. The Act of Union, passed in 1840, united the two colonies in the Province of Canada. Many Canadians felt that these reforms did not

Papineau

Louis Joseph Papineau (1786–1871) was a French-Canadian politician. He led the French-speaking Canadians' demands for reform. When rebellions broke out, he fled to the United States. He returned to Canada in 1847, and continued to campaign for independence.

Mackenzie

William Lyon Mackenzie (1795–1861), was a member of Canada's Reform Party. He wanted Canada to have more freedom from British rule and more democracy. He led the 1837 rebellion in Upper Canada. When defeated, he escaped to the U.S.

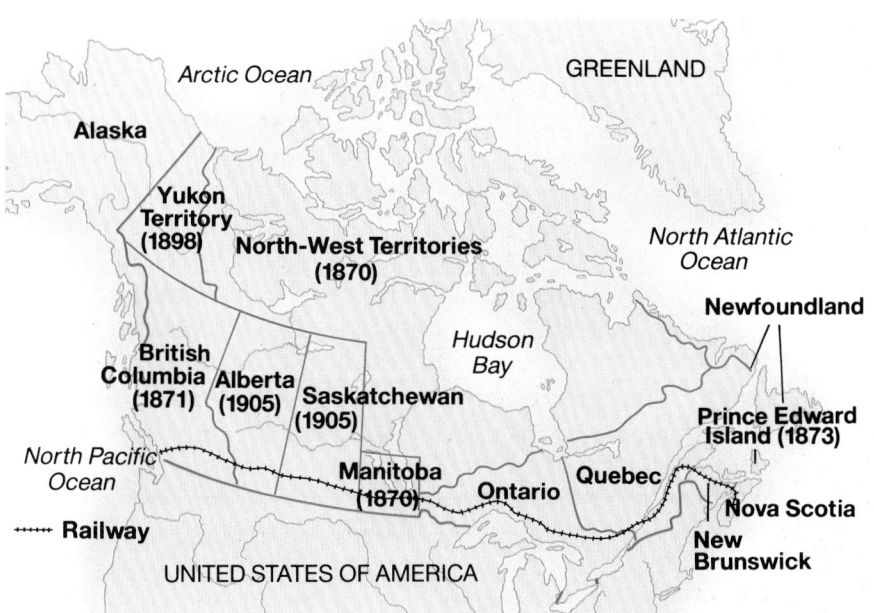

◀ The British North America Act of 1867 united the provinces of Nova Scotia, New Brunswick, Ontario (formerly Upper Canada), and Quebec (Lower Canada) in the Dominion of Canada. They were joined by the provinces of Manitoba, British Columbia, and Prince Edward Island during the 1870s. The provinces of Saskatchewan and Alberta joined in 1905. Newfoundland was the last to join, in 1949.

go far enough, partly because they were afraid that the United States might invade if Canada looked weak.

In 1867, the British North America Act was passed. It united four Canadian provinces in a dominion. The French Canadians of Quebec were promised equality (*see* pages 498–499). French and English became official languages.

The huge lands to the west, which belonged to the Hudson's Bay Company, later became part of Canada too. The Northwest Territories joined the dominion in 1870, followed by Yukon Territory in 1898. Completion of the Canadian Pacific Railway in 1885 linked Canada's east and west coasts.

▼ Winnipeg, a center of the fur trade, was still a small town in 1870. In that year, the province of Manitoba became part of the Dominion of Canada, and Winnipeg became the province's capital.

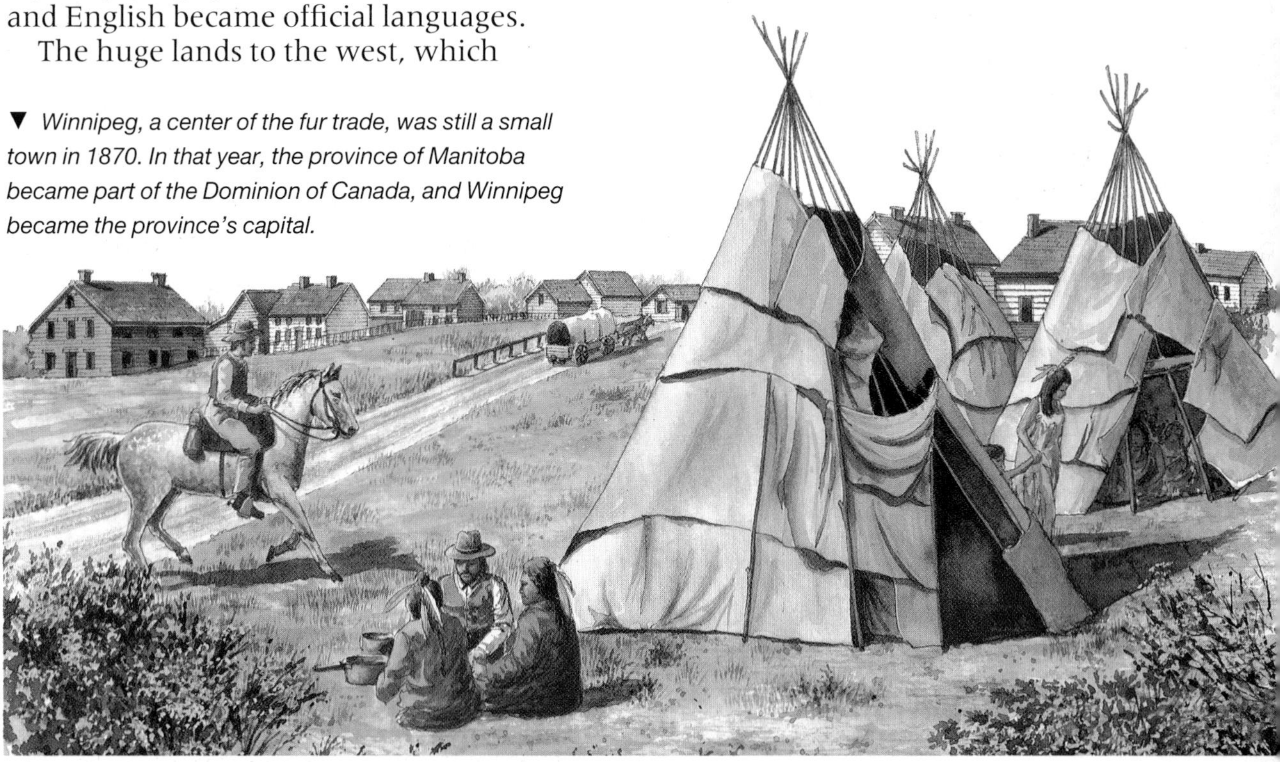

Communications

Advances in transportation and communications made it easier for people to travel and keep in touch. No public railroads existed in 1820, but by 1900 every large country was building them. People could travel faster and goods were carried more cheaply. Steam engines also powered large ships.

In 1800 it took weeks for news to travel between countries. After electric telegraph wires were laid, it took only seconds. The invention of the telephone made a two-way conversation possible between people in different towns. The radio meant that spoken words could be broadcast to any receiver within range. Magazines became popular as more people learned to read.

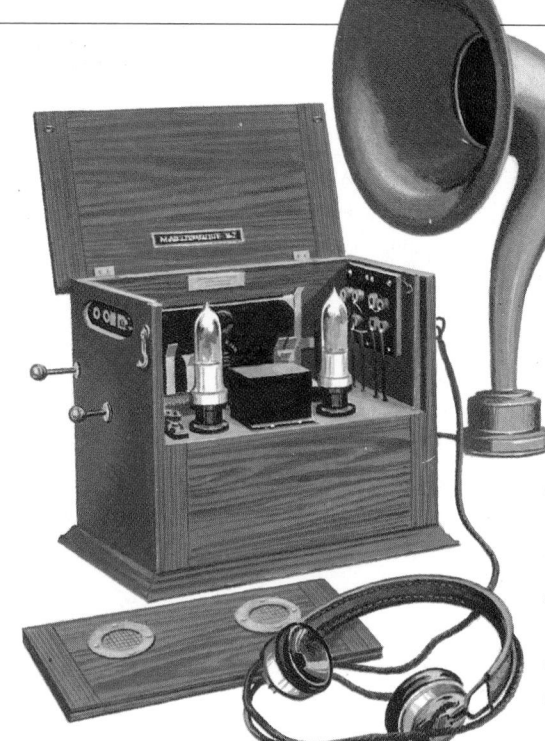

◀ An early radio, called a "wireless," had glass tubes instead of the tiny transistors used today. It could be used either with headphones or a large trumpet-like loudspeaker.
No one knew that radio waves existed until Heinrich Hertz (1857–1894), the German scientist, proved it in 1888 by transmitting and receiving them in his laboratory.

▶ In 1840 the British Post Office issued the "penny black." This was the first stamp on which the postage was prepaid by the sender. Before that a letter was paid for when it was delivered.

▼ This German trolley car first ran in Berlin in 1881. Power came from the overhead electricity cables.

▼ The rickshaw was still the most successful "taxi" in many Eastern cities.

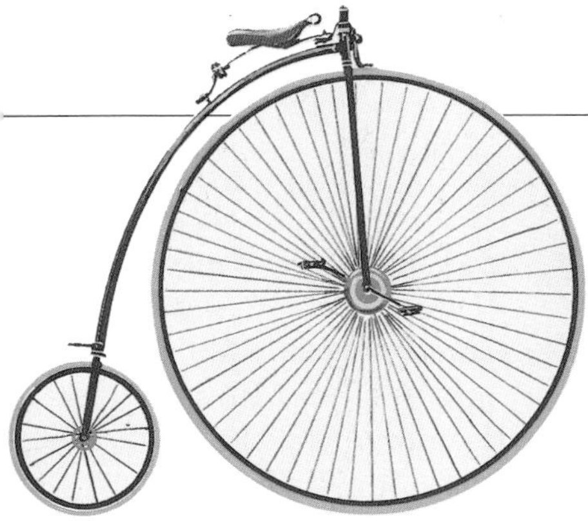

▲ *The first bicycles were uncomfortable and dangerous. This "high wheeler" of 1883 had solid tires and no brakes.*

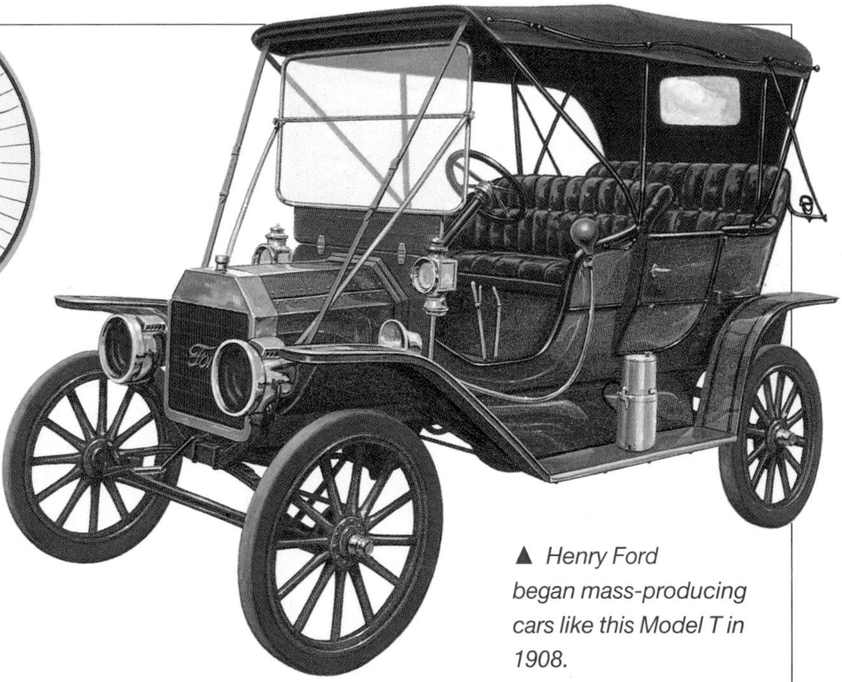

▲ *Henry Ford began mass-producing cars like this Model T in 1908.*

▼ *In 1901 Marconi sent the first Morse code radio signals across the Atlantic.*

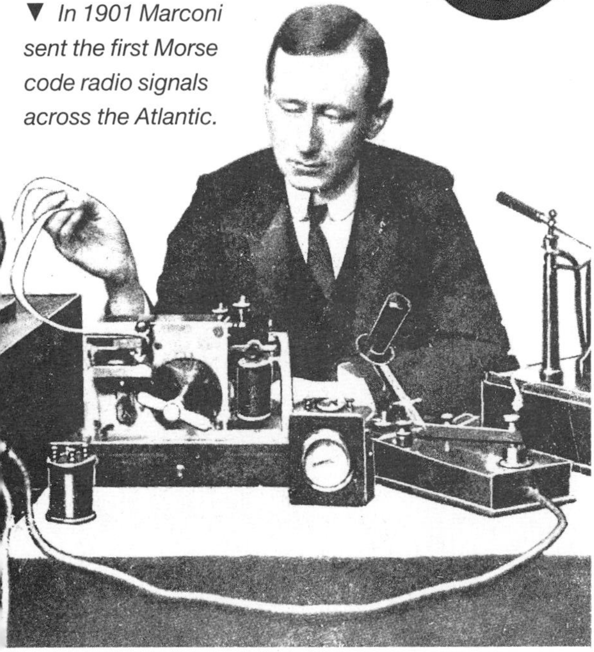

WHEN IT HAPPENED

1837	Samuel Morse invents the Morse code.
1869	The east and west coasts of the U.S. are linked by railroad.
1860	The Pony Express mail riders make their first deliveries in the U.S..
1875	Bell makes the first telephone call.
1885	Earliest automobiles built in Germany.
1894	First motorcycle sold.
1903	The Wright brothers invent a successful powered aircraft.

► *The telephone was invented by Alexander Graham Bell, a teacher of the deaf. The first public telephone exchange opened in Pittsburgh in 1877, and all calls were connected by someone at a switchboard. However, few private houses had a telephone until the 1920s. This phone was made about 1905.*

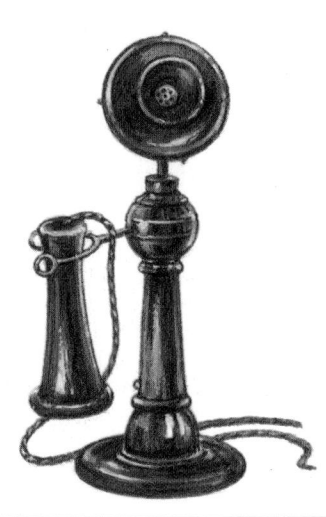

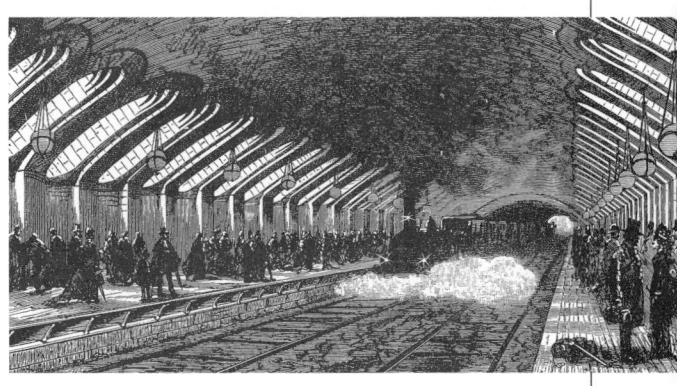

▲ *Underground railways did not take up space on city streets. People could travel further to find work.*

1869 The Suez Canal opens, joining the Mediterranean and Red seas. U.S.: The first transcontinental railroad, Union Pacific Railroad, is completed. The state of Wyoming is the first to grant women's suffrage (right to vote). Regular weather forecasting begun at Cincinnati observatory. Canada: Red River Rebellion; settlers resist British rule (to 1870). Germany: Social Democratic Labor Party is first political party to adopt socialist (Marxist) policies. Russia: Chemist Dimitri Mendeleyev compiles the periodic table of elements. Author Leo Tolstoy completes his mammoth novel *War and Peace*. France: Margarine is made as a cheap substitute for butter.

1870 Franco-Prussian War begins (to 1871): Napoleon III is captured at Sedan,

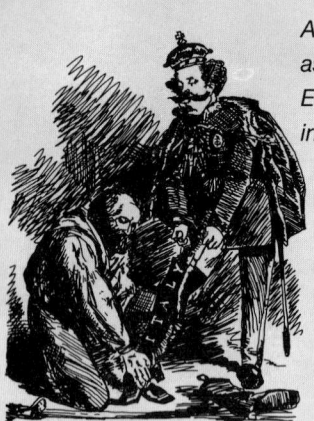

A cartoon of Garibaldi assisting King Victor Emmanuel II as he steps into his boot; Italy.

ending Second Empire; French Third Republic is founded; Prussians besiege Paris. Italy: Papal States annexed; Rome becomes Italian capital. U.S.: The 15th Amendment is passed requiring all Southern states to allow Blacks to vote. Russia: Limited local government introduced in cities. South America: End of Paraguayan War. Czechoslovakia: Composer Bedrich Smetana's opera *The Bartered Bride* is produced. France: Novelist Jules Verne publishes early science fiction story *20,000 Leagues Under the Sea*.

Italy

In the early 1800s Italy was made up of a number of small states. Apart from the kingdom of Piedmont Sardinia, and Rome (ruled by the pope), these states were ruled by a number of different foreign countries. An independence movement (known as the Risorgimento) began in the 1830s. In 1848, revolutions against foreign rule broke out in many Italian cities and states, but they were quickly defeated.

Count Cavour, the chief minister of the kingdom of Piedmont Sardinia made an alliance with France in 1858, and together they defeated the Austrians in 1859. Most of northern Italy then joined with Piedmont Sardinia.

In 1860, rebellion broke out in southern Italy, which was part of the

Victor Emmanuel II

1820 Born.
1848 Fights against Austrian rule in Italy.
1849 Becomes king of Piedmont Sardinia.
1853–1856 Supports Britain and France in Crimean War.
1861 Becomes king of unified Italy.
1866 Backs Prussia in Austro-Prussian War.
1878 Dies.

Cavour

Count Camillo Cavour (1810–1861) made most of the plans for Italian unity. He cleverly used the rivalries of France and Austria to increase the power of the kingdom of Piedmont Sardinia. He also made the most of the successes of Garibaldi to help his own plans.

Garibaldi was an Italian patriot who fought against foreign rule in Italy. Along with his force of "Redshirts" he conquered the kingdom of the Two Sicilies in 1860, and it became part of the kingdom of Italy.

kingdom of the Two Sicilies. Giuseppe Garibaldi led a revolt and conquered the kingdom. Cavour was afraid that Garibaldi would attack Rome, which might lead Austria or France to come to the aid of the pope. Cavour invaded the Papal States and reached an agreement with Garibaldi. The kingdom of Italy was declared in 1861.

Two small areas were not included. Venice was still part of the Austrian empire, and Rome was ruled by the pope but occupied by France. Venice was given to Italy after Austria was defeated in the Austro-Prussian War (1866). The French left Rome after their defeat in the Franco-Prussian War in 1871, and the kingdom of Italy was complete.

▶ Piedmont Sardinia took the lead in uniting Italy in 1859–1860. Nice and Savoy were given to France.

Savoy (to France 1860)
Lombardy (1859)
Venetia (1866)
Kingdom of Sardinia
Parma (1860)
Modena (1860)
San Marino
Nice (to France 1860)
Tuscany (1860)
Corsica (to France 1768)
Papal States (1870)
Papal States (1860)
Kingdom of Sardinia
Kingdom of the Two Sicilies (1860)

The German State

The German Confederation (which was founded in 1815) contained 38 different states. Austria and Prussia were the most powerful states, and they competed for the leadership. This contest came into the open when Austria and Prussia went to war against Denmark over control of the duchies of Schleswig and Holstein. After beating Denmark, Austria and Prussia disagreed over how they should be run, and Prussia declared war on Austria in 1866. After beating Austria at the battle of Sadowa, Prussia's chief minister, Otto von Bismarck, set up the North German confederation, with Prussia as the most powerful member.

France felt threatened by Prussia's increasing power. Bismarck provoked the French when he altered the report of a conversation between the Prussian king and the French ambassador so that it looked like an insult to France. When the document, the "Ems Telegram," was published, the French emperor Napoleon

III was furious and declared war. Prussia defeated France in 1871, and took over Alsace and Lorraine. The remaining German states also joined in 1871. Bismarck then formed the German Second empire with the king of Prussia, (William I), as emperor.

◀ The North German Confederation was formed in 1867. It was a union of states in which the members kept their own governments, but military and foreign policy was decided by a federal government. Prussia dominated the confederation. Lorraine and Alsace were won from France in the Franco-Prussian War.
The German Second empire was created in 1871. Schleswig-Holstein was taken over by Prussia in 1866.

DENMARK
Schleswig
Holstein
NETHERLANDS
RUSSIA
BELGIUM
Dominated by Prussia
POLAND
Sedan
LUXEMBOURG
Lorraine Bavaria and
AUSTRIA
Alsace Southern States
FRANCE
SWITZERLAND

— German Confederation
— North German Confederation 1866
— German Second empire 1871

▲ *Napoleon III of France was captured at the battle of Sedan. Prussia won the Franco-Prussian War in 1871.*

1871 End of Franco-Prussian War after the surrender of Paris; Alsace-Lorraine, is ceded to Germany. The Socialist Commune is founded in Paris; it is crushed by government troops. Germany: The Second Empire is created with William I of Prussia as emperor and Bismarck as chancellor. Bismarck introduces his *Kulturkampf* (conflict of beliefs) policy. He seeks to restrict the powers of the Roman Catholic Church in southern Germany, Alsace-Lorraine, and the Polish provinces. Opponents are punished. Britain: trade unions are legalized. East Africa: explorer Sir Henry Stanley meets David Livingstone at Lake Tanganyika. Canada: British Columbia, including Vancouver Island, joins the Dominion. Switzerland: The Mont Cenis Tunnel (rail) through the Alps is finally completed. South Africa: Britain annexes the Kimberley diamond region. Egypt: The Cairo Opera House opens with a performance of Giuseppe Verdi's *Aida*.

1872 League of Three Emperors (Austrian, German, and Russian) is formed. British ship *Challenger* begins the first large study of the oceans (to 1876). Britain: Librettist William Gilbert and composer Arthur Sullivan write their first light opera, *Trial by Jury*, together.

Bismarck

Otto von Bismarck (1815–1898), the German aristocrat and monarchist, was the chief minister of Prussia. His policy of "blood and iron" was brutal. His skillful diplomacy kept his enemies isolated. In 1871 he became the chancellor of the new German empire.

Napoleon III

1808 Born.
1852 Becomes emperor of the French.
1870 Outbreak of Franco-Prussian War. Captured at the battle of Sedan during the Franco-Prussian War.
1871 Ceases to be emperor when France loses Franco-Prussian War.
1873 Dies in exile.

Germany and Austria-Hungary made many protective treaties with the various European nations in an attempt to isolate France.

Food and Farming

As a result of fewer plagues and better health, the population of industrial countries grew in the 19th century. More people meant that more food had to be produced.

In some parts of the world, farms grew larger and more specialized. In the United States, crops of wheat and corn stretched as far as the eye could see. Better methods of transportation meant that crops could be exported.

Breeding experiments produced bigger crops and fatter animals. New farm machinery became available. At first the machines were horse-drawn, but by the turn of the century gasoline-driven tractors were in general use.

▲ Cyrus McCormick, invented this reaping machine in the U.S.. It was first seen in London at the Great Exhibition in 1851, 20 years after its invention. Only rich farmers could afford such machines. Most people still harvested their crops using scythes or sickles.

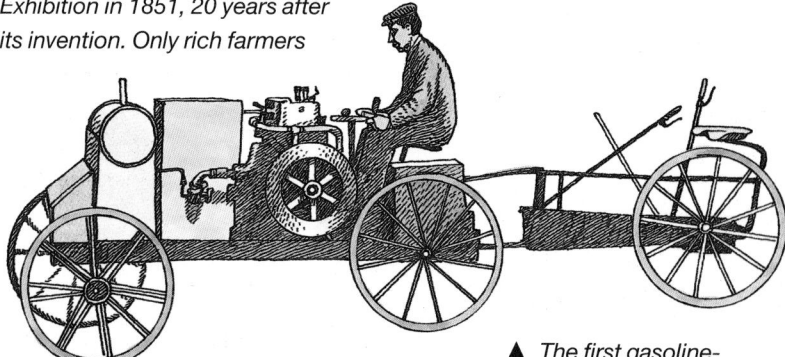

▲ The first gasoline-driven tractors were produced in the U.S. in 1901, but they weighed 5 to 10 tons. A lighter tractor weighing 1.5 tons was produced in 1902, but most farms used horses to pull plows.

◄ Food from abroad started flooding into Europe in the 1870s. One of the main reasons was the invention of refrigerated ships. They could transport frozen food from countries as far away as New Zealand. Mechanical refrigerators had not yet been invented for use in the home.

1840 Justus von Liebig's book *Chemistry in its Application to Agriculture* starts the movement for scientific farming.

1845 Potato crop fails in Ireland. Start of Irish potato famine.

1853 First U.S. state agricultural college founded in New York.

1875 Beginning of a serious slump in European farming due to food imports from Australia and the U.S.

1876 Rubber seedlings planted in Malaysia.

1889 First gasoline-driven tractor built.

▶ In the 19th century, people had a wider choice of food as new crops were imported into Europe. One of the new crops was the peanut which was grown in South America and West Africa. Another new discovery was that tomatoes could be eaten raw. Until the 19th century they had always been cooked first. Advances in chemistry meant that new ways of treating food were discovered. This included the extraction of sugar from sugar beet, a crop that grows in cool climates.

FERTILIZERS

Advances in the study of plants led to farming becoming more scientific in the 19th century. Fertilizers containing the chemicals phosphorus and potassium began to be produced in the U.S. in about 1850. The fertilizers helped to double the U.S. cereal crop between 1870 and 1900.

◀ This threshing machine, which was made about 1860, removed grain from its stalks. As the machines were expensive to buy, one machine was often owned by a group of farmers and moved about from farm to farm. Threshers were powered by stationary steam engines that stood on the edge of fields.

1873 Spain: Republican government established (to 1874); renewal of wars over rightful heir to throne. Africa: British-Asante war; the British win. Zanzibar: Slave market closed. Dutch East Indies: Acheh War (to 1903) between Dutch and Achenese. Germany: Mark is adopted as standard currency. Britain: Scottish physicist James Clerk Maxwell explains laws of electromagnetism. Turkey: German archaeologist Heinrich Schliemann discovers site of ancient Troy. U.S.: First commercial typewriters are manufactured.

Much of Africa's interior was only accessible on foot, so ivory was transported between trading posts by hired porters. They often traveled hundreds of miles, carrying loads of 55 pounds (25 kg) or more.

1874 Spain: Monarchy restored. Britain annexes Fiji and establishes colony of Gold Coast (Ghana). Britain: Factory Act reduces working day to ten hours. Lawn tennis invented. Author Thomas Hardy publishes *Far from the Madding Crowd*. France: First exhibition of Impressionist paintings in Paris. Austria: Composer Johann Strauss's operetta *Die Fledermaus* first performed.

1875 The British buy Egypt's shares in the Suez Canal Company to control the route to India. Balkans: Revolt in Bosnia-Herzegovina against Turks. Switzerland: Universal Postal Union is set up in Berne; it provides an international mail service. Britain: New sewers in London reduce cholera threat. France: Georges Bizet's opera *Carmen* is first performed. U.S.: Scottish-born inventor Alexander Graham Bell invents the telephone.

Africa

Europeans knew almost nothing about the interior of Africa, which they called the "Dark Continent." In the 1800s missionaries began to travel farther inland. They thought that they were doing the Africans a favor by bringing them Christianity. They also brought corn and cassava, which became important food crops.

Between 1850 and 1880 a number of European explorers including Burton and Speke, and Livingstone and Stanley followed the courses of the major rivers into the center of Africa.

Gradually, some European countries began to establish larger areas of influence. The French conquered most of Algeria, while the British and Dutch spread northward from Cape Colony.

In some parts of Africa, the slave trade had almost destroyed the structure of African society, and this reduced the ability of the Africans to resist invasion. Elsewhere, well trained and organized

▼ *In 1850, only a few small regions were under European rule. The British, Dutch, French, and Portuguese had established coastal areas of influence.*

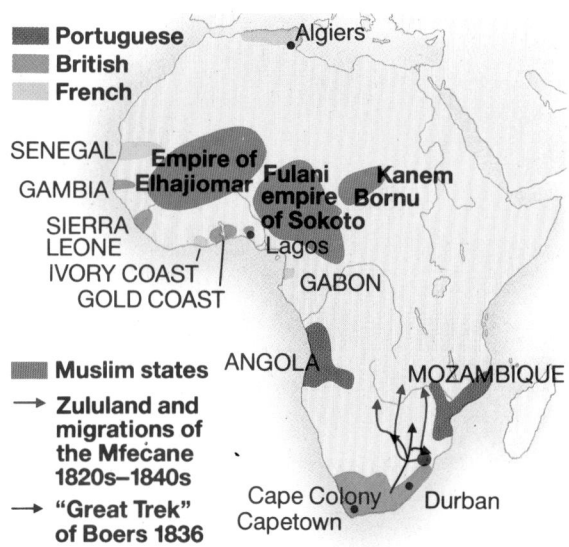

Portuguese
British
French

Algiers

SENEGAL
GAMBIA
SIERRA LEONE
IVORY COAST
GOLD COAST

Empire of Elhajiomar

Fulani empire of Sokoto

Kanem Bornu

Lagos

GABON

Muslim states
Zululand and migrations of the Mfecane 1820s–1840s
"Great Trek" of Boers 1836

ANGOLA

MOZAMBIQUE

Cape Colony
Capetown
Durban

LIBERIA

Liberia was the first African country to become independent (in 1847). It had been founded by freed American slaves. New settlers did not mix easily with the local people, who were not allowed to become citizens until 1902.

Kingsley

Mary Kingsley (1862–1900) traveled in West Africa. She explored many rivers by canoe and brought insects, reptiles, and fish back to England. She once said that a good thick skirt saved her life when she fell into a trap. Europeans were surprised at the idea of a woman traveling alone, but her books about Africa became very popular.

Livingstone

David Livingstone (1813–1873) made three great journeys to Africa. His first journey took him to southern Africa, where he became fascinated by the land and people. He crossed the African continent in 1852–1856, following the Zambezi River, and named the Victoria Falls. His last journey was a search for the source of the Nile.

tribal groups tried to prevent the advance of Europeans. As the British and French advanced into West Africa, they came into conflict with well-established Islamic kingdoms, which were strong enough to repel the invaders.

By 1880, advances in medicine made travel in Africa easier. Steamships and the opening of the Suez Canal brought distant parts of Africa within easy reach. The discovery of gold and diamonds in South Africa made Europeans even more eager to claim colonies.

▶ *The abolition of the slave trade in the 1800s did not end trade between Europe and Africa. Europeans wanted African gold and ivory, which the Africans traded for guns. The guns had a devastating effect in Africa. They were used in conflicts between Africans and Europeans, and between Africans and other Africans.*

Scramble for Africa

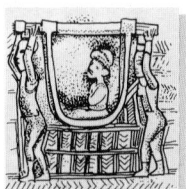

Rival European nations rushed to carve out colonies in Africa. This process became known as the "scramble for Africa." Britain and France led the scramble, with Germany, Belgium, and Italy close behind. Conflicts flared up between Britain and France over colonies in West Africa, and relations between the two countries worsened when the British occupied Egypt in 1882. The Italians invaded Eritrea (now part of Ethiopia), and King Leopold of the Belgians took over the Congo, which

SPANISH MOROCCO
MOROCCO
TUNISIA
ALGERIA LIBYA EGYPT
FRENCH WEST AFRICA
ANGLO EGYPTIAN SUDAN
GAMBIA
TOGO
SIERRA LEONE NIGERIA
KAMERUN
FRENCH EQUATORIAL AFRICA
ETHIOPIA
LIBERIA GOLD COAST
BELGIAN CONGO
FRENCH EQUATORIAL AFRICA
GERMAN EAST AFRICA
ANGOLA NORTH RHODESIA
MOZAMBIQUE
GERMAN SOUTH-WEST AFRICA BECHUANALAND
UNION OF SOUTH AFRICA

- British
- French
- German
- Italian
- Belgian
- Portuguese
- Spanish
- Independent

▲ Rivalry between the different European powers played a large part in the scramble for Africa. Control of African lands depended on reaching the area before the rival European power. The French hurried to extend their territory in northern Africa to prevent the British gaining control. The British conquered parts of West Africa to stop them falling to the French. The Germans took control of parts of southwestern and eastern Africa, but they lost control after World War I.

◄ The French conquest of Mali in West Africa was symbolized by the raising of the French flag in Timbuktu in 1893. Their advance along the Niger River was held up by the resistance of the local people, the Mande.

he considered to be his personal possession. Britain increased its empire when it took over the republics of the Transvaal and Orange Free State after the Boer wars (*see* pages 564–565).

The scramble for Africa became a formal process at a conference in Berlin in 1884. The rival European countries cut up Africa like a cake. Only Liberia and Ethiopia, which defeated an Italian invasion, remained independent.

The colonization of Africa had a number of effects on Africans. The different African nations and tribal boundaries were not recognized when the Europeans drew the new country borders. The Europeans brought new forms of government to Africa, but few Africans could vote. Profits made in the colonies went back to Europe, and European colonists often took the best farmland. Different European powers ruled their colonies in different ways, so the effects varied from place to place, but all Africans lost political power.

▲ *European heads of state attended a conference in Berlin in 1884. They drew lines across a map of Africa to stake their claims to different parts of the continent. Africans were not consulted or given any say in what happened to their countries.*

1876 Balkans: Turks massacre Bulgarian rebels; Serbia and Montenegro attack Turks. Africa: Leopold II of Belgium founds Association of the Congo. France and Britain share control of bankrupt Egypt. Mexico: Porfirio Diaz gains power. U.S.: Rutherford B. Hayes wins disputed presidential election. Sioux and allies defeat General Custer's troops at Little Big Horn. Author Mark Twain (Samuel Clemens) writes *Tom Sawyer*. Germany: N. A. Otto invents four-stroke engine. Composer Richard Wagner produces his opera series *The Ring of the Nibelung* at Bayreuth. Queen Victoria is proclaimed empress of India.

A cartoon of the German eagle, poised to take as much of Africa as it can.

1877 Russo-Turkish War (to 1878) over Balkans. Romania is officially recognized as independent from Turkey. South Africa: Britain annexes Transvaal. Last Xhosa War (to 1879) against Europeans. Japan: Samurai are defeated in Satsuma Rebellion. U.S.: Inventor Thomas Edison patents his phonograph. Russia: Composer Peter Ilyich Tchaikovsky's music for the ballet *Swan Lake* is performed.

1878 End of Russo-Turkish War. Congress of Berlin reduces Russian gains, places Bosnia-Herzegovina under Austrian protection, and confirms independence of Serbia, Romania, and Montenegro. Bulgaria is granted self-government. Afghanistan: Second Anglo-Afghan War (to 1880).

Ireland

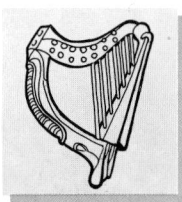

Most of the people of Ireland made a living by farming small plots of rented land, or working large estates for Anglo-Irish landlords. They rarely had enough to eat. Most people lived on potatoes because they could not afford to eat bread.

The Corn Laws kept the price of wheat high by taxing imported wheat. Powerful Anglo-Irish landlords favored the Corn Laws because they made large profits from the wheat grown on their land.

Disaster struck in 1845 and 1846 when disease ruined the potato crop. People were starving to death. The British prime minister, Sir Robert Peel, ended the Corn Laws, which gradually brought the price of bread down. But it was too late to save the Irish people. About one million died and one million more emigrated.

The potato famine increased Irish feelings of hatred toward their British rulers. In 1870, they began to demand their own parliament, which had been abolished in 1801.

The demands of Irish politicians, particularly Charles Parnell, and the

▲ Irish tenant farmers were ruined when the potato blight struck in 1845. The harvest was poor and they could not pay the rent. Many were thrown off their farms.

▶ During the potato famine, many Irish people had to choose between starving or leaving the country. About one million people starved to death, and another million emigrated over the next five years, mostly to the U.S. A typhoid epidemic in 1846–1847 killed another 350,000.

O'Connell

Daniel O'Connell (1775–1847), was called the Liberator, because he fought for Catholics to have political rights in Britain. He was the first Irish Catholic to be elected to the British parliament, and served from 1829–1847.

Parnell

Charles Stewart Parnell (1846–1891) was the leader of the Irish nationalists in the British parliament, and led the struggle for home rule. He also supported the Irish Land League, which wanted land to be given to Irish farmers.

strength of feeling among the Irish people led to many law reforms, especially relating to the right to own land. But these reforms were not enough. Most Irish people wanted home rule, or self-government (*see* pages 648–649). After the failure of the 1886 and 1893 Home Rule Bills, the British parliament finally passed the third Home Rule Bill in 1912, but it was not put into operation because World War I started.

▼ *The Fenians, an organization that aimed to set up a new Irish republic, attacked a police van in Manchester in 1867 to rescue their comrades.*

1879 South Africa: Zulu War; Zulus defeat British at Isandhlwana but are crushed at Ulundi. Afghanistan: British occupy Kabul and control Afghan affairs. Germany: Free-trade policy abandoned. Austria-Hungary and Germany form Dual Alliance. Ireland: Irish Land League formed; calls for land to be returned to Irish people. South America: War of the Pacific (to 1884) begins between Chile, Bolivia and Peru. U.S.: First Christian Science Church founded. Edison develops the electric light bulb. Britain: Scientist William Crookes demonstrates cathode rays. Norway: Dramatist Henrik Ibsen writes *A Doll's House*.

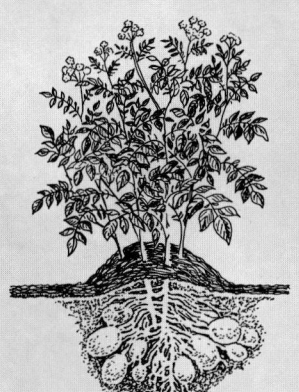

The potato was a staple food for many Irish people. The attack of potato blight lasted three years, during which time many starved to death or were forced to emigrate.

1880 Afghanistan: Rebels lay siege to British at Kandahar; pro-British Abd-er-Rahman Khan comes to power. South Africa: First Boer War against the British (to 1881). Ireland: Land agent Charles Boycott tries to evict tenants for non-payment of rents, but tenants "boycott" and triumph. France: Socialist Party founded.

1881 "Scramble for Africa" begins. France occupies Tunisia. South Africa: Boers defeat British at Majuba Hill; Transvaal self-government restored. Sudan: The Mahdi leads a Muslim revolt against the Egyptian government. Prussia: Bismarck introduces social security benefits. Russia: Tsar Alexander II assassinated. U.S.: President James Garfield assassinated. Britain: Novelist Henry James publishes *Portrait of a Lady*.

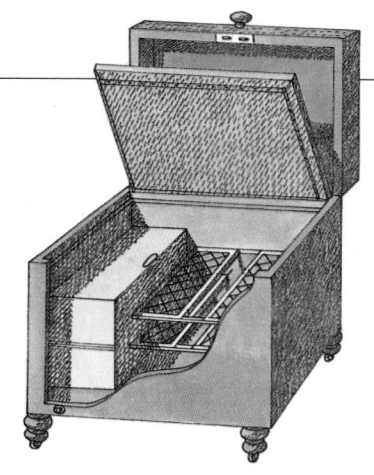

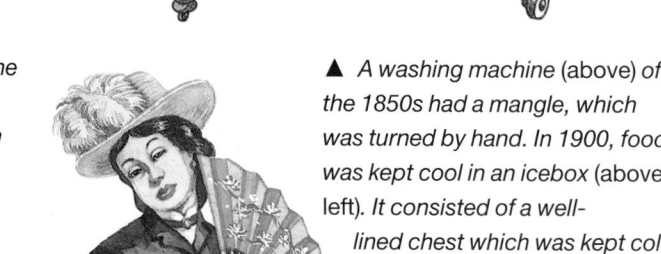

Mangle

Drum

People

The increase and success of industry meant that middle-class people had more money to spend. Some people, like bank managers or clergymen, could afford servants, so they had more spare time.

In many ways life was easier, but for middle-class women life had its problems. They were expected to marry, and obey their husbands. They had to know how to manage their servants so the house was run properly. They could not take a job because it was not considered "respectable" to work, except for charities, so they had to find other diversions to occupy their time. In contrast, a maid might work 60 or 70 hours a week but in return receive very little in wages.

► In the 1870s, women wore bustle gowns. The bustle made the back of the skirt stick out.

▲ *A washing machine* (above) *of the 1850s had a mangle, which was turned by hand. In 1900, food was kept cool in an icebox* (above left). *It consisted of a well-lined chest which was kept cold by blocks of ice.*

► *Prince Albert had an influence on men's fashion. Tartan pants and the black frock coat were introduced by him.*

◄ *The Lumière brothers added a projector to the kinetoscope (a one-person peepshow) and showed their first short film in Paris in 1895. It was silent and in black and white.*

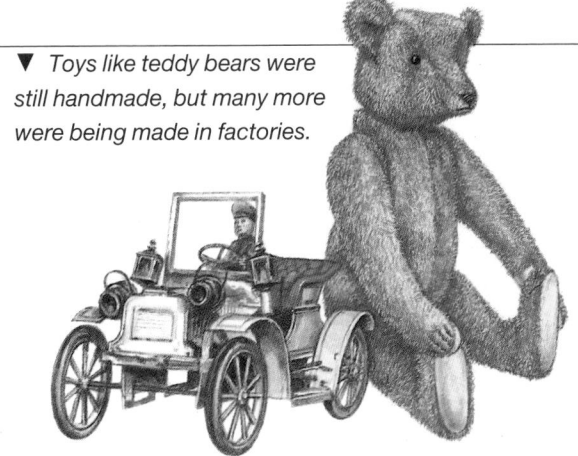

▼ *Toys like teddy bears were still handmade, but many more were being made in factories.*

WHEN IT HAPPENED

1855	Rayon, the first artificial fiber, invented.
1860	Brighter clothes made with chemical dyes.
1871	A large part of Chicago is destroyed by fire.
1877	U.S. inventor Robert Edison patents his "phonograph" or gramophone.
1891	Otto Lilienthal demonstrates hang-gliding.
1896	Olympic Games revived in Athens.
1907	First electric washing machine invented.

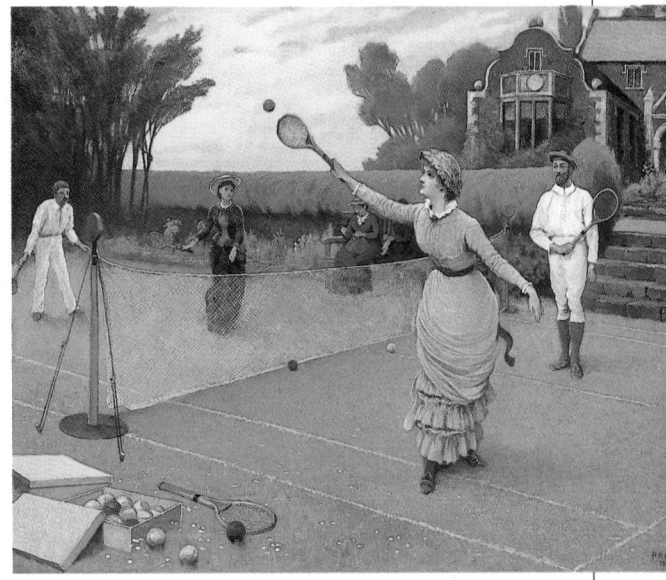

▲ *More leisure meant more time for sports. Many middle-class houses had large gardens, and lawn tennis became popular in the 1870s. Basketball was first played in North America in 1891, using a soccer ball and two peach baskets as nets. Proper rules for football and baseball were also introduced.*

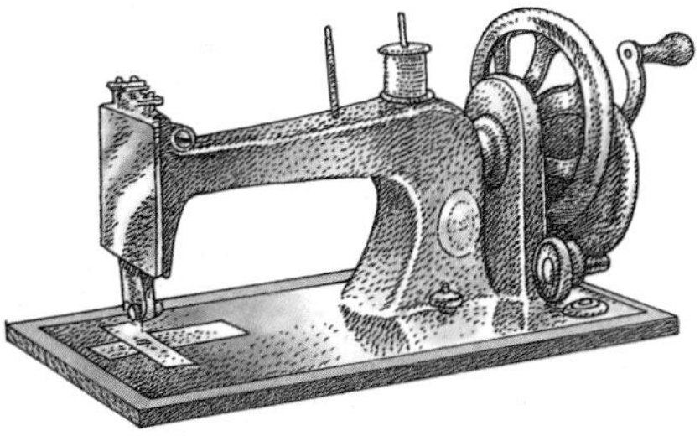

▲ *In 1846, sewing machines were made that cut down the amount of time women spent sewing.*

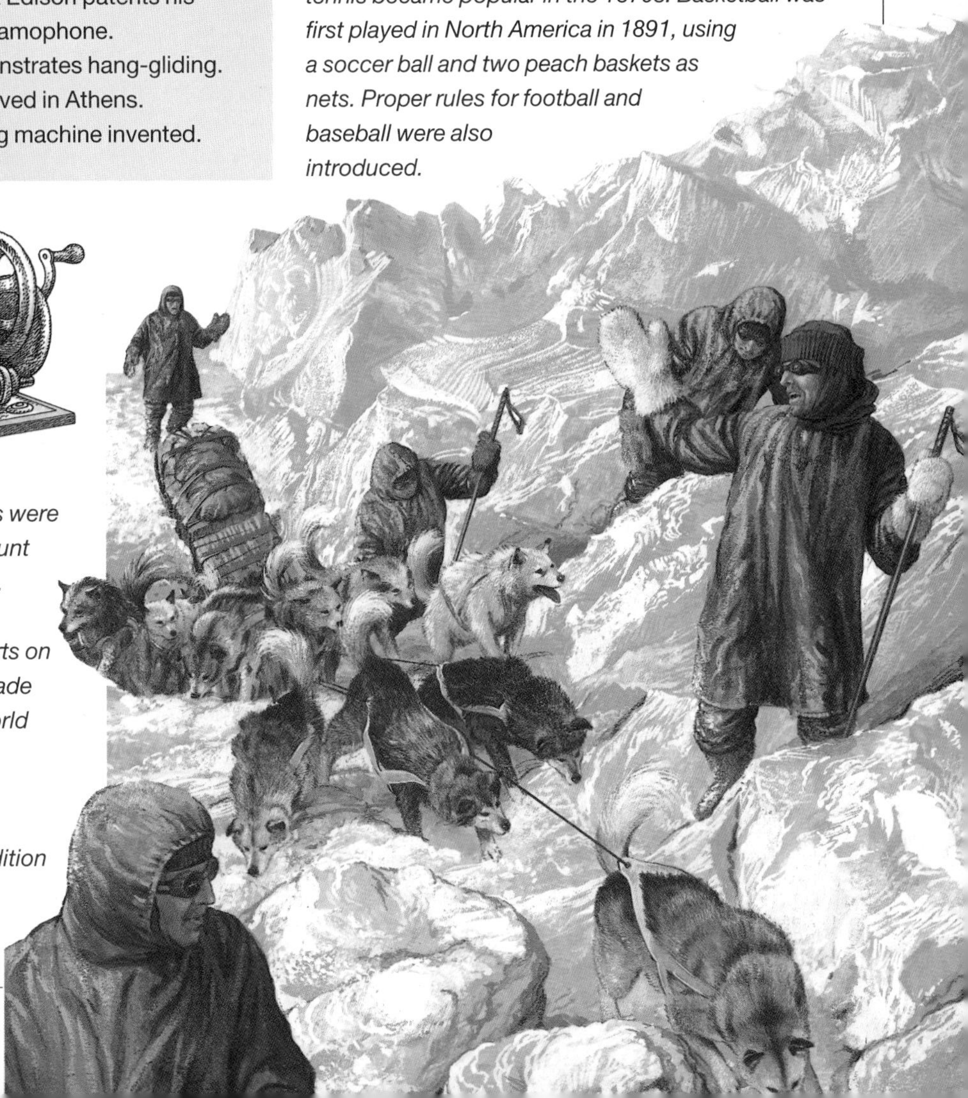

► *In 1911, newspaper reports on the race to the South Pole made more people interested in world events. Norway's Roald Amundsen arrived there first, using dogs to pull the sleds. Captain Scott's British expedition used ponies for the sleds and arrived five weeks later.*

Southeast Asia

Southeast Asia was colonized by Europeans who set up plantations and became rich on the profits from the crops grown by the local people. The French colony of Indochina included Cambodia, Laos, and Vietnam (which was divided into three areas called Cochin-China, Annam, and Tonkin). They gradually conquered the area during the 1800s, but local people resisted. In Annam, the emperor Ham Nghi waged a guerrilla war from the mountains until 1888.

The Dutch had been established in Indonesia since the 1620s (*see* pages 516–517). They had already taken over Indonesian trade, and from 1830 they took over agriculture too. The peasant farmers were forced to grow the crops the Dutch wanted, especially coffee and indigo (a plant from which a blue dye was made). By 1900 a nationalist movement was growing inside Indonesia itself. The Indonesians made efforts to improve education, and to regain some control over their business and trade.

The British colonized Burma and the

Malay Peninsula in the late 19th century because they wanted to protect India, which they regarded as the most valuable part of the British empire. The Burmese resisted British rule in a series of bloody battles. The situation in Malaya was calmer because the British ruled through the local sultans. They set up rubber plantations and improved the techniques used for mining the large deposits of tin in the country.

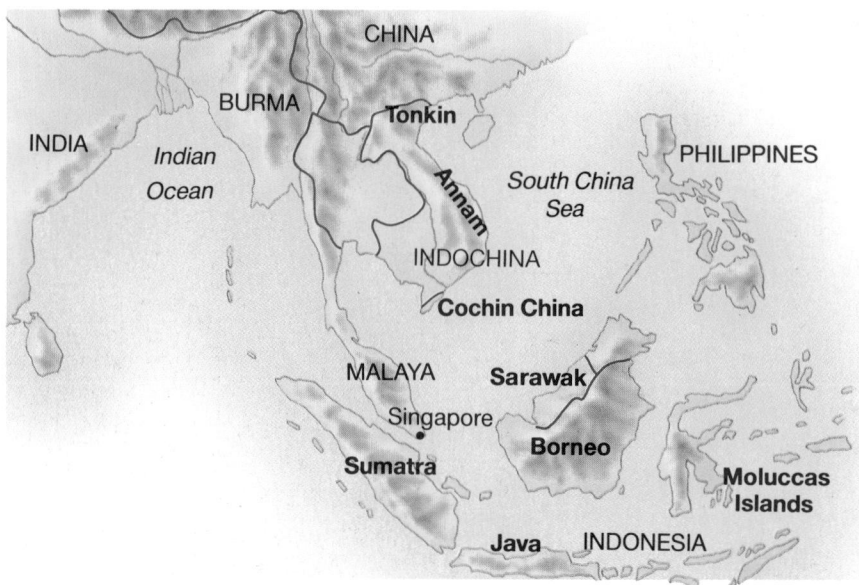

◀ *Southeast Asia was dominated by three European powers in the late 19th century. The French controlled Indo-China. The British controlled most of Burma, and Malaya from its capital on the island of Singapore. Singapore later became independent of Malaya. The Dutch ruled most of the Indonesian islands from their main base in Java, but shared Borneo with the British.*

◄ *The French won the battle of Bac-Ninh in Indochina in 1884. At the Treaty of Tientsin (Tianjin) in 1885, the Chinese rulers of Annam recognized the French protectorates in Annam and Tonkin.*

▼ *Both the Indonesian princes and Dutch colonists benefited from the profits made by growing cash crops on the islands. But for ordinary Indonesians, this way of life meant great hardship.*

This beautiful mural of the tree of life comes from a family home in Sarawak.

1882 British occupy Egypt; France withdraws. Italy joins Germany and Austria-Hungary in Triple Alliance. Indochina: French take Hanoi. Russia: Anti-Semitic laws passed. U.S.: First American hydroelectric generating station opens in Wisconsin. Germany: Robert Koch identifies the germ that causes tuberculosis. Britain: First electric train services run. Scottish writer Robert Louis Stevenson publishes *Treasure Island*.

1883 Africa: France occupies Madagascar. Indonesia: Huge volcanic explosion of Mount Krakatoa, near Java. U.S.: Pendelton Act reforms system of job appointments in the civil service. Spain: Architect Antoni Gaudi begins building the church of the *Holy Family* at Barcelona in the Art Nouveau style.

1884 Sudan: British General Gordon arrives to evacuate Egyptian forces. Pacific: Britain annexes southeast New Guinea. Berlin Conference decides colonial divisions in Africa; Belgian king Leopold II is recognized as ruler of the Congo; Germany gains colonies in southwest and West Africa. Asia: War between China and France (to 1885) over Annam. Britain: Third Reform Act gives male farm workers and domestic servants the vote. France: Artist Georges Seurat paints *Bathers at Asnières* in the Pointillist style (painting made up of tiny spots of color). U.S.: Construction starts on the first skyscraper, in Chicago.

Science and Medicine

In medicine, the greatest single advance was made in the 1840s when Louis Pasteur and Robert Koch discovered that bacteria and viruses lead to infection and cause certain diseases. This led to over 20 fatal diseases being prevented by immunization. Serious epidemics such as the outbreak of cholera that had killed 16,000 people in London in 1849 could be prevented.

Major developments in surgery included the introduction of ether as an anesthetic in 1847. It helped to reduce the pain and shock of operations. Also the use of antiseptics in 1865 helped to reduce the risk of death due to infection after surgery.

▶ Sigmund Freud (1856-1939) was an Austrian doctor. He became interested in illnesses that had no physical cause. Freud believed they came from an unconscious level of the mind, and developed psychoanalysis to treat neurotic mental disorders.

▲ The discovery of quinine, a cure for malaria, in 1854 was a great medical advance. But not many of the pills and potions carried by Livingstone in Africa, or Scott in the Antarctic would be found in a modern chemist's shop.

▼ The Polish-born Marie Curie and her French husband Pierre discovered the element radium during their research into radioactivity.

◀ Charles Darwin was a biologist. His theory of natural selection explained how different kinds of animals had evolved, or developed since life began. This cartoon makes fun of his idea that humans were descended from apes. Most people believed that the Earth, and everything on it, had not changed since God created them.

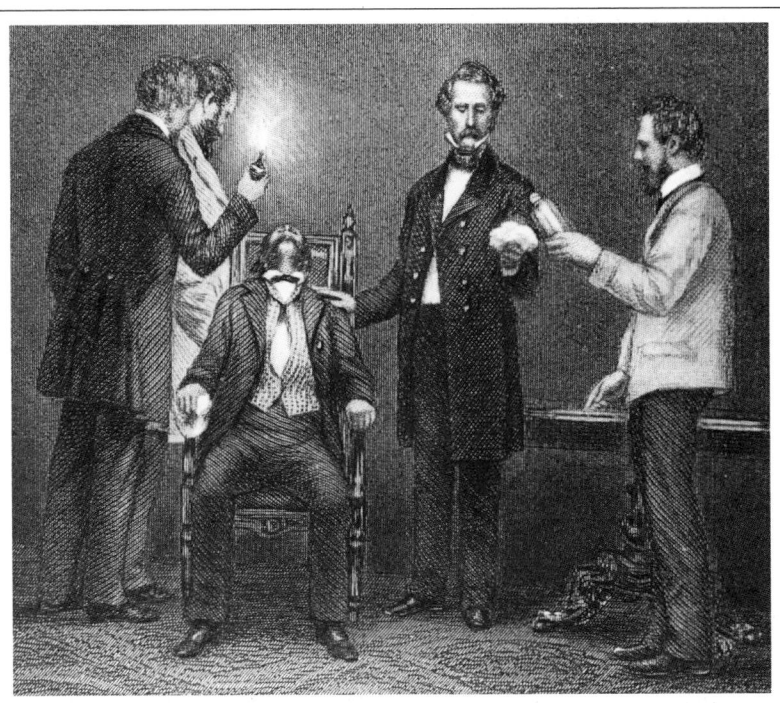

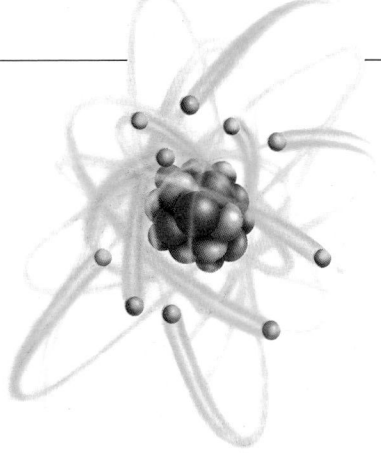

▲ Scientists believed that all things were made up of atoms. Proof was provided by Rutherford's discovery of the atomic nucleus in 1911.

▼ The chemist Louis Pasteur proved by experiment that food goes bad due to airborne germs. This discovery led to pasteurization (the treatment of foods to prevent them being infected by bacteria).

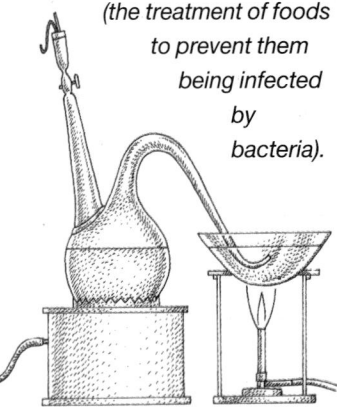

▲ The horrors of a visit to the dentist were greatly reduced by an American, William Morton (1819–1868). He gave a public exhibition of ether, the first anesthetic, in 1846. Soon, surgeons were also using anesthetics for operations.

▼ New medical instruments included the hypodermic syringe. A liquid vaccine could be injected into the body through a hollow needle. Advances in precision engineering (making small objects with perfect accuracy) made such instruments possible.

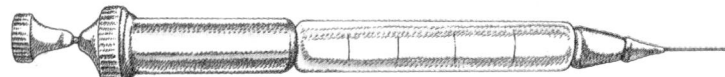

◄ The surgeon Joseph Lister experimented with antiseptics which would prevent germs infecting a wound. He found that carbolic acid worked as an antiseptic, and used it as a spray to disinfect the air during operations. The use of antiseptics reduced death after surgery.

WHEN IT HAPPENED

1854 Florence Nightingale leaves for the Crimea, where she improves hospital conditions.

1864 Henri Dunant founds the Red Cross.

1869 Dimitri Mendeleyev works out the periodic table of elements.

1882 Robert Koch isolates the bacteria responsible for tuberculosis.

1895 Wilhelm Röntgen discovers X rays, which are used in diagnosing injury and illness.

1900s Christiaan Eijkman and Frederick Hopkins demonstrate the importance of vitamins.

India

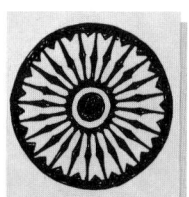

In 1850, the 200 million people of India remained under the rule of the British East India Company (*see* pages 528–529). The Company had lost its monopoly of trade. Its income now came from taxes. The Company had turned into a government ruling a huge area with people who had different languages and religions.

To the British, India seemed to be doing well under their rule, so the rebellion that broke out in 1857 came as a great shock to them. It started with a rumor in the army in Bengal that the gun cartridges were greased with animal fats. This offended the *sepoys* (soldiers) as the cow was sacred to the Hindus and the pig was considered unclean by the Muslims. The rebellion spread, fueled by

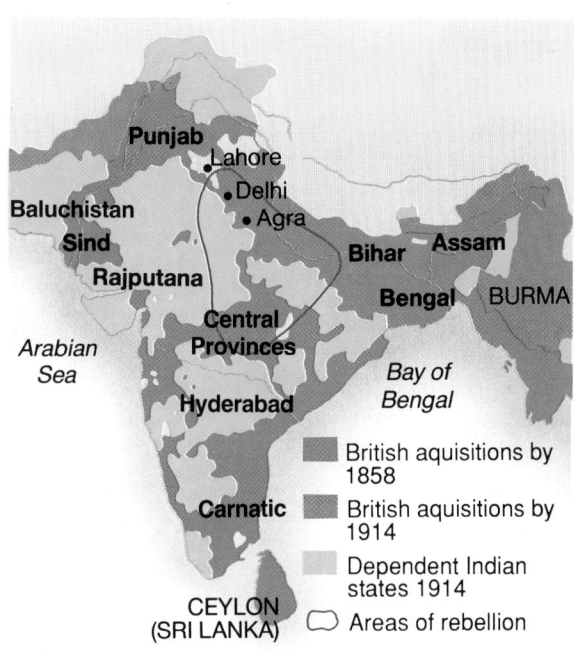

▼ During the Indian Mutiny bitter fighting took place at Delhi, Cawnpore, and Lucknow. The rebellion ended in 1858 because the rebels were not united.

◄ *Successful wars with neighboring states increased British territory, but fighting continued on the northwest frontier.*

▶ *The maharajah (ruler) Ranjit Singh united the Sikh empire in the Punjab, in northwest India. Its capital was at Lahore. He died in 1839.*

the discontent felt by the Indians against British interference in their customs. For a few months British rule in the north was in danger of collapsing.

After the rebellion ended in 1858, India was placed under the rule of the British government, and its policy became more cautious. British officials left control of local affairs to the princes. In return for their allegiance the British promised their support.

Nationalism grew after the rebellion. Young educated Indians wanted more say in government. They also felt that India was being held back. They were angered by Britain's failure to encourage Indian industries, like cotton, because it could compete with industry in Britain.

▲ *The British brought their own customs and traditions to India, and they lived their lives much as they would have done at home. Christmas was always celebrated as a major family occasion.*

1885 Sudan: General Gordon killed by Mahdist forces in Khartoum. Burma: Third British-Burmese War leads to British control. Indochina: China accepts French protectorate of Annam (central Vietnam). Ethiopia: Italians occupy Massawa and begin to advance inland. India: Indian National Congress founded. Canadian Pacific Railway completed. Germany: Karl Benz builds automobile; Gottlieb Daimler invents the gasoline engine. France: Artist Henri de Toulouse-Lautrec begins work in Paris. U.S.: Washington Monument is completed.

The merchant ships of the British East India Company were known as "East Indiamen."

1886 South Africa: Discovery of gold in Transvaal; Johannesburg is founded. Britain: Parliament rejects Irish Home Rule Bill. Balkans: Treaty of Bucharest ends 14-day Serbian-Bulgarian conflict. Cuba: Slavery abolished. U.S.: The Statue of Liberty, a gift from the French, is unveiled in New York harbor.

1887 Ethiopia: Italians defeated at Dogali. Southeast Asia: Britain annexes Burma. French complete union of Indochina. Britain: Writer Sir Arthur Conan Doyle's first Sherlock Holmes detective story is published. U.S.: Inventors Edison and Swan combine to produce "Ediswan" household electric lamp. New electrolysis process for cheaper production of aluminum invented by chemist Charles Martin Hall.

The British Empire

At its height during the reign of Queen Victoria, the British empire included a quarter of the world's land and people. Colonies in the Caribbean, Africa, Asia, Australasia, and the Pacific were ruled from London and were all united under the British monarch. The empire provided the British with raw materials for manufacturing industry, and British demand for colonial products such as silk, spices, rubber, cotton, tea, coffee, and sugar led to the gradual takeover of many countries.

Several countries became colonies when the British government took over from a trading company that had gone bankrupt. India was an example of a country where the British had come to trade and stayed to rule. It was the most prized colony in the empire. The British took over Egypt to guard the route to India. Then, after a rebellion to the south of Egypt led by a religious leader, the Mahdi, Britain took over Sudan as well.

▼ Between 1870 and 1913 the British empire expanded farther to take in land in Africa and Southeast Asia, providing jobs for many British people.

▲ The rich splendor of life in India for the British is reflected by this ceremonial occasion at the court of an Indian prince. But few learned about Indian customs.

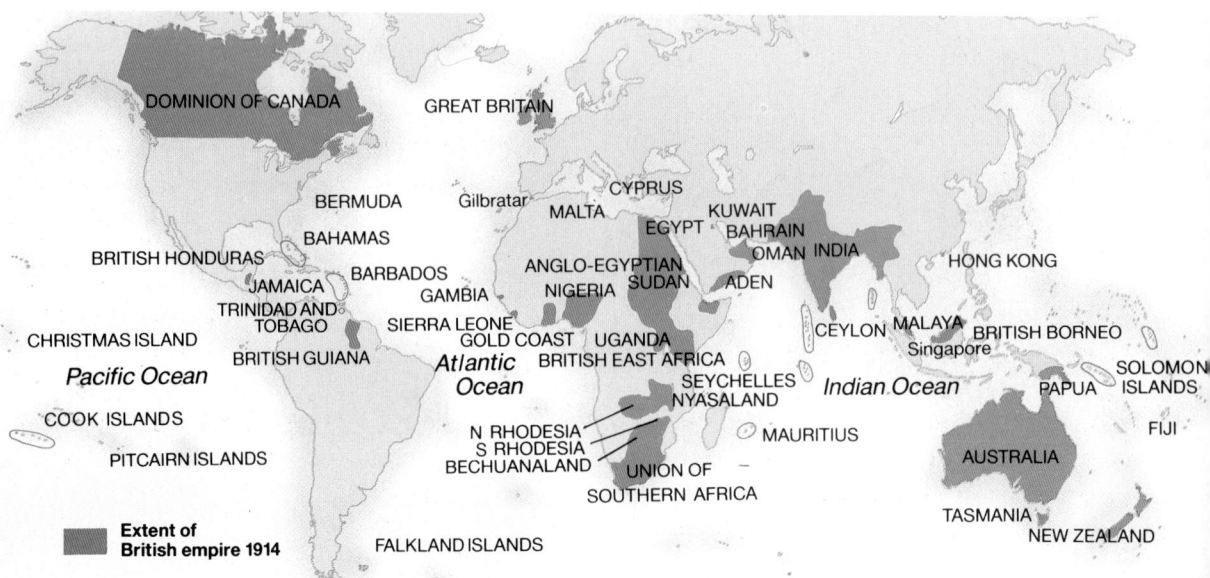

DOMINION OF CANADA
GREAT BRITAIN
BERMUDA
Gilbratar
CYPRUS
MALTA
KUWAIT
EGYPT
BAHRAIN
BAHAMAS
OMAN INDIA
BRITISH HONDURAS
ANGLO-EGYPTIAN
HONG KONG
JAMAICA
BARBADOS
NIGERIA
SUDAN
ADEN
TRINIDAD AND
TOBAGO
GAMBIA
CHRISTMAS ISLAND
SIERRA LEONE
CEYLON
MALAYA
BRITISH BORNEO
GOLD COAST
UGANDA
Singapore
Pacific Ocean
BRITISH GUIANA
Atlantic
Ocean
BRITISH EAST AFRICA
SEYCHELLES
SOLOMON
ISLANDS
PAPUA
COOK ISLANDS
NYASALAND
Indian Ocean
FIJI
MAURITIUS
PITCAIRN ISLANDS
N RHODESIA
S RHODESIA
BECHUANALAND
UNION OF
SOUTHERN AFRICA
AUSTRALIA
TASMANIA
NEW ZEALAND

Extent of
British empire 1914
FALKLAND ISLANDS

Britain established trade links throughout the empire by appointing an agent in every port and island. The agents organized local products for export to Britain and markets for British imports. The British navy protected British interests and kept the sea routes safe for merchant ships.

Toward the end of the 19th century, some colonies began to break away from British rule. Home rule was granted to Canada in 1867, and independence to Australia in 1901. Both countries became dominions, although they remained part of the British empire. The loosening of ties with the British empire reflected the fact that Britain had ceased to be the leading industrial nation. Germany and the United States had overtaken it, with France and Russia close behind.

A cartoon showing the colonies of the British empire constantly worrying the imperial lion.

1888 Germany: William II becomes emperor (to 1918). Physicist Heinrich Hertz discovers electromagnetic waves. Britain: John Boyd Dunlop invents the pneumatic tire. Brazil: Slavery abolished. U.S.: George Eastman makes roll film for cameras. France: Dutch post-Impressionist artist Vincent Van Gogh paints *Sunflowers*. Sweden: Dramatist August Strindberg writes *Miss Julie*. China: The first Chinese railroad is opened, running from Tianjin to Tanghshan.

1889 The Republic of Brazil is proclaimed. Italy gains protectorate over Ethiopia. Japan: New Meiji Constitution is published. France: Former minister Georges Boulanger flees to escape treason charge. Central America: Panama Canal Company goes bankrupt, ending work on canal. Britain: dockers on strike. U.S. Edison invents kinetoscope for viewing moving pictures.

1890 Germany: Bismarck is dismissed as chancellor. U.S.: Massacre of Sioux Indians by U.S. cavalry at Wounded Knee. Oklahoma Territory is created. The U.S. population reaches 63 million, a 25 percent increase in a decade. Britain: Scottish anthropologist James Frazer publishes *The Golden Bough*. A telephone line is laid between London and Paris. Russia: Alexander Borodin's opera *Prince Igor* has its first performance.

▲ *The Suez Canal was built by a French company and opened in 1869. It reduced the sea voyage from Britain to India by 4,000 miles (6,400 km). The canal was therefore vitally important to Britain. In 1875, the British government gained control of it by buying shares in the company from the Egyptian government. To protect the canal, Britain took over yet another colony, Cyprus.*

Science and Technology

Industry continued to develop, with new inventions, new products, and factories producing new types of goods. In 1850 coal and steam engines still provided the power for machinery. By 1900 electricity and oil were being used.

Oil provided the fuel for the internal combustion engine, which led to the first automobiles. Oil products also played a large part in the new chemical industry. They made possible the development of materials such as plastics and artificial rubber.

▼ The German engineer Rudolph Diesel invented his internal-combustion engine in 1897. Diesel's engine was used in factories because it was cheaper to run than other engines.

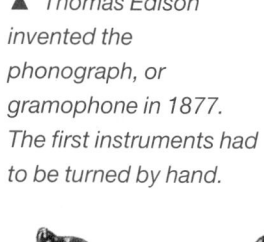

▲ Thomas Edison invented the phonograph, or gramophone in 1877. The first instruments had to be turned by hand.

▶ An American, Whitcomb Judson, invented the zipper in 1891. The first ones were clumsy and looked like the hooks and eyes they replaced.

▼ Prince Albert helped to organize the Great Exhibition in London in 1851. All the latest inventions were shown. Factory machines were the main exhibits.

▲ Typewriters that really worked appeared in the 1870s. Until 1878 they typed only capital letters.

1859 First oil well drilled in Pennsylvania.

1867 Dynamite invented by Swedish chemist Alfred Nobel.

1868 Frenchman Georges Leclanché invents a dry-cell battery, as used in flashlights.

1876 Nikolaus Otto invents a four-stroke gasoline engine, later used in automobiles.

1882 First hydroelectric power station built, using the force of water to generate electricity.

1888 Scottish inventor John Dunlop fits an air-filled tire to a bicycle to give a softer ride.

1909 American chemist Leo Baekeland invents the first plastic, bakelite.

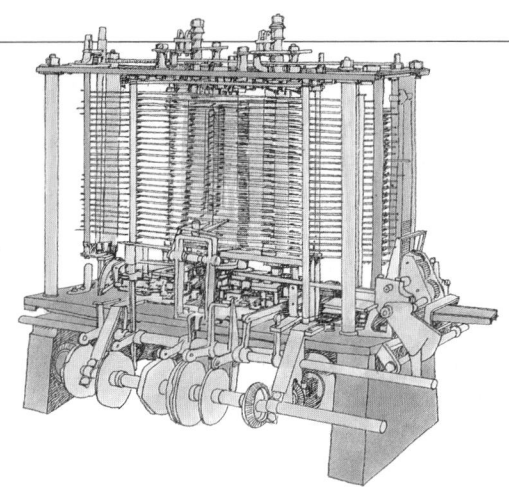

▲ *The mathematician Charles Babbage spent years working on his "Analytical Engine." It was a mechanical calculating machine, a forerunner of the computer.*

▼ *Thomas Edison was also a pioneer of the electric light bulb. In 1880, his system was first used to light a steamship. But when electric light was installed in public buildings, people were afraid that the light would damage their eyes. By 1900, a few homes had electric lights. They were fitted to brackets that were attached to the wall.*

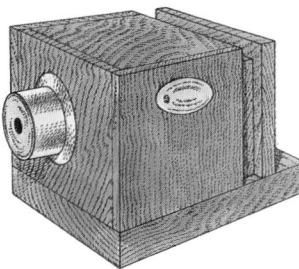

▲ *The daguerreotype camera appeared in 1838, but it was slow to operate. It was not until 1888 when George Eastman introduced the first roll film camera that photography was available to everyone.*

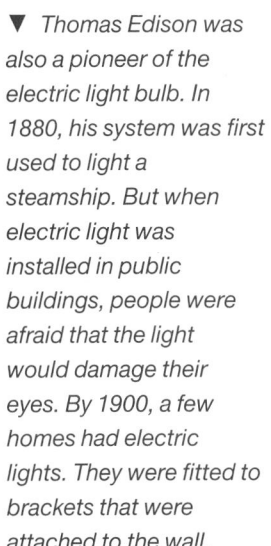

▶ *A big step forward in steel-making was made by Henry Bessemer. In a Bessemer Converter hot air was blasted through melted iron to convert it into steel. Steel was stronger and more useful than iron, but before Bessemer's invention in 1856, it was very expensive to make.*

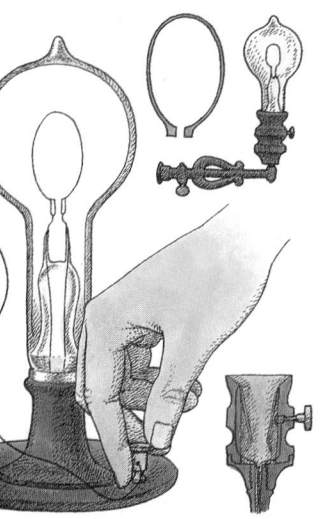

North America

After the civil war (*see* pages 582–585), the land west of the Mississippi River was steadily settled by white Americans. The gold rush of 1848–1849 had already brought thousands to California hoping to find gold.

The government encouraged people to migrate westward. Under the Homestead Act of 1862, a family could have 160 acres (65 ha) for a small fee, provided they did not sell the land for five years. More land was given to those who made improvements by drilling wells or planting trees. The Act encouraged farmers to move into the Great Plains.

The government also encouraged the building of railroads, which carried people into unsettled regions. It gave land to the railroads so generously that many lines were built just to gain land.

By 1900, the United States was already producing more food than it needed. Industry and business developed rapidly, making the United States the richest country in the world. It produced and

traded more goods than any other. It also began to play a larger part in world affairs.

Poor Europeans saw the United States as a land of freedom, democracy, and riches. Not everyone grew rich, however. The Native Americans lost land to settlers. Workers in the booming cities were not much better off than industrial workers in Europe. Black Americans especially, had little chance of improving their lives.

◀ Railroads made the settlement of the West relatively rapid. This poster shows the Union Pacific Railroad which was finished in 1869, joining America from coast to coast. Other lines soon spread out across the plains. As well as carrying passengers, and transporting goods to the farmers, railroads carried cattle and crops to towns. Cheap, quick transportation allowed new mines and new industries to open up in other areas.

▲ *Between 1830 and 1910, 28 million immigrants entered America. Most were poor Europeans who came to escape from poverty and unemployment. They came from Ireland, Germany, Britain, and Scandinavia. Later, more came from southern and eastern Europe.*

▼ *The U.S. government gained land in the west mainly by agreement from France and Britain, who had colonies there. As well as the land shown on the map, the United States expanded to include Alaska in 1867. In 1898 it took over Hawaii in the Pacific Ocean. It also took over Cuba, Puerto Rico, and the Philippines from Spain.*

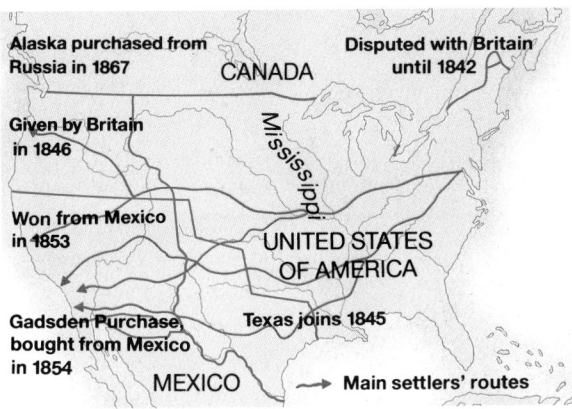

Alaska purchased from Russia in 1867

Disputed with Britain until 1842

CANADA

Given by Britain in 1846

Mississippi

Won from Mexico in 1853

UNITED STATES OF AMERICA

Gadsden Purchase, bought from Mexico in 1854

Texas joins 1845

MEXICO → Main settlers' routes

1891 France and Russia form entente (alliance). Africa: Britain stakes its claims to East and Central Africa. Turkey: Young Turk movement is founded to seek political reforms. Russia: Construction begins of Trans-Siberian railroad. Famine follows harvest failure. Britain: Factory Act forbids employment of children under 11. Tahiti: French artist Paul Gauguin paints his first South Sea paintings. Australia: Sheepshearers go on strike. U.S.: Zipper is invented. The game of basketball is devised.

1892 U.S.: Federal Bureau of Immigration opens a receiving station for immigrants on Ellis Island, in New York harbor. Rival firms controlled by Edison and Westinghouse combine to form General Electric. West Africa: French occupy Dahomey (now Benin).

Wood was scarce in the lands west of the Mississippi, so settlers often used clods of earth and grass as a roofing material.

1893 Hawaii: U.S. forces depose queen; provisional government is set up. Africa: Matabele War against the British. West Africa: Ivory Coast becomes a French colony. New Zealand: Women are granted the right to vote (the first nation to do so). Far East: France annexes Laos. U.S.: Czech composer Antonin Dvořák's "*New World*" Symphony is performed in New York. Norway: Artist Edvard Munch paints *The Scream*, which influences the Expressionist movement. Britain: Second Irish Home Rule Bill fails.

1894 France: Conviction of Jewish army officer Dreyfus for treason causes conflict. President Sadi-Carnot is assassinated. France and Russia form a military alliance. China and Japan at war over Korea (to 1895). Russia: Nicholas II becomes tsar. Britain: Writer Rudyard Kipling publishes *The Jungle Book*. Irish playwright George Bernard Shaw writes *Arms and the Man*.

During the 1850s, a tailor in San Francisco began making practical, hardwearing pants for the gold miners. He made them out of a brown canvas material originally intended for tents. His name was Levi Strauss and his pants became known as jeans.

1895 Treaty of Shimonoseki ends war between China and Japan; Korea remains independent; Japan takes Taiwan. South Africa: British South African Company's territory is named Rhodesia. Cecil Rhodes authorizes Jameson Raid against Boers in the Transvaal (to 1896). Turkey: Armenians are massacred by Turks and Kurds. Cuba: Revolt against Spanish rule. Germany: Wilhelm Röntgen discovers X rays. Britain: H. G. Wells publishes science fiction novel *The Time Machine*. France: The Lumière brothers give first public showing of motion pictures. U.S.: The first U.S. Open Golf Championship is won by Horace Rawlins, a British professional.

1896 Ethiopia: Italy recognizes Ethiopian independence. Sudan: General Kitchener leads British forces against Mahdists in Sudan. France annexes Madagascar. Greece: Olympic Games held. France: Hungarian Theodore Herzl calls for a Jewish state and founds Zionism.

Gold Rushes

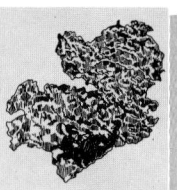

During the 1820s, gold was discovered in Georgia in the United States. People came from around the world hoping to make their fortune. This was the first of many gold rushes. After the find in Georgia large amounts of gold were found elsewhere in the United States. Discoveries were also made in Canada, Australia, and South Africa. Populations increased and cities grew up in areas where gold was found.

One of the most famous gold rushes was to California. Gold was unearthed near the sawmill of a Swiss settler, John Sutter in 1848. Over 100,000 prospectors (people who look for gold) entered California in 1849, including many from overseas. They became known as the "forty-niners." In a few years new cities were founded, and the area began a period of rapid growth and prosperity.

One of the gold prospectors in California was an Australian, Edward Hargraves. He noticed that the land was similar to his home country. Returning home, he washed a pan of gravel in a

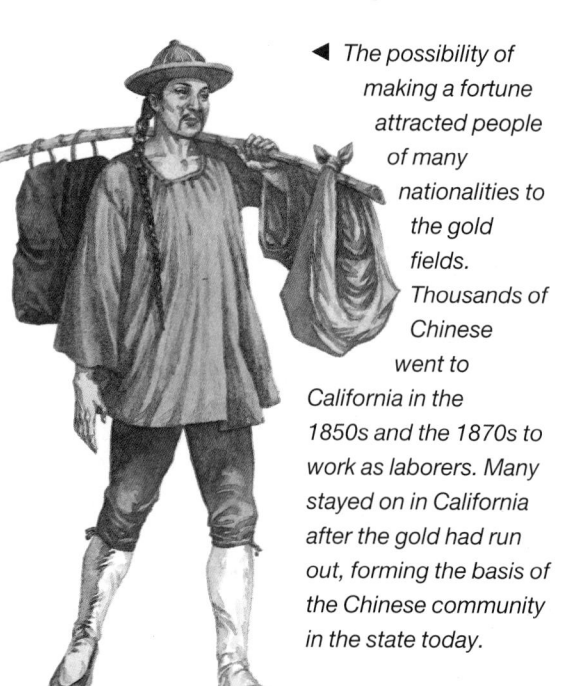

◄ *The possibility of making a fortune attracted people of many nationalities to the gold fields. Thousands of Chinese went to California in the 1850s and the 1870s to work as laborers. Many stayed on in California after the gold had run out, forming the basis of the Chinese community in the state today.*

creek, and found gold. Soon after, gold was also found in Melbourne. Gold fever hit Australia. In ten years the country's population almost tripled.

In 1886, gold was discovered in South Africa. *Uitlanders* (foreigners) poured into the Transvaal republic in thousands. The last of the big gold rushes took place in Alaska and Canada. Prospectors in the Klondike region extracted over 22 million dollars' worth of gold in the year 1900.

▲ Prospectors "panned" the river, hoping to find gold in the gravel. Some were lucky, but many others left empty-handed. Traders who sold supplies to the gold diggers grew rich by charging high prices for food, drink, and clothing.

► Towns grew with amazing speed during the gold-rush days. Sometimes they disappeared just as quickly. Virginia City in Nevada did not exist until 1859, when gold and silver were found nearby. By 1876 it was a large town. When the gold and silver had all gone, people left as quickly as they had come and it became a ghost town.

Society and Government

Most people in the late 19th century knew they were living in a world of change. By 1900, Europeans, at home or in countries where they had settled, had cut their ties with the past and created a new kind of society.

Monarchs with absolute powers no longer ruled in most countries. For some people, "democracy" still meant rule by the mob. Yet some of the deepest divisions in society were growing smaller. After 1848, fewer political revolts broke out, partly because many of the rebels' demands had been granted. Workers gained better conditions. People were better educated.

The changes were not limited to the industrial countries. European influence in their colonies also changed the lives of local people.

▲ People without a home or job had to depend on charity. The Salvation Army offered practical help to the poor so they could improve their lives.

► In 1868, only 15 percent of Japanese could read and write. The Meiji government made all children go to elementary school, and increased the number of secondary schools and universities. By 1914, the Japanese were among the best-educated people in the world.

▼ In the 19th century many children worked long hours in factories and coal mines. By 1900, most industrial countries had passed laws to ensure children went to school, not to work.

◀ *Booker T. Washington led the fight for better education for Black Americans. He headed the Tuskegee Institute where students trained as farmers, mechanics, and domestics.*

▶ *In 1848 trade unions were illegal in most countries, but that did not stop workers forming them. By the 1890s trade unions were recognized in Germany, Britain, and France, and they continued to strive for better pay and conditions.*

▶ *Friedrich Engels was one of the founders of modern communism. In 1848 he worked with Karl Marx in Brussels to provide a political program for the working-class movement against capitalism.*

8 HOURS LABOUR!

NATIONAL UNION
of GAS WORKERS & GENERAL LABOURERS
OF GREAT BRITAIN AND IRELAND

◀ *A woodcarving of an African ruler sitting in state, ready to receive his new masters. Some Africans fought against foreign rule, but by 1914 most of Africa was controlled by Europeans, who tried to impose their own way of life there.*

WHEN IT HAPPENED

1833 In Britain, the Factory Act prohibits children from working in textile mills.

1866 Civil Rights Act makes Black Americans citizens of the United States.

1869 U.S. has coast-to-coast railroad system.

1871 All men in Germany gain the right to vote.

1875–1885 Socialist parties founded in many European countries.

1902 French laws improve working conditions.

1897 Brief war between Greece and Turkey (to 1898). U.S.: Last Apache groups continue to resist government forces (to 1900) to place them on reservations. Britain: Physicist Joseph John Thomson discovers the electron. Doctor Ronald Ross identifies a species of mosquito as the cause of malaria. Irish writer Bram Stoker publishes the horror story *Dracula*. France: Playwright Edmond Rostand's *Cyrano de Bergerac* is produced. Austria: Artist Gustav Klimt founds a group for painters influenced by Art Nouveau.

Plains Indians believed that ghost shirts would protect them from the white man's bullets.

1898 Sudan: Mahdists defeated at Omdurman. Egypt: Britain and French both claim ownership of Fashoda; event which is known as the Fashoda incident. U.S.: Annexes Hawaii. American battleship *Maine* destroyed at Havana, Cuba, provoking Spanish-American War; Cuba becomes independent; U.S. gains Philippines, Guam, and Puerto Rico. China: "Hundred Days of Reform" end when empress dowager Cixi deposes the emperor. Russia leases Port Arthur from China. China: Britain gains the Kowloon Peninsula and the New Territories, on a 99-year lease. France: Pierre and Marie Curie discover radium. Artist Auguste Rodin sculpts *The Kiss*.

The Plains Wars

Many groups of Native Americans lived on the Great Plains of the American west. Some of the larger groups became known as the "Plains nations." White settlers had forced some groups to move west from their original homelands east of the Mississippi River (*see* page 556).

During the 19th century, the number of white settlers spreading westward increased, especially after the Homestead Act of 1862 (*see* page 614). The two different kinds of society came into conflict. When local Native American chiefs signed land agreements with the settlers, the agreements meant different things to the two sides. The settlers' idea of private property meant nothing to the Native Americans who thought they could still use the land to hunt on. A struggle for survival began. Many Native Americans bought guns and attacked the settlers' homesteads, the wagon trains, and the U.S. cavalry.

As the U.S. president Rutherford B. Hayes said in 1877, "Many, if not most, of our Indian wars had their origin in broken promises and acts of injustice." Some army officers advised killing all the Native Americans. Killing the bison, on

▼ At the end of the Civil War, the expanse of land between the Mississippi River and the Rocky Mountains was thought of as a wilderness of plains and mountains. Settlers traveled in long wagon trains to the lands of the West.

▲ *The Native Americans depended on the vast herds of bison for food, clothing, shelter, and fuel. Many bison were killed to supply meat for the railroad gangs.*

Custer

George Custer (1839–1876) became a general during the Civil War. In June 1876 he headed an attack against the Sioux, led by Sitting Bull and Crazy Horse, on the Little Bighorn River in Montana. Custer and 200 of his men died.

Sitting Bull

Sitting Bull (died 1890), was a Sioux chief. He gathered about 4,000 men from the Sioux, Cheyenne, and Arapaho who refused to be herded onto reservations, to fight the U.S. troops. After defeating Custer, he fled to Canada.

which the Plains nations depended for food, was enough. There were about 15 million bison in 1860, but by 1885 only 2,000 were left.

Survivors of the Plains nations were forced onto reservations, often on poor land. They were expected to grow crops. But they resisted government efforts to make them change their way of life. They were used to hunting, and regarded farming as too lowly for them. They were not allowed to become American citizens and had few civil rights. Some of the Plains nations almost died out.

The Boxer Rebellion

Under the weak Qing (Manchu) government, the Chinese empire seemed to be breaking up (*see* page 569). Much of China was dominated by European powers. Powerful groups in China struggled to preserve the country from the Westerners, but they recognized that they would have to copy Western ways and set up new industries.

In 1898, the reformers gained power for a brief time. New laws were passed to turn China into a modern state. But the "Hundred Days of Reform" ended when the empress dowager, Cixi, regained power. Many reformers were executed.

In 1900, a revolt began in northern China against all foreigners. It was led by a secret society called the Society of Harmonious Fists, or "Boxers." They were secretly supported by the Manchu government. The Boxers attacked the European embassies in Peking (Beijing), and killed many Europeans, especially missionaries, as well as Chinese Christians. An international force of eight nations crushed the

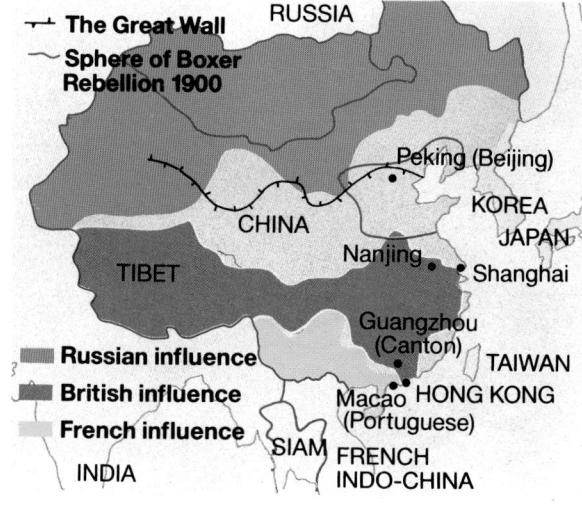

▲ Much of China was under foreign influence by 1905. Russia had taken large border territories in the north and west. The Chinese (Manchu) empire finally collapsed in 1911.

▼ The siege of the embassies in Peking (Beijing) by the Boxers in 1900 ended when American, Japanese, and European soldiers arrived from the coast. The troops quickly put an end to the rebellion before looting the city.

Cixi

The Empress Cixi (1835–1908) was also known as Tz'u-hsi. She seized power from a weak emperor. She prevented reform and encouraged the Boxers. The empress fled from Peking (Beijing) after the Boxer Rebellion.

The last Emperor

P'u-yi (1906–1967) was appointed emperor in 1908 at the age of two. His father, who acted as regent, was a typical Manchu prince, blind to the need for reform. On February 12, 1912, at the age of six, the last emperor of China gave up his throne.

Boxer Rebellion and forced the Chinese government to allow more foreign interference in the country.

Educated Chinese began to plot the overthrow of the Manchu government. In 1905, Sun Yat-sen founded what became the Chinese Nationalist Party, or Kuomintang. Plots and rebellions were organized by other groups too. The Manchu government steadily lost control of the country. In 1911, a powerful general, Yuan Shikai, gave his support to a nationalist rebellion. Manchu authority collapsed, and a republic was declared.

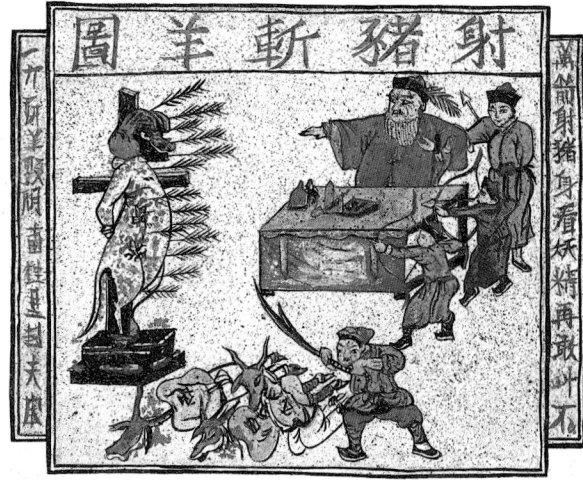

▲ Some Chinese felt extreme hatred for Christianity and Christians. At the time of the rebellion, propaganda cartoons encouraged the murder of Christians.

1899 South Africa: Second Boer War begins (to 1902). Sudan: British-French agreement ends tension over the Fashoda incident. British-Egyptian rule of Sudan established. Netherlands: The Russian tsar, Nicholas II, suggests setting up a permanent court at the Hague to handle international disputes. Finland: Composer Jean Sibelius writes the popular symphony *Finlandia*.

1900 China: In the Boxer Rebellion, nationalists besiege foreign embassies in Peking (Beijing) for two months before international forces relieve the Europeans. Nigeria: Britain establishes protectorates over northern and southern Nigeria. South Africa: The Boers are defeated; Britain annexes the Transvaal and Orange Free State. Germany: The Navy Act leads to faster warship construction, which starts an arms race with Britain.

Britain, Germany, Russia, Italy, and Japan carve up the Chinese "cake" among them, while China looks on, angry and rebellious.

1901 China: Russia occupies Manchuria, an area in northeast China. Australia: Commonwealth established. U.S.: Britain and the U.S. sign Hay-Pauncefort Treaty giving the U.S. authority to build Panama Canal. President McKinley is assassinated; Theodore Roosevelt becomes president. Britain: Queen Victoria dies; Edward VII succeeds her as king. Italian Guglielmo Marconi sends radio signals across the Atlantic. The first Pan-African Conference is held in London. Germany: Novelist Thomas Mann publishes *Buddenbrooks*.

Trade

In 1846 Britain adopted a free trade policy, with no customs duties. This helped to make London into the center of the world's trading system, with much of the business being carried out in pounds sterling. However, when an economic recession began in the 1870s, countries started to protect their own industries by introducing taxes on imports.

The world was roughly divided into producers and manufacturers. The industrial countries of Europe exported manufactured goods and imported raw materials from the producers. However, there were exceptions; the U.S. was a big manufacturer as well as a producer.

▲ In the cities, small shops opened new departments to sell different types of goods. In France, the department store Bon Marché opened in 1850, and by 1900 department stores had opened throughout the U.S.

▼ Cotton was one of the biggest cash crops produced on the plantations of southern U.S. Much of the cotton was exported to Britain, where it was spun into yarn and then woven into cloth in the cotton mills of Lancashire.

▲ Guns were a large item of trade between Europe and non-industrial countries. In the 19th century, increasing numbers were sold to the peoples of Africa. Although they still continued to use their traditional weapons in wars against each other and against Europeans, guns began to have an increasing influence on events.

WHEN IT HAPPENED

1838 British Anti-Corn Law League founded in Manchester to press for free trade.

1854 American clipper *James Baines* sails from London to Melbourne in 63 days.

1859 First A & P (Great Atlantic and Pacific Tea Company) chain store opens in New York.

1860 British-French treaty lays the basis for free trade between the two countries.

1867 Regular steamship service begins between California and the Far East.

1870s–1880s European countries introduce "protection" for their goods against imports.

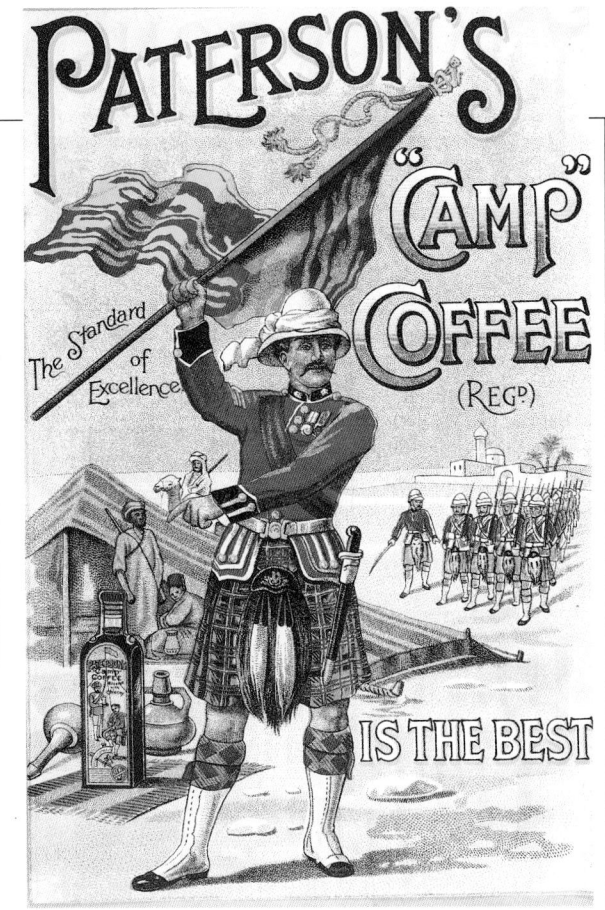

► *Advances in food processing led to the first "convenience foods." Methods of canning food were improving, and millions of cans of food were supplied to the troops during the American Civil War (1861–1865). Soldiers in camp used instant coffee in liquid form. Meat, fish, and fruit could all be frozen by 1908.*

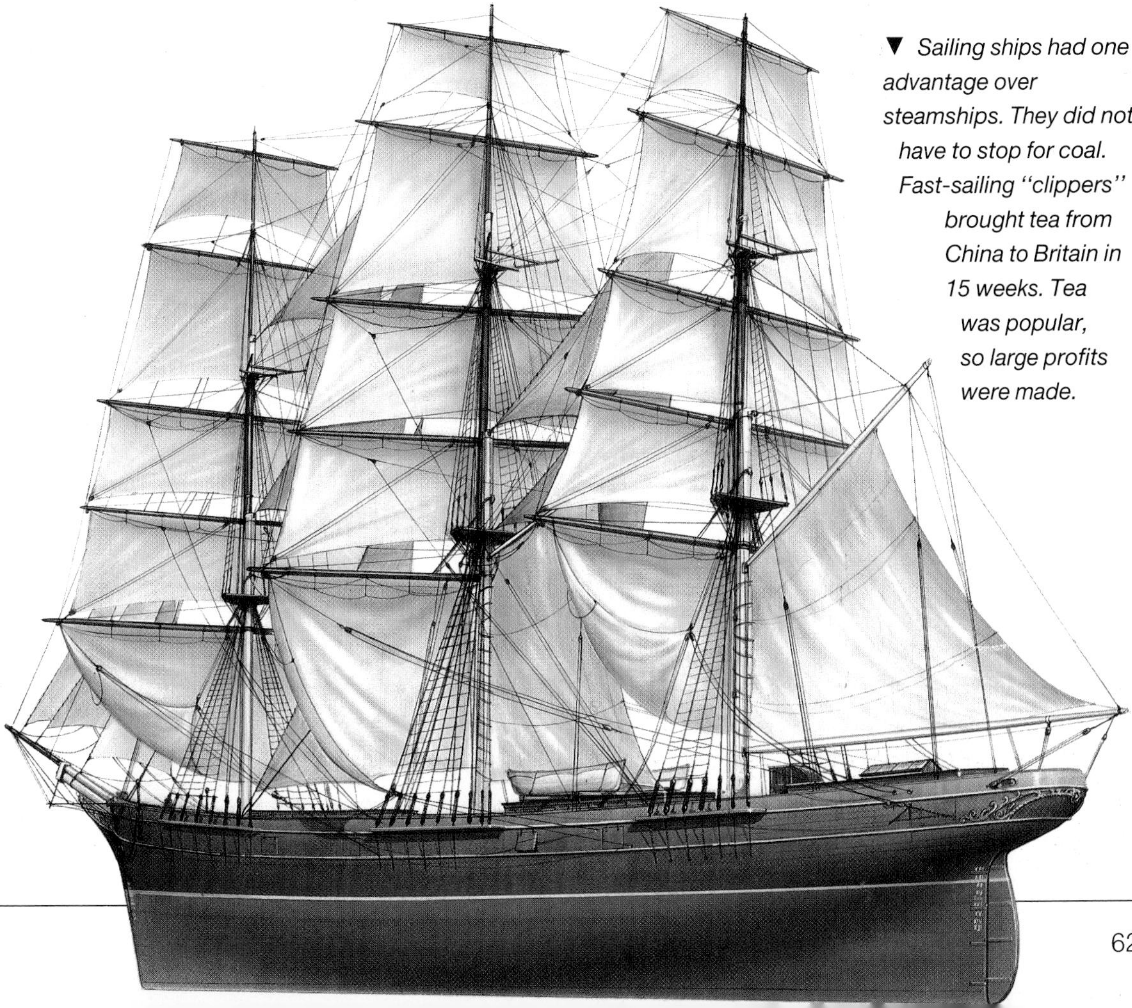

▼ *Sailing ships had one advantage over steamships. They did not have to stop for coal. Fast-sailing "clippers" brought tea from China to Britain in 15 weeks. Tea was popular, so large profits were made.*

1902 Second Boer War ends with the Treaty of Vereeniging. Britain makes a defensive alliance with Japan. Cuba: Republic is declared. Venezuela: British, German, and Italian warships mount a blockade to enforce debt payment. Turks agree to Germans' building Baghdad Railroad, linking Germany to the Persian Gulf. Britain: Beatrix Potter publishes *The Tale of Peter Rabbit*. Ireland: Poet W. B. Yeats writes play *Cathleen ni Houlihan*.

Suffragettes publicized the injustice of the voting system through poster campaigns.

1903 Talks between Britain and France lead to Entente Cordiale (friendly alliance). Central America: Panama becomes independent from Colombia; U.S. leases 10 mile (16km) wide Panama canal zone. Serbia: King is assassinated. West Africa: Britain captures Kano and Sokoto, both part of the Fulani empire. Britain: Women's Social and Political Union formed to fight for votes for women. Russia: Vladimir Lenin leads the Bolsheviks in split from Mensheviks. U.S.: Wright brothers fly their aircraft in North Carolina.

1904 Entente Cordiale is confirmed by settlement of outstanding colonial disputes. Far East: Japan attacks Russians at Port Arthur, starting Russo-Japanese War (to 1905). Britain: writer J. M. Barrie's play *Peter Pan* performed. Russia: Dramatist Anton Chekhov's play *The Cherry Orchard* is performed. U.S.: The first cars start running in the New York City subway.

Votes for Women

During the early 19th, century only men who owned property had the right to vote for an elected government. This meant that poor people, as well as women and American slaves were excluded. The Chartist movement in Britain led the way for political reform, but only demanded votes for men.

In the middle of the 19th century a worldwide movement began with the aim of winning the vote for women. In 1848 a women's rights convention was held in New York State by two famous American reformers, Lucretia Mott and Elizabeth Cady Stanton. This was the first of many public meetings in the U.S.

Supporters of votes for women were given the name suffragettes. "Suffrage" means the right to vote. A famous British suffragette, Emmeline Pankhurst set up the Women's Social and Political Union (WSPU) in 1903. She believed in "deeds,

AMERICAN SUFFRAGE

The women's rights movement in the U.S. developed from the crusade of antislavery reformers. Sojourner Truth (*left*) was a Black American who became famous for her stand against slavery and support of women's rights. Born a slave in 1771, she escaped and moved north. In 1843, prompted by a religious urge to preach, she traveled around the country, drawing large crowds to her lectures. Harriet Tubman was also a noted speaker on these issues. These women, together with others, including Lucretia Mott, Elizabeth Cady Stanton, Susan B. Anthony, and Lucy Stone, helped to lay the foundations for women's suffrage in the U.S., often in the face of fierce opposition.

not words." Her campaign involved attacks against property, nonpayment of taxes, and public demonstrations. In 1913, at the Derby (an important horse race), one suffragette, Emily Davison, threw herself under a horse owned by the British king and was killed. The outbreak of World War I interrupted the activities of the WSPU but other groups continued to support the movement.

New Zealand gave voting rights to everyone in 1893. In 1918, Britain granted the vote to women aged over 30. In 1920, the 19th Amendment to the U.S. Constitution gave suffrage to women, although several states already permitted women to vote in local elections.

◄ *Many suffragettes were sent to prison for disturbing the peace, often going on hunger strike to continue to draw attention to their cause. Many were forcibly fed, which was both painful and dangerous.*

▼ *In Britain and the United States women took to the streets in peaceful demonstrations to gain public support for their campaign to give women the vote.*

1905 Far East: Japanese defeat Russians on land and at sea; war ended by Treaty of Portsmouth. Russia: Revolution starts; tsar issues manifesto promising reforms. Morocco: Germany seeks to limit French influence. Norway: Independence from Sweden is gained. India: Muslim League is founded. British partition of Bengal provokes nationalist riots. Ireland: Sinn Fein Party founded. Switzerland: German physicist Albert Einstein forms the theory of relativity. France: Henri Matisse and other artists nicknamed Fauves (wild beasts) exhibit their work.

1906 French rights in Morocco confirmed by Algeciras Conference. Australia: Protective duties introduced on some imports. France: Convicted Jewish army officer Dreyfus declared innocent of treason by appeal court. Persia (Iran): Liberal revolution. Russia: First national assembly (Duma) meets.

1907 At the Hague peace conference Germany rejects limits on arms. British entente with Russia leads to Triple Entente with Britain, France, and Russia. Russia: Second Duma dismissed; third Duma starts (to 1912). Nicaragua: U.S. supports revolution. South Africa: Gandhi leads a civil disobedience campaign in support of Indian rights. New Zealand becomes a dominion of the British empire. Spain: Pablo Picasso completes *Les Demoiselles d'Avignon*, first Cubist painting.

Peter Fabergé was a jeweler for the tsars of Russia. His most well-known pieces are the gold and jewel-encrusted Easter eggs he made for Alexander II and Nicolas II.

Russia

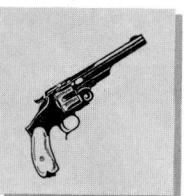

After Russia lost the Crimean War (*see* pages 576–577), the tsar, Alexander II, realized that his country was lagging behind the rest of Europe and needed reform. The economy was based on agriculture which depended on the labor of serfs (peasants tied to the land and who had few rights).

Alexander II introduced a number of reforms. The serfs were freed, and education was improved. Some steps were taken toward democracy in local government. Some radical groups felt that the reforms did not go far enough. Riots, strikes, and outbreaks of violence were common. Some people wanted an

Marx

Karl Marx (1818–1883) was a political thinker of the 19th century, and a founder of communism. Marx's theories (Marxism) taught that capitalist governments (who allow private business) could be overthrown by the working class. The Bolsheviks were followers of Marxism, which later inspired communists all over the world.

Nicholas II

1868 Born.
1894 Becomes tsar. Marries Alexandra.
1898 Forms an alliance with France.
1905 Forced to issue the October Manifesto granting constitutional and democratic rights.
1917 The Russian Revolution. Nicholas is forced to abdicate and imprisoned.
1918 Murdered by the Bolsheviks, together with his family.

◄ The peasants formed the mass of the Russian people. To reformers in St. Petersburg, the peasants were of great importance. They wanted to end their backwardness and make them part of educated Russian society. The peasants themselves, however, were not rebellious. They were too busy trying to scratch a living, like these women hauling barges down the Volga River.

end to the imperial system, and this led to the assassination of the tsar in 1881.

When the new tsar Alexander III came to the throne, he wanted a return to the old system, and reversed all Alexander II's reforms. Local assemblies were abolished. Books and newspapers were censored, and police power increased.

Meanwhile, Russian expansion into Manchuria (now part of China) led to the outbreak of the Russo-Japanese War in 1904. Japan attacked and drove the Russians out. The defeat showed the government to be inefficient, as well as harsh. In January 1905, troops fired on striking workers in St. Petersburg, and riots broke out. The new tsar, Nicholas II, issued a declaration promising civil rights and a national parliament (Duma).

The government did not keep its promises. Elections were managed so that reformers were kept out of the Duma. Opponents of the government were arrested, and the leaders fled.

▼ The Russo-Japanese War (1904–1905) began with a Japanese attack on Port Arthur (Lushun). At the battle of Tsushima the Russian fleet was totally destroyed.

1908 Congo Free State (now Zaire): Belgian state takes over from personal rule of King Leopold. Morocco: The sultan is deposed. Balkans: Austria-Hungary empire annexes Bosnia-Herzegovina. Crete: Island proclaims union with mainland Greece. Turkey: The Young Turks lead a revolt for a more liberal government (to 1909). Bulgaria proclaims full independence. Australia: Parliament passes the Pensions Act and introduces the general Customs Tariff Act. Britain: Boy Scouts movement founded by Robert Baden-Powell. Writer Kenneth Grahame publishes *The Wind in the Willows.*

1909 Turkey: The sultan is deposed. American explorer Robert Peary reaches the North Pole. Iran: Oil drilling begins. France: aviator Louis Blériot flies across the English Channel. Russian ballet master Sergei Diaghilev sets up the Ballets Russes company in Paris.

1910 Union of South Africa founded as British dominion. Mexico: Outbreak of revolution (to 1940). Portugal: Revolution; republic proclaimed. Far East: Japan officially annexes Korea. Britain: Suffragettes adopt violent tactics in campaign for women's right to vote. Girl Guides founded. Russia: Artist Wassily Kandinsky adopts abstract style in painting. Composer Igor Stravinsky writes the ballet music *The Firebird.*

An Aborigine ritual dance. Aborigines expressed their close relationship with the environment through dance, music, songs, and their religion.

Australia

During the 19th century, the new nation of Australia was created. The white population had expanded from small settlements of convicts (*see* pages 512–513) into colonies of free settlers, administered from Great Britain.

Early settlements were founded along the coast, but explorers gradually opened up the interior, closely followed by pioneers looking for new grazing land for their sheep. As the wool industry grew, so did the demand for land. Many drove their sheep beyond the official settlement limits, earning the name "squatters."

▼ *Aborigines led a way of life based around tribal territories and customs. Although the spread of European settlement destroyed much of this, they retained a strong cultural identity.*

Though later granted grazing rights, the name stuck. They gradually spread into the interior, acquiring land as they went.

As the squatters moved across the country, they came into conflict with the Aborigines. The Aboriginal culture was threatened and their land was taken over by the squatters. In Van Diemen's Land, later renamed Tasmania, the whole

The Kelly Gang

Ned Kelly (*left*) and his gang were bushrangers (bandits) who roamed the country staging hold-ups and raiding banks. The Kelly Gang were notorious outlaws, but were seen by some as heroes, fighting the rich to help the poor. Ned, who often wore homemade armor, was captured in 1880 and hanged.

Aboriginal population was wiped out.

Squatter settlement also created problems later on when immigrants, attracted by the gold rushes of the 1850s, and ex-convicts demanded that land be made available for smallholdings. Many failed to gain land because of opposition from squatters and the unsuitability of much of the land for farming.

Britain had granted self-government to all colonies by the 1890s. At the same time, a sense of nationalism was growing. In 1900 after fierce arguments, the colonies agreed to unite in a federation. The Commonwealth of Australia was proclaimed on the first day of 1901 and Canberra was chosen as the federal capital.

▶ Robert O'Hara Burke and William Wills were the first Europeans to cross Australia. Their expedition of 18 men set out in 1860 to travel from Melbourne to the Gulf of Carpentaria. They suffered terribly from starvation and exhaustion on the journey back. Only one man, who had been helped by the Aborigines, was found alive by the search party.

▼ The colonies were granted self-government before 1890. New South Wales originally occupied the whole of eastern Australia, but was eventually divided.

War and Weapons

In this period, improvements to guns meant they could be fired faster. The power of ammunition also increased. The improvements in communications and transportation changed the ways in which battles could be fought. However, cavalry (soldiers on horseback) was still an important part of any army, and soldiers still carried swords. Changes in naval warfare were even greater. Ships were made from steel instead of wood, and coal or oil took over from sails. The firepower of the first *Dreadnought* battleship (1906) was greater than the whole British fleet 100 years earlier.

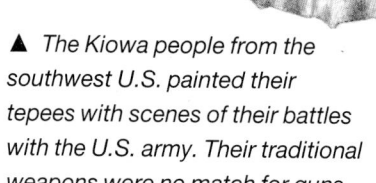

▲ The Kiowa people from the southwest U.S. painted their tepees with scenes of their battles with the U.S. army. Their traditional weapons were no match for guns.

▶ The Gatling gun was invented during the American Civil War. It had a cluster of barrels which fired one after another as a handle was turned.

▶ The biggest weapons' maker in Europe was the Krupp works at Essen in Germany. This 50-ton steel cannon was shown at the Paris Exhibition in 1867. Three years later it was being used in the war against the French.

◀ Balloons were used for observation in the American Civil War. One of the observers was a retired German army officer named Zeppelin. He was an inventor of airships that are sometimes called Zeppelins after him. Airships were better than balloons because they could move under their own power. By 1913 several countries had them.

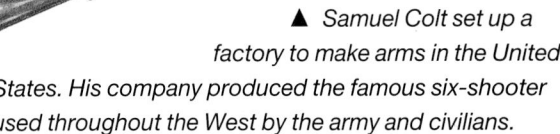

▲ Samuel Colt set up a factory to make arms in the United States. His company produced the famous six-shooter used throughout the West by the army and civilians.

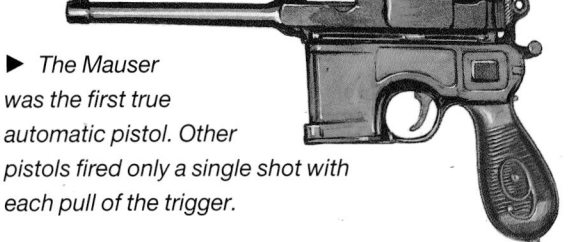

► The Mauser was the first true automatic pistol. Other pistols fired only a single shot with each pull of the trigger.

▲ Alfred Nobel (1833–1896) was a Swedish chemist and explosives expert. Dynamite was his most famous invention. On his death, he left his fortune to found the Nobel prizes, including the peace prize.

WHEN IT HAPPENED

1850 Krupp produces the first all-steel guns.

1854 First use of mines to protect a harbor.

1859 French frigate *Gloire* is first warship with armor-plated hull.

1864 A Union warship is sunk by a torpedo from a Confederate "submersible."

1884 Maxim perfects the first true machine gun.

1899 International agreement at the Hague not to drop bombs or use poison gas.

1902 John M. Browning develops the Browning automatic pistol.

1914 Tear-gas shells developed in Germany.

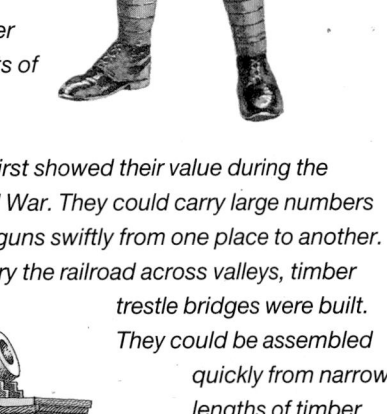

► Soldiers' uniforms used to be colorful and uncomfortable. The British army, for example, was famous for its red uniforms. Khaki was adopted by troops in India by 1857 and was later used in other parts of the empire.

▼ Railroads first showed their value during the American Civil War. They could carry large numbers of troops and guns swiftly from one place to another. To carry the railroad across valleys, timber trestle bridges were built. They could be assembled quickly from narrow lengths of timber.

The Balkan Wars

As the Ottoman empire shrank, the Balkan states in the southeast corner of Europe began to want independence. They were encouraged by Russia and Austria-Hungary who each did not want the other to increase its influence there. Britain and Germany also supported Austria-Hungary to stop Russia's getting access to ice-free ports and the Mediterranean.

Greece was the first to rebel (*see* page 552), becoming independent in 1829. In 1878, Montenegro, Serbia, and Romania became independent, and Bulgaria gained self-government. Austria-Hungary occupied the Ottoman territory of Bosnia-Herzegovina in 1908 so that it would not fall under the growing power of Serbian nationalists in the region. Albania and Macedonia remained under Ottoman control.

In March 1912 Serbia and Bulgaria made a secret treaty to attack Turkey and divide the Ottoman territory between themselves. The Balkan League of Serbia, Bulgaria, Greece, and Montenegro was formed in October and by the end of

Peter I

1844 Born.
1870 Fights in Franco-Prussian War.
1903 Elected king.
1916 Exiled to Greece.
1918 Returns, and is proclaimed king of Serbs, Croats, and Slovenes.
1921 Dies.

Ferdinand I

1861 Born.
1908 Proclaims Bulgaria independent from Ottoman empire and becomes king.
1912 Joins Balkan League against Turkey.
1918 Abdicates.
1948 Dies.

▼ *The Balkans had long been a dangerous and violent area. The power of the Ottoman empire was fading, and Russian power was growing. Austria-Hungary was trying to hold its own.*

▶ *The Ottoman Turks were defeated in 1912, because they were also fighting the Italians in North Africa. The Young Turks movement was also battling against the old regime of the sultan.*

The Balkan Peninsula 1912

RUSSIA
AUSTRIA-HUNGARY
Belgrade
ROMANIA
• Bucharest
Bosnia
SERBIA
BULGARIA
MONTENEGRO
Sofia •
Albania
Istanbul •
ITALY
Macedonia
Ottoman empire
GREECE
Ionian Sea
Athens •
Mediterranean Sea

The Balkan Peninsula 1914

RUSSIA
AUSTRIA-HUNGARY
Belgrade
ROMANIA
• Bucharest
SERBIA
BULGARIA
MONTENEGRO
Sofia •
Albania
Istanbul •
Macedonia
TURKEY
Ionian Sea
GREECE
• Athens
Mediterranean Sea

the month they were all at war with Turkey. The First Balkan War ended in 1913 after the defeat of the Turks. Serbia and Greece gained territory in Macedonia, while Bulgaria extended its territory to the Aegean Sea. Albania declared itself an independent Muslim principality in December 1912. Austria-Hungary supported Albanian independence because it wanted to stop

Serbia's expanding to the Adriatic.

The peace settlement led to disagreements among the victors. Bulgaria had gained far more territory than Serbia, which wanted more territory in Macedonia. Bulgaria's three former allies combined against it. The Second Balkan War broke out in June 1913 when Bulgaria declared war on Serbia and Greece. Romania and Turkey joined against Bulgaria. The Bulgarians were surrounded and overpowered. In the Treaty of Bucharest (August 1913), Macedonia was divided between Greece and Serbia, and Romania gained some of Bulgaria. This settlement greatly increased the size of Serbia.

1911 Morocco: Germany sends gunboat to Agadir but withdraws as France stands firm. Italy conquers Libya, leading to Italian-Turkish War (to 1912). Mexico: Dictator Porfirio Diaz resigns. China: Revolution leads to fall of Qing dynasty; Sun Yat-sen proclaimed provisional president. Russia: Prime minister Peter Stolypin is assassinated. Britain: Scientist Ernest Rutherford discovers structure of the atom. Roald Amundsen's Norwegian expedition reaches the South Pole ahead of Captain Robert Scott's British team.

1912 Italian-Turkish war ended by Treaty of Ouchy: Italy gains Tripoli (Libya). First Balkan War (to 1913): Ottoman Turks defeated by Balkan League. South Africa: African National Congress founded. North Atlantic liner *Titanic* sinks. Britain and France agree naval strategy. U.S.: Woodrow Wilson becomes president. The American Indian Jim Thorpe is star of the Stockholm Olympics.

1913 Ireland: Ulster Volunteers formed to oppose home rule. Treaty of London ends First Balkan War: Albania gains independence. Second Balkan War: Bulgaria defeated by former allies. Britain: Novelist D. H. Lawrence publishes *Sons and Lovers*. U.S.: Charlie Chaplin makes his first film. Henry Ford opens his first assembly line.

1914 German East Africa: Railway built from Lake Tanganyika to Dar es Salaam.

The Balkan countries were seen by Europe as a boiling pot of troubles.

The Brink of War

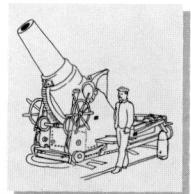

Serbia's success in the Balkan Wars had made it powerful. This alarmed Austria-Hungary who feared that Serbia wanted to create a Slav state, including the large Slav population living in Austria-Hungary. Other Balkan people, Croatians, Bosnians, and Slovenes, also feared the Serbians.

At the same time, the newly unified Germany (*see* pages 592–593) was increasing its power and threatening its neighbors. Germany's plans to expand its African empire led it into a dispute with France over Morocco. The German navy was threatening British supremacy at sea. Russia also became alarmed at Germany's military power.

These threats split Europe into two powerful opposing groups of countries. Britain and France formed the Entente Cordiale in 1904. When Russia joined in 1907 it became known as the Triple Entente. Germany, Italy, and Austria-Hungary were members of the Triple Alliance. Most other European nations were either allied with or under the control of one of these alliances.

▲ In response to the fast-growing German navy, the British produced Dreadnought. It was the first of the modern battleships and had immense firepower. Other countries soon started building similar ships.

Triple Alliance (Germany, Austria-Hungary and Italy)

Triple Entente (Great Britain, Russia and France)

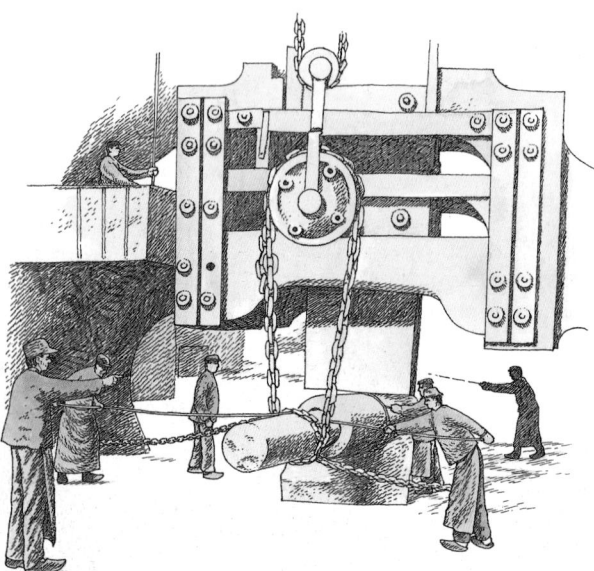

◄ A huge armaments' industry was built up in Europe. Guns fired more rapidly and accurately than before. Armies were expanded to meet the increased threat.

▲ By 1914, Europe was split into two opposing groups, The Triple Alliance and the Triple Entente. If two countries went to war, others were likely to be drawn in.

The World at War

The years from 1914 to 1949 saw the world go through a period of rapid change. When World War I broke out in 1914, it made use of all the latest technology, and speeded up the change in the role of women in society. While World War I was taking place, there was a revolt against British rule in Ireland and there were two revolutions in Russia. The first Russian Revolution forced the tsar to abdicate, while the second turned Russia into a communist country. After the war, the borders of Europe were redrawn and a number of new states emerged. Between the wars, two political beliefs had a great influence in some parts of the world. The first was communism, the second was fascism.

However, perhaps the most far-reaching event of the time between the wars was the Wall Street Crash of 1929. Many people and companies went bankrupt, and millions became unemployed all over the world as buyers could no longer afford their products. However, the years from 1914 to 1949 saw many improvements in education, medicine, and health care. In agriculture, the development of fertilizers and chemicals made higher yields possible. New household appliances meant that housework took less time and was easier. Transportation also improved, enabling people to travel farther and faster.

The changes were speeded up by World War II, from which both the U.S. and the USSR emerged as superpowers. The jet engine and the atomic bomb were developed, and advances in medicine helped civilians and soldiers who were injured in the conflicts.

When peace came again, it brought with it demands for greater equality. It also brought demands for independence from many of the countries which were still ruled as colonies of European powers. In some countries these demands were met peacefully, but in others they led to war and bloodshed.

▼ *In World War I soldiers had to go "over the top" of a trench and face enemy bullets. Although World War I was known as "the war to end all wars," World War II broke out just over 20 years later.*

The Americas

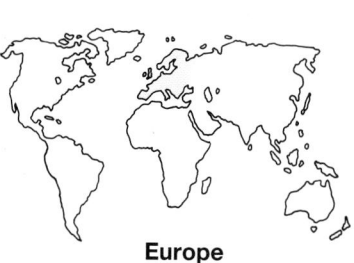

Europe

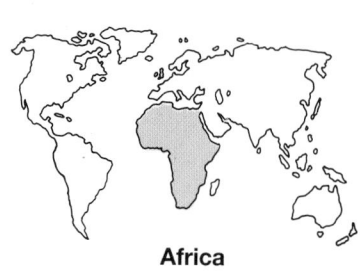

Africa

1914 The Panama Canal is opened.
1917 U.S.A. declares war on Germany.

1920 Congress rejects Versailles Treaty.

1926 U.S. troops land in Nicaragua.
1927 First solo Atlantic crossing by Charles Lindbergh.
1929 The Wall Street Crash.
1930 Revolutions in Brazil and Argentina.
1932–1935 War between Paraguay and Bolivia.
1933–1945 Franklin Delano Roosevelt is U.S. president.
1939 Battle of the River Plate.
1941 U.S.A. enters World War II.

1943 Juan Perón leads a revolt in Argentina.
1945 The United Nations Organization is founded.
1946 Juan Perón is elected president of Argentina.
1948 The Marshall Plan for economic recovery in Europe is set up by the U.S.A.
1949 The U.S. Senate ratifies the North Atlantic Treaty.

1914–1918 World War I.
1916 The Easter Rising in Ireland against British rule.
1917 The Russian Revolution.
1919 The Versailles Peace Settlement establishes new countries in eastern Europe. League of Nations is formed.
1922 Irish Free State is established.
1923 Italy becomes a fascist state.
1929 Yugoslavia becomes name of the kingdom of Croats, Serbs, and Slovenes.
1933 Hitler takes power in Germany.
1936–1939 Spanish Civil War.
1938 Germany annexes Austria. Germany, Britain, France, and Italy sign the Munich Pact.
1939 Germany invades Poland.
1939–1945 World War II.
1941 Germany invades USSR.
1945 By the end of the war the Nazis had killed about 6 million Jews – the Holocaust.
1945 Germany surrenders, ending World War II.
1945–1946 Nuremberg war trials.
1948 Communist governments take power in Eastern Europe.
1948–1949 Berlin Airlift.
1949 NATO is formed. Ireland becomes a republic. Germany is divided into East and West.

1914–1918 World War I.

1922 Egypt is declared independent from British and French influence.
1925–1926 Abd-el-Krim leads an Arab uprising in Morocco. It is crushed by France and Spain.

1935 Italian forces invade Ethiopia.

1939–1945 World War II.

1941 Allied troops take Benghazi.
1942 The battle of El Alamein in Egypt.

1949 The apartheid policy is introduced in South Africa.

Middle East

1914-1918 World War I.

1917 Britain issues the Balfour Declaration, promising a Jewish homeland in Palestine.

1923 The Ottoman empire ends. Turkish Republic established under Mustafa Kemal (Atatürk).

1932 Saudi Arabia united.

1939–1945 World War II.

1943 Lebanon gains independence from France.

1946 Syria becomes independent of France.
1947–1948 Palestine is partitioned and the Jewish state of Israel is set up.
1948 War between the Arab League and Israel.

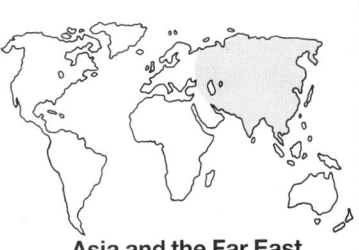

Asia and the Far East

1914-1918 World War I.

1919 Amritsar massacre in India.
1920 Nationalist movement formed in India.

1924 New government in China under Sun Yat-sen.
1926 Emperor Hirohito ascends the Japanese throne.
1927–1937 Chinese Civil War.
1931 The Japanese occupy Manchuria.
1934–1935 Mao Zedong's Long March.
1935 The Government of India Act creates a new Indian constitution.
1937 The Japanese capture Shanghai and Beijing.
1939-1945 World War II.
1940 Japan joins the Axis Powers.
1944 The battle of Leyte Gulf off the Philippines.
1945 Atomic bombs dropped on Hiroshima and Nagasaki.
1946–1954 War over French control of Indochina.
1947 India and Pakistan gain independence from Britain.
1948 Gandhi is assassinated.
1949 The Dutch grant independence to Indonesia. The Communist Party takes control in China.

Australasia and Pacific

1914–1918 World War I.

1920 Australia and Japan acquire former German colonies in the Pacific.

1927 The federal capital of Australia is transferred from Melbourne to Canberra.

1939–1945 World War II.
1941 The Japanese bomb Pearl Harbor, Hawaii, and bring the U.S. into World War II.
1942 The Japanese capture islands in the Pacific and threaten Australia.

The World

Almost the whole world was affected by World War I, the Great Depression, and World War II. In **North America**, the United States adopted a policy of isolation between the wars, but joined the Allied side in World War II. In **South America**, right wing governments came to power in Argentina and Brazil.

In **Europe**, civil wars broke out in Ireland, Spain, and Greece, and revolution in Russia led to civil war there, too.

In the **Middle East**, the Ottoman empire collapsed after World War I, and Israel was founded in 1948 as a homeland for the Jewish people.

In **Africa**, Italy's attempts to build an empire failed, and many countries began campaigning for independence. **India** gained independence from Britain but part of it was partitioned to form Pakistan.

Civil war divided **China**, while **Japanese** expansion was one of the causes of World War II. Many people emigrated to **Australia** and **New Zealand**, while the Pacific became a battle zone in World War II.

▶ Some of the most savage fighting in World War I took place in northwestern Europe, but the consequences of the war reached right around the world.

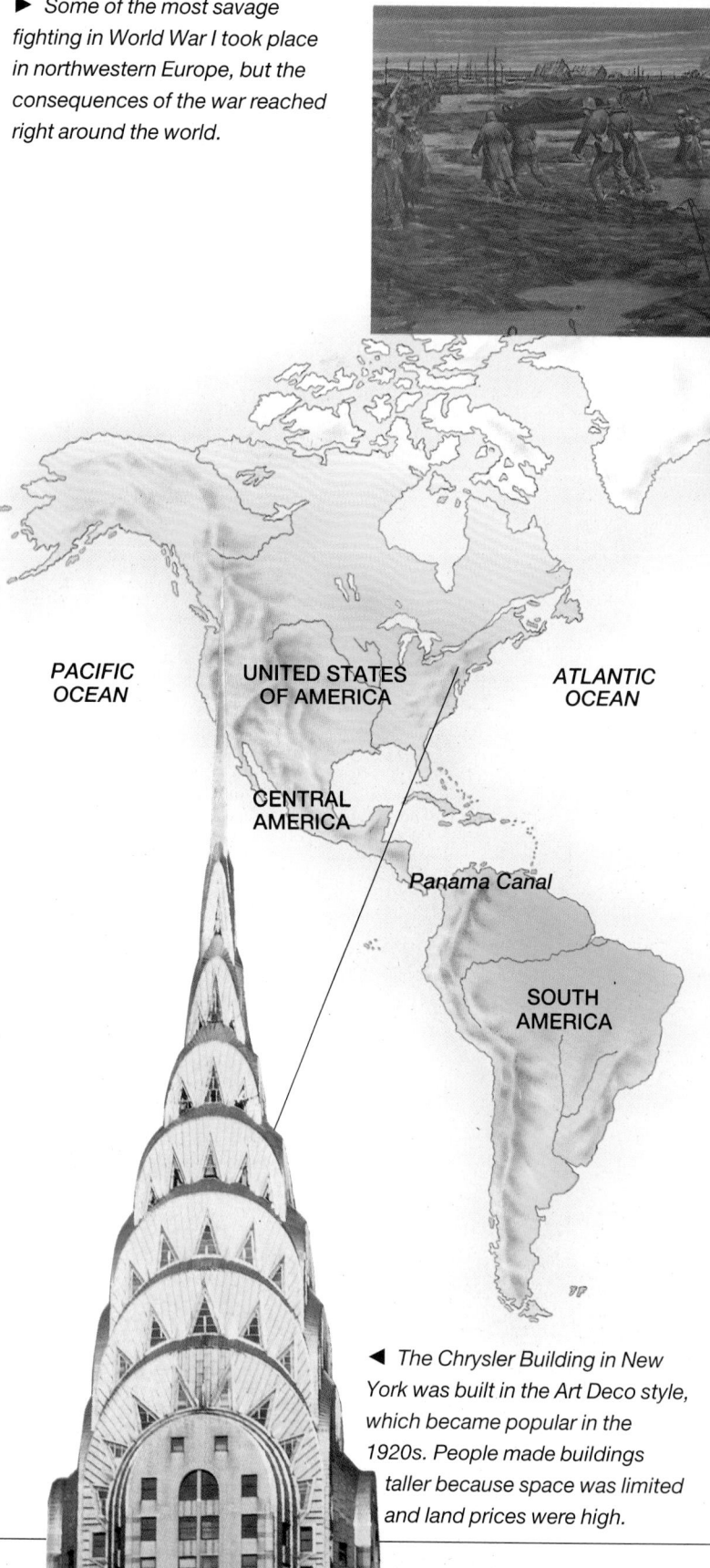

PACIFIC OCEAN

UNITED STATES OF AMERICA

ATLANTIC OCEAN

CENTRAL AMERICA

Panama Canal

SOUTH AMERICA

◀ The Chrysler Building in New York was built in the Art Deco style, which became popular in the 1920s. People made buildings taller because space was limited and land prices were high.

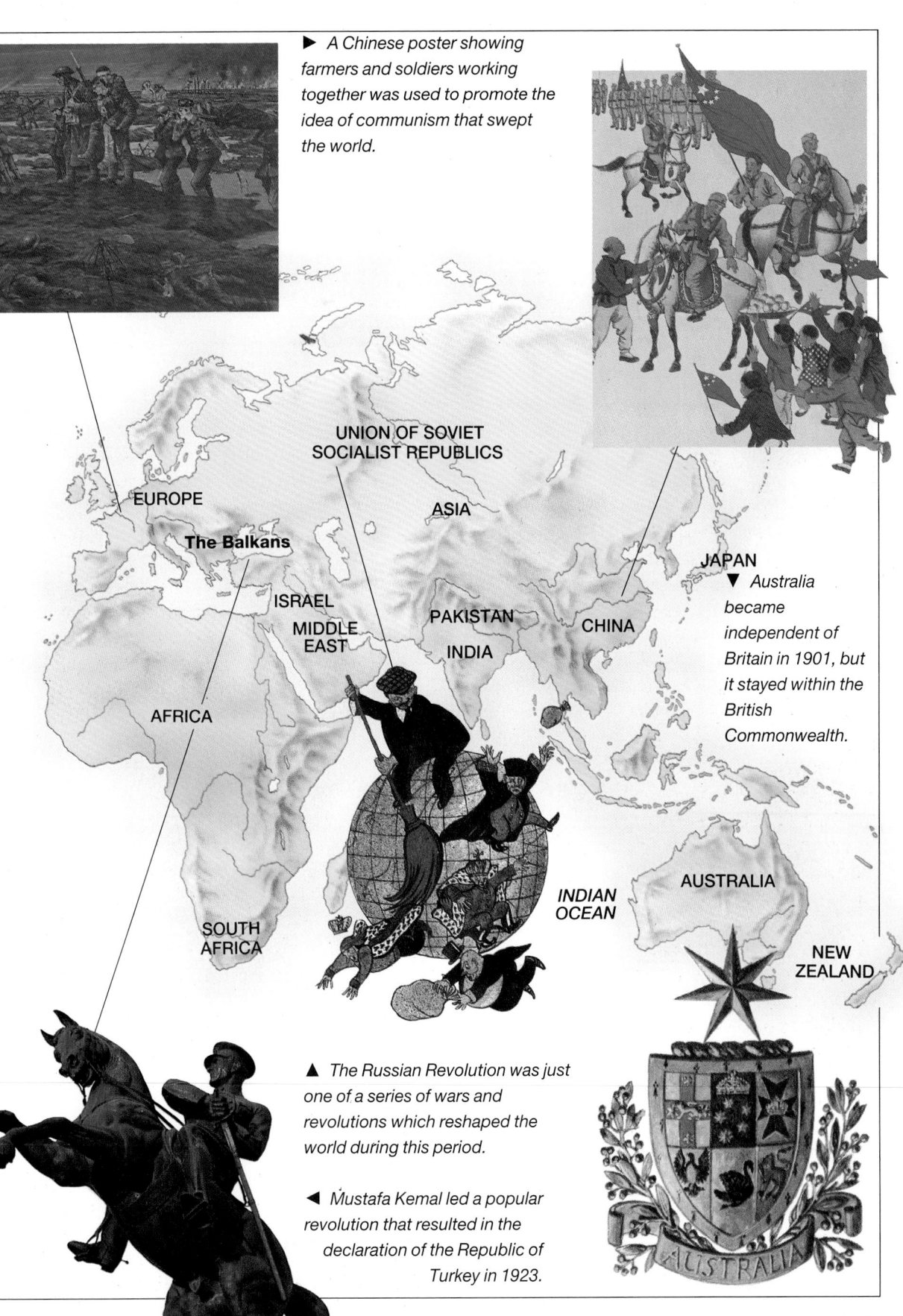

▶ A Chinese poster showing farmers and soldiers working together was used to promote the idea of communism that swept the world.

UNION OF SOVIET
SOCIALIST REPUBLICS

EUROPE

The Balkans

ASIA

JAPAN

▼ Australia became independent of Britain in 1901, but it stayed within the British Commonwealth.

ISRAEL

MIDDLE EAST

PAKISTAN

INDIA

CHINA

AFRICA

INDIAN OCEAN

AUSTRALIA

SOUTH AFRICA

NEW ZEALAND

▲ The Russian Revolution was just one of a series of wars and revolutions which reshaped the world during this period.

◀ Mustafa Kemal led a popular revolution that resulted in the declaration of the Republic of Turkey in 1923.

AUSTRALIA

1914 Central America: Panama Canal opens to shipping. It is controlled by the United States and links the Atlantic and Pacific Oceans. Europe: Archduke Franz Ferdinand, heir to the Austro-Hungarian empire, is assassinated at Sarajevo by a Serbian student on June 28. Austria declares war on Serbia on July 28. Russia mobilizes its troops to defend Serbia. Germany declares war on Russia on August 1, and on France on August 3. Britain declares war on Germany on August 4. World War I starts (to 1918).

Germany invades Belgium. The battle of Mons is the first of the frontier battles, most of which end in favor of Germany. Eastern Front: Germans defeat Russians at the battles of Tannenberg and Masurian Lakes, forcing Russians to retreat from East Prussia.

Western Front: At battle of the Marne, Allies halt German advance on Paris.

First battle of Ypres prevents German army reaching the Channel ports. By the end of 1914, armies from both sides are locked in trench warfare on Eastern and Western Fronts. British troops arrive from all parts of the empire to help the Allied cause. The Irish Home Rule Bill, which provides for a separate parliament in Ireland, is suspended until after the war. The first single-seater fighter planes are built. Middle East: Mesopotamian Campaign to protect oil supply begins.

A wartime propaganda poster showing Germany grabbing at Europe.

Start of World War I

By 1914, there was much rivalry among the European powers over trade and colonies, as well as over military and naval strength. This rivalry led some countries to form alliances to defend themselves. The main alliance was the Triple Alliance, made up of Germany, Italy, and Austria-Hungary (*see* page 636). In this alliance, an attack on any one country would bring its allies to its defense. Another agreement, the Triple Entente, was made between Britain, France, and Russia. It was not a military alliance, but its members had agreed to cooperate against Germany.

The Triple Alliance was tested after the assassination of Archduke Franz Ferdinand, heir to the Austro-Hungarian empire, and his wife in Sarajevo on June 28, 1914. The assassination led Austria to declare war on Serbia on 28 July. Russia mobilized its troops to defend Serbia from Austria. This led

▼ *Gavrilo Princip told police that he shot Franz Ferdinand as a protest against the oppression of the Serbian people who lived in Bosnia.*

◄ *When the war began, thousands of men on each side rushed to volunteer for the armed forces. They were encouraged by recruitment posters like this British one. At the beginning of the war, people on all sides thought that it would be brief, but instead it lasted for four years.*

THE BUILDUP TO WAR

Before World War I broke out, Britain and Germany competed to build bigger and better ships for their navies. Their armies started out less evenly matched, with the British forces sometimes outnumbered by the Germans. Both sides raced to make more and more deadly weapons, such as machine guns and poison gas. They thought that using these weapons would make the war shorter than other wars, but it lasted for four years and was the bloodiest conflict in human history.

Germany to declare war on Russia on August 1. On August 3 Germany declared war on Russia's ally, France. On August 4 the German army invaded Belgium on their way to France.

The German invasion of a neutral country, Belgium, brought Britain into the war. Britain went to Belgium's defense and declared war on Germany on August 4. During the war, Britain, France, and Russia were known as the Allies, or Allied Powers. Germany, Italy, Austria-Hungary, and their allies were known as the Central Powers.

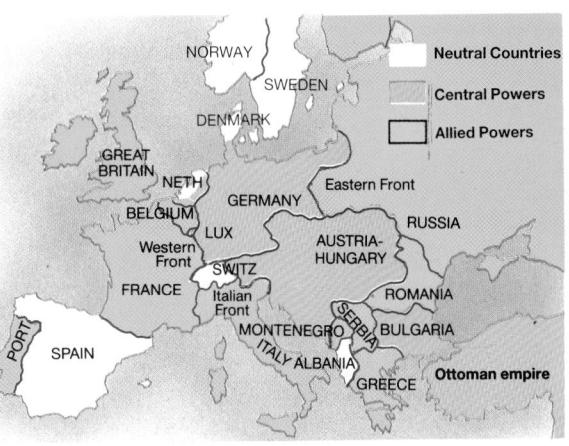

▲ *World War I divided Europe into two, with fighting taking place on an Eastern Front and a Western Front.*

▼ *When war broke out, men on all sides were eager to "do their duty" and volunteer.*

Battles of World War I

During World War I, fighting took place in several areas. There was a Western Front between Germany and northern France, and an Eastern Front between Germany and the Russian forces. There was also fighting at sea and in the Middle East, where the Allied Powers attacked the Ottoman empire.

On the Western Front, French and British troops, together with thousands of men from Australia, Canada, New Zealand, and South Africa, occupied a network of deep trenches from September 1914. Facing them, across a few hundred yards of ground known as No Man's Land, were trenches occupied by the Germans. Millions of men were killed on the Western Front in battles such as Ypres, Verdun, and the Somme, and on routine patrols.

The Eastern Front ran from the Baltic to the Black Sea and also had its lines of trenches to which the Russians retreated after being defeated in Germany in September 1914. In an attempt to send reinforcements to Russia through the

▲ At the third battle of Ypres in 1917 many drowned in a sea of mud caused by heavy rain and the effects of bombardment. These Australian troops are using duckboards to cross what was once woods.

▼ Troops landing at Gallipoli to try to capture the Dardanelles. The Allied Powers had underestimated the strength of the Turkish forces and the Australians alone suffered 8,587 men killed and 19,367 wounded.

▲ *Jutland was the only major sea battle of World War I. Britain and Germany both claimed victory, but after the battle the German fleet stayed in the Baltic.*

Black Sea, British, Australian, and New Zealand troops attacked the Dardanelles Strait in 1915. Politicians and military commanders bungled this campaign, however, and thousands of men were killed without the Dardanelles' being captured. The war had reached a stalemate. Then the U.S.A. declared war on Germany in April 1917 and prepared to send troops to Europe.

▼ *The Western Front stretched across Belgium and northeast France. Millions of men were killed along it between 1914 and 1918, but its line never moved more than 10 miles (15 km) in any direction.*

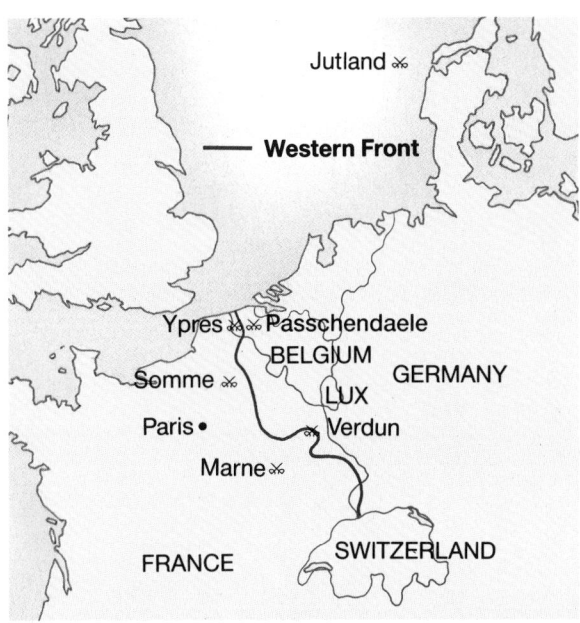

1915 Britain announces a naval blockade of Germany in the hope of preventing food and supplies getting in. Germany retaliates by starting a submarine blockade of Britain. Gallipoli Campaign: Joint British and French fleet tries to force a way through the Dardanelles. Allied troops, mainly from Australia and New Zealand, are landed on the beaches of Gallipoli, Turkey. Strong Turkish opposition leaves thousands of Allied troops dead or wounded. The Campaign fails and all remaining troops are withdrawn. Western Front: At the second battle of Ypres, the Germans use poison gas for the first time. A German submarine sinks the British liner *Lusitania* in the Atlantic Ocean; 1,153 passengers, including many Americans, are drowned. Italy joins the Allied Powers on May 22. In September, an Allied offensive (attack) starts in the French regions of Artois and Champagne. The British use poison gas for the first time at the battle of Loos, but stalemate situation continues. On October 15 Bulgaria joins the war on the side of the Central Powers. There is growing economic disorder in Russia because of the war. Britain: First automatic telephone exchange in use. Author D. H. Lawrence publishes his novel *The Rainbow*; it is declared obscene and all copies are destroyed. A collection of English poet Rupert Brooke's poems is published after he dies on his way to fight at the Dardanelles. Switzerland: Albert Einstein prepares his papers on the general theory of relativity for publication.

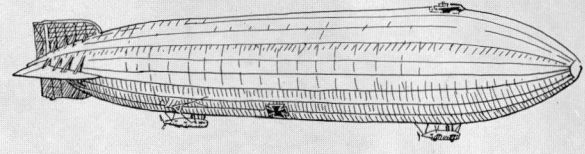

Germany was the only country during World War I to use zeppelin airships for strategic bombing. Bombing raids were made over southeast England and London.

The Arts

In this period the arts were influenced by what was going on all over the world. From 1914 to 1918 the world was dominated by World War I and the period is famous for its anti-war poets, such as Wilfred Owen.

The "Roaring Twenties" is known for its wildness and gaiety as people of all ages tried to forget the horrors of war.

The Thirties were dominated by the Depression and the threat of war. During World War II the arts leaned toward patriotism (support of your country). Then after 1945, both art and sculpture became quite abstract in form.

▼ The Spaniard Salvador Dali (1904–1989) was an artist who also designed jewelry. This jeweled watch called The Eye of Time is in the Surrealist style of the 1920s, which showed objects as if they were influenced by dreams and by the subconscious mind.

◄ Ballet was a popular form of entertainment in Russia before and after the Revolution of 1917. One of the most famous dancers was Vaslav Nijinsky (1890–1950) who was known for his amazing leaps. One of his most famous interpretations was the role of the faun in The Afternoon of a Faun by the French composer Claude Debussy.

▲ Art Deco was a popular art style between 1925 and 1935. It used geometric shapes and bright colors to decorate objects such as this woman's powder compact.

▲ The film All Quiet on the Western Front describes the experiences of soldiers during World War I.

► In Nazi Germany all the arts had to reflect approved ideas. This sculpture, called Comrades, is by the official Nazi sculptor Arno Breker and was commissioned for the headquarters of the Nazi Party. In the sculpture Breker tried to imitate the graceful statues of ancient Greece, but failed.

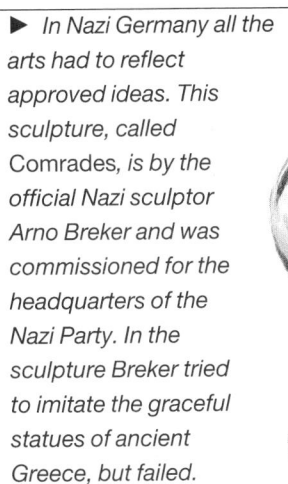

▲ The abstract figure Man Pointing by the Swiss sculptor Alberto Giacometti was made in bronze in 1947. It is one of several "thin man" bronzes made by him.

▼ Otto Dix's 1928 painting Large Towns makes fun of the way of life led by many young people in the "Roaring Twenties" in Germany.

WHEN IT HAPPENED

1925 F. Scott Fitzgerald, famous for writing about the "Jazz Age" of the Twenties, publishes his best-known novel, The Great Gatsby.

1929 Robert Graves publishes Goodbye To All That, an autobiographical account of his experiences in World War I.

1935 George Gershwin's Black American folk opera Porgy and Bess is completed.

1937 Picasso's painting Guernica shows the town's destruction in the Spanish Civil War.

1916 Western Front: A German offensive starts with the battle of Verdun. The five-month battle ends in appalling losses on both sides, but stalemate continues. Ireland: In the Easter Rising Nationalists, led by Pádraic Pearse and James Connolly, take control of public buildings in Dublin. The uprising is put down after a week.

North Sea: The battle of Jutland is the only major sea battle of the war. Both sides claim victory, but after the battle the German fleet returns to its home ports and most of it stays there for the rest of the war. Eastern Front: Russian Brusilov offensive against the Germans fails, increasing the discontent of the people in Russia. North Sea: Lord Kitchener, who had been responsible for the recruiting campaign in Britain, is killed when the ship he is traveling on hits a mine. Middle East: Grand Sharif Ali ibn Hussein of Mecca (a descendent of the prophet Muhammad) starts the Arab revolt (to 1918) against the Turks. Western Front: In the first battle of the Somme, a mainly British attack, more than one million men are killed. Tanks make their first appearance in battle. Britain: New prime minister Lloyd George introduces vigorous policies to help win the war, including the convoy system to

 protect merchant shipping. Romania: Bucharest falls to the Central Powers. U.S.: Woodrow Wilson is re-elected president. The first birth control clinic is opened in Brooklyn.

The General Post Office building in Dublin.

The Easter Rising

 By the early 20th century many Irish people wanted Home Rule. After two earlier Home Rule Bills had been defeated in Parliament, a third Bill was approved in 1912. This would have become law, giving Ireland its own parliament to deal with domestic affairs, but it was suspended when World War I broke out in Europe in 1914.

At this time Ireland was on the brink of civil war. In the north, Protestants opposed Home Rule because it would make them a minority in a country run by Roman Catholics, and would mean that they had less power. Some people (known as Republicans) wanted Ireland to become an independent republic. Many of them supported a political party called Sinn Féin. Some belonged to the Irish Republican Brotherhood, the Irish

▼ *The Republicans made their headquarters inside Dublin Post Office. The British army fired heavy guns on the building, and it caught fire. The Republicans fled the building when it became red hot.*

Connolly

James Connolly (1870–1916) led the Irish Citizen Army. A laborer's son, he was born in County Monaghan. In 1896 he founded the Irish Socialist Republican Party. After the Easter Rising, he was shot in jail, even though he was already mortally wounded.

▲ *Barricades were set up in the streets of Dublin in 1916. On one side were the British forces, and on the other were the Republicans. Many civilians died in the Easter Rising.*

Volunteers, and the Irish Citizen Army.

On Easter Monday 1916 about 1,600 members of the Irish Volunteers and the Irish Citizen Army, led by Pádraic Pearse and James Connolly, took control of several public buildings in Dublin. The event became known as the Easter Rising. From their headquarters in the General Post Office, Pearse and Connolly declared a republic, but they were soon defeated by the British.

However, after 15 of the leaders were shot and many suspects arrested, support for the republican cause grew. In the 1918 election, members of the Sinn Féin party won 73 of the 105 Irish seats in the British Parliament. They set up their own parliament, called the Dáil Éireann, and declared Ireland to be an independent republic in 1919. This led to war between the Irish Republican Army (IRA), led by Michael Collins, and the Royal Irish Constabulary (RIC), the armed police force. The British sent extra armed police to support the RIC. They were known as the Black-and-Tans because of the colors of their uniforms and belts. The fighting continued until 1921 (*see* pages 662–663).

◄ *Republican campaigners urged their supporters to join the fight for Ireland, rather than fight in the trenches in France alongside the English.*

The Russian Revolution

Although the 1905 revolution had been crushed (*see* pages 628–629), many of the Russian people still wanted reforms. They thought that the tsar was out of touch with the population and that his advisers were corrupt. The government, which had not been very efficient in peacetime, became even worse as World War I went on. Soldiers who thought that they would be sent to fight in the war began to feel disloyal to their country.

Because the railroads were being used to take supplies to soldiers at the Eastern Front, food and fuel were not reaching the cities. The economy was on the way to collapse and many people in the cities began to starve. In March 1917 riots broke out in the capital, St. Petersburg, which had been renamed Petrograd at the start of World War I. Rioting crowds were usually broken up by troops, but they

▲ Barricades were set up on the streets of Petrograd during the March 1917 revolution. The city was the focal point for strikes, riots, and a mutiny by army troops. Many people in the city were starving.

▼ Tsar Nicholas II with his wife Alexandra and their children. The tsar belonged to the Romanov family, who ruled Russia for 300 years. The tsar and his family were arrested during the March revolution. They are believed to have been killed by revolutionaries in July 1918.

Vladimir Lenin

1870 Born in Russia.
1887 Becomes a Marxist after his brother is executed for trying to assassinate the tsar.
1917 Returns from exile to lead the Communists to victory.
1922 Forms the USSR.
1924 Dies.

► Lenin tried to persuade people to support the Bolshevik Party. This was hard at first, but he finally succeeded.

Rasputin

Grigori Rasputin
(1871–1916) was an
adviser to Tsar
Nicholas II and his wife
Alexandra. They
thought he was a holy
man who could help
make their sick son
better. Rasputin was
selfish and greedy and
was hated by the
people of Russia.

Kerensky

Alexander Kerensky
(1881–1970) was a
member of the
Socialist Revolutionary
Party. After the
March revolution,
he was minister of war.
He became leader of
the government in
July, but fled to Paris
after the October
Revolution.

refused to obey their orders. When the
troops joined the rioters, the tsar
abdicated and his advisers resigned. A
temporary government was set up, led
by Prince George Lvov.

People were still short of food and fuel,
and the transportation system was in
chaos. The government found it
increasingly difficult to carry on with the
war. Alexander Kerensky succeeded
Prince Lvov as chief minister. After the
March revolution the Bolshevik Party was
still determined to seize power. Their
leader, Lenin came back to Petrograd.

1917 Russia: In the February revolution
strikes and riots force Tsar Nicholas II
and his generals to resign. He is
replaced by a provisional government,
led first by Prince Lvov, then by
Kerensky, but discontent continues. The
Bolsheviks, led by Lenin, overthrow the
provisional government in the October
revolution. Lenin promises the Russian
people "Peace, Land, and Bread" and
starts talks for peace with Germany.
Turkey: British troops capture Baghdad,
in Iraq, from the Turks. U.S.: On April 6
U.S. declares war on Germany as a
result of Germany's policy of attacking
any ships in British waters, including
those from neutral countries. American
troops join the Allies on the Western
Front. All American males between the
ages of 21 and 30 to be drafted. Middle
East: British soldier T. E. Lawrence, later
known as Lawrence of Arabia, takes over
as leader of the Arab revolt against
Turkey. Western Front: A major Allied
offensive starts at Ypres; the Allies gain 5
miles (8 km), which they lose in a German
counterattack the following spring. Bad
weather turns the battlefield into a sea of
mud. Britain: The Balfour Declaration
supports a Jewish homeland in Palestine.
Middle East: British capture Jerusalem
from Turks.

A Bolshevik poster of 1919 entitled To Horse,
Workers! *with the red flag of communism
flying in the background.*

1918 Russia and Germany sign the Treaty of Brest-Litovsk; Russia withdraws from the war. This releases thousands of German soldiers from the Eastern Front and makes them available to fight on the Western Front. The Germans take advantage of this by launching a spring offensive against the Allies. The Germans are successful at first, but are defeated at the second battle of the Marne. The Allies break through German defenses on the Hindenburg Line, forcing the Germans to retreat. Following the Italian victory at the battle of Vittorio Veneto, Austria-Hungary surrenders on October 24. Germany: On November 7 starving people start a revolution, the German navy mutinies, the emperor abdicates and a republic is declared. At 5 o'clock on the morning of November 11 Germany signs the armistice and fighting ends at 11 o'clock. U.S.: President Wilson proposes 14-point peace plan. Russia: Lenin's new regime adopts the Gregorian calendar and brings the country in line with the rest of the world. Tsar Nicholas II and his family are murdered. Civil war begins with fighting between the Bolshevik Red Army and White Russian troops (to 1921). Middle East: Arab revolt ends. Britain: Women over 30 (property owners and the wives of property owners) are given the vote for the first time. A worldwide epidemic of influenza begins.

The Bolsheviks in Petrograd (St. Petersburg) wanted Russia to become a communist state. After struggling with the government, the Bolsheviks, led by Lenin, seized power in November 1917. This was called the October Revolution because the Russians used a different calendar at the time.

The new government signed the Treaty of Brest-Litovsk which made peace with Germany in March 1918. It moved the capital from Petrograd to Moscow and broke up the large estates, giving the farmland to the peasants. Control of factories was given to workers. Banks were taken into state control, and Church property was confiscated.

The White Russians (anti-Communists) opposed these moves, and later in 1918 the Russian Civil War broke out between the Bolshevik Red Army and the White Russians. The White Russians were finally defeated in 1921. By this time around 100,000 people had been

▲ After the October revolution, the country was governed by soviets (elected governing councils), many of whom were ordinary working men and women, like these being addressed by Lenin.

▶ Armed workers with Bolshevik-led soldiers and sailors attacked the Winter Palace in Petrograd on November 6, 1917. Although it was the headquarters of the tsar's government, it was weakly defended and was soon in Bolshevik hands.

A poster of 1920 shows a Russian worker plowing ground covered with crowns and money, symbols of the old world of the tsar and capitalism.

Trotsky

Leon Trotsky (1879–1940) was the most important person after Lenin in the October Revolution. In the Russian Civil War he directed the Red Army to victory. He hoped to become president after Lenin's death, but lost to Stalin. He went into exile in Mexico.

Josef Stalin

1879 Born in Georgia as Josef Dzhugashvili (later changes his name to Stalin, meaning "man of steel").
1903 Joins the Bolshevik Party.
1922 Becomes general secretary of the Communist Party.
1924 Becomes leader of the USSR.
1953 Dies.

▲ *This early Soviet cartoon shows Lenin ridding the world of kings, emperors, priests, and capitalists (rich moneymakers). The original caption read, "Comrade Lenin sweeps the world of its rubbish."*

killed and 2 million had emigrated. In 1922, the country's name was changed to the Union of Soviet Socialist Republics (USSR) or Soviet Union.

Lenin led the USSR until his death in 1924, when a new power struggle began between Leon Trotsky and Josef Stalin. Stalin won and went on to dominate Soviet politics until 1953. Many people opposed his policies in the late 1930s. To crush this opposition Stalin carried out the Great Purge, in which millions of people were arrested and murdered.

Buildings

Many buildings designed by architects in Europe and North America at this time were made from reinforced concrete and steel. They were built in the International style which featured large areas of windows that let in plenty of light, but left very little room on the outside walls for external decoration. They often had white walls and were geometric in shape.

A shortage of space in the major cities led to the construction of tall skyscrapers. Many reflected the work of architect Mies van der Rohe. He designed metal-framed skyscrapers with thin metal and glass walls.

Slum clearance schemes in many towns and cities led to the worst of the old houses being replaced by apartment buildings.

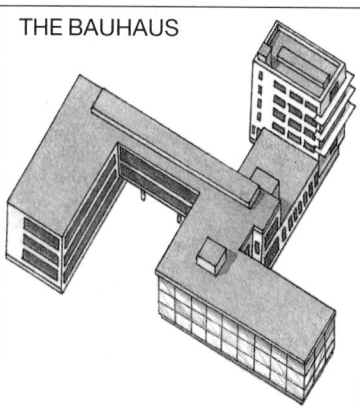

THE BAUHAUS

The Bauhaus was a German school of design founded in 1919. The first director, Walter Gropius, designed this building for the school. The influence of the Bauhaus continued even after the Nazis closed it in 1933.

▲ Le Corbusier used features on the Villa Savoye (above) at Poissy, France, which are typical of buildings of the 1920s. The building is on stilts, the rooms flow into each other, and the windows are in horizontal strips. The outer walls do not bear the load of the structure, and the roof is flat so it can be used as a garden.

▼ Sydney Harbour Bridge, Australia was built in 1932 to connect the suburbs with the city center. It has a main span of 1,670 feet (509 m). Other bridges from this period are the Quebec Bridge in Canada (1917) with a main span of 1,800 feet (549 m), and the Golden Gate Bridge in San Francisco (1937) with a main span of 4,200 feet (1,280 m).

▲ This house is called Fallingwater, and it is built over a natural waterfall. It was designed in 1936 by the American architect Frank Lloyd Wright.

▶ The Chrysler Building in New York is an example of the Art Deco style that influenced building design between 1925 and 1935. Inside, geometric shapes, bright color schemes and manmade materials, such as plastics and chrome, were used. Art Deco was influenced by the Bauhaus school of art.

◀ The Art Nouveau style was still popular. Buildings like the Einstein Tower at Potsdam, Germany, had flowing lines and shapes that were based on natural forms.

WHEN IT HAPPENED

1925 The Bauhaus moves from Weimar to Dessau, Germany.

1931 The Empire State Building is completed.

1932 *The International Style* is published, a book which introduces the International style of architecture.

1936 The Hoover Dam is completed.

1937 Repairs are completed on Rheims Cathedral, France, after heavy damage during World War I.

1919 Versailles Peace Settlement meets to bring a formal end to World War I. Five treaties are signed by 1923. Germany and the Allies sign the Treaty of Versailles; Germany is to give Alsace-Lorraine back to France, return lands to Belgium, Czechoslovakia, and Poland, accept guilt for beginning the war, pay heavy reparations, strictly limit its armed forces, give up its overseas colonies and abandon hopes of a union with Austria. The League of Nations is formed. The Austrians sign the Treaty of Saint-Germain-en-Laye. It ends the Habsburg monarchy and recognizes the new states of Czechoslovakia, Poland, Yugoslavia, and Hungary. Other treaties are signed by Ireland: Sinn Féin members set up a parliament, the Dáil Éireann, and declare the country a republic. Michael Collins forms the Irish Republican Army (IRA). U.S.: The U.S. Senate votes against the Versailles Treaty. Germany: A Spartakist (communist) uprising in Berlin is crushed. The Weimar Constitution is adopted. Italy: Benito Mussolini sets up the Fascist movement. Italian Nationalist, Gabriel d'Annunzio, seizes the port of Fiume from Yugoslavia. India: Mahatma (Mohandas) Gandhi begins a campaign of passive resistance to British rule; others protest violently. British troops fire on Nationalist rioters in Amritsar; killing 379 people and wounding over 1,200.

Gas masks were needed in World War I to protect the troops against gas attacks by the enemy.

End of World War I

During World War I, both France and Britain relied on the U.S. and Canada for arms and food. The Germans therefore used submarines, or U-boats, to attack the supply ships in the Atlantic. Then from February 1917 they began to attack any ship in the seas around Britain, even if it belonged to a neutral country. They knew this would probably bring the United States into the war, but hoped to starve Britain and France into surrender before that happened. They did not succeed, however, because a convoy system protected the merchant ships.

The arrival of American troops in 1917 meant that the Allies could launch fresh attacks on the Western Front. In 1918, Russia withdrew from the war (*see* pages 652–653) and so German soldiers were no longer needed on the Eastern Front.

By 1918, there were more than 3.5 million German soldiers on the Western Front. In March they broke through the trenches and advanced toward Paris. The French counterattacked in July and in August British tanks broke through the German line at Amiens. As the U.S. poured more troops into France, the

▲ World War I involved whole populations. Many women went to work producing armaments and keeping industry going while the men were at war.

WEAPONS

World War I saw the first widespread use of aerial warfare. At first the airplanes were used to spy on the enemy trenches. Later they were used for

Sopwith Camel

fighting and for dropping bombs. The Germans also tried using airships, but these were too easy to shoot down. The first tank appeared at the Somme in September 1916. Tanks could travel through barbed wire and across trenches and rough ground. They were not stopped by machine-gun fire.

Mark IV tank

▲ The horrors of World War I shocked many people. The soldiers who survived never forgot their terrible experiences or their comrades.

◄ World War I left parts of France and Belgium devastated. Cities such as Ypres were left in ruins. Before 1939, World War I was known as the Great War and the War To End All Wars.

Germans retreated. By October, the fighting was nearing the German border and a naval blockade was leading to starvation in Germany. Early in the morning of November 11, Germany signed the armistice. William II, the German emperor, abdicated and at 11 o'clock fighting in World War I ended.

Almost 10 million people had been killed and over 20 million wounded. Most were young men. Their loss changed the social structure of many countries. As a result, many women gained more equality and freedom than they had before the war. Many also gained the right to vote.

Aftermath of World War I

World War I was formally ended by the Versailles Peace Settlement which was discussed from 1919 to 1923. All the nations that had been involved in the war (except Germany) met to draw up a peace agreement, but the United States, Britain, France, and Italy were dominant. Five treaties were drawn up altogether. The most important was the Treaty of Versailles, which punished Germany for its part in World War I. As well as having to accept the guilt for starting the war, Germany lost some of its territory and its colonies, and had to pay large sums of money (called reparations) to the Allies. The German economy collapsed. Other nations also suffered as they tried to pay back money they had borrowed during the war. This led to political and economic upheaval in many places.

Further strife was caused by the

▼ On June 28, 1919, the Treaty of Versailles was signed in the Hall of Mirrors in the Palace of Versailles, near Paris in France.

▲ Many countries suffered economic upheaval and difficulties after World War I. A General Strike broke out in Britain in 1926 in support of coal miners.

HYPERINFLATION

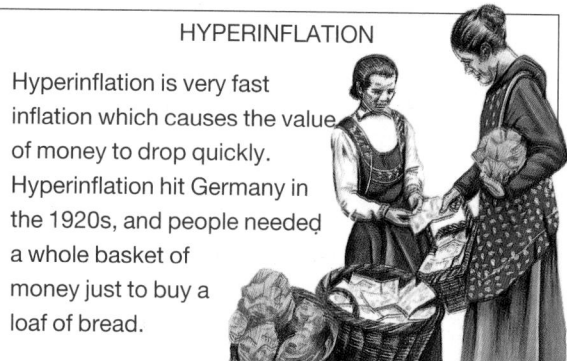

Hyperinflation is very fast inflation which causes the value of money to drop quickly. Hyperinflation hit Germany in the 1920s, and people needed a whole basket of money just to buy a loaf of bread.

MANDATES

The League of Nations set up a series of mandates (agreements that made one country the trustee of another) after World War I. The mandates gave control of former German and Turkish possessions to one of the Allied Powers. Britain became responsible for Iraq from 1920 to 1932, for Palestine from 1922 to 1948, for Transjordan (now known as Jordan) until 1946, and for Tanganyika (Tanzania) until 1961. South Africa became responsible for German South-West Africa (now Namibia). France became responsible for Syria from 1920 to 1946. At first this included Lebanon, but it became a republic in 1926. Australia and Japan were given former German colonies in the Pacific.

▲ *There were many newly independent countries in Europe after World War I. They included Finland, Estonia, Latvia, Lithuania, Poland, Czechoslovakia, Hungary, and Yugoslavia.*

redrawing of international boundaries in Europe following the collapse of the German, Austro-Hungarian, Russian, and Ottoman (Turkish) empires.

The Versailles Peace Settlement also set up the League of Nations. This aimed to help keep world peace by settling disputes by discussion and agreement rather than fighting, but it failed. One reason for this was that it had little power because the U.S. refused to join. Another reason was that there were still rivalries between some of the 53 members. These weakened the League and reduced its power, so that by the late 1930s few countries took any notice of it. Eventually it was disbanded and was replaced by the United Nations in 1946.

1920 The Allies and Turkey sign the Treaty of Sèvres. This breaks up the remains of the Ottoman empire and confines the Ottoman Turks to Anatolia and a small area around Istanbul. Turkish Nationalists, led by Mustafa Kemal, start a revolution. Ireland: British government passes the Government of Ireland Act, offering Home Rule to both northern and southern communities. Northern Ireland accepts this, but Dáil Éireann does not; fighting breaks out. Italy and Yugoslavia sign the Treaty of Rapallo. Italy: Industrial unrest leads to fears of revolution. Eastern Europe: State of civil war in Russia; in some areas there is famine, in others there are peasant uprisings and anti-Bolshevik campaigns. There are nationalist rebellions in Estonia, Finland, Latvia, and Lithuania. Russia is at war with Poland, which has taken over much Russian territory. Germany: Adolf Hitler joins the National Socialist German Workers' Party, or Nazi Party. Switzerland: League of Nations meets for the first time. Pacific: Australia and Japan acquire former German colonies. U.S.: Warren Harding becomes president. The making, selling, and transporting of alcohol is prohibited. Chicago becomes the center of jazz music. Women are given the right to vote as the 19th Amendment to the Constitution is signed. Woodrow Wilson wins Nobel Peace Prize. The Senate rejects the Versailles Treaty. John Thompson patents the Thompson sub-

A German banknote of 1923 with a value of one million marks.

machine gun, known as the "Tommy" gun. Middle East: Britain establishes Palestine as a Jewish homeland.
Britain: The poems of Wilfred Owen, who died in World War I, are published.

Communications

New methods of communication were being used to entertain people and keep them in touch with world events. Radio was the main form of family entertainment, and movies, including the news, were popular. By 1949, televisions in the U.S. and Britain were becoming widespread. In times of war the new methods of communication could be used for propaganda purposes. Advertising became more common in the 1930s, especially in magazines, newspapers, and in public places.

Cars and motorcycles became more widely available, but many people relied on buses, trolley cars and trains. For the rich there were huge cruise liners or aircraft.

◄ Motorcycles, like this one from 1926, were popular with people who could not afford a car. Passengers traveled in a sidecar.

▶ Huge crowds watch the launch of the liner Queen Elizabeth on September 27, 1938. At the time it was one of the most luxurious ships ever built, and had all the facilities of a first-class hotel. The ship could cross the Atlantic in four days.

▼ On long-distance rail journeys, some steam locomotives were being replaced by diesel, such as this United States diesel locomotive of 1943. Diesel engines could climb hills faster, had better acceleration than steam, and needed fewer people to run them.

WHEN IT HAPPENED

1927 Japan's first underground railroad opens.

1928 The development of a Morse radio transmitter-receiver makes it possible to set up the Royal Flying Doctor Service of Australia to help people in remote areas.

1937 The German airship *Hindenburg* bursts into flames at Lakehurst, N.J. after crossing the Atlantic.

1938 The British passenger liner *Queen Mary* crosses the Atlantic in 3 days, 20 hours, and 42 minutes.

▲ In Germany, Ferdinand Porsche designed the Volkswagen in 1937. He wanted to produce a car that could be sold at a price people could afford.

◀ John Logie Baird invented an early television system. In 1926, he transmitted the first pictures of moving objects, but his system was soon replaced by a more practical one developed by Vladimir Zworykin.

▲ Early radios were quite big. Some were bought ready-made, others were made from kits. People could listen to news, drama, comedy, and dance music.

▶ By the 1930s, airlines regularly flew passengers to most parts of the world. This poster is advertising the German airline, Lufthansa. Flying boats were also popular.

◀ Army photographers in the 1930s. The advances in photography meant that better film gave clearer pictures that could be taken by smaller cameras. The Leica was introduced in 1924 and was small enough to put in a pocket. In 1931, the electronic flash made it possible to take a wider choice of subjects. By 1947, Polaroid cameras could produce pictures instantly, as the film was developed and printed inside the camera immediately after each picture had been taken.

Republic of Ireland

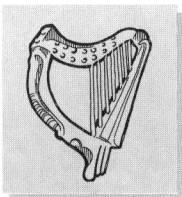

The British government did not agree with Dáil Éireann's declaration of an independent republic of all Ireland (*see* pages 648–649). Instead it wanted to divide Ireland into two countries, with six of the counties of Ulster separate from the rest. Under the 1920 Government of Ireland Act, each of the two countries would have some form of self-government. The six Ulster counties had a Protestant majority who did not want to be ruled from Dublin. They agreed to the Act and formed the new state of Northern Ireland. Dáil Éireann, led by Eamon de Valera, opposed the Act because they wanted full independence for all Ireland.

To try and bring peace to the country, the Anglo-Irish Treaty of 1921 made southern Ireland into a dominion (or self-governing country) of Great Britain. Called the Irish Free State, the new dominion was established in 1922. But instead of bringing peace, this action led to civil war. On one side were the Free Staters who agreed to the treaty's terms. They were led first by Michael Collins and then by William Cosgrave. On the other side were the Republicans, led by de Valera, who still wanted full independence for a united Ireland.

The civil war lasted until 1923 when de Valera ordered his followers to stop fighting. In 1926, he founded a new political party, called Fiànna Fáil, and in the general election of 1932, he defeated Cosgrave. His government wanted to end most ties between their country and Britain. The new constitution of 1937 renamed the country Eire, but it stayed within the British Commonwealth.

Although Ireland remained neutral during World War II, thousands of Irish soldiers fought in the British armed forces. It became independent of Britain in 1949, and left the Commonwealth.

Ulster

◀ *Northern Ireland consists of six of the nine counties of Ulster. The rest of the island forms the Republic of Ireland.*

◀ *The civil war brought fierce fighting back to the streets of Dublin. Many buildings were damaged or destroyed. These people are sheltering behind a barricade made from trucks.*

▼ *Both the Free Staters and the Republicans were well-supplied with weapons during the civil war. This field gun belonged to the Free Staters and was used in County Limerick. An early victim of the war was Michael Collins, who was shot by Republicans in 1922 for signing the treaty which created the Irish Free State.*

Eamon de Valera

1882 Born in the U.S.
1916 Imprisoned after the Easter Rising.
1926 Founds Fiànna Fáil Party.
1937–1948 Serves as prime minister of the Republic of Ireland. (Holds this post three times 1937–1959).
1959–1973 President.
1975 Dies.

1921 U.S.: Government follows policy of isolationism and refuses to join the League of Nations. The Washington Conference is held to discuss naval armament (weapons) reductions. The U.S. economy is depressed, with almost five million workers unemployed. Germany: Economy begins to feel the strain of making war reparation payments to the Allies. The first superhighway is built in Berlin. Spain: State of crisis, following assassination of the prime minister and the loss of 12,000 Spanish troops in battle of Anual in Morocco. Ireland: The Anglo-Irish Treaty establishes the Irish Free State as a dominion of the British Commonwealth. It allows the withdrawal of six of the counties of Ulster which, as Northern Ireland, remain part of the U.K. British police recruits (Black-and-Tans) are withdrawn. Britain: Coal miners strike over poor working conditions and low pay. Eastern Europe: Treaty of Riga ends war between Russia and Poland. Mutiny of Russian sailors at Kronshtadt, Russia, is put down. Russia: White Russians are defeated. Turkey: Turks continue fighting against invading Greeks. Switzerland: Psychologist Carl Jung publishes his theories on human psychology. Italy: Luigi Pirandello writes his play *Six Characters in Search of an Author*. China: The Communist Party is formed.

The coat of arms of Northern Ireland. The red cross of St. George appears in the background.

1922 Italy: Mussolini and his Fascist followers march on Rome to demand a place for their party in the government. King Victor Emmanuel III invites Benito Mussolini to be prime minister. Britain: Unemployment grows in old industrial areas of the north and Scotland. Many men take temporary work in Canada where there is a bumper grain harvest. Scottish trade unionists and socialists organize first Hunger March. American-born poet, dramatist, and critic T. S. Eliot publishes his poem *The Waste Land*. The Union of Soviet Socialist Republics (USSR) is established with Lenin as its leader. Egypt: Independence declared. British archaeologist Howard Carter uncovers the tomb of ancient Egyptian boy-king Tutankhamun. Turkey: End of the Ottoman empire. The sultan is deposed by Mustafa Kemal. Kemal's army drives Greeks out of Turkish city of Smyrna (Izmir); the city is destroyed and many Greek civilians are killed. U.S.: The Washington Conference agrees Pacific Treaty between Britain, France, Japan, and U.S.A. Sinclair Lewis publishes *Babbitt*, and H. L. Mencken, *Defense of Women*. Ireland: A civil war is fought between Free Staters and Republicans (to 1923). Author James Joyce publishes his novel *Ulysses*, which influences the development of the modern novel. W. B. Yeats publishes his *Later Poems*.

The magnificent throne of Tutankhamun, found buried among other treasures in his tomb.

The Turkish Revolution

As the Ottoman empire gradually became weaker and weaker, Turkish nationalism grew. The most important nationalist group was called the "Young Turks." They had succeeded in deposing the sultan, Abdul Hamid II, in 1909.

The Nationalists, under their leader Mustafa Kemal, formed a temporary government in April 1920, and founded the Turkish Grand National Assembly in the town of Ankara. Later the same year, the new sultan, Muhammad V, signed the Treaty of Sèvres. This was one of the treaties imposed on the Ottoman empire by the Allied Powers when it was

▼ *An election scene in Istanbul in 1923. Mustafa Kemal was elected first president of the Republic of Turkey. The votes were collected in urns, which were carried in triumph through the streets.*

defeated in World War I (*see* pages 658–659). Under the terms of the treaty, the Ottoman empire was divided up. Only Istanbul and Anatolia remained. Ankara was made the new capital of Turkey in 1923.

Many Turkish people did not want their country to be broken up and so they began to support the nationalists. In 1920 their leader, General Mustafa Kemal, started a revolution. In 1922, he abolished the sultanate, and in 1923 he declared Turkey a republic with himself as president. He then defeated the Greeks who were attacking Turkey and negotiated better terms with the Allies. He ruled until his death in 1938 and did much to make Turkey into a modern state. In 1934, he took the surname Atatürk, meaning "Father of the Turks."

▶ *Atatürk worked hard to modernize his country. He introduced new technology and improved the rights of women.*

◀ *After the revolution, Turkey was still split between Europe and Asia. The capital was moved from Istanbul to Ankara in 1923.*

▼ *Atatürk introduced language reforms and fought against illiteracy.*

Ataturk

1881 Born Mustafa Kemal in Salonika.
1914–1918 Fights as a general for Turkey in World War I.
1920 Elected president of Turkish Grand National Assembly.
1922 Marries Latifeh Hanoum.
1923 Founds Republic of Turkey.
1938 Dies.

The Rise of Fascism

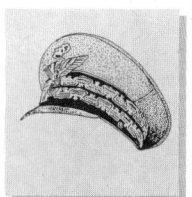

The political movement known as fascism became popular in a number of countries during the 1930s. Fascist leaders including Benito Mussolini in Italy and Adolf Hitler in Germany opposed communism and encouraged national pride. Fascism often involved racism (prejudice against other races), especially in Germany where hatred was directed at Jews and Gypsies. Many people supported fascism because it seemed to offer a way out of the economic decline and the Great Depression which many countries experienced during the 1930s. Many others supported socialists or communists.

In Italy, the Fascists came to power in 1922. Mussolini became prime minister, but from 1925 he ruled as a dictator, and was known as *Il Duce*. His social policies won him the approval of the people.

Adolf Hitler brought the fascists (called Nationalists or Nazis) to power in

▲ *Italy wanted to expand its colonies in Africa, so it invaded Ethiopia in 1935. Under Mussolini's orders, Italian troops occupied the country until 1941.*

Germany in 1933. He promised to build the country into a great state after its humiliation in World War I. In the same year, Primo de Rivera created the Fascist (Falangist) Party in Spain. Fascism also won support in Portugal, Austria, the Balkan states, and South America in the years before World War II.

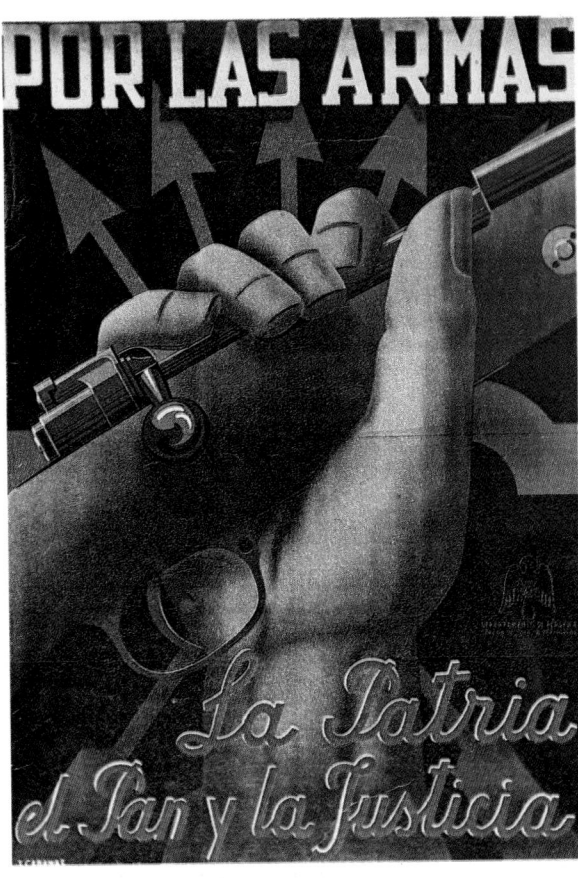

▲ This Spanish poster shows red arrows which were a Falangist (Fascist) symbol. The Falangists fought against the Republicans in the Spanish Civil War (1936–1939). The slogan across the bottom translates as "Country, Bread, and Justice."

◄ Mussolini reviews his troops in Naples on October 30, 1922 before his march on Rome to seize power for the Fascists. His followers were officially called Fasci de Combattimento, but were known as "Blackshirts" because of the color of their uniforms.

Benito Mussolini

1883 Born in Italy.
1914 Expelled from the Socialist Party for his support of Italy's role in World War I.
1922 Becomes dictator after march on Rome.
1940 Italy enters World War II on Axis side.
1945 Captured and shot by Italians.

1923 Germany: French and Belgian troops occupy the Ruhr district after Germany fails to pay reparations. Germany suffers from hyperinflation. Adolf Hitler fails in an armed bid to overthrow the government of Bavaria; he is jailed. In prison, he writes *Mein Kampf* (My Struggle). Spain: General Primo de Rivera rules as a virtual dictator (to 1930). Italy: Mussolini creates a fascist state. Ireland: End of civil war. Middle East: Treaty of Lausanne is signed between Greece and Turkey. Turkey is declared a republic with Mustafa Kemal as president; capital is moved from Istanbul to Ankara. China: Support grows for the Communist Party. Ethiopia joins the League of Nations. France: Le Corbusier, architect and town planner, publishes book on architecture.

1924 The Dawes Plan spreads the load of Germany's reparations. Germany: Novelist Thomas Mann publishes *The Magic Mountain*. Italy: Giocomo Matteotti, a socialist, is murdered by Fascists. USSR: Lenin dies; Leon Trotsky struggles unsuccessfully for power with Josef Stalin. China: A new government, including Communists, is set up at Guangzhou (Canton) under Sun Yat-sen. Ireland: Dramatist Sean O'Casey writes *Juno and the Paycock*. U.S.: Congress passes Johnson-Reed Act restricting immigration. George Gershwin composes *Rhapsody in Blue*. U.S. dominates the Paris Olympics.

An anti-fascism poster that was issued by the Socialist Party of Catalonia, Spain.

Food and Farming

Great efforts were being made to produce more food that was of better quality. These efforts were helped by the development of chemical fertilizers to improve the soil, herbicides to kill the weeds, and pesticides to kill the insects that damaged the crops.

Although food production went up, fewer people were needed on the farms as many more jobs could be done by machinery. This meant that many farm laborers and their families left the land to look for work in the cities.

The production of more food meant that countries like Australia and the U.S. could grow food for export as well as for their home markets. But unusual drought, wind, and poor soil conservation badly affected crops grown in the U.S. in the 1930s.

▶ *In the 1920s and 1930s, collective farming had some disastrous results in the USSR. Decisions came from Moscow and not from local committees. Sometimes the crops failed, while at other times they were harvested and sent for export, while children like these were starving.*

▶ *Insecticides and herbicides were sprayed onto crops to kill pests and weeds. Not many farmers had planes, so they hired pilots to spray their crops for them.*

▼ *The importance of chemical fertilizers became widely recognized. The added nutrients produced more and better crops.*

▲ *The Communists introduced collective farming to China. This meant that all the land, the buildings, and machinery belonged to the community, and committees in each village decided what to grow. One improvement was replacing their oxen with tractors, which they called "Iron Oxen."*

THE HIGHEST GUARANTEED ANALYSIS.

THE
STANDARD FERTILIZERS

SUPERIOR IN FINE AND DRY CONDITION.

DON'T BUY WATER ON BASIS OF HIGH VALUATION

GROWN WITH STANDARD FERTILIZERS

GROWN WITHOUT

MANUFACTURED BY
STANDARD FERTILIZER CO.
BOSTON, MASS. · WORKS, DUXBURY, MASS, BRISTOL, ME.
FOR SALE BY
A. F. SANBORN, FREMONT.

THE LOWEST IN MOISTURE.

▲ The Great Depression hit farmers all over the world as prices fell. In parts of the U.S. drought added to the problems. Many poor families were forced to leave the land and look for other work.

◄ Combine harvesters had to be pulled by tractors, but they could reap, thresh, and store the grain, and bale the straw. This meant that fewer people were needed to bring in the harvest.

1925 At the Locarno Conference, the great powers agree to put disputes to arbitration, rather than going to war. Italy: Mussolini bans all non-Fascist parties. Morocco: Abd-el-Krim leads an Arab uprising (to 1926). China: Sun Yat-sen dies; Chiang Kai-shek becomes leader of the Kuomintang or Nationalist Party. U.S.: Al Capone takes over Chicago's South Side gang. Charlie Chaplin stars in the film *The Gold Rush*. Czechoslovakia: The novel *The Trial* is published after the death of its author, Franz Kafka. France: Surrealist painters put on an exhibition in Paris.

A German cartoon of Roosevelt fighting Prohibition, shown as a dragon.

1926 Nicaragua: The U.S. sends troops to protect its interests after a popular revolt. Britain: The army is called in to run essential services during the General Strike. The Trade Union Council (TUC) calls off the strike. Author A. A. Milne publishes the children's book *Winnie the Pooh*. Scottish inventor John Logie Baird demonstrates how television works. Ireland: Eamon de Valera founds the Fiànna Fáil Party. Portugal: Army overthrows the government. Germany is admitted to the League of Nations. Middle East: French bombard Damascus in Syria after a Druse uprising. Morocco: Arab uprising crushed by France and Spain. U.S.: Comedians Stan Laurel and Oliver Hardy begin working together. The first liquid-fueled rocket is launched. Ernest Hemingway publishes his novel, *The Sun Also Rises*. Rudolph Valentino dies. Japan: Hirohito becomes emperor.

U.S.A. Between the Wars

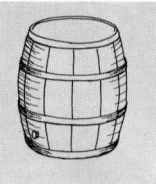

Even before the outbreak of World War I in Europe, the U.S. had a policy of isolationism. This meant that the country did not become involved in world affairs, except when it was necessary for self-defense. The geographic insularity of the United States and its preoccupation with domestic affairs made it possible for U.S. leaders to stay out of entangling alliances with European states. The U.S. only entered World War I after some of its ships had been attacked by German submarines in 1917.

After World War I, the desire for isolationism grew stronger, and the U.S. Senate voted not to join the League of Nations in 1919. A year later a new president, Warren Harding, was elected. He promised "a return to normalcy." To Harding this meant not taking part in

Capone

Al Capone (1899–1947) was born in Italy. From 1925, he led Chicago's South Side gang, dominating the city's underworld and dealing in illegal (bootleg) liquor. In 1929, his gang killed seven of their rivals in the St. Valentine's Day massacre. He was jailed in 1931.

Warren Harding

1865 Born near Blooming Grove, Ohio, U.S.
1915 Becomes Republican senator.
1920 Elected president.
1921 Signs peace treaties with Germany, Austria, and Hungary.
1923 Health affected when several cabinet ministers are involved in scandal, and dies.

international relations, and bringing more law and order to the country in general, and to people's lives.

This policy included the 18th Amendment to the Constitution. It became law in 1920 and banned the making, sale, and transportation of alcoholic drinks, and led to an era known as Prohibition. Many thought this would reduce crime, but the opposite happened. Illegal bars, known as "speakeasies," were controlled by gangsters. Gangs also demanded money from businesses (protection rackets) and many people were shot in rival gangland warfare. Prohibition was ended in 1933.

The U.S. continued its policy of isolationism into the 1930s (*see* pages 678–679) and even introduced restrictions on immigration. It was forced into World War II in 1941, however, when Japanese aircraft attacked the U.S. fleet at Pearl Harbor, Hawaii.

▲ *In the 1920s the New York skyline kept changing as ever taller buildings were constructed. The Empire State Building, opened in 1931, towered above them all at a height of 1,250 feet (381 m).*

▼ *In the Prohibition period, alcohol could only be made and sold illegally. Here law officers are raiding a speakeasy in Washington D.C.*

1927 American Charles Lindbergh makes the first solo flight across the Atlantic. China: Chiang Kai-shek sets up a government at Nanjing (Nanking) and purges Communists from it; civil war between Communists and Nationalists (to 1937). Australia: Canberra becomes the federal capital. U.S.: *The Jazz Singer* is the first "talkie" (movie with sound). Germany: Dramatist Bertolt Brecht produces play *The Threepenny Opera*.

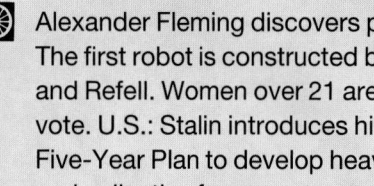

The tomb of Sun Yat-sen on Zijin Mountain, just east of Nanjing (Nanking).

1928 In Paris world powers sign the Kellogg-Briand Pact in which they denounce war. Britain: Scottish scientist Alexander Fleming discovers penicillin. The first robot is constructed by Rickards and Refell. Women over 21 are given the vote. U.S.: Stalin introduces his first Five-Year Plan to develop heavy industry and collective farms; many peasants are executed for opposing government plans. Australian pilot Charles Kingsford-Smith makes the first crossing of the Pacific. U.S.: The Walt Disney cartoon character Mickey Mouse first appears in the film *Steamboat Willie*.

1929 Following the collapse of the German economy, the Young Plan reassesses reparation payments. U.S.: Wall Street Crash: The U.S. stock market collapses, causing bankruptcies and worldwide economic depression. The Academy of Motion Picture Arts and Sciences gives its first awards. Ernest Hemingway publishes his novel *A Farewell to Arms*. Palestine: First major conflict between Jews and Arabs. Antarctic: American explorer Richard Byrd flies over the South Pole.

The Long March

The Republic of China (*see* pages 622–623) was led by Sun Yat-sen, who was named provisional president. When he died in 1925, leadership of China and the Kuomintang (Nationalist) Party passed to Chiang Kai-shek.

In 1926, Chiang Kai-shek launched an expedition against the warlords in the north of the country who wanted to overthrow the Nationalist government. He was helped in this by the Chinese Communist Party. Together they defeated the warlords, but in 1927 the Communist-Kuomintang alliance ended and the two sides started fighting each other. This fighting became known as the Chinese Civil War. Chiang Kai-shek set up his capital in Nanjing (Nanking) in 1927. In that same year the Nationalists drove the Communists out of Shanghai

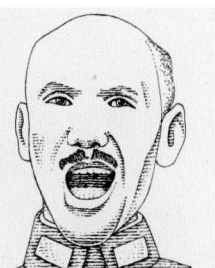

Chiang Kai-shek

1887 Born.
1926 Takes control of Kuomintang.
1927 Sets up Nationalist government in Nanjing (Nanking).
1937 Japanese invade. Republic of China collapses.
1949 Flees to Taiwan. Establishes Republic of China in Taiwan.
1975 Dies.

Mao Zedong

1893 Born.
1919–1921 Becomes involved with Chinese Communist Party.
1931 Becomes chairman of Jiangxi soviet.
1934–1935 Leads Long March.
1949 Proclaims People's Republic of China.
1976 Dies.

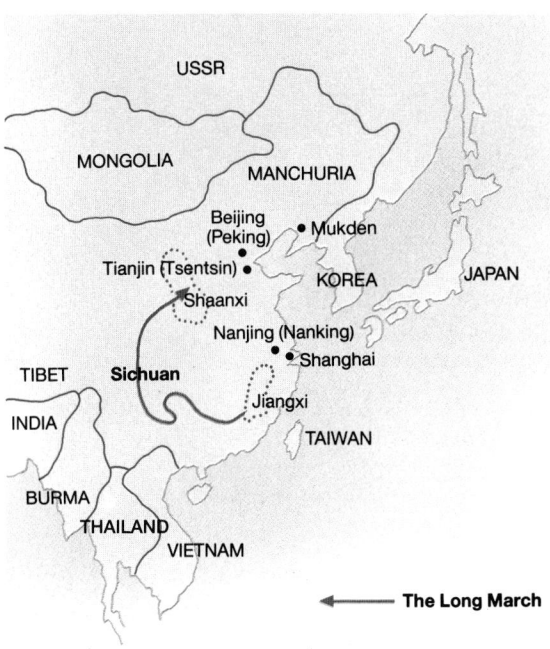

USSR

MONGOLIA

MANCHURIA

Beijing (Peking)

Mukden

Tianjin (Tsentsin)

Shaanxi

KOREA

JAPAN

Nanjing (Nanking)

TIBET   Sichuan

Shanghai

INDIA

Jiangxi

TAIWAN

BURMA

THAILAND

VIETNAM

⟵ The Long March

▲ *The Long March took the Communists from Jiangxi in the south to Shaanxi Province in the north. The journey took more than a year.*

▼ *The Communists had to endure terrible conditions on the Long March. More than three-fourths of them died of cold and hunger.*

and forced them to flee into the Jiangxi hills. The Nationalists claimed to have united China, but they still did not have full control of the country.

By 1931, the Communists had set up a rival government (the Jiangxi soviet) in southern China. They built up their forces in Jiangxi and withstood four attempts by the Kuomintang to defeat them. In October 1933, however, Chiang Kai-shek launched a massive attack against the Communists with the intention of exterminating them. The Communists resisted for a year, then in October 1934 100,000 of them left Jiangxi and set out on the "Long March."

Mao Zedong led the Long March for almost 6,000 miles (10,000 km) at the rate of about 40 to 60 miles (60 to 100 km) a day until they reached Yan'an in Shaanxi Province in northern China. It took them until October 1935 and only about 20,000 of the original 100,000 marchers reached their destination. The Long March established Mao Zedong as the leader of the Chinese Communists.

India

The Indian people had disliked British rule since the 19th century. To counter this, Britain began to give the Indian people more power in local government. After World War I, Britain promised India a major role in running its own government, in return for the support India had given during World War I. Although reforms were announced, the British governors and viceroys still held supreme power. Some Indian nationalists protested violently about this and many were killed. Then in 1919 the Government of India Act was passed. This allowed the election of Indian ministers to an Indian parliament, but the appointed British governors still held the real power. The Indians felt that the Act did not go far enough.

There was also a campaign of civil disobedience and noncooperation with the British by some members of the Indian Congress Party, such as Jawarhalal Nehru. They took up the cause of Home Rule in 1917 and were guided in their campaign by Mahatma (Mohandas) Gandhi. He encouraged the boycotting of British goods and the non-payment of taxes. He also encouraged passive, or nonviolent, resistance to the British. In 1930 he led a protest against the British tax on salt. With thousands of followers he marched over 200 miles (320 km) to the coast to make salt from seawater. This was illegal and over 60,000 people were imprisoned as a result. This and other events in the nonviolent campaign helped to convince the British authorities of the strength of Indian feeling and so helped to achieve Indian independence in 1947 (*see* pages 708–709).

▼ *As the demands for Indian independence increased, anti-British feeling also grew. In this picture from around 1930, troops are dispersing anti-British demonstrators (nationalists) in Peshawar, northern India.*

▲ *The Salt March in 1930 was one of Gandhi's non-violent campaigns. After his arrest, his followers continued the campaign of civil disobedience.*

Gandhi

Mahatma (Mohandas) Gandhi (1869–1948) was born in India, studied law in England, then worked in South Africa. He went back to India in 1914. He was jailed many times for his campaigns. His work toward Indian independence and his philosophy of nonviolence made him very popular.

AMRITSAR

One of the most violent incidents in the campaign for Indian Home Rule occurred in Amritsar in the Punjab in 1919. Troops under the command of the British brigadier Dyer were brought into the town to deal with large numbers of Indian rioters. The troops started shooting, and did not give the Indians enough time to run for cover. As a result, 379 Indians were killed and over 1,200 were injured. This incident helped to turn opinion more firmly against British rule.

1930 At a conference in London, world powers fail to agree on naval limitations. Greece and Turkey sign the Treaty of Ankara. South America: Right-wing dictatorships set up in Argentina and Brazil. Ethiopia: Ras Tafari is crowned as Haile Selassie I. India: Gandhi leads Salt March in protest against British; the Civil Disobedience movement (to 1934) demands independence. France: Singer Edith Piaf begins appearing in cabaret. Spain: Primo de Rivera resigns. English pilot Amy Johnson flies solo to Australia. U.S.: Art Deco style Chrysler Building is built in New York. Clarence Birdseye develops a technique for preserving foods by freezing. Clyde Tombaugh discovers the planet Pluto. Census puts the U.S. population at 122.7 million, 30 million more than in 1920.

1931 Britain: The Statute of Westminster clarifies the relationship between Britain and its dominions; The Commonwealth of Nations replaces the British empire. U.S.: Vaccine production becomes possible through the work of Ernest Goodpasture. President Hoover opens the Empire State Building. Spain: King Alfonso XIII flees; a republic is proclaimed. Germany: Support for Adolf Hitler and the Nazi Party grows. The electron microscope is invented. China: The Communists set up a rival government in Jiangxi. Japanese occupy Manchuria.

In 1930 Amy Johnson completed her solo flight to Australia.

Refrigerator   Washing machine   Vacuum cleaner

People

A period that saw two world wars and a worldwide slump in trade brought many changes to the lives of most people. In some countries the rigid class system was beginning to break down, and it became easier to move between social classes. There was better access to education for everyone. However, many people suffered unemployment or lost their homes in the wars and the Great Depression. Some people lost their family in the wars.

    Entertainments included dancing and the movies, which were quite cheap. Movies offered a brief escape from everyday life.

▲ *Fewer people had servants, but better equipment made domestic chores easier. These included more efficient vacuum cleaners and washing machines.*

◀ *Fruit machines, or ''one-armed bandits'' were first introduced in the U.S.. They soon became a popular form of entertainment in many public places.*

▼ *Jazz music became very popular in the U.S. in the 1920s. Many of the stars were Black Americans, like Louis Armstrong. Later, large dance bands emerged and were very popular in World War II.*

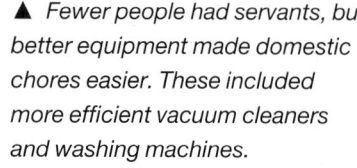

▶ During this period, hemlines gradually went higher, and in the 1920s fashionable women liked to appear flat-chested and had their hair cut short. After 1938 synthetic materials such as nylon made some clothes easier to wash.

◀ Charlie Chaplin appeared in the film The Kid in 1920. It was made in black and white and was silent. By 1930, films had soundtracks and some were filmed in color. Many were produced in Hollywood. They included comedies, cartoons, and musicals.

▶ Refugees fleeing before the German advance into the Netherlands and Belgium in 1940. Many people were forced to leave their homes in both world wars. They put what possessions they could carry on bicycles, carts, or even wheelbarrows and just kept moving until they found a place where they could be safe and start a new life.

WHEN IT HAPPENED

1927 *The Jazz Singer* starring Al Jolson, is the first full-length movie with sound.

1928 The cartoon character Mickey Mouse appears.

1930 Sliced bread is introduced.

1939 First precooked frozen foods are sold.

1940 Charlie Chaplin receives a death threat from Hitler after the release of his film *The Great Dictator*.

1945 After World War II, many Eastern Europeans flee to the West as refugees from communism.

1947 First microwave oven sold in the U.S.

1947 French fashion designer Christian Dior introduces the long-skirted "new look" for women's clothes.

▼ At the start of World War II, British children were evacuated to the country. People in London slept in subway stations to escape the bombing.

The Great Depression

In the late 1920s the price of shares in the U.S. had been forced up beyond their real value by reckless speculators. Then in October 1929 people started to sell shares rapidly. People began to panic. On a single day, 13 million shares were sold on the New York Stock Exchange. This started an economic crisis which soon affected the whole world. Many people lost all their money. Banks and businesses closed and unemployment began to increase. By 1932 there were 12 million people unemployed in the U.S. alone. The situation was made worse by a drought in the agricultural center of the country. The soil turned to dust in many places and blew away in the wind and thousands of farmers left their land to start a new life in California and other states.

▼ The Wall Street Crash caused panic on the streets of New York in October 1929. Share prices dropped so rapidly that many people lost all their money. This meant that there was no money for investments or purchasing new goods. This in turn led to severe cuts both in exports and in the U.S. domestic market.

Roosevelt

1882 Born Franklin D. Roosevelt in New York State.

1928 Elected governor of New York.

1932 Wins presidential election.

1933 Introduces the "New Deal."

1944 Becomes only U.S. president to be re-elected three times.

1945 Dies.

◀ *The Great Depression meant that people in many countries lost their jobs. Without government support, many unemployed people were homeless and hungry.*

In 1933 the new U.S. President, Franklin D. Roosevelt promised a "New Deal." This introduced protection for people's savings and new regulation of banks. Farm prices were supported and a huge program of construction was started to create employment.

In some parts of the world the Depression lasted until the end of the 1930s. High unemployment led to social and political unrest. This was especially true in Germany where six million people were out of work by 1933.

WORLD EFFECTS

The Wall Street Crash led to the collapse of the system of international loans which had been set up to handle reparations (*see* pages 658–659). This affected Europe and North America directly. Other parts of the world, especially the colonies, were also badly hit since much of their trade and business relied on selling food and raw materials to Europe and North America. As these overseas markets collapsed, many people around the world also lost their jobs. As a result, unrest increased, and nationalism grew in many countries.

▲ *In October 1935, 200 men from Jarrow in northern England marched to London with a petition, drawing attention to unemployment in their home town.*

1932 At the Imperial Economic Conference in Ottawa, Britain gives limited trading preference to the Commonwealth countries. U.S.: Unemployment tops 12 million as a result of the Great Depression. South America: War breaks out between Paraguay and Bolivia over Chaco region (to 1935). Saudi Arabia: Country is united. Europe: Disarmament conference at Geneva, but achieves nothing. Portugal: Finance minister Antonio de Oliveira Salazar becomes dictator (to 1968). China: Japanese set up puppet state of Manchukuo in Manchuria. Britain: Novelist and essayist Aldous Huxley publishes his science fiction novel *Brave New World*. American Amelia Earhart becomes the first woman to fly solo across the Atlantic.

1933 U.S.: Prohibition ends. Franklin D. Roosevelt becomes president, having promised a "New Deal" to help the U.S. out of the Depression. He removes U.S. currency from gold standard. Germany: President Paul von Hindenburg appoints Hitler as chancellor. The Reichstag (German parliament) building is set on fire. The Nazis allege it is a Communist plot. Hitler and the Nazi Party begin to eliminate opposition and gradually gain control through the Enabling Act, giving the government dictatorial powers. This is the start of the Third Reich (empire). The first concentration camps for "political and racial enemies" set up at Dachau and Oranienburg. Nazis make Jews and other minorities "scapegoats" for their troubles. Germany withdraws from the League of Nations.

A cartoon ridiculing Roosevelt's "New Deal."

Weimar and Hitler

After Emperor William II abdicated in 1918, Germany became a republic. Its new government ruled from Weimar, instead of Berlin. From 1919 to 1933 Germany was known as the Weimar Republic. Its first president was Friedrich Ebert, a Socialist. He died in 1925 and was succeeded by Field Marshal Paul von Hindenburg who was by then 78 years old.

The next presidential election was in 1932, when Germany was in economic crisis, with massive inflation and high unemployment. Hindenburg was elected as president again, with Adolf Hitler, leader of the National Socialist (Nazi) Party, in second place. The Nazi Party won the most seats in the Reichstag (German parliament), and Hindenburg appointed Hitler as chancellor in January 1933. By April 1933 the Nazi Party had gained absolute power in Germany.

When Hindenburg died in 1934, Hitler set out to avenge the humiliation brought to Germany by the Versailles Peace Settlement. He wanted Germany to become a powerful empire (called the Third Reich) which would dominate Europe.

▲ Hindenburg appointed Hitler as Chancellor in 1933. Hitler became the country's leader in 1934.

▶ In 1933, the Nazis burned all books that opposed their views or were written by Jews.

▼ A Nazi party rally at Nuremburg in 1933. At first Nazi policies were popular because they promised to make Germany powerful. But by 1939 Germany had become a police state dominated by the Nazis. People lived in fear of the Gestapo, the secret police.

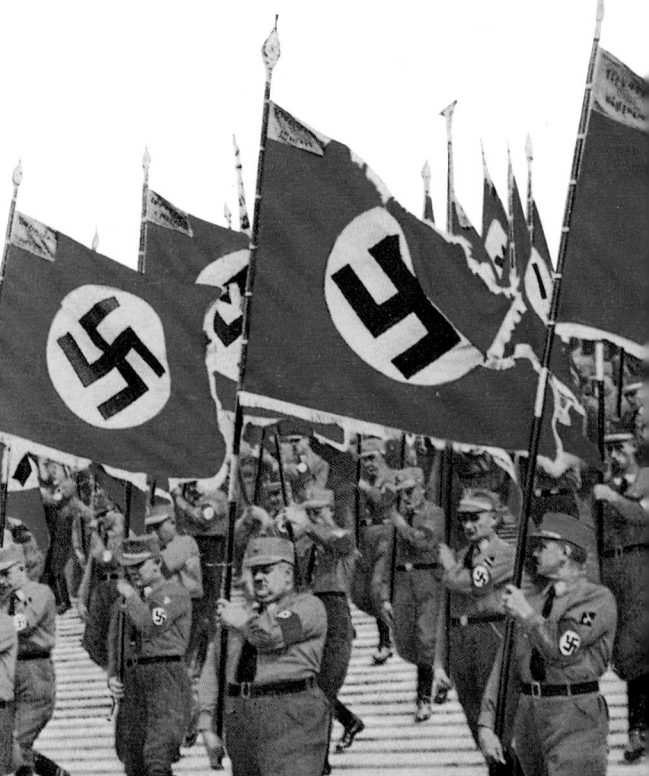

On the "Night of the Long Knives" Hitler had his rivals killed and became Führer, or leader, of Germany. He withdrew from the League of Nations and started to rearm the country. Blaming the Jews and the labor unions for Germany's problems, he began persecuting them. He banned strikes and built concentration camps (*see* page 694) in which Jews and others were killed.

ANTI-SEMITISM

Hitler's Nazis persecuted the Jews. They attacked Jewish homes, stores, and synagogues. Many Jews were forced to live in ghettos and wear a yellow star to show that they were Jews. Some escaped, but millions were killed in concentration camps.

Adolf Hitler

1889 Born in Austria.
1914–1918 Serves in the German army and wins the Iron Cross.
1921 Becomes leader of the Nazi Party.
1925 Publishes *Mein Kampf*, setting out his political theories.
1933 Is chancellor.
1934–1945 Rules Germany as dictator.
1945 Commits suicide.

1934 Turkey, Greece, Romania, and Yugoslavia form the Balkan Pact. Turkey: Mustafa Kemal chooses the surname "Atatürk," meaning Father of the Turks. Austria: Chancellor Engelbert Dollfuss is killed by Nazis. Germany: President Hindenburg dies and Hitler becomes Führer, or leader. On the "Night of the Long Knives" SS troops murder Hitler's rivals. U.S.: Stalin starts to rid the Communist Party of any possible rivals. China: Mao Zedong leads Chinese Communists northward on the Long March from Jiangxi (to 1935). U.S.: After nine months without rain, severe drought hits Midwest. Bank robbers Bonnie and Clyde are shot dead at a police roadblock.

1935 Germany: Hitler renounces Treaty of Versailles and begins a policy of rearmament. He passes the Nuremberg Laws which classify Jews as second-class citizens; persecution of Jews begins. Greece: The monarchy is restored. Middle East: Persia officially changes its name to Iran. Africa: Italian forces invade Ethiopia in an attempt to set up an African empire; League of Nations fails to take any effective action. India: British Parliament passes Government of India Act, which allows provincial councils to be set up in India as a step toward independence. China: Survivors of the Long March reach Yan'an. South America: Paraguay defeats Bolivia. U.S.: Dancer Fred Astaire stars in the film *Top Hat*.

Dancer Fred Astaire seen here with his partner Ginger Rogers. His graceful style inspired many young dancers.

1936 Britain: King George V dies; succeeded by his son as Edward VIII. Edward VIII abdicates to marry Wallis Simpson, a twice-divorced American. His younger brother becomes King George VI (to 1952). Germany: German troops break the Treaty of Versailles by occupying the Rhineland. Hitler opens the Olympic games in Berlin, but is furious when Black athletes are victorious. Professor Heinrich Focke designs the first practical helicopter. Spain: A military revolt led by General Francisco Franco against the left-wing Republican government starts the Spanish Civil War (to 1939). Italy and Germany support the Falange (Fascist) rebels under Franco and use the war to test weapons and men in the field. U.S. sends aid to the Republicans, who are also supported by volunteers from other countries. An agreement known as the Rome-Berlin Axis is set up between Italy and Germany. Ethiopia: Italian troops take Addis Ababa and annex Ethiopia. France: The Popular Front, a left-wing coalition government headed by Leon Blum, is elected. China: Chiang Kai-shek is kidnapped by Nationalist troops. They want an end to the civil war with the Communists and a united front against Japan. USSR: Composer Sergei Prokofiev writes *Peter and the Wolf*. U.S.: The Hoover Dam is opened. President Roosevelt is elected for a second term.

The Spanish Civil War

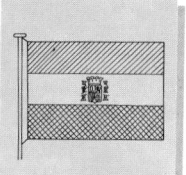

Following a successful coup in 1923, Primo de Rivera ruled Spain as a dictator until he fell from power in 1930. In the following year, King Alfonso XIII gave in to the demand for elections. The Republican Party won and the monarchy was overthrown. A new Republican government was elected in February 1936. Supported by Socialists and Communists, it opposed the power of the Roman Catholic Church in Spanish affairs. The Church was supported by the army and by the Fascists, including the Falange Party.

On July 17, 1936, Spanish army generals in Morocco began a rebellion which spread to the mainland. Led by

▲ *Nationalist troops march through the snow in Catalonia in northeastern Spain. At the beginning of the war, the northeast was a Republican stronghold, but Nationalists gradually swept across the country from the west.*

A poster of a soldier going off to fight a war against the Fascists saying to his child "I Go to Fight for Your Future."

Francisco Franco

1892 Born.
1906 Attends the Infantry Academy.
1915 Is youngest captain in the army.
1936 Leads uprising against the Republican government.
1939–1975 Rules as a dictator.
1975 Dies.

GUERNICA

The town of Guernica in northern Spain became a symbol of the Spanish Civil War. It was a traditional meeting place for the Basque parliament. On April 27, 1937, German aircraft supporting the Nationalists bombed the town. Hundreds of civilians died, and the event is remembered for the ruthlessness of the attack. The attack on Guernica is the subject of a painting by Pablo Picasso.

General Franco, they were called the Nationalists or Falange Party. They had the support of the Fascist governments of Italy and Germany. The rebellion led to a bitter civil war. By the end of 1936 the Nationalists controlled most of western and southern Spain, while Republicans held the urban areas to the north and east, including Barcelona, Bilbao, Madrid, and Valencia. The Nationalists captured Bilbao in 1937.

The fighting ended in 1939 when Barcelona, Valencia, and Madrid fell to the Nationalists. General Franco was declared "Caudillo of the Realm and Head of State." He ruled Spain until 1975. Although sympathetic to Hitler, he kept Spain neutral during World War II.

▼ *German aircraft bombed Spanish towns. People had to search through the rubble to find survivors.*

▼ *Both men and women took part in the civil war. These three members of the republican forces are holding a high position from which they can fire on Nationalists. The USSR and the International Brigade of foreign volunteers helped the Republicans.*

Science and Medicine

Cures and preventions were being found for some of the diseases that had previously killed thousands. As a result of the two world wars, many advances were made in the treatment of injuries.

During World War II, Alexander MacIndoe made great advances in plastic surgery to reconstruct the faces and bodies of airmen who had been badly burned.

Developments in peacetime included the discovery of insulin for the treatment of diabetics in 1921, and the first antibiotic in 1928. In 1937, the first blood bank opened in the U.S. and plasma started to be used in 1940.

▲ A Red Cross man giving first aid to an injured soldier in Russia during World War I. Doctors realized that if wounds were treated quickly people had a better chance of surviving.

▶ Liberated prisoners of war in Singapore in 1945 receive the first medical treatment they have had for several years. Apart from disease, malnutrition (lack of proper food) was a major problem.

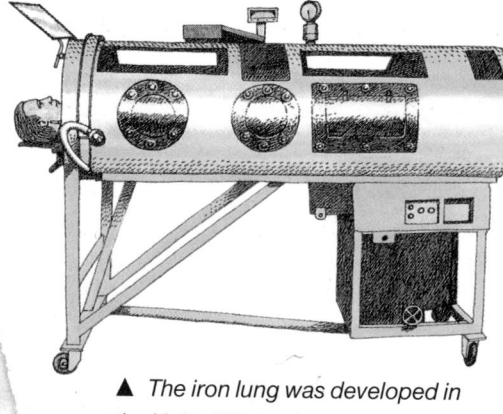

▲ The iron lung was developed in the United States in 1928. It helped people to breathe when their chest muscles were paralyzed and saved many lives during polio epidemics.

◀ Penicillin was discovered by Alexander Fleming in 1928 when a mold he grew in his laboratory killed the bacteria around it.

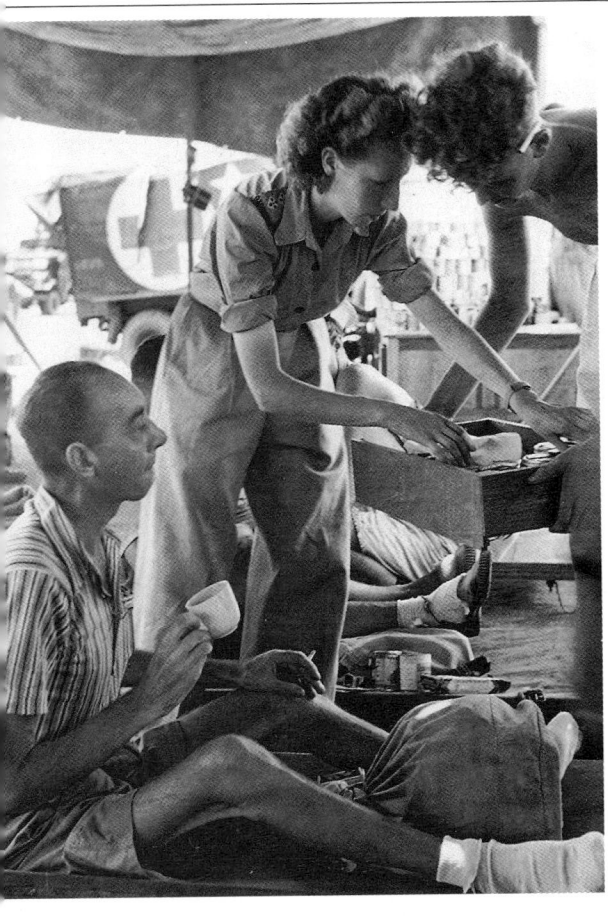

WHEN IT HAPPENED

1921 Alfred Adler, an early associate of psychoanalyst Sigmund Freud, opens his first child guidance clinic in Vienna, Austria.

1922 BCG tuberculosis vaccine is used in France.

1930 Karl Landsteiner wins a Nobel Prize for his discovery of different human blood groups. His work makes transfusions more successful.

1940 Large-scale production of penicillin begins.

1945 Fluoride is added to the water supply in the United States.

1949 The Labor government in Britain sets up the National Health Service to provide free health care for everybody.

▼ *(Left) A refugee is innoculated against disease at a relief station along the migration route between India and Pakistan in 1947. (Right) U.S. doctors prepare donated blood plasma for the treatment of British war wounded. Increased availability of blood products gave badly injured people and premature babies a better chance of survival.*

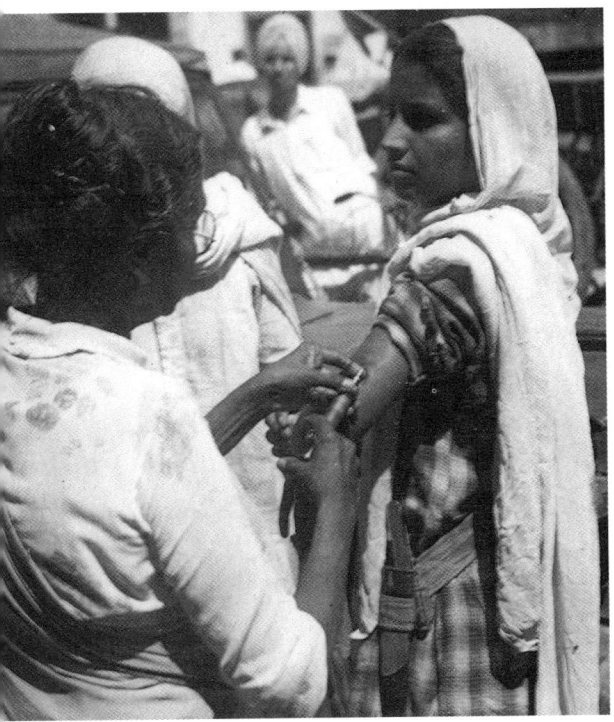

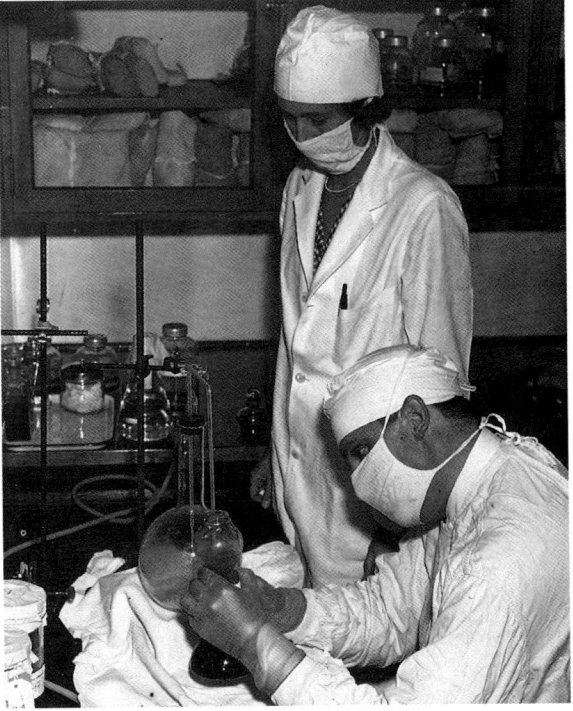

China and Japan at War

Both industry and population expanded rapidly in Japan from 1900 to 1925. However, the industry depended largely on foreign markets. During the Great Depression, these markets collapsed and many Japanese factories were at a standstill.

At the same time, China seemed ready to try and reclaim Manchuria, which Japan had dominated since 1905. An explosion on the south Manchurian railroad in 1931 led the Japanese to occupy the city of Mukden in Manchuria. They set up a puppet state called Manchukuo there in 1932. Officially it was ruled by P'u-yi, the last Chinese emperor (*see* pages 622–623), but in fact, the Japanese

▲ Japanese troops march through a city in Manchuria in 1933. In 1937, they attacked Beijing (Peking) and took control of many other cities in 1938.

▼ Japanese marines examine a brand-new armored car for use against China. Japanese forces had better equipment and weapons than the Chinese. This helped them take over much of eastern China by 1937.

army was in control.

In China itself, the civil war between the Nationalists and the Communists continued. The two sides became allies, however, when the Chinese-Japanese War started in 1937. The Japanese attacked Chinese cities, including Tianjin, Beijing, Shanghai, and Nanjing. Despite resistance, by 1938 they controlled most of eastern China. Chiang Kai-shek and his government had to leave Nanjing, which had been their capital since 1927. They moved to Sichuan and set up a base at Chongqing. Here they received supplies from the U.S. and Britain.

Meanwhile Mao Zedong's Communists still controlled much of northwest China. When the Japanese tried to advance westward in 1939, the Soviet army stopped them. The Chinese-Japanese War lasted until 1945 when World War II ended.

▼ *Chinese troops prepare to fire on Japanese soldiers and tanks, protected by a barricade made from logs. The Chinese-Japanese War eventually became part of World War II in the Pacific, and ended when Japan surrendered in 1945.*

1937 Spain: German planes bomb the Basque town of Guernica. Many civilians are killed and the town is almost completely destroyed. Cubist artist Pablo Picasso paints *Guernica* as a memorial to the town. Britain: Neville Chamberlain continues a coalition government and adopts a policy of appeasement toward Hitler. Engineer Frank Whittle designs the first experimental jet aircraft engine. Ireland: Eamon de Valera establishes a new constitution with an elected president. Africa: Anglo-Egyptian Treaty is set up to restrict British forces to the Canal Zone for 20 years. Far East: Chinese-Japanese War begins (to 1945) as the Japanese invade China, capturing Shanghai and Beijing (Peking); Chinese Nationalists and Communists unite to fight them. Nanjing (Nanking) falls to the Japanese in mid-December. Over 100,000 Chinese are massacred by Japanese troops in the "Rape of Nanking." U.S.: Walt Disney produces the first full-length cartoon film, *Snow White and the Seven Dwarfs*. Wallace Carothers invents nylon. German airship *Hindenburg* explodes in New Jersey, killing 35 of the 97 people on board. The Golden Gate Bridge in San Francisco is opened. Germany: Catholic and Protestant leaders are persecuted. The Nazis hold a rally at Nuremberg to open the Nazi congress.

A German cartoon showing Japanese brutality toward Chinese opposition during the invasion of Manchuria.

1938 Austria: Chancellor Kurt von Schuschnigg resigns over the issue of Austrian independence. He is succeeded by Artur von Seyss-Inquart, a Nazi supporter. German troops march into Austria at the invitation of the Austrian Nazi Party. Hitler declares Anschluss, the union of Austria with Germany. The Munich Pact is signed by Hitler, Mussolini, Neville Chamberlain (prime minister of Britain), and Edouard Daladier of France. It gives the Sudetenland (German-speaking part of Czechoslovakia) to Germany. Germany: A day of widespread riots against the Jews becomes known as *Kristallnacht* (the night of broken glass). Chinese-Japanese War: Japan wins a series of victories over the Chinese and captures Guangzhou (Canton) and Hankou. U.S.: Child labor is abolished. Australian-born Errol Flynn stars in the film *The Adventures of Robin Hood*. Orson Welles directs a radio production of H. G. Wells' science fiction novel *War of the Worlds*, about an invasion from Mars; listeners panic because it is so realistic. Hungary: Journalist Lazlo Biro invents the ballpoint pen. France: Philosopher and writer Jean-Paul Sartre publishes his novel *Nausea*. Britain: Surgeon Philip Wiles develops the first complete artificial hip replacement.

A cartoon of 1934 which comments on Hitler's claim that his only aim is peace.

Anschluss and Munich

One of Adolf Hitler's ambitions was to unite Germany and Austria. This union (called the Anschluss) had been forbidden by the Treaty of Versailles in 1919 as France and other countries thought it would make Germany more powerful. By the early 1930s, however, many people in Germany and Austria wanted their countries to unite, but in 1934 an attempted Nazi coup in Austria failed.

In 1938, Hitler met with the Austrian chancellor, Kurt von Schuschnigg, and made new demands. With chaos and German troops threatening his country, Schuschnigg resigned in favor of Artur von Seyss-Inquart, leader of the Austrian Nazis. He invited German troops to occupy Austria and the union, or Anschluss, of the two countries was formally announced on March 13, 1938.

Hitler also wanted to reclaim the areas of Europe that had been ceded to other states by the Treaty of Versailles and

▼ *Neville Chamberlain, the British prime minister, with the Munich Agreement. It was also signed by Daladier of France, Hitler, and Mussolini. Giving what were seen as reasonable concessions to Hitler was called appeasement.*

German troops marching into Vienna in 1938. Hitler wanted to unite all German-speaking peoples into a "Greater Germany," an important part of his vision of the third German empire (Third Reich).

Many Austrians welcomed the union of their country with Germany. Here, an Austrian woman greets a German soldier by giving him a flower. For the Jewish people of Austria, the Anschluss meant that they had to go into hiding or leave the country.

which contained many people of German descent. One of these areas was the Sudetenland of Czechoslovakia. In an attempt to keep peace in Europe, the Munich Agreement was signed on September 29, 1938. It gave the Sudetenland to Germany. This was not enough for Hitler, however, and in March 1939 his troops took over the whole of Czechoslovakia. There were many protests, but no action was taken.

Nazis salute Adolf Hitler. Hitler's forceful personality and rousing speeches won him the support of many German people. He wanted to create a third German empire which would last one thousand years. People who opposed him were beaten, imprisoned, or murdered by the army or the secret police.

Science and Technology

This period saw the introduction of many new products. The development of plastics and synthetic fibers meant that many consumer goods and clothes could be mass-produced at prices which most people could afford.

Major advances were made in the development of computers. Robots also appeared, but they were not yet used for industrial work. After 1948, the transistor brought about a revolution in electronics, while developments in atomic physics led to the discovery of the most accurate method of measuring time, as well as the atomic bomb.

▲ *In 1934, the physicist Enrico Fermi found that a chain reaction of nuclear fission could be achieved using uranium. This later led to the development of the atomic bomb at Los Alamos, New Mexico.*

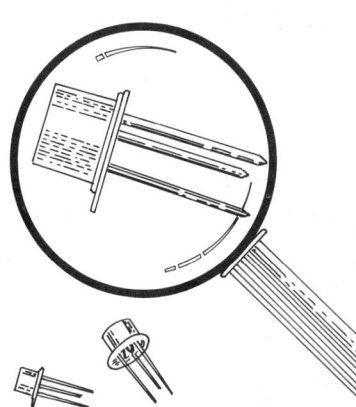

◄ *The transistor was developed by the Bell Telephone Company in 1948. It amplified sound, and revolutionized electronics because it was so small.*

▼ *As more types of plastic became available, they began to be used to make household goods, like these elaborate salt and pepper shakers. In World War II the shortages of raw materials, such as rubber and silk, led to farther advances and plastics were used for electrical equipment and food packaging.*

WHEN IT HAPPENED

1919 In Britain the physicist Ernest Rutherford becomes the first person to split the atom.

1919 Alcock and Brown make the first non-stop flight across the Atlantic.

1926 The first liquid-fueled rocket is launched in the U.S.

1937 The first experimental jet engine for an aircraft is made by Frank Whittle.

1938 Lazlo Biro introduces the first ballpoint pen.

1939 The first nylon stockings are sold in the U.S.

1948 The invention of the atomic clock allows the first truly accurate measurement of time.

► In 1943, the first completely electronic computer was used in Britain for code-breaking. As the work was secret, the American ENIAC computer, completed in 1946, is better known. Early computers were enormous. ENIAC needed 18,000 tubes and large amounts of electricity to handle a very small amount of data. However, it could do 5,000 calculations a second. The development of transistors led to smaller and more powerful computers being built after 1948.

◄ Albert Einstein won the Nobel prize for Physics in 1921. Although he intended his work to be used for peaceful purposes, it led to the development of the atomic bomb.

◄ Research on synthetic fibers continued during the 1930s. This dress is made from rayon, which was in use by the 1920s. At the time it was called artificial silk. The first nylon products appeared in 1939.

► This robot, called Maria, appeared in Fritz Lang's film Metropolis in 1926. People's ideas about robots were influenced by science fiction, where robots threatened to take over from humans.

World War II

World War II was fought by the Axis Powers and the Allied Powers. The main Axis Powers were Germany, Italy, and Japan. The Allied Powers included Britain, France, the United States, and the USSR (Soviet Union).

The three Axis Powers all wanted more territory. Germany had already taken over Austria and Czechoslovakia (*see* pages 688–689). Italy had conquered land in East Africa and Albania, and a Japanese-controlled state had been set up in China. After his invasion (*see* pages 688–689) of Czechoslovakia, Hitler did not expect any international military action against his plans to expand further. But when he invaded Poland on September 1, 1939, both Britain and France declared war on Germany two days later.

Troops from the Soviet Union, which had signed a non-aggression pact

▼ *By 1941 Germany had conquered most of Europe apart from Britain, and was expanding into North Africa. Spain, devastated by its own civil war, managed to remain neutral, as did Portugal, Ireland, Sweden, Switzerland, and Turkey.*

▶ *German infantry troops under fire in Warsaw in 1939. Poland was not prepared for a 20th-century war. It had 370,000 troops, but their equipment was out of date. They had to attack the German tanks with cavalry.*

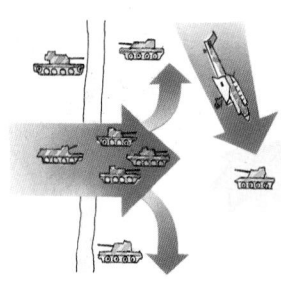

BLITZKRIEG

Blitzkrieg is the name given to the system of warfare which Hitler used in 1940. It means "lightning war" and was a fast way of eliminating opposing forces. It relied on a surprise attack with overwhelming numbers of tanks to overrun a country's ground defenses. While the tanks pushed ahead, aircraft moved in behind to bomb any defenses the tanks missed. Then infantry units moved in to wipe out any remaining pockets of resistance. Hitler used the system successfully against Norway, Denmark, the Netherlands, Belgium, and France.

▶ *Between May 29 and June 4, 1940 more than 330,000 Allied troops were rescued from the beaches at Dunkirk.*

German domination at its greatest extent in 1941

Neutral countries

FINLAND
NORWAY
SWEDEN
DENMARK
IRELAND
UNITED KINGDOM
NETH
BELGIUM
GERMANY
POLAND
RUSSIA
CZECHOSLOVAKIA
FRANCE
SWITZ
AUSTRIA
HUNGARY
ITALY
YUGOSLAVIA
ROMANIA
PORT
SPAIN
BULGARIA
ALBANIA
GREECE
TURKEY
NORTH AFRICA

with Germany, invaded Poland from the east on September 17, 1939. Poland was divided between Germany and the USSR. The USSR then invaded Finland in November 1939. In April 1940 German troops invaded Denmark and Norway, and in May they invaded Belgium, the Netherlands, and France. In June Italy declared war on the Allies. With almost all of Europe under fascist control, Hitler planned to invade Britain while the United States stayed in isolation.

1939 Spain: Franco's forces capture Barcelona from the Republicans. Madrid, the last Republican stronghold, surrenders, bringing the Spanish Civil War to an end. General Franco becomes dictator of Spain (to 1975). Germany: Membership of the Hitler Youth and the League of German Maidens becomes compulsory for all children over 14. Germany annexes Czechoslovakia. Britain and France confirm they will defend Poland against attack. Italian troops invade Albania. Hitler and Stalin sign a non-aggression Nazi-Soviet pact. The pact also partitions (divides) Poland between Germany and USSR. Germany invades Poland on September 1, starting World War II (to 1945). Norway, Switzerland, and Finland declare their neutrality; France and Britain give Germany an ultimatum to leave Poland. On September 3 they declare war on Germany. USSR invades Poland from the east. In a period known as the "Phony War" everyone waits for something to happen. On November 30 USSR attacks Finland. The first real action of war is the battle of the Plate River in the South Atlantic. Outer Mongolia: Clash between Soviet and Japanese troops. Palestine: Britain announces limitations on Jewish immigration following Arab unrest at the large numbers arriving there. U.S.: Premieres of films *Gone with the Wind* and *The Wizard of Oz*.

During World War II midget submarines were used to attack large warships.

1940 Japan joins the Axis Powers. Europe: German troops invade Denmark and Norway, Belgium, the Netherlands, and Luxembourg. Winston Churchill replaces Neville Chamberlain as prime minister. France: Germans invade France; British and other Allied troops are evacuated from Dunkirk. Germans occupy Paris and France surrenders. Marshal Pétain signs armistice with Hitler. Pétain sets up a new French government at Vichy under German control. General de Gaulle leads the Free French (organization of French men and women in exile) from London. German troops invade Channel Islands. They plan a *Blitzkrieg* (lightning war) on Britain. In the Battle of Britain many cities are bombed. The RAF finally defeats the Luftwaffe (German air force). Italy declares war on Britain and France. North Africa: British troops capture 62 Italians in the first skirmish of the campaign. Italian troops invade Greece.

1941 North Africa: Australian and British troops capture port of Tobruk in Libya. Italian and German troops invade Egypt. Europe: Germany invades USSR, besieging Leningrad (St. Petersburg) and Stalingrad (Volgograd). They advance on Moscow, but are defeated by Soviet forces and a cold winter. The Soviet army attacks the Germans in the Ukraine. Pacific: The Japanese launch an air attack on the U.S. navy in Pearl Harbor, Hawaii. United States declares war on the Axis Powers. Malaya and Hong Kong are captured by the Japanese.

An airgraph from World War II. To speed mail delivery, letters to the forces were photographed, developed onto sheets, then sent out.

War in the West

On July 10, 1940 the battle of Britain began. It lasted until October 31 and forced Hitler to abandon his plan to invade Britain. Instead he turned his attention elsewhere. In April 1941 Hitler's troops occupied Greece and Yugoslavia to help Mussolini's troops who were fighting there. In June, Hitler invaded the USSR. After some initial successes, the Germans were turned back at the battle of Stalingrad in 1943.

In December 1941 the United States entered the war after a Japanese attack on Pearl Harbor, Hawaii (*see* pages 696–697). Meanwhile Allied troops had been sent to Africa and the Middle East. They took Ethiopia from the Italians and gained control of Iraq, Syria, Lebanon, and Iran. In 1942, the Allies won the battle of El Alamein in Egypt against the

---

CONCENTRATION CAMPS

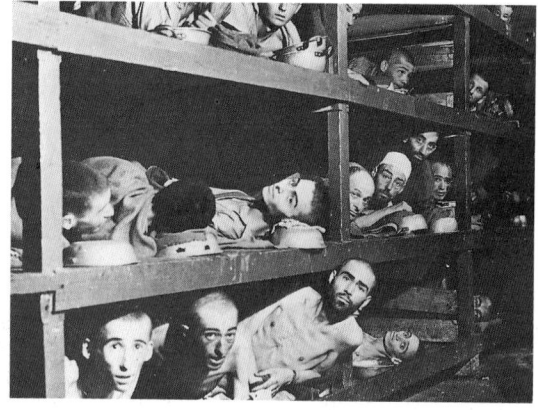

Hitler blamed the Jews for all Germany's problems. When he came to power he planned to destroy the whole Jewish population of Europe. Millions of Jews were sent to concentration camps, such as this one at Buchenwald. In the camps, over 6 million Jews were tortured, used in medical experiments, or gassed to death. Their ordeal was known as the Holocaust.

▶ *Vichy France (the part not occupied by Germany) was ruled from the town of Vichy from 1940. Germany occupied the rest of France. The French Resistance movement worked against the German occupation.*

Winston Churchill

1874 Born.
1900 Elected to British Parliament.
1940 Becomes British prime minister and leads Britain during World War II.
1945 Defeated in election.
1951 Re-elected.
1965 Dies.

BATTLE OF BRITAIN

On July 10, 1940 the German air force (the Luftwaffe) began to bomb British cities. On July 13, Hitler ordered the destruction of the British air force (the RAF). While the battle of Britain took to the skies, German bombers kept attacking British cities, hoping to lower the morale of the people. Altogether, the RAF destroyed 1,733 Luftwaffe planes and the RAF lost 915, but by October 31, they had won the battle.

German
occupied

Vichy France

Present day
boundary

BRITAIN
NETH
BELG
GERMANY
Paris
SWITZ
Vichy
ITALY
CORSICA

Germans and the Italians. Italy surrendered in September 1943.

Early in 1944 the Allies attacked Nazi-held areas of Italy, and on June 6, 1944 the D-Day invasion of Normandy, France, began the end of Nazi Germany. German troops launched a counter-offensive in December 1944, but had to retreat in January 1945. Having forced German troops off its territory in August 1944, the Soviet army began to march toward Germany. After heavy bomb attacks on Germany, opposition to Hitler grew. He killed himself on April 30, 1945.

▼ *British and Commonwealth troops fought together against the Axis powers in Africa and the Middle East. Much of the fighting took place in the desert.*

1942 Far East: Japanese capture Manila and Singapore, where they take 90,000 British and Commonwealth troops prisoner. Many of these prisoners die from ill-treatment in prison camps and on the Burma railroad. Japanese take the Dutch East Indies (Indonesia), the Philippines, and Burma. India and Australia are also threatened, but U.S. victories at the battles of the Coral Sea, Midway, and Guadalcanal stop the Japanese advance. Europe: Battle for the besieged city of Stalingrad (Volgograd) starts. North Africa: The Germans under General Rommel are defeated by the Allies at the battle of El Alamein. The Germans start to retreat from North Africa. Allied forces go on to take Tripoli and Tunis. Humphrey Bogart and Ingrid Bergman star in the film *Casablanca*.

1943 Argentina: Juan Perón leads a revolt. Lebanon becomes independent from France. North Africa: All Axis resistance ends by May. USSR: German forces at Stalingrad (Volgograd) surrender after losing 200,000 troops in the siege of the city. Italy: The Fascist government surrenders. The Fascists cling to power in the north where the Germans help Mussolini to set up a separate government in Salo. The official Italian government, led by Badoglio, declares war on Germany. Pacific: U.S. begins to recapture Japanese-held islands. Britain: American-born poet T. S. Eliot publishes his series of poems *The Four Quartets*.

Japanese kamikaze *pilots crashed their planes, loaded with bombs, into U.S. warships.*

War in the Pacific

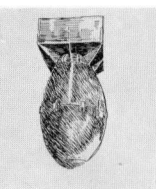

The war in the Pacific really began on December 7, 1941 when the Japanese carried out an unprovoked attack on the U.S. naval base at Pearl Harbor, Hawaii. Japanese forces invaded Thailand on the same day. Within five months, the Japanese had overrun Burma, Hong Kong, Singapore, Malaya, the Dutch East Indies (Indonesia), Thailand, and the Philippines. They also invaded New Guinea and threatened the north coast of Australia. With most of its own troops and equipment helping the Allies fight the war in the West, Australia had to look to the U.S. for defense.

Japanese hopes of further expansion were stopped in 1942 by U.S. victories in the battles of the Coral Sea (May 4–8), Midway Island (June 4–6) and Guadalcanal (August). With the Japanese advance halted, the task of

◄ *The Japanese bombed the U.S. naval base at Pearl Harbor without any warning. Four battleships were lost. Many other ships were damaged and 3,300 people were killed.*

▼ *World War II ended on September 2, 1945. The statement of surrender was signed by several Japanese representatives and General Douglas MacArthur of the United States.*

▼ *The atomic bomb totally destroyed about 5 square miles (13 sq. km) of the city of Hiroshima. Between 70,000 and 100,000 people died in the explosion and thousands more died later from injuries and radiation sickness. The bomb dropped on Nagasaki had similar effects. The development of the bomb had been kept secret, and many people all over the world were shocked when they saw pictures of the ruined cities, and learned what had happened to the people.*

recapturing the territory began. In a series of battles in 1943 and 1944, U.S. troops retook the Gilbert, Marshall, Caroline, and Mariana islands. They could bomb Japan from these bases.

In September 1944, U.S. forces began to reconquer the Philippines, while the British Fourth Army began to reconquer Burma. Other Allied troops fought a way through to China. The Allies had planned to invade Japan in late 1945, but on August 6, 1945 the U.S. dropped the first atomic bomb on the Japanese city of Hiroshima. On August 9 a second bomb was dropped on Nagasaki. Five days later, the Japanese surrendered.

Society and Government

The gradual spread of education led people to expect more from life. At the same time, better communications led to the spread of ideas. Some people began to question their lot in life, instead of just accepting it. In the 1930s protest marchers in Britain tried to bring the government's attention to unemployment, and as a result the Labor Party grew in strength.

In other countries, especially those recovering from the effects of World War I, people looked for scapegoats to take the blame for the state their country was in. Often, those who looked for people to blame were willing to follow any strong leader who offered a solution to their problems. Dictatorships in fascist Germany and Italy, and the totalitarian (all-controlling) system in the communist USSR were all able to flourish.

◀ When the American athlete Jesse Owens won four gold medals at the Berlin Olympics in 1936, Hitler refused to congratulate him as he thought black people were inferior to Aryans (Hitler's master race). Black people had few rights in many parts of the world in the 1930s, but after World War II the idea of Black Power began to make itself felt.

▶ Over 30 million people faced starvation after a bad harvest in parts of Russia in 1921. This poster from the government campaign to help them says "Remember the starving." During the winter, aid from other parts of Russia and overseas poured into the worst-affected areas and in 1922 the harvest was small but successful.

▶ Women demonstrating against war in Hyde Park, London, in 1923. The suffragist movement successfully campaigned for votes for women, and the 1920s were a time of greater freedom for them.

▶ After the U.S. stock market crash in 1929 economic conditions grew worse, and by 1932 12 million Americans were out of work. Many of the unemployed lost their homes as well as their jobs. There was no government support and many of them ended up in shantytowns like this one in New York. They were also called "Hoovervilles," after President Hoover who people saw as responsible for their plight.

◀ While the European powers dominated Africa, children there were taught to copy European ways, rather than follow their own cultures. They also had to wear European clothing instead of their own which suited the climate.

▼ British women over 30 who owned property or whose husbands were property owners given the vote in 1918. The age was reduced to 21 in 1928. After a long campaign women in the U.S. won the vote in 1920.

WHEN IT HAPPENED

1927 Canberra is made the federal capital of Australia.

1926 The General Strike begins in Britain.

1929 The Wall Street crash in the U.S. marks the start of a world economic depression.

1930 Gandhi begins a campaign of civil disobedience against British rule in India.

1932 Sir Oswald Mosley founds the British Union of Fascists. Its followers stir up anti-Semitism (anti-Jewish feeling), especially in the East End of London.

1942 In Britain the Beveridge Report lays the foundations of the welfare state.

1949 The Republic of South Africa introduces its policy of apartheid, which gives different rights to Coloreds, Whites, and Blacks.

End of World War II

At the Yalta Conference in February 1945, the "Big Three" Allied powers, represented by their leaders Churchill, Roosevelt, and Stalin, decided to divide Germany into four zones after the war. These zones were to be occupied by troops from Britain, the U.S.A., the USSR, and France. This division was confirmed on August 2, 1945 at the Potsdam Conference. By this time, Roosevelt had died and he was replaced by Harry S. Truman, the new U.S. president. Britain was represented by Clement Attlee. The Potsdam Conference made it possible to set up the United Nations and bring Nazi war criminals to justice in war trials held in the German city of Nuremburg. As well as being divided, Germany also lost some of its territory to Poland and the USSR.

Countries conquered by Germany and

▼ At the end of the war, all prisoners of war were released. These men had been captured by the Japanese in 1942. In Singapore alone 50,000 Allied troops, including 15,000 from Australia, had become Japanese prisoners.

Harry S. Truman

1884 Born in Missouri.
1944 Elected vice president.
1945 Becomes president.
1948 Berlin Airlift.
1949 Establishes North Atlantic Treaty Organization (NATO).
1972 Dies.

◀ *Attlee, Truman, and Stalin attended the Potsdam Conference in July and August 1945. The division between the communist and capitalist worlds became clear.*

▼ *On June 25, 1948, the USSR set up a blockade around Berlin to try and force France, Britain, and the U.S. to give up their rights to the western part of the city. Britain and the U.S. flew supplies in for 15 months.*

Charles de Gaulle

1890 Born in Lille.
1940 Becomes leader of the Free French.
1945 Paris is liberated.
1945 and **1959** Serves as President of France.
1970 Dies.

Japan regained their former status, but the influence of the USSR increased when Bulgaria, Hungary, Poland, Romania, Czechoslovakia, Yugoslavia (*see* pages 704–705), and eastern Germany became communist states. The U.S. promised to help all free peoples who felt threatened (the Truman Doctrine) and provided the Marshall Plan for economic recovery.

1944 Europe: Allied forces enter Rome on their way to defeat remaining Fascists in the north. Allied troops land in Normandy, France, on what is known as D-Day (6 June). German forces begin to retreat. A German plot to assassinate Hitler with a briefcase bomb in his operations room fails. Allied forces liberate Paris and Brussels. V-1 flying bombs and V-2 rocket bombs, launched by German troops, land on London. The German army crushes all resistance in Warsaw, Poland. Pacific: The Japanese navy is defeated by the U.S. navy at the battle of Leyte Gulf.

1945 Europe: Soviet troops marching west to Germany capture Warsaw. At the Yalta Conference in the USSR, Churchill, Roosevelt, and Stalin meet to discuss post-war settlements. Allied troops cross into Germany at Remagen. Dresden is heavily bombed. U.S.: Franklin D. Roosevelt dies and Harry S. Truman becomes President. Europe: Mussolini is assassinated by Italian partisans (armed resistance fighters). The Soviet army reaches the outskirts of Berlin and the rest of the Allied forces approach from the west. Hitler commits suicide. On 7 May Germany surrenders. Celebrations are held on 8 May (VE Day or Victory in Europe) to mark the end of the war in Europe. Britain: Churchill loses the general election to Clement Attlee (to 1951). (*continued* page 703).

The foreign ministers of Britain and the USSR, Bevin and Molotov, dispute Germany's future.

The United Nations

The term "United Nations" was first used on January 1, 1942 to describe the main group of countries fighting against the Axis Powers (*see* pages 692–693). On that date they signed the Atlantic Charter which Roosevelt and Churchill had drafted in 1941. In the Charter they agreed to fight the Axis countries and not to make any separate peace agreements. As well as the United States, Britain, the USSR, and China, the Charter was signed by Australia, Canada, India, New Zealand, South Africa, eight European countries, and nine South American republics.

On April 25, 1945 the United Nations Organization was set up formally at a conference in San Francisco. It aimed to keep international peace and to solve problems by international cooperation instead of by fighting. A charter was signed by 50 countries and the United Nations came into being on October 24.

The UN was planned to be stronger than the League of Nations had been. It had a powerful Security Council which

▶ *The United Nations General Assembly meets in this huge auditorium. It is large enough to allow representatives from all member countries to take part in debates. Each member has one vote.*

UN FORCES

The United Nations symbol appears on the UN flag. It shows a map of the world inside a circle of olive branches to represent peace. Keeping international peace is the job of the UN Security Council. It is made up of China, France, Britain, the United States, and Russia, plus ten other members who are elected for two-year terms. The Security Council has the power to send UN troops to troubled areas. The UN forces are made up of soldiers of different nationalities.

◀ *Members of the UN have to sign the UN Charter which lays out the principles of the organization. The UN allows each member to have one equal vote in the General Assembly which meets for three months every year. It also allows the UN to set up various agencies, which include the World Health Organization (WHO), the International Court of Justice, and the International Monetary Fund (IMF).*

would decide what should be done if international disputes broke out. All members were to contribute arms and personnel to peace-keeping missions organized by the UN. In 1948 the UN made a Universal Declaration of Human Rights which was not binding. However, it has become the basis for other agreements that are binding.

▶ *The United Nations' headquarters building in New York City was built in 1951.*

1945 (*continued* from page 701). On August 2 Harry S. Truman (American president), Attlee (British prime minister), and Stalin (leader of the USSR) meet at Potsdam, near Berlin, to continue the discussions on post-war settlements started at Yalta earlier in the year. On August 6 United States drops the first atomic bomb on Hiroshima, Japan. A second atomic bomb is dropped on Nagasaki. The two cities are devastated and thousands of people are killed and injured. Japan surrenders on August 15, ending World War II. Chinese-Japanese War ends. The United Nations Organization (UN) is established; 50 member states sign the UN charter. Dutch East Indies (Indonesia): The Nationalists declare war on the Netherlands. French Indochina: Ho Chi Minh declares Vietnam a republic. Cambodia also becomes independent. Yugoslavia: Tito's party wins the general election and declares the country a republic. Bulgaria: Communists win the general election. France: Charles de Gaulle is elected president. Germany: The International War Crimes' Tribunal opens at Nuremberg (to 1946). Former Nazi leaders appear before a tribunal of British, French, Soviet, and U.S. jurors. Britain: Novelist and essayist George Orwell publishes *Animal Farm*, a novel mocking the Russian Revolution. U.S.: The first electronic computer is built, at the University of Pennsylvania.

The UN International Children's Emergency Fund (UNICEF) was set up to help child victims of the war. Today it provides education and healthcare throughout the world.

1946 The Norwegian statesman, Trygve Lie, is elected as the first secretary-general of the United Nations and the League of Nations is formally ended. A peace conference opens in Paris to end the war formally. Argentina: Juan Perón is elected president. He is helped by the popularity of his wife, Evita, who is idolized by the poor for her charitable work. She persuades him to make many social reforms, including giving women the right to vote. Greece: Civil war breaks out between Communists and Royalists (to 1949). Hungary: A republic is proclaimed. Germany: Britain and United States agree on an economic union of the British and American zones in Germany. Middle East: Zionist terrorists, (those who want to establish a Jewish state in Palestine by violent means) blow up the King David Hotel in Jerusalem, the headquarters of the British administration; 91 people are killed. Transjordan (Jordan) gains independence from Britain. Syria gains independence from France. French Indochina: Civil war starts between Vietnamese nationalists led by Ho Chi Minh, and the French. India: Hindus and Muslims riot. Britain: The Bank of England is nationalized. Bread rationing is introduced, partly as a result of a worldwide wheat shortage. Pacific: U.S. atomic tests are carried out at Bikini and Eniwetok atolls.

The Yugoslavian coat of arms showing the red star of communism and six torches symbolizing the six republics.

U.S.: Dr. Benjamin Spock publishes *The Commonsense Book of Baby and Child Care.*

Italy and the Balkans

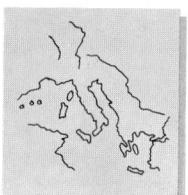

After its surrender to the Allies in 1943, Italy had two governments. In the south the king, Victor Emmanuel III, and his prime minister Badoglio ruled with Allied support. In the north the Germans rescued Mussolini from prison and set up a Fascist Italian state (Salo). This lasted until April 28, 1945 when Mussolini was shot by Italian partisans (armed resistance fighters). After that the king and his new prime minister, Alcide de Gasperi, ruled the whole of Italy. By that time, however, Victor Emmanuel was 75 years old and in May 1946 he abdicated in favor of his son Umberto II. A month later a national referendum voted for a republic and the royal family left the country. De Gasperi remained as prime minister and led a series of governments.

Tito

1892 Born Josip Broz, in Croatia.
1915 Fights in World War I.
1937 Becomes secretary-general of Communist Party.
1941 Organizes resistance to German occupation of Yugoslavia.
1953 Becomes president.
1980 Dies.

Mediterranean Sea

▲ *After World War II, Italy, Greece, and Yugoslavia changed from monarchies to republics. Yugoslavia became a communist state led by Tito.*

▼ *In Greece the Communists put up a strong resistance to the Germans, but they had less success against the U.S.-backed Monarchists.*

Alcide de Gasperi

1881 Born in Trento.
1919 Becomes secretary-general of Italian People's Party.
1929 Takes refuge from Mussolini in the Vatican.
1945 Organizes the Christian Democratic Party, and becomes prime minister.
1954 Dies.

During the German occupation of Greece, the communists built up a powerful armed force. After World War II, they hoped to make Greece into a communist state. In 1946, however, a royalist government was elected which returned King George II to the throne. The communists started a revolt and civil war broke out. Under the Truman Doctrine, the U.S. gave massive amounts of aid to the army, which supported the king. Fighting continued until 1949, when the Communists were defeated.

Yugoslavia was formed in 1918 from Serbia, Montenegro, Croatia, Slovenia, and Bosnia-Herzegovina, and ruled by Alexander I. The country was occupied by the Germans in World War II and the king fled to London. Resistance to the Germans was organized by Chetniks (Serbian nationalists) and communist partisans, but the two groups ended up fighting each other. After World War II, the partisan leader Tito became head of a Communist government.

Trade

After the Wall Street Crash in 1929, trade was hit hard by the effects of a worldwide recession. Unemployment was high as many factories closed down. Heavy industries such as mining, ship-building, and steel-making were badly affected.

The start of World War II and the need for armaments, however, soon made industry and employment thrive again. But international trade was badly hit with trade embargoes and blockades preventing the free movement of goods. This meant that countries had to try and produce the goods they needed, rather than rely on imports. Trade grew after World War II as countries began to rebuild their economies.

▲ By 1941 some foods were in short supply; to make sure people could obtain basic food supplies everyone in Britain had a ration book. Two weeks' supply of rationed foods for one person is shown here.

▶ The Panama Canal connecting the Atlantic to the Pacific opened in 1914. Before 1914 ships had to sail around South America adding 7,800 miles (12,600 km) to their journey.

◀ The Anglo-Persian Oil Company (later British Petroleum) developed one of the world's largest oil fields in what is now Iran after World War I. Other oil fields were soon operating in Iraq, Saudi Arabia, and the Gulf. Demand for oil and petroleum products increased after World War I as farmers began to use tractors and other oil-powered equipment.

▼ After World War II, Australia increased its production of table wines for consumers both at home and abroad. The government promoted the sales of wine and fruits to encourage the export trade. Immigration from Europe also increased after the war.

BUY EMPIRE GOODS FROM HOME AND OVERSEAS

▲ This poster was issued in 1929 to encourage people in the British empire, and later the British Commonwealth, to buy goods from other empire countries. They hoped this would increase trade and help to develop the economies of those countries. If goods were imported from countries outside the empire it meant that money left the empire, so taxes were added to the price of imported goods. Many countries tried to produce all the goods they needed themselves.

WHEN IT HAPPENED

1930 After a fishing trip to Alaska, Clarence Birdseye experiments with freezing food to keep it fresh.

1932 First self-service supermarket opens.

1939–1945 As wartime rationing leads to shortages, a vigorous black market trade develops in Europe.

1941 The Japanese attack on American ships at Pearl Harbor, Hawaii, is partly motivated by resentment over U.S. trade embargoes against Japanese goods.

▼ There was a rapid growth in advertising between the wars. Advertisers began to aim at young people and women in particular, because these two groups of people were seen by advertisers as potential new customers. This Coca-Cola advertisement emphasizes youth and enjoyment.

Indian Independence

In 1945, the British government under Clement Attlee decided to grant India independence within the British Commonwealth (*see* pages 674–675). The situation was complicated because India contained two major religious groups, the Hindus and the Muslims. There were fewer Muslims than Hindus but the Muslims would not agree to any form of government which would put them under Hindu rule. As independence came closer, however, the Muslims, led by Muhammad Ali Jinnah, started to press for a separate state for Indian Muslims. When Britain first offered independence to India as a whole in 1946, the leaders could not agree on a form of government which would please both sides. After riots broke out and many people were killed, the British

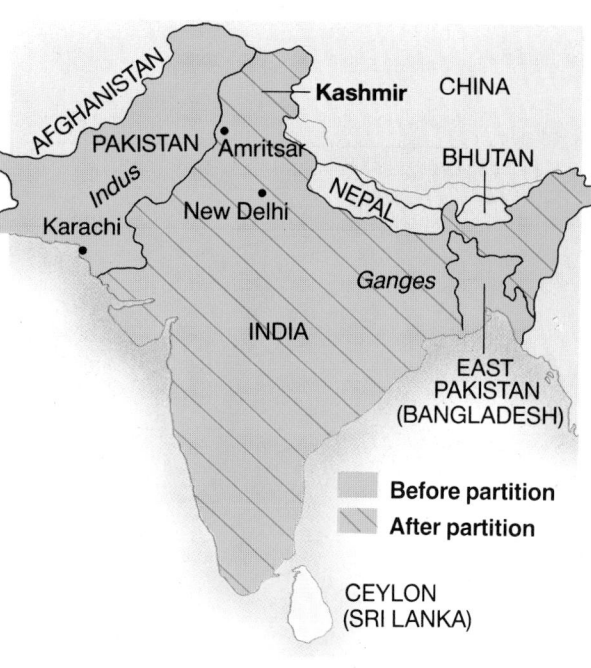

▲ After partition, both parts of Pakistan were governed from Karachi, while India was governed from New Delhi. East Pakistan broke away and became the separate state of Bangladesh in 1971.

government finally agreed to partitioning (dividing) India.

On August 14, 1947 the northeast and northwest of India, which were mostly Muslim, became the independent country of Pakistan. Muhammad Ali Jinnah became the first governor-general. The next day the remaining area became independent India with Jawaharlal Nehru as its first prime minister. When India was partitioned a massive migration took place. Millions of Muslims moved from India to East or West Pakistan and millions of Hindus moved from Pakistan to India. Many people were killed in the violence that followed. Mahatma (Mohandas) Gandhi himself was assassinated by a Hindu extremist in 1948.

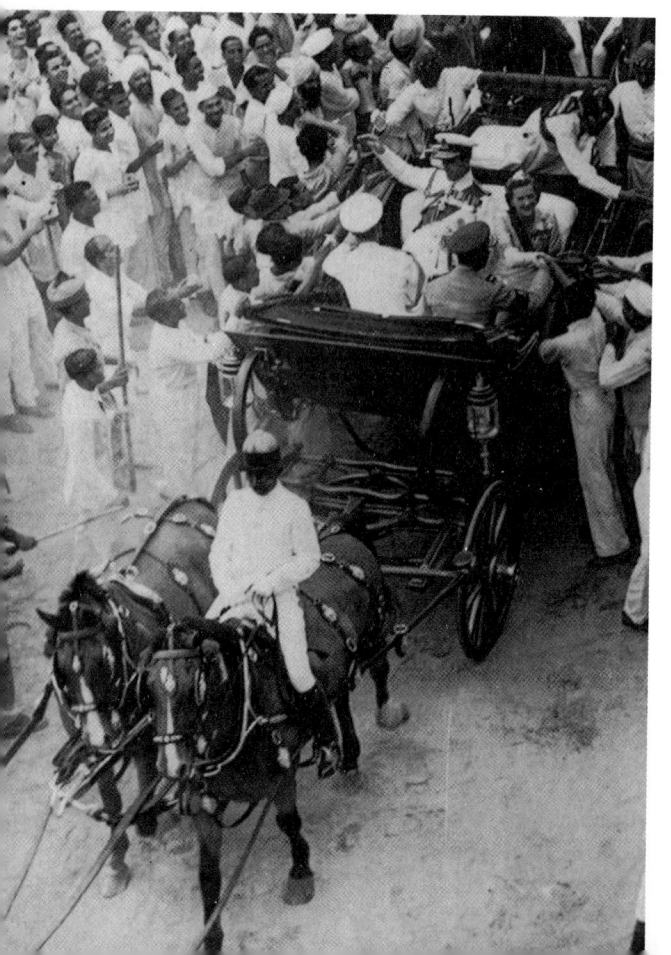

◀ Lord and Lady Mountbatten in their state coach. Lord Mountbatten was the last viceroy of India, and oversaw the transfer of power from Britain to Pakistan and India. He was governor general of India until 1948.

▲ *In the large-scale migrations that followed partition over one million people were killed. These people arrived in Amritsar, India on a refugee train. Their families had been killed in the violence.*

1947 Allied peace treaties are signed in Paris with Italy, Romania, Hungary, Bulgaria, and Finland. A four-power conference of foreign ministers on Germany fails to reach agreement. A program of aid for the parts of Europe which have been devastated by the war is suggested by the U.S. Secretary of State, George Marshall. It becomes known as the Marshall Plan. Eastern Europe: The Communist Information Bureau, known as Cominform, is set up with headquarters at Belgrade, Yugoslavia. Palestine: The partition into Arab and Jewish states is agreed by the United Nations, but the Arabs reject the proposals. Britain: Parliament passes the India Independence Act, which creates two dominions: India with a mainly Hindu population; and Pakistan, which is mainly Muslim. A dispute then arises between India and Pakistan over Kashmir. Burma (Myanmar): Becomes independent from Britain and leaves the Commonwealth. Indonesia: The United States of Indonesia are established. France: Writer Albert Camus publishes his novel *The Plague*. U.S.: Dramatist Tennessee Williams writes *A Streetcar* *Named Desire*. Chuck Yeager becomes first pilot to pass through the sound barrier. Pacific: Norwegian Thor Heyerdahl makes a successful sea voyage on *Kon Tiki* to show that Polynesian islanders may originally have come from South America.

Nehru

1889 Born Jawaharlal Nehru in India.
1921 Imprisoned for civil disobedience.
1928 Becomes leader of Indian National Congress.
1942 Refuses to make India a dominion.
1947 Becomes prime minister of India.
1964 Dies.

Jinnah

1876 Born Muhammad Ali Jinnah in Karachi.
1896 Studies law.
1930 Opposes Gandhi's policies.
1934 Becomes President of the Indian Muslim League.
1947 Becomes governor-general of Pakistan.
1948 Dies.

The coat of arms of independent Pakistan.

1948 Czechoslovakia: The Communists come to power and form a people's republic. Berlin: The USSR blockades West Berlin in an attempt to gain control of the whole city. Britain and the U.S. beat the blockade with an airlift of food and fuel which goes on until 1949. Israel: The State of Israel is declared in Palestine and is attacked by members of the Arab League. David Ben-Gurion becomes the first prime minister of the new state. India: Mahatma Gandhi is assassinated by a Hindu extremist. Ceylon (now Sri Lanka): Becomes a self-governing dominion. China: The country is split by renewed conflict between Communists and Nationalists. Southeast Asia: Korea is divided into the Republic of Korea (South Korea) and the People's Republic of Korea (North Korea). The Federation of Malaya is set up by the British. Minority Chinese, resentful of Malay dominance of the Federation, begin an armed uprising, known as the Malayan Emergency (to 1960). Switzerland: The World Health Organization (WHO) is established at Geneva as part of the United Nations Organization. The UN accepts the Universal Declaration of Human Rights. U.S.: The Marshall Plan is passed by Congress. Over $13.5 billion is distributed by 1951. Ukrainian-born physicist George Gamow, together with Ralph Alpher and Robert Herman, puts forward the Big Bang theory of the universe's creation. Peter Goldmark and his team develops the first fine-grooved, vinyl, long-playing record (LP). Margaret Chase Smith from Maine is elected first woman senator.

The rise of nationalist feeling among Arabs led the Young Arab Society to design a flag in 1914. The triangle was added in 1917.

Israel

 Until the end of World War I, Palestine was part of the Ottoman empire. It was inhabited by Arabs and a growing number of Jews who wanted to settle in a Jewish homeland. When the Ottoman empire collapsed, Palestine was ruled by Britain under a League of Nations' mandate (*see* page 658). In 1917, Britain had promised its support to establish a Jewish homeland in Palestine. However, more Jews began arriving during the 1930s as problems grew in Europe. The Arabs resented this and fighting often broke out between the two groups. After World War II, more Jewish people wanted to move to Palestine. Under pressure from the Arabs, Britain restricted the number of new settlers allowed in. This led Jewish terrorists to attack both the Arabs and the British.

Britain took the matter to the United Nations. In 1947, the UN voted to divide Palestine into two states. One would be

◀ *The Israeli flag was raised at Eilat on the Gulf of Aqaba in 1949. It is Israel's most southerly point and is its only port on the Red Sea, giving Israel access to the Indian Ocean.*

David Ben-Gurion

1886 Born in Poland.
1906 Goes to live in Palestine.
1930 Becomes leader of Labor (Mapai) Party.
1948 Announces state of Israel and becomes its first prime minister.
1973 Dies.

◀ *When Israel was founded, Jewish settlers made their way there from all over the world. Some tried to reach Israel by boat, others traveled on trains. Many tried to enter illegally.*

▶ *The new state of Israel was surrounded by Arab states. On May 14, 1948, the Arab League of Lebanon, Syria, Iraq, Transjordan, and Egypt all declared war on Israel and attacked it.*

PALESTINIAN REFUGEES

One result of the hostility between the Arabs and the Jews was the migration of nearly one million Arabs from Palestine. They left their homes and became refugees because they were afraid of the actions Israel might take after the war with the Arab League in 1948.

Jewish and the other one Arab. Jerusalem, which was sacred to Jews, Muslims, and Christians, would be international. The Jews agreed, but the Arabs did not. On May 14, 1948 Britain gave up its mandate and withdrew its troops. On the same day the Jews, led by David Ben-Gurion, proclaimed the state of Israel. It was immediately attacked by the surrounding Arab states. Israel defeated them and increased its territory by a quarter. The UN negotiated a cease-fire in 1949, but conflicts between Israel and its Arab neighbors continued.

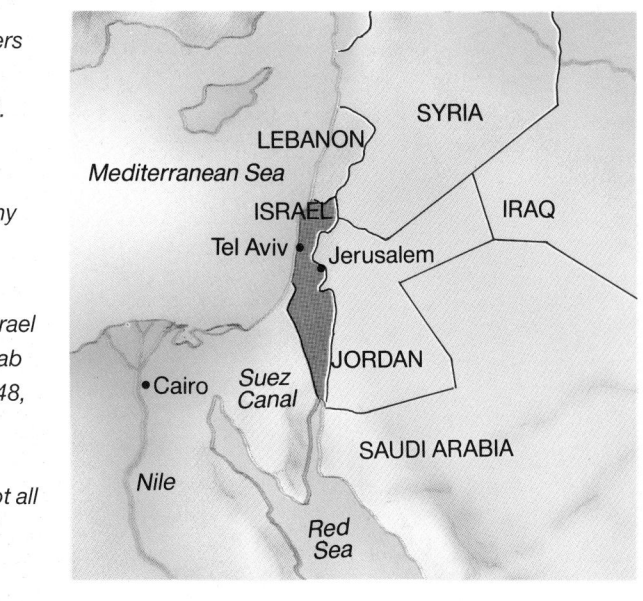

◀ At the start of World War I, planes were only used for observation, but by 1918 guns had been fitted and the conflict was being fought from the air as well.

◀ Germany used submarines during World War I. They attacked surface shipping by firing torpedoes at them from under the water.

War and Weapons

Between 1914 and 1949, the way wars were fought changed a great deal. World War I was dominated by trench warfare, while in World War II the development of weaponry meant that more people, including civilians, could be killed more quickly and with less effort.

World War I saw the first chemical warfare and the first use of tanks on the battlefield. Aircraft were used for observation, aerial combat, and bombing.

By World War II, most weapons were far more sophisticated. Aircraft could fly faster and carry more bombs. Large aircraft carriers allowed planes to be used in sea battles. Submarines and tanks were larger and more efficient. In 1942 missiles reached their targets under their own power. The use of atomic bombs brought World War II to an end in 1945.

▼ Two military policemen walking through a French town in 1918. Both men are wearing gas masks. Poison gas was first used as a weapon by Germany in April 1915, and the Allies started using it shortly afterward. Soldiers on both sides had to wear protective masks because no one could be sure which way the fumes would blow in a gas attack. The gas caused sickness and suffocation.

◀ From 1917 onward, the tank was used successfully to break the stalemate of trench warfare along the Western Front. This British tank was used in World War I. It had two large guns and four machine guns. The caterpillar tracks helped it to deal with any obstacles, such as barbed wire or trenches.

Messerschmidt

P51 Mustang

Spitfire

Britain Russia Japan

USA Germany

FRIEND OR FOE

In World War I, aircraft were marked with their national flags to help identification. Symbols soon replaced flags as they were clearer.

WHEN IT HAPPENED

1914–1918 The Germans use airships for spying and dropping bombs.

1915 The sonar system is developed to detect submarines under the water.

1937 First saturation bombing raid on Guernica, Spain by the Germans.

1940 The battle of Britain.

1940 The radar system is developed to locate distant objects such as enemy aircraft.

1941 American scientists start work on the Manhattan project to make an atomic bomb.

1944 Both Britain and Germany start using jet-engined fighter planes.

1947 The AK 47 Kalashnikov rifle is developed from the assault rifle of 1944.

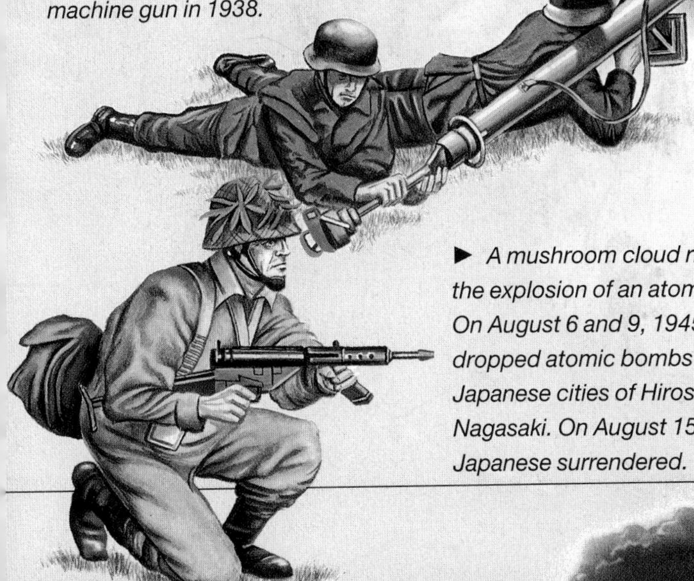

▲ *By World War II, planes were much improved. The eight-gun Spitfire (right) was the best fighter aircraft in the battle of Britain. The German Messerschmidt (top)* had a top speed of 357 mph (575 km/h). Many American pilots gave *their planes names, such as Dallas Doll.*

▼ *The antitank gun appeared in 1918, and the bazooka (right) in 1940. The submachine gun (below) was invented in 1915, and the heavy machine gun in 1938.*

▶ *A mushroom cloud rising after the explosion of an atomic bomb. On August 6 and 9, 1945 the U.S. dropped atomic bombs on the Japanese cities of Hiroshima and Nagasaki. On August 15, 1945 the Japanese surrendered.*

1949 The North Atlantic Treaty Organization (NATO) is formed as a defensive alliance by the Western nations. Germany: The blockade of Berlin ends and airlift is halted. The country is divided into the Federal Republic (West) and the German Democratic Republic (East). Dramatist Bertolt Brecht sets up a theater company in Berlin. Eastern Europe: The Council for Mutual Economic Assistance (COMECON) is founded by the USSR and other communist states. South Africa: Government adopts apartheid (the separate development, or segregation, of Whites and Nonwhites) as official policy. Britain: The National Health Service begins, providing free health care for all. The Republic of Ireland withdraws from the British Commonwealth. China: Mao Zedong sets up the People's Republic of China. Nationalist government flees to Formosa (Taiwan). Southeast Asia: France recognizes the independence of Vietnam and Cambodia. Dutch grant Indonesia independence. Middle East: The UN negotiates a ceasefire to end the Israeli and Arab League war. Greece: Civil war ends when Communists are defeated. France: Novelist and essayist Simone de Beauvoir writes a feminist essay called *The Second Sex*. U.S.: Film director and actor Orson Welles stars in the film *The Third Man*. Britain: Writer George Orwell publishes grim, futuristic novel *1984*.

A poster showing soldiers from various countries of the Commonwealth united under the flag of Great Britain.

British Commonwealth

The relationship between Britain and parts of its empire had started to change by the beginning of the 20th century. Some countries were given a form of independence as British dominions. They looked after their own internal affairs, but their defense and foreign policy were still mainly controlled by Britain.

By the time the Imperial Conference met in London in 1926, however, the dominions wanted to control their own external affairs too. They also asked for a clear definition of their relationship with Britain. This was given in 1931 in the Statute of Westminster when dominions were defined as "autonomous (self-ruling) communities within the British empire, equal in status . . . united by a common allegiance to the Crown and freely associated as members of the British Commonwealth of Nations." After this statute the name British Commonwealth of Nations was used instead of British empire and many

INDEPENDENT MEMBERS OF THE COMMONWEALTH			
Antigua and Barbuda	1981	Mauritius	1968
Australia	1901	Nauru	1968
Bahamas	1973	New Zealand	1907
Bangladesh	1972	Nigeria	1960
Barbados	1966	Papua New Guinea	1975
Belize	1981	St. Kitts-Nevis	1983
Botswana	1966	St. Lucia	1979
Brunei	1984	St. Vincent and	
Canada	1867	the Grenadines	1979
Cyprus	1960	Seychelles	1976
Dominica	1978	Sierra Leone	1961
Gambia	1965	Singapore	1965
Ghana	1957	Solomon Islands	1978
Grenada	1974	Sri Lanka	1948
Guyana	1966	Swaziland	1968
India	1947	Tanzania	1961
Jamaica	1962	Tonga	1970
Kenya	1963	Trinidad and Tobago	1962
Kiribati	1979	Tuvalu	1978
Lesotho	1966	Uganda	1962
Malawi	1964	Vanuatu	1980
Malaysia	1957	Western Samoa	1962
Maldives	1965	Zambia	1964
Malta	1964	Zimbabwe	1980

▲ *The British West Indian regiment fought with the Allied troops in World War I. Commonwealth soldiers fought on the side of Britain in both World Wars.*

colonies wanted independence.

Canada, Australia, New Zealand, and South Africa had all become dominions before World War I. The Irish Free State also became a dominion in 1921. The first three to gain their independence after World War II were India (1947), Ceylon (1948), and Burma (1948). India and Ceylon (Sri Lanka) stayed in the Commonwealth, but Burma did not join and the Republic of Ireland left in 1949.

▼ *A lavish ceremony was held when the new parliament building in Canberra, the federal capital of the Commonwealth of Australia, opened in 1927.*

INDEPENDENCE

Although Canada, Australia, New Zealand, and South Africa had become independent by 1914, they all joined the other empire and Commonwealth countries in sending troops and equipment to help Britain in both World Wars. Also, following the economic conference at Ottawa in 1932, the dominions received better terms for trading with Britain than countries outside the Commonwealth were offered. The independent countries also had their own flags and emblems: South Africa (*top left*), Australia (*top right*), New Zealand (*bottom left*), and Canada (*bottom right*).

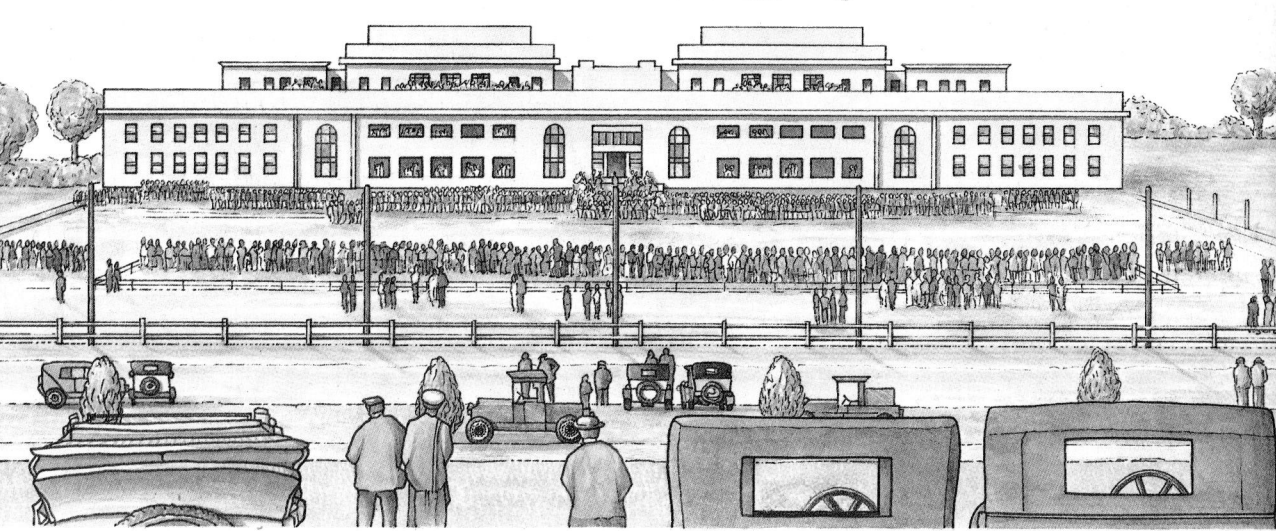

Communist China

In 1936 the Chinese Nationalist leader, Chiang Kai-shek, was forced to make an alliance with the Communist Party to fight against the Japanese in Manchuria. This alliance lasted until 1945 and brought China into World War II on the Allies' side. While the Chinese were fighting the Japanese, Britain and the U.S. provided them with aid. After the defeat of Japan in 1945, the alliance collapsed and civil war broke out in 1946. The Nationalists were weak and divided, but Mao Zedong's Communists had the support of the people. The Communists also had a large army and by January 1949 they had taken Tianjin and Beijing (Peking). From there they moved south, pushing the Nationalists onto the island of Taiwan (Formosa) which became known as the Republic of China. It held a seat in the United Nations until 1971. The People's Republic of China was declared on October 1, 1949 on the mainland, but many countries refused to recognize it.

▲ Mao Zedong introduced reforms in the countryside in order to gain the support of the people. This 1949 poster for the Chinese Communist Party shows farmers and soldiers working together.

▼ Large posters of Party leaders formed the backdrop to speeches at a meeting of the Communist Party in Shanghai in 1949.

1950 to the Present Day

The Modern World

The years between 1950 and the present day are recent history and concern people many of whom are still alive. Some of the events may have occurred during our lifetime, or we may have seen them on television. Also social, technological, and environmental changes are taking place all the time. This makes it difficult for historians to select the really important events from the vast amount of information that is available in the modern world. Many of the events that seem important today may not be thought important in fifty or a hundred years from now.

Some events seem too important to leave out. Since 1950 there have been many "firsts." The first astronauts, the first test-tube babies, the first VCRs, and the first personal computers.

There have been major political changes, including independence for many new nations in Africa and other continents, and the breakup of the once-powerful USSR. There have been tragic wars in the Far East and Middle East. Economic power is moving away from Europe and North America toward the Far East.

Politicians and policymakers, as well as historians, have identified several important trends that seem to be transforming our world: the long-term effects of environmental pollution, increasing population, changing family structures, and the growing gap between rich and poor people and countries.

All these concerns have yet to be assessed, but that is the future, not the past.

▼ *Joyful Berliners pull down the wall which overshadowed their lives for nearly 30 years. It was built to prevent the East Germans traveling to the West.*

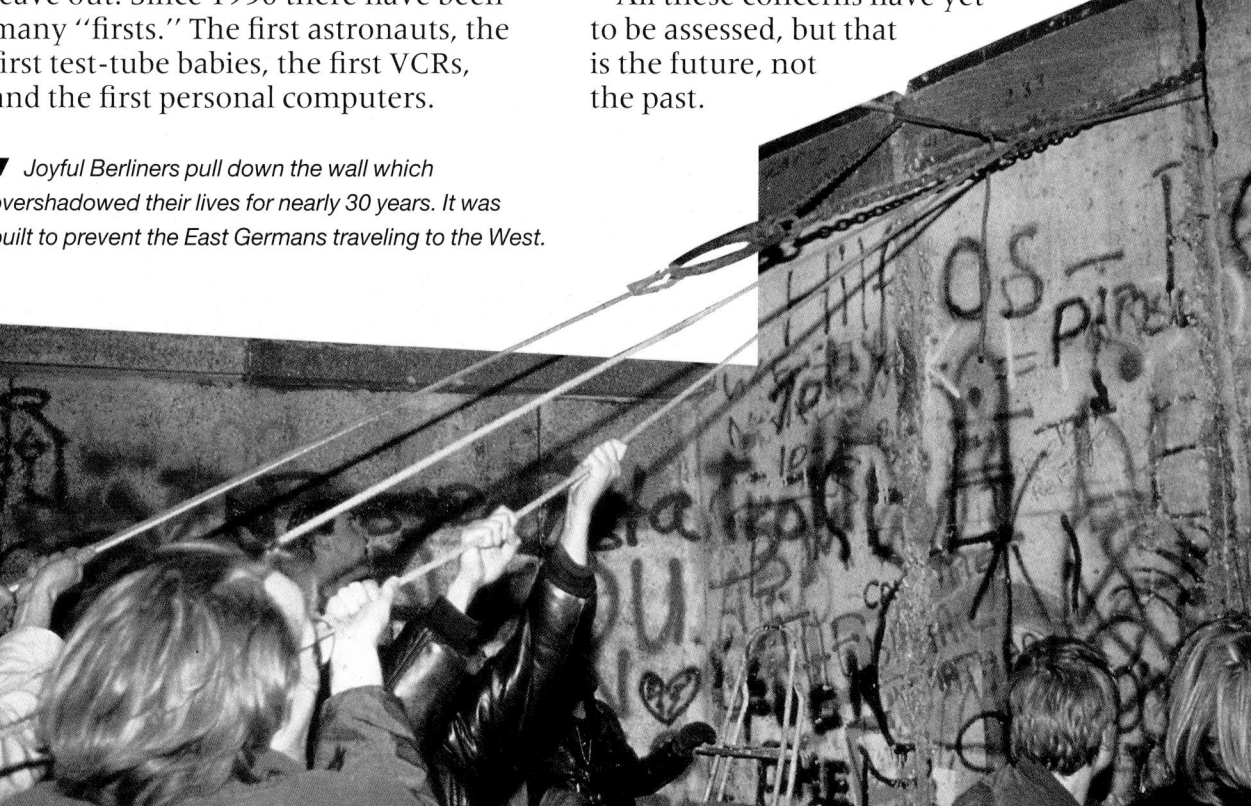

The Americas

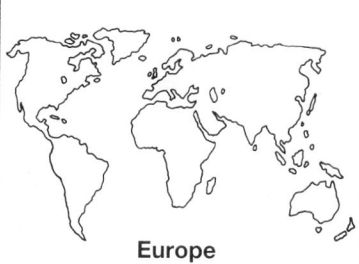

Europe

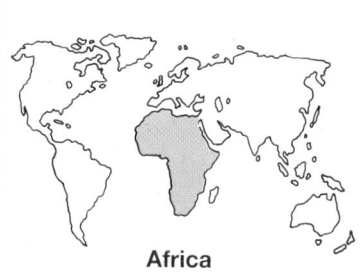

Africa

1951 First U.S. nuclear power stations.

1959 Revolution in Cuba, Fidel Castro in power.
1962 Cuban missile crisis.
1962–1966 Civil rights protests. Growth of Black power movement.
1963 President Kennedy is assassinated.

1968 Martin Luther King is assassinated.
1969 American astronaut walks on the Moon.
1970 Communist Salvador Allende becomes president of Chile.
1974 President Nixon resigns.
1979 Civil war in Nicaragua and El Salvador.
1981 First U.S. space shuttle flight.
1982 Falklands War.
1983 Argentinean government is overthrown. New democratic leadership.
1987 U.S. signs INF treaty with USSR. They agree to ban all intermediate nuclear weapons.
1988 George Bush is elected president.
1992 Representatives of all nations meet at Earth summit in Rio to discuss future of planet.
1993 Bill Clinton is inaugurated as president.

1955 Warsaw Pact is signed.
1956 Hungarian Rising is put down by USSR.
1957 Common Market (EEC) is established.

1961 Berlin Wall is built. Russian cosmonaut is first man to orbit in space.
1968 Soviet troops invade Czechoslovakia.
1969 Irish Republican Army (IRA) begins campaign for a united Ireland.
1973 Britain, Ireland, and Denmark join the European Community (EC).
1975 Death of Franco ends dictatorship in Spain.

1980 Polish trade union, Solidarity, is created.
1981 Greece joins EC. IRA hunger strikes in Ireland.
1985 Gorbachev becomes leader of the USSR.
1986 Chernobyl nuclear disaster in Ukraine. Spain and Portugal join EC.
1989 Ceaucescu is overthrown in Romania.
1990 East and West Germany are reunited.
1991 Gorbachev resigns. Communist Party is outlawed in USSR. USSR breaks up. Civil war in Yugoslavia.

1952 Mau Mau fighters in Kenya seek independence.
1957 Ghana becomes independent.
1960 Nigeria and Zaire become independent. Sharpeville massacre in South Africa.
1961 Tanzania becomes independent.
1962 Algeria and Uganda become independent.
1963 Kenya becomes independent.
1964 Zambia and Malawi become independent.
1965 White minority government in Rhodesia (now Zimbabwe) declares itself independent from Britain.
1967–1970 Civil war in Nigeria. Many die of starvation in Biafra.
1974 Emperor Haile Selasse of Ethiopia is overthrown by military leaders.
1975 Angola and Mozambique become independent.
1980 Black majority rule is achieved in Zimbabwe.
1986 Fighting in South African townships between rival Black groups.

1990 African National Congress (ANC) leader Nelson Mandela is released from South African prison.

Middle East

1952 Military takeover in Egypt.
1953 Egypt becomes independent.
1956 Suez Crisis.
1967 Six Day War.

1972 Palestine Liberation Organization (PLO) stages terrorist attacks.
1973 Yom Kippur War.
1973–1974 OPEC countries, led by Arab states, rapidly increase oil prices.
1976–1982 Civil war between Christians and Muslims in Lebanon.
1979 Egypt and Israel sign peace treaty. Shah of Iran is overthrown.
1980–1988 Iran-Iraq War.
1981 President Sadat of Egypt is assassinated.
1982 Israel invades Lebanon.

1986 U.S. bombs Libya.

1990 Iraq invades Kuwait. Soviet troops intervene to try to end ethnic dispute between Armenia and Azerbaijan.
1991 UN forces Iraq to withdraw from Kuwait.

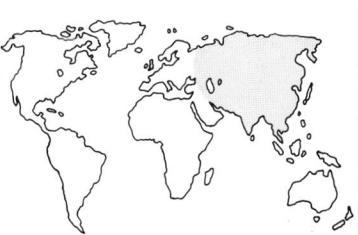

Asia and the Far East

1950–1953 Korean War.

1962 War between India and China.
1963 Malaysia becomes independent.
1964–1975 War in Vietnam.
1965 America sends troops to Vietnam. War between India and Pakistan. Singapore becomes independent.
1966 Cultural Revolution begins in China.
1971 Bangladesh becomes independent.
1973 American troops withdraw from Vietnam.
1975 Communists control Vietnam, Laos, and Cambodia.
1976 Death of Mao Zedong.
1978 Vietnam invades Cambodia.
1979 USSR invades Afghanistan.
1984 Indira Gandhi, Indian prime minister, is assassinated. Agreement between Britain and China that Hong Kong will be returned to China in 1997.

1988–1990 Benazir Bhutto is prime minister of Pakistan.
1989 Demonstrators calling for democracy are attacked by Chinese government troops in Tiananmen Square, Beijing.

Australasia and Pacific

1951 ANZUS alliance is signed between Australia, New Zealand, and U.S.
1954 U.S. tests atomic bombs in the Pacific.

1959 Hawaii becomes the 50th state of the U.S.

1966 Australian troops fight alongside Americans in Vietnam.

1972 Labor party victories in general elections in Australia and New Zealand after many years of Conservative rule.
1975 Papua New Guinea becomes independent.

1978 Solomon Islands and Tuvalu become independent.
1985 South Pacific Forum draws up Nuclear Free Zone Treaty. French agents blow up Greenpeace ship *Rainbow Warrior*.

1987 Scientists confirm existence of a hole in the ozone layer above Antarctica.

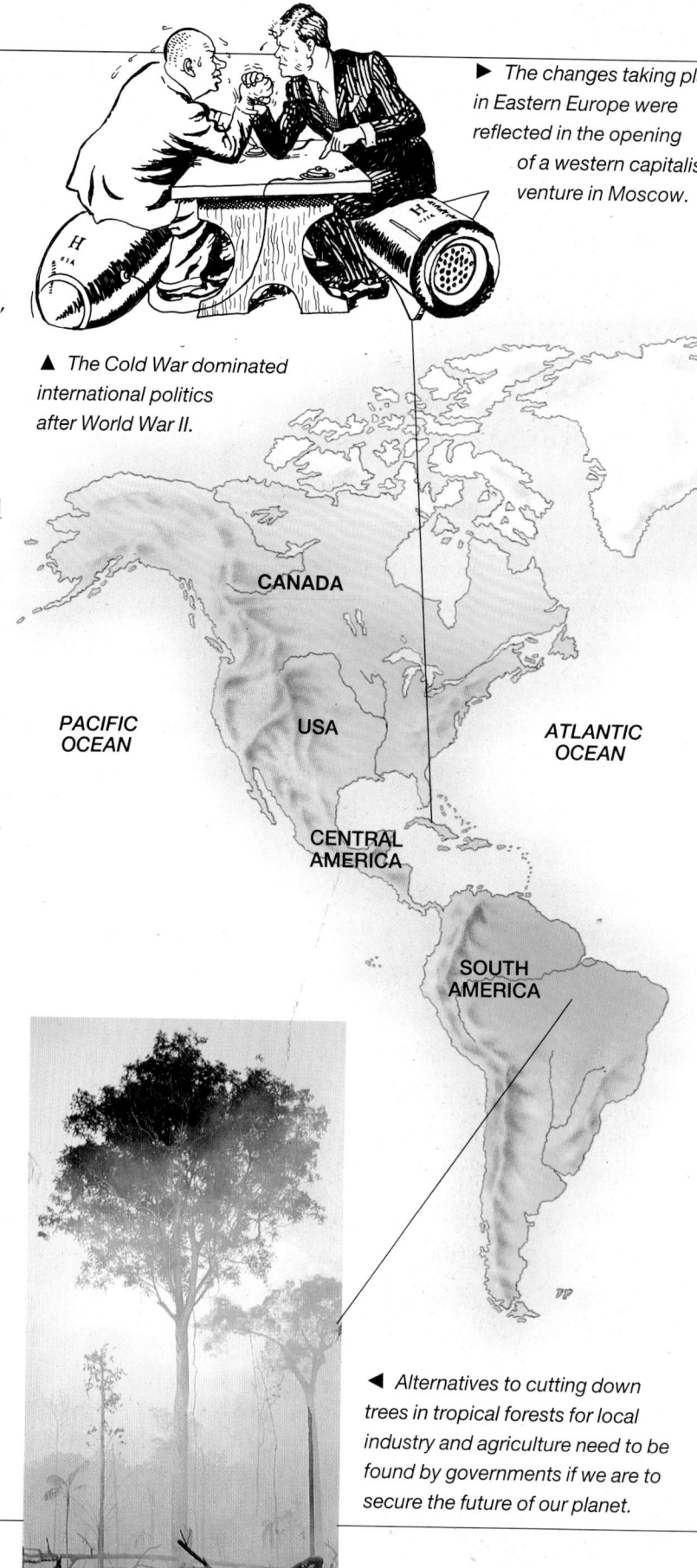

The World

This period was dominated by the Cold War between communism and the West, in which the **United States** and the **Soviet Union** played the leading parts. These two were also involved in the space race. The USSR was the first to send a man into space, and the United States the first to put a man on the Moon. Changes in the USSR led to the end of the Cold War, but created uncertainty about the future as nationalists demanded independence.

In western **Europe**, the European Community encouraged economic growth and worked toward political union. In **Africa**, many nations became independent, but faced severe economic problems as well as drought and famine. In some countries militant Islamic groups have risen to power causing conflict.

In **Southeast Asia**, industry and technology developed, and Japanese business has become the most successful in the world. **China** experienced a cultural revolution and tried to reduce its population. Indochina (Southeast Asia) was devastated by wars.

▶ The changes taking place in Eastern Europe were reflected in the opening of a western capitalist venture in Moscow.

▲ The Cold War dominated international politics after World War II.

CANADA

PACIFIC OCEAN

USA

ATLANTIC OCEAN

CENTRAL AMERICA

SOUTH AMERICA

◀ Alternatives to cutting down trees in tropical forests for local industry and agriculture need to be found by governments if we are to secure the future of our planet.

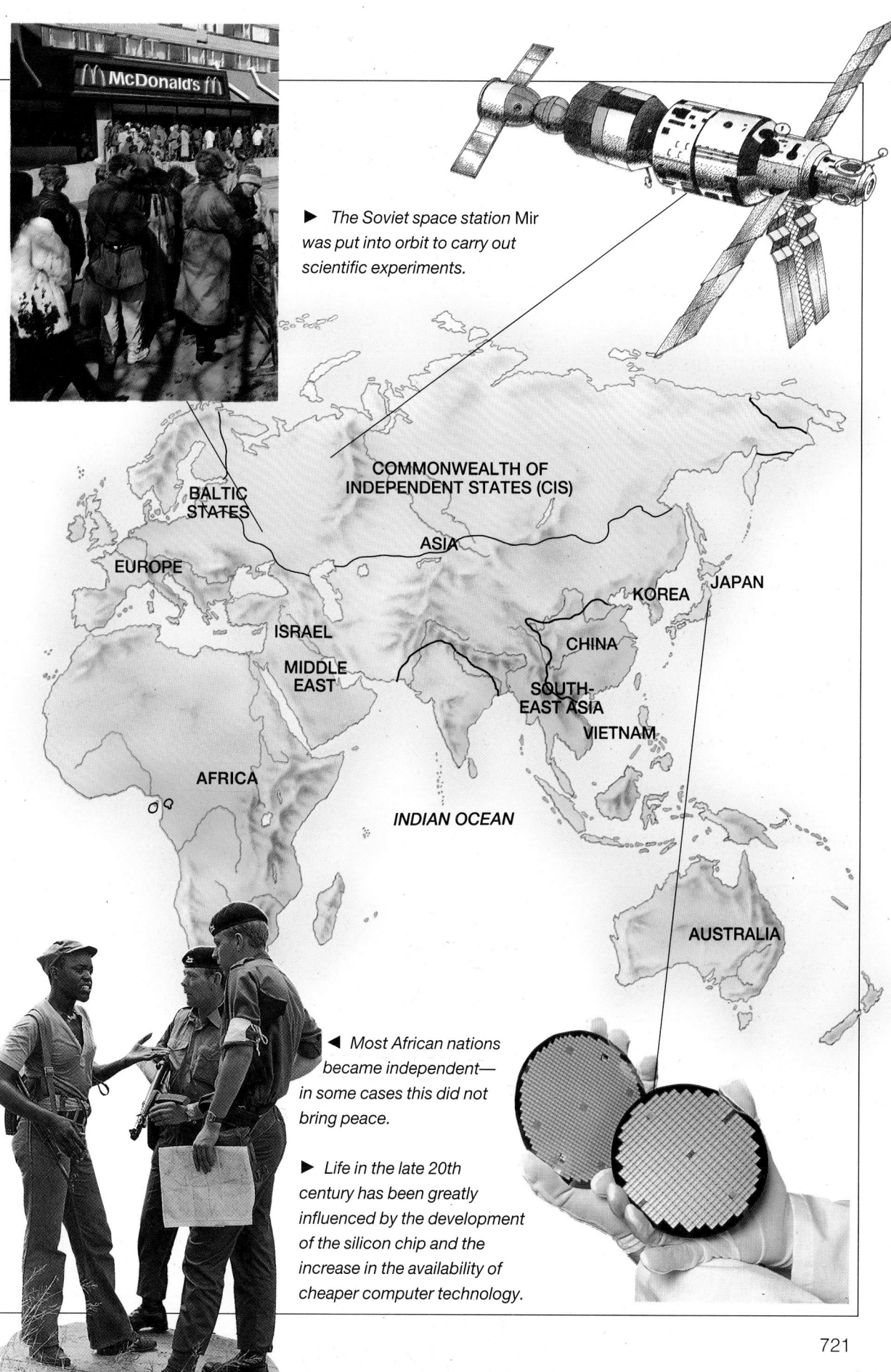

▶ *The Soviet space station Mir was put into orbit to carry out scientific experiments.*

COMMONWEALTH OF
INDEPENDENT STATES (CIS)

BALTIC
STATES

ASIA

EUROPE

KOREA   JAPAN

ISRAEL

CHINA

MIDDLE
EAST

SOUTH-
EAST ASIA

VIETNAM

AFRICA

INDIAN OCEAN

AUSTRALIA

◀ *Most African nations became independent— in some cases this did not bring peace.*

▶ *Life in the late 20th century has been greatly influenced by the development of the silicon chip and the increase in the availability of cheaper computer technology.*

1950 USSR and Communist China sign a 30-year friendship treaty. Korean War: Invasion of South Korea by North Korean forces (to 1953).

1951 ANZUS security treaty is signed by Australia, New Zealand, and U.S. First U.S. nuclear power station built.

One of the first postage stamps to feature the head of the new queen, Elizabeth II, in the first years of her reign.

1952 Britain: Elizabeth II becomes queen. Kenya: Mau Mau terrorist groups seek independence from Britain.

1953 End of the Korean War. U.S.: Dwight D. Eisenhower becomes president (to 1961). USSR: Nikita Khrushchev becomes leader (to 1964). Nepal: Edmund Hilary and Tensing Norgay reach top of Mount Everest. U.S.: Arthur Miller's play *The Crucible* draws parallel between witch hunts and Senator Joseph McCarthy's campaign against alleged Communists. Ernest Hemingway wins Pulitzer Prize for *The Old Man and the Sea*.

1954 France, U.S., USSR, and Britain discuss the future of Germany; USSR insists on a division between east and west Germany. Vietnam: French colonial troops defeated by Communists at Dien Bien Phu. U.S.: Supreme Court rules whites-only schools unlawful. U.S. tests nuclear bombs in Pacific. Egypt: General Nasser elected president (to 1970). Britain: Roger Bannister runs mile (1.6 km) in under four minutes.

1955 West Germany becomes a member of North Atlantic Treaty Organization (NATO). Eastern Europe: Communist countries sign Warsaw Pact. Middle East: Tension increases on Israel-Jordan border. U.S.: Martin Luther King leads civil rights protest.

The Cold War

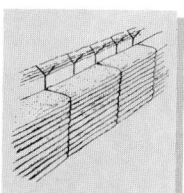

The USSR and the U.S. fought together as allies in World War II, but in 1945 these two superpowers became enemies. This division became known as the Cold War – a war without fighting. The United States and USSR "fought" by making threats and by strengthening their armed forces. They stockpiled nuclear weapons. Peaceful, friendly contacts between their peoples ceased. The USSR became shut off from the rest of the world. The British statesman Winston Churchill described the frontier between East and West as the "iron curtain."

The Cold War dominated politics for many years. On one side, the United States became leader of NATO (an alliance of Western nations against the communist powers). On the other side, the USSR dominated the Warsaw Pact, a military alliance of East European states that supported communism. When the Hungarians in 1956 and the Czechs in 1968 tried to act independently, Soviet forces were sent in to regain control.

▲ *Rebel guerrillas in Afghanistan fought against government and Soviet troops in the 1980s. They wanted to free their country from Soviet control.*

▶ *Czech students trying to stop Soviet tanks in Prague, in August 1968. The USSR feared that independent actions by Warsaw Pact members might weaken its power, so it moved troops into Czechoslovakia.*

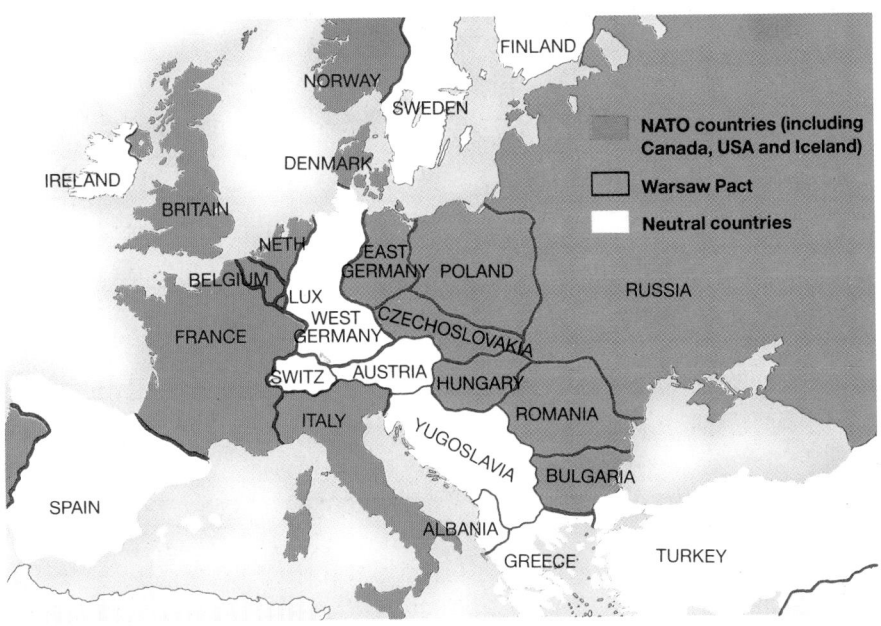

◀ *By 1949, most European states had joined rival alliances. Warsaw Pact states supported the USSR. Members of the North Atlantic Treaty Organization (NATO) supported the U.S.A.*

▼ *A 1962 cartoon shows the two superpower leaders arm-wrestling for power: USSR's Nikita Khrushchev (left) facing the U.S. President John F. Kennedy. They are sitting on nuclear weapons.*

Although the U.S. and USSR never fought, they came close to it in 1962 when Soviet missiles were based in Cuba. Both sides have sent money and arms to encourage fighting in Korea, Vietnam, Iraq, Cambodia, Nicaragua, and Afghanistan. In 1969, the two first met to discuss disarmament and by 1987 they had agreed to abolish medium-range nuclear missiles. The Cold War was over.

The Space Race

The development of technology during World War II helped scientists to realize that one day it might be possible for people to travel in space. Cold War rivalry between the United States and the USSR helped the space race to get going. Both sides felt that being the first nation in space would increase their prestige. They also hoped that space science would help them develop new, more powerful weapons.

The Soviets achieved the first "space first" when they sent a satellite into orbit around the world in 1957. Soon both sides were investing enormous amounts of time and money in space science. Notable achievements included the first manned flights, probes sent to the Moon and past Venus, and the launch of weather and communications satellites.

In 1961, President John F. Kennedy said that American scientists would get a man to the Moon by 1970. In fact, United States' astronauts landed on the Moon in 1969. By 1975, five other countries (France, China, Japan, Britain, and India) had launched their own spacecraft in the space race.

More recently, competition between the two superpowers has turned to co-operation, with scientists sharing ideas and inventions. They have concentrated on long-distance, unmanned space probes, designed to investigate distant planets in the solar system, rather than trying to achieve expensive, eye-catching firsts. International cooperation has also helped to produce orbiting space stations where peaceful scientific experiments can be performed under conditions very different from those on Earth.

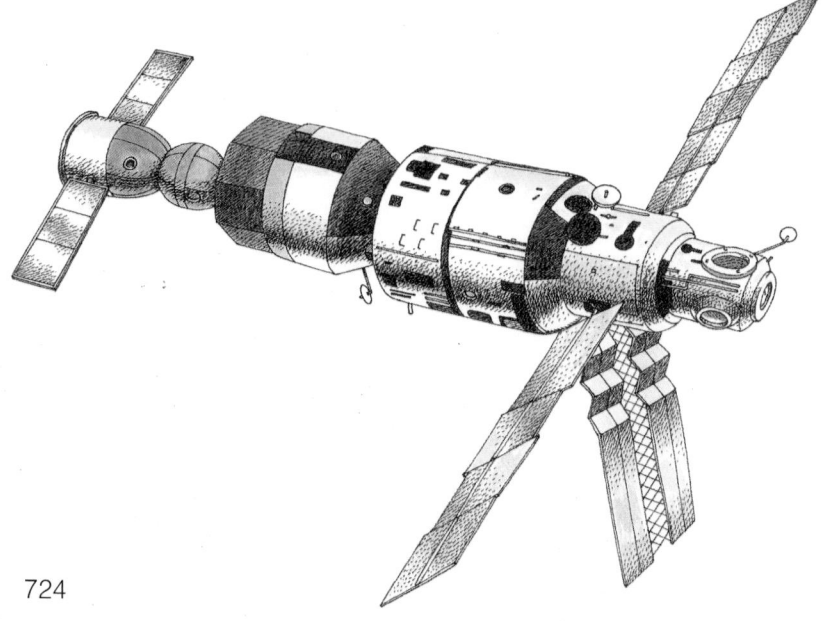

▲ The first man on the Moon was the American astronaut Neil Armstrong. He described walking on the Moon as "one small step for a man, one giant leap for mankind."

◄ The Soviet space station Mir was launched in 1986. It was designed to stay in orbit for long periods, so that complicated scientific experiments could be carried out on board.

EXPERIMENTS IN SPACE

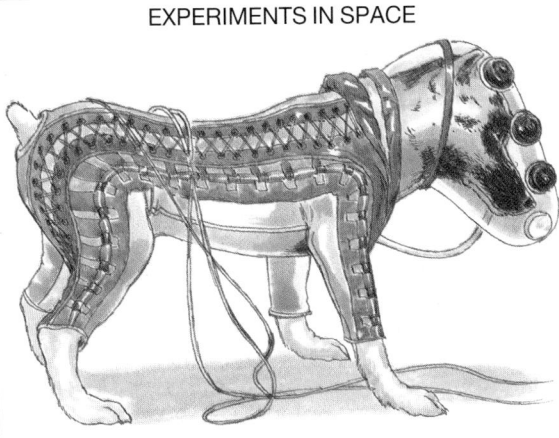

Laika, a Soviet dog, was the first animal in space. She left Earth on November 3, 1957, in a capsule on board *Sputnik 2*. It contained an air supply, food and water, together with instruments for recording her heartbeat, breathing, and blood pressure. They transmitted data back to scientists on Earth. At that time, engineers did not know how to bring a spacecraft safely back to Earth, so sadly Laika died in space. Experiments like these provided vital information for human space travel.

SPACE FIRSTS

1957 USSR launches first satellite, *Sputnik 1*.

1959 *Luna 2* probe (USSR) hits the Moon.

1961 Yuri Gagarin (USSR) is first man in space.

1962 U.S.A. launches first communications satellite.

1963 Valentina Tereshkova (USSR) is first woman cosmonaut.

1969 *Apollo 11* astronauts Neil Armstrong and Edwin Aldrin (U.S.A.) land on the Moon.

1971 USSR sends two probes to Mars.

1975 U.S.A. and USSR cooperate in space; *Apollo* and *Soyuz* craft dock (link) in orbit.

1977 U.S.A. sends *Voyager 2* mission to fly past Jupiter, Saturn, Uranus, and Neptune.

1981 Flight of first space shuttle (U.S.A.).

1983 Flight of first *Spacelab* (U.S.A.).

1986 *Pioneer* spacecraft (U.S.A.) leaves solar system.

1986 Shuttle *Challenger* (U.S.A.) explodes; crew is killed and U.S. shuttle program is delayed.

1990 Hubble Space Telescope (U.S.A.) launched.

1956 Pakistan becomes an Islamic republic. Egypt takes control of Suez Canal which leads to war with France and Britain. Hungary: Soviet troops invade to stop movement toward independence. US.: Segration on buses is declared unconstitutional. Elvis Presley and rock and roll music are popular.

1957 Treaty of Rome sets up European Economic Community (EEC). USSR: Launch of the first space satellite *Sputnik 1*. Italy: Russian author Boris Pasternak publishes his novel *Doctor Zhivago*. U.S.: Riots in Little Rock, Arkansas, over government policy requiring the end of whites-only schools. Composer Leonard Bernstein writes the musical *West Side Story*. Novelist Jack Kerouac publishes *On the Road*.

1958 West Indian Federation is formed to protect trade and political interests. Cuba: Fidel Castro leads a revolution. France: Charles de Gaulle becomes president (to 1969). U.S.: National Aeronautics and Space Administration (NASA) launches first satellite. Marilyn Monroe stars in the film *Some Like It Hot*. Britain: Its first superhighway opens. Dramatist Harold Pinter writes *The Birthday Party*.

1959 USSR launches rocket with monkeys aboard. Canada: St. Lawrence Seaway is opened. Cuba: Castro in power. U.S.: Hawaii becomes 50th state.

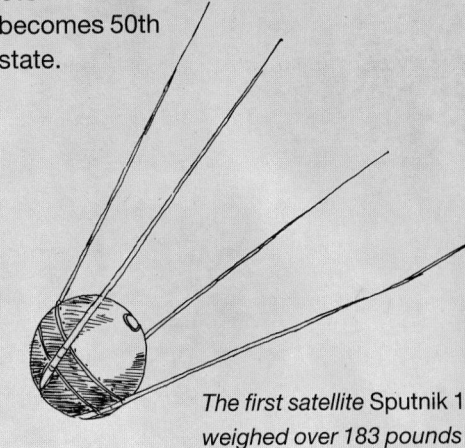

The first satellite Sputnik 1 weighed over 183 pounds (83 kg) and carried a radio transmitter.

1960 Nigeria and Zaire become independent. USSR: Soviets shoot down American U-2 spy plane. Egypt: Work starts on Aswan High Dam, financed by USSR. South Africa: Police kill 67 black people in the Sharpeville massacre. U.S.: John F. Kennedy elected president (to 1963). American scientists develop lasers. First weather observation satellite launched.

1961 Tanzania becomes independent. Germany: Berlin Wall is built. USSR: Launches first manned spacecraft with Yuri Gagarin. Middle East: Organization of Petroleum Exporting Countries (OPEC) is formed. International crisis after the U.S. backs Bay of Pigs invasion (which fails) of communist Cuba.

1962 Tension between U.S. and USSR after discovery of Soviet missile bases on Cuba. South Vietnam: U.S. sets up military council to support government against Communists. Asia: India and China at war. U.S.: Riots when a Black student is admitted to University of Mississippi. Britain: Immigration is limited. Uganda becomes independent.

1963 France stops Britain joining EEC. U.S.: Freedom marches by civil rights' protesters. President Kennedy is assassinated. South Vietnam: Government overthrown; U.S. sends aid. Kenya, led by Jomo Kenyatta, and Malaysia, led by Tunku Abdul Rahman, become independent.

The assassination of John Kennedy touched the hearts of many people worldwide.

Wars in Asia

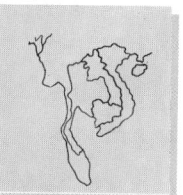

In 1950, many countries in the East had not yet recovered from Japanese invasions during World War II. People were exhausted, farms were neglected, and businesses were in ruins. They needed peace and stability, but many states were soon at war. These wars caused further damage, to people, cities, and the land. In some parts of the East, for example the Philippines, the political situation is still unstable.

Eastern countries fought for independence. They no longer wished to be colonies of some distant European power. The old colonial "masters" (France, Britain, and the Netherlands) wanted to hold on to these potentially rich lands. Fighting broke out in Vietnam (and its neighbors, Laos, Thailand, and Cambodia), Indonesia, Malaysia, Burma, and the Philippines.

These wars were often complicated by political differences between rival groups seeking independence. Some local

---

CAMBODIA

In 1970 the United States helped put Lon Nol in power in Cambodia. A rebel communist group, the Khmer Rouge, began fighting against the new rulers. By 1975 they had gained control. They enforced a brutal regime, resulting in the death of two million people. In 1978 Vietnamese forces invaded and overthrew the Khmer Rouge.

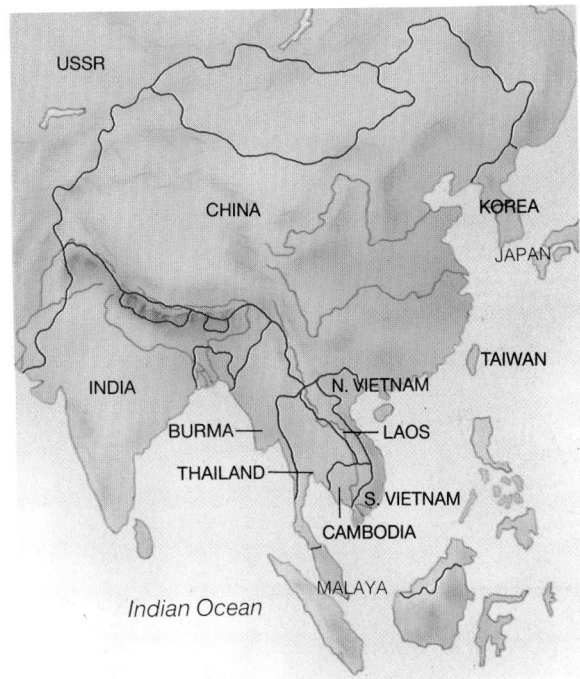

◀ American troops fought with the South Koreans against the North Koreans and Chinese during the Korean War (1950–1953). Helicopters were used intensively for the first time in this war (as they were later in Vietnam) to transport troops across difficult, mountainous territory in poor weather conditions.

▼ Fighting between rival political groups flared up in many parts of Asia between 1946 and 1988, following Japan's defeat in World War II and the collapse of European colonial power. Opponents were backed by superpowers: the U.S., USSR and, sometimes, China.

leaders wanted to set up a capitalist state after the colonial power had gone, others hoped to introduce a communist government. The situation became even more dangerous when the Soviet and U.S. superpowers joined in, offering money, weapons, or technical advice to these rival groups.

For example, in Korea, the country was divided into a communist north and a capitalist south. Troops from the north, helped by China, overran the south in 1950. So the Americans sent a large army to the south. In all over 3 million people were killed or made homeless before peace terms were agreed in 1953.

▶ During the Vietnam War (1964–1975), many parts of the country were devastated. The forests were sprayed with deadly chemicals to kill the undergrowth where rebels were hiding. Mines were planted as booby traps. Many civilians were killed and injured. Others were made homeless and fled as refugees to neighboring lands.

Common Markets

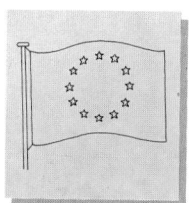

Throughout the world, neighboring states, or states with shared economic interests, have joined together to form powerful international associations. OPEC is probably the best known international trading association.

Some groups of states have also set up cooperative economic communities, known as "common markets." Within these markets, members buy and sell at favorable rates. They agree to protect one another from economic competition from outside. Often, strong political links develop between members.

Today's European Community (EC) is based on the former European Economic Community (EEC), set up in 1957 by the Treaty of Rome. Since then the original membership (France, Italy, West Germany, Netherlands, Belgium, and Luxembourg) has grown to include Britain, Ireland, Denmark, Greece, Spain,

OPEC

The Organization of Petroleum (oil) Exporting Countries was founded in 1961 to get the best price possible on world markets for its member states' oil. OPEC members include many Middle Eastern Arab states as well as Algeria, Indonesia, Nigeria, Ecuador, Gabon, and Venezuela. Between 1973 and 1974 OPEC quadrupled the price of crude oil. This led to a worldwide energy crisis.

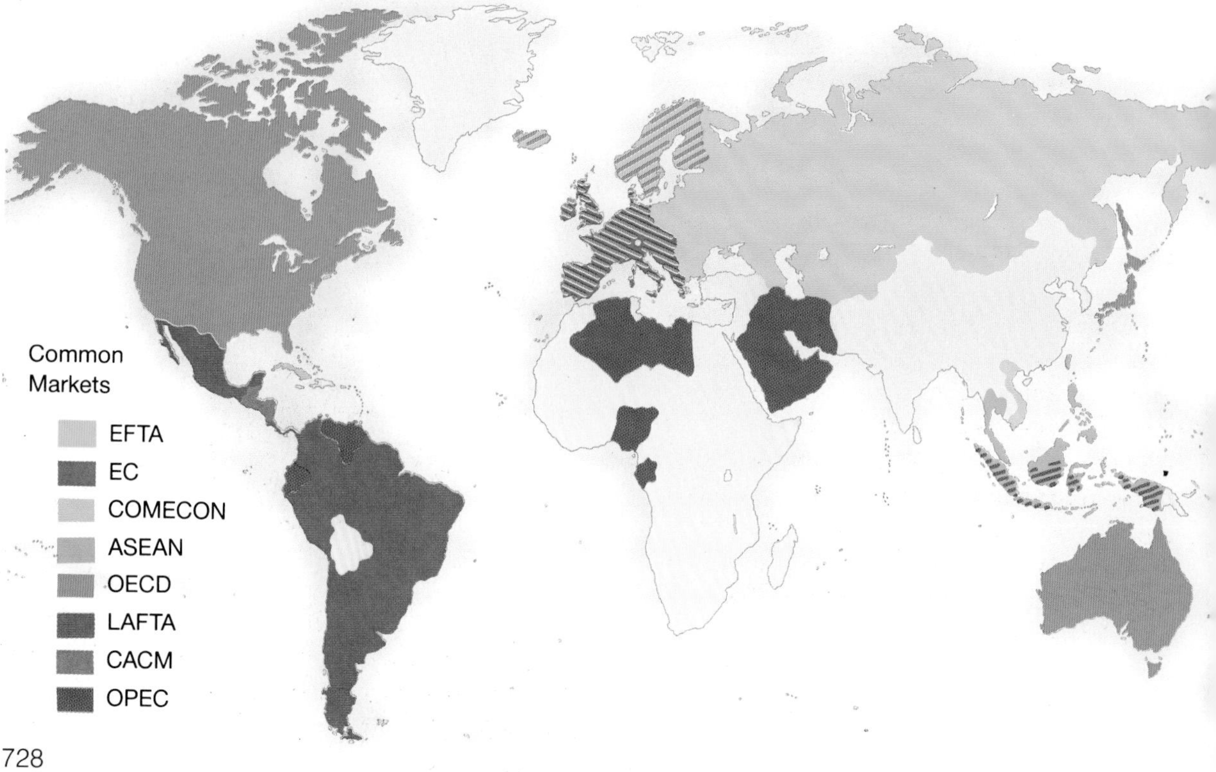

Common Markets

- EFTA
- EC
- COMECON
- ASEAN
- OECD
- LAFTA
- CACM
- OPEC

▲ *The EC headquarters building in Brussels, Belgium. The Community's administration is based there, and the parliament is in Strasbourg, France.*

and Portugal. There are plans for a single European currency, taxation, and law. There is already a European Parliament.

COMECON is a similar organization run by communist states. There are also "common markets" in Asia and Latin America. International groups, such as OECD, aim to protect weaker nations against powerful market forces, and to aid economic development.

◀ *International common markets and groupings of states with shared economic interests are found in all continents. In Europe the main common markets are the European Community (EC), the European Free Trade Association (EFTA), and the Soviet equivalent, the Council for Mutual Economic Assistance (COMECON), formed in 1949. The Central American Common Market (CACM) was set up in 1960, but was suspended in the 1980s. The Latin American Free Trade Association (LAFTA) was founded in 1961. The Association of Southeast Asian Nations (ASEAN) was set up in 1967 and includes non-communist countries. The Organization for Economic Cooperation and Development (OECD) started in Europe in 1948 and now includes the U.S.A. and Australia.*

1964 Malawi and Zambia become independent. Vietnam: War between North (backed by Communists) and South (backed by the U.S.). U.S.: Martin Luther King wins Nobel Peace Prize. Race riots in U.S. cities. British pop group The Beatles tour the U.S. Civil Rights Act becomes law. Britain: Exploration for North Sea oil and gas begins.

1965 Vietnam: U.S. troops arrive in South Vietnam. Rhodesia (Zimbabwe): Prime minister Ian Smith declares independence from Britain, and leads a white minority government which ignores Black Africans' rights. Britain: Designer Mary Quant launches the miniskirt.

1966 China: Cultural Revolution (to 1976). Vietnam: Australian troops fight alongside the Americans. Italy: Floods damage art treasures. U.S.: Anti-war demonstrations and race riots.

1967 Middle East: Six Day War between Israel and Arab states. Israel gains territory. Vietnam War: Efforts toward peace, but fighting starts again. Mass anti-war demonstrations in the U.S. and Europe. South Africa: first successful heart transplant operation performed. Europe: EEC becomes the European Community (EC). France again stops Britain joining. Caribbean: Anguilla becomes independent. Nigeria: Fighting begins in Biafra (to 1970); many die of starvation.

An offshore oil platform houses the drilling and extraction equipment and is used to store oil before it is pumped ashore.

1968 U.S.: Martin Luther King and Senator Robert Kennedy (presidential candidate) are assassinated. More race riots. Shirley Chisholm is first black woman to be elected to U.S. Congress. Vietnam War: Efforts toward peace, but fighting starts again. Czechoslovakia: Leader Alexander Dubček encourages free speech and independence from Soviets. USSR invades. Rhodesia: Talks between British prime minister Harold Wilson and Ian Smith of Rhodesia, fail. France: Student uprising in Paris.

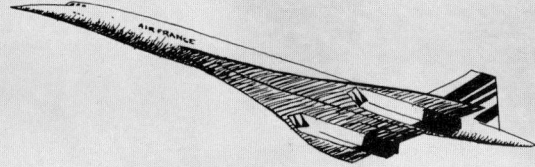

The British- and French-built supersonic aircraft, Concorde, *is capable of traveling at over twice the speed of sound.*

1969 Northern Ireland: Fighting between Catholics and Protestants. Irish Republican Army (IRA) campaigns for an independent, united Ireland and the end of British rule. Czechoslovakia: USSR sets up new government which is loyal to Moscow. Nigeria: Red Cross leads international aid mission to relieve famine caused by the war between Biafrans, seeking independence, and the Nigerian government. Vietnam War: U.S. begins to withdraw troops from South Vietnam, but fighting (and anti-war protests) continues. U.S.: *Apollo 11* lands on the Moon and Neil Armstrong becomes the first man to walk on the Moon. Television pictures of his moonwalk are transmitted to Earth. Over 400,000 people attend a pop concert at Woodstock, New York State. Over 250,000 attend anti-war rally in Washington D.C. France: Supersonic aircraft *Concorde* makes first flight. President de Gaulle resigns. Georges Pompidou becomes president (to 1974).

New Nations

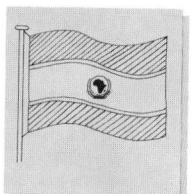

In the 1950s many military and political leaders in European colonies in Africa and the Far East campaigned for independence. They demanded the right to run their countries for themselves. Many of the independence movements were led by men of courage and vision. Often, they were imprisoned before gaining power.

Many countries used military force to win independence from colonial rule. During the 1950s and 1960s, many peoples in Africa and Southeast Asia were at war. European nations would not give up their power, and so freedom fighters, like the Mau Mau in Kenya, launched terrorist campaigns. In some states, as in Egypt in 1952–1953, independence came after the army took control. There were also civil wars, when minority tribal or religious groups within former European colonies sought to

◄ *Countries that have gained independence since 1950 include many former European colonies in Africa and Southeast Asia, as well as territories in the Pacific, South America, the Middle East, and the Caribbean. In some cases, independence was won only after a bloody struggle. Life for new nations has been hard. Today, many of them are among the poorest in the world.*

Countries that have gained independence since 1950

► *Before Zimbabwe was born, there was conflict in the country (then Rhodesia). British soldiers, here talking to a commander in Robert Mugabe's army, formed part of a Commonwealth ceasefire-monitoring force.*

▼ *In 1961, protesters in the French colony of Algeria called for talks on independence between the French president, De Gaulle, and their leader Ferhat Abbas.*

break free from majority control. In the civil war between Nigeria and the Biafra region (1967–1970) millions died.

Today most former colonies are independent. Some maintain ties, as do members of the British Commonwealth (*see* pages 714–715). Others have formed new alliances, such as the Organization for African Unity (OAU).

However, many former colonies are economically dependent. World trade is controlled by Europe, the United States, and Japan, and by multinational companies based largely in the West. It is hard for new nations not to fall into debt.

Wars in the Middle East

The area around the city of Jerusalem has been described for centuries as the traditional homeland of the Jewish people. However, Muslims and Christians have also lived there for hundreds of years. After World War II, over a million Jewish refugees from Europe settled in Palestine, although the area was occupied by Arab peoples. Following the formation of the state of Israel (*see* pages 710–711), fighting broke out with neighboring Arab countries and again in 1956, 1967, 1973, 1978, and 1982. Israel's occupation of the Gaza Strip and the West Bank were the cause of violent demonstrations which intensified in 1988, and the Palestine Liberation Organization (PLO) continues to fight for an Arab state in Palestine.

Between 1980 and 1988, Iran and Iraq were at war. Iraq (backed by the USSR and sometimes the U.S.) feared the power of the new Iranian government, set up by Ayatollah Khomeini after the shah had been overthrown.

▲ *Iranian protesters support the religious revolutionary leader, Ayatollah Khomeini (1900–1989), in 1979 during an anti-U.S. demonstration.*

▼ *The Six Day War took place between June 5 and 10, 1967. In a surprise attack, Israeli bombers destroyed Egyptian planes on the ground and followed this immediately with sending in troops to capture the Egyptian soldiers left in Sinai.*

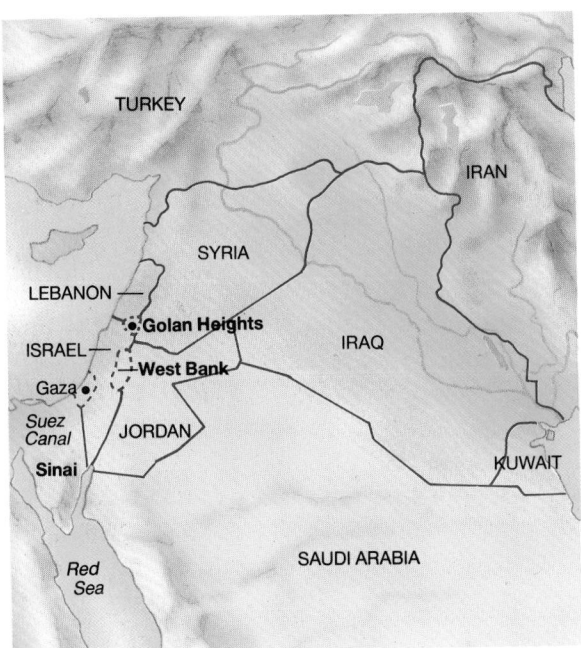

▲ *There have been conflicts between Israeli, Palestinian, and Arab peoples, particularly since 1948. Some areas of territory are still in dispute.*

Rivalries within the Arab world have been caused by the region's oil deposits. In 1990 Iraq invaded Kuwait to improve its sea access, and United Nations' forces fought to free Kuwait and safeguard oil supplies. Other tensions are caused by religious differences. There are two main forms of Islam, Sunni and Shiite. Sunni Muslims follow the "practice of the Prophet," Shiites follow the teachings of Muhammad's son-in-law, Ali.

THE SUEZ CRISIS

In July 1956, Egypt took over the Suez Canal which was owned by Britain and France. Because it felt threatened, Israel invaded Egyptian territory in Sinai, and Britain and France attacked the canal area. There was international disapproval and the United States and USSR both called for a ceasefire. After the withdrawal of Israeli, British, and French troops, a United Nations peace-keeping force arrived in Sinai. The UN troops were able to stop the Israelis and Arabs fighting for another ten years.

1970 Nigeria: Biafran war ends. Middle East: Truce between Israeli and Arab governments along borders of Suez Canal. Arab terrorists (protesting at U.S. support for Israel) hijack three passenger aircraft bound for U.S.. Egypt: Anwar Sadat becomes president (to 1981). Vietnam War: U.S. army invades Cambodia. U.S.: Student protest riots at 448 universities. Chile: Communist Salvador Allende becomes president. USSR: Soviet spacecraft lands on Venus.

1971 Vietnam War: Fighting spreads to Laos. U.S. bombs North Vietnam. Growing friendship between U.S. and China. Northern Ireland: Britain introduces internment (imprisonment without trial) following rioting. Bangladesh (formerly East Pakistan) becomes independent. Pakistan: War with India. USSR: Soviet spacecraft lands on Mars. Switzerland: Women get the vote.

1972 Germany: Arab terrorists kill Israeli athletes at Munich Olympics. Sri Lanka (formerly Ceylon) becomes independent. Northern Ireland: 13 Catholics are killed by British troops on "Bloody Sunday." Britain imposes direct rule. Vietnam War: Peace talks continue. Labor Party victories in elections in Australia and New Zealand lead to major changes. U.S.: Bobby Fischer becomes first American world chess champion. DDT insect-killer banned; start of government concern for environment.

Aircraft are frequently used to spray crops with plant food or insecticides (to prevent disease and attacks by insects) and herbicides (to kill weeds). Most of the sprays are bad for people if they breathe them in.

1973 World energy crisis after Arab oil producers stop oil supplies to U.S., western Europe, and Japan. OPEC raises oil prices greatly. Middle East: Yom Kippur War between Israel and Egypt and Syria. Vietnam War: Ceasefire agreed; U.S. withdraws troops, but some fighting continues. Europe: Britain, Ireland, and Denmark join the European Community.

1974 Energy crisis leads to economic problems in the U.S., Europe, and Japan. India and China test nuclear weapons. Africa: Drought causes famine. U.S.: President Nixon resigns over the Watergate affair, a political scandal. Ella Grasso of Connecticut becomes first elected female state governor. Cyprus: Turks invade and occupy north of island. Ethiopia: Communists overthrow Emperor Haile Selasse.

1975 Terrorism and kidnappings worldwide. Southeast Asia: Khmer Rouge rebels, backed by China, seize power in Cambodia. Communist forces take control of the whole of Vietnam. Pathet Lao troops (communist-led) rule Laos. Taiwan: Chiang Kai-shek dies. U.S. withdraws all troops and civilians from Vietnam, and reduces army in Taiwan. Nepal: Japanese Junko Tabei becomes first woman to climb Mount Everest. Angola, Mozambique, Surinam, and Papua New Guinea gain independence. Spain: Death of Franco ends dictatorship.

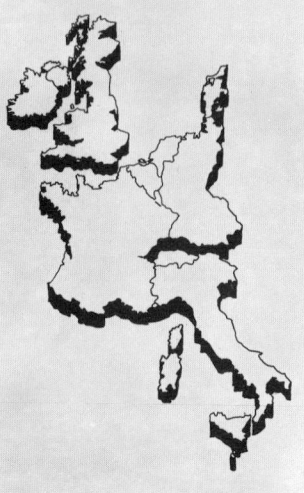

A map outlining the member countries of the European Community in 1973. Spain, Portugal, and Greece have since become members.

China and Japan

When Mao Zedong became chairman of the People's Republic of China in 1949, the civil war (*see* pages 672–673) had left the land poor and war-torn. The people were starving. Roads, railroads, schools, and hospitals could not meet the people's needs. Over the next 25 years, Mao transformed China. Collective farms grew basic foods, like rice, to feed the people. Industry produced more iron and steel. "Barefoot doctors" provided medical care to people in the countryside, and children learned to read and write. However, Mao's political opponents were executed, scholars were tortured, families were split up, and millions of people still died from famine. This was known as the

▲ The Thoughts of Chairman Mao *were studied by people all over China. They gave the required action for any situation. Here students chant from the book.*

JAPANESE TECHNOLOGY

Since the 1960s, Japanese manufacturers have pioneered the development of many new high-technology products. Japan manufactures a wide variety of objects including cars, computers, radios and televisions, and other electrical machines used in offices and factories throughout the world. Their factories are highly automated and robots are used on assembly lines to make production more efficient.

▲ In the spring of 1989 student demonstrators in Beijing and other cities in China called for freedom and democracy. The government sent in troops and tanks to crush the protests.

▼ When Mao came to power, many people in China were hungry. His government reorganized agriculture and created collective farms. Peasants and townspeople were put to work growing food.

Cultural Revolution. Mao was reacting because educated people criticized communism in the early 1960s. He was afraid that they would resist his extreme communist views. After Mao's death, the Chinese government became more open, and began to encourage contacts with the rest of the world. But the massacres that followed the student demonstrations in 1989 showed that full political freedom had not been achieved.

In Japan, government and business had to rebuild their economy after their defeat in World War II. They followed a different approach to China and planned a complete industrial redevelopment of their country, and rapid capitalist growth. Through the hard work and discipline of their people, they have been very successful. By 1990, Japan was one of the richest nations in the world.

In Hong Kong, one of the last British colonies, there was also fast economic growth. In 1984, Britain agreed to return Hong Kong to China in 1997 when the lease on the land runs out.

A Troubled World

Many parts of the world have been troubled by border disputes and civil wars. Families have been divided, economies have been weakened and torn apart by famine, disease, and death.

These conflicts have occurred because political boundaries between nations sometimes do not fit with traditional geographical, cultural, language, or religious frontiers. Groups like the Basques in Spain or the Shan peoples in Myanmar (Burma) can feel trapped within a larger state. Other peoples, such as the Eritreans and the Ethiopians in northeast Africa, who have different histories and traditions, have found themselves together in one "new nation" as a result of peace treaties or decisions made by former colonial powers.

▲ The Kurds' traditional homelands cross the borders of Turkey, Iran, and Iraq. When these countries are at war, suspicion falls on the Kurds. In 1990, many Kurds became refugees as they fled from Iraqi troops.

▼ After World War II, border disputes and wars between countries continued. Sometimes the wars, such as the Gulf War, involved other nations as well.

Many border disputes resulted from frontiers being drawn with no regard for the people in these regions. Civil wars have broken out, usually after years of discontent.

Area of conflict
1. Cyprus
2. Lebanon
3. Israeli occupied territories (West Bank, Golan Heights Gaza Strip)
4. Yugoslavian Republics

Some groups of people use violence (terrorism) to gain publicity and win support for a political cause. They are often called freedom fighters by their supporters. Terrorists murder and kidnap people, set off bombs, and hijack aircraft. The reasons behind terrorism are not always the same. Some want to spread their own political beliefs, while others (nationalists or liberationists) want to establish a separate state for peoples who do not have a country of their own. For example, in the Middle East, terrorists have kidnapped people and carried out bombing campaigns to draw attention to the cause of the Palestinian people, who do not have a homeland. In Spain, a group known as ETA tries to pressurize the Spanish government into creating a separate state for the Basque people in the north of the country. But not all Palestinian or Basque people support the use of violence for political purposes.

▼ *A woman soldier in the Eritrean army. Since 1962 the Eritrean people have been fighting for independence from Ethiopia.*

1976 North and South Vietnam are united under communist rule. Cambodia: Pol Pot comes to power; he and his followers massacre many civilians. Thailand: Military coup. Earthquakes in China, the Philippines, Bali, Turkey, and Guatemala kill 780,000 people. China: Chairman Mao Zedong dies. South Africa: Riots against apartheid in Soweto and other Black townships. Nicaragua: Civil war (to 1979). Lebanon: Fighting among Syrians, Palestinians, Lebanese Christians, and Muslims. Canada: French-Canadians campaign for independent Quebec state. Angola: Outbreak of civil war. U.S.: First fears expressed by U.S. scientists about damage to ozone layer. Episcopal Church approves ordination of women to priesthood. France: The Pompidou Center is built in Paris.

1977 Czechoslovakia: New protests against Soviet control. USSR: Civil rights' protesters arrested. Ethiopia: Civil war. Zaire: Katanga rebels from Angola invade, but are defeated (and in 1978). U.S.: Tests neutron bomb. Rhodesia (now Zimbabwe): White rebels agree to Black majority rule.

1978 Nicaragua: Sandinista rebels fight against U.S.-backed government. Italy: Former prime minister, Aldo Moro, is killed by Red Brigades' terrorists (left-wing). Britain: First test-tube baby is born. Vietnam invades Cambodia.

The Pompidou Center was designed by Piano and Rogers to have its pipes and ducts on the outside, to create more interior space.

1979 Israel and Egypt sign peace treaty. Central America: Sandinistas win civil war in Nicaragua. Rebellion in El Salvador. Iran: Shah is replaced by Islamic republican government led by Ayatollah Khomeini. Iranian students seize American embassy and take hostages. Afghanistan: Soviet invasion. Fighting between Vietnam and China. Margaret Thatcher becomes first woman prime minister of Britain.

1980 Turkey: Military coup. Middle East: War between Iran and Iraq (to 1988). Poland: Solidarity, the independent trade union led by Lech Walesa, is formed. Yugoslavia: Marshal Tito, the president, dies. Communist government faces demands for regional independence. U.S.: Illnesses caused by AIDS virus first recognized. Beginning of "silicon revolution;" computers widely used in business and industry.

1981 Poland: Government crackdown on all trade unions. Egypt: President Sadat assassinated. Northern Ireland: IRA hunger strikes. Greece joins EC. U.S.: First space shuttle flight. France: François Mitterand becomes president.

1982 Argentina occupies Falkland Islands. Britain sends troops to force Argentinians to leave. West Germany: Helmut Kohl becomes chancellor. Spain joins NATO.

1983 Caribbean: U.S. invades Grenada to stop army taking control. Argentina: New democratic leadership elected.

The personal computer has revolutionized the end of the 20th century and greatly affected the way we live our lives today.

Change in Eastern Europe

Mikhail Gorbachev became leader of the USSR in 1985. His appointment led to enormous changes as he tried to strengthen the Soviet economy and to reduce corruption. He dismissed inefficient local officials, reformed the way elections were carried out, encouraged private enterprise in agriculture, and introduced policies of "perestroika" (economic reform) and "glasnost" (openness). He called for cuts in army spending and for friendship between the Warsaw Pact countries and the West.

Gorbachev's reforms were welcomed by most of the Soviet people as they had more freedom, but this new freedom uncovered problems. The republics of Estonia, Latvia, and Lithuania, and Georgia demanded freedom from Communist Party control. In Armenia

SOLIDARITY

Solidarity was formed in 1980 in Poland, to campaign for workers' rights, better conditions, and freedom from communist control. At first it was banned and its leader, Lech Walesa, arrested. The people continued to press for reforms and Solidarity was finally recognized in 1989.

and Azerbaijan there were violent clashes between Christians and Muslims.

Powerful Soviet politicians feared that Gorbachev's reforms would lead to the collapse of the USSR and tried to take over the government in 1991. They failed and at the end of the year the old USSR was abolished and replaced by an alliance of independent states. Gorbachev resigned and Boris Yeltsin became president of Russia.

Similar upheavals were taking place in other parts of Europe. After almost 30 years, the Berlin Wall was demolished and East and West Germany were reunited in 1990. The reunification caused problems for the strong West German economy as efforts were made to modernize equipment and industry throughout eastern Germany.

In the previously communist countries of Hungary, Poland, Czechoslovakia, Romania, and Bulgaria, new liberal groups came to power and struggled to adapt to a capitalist economy. Yugoslavia also struggled with a bitter civil war as three provinces, Bosnia, Croatia, and Slovenia fought for independence from a Yugoslav state dominated by Serbia.

▲ Crowds lining outside a McDonald's restaurant in Moscow in 1989. It was one of the first Western enterprises to open in the USSR, which had previously been very against Western influences.

▼ The Berlin Wall was built in 1961 to isolate the western part of the city from the east. Anyone trying to cross it from the east was killed. In 1989 Berliners celebrated as the wall came down and the guards left.

The Scientific Revolution

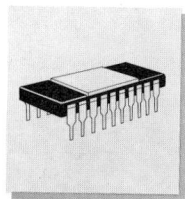

The second half of the 20th century has been a period of rapid development in science and technology. Scientists and business people have been able to develop the discoveries made earlier in the century, and put them to practical use. One of the most important inventions was the silicon chip, a tiny component which could be cheaply mass-produced. It replaced old, bulky, and fragile pieces of equipment, and enabled machines such as smaller calculators and computers to be built. Machines like these, along with photocopiers and faxes, meant that office workers could handle vast amounts of information more quickly than before. They could also communicate rapidly with other offices around the world.

Lasers were used in surgery to burn away diseased tissue. They also had many military uses. British and American scientists discovered the structure of DNA, the basic building blocks from which living cells are made. This knowledge led eventually to the

SILICON WAFERS

Silicon wafers or chips are "printed" with tiny electric circuits that enable computers to process and store information. The first silicon chip microprocessor was developed in 1971 in the U.S.A. Since then new industries have grown up, using silicon-chip based technology. These include control systems for factories, aircraft, and cars.

SCIENTIFIC ACHIEVEMENTS

1950 First color television program is broadcast in the United States.

1952 Acrilan, a synthetic fiber used for making cloth, is discovered.

1955 The first anti-polio vaccine is made available after being declared safe and effective.

1959 First photocopier is introduced.

1962 Launch of the communications satellite, *Telstar*. It is used to transmit the first trans-Atlantic television pictures.

1967 First tidal power station opens across the Rance river estuary in France.

1968 Regular hovercraft service starts across the English Channel.

1978 Solar-powered calculators are first sold in the U.S.

1979 Personal computers are launched.

1982 Compact disc players are first introduced.

1983 HIV retrovirus, from which AIDS can result, first identified in France and U.S.

1987 First criminal convicted as a result of genetic fingerprinting.

▶ *The green revolution aims to help farmers grow more food using better seeds and fertilizers. Higher-yielding crops are being produced but the cost of fertilizer presents a problem in some countries.*

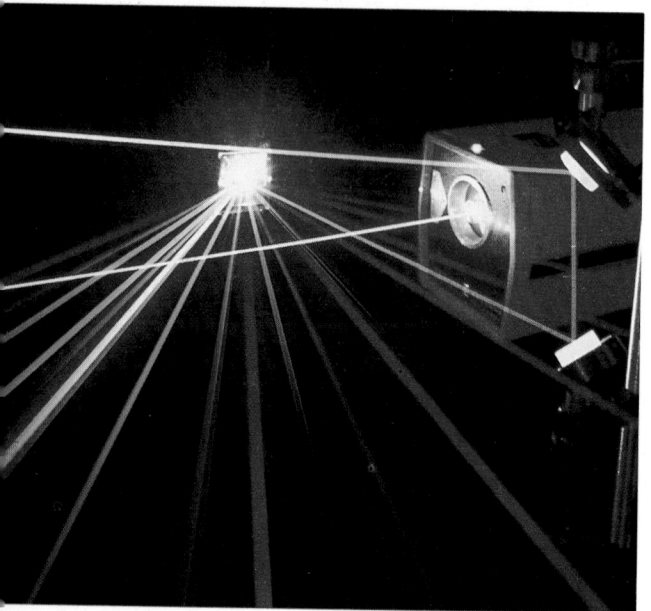

◀ *Since lasers were invented in 1960 they have been used for a wide range of purposes including eye surgery, construction work, and light shows.*

▲ Concorde *went into service in 1976. It was the world's first supersonic passenger aircraft, and was built by a team of French and English engineers.*

production of new drugs by genetic engineering which helped cure serious diseases. It also raised the possibility of new or improved strains of plants and animals being created in laboratories.

In some countries, new technology made life easier. Many people owned washing machines, refrigerators, and freezers. Home entertainment was transformed by televisions, VCRs, music tapes, and compact discs.

1984 India: President Indira Gandhi is assassinated by Sikh militants. Famine in Ethiopia. Britain agrees to return Hong Kong to China in 1997.

1985 USSR: President Chernenko, succeeded by Mikhail Gorbachev (to 1991) who introduces major reforms. South Africa: Apartheid policies slowly being relaxed. Marriages between black and white people become legal. South Pacific Forum draws up Nuclear Free Zone Treaty. New Zealand bans nuclear weapons; France continues nuclear tests. Pop singer Bob Geldof organizes Live Aid charity pop concerts in Britain and United States to raise money for famine victims in Ethiopia; they are seen by the largest-ever TV audience. World population now 4.5 billion; scientists predict that it will reach 6–9 billion by the year 2000.

1986 Libya: U.S. bombs Tripoli and Benghazi in retaliation for Libyan support for anti-American terrorist campaigns. Europe: Spain and Portugal join the EC. South Africa: Widespread fighting in Black townships by civil rights' protesters. Rival Black political groups (ANC and Inkatha) also clash. USSR: Accident at Chernobyl nuclear reactor causes massive leak of radioactive particles. U.S.: Space shuttle *Challenger* explodes after takeoff, killing the crew of seven. Airplane *Voyager* becomes first to circumnavigate the globe without refueling. USSR: *Mir* space station is launched.

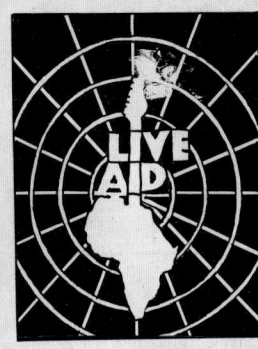

The logo used to promote the Live Aid concerts that raised money for famine victims.

1987 U.S. and USSR agree to ban medium-range nuclear weapons. Middle East: Violent rioting by Palestinians and attacks in return by Israeli troops cause widespread international concern. European Community (EC): Members meet to plan eventual European union. New rules (to be introduced in 1992) aim to achieve unified laws, taxes, welfare benefits, and currency, also a European army and police force. Bangladesh: Monsoon makes 24 million people homeless. Scientists confirm existence of a hole in the ozone layer above Antarctica.

1988 End of Iran-Iraq War. USSR: New constitution (system of government) introduced allowing greater freedom of speech and less Communist Party control. Pakistan: Benazir Bhutto becomes prime minister (to 1990) and the first woman to govern an Islamic republic. Israel occupies Gaza Strip.

1989 USSR: Demonstrations in Estonia by local Communist Party and nationalist groups wanting freedom from Soviet control. Demands for independence in Lithuania. Afghanistan: Soviet president Gorbachev decides to withdraw Soviet troops from Afghanistan. Romania: Dictator Ceaucescu is overthrown. China: Student demonstrations in Beijing calling for greater freedom and democracy are crushed by government troops. Namibia: First free elections are held. Muslims call for death of British author Salman Rushdie after publication of his novel *The Satanic Verses*. Iran: Ayatollah Khomeini dies.

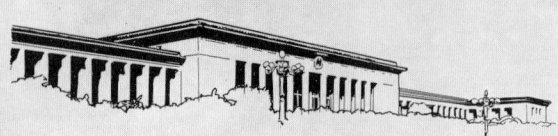

Chinese Government buildings beside Tiananmen Square, Beijing, where many people lost their lives when government troops suppressed a student demonstration.

Social Change

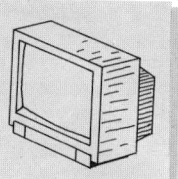

During the late 1960s, many young people took part in protest movements. They were calling for a social revolution based on peace, freedom, and understanding. Few of their aims were achieved. However, there were other, slower changes taking place in society.

The number of people in the world was growing fast and there was an increasing awareness of the problems of feeding them all. International bodies such as the United Nations gave aid, along with charities in wealthy countries but the gap between rich and poor got wider.

In rich countries, the power of the press, television, and advertising grew rapidly. As a result a consumer society

▼ *Signs like this were widespread in South Africa while the government encouraged the policy of apartheid (separation of black and white people). It was finally abolished in 1990.*

▶ One of the largest fund-raising pop concerts was organized by Bob Geldof in 1985. He was appalled by reports of the 1984 famine in Ethiopia, and planned the Live Aid concert to raise money to send food and expert help. It was broadcast live in many countries.

developed, concerned with quality of life, fashion, and style. Education led to improved opportunities for many young people, but there was still inequality between and within different racial groups, in spite of the activities of civil rights campaigners. With the greater ability to travel and greater distances between people, communities changed as did families as divorce and single-parent families became more common.

The position of women is changing and improving as their equal social and legal rights are clarified and reinforced.

POP CULTURE

The American pop singer, Michael Jackson became famous as a solo singer in the 1980s. The pop music industry developed in the 1950s and 1960s, after records and record players became cheaper through mass production. Today, pop music is very big business.

EDUCATION

In many countries, people were better educated than before. School graduation ages were raised and higher education was available for more students. Education and qualifications were seen as essential, as a pathway to a good job. In other countries the lack of teachers and facilities meant that children received only a basic education. Opportunities for adult education increased.

WOMEN

The 1960s and 1970s saw the rise of the women's movement. Women demanded equal opportunities and the same pay as men and an end to discrimination based on sexism. Women took traditionally male jobs and proved they could succeed. Women also campaigned for recognition of the important job they did as homemakers and child-carers.

▲ A Chinese government poster, encouraging couples to have only one child. For several years, it has been illegal for Chinese people to have more children. Other governments tried to restrict population growth but only some have been successful.

1990 Gulf War: Iraq invades Kuwait. UN forces sent to the area. Eastern Europe: Political unrest continues. Soviet troops intervene in ethnic violence between Armenia and Azerbaijan. East and West Germany are reunited as one nation. South Africa: Veteran anti-apartheid campaigner Nelson Mandela is released from prison; he continues his leadership of African National Congress (ANC). Apartheid abolished. Britain: Margaret Thatcher resigns after 11 years in power.

1991 UN forces Iraq to withdraw from Kuwait. USSR: Hardline Communists attempt a coup, but meet resistance led by Russian leader Boris Yeltsin. Mikhail Gorbachev resigns as leader, the USSR is officially dissolved. Yugoslavia: Civil war breaks out as individual states fight about independence (Slovenia and Croatia) and federation. Lebanon: Remaining U.S. and British hostages held by Muslim groups are released.

1992 European Community: Single European Act brings unity closer, although states disagree on some issues. Africa: Famine threat. Fears that ozone layer over Europe is thinning rapidly. Brazil: UN Earth summit is held to discuss world environmental concerns. Czechoslovakia: Czechs and Slovaks agree to form separate governments.

1993 Yugoslavia: Civil war intensifies as Serbia fights to maintain federation. US: Bill Clinton is inaugurated as president.

Nelson Mandela was released from prison after 27 years, having been convicted of sabotage and conspiracy.

Environmental Concerns

For centuries, people believed that nature should be tamed and controlled. In the latter half of the 20th century, people realized the Earth was in danger, threatened with pollution and over-exploitation as a result of ignorance and greed. At first, only a few naturalists, like Rachel Carson, whose book *Silent Spring* caused a sensation when it was published in the 1950s, dared to speak up. Then pressure groups, such as Greenpeace, also began to campaign. By the 1980s, some governments passed laws to protect the environment, but some scientists believed that these attempts to protect our planet might be too little and too late.

Change was slow to take effect because at first people did not believe that the Earth was really in danger. New information was collected by scientists which proved that the threat was real. Clean (non-polluting) products started to appear but they proved expensive to buy and less profitable to produce. It took environmental disasters such as accidents at nuclear reactors in the U.S. and the

▲ *In the Mato Grosso in Brazil, huge areas of rain forest are being destroyed so that local farmers can graze cattle on the land, and to sell the valuable timber.*

USSR, explosions at chemical plants in Italy and India, and oil spillages at sea to show people that new technology could be deadly. Then public opinion forced governments to take action and try to halt pollution. The discovery of holes in the ozone layer around the Earth, and possible worldwide climatic change have encouraged environmental concern.

In environmental matters we have, unfortunately, little to learn from the past, but there is much in history that we must continue to remember in order to avoid disaster. We must also be ruthless in remembering ideas and practices that have been important in the past but which would be fatal for all our futures.

▲ Seas around the world have been polluted because they are used to dump household and industrial waste. It is either discharged directly into the sea or dumped from boats.

► Oil spills are caused either by accidents involving oil tankers, or as waste-oil is discharged into the sea when ships clean out their tanks. The oil floats on the sea's surface, forming a slow-moving slick covering fish, birds, and sea creatures. Most of them die.

▼ After the explosion at the nuclear power station at Chernobyl, USSR, in 1986, houses nearby were hosed down to get rid of the contamination. The people were moved away but many still suffer from the after-effects.

ACID RAIN

In northern Europe, the U.S., and Canada, waste gases from power stations burning oil and coal drift over lakes and forests and mix with rain to produce a weak acid. Scientists think that this acid rain has damaged and killed millions of trees, polluted waterways, and killed fish.

RECYCLING

Many of the resources on the Earth are non-renewable (cannot be recreated). These include most of our energy sources such as coal and oil, and the raw materials that go to make goods. It is now economic to recycle (use again) many things we use daily, such as paper, cans, and glass.

Ready Reference

ANCIENT EGYPTIAN DYNASTIES

Period	Dynasty	Dates (B.C.)	Principal pharaohs
Early Dynastic	1–3	c. 2920–2575	Menes (Aha)
			Zoser (Djoser)
Old Kingdom	4–7/8	c. 2575–2134	Cheops (Khufu)
First Intermediate Period	9–11	c. 2134–2040	
Middle Kingdom	11–14	c. 2040–1532	Mentuhotep II
Second Intermediate Period	15–17	1640–1532	Hyksos kings in north Kamose reunites Egypt
New Kingdom	18–20	1550–1070	Amenhotep I–III (Amenophis)
			Thutmosis I–IV
			Queen Hatshepsut
			Akhenaten (Amenhotep IV)
			Tutankhamun
			Rameses I–XI
Third Intermediate Period	21–25	1070–712	Sheshonq I
			Rule of Nubians
Late Period	25–31	712–332	Psammetichus I
			Rule of Persians
			Nectanebo II
			Conquest of Alexander the Great

CHINESE DYNASTIES

Dynasty	Date	Details
Hsia	c. 2205–1500 B.C.	
Shang	1500–1122	
Zhou	1122–256	
Qin	221–207	Shi Huangdi, first emperor of unified China
Early Han	202 B.C.–A.D. 9	Emperor Wu-ti also rules Korea and north Vietnam
Hsin	5–23	Usurpation of Wang Mang
Later Han	25–220	
The Three Kingdoms	220–265	China breaks into three kingdoms – the Wei, Shu, and Wu
Western Chin	265–317	
Eastern Chin	317–420	
Southern dynasties	420–589	
Sui	581–618	China reunified
Tang	618–907	Golden age of culture; includes reign of Emperor T'ai Tsung the Great
The five dynasties and ten kingdoms	907–960	Period of disunity
Liao	947–1125	Part of northern China ruled by Khitan Mongols
Song	960–1279	Dynasty rules parts of China only
Northern Song	960–1126	
Western Hsia	990–1227	
Chin	1115–1234	
Southern Song	1127–1279	
Yuan (Mongol)	1279–1368	All China ruled by the Mongols led by Kublai Khan
Ming	1368–1644	Reestablishment of a native Chinese dynasty
Qing (Manchu)	1644–1911	
Republic of China	1911–1949	Government set up under Sun Yat-sen, followed by disunity and the warlord era
People's Republic	1949–	Mao Zedong is first chairman of Communist Party

ROMAN RULERS

Kings of Rome

Romulus	753–716 B.C.	Tarquinius Priscus	616–579
Numa Pompilius	716–673	Servius Tullius	579–534
Tullus Hostilius	673–640	Tarquinius Superbus	534–509
Ancus Martius	640–616		

The Republic of Rome

Dictatorship of Sulla	82–78	Dictatorship of Julius Caesar	45–44
First Triumvirate (Julius Caesar, Pompey, and Crassus)	60–53	Second Triumvirate (Octavian, Mark Anthony and Marcus Lepidus)	43–27
Dictatorship of Pompey	52–47		

Emperors of the Roman Empire

Augustus (previously Octavian)	27 B.C.–A.D. 14	Gallus and Hostilianus (Volusianus)	251–253
Tiberius I	AD 14–37	Aemilianus	253
Caligula (Gaius Caesar)	37–41	Valerian and Gallienus	253–260
Claudius I	41–54	Gallienus	260–268
Nero	54–68	Claudius II (Gothicus)	268–270
Galba	68–69	Quintillus	270
Otho	69	Aurelianus	270–275
Vitellius	69	Tacitus	275–276
Vespasian	69–79	Florianus	276
Titus	79–81	Probus	276–282
Domitian	81–96	Carus	282–283
Nerva	96–98	Carinus and Numerianus	283–284
Trajan	98–117	Diocletian (divides empire)	284–305
Hadrian	117–138	Maximian (jointly)	286–305
Antoninus Pius	138–161	Constantius I	305–306
Marcus Aurelius	161–180	Severus	306–307
Lucius Verus (jointly)	161–169	Licinius (jointly)	307–323
Commodus	180–192	Constantine I (reunites empire)	308–337
Pertinax	193	Constantine II (jointly)	337–340
Didius Julianus	193	Constans (jointly)	337–350
Septimus Severus	193–211	Constantius II (jointly)	337–361
Caracalla	211–217	Magnentius (jointly)	350–353
Geta (jointly)	211–212	Julian (the Apostate)	361–363
Macrinus	217–218	Jovianus	363–364
Elagabulus (Heliogabalus)	218–222	Valentinian I (rules West)	364–375
Alexander Severus	222–235	Valens (rules East)	364–378
Maximinius I (the Thracian)	235–238	Gratian (rules West)	375–383
Gordian I	238	Magnus Maximus (usurper in West)	383–388
Gordian II	238	Valentinian II (rules West)	375–392
Balbinus and Pupienus Maximus	238	Eugenius (usurper in West)	392–394
Gordian III	238–244	Theodosius I (the Great) (rules East, then unites East and West)	378–395
Philip (the Arab)	244–249		
Decius	249–251		

Emperors of the Eastern Roman Empire

Arcadius	395–408	Leo II	474
Theodosius II	408–450	Zeno	474–491
Marcian	450–457	Anastasius	491–518
Leo I	457–474		

Emperors of the Western Roman Empire

Honorius	395–423	Majorian	457–461
Maximus	410–411	Severus III	461–465
Constantius III	421	Anthemius	467–472
John	423–425	Olybrius	472
Valentinian III	425–455	Glycerius	473
Petronius Maximus	455	Julius Nepos	473–480
Avitus	455–456	Romulus Augustus	475–476

ARGENTINA

Presidents (since 1854)

Justo José Urquiza	1854–1860	Augustín P. Justo	1932–1938
Santiago Derqui	1860–1862	Roberto M. Ortiz	1938–1942
Bartolomé Mitre	1862–1868	Ramón S. Castillo	1942–1943
Domingo Faustino Sarmiento	1868–1874	Pedro Ramirez	1943–1944
Nicolás Avellaneda	1874–1880	Edelmiro J. Farrell	1944–1946
Julio Argentino Roca	1880–1886	Juan Domingo Perón	1946–1955
Miguel Juárez Celmán	1886–1890	Pedro Eugenion Aramburu (provisional)	1955–1958
Carlos Pellegrini	1890–1892	Arturo Frondizi	1958–1962
Luis Sáenz Peña	1892–1895	José María Guido	1962–1963
José Evaristo Uriburu	1895–1898	Arturo Umberto Illia	1963–1966
Julio Argentino Roca	1898–1904	Juan Carlos Onganía	1966–1970
Manuel Quintana	1904–1906	Roberto Marcelo Levingston	1970–1971
José Figueroa Alcorta	1906–1910	Alejandro Agustin Lanusse	1971–1973
Roque Sáenz Peña	1910–1914	Héctor J. Cámpora	1973
Victorino de la Plaza	1914–1916	Juan Domingo Perón	1973–1974
Hipólito Irigoyen	1916–1922	Isabel Perón	1974–1976
Marcelo Torcuato de Alvear	1922–1928	Military Junta	1976–1983
Hipólito Irigoyen	1928–1930	Raúl Alfonsín	1983–1989
José Francisco Uriburu (provisional)	1930–1932	Carlos Menem	1989–

BRAZIL

Presidents

Manuel Deodoro da Fonesca	1889–1891	José Linhares (provisional)	1945–1946
Floriano Peixoto	1891–1894	Enrico Gaspar Dutra	1946–1951
Prudente José de Moraes Barros	1894–1898	Getúlio Dornelles Vargas	1951–1954
Manuel Ferraz de Campos Salles	1898–1902	João Café Filho	1954–1955
Francisco de Paula Rodrigues Alves	1902–1906	Nereú Ramos (acting)	1955–1956
Affonso Augusto Moreira Penna	1906–1909	Jusceline Kubitschek de Oliveira	1956–1961
Nilo Peçanha	1909–1910	Jânio Quadros	1961
Hermes da Fonseca	1910–1914	João Belchior Marques Goulart	1961–1964
Wenceslau Braz Pereira Gomes	1914–1918	Humberto Castelo Branco	1964–1967
Francisco de Paula Rodrigues Alves	1918–1919	Arthur Costa e Silva	1967–1969
Delfim Moreira (acting)	1918–1919	Emilio Garrastazú Médici	1969–1974
Epitacio da Silva Pessôa	1919–1922	Ernesto Geisel	1974–1979
Arthur da Silva Bernardes	1922–1926	João Baptista Figueiredo	1979–1985
Washington Luiz Pereira de Souza (deposed)	1926–1930	José Sarney	1985–1990
		Fernando Collor de Mello	1990–1992
Getulio Dornelles Vargus	1930–1945	Itamar Franco	1992–

MEXICO

Presidents (since 1824)

Guadalupe Victoria	1824–1829	José Joaquin Herrera	1844–1845
Vicente Guerrero	1829	Mariano Paredes y Arrillaga	1846
José María de Bocanegra (acting)	1829	Nicolás Bravo	1846
Anastasio Bustamante	1829–1832	José Mariano Salas (acting)	1846
Melchor Múzquiz (acting)	1832	[War with the United States, 1846–1848]	
Manuel Gómez Pedraza	1832–1833	Valentin Gómez Farias (acting)	1846–1847
Antonio López de Santa Anna	1833–1835	Antonio López de Santa Anna	1847
Miguel Barragán	1835–1836	Pedro María Anaya	1847
José Justo Corro	1836–1837	Antonio López de Santa Anna	1847
Anastasio Bustamente*	1837–1841	Manuel de la Peña y Peña (provisional)	1847
Javier Echeverria (acting)	1841	Pedro María Anaya (acting)	1847–1848
Antonio López de Santa Anna	1841–1842	Manuel de la Peña y Peña	1848
Nicolás Bravo	1842–1843	José Joaquin Herrera	1848–1851
Antonio López de Santa Anna (provisional)	1843	Mariano Arista	1851–1853
		Juan Bautista Ceballos (acting)	1853
Valentín Canalizo	1843–1844	Manuel M. Lombardine (acting)	1853
Antonio López de Santa Anna	1844	Antonio López de Santa Anna (dictator)	1853–1855
José Joaquin Herrera (acting)	1844	Martin Carrera (acting)	1855
Valentín Canalizo (acting)	1844	Juan Alvarez (acting)	1855

Ignacio Comonfort	1855–1857	Francisco Lagos Cházaro (provisional)	1915
Benito Juárez (provisional)	1857–1861	Venustiano Carranza (provisional)	1915–1917
Benito Juárez	1861–	Venustiano Carranza	1917–1920
[Period of French intervention, 1861–1867.		Adolfo de la Huerta (provisional)	
Austrian Archduke Maximilian crowned Emperor,		Alvaro Obregón	1920–1924
June 12, 1864; executed June 19, 1867]		Plutarco Elías Calles	1924–1928
Sebastian Lerdo de Tejada	1872–	Emilio Portes Gil (provisional)	1928–1930
Porfirio Díaz (provisional)		Pascual Ortiz Rubio	1930–1932
Juan N. Méndez (acting)	1876–	Abelardo L. Rodriquez (provisional)	1932–1934
Porfirio Díaz (provisional)		Lázaro Cárdenas	1934–1940
Porfirio Díaz	1877–1880	Manuel Avila Camacho	1940–1946
Manuel González	1880–1884	Miguel Alemán Valdés	1946–1952
Porfirio Díaz	1884–	Adolfo Ruiz Cortines	1952–1958
Francisco León de la Barra (provisional)		Adolfo López Mateos	1958–1964
Francisco Indalecio Madero	1911–1913	Gustavo Díaz Ordaz	1964–1970
Victoriano Huerta (provisional)	1913–1914	Luis Echeverría Alvarez	1970–1976
Francisco Carbajal (provisional)	1914	José López Portillo	1976–1982
Venustiano Carranza ("first chief")	1914	Miguel de la Madrid Huertad	1982–1988
Eulalio Martin Gutiérrez (provisional)	1914–1915	Carlos Salinas de Gortari	1988–
Roque Gonzalez Garza	1915		

*From March 18 to July 10, 1839, Santa Anna was in control; from July 10 to 17, 1839, Nicolas Bravo was acting president.

PERU

Presidents (since 1821)

José de San Martín	1821–1822	Manuel Candamo	1903–1904
José de la Riva Aguero	1823	Serapio Calderón (acting)	May–Sept. 1904
Simón Bolívar (dictator)	1824–1827	José Pardo y Barreda	1904–1908
José de Lamar	1827–1829	Augusto Bernardino Leguía y Salcedo	1908–1912
Agustin Gamarra	1829–1833	Guillermo Enrique Billinghurst	1912–1914
Luis José Orbegosa	1833–1835	Oscar Raimundo Benavides	1915
Felipe Santiago Salaverry	1835–1836	(provisional)	
Andrés Santa Cruz	1836–1839	José Pardo y Barreda	1915–1919
Agustin Gamarra	1839–1841	Augusto Bernardino Leguía y Salcedo	1919–1930
Manuel Menéndez* (acting)	1841–1845	Manuel Ponce (provisional)	1930
Ramón Castilla	1845–1851	Luis M. Sánchez Cerro (provisional)	1930–1931
José Rufino Echenique	1851–1855	Ricardo Leoncio Elías (provisional)	1931
Ramón Castilla	1855–1862	Gustavo Jiménez (provisional)	1931
Miguel San Román	1862–1863	David Samánez Ocampo (provisional)	1931
Juan Antonio Pezet	1863–1865	Luis M. Sánchez Cerro	1931–1933
Mariano Ignacio Prado (dictator)	1865–1868	Oscar Raimundo Benavides	1833–1939
José Balta	1868–1872	Manuel Prado Ugarteche	1939–1945
Manuel Pardo	1872–1876	José Luis Bustamente Rivero	1945–1948
Mariano Ignacio Prado	1876–1879	Manuel Odría (provisional)	1948–1950
Nicolás de Piérola	1879–1881	Zenón Noriega	1950
Francisco García Calderón	1881	Manuel Odría	1950–1956
Lizardo Montero	1881–1883	Manuel Prado y Ugarteche	1956–1962
Miguel Iglesias	1883–1886	Ricardo Pérez Godoy (provisional)	1962
Andrés Avelino Cáceres	1886–1890	Fernando Belaúnde Terry	1963–1968
Remigio Morales Bermúdez	1890–1894	Military rule	1968–1980
Justíniano Borgoño	1894	Fernando Belaúnde Terry	1980–1985
Andrés Avelino Cáceres	1894–1895	Alan Garcia Pérez	1985–1990
Nicolás de Piérola	1895–1899	Alberto Fujimori	1990–
Eduardo Lopez de Romaña	1899–1903		

*The period 1841–1844 was one of civil war and confusion. Juan Crisóstomo Terrico and Manuel Vivanco were each for a short time in power.

RULERS OF ENGLAND

Saxons

Egbert	827–839	Ethelbert	860–865
Ethelwulf	839–858	Ethelred I	865–871
Ethelbald	858–860	Alfred the Great	871–899

Edward the Elder	899–924	Edgar	959–975
Athelstan	924–939	Edward the Martyr	975–978
Edmund	939–946	Ethelred II, the Unready	978–1016
Edred	946–955	Edmund Ironside	
Edwy	955–959		

Danes

Canute	1016–1035	Harthacanute	1040–1042
Harold I Harefoot	1035–1040		

Saxons

Edward the Confessor	1042–1066	Harold II	1066

House of Normandy

William I, the Conqueror	1066–1087	Henry I	1100–1135
William II	1087–1100	Stephen	1135–1154

House of Plantagenet

Henry II	1154–1189	Edward I	1272–1307
Richard I, the Lionheart	1189–1199	Edward II	1307–1327
John	1199–1216	Edward III	1327–1377
Henry III	1216–1272	Richard II	1377–1399

House of Lancaster

Henry IV	1399–1413	Henry VI	1422–1461
Henry V	1413–1422		

House of York

Edward IV	1461–1483	Richard III	1483–1485
Edward V	1483		

House of Tudor

Henry VII	1485–1509	Mary I	1553–1558
Henry VIII	1509–1547	Elizabeth I	1558–1603
Edward VI	1547–1553		

RULERS OF SCOTLAND

Malcolm II	1005–1034	Alexander II	1214–1249
Duncan I	1034–1040	Alexander III	1249–1286
Macbeth (usurper)	1040–1057	Margaret of Norway	1286–1290
Malcolm III (Cranmore)	1057–1093		
Donald Bane	1093–1094	(Interregnum	1290–1292)
Duncan II	1094		
Donald Bane (restored)	1094–1097	John Balliol	1292–1296
Edgar	1097–1107		
Alexander I	1107–1124	(Interregnum	1296–1306)
David I	1124–1153		
Malcolm IV	1153–1165	Robert I, the Bruce	1306–1329
William the Lion	1165–1214	David II	1329–1371

House of Stuart

Robert II	1371–1390	James IV	1488–1513
Robert III	1390–1406	James V	1513–1542
James I	1406–1437	Mary, Queen of Scots	1542–1567
James II	1437–1460	James VI (I of Great Britain)	1567–1625
James III	1460–1488		

RULERS OF ENGLAND AND SCOTLAND

House of Stuart

James I	1603–1625	Charles I	1625–1649

Commonwealth	**1649–1653;**		
Protectorate	**1653–1660**		
Oliver Cromwell	1649–1658		
Richard Cromwell	1658–1659		

House of Stuart

Charles II	1660–1685	William III (jointly)	1689–1702
James II	1685–1688	Anne	1702–1714
Mary II (jointly)	1689–1694		

RULERS OF GREAT BRITAIN

House of Hanover

George I	1714–1727	George IV	1820–1830
George II	1727–1760	William IV	1830–1837
George III	1760–1820	Victoria	1837–1901

House of Saxe-Coburg

Edward VII	1901–1910		

House of Windsor

George V	1910–1936	George VI	1936–1952
Edward VIII	1936	Elizabeth II	1952–

PRIME MINISTERS OF GREAT BRITAIN

	In office	Party
Sir Robert Walpole	1721–1742	Whig
Earl of Wilmington	1742–1743	Whig
Henry Pelham	1743–1754	Whig
Duke of Newcastle	1754–1756	Whig
Duke of Devonshire	1756–1757	Whig
Duke of Newcastle	1757–1762	Whig
Earl of Bute	1762–1763	Tory
George Grenville	1763–1765	Whig
Marquess of Rockingham	1765–1766	Whig
William Pitt the Elder (Earl of Chatham)	1766–1768	Whig
Duke of Grafton	1767–1770	Whig
Lord North	1770–1782	Tory
Marquess of Rockingham	1782	Whig
Earl of Shelburne	1782–1783	Whig
Duke of Portland	1783	Coalition
William Pitt the Younger	1783–1801	Tory
Henry Addington	1801–1804	Tory
William Pitt the Younger	1804–1806	Tory
Lord Grenville	1806–1807	Whig
Duke of Portland	1807–1809	Tory
Spencer Perceval	1809–1812	Tory
Earl of Liverpool	1812–1827	Tory
George Canning	1827	Tory
Viscount Goderich	1827–1828	Tory
Duke of Wellington	1828–1830	Tory
Earl Grey	1830–1834	Whig
Viscount Melbourne	1834	Whig
Sir Robert Peel	1834–1835	Tory
Viscount Melbourne	1835–1841	Whig
Sir Robert Peel	1841–1846	Tory
Lord John Russell	1846–1852	Whig
Earl of Derby	1852	Tory
Earl of Aberdeen	1852–1855	Peelite
Viscount Palmerston	1855–1858	Liberal
Earl of Derby	1858–1859	Conservative
Viscount Palmerston	1859–1865	Liberal
Earl Russell	1865–1866	Liberal

Earl of Derby	1866–1868	Conservative
Benjamin Disraeli	1868	Conservative
William Gladstone	1868–1874	Liberal
Benjamin Disraeli	1874–1880	Conservative
William Gladstone	1880–1885	Liberal
Marquess of Salisbury	1885–1886	Conservative
William Gladstone	1886	Liberal
Marquess of Salisbury	1886–1892	Conservative
William Gladstone	1892–1894	Liberal
Earl of Rosebery	1894–1895	Liberal.
Marquess of Salisbury	1895–1902	Conservative
Arthur Balfour	1902–1905	Conservative
Sir Henry Campbell-Bannerman	1905–1908	Liberal
Herbert Asquith	1908–1915	Liberal
Herbert Asquith	1915–1916	Coalition
David Lloyd-George	1916–1922	Coalition
Andrew Bonar Law	1922–1923	Conservative
Stanley Baldwin	1923–1924	Conservative
James Ramsay MacDonald	1924	Labour
Stanley Baldwin	1924–1929	Conservative
James Ramsay MacDonald	1929–1931	Labour
James Ramsay MacDonald	1931–1935	National Coalition
Stanley Baldwin	1935–1937	National Coalition
Neville Chamberlain	1937–1940	National Coalition
Winston Churchill	1940–1945	Coalition
Winston Churchill	1945	Conservative
Clement Atlee	1945–1951	Labour
Sir Winston Churchill	1951–1955	Conservative
Sir Anthony Eden	1955–1957	Conservative
Harold Macmillan	1957–1963	Conservative
Sir Alec Douglas-Home	1963–1964	Conservative
Harold Wilson	1964–1970	Labour
Edward Heath	1970–1974	Conservative
Harold Wilson	1974–1976	Labour
James Callaghan	1976–1979	Labour
Margaret Thatcher	1979–1990	Conservative
John Major	1990–	Conservative

HOLY ROMAN EMPERORS

Dates given are period of reign.

Charlemagne	800–814		
Louis I (the Pious)	814–840	Lothair I	840–855

Saxon dynasty

Otto I, the Great	936–973	Otto III	983–1002
Otto II	973–983	Henry II	1002–1024

Franconian dynasty

Conrad II	1024–1039	Henry V	1106–1125
Henry III	1039–1056	Lothair III, Duke of Saxony	1125–1137
Henry IV	1056–1106		

Hohenstaufen dynasty

Conrad III	1138–1152	Otto IV of Brunswick	1198–1212
Frederick I, Barbarossa	1152–1190	Frederick II	1212–1250
Henry VI	1190–1197	Conrad IV	1250–1254
Philip of Swabia	1197–1208		

Interregnum
Electors gain power — 1254–1273

Transition period

Rudolf I of Habsburg	1273–1292	Frederick of Austria (co-regent)	1314–1322
Adolf of Nassau	1292–1298	Charles IV, of Luxembourg	1347–1378
Albert I, King of Germany	1298–1308	Wenceslas of Luxembourg	1378–1400
Henry VII of Luxembourg	1308–1314	Rupert, Duke of Palatine	1400–1410
Louis IV of Bavaria (co-regent)	1314–1347	Sigismund of Luxembourg	1410–1434

Habsburg dynasty

Albert II	1437–1439	Leopold I	1658–1705
Frederick III	1440–1493	Joseph I	1705–1711
Maximilian I	1493–1519	Charles VI	1711–1740
Charles V, King of Spain	1519–1556	War of Austrian Succession	1740–1748
Ferdinand I	1556–1564	Charles VII of Bavaria	1742–1745
Maximilian II	1564–1576	Francis I of Lorriane	1745–1765
Rudolf II	1576–1612	Joseph II	1765–1790
Matthias	1612–1619	Leopold II	1790–1792
Ferdinand II	1619–1637	Francis II	1792–1806
Ferdinand III	1637–1657		

HABSBURG EMPERORS OF AUSTRIA

Francis II	1804–1835	Francis Joseph	1848–1916
Ferdinand	1835–1848	Charles	1916–1918

HOHENZOLLERN EMPERORS OF GERMANY

William I (of Prussia)	1871–1888	William II	1888–1918
Frederick III	1888		

RULERS OF GERMANY

Weimar Republic

Friedrich Ebert	1919–1925	Paul von Hindenburg	1925–1934

Third Reich
Adolf Hitler — 1934–1945

Post World War II
Germany under Allied control — 1945–1949

CHANCELLORS OF THE FEDERAL REPUBLIC OF GERMANY (WEST GERMANY)

Konrad Adenauer	1949–1963	Willy Brandt	1969–1974
Dr. Ludwig Erhard	1963–1966	Helmut Schmidt	1974–1982
Kurt Georg Kiesinger	1966–1969	Helmut Kohl	1982–1990

CHAIRMEN OF THE DEMOCRATIC REPUBLIC OF GERMANY (EAST GERMANY)

Walter Ulbricht	1949–1971	Egon Krenz	1989–1990
Erich Honecker	1971–1989		

CHANCELLORS OF UNITED GERMANY

Helmut Kohl — 1990–

RULERS OF FRANCE

The Carolingians

Charles I, the Bald	843–877	Charles II	885–888
Louis II	877–879	Eudes	888–898
Louis III	879–882	Charles III	898–922

Robert	922–923	Lothair	954–986
Rudolph	923–936	Louis V	986–987
Louis IV	936–954		

The Capets

Hugh Capet	987–996	Louis VIII	1223–1226
Robert II, the Pious	996–1031	Louis IX	1226–1270
Henry I	1031–1060	Philip III	1270–1285
Philip I	1060–1108	Philip IV	1285–1314
Louis VI	1108–1137	Louis X	1314–1316
Louis VII	1137–1180	Philip V	1316–1322
Philip II	1180–1233	Charles IV	1322–1328

House of Valois

Philip VI	1328–1350	Louis XII	1498–1515
John II	1350–1364	Francis I	1515–1547
Charles V	1364–1380	Henry II	1547–1559
Charles VI	1380–1422	Francis II	1559–1560
Charles VII	1422–1461	Charles IX	1560–1574
Louis XI	1461–1483	Henry III	1574–1589
Charles VIII	1483–1498		

House of Bourbon

Henry IV, of Navarre	1589–1610	Louis XV	1715–1774
Louis XIII	1610–1643	Louis XVI	1774–1793
Louis XIV	1643–1715		

The First Republic and First Empire

Napoleon Bonaparte (first consul)	1799–1804	Napoleon I (emperor)	1804–1814

Restoration of monarchy

Louis XVIII	1814–1824	Louis-Philippe	1830–1848
Charles X	1824–1830		

Second Republic

Louis Napoleon Bonaparte (president)	1848–1852	Napoleon III (emperor)	1852–1870

Third Republic

Louis Adolphe Thiers	1871–1873	Paul Deschanel	1920
Marshal Patrice de MacMahon	1873–1879	Alexandre Millerand	1920–1924
Paul Grévy	1879–1887	Gaston Doumergue	1924–1931
Marie Carnot	1887–1894	Albert Lebrun	1932–1940
Jean Casimir-Périer	1894–1895		
François Faure	1895–1899	Vichy government (under Germans)	1940–1944
Émile Loubet	1899–1906		
Armand C. Fallières	1906–1913	Provisional government	1944–1946
Raymond Poincaré	1913–1920		

Fourth Republic

Vincent Auriol	1947–1954	René Coty	1954–1959

Fifth Republic

Charles de Gaulle	1959–1969	Valéry Giscard d'Estaing	1974–1981
Georges Pompidou	1969–1974	François Mitterrand	1981–

RULERS OF SPAIN

Habsburg dynasty

Charles I (V of Germany)	1516–1556		
Philip II	1556–1598	Philip IV	1621–1665
Philip III	1598–1621	Charles II	1665–1700

Bourbon dynasty

Philip V	1700–1724	Charles IV	1788–1808
Louis I	1724	Joseph Bonaparte	1808–1814
Philip V (restored)	1724–1746	Ferdinand II	1814–1833
Ferdinand VI	1746–1759	Isabella II	1833–1868
Charles II	1759–1788		

Other monarchs

Amadeus of Savoy	1870–1873

First republic 1873–1874

Restoration of Monarchy

Alfonso XII	1874–1885	Alfonso XIII	1886–1931
Primo de Rivero (dictator)	1923–1930		

Second Republic

Niceto Alcalá Zamora	1931–1936	General Francisco Franco	1939–1975
Manuel Azaña	1936–1939		

Restoration of monarchy

Juan Carlos	1975–

Prime ministers

Admiral Luis Blanco	1973	Adolfo Suárez	1976–1982
Carlos Navarro	1973–1976	Felipe González	1982–

PERIODS OF JAPAN

Yamato	c. 300–592	
Asaka	592–710	Empress Suiko (592–628)
		Emperor Temmu (673–686)
Nara	710–794	Emperor Kammu (781–806)
Heian	794–1185	Japan ruled from Heian (now called Kyoto)
Fujiwara	858–1160	Fujiwara clan rules
Taira	1159–1185	Taira clan take control
Kamakura	1185–1333	Minamoto Yoritomo defeats Taira clan; in 1192 he becomes shogun
Namboku	1334–1392	End of shogun rule in 1333; Emperor Godaigo rules alone 1333–1339; imperial line splits into northern and southern courts
Ashikaga	1338–1573	Ashikaga Takauji becomes shogun in 1338
Muromachi	1392–1573	Two rival courts are unified
Sengoku	1467–1600	Emperor Gonara (1527–1557)
Momoyama	1573–1603	Oda Nobunaga, a daimyo (baron), deposes the shogun and becomes dictator to 1582
Edo	1603–1867	Ieyasu Tokugawa becomes shogun in 1603; Tokugawa shoguns rule until 1867
Meiji	1868–1912	Emperor Mutsuhito (Meiji) is restored; he ends the shogunate and modernizes Japan
Taisho	1912–1926	Emperor Yoshihito
Showa	1926–1989	Emperor Hirohito
Heisei	1989–	Emperor Akihoto

TSARS OF RUSSIA

Ivan III, the Great	1462–1505	Basil (IV) Shuiski	1606–1610
Basil III	1505–1533	(Interregnum	1610–1613)
Ivan IV, the Terrible	1533–1584	Michael Romanov	1613–1645
Fyodor I	1584–1598	Alexis	1645–1676
Boris Godunov	1598–1605	Fyodor III	1676–1682
Fyodor II	1605	Ivan V & Peter I, the Great	1682–1689
Demetrius	1605–1606	Peter I	1689–1725

Catherine I	1725–1727	Paul I	1796–1801
Peter II	1727–1730	Alexander I	1801–1825
Anna	1730–1740	Nicholas I	1825–1855
Ivan VI	1740–1741	Alexander II	1855–1881
Elizabeth	1741–1762	Alexander III	1881–1894
Peter III	1762	Nicholas II	1894–1917
Catherine II, the Great	1762–1796		

EFFECTIVE RULERS OF THE UNION OF SOVIET SOCIALIST REPUBLICS

Vladimir Lenin	1917–1922	Yuri Andropov	1982–1984
Joseph Stalin	1922–1953	Konstantin Chernenko	1984–1985
Nikita Khrushchev	1953–1964	Mikhail Gorbachev	1985–1992
Leonid Brezhnev	1964–1982		

PRESIDENTS OF RUSSIA

Boris Yeltsin	1992–

PRESIDENTS OF THE UNITED STATES OF AMERICA

George Washington	1789–1797	None
John Adams	1797–1801	Federalist
Thomas Jefferson	1801–1809	Democratic-Republican
James Madison	1809–1817	Democratic-Republican
James Monroe	1817–1825	Democratic-Republican
John Quincy Adams	1825–1829	Democratic-Republican
Andrew Jackson	1829–1837	Democratic
Martin Van Buren	1837–1841	Democratic
William H. Harrison	1841	Whig
John Tyler	1841–1845	Whig
James K. Polk	1845–1849	Democratic
Zachary Taylor	1849–1850	Whig
Millard Fillmore	1850–1853	Whig
Franklin Pierce	1853–1857	Democratic
James Buchanan	1857–1861	Democratic
Abraham Lincoln	1861–1865	Republican
Andrew Johnson	1865–1869	National Union
Ulysses S. Grant	1869–1877	Republican
Rutherford Hayes	1877–1881	Republican
James Garfield	1881	Republican
Chester Arthur	1881–1885	Republican
Grover Cleveland	1885–1889	Democratic
Benjamin Harrison	1889–1893	Republican
Grover Cleveland	1893–1897	Democratic
William McKinley	1897–1901	Republican
Theodore Roosevelt	1901–1909	Republican
William Taft	1909–1913	Republican
Woodrow Wilson	1913–1921	Democratic
Warren Harding	1921–1923	Republican
Calvin Coolidge	1923–1929	Republican
Herbert Hoover	1929–1933	Republican
Franklin D. Roosevelt	1933–1945	Democratic
Harry S. Truman	1945–1953	Democratic
Dwight Eisenhower	1953–1961	Republican
John F. Kennedy	1961–1963	Democratic
Lyndon Johnson	1963–1969	Democratic
Richard Nixon	1969–1974	Republican
Gerald Ford	1974–1977	Republican
Jimmy Carter	1977–1981	Democratic
Ronald Reagan	1981–1989	Republican
George Bush	1989–1993	Republican
Bill Clinton	1993–	Democratic

PRIME MINISTERS OF CANADA

Sir John MacDonald	1867–1873	Richard Bennett	1930–1935
Alexander MacKenzie	1873–1878	William King	1935–1948
Sir John MacDonald	1878–1891	Louis St Laurent	1948–1957
Sir John Abbott	1891–1892	John Diefenbaker	1957–1963
Sir John Thompson	1892–1894	Lester Pearson	1963–1968
Sir Mackenzie Bowell	1894–1896	Pierre Trudeau	1968–1979
Sir Charles Tupper	1896	Joe Clark	1979–1980
Sir Wilfrid Laurier	1896–1911	Pierre Trudeau	1980–1984
Sir Robert Borden	1911–1920	John Turner	1984
Arthur Meighen	1920–1921	Brian Mulroney	1984–1993
William King	1921–1926	Kim Campbell	1993
Arthur Meighen	1926	Jean Chrétien	1993–
William King	1926–1930		

PRIME MINISTERS OF AUSTRALIA

Australia was established as a Commonwealth in 1901.

Sir Edmund Barton	1901–1903	Sir Robert Menzies	1939–1941
Alfred Deakin	1903–1904	Sir Arthur Fadden	1941
John Watson	1904	John Curtin	1941–1945
Sir George Reid	1904–1905	Francis Forde	1945
Alfred Deakin	1905–1908	Joseph Chifley	1945–1949
Andrew Fisher	1908–1909	Sir Robert Menzies	1949–1966
Alfred Deakin	1909–1910	Harold Holt	1966–1967
Andrew Fisher	1910–1913	Sir John McEwen	1967–1968
Sir Joseph Cook	1913–1914	John Gorton	1968–1971
Andrew Fisher	1914–1915	William McMahon	1971–1972
William Hughes	1915–1923	Edward Gough Whitlam	1972–1975
Stanley Bruce	1923–1929	John Fraser	1975–1983
James Scullin	1929–1932	Robert Hawke	1983–1991
Joseph Lyons	1932–1939	Paul Keating	1991–
Sir Earle Page	1939		

PRIME MINISTERS OF NEW ZEALAND

Sir Joseph Ward	1906–1912	Sir Walter Nash	1957–1960
Thomas MacKenzie	1912–1915	Keith Holyoake	1960–1972
William Massey	1915–1925	Sir John Marshall	1972
Sir Francis Bell	1925	Norman Kirk	1972–1974
Joseph Coates	1925–1928	Hugh Watt	1974
Sir Joseph Ward	1928–1930	Wallace (Bill) Rowling	1974–1975
George Forbes	1930–1935	Robert Muldoon	1975–1984
Michael Savage	1935–1940	David Lange	1984–1989
Peter Fraser	1940–1949	Geoffrey Palmer	1989–1990
Sir Sidney Holland	1949–1957	Michael Moore	1990
Keith Holyoake	1957	James Bolger	1990–

PRESIDENTS OF THE REPUBLIC OF ITALY

Alcide de Gasperi (acting head of state)	1946	Giovanni Leone	1971–1978
Enrico de Nicola (provisional president)	1946–1948	Amintore Fanfani	1978
Luigi Einaudi	1948–1955	Alessandro Pertini	1978–1985
Giovanni Gronchi	1955–1962	Francesco Cossiga	1985–1992
Antonio Segni	1962–1964	Oscar Luigi Scalfaro	1992–
Giuseppe Saragat	1964–1971		

Prime Ministers

Alcide de Gasperi	1946–1953	Adone Zoli	1957–1958
Guiseppe Pella	1953–1954	Amintore Fanfani	1958–1959
Amintore Fanfani	1954	Antonio Segni	1959–1960
Mario Scelba	1954–1955	Fernando Tambroni	1960
Antonio Segni	1955–1957	Amintore Fanfani	1960–1963

Giovanni Leone	1963	Francesco Cossiga	1979–1980
Aldo Moro	1963–1968	Arnaldo Forlani	1980–1981
Giovanni Leone	1968	Giovanni Spadolini	1981–1982
Mariano Rumor	1968–1970	Armintore Fanfani	1982–1983
Emilio Colombo	1970–1972	Bettino Craxi	1983–1987
Giulio Andreotti	1972–1973	Giovanni Goria	1987–1988
Mariano Rumor	1973–1974	Luigi Ciriaco de Mita	1988–1989
Aldo Moro	1974–1976	Giulio Andreotti	1989–
Giulio Andreotti	1976–1979		

PRESIDENTS OF REPUBLIC OF INDIA

Dr. Rajendra Prasad	1949–1962	Basappa Jatti	1977
Dr. Sarvapalli Radhakrishnan	1962–1967	Neelam Reddy	1977–1982
Dr. Zahir Hussain	1967–1969	Giani Zail Singh	1982–1987
Varahgiri Girir	1969–1974	Ramaswamy Venkataraman	1987–
Fakhruddin Ahmed	1974–1977		

Prime Ministers

Jawaharlal Nehru	1949–1964	Charan Singh	1979–1980
Gulzarilal Nanda	1964	Indira Gandhi	1980–1984
Lal Shastri	1964–1966	Rajiv Gandhi	1984–1989
Gulzarilal Nanda	1966	V.P. Singh	1989–1990
Indira Gandhi	1966–1977	Chandra Shekhar	1990–1991
Shri Desai	1977–1979	P.V. Narasimha Rao	1991–

MAJOR WARS

Date	Name of war	Warring parties
c. 1250 B.C.	Trojan wars	Mycenaeans v. Trojans
431–404 B.C.	Peloponnesian War	Athens v. Sparta
264–241 B.C.	First Punic War	
218–101 B.C.	Second Punic War	Rome v. Carthage
149–146 B.C.	Third Punic War	
1096–1099	First Crusade	
1147–1149	Second Crusade	Saracens v. Christians over Palestine
1189–1192	Third Crusade	
1202–1204	Fourth Crusade	
1337–1453	Hundred Years War	England v. France
1455–1485	Wars of the Roses	House of York v. House of Lancaster
1562–1598	French Wars of Religion	Huguenots v. Catholics
1642–1648	English Civil War	Cavaliers v. Roundheads
1618–1648	Thirty Years War	Catholic League (Germany, Austria, Spain) v Denmark, Sweden, France
1689–1697	War of League of Augsburg	France v. the League, England, and the Netherlands
1700	Great Northern War	Sweden v. Russia, Denmark, Poland, Holland
1701–1713	War of Spanish Succession	Spain, France and Bavaria v. England, Holland, Austrian empire and Portugal
1730–1738	War of Polish Succession	Russia, Poland v. France
1740–1748	War of Austrian Succession	Austria, Britain v. Prussia, Bavaria, France, Spain
1756–1763	Seven Years War	Britain and Prussia v. France, Austria, and Russia
1775–1783	Revolutionary War (American)	American colonies v. Britain
1793–1815	Napoleonic wars	France v. Britain, Austria, Sweden, Russia, and Prussia
1821–1829	Greek War of Independence	Greece v. Ottoman Turkey
1846–1848	Mexican–American War	Mexico v. U.S.
1854–1856	Crimean War	Russia v. Britain, France and Turkey
1859	War for Italian Independence	France, Piedmont-Sardinia v. Austria
1861–1865	U.S. Civil War	Confederates v. Unionists
1866	Austro–Prussian War	Prussia v. Austria
1870	Franco–Prussian War	France v. Prussia
1894–1895	Chinese–Japanese War	China v. Japan
1899–1902	Boer War	Britain v. Boers (Dutch) in South Africa
1904–1905	Russo-Japanese War	Russia v. Japan

1914–1918	World War I	Germany and Austria-Hungary v. France, Russia, Britain and other nations
1918–1921	Russian Civil War	Bolsheviks v. White Russians
1931–1933	Chinese–Japanese War	Japan v. China
1936–1939	Spanish Civil War	Nationalists (Franco) v. Republicans
1939–1945	World War II	Britain, France, USSR, U.S.A., and other nations v. Germany, Italy, and Japan
1967	Six Day War	Israel v. Arab states
1950–1953	Korean War	N. Korea v. S. Korea
1964–1973	Vietnam War	N. Vietnam v. S. Vietnam and U.S.A.
1980–1988	Iran–Iraq War	Iran v. Iraq

EXPLORATION AND DISCOVERY

Place	Achievement	Explorer	Date
World	circumnavigated	Ferdinand Magellan (Portuguese for Spain)	1519–1521
Pacific Ocean	discovered	Vasco Nuñez de Balboa (Spanish)	1513
Africa			
River Congo (mouth)	discovered	Diogo Cão (Portuguese)	c. 1483
Cape of Good Hope	sailed round	Bartolomeu Diaz (Portuguese)	1488
River Niger	explored	Mungo Park (British)	1795
River Zambezi	discovered	David Livingstone (British)	1851
Sudan	explored	Heinrich Barth (German for Britain)	1852–1855
Victoria Falls	discovered	Livingstone	1855
Lake Tanganyika	discovered	Richard Burton and John Speke (British)	1858
River Congo	traced	Sir Henry Stanley (British)	1877
Asia			
China	visited	Marco Polo (Italian)	c. 1272
Asia, India (Africa)	explored	Cheng Ho (Chinese)	1405–1433
India (Cape route)	visited	Vasco da Gama (Portuguese)	1498
Japan	visited	St. Francis-Xavier (Spanish)	1549
China	explored	Ferdinand Richthofen (German)	1868
North and Central America			
North America	settled	Leif Ericsson (Norse)	c. 1003
Caribbean	discovered	Christopher Colombus (Italian for Spain)	1492
Newfoundland	discovered	John Cabot (Italian for England)	1497
Central America	explored	Rodrigo de Bastidas (Spanish)	1501
Mexico	conquered	Hernando Cortés (Spanish)	1519–21
St. Lawrence River	explored	Jacques Cartier (French)	1534–1536
Mississippi River	discovered	Hernando de Soto (Spanish)	1541
Canadian interior	explored	Samuel de Champlain (French)	1603–1609
Hudson Bay	discovered	Henry Hudson (English)	1610
Alaska	discovered	Vitus Bering (Danish for Russia)	1728
South America			
South America	visited	Columbus	1498
Venezuela	explored	Alonso de Ojeda (Spanish)	1499
Brazil	discovered	Pedro Alvares Cabral (Portuguese)	1500
Tierra del Fuego	discovered	Magellan	1520
Peru	conquered	Francisco Pizarro (Spanish)	1530–1538
River Amazon	explored	Francisco de Orellana (Spanish)	1541
Cape Horn	discovered	Willem Schouten (Dutch)	1616
Australasia, Polar regions etc.			
Greenland	visited	Eric the Red (Norse)	c. 982
Spitsbergen	discovered	Willem Barents (Dutch)	1596
Tasmania	visited	Abel Tasman (Dutch)	1642
New Zealand	sighted	Tasman	1642
New Zealand	visited	James Cook (British)	1769
Antarctica	sighted	Nathaniel Palmer (American)	1820

Antarctica	circumnavigated	Fabian von Bellingshausen (Russian)	1819–1821
Australian	explored	Charles Wilkes (American)	c. 1838–1842
Australia	crossed (S–N)	Robert Burke (Irish) and William Wills (British)	1860–1861
Greenland	explored	Fridtjof Nansen (Norwegian)	1888
North Pole	reached	Robert Peary (American)	1909
South Pole	reached	Roald Amundsen (Norwegian)	1911
Antarctica	crossed	Sir Vivian Fuchs (British)	1957–1958

Space

| Earth | orbited | Yuri Gagarin (Russian) | 1961 |
| Moon | visited | Neil Armstrong (American) | 1969 |

UNITED NATIONS MEMBER COUNTRIES

Country	Joined		
Afghanistan	1946	Ecuador	1945
Albania	1955	Egypt	1945
Algeria	1962	El Salvador	1945
Angola	1976	Equatorial Guinea	1968
Antigua and Barbuda	1981	Estonia	1991
Argentina	1945	Ethiopia	1945
Armenia	1992	Fiji	1970
Azerbaijan	1992	Finland	1955
Australia	1945	France	1945
Austria	1955	Gabon	1960
Bahamas	1973	Gambia	1965
Bahrain	1971	Germany	1973
Bangladesh	1974	Ghana	1957
Barbados	1966	Greece	1945
Belarus	1945	Grenada	1974
Belgium	1945	Guatemala	1945
Belize	1981	Guinea	1958
Benin	1960	Guinea-Bissau	1974
Bhutan	1971	Guyana	1966
Bolivia	1945	Haiti	1945
Bosnia-Herzegovina	1992	Honduras	1945
Botswana	1966	Hungary	1955
Brazil	1945	Iceland	1946
Brunei	1984	India	1945
Bulgaria	1955	Indonesia	1950
Burkina Faso	1960	Iran	1945
Burundi	1962	Iraq	1945
Cambodia	1955	Ireland, Republic of	1955
Cameroon	1960	Israel	1949
Canada	1945	Italy	1955
Cape Verde	1975	Ivory Coast	1960
Central African Republic	1960	Jamaica	1962
Chad	1960	Japan	1956
Chile	1945	Jordan	1955
China	1945	Kazakhstan	1992
Colombia	1945	Kenya	1963
Comoros	1975	Korea, DPR	1991
Congo	1960	Korea, Republic of	1991
Costa Rica	1945	Kuwait	1963
Croatia	1992	Kirghizia	1992
Cuba	1945	Laos	1955
Cyprus	1960	Latvia	1991
Czechoslovakia	1945	Lebanon	1945
Denmark	1945	Lesotho	1966
Djibouti	1977	Liberia	1945
Dominica	1978	Libya	1955
Dominican Republic	1945	Liechtenstein	1990

Country	Year
Lithuania	1991
Luxembourg	1945
Madagascar	1960
Malawi	1964
Malaysia	1957
Maldives, Republic of	1965
Mali	1960
Malta	1964
Marshall Islands	1991
Mauritania	1961
Mauritius	1968
Mexico	1945
Micronesia	1991
Moldova	1992
Mongolian PR	1961
Morocco	1956
Mozambique	1975
Myanmar	1948
Namibia	1990
Nepal	1955
Netherlands	1945
New Zealand	1945
Nicaragua	1945
Niger	1960
Nigeria	1960
Norway	1945
Oman	1971
Pakistan	1947
Panama	1945
Papua New Guinea	1975
Paraguay	1945
Peru	1945
Philippines	1945
Poland	1945
Portugal	1955
Qatar	1971
Romania	1955
Russia	1945
Rwanda	1962
San Marino	1992
St Kitts-Nevis	1983
St Lucia	1979

Country	Year
St Vincent & the Grenadines	1980
Sao Tome & Principe	1975
Saudi Arabia	1945
Senegal	1960
Seychelles	1976
Sierra Leone	1961
Singapore	1965
Slovenia	1992
Solomon Islands	1978
Somali Republic	1960
South Africa	1945
Spain	1955
Sri Lanka	1955
Sudan	1956
Surinam	1975
Swaziland	1968
Sweden	1946
Syria	1945
Tadzhikstan	1992
Tanzania	1961
Thailand	1946
Togo	1960
Trinidad & Tobago	1962
Tunisia	1956
Turkmenistan	1992
Turkey	1945
Uganda	1962
Ukraine	1945
United Arab Emirates	1971
United Kingdom	1945
United States	1945
Uruguay	1945
Uzbekistan	1992
Vanuatu	1981
Venezuela	1945
Vietnam	1977
Western Samoa	1976
Yemen (as separate states)	1947 and 1967
Yugoslavia	1945
Zaire	1960
Zambia	1964
Zimbabwe	1980

Index

This index has been designed to help you find easily the information you are looking for. You may find that the subject you are interested in has no article to itself but is mentioned in several places. For example, the start of radio can be found on a Communications special and later on, early radios in the home can be found on a People special. Page numbers in **boldface type** (heavy and dark) indicate where the main reference to a subject can be found. Page numbers in *italic type* (slanting) refer to pages on which there are illustrations. Take the entry on

Alexander the Great for example:
Alexander the Great 77, 78, 79, 86, **90–91**, 94, 138, *154*, 155
The main entry on Alexander is on pages 90 to 91. On page 154 is an illustration of the battle formation he used with great success. On the other pages listed you will find information in the main or boxed text or in the timeline about his victories, his successors, and the effect his actions had on spreading Greek culture and thought throughout the ancient world.

Thirty Years' War 414–415, 417, 419, 424, 433
war with Denmark 433
war with Poland 438
Treaty of Kardis 443
Great Northern War 456–457, 466–467, 471, 473
Seven Years' War 496
Sweyn I Forkbead, King of Denmark 211, 214, 217, 218, 222
Sweyn I, King of Norway 222
Sweyn II, King of Denmark 222
Swift, Jonathan 494
Swiss Confederation 331, 332, 353
Switzerland:
Reformation 355
civil war 361
Calvinism 366
Villmergen wars 438
World War II 693
Swords 235, 314, *314*
Syagrius 152
Sydney *541*
Sydney Harbour Bridge *654*
Sylvester, Pope 200, *201*
Syria:
Hittite invasion 40
Seleucid dynasty 79, 94
Romans conquer 103, 112
Arabs conquer 176, 177
in Ottoman empire 355
war with Ottoman Turks 565
independence from France 639, 704
French mandate 658
Druse uprising 670
World War II 694
Szalankemen, battle of (1691) 465

T

Tabei, Junko 734
Tabriz, battle of (1604) 399, 402
Tacitus, Emperor 135
Tahiti 79, 152, 239, 257, 559, 569, 615
T'ai Tsung the Great, Emperor of China 177, 211
Taikwa reforms, Japan 178
Taiping rebellion 559, *568*, 569, 572
Taira clan 254–255
Taiwan 616, 716, 734
see also Formosa
Taj Mahal *401*, 413, 423, 440, *441*
The Tale of Genji **199**
Talleyrand, Charles Maurice de 542
Talmud 178
Tamerlane *241*, **272–273**, *272–273*, 291, 295, 299, 302, 304, 360
Tammany Hall 541
Tamyris 74
T'ang, Emperor of China 43
Tang dynasty 159, *159*, *161*, **170–171**, 174, *181*, *197*, 203, 232
Tanganyika 658
see also Tanzania
Tanganyika, Lake 593, 635
Tangier 182, 329, 443

Tanis 50
Tanks 657, 712, *712*
Tannenberg, battle of (1914) 642
Tanzania 658, 714, 718, 726
Taoism 104
Tapestries 246, **436**, *436*
Tarquinius Superbus, King of Rome 111
Tartars 290, 318, 336, 382, 383
Taruga 133
Tarxien 31
Tasman, Abel 399, 430, **454**, *454*
Tasmania 76, 399, 454, *540*, 559, 579, 630–631
Tassili-n-Ajjer *59*
Taxation:
Poll Tax 299
window-tax *493*
Taxila 90, 149
Tchaikovsky, Peter Ilyich 599
Tea 427, **429**, *429*, 433, 450, 503, 515, *549*
Tea ceremony 393
Tear gas 633
Technology *see* Science and technology
Tecumseh *538*, *538*, 539
Tehuacan Valley 31
Telamon, battle of (225 B.C.) 98
Telegraph 501, *501*, 529, 588
Telephones 588, 589, *589*, 596, 611, 645
Telescopes 408, *446*, *452*, 453
Television 660, *661*, 670, 740
Telstar 740
Temple of Heaven, Beijing *481*, *493*
Temple Mound culture 158, 182, *182*
Temples:
Egyptian *21*
ancient Greece *93*
Mayan *93*
Temujin *see* Genghis Khan
Temur Oljaitu, Emperor of China 279
Teng, Dowager Empress 126
Tennis 357, 596
Tennyson, Alfred 572
Tenochtitlán 238, 240, *278*, 279, 283, 320, 322–323, *322*, 340, 358, 362–363, *362*, *380*
Tensing Norgay 722
Teotihuacán 77, 78, 93, 134, *134*, 135, 158, 208
Tereshkova, Valentina 725
Terracotta army *99*
Terrorism 730, 733, 737
Tertry, battle of (687) 182
Test Acts 443, 450, 458
Test-tube baby 737
Teusina, Treaty of (1595) 393
Teutonic Knights 326
Teutonic tribes 57
Tewkesbury, battle of (1471) 329
Texas 368, 491, 557, 558, **562–563**, *563*
Texcoco, Lake 279
Thai peoples 120
Thailand 726
prehistory 11, 79

ancient history 27
invades Cambodia *241*, 310, 311
World War II 696
military coup 737
see also Siam
Thames river 12, 214, 418, 449, *449*
Thanksgiving Day 397, **409**
Thatcher, Margaret 738, 744
Theater:
Greek and Roman *116*, 117
Middle Ages *246*
Elizabethan England *325*
commedia dell'arte 435
actresses 443
pantomime 471
18th century 484
19th century 566
Thebes (Egypt) 42, 54, 70
Thebes (Greece) 89
Theodora, Empress 162, **163**, *164*
Theodoric the Great, King of the Ostrogoths 151, 152, 156
Theodosius, General 143
Theodosius I the Great, Emperor 143
Theodosius II, Emperor 144
Thera 10, 38, 39, 42
Thermometers 453, *453*, 487
Thermopylae, battle of (480 B.C.) 82, 83
Thevenot, Jean 446
Thirty-Nine Articles 379
Thirty Tyrants 135
Thirty Years' War 371, 397, 398, 414–415, **416–417**, 418, 419, 423, 424, 430, 433, 435, 437, 473
Thompson, John 659
Thomson, Joseph John 620
Thor 204, 217
Thorn, Peace of (1466) 326
Thorpe, Jim 635
The Thousand and One Nights 191, *191*, 201
Thrace 90
Thucydides 1, 88
Thuringia 182
Thutmosis I, Pharaoh 40
Thutmosis II, Pharaoh 42
Thutmosis III, Pharaoh 42, 54
Tiahuanaco 158, 208–209, 229
Tianjin 687, 716
Tiber River 66
Tiberius, Emperor 119, 121
Tibet:
Mongol invasions 270, 488
Dalai Lama **433**, 445
China takes control of 491
Tientsin Treaty (1858) 581
Tientsin Treaty (1885) 605
Tiffany, Louis 566
Tiglathpileser I, King of Assyria 48, 55
Tiglathpileser III, King of Assyria 48, 64
Tigris River 9, 18, 24, 25, 48, 126, 135
Tikal 80, 93
Tilly, Count 423, 424
Timbuktu 264, *264*, 310, 326, 340, 344–345, *345*, *598*
Time bombs 391
The Times 520

Timur *360*
Tinchebrai, battle of (1106) 242
Tintoretto *324*
Tipu Sultan 479, 519, *528*, *529*, 532
Titanic 635
Titian 324
Titicaca, Lake 208
Titicaca basin 327
Tito, Marshal 703, **705**, *705*, 738
Titus, Emperor 122, 126
Tiwanaku culture 78
Tlaloc 16, *134*
Tobacco 376, 379, 408, **409**, 414, *469*, 476, 549, *549*
Tobago 446
Tobruk 694
Toghril Beg 230
Tokugawa shoguns 514, 578, 586
Tokyo 586
see also Edo
Tolbiac, battle of (496) 152
Toledo 144, 232
Toleration Act (1689) 463
"Tollund Man" 3
Tolstoy, Leo 567, 590
Toltecs 158, 160, *160*, 165, 208, *208*, 209, 238, 248
Tombaugh, Clyde 675
Tombs:
prehistoric 20
Egyptian 5
mastabas 27, *27*
megaliths *31*
barrows 31
"beehive" 40–41, *40*
Tomsk 402
Tonga 11, 152, 399, 454, 714
Tonkin 121, 482, 604, *605*
Tonle Sap 310
Tools:
prehistoric *14*
for building *20*
in the ancient world *52*
in the classical world **92**, *92*
farming 188
see also Science and technology
Topa, Sapa Inca 318, 322, 326, 327, 329
Topiltzin Quetzalcoatl 208
Toqtamish 299
Tordesillas, Treaty of (1494) 318, 344
Tories 455
Toronto 539
Torpedoes 555
Torres, Luis Vaez de 399
Torres Strait 399
Torricelli, Evangelista 433, 453
Tostig, Earl of Northumbria 225, 227
Totem poles *164*
Toul 371, 376
Toulouse 263
Toulouse-Lautrec, Henri de 609
Touraine 248, 258
Tournaments *244*, 245
Toussaint L'Ouverture, Pierre Dominique *480*, 526–527, *526–527*, 544
Toutswe state 158
Tower of London 173, 227, 326, 329, 339

Acknowledgments

The publishers would like to thank the following artists for their contribution to this book:

Jonathan Adams 441*b*; Hemesh Alles (Maggie Mundy) 260*b*, 356*b*, 393*m*, 405*tr*, 421*br*, 425*m*, 434*br*, 435*b*, 453*r*, 459*tl*, 460*t*, 461*r*, 464*b*, 468*t*, 495*t*, 503*mr*, 514*b*, 521*t*, 523*t*, 525*ml*, 546, 571*t*, 583, 591, 592–593, 598*b*, 602*mr*, 605, 616*b*, 618*t*, 623*t*, 631*b*, 633*mr*, 665*b*, 704*b*, 716*br*; Marion Appleton 63*tr*, 101*ml*, 148*t*, 164*m*, 166*t*, 170*t*, 181*b*, 233*br*, 259*br*, 323*tl*, 324, 356*l*, 394*m*, 404*m*, 439*b*, 444*t*, 446*b*, 453*l*, 457*tr*, 460*bl*, 484*m,b*, 485*t*, 505*b*, 514*ml*, 516*t*, 519*l*, 530*m,l*, 531*t*, 544*b*, 566*tl*, 566*bl*, 567*l*, 573*m*, 589*b*, 603*tl*, 606*m*, 612*mr*, 619*m*, 624*m*, 632*t,m*, 633*tl*, 646*t,b*, 647*m*, 676*t*, 681, 690*t*, 715*tr*; Sue Barclay 123*b*; R. Barnett 431*b*; Noel Bateman 205*r*; Simon Bishop 662*b*; Richard Bonson 96*bl*, 153*m*, 269*m*, 279*b*, 316*t*, 323*b*, 426*r,b*, 468*m*, 508*m*, 595*tl*; Nick Cannan 28*b,l*; Vanessa Card 12, 17*t*, 28*t*, 29*b*, 45*tl*, 47*tb*, 51*tr*, 59*tr*, 59*b*, 87*mr*, 89*bl*, 116*t*, 129*t*, 137*t*, 138*t*, 163*b*, 164*br*, 165*m*, 167*b*, 175*t*, 179*tl*, 180*t*, 185*bl*, 187*ml*, 188*b*, 191*tl*, *br*, 198*b*, 200*b*, 204*ml*, 221*t*, 226*t*, 229*b*, 245*t*, 249*b*, 254*b*, 266*t*, 276*br*, 279, 292*t,b*, 300*b*, 308*b*, 309*b*, 311*t*, 349*m*, 351*t*, 357*t*, 358*b*, 361*b*, 364*m*, 372*tr*, 376*t*, 392*t*, 396, 402*b*, 422*t*, 424*m*, 425*b*, 435*tl*, 436*m*, 441*t*, 445*br*, 455*b*, 457*l*, 469*t*, 503*b*, 505*tr*, 515*m*, 524*b*, 526*b*, 529, 541*t,ml*, 555, 568*m,b*, 609, 610, 618*m*, 623*b*, 653*tr*, 668*t*, 698*m*; Tony Chance (Garden Studio) 601*b*, 631*br*; Harry Clow 565*b*, 673*b*; Stephen Conlin 20*b*, 25*t*, 33*m*, 45*mr*, 60*mr*, 166*b*, 278*m*, 468*m*, 476*b*, 507*b*, 575*m*; Peter Dennis (Linda Rogers Assoc.) 500*m*, 501*mr*, 509*l*, 543, 549*l*, 553*b*; Dave Etchell 252*m*, 530*br*; James Field (Simon Girling Assoc.) 108*bl*, 109*mr*, 250*b*, 275*b*, 289*b*, 294*b*, 487*ml*, 496–497*t*, 534-535*b*; Michael Fisher 31*b*, 413*b*; Eugene Fleury All maps; Chris Forsey 37*t,br*, 60*tr,br*, 61*m*, 86*mr*, 87*tl*, 125*b*, 134*t,bl*, 145*t*, 196*m*, 234*m*, 235*mr*, 262*t*, 282*b*, 469*m*, 492*m*, 508*b*, 548, 555, 692*t*; Dewey Franklin (Garden Studio) 562*b*, 567*t*; Terry Gabbey (Eva Morris A.F.A) 16*m*, 17*m*, 22*b*, 23*ml*, 42*br*, 43*bl*, 44*tr,tl,bl*, 45*ml*, 51*b*, 62*b*, 84*t*, 87*ml*, 91*t*, 101*ml*, 111*br*, 113*m*, 124*b*, 130*t*, 140*b* 154*b*, 164*bl*, 165*tl*, 187*r*, 193*b*, 199*r*, 201*t*, 204*br*, 207*t*, 208*t*, 212*bl*, 231*t*, 234, 235*b,tr*, 236*b*, 247*tl*, 253*br*, 256*b*, 259*bl*, 280*t*, 293*m*, 295*m*, 303*tr*, 313*b*, 326*bl*, 331*t*, 349*b*, 369*b*, 388*m*, 405*m*, 432*t*, 447*m*, 451*t*, 473*mr*, 482*b*, 554, 527*t*, 538*b*, 570*b*, 600*b*, 617*b*; Fred Gambino 573*t*; John Gillatt 490*t*; Jeremy Gower 132*br*; Neil Gower 172*m*; Ray Grinaway 285*ml*, 517*m*, 585*b*, 621*t*, 632*bl*, 635, 653*b*, 658*m*, 711*tr*, 713*bl*; Allan Hardcastle 120*t*, 275*mr*, 295*b*, 305*tl*, 371*b*; Nick Harris 11; Nicholas Hewetson 2, 5*m*, 36*m*, 37*ml*, 43*tr*, 52*l*, 53*br*, 61*t*, 86*ml*, 99*m*, 100*bl*, 106*bl*, 130*b*, 132*ml*, 145*b*, 150*b*, 154*t*, 169*b*, 195*b*, 206*b*, 211*t*, 213*tr,b*, 220*b*, 224, 235*tl*, 244*t*, 247*tr*, 255*t*, 276*bl*, 277*b*, 284*t*, 293*b,tr*, 301*tr*, 315*tr*, 323*tl*, 342*tl* 353*b*, 355*t*, 357*ml*, 369*tr*, 370*t*, 393*b*, 404*b*, 416*t*, 434*t*, 450*m*, 460*m*, 462*b*, 472*m*, 473*tl*, 515*b*,

525*mr*, 664*b*, 711*tl*, 725; Bruce Hogarth 620–621*b*; Richard Hook 95*b*, 116*b*, 119*t*, 120*b*, 123*t*, 243*bl*, 244*b*, 316*b*, 377*b*, 436*b*, 577; Simon Huson 15*t*, 16*b*, 63*b*, 124*ml*, 741*b*; John James (Pat Kelliner) 183*t*, 219*b*, 364*t*, 380*t*, 390*l*, 391*m*, 397, 409*t*, 410*b*, 475*b*, 518*b*, 557; Peter Jarvis (Simon Girling Assoc.) 384*b*, 587*b*, 624*b*; Deborah Kindred (Simon Girling Assoc.) 92*t*, 93*b*, 119*b*, 128*t*, 135*b*, 173*ml*, 175*b*, 189*mr*, 253*tr*, 261*t*, 280*bl*, 284*m*, 285*t*, 290*b*, 297*t*, 330*t*, 347*b*, 383*t*, 597*b*, 614*t*; Adrian Lascome 366*b*; Jason Lewis 152*b*, 263*t*, 266*b*, 273*b*, 287*tl*, 292*m*, 301*tl*, 325*t*, 334*tl*, 341*b*, 348*t*, 372*tl*, 381*t*, 410*m*, 413*t*, 420–421*m*; Chris Lyon 713*br*; Kevin Maddison 5*b*, 14*m*, 18*b*, 19*b*, 22*m*, 22*b*, 27*b*, 36*t*, 37*mr*, 52*m*, 53*t*, 54*bl*, 56*t*, 57*bl*, 59*tl*, 63*t*, 73*b*, 75*m*, 86*b*, 89*bl*, 92*bl*, 102*b*, 103*b*, 105*tr*, 116*tr*, 117*tr*, *tl*, 121*t*, 131*b*, 132*b*, 142*m*, 151*b*, 163*ml*, 189*b*, 202*t*, 208*br*, 218, 219, 245*b*, 247*ml*, 294*t*, 302*b*, 345*t*, 348*bl*, 362*b*, 527, 536*b*, 544*mr*, 578*t*, 583; Shirley Mallinson 506*b*; Shane Marsh 407*b*; David MacAllister 328*b*, 389*b*, 419*t*; Angus McBride (Linden Artists) 9*b*, 14*t*, 15*b*, 21*b*, 25*b*, 31*b*, 35*t*, 44–45*b*, 48*b*, 61*b*, 68*b*, 69*b*, 113*b*, 128*b*, 303*br*; Frank Nichols 389*r*; Chris D. Orr 364*b*, 365*b*, 373*b*, 394*t*, 403*m*, 407*m*, 412*t*, *b*, 433*t*, 444*m*, 475*t*, 493*tl*, *b*, 550, 575*t*, 654*m*, 715*b*; Sharon Pallent 41*tr*; R. Payne 305*tr*; R. Philips 317*b*; Jayne Pickering 409*m*; Melvyn Pickering 39*b*, 46*mr*, 66*t*, 68*tl*, 132*t*, 138*ml*, 148*mr*; Malcolm Porter 13, 29; Mike Posen 608; John Ridyard 490*b*, 509*br*; Mike Roffe 489*m*, 496*mr*, 500*t*, 501*br*, 549, 528*t*, 534*m*, 712*m*; Chris Rothero 63*ml*; David Salarya 24, 26, 41, 54, 72, 84, 85, 86, 105, 108, 109, 117, 126, 139, 148, 157, 165, 169, 194, 196, 197, 202, 204, 221, 226, 229; Mike Saunders 607*tr*; Rodney Shackell All biography box heads, 32*b*, 53*m*, 63*ml*, 64*b*, 101*b*, 104*b*, 106*t*, 107*t*, 115*bl*, 125*r*, 132*ml*, 133*ml*, 172*t*, 173*b*, 210, 243*br*, 257, 277*t*, 288*b*, 293*tl*, 296*b*, 308*m*, 325*bl*, 367*t*, 372*b*, 378*t*, 406*b*, 439*r*, 441*mr*, 456*b*; Rob Shone 5*t*, 21*t*, 52*tr*, 52*br*, 54*t*, 65*t*, 95*tl*, 96*bl*, 101*t*, 102*t*, 109*t*, 124*mr*, 133*mr*, 137*m*, 139*t*, 147*ml*, 149*t*, 151*t*, 155*m*, 156*b*, 174*b*, 179*br*, 181*ml*, 188*m*, 189*ml*, 190*b*, 191*mr*, 196*bl*, 208*b*, 212*t*, 220*t*, 230*b*, 233*bl*, 249*tr*, 258*b*, 261*b*, 269*t*, 291*b*, 309*mr*, 343*tr*, 365*ml*, 387*b*, 417*b*, 435*tr*, 446*m*, 447*t*, 452*t*, 474*b*, 576, 579*t*, 588*bl*, 593, 594*m*, 595*b*, 597*t*, 602*t*, 607*b*, 612*ml*, 613, 618–619*b*, 626*b*, 633*b*, 636, 684*m*, 724*b*, *t*, 735*t*; Mark Stacey 511, 540*b*; Paul Stangroom 499*b*, 516*b*, 524*t*, 541*br*; Stephen Sweet 669*t*, *b*; Mike Taylor (Simon Girling Assoc.) 261*m*, 306*t*, 415*t*, 428*bl*, 434*bl*; George Thompson 122*b*, 356*m*, 429*r*; David Wright (Kathy Jakeman) 189*ml*, 237*t*; Paul Wright 365*mr*, 555, 564*t*, 630*m*.

Additional black and white illustrations by: Chris Lenthall, Stefan Morris, Jackie Moore, Branka Surla, Smiljka Surla, John Kelly, Martin Wilson, Teresa Morris, Matthew Gore, Ian Fish.

The publishers wish to thank the following for supplying photographs for this book:

Page 1 *t* ZEFA, *b* Press Association; 2 ZEFA; 3 National Museum, Denmark; 4 *t* Michael Holford, *b* Cambridge University Collection of Air Photographs; 6 British Museum; 7 *t* Peter Newark Photographs, *b* ZEFA; 8 *l* E.T. Archive, *r* Mansell Collection; 12 ZEFA; 16 Reunion des Musees Nationaux; 17 *l* Brooklyn Museum, *r* Reunion des Musees Nationaux; 25 ZEFA; 26 Peter Clayton; 28 Peter Clayton; 30 ZEFA; 60 British Museum; 69 Ancient Art and Architecture Collection; 76 ZEFA; 81 Michael Holford; 88 Ancient Art and Architecture Collection; 110 and 111 Sonia Halliday Photographs; 125 Sonia Halliday Photographs; 133 Mansell Collection; 142 Sonia Halliday Photographs; 149 C.M. Dixon; 156 Trinity College, Cambridge; 164 Sonia Halliday Photographs; 169 Trinity College, Dublin; 177 Sonia Halliday Photographs; 179 Ancient Art and Architechture Collection; 180 Mansell Collection; 181 British Library; 183 ZEFA; 185 Michael Holford; 192 British Museum; 196 Michael Holford; 197 Werner Forman Archive; 205 ZEFA; 212 Bodleian Library; 215 Mansell Collection; 222 and 223 Town of Bayeux; 227 Public Record Office; 228 Seattle Art Museum; 229 Werner Forman Archive; 233 E.T. Archive; 235 Werner Forman Archive; 241 Giraudon; 243 Sonia Halliday Photographs; 246 Sonia Halliday Photo graphs; 247 National Gallery, London; 251 National Gallery of Ireland; 259 Bodlerian Library; 262 Mary Evans Picture Library; 264 British Library; 274 Scottish National Portrait Gallery; 277 National Gallery, London; 284 Michael Holford; 287 Bodleian Library; 291 SCALA; 298 British Library; 299 Giraudon; 300 Windsor Castle, Royal Library 1992 Her Majesty The Queen; 303 ZEFA; 308 Giraudon; 309 British Library; 314 Werner Forman Archive; 321 Michael Holford; 323 SCALA; 324 *t* National Gallery, *b* V & A/Bridgeman Art Library; 327 South American Pictures; 329 Michael Holford; 332 SCALA; 333 *t* Galleria degli Uffizi/Bridgeman Art Library, *m* Mary Evans Picture Library; 334 Michael Holford; 337 SCALA; 343 *l* St. Bride Library, *r* SCALA; 345 Mary Evans Picture Library; 347 E.T. Archive; 348 Michael Holford; 349 Christie's/Bridgeman Art Library; 351 National Portrait Gallery; 352 Michael Holford; 353 Werner Forman Archive; 357 V & A/Bridgeman Art Library; 360 Michael Holford; 365 British Museum; 368 Mary Evans Picture Library; 372 Mary Evans Picture Library; 373 Ann Ronan Picture Library; 375 By kind permission of the Marquess of Tavistock and the Trustees of the Bedford Estates; 378 Giraudon; 381 *m* National Gallery, *b* Mansell Collection; 382 fotomas Index; 385 National Maritime Museum; 387 E.T. Archive; 388 *t* Giraudon/Bridgeman Art Library, *b* Bibliotheque Nationale/Bridgeman Art Library; 389 Bridgeman Art Library; 391 Mary Evans Picture Library; 395 *t* Werner Forman Archive, *b* The Royal Collection/St. James' Palace c H M Queen; 401 Mary Evans Picture Library; 403 Mary Evans Picture Library; 404 *t*, Rijkmuseum, *b* Bridgeman Art Library; 405 *b* British Museum; 406 National Portrait Gallery; 410 Mansell Collection; 412 Spectrum; 420 Michael Holford; 421 Hulton-Deutsch Collection; 422 *l* Mansell Collection, *r* Michael Holford; 423 Prado/Bridgeman Art Library; 47 Rijkmuseum; 428 Mansell Collection; 429 Staatliche Kunstsammlungen/Bridgeman Art Library; 431 British Museum; 432 Fotomas Index; 435 V&A/Bridgeman Art Library; 437 Mary Evans Picture Library; 440 Mary Evans Picture Library; 444 Fotomas Index; 445 *t* Sonia Halliday Photo graphs, *b* Peter Newark Photographs; 447 The Hague; 448 National Maritime Museum; 451 National Maritime Museum; 452 *bl* Michael Holford, *br* Ann Ronan Picture Library; 453 Mansell Collection; 454 Mansell Collection; 457 Spectrum; 458 Peter Clayton; 459 Mansell Collection; 461 *t* E.T. Archive, *b* Giraudon/Bridgeman Art Library; 463 Peter Newark Photographs; 465 National Portrait Gallery; 467 Kungil Armemuseum; 469 *l* Bank of England, *b* Mansell Collection; 472 National Army Museum; 473 Fotomas Index; 477 Mansell Collection; 483 V&A/Bridgeman Art Library; 484 *t* Michael Holford, *b* SCALA; 485 *r* British Library/Bridgeman Art Library, *l* V&A/Bridgeman Art Library; 486 E.T. Archive; 489 *t* Ann Ronan Picture Library, *b* Holkham Estate; 491 Mansell Collection; 493 Mary Evans Picture Library; 494 Ancient Art & Architecture Collection; 495 India Office Library/Bridgeman Art Library; 499 National Army Museum; 501 Mansell Collection; 504 Tate Gallery/Bridgeman Art Library; 505 Giraudon; 507 Mary Evans Picture Library; 508 E.T. Archive; 509 Ann Ronan Picture Library; 510 Michael Holford; 512 Michael Holford; 514 *t* V&A/Bridgeman Art Library, *b* Mansell Collection; 515 National Gallery; 517 Michael Holford; 521 Peter Newark Pictures; 523 Giraudon; 524 Mansell Collection; 525 E.T. Archive; 528 Guildhall Library/Bridgeman Art Library, 534 Mansell Collection; 535 *ml*

E.T. Archive, *mr* Lindley Library, R H S/Bridgeman Art Library, *br* Science Museum; 539 Bettiman Archive; 50 *t* Prado/Bridgeman Art Library, *m* E.T. Archive; 541 Mansell Collection; 544 Peter Newark Pictures; 545 Peter Newark Pictures; 546 Mansell Collection; 547 Mansell Collection; 548 Mansell Collection; 549 *l* Werner Forman Archive, *b* City of Bristol Museum & Art Gallery/Bridgeman Art Library; 551 Guildhall Library/Bridgeman Art Library; 552 Windsor Castle, Royal Library 1992 Her Majesty The Queen; 554 Peter Newark Pictures; 556 Peter Newark Pictures; 561 Mary Evans Picture Library; 563 Betmann Archive; 564 Mary Evans Picture Library; 566 *t* Allans of Duke Street, London, DACS/Hermitage, St. Petersburg,*r* Bridgeman Art Library; 569 National Army Musem; 572 New Zealand High Commission/Bridgeman Art Library; 573 Royal Geographical Society/Bridgeman Art Library; 574 Mary Evans Picture Library; 575 Mary Evans Picture; 578 Kyoto Costume Institute; 580 Windsor Castle, Royal Library Her Majesty The Queen; 585 Peter Newark Pictures; 588 *r* Mansell Collection, *b* Mary Evans Picture Library; 589 *ml, br* Mary Evans Picture Library; 594 *t* Science Museum, *b* Mansell Collection; 599 Mary Evans Picture Library; 600 Mary Evans Picture Library; 602 *bl* Science Museum; 603 Christopher Wood Gallery/Bridgeman Art Library; 604 Giraudon; 606 Mary Evans Picture Library; 607 Mansell Collection; 609 Mary Evans Picture Library; 611 Mary Evans Picture Library; 612 Mansell Collection; 613 Peter Newark Pictures; 614 Library of Congress; 617 Peter Newark Pictures; 619 Trades Union Congress; 622 Bettmann Archive; 624 Mary Evans Pic ture Library; 625 Mary Evans Picture Library; 627 *t* Mary Evans Picture Library, *b* E.T. Archive; 629 *t* Novosti Press Agency, *b* Victoria & Albert Museum; 636 Mansell Collection; 637 Peter Newark Pictures; 640 *t* Imperial War Museum, *b* ZEFA; 641 *t* E.T. Archive, *bl* Sonia Halliday Photographs; 642 E.T. Archive; 643 *t* E.T. Archive, *b* Mary Evans Picture Library; 644 *t* Imperial War Museum, *b* E.T. Archive; 645 E.T. Archive; 646 *r* E.T. Archive, *br* Ronald Grant Archive; 647 *tr* Visual Arts Library, *b* Galerie Der Stadt Stuttgart; 648 Hulton-Deutsch Collection; 649 *t* Mary Evans Pic ture Library, *b* Hulton-Deutsch Collection; 650 Novosti Press Agency; 652 Bettmann Archive; 654 *t* Architectural Association/Taylor Galyean, *b* E.T. Archive; 655 *l* Architectural Association/Andrew Higgot, *r* ZEFA; 656 Imperial War Museum; 657 Imperial War Museum; 658 *t* Illustrated London News, *b* Bettmann Archive; 660 *t* Mary Evans Picture Library, *m* Illustrated London News, *b* Peter Newark Pictures; *tl* 661 B.B.C., *tr* Hulton-Deutsch Collection, *ml/bl* ZEFA, *mr* E.T. Archive; 662 Peter Newark Pictures; 665 Sonia Halliday Photographs; 666 *t* E.T. Archive, *b* Popperfoto; 667 Peter Newark Photographs; 668 Bettmann Archive; 669 Bettmann Archive; 671 Bettmann Archive; 674 Bettmann Archive; 675 Popperfoto; 676 *m* E.T. Archive, *b* Peter Newark Pictures; 677 *tl* Ronald Grant Archive, *tr* Mary Evans Picture Library, *m* Peter Newark Pictures, *b* Imperial War Museum; 678 Bettmann Archive; 679 Popperfoto; 680 *t* Imperial War Museum, *b* Peter Newark Pictures; 681 Bettmann Archive; 682 E.T. Archive; 683 *m* Bettmann Archive, *b* Popperfoto; 684 *t* ZEFA, *b* Science Photo Library; 685 *t* Popperfoto, *b* Bettmann Archive; 686 Bettmann Ar chive; 687 Bettmann Archive; 688 Popperfoto; 689 *t* E.T. Archive, *m* Peter Newark Pictures, *b* Hulton-Deutsch Collection; 690 E.T. Archive; 691 *t* IBM/ENIAC, *m* Popperfoto, *bl* Liberty Archive, Victoria Library/Bridgeman Art Library, *br* Ronald Grant Archive; 693 Imperial War Museum; 694 Imperial War Museum; 695 Peter Newark Pictures; 696 Bettmann Archive; 697 *l* E.T. Archive, *r* Bettmann Archive; 698 *t* Popperfoto, *b* Hulton-Deutsch Collection; 699 *t,m* Bettmann Archive, *b* Hul ton-Deutsch Collection; 700 Bettmann Archive; 701 Imperial War Museum; 702 *l* United Nations, *r* Bettmann Archive; 703 *t* United Nations, *b* ZEFA; 706 *t,m* Mary Evans Picture Library, *b* British Petroleum; 707 *t,m* E.T. Archive, *b* Robert Opie Collection; 708 Bettmann Archive; 709 Bettmann Archive; 710 Wiener Library/Bergen-Belsen Memorial Press; 712 Imperial War Museum; 715 Imperial War Museum; 716 E.T. Archive; 717 Frank Spooner Pictures/FERRY; 720 Panos Pictures; 721 *t* TRIP/Eye Ubiquitous, *bl* Camera Press, *br* ZEFA; 722 Camera Press; 723 Hulton-Deutsch Collection; 24 NASA; 726 Camera Press; 727 *t* Hulton-Deutsch Collection, *b* Camera Press; 728 ZEFA; 729 B.N.TO.; 730 Popperfoto; 73 Camera Press; 732 *t* Frank Spooner Pictures/GAMMA, *b* Hulton-Deutsch Collection; 734 Camera Press; 735 *t* Associated Press, *b* ZEFA; 736 Camera Press; 737 Camera Press; 738 Frank Spooner Pictures/GAMMA; 739 *t* TRIP/Eye Ubiquitous, *b* Frank Spooner Pictures/GAMMA; 740 ZEFA; 74 ZEFA; 74 Camera Press; 743 *t* Live Aid *m* Associated Press, *b* Panos Pictures; 744 NHPA/Martin Wendler; 745 *t* ZEFA, *m* NHPA/K. Ghani, Frank Spooner Pictures/GAMMA.